Lecture Notes in Computer Science 12225

More information about this series at http://www.springer.com/series/7407

Shuvendu K. Lahiri · Chao Wang (Eds.)

Computer Aided Verification

32nd International Conference, CAV 2020
Los Angeles, CA, USA, July 21–24, 2020
Proceedings, Part II

 Springer

Editors
Shuvendu K. Lahiri
Microsoft Research Lab
Redmond, WA, USA

Chao Wang
University of Southern California
Los Angeles, CA, USA

ISSN 0302-9743   ISSN 1611-3349   (electronic)
Lecture Notes in Computer Science
ISBN 978-3-030-53290-1   ISBN 978-3-030-53291-8   (eBook)
https://doi.org/10.1007/978-3-030-53291-8

LNCS Sublibrary: SL1 – Theoretical Computer Science and General Issues

This Springer imprint is published by the registered company Springer Nature Switzerland AG
The registered company address is: Gewerbestrasse 11, 6330 Cham, Switzerland

Preface

It was our privilege to serve as the program chairs for CAV 2020, the 32nd International Conference on Computer-Aided Verification. CAV 2020 was held as a virtual conference during July 21–24, 2020. The tutorial day was on July 20, 2020, and the pre-conference workshops were held during July 19–20, 2020. Due to the coronavirus disease (COVID-19) outbreak, all events took place online.

CAV is an annual conference dedicated to the advancement of the theory and practice of computer-aided formal analysis methods for hardware and software systems. The primary focus of CAV is to extend the frontiers of verification techniques by expanding to new domains such as security, quantum computing, and machine learning. This puts CAV at the cutting edge of formal methods research, and this year's program is a reflection of this commitment.

CAV 2020 received a very high number of submissions (240). We accepted 18 tool papers, 4 case studies, and 43 regular papers, which amounts to an acceptance rate of roughly 27%. The accepted papers cover a wide spectrum of topics, from theoretical results to applications of formal methods. These papers apply or extend formal methods to a wide range of domains such as concurrency, machine learning, and industrially deployed systems. The program featured invited talks by David Dill (Calibra) and Pushmeet Kohli (Google DeepMind) as well as invited tutorials by Tevfik Bultan (University of California, Santa Barbara) and Sriram Sankaranarayanan (University of Colorado at Boulder). Furthermore, we continued the tradition of Logic Lounge, a series of discussions on computer science topics targeting a general audience.

In addition to the main conference, CAV 2020 hosted the following workshops: Numerical Software Verification (NSV), Verified Software: Theories, Tools, and Experiments (VSTTE), Verification of Neural Networks (VNN), Democratizing Software Verification, Synthesis (SYNT), Program Equivalence and Relational Reasoning (PERR), Formal Methods for ML-Enabled Autonomous Systems (FoMLAS), Formal Methods for Blockchains (FMBC), and Verification Mentoring Workshop (VMW).

Organizing a flagship conference like CAV requires a great deal of effort from the community. The Program Committee (PC) for CAV 2020 consisted of 85 members – a committee of this size ensures that each member has to review a reasonable number of papers in the allotted time. In all, the committee members wrote over 960 reviews while investing significant effort to maintain and ensure the high quality of the conference program. We are grateful to the CAV 2020 PC for their outstanding efforts in evaluating the submissions and making sure that each paper got a fair chance. Like last year's CAV, we made the artifact evaluation mandatory for tool paper submissions and optional but encouraged for the rest of the accepted papers. The Artifact Evaluation Committee consisted of 40 reviewers who put in significant effort to evaluate each artifact. The goal of this process was to provide constructive feedback to tool developers and help make the research published in CAV more reproducible. The Artifact

Evaluation Committee was generally quite impressed by the quality of the artifacts, and, in fact, all accepted tools passed the artifact evaluation. Among the accepted regular papers, 67% of the authors submitted an artifact, and 76% of these artifacts passed the evaluation. We are also very grateful to the Artifact Evaluation Committee for their hard work and dedication in evaluating the submitted artifacts. The evaluation and selection process involved thorough online PC discussions using the EasyChair conference management system, resulting in more than 2,000 comments.

CAV 2020 would not have been possible without the tremendous help we received from several individuals, and we would like to thank everyone who helped make CAV 2020 a success. First, we would like to thank Xinyu Wang and He Zhu for chairing the Artifact Evaluation Committee and Jyotirmoy Deshmukh for local arrangements. We also thank Zvonimir Rakamaric for chairing the workshop organization, Clark Barrett for managing sponsorship, Thomas Wies for arranging student fellowships, and Yakir Vizel for handling publicity. We also thank Roopsha Samanta for chairing the Mentoring Committee. Last but not least, we would like to thank members of the CAV Steering Committee (Kenneth McMillan, Aarti Gupta, Orna Grumberg, and Daniel Kroening) for helping us with several important aspects of organizing CAV 2020.

We hope that you will find the proceedings of CAV 2020 scientifically interesting and thought-provoking!

June 2020

Shuvendu K. Lahiri
Chao Wang

Organization

Program Chairs

Shuvendu K. Lahiri   Microsoft Research, USA
Chao Wang   University of Southern California, USA

Workshop Chair

Zvonimir Rakamaric   University of Utah, USA

Sponsorship Chair

Clark Barrett   Stanford University, USA

Publicity Chair

Yakir Vizel   Technion - Israel Institute of Technology, Israel

Fellowship Chair

Thomas Wies   New York University, USA

Local Arrangements Chair

Jyotirmoy Deshmukh   University of Southern California, USA

Program Committee

Aws Albarghouthi   University of Wisconsin-Madison, USA
Jade Alglave   University College London, UK
Christel Baier   Technical University of Dresden, Germany
Gogul Balakrishnan   Google, USA
Sorav Bansal   India Institute of Technology, Delhi, India
Gilles Barthe   Max Planck Institute, Germany
Josh Berdine   Facebook, UK
Per Bjesse   Synopsys, USA
Sam Blackshear   Calibra, USA
Roderick Bloem   Graz University of Technology, Austria
Borzoo Bonakdarpour   Iowa State University, USA
Ahmed Bouajjani   Paris Diderot University, France
Tevfik Bultan   University of California, Santa Barbara, USA
Pavol Cerny   Vienna University of Technology, Austria

Sagar Chaki	Mentor Graphics, USA
Swarat Chaudhuri	University of Texas, Austin, USA
Hana Chockler	King's College London, UK
Maria Christakis	Max Planck Institute, Germany
Eva Darulova	Max Planck Institute, Germany
Cristina David	University of Cambridge, UK
Ankush Desai	Amazon, USA
Jyotirmoy Deshmukh	University of Southern California, USA
Cezara Dragoi	Inria, France
Kerstin Eder	University of Bristol, UK
Michael Emmi	Amazon, USA
Constantin Enea	Université de Paris, France
Lu Feng	University of Virginia, USA
Yu Feng	University of California, Santa Barbara, USA
Bernd Finkbeiner	Saarland University, Germany
Dana Fisman	Ben-Gurion University, Israel
Daniel J. Fremont	University of California, Santa Cruz, USA
Malay Ganai	Synopsys, USA
Ganesh Gopalakrishnan	University of Utah, USA
Orna Grumberg	Technion - Israel Institute of Technology, Israel
Arie Gurfinkel	University of Waterloo, Canada
Alan J. Hu	The University of British Columbia, Canada
Laura Humphrey	Air Force Research Laboratory, USA
Franjo Ivancic	Google, USA
Joxan Jaffar	National University of Singapore, Singapore
Dejan Jovanovié	SRI International, USA
Zachary Kincaid	Princeton University, USA
Laura Kovacs	Vienna University of Technology, Austria
Daniel Kroening	University of Oxford, UK
Ori Lahav	Tel Aviv University, Israel
Akash Lal	Microsoft, India
Anthony Lin	TU Kaiserslautern, Germany
Yang Liu	Nanyang Technological University, Singapore
Francesco Logozzo	Facebook, USA
Ruben Martins	Carnegie Mellon University, USA
Anastasia Mavridou	NASA Ames Research Center, USA
Jedidiah McClurg	Colorado School of Mines, USA
Kenneth McMillan	Microsoft, USA
Kuldeep S. Meel	National University of Singapore, Singapore
Sayan Mitra	University of Illinois at Urbana-Champaign, USA
Ruzica Piskac	Yale University, USA
Xiaokang Qiu	Purdue University, USA
Mukund Raghothaman	University of Southern California, USA
Jan Reineke	Saarland University, Germany
Kristin Yvonne Rozier	Iowa State University, USA
Philipp Ruemmer	Uppsala University, Sweden

Krishna S	India Institute of Technology, Bombay, India
Sriram Sankaranarayanan	University of Colorado at Boulder, USA
Natarajan Shankar	SRI International, USA
Natasha Sharygina	University of Lugano, Switzerland
Sharon Shoham	Tel Aviv University, Israel
Alexandra Silva	University College London, UK
Anna Slobodova	Centaur Technology, USA
Fabio Somenzi	University of Colorado at Boulder, USA
Fu Song	ShanghaiTech University, China
Aditya Thakur	University of California, Davis, USA
Ashish Tiwari	Microsoft, USA
Aaron Tomb	Galois, Inc., USA
Ashutosh Trivedi	University of Colorado at Boulder, USA
Caterina Urban	Inria, France
Niki Vazou	IMDEA, Spain
Margus Veanes	Microsoft, USA
Yakir Vizel	Technion - Israel Institute of Technology, Israel
Xinyu Wang	University of Michigan, USA
Georg Weissenbacher	Vienna University of Technology, Austria
Fei Xie	Portland State University, USA
Jin Yang	Intel, USA
Naijun Zhan	Chinese Academy of Sciences, China
He Zhu	Rutgers University, USA

Artifact Evaluation Committee

Xinyu Wang (Co-chair)	University of Michigan, USA
He Zhu (Co-chair)	Rutgers University, USA
Angello Astorga	University of Illinois at Urbana-Champaign, USA
Subarno Banerjee	University of Michigan, USA
Martin Blicha	University of Lugano, Switzerland
Brandon Bohrer	Carnegie Mellon University, USA
Jose Cambronero	Massachusetts Institute of Technology, USA
Joonwon Choi	Massachusetts Institute of Technology, USA
Norine Coenen	Saarland University, Germany
Katherine Cordwell	Carnegie Mellon University, USA
Chuchu Fan	Massachusetts Institute of Technology, USA
Yotam Feldman	Tel Aviv University, Israel
Timon Gehr	ETH Zurich, Switzerland
Aman Goel	University of Michigan, USA
Chih-Duo Hong	University of Oxford, UK
Bo-Yuan Huang	Princeton University, USA
Jeevana Priya Inala	Massachusetts Institute of Technology, USA
Samuel Kaufman	University of Washington, USA
Ratan Lal	Kansas State University, USA
Stella Lau	Massachusetts Institute of Technology, USA

Juneyoung Lee	Seoul National University, South Korea
Enrico Magnago	Fondazione Bruno Kessler, Italy
Umang Mathur	University of Illinois at Urbana-Champaign, USA
Jedidiah McClurg	Colorado School of Mines, USA
Sam Merten	Ohio University, USA
Luan Nguyen	University of Pennsylvania, USA
Aina Niemetz	Stanford University, USA
Shankara Pailoor	The University of Texas at Austin, USA
Brandon Paulsen	University of Southern California, USA
Mouhammad Sakr	Saarland University, Germany
Daniel Selsam	Microsoft Research, USA
Jiasi Shen	Massachusetts Institute of Technology, USA
Xujie Si	University of Pennsylvania, USA
Gagandeep Singh	ETH Zurich, Switzerland
Abhinav Verma	Rice University, USA
Di Wang	Carnegie Mellon University, USA
Yuepeng Wang	The University of Texas at Austin, USA
Guannan Wei	Purdue University, USA
Zikang Xiong	Purdue University, USA
Klaus von Gleissenthall	University of California, San Diego, USA

Mentoring Workshop Chair

| Roopsha Samanta | Purdue University, USA |

Steering Committee

Kenneth McMillan	Microsoft Research, USA
Aarti Gupta	Princeton University, USA
Orna Grumberg	Technion - Israel Institute of Technology, Israel
Daniel Kroening	University of Oxford, UK

Additional Reviewers

Shaull Almagor
Sepideh Asadi
Angello Astorga
Brandon Bohrer
Vincent Cheval
Javier Esparza
Marie Farrell
Grigory Fedyukovich
Jerome Feret
James Hamil

Antti Hyvarinen
Matteo Marescotti
Rodrigo Ottoni
Junkil Park
Sean Regisford
David Sanan
Aritra Sengupta
Sadegh Soudjani
Tim Zakian

Contents – Part II

Model Checking

Automata Tutor v3 3
  Loris D'Antoni, Martin Helfrich, Jan Kretinsky, Emanuel Ramneantu,
  and Maximilian Weininger

Seminator 2 Can Complement Generalized Büchi Automata via Improved
Semi-determinization 15
  František Blahoudek, Alexandre Duret-Lutz, and Jan Strejček

RTLola Cleared for Take-Off: Monitoring Autonomous Aircraft 28
  Jan Baumeister, Bernd Finkbeiner, Sebastian Schirmer,
  Maximilian Schwenger, and Christoph Torens

Realizing ω-regular Hyperproperties 40
  Bernd Finkbeiner, Christopher Hahn, Jana Hofmann,
  and Leander Tentrup

AdamMC: A Model Checker for Petri Nets with Transits against Flow-LTL . . . 64
  Bernd Finkbeiner, Manuel Gieseking, Jesko Hecking-Harbusch,
  and Ernst-Rüdiger Olderog

Action-Based Model Checking: Logic, Automata, and Reduction 77
  Stephen F. Siegel and Yihao Yan

Global Guidance for Local Generalization in Model Checking 101
  Hari Govind Vediramana Krishnan, YuTing Chen, Sharon Shoham,
  and Arie Gurfinkel

Towards Model Checking Real-World Software-Defined Networks 126
  Vasileios Klimis, George Parisis, and Bernhard Reus

Software Verification

Code2Inv: A Deep Learning Framework for Program Verification. 151
  Xujie Si, Aaditya Naik, Hanjun Dai, Mayur Naik, and Le Song

MetaVal: Witness Validation via Verification 165
  Dirk Beyer and Martin Spiessl

Recursive Data Structures in SPARK. 178
  Claire Dross and Johannes Kanig

Ivy: A Multi-modal Verification Tool for Distributed Algorithms   190
   Kenneth L. McMillan and Oded Padon

Reasoning over Permissions Regions in Concurrent Separation Logic   203
   James Brotherston, Diana Costa, Aquinas Hobor, and John Wickerson

Local Reasoning About the Presence of Bugs: Incorrectness
Separation Logic.   225
   Azalea Raad, Josh Berdine, Hoang-Hai Dang, Derek Dreyer,
   Peter O'Hearn, and Jules Villard

Stochastic Systems

Maximum Causal Entropy Specification Inference from Demonstrations   255
   Marcell Vazquez-Chanlatte and Sanjit A. Seshia

Certifying Certainty and Uncertainty in Approximate Membership
Query Structures.   279
   Kiran Gopinathan and Ilya Sergey

Global PAC Bounds for Learning Discrete Time Markov Chains   304
   Hugo Bazille, Blaise Genest, Cyrille Jegourel, and Jun Sun

Unbounded-Time Safety Verification of Stochastic Differential Dynamics . . .   327
   Shenghua Feng, Mingshuai Chen, Bai Xue, Sriram Sankaranarayanan,
   and Naijun Zhan

Widest Paths and Global Propagation in Bounded Value Iteration
for Stochastic Games.   349
   Kittiphon Phalakarn, Toru Takisaka, Thomas Haas, and Ichiro Hasuo

Checking Qualitative Liveness Properties of Replicated Systems
with Stochastic Scheduling.   372
   Michael Blondin, Javier Esparza, Martin Helfrich, Antonín Kučera,
   and Philipp J. Meyer

Stochastic Games with Lexicographic Reachability-Safety Objectives   398
   Krishnendu Chatterjee, Joost-Pieter Katoen, Maximilian Weininger,
   and Tobias Winkler

Qualitative Controller Synthesis for Consumption Markov
Decision Processes   421
   František Blahoudek, Tomáš Brázdil, Petr Novotný, Melkior Ornik,
   Pranay Thangeda, and Ufuk Topcu

STMC: Statistical Model Checker with Stratified and Antithetic Sampling . . .   448
   Nima Roohi, Yu Wang, Matthew West, Geir E. Dullerud,
   and Mahesh Viswanathan

AMYTISS: Parallelized Automated Controller Synthesis for Large-Scale
Stochastic Systems   461
    Abolfazl Lavaei, Mahmoud Khaled, Sadegh Soudjani, and Majid Zamani

PRISM-games 3.0: Stochastic Game Verification with Concurrency,
Equilibria and Time.   475
    Marta Kwiatkowska, Gethin Norman, David Parker, and Gabriel Santos

Optimistic Value Iteration   488
    Arnd Hartmanns and Benjamin Lucien Kaminski

PrIC3: Property Directed Reachability for MDPs.   512
    Kevin Batz, Sebastian Junges, Benjamin Lucien Kaminski,
    Joost-Pieter Katoen, Christoph Matheja, and Philipp Schröer

Synthesis

Good-Enough Synthesis.   541
    Shaull Almagor and Orna Kupferman

Synthesizing JIT Compilers for In-Kernel DSLs   564
    Jacob Van Geffen, Luke Nelson, Isil Dillig, Xi Wang, and Emina Torlak

Program Synthesis Using Deduction-Guided Reinforcement Learning   587
    Yanju Chen, Chenglong Wang, Osbert Bastani, Isil Dillig, and Yu Feng

Manthan: A Data-Driven Approach for Boolean Function Synthesis   611
    Priyanka Golia, Subhajit Roy, and Kuldeep S. Meel

Decidable Synthesis of Programs with Uninterpreted Functions.   634
    Paul Krogmeier, Umang Mathur, Adithya Murali, P. Madhusudan,
    and Mahesh Viswanathan

Must Fault Localization for Program Repair.   658
    Bat-Chen Rothenberg and Orna Grumberg

Author Index   681

Contents – Part I

AI Verification

NNV: The Neural Network Verification Tool for Deep Neural Networks
and Learning-Enabled Cyber-Physical Systems 3
    Hoang-Dung Tran, Xiaodong Yang, Diego Manzanas Lopez,
    Patrick Musau, Luan Viet Nguyen, Weiming Xiang, Stanley Bak,
    and Taylor T. Johnson

Verification of Deep Convolutional Neural Networks Using ImageStars 18
    Hoang-Dung Tran, Stanley Bak, Weiming Xiang, and Taylor T. Johnson

An Abstraction-Based Framework for Neural Network Verification 43
    Yizhak Yisrael Elboher, Justin Gottschlich, and Guy Katz

Improved Geometric Path Enumeration for Verifying ReLU
Neural Networks 66
    Stanley Bak, Hoang-Dung Tran, Kerianne Hobbs,
    and Taylor T. Johnson

Systematic Generation of Diverse Benchmarks for DNN Verification 97
    Dong Xu, David Shriver, Matthew B. Dwyer, and Sebastian Elbaum

Formal Analysis and Redesign of a Neural Network-Based Aircraft
Taxiing System with VERIFAI 122
    Daniel J. Fremont, Johnathan Chiu, Dragos D. Margineantu,
    Denis Osipychev, and Sanjit A. Seshia

Blockchain and Security

The Move Prover 137
    Jingyi Emma Zhong, Kevin Cheang, Shaz Qadeer, Wolfgang Grieskamp,
    Sam Blackshear, Junkil Park, Yoni Zohar, Clark Barrett,
    and David L. Dill

End-to-End Formal Verification of Ethereum 2.0 Deposit Smart Contract 151
    Daejun Park, Yi Zhang, and Grigore Rosu

Stratified Abstraction of Access Control Policies.   165
    John Backes, Ulises Berrueco, Tyler Bray, Daniel Brim, Byron Cook,
    Andrew Gacek, Ranjit Jhala, Kasper Luckow, Sean McLaughlin,
    Madhav Menon, Daniel Peebles, Ujjwal Pugalia, Neha Rungta,
    Cole Schlesinger, Adam Schodde, Anvesh Tanuku, Carsten Varming,
    and Deepa Viswanathan

Synthesis of Super-Optimized Smart Contracts Using Max-SMT.   177
    Elvira Albert, Pablo Gordillo, Albert Rubio, and Maria A. Schett

Verification of Quantitative Hyperproperties Using Trace
Enumeration Relations.   201
    Shubham Sahai, Pramod Subramanyan, and Rohit Sinha

Validation of Abstract Side-Channel Models for Computer Architectures   225
    Hamed Nemati, Pablo Buiras, Andreas Lindner, Roberto Guanciale,
    and Swen Jacobs

Concurrency

Semantics, Specification, and Bounded Verification of Concurrent Libraries
in Replicated Systems   251
    Kartik Nagar, Prasita Mukherjee, and Suresh Jagannathan

Refinement for Structured Concurrent Programs   275
    Bernhard Kragl, Shaz Qadeer, and Thomas A. Henzinger

Parameterized Verification of Systems with Global
Synchronization and Guards.   299
    Nouraldin Jaber, Swen Jacobs, Christopher Wagner, Milind Kulkarni,
    and Roopsha Samanta

HAMPA: Solver-Aided Recency-Aware Replication.   324
    Xiao Li, Farzin Houshmand, and Mohsen Lesani

Root Causing Linearizability Violations   350
    Berk Çirisci, Constantin Enea, Azadeh Farzan,
    and Suha Orhun Mutluergil

Symbolic Partial-Order Execution for Testing Multi-Threaded Programs   376
    Daniel Schemmel, Julian Büning, César Rodríguez, David Laprell,
    and Klaus Wehrle

Hardware Verification and Decision Procedures

fault: A Python Embedded Domain-Specific Language
for Metaprogramming Portable Hardware Verification Components   403
   Lenny Truong, Steven Herbst, Rajsekhar Setaluri, Makai Mann,
   Ross Daly, Keyi Zhang, Caleb Donovick, Daniel Stanley,
   Mark Horowitz, Clark Barrett, and Pat Hanrahan

Nonlinear Craig Interpolant Generation   415
   Ting Gan, Bican Xia, Bai Xue, Naijun Zhan, and Liyun Dai

Approximate Counting of Minimal Unsatisfiable Subsets   439
   Jaroslav Bendík and Kuldeep S. Meel

Tinted, Detached, and Lazy CNF-XOR Solving and Its Applications
to Counting and Sampling   463
   Mate Soos, Stephan Gocht, and Kuldeep S. Meel

Automated and Scalable Verification of Integer Multipliers   485
   Mertcan Temel, Anna Slobodova, and Warren A. Hunt Jr.

Interpolation-Based Semantic Gate Extraction and Its Applications
to QBF Preprocessing   508
   Friedrich Slivovsky

TarTar: A Timed Automata Repair Tool   529
   Martin Kölbl, Stefan Leue, and Thomas Wies

Hybrid and Dynamic Systems

SAW: A Tool for Safety Analysis of Weakly-Hard Systems   543
   Chao Huang, Kai-Chieh Chang, Chung-Wei Lin, and Qi Zhu

PIRK: Scalable Interval Reachability Analysis for High-Dimensional
Nonlinear Systems   556
   Alex Devonport, Mahmoud Khaled, Murat Arcak, and Majid Zamani

AEON: Attractor Bifurcation Analysis of Parametrised Boolean Networks . . .   569
   Nikola Beneš, Luboš Brim, Jakub Kadlecaj, Samuel Pastva,
   and David Šafránek

A Novel Approach for Solving the BMI Problem in Barrier
Certificates Generation   582
   Xin Chen, Chao Peng, Wang Lin, Zhengfeng Yang, Yifang Zhang,
   and Xuandong Li

Reachability Analysis Using Message Passing over Tree Decompositions. . . .   604
  Sriram Sankaranarayanan

Fast and Guaranteed Safe Controller Synthesis for Nonlinear
Vehicle Models.   629
  Chuchu Fan, Kristina Miller, and Sayan Mitra

SeQuaiA: A Scalable Tool for Semi-Quantitative Analysis of Chemical
Reaction Networks   653
  Milan Češka, Calvin Chau, and Jan Křetínský

Author Index   667

Model Checking

Automata Tutor v3

Loris D'Antoni[1], Martin Helfrich[2],
Jan Kretinsky[2], Emanuel Ramneantu[2],
and Maximilian Weininger[2(✉)]

[1] University of Wisconsin, Madison, USA
`loris@cs.wisc.edu`
[2] Technical University of Munich, Munich, Germany
{`martin.helfrich,jan.kretinsky,emanuel.ramneantu,maxi.weininger`}`@tum.de`

Abstract. Computer science class enrollments have rapidly risen in the past decade. With current class sizes, standard approaches to grading and providing personalized feedback are no longer possible and new techniques become both feasible and necessary. In this paper, we present the third version of Automata Tutor, a tool for helping teachers and students in large courses on automata and formal languages. The second version of Automata Tutor supported automatic grading and feedback for finite-automata constructions and has already been used by thousands of users in dozens of countries. This new version of Automata Tutor supports automated grading and feedback generation for a greatly extended variety of new problems, including problems that ask students to create regular expressions, context-free grammars, pushdown automata and Turing machines corresponding to a given description, and problems about converting between equivalent models - e.g., from regular expressions to nondeterministic finite automata. Moreover, for several problems, this new version also enables teachers and students to automatically generate new problem instances. We also present the results of a survey run on a class of 950 students, which shows very positive results about the usability and usefulness of the tool.

Keywords: Theory of computation · Automata theory · Personalized education · Automata tutor · Automated grading

1 Introduction

Computer science (CS) class enrollments have been rapidly rising, e.g., CS enrollment roughly triples per decade at Berkeley and Stanford [12] or TU Munich.

We thank Emil Ratko-Dehnert from ProLehre TUM for the professional help with the student survey; Tobias Nipkow and his team for allowing us to conduct the user survey in his class; Christian Backs, Vadim Goryainov, Sebastian Mair and Jan Wagener for the exercises they added as part of their Bachelor's theses; Julia Eisentraut and Salomon Sickert-Zehnter for their help in developing this project; the TUM fund "Verbesserung der Lehrmittelsituation" and the CAV community for caring about good teaching. Loris D'Antoni was supported, in part, by NSF under grants CNS-1763871, CCF-1750965, CCF-1744614, and CCF-1704117; and by the UW-Madison OVRGE with funding from WARF.

S. K. Lahiri and C. Wang (Eds.): CAV 2020, LNCS 12225, pp. 3–14, 2020.
https://doi.org/10.1007/978-3-030-53291-8_1

Both online and offline courses and degrees are being created to educate students and professionals in computer science and these courses may soon have thousands of students attending a lecture, or tens of thousands following a Massive Online Open Course (MOOC). At these scales, standard approaches to grading and providing personalized feedback are no longer possible and new techniques become both feasible and necessary. Current approaches for handling this growing student volume include reducing the complexity of assignments or relying on imprecise feedback and grading mechanisms. Simpler assessment mechanisms, e.g., multiple-choice questions, are easier to grade automatically but lack realism [8]. Designing better techniques for automated grading and feedback generation is therefore a necessity.

Recent advances in formal methods, including program synthesis and verification, can help teachers and students in verifiably correct ways that statistical or rule-based techniques cannot. For example, formal methods have been used to identify student errors and provide feedback for problems related to introductory Python programming assignments [17] geometry [9,11], algebra [16], logic [2], and automata [3,6]. In particular, for this last topic, the tool Automata Tutor v2 [7] has already been used by more than 9,000 students at more than 30 universities in North America, South America, Europe, and Asia.

In this paper, we present Automata Tutor v3, an online[1] tool that extends Automata Tutor v2 and uses techniques from program synthesis and decision procedures to improve the quality and effectiveness of teaching courses on automata and formal languages. Besides being part of the standard CS curriculum, the concepts taught in these courses are rich in structure and applications, e.g., in control theory, text editors, lexical analyzers, or models of software interfaces. Concrete topics in such curricula include automata, regular expressions, context-free grammars, and Turing machines. For problems and assignments related to these topics Automata Tutor v3 can automatically: (1) Detect whether the student's solution is correct. (2) Detect different types of student's mistakes and translate them into explanatory feedback. (3) If possible, generate new problems together with the corresponding solutions for teachers to use in class.

Automata Tutor v3 greatly expands its predecessor Automata Tutor v2, which only provides ways to pose and solve problems for deterministic and nondeterministic finite automata constructions. This paper describes the new components introduced by Automata Tutor v3 and how this new version improves on its previous one. The key advantages to its competitors are the breadth, automatic generation and grading of exercises, infrastructure allowing for use in large courses and a useful feedback to the students, compared to text-based interfaces used by Autotool [13], rudimentary feedback in JFLAP [14] and none in Gradience [1].

Since Automata Tutor has already been well received by teachers around the world, we believe that the readers from the CAV community will find great value in knowing about this new and fundamentally richer version of the tool and how

---

[1] https://automata.model.in.tum.de.

it can extensively help with teaching the automata and formal languages courses, a task we know many of the attendees have to face on a yearly basis.

Our contributions are the following:

- **Twelve new types of problems** (added to the four problems from the previous version) that can be created by teachers and for which the *tool can assign grades together with feedback* to student attempts. While the previous version of Automata Tutor could only support problems involving finite automata constructions, Automata Tutor v3 now supports problems for proving language non-regularity using the pumping lemma, building regular expressions, context free grammars, pushdown automata and Turing machines, and conversions between such models.
- **Automatic problem generation** for five types of problems, with the code modularity allowing to add it for all the others. This feature allows teachers to effortlessly create new assignments, or students to practice by themselves with potentially infinitely many exercises.
- A new and **improved user interface** that allows teachers and students to navigate the increased number of problem types and assignments. Furthermore, each problem type comes with an intuitive user interface (e.g., for drawing pushdown automata).
- An improved **infrastructure** for the use in large courses, in particular, incorporating login systems (e.g. *LDAP* or *OAuth*), getting a certified mapping from users to students and enabling teachers to grade homework or exams.
- A **user study** run on a class of 950 students to assess the effectiveness and usability of Automata Tutor v3. In our survey, students report to have *learned quickly, felt confident,* and *enjoyed* using Automata Tutor v3, and found it *easy to use.* Most importantly, students found the feedback given by the tool to be *useful* and claimed they *understood more* after using the tool and felt *better prepared* for an upcoming exam. In our personal experience, the tool saves us dozens of thousands of corrections in each single course.

2   Automata Tutor in a Nutshell

Automata Tutor is an online education tool created to support courses teaching basic concepts in automata and formal languages [7]. In this section, we describe how Automata Tutor helps teachers run large courses and students learn efficiently in such courses.

Learning Without Automata Tutor. Figure 1 schematically shows a student-teacher interaction in a course taught without an online tutoring system. The teacher creates exercises, grades them manually, and (sometimes) manually provides personalized feedback to the students. This type of interaction has many limitations: (1) it is asynchronous (i.e., the student has to wait a long time for what is often little feedback) and does not scale to large classrooms, posing strenuous amount of work on teachers, (2) it does not guarantee consistency in the assigned grades and feedback, and (3) it does not allow students to revise

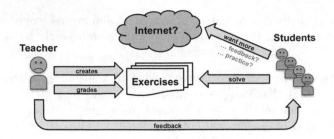

Fig. 1. Common structure of practical sessions for CS classes.

their solutions upon receiving feedback as the teachers often release a solution to all students as part of the feedback and do not grade new submissions.

Another drawback of this interaction is the limited number of problems students can practice on. Because teachers do not have the resources to create many practice problems and provide feedback for them, students are often forced to search the Internet for old exams and practice sheets or even exercises from other universities. Due to the lack of feedback, this chaotic search for practice problems often ends up confusing the students rather than helping them.

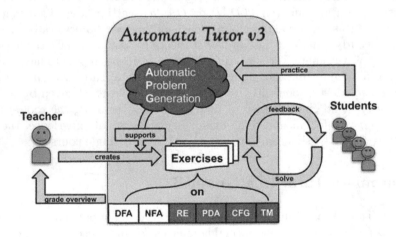

Fig. 2. Overview of Automata Tutor v3 (our contributions in green). The teacher creates exercises on various topics. The students solve the exercises in a feedback cycle: After each attempt they are automatically graded and get personalized feedback. The teacher has access to the grade overview. For additional practice, students can generate an unlimited number of new exercises using the automatic problem generation. (Color figure online)

Learning with Automata Tutor. Figure 2 shows the improved interaction offered by Automata Tutor v3. Here, a teacher creates the problem instances with the

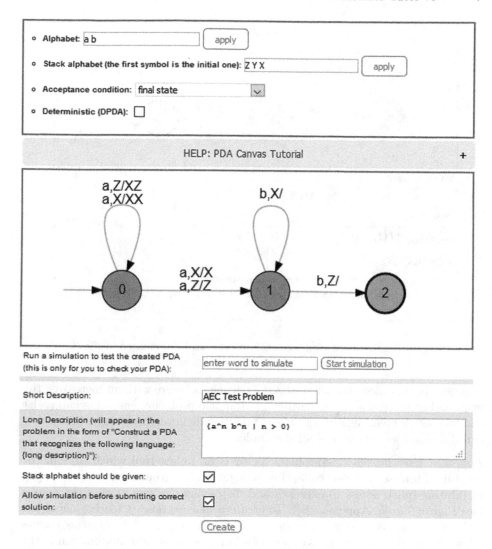

Fig. 3. Creating a new problem of type "PDA Construction".

help of the tool. The problems are then posed to the students and, *no matter how large a class is*, Automata Tutor automatically grades the solution attempts of students right when they are submitted and immediately gives detailed and personalized feedback for each submission. If required, e.g. for a graded homework, it is possible to restrict the number of attempts. Using this feedback, the students can immediately try the problem again and learn from their mistakes. As shown in a large user study run on the first version of Automata Tutor [6], this fast feedback cycle is encouraging for students and results in students spontaneously exploring more practice problems and engaging with the course material. Additional practice is supported by the automatic problem generation, with the

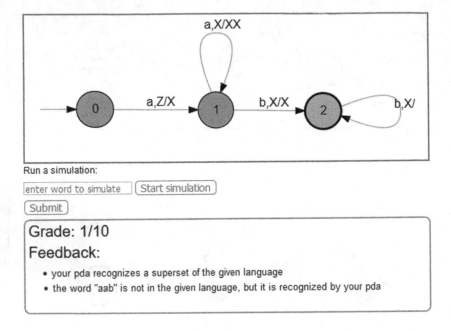

Run a simulation:

| enter word to simulate | Start simulation |

Submit

Grade: 1/10
Feedback:
  • your pda recognizes a superset of the given language
  • the word "aab" is not in the given language, but it is recognized by your pda

Fig. 4. Feedback received when solving the problem created in Fig. 3.

same level of detailed and personalized feedback as before without increasing the workload of the teacher. Furthermore, automatic problem generation can assist the teacher in creating new exercises. Finally, whenever necessary, the teacher can download an overview of all the grades.

Improved User interface. Automata Tutor is an online tool which runs in the most used browsers. A new collapsible navigation bar groups problems by topic, facilitating quick access to exercises and displaying the structure of the course (see Figure 6 in [5, Appendix B]). To create a new exercise, a teacher clicks the "+"-button and is presented the view of Fig. 3. In this case, the drawing canvas allows to easily specify the sample solution pushdown automaton. Similarly, when students solve this exercise, they draw their solution attempt also on the canvas. After submitting, they receive their personalized feedback and grade (see example in Fig. 4). For the automatic problem generation, a dropdown menu to select the problem type and a slider to select the difficulty is displayed together with the list of all problems the user has generated so far (see the screenshot in Figure 7 in [5, Appendix B]).

3   Design

3.1   University and Course Management

While Automata Tutor can be used for independent online practice, one of the main advantages is its infrastructure for large university courses. To this end, it is organized in *courses*. A course is created and supervised by one or more teachers. Together, they can create, test and edit exercises. The students cannot immediately see the problems, but only after the teachers have decided to pose them. This involves setting the maximum number of points, the number of allowed attempts as well as the start and end date.

To use Automata Tutor, students must have an account. One can either register by email or, in case the university supports it, login with an external login service like *LDAP* or *Oauth*. When using the login service of their university, teachers get a certified mapping from users to students and enabling teachers to use Automata Tutor v3 for grading homework or exams.

Students can enroll in a course using a password. Enrolled students see all posed problems and can solve them (using the allowed number of attempts). The final grade can be accessed by the teachers in the grade overview.

3.2   New Problem Types

In this section, we list the problem types newly added to Automata Tutor v3. They are all part of the course [10] and a detailed description of each problem can be found in [5, Appendix A], including the basic theoretical concept, how a student can solve such a problem, what a teacher has to provide to create a problem, the idea of the grading algorithm, and what feedback the tool gives.

RE/CFG/PDA Words: Finding words in or not in the language of a regular expression, context free grammar or pushdown automaton.

RE/CFG/PDA Construction: Given a description of a language, construct a regular expression, context free grammar or pushdown automaton.

RE to NFA: Given a regular expression, construct a nondeterministic-finite automaton.

Myhill-Nerode Equivalence Classes: There are two subtypes: either, given a regular expression and two words, find out whether they are equivalent w.r.t. the language, or, given a regular expression and a word, find further words in the same equivalence class.

Pumping-Lemma Game: Given a language, the student has to guess whether it is regular or not and then plays the game as one of the quantifiers.

Find Derivation: Given a context free grammar and a word, the student has to specify a derivation of that word.

CNF: Given a context free grammar, the student has to transform it into Chomsky Normal Form.

CYK: Given a context free grammar in CNF and a word, the student has to decide whether the word is in the language of the grammar by using the Cocke–Younger–Kasami algorithm.

While to TM: Given a while-program (a Turing-complete programming language with very restricted syntax), construct a (multi-tape) Turing machine with the same input-output behaviour.

3.3 Automatic Problem Generation

Automatic Problem Generation (APG) allows one to generate new exercises of a requested *difficulty* level and problem type. This allows students to practice independently and supports teachers when creating new exercises. While APG is currently implemented for four CFG problem types and for the problem type "While to TM", it can be easily extended to other problem types by providing the following components:

- **Procedure for generating exercises at random** either from given basic building blocks or from scratch.
- **A "quality" metric** $qual(E)$ for assessing the quality of the generated exercise E, ranging from trivial or infeasible to realistic.
- **A "difficulty" metric** $diff(E)$ for assessing the difficulty of E.

Given these components, Automata Tutor generates a new problem with a given minimum difficulty $d_{\min}$ and maximum difficulty $d_{\max}$ as follows. Firstly, 100 random exercises are generated. Secondly, Automata Tutor chooses exercises E with the best quality such that $d_{\min} \leq diff(E) \leq d_{\max}$.

Concretely, for the CFG problem types, CFGs with random productions are generated and sanitized. Resulting CFGs that do not accept any words or have too few productions are excluded using the quality metric. The difficulty metric always depends on the number of productions; additionally, depending on the exact problem type, further criteria are taken into account.

For the problem type "While to TM" we use an approach similar to the one suggested in existing tools for automatic problem generation [15,18]: We handcrafted several *base programs* which are of different difficulty level. In the generation process, the syntax tree of such a base program is abstracted and certain modifying operations are executed; these change the program without affecting the difficulty too much. E.g. we choose different variables, switch the order of if-else branches or change arithmetic operators. Then several programs are generated and those of bad quality are filtered out. A program is of bad quality if its language is trivially small or if it contains infinite loops; since detecting these properties is undecidable, we employ heuristics such as checking that the loops terminate for all inputs up to a certain size with a certain timeout.

4 Implementation and Scalability

Automata Tutor v3 is open source and it consists of a frontend, a backend, and a database. It also provides a developer's manual for creating new exercises.

The frontend, written in `scala`, renders the webpage. The drawing canvases for the different automata and the Turing machines rely on javascript. The frontend and backend communicate using XML objects.

The backend, written in C#, contains methods to unpack the xml of the frontend to compute the grade and feedback for solutions. It is also used to check the syntax of exercises and for the automatic problem generation. It relies on AutomataDotNet[2], a library that provides efficient algorithms for automata and regular expressions.

The database keeps track of existing users, problems and courses. It uses the H2 Database Engine.

All the new parts of Automata Tutor v3 were developed and tested over the last 3 years at TU Munich, where they were used to support the introductory theoretical computer science course. This local deployment served as an important test-bed before publicly deploying the tool online at large scale. Due to its modular structure, the tool is easily scalable by having multiple frontends and backends together with a load distributor. This approach has successfully scaled to 950 concurrent student users; for this, we used 7 virtual machines: 3 hosting frontends, 3 hosting backends (each with 2 cores 2.60 GHz Intel(R) Xeon(R) CPU and 4 GB RAM), and 1 for load distribution and the database (with 4 such cores and 8 GB RAM). We will scale the number of machines based on need.

5   Evaluation and User Study

Large-Class Deployment. In the latest iteration of the TU Munich course in 2019, we used Automata Tutor v3 (in the following denoted as AT) in a mandatory homework system for a course with about 950 students; the homework system also included written and programming exercises. In total, we posed 79 problems consisting of 18 homework and 61 practice problems. The teachers saved themselves the effort of correcting 26,535 homework exercises, and the students used AT to get personalized feedback for their work 76,507 times. On average, each student who used AT did so 107 times.

Student Survey Results. At the end of the course, we conducted an anonymized survey, based on the System Usability Survey [4]. 14.6% of the students in the course answered the survey, which is an ordinary rate of return for an online questionnaire, especially given that there was no incentive. The students were given statements to judge on a Likert scale from 1 to 5 (strongly disagree to strongly agree). We define "The students agreed with the following statement" to mean that the average and median scores were at least 4 and less than 10% of the students chose a score below 3. Dually, if the students disagreed with the statement with median and average score that was at most 2 and less than 10% having a score greater than 3, we say that they "agreed with the negation of the statement". For all statements that do not satisfy either of the criteria, we report mixed answers. The full survey results can be found in [5, Appendix C].

Usability. Regarding the usability of the tool, the students agreed with the following statements:

---

[2] https://github.com/AutomataDotNet/Automata.

- I quickly learned to use the AT.
- I do *not* need assistance to use the AT.
- I feel confident using the AT.
- The AT is easy to use.
- I enjoy using the AT/the AT is fun to use.

However, there were lots of valuable suggestions for improvements, many of which we have implemented since then. Moreover, the survey also revealed space for improvement, in particular for streamlining as documented by the following statements where the answers were more mixed:

- The AT is unnecessarily complex.
- The canvas for drawing is intuitive.
- The use of AT is self-explanatory.

Usefulness. Regarding how useful AT was for learning, the students agreed with the following statements:

- I understand more after using the AT.
- I prefer using the AT to using pen and paper exercises (12.9% disagreed, but median and average are 4).
- The feedback of the AT was helpful and instructive.
- The exercises within the AT are well-designed.
- The AT fits in well with the programming tasks and written homework.
- The AT did *not* hinder my learning.
- I feel better prepared for the exam after using AT.
- The feedback of the AT was *not* misleading/confusing.

Note that there are no statements with mixed or negative answers regarding the usefulness. Additionally, as shown in Fig. 5, when we asked students about their preferred means of learning, AT gets the highest approval rate, being preferred to written or programming exercises as well as lectures.

What are your preferred means of learning?
(Multiple answers possible.)

		n=139
Lecture		30.2%
Written exercises		67.6%
Programming		56.8%
Automata Tutor Tool		76.3%
Individual learning (via script, book, or videostream)		56.8%
Group discussion/ learning group		32.4%

Fig. 5. Question from the survey we conducted to evaluate Automata Tutor, showing that the tool is preferred by a majority of students.

Overall, this class deployment of Automata Tutor v3 and the accompanying surveys were great successes, and showed how the tool is of extreme value for both students and teachers, in particular for such large a course.

6 Conclusion

This paper presents the third version of Automata Tutor, an online tool helping teachers and students in large automata/computation theory courses. Automata Tutor v3 now supports automated grading and feedback generation for a wide variety of problems and, for some of them, even automatic generation of new problem instances. Furthermore, it is easy to extend and we invite the community to contribute by implementing further exercises. Finally, our experience shows that Automata Tutor v3 improves the economical aspects of teaching greatly as it scales effortlessly with the number of students.

Earlier versions of Automata Tutor have already been adopted by thousands of students at dozens of schools and we hope this paper allows Automata Tutor v3 to help even more students and teachers around the world.

References

1. Gradiance online accelerated learning. http://www.newgradiance.com/
2. Ahmed, U.Z., Gulwani, S., Karkare, A.: Automatically generating problems and solutions for natural deduction. In: IJCAI 2013, Proceedings of the 23rd International Joint Conference on Artificial Intelligence, 3–9 August 2013, Beijing, China (2013)
3. Alur, R., D'Antoni, L., Gulwani, S., Kini, D., Viswanathan, M.: Automated grading of DFA constructions. In: Proceedings of the Twenty-Third International Joint Conference on Artificial Intelligence, IJCAI 2013, pp. 1976–1982. AAAI Press (2013)
4. Brooke, J., et al.: Sus-a quick and dirty usability scale. In: Jordan, P.W., Thomas, B., McClelland, I.L., Weerdmeester, B. (eds.) Usability Evaluation in Industry, vol. 189(194), pp. 4–7. CRC Press, Ohio (1996)
5. D'Antoni, L., Helfrich, M., Kretinsky, J., Ramneantu, E., Weininger, M.: Automata tutor v3. CoRR, abs/2005.01419 (2020)
6. D'antoni, L., Kini, D., Alur, R., Gulwani, S., Viswanathan, M., Hartmann, B.: How can automatic feedback help students construct automata? ACM Trans. Comput. Hum. Interact. 22(2), 1–24 (2015)
7. D' Antoni, L., Weavery, M., Weinert, A., Alur, R.: Automata tutor and what we learned from building an online teaching tool. Bull. EATCS, 3(117), 144–158 (2015)
8. National Research Council: How People Learn: Brain, Mind, Experience, and School: Expanded Edition. The National Academies Press, Washington, D.C (2000)
9. Gulwani, S., Korthikanti, V.A., Tiwari, A.: Synthesizing geometry constructions. SIGPLAN Not. 46(6), 50–61 (2011)
10. Hopcroft, J.E., Motwani, R., Ullman, J.D.: Introduction to Automata Theory, Languages, and Computation, 3rd edn. Addison-Wesley, Boston (2007)
11. Itzhaky, S., Gulwani, S., Immerman, N., Sagiv, M.: Solving geometry problems using a combination of symbolic and numerical reasoning. In: McMillan, K., Middeldorp, A., Voronkov, A. (eds.) LPAR 2013. LNCS, vol. 8312, pp. 457–472. Springer, Heidelberg (2013). https://doi.org/10.1007/978-3-642-45221-5_31
12. Patterson, D.: Why are English majors studying computer science? November 2013

13. Rahn, M., Waldmann, J.: The leipzig autotool system for grading student homework. Functional and Declarative Programming in Education (FDPE) (2002)
14. Shekhar, V.S., Agarwalla, A., Agarwal, A., Nitish, B., Kumar, V.: Enhancing JFLAP with automata construction problems and automated feedback. In: Parashar, M., et al. (ed.) Seventh International Conference on Contemporary Computing, IC3 2014, Noida, India, 7–9 August 2014, pp. 19–23. IEEE Computer Society (2014)
15. Shenoy, V., Aparanji, U., Sripradha, K., Kumar, V.: Generating DFA construction problems automatically. In: 2016 International Conference on Learning and Teaching in Computing and Engineering, LaTICE, pp. 32–37. IEEE (2016)
16. Singh, R., Gulwani, S., Rajamani, S.K.: Automatically generating algebra problems. In: Proceedings of the Twenty-Sixth AAAI Conference on Artificial Intelligence, 22–26 July 2012 Toronto, Ontario, Canada (2012)
17. Singh, R., Gulwani, S., Solar-Lezama, A.: Automated feedback generation for introductory programming assignments. In: Proceedings of PLDI 2013, New York, NY, USA, pp. 15–26. ACM (2013)
18. Weinert, A.: Problem generation for DFA construction (2014). https://alexanderweinert.net/papers/2014dfageneration.pdf. Accessed 04 May 2020

Seminator 2 Can Complement Generalized Büchi Automata via Improved Semi-determinization

František Blahoudek[1], Alexandre Duret-Lutz[2(✉)], and Jan Strejček[3]

[1] University of Texas at Austin, Austin, USA
frantisek.blahoudek@gmail.com
[2] LRDE, EPITA, Le Kremlin-Bicêtre, France
adl@lrde.epita.fr
[3] Masaryk University, Brno, Czech Republic
strejcek@fi.muni.cz

Abstract. We present the second generation of the tool Seminator that transforms transition-based generalized Büchi automata (TGBAs) into equivalent semi-deterministic automata. The tool has been extended with numerous optimizations and produces considerably smaller automata than its first version. In connection with the state-of-the-art LTL to TGBAs translator Spot, Seminator 2 produces smaller (on average) semi-deterministic automata than the direct LTL to semi-deterministic automata translator ltl2ldgba of the Owl library. Further, Seminator 2 has been extended with an improved NCSB complementation procedure for semi-deterministic automata, providing a new way to complement automata that is competitive with state-of-the-art complementation tools.

1 Introduction

Semi-deterministic [24] automata are automata where each accepting run makes only finitely many nondeterministic choices. The merit of this interstage between deterministic and nondeterministic automata comes from two facts known since the late 1980s. First, every nondeterministic Büchi automaton with n states can be transformed into an equivalent semi-deterministic Büchi automaton with at most 4^n states [7,24]. Note that asymptotically optimal determinization procedures transform nondeterministic Büchi automata to deterministic automata with $2^{\mathcal{O}(n \log n)}$ states [24] and with a more complex (typically Rabin) acceptance condition, as deterministic Büchi automata are strictly less expressive. Second, some algorithms cannot handle nondeterministic automata, but they can handle semi-deterministic ones; for example, algorithms for qualitative model checking of *Markov decision processes* (MDPs) [7,29].

For theoreticians, the difference between the complexity of determinization and semi-determinization is not dramatic—both constructions are exponential. However, the difference is important for authors and users of practical automata-based tools—automata size and the complexity of their acceptance condition often have a significant impact on tool performance. This latter perspective has recently

© The Author(s) 2020
S. K. Lahiri and C. Wang (Eds.): CAV 2020, LNCS 12225, pp. 15–27, 2020.
https://doi.org/10.1007/978-3-030-53291-8_2

initiated another wave of research on semi-deterministic automata. Since 2015, many new results have been published: several direct translations of LTL to semi-deterministic automata [11,15,16,26], specialized complementation constructions for semi-deterministic automata [4,6], algorithms for quantitative model checking of MDPs based on semi-deterministic automata [13,25], a transformation of semi-deterministic automata to deterministic parity automata [10], and reinforcement learning of control policy using semi-deterministic automata [21].

In 2017, we introduced Seminator 1.1 [5], a tool that transforms nondeterministic automata to semi-deterministic ones. The original semi-determinization procedure of Courcoubetis and Yannakakis [7] works with standard *Büchi automata* (BAs). Seminator 1.1 extends this construction to handle more compact automata, namely *transition-based Büchi automata* (TBAs) and *transition-based generalized Büchi automata* (TGBAs). TBAs use accepting transitions instead of accepting states, and TGBAs have several sets of accepting transitions, each of these sets must be visited infinitely often by accepting runs. The main novelty of Seminator 1.1 was that it performed degeneralization and semi-determinization of a TGBA simultaneously. As a result, it could translate TGBAs to smaller semi-deterministic automata than (to our best knowledge) the only other tool for automata semi-determinization called nba2ldba [26]. This tool only accepts BAs as input, and thus TGBAs must be degeneralized before nba2ldba is called.

Moreover, in connection with the LTL to TGBAs translator ltl2tgba of Spot [8], Seminator 1.1 provided a translation of LTL to semi-deterministic automata that can compete with the direct LTL to semi-deterministic TGBAs translator ltl2ldba [26]. More precisely, our experiments [5] showed that the combination of ltl2tgba and Seminator 1.1 outperforms ltl2ldba on LTL formulas that ltl2tgba translates directly to deterministic or semi-deterministic TGBA (i.e., when Seminator has no work to do), while ltl2ldba produced (on average) smaller semi-deterministic TGBAs on the remaining LTL formulas (i.e., when the TGBA produced by ltl2tgba has to be semi-determinized by Seminator).

This paper presents Seminator 2, which changes the situation. With many improvements in semi-determinization, the combination of ltl2tgba and Seminator 2 now translates LTL to smaller (on average) semi-deterministic TGBAs than ltl2ldba even for the cases when ltl2tgba produces a TGBA that is not semi-deterministic. Moreover, this holds even when we compare to ltl2ldgba, which is the current successor of ltl2ldba distributed with Owl [19].

Further, Seminator 2 now provides a new feature: *complementation of TGBAs*. Seminator 2 chains semi-determinization with the complementation algorithm called NCSB [4,6], which is tailored for semi-deterministic BAs. Our experiments show that the complementation in Seminator 2 is fully competitive with complementations implemented in state-of-the-art tools [1,8,20,23,30].

2   Improvements in Semi-determinization

First of all, we recall the definition of semi-deterministic automata and principles of the semi-determinization procedure implemented in Seminator 1.1 [5].

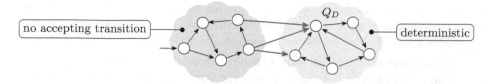

Fig. 1. Structure of a semi-deterministic automaton. The deterministic part contains all accepting transitions and states reachable from them. Cut-transitions are magenta.

Let $\mathcal{A} = (Q, \Sigma, \delta, q_0, \{F_1, \ldots, F_n\})$ be a TGBA over alphabet Σ, with a finite set of states Q, a transition relation $\delta \subseteq Q \times \Sigma \times Q$, an initial state $q_0 \in Q$, and sets of accepting transitions $F_1, \ldots, F_n \subseteq \delta$. Then $\mathcal{A}$ is *semi-deterministic* if there exists a subset $Q_D \subseteq Q$ such that (i) each transition from Q_D goes back to Q_D (i.e., $\delta \cap (Q_D \times \Sigma \times (Q \setminus Q_D)) = \emptyset$), (ii) all states of Q_D are deterministic (i.e., for each $q \in Q_D$ and $a \in \Sigma$ there is at most one q' such that $(q, a, q') \in \delta$), and (iii) each accepting transition starts in a state of Q_D (i.e., $F_1, \ldots, F_n \subseteq Q_D \times \Sigma \times Q_D$).

The part of $\mathcal{A}$ delimited by states of Q_D is called *deterministic*, while the part formed by the remaining states $Q \setminus Q_D$ is called *nondeterministic*, although it could contain deterministic states too. The transitions leading from the nondeterministic part to the deterministic one are called *cut-transitions*. The structure of a semi-deterministic automaton is depicted in Fig. 1.

Intuitively, a TGBA $\mathcal{A}$ with a set of states Q and a single set of accepting transitions F can be transformed into a semi-deterministic TBA $\mathcal{B}$ as follows. First, we use a copy of $\mathcal{A}$ as the nondeterministic part of $\mathcal{B}$. The deterministic part of $\mathcal{B}$ has states of the form (M, N) such that $Q \supseteq M \supseteq N$ and $M \neq \emptyset$. Every accepting transition $(q, a, q') \in F$ induces a cut-transition $(q, a, (\{q'\}, \emptyset))$ of $\mathcal{B}$. The deterministic part is then constructed to track all runs of $\mathcal{A}$ from each such state q' using the powerset construction. More precisely, the first element of (M, N) tracks all runs while the second element tracks only the runs that passed some accepting transition of F. Each transition of the deterministic part, that would reach a state where $M = N$ (so-called *breakpoint*) is replaced with an accepting transition of $\mathcal{B}$ leading to state (M, N'), where N' tracks only the runs of $\mathcal{A}$ passing an accepting transition of F in the current step.

Seminator 1.1 extended this procedure to construct a semi-deterministic TBA even for a TGBA with multiple acceptance sets $F_1, \ldots, F_n$. States of the deterministic part are now triples (M, N, i), where $i \in \{0, \ldots, n-1\}$ is called *level* and it has a similar semantics as in degeneralization. Cut-transitions are induced by transitions of F_n and they lead to states of the form $(\{q'\}, \emptyset, 0)$. The level i says that N tracks runs that passed a transition of F_{i+1} since the last level change. When the deterministic part reaches a state (M, N, i) with $M = N$, we change the level to $i' = (i + 1) \bmod n$ and modify N to track only runs passing $F_{i'+1}$ in the current step. Transitions changing the level are accepting.

A precise description of these semi-determinization procedures and proofs of their correctness can be found in Blahoudek's dissertation [3]. Now we briefly explain the most important optimizations added in Seminator 2 (we work on a journal paper with their formal description). Each optimization can be enabled/disabled by the corresponding option. All of them are enabled by default.

--scc-aware approach identifies, for each cut-transition, the strongly connected component (SCC) of A that contains the target of the transition triggering the cut-transition. The sets M, N then track only runs staying in this SCC.

--reuse-deterministic treats in a specific way each deterministic SCC from which only deterministic SCCs are reachable in A: it (i) does not include them in the nondeterministic part, and (ii) copies them (and their successors) in the deterministic part as they are, including the original acceptance transitions. This optimization can result in a semi-deterministic TGBA with multiple acceptance sets on output.

--cut-always changes the policy *when* cut-transitions are created: they are now triggered by all transitions of A with the target state in an accepting SCC.

--powerset-on-cut applies the powerset construction when computing targets of cut-transitions. The target of a cut-transition leading from q is constructed in the same way as the successor of the hypothetical state $(\{q\}, \emptyset, 0)$ of the deterministic part.

--skip-levels is a variant of the level jumping trick from TGBA degeneralization [2]. Roughly speaking, a single transition in the deterministic part can change the level i directly to $i + j$ where $j \geq 1$ if all runs passed acceptance transitions from all the sets $F_{i+1}, \ldots, F_{i+j}$ in the current step.

--jump-to-bottommost makes sure that all cut-transitions leading to states with the same M component lead to the same state (M, N, i) for some N and i. It relies on the fact that each run takes only one cut-transition, and thus only the component M of the cut-transition's target state is important for determining the acceptance of the run. During the original construction, many states of the form (M, N', i') may appear in different SCCs. After the construction finishes, this optimization redirects each cut-transition leading to (M, N', i') to some state of the form (M, N, i) that belongs to the bottommost SCC (in a topological ordering of the SCCs) that contains such a state. This is inspired by a similar trick used by Křetínský et al. [18] in a different context.

--powerset-for-weak simplifies the construction for weak accepting SCCs (i.e., SCCs where all cycles are accepting) of A. For such SCCs it just applies the powerset construction (builds states of the form M instead of triples (M, N, i)) with all transitions accepting in the deterministic part.

Note that Seminator 1.1 can produce a semi-deterministic TGBA with multiple acceptance sets only when it gets a semi-deterministic TGBA as input. Seminator 2 produces such automata more often due to --reuse-deterministic.

3   Implementation and Usage

Seminator 2 is an almost complete rewrite of Seminator [5], and is still distributed under the GNU GPL 3.0 license. Its distribution tarball and source code history

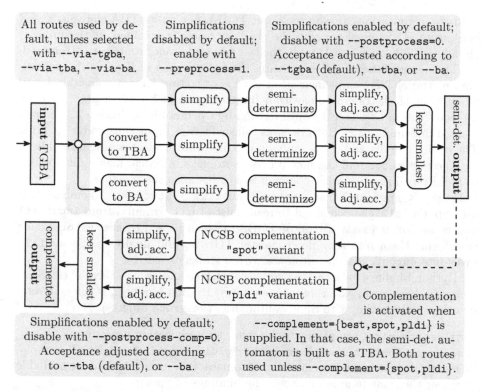

Fig. 2. Workflow for the two operation modes of `seminator`: semi-determinizing and complementing via semi-determinization.

are hosted on GitHub (https://github.com/mklokocka/seminator). The package contains sources of the tool with two user-interfaces (a command-line tool and Python bindings), a test-suite, and some documentation.

Seminator is implemented in C++ on top of the data-structures provided by the Spot library [8], and reuses its input/output functions, simplification algorithms, and the NCSB complementation. The main implementation effort lies in the optimized semi-determinization and an alternative version of NCSB.

The first user interface is a command-line tool called `seminator`. Its high-level workflow is pictured in Fig. 2. By default (top-part of Fig. 2) it takes a TGBA (or TBA or BA) on input and produces a semi-deterministic TGBA (or TBA or BA if requested). Figure 2 details various switches that control the optional simplifications and acceptance transformations that occur before the semi-determinization itself. The pre- and post-processing are provided by the Spot library. The semi-determinization algorithm can be adjusted by additional command-line options (not shown in Fig. 2) that enable or disable optimizations of Sect. 2. As Spot simplification routines are stronger on automata with simpler acceptance conditions, it sometimes pays off to convert the automaton to TBA or BA first. If the input is a TGBA, `seminator` attempts three semi-determinizations, one on the input TGBA, one on its TBA equivalent, and one on its BA equivalent; only the smallest result is retained. If the input is already a TBA (resp. a BA), only the last two (resp. one) routes are attempted.

The `--complement` option activates the bottom part of Fig. 2 with two variants of the NCSB complementation [4]: `"spot"` stands for a transition-based adaptation of the original algorithm (implemented in Spot); `"pldi"` refers to its modification based on the optimization by Chen et al. [6, Section 5.3] (implemented in Seminator 2). Both variants take a TBA as input and produce a TBA. The options `--tba` and `--ba` apply on the final complement automaton only.

The `seminator` tool can now process automata in batch, making it possible to build pipelines with other commands. For instance the pipeline

`ltl2tgba <input.ltl | seminator | autfilt --states=3.. >output.hoa`

uses Spot's `ltl2tgba` command to read a list of LTL formulas from `input.ltl` and transform it into a stream of TGBAs that is passed to `seminator`, which transforms them into semi-deterministic TGBAs, and finally Spot's `autfilt` saves into `output.hoa` the automata with 3 states or more.

Python bindings form the second user-interface and are installed by the Seminator package as an extension of Spot's own Python bindings. It offers several functions, all working with Spot's automata (`twa_graph` objects):

`semi_determinize()` implements the semi-determinization procedure;

`complement_semidet()` implements the `"pldi"` variant of the NCSB complementation for semi-deterministic automata (the other variant is available under the same function name in the bindings of Spot);

`highlight_components()` and `highlight_cut()` provide ways to highlight the nondeterministic and the deterministic parts of a semi-deterministic automaton, and its cut-transitions;

`seminator()` provides an interface similar to the command-line `seminator` tool with options that selectively enable or disable optimizations or trigger complementation.

The Python bindings integrate well with the interactive notebooks of Jupyter [17]. Figure 3 shows an example of such a notebook, using the `seminator()` and `highlight_components()` functions. Additional Jupyter notebooks, distributed with the tool, document the effect of the various optimization options.[1]

4 Experimental Evaluation

We evaluate the performance of Seminator 2 for both semi-determinization and complementation of TGBAs. We compare our tool against several tools listed in Table 1. As `ltl2ldgba` needs LTL on input, we used the set of 221 LTL formulas already considered for benchmarking in the literature [9,12,14,22,27]. To provide TGBAs as input for Seminator 2, we use Spot's `ltl2tgba` to convert the LTL formulas. Based on the automata produced by `ltl2tgba`, we distinguish three

---

[1] https://nbviewer.jupyter.org/github/mklokocka/seminator/tree/v2.0/notebooks/.

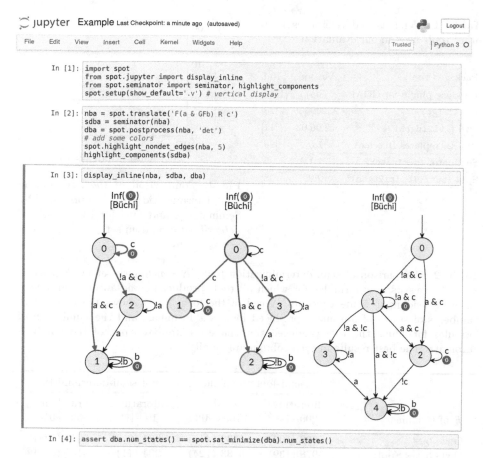

Fig. 3. Jupyter notebook illustrating a case where a nondeterministic TBA (**nba**, left) has an equivalent semi-deterministic TBA (**sdba**, middle) that is smaller than a minimal deterministic TBA (**dba**, right). Accepting transitions are labeled by ⓪.

categories of formulas: *deterministic* (152 formulas), *semi-deterministic* but not deterministic (49 formulas), and *not semi-deterministic* (20 formulas). This division is motivated by the fact that Seminator 2 applies its semi-determinization only on automata that are not semi-deterministic, and that some complementation tools use different approaches to deterministic automata. We have also generated 500 random LTL formulas of each category.

The scripts and formulas used in those experiments can be found online,[2] as well as a Docker image with these scripts and all the tools installed.[3] All experiments were run inside the supplied Docker image on a laptop Dell XPS13 with Intel i7-1065G7, 16 GB RAM, and running Linux.

---

[2] https://github.com/xblahoud/seminator-evaluation/.

[3] https://hub.docker.com/r/gadl/seminator.

Table 1. Versions and references to the other tools used in our evaluation.

Package (Tool)	Version	Ref.
Fribourg plugin for GOAL	(na)	[1,30]
GOAL (gc)	20200506	[28]
Owl (ltl2ldgba)	19.06.03	[11]
ROLL (replaces Buechic)	1.0	[20]
Seminator (seminator)	1.1	[5]
Spot (autfilt, ltl2tgba)	2.9	[8]

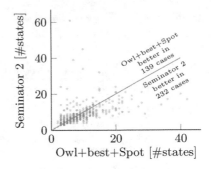

Fig. 4. Comparison of the sizes of the semi-deterministic automata produced by Seminator 2 and Owl for the *not semi-deterministic* random set.

Table 2. Comparison of semi-determinization tools. A benchmark set marked with $x + y$ ⏱ consists of x formulas for which all tools produced some automaton, and y formulas leading to some timeouts. A cell of the form $s\,(m)$ shows the cumulative number s of states of automata produced for the x formulas, and the number m of formulas for which the tool produced the smallest automaton out of the obtained automata. The best results in each column are highlighted.

# of formulas	(semi-)deterministic		not semi-deterministic	
	literature 200+1⏱	random 1000+0⏱	literature 19+1⏱	random 500+0⏱
Owl+best	1092 (102)	6335 (454)	281 (6)	5041 (144)
Owl+best+Spot	978 (139)	5533 (724)	234 (11)	4153 (268)
Seminator 1.1	787 (201)	4947 (963)	297 (7)	7020 (60)
Seminator 2	787 (201)	4947 (963)	230 (16)	3956 (356)

4.1 Semi-determinization

We compare Seminator 2 to its older version 1.1 and to ltl2ldgba of Owl. We do not include Buchifier [16] as it is available only as a binary for Windows. Also, we did not include nba2ldba [26] due to the lack of space and the fact that even Seminator 1.1 performs significantly better than nba2ldba [5].

Recall that Seminator 2 calls Spot's automata simplification routines on constructed automata. To get a fair comparison, we apply these routines also to the results of other tools, indicated by *+Spot* in the results. Further, ltl2ldgba of Owl can operate in two modes: --symmetric and --asymmetric. For each formula, we run both settings and pick the better result, indicated by *+best*.

Table 2 presents the cumulative results for each semi-determinization tool and each benchmark set (we actually merged *deterministic* and *semi-deterministic* benchmark sets). The timeout of 30 s was reached by Owl for one formula in

Table 3. Comparison of tools complementing Büchi automata, using the same conventions as Table 2.

# of formulas	deterministic		semi-detereministic		not semi-deterministic	
	literature 147+5🕕	random 500+0🕕	literature 47+2🕕	random 499+1🕕	literature 15+5🕕	random 486+14🕕
ROLL+Spot	1388 (0)	3687 (0)	833 (0)	5681 (4)	272 (0)	6225 (58)
Fribourg+Spot	627 (137)	2493 (464)	290 (26)	3294 (258)	142 (14)	5278 (238)
GOAL+Spot	617 (143)	2490 (477)	277 (28)	3676 (125)	206 (5)	7713 (96)
Spot	611 (150)	2477 (489)	190 (40)	2829 (354)	181 (9)	5310 (202)
Seminator 2	622 (142)	2511 (465)	210 (37)	2781 (420)	169 (8)	4919 (277)

the *(semi-)deterministic* category and by Seminator 1.1 for one formula in the *not semi-deterministic* category. Besides timeouts, the running times of all tools were always below 3 s, with a few exceptions for Seminator 1.1.

In the *(semi-)deterministic* category, the automaton produced by `ltl2tgba` and passed to both versions of Seminator is already semi-deterministic. Hence, both versions of Seminator have nothing to do. This category, in fact, compares `ltl2tgba` of Spot against `ltl2ldgba` of Owl.

Figure 4 shows the distribution of differences between semi-deterministic automata produced by Owl+best+Spot and Seminator 2 for the *not semi-deterministic* random set. A dot at coordinates (x, y) represents a formula for which Owl and Seminator 2 produced automata with x and y states, respectively.

We can observe a huge improvement brought by Seminator 2 in *not semi-deterministic* benchmarks: while in 2017 Seminator 1.1 produced a smaller automaton than Owl in only few cases in this category [5], Seminator 2 is now more than competitive despite the fact that also Owl was improved over the time.

4.2 Complementation

We compare Seminator 2 with the complementation of ROLL based on automata learning (formerly presented as Buechic), the determinization-based algorithm [23] implemented in GOAL, the asymptotically optimal Fribourg complementation implemented as a plugin for GOAL, and with Spot (`autfilt --complement`). We apply the simplifications from Spot to all results and we use Spot's `ltl2tgba` to create the input Büchi automata for all tools, using transition-based generalized acceptance or state-based acceptance as appropriate (only Seminator 2 and Spot can complement transition-based generalized Büchi automata). The timeout of 120 s was reached once by both Seminator 2 and Spot, 6 times by Fribourg, and 13 times by GOAL and ROLL.

Table 3 shows results for complementation in the same way as Table 2 does for semi-determinization. For the *deterministic* benchmark, we can see quite

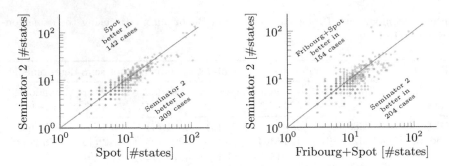

Fig. 5. Comparison of Seminator 2 against Spot and Fribourg+Spot in terms of the sizes (i.e., number of states) of complement automata produced for the *not semi-deterministic* random benchmark. Note that axes are logarithmic.

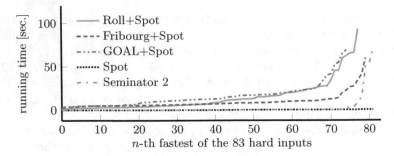

Fig. 6. Running times of complementation tools on the 83 hard cases of the *not semi-deterministic* random benchmark. The running times of each tool on these cases are sorted increasingly before being plotted.

similar results from all tools but ROLL. This is caused by the fact that complementation of deterministic automata is easy. Some tools (including Spot) even apply a dedicated complementation procedure. It comes at no surprise that the specialized algorithm of Seminator 2 performs better than most other complementations in the *semi-deterministic* category. Interestingly, this carries over to the *not semi-deterministic* category. The results demonstrate that the 2-step approach of Seminator 2 to complementation performs well in practice. Figure 5 offers more detailed insight into distribution of automata sizes created by Seminator 2, Spot, and Fribourg+Spot for random benchmarks in this category.

Finally, Fig. 6 compares the running times of these tools over the 83 hard cases of *not semi-deterministic* random benchmark (a case is *hard* if at least one tool did not finish in 10 s). We can see that Seminator 2 and Spot run significantly faster than the other tools.

5   Conclusion

We have presented Seminator 2, which is a substantially improved version of Seminator 1.1. The tool now offers a competitive complementation of TGBA. Furthermore, the semi-determinization code was rewritten and offers new optimizations that significantly reduce the size of produced automata. Finally, new user-interfaces enable convenient processing of large automata sets thanks to the support of pipelines and batch processing, and versatile applicability in education and research thanks to the integration with Spot's Python bindings.

Acknowledgment. F. Blahoudek has been supported by the DARPA grant D19AP00004 and by the F.R.S.-FNRS grant F.4520.18 (ManySynth). J. Strejček has been supported by the Czech Science Foundation grant GA19-24397S.

References

1. Allred, J.D., Ultes-Nitsche, U.: A simple and optimal complementation algorithm for Büchi automata. In: LICS 2018, pp. 46–55. ACM (2018)
2. Babiak, T., Badie, T., Duret-Lutz, A., Křetínský, M., Strejček, J.: Compositional approach to suspension and other improvements to LTL translation. In: Bartocci, E., Ramakrishnan, C.R. (eds.) SPIN 2013. LNCS, vol. 7976, pp. 81–98. Springer, Heidelberg (2013). https://doi.org/10.1007/978-3-642-39176-7_6
3. Blahoudek, F.: Automata for formal methods: little steps towards perfection. PhD thesis, Masaryk University, Brno, Czech Republic (2018)
4. Blahoudek, F., Heizmann, M., Schewe, S., Strejček, J., Tsai, M.-H.: Complementing semi-deterministic Büchi automata. In: Chechik, M., Raskin, J.-F. (eds.) TACAS 2016. LNCS, vol. 9636, pp. 770–787. Springer, Heidelberg (2016). https://doi.org/10.1007/978-3-662-49674-9_49
5. Blahoudek, F., Duret-Lutz, A., Klokočka, M., Křetínský, M., Streček, J.: Seminator: a tool for semi-determinization of omega-automata. In: LPAR 2017, vol. 46 of EPiC Series in Computing, pp. 356–367. EasyChair (2017). https://easychair.org/publications/paper/340360
6. Chen, Y.-F., Heizmann, M., Lengál, O., Li, Y., Tsai, M.-H., Turrini, A., Zhang, L.: Advanced automata-based algorithms for program termination checking. In: PLDI 2018, pp. 135–150 (2018)
7. Courcoubetis, C., Yannakakis, M.: Verifying temporal properties of finite-state probabilistic programs. In: FOCS 1988, pp. 338–345. IEEE Computer Society (1988)
8. Duret-Lutz, A., Lewkowicz, A., Fauchille, A., Michaud, T., Renault, É., Xu, L.: Spot 2.0 — a framework for LTL and ω-automata manipulation. In: Artho, C., Legay, A., Peled, D. (eds.) ATVA 2016. LNCS, vol. 9938, pp. 122–129. Springer, Cham (2016). https://doi.org/10.1007/978-3-319-46520-3_8
9. Dwyer, M.B., Avrunin, G.S., Corbett, J.C.: Property specification patterns for finite-state verification. In: FMSP 1998, pp. 7–15. ACM (1998)
10. Esparza, J., Křetínský, J., Raskin, J.-F., Sickert, S.: From LTL and limit-deterministic Büchi automata to deterministic parity automata. In: Legay, A., Margaria, T. (eds.) TACAS 2017. LNCS, vol. 10205, pp. 426–442. Springer, Heidelberg (2017). https://doi.org/10.1007/978-3-662-54577-5_25

11. Esparza, J., Křetínský, J., Sickert, S.: One theorem to rule them all: a unified translation of LTL into ω-automata. In: LICS 2018, pp. 384–393. ACM (2018)
12. Etessami, K., Holzmann, G.J.: Optimizing Büchi automata. In: Palamidessi, C. (ed.) CONCUR 2000. LNCS, vol. 1877, pp. 153–168. Springer, Heidelberg (2000). https://doi.org/10.1007/3-540-44618-4_13
13. Hahn, E.M., Li, G., Schewe, S., Turrini, A., Zhang, L.: Lazy probabilistic model checking without determinisation. In: CONCUR 2015, vol. 42 of LIPIcs, pp. 354–367. Schloss Dagstuhl - Leibniz-Zentrum für Informatik (2015)
14. Holeček, J., Kratochvíla, T., Řehák, V., Šafránek, D., Šimeček, P.: Verification results in Liberouter project. Technical Report 03, p. 32 CESNET, 9 (2004)
15. Kini, D., Viswanathan, M.: Limit Deterministic and Probabilistic Automata for LTL\ GU. In: Baier, Christel, Tinelli, Cesare (eds.) TACAS 2015. LNCS, vol. 9035, pp. 628–642. Springer, Heidelberg (2015). https://doi.org/10.1007/978-3-662-46681-0_57
16. Kini, D., Viswanathan, M.: Optimal translation of LTL to limit deterministic automata. In: Legay, A., Margaria, T. (eds.) TACAS 2017. LNCS, vol. 10206, pp. 113–129. Springer, Heidelberg (2017). https://doi.org/10.1007/978-3-662-54580-5_7
17. Kluyver, T., et al.: Jupyter notebooks – a publishing format for reproducible computational workflows. In: ELPUB 2016, pp. 87–90. IOS Press (2016)
18. Křetínský, J., Meggendorfer, T., Waldmann, C., Weininger, M.: Index appearance record for transforming rabin automata into parity automata. In: Legay, A., Margaria, T. (eds.) TACAS 2017. LNCS, vol. 10205, pp. 443–460. Springer, Heidelberg (2017). https://doi.org/10.1007/978-3-662-54577-5_26
19. Křetínský, J., Meggendorfer, T., Sickert, S.: Owl: a library for ω-Words, automata, and LTL. In: Lahiri, S.K., Wang, C. (eds.) ATVA 2018. LNCS, vol. 11138, pp. 543–550. Springer, Cham (2018). https://doi.org/10.1007/978-3-030-01090-4_34
20. Li, Y., Turrini, A., Zhang, L., Schewe, S.: Learning to complement Büchi automata. VMCAI 2018. LNCS, vol. 10747, pp. 313–335. Springer, Cham (2018). https://doi.org/10.1007/978-3-319-73721-8_15
21. Oura, R., Sakakibara, A., Ushio, T.: Reinforcement learning of control policy for linear temporal logic specifications using limit-deterministic Büchi automata. CoRR, abs/2001.04669 (2020)
22. Pelánek, R.: BEEM: benchmarks for explicit model checkers. In: Bošnački, D., Edelkamp, S. (eds.) SPIN 2007. LNCS, vol. 4595, pp. 263–267. Springer, Heidelberg (2007). https://doi.org/10.1007/978-3-540-73370-6_17
23. Piterman, N.: From nondeterministic Büchi and Streett automata to deterministic parity automata. In: LICS 2006, pp. 255–264. IEEE Computer Society (2006)
24. Safra, S.: On the complexity of omega-automata. In: FOCS 1988, pp. 319–327. IEEE Computer Society (1988)
25. Sickert, S., Křetínský, J.: MoChiBA: probabilistic LTL model checking using limit-deterministic Büchi automata. In: Artho, C., Legay, A., Peled, D. (eds.) ATVA 2016. LNCS, vol. 9938, pp. 130–137. Springer, Cham (2016). https://doi.org/10.1007/978-3-319-46520-3_9
26. Sickert, S., Esparza, J., Jaax, S., Křetínský, J.: Limit-deterministic Büchi automata for linear temporal logic. In: Chaudhuri, S., Farzan, A. (eds.) CAV 2016. LNCS, vol. 9780, pp. 312–332. Springer, Cham (2016). https://doi.org/10.1007/978-3-319-41540-6_17
27. Somenzi, F., Bloem, R.: Efficient Büchi automata from LTL formulae. In: Emerson, E.A., Sistla, A.P. (eds.) CAV 2000. LNCS, vol. 1855, pp. 248–263. Springer, Heidelberg (2000). https://doi.org/10.1007/10722167_21

28. Tsai, M.-H., Tsay, Y.-K., Hwang, Y.-S.: GOAL for games, omega-automata, and logics. In: Sharygina, N., Veith, H. (eds.) CAV 2013. LNCS, vol. 8044, pp. 883–889. Springer, Heidelberg (2013). https://doi.org/10.1007/978-3-642-39799-8_62
29. Vardi, M.Y.: Automatic verification of probabilistic concurrent finite-state programs. In: FOCS 1985, pp. 327–338. IEEE Computer Society (1985)
30. Weibel, D.: Empirical performance investigation of a Büchi complementation construction. Master's thesis, University of Fribourg (2015)

RTLola Cleared for Take-Off: Monitoring Autonomous Aircraft

Jan Baumeister[1] , Bernd Finkbeiner[1] , Sebastian Schirmer[2],
Maximilian Schwenger[1(✉)] , and Christoph Torens[2]

[1] Department of Computer Science, Saarland University,
66123 Saarbrücken, Germany
{jbaumeister,finkbeiner,schwenger}@react.uni-saarland.de
[2] German Aerospace Center (DLR), 38108 Braunschweig, Germany
{sebastian.schirmer,christoph.torens}@dlr.de

Abstract. The autonomous control of unmanned aircraft is a highly safety-critical domain with great economic potential in a wide range of application areas, including logistics, agriculture, civil engineering, and disaster recovery. We report on the development of a dynamic monitoring framework for the DLR ARTIS (Autonomous Rotorcraft Testbed for Intelligent Systems) family of unmanned aircraft based on the formal specification language RTLola. RTLola is a stream-based specification language for real-time properties. An RTLola specification of hazardous situations and system failures is statically analyzed in terms of consistency and resource usage and then automatically translated into an FPGA-based monitor. Our approach leads to highly efficient, parallelized monitors with formal guarantees on the noninterference of the monitor with the normal operation of the autonomous system.

Keywords: Runtime verification · Stream monitoring · FPGA · Autonomous aircraft

1 Introduction

An unmanned aerial vehicle, commonly known as a drone, is an aircraft without a human pilot on board. While usually connected via radio transmissions to a base station on the ground, such aircraft are increasingly equipped with decision-making capabilities that allow them to autonomously carry out complex missions in applications such as transport, mapping and surveillance, or crop and irrigation monitoring. Despite the obvious safety-criticality of such systems, it is impossible to foresee all situations an autonomous aircraft might encounter and thus make a safety case purely by analyzing all of the potential behaviors in advance. A critical part of the safety engineering of a drone is therefore to carefully monitor the actual behavior during the flight, so that the health status of the system can be assessed and mitigation procedures (such as a return to the base station or an emergency landing) can be initiated when needed.

S. K. Lahiri and C. Wang (Eds.): CAV 2020, LNCS 12225, pp. 28–39, 2020.
https://doi.org/10.1007/978-3-030-53291-8_3

In this paper, we report on the development of a dynamic monitoring framework for the DLR ARTIS (Autonomous Rotorcraft Testbed for Intelligent Systems) family of aircraft based on the formal specification language RTLOLA. The development of a monitoring framework for an autonomous aircraft differs significantly from a monitoring framework in a more standard setting, such as network monitoring. A key consideration is that while the specification language needs to be highly *expressive*, the monitor must operate within strictly limited resources, and the monitor itself needs to be highly *reliable*: any interference with the normal operation of the aircraft could have fatal consequences.

A high level of expressiveness is necessary because the assessment of the health status requires complex analyses, including a cross-validation of different sensor modules such as the agreement between the GPS module and the accelerometer. This is necessary in order to discover a deterioration of a sensor module. At the same time, the expressiveness and the precision of the monitor must be balanced against the available computing resources. The reliability requirement goes beyond pure correctness and robustness of the execution. Most importantly, reliability requires that the peak resource consumption of the monitor in terms of energy, time, and space needs to be known ahead of time. This means that it must be possible to compute these resource requirements statically based on an analysis of the specification. The determination whether the drone is equipped with sufficient hardware can then be made before the flight, and the occurrence of dynamic failures such as running out of memory or sudden drops in voltage can be ruled out. Finally, the collection of the data from the on-board architecture is a non-trivial problem: While the monitor needs access to almost the complete system state, the data needs to be retrieved non-intrusively such that it does not interfere with the normal system operation.

Our monitoring approach is based on the formal stream specification language RTLOLA [11]. In an RTLOLA specification, input streams that collect data from sensors, networks, etc., are filtered and combined into output streams that contain data aggregated from multiple sources and over multiple points in time such as over sliding windows of some real-time length. Trigger conditions over these output streams then identify critical situations. An RTLOLA specification is translated into a monitor defined in a hardware description language and subsequently realized on an FPGA. Before deployment, the specification is checked for consistency and the minimal requirements on the FPGA are computed. The hardware monitor is then placed in a central position where as much sensor data as possible can be collected; during the execution, it then extracts the relevant information. In addition to requiring no physical changes to the system architecture, this integration incurs no further traffic on the bus.

Our experience has been extremely positive: Our approach leads to highly efficient, parallelized monitors with formal guarantees on the non-interference of the monitor with the normal operation of the autonomous system. The monitor is able to detect violations to complex specifications without intruding into the system execution, and operates within narrow resource constraints. RTLOLA is cleared for take-off.

1.1 Related Work

Stream-based monitoring approaches focus on an expressive specification language while handling non-binary data. Its roots lie in synchronous, declarative stream processing languages like Lustre [13] and Lola [9]. The *Copilot* framework [19] features a declarative data-flow language from which constant space and constant time C monitors are generated; these guarantees enable usage on an embedded device. Rather than focusing on data-flow, the family of Lola-languages puts an emphasis on statistical measures and has successfully been used to monitor synchronous, discrete time properties of autonomous aircraft [1,23]. In contrast to that, RTLOLA [12,22] supports real-time capabilities and efficient aggregation of data occurring with arbitrary frequency, while forgoing parametrization for efficiency [11]. RTLOLA can also be compiled to VHDL and subsequently realized on an FPGA [8].

Apart from stream-based monitoring, there is a rich body of monitoring based on real-time temporal logics [2,10,14–16,20] such as Signal Temporal Logic (STL) [17]. Such languages are a concise way to describe temporal behaviors with the shortcoming that they are usually limited to qualitative statements, i.e. boolean verdicts. This limitation was addressed for STL [10] by introducing a quantitative semantics indicating the robustness of a satisfaction. To specify continuous signal patterns, specification languages based on regular expressions can be beneficial, e.g. Signal Regular Expressions (SRE) [5]. The R2U2 tool [18] stands out in particular as it successfully brought a logic closely related to STL onto unmanned aerial systems as an external hardware implementation.

2 Setup

The Autonomous Rotorcraft Testbed for Intelligent Systems (ARTIS) is a platform used by the Institute of Flight Systems of the German Aerospace Center (DLR) to conduct research on autonomous flight. It consists of a set of unmanned helicopters and fixed-wing aircraft of different sizes which can be used to develop new techniques and evaluate them under real-world conditions.

The case study presented in this paper revolves around the superARTIS, a large helicopter with a maximum payload of 85 kg, depicted in Fig. 1. The high payload capabilities allow the aircraft to carry multiple sensor systems, computational resources, and data links. This extensive range of avionic equipment plays an important role in improving the situational awareness of the aircraft [3] during the flight. It facilitates safe autonomous research missions which include flying in urban or maritime areas, alone or with other aircraft. Before an actual flight test, software- and hardware-in-the-loop simulations, as well as real-time logfile replays strengthen confidence in the developed technology.

2.1 Mission

One field of application for unmanned aerial vehicles (UAVs) is reconnaissance missions. In such missions, the aircraft is expected to operate within a fixed area in which it can cause no harm. The polygonal boundary of this area is called a geo-fence. As soon as the vehicle passes the geo-fence, mitigation procedures need to be initiated to ensure that the aircraft does not stray further away from the safe area.

The case study presented in this paper features a reconnaissance mission. Figure 2 shows the flight path (blue line) within a geo-fence (red line). Evidently, the aircraft violates the fence several times temporarily. A reason for this can be flawed position estimation: An aircraft estimates its position based on several factors such as landmarks detected optically or GPS sensor readings. In the latter case, GPS satellites send position and time information to earth. The GPS module uses this data to compute the aircraft's absolute position with trilateration. However, signal reflection or a low number of GPS satellites in range can result in imprecisions in the position approximation. If the aircraft is continuously exposed to imprecise position updates, the error adds up and results in a strong deviation from the expected flight path.

The impact of this effect can be seen in Fig. 3. It shows the velocity of a ground-borne aircraft in an enclosed backyard according to its GPS module.[1] During the reported period of time, the aircraft was pushed across the backyard by hand. While the expected graph is a smooth curve, the actual measurements show an erratic curve with errors of up to $\pm 1.5\,\mathrm{ms}^{-1}$, which can be mainly attributed to signals being reflected on the enclosure. The strictly positive trend of the horizontal velocity can explain strong deviations from the desired flight path seen in Fig. 3.

A counter-measure to these imprecisions is the cross-validation of several redundant sensors. As an example, rather than just relying on the velocity reported by a GPS module, its measured velocity can be compared to the integrated output of an accelerometer. When the values deviate strongly, the values can be classified as less reliable than when both sensors agree.

2.2   Non-Intrusive Instrumentation

When integrating the monitor into an existing system, the system architecture usually cannot be altered drastically. Moreover, the monitor should not interfere with the regular execution of the system, e.g. by requiring the controller to send explicit messages to it. Such a requirement could offset the timing behavior and thus have a negative impact on the overall performance of the system.

The issue can be circumvented by placing the monitor at a point where it can access all data necessary for the monitoring process non-intrusively. In the case of the superARTIS, the logger interface provides such a place as it compiled the data of all position-related sensors as well as the output of the position estimation [3,4]. Figure 4 outlines the relevant data lines of the aircraft. Sensors were polled with fixed frequencies of up to 100 Hz. The schematic shows that the logger explicitly sends data to the monitor. This is not a strict requirement of

---

[1] GPS modules only provide absolute position information; the first derivative thereof, however, is the velocity.

Fig. 1. DLR's autonomous superAR-TIS equipped with optical navigation.

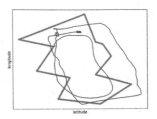

Fig. 2. Reconnaissance mission for a UAV. The thin blue line represents its trajectory, the thick red line a geofence.

the monitor as it could be connected to the data buses leading to the logger and passively read incoming data packets. However, in the present setting, the logger did not run at full capacity. Thus sending information to the monitor came at no relevant cost while requiring few hardware changes to the bus layout.

In turn, the monitor provides feedback regarding violations of the specification. Here, we distinguish between different timing behaviors of triggers. The monitor evaluates event-based triggers whenever the system passes new events to the monitor and immediately replies with the results. For periodic triggers, i.e. , those annotated with an evaluation frequency, the evaluation is decoupled from the communication between monitor and system. Thus, the monitor needs to wait until it receives another event until reporting the verdict. This incurs a short delay between detection and report.

2.3   StreamLAB

StreamLAB[2] [11] is a monitoring framework revolving around the stream-based specification language RTLola. It emphasizes on analyses conducted before deployment of the monitor. This increases the confidence in a successful execution by providing information to aid the specifier. To this end, it detects inconsistencies in the specification such as type errors, e.g. an lossy conversion of a floating point number to an integer, or timing errors, e.g. accessing values that might not exist. Further, it provides two execution modes: an interpreter and an FPGA compilation. The interpreter allows the specifier to validate their specification. For this, it requires a *trace*, i.e. a series of data that is expected to occur during an execution of the system. It then checks whether a trace complies with the specification and reports the points in time when specified bounds are violated. After successfully validating the specification, it can be compiled into VHDL code. Yet again, the compiled code can be analyzed with respect to the space and power consumption. This information allows for evaluating whether the available hardware suffices for running the RTLola monitor.

---

[2] www.stream-lab.eu.

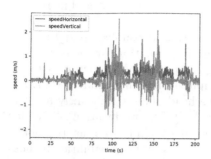

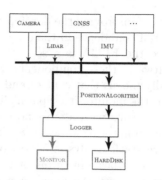

Fig. 3. Line plot of the horizontal and vertical speed calculated by a GPS receiver.

Fig. 4. Overview of data flow in system architecture.

An RTLOLA specification consists of input and output streams, as well as trigger conditions. *Input* streams describe data the system produces asynchronously and provides to the monitor. *Output* streams use this data to assess the health state of the system e.g. by computing statistical information. *Trigger* conditions distinguish desired and undesired behavior. A violation of the condition issues an alarm to the system.

The following specification declares a floating point input stream `height` representing sensor readings of an altimeter. The output stream `avg_height` computes the average value of the `height` stream over two minutes. The aggregation is a sliding window computed once per second, as indicated with the `@1Hz` annotation.[3] The stream δheight computes the difference between the average and the current height. A strong deviation of these values constitutes a suspicious jump in sensor readings, which might indicate a faulty sensor or an unexpected loss or gain in height. In this case, the trigger in the specification issues a warning to the system, which can initiate mitigation measures.

```
input height: Float32
output avg_height @1Hz := height.aggregate(over: 2min, using: avg)
output δheight := abs(avg_height.hold().defaults(to: height) - height)
trigger δheight > 50.0 "WARNING: Suspicious jump in height."
```

Note that this is just a brief introduction to RTLOLA and the STREAMLAB framework. For more details, the authors refer to [8,11,12,22].

2.4   FPGA as Monitoring Platform

An RTLOLA specification can be compiled into the hardware description language VHDL and subsequently realized on an FPGA as proposed by Baumeister et al. [8]. An FPGA as target platform for the monitor has several advantages

---

[3] Details on how such a computation can cope with a statically-bounded amount of memory can be found in [12,22].

in terms of improving the development process, reducing its cost, and increasing the overall confidence in the execution.

Since the FPGA is a separate module and thus decoupled from the control software, these components do not share processor time or memory. This especially means that control and monitoring computations happen in parallel. Further, the monitor itself parallelizes the computation of independent RTLOLA output streams with almost no additional overhead. This significantly accelerates the monitoring process [8]. The compiled VHDL specification allows for extensive static analyses. Most notably, the results include whether the board is sufficiently large in terms of look-up tables and storage capabilities to host the monitor, and the power consumption when idle or at peak performance. Lastly, an FPGA is the sweet spot between generality and specificity: it runs faster, is lighter, and consumes less energy than general purpose hardware while retaining a similar time-to-deployment. The latter combined with a drastically lower cost renders the FPGA superior to application-specific integrated circuits (ASIC) during development phase. After that, when the specification is fixed, an ASIC might be considered for its yet increased performance.

2.5   RTLola Specifications

The entire specification for the mission is comprised of three sub-specifications. This section briefly outlines each of them and explains representative properties in Fig. 5. The complete specifications as well as a detailed description were presented in earlier work [6, 21] and the technical report of this paper [7].

Sensor Validation. Sensors can produce incorrect values, e.g. when too few GPS satellites are in range for an accurate trilateration or if the aircraft flies above the range of a radio altimeter. A simple exemplary validation is to check whether the measured altitude is non-negative. If such a check fails, the values are meaningless, so the system should not take them into account in its computations.

Geo-Fence. During the mission, the aircraft has permission to fly inside a zone delimited by a polygon, called a geo-fence. The specification checks whether a face of the fence has been crossed, in which case the aircraft needs to ensure that it does not stray further from the permitted zone.

Sensor Cross-Validation. Sensor redundancy allows for validating a sensor reading by comparing it against readings of other sensors. An agreement between the values raises the confidence in their correctness. An example is the cross-validation of the GPS module against the accelerometer. Integrating the readings of the latter twice yields an absolute position which can be compared against the GPS position.

Figure 5 points out some representative sub-properties of the previously described specification in RTLOLA, which are too long to discuss them in detail. It contains a validation of GPS readings as well as a cross-validation of the GPS module against the Inertial Measurement Unit (IMU). The specification declares

```
input gps_x: Float16 // Absolute x positive from GPS module
input num_sat : UInt8 // Number of GPS satellites in range
input imu_acc_x: Float32 // Acceleration in x direction from IMU
// Check if the GPS module emitted few readings in the last 3s.
trigger @1Hz gps_x.aggregate(over: 3s, using: count) < 10
    "VIOLATION: Few GPS updates "
// 1 if there are few GPS Satellites in range, otherwise 0.
output few_sat: UInt8 := Int(num_sat < 9)
// Check if there rarely were enough GPS satellites in range.
trigger @1Hz few_sat.aggregate(over: 5s, using: Σ) > 12 "WARNING:
    Unreliable GPS data."
// Integrate acceleration twice to obtain absolute position.
output imu_vel_x@1Hz := imu_acc_x.aggregate(over: ∞, using: ∫)
output imu_x@1Hz := imu_vel_x.aggregate(over: ∞, using: ∫)
// Issue an alarm if readings from GPS and IMU disagree.
trigger abs(imu_x − gps_x) > 0.5 "VIOLATION: GPS and IMU readings
    deviate."
```

Fig. 5. An RTLOLA specification validating GPS sensor data and cross validating readings from the GPS module and IMU.

three input streams, the x-position and number of GPS satellites in range from the GPS module, and the acceleration in x-direction according to the IMU.

The first trigger counts the number of updates received from the GPS module by counting how often the input stream `gps_x` gets updated to validate the timing behavior of the module.

The output stream `few_sat` computes the indicator function for `num_sat < 9`, which indicates that the GPS module might report unreliable data due to few satellites in reach. If this happens more than 12 times within five seconds, the next trigger issues a warning to indicate that the incoming GPS values might be inaccurate. The last trigger checks whether the double integral of the IMU acceleration coincides with the GPS position up to a threshold of 0.5 m.

2.6   VHDL Synthesis

The specifications mentioned above were compiled into VHDL and realized on the Xilinx ZC702 Base Board[4]. The following table details the resource consumption of each sub-specification reported by the synthesis tool Vivado. The number of flip-flops (FF) indicates the memory consumption in bits; neither specification requires more than 600B of memory. The number of LUTs (Lookup Tables) is an indicator for the complexity of the logic. The sensor validation, despite being significantly longer than the cross-validation, requires the least

---

[4] https://www.xilinx.com/support/documentation/boards_and_kits/zc702_zvik/ug8 50-zc702-eval-bd.pdf.

Spec	FF	FF[%]	LUT	LUT[%]	MUX	Idle [mW]	Peak [W]
Geo-fence	2,853	3	26,181	71	4	149	1.871
Validation	4,792	5	34,630	67	104	156	2.085
Cross	3,441	4	23,261	46	99	150	1.911

amount of LUTs. The reason is that its computations are simple in comparison: Rather than computing sliding window aggregations or line intersections, it mainly consists of simple thresholding. The number of multiplexers (MUX) reflects this as well: Since thresholding requires comparisons, which translate to multiplexers, the validation requires twice as many of them. Lastly, the power consumption of the monitor is extremely low: When idle, neither specification requires more than 156mW and even under peak pressure, the power consumption does not exceed 2.1W. For comparison, a Raspberry Pi needs between 1.1W (Model 2B) and 2.7W (Model 4B) when idle and roughly twice as much under peak pressure, i.e., 2.1W and 6.4W, respectively.[5]

Note that the geo-fence specification checks for 12 intersections in parallel, one for each face of the fence (cf. Fig. 2). Adapting the number of faces allows for scaling the amount of FPGA resources required, as can be seen in Fig. 6a. The graph does not grow linearly because the realization problem of VHDL code onto an FPGA is a multi-dimensional optimization problem with several pareto-optimal solutions. Under default settings, the optimizer found a solution for four faces that required fewer LUTs than for three faces. At the same time, the worst negative slack time (WNST) of the four-face solution was lower than the WNST for the three-face solution as well (cf. Fig. 6b), indicating that the former performs worst in terms of running time.

3   Results

As the title of the paper suggests, the superARTIS with the RTLOLA monitor component is cleared to fly and a flight test is already scheduled. In the meantime, the monitor was validated on log files from past missions of the superARTIS replayed under realistic conditions. During a flight, the controller polls samples from sensors, estimates the current position, and sends the respective data to the logger and monitor. In the replay setting, the process remains the same except for one detail: Rather than receiving data from the actual sensors, the data sent to the controller is read from a past log file in the same frequency in which they were recorded. The timing and logging behavior is equivalent to a real execution. This especially means that the replayed data points will be recorded again in the same way. Control computations take place on a machine identical to the one on the actual aircraft. As a result, from the point of view of the monitor, the replay mode and the actual flight are indistinguishable. Note that the setup

---

[5] Information collected from https://www.pidramble.com/wiki/benchmarks/power-consumption in January, 2020.

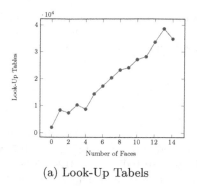

(a) Look-Up Tabels

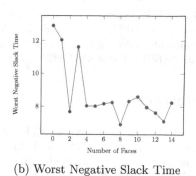

(b) Worst Negative Slack Time

Fig. 6. Result of the static analysis for different amounts of face of the geo-fence.

is open-loop, i.e. , the monitor cannot influence the running system. Therefore, the replay mode using real data is more realistic than a high-fidelity simulation.

When monitoring the geo-fence of the reconnaissance mission in Fig. 2, all twelve face crossings were detected successfully. Additionally, when replaying the sensor data of the experiment in the enclosed backyard from Sect. 2.1, the erratic GPS sensor data lead to 113 violations regarding the GPS module on its own. Note that many of these violations point to the same culprit: a low number of available GPS satellites, for example, correlates with the occurrence of peaks in the GPS velocity. Moreover, the cross validation issued another 36 alarms due to a divergence of IMU and GPS readings. Other checks, for example detecting a deterioration of the GPS module based on its output frequency, were not violated in either flight and thus not reported.

4 Conclusion

We have presented the integration of a hardware-based monitor into the super-ARTIS UAV. The distinguishing features of our approach are the high level of expressiveness of the RTLOLA specification language combined with the formal guarantees on the resource usage. The comprehensive tool framework facilitates the development of complex specifications, which can be validated on log data before they get translated into a hardware-based monitor. The automatic analysis of the specification derives the minimal requirements on the development board needed for safe operation. If they are met, the specification is realized on an FPGA and integrated into the superARTIS architecture. Our experience shows that the overall system works correctly and reliably, even without thorough system-level testing. This is due to the non-interfering instrumentation, the validated specification, and the formal guarantees on the absence of dynamic failures of the monitor.

Acknowledgments. This work was partially supported by the German Research Foundation (DFG) as part of the Collaborative Research Center Foundations of Perspicuous Software Systems (TRR 248, 389792660), and by the European Research Council (ERC) Grant OSARES (No. 683300).

References

1. Adolf, F.-M., Faymonville, P., Finkbeiner, B., Schirmer, S., Torens, C.: Stream runtime monitoring on UAS. In: Lahiri, S., Reger, G. (eds.) RV 2017. LNCS, vol. 10548, pp. 33–49. Springer, Cham (2017). https://doi.org/10.1007/978-3-319-67531-2_3
2. Alur, R., Henzinger, T.A.: Real-time logics: complexity and expressiveness. In: [1990] Proceedings Fifth Annual IEEE Symposium on Logic in Computer Science, pp. 390–401, June 1990. https://doi.org/10.1109/LICS.1990.113764
3. Ammann, N., Andert, F.: Visual navigation for autonomous, precise and safe landing on celestial bodies using unscented kalman filtering. In: 2017 IEEE Aerospace Conference, pp. 1–12, March 2017. https://doi.org/10.1109/AERO.2017.7943933
4. Andert, F., Ammann, N., Krause, S., Lorenz, S., Bratanov, D., Mejias, L.: Optical-aided aircraft navigation using decoupled visual SLAM with range sensor augmentation. J. Intell. Robot. Syst. **88**(2), 547–565 (2017). https://doi.org/10.1007/s10846-016-0457-6
5. Bakhirkin, A., Ferrère, T., Maler, O., Ulus, D.: On the quantitative semantics of regular expressions over real-valued signals. In: Abate, A., Geeraerts, G. (eds.) FORMATS 2017. LNCS, vol. 10419, pp. 189–206. Springer, Cham (2017). https://doi.org/10.1007/978-3-319-65765-3_11
6. Baumeister, J.: Tracing correctness: a practical approach to traceable runtime monitoring. Master thesis, Saarland University (2020)
7. Baumeister, J., Finkbeiner, B., Schirmer, S., Schwenger, M., Torens, C.: Rtlola cleared for take-off: Monitoring autonomous aircraft. CoRR abs/2004.06488 (2020). https://arxiv.org/abs/2004.06488
8. Baumeister, J., Finkbeiner, B., Schwenger, M., Torfah, H.: FPGA stream-monitoring of real-time properties. ACM Trans. Embedded Comput. Syst. **18**(5s), 88:1–88:24 (2019). https://doi.org/10.1145/3358220
9. D'Angelo, B., et al.: Lola: Runtime monitoring of synchronous systems. In: TIME 2005, pp. 166–174. IEEE Computer Society Press, June 2005
10. Donzé, A., Maler, O.: Robust satisfaction of temporal logic over real-valued signals. In: Chatterjee, K., Henzinger, T.A. (eds.) FORMATS 2010. LNCS, vol. 6246, pp. 92–106. Springer, Heidelberg (2010). https://doi.org/10.1007/978-3-642-15297-9_9
11. Faymonville, P., et al.: StreamLAB: stream-based monitoring of cyber-physical systems. In: Dillig, I., Tasiran, S. (eds.) CAV 2019. LNCS, vol. 11561, pp. 421–431. Springer, Cham (2019). https://doi.org/10.1007/978-3-030-25540-4_24
12. Faymonville, P., Finkbeiner, B., Schwenger, M., Torfah, H.: Real-time stream-based monitoring. CoRR abs/1711.03829 (2017). http://arxiv.org/abs/1711.03829
13. Halbwachs, N., Caspi, P., Raymond, P., Pilaud, D.: The synchronous dataflow programming language LUSTRE. In: Proceedings of the IEEE, pp. 1305–1320 (1991)
14. Harel, E., Lichtenstein, O., Pnueli, A.: Explicit clock temporal logic. In: LICS 1990, pp. 402–413. IEEE Computer Society (1990). https://doi.org/10.1109/LICS.1990.113765

15. Jahanian, F., Mok, A.K.L.: Safety analysis of timing properties in real-time systems. IEEE Trans. Softw. Eng. SE **12**(9), 890–904 (1986). https://doi.org/10.1109/TSE.1986.6313045

16. Koymans, R.: Specifying real-time properties with metric temporal logic. Real Time Syst. **2**(4), 255–299 (1990). https://doi.org/10.1007/BF01995674

17. Maler, O., Nickovic, D.: Monitoring properties of analog and mixed-signal circuits. STTT **15**(3), 247–268 (2013). https://doi.org/10.1007/s10009-012-0247-9

18. Moosbrugger, P., Rozier, K.Y., Schumann, J.: R2U2: monitoring and diagnosis of security threats for unmanned aerial systems. Formal Methods Syst. Des. **51**(1), 31–61 (2017). https://doi.org/10.1007/s10703-017-0275-x

19. Pike, L., Goodloe, A., Morisset, R., Niller, S.: Copilot: a hard real-time runtime monitor. In: Barringer, H., et al. (eds.) RV 2010. LNCS, vol. 6418, pp. 345–359. Springer, Heidelberg (2010). https://doi.org/10.1007/978-3-642-16612-9_26

20. Raskin, J.-F., Schobbens, P.-Y.: Real-time logics: fictitious clock as an abstraction of dense time. In: Brinksma, E. (ed.) TACAS 1997. LNCS, vol. 1217, pp. 165–182. Springer, Heidelberg (1997). https://doi.org/10.1007/BFb0035387

21. Schirmer, S., Torens, C., Adolf, F.: Formal monitoring of risk-based geofences. https://doi.org/10.2514/6.2018-1986

22. Schwenger, M.: Let's not Trust Experience Blindly: Formal Monitoring of Humans and other CPS. Master thesis, Saarland University (2019)

23. Torens, C., Adolf, F., Faymonville, P., Schirmer, S.: Towards intelligent system health management using runtime monitoring. In: AIAA Information Systems-AIAA Infotech @ Aerospace. American Institute of Aeronautics and Astronautics (AIAA), January 2017. https://doi.org/10.2514/6.2017-0419

Realizing ω-regular Hyperproperties

Bernd Finkbeiner[iD], Christopher Hahn[iD], Jana Hofmann[✉][iD], and Leander Tentrup[iD]

Reactive Systems Group, Saarland University,
Saarbrücken, Germany
{finkbeiner,hahn,hofmann,
tentrup}@react.uni-saarland.de

Abstract. We study the expressiveness and reactive synthesis problem of HyperQPTL, a logic that specifies ω-regular hyperproperties. HyperQPTL is an extension of linear-time temporal logic (LTL) with explicit trace and propositional quantification and therefore *truly* combines trace relations and ω-regularity. As such, HyperQPTL can express promptness, which states that there is a common bound on the number of steps up to which an event must have happened. We demonstrate how the HyperQPTL formulation of promptness differs from the type of promptness expressible in the logic Prompt-LTL. Furthermore, we study the realizability problem of HyperQPTL by identifying decidable fragments, where one decidable fragment contains formulas for promptness. We show that, in contrast to the satisfiability problem of HyperQPTL, propositional quantification has an immediate impact on the decidability of the realizability problem. We present a reduction to the realizability problem of HyperLTL, which immediately yields a bounded synthesis procedure. We implemented the synthesis procedure for HyperQPTL in the bounded synthesis tool BoSy. Our experimental results show that a range of arbiter satisfying promptness can be synthesized.

1 Introduction

Hyperproperties [5], which are mainly studied in the area of secure information flow control, are a generalization from trace properties to *sets* of trace properties. That is, they relate multiple execution traces with each other. Examples are noninterference [20], observational determinism [34], symmetry [16], or promptness [24], i.e., properties whose satisfaction cannot be determined by analyzing each execution trace in isolation.

A number of logics have been introduced to express hyperproperties (examples are [4,19,25]). They either add explicit trace quantification to a temporal logic or build on monadic first-order or second-order logics and add an equal-level predicate, which connects traces with each other. A comprehensive study comparing such hyperlogics has been initiated in [6].

This work was partially supported by the Collaborative Research Center "Foundations of Perspicuous Software Systems" (TRR 248, 389792660) and by the European Research Council (ERC) Grant OSARES (No. 683300).

S. K. Lahiri and C. Wang (Eds.): CAV 2020, LNCS 12225, pp. 40–63, 2020.
https://doi.org/10.1007/978-3-030-53291-8_4

The most prominent hyperlogic is HyperLTL [4], which extends classic linear-time temporal logic (LTL) [26] with trace variables and explicit trace quantification. HyperLTL has been successfully applied in (runtime) verification, (e.g., [15,21,32]), specification analysis [11,14], synthesis [12,13], and program repair [1] of hyperproperties. As an example specification, the following HyperLTL formula expresses observational determinism by stating that for every pair of traces, if the observable inputs I are the same on both traces, then also the observable outputs O have to agree

$$\forall \pi \forall \pi'. \Box(I_\pi = I_{\pi'}) \rightarrow \Box(O_\pi = O_{\pi'}) \ . \tag{1}$$

Thus, hyperlogics can not only specify functional correctness, but may also enforce the absence of information leaks or presence of information propagation. There is a great practical interest in information flow control, which makes synthesizing implementations that satisfy hyperproperties highly desirable. Recently [12], it was shown that the synthesis problem of HyperLTL, although undecidable in general, remains decidable for many fragments, such as the $\exists^*\forall$ fragment. Furthermore, a *bounded synthesis* procedure was developed, for which a prototype implementation based on BoSy [7,9,12] showed promising results.

HyperLTL is, however, intrinsically limited in expressiveness. For example, promptness is not expressible in HyperLTL. Promptness is a property stating that there is a bound b, common for all traces, on the number of steps up to which an event e must have happened. Additionally, just like LTL, HyperLTL can express neither ω-regular nor epistemic properties [2,29]. Epistemic properties are statements about the transfer of knowledge between several components. An exemplary epistemic specification is described by the *dining cryptographers problem* [3]: three cryptographers sit at a table in a restaurant. Either one of the cryptographers or, alternatively, the NSA must pay for their meal. The question is whether there is a protocol where each cryptographer can find out whether the NSA or one of the cryptographers paid the bill, without revealing the identity of the paying cryptographer.

In this paper, we explore HyperQPTL [6,29], a hyperlogic that is more expressive than HyperLTL. Specifically, we study its expressiveness and reactive synthesis problem. HyperQPTL extends HyperLTL with quantification over sequences of new propositions. What makes the logic particularly expressive is the fact that the trace quantifiers and propositional quantifiers can be freely interleaved. With this mechanism, HyperQPTL can not only express all ω-regular properties over a sequences of n-tuples; it truly interweaves trace quantification and ω-regularity. For example, promptness can be stated as the following HyperQPTL formula:

$$\exists b. \forall \pi. \ \Diamond b \wedge (\neg b \ \mathcal{U} e_\pi) \ . \tag{2}$$

The formula states that there exists a sequence $s \in (2^{\{q\}})^\omega$, such that event e holds on all traces before the first occurrence of b in s. In this paper, we argue that the type of promptness expressible in HyperQPTL is incomparable to the expressiveness of Prompt-LTL [24], a logic introduced to express promptness

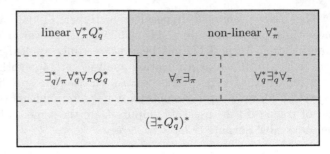

multiple universal trace quantifiers (Sec. 4.3)	linear $\forall_\pi^* Q_q^*$	non-linear $\forall_\pi^*$	
single universal trace quantifier (Sec. 4.2)	$\exists_{q/\pi}^* \forall_q^* \forall_\pi Q_q^*$	$\forall_\pi \exists_\pi$	$\forall_q^* \exists_q^* \forall_\pi$
no universal trace quantifier (Sec. 4.1)	$(\exists_\pi^* Q_q^*)^*$		

Fig. 1. The realizability problem of HyperQPTL. Left and below of the solid line are the decidable fragments, right above the solid line the undecidable fragments.

properties. It is further known that HyperQPTL also subsumes epistemic extensions of temporal logics such as LTL$_\mathcal{K}$ [22], as well as the first-order hyperlogic FO[$<, E$] [6,19,29]. Its expressiveness makes HyperQPTL particularly interesting. The model checking problem of HyperQPTL is, despite the logic being quite expressive, decidable [29]. We also explore an alternative definition of HyperQPTL that would result in an even more expressive logic. However, we show that the logic would have an undecidable model checking problem, which constitutes a major drawback in the context of computer-aided verification. Furthermore, satisfiability is decidable for large fragments of the logic [6]. Decidable HyperQPTL fragments can be described solely in terms of their *trace* quantifier prefix. This indicates that propositional quantification has no negative impact on the decidability, although it greatly increases the expressiveness. We establish that propositional quantification, in contrast to the satisfiability problem, has an impact on the realizability problem: it becomes undecidable when combining a propositional $\forall\exists$ quantifier alternation with a single universal trace quantifier. However, we show that the synthesis problem of large HyperQPTL fragments remains decidable, where one of these fragments contains promptness properties. We partially obtain these results by reducing the HyperQPTL realizability problem to the HyperLTL realizability problem. Based on this reduction, we extended the BoSy bounded synthesis tool to also synthesize systems respecting HyperQPTL specifications. We provide promising experimental results of our prototype implementation: using BoSy and HyperQPTL specifications, we were able to synthesize arbiters that respect promptness.

This paper is structured as follows. In Sect. 2, we give necessary preliminaries. In Sect. 3, we define HyperQPTL. We discuss an alternative approach to define a logic expressing ω-regular hyperproperties, before pointing out that its model checking problem is undecidable. Subsequently, we give examples for the expressiveness of HyperQPTL, namely by characterizing the type of promptness properties HyperQPTL can express. Additionally, we recapitulate how HyperQPTL also subsumes epistemic properties. Section 4 discusses the realizability problem of HyperQPTL. We describe HyperQPTL fragments in terms of their quantifier prefixes. To present our results, we use the following notation. We write $\forall_\pi$

and $\forall_q$ for a single universal trace and propositional quantifier, respectively. To denote a sequence of universal trace and propositional quantifiers, we write $\forall_\pi^*$ and $\forall_q^*$. Furthermore, we use $\forall_{\pi/q}^*$ for a sequence of mixed universal quantification. We use the analogous notation for existential quantifiers. Lastly, Q_π^* and Q_q^* denote a sequence of mixed universal and existential trace and propositional quantifiers, respectively. As an example, the $\forall_\pi^* Q_q^*$ fragment denotes all formulas of the form $\forall \pi_1 \ldots \forall \pi_m . \exists/\forall q_1 \ldots \exists/\forall q_n . \varphi$, where φ is quantifier free. Figure 1 summarizes our results. We establish that a major factor for the decidability of the realizability problem consists in the number of universal trace occurring in a formula. Realizability of HyperQPTL formulas without $\forall \pi$ quantifiers is decidable (Sect. 4.1). Formulas with a single $\forall \pi$ are decidable if they belong to the $\exists_{q/\pi}^* \forall_q^* \forall_\pi Q_q^*$ fragment. This fragment also contains promptness. For more than one universal trace quantifier, we show that decidability can be guaranteed for a fragment that we call the linear $\forall_\pi^* Q_q^*$ fragment. We also show that all the above fragments are tight, i.e., realizability of all other formulas is in general undecidable. Lastly, Sect. 5 presents experiments for the prototype implementation of our bounded synthesis algorithm for HyperQPTL.

2   Preliminaries

We use AP for a set of atomic propositions. A *trace* over AP is an infinite sequence $t \in (2^{\text{AP}})^\omega$. For $i \in \mathbb{N}$, we write $t[i]$ for the ith element of t and $t[i, \infty]$ for the suffix of t starting from position i. For two traces t, t' over AP and a set $\text{AP}' \subseteq \text{AP}$, we write $t =_{\text{AP}'} t'$ to indicate that t and t' agree on all $a \in \text{AP}'$, and respectively $T =_{\text{AP}'} T'$ for two sets of traces T and T'. Furthermore, we define a replacement function $t[q \mapsto t_q]$ that given a trace t and a trace $t_q \in (2^{\{q\}})^\omega$, replaces the occurrences of q in t according to t_q, such that $t[q \mapsto t_q] =_{\{q\}} t_q$ and $t[q \mapsto t_q] =_{\text{AP}\setminus\{q\}} t$. We also lift this notation to sets of traces and define $T[q \mapsto t_q] = \{t[q \mapsto t_q] \mid t \in T\}$.

QPTL [31] extends Linear Temporal Logic (LTL) with quantification over propositions. QPTL formulas φ are defined as follows.

$$\varphi ::= \exists q . \varphi \mid \forall q . \varphi \mid \psi$$
$$\psi ::= q \mid \neg \psi \mid \psi \vee \psi \mid \bigcirc \psi \mid \Diamond \psi$$

where $q \in \text{AP}$ and AP is a set of atomic propositions. For simplicity, we assume that variable names in formulas are cleared of double occurrences. The semantics of φ over AP is defined with respect to a trace $t \in (2^{\text{AP}})^\omega$.

$$
\begin{array}{lll}
t \models q & \text{iff} & q \in t[0] \\
t \models \neg\psi & \text{iff} & t \not\models \psi \\
t \models \psi_1 \vee \psi_2 & \text{iff} & t \models \psi_1 \text{ or } t \models \psi_2 \\
t \models \bigcirc\psi & \text{iff} & t[1, \infty] \models \psi \\
t \models \Diamond\psi & \text{iff} & \exists i \geq 0.\ t[i, \infty] \models \psi \\
t \models \exists q.\ \varphi & \text{iff} & \exists t_q \in (2^{\{q\}})^\omega.\ t[q \mapsto t_q] \models \varphi \\
t \models \forall q.\ \varphi & \text{iff} & \forall t_q \in (2^{\{q\}})^\omega.\ t[q \mapsto t_q] \models \varphi
\end{array}
$$

We did not define the until operator $\mathcal{U}$ as native part of the logic. It can be derived using propositional quantification [23]. The boolean connectives $\wedge, \rightarrow, \leftrightarrow$ and the temporal operators globally $\square$ and release $\mathcal{R}$ are derived as usually.

3 ω-Regular Hyperproperties

Just like LTL, HyperLTL cannot express ω-regular languages [29]. LTL can be extended to QPTL by adding quantification over atomic propositions. In QPTL, ω-regular languages become expressible. We therefore study HyperQPTL [6,29], the extension of HyperLTL with propositional quantification, to express ω-regular hyperproperties. Given a set AP of atomic propositions and a set $\mathcal{V}$ of trace variables, the syntax of HyperQPTL is defined as follows

$$
\begin{aligned}
\varphi &::= \forall\pi.\ \varphi \mid \exists\pi.\ \varphi \mid \forall q.\ \varphi \mid \exists q.\ \varphi \mid \psi \\
\psi &::= a_\pi \mid q \mid \neg\psi \mid \psi \vee \psi \mid \bigcirc\psi \mid \Diamond\psi ,
\end{aligned}
$$

where $a, q \in \text{AP}$ and $\pi \in \mathcal{V}$. As for QPTL, we assume that formulas are cleared of double occurrences of variable names. We require that in well-defined HyperQPTL formulas, each a_π is in the scope of a trace quantifier binding π and each q is in the scope of a propositional quantifier binding q. Note that atomic propositions a_π refer to a quantified trace π, whereas quantified propositional variables q are independent of the traces. The semantics of a well-defined HyperQPTL formula over AP is defined with respect to a set of traces $T \subseteq (2^{\text{AP}})^\omega$ and an assignment function $\Pi : \mathcal{V} \to T$. We define the satisfaction relation $\Pi, i \models_T \varphi$ as follows:

$$\Pi, i \models_T a_\pi \qquad \text{iff} \qquad a \in \Pi(\pi)[i]$$

$$\Pi, i \models_T q \qquad \text{iff} \qquad \forall t \in T. \, q \in t[i]$$

$$\Pi, i \models_T \neg\psi \qquad \text{iff} \qquad \Pi, i \not\models_T \psi$$

$$\Pi, i \models_T \psi_1 \vee \psi_2 \qquad \text{iff} \qquad \Pi, i \models_T \psi_1 \vee \Pi, i \models_T \psi_2$$

$$\Pi, i \models_T \bigcirc\psi \qquad \text{iff} \qquad \Pi, i+1 \models_T \psi$$

$$\Pi, i \models_T \Diamond\psi \qquad \text{iff} \qquad \exists j \geq i. \, \Pi.j \models_T \psi$$

$$\Pi, i \models_T \exists\pi.\,\varphi \qquad \text{iff} \qquad \exists t \in T. \, \Pi[\pi \mapsto t], i \models_T \varphi$$

$$\Pi, i \models_T \forall\pi.\,\varphi \qquad \text{iff} \qquad \forall t \in T. \, \Pi[\pi \mapsto t], i \models_T \varphi$$

$$\Pi, i \models_T \exists q.\,\varphi \qquad \text{iff} \qquad \exists t_q \in (2^{\{q\}})^\omega. \, \Pi, i \models_{T[q \mapsto t_q]} \varphi$$

$$\Pi, i \models_T \forall q.\,\varphi \qquad \text{iff} \qquad \forall t_q \in (2^{\{q\}})^\omega. \, \Pi, i \models_{T[q \mapsto t_q]} \varphi \, .$$

Note that the semantics of propositional quantification is defined in such a way that in the scope of a quantifier binding q, all traces agree on their q-sequence. We say that a set of traces T satisfies a HyperQPTL formula φ if $\emptyset, 0 \models_T \varphi$, where $\emptyset$ is the empty trace assignment. QPTL formulas can be expressed in HyperQPTL using a single universal trace quantifier. Furthermore, HyperLTL [4] is the syntactic subset of HyperQPTL that does not contain propositional quantification.

While HyperQPTL can express a wide range of properties (see Sect. 3.1), its model checking problem is still decidable [29]. Furthermore, the syntactic fragments for which satisfiability is decidable can be expressed solely in terms of the occurring trace quantifiers: Just like for HyperLTL, satisfiability of a HyperQPTL formula is decidable if no $\forall\pi$ is followed by an $\exists\pi$ [6].

The definition of HyperQPTL is straightforward, however, one could argue that it is not the only way to extend QPTL to a hyperlogic. The original idea of QPTL is to "color" the trace by introducing additional atomic propositions. The way HyperQPTL is defined, that idea is translated to sets of traces by coloring the traces uniformly. An alternative approach could be to color every trace individually by introducing a full atomic proposition for every propositional quantification. This resembles full second-order quantification and would therefore result in a considerably more expressive logic. In particular, we show that the model checking problem would become undecidable, which is, especially in the context of automatic verification, unfavorable. For the remainder of this section, we call the logic resulting from the alternative definition HyperQPTL$^+$. The syntax of HyperQPTL$^+$ is similar to the one of HyperQPTL, just without the rule q for the evaluation of the propositional variables. This accounts for the idea that the propositional quantification can freely reassign atomic propositions; thus, there is no need to distinguish between free atomic propositions and quantified atomic propositions:

$$\varphi ::= \forall\pi.\,\varphi \mid \exists\pi.\,\varphi \mid \forall a.\,\varphi \mid \exists a.\,\varphi \mid \psi$$
$$\psi ::= a_\pi \mid \neg\psi \mid \psi \vee \psi \mid \bigcirc\psi \mid \Diamond\psi \, .$$

Semantically, only the rules for the quantification of the propositional quantifiers change:

$$\Pi, i \models_T \exists a.\, \varphi \qquad \text{iff} \qquad \exists T' \subseteq (2^{\mathrm{AP}})^\omega.\, T' =_{\mathrm{AP}\setminus\{a\}} T \wedge \Pi, i \models_{T'} \varphi$$

$$\Pi, i \models_T \forall a.\, \varphi \qquad \text{iff} \qquad \forall T' \subseteq (2^{\mathrm{AP}})^\omega.\, T' =_{\mathrm{AP}\setminus\{a\}} T \rightarrow \Pi, i \models_{T'} \varphi\ .$$

Lemma 1. *The HyperQPTL$^+$ model checking problem is undecidable.*

Proof. Given a finite Kripke structure K and a HyperQPTL$^+$ formula φ, the model checking problem asks whether the trace set T produced by K satisfies φ. The proof follows the undecidability proof for the model checking problem of S1S[E] [6], a logic which lifts S1S to the level of hyperlogics. We describe a reduction from the halting problem of 2-counter machines (which are Turing complete) to the HyperQPTL$^+$ model checking problem. A 2-counter machine (2CM) consists of a finite set of serially numbered instructions that modify two counters. A configuration of a 2CM is a triple $(n, v_1, v_2) \in \mathbb{N}^3$, where n determines the next instruction to be executed, and v_1 and v_2 assign the counter values. Each instruction can either increase or decrease one of the counters; or test either of the counters for zero and, depending on the outcome, jump to another instruction. Furthermore, we assume a special instruction i_{halt}, which indicates that the machine has reached a halting state. A 2CM halts from initial configuration s_0 if there is a finite sequence $s_0, \ldots, s_n$ of configurations such that s_n is a halting configuration and s_{i+1} is a result of applying the instruction in s_i to configuration s_i. Let $\mathcal{M}$ be a 2CM. We describe T and φ such that $T \models \varphi$ iff $\mathcal{M}$ halts. We choose $\mathrm{AP} = \{i, c_1, c_2\}$ and T is the set of all traces where each atomic proposition holds exactly once. That way, a trace t encodes a configuration of the machine: If $i \in t[n]$, $c_1 \in t[v_1]$, and $c_2 \in t[v_2]$, the machine is in configuration (n, v_1, v_2). It is easy to see that T can be produced by a finite Kripke structure. To describe φ, we make two helpful observations. First, using propositional quantification, we can quantify a trace set $T_q \subseteq T$: a trace t is in T_q iff the quantified proposition q eventually occurs on t. Second, for two traces $t, t' \in T$, we can state that t' encodes a configuration which is the successor of the configuration encoded by t. Using these observations, we define $\varphi = \exists q.\, \varphi'$, where q encodes a set $T_q \subseteq T$ that is supposed to describe a halting computation. To ensure that T_q describes a halting computation, φ' is a conjunction of the following requirements: T_q must

1. be finite,
2. contain a halting configuration and the initial configuration,
3. be predecessor closed with respect to the encoded configurations it contains (except for the initial configuration).

Finiteness of T_q can be expressed by stating that there is an upper bound on the values of i, c_1, and c_2 on the traces in T_q. With the observations made before, stating the above requirements in HyperQPTL$^+$ now remains a straightforward exercise. □

Since the model checking problem of HyperQPTL$^+$ is undecidable, we focus on HyperQPTL to express ω-regular hyperproperties. In particular, we show that HyperQPTL can express a range of relevant properties that are neither expressible in HyperLTL, nor in QPTL.

3.1   The Expressiveness of HyperQPTL

HyperQPTL combines trace quantification with ω-regularity. The interplay between the two features enables HyperQPTL to express a variety of properties. In Sect. 1, we showed how HyperQPTL can express a form of promptness. In this section, we further elaborate on the type of properties HyperQPTL can express. In particular, we compare it to Prompt-LTL, a logic that extends LTL with bounded eventualities. Furthermore, HyperQPTL is also able to express epistemic properties by emulating the knowledge operator known from LTL$_\mathcal{K}$.

A straightforward class of properties HyperQPTL can express are ω-regular properties over n-tuples of quantified traces. Formulas expressing this type of properties first have a trace quantifier prefix followed by a QPTL formula, i.e., they lie in the $Q_\pi^* Q_q^*$ fragment. This fragment of HyperQPTL corresponds to the extension of QPTL with *prenex* trace quantification. However, the true expressive power of HyperQPTL originates from the fact that we allow the trace quantifiers and propositional quantifiers to alternate.

Promptness Properties. Promptness properties are an example for HyperQPTL's interplay between trace quantification and propositional quantification. Promptness expresses that eventualities are fulfilled within a bounded number of steps. One way to express promptness properties is the logic Prompt-LTL, which extends LTL with the promptness operator $\Diamond_p$. A system satisfies a Prompt-LTL formula φ if there is a bound k such that all traces of the system fulfill the formula where each $\Diamond_p$ in φ is replaced by $\Diamond^{\leq k}$, i.e., the system must fulfill all prompt eventualities within k steps. For example, $\varphi = \Box \Diamond_p \psi$ holds in a system if there is a bound k such that all traces of the system at all times satisfy ψ within k steps. HyperQPTL can express a different type of promptness properties. In Sect. 1, Formula 2, we showed how one can state in HyperQPTL that there is a bound, common for all traces, until which an eventuality has to be fulfilled. The idea is to quantify a new proposition b, such that the first position in which b is true serves as the bound. Compared to Prompt-LTL, HyperQPTL thus expresses a weaker form of promptness, while still being stronger than pure eventuality. This type of promptness only becomes meaningful when comparing several traces of the system: HyperQPTL can enforce that there is a common bound for all traces (the system cannot starve), but it does not make the bound explicit. The following example shows a more involved promptness property expressible in HyperQPTL.

Example 1. HyperQPTL can express *bounded waiting for a grant*. It states that if the system requests access to a shared resource at point in time t, then it will be granted access within a bounded amount of time. The bound may depend on the point in time t where access to the resource was requested. However, it may not depend on the current trace. We express this property in HyperQPTL as follows, also adding that the system will not request access twice without being granted access in between.

$$\forall \pi. \Box(r_\pi \rightarrow \bigcirc(\neg r_\pi \, \mathcal{W} \, g_\pi)) \tag{1}$$

$$\forall \pi. \exists b. \forall \pi'. \Box(r_\pi \wedge r_{\pi'} \rightarrow \bigcirc(\Diamond b \wedge (\neg b \, \mathcal{U} \, g_\pi) \wedge (\neg b \, \mathcal{U} \, g_{\pi'}))) \tag{2}$$

Formula 1 states that no second request is posed before being given a grant. Formula 2 expresses the bounded waiting property by universally quantifying a trace, then existentially quantifying a sequence of bounds b. Now, for every trace π', whenever π and π' pose a request at the same point in time, both have to get access to the resource before b holds next. Therefore, for each point in time, there is a bound such that all traces posing a request at that point in time get access within a bounded number of steps. Note that this property differs from saying "all traces are eventually granted access", where the bound may also depend on the trace under consideration. In this scenario, each of the infinitely many traces could wait arbitrarily long for the grant. In particular, it could happen that with each trace the waiting time is longer than before.

The above example shows how the interplay of trace quantifiers and propositional quantifiers can be leveraged to express a new class of promptness properties. We finally note that compared to Prompt-LTL, HyperQPTL cannot express that all eventualities must be fulfilled within a fixed k number of steps.

Corollary 1. *The expressiveness of HyperQPTL and Prompt-LTL is incomparable.*

Epistemic Properties. Another interesting class of properties that are not expressible in HyperLTL are epistemic properties. Epistemic properties describe the knowledge of agents that interact with each other in a system. Logics that express epistemic properties are often equipped with a so-called knowledge operator, e.g., $\text{LTL}_\mathcal{K}$, which is LTL extended with the knowledge operator $\mathcal{K}_A \, \varphi$. The operator denotes that an agent $A \subseteq AP$ knows φ. An agent A is characterized in terms of the atomic propositions he can observe. The semantics of the operator is described with the following rule

$$t, i \models \mathcal{K}_A \, \varphi \quad \text{iff} \quad \forall t'. t[0, i] =_A t'[0, i] \rightarrow t', i \models \varphi \,.$$

The formula is evaluated with respect to a trace t and a position i. We omit the semantic definition for the rest of the logic, which corresponds to plain LTL. The semantic definition of the operator captures the idea that an agent knows some fact φ if φ holds on all traces that are indistinguishable for the agent.

Example 2 (Dining Cryptographers). The dining cryptographers problem [3] is an interesting example of how epistemic properties can characterize non-trivial

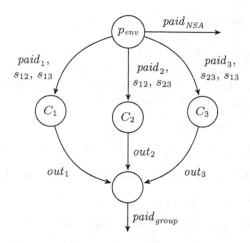

Fig. 2. The dining cryptographers problem with three cryptographers.

protocols. The problem describes the following situation (see Fig. 2): three cryptographers C_1, C_2, and C_3 sit at a table in a restaurant and either one of cryptographers or, alternatively, the NSA paid for their meal. The task for the cryptographers is to figure out whether the NSA or one of the cryptographers paid. However, if one of the cryptographers paid, then the others must not be able to infer who it was. Each cryptographer C_i receives several bits of information: $paid_i$ indicating whether or not he pays the bill, and two secrets, each shared with one of the other cryptographers. The secrets can be used to encode the information they share as output out_i. By combining the outputs of all cryptographers, it must become clear whether the NSA or one of the group paid. The specification of the protocol can be easily formalized in $LTL_\mathcal{K}$. The following formula describes the desired behavior of agent C_1:

$$DC\,agent1 :=$$
$$(paid_{group} \wedge \neg paid_1 \rightarrow (\mathcal{K}_{C_1}(paid_2 \vee paid_3) \wedge \neg \mathcal{K}_{C_1}\, paid_2 \wedge \neg \mathcal{K}_{C_1}\, paid_3))$$
$$\wedge\, (paid_{NSA} \rightarrow \mathcal{K}_{C_1}(\neg paid_1 \wedge \neg paid_2 \wedge \neg paid_3))\ .$$

The knowledge operator can also be defined for hyperlogics [29]. It receives an additional parameter π, indicating the trace the knowledge refers to. When added to HyperQPTL, it has the following semantics:

$$\Pi, i \models_T \mathcal{K}_{A,\pi}\varphi \qquad \text{iff} \qquad \forall t' \in T.\ \Pi(\pi)[0,i] =_A t'[0,i] \rightarrow \Pi[\pi \mapsto t'], i \models_T \varphi\ .$$

The knowledge operator, however, can be encoded in HyperQPTL using propositional quantification. Epistemic problems, such as the dining cryptographers problem, can thus be expressed in HyperQPTL.

Theorem 1 (*[29]*). *HyperQPTL can emulate the knowledge operator.*

Proof. We recap the proof from [29]: Let $\varphi = Q_{\pi/q} \ldots Q_{\pi/q}. \varphi'$ be a HyperQPTL formula, equipped with the knowledge operator as defined above. We assume that φ is given in negated normal form, i.e. each $\mathcal{K}_{A,\pi}$ occurs either in positive position or in negated form. Let u and t be fresh propositions and let π' be a fresh trace variable. Recursively, we replace each knowledge operator $\mathcal{K}_{A,\pi}$ occurring in φ in positive position with the following formula

$$Q_{\pi/q} \ldots Q_{\pi/q}. \exists u. \forall r. \forall \pi'. \ \varphi'[\mathcal{K}_{A,\pi}\psi \mapsto u] \wedge$$
$$((r \ \mathcal{U} \ (u \wedge r \wedge \bigcirc \square \neg r)) \wedge \square(r \rightarrow A_\pi = A_{\pi'}) \rightarrow \square(r \wedge \bigcirc \neg r \rightarrow \psi[\pi \mapsto \pi']))$$

and each $\mathcal{K}_{A,\pi}$ occurring negatively with the following formula

$$Q_{\pi/q} \ldots Q_{\pi/q}. \exists u. \forall r. \exists \pi'. \ \varphi'[\neg \mathcal{K}_{A,\pi}\psi \mapsto u] \wedge$$
$$((r \ \mathcal{U} \ (u \wedge r \wedge \bigcirc \square \neg r)) \rightarrow \square(r \rightarrow A_\pi = A_{\pi'}) \wedge \square(r \wedge \bigcirc \neg r \rightarrow \neg\psi[\pi \mapsto \pi'])),$$

where we use $\varphi'[\mathcal{K}_{A,\pi}\psi \mapsto u]$ to denote that in φ', a *single* occurrence of the knowledge operator is replaced by u, and $\psi[\pi \mapsto \pi']$ to denote the formula where π is replaced by π'. The existentially quantified proposition u indicates the points in time where the knowledge operator is supposed to hold/not hold. The universally quantified proposition r is assumed to change once from r to $\neg r$ and thereby point at one of the points in time picked by u. It is then used to compare the prefix of the old trace π and an alternative trace quantified by the trace variable π'.   □

4 HyperQPTL Realizability

In reactive synthesis, the task is, given a specification φ, to construct a system that satisfies the specification. More precisely, the system is assumed to receive some inputs from an environment and has to react with outputs such that the specification is fulfilled. The realizability problem asks for the existence of a so-called *strategy tree*, where the edges are labeled with all possible inputs and the task is to find a function f that labels the nodes with the corresponding outputs. Figure 3 shows a strategy tree for a single input bit i. We define strategies following [12]. Let a set $\text{AP} = I \mathbin{\dot\cup} O$ be given. A *strategy* $f: (2^I)^* \rightarrow 2^O$ maps sequences of input valuations 2^I to an output valuation 2^O. For an infinite word $w = w_0 w_1 w_2 \cdots \in (2^I)^\omega$, the trace corresponding to a strategy f is defined as $(f(\epsilon) \cup w_0)(f(w_0) \cup w_1)(f(w_0 w_1) \cup w_2) \ldots \in (2^{I \cup O})^\omega$. For any trace $w = w_0 w_1 w_2 \ldots \in (2^{I \cup O})^\omega$ and strategy $f: (2^I)^* \rightarrow 2^O$, we lift the set containment operator $\in$ defining that $w \in f$ iff $f(\epsilon) = w_0 \cap O$ and $f((w_0 \cap I) \cdots (w_i \cap I)) = w_{i+1} \cap O$ for all $i \geq 0$. We say that a strategy f satisfies a HyperQPTL formula φ over $\text{AP} = I \mathbin{\dot\cup} O$ iff $\{w \mid w \in f\}$ satisfies φ.

With the definition of a strategy at hand, we can define the realizability problem of HyperQPTL formally.

Definition 1 (HyperQPTL Realizability). *A HyperQPTL formula φ over atomic propositions $AP = I \mathbin{\dot\cup} O$ is realizable if there is a strategy $f: (2^I)^* \rightarrow 2^O$ that satisfies φ.*

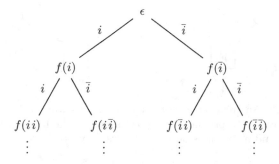

Fig. 3. A strategy tree for the reactive realizability problem.

For technical reasons, we assume (without loss of generality) that quantified atomic propositions are classified as outputs, not inputs. This complies with the intuition that propositional quantifiers should be a means for additional expressiveness; they should not overwrite the inputs received from the environment. The definition of realizability of QPTL and HyperLTL specifications is inherited from the definition for HyperQPTL.

Compared to the standard realizability problem, the distributed realizability problem is defined over an architecture, containing a number of processes interacting with each other. The goal is to find a strategy for each of the processes. In the following proofs, we will make use of the distributed realizability problem of QPTL, which we therefore also define formally.

A *distributed architecture* [17,27] A over atomic propositions AP is a tuple $\langle P, p_{env}, \mathcal{I}, \mathcal{O} \rangle$, where P is a finite set of processes and $p_{env} \in P$ is a designated environment process. The functions $\mathcal{I} : P \to 2^{AP}$ and $\mathcal{O} : P \to 2^{AP}$ define the inputs and outputs of processes. The output of one process can be the input of another process. The output of the processes must be pairwise disjoint, i.e., for all $p \neq p' \in P$ it holds that $\mathcal{O}(p) \cap \mathcal{O}(p') = \emptyset$. We assume that the environment process forwards inputs to the processes and has no input of its own, i.e., $\mathcal{I}(p_{env}) = \emptyset$.

Definition 2 (Distributed QPTL Realizability [17]). *A QPTL formula φ over free atomic propositions AP is realizable in an architecture $A = \langle P, p_{env}, \mathcal{I}, \mathcal{O} \rangle$ if for each process $p \in P$, there is a strategy $f_p \colon (2^{\mathcal{I}(p)})^* \to 2^{\mathcal{O}(p)}$ such that the combination of all f_p satisfies φ.*

The distributed realizability problem for QPTL is (inherited from LTL) in general undecidable [27]. However, we will use the result that the problem remains decidable for architectures without *information forks*[17]. The notion of information forks captures the flow of data in the system. Intuitively, an architecture contains an information fork if the processes cannot be ordered linearly according to their informedness. Formally, an information fork in an architecture $A = \langle P, p_{env}, \mathcal{I}, \mathcal{O} \rangle$ is defined as a tuple (P', V', p, p'), where p, p' are two different processes, $P' \subseteq P$, and $V' \subseteq AP$ is disjoint from $\mathcal{I}(p) \cup \mathcal{I}(p')$. (P', V', p, p')

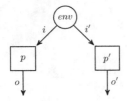   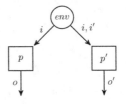

(a) Information fork: An architecture with two processes; process p to produces output o from input i and p' produces output o' from input i'.

(b) No information fork: The same architecture as on the left, where the inputs of process p' are changed to i and i'.

Fig. 4. Distributed architectures

is an information fork if P' together with the edges that are labeled with at least one variable from V' forms a subgraph rooted in the environment and there exist two nodes $q, q' \in P'$ that have edges to p, p', respectively, such that $\mathcal{O}(q) \cap \mathcal{I}(p) \not\subseteq \mathcal{I}(p')$ and $\mathcal{O}(q') \cap \mathcal{I}(p') \not\subseteq \mathcal{I}(p)$. The definition formalizes the intuition that p and p' receive incomparable input bits, i.e., they have incomparable information.

Example 3. Two example architectures are depicted in Fig. 4 [12]. The processes in Fig. 4a receive distinct inputs and thus neither process is more informed than the other. The architecture therefore contains an information fork with $P' = \{env, p, p'\}, V' = \{i, i'\}, q = env, q' = env$. The processes in Fig. 4b can be ordered linearly according to the subset relation on the inputs and thus the architecture contains no information fork.

In the following sections, we identify tight syntactic fragments of HyperQPTL for which the standard realizability problem is decidable. We give decidability proofs and show that formulas outside the decidable fragments are in general undecidable. An important aspect for decidability is the number of universal trace quantifiers that appear in the formula. We thus present our findings in three categories, depending on the number of universal trace quantifiers a formula has.

4.1 No Universal Trace Quantifier

We show that the realizability problem of any HyperQPTL formula without a $\forall_\pi$ quantifier is decidable. The problem is reduced to QPTL realizability.

Theorem 2. *Realizability of the $(\exists_\pi^* Q_q^*)^*$ fragment of HyperQPTL is decidable.*

Proof. Let a $(\exists_\pi^* Q_q^*)^*$ HyperQPTL formula φ over AP $= I \mathbin{\dot\cup} O = \{a^0, \ldots, a^k\}$ with trace quantifiers $\pi_0, \ldots \pi_n$ be given. We reduce the problem to the realizability problem of QPTL, which is known to be decidable (since QPTL formulas can be translated to Büchi automata). The idea is to replace each existential trace quantifier $\exists \pi_i$ with quantification of propositions $a_{\pi_i}^0, a_{\pi_i}^1, \ldots, a_{\pi_i}^k$, one for each $a^j \in \text{AP}$, thereby mimicking the quantification of a trace. To make sure that only traces from an actual strategy tree are chosen, we add a dependency formula which forces the outputs to be dependent on the inputs. The following QPTL formula implements the idea.

$$\varphi_{QPTL} := \varphi[i \leq n : \exists \pi_i \mapsto \exists a^0_{\pi_i}. \ldots \exists a^k_{\pi_i}.] \wedge$$

$$\bigwedge_{i \leq n} \bigwedge_{j \leq n} (I_{\pi_i} \neq I_{\pi_j}) \mathcal{R} (O_{\pi_i} = O_{\pi_j})$$

We use the notation $[i \leq n : \exists \pi_i \mapsto \exists a^0_{\pi_i}. \ldots \exists a^k_{\pi_i}.]$ to indicate that each π_i for $0 \leq i \leq n$ is replaced with the respective series of existential propositional quantification. Furthermore, we write $I_{\pi_i} \neq I_{\pi_j}$ as syntactic sugar for $\bigvee_{a \in I} a_{\pi_i} \nleftrightarrow a_{\pi_j}$ (and similarly for $O_{\pi_i} = O_{\pi_j}$). We show that φ and φ_{QPTL} are equirealizable. For the first direction, assume that φ is realizable by a strategy f. Notice that all atomic propositions in φ_{QPTL} are bound by a propositional quantifier. Therefore, if the witness sequences for the quantified propositions can be chosen correctly, any strategy realizes φ_{QPTL}. Propositions $a^j_{\pi_i}$ are chosen according to the witness traces of $f \models \varphi$. Witnesses for the remaining atomic propositions are also chosen according to their witnesses from $f \models \varphi$. Now, the first conjunct of φ_{QPTL} is fulfilled since $f \models \varphi$ holds. The second conjunct is fulfilled since any two traces π_i, π_j of a strategy tree fulfill by construction $(I_{\pi_i} \neq I_{\pi_j}) \mathcal{R} (O_{\pi_i} = O_{\pi_j})$. For the other direction, assume that φ_{QPTL} is realizable (by construction independently from the strategy). Let $t_{a^0_{\pi_0}}, \ldots, t_{a^k_{\pi_n}}$ be the witness sequences for the respective quantified atomic propositions. The following strategy realizes φ.

$$f(\sigma) = \begin{cases} \{t_{a_{\pi_i}}[|\sigma|] \mid a \in O\} & \text{if for some } i \leq n, \\ & \sigma = \{t_{a_{\pi_i}}[0] \mid a \in I\} \ldots \{t_{a_{\pi_i}}[|\sigma|] \mid a \in I\} \\ \emptyset & \text{otherwise} \end{cases}$$

Strategy f chooses the outputs according to the witnesses for the propositions encoding the traces. Note that because of the second conjunct in φ_{QPTL}, the output is always unique, even if several encoded traces start with the same input sequence. Now, $f \models \varphi$ holds because of the first conjunct of φ_{QPTL}. $\quad\square$

4.2   Single Universal Trace Quantifier

In this fragment, we allow exactly one universal trace quantifier. It is particularly interesting as it contains many promptness properties. For example, the following promptness formulation mentioned in the introduction lies within the fragment:

$$\exists b. \forall \pi. \ \Diamond b \wedge (\neg b \ \mathcal{U} \ e_\pi) .$$

Theorem 3. *Realizability of the $\exists^*_{q/\pi} \forall^*_q \forall_\pi Q^*_q$ fragment is decidable.*

We show the theorem in two steps. First, we generalize a proof from [12], showing that realizability of the $\exists^*_\pi \forall_\pi Q^*_q$ fragment is decidable. Second, we show that we can reduce the realizability problem of any HyperQPTL formula to a formula where some propositional quantifiers are replaced with trace quantifiers.

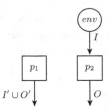

Fig. 5. Distributed architecture encoding existential choice of traces.

Lemma 2. *Realizability of the $\exists_\pi^* \forall_\pi Q_q^*$ fragment is decidable.*

Proof. The reasoning generalizes the proof in [12] showing that realizability $\exists_\pi^* \forall_\pi$ HyperLTL formulas is decidable. We reduce the problem to the distributed realizability problem of QPTL without information forks, which is—since QPTL is subsumed by the μ-calculus—decidable [17]. Let a HyperQPTL formula $\varphi = \exists\pi_1 \dots \exists\pi_n . \forall\pi . \psi$ over $AP = I \mathbin{\dot\cup} O$ be given, where ψ is from the Q_q^* fragment. We define a distributed architecture $\mathcal{A}$ over an extended set of atomic propositions $AP' = I \cup O \cup I' \cup O'$. Similarly to the proof in Theorem 2, I' and O' are composed of a copy of the atomic propositions for each existentially quantified variable π_j. Formally, $I' = \bigcup_{1 \le j \le n} \{i_{\pi_j} \mid i \in I\}$ and $O' = \bigcup_{1 \le j \le n} \{o_{\pi_j} \mid o \in O\}$. Now we define $\mathcal{A}$ as follows.

$$\mathcal{A} := \langle (p_{env}, p_1, p_2), p_{env}, \mathcal{I}, \mathcal{O}, \rangle$$
$$\mathcal{I} := (p_1 \mapsto \emptyset, p_2 \mapsto I)$$
$$\mathcal{O} := (p_{env} \mapsto I, p_1 \mapsto I' \cup O', p_2 \mapsto O)$$

The architecture is displayed in Fig. 5. The idea is that process p_1 sets the values of all i_{π_j} and o_{π_j} (for $j \le n$) and thereby determines the choice for the existentially quantified traces. Process p_1 receives no input and therefore needs to make a deterministic choice. Process p_2 then solves the realizability of formula $\forall\pi . \psi$. The following QPTL formula φ' encodes the idea.

$$\varphi' := \psi' \wedge \left(\bigwedge_{1 \le j \le n} (I_{\pi_j} \ne I)\, \mathcal{R}(O_{\pi_j} = O) \right) ,$$

where ψ' is defined as ψ, where all a_π are replaced by a (but atomic propositions a_{π_j} are still part of ψ'!). Note that QPTL formulas implicitly quantify over all traces universally. Similarly to the proof in Theorem 2, the second conjunct ensures that process p_1 encodes actual paths from the strategy tree of process p_2 (which is also the strategy tree for formula φ). Thus, φ' is realizable for the distributed architecture $\mathcal{A}$ iff φ is realizable. $\square$

To state the second lemma, we need to define what it means to replace quantifiers in a formula. Let $\varphi = Q_{\pi/q}, \dots, Q_{\pi/q} . \psi$ be a HyperQPTL formula, and J be a set of indices such that for all $j \in J$, there exists a propositional quantifier

$\exists q_j$ or $\forall q_j$ in φ. Furthermore, assume that no π_j with $j \in J$ occurs in φ and that $a \in AP$. We denote by $\varphi[J \hookrightarrow_a \pi]$ the formula where each propositional quantifier $\exists q_j$ (or $\forall q_j$, respectively) with $j \in J$ is replaced with the corresponding trace quantifier $\exists \pi_j$ (or $\forall \pi_j$, respectively); and each q_j in ψ is replaced by a_{π_j}.

Lemma 3. *Let any HyperQPTL formula φ over $AP = I \dot\cup O$ and a set of indices J be given. If $\varphi[J \hookrightarrow_i \pi]$ is realizable, then so is φ, where $i \in I$ is an arbitrary input, assuming w.l.o.g., that I is non-empty.*

Proof. Let φ and J be given. Formula $\varphi[J \hookrightarrow_i \pi]$ replaces the quantification over sequences $(2^{\{q\}})^\omega$ with trace quantification, where the trace is only used for statements about a single input i. We thus exploit the fact that in the realizability problem, there is a trace for every input sequence. Therefore, the transformed formula is equirealizable. $\qquad\square$

Now, we have everything we need to prove Theorem 3.

Proof (of Theorem 3). Let φ be a HyperQPTL formula of the $\exists^*_{q/\pi} \forall^*_q \forall_\pi Q^*_q$ fragment. First, observe that in the quantifier prefix of φ, the $\forall^*_q$ quantifiers and the $\forall_\pi$ can be swapped. The resulting formula belongs to the $\exists^*_{q/\pi} \forall_\pi Q^*_q$ fragment. By Lemma 3, the formula can be transformed to a equirealizable formula of the $\exists^*_\pi \forall_\pi Q^*_q$ fragment, for which realizability is decidable by Lemma 2. $\qquad\square$

Lemma 3 allows us to decide realizability of a HyperQPTL formula by replacing propositional quantifiers with trace quantifiers. Thus, we can reduce HyperQPTL realizability to HyperLTL realizability, a fact that we use in Sect. 5 to describe a bounded synthesis algorithm for HyperQPTL.

Corollary 2. *The realizability problem of HyperQPTL can be soundly reduced to the realizability problem of HyperLTL.*

Lastly, we show that the decidable fragment is tight in the class of formulas with a single universal trace quantifier. We do so by showing that a propositional $\forall^*_q \exists^*_q$ quantifier alternation followed by a single trace quantifier $\forall_\pi$ leads to an undecidable realizability problem. The proof is carried out by a reduction from Post's Correspondence Problem.

Theorem 4. *Realizability is undecidable for HyperQPTL formulas with a single $\forall_\pi$ quantifier outside the $\exists^*_{q/\pi} \forall^*_q \forall_\pi Q^*_q$ fragment.*

Proof. Inherited from HyperLTL, realizability of formulas with a $\forall_\pi$ quantifier followed by an $\exists_\pi$ quantifier is undecidable [12]. It remains to show that realizability of formulas from the $\forall^*_q \exists^*_q \forall_\pi$ fragment is in general undecidable. We give a reduction from Post's Correspondence Problem (PCP) [28] to a HyperQPTL formula from the $\forall^*_q \exists^*_q \forall_\pi$ fragment. In PCP, we are given two equally long lists α and β consisting of finite words from some alphabet Σ of size n. PCP is the problem to find an index sequence $(i_k)_{1 \le k \le K}$ with $K \ge 1$ and $1 \le i_k \le n$, such that $\alpha_{i_1} \ldots \alpha_{i_K} = \beta_{i_1} \ldots \beta_{i_K}$. Intuitively, PCP is the problem of choosing an infinite sequence of domino stones (with finitely many different stones), where each stone

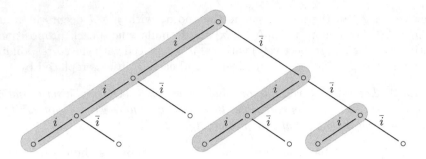

Fig. 6. A sketch of the strategy tree of our PCP reduction: relevant traces are marked in green. (Color figure online)

consists of two words α_i and β_i. Let a PCP instance with $\Sigma = \{a_1, a_2, ..., a_n\}$ and two lists α and β be given. We choose our set of atomic propositions as follows: AP $:= I \,\dot\cup\, O$ with $I := \{i\}$ and $O := (\Sigma \cup \{\dot{a}_1, \dot{a}_2, ..., \dot{a}_n\} \cup \#)^2$, where we use the dot symbol to encode that a stone starts at this position of the trace. We write $\tilde{a}$ to denote either a or $\dot{a}$. The single input i spans a binary strategy tree. We encode the PCP instance into a HyperQPTL formula that is realizable if and only if the PCP instance has a solution:

$$\forall q_i. \forall \boldsymbol{q}. \exists p_i. \exists \boldsymbol{p}. \forall \pi. \left((\Box \pi = p_i) \to (\Box \pi = \boldsymbol{p}) \right) \wedge$$
$$\left((\Box \pi = (q_i, \boldsymbol{q})) \to \varphi_{reduc}(q_i, \boldsymbol{q}, p_i, \boldsymbol{p}) \right) ,$$

where $\boldsymbol{q}$ and $\boldsymbol{p}$ are sequences of universally and existentially quantified propositional variables, such that for each $(o, o') \in O$, there is a $q_{(o,o')} \in \boldsymbol{q}$ and a $p_{(o,o')} \in \boldsymbol{p}$. Together with q_i and p_i for the input i, they simulate a universally and an existentially quantified trace from the model. The notation $\pi = \boldsymbol{q}$ denotes that for every $q_a \in \boldsymbol{q}$, it holds that $a_\pi \leftrightarrow q_a$. As seen before, the premise $(\Box \pi = (q_i, \boldsymbol{q}))$ and the conjunct $(\Box \pi = p_i) \to (\Box \pi = \boldsymbol{p})$ ensure that the propositions $(q_i, \boldsymbol{q})$ and $(p_i, \boldsymbol{p})$ are chosen to represent actual traces from the model. The universal quantification π thus only ensures that $(q_i, \boldsymbol{q})$ and $(p_i, \boldsymbol{p})$, which are used for the main reduction, are chosen correctly. The reduction is implemented in the formula φ_{reduc} and follows the construction in [10], where it is shown that the satisfiability and realizability problem of HyperLTL are undecidable for a $\forall \exists$ trace quantifier prefix.

$$\varphi_{reduc}(q_i, \boldsymbol{q}, p_i, \boldsymbol{p}) := \varphi_{rel}(q_i) \to \varphi_{is++}(q_i, p_i)$$
$$\wedge \; \varphi_{start}(\varphi_{stone\&shift}(\boldsymbol{q}, \boldsymbol{p}), q_i) \wedge \varphi_{sol}(q_i, \boldsymbol{q})$$

- $\varphi_{rel}(q_i) := \neg q_i \,\mathcal{U}\, \Box q_i$ defines the set of *relevant* traces trough the binary strategy tree (see Fig. 6).
- $\varphi_{is++}(q_i, p_i) := (\neg q_i \wedge \neg p_i) \,\mathcal{U}\, (\Box q_i \wedge \neg p_i \wedge \bigcirc \Box p_i)$ defines that a relevant trace is the direct successor trace of another relevant trace.

- $\varphi_{\mathrm{sol}}(q_i, \boldsymbol{q}) := \Box q_i \rightarrow ((\bigvee_{i=1}^n q_{(\dot{a}_i, \dot{a}_i)}) \wedge (\bigvee_{i=1}^n q_{(\tilde{a}_i, \tilde{a}_i)})) \, \mathcal{U} \Box q_{(\#, \#)}$ ensures that the path on which globally i holds is a "solution" trace, i.e., encodes the PCP solution sequence.
- $\varphi_{start}(\varphi, q_i) := \neg q_i \, \mathcal{U} (\varphi \wedge \Box q_i)$ cuts off an irrelevant prefix until φ starts.
- $\varphi_{stone\&shift}(\boldsymbol{q}, \boldsymbol{p})$ encodes that the trace simulated by $\boldsymbol{q}$ starts with a valid encoding of a stone from the PCP instance and that the trace simulated by $\boldsymbol{p}$ encodes the same trace but with the first stone removed (see [10]).

For example, let α with $\alpha_1 = a$, $\alpha_2 = ab$, $\alpha_3 = bba$, and β with $\beta_1 = baa$, $\beta_2 = aa$ and $\beta_3 = bb$ be given. A possible solution for this PCP instance is be $(3, 2, 3, 1)$, since $bbaabbbaa = i_\alpha = i_\beta$. The full sequence at the trace $\Box i$ represents the solution with the outputs

$$(\dot{b}, \dot{b})(b, b)(a, \dot{a})(\dot{a}, a)(b, \dot{b})(\dot{b}, b)(b, \dot{b})(a, a)(\dot{a}, a)(\#, \#)(\#, \#) \cdots$$

The next relevant trace, therefore, contains

$$(\dot{a}, \dot{a})(b, a)(\dot{b}, \dot{b})(b, b)(a, \dot{b})(\dot{a}, a)(\#, a)(\#, \#)(\#, \#) \cdots$$

Continuing this, the following relevant traces are:

$$(\dot{b}, \dot{b})(b, b)(a, \dot{b})(\dot{a}, a)(\#, a)(\#, \#)(\#, \#) \cdots$$
$$(\dot{a}, \dot{b})(\#, a)(\#, a)(\#, \#)(\#, \#) \cdots$$
$$(\#, \#)(\#, \#) \cdots$$

The relevant traces verify the solution provided on the $\Box i$ trace by removing one stone after the other. Thus, the formula is realizable iff the PCP instance has a solution. $\qquad \Box$

4.3 Multiple Universal Trace Quantifiers

When considering multiple universal trace quantifiers $\forall_\pi^*$, the problem becomes undecidable. This is because in HyperLTL, one can encode distributed architectures – for which the problem is undecidable – directly into the formula without using any propositional quantification [12].

Corollary 3. *Realizability of the $\forall_\pi^*$ fragment is in general undecidable.*

However, we show that the realizability problem for formulas with more than one universal trace quantifier is decidable if we restrict ourselves to formulas in the so-called *linear fragment*, i.e., that does not allow an encoding of a distributed architecture. We define the linear fragment of HyperQPTL, where the definitions are adopted from [12].

Let $A, C \subseteq \mathrm{AP}$. We define that atomic propositions $c \in C$ do solely depend on propositions $a \in A$ as the HyperQPTL formula

$$D_{A \mapsto C} := \forall \pi \forall \pi'. \left(\bigvee_{a \in A} (a_\pi \leftrightarrow a_{\pi'}) \right) \mathcal{R} \left(\bigwedge_{c \in C} (c_\pi \leftrightarrow c_{\pi'}) \right).$$

We define a *collapse* function, which collapses a HyperQPTL formula with a $\forall_\pi^*$ universal quantifier prefix into a formula with a single $\forall_\pi$ quantifier. Propositional quantifiers are preserved by the operation. Let φ be $\forall\pi_1 \cdots \forall\pi_n . Q_q^* . \psi$. We define the collapsed formula of φ as $collapse(\varphi) := \forall\pi . Q_q^* . \psi[\pi_1 \mapsto \pi][\pi_2 \mapsto \pi] \ldots [\pi_n \mapsto \pi]$ where $\psi[\pi_i \mapsto \pi]$ replaces all occurrences of π_i in ψ with π.

Lemma 4. *Either $\varphi \equiv collapse(\varphi)$ or φ has no equivalent $\forall_\pi^1 . Q_q^*$ formula.*

Proof. The collapse function solely works on the trace quantification mechanism of the HyperQPTL formula, by reducing them to a single universal quantification. The theorem has been proven for $\forall^*$ HyperLTL formulas in [12]. Inner propositional quantification does not interfere with this mechanism, hence, the proof can be carried out identically.   □

Now we can formally define the linear $\forall_\pi^*$ fragment. Intuitively, we require that every input-output dependency can be ordered linearly, i.e., we are restricted to linear architectures without information forks (see Example 3).

Definition 3. *Let $O = \{o_1, \ldots, o_n\}$. A HyperQPTL formula φ is called linear if for all $o_i \in O$ there is a $J_i \subseteq I$ such that $\varphi \wedge D_{I \mapsto O} \equiv collapse(\varphi) \wedge \bigwedge_{o_i \in O} D_{J_i \mapsto \{o_i\}}$ and $J_i \subseteq J_{i+1}$ for all $i \leq n$.*

This results in the following corollary. Since the universal quantifiers can be collapsed, the resulting problem is the realizability problem of QPTL in a linear architecture, which is decidable [17].

Corollary 4. *Realizability of the linear $\forall_\pi^* Q_q^*$ fragment is decidable.*

Remark on Complexities. Our aim was to work out the largest possible fragments for which the realizability problem of HyperQPTL remains decidable. The three fragments for which we could prove decidability all subsume the logic QPTL, for which the realizability problem is known to be non-elementary (already its satisfiability problem is non-elementary [30]). Hence, realizability of the discussed HyperQPTL fragments has a non-elementary lower bound. Finding interesting fragments for which the problem has a more feasible complexity therefore remains an open challenge.

5   Experiments

We have implemented a prototype tool that can solve the HyperQPTL realizability problem using the bounded synthesis approach [18]. More concretely, we extended the HyperLTL synthesis tool BoSy [7,9,12]. Bosy reduces the HyperLTL synthesis problem to a SMT constraint system which is then solved by z3 [8] (for more see [12]). We implemented the reduction of HyperQPTL synthesis to HyperLTL synthesis (Corollary 2) in BoSy, such that the tool can also handle HyperQPTL formulas. We evaluated the tool against a range of

Table 1. Experimental results for prompt arbiter

Instance	Bound on system	Bound on ∃-strategy	Result	Time [sec.]
arbiter-2-prompt	2	1	unsat	<1
	2	2	sat	<1
arbiter-2-full-prompt	3	1	unsat	2.4
	3	2	sat	6.0
arbiter-3-prompt	3	1	unsat	4.2
	3	2	sat	9.5
arbiter-4-prompt	4	1	unsat	97
	4	2	?	TO

benchmarks sets, shown in Table 1. The first column indicates the parameterized benchmark name. The second and third columns indicate the bounds given to the bounded synthesis procedure. The second column is the bound on the size of the system. The newest version of BoSy also bounds the size of the strategy for the existential player, this bound is given in column three. For a detailed explanation of how existential strategies are bounded in BoSy, we refer to [7].

We synthesized a range of resource arbiters. Our benchmark set is parametric in the number of clients that can request access to the shared resource (written arbiter-k-prompt where k is the number of clients in Table 1). Unlike normal arbiters, we require the arbiter to fulfill promptness for some of the clients, i.e., requests must be answered within a bounded number of steps [33]. We state the promptness requirement in HyperQPTL by applying the *alternating-color technique* from [24]. Intuitively, the alternating-color technique works as follows: We quantify a q-sequence that "changes color" between q and $\neg q$. Each change of color is used as a potential bound. Once a request occurs, the grant must be given withing two changes of color. Thus, the HyperQPTL formulation amounts to the following specifications, here exemplary for 2 clients, where we require promptness only for client 1.

$$\forall \pi. \Box \neg (g_\pi^1 \wedge g_\pi^2) \tag{1}$$

$$\forall \pi. \Box (r_\pi^2 \rightarrow \Diamond g_\pi^2) \tag{2}$$

$$\exists q. \forall \pi. \Box \Diamond q \wedge \Box \Diamond \neg q \tag{3}$$

$$\begin{aligned} &\wedge \Box (r_\pi^1 \rightarrow (q \rightarrow (q\,\mathcal{U}(\neg q\,\mathcal{U}\,g_\pi^1)))) \\ &\quad \wedge (\neg q \rightarrow (\neg q\,\mathcal{U}(q\,\mathcal{U}\,g_\pi^1)))) \\ \forall \pi. (\neg g_\pi^1\,\mathcal{W}\,r_\pi^1) &\wedge (\neg g_\pi^2\,\mathcal{W}\,r_\pi^2) \end{aligned} \tag{4}$$

Formula 1 states mutual exclusion. Formula 2 states that client 2 must be served eventually (but not within a bounded number of steps). Formula 3 states the promptness requirement for client 1. It quantifies an alternating q-sequence, which serves as a sequence of global bounds that must be respected on all traces π. Then, if client 1 poses a request, the grant must be given within two changes of the value of q. Formula 4 is only added in benchmarks named arbiter-k-full-prompt. It specifies that no spurious grants should be given.

BoSy successfully synthesizes prompt arbiter of up to 3 states. For a 4-state prompt arbiter BoSy did not return in reasonable time.

6   Conclusion

We studied the hyperlogic HyperQPTL, which combines the concepts of trace relations and ω-regularity. We showed that HyperQPTL is very expressive, it can express properties like *promptness, bounded waiting for a grant, epistemic* properties, and, in particular, any ω-*regular* property. Those properties are not expressible in previously studied hyperlogics like HyperLTL. At the same time, we argued that the expressiveness of HyperQPTL is optimal in a sense that a more expressive logic for ω-regular hyperproperties would have an undecidable model checking problem. We furthermore studied the realizability problem of HyperQPTL. We showed that realizability is decidable for HyperQPTL fragments that contain properties like promptness. But still, in contrast to the satisfiability problem, propositional quantification does make the realizability problem of hyperlogics harder. More specifically, the HyperQPTL fragment of formulas with a universal-existential propositional quantifier alternation followed by a single trace quantifier is undecidable in general, even though the projection of the fragment to HyperLTL has a decidable realizability problem. Lastly, we implemented the bounded synthesis problem for HyperQPTL in the prototype tool BoSy. Using BoSy with HyperQPTL specifications, we have been able to synthesize several resource arbiters. The synthesis problem of non-linear-time hyperlogics is still open. For example, it is not yet known how to synthesize systems from specifications given in branching-time hyperlogics like HyperCTL*.

References

1. Bonakdarpour, B., Finkbeiner, B.: Program repair for hyperproperties. In: Chen, Y.-F., Cheng, C.-H., Esparza, J. (eds.) ATVA 2019. LNCS, vol. 11781, pp. 423–441. Springer, Cham (2019). https://doi.org/10.1007/978-3-030-31784-3_25
2. Bozzelli, L., Maubert, B., Pinchinat, S.: Unifying hyper and epistemic temporal logics. In: Pitts, A. (ed.) FoSSaCS 2015. LNCS, vol. 9034, pp. 167–182. Springer, Heidelberg (2015). https://doi.org/10.1007/978-3-662-46678-0_11
3. Chaum, D.: Security without identification: transaction systems to make big brother obsolete. Commun. ACM **28**(10), 1030–1044 (1985). https://doi.org/10.1145/4372.4373

4. Clarkson, M.R., Finkbeiner, B., Koleini, M., Micinski, K.K., Rabe, M.N., Sánchez, C.: Temporal logics for hyperproperties. In: Abadi, M., Kremer, S. (eds.) POST 2014. LNCS, vol. 8414, pp. 265–284. Springer, Heidelberg (2014). https://doi.org/10.1007/978-3-642-54792-8_15

5. Clarkson, M.R., Schneider, F.B.: Hyperproperties. J. Comput. Secur. **18**(6), 1157–1210 (2010). https://doi.org/10.3233/JCS-2009-0393

6. Coenen, N., Finkbeiner, B., Hahn, C., Hofmann, J.: The hierarchy of hyperlogics. In: 34th Annual ACM/IEEE Symposium on Logic in Computer Science (LICS 2019), pp. 1–13 (2019). https://doi.org/10.1109/LICS.2019.8785713

7. Coenen, N., Finkbeiner, B., Sánchez, C., Tentrup, L.: Verifying hyperliveness. In: Dillig, I., Tasiran, S. (eds.) CAV 2019. LNCS, vol. 11561, pp. 121–139. Springer, Cham (2019). https://doi.org/10.1007/978-3-030-25540-4_7

8. de Moura, L., Bjørner, N.: Z3: an efficient SMT solver. In: Ramakrishnan, C.R., Rehof, J. (eds.) TACAS 2008. LNCS, vol. 4963, pp. 337–340. Springer, Heidelberg (2008). https://doi.org/10.1007/978-3-540-78800-3_24

9. Faymonville, P., Finkbeiner, B., Tentrup, L.: BoSy: an experimentation framework for bounded synthesis. In: Majumdar, R., Kunčak, V. (eds.) CAV 2017. LNCS, vol. 10427, pp. 325–332. Springer, Cham (2017). https://doi.org/10.1007/978-3-319-63390-9_17

10. Finkbeiner, B., Hahn, C.: Deciding hyperproperties. In: Proceedings of CONCUR. LIPIcs, vol. 59, pp. 13:1–13:14. Schloss Dagstuhl - Leibniz-Zentrum fuer Informatik (2016). https://doi.org/10.4230/LIPIcs.CONCUR.2016.13

11. Finkbeiner, B., Hahn, C., Hans, T.: MGHYPER: checking satisfiability of hyperltl formulas beyond the $\exists^*\forall^*$ fragment. In: Lahiri, S.K., Wang, C. (eds.) ATVA 2018. LNCS, vol. 11138, pp. 521–527. Springer, Cham (2018). https://doi.org/10.1007/978-3-030-01090-4_31

12. Finkbeiner, B., Hahn, C., Lukert, P., Stenger, M., Tentrup, L.: Synthesizing reactive systems from hyperproperties. In: Chockler, H., Weissenbacher, G. (eds.) CAV 2018. LNCS, vol. 10981, pp. 289–306. Springer, Cham (2018). https://doi.org/10.1007/978-3-319-96145-3_16

13. Finkbeiner, B., Hahn, C., Lukert, P., Stenger, M., Tentrup, L.: Synthesis from hyperproperties. Acta Inf. **57**(1), 137–163 (2020). https://doi.org/10.1007/s00236-019-00358-2

14. Finkbeiner, B., Hahn, C., Stenger, M.: EAHyper: satisfiability, implication, and equivalence checking of hyperproperties. In: Majumdar, R., Kunčak, V. (eds.) CAV 2017. LNCS, vol. 10427, pp. 564–570. Springer, Cham (2017). https://doi.org/10.1007/978-3-319-63390-9_29

15. Finkbeiner, B., Hahn, C., Torfah, H.: Model checking quantitative hyperproperties. In: Chockler, H., Weissenbacher, G. (eds.) CAV 2018. LNCS, vol. 10981, pp. 144–163. Springer, Cham (2018). https://doi.org/10.1007/978-3-319-96145-3_8

16. Finkbeiner, B., Rabe, M.N., Sánchez, C.: Algorithms for model checking hyperLTL and hyperCTL*. In: Kroening, D., Păsăreanu, C.S. (eds.) CAV 2015. LNCS, vol. 9206, pp. 30–48. Springer, Cham (2015). https://doi.org/10.1007/978-3-319-21690-4_3

17. Finkbeiner, B., Schewe, S.: Uniform distributed synthesis. In: Proceedings of LICS, pp. 321–330. IEEE Computer Society (2005). https://doi.org/10.1109/LICS.2005.53

18. Finkbeiner, B., Schewe, S.: Bounded synthesis. STTT **15**(5–6), 519–539 (2013). https://doi.org/10.1007/s10009-012-0228-z

19. Finkbeiner, B., Zimmermann, M.: The first-order logic of hyperproperties. In: Proceedings of STACS. LIPIcs, vol. 66, pp. 30:1–30:14. Schloss Dagstuhl - Leibniz-Zentrum fuer Informatik (2017). https://doi.org/10.4230/LIPIcs.STACS.2017.30

20. Goguen, J.A., Meseguer, J.: Security policies and security models. In: Proceedings of S&P, pp. 11–20. IEEE Computer Society (1982). https://doi.org/10.1109/SP.1982.10014

21. Hahn, C.: Algorithms for monitoring hyperproperties. In: Finkbeiner, B., Mariani, L. (eds.) RV 2019. LNCS, vol. 11757, pp. 70–90. Springer, Cham (2019). https://doi.org/10.1007/978-3-030-32079-9_5

22. Halpern, J.Y., Vardi, M.Y.: The complexity of reasoning about knowledge and time. i. lower bounds. J. Comput. Syst. Sci. 38(1), 195–237 (1989). https://doi.org/10.1016/0022-0000(89)90039-1

23. Kaivola, R.: Using automata to characterise fixed point temporal logics. Ph.D. thesis (1997)

24. Kupferman, O., Piterman, N., Vardi, M.Y.: From liveness to promptness. Formal Methods Syst. Des. 34(2), 83–103 (2009). https://doi.org/10.1007/s10703-009-0067-z

25. Nguyen, L.V., Kapinski, J., Jin, X., Deshmukh, J.V., Johnson, T.T.: Hyperproperties of real-valued signals. In: Proceedings of MEMOCODE, pp. 104–113. ACM (2017). https://doi.org/10.1145/3127041.3127058

26. Pnueli, A.: The temporal logic of programs. In: Proceedings of FOCS, pp. 46–57. IEEE Computer Society (1977). https://doi.org/10.1109/SFCS.1977.32

27. Pnueli, A., Rosner, R.: Distributed reactive systems are hard to synthesize. In: Proceedings of FOCS, pp. 746–757. IEEE Computer Society (1990). https://doi.org/10.1109/FSCS.1990.89597

28. Post, E.L.: A variant of a recursively unsolvable problem. Bull. Am. Math. Soc. 52(4), 264–268 (1946)

29. Rabe, M.N.: A temporal logic approach to information-flow control. Ph.D. thesis, Saarland University (2016)

30. Sistla, A.P., Vardi, M.Y., Wolper, P.: The complementation problem for Büchi automata with applications to temporal logic. In: Brauer, W. (ed.) ICALP 1985. LNCS, vol. 194, pp. 465–474. Springer, Heidelberg (1985). https://doi.org/10.1007/BFb0015772

31. Sistla, A.P.: Theoretical issues in the design and verification of distributed systems, Ph.D. thesis (1983)

32. Stucki, S., Sánchez, C., Schneider, G., Bonakdarpour, B.: Gray-box monitoring of hyperproperties. In: ter Beek, M.H., McIver, A., Oliveira, J.N. (eds.) FM 2019. LNCS, vol. 11800, pp. 406–424. Springer, Cham (2019). https://doi.org/10.1007/978-3-030-30942-8_25

33. Tentrup, L., Weinert, A., Zimmermann, M.: Approximating optimal bounds in prompt-ltl realizability in doubly-exponential time. In: Proceedings of GandALF, EPTCS, vol. 226, pp. 302–315 (2016). https://doi.org/10.4204/EPTCS.226.21

34. Zdancewic, S., Myers, A.C.: Observational determinism for concurrent program security. In: Proceedings of CSFW, p. 29. IEEE Computer Society (2003). https://doi.org/10.1109/CSFW.2003.1212703

AdamMC: A Model Checker for Petri Nets with Transits against Flow-LTL

Bernd Finkbeiner[1], Manuel Gieseking[2]($^{\boxtimes}$),
Jesko Hecking-Harbusch[1],
and Ernst-Rüdiger Olderog[2]

[1] Saarland University, Saarbrücken, Germany
{finkbeiner,hecking-harbusch}@react.uni-saarland.de
[2] University of Oldenburg, Oldenburg, Germany
{gieseking,olderog}@informatik.uni-oldenburg.de

Abstract. The correctness of networks is often described in terms of the individual data flow of components instead of their global behavior. In software-defined networks, it is far more convenient to specify the correct behavior of packets than the global behavior of the entire network. Petri nets with transits extend Petri nets and Flow-LTL extends LTL such that the data flows of tokens can be tracked. We present the tool AdamMC as the first model checker for Petri nets with transits against Flow-LTL. We describe how AdamMC can automatically encode concurrent updates of software-defined networks as Petri nets with transits and how common network specifications can be expressed in Flow-LTL. Underlying AdamMC is a reduction to a circuit model checking problem. We introduce a new reduction method that results in tremendous performance improvements compared to a previous prototype. Thereby, AdamMC can handle software-defined networks with up to 82 switches.

1 Introduction

In networks, it is difficult to specify correctness in terms of the global behavior of the entire system. Instead, the individual *flow* of components is far more convenient to specify correct behavior. For example, loop and drop freedom can be easily specified for the flow of each packet. Petri nets and LTL lack this local view. Petri nets with transits and Flow-LTL have been introduced to overcome this restriction [10]. A transit relation is introduced to follow the *flow* induced by tokens. *Flow-LTL* is a temporal logic to specify both the *local* flow of data and the *global* behavior of markings. The global behavior as in Petri nets and LTL is still important for maximality and fairness assumptions. In this paper,

---

[1] AdamMC is available online at https://uol.de/en/csd/adammc [12].

This work was supported by the German Research Foundation (DFG) Grant Petri Games (392735815) and the Collaborative Research Center "Foundations of Perspicuous Software Systems" (TRR 248, 389792660), and by the European Research Council (ERC) Grant OSARES (683300).

S. K. Lahiri and C. Wang (Eds.): CAV 2020, LNCS 12225, pp. 64–76, 2020.
https://doi.org/10.1007/978-3-030-53291-8_5

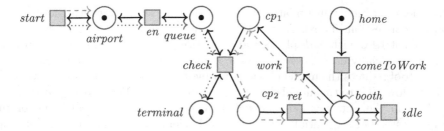

Fig. 1. Access control at an airport modeled as Petri net with transits. Colored arrows display the transit relation and define flow chains to model the passengers.

we present the tool ADAMMC[1] as the first model checker for Petri nets with transits against Flow-LTL and its application to software-defined networking.

In Fig. 1, we present an example of a Petri net with transits that models the security check at an airport where passengers are checked by a security guard. The number of passengers entering the airport is unknown in advance. Rather than introducing the complexity of an infinite number of tokens, we use a fixed number of tokens to model possibly infinitely many *flow chains*. This is done by the transit relation which is depicted with colored arrows.

The left-hand side of Fig. 1 models passengers who want to reach the terminal. There are three tokens in the places *airport*, *queue*, and *terminal*. Thus, transitions *start* and *en* are always enabled. Each firing of *start* creates a new flow chain as depicted by the green arrow. This models a new person arriving at the *airport*. Meanwhile, the double-headed blue arrow maintains all flow chains that are still in place *airport*. Passengers have to *en*ter the *queue* and wait until the security *check* is performed. Therefore, transition *en* continues every flow chain in *airport* to *queue*. Checking the passengers is carried out by transition *check* which becomes enabled if the security guard *work*s. Thus, passengers residing in *queue* have to wait until the guard *check*s them. Afterwards, they reach the *terminal*. The security guard is modeled on the right-hand side of Fig. 1. By firing *comeToWork* and thus moving the token in place *home*, her flow chain starts and she can repeatedly either *idle* or *work*, *check* passengers, and *ret*urn. Her transit relation is depicted in orange and models exactly one flow chain.

In Fig. 1, we define the checkpoints cp_1 and cp_2 and the *booth* as a security zone and require that passengers never enter the security zone and eventually reach the *terminal*. The flow formula $\varphi = \mathbb{A}(airport \rightarrow (\Box\neg(cp_1 \vee cp_2 \vee booth) \wedge \Diamond terminal))$ specifies this. ADAMMC verifies the example from Fig. 1 against the formula $\Box\Diamond check \rightarrow \varphi$ specifying that if passengers are checked regularly then they cannot access the security zone and eventually reach the terminal.

In this paper, we present ADAMMC as a full-fledged tool. First, ADAMMC can handle Petri nets with transits and Flow-LTL formulas in general. Second, ADAMMC has an input interface for a concurrent update and a software-defined network and encodes both of them as a Petri nets with transits. Common assumptions on fairness and requirements for network correctness are also provided as Flow-LTL formulas. This allows users of the tool to model check the correctness of concurrent updates and to prevent packet loss, routing loops, and network congestion. Third, ADAMMC provides algorithms to check safe Petri nets against LTL with *both* places and transitions as atomic propositions which makes it especially easy to specify fairness and maximality assumptions.

The tool reduces the model checking problem for safe Petri nets with transits against Flow-LTL to the model checking problem for safe Petri nets against LTL. We develop the new *parallel approach* to check global and local behavior in parallel instead of sequentially. This approach yields a tremendous speed-up for a few local requirements and realistic fairness assumptions in comparison to the sequential approach of a previous prototype [10]. In general, the parallel approach has worst-case complexity inferior to the sequential approach even though the complexities of both approaches are the same when using only one flow formula.

As last step, ADAMMC reduces the model checking problem of safe Petri nets against LTL to a circuit model checking problem. This is solved by ABC [2,4] with effective verification techniques like IC3 and bounded model checking. ADAMMC verifies concurrent updates of software-defined networks with up to 38 switches (31 more than the prototype) and falsifies concurrent updates of software-defined networks with up to 82 switches (44 more than the prototype).

The paper is structured as follows: In Sect. 2, we recall Petri nets with transits and Flow-LTL. In Sect. 3, we outline the three application areas of ADAMMC: checking safe Petri nets with transits against Flow-LTL, checking concurrent updates of software-defined networks against common assumptions and specifications, and checking safe Petri nets against LTL. In Sect. 4, we algorithmically encode concurrent updates of software-defined networks in Petri nets with transits. In Sect. 5, we introduce the parallel approach for the underlying circuit model checking problem. In Sect. 6, we present our experimental evaluation.

Further details can be found in the full paper [13].

2 Petri Nets with Transits and Flow-LTL

A safe *Petri net with transits* $\mathcal{N} = (\mathcal{P}, \mathcal{T}, \mathcal{F}, In, \Upsilon)$ [10] contains the set of *places* $\mathcal{P}$, the set of *transitions* $\mathcal{T}$, the *flow relation* $\mathcal{F} \subseteq (\mathcal{P} \times \mathcal{T}) \cup (\mathcal{T} \times \mathcal{P})$, and the *initial marking* $In \subseteq \mathcal{P}$ as in safe Petri nets [27]. In a *safe* Petri net, reachable markings contain at most one token per place. The *transit relation* Υ is for every transition $t \in \mathcal{T}$ of type $\Upsilon(t) \subseteq (pre^{\mathcal{N}}(t) \cup \{\triangleright\}) \times post^{\mathcal{N}}(t)$. With $p \; \Upsilon(t) \; q$, we define that firing transition t *transits* the flow in place p to place q. The symbol $\triangleright$ denotes a *start* and $\triangleright \Upsilon(t) \; q$ defines that firing transition t *starts* a new flow for the token in place q. Note that the transit relation can split, merge, and end flows. A sequence of flows leads to a *flow chain* which is a sequence of the current place and the fired outgoing transition. Thus, Petri nets with transits can describe both the global progress of tokens and the local flow of data.

Flow-LTL [10] extends Linear-time Temporal Logic (LTL) and uses places and transitions as atomic propositions. It introduces $\mathbb{A}$ as a new operator which uses LTL to specify the flow of data for *all* flow chains. For Fig. 1, the formula $\mathbb{A}(booth \rightarrow \Diamond check)$ specifies that the guard performs at least one check. We call

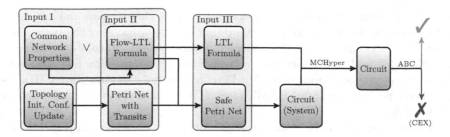

Fig. 2. Overview of the workflow of ADAMMC: The application areas of the tool are given by three different input domains: software-defined network/Flow-LTL (Input I), Petri nets with transits/Flow-LTL (Input II), and Petri nets/LTL (Input III). ADAMMC performs all unlabeled steps. MCHyper creates the final circuit which ABC checks to answer the initial model checking problem.

formulas starting with A *flow formulas*. Formulas around flow formulas specify the global progress of tokens in the form of markings and fired transitions to formalize maximality and fairness assumptions. These formulas are called *run formulas*. Often, Flow-LTL formulas have the form *run formula* → *flow formula*.

3   Application Areas

ADAMMC consists of modules for three application areas: checking safe Petri nets with transits against Flow-LTL, checking concurrent updates of software-defined networks against common assumptions and specifications, and checking safe Petri nets against LTL. The general architecture and workflow of the model checking procedure is given in Fig. 2. ADAMMC is based on the tool ADAM [14].
Petri Nets with Transits.   Petri nets with transits follow the progress of tokens and the flow of data. Flow-LTL allows to specify requirements on both. For Petri nets with transits and Flow-LTL (Input II), ADAMMC extends a parser for Petri nets provided by APT [30], provides a parser for Flow-LTL, and implements two reduction methods to create a safe Petri net and an LTL formula. The sequential approach is outlined in [10] and the parallel approach in Sect. 5.
Software-Defined Networks.   Concurrent updates of software-defined networks are the second application area of ADAMMC. The tool automatically encodes an initially configured network topology and a concurrent update as a Petri net with transits. The concurrent update renews the forwarding table. We provide parsers for the *network topology*, the *initial configuration*, the *concurrent update*, and Flow-LTL (Input I). In Sect. 4, we present the creation of a Petri net with transits from the input and Flow-LTL formulas for *common network properties* like *connectivity*, *loop freedom*, *drop freedom*, and *packet coherence*.
Petri Nets.   ADAMMC supports the model checking of safe Petri nets against LTL with both places *and* transitions as atomic propositions. It provides dedicated algorithms to check *interleaving-maximal* runs of the system. A run is interleaving-maximal if a transition is fired whenever a transition is

enabled. Furthermore, ADAMMC allows a concurrent view on runs and can check *concurrency-maximal* runs which demand that each subprocess of the system has to progress maximally rather than only the entire system. State-of-the-art tools like LoLA [32] and ITS-Tools [29] are restricted to interleaving-maximal runs and places as atomic propositions. For Petri net model checking (Input III), we allow Petri nets in APT and PNML format as input and provide a parser for LTL formulas.

The construction of the circuit in Aiger format [3] is defined in [11]. MCHyper [15] is used to create a circuit from a given circuit and an LTL formula. This circuit is given to ABC [2,4] which provides a toolbox of modern hardware verification algorithms like IC3 and bounded model checking to decide the initial model checking question. As output for all three modules, ADAMMC transforms a possible counterexample (CEX) from ABC into a counterexample to the Petri net (with transits) and visualizes the net with Graphviz and the dot language [9]. When no counterexample exists, ADAMMC verified the input successfully.

4   Verifying Updates of Software Defined Networks

We show how ADAMMC can check concurrent updates of realistic examples from software-defined networking (SDN) against typical specifications [19]. SDN [6,25] separates the *data plane* for forwarding packets and the *control plane* for the routing configuration. A central controller initiates updates which can cause problems like routing loops or packet loss. ADAMMC provides an input interface to automatically encode software-defined networks and concurrent updates of their configuration as Petri nets with transits. The tool checks requirements like loop and drop freedom to find erroneous updates before they are deployed.

4.1   Network Topology, Configurations, and Updates

A *network topology* T is an undirected graph $T = (Sw, Con)$ with *switches* as vertices and *connections* between switches as edges. Packets enter the network at *ingress* switches and they leave at *egress* switches. *Forwarding* rules are of the form x.fwd(y) with x, y $\in$ Sw. A concurrent *update* has the following syntax:

switch update   ::= upd(x.fwd(y/z)) | upd(x.fwd(y/-)) | upd(x.fwd(-/z))
sequential update ::= (update >> update >> ... >> update)
parallel update   ::= (update || update || ... || update)
update   ::= switch update | sequential update | parallel update

where a switch update can renew the forwarding rule of switch x from switch z to switch y, introduce a new forwarding rule from switch x to switch y, or remove an existing forwarding rule from switch x to switch z.

4.2 Data Plane and Control Plane as Petri Net with Transits

For a network topology $T = (Sw, Con)$, a set of *ingress* switches, a set of *egress* switches, an initial *forwarding* table, and a concurrent *update*, we show how data and control plane are encoded as Petri net with transits. Switches are modeled by tokens remaining in corresponding places **s** whereas the flow of packets is modeled by the transit relation Υ. Specific transitions i_s model ingress switches where new data flows begin. Tokens in places of the form **x.fwd(y)** configure the forwarding. Data flows are extended by firing transitions **(x,y)** corresponding to configured forwarding without moving any tokens. Thus, we model any order of newly generated packets and their forwarding. Assuming that each existing direction of a connection between two switches is explicitly given in Con, we obtain Algorithm 1 which calls Algorithm 2 to obtain the control plane.

input : $T = (Sw, Con)$, ingress, forwarding, update
output: Petri net with transits
$\mathcal{N} = (\mathcal{P}, \mathcal{T}, \mathcal{F}, In, \Upsilon)$ for update of topology T with ingress and forwarding
create empty $\mathcal{N} = (\mathcal{P}, \mathcal{T}, \mathcal{F}, In, \Upsilon)$;
for switch $s \in Sw$ **do**
    add place **s** to $\mathcal{P}$;
    add place **s** to In;
    if $s \in$ ingress **then**
       add transition i_s to $\mathcal{T}$;
       add **s** to $pre(i_s)$, $post(i_s)$;
       add creating data flow
       $\triangleright \Upsilon(i_s)$ **s** to Υ;
       add maintaining data flow
       s $\Upsilon(i_s)$ **s** to Υ;
for connection $(x, y) \in Con$ **do**
    add place **x.fwd(y)** to $\mathcal{P}$;
    if **x.fwd(y)** $\in$ forwarding **then**
       add place **x.fwd(y)** to In;
    add transition **(x,y)** to $\mathcal{T}$;
    add **x, y, x.fwd(y)** to
       $pre((x,y))$, $post((x,y))$;
    add connecting data flow
       x $\Upsilon((x,y))$ **y** to Υ;
    add maintaining data flow
       y $\Upsilon((x,y))$ **y** to Υ;
$\mathcal{N} = $ call Algorithm 2 with T, update, $\mathcal{N}$ as input;
add place $update^s$ to In;

Algorithm 1: Data plane

input : $T = (Sw, Con)$, update, $\mathcal{N}$
output: $\mathcal{N} = (\mathcal{P}, \mathcal{T}, \mathcal{F}, In, \Upsilon)$
for switch update $u \in SwU$ **do**
    // $u = $ upd(x.fwd(y/z))
    add places u^s, u^f to $\mathcal{P}$;
    add transition u to $\mathcal{T}$;
    add u^s to $pre(u)$, u^f to $post(u)$;
    if $z \neq -$ **then**
       add **x.fwd(z)** to $pre(u)$;
    if $y \neq -$ **then**
       add **x.fwd(y)** to $post(u)$;
for sequential update $s \in SeU$ **do**
    // $s = [s_1, ..., s_i, ..., s_{|s|}]$
    add places s^s, s^f to $\mathcal{P}$;
    for $i \in \{0, ..., |s|\}$ **do**
       add transition s^i to $\mathcal{T}$;
       if $i = 0$ **then**
          add s^s to $pre(s^i)$;
       else
          add s_i^f to $pre(s^i)$;
       if $i = |s|$ **then**
          add s^f to $post(s^i)$;
       else
          add s_{i+1}^s to $post(s^i)$;
for parallel update $p \in PaU$ **do**
    add places p^s, p^f to $\mathcal{P}$;
    add transitions p^o, p^c to $\mathcal{T}$;
    add p^s to $pre(p^o)$, p^f to $post(p^c)$;
    for sub-update u_i of p **do**
       add u_i^s to $post(p^o)$, u_i^f to $pre(p^c)$;

Algorithm 2: Control plane

For the *update*, let SwU be the set of switch updates in it, SeU the set of sequential updates in it, and PaU the set of parallel updates in it. Depending on *update*'s type, it is also added to the respective set. The subnet for the *update* has an empty transit relation but moves tokens from and to places of the form x.fwd(y). Tokens in these places correspond to the forwarding table. The order of the switch updates is defined by the nesting of sequential and parallel updates. The *update* is realized by a specific token moving through unique places of the form $u^s, u^f, s^s, s^f, p^s, p^f$ for start and finish of each switch update $u \in SwU$, each sequential update $s \in SeU$, and each parallel update $p \in PaU$. A parallel update temporarily increases the number of tokens and reduces it upon completion to one. Algorithm 2 defines the update behavior between start and finish places and connects finish and start places depending on the subexpression structure.

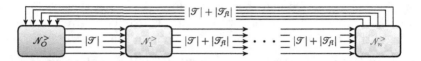

Fig. 3. Overview of the *sequential approach*: Each firing of a transition of the original net is split into first firing a transition in the subnet for the run formula and subsequently firing a transition in each subnet tracking a flow formula. The constructed LTL formula skips the additional steps with until operators.

Fig. 4. Overview of the *parallel approach*: The n subnets are connected such that for every transition $t \in \mathscr{T}$ there are $(|\Upsilon(t)| + 1)^n$ transitions, i.e., there is one transition for every combination of which transit of t (or none) is tracked by which subnet. We use until operators in the constructed LTL formula to only skip steps not involving the tracking of the guessed chain in the flow formula.

4.3 Assumptions and Requirements

We use the run formula $\lozenge \square pre(t) \rightarrow \square \lozenge t$ to assume weak fairness for every transition t in our encoding $\mathcal{N}$. Transitions, which are always enabled after some point, are ensured to fire infinitely often. Thus, packets are eventually forwarded and the routing table is eventually updated. We use flow formulas to test specific requirements for all packets. Connectivity $(\mathbb{A}(\lozenge \bigvee_{s \in egress} s))$ ensures that all packets reach an egress switch. Packet coherence $(\mathbb{A}(\square (\bigvee_{s \in initial} s) \vee \square(\bigvee_{s \in final} s)))$ tests that packets are either routed according to the initial or final configuration. Drop freedom $(\mathbb{A} \square (\bigwedge_{e \in egress} \neg e \rightarrow \bigvee_{f \in Con} f))$ forbids dropped packets whereas loop freedom $(\mathbb{A} \square (\bigwedge_{s \in Sw \setminus egress} s \rightarrow (s \cup \square \neg s)))$ forbids routing loops. We combine run and flow formula into *fairness* $\rightarrow$ *requirement*.

5 Algorithms and Optimizations

Central to model checking a Petri net with transits $\mathcal{N}$ against a Flow-LTL formula φ is the reduction to a safe Petri net $\mathcal{N}^>$ and an LTL formula $\varphi^>$. The infinite state space of the Petri net with transits due to possibly infinitely many flow chains is reduced to a finite state model. The key idea is to guess and track a violating flow chain for each flow subformula $\mathbb{A}\,\psi_i$, for $i \in \{1, \ldots, n\}$, and to only once check the equivalent future of flow chains merging into a common place.

AdamMC provides two approaches for this reduction: Fig. 3 and Fig. 4 give an overview of the *sequential* approach and the *parallel* approach, respectively. Both algorithms create one subnet $\mathcal{N}_i^>$ for each flow subformula $\mathbb{A}\,\psi_i$ to track the corresponding flow chain and have one subnet $\mathcal{N}_O^>$ to check the run part of the formula. The places of $\mathcal{N}_O^>$ are copies of the places in $\mathcal{N}$ such that the current state of the system can be memorized. The subnets $\mathcal{N}_i^>$ also consist of the original places of $\mathcal{N}$ but only use one token (initially residing on an additional place) to track the current state of the considered flow chain. The approaches differ in how these nets are connected to obtain $\mathcal{N}^>$.

Sequential Approach.   The places in each subnet $\mathcal{N}_i^>$ are connected with one transition for each transit ($\mathcal{T}_{\mathit{fl}} = \bigcup_{t \in \mathcal{T}} \Upsilon(t)$). An additional token iterates sequentially through the subnets to activate or deactivate the subnet. This allows each subnet to track a flow chain corresponding to firing a transition in $\mathcal{N}_O^>$. The formula $\varphi^>$ takes care of these additional steps by means of the until operator: In the run part of the formula, all steps corresponding to moves in a subnet $\mathcal{N}_i^>$ are skipped and, for each subformula $\mathbb{A}\,\psi_i$, all steps are skipped until the next transition of the corresponding subnet is fired which transits the tracked flow chain. This technique results in a polynomial increase of the size of the Petri net and the formula: $\mathcal{N}^>$ has $\mathcal{O}(|\mathcal{N}| \cdot n + |\mathcal{N}|)$ places and $\mathcal{O}(|\mathcal{N}|^3 \cdot n + |\mathcal{N}|)$ transitions and the size of $\varphi^>$ is in $\mathcal{O}(|\mathcal{N}|^3 \cdot n \cdot |\varphi| + |\varphi|)$. We refer to [11] for formal details.

Parallel Approach.   The n subnets are connected such that the current chain of each subnet is tracked simultaneously while firing an original transition $t \in \mathcal{T}$. Thus, there are $(|\Upsilon(t)| + 1)^n$ transitions. Each of these transitions stands for exactly one combination of which subnet is tracking which (or no) transit. Hence, firing one transition of the original net is directly tracked in one step for all subnets. This significantly reduces the complexity of the run part of the constructed formula, since no until operator is needed to skip sequential steps. A disjunction over all transitions corresponding to an original transition suffices to ensure correctness of the construction. Transitions and next operators in the flow parts of the formula still have to be replaced by means of the until operator to ensure that the next step of the tracked flow chain is checked at the corresponding step of the global timeline of $\varphi^>$. In general, the parallel approach results in an exponential blow-up of the net and the formula: $\mathcal{N}^>$ has $\mathcal{O}(|\mathcal{N}| \cdot n + |\mathcal{N}|)$ places and $\mathcal{O}(|\mathcal{N}|^{3n} + |\mathcal{N}|)$ transitions and the size of $\varphi^>$ is in $\mathcal{O}(|\mathcal{N}|^{3n} \cdot |\varphi| + |\varphi|)$. For the practical examples, however, the parallel approach allows for model checking Flow-LTL with few flow subformulas with a tremendous speed-up in comparison to the sequential approach. Formal details are in the full version of the paper [13].

Table 1. Overview of optimization parameters of ADAMMC: The three reduction steps depicted in the first column can each be executed by different algorithms. The first step allows to combine the optimizations of the first and second row.

1) Petri Net with Transits ⤳ Petri Net	sequential		parallel	
	inhibitor	act. token	inhibitor	act. token
2) Petri Net ⤳ Circuit	explicit		logarithmic	
3) Circuit ⤳ Circuit	gate optimizations			

Optimizations. Various optimizations parameters can be applied to the model checking routine described in Sect. 3 to tweak the performance. Table 1 gives an overview of the major parameters.

We found that the versions of the sequential and the parallel approach with inhibitor arcs to track flow chains are generally faster than the versions without. Furthermore, the reduction step from a Petri net into a circuit with logarithmically encoded transitions had oftentimes better performance than the same step with explicitly encoded transitions. However, several possibilities to reduce the number of gates of the created circuit worsened the performance of some benchmark families and improved the performance of others. Consequently, all parameters are selectable by the user and a script is provided to compare different settings. An overview of the selectable optimization parameters can be found in the documentation of ADAMMC [12]. Our main improvement claims can be retraced by the case study in Sect. 6.

6   Evaluation

We conduct a case study based on SDN with a corresponding artifact [16]. The performance improvements of ADAMMC compared to the prototype [10] are summarized in Table 2. For realistic software-defined networks [19], one ingress and one egress switch are chosen at random. Two forwarding tables between the two switches and an update from the first to the second configuration are chosen at random. ADAMMC verifies that the update maintained *connectivity* between ingress and egress switch. The results are depicted in rows starting with T. For rows starting with F, we required *connectivity* of a random switch which is not in the forwarding tables. ADAMMC falsified this requirement for the update.

The prototype implementation based on an *explicit encoding* can verify updates of networks with 7 switches and falsify updates of networks with 38 switches. We optimize the explicit encoding to a *logarithmic encoding* and the number of switches for which updates can be verified increases to 17. More significantly, the *parallel approach* in combination with the logarithmic encoding leads to tremendous performance gains. The performance gains of an approach with inferior worst-case complexity are mainly due to the smaller complexity of the LTL formula created by the reduction. The encoding of SDN requires fairness assumptions for each transition. These assumptions (encoded in the run

Table 2. We compare the explicit and logarithmic encoding of the sequential approach with the parallel approach. The results are the average over five runs from an Intel i7-2700K CPU with 3.50 GHz, 32 GB RAM, and a timeout (TO) of 30 min. The runtimes are given in seconds.

T / F	Network	#Sw	expl. enc.			log. enc.			parallel appr.		
			Alg.	Time	$\models$	Alg.	Time	$\models$	Alg.	Time	$\models$
T	Arpanet196912	4	IC3	12.08	✓	IC3	9.89	✓	IC3	**2.18**	✓
T	Napnet	6	IC3	146.49	✓	IC3	96.06	✓	IC3	**4.75**	✓
	...			...			...			...	
T	Heanet	7	IC3	806.81	✓	IC3	84.62	✓	IC3	**30.30**	✓
T	HiberniaIreland	7	-	TO	?	-	TO	?	IC3	**26.58**	✓
T	Arpanet19706	9	-	TO	?	IC3	362.21	✓	IC3	**11.33**	✓
T	Nordu2005	9	-	TO	?	-	TO	?	IC3	**12.67**	✓
	...			...			...			...	
T	Fatman	17	-	TO	?	IC3	1543.34	✓	IC3	**162.17**	✓
	...			...			...			...	
T	Myren	37	-	TO	?	-	TO	?	IC3	**1309.23**	✓
T	KentmanJan2011	38	-	TO	?	-	TO	?	IC3	**1261.32**	✓
F	Arpanet196912	4	BMC3	2.18	✗	BMC3	**1.85**	✗	BMC3	1.97	✗
F	Napnet	6	BMC2	4.17	✗	BMC2	5.22	✗	BMC3	**1.48**	✗
	...			...			...			...	
F	Fatman	17	BMC3	168.78	✗	BMC3	169.82	✗	BMC3	**6.72**	✗
	...			...			...			...	
F	Belnet2009	21	BMC2	1146.26	✗	BMC2	611.81	✗	BMC3	**24.26**	✗
	...			...			...			...	
F	KentmanJan2011	38	BMC3	167.92	✗	BMC3	86.44	✗	BMC2	**9.35**	✗
	...			...			...			...	
F	Latnet	69	-	TO	?	-	TO	?	BMC2	**209.20**	✗
F	Ulaknet	82	-	TO	?	-	TO	?	BMC2	**1043.74**	✗
Sum of runtimes (in hours):				82.99			79.15			30.31	
Nb of TOs (of 230 exper.):				146			138			6	

part of the formula) experience a blow-up with until operators by the sequential approach but only need a disjunction in the parallel approach. Hence, the size of networks for which ADAMMC can verify updates increases to 38 switches and the size for which it can falsify updates increases to 82 switches. For rather small networks, the tool needs only a few seconds to verify and falsify updates which makes it a great option for operators when updating networks.

7   Related Work

We refer to [21] for an introduction to SDN. Solutions for correctness of updates of software-defined networks include *consistent updates* [7,28], *dynamic scheduling* [17], and *incremental updates* [18]. Both explicit and SMT-based model checking [1,5,22,23,26,31] is used to verify software-defined networks. Closest to our approach are models of networks as Kripke structures to use model checking for synthesis of correct network updates [8,24]. The model checking subroutine of the synthesizer assumes that each packet sees at most one updated switch. Our model checking routine does not make such an assumption.

There is a significant number of model checking tools (e.g., [29,32]) for Petri nets and an annual model checking contest [20]. ADAMMC is restricted to safe Petri nets whereas other tools can handle bounded and colored Petri nets. At the same time, only ADAMMC accepts LTL formulas with places *and* transitions as atomic propositions. This is essential to express fairness in our SDN encoding.

8   Conclusion

We presented the tool ADAMMC with its three application domains: checking safe Petri nets with transits against Flow-LTL, checking concurrent updates of software-defined networks against common assumptions and specifications, and checking safe Petri nets against LTL. New algorithms allow ADAMMC to model check software-defined networks of realistic size: it can verify updates of networks with up to 38 switches and can falsify updates of networks with up to 82 switches.

References

1. Ball, T., et al.: Vericon: towards verifying controller programs in software-defined networks. In: Proceedings of PLDI, pp. 282–293 (2014). https://doi.org/10.1145/2594291.2594317
2. Berkeley Logic Synthesis and Verification Group: ABC: A system for sequential synthesis and verification. http://www.eecs.berkeley.edu/~alanmi/abc/, version 1.01 81030
3. Biere, A., Heljanko, K., Wieringa, S.: AIGER 1.9 and beyond. Technical report (2011)
4. Brayton, R.K., Mishchenko, A.: ABC: an academic industrial-strength verification tool. In: Proceedings of CAV, pp. 24–40 (2010). https://doi.org/10.1007/978-3-642-14295-6_5
5. Canini, M., Venzano, D., Peresíni, P., Kostic, D., Rexford, J.: A NICE way to test openflow applications. In: Proceedings of NSDI, pp. 127–140 (2012). https://www.usenix.org/conference/nsdi12/technical-sessions/presentation/canini
6. Casado, M., Foster, N., Guha, A.: Abstractions for software-defined networks. Commun. ACM **57**(10), 86–95 (2014). https://doi.org/10.1145/2661061.2661063
7. Cerný, P., Foster, N., Jagnik, N., McClurg, J.: Optimal consistent network updates in polynomial time. In: Proceedings of DISC, pp. 114–128 (2016). https://doi.org/10.1007/978-3-662-53426-7_9
8. El-Hassany, A., Tsankov, P., Vanbever, L., Vechev, M.T.: Network-wide configuration synthesis. In: Proceedings of CAV, pp. 261–281 (2017). https://doi.org/10.1007/978-3-319-63390-9_14
9. Ellson, J., Gansner, E.R., Koutsofios, E., North, S.C., Woodhull, G.: Graphviz and dynagraph - static and dynamic graph drawing tools. In: Jünger M., Mutzel P. (eds.) Graph Drawing Software, pp. 127–148. Springer, Heidelberg (2004). https://doi.org/10.1007/978-3-642-18638-7_6

10. Finkbeiner, B., Gieseking, M., Hecking-Harbusch, J., Olderog, E.: Model checking data flows in concurrent network updates. In: Proceedings of ATVA, pp. 515–533 (2019). https://doi.org/10.1007/978-3-030-31784-3_30

11. Finkbeiner, B., Gieseking, M., Hecking-Harbusch, J., Olderog, E.: Model checking data flows in concurrent network updates (full version). Technical report (2019). http://arxiv.org/abs/1907.11061

12. Finkbeiner, B., Gieseking, M., Hecking-Harbusch, J., Olderog, E.: AdamMC - A Model Checker for Petri Nets with Transits against Flow-LTL. University of Oldenburg and Saarland University (2020). https://uol.de/en/csd/adammc

13. Finkbeiner, B., Gieseking, M., Hecking-Harbusch, J., Olderog, E.: AdamMC: A model checker for Petri nets with transits against Flow-LTL (full version). Technical report (2020). https://arxiv.org/abs/2005.07130

14. Finkbeiner, B., Gieseking, M., Olderog, E.: Adam: causality-based synthesis of distributed systems. In: Proceedings of CAV, pp. 433–439 (2015). https://doi.org/10.1007/978-3-319-21690-4_25

15. Finkbeiner, B., Rabe, M.N., Sánchez, C.: Algorithms for model checking HyperLTL and HyperCTL*. In: Proceedings of CAV, pp. 30–48 (2015). https://doi.org/10.1007/978-3-319-21690-4_3

16. Gieseking, M., Hecking-Harbusch, J.: AdamMC: A Model Checker for Petri Nets with Transits against Flow-LTL (Artifact) (2020). https://doi.org/10.6084/m9.figshare.11676171

17. Jin, X., et al.: Dynamic scheduling of network updates. In: Proceedings of SIGCOMM, pp. 539–550 (2014). https://doi.org/10.1145/2619239.2626307

18. Katta, N.P., Rexford, J., Walker, D.: Incremental consistent updates. In: Proceedings of HotSDN, pp. 49–54 (2013). https://doi.org/10.1145/2491185.2491191

19. Knight, S., Nguyen, H.X., Falkner, N., Bowden, R.A., Roughan, M.: The internet topology zoo. IEEE J. Selected Areas Commun. **29**(9), 1765–1775 (2011). https://doi.org/10.1109/JSAC.2011.111002

20. Kordon, F., et al.: Complete Results for the 2019 Edition of the Model Checking Contest. http://mcc.lip6.fr/2019/results.php, April 2019

21. Kreutz, D., Ramos, F.M.V., Veríssimo, P.J.E., Rothenberg, C.E., Azodolmolky, S., Uhlig, S.: Software-defined networking: a comprehensive survey. Proc. IEEE **103**(1), 14–76 (2015). https://doi.org/10.1109/JPROC.2014.2371999

22. Mai, H., Khurshid, A., Agarwal, R., Caesar, M., Godfrey, B., King, S.T.: Debugging the data plane with anteater. In: Proceedings of SIGCOMM, pp. 290–301 (2011). https://doi.org/10.1145/2018436.2018470

23. Majumdar, R., Tetali, S.D., Wang, Z.: Kuai: a model checker for software-defined networks. In: Proceedings of FMCAD, pp. 163–170 (2014). https://doi.org/10.1109/FMCAD.2014.6987609

24. McClurg, J., Hojjat, H., Cerný, P.: Synchronization synthesis for network programs. In: Proceedings of CAV, pp. 301–321 (2017). https://doi.org/10.1007/978-3-319-63390-9_16

25. McKeown, N., et al.: Openflow: enabling innovation in campus networks. Comput. Commun. Rev. **38**(2), 69–74 (2008). https://doi.org/10.1145/1355734.1355746

26. Padon, O., Immerman, N., Karbyshev, A., Lahav, O., Sagiv, M., Shoham, S.: Decentralizing SDN policies. In: Proceedings of POPL, pp. 663–676 (2015). https://doi.org/10.1145/2676726.2676990

27. Reisig, W.: Petri Nets: An Introduction. Springer, Heidelberg (1985). https://doi.org/10.1007/978-3-642-69968-9

28. Reitblatt, M., Foster, N., Rexford, J., Schlesinger, C., Walker, D.: Abstractions for network update. In: Proceedings of SIGCOMM, pp. 323–334 (2012). https://doi.org/10.1145/2342356.2342427
29. Thierry-Mieg, Y.: Symbolic model-checking using ITS-tools. In: Proceedings of TACAS, pp. 231–237 (2015). https://doi.org/10.1007/978-3-662-46681-0_20
30. University of Oldenburg: APT - Analyse von Petri-Netzen und Transitionssystemen. https://github.com/CvO-Theory/apt (2012)
31. Wang, A., Moarref, S., Loo, B.T., Topcu, U., Scedrov, A.: Automated synthesis of reactive controllers for software-defined networks. In: Proceedings of ICNP, pp. 1–6 (2013). https://doi.org/10.1109/ICNP.2013.6733666
32. Wolf, K.: Petri net model checking with LoLA 2. In: Proceedings of PETRI NETS, pp. 351–362 (2018). https://doi.org/10.1007/978-3-319-91268-4_18

Action-Based Model Checking: Logic, Automata, and Reduction

Stephen F. Siegel[✉] and Yihao Yan

University of Delaware, Newark, DE 19716, USA
{siegel,yihaoyan}@udel.edu

Abstract. Stutter invariant properties play a special role in state-based model checking: they are the properties that can be checked using partial order reduction (POR), an indispensable optimization. There are algorithms to decide whether an LTL formula or Büchi automaton (BA) specifies a stutter-invariant property, and to convert such a BA to a form that is appropriate for on-the-fly POR-based model checking.

The *interruptible* properties play the same role in action-based model checking that stutter-invariant properties play in the state-based case. These are the properties that are invariant under the insertion or deletion of "invisible" actions. We present algorithms to decide whether an LTL formula or BA specifies an interruptible property, and show how a BA can be transformed to an *interrupt normal form* that can be used in an on-the-fly POR algorithm. We have implemented these algorithms in a new model checker named McRERS, and demonstrate their effectiveness using the RERS 2019 benchmark suite.

Keywords: Model checking · Action · Event · LTL · Stutter-invariant

1 Introduction

To apply model checking to a concurrent system, one must formulate properties that the system is expected to satisfy. A property may be expressed by specifying acceptable sequences of states, or by specifying acceptable sequences of actions—the events that cause the state to change. Each approach has advantages and disadvantages, and in any particular context one may be more appropriate than the other.

In the state-based context, there is a rich theory involving automata, logic, and reduction for model checking. Some of the core ideas in this theory can be summarized as follows. First, the behavior of the concurrent system is represented by a state-transition system T. One identifies a set AP of atomic propositions, and each state of T is labeled by the set of propositions which hold at that state. An execution passes through an infinite sequence of states, which defines a *trace*, i.e., a sequence of subsets of AP. A *property* is a set of traces, and T satisfies the property if every trace of T is in P.

Y. Yan—Currently employed at Google.

S. K. Lahiri and C. Wang (Eds.): CAV 2020, LNCS 12225, pp. 77–100, 2020.
https://doi.org/10.1007/978-3-030-53291-8_6

Properties may be specified by formulas in a temporal logic, such as LTL [26]. There are algorithms (e.g., [37]) to convert an LTL formula ϕ to an equivalent Büchi automaton (BA) B_ϕ with alphabet 2^{AP}. (Properties may also be specified directly using BAs.) The system T satisfies ϕ if and only if the language of the synchronous product $T \otimes B_{\neg\phi}$ is empty. The emptiness of the language can be determined on-the-fly, i.e., while the reachable states of the product are being constructed.

A property P is *stutter-invariant* if it is closed under the insertion and deletion of repetitions, i.e., $s_0 s_1 \cdots \in P \iff s_0^{i_0} s_1^{i_1} \cdots \in P$ holds for any positive integers $i_0, i_1, \cdots$. Many algorithms are known for deciding whether an LTL formula or a BA specifies a stutter-invariant property [22,24]. There is also an argument that only stutter-invariant properties should be used in practice. For example, suppose that a trace is formed by sampling the state of a system once every millisecond. If we sample the same system twice each millisecond, and there are no state changes in the sub-millisecond intervals, the second trace will be stutter-equivalent to the first. A meaningful property should be invariant under this choice of time resolution.

Stutter-invariant properties are desirable for another reason: they admit the most significant optimization in model checking, partial order reduction (POR, [15,23,25]). At each state encountered in the exploration of the product space, an on-the-fly POR scheme produces a subset of the enabled transitions. Restricting the search to the transitions in those subsets does not affect the language emptiness question. Recent work has revealed that the BA must have a certain form—"SI normal form"—when POR is used with on-the-fly model checking, but any BA with a stutter-invariant language can be easily transformed into SI normal form [27].

The purpose of this paper is to elaborate an analogous theory for event-based models. Event-based models of concurrency are widely used and have been extremely influential for over three decades. For example, process algebras, such as CSP, are event-based and use *labeled transition systems* (LTSs) for the semantic model. Event-based models are the main formalism used in assume-guarantee reasoning (e.g, [10]), and in many other areas. There are mature model checking and verification tools for process algebras and LTSs, and which have significant industrial applications; see, e.g., [13]. Temporal logics, including LTL, CTL, and CTL*, have long been used to specify event-based systems [3,7,12].

We call the class of properties in the action context that are analogous to the stutter-invariant properties in the state context the *interruptible* properties (Sect. 3). These properties are invariant under "action stuttering" [34], i.e., the insertion or deletion of "invisible" actions. We present algorithms for deciding whether an LTL formula or a BA specifies an interruptible property (Theorems 1 and 2); to the best of our knowledge, these are the first published algorithms for deciding this property of formulas or automata.

Interruptible properties play the same role in action-based POR that stutter-invariant properties play in state-based POR. In particular, we present an action-based on-the-fly POR algorithm that works for interruptible properties (Sect. 4).

As with the state-based case, the algorithm requires that the BA be in a certain normal form. We introduce a novel *interrupt normal form* (Definition 11) for this purpose, and show how any BA with an interruptible language can be transformed into that form. The relation to earlier work is discussed in Sect. 5. The effectiveness of these reduction techniques is demonstrated by applying them to problems in the 2019 RERS benchmark suite (Sect. 6).

2 Preliminaries

Let S be a set. 2^S denotes the set of all subsets of S. S^* denotes the set of finite sequences of elements of S; S^ω the infinite sequences. Let $\zeta = s_0 s_1 \cdots$ be a (finite or infinite) sequence and $i \geq 0$. If ζ is finite of length n, assume $i < n$. Then $\zeta(i)$ denotes the element s_i. For any $i \geq 0$, ζ^i denotes the suffix $s_i s_{i+1} \cdots$. (ζ^i is empty if ζ is finite and $i \geq n$).

For $\zeta \in S^*$ and $\eta \in S^* \cup S^\omega$, $\zeta \circ \eta$ denotes the concatenation of ζ and η.

If $S \subseteq T$ and η is a sequence of elements of T, $\eta|_S$ denotes the sequence obtained by deleting from η all elements not in S.

2.1 Linear Temporal Logic

Let Act be a universal set of actions. We assume Act is infinite.

Definition 1. Form (the *LTL formulas over* Act) is the smallest set satisfying:

- true $\in$ Form,
- if $a \in$ Act then $a \in$ Form, and
- if f and g are in Form, so are $\neg f$, $f \wedge g$, $\mathbf{X}f$, and $f\mathbf{U}g$.

Additional operators are defined as shorthand for other formulas: false $= \neg$true, $f \vee g = \neg((\neg f) \wedge \neg g)$, $f \rightarrow g = (\neg f) \vee g$, $\mathbf{F}f = \text{true}\mathbf{U}f$, $\mathbf{G}f = \neg\mathbf{F}\neg f$, and $f\mathbf{W}g = (f\mathbf{U}g) \vee \mathbf{G}f$. □

Definition 2. The *alphabet* of an LTL formula f, denoted αf, is the set of actions that occur syntactically within f. □

Definition 3. The *action-based semantics* of LTL is defined by the relation $\zeta \models_A f$, where $\zeta \in \text{Act}^\omega$ and $f \in$ Form, which is defined as follows:

- $\zeta \models_A$ true,
- $\zeta \models_A a$ iff $\zeta(0) = a$,
- $\zeta \models_A \neg f$ iff $\zeta \not\models_A f$,
- $\zeta \models_A f \wedge g$ iff $\zeta \models_A f$ and $\zeta \models_A g$,
- $\zeta \models_A \mathbf{X}f$ iff $\zeta^1 \models_A f$, and
- $\zeta \models_A f\mathbf{U}g$ iff $\exists i \geq 0 . (\zeta^i \models_A g \wedge \forall j \in 0..i - 1 . \zeta^j \models_A f)$. □

When using the action-based semantics, the logic is sometimes referred to as "Action LTL" or ALTL [11,12].

The *state-based semantics* is defined by a relation $\xi \models_s f$, where $\xi \in (2^{\text{Act}})^\omega$. The definition of $\models_s$ is well-known, and is exactly the same as Definition 3, except that $\xi \models_s a$ iff $a \in \xi(0)$. The action semantics are consistent with the state semantics in the following sense. Let $f \in$ Form, and $\zeta = a_0 a_1 \cdots \in$ Act$^\omega$. Let $\xi = \{a_0\}\{a_1\} \cdots \in (2^{\text{Act}})^\omega$. Then $\zeta \models_A f$ iff $\xi \models_s f$. The main difference between the state- and action-based formalisms is that in the state-based formalism, any number of atomic propositions can hold at each step. In the action-based formalism, precisely one action occurs in each step.

Definition 4. Let $f, g \in$ Form. Define

- (action equivalence) $f \equiv_A g$ if $(\zeta \models_A f \Leftrightarrow \zeta \models_A g)$ for all $\zeta \in$ Act$^\omega$
- (state equivalence) $f \equiv_s g$ if $(\xi \models_s f \Leftrightarrow \xi \models_s g)$ for all $\xi \in (2^{\text{Act}})^\omega$.   □

The following fact about the state-based semantics can be proved by induction on the formula structure:

Lemma 1. Let $f \in$ Form and $\xi = s_0 s_1 \cdots \in (2^{\text{Act}})^\omega$. Let $\xi' = s'_0 s'_1 \cdots$, where $s'_i = \alpha f \cap s_i$. Then $\xi \models_s f$ iff $\xi' \models_s f$.

The following shows that action LTL, like ordinary state-based LTL, is a decidable logic:

Proposition 1. Let $f, g \in$ Form, $A = \alpha f \cup \alpha g$, and

$$h = \mathbf{G}\Big[\Big(\bigwedge_{a \in A} \neg a\Big) \vee \bigvee_{a \in A}\Big(a \wedge \bigwedge_{b \in A \setminus \{a\}} \neg b\Big)\Big].$$

Then $f \equiv_A g \Leftrightarrow f \wedge h \equiv_s g \wedge h$. In particular, action equivalence is decidable.

Proof. Note the meaning of h: at each step in a state-based trace, at most one element of A is true.

Suppose $f \wedge h \equiv_s g \wedge h$. Let $\zeta = a_0 a_1 \cdots \in$ Act$^\omega$. Let $\xi = \{a_0\}\{a_1\} \cdots$. We have $\xi \models_s h$. By the consistency of the state and action semantics, we have

$$\zeta \models_A f \Leftrightarrow \xi \models_s f \Leftrightarrow \xi \models_s f \wedge h \Leftrightarrow \xi \models_s g \wedge h \Leftrightarrow \xi \models_s g \Leftrightarrow \zeta \models_A g,$$

hence $f \equiv_A g$.

Suppose instead that $f \equiv_A g$. We wish to show $\xi \models_s f \wedge h \Leftrightarrow \xi \models_s g \wedge h$ for any $\xi = s_0 s_1 \cdots \in (2^{\text{Act}})^\omega$. By Lemma 1, it suffices to assume $s_i \subseteq A$ for all i.

Let τ be any element of Act $\setminus A$. (Here we are using the fact that Act is infinite, while A is finite.) If $|s_i| > 1$ for some i, then ξ violates h and therefore violates both $f \wedge h$ and $g \wedge h$. So suppose $|s_i| \leq 1$ for all i, which means $\xi \models_s h$. Let $\zeta = a_0 a_1 \cdots$, where a_i is the sole member of s_i if $|s_i| = 1$, or τ if $|s_i| = 0$. By Lemma 1, $\xi \models_s f$ iff $\{a_0\}\{a_1\} \cdots \models_s f$. By the consistency of the action and state semantics, this is equivalent to $\zeta \models_A f$. A similar statement holds for g. Hence

$$\xi \models_s f \wedge h \Leftrightarrow \xi \models_s f \Leftrightarrow \zeta \models_A f \Leftrightarrow \zeta \models_A g \Leftrightarrow \xi \models_s g \Leftrightarrow \xi \models_s g \wedge h.$$

The proposition reduces the question of action equivalence to one of ordinary (state) equivalence of LTL formulas, which is known to be decidable ([26], see also [36, Thm. 24]).   □

Definition 5. For $A \subseteq \mathsf{Act}$ and $f \in \mathsf{Form}$ with $\alpha f \subseteq A$, let

$$\mathcal{L}(f, A) = \{\zeta \in A^\omega \mid \zeta \models f\}.$$

$\square$

2.2   Büchi Automata

Definition 6. A *Büchi Automaton* (BA) over Act is a tuple $(S, \Sigma, \rightarrow, S^0, F)$ where

1. S is a finite set of *states*,
2. Σ, the *alphabet*, is a finite subset of Act,
3. $\rightarrow \subseteq S \times \Sigma \times S$ is the *transition relation*,
4. $S^0 \subseteq S$ is the set of *initial states*, and
5. $F \subseteq S$ is the set of *accepting states*. $\square$

We will use the following notation and terminology for a BA B. The *source* of a transition (s, a, s') is s, the *destination* is s', and the *label* is a. We write $s \xrightarrow{a} s'$ as shorthand for $(s, a, s') \in \rightarrow$, and $s \xrightarrow{a_0 a_1 \ldots a_n} s'$ for $\exists s_1, s_2, \ldots s_n \in S . s \xrightarrow{a_0} s_1 \xrightarrow{a_1} s_2 \ldots s_n \xrightarrow{a_n} s'$. For $a \in A$ and $s \in S$, we say a is *enabled at* s if $s \xrightarrow{a} s'$ for some $s' \in S$. The set of all actions enabled at s is denoted $\mathsf{enabled}(B, s)$.

For $s \in S$, a *path in B starting from* s is a (finite or infinite) sequence π of transitions such that (1) if π is not empty, the source of $\pi(0)$ is s, and (2) the destination of $\pi(i)$ is the source of $\pi(i + 1)$ for all i for which these are defined. If π is not empty, define $\mathsf{first}(\pi)$ to be s; if π is finite, define $\mathsf{last}(\pi)$ to be the destination of the last transition of π. We say π *spells the word* $a_0 a_1 \cdots$, where a_i is the label of $\pi(i)$.

An infinite path is *accepting* if it visits a state in F infinitely often. An *(accepting) trace starting from* s is a word spelled by an (accepting) path starting from s. An *(accepting) trace of* B is an (accepting) trace starting from an initial state. The *language of* B, denoted $\mathcal{L}(B)$, is the set of all accepting traces of B.

Proposition 2. *There is an algorithm that consumes any finite subset A of Act and an $f \in \mathsf{Form}$ with $\alpha f \subseteq A$, and produces a BA B with alphabet A such that $\mathcal{L}(B) = \mathcal{L}(f, A)$.*

Proof. There are well-known algorithms to produce a BA C with alphabet 2^A which accepts exactly the words satisfying f under the state semantics (e.g., [37]). Let B be the same as C, except the alphabet is A and there is a transition $s \xrightarrow{a} s'$ in B iff there is a transition $s \xrightarrow{\{a\}} s'$ in C. We have

$$a_0 a_1 \cdots \in \mathcal{L}(B) \iff \{a_0\}\{a_1\} \cdots \in \mathcal{L}(C)$$
$$\iff \{a_0\}\{a_1\} \cdots \models_s f$$
$$\iff a_0 a_1 \cdots \in \mathcal{L}(f, A).$$

$\square$

In practice, tools that convert LTL formulas to BAs produce an automaton in which an edge is labeled by a propositional formula ϕ over αf. Such an edge represents a set of transitions, one for each $P \subseteq A$ for which ϕ holds for the valuation that assigns *true* to each element of P and *false* to each element of $A \setminus P$. In this case, the conversion to B entails creating one transition for each $a \in A$ for which ϕ holds when *true* is assigned to a and *false* is assigned to all other actions.

Definition 7. Let $B_i = (S_i, \Sigma_i, \rightarrow_i, S_i^0, F_i)$ $(i = 1, 2)$ denote two BAs over Act. The *parallel composition of* B_1 *and* B_2 is the BA

$$B_1 \parallel B_2 \equiv (S_1 \times S_2, \Sigma_1 \cup \Sigma_2, \rightarrow, S_1^0 \times S_2^0, F_1 \times F_2),$$

where $\rightarrow$ is defined by

$$\frac{s_1 \xrightarrow{a}_1 s_1' \quad a \notin \Sigma_2}{\langle s_1, s_2 \rangle \xrightarrow{a} \langle s_1', s_2 \rangle} \qquad \frac{s_2 \xrightarrow{a}_2 s_2' \quad a \notin \Sigma_1}{\langle s_1, s_2 \rangle \xrightarrow{a} \langle s_1, s_2' \rangle} \qquad \frac{s_1 \xrightarrow{a}_1 s_1' \quad s_2 \xrightarrow{a}_2 s_2'}{\langle s_1, s_2 \rangle \xrightarrow{a} \langle s_1', s_2' \rangle}.$$

$\square$

If we flatten all tuples (e.g., identify $(S_1 \times S_2) \times S_3$ with $S_1 \times S_2 \times S_3$) then $\parallel$ is an associative operator.

Note that in the special case where the two automata have the same alphabet $(\Sigma_1 = \Sigma_2)$, every action is synchronizing, and the parallel composition is the usual "synchronous product." In this case, $\mathcal{L}(B_1 \parallel B_2) = \mathcal{L}(B_1) \cap \mathcal{L}(B_2)$.

2.3 Labeled Transition Systems

Definition 8. A *labeled transition system* (LTS) over Act is a tuple $(Q, A, \rightarrow, q^0)$ for which $(Q, A, \rightarrow, \{q^0\}, Q)$ is a BA over Act. In other words, it is a BA in which all states are accepting and there is only one initial state. $\square$

Definition 9. Let M be an LTS with alphabet A, and f an LTL formula with $\alpha f \subseteq A$. We write $M \models f$ if $\mathcal{L}(M) \subseteq \mathcal{L}(f, A)$. $\square$

The following observation is the basis of the automata-theoretic approach to model checking (cf. [36, §4.2]):

Proposition 3. *Let* M *be an LTS with alphabet* A *and* f *an LTL formula with* $\alpha f \subseteq A$. *Let* B *be a BA with* $\mathcal{L}(B) = \mathcal{L}(\neg f, A)$. *Then* $M \models f \Leftrightarrow \mathcal{L}(M \parallel B) = \emptyset$.

Proof. M and B have the same alphabet, so $\mathcal{L}(M \parallel B) = \mathcal{L}(M) \cap \mathcal{L}(B)$, hence

$$\mathcal{L}(M \parallel B) = \mathcal{L}(M) \cap \mathcal{L}(\neg f, A) = \mathcal{L}(M) \cap (A^\omega \setminus \mathcal{L}(f, A)) = \mathcal{L}(M) \setminus \mathcal{L}(f, A).$$

This set is empty iff $\mathcal{L}(M) \subseteq \mathcal{L}(f, A)$. $\square$

There are various algorithms to determine language emptiness of a BA; in this paper we use the well-known Nested Depth First Search (NDFS) algorithm [2].

3 Interruptible Properties

3.1 Definition and Examples

An LTS comes with an alphabet, which is a subset A of Act. By a *property over A* we simply mean a subset P of A^ω. We say a trace $\zeta \in A^\omega$ *satisfies* P if $\zeta \in P$. We have already seen two ways to specify properties. An LTL formula f with $\alpha f \subseteq A$ specifies the property $\mathcal{L}(f, A)$. A Büchi automaton B with alphabet A specifies the property $\mathcal{L}(B)$. We next define a special class of properties:

Definition 10. Given sets $V \subseteq A \subseteq$ Act, we say a property P over A is *V-interruptible* if

$$\zeta|_V = \eta|_V \Rightarrow (\zeta \in P \Leftrightarrow \eta \in P) \qquad \text{for all } \zeta, \eta \in A^\omega.$$

An LTL formula f is *V-interruptible* if $\mathcal{L}(f, \text{Act})$ is V-interruptible. We say f is *interruptible* if f is αf-interruptible. The set of all interruptible LTL formulas is denoted Intrpt. □

The set V is known as the *visible set*. The definition essentially says that the insertion or deletion of invisible actions (those in $A \backslash V$) has no bearing on whether a trace satisfies P. Put another way, the question of whether a trace belongs to P is determined purely by its visible actions. The following collects some basic facts about interruptibility. All follow immediately from the definitions.

Proposition 4. *Let $V \subseteq A \subseteq$ Act, $P \subseteq A^\omega$ and $f, g \in$ Form. Then all of the following hold:*

1. *P is A-interruptible.*
2. *If P is V-interruptible, and $V \subseteq V'$, then P is V'-interruptible.*
3. *If f is interruptible and $\alpha f \subseteq A$, then $\mathcal{L}(f, A)$ is αf-interruptible.*
4. *f is interruptible iff the following holds:*

$$\forall \zeta, \eta \in \text{Act}^\omega . (\zeta|_{\alpha f} = \eta|_{\alpha f} \wedge \zeta \models_A f) \Rightarrow \eta \models_A f.$$

5. *If $\alpha f = \alpha g$ and $f \equiv_A g$ then f is interruptible iff g is interruptible.*

Many, if not most, properties that arise in practice are V-interruptible for the set V of actions that are mentioned in the property. Assuming a, b, and c are distinct actions, we have:

– For any $n \geq 0$, the property "a occurs at most n times" is $\{a\}$-interruptible, since the insertion or deletion of actions other than a cannot affect whether a word satisfies that property. The same is true for the properties "a occurs at least n times" and "a occurs exactly n times." These are examples of the *bounded existence pattern with global scope* in a widely used property specification pattern system [5]. LTL formulas in this category include $\mathbf{G}\neg a$ (a occurs 0 times), $\mathbf{F}a$ (a occurs at least once), and $\mathbf{F}(a \wedge \mathbf{XF}a)$ (a occurs at least twice).

– The property "after any occurrence of a, b eventually occurs", $\mathbf{G}(a \to \mathbf{F}b)$, is $\{a, b\}$-interruptible. This is the *response pattern with global scope* [5].
– The property "after any occurrence of a, c will eventually occur, and no b will occur until c", $\mathbf{G}(a \to ((\neg b)\mathbf{U}c))$, is $\{a, b, c\}$-interruptible. This is a variation on the *absence pattern with after-until scope*, and is used to specify mutual exclusion [5].

On the other hand, the property "a occurs at time 0", (LTL formula a) is not $\{a\}$-interruptible. Neither is "an event other than a occurs at least once" ($\mathbf{F}\neg a$) nor "only a occurs" ($\mathbf{G}a$). The property "every occurrence of a is followed immediately by b," formula $\mathbf{G}(a \to \mathbf{X}b)$, is not $\{a, b\}$-interruptible. The property "after any occurrence of a, c eventually occurs and until then only b occurs," $\mathbf{G}(a \to \mathbf{X}(b\mathbf{U}c))$, is not $\{a, b, c\}$-interruptible.

The following provides a useful way to show that two interruptible properties are equal:

Lemma 2. *Suppose $V \subseteq A \subseteq \mathsf{Act}$ and P_1 and P_2 are V-interruptible properties over A. Let $\mathcal{F} = V^\omega \cup V^* \circ (A \setminus V)^\omega$. Then $P_1 = P_2$ iff $P_1 \cap \mathcal{F} = P_2 \cap \mathcal{F}$.*

Proof. Assume $P_1 \cap \mathcal{F} = P_2 \cap \mathcal{F}$. Let $\zeta \in P_1$. If $\zeta|_V$ is infinite, then since $\zeta|_V|_V = \zeta|_V$, and P_1 is V-interruptible, $\zeta|_V \in P_1$. But $\zeta|_V \in V^\omega$, so $\zeta|_V \in P_1 \cap \mathcal{F}$, and therefore $\zeta|_V \in P_2$. Since P_2 is V-interruptible, $\zeta \in P_2$.

If $\zeta|_V$ is finite, there is a prefix θ of ζ such that $\zeta = \theta \circ \eta$, with $\eta \in (V \setminus A)^\omega$. Let $\xi = \theta|_V \circ \eta$. We have $\xi \in V^* \circ (A \setminus V)^\omega$ and $\xi|_V = \zeta|_V$, hence $\xi \in P_1 \cap \mathcal{F}$. Therefore $\xi \in P_2$, and since P_2 is V-interruptible, $\zeta \in P_2$.   □

The elements of $\mathcal{F}$ are known as the *V-interrupt-free* words over A.

3.2   Decidability of Interruptibility of LTL Formulas

We next show that interruptibility is a decidable property of LTL formulas. Define $\mathsf{intrpt}\colon \mathsf{Form} \to \mathsf{Form}$ as follows. Given $f \in \mathsf{Form}$, let $V = \alpha f$ and $\hat{V} = \bigvee_{a \in V} a$, and define $\beta\colon \mathsf{Form} \to \mathsf{Form}$ by

$$\beta(\mathsf{true}) = \mathsf{true}$$
$$\beta(a) = (\neg \hat{V})\mathbf{U}a$$
$$\beta(\neg f_1) = \neg\beta(f_1)$$
$$\beta(f_1 \wedge f_2) = \beta(f_1) \wedge \beta(f_2)$$
$$\beta(\mathbf{X}f_1) = ((\neg \hat{V})\mathbf{U}(\hat{V} \wedge \mathbf{X}\beta(f_1))) \vee ((\mathbf{G}\neg\hat{V}) \wedge \mathbf{X}\beta(f_1))$$
$$\beta(f_1 \mathbf{U} f_2) = \beta(f_1)\mathbf{U}\beta(f_2).$$

for $a \in \mathsf{Act}$ and $f_1, f_2 \in \mathsf{Form}$. Let $\mathsf{intrpt}(f) = \beta(f)$.

Theorem 1. *Let f be an LTL formula over Act. The following hold:*

1. $\mathsf{intrpt}(f)$ is interruptible.
2. f is interruptible iff $\mathsf{intrpt}(f) \equiv_A f$.

In particular, interruptibility of LTL formulas is decidable.

Before proving Theorem 1, we give some intuition regarding the definition of intrpt. Function β can be thought of as consuming a property on V-interrupt-free words (i.e., words in $V^\omega \cup V^* \circ (A \setminus V)^\omega$) and extending it to a property on all words (A^ω). It is designed so that $\beta(g)$ is V-interruptible and agrees with g on V-interrupt-free words. For example, the formula a means "a is the first action" (in an interrupt-free word), which extends to the property "a is the first visible action" (in an arbitrary word). The formula $\mathbf{X}f_1$ states "f_1 holds after removing the first action," so $\beta(\mathbf{X}f_1)$ should declare "$\beta(f_1)$ holds after removing the prefix ending in the first visible action." That is almost correct, but there is also the possibility that an element of A^ω has no visible action, which is the reason for the second clause in the definition of $\beta(\mathbf{X}f_1)$.

The remainder of this subsection is devoted to the proof of Theorem 1. First note that intrpt(f) and f have the same alphabet, i.e., αintrpt$(f) = V$.

Proof of Part 1. Say a subformula g of f is *good* if $\beta(g)$ is V-interruptible, i.e.,

$$\forall \zeta, \eta \in \mathsf{Act}^\omega . \zeta|_V = \eta|_V \Rightarrow (\zeta \models_\mathsf{A} \beta(g) \Leftrightarrow \eta \models_\mathsf{A} \beta(g)).$$

We show by induction on formula structure that every subformula of f is good. The case $g = f$ will show that intrpt(f) is interruptible. Assume throughout that $\zeta|_V = \eta|_V$.

If $g = \mathsf{true}$ then $\beta(g) = \mathsf{true}$, so g is clearly good.

If $g = a$ for some $a \in \mathsf{Act}$, then $\zeta \models_\mathsf{A} \beta(g) = (\neg \hat{V})\mathbf{U}a$ iff $\zeta|_V$ is non-empty and $\zeta|_V(0) = a$. Since this depends only on $\zeta|_V$, g is good.

If $g = \neg f_1$ and f_1 is good, then g is good because

$$\zeta \models_\mathsf{A} \beta(g) \Leftrightarrow \zeta \not\models_\mathsf{A} \beta(f_1) \Leftrightarrow \eta \not\models \beta(f_1) \Leftrightarrow \eta \models_\mathsf{A} \beta(g).$$

If $g = f_1 \wedge f_2$, and f_1 and f_2 are good, then g is good because

$$\zeta \models_\mathsf{A} \beta(g) \Leftrightarrow \zeta \models_\mathsf{A} \beta(f_1) \wedge \zeta \models_\mathsf{A} \beta(f_2)$$
$$\Leftrightarrow \eta \models_\mathsf{A} \beta(f_1) \wedge \eta \models_\mathsf{A} \beta(f_2) \Leftrightarrow \eta \models_\mathsf{A} \beta(g).$$

Suppose $g = \mathbf{X}f_1$ and f_1 is good. There are two cases:

- **Case 1:** $\zeta|_V$ is empty. Then no suffix of ζ or η satisfies $\hat{V}$. Hence

$$\theta \models_\mathsf{A} \beta(g) \Leftrightarrow \theta \models_\mathsf{A} \mathbf{X}\beta(f_1) \Leftrightarrow \theta^1 \models_\mathsf{A} \beta(f_1) \quad (\theta \in \{\zeta, \eta\}).$$

  Moreover, $\zeta^1|_V = \eta^1|_V$ (as both are empty), and $\beta(f_1)$ is good, so we have $\zeta^1 \models_\mathsf{A} \beta(f_1) \Leftrightarrow \eta^1 \models_\mathsf{A} \beta(f_1)$. These show $\zeta \models_\mathsf{A} \beta(g) \Leftrightarrow \eta \models_\mathsf{A} \beta(g)$.
- **Case 2:** $\zeta|_V$ is nonempty. Let i be the index of the first occurrence of an element of V in ζ, and j the similar index for η. We have

$$\zeta^{i+1}|_V = (\zeta|_V)^1 = (\eta|_V)^1 = \eta^{j+1}|_V.$$

As f_1 is good, it follows that $\zeta^{i+1} \models_\mathsf{A} \beta(f_1) \Leftrightarrow \eta^{j+1} \models_\mathsf{A} \beta(f_1)$. Hence

$$\zeta \models_\mathsf{A} \beta(g) \Leftrightarrow \zeta^{i+1} \models_\mathsf{A} \beta(f_1) \Leftrightarrow \eta^{j+1} \models_\mathsf{A} \beta(f_1) \Leftrightarrow \eta \models_\mathsf{A} \beta(g).$$

Suppose $g = f_1 \mathbf{U} f_2$ and f_1 and f_2 are good. We have $\beta(g) = \beta(f_1)\mathbf{U}\beta(f_2)$. If $\zeta \models_A \beta(g)$ then there exists $i \geq 0$ such that $\zeta^i \models_A \beta(f_2)$ and $\zeta^j \models_A \beta(f_1)$ for $j < i$. Now there is some $i' \geq 0$ such that $\eta^{i'}|_V = \zeta^i|_V$ and for all $j' < i'$, there is some $j < i$ such that $\eta^{j'}|_V = \zeta^j|_V$. It follows that $\eta \models \beta(g)$. Hence g is good.

Proof of Part 2. Suppose first that $\mathsf{intrpt}(f) \equiv_A f$. From part 1, $\mathsf{intrpt}(f)$ is interruptible, so Proposition 4(5) implies f is interruptible.

Suppose instead that f is interruptible. We wish to show $\mathsf{intrpt}(f) \equiv_A f$. By Lemma 2, it suffices to show the two formulas agree on V-interrupt-free words. We will show by induction that for each subformula g of f, $\zeta \models_A g \Leftrightarrow \zeta \models_A \beta(g)$ for all V-interrupt-free ζ. The case $g = f$ will complete the proof.

If $g = \mathsf{true}$, $\beta(g) = \mathsf{true}$ and the condition clearly holds.

If $g = a$ for some $a \in \mathsf{Act}$, $\zeta \models_A \beta(g) \Leftrightarrow \zeta \models_A (\neg \hat{V})\mathbf{U}a \Leftrightarrow \zeta \models_A a$, as ζ is V-interrupt-free.

If $g = \neg f_1$ and the inductive hypothesis holds for f_1, then

$$\zeta \models_A \beta(g) \Leftrightarrow \zeta \not\models_A \beta(f_1) \Leftrightarrow \zeta \not\models_A f_1 \Leftrightarrow \zeta \models_A g.$$

If $g = f_1 \wedge f_2$ and the inductive hypothesis holds for f_1 and f_2 then

$$\zeta \models_A \beta(g) \Leftrightarrow \zeta \models_A \beta(f_1) \wedge \zeta \models_A \beta(f_2) \Leftrightarrow \zeta \models_A f_1 \wedge \zeta \models_A f_2 \Leftrightarrow \zeta \models_A g.$$

Suppose $g = \mathbf{X}f_1$ and the inductive hypothesis holds for f_1. Note that any suffix of a V-interrupt-free word, e.g., ζ^1, is also V-interrupt-free. If $\zeta|_V$ is empty,

$$\zeta \models_A \beta(g) \Leftrightarrow \zeta \models_A \mathbf{X}\beta(f_1) \Leftrightarrow \zeta^1 \models_A \beta(f_1) \Leftrightarrow \zeta^1 \models_A f_1 \Leftrightarrow \zeta \models_A g.$$

If $\zeta|_V$ is nonempty, then $\zeta \models_A \hat{V}$, so

$$\zeta \models_A \beta(g) \Leftrightarrow \zeta \models_A (\neg\hat{V})\mathbf{U}(\hat{V} \wedge \mathbf{X}\beta(f_1)) \Leftrightarrow \zeta \models_A \mathbf{X}\beta(f_1)$$
$$\Leftrightarrow \zeta^1 \models_A \beta(f_1) \Leftrightarrow \zeta^1 \models_A f_1 \Leftrightarrow \zeta \models_A g.$$

If $g = f_1 \mathbf{U} f_2$, then applying the inductive hypothesis to f_1 and f_2 yields

$$\zeta \models_A g \Leftrightarrow \exists i > 0\,.\,\zeta^i \models_A f_2 \wedge \forall j < i\,.\,\zeta^j \models_A f_1$$
$$\Leftrightarrow \exists i > 0\,.\,\zeta^i \models_A \beta(f_2) \wedge \forall j < i\,.\,\zeta^j \models_A \beta(f_1)$$
$$\Leftrightarrow \zeta \models_A \beta(g).$$

Decidability follows from part 2 and Proposition 1. This completes the proof of Theorem 1.

Remark 1. The definition of $\beta(\mathbf{X}f_1)$ is convenient for the proof but shorter definitions also work. If the formula f_1 is satisfied by some word $\zeta \in (A \setminus V)^\omega$, then all such ζ satisfy f_1, and the clause $(\mathbf{G}\neg\hat{V}) \wedge \mathbf{X}\beta(f_1)$ can be replaced by $\mathbf{G}\neg\hat{V}$. Otherwise, that clause can be removed altogether. One can determine whether a formula is satisfied by such a word by replacing every occurrence of every action with false.

3.3   Generation of Interruptible LTL Formulas

The following can be used to show that many formulas are interruptible. It establishes a kind of parity pattern involving a class of *positive* formulas (Pos) and a class of *negative* formulas (Neg). It is proved in [28].

Proposition 5. *There exist* Pos, Neg $\subseteq$ Form *such that (i) for all* $f, f' \in$ Form,

$$(f \in \mathsf{Pos} \wedge f' \equiv_{\mathsf{A}} f) \Rightarrow f' \in \mathsf{Pos}$$
$$(f \in \mathsf{Neg} \wedge f' \equiv_{\mathsf{A}} f) \Rightarrow f' \in \mathsf{Neg},$$

and (ii) for all $a \in$ Act, $f_1, f_2 \in$ Intrpt, $g_1, g_2 \in$ Pos, *and* $h_1, h_2 \in$ Neg,

$$\mathit{false}, \; a, \; \neg h_1, \; g_1 \wedge g_2, \; g_1 \vee g_2, \; a \wedge f_1, \; a \wedge \mathbf{X} f_1 \; \in \; \mathsf{Pos}$$
$$\mathit{true}, \; \neg a, \; \neg g_1, \; h_1 \wedge h_2, \; h_1 \vee h_2, \; \neg a \vee f_1, \; \neg a \vee \mathbf{X} f_1 \; \in \; \mathsf{Neg}$$
$$\mathit{true}, \mathit{false}, \; f_1 \wedge f_2, \; f_1 \vee f_2, \; \neg f_1, \; \mathbf{F} g_1, \; \mathbf{G} h_1, \; f_1 \mathbf{U} f_2, \; h_1 \mathbf{U} g_1, \; h_1 \mathbf{U} f_1 \; \in \; \mathsf{Intrpt}.$$

Consider the examples from Sect. 3.1. The formula a is positive, so $\mathbf{F}a$ is interruptible. Since $\neg a$ is negative, $\mathbf{G}\neg a$ is interruptible. Since $\mathbf{F}a$ is interruptible, $a \wedge \mathbf{X}\mathbf{F}a$ is positive, hence $\mathbf{F}(a \wedge \mathbf{X}\mathbf{F}a)$ is interruptible.

Formula $\mathbf{G}(a \to \mathbf{F}b)$ is seen to be interruptible as follows. Since $b \in$ Pos, $\mathbf{F}b \in$ Intrpt, whence $\neg a \vee \mathbf{F}b \in$ Neg. Since this last formula is action-equivalent to $a \to \mathbf{F}b$, we have $a \to \mathbf{F}b \in$ Neg. Therefore $\mathbf{G}(a \to \mathbf{F}b) \in$ Intrpt.

Similarly, $(\neg b)\mathbf{U}c \in$ Intrpt, so $a \to \mathbf{X}((\neg b)\mathbf{U}c) \in$ Neg. This negative formula is action-equivalent to $a \to ((\neg b)\mathbf{U}c)$, whence $\mathbf{G}(a \to ((\neg b)\mathbf{U}c)) \in$ Intrpt.

Note that Intrpt and the set of stutter-invariant formulas are not comparable. For example, $f = \mathbf{F}(a \wedge \mathbf{X}\mathbf{F}a)$ is interruptible, but not stutter-invariant. In fact f is not action-equivalent to any stutter-invariant formula g, since if there were such a g, the sequence aab^ω would satisfy g, but the stutter-equivalent sequence ab^ω cannot satisfy g. Conversely, the formulas a and $\mathbf{G}a$ are both stutter-invariant, but neither is interruptible. The formula $\mathbf{F}a$ is both stutter-invariant and interruptible. Finally, the formula $\mathbf{X}a$ is neither stutter-invariant nor interruptible.

3.4   Decidability of Interruptibility of Büchi Automata

Definition 11. Let B be a BA with alphabet A, $V \subseteq A$ (the *visible* actions), and $I = A \setminus V$ (the *invisible* actions). We say B is in V-*interrupt normal form* if the following hold for any $x \in I$, $a \in A$, and states s_1, s_2, and s_3:

1. If $s_1 \overset{a}{\to} s_2$ then B has a state s_1' such that $s_1 \overset{x}{\to} s_1' \overset{a}{\to} s_2$.
2. If $s_1 \overset{x}{\to} s_2 \overset{a}{\to} s_3$ then $s_1 \overset{a}{\to} s_3$ and if s_2 is accepting then s_1 or s_3 is accepting.
3. If $s_1 \overset{x}{\to} s_2$ then $s_1 \overset{y}{\to} s_2$ for all $y \in I$.

Proposition 6. *Suppose B is in V-interrupt normal form. Then $\mathcal{L}(B)$ is V-interruptible.*

Proof. Suppose $\zeta, \eta \in A^\omega$, $\zeta \in \mathcal{L}(B)$, and $\zeta|_V = \eta|_V$. We wish to show $\eta \in \mathcal{L}(B)$. Let π be an accepting path for ζ.

Assume $\zeta|_V$ is infinite. By Definition 11(2), we can remove all invisible transitions from the accepting path π, and the result is an accepting path that spells $\zeta|_V$. By Definition 11(1), we can insert any arbitrary finite sequence of invisible transition between two consecutive visible transitions; we can therefore construct an accepting path for η.

If $\zeta|_V$ is finite, proceed as above to form an accepting path which spells a finite prefix of η followed by an infinite word of invisible actions. By Definition 11(3), that infinite suffix can be transformed to spell any infinite word of invisibles, and in that way one obtains an accepting path for η. $\square$

Given any BA $B = (S, A, T, S^0, F)$ and a visible set $V \subseteq A$, define a BA $\mathsf{norm}(B, V)$ as follows: if $V = A$, $\mathsf{norm}(B, V) = B$, otherwise $\mathsf{norm}(B, V)$ is $\hat{B} = (\hat{S}, A, \hat{T}, \hat{S}^0, \hat{F})$, where

$$D = \{s \in S \mid \text{there is an accepting path from } s \text{ with all labels in } I\}$$

$$\hat{S} = \{\hat{u} \mid u \in S\} \cup \{u^\sharp \mid u \in F \setminus D\} \cup \{\mathsf{DIV}\}$$

$$\hat{S}^0 = \{\hat{u} \mid u \in S^0\}$$

$$\hat{F} = \{\hat{u} \mid u \in F\} \cup \{\mathsf{DIV}\}$$

$$
\begin{aligned}
\hat{T} = \quad &\{(\hat{u}, a, \hat{v}) && \mid a \in V \wedge u, v \in S \wedge (u, a, v) \in T && \} \cup \\
&\{(\hat{u}, x, \hat{u}) && \mid x \in I \wedge u \in D \cup (S \setminus F) && \} \cup \\
&\{(\mathsf{DIV}, x, \mathsf{DIV}) && \mid x \in I && \} \cup \\
&\{(\hat{u}, x, \mathsf{DIV}) && \mid x \in I \wedge u \in D \setminus F && \} \cup \\
&\{(\hat{u}, x, u^\sharp), (u^\sharp, x, u^\sharp) && \mid x \in I \wedge u \in F \setminus D && \} \cup \\
&\{(u^\sharp, a, \hat{v}) && \mid a \in V \wedge u \in F \setminus D \wedge v \in S \wedge (u, a, v) \in T && \}
\end{aligned}
$$

The set $\hat{S}$ consists of the *original states* $\hat{u}$, the *sharp states* $u^\sharp$, and one additional state DIV. The mapping from S to $\hat{S}$ defined by $u \mapsto \hat{u}$ is injective and preserves acceptability and visible transitions, i.e., for any $u, v \in S$ and $a \in V$, $u \xrightarrow{a} v \Leftrightarrow \hat{u} \xrightarrow{a} \hat{v}$. It follows that paths in B in which all labels are visible correspond one-to-one with paths through original states in $\hat{B}$ in which all labels are visible. Note that every invisible transition in $\hat{B}$ is a self-loop or ends in a sharp state or DIV. Moreover, all transitions in $\hat{B}$ ending in a sharp state or DIV are invisible.

Proposition 7. *For any BA B with alphabet A, and any visible set $V \subseteq A$, $\mathsf{norm}(B, V)$ is in V-interrupt normal form.*

Proof. To see Definition 11(1), suppose $s_1 \xrightarrow{a} s_2$. If $s_1 \xrightarrow{x} s_1$, take $s_1' = s_1$. Otherwise, $s_1 = \hat{u}$ for some $u \in F \setminus D$, and we can take $s_1' = u^\sharp$.

For Definition 11(2), suppose $s_1 \xrightarrow{x} s_2 \xrightarrow{a} s_3$. We need to show $s_1 \xrightarrow{a} s_3$ and if s_2 is accepting then s_1 or s_3 is accepting. If $s_1 = s_2$, the result is clear, so assume $s_1 \neq s_2$. There are then two cases: $s_2 = \mathsf{DIV}$ or $s_2 = u^\sharp$ for some $u \in F \setminus D$.

If $s_2 = \mathsf{DIV}$, then $a \in I$ and $s_3 = \mathsf{DIV}$, and we have $s_1 \xrightarrow{a} \mathsf{DIV}$. As DIV is accepting, the desired conclusion holds.

If $s_2 = u^\sharp$, then $s_1 = \hat{u}$, which is accepting. There are again two cases: either $s_3 = u^\sharp$ or $s_3 = \hat{v}$ for some $v \in S$. If $s_3 = u^\sharp$ then $a \in I$ and $\hat{u} \xrightarrow{a} u^\sharp$, as required. If $s_3 = \hat{v}$, then $a \in V$ and therefore $u \xrightarrow{a} v$, hence $\hat{u} \xrightarrow{a} \hat{v}$, as required.

Definition 11(3) is clear from the definition of $\hat{T}$.   □

Theorem 2. $\mathcal{L}(B)$ *is* V-*interruptible iff* $\mathcal{L}(\mathsf{norm}(B, V)) = \mathcal{L}(B)$. *In particular interruptibility for Büchi Automata is decidable.*

Proof. Let $P_1 = \mathcal{L}(B)$ and $P_2 = \mathcal{L}(\mathsf{norm}(B, V))$. By Proposition 7, $\mathsf{norm}(B, V)$ is in V-interrupt normal form, so by Proposition 6, P_2 is V-interruptible. Hence one direction is clear: if $P_1 = P_2$, then P_1 is V-interruptible.

So suppose P_1 is V-interruptible. We wish to show $P_1 = P_2$. By Lemma 2, it suffices to show the two languages contain the same V-interrupt-free words.

Suppose ζ is a V-interrupt-free word in P_1. If $\zeta \in V^\omega$ then an accepting path θ in B maps to the accepting path $\hat{\theta}$ in $\hat{B}$, and $\zeta \in P_2$. So assume $\zeta \in V^*I^\omega$. Then an accepting path in B has a prefix θ of visible transitions ending in a state $u \in D$. That prefix corresponds to a path $\hat{\theta}$ in $\hat{B}$ ending in $\hat{u}$. As $u \in D$, $\hat{u} \xrightarrow{x} \hat{u}$ for all $x \in I$. If u is accepting, we get an accepting path for ζ that follows $\hat{\theta}$ and then loops at $\hat{u}$. If u is not accepting then $u \in D \setminus F$, and $\hat{u} \xrightarrow{x} \mathsf{DIV}$ for all $x \in I$. Since DIV is accepting and $\mathsf{DIV} \xrightarrow{x} \mathsf{DIV}$ for all $x \in I$, we again get an accepting path for ζ in $\hat{B}$.

Suppose now that ζ is a V-interrupt-free word in P_2. Assume $\zeta \in V^\omega$. An accepting path for ζ cannot pass through a sharp state or DIV, because only invisible transitions end in those states. So the path passes through only original states, and therefore corresponds to an accepting path in B.

Suppose $\zeta \in V^*I^\omega$. An accepting path for ζ in $\hat{B}$ consists of a prefix $\hat{\theta}$ of visible transitions followed by an infinite accepting path ξ of invisible transitions. As above, $\hat{\theta}$ corresponds to a path θ in B ending in a state u.

We claim that ξ cannot pass through a sharp state. This is because all invisible transitions departing from a sharp state are self loops. But sharp states are not accepting, while ξ is an accepting path of invisible transitions. It follows that each transition in ξ is a self-loop or terminates in DIV.

We now claim $u \in D$. For suppose the first transition in ξ is a self-loop on $\hat{u}$. According to the definition of $\hat{T}$, this implies $u \in D \cup (S \setminus F)$. Hence, if $u \notin D$ then u is not accepting, and all invisible transitions departing from $\hat{u}$ are self-loops, contradicting the fact that ξ is an accepting path. If, on the other hand, the first transition in ξ is $\hat{u} \xrightarrow{x} \mathsf{DIV}$, for some $x \in I$, then the definition of $\hat{T}$ implies $u \in D$, establishing the claim.

So $u \in D$, i.e., there is an accepting path ρ in B starting from u and consisting of all invisible transitions. The accepting path obtained by concatenating θ and ρ spells a word which, projected onto V, equals $\zeta|_V$. Since P_1 is V-interruptible, $\zeta \in P_1$. This completes the proof that $P_1 = P_2$.

The theorem reduces the problem of determining V-interruptibility to a problem of determining equivalence of two Büchi Automata, which can be done using language intersection, complement, and emptiness algorithms for BAs [37].   □

4 On-the-Fly Partial Order Reduction

4.1 General Theory and Soundness Theorem

Let $M = (Q, A, T, q^0)$ be an LTS, $V \subseteq A$, and $B = (S, A, \delta, S^0, F)$ a V-interruptible BA. The goal of on-the-fly POR is to explore a sub-automaton R' of $R = M \parallel B$ with the property that $\mathcal{L}(R) = \emptyset \Leftrightarrow \mathcal{L}(R') = \emptyset$.

A function amp: $Q \times S \to 2^A$ is an *ample selector* if $\mathsf{amp}(q, s) \subseteq \mathsf{enabled}(M, q)$ for all $q \in Q, s \in S$. Each $\mathsf{amp}(q, s)$ is an *ample set*. An ample selector determines a BA $R' = \mathsf{reduced}(R, \mathsf{amp})$ which has the same states, accepting states, and initial state as R, but only a subset of the transitions:

$$R' = (Q \times S, A, \delta', \{q^0\} \times S^0, Q \times F)$$
$$\delta' = \{((q, s), a, (q', s')) \mid a \in \mathsf{amp}(q, s) \wedge (q, a, q') \in T \wedge (s, a, s') \in \delta\}.$$

We now define some constraints on an ample selector that will be used to guarantee the reduced product space has nonempty language if the full space does. First we need the usual notion of independence:

Definition 12. Let M be an LTS with alphabet A, and $a, b \in A$. We say a and b are *independent* if both of the following hold for all states q and q' of M:

1. $(q \xrightarrow{a} q' \wedge b \in \mathsf{enabled}(M, q)) \Rightarrow b \in \mathsf{enabled}(M, q')$
2. $q \xrightarrow{ab} q' \Leftrightarrow q \xrightarrow{ba} q'$.

We say a and b are *dependent* if they are not independent. □

Note that, in contrast with [1], we do not assume actions are deterministic. We can now define the four constraints:

C0 For all $q \in Q$, $s \in S$: $\mathsf{enabled}(M, q) \neq \emptyset \Rightarrow \mathsf{amp}(q, s) \neq \emptyset$.
C1 For all $q \in Q$, $s \in S$: on any trace in M starting from q, no action outside of $\mathsf{amp}(q, s)$ but dependent on an action in $\mathsf{amp}(q, s)$ can occur without an action in $\mathsf{amp}(q, s)$ occurring first.
C2 For all $q \in Q$, $s \in S$: if $\mathsf{amp}(q, s) \neq \mathsf{enabled}(M, q)$, then $\mathsf{amp}(q, s) \cap V = \emptyset$.
C3 For all $a \in A$: on any cycle in R' for which a is enabled in R at each state, there is some state (q, s) on the cycle for which $a \in \mathsf{amp}(q, s)$.

Theorem 3. *Let M be an LTS with alphabet A, $V \subseteq A$, B a BA with alphabet A in V-interrupt normal form, $R = M \parallel B$, and amp an ample selector satisfying* **C0–C3**. *Then* $\mathcal{L}(\mathsf{reduced}(R, \mathsf{amp})) = \emptyset \Leftrightarrow \mathcal{L}(R) = \emptyset$.

The requirement that B be in interrupt normal form is necessary. A counterexample when that condition is not met is given in Fig. 1. Note a and b are independent, and a is invisible. The ample set for product states 0 and 1 is $\{a\}$; the ample set for product state 2 is $\{a, b\}$. Hence **C3** holds because a state on the sole cycle is fully enabled. After normalizing B (and removing unreachable states), this problem goes away: in any reduced space, the ample sets must retain the a-transitions, and state $0^\sharp$ must be fully enabled since it has an a-self-loop, so the accepting cycle involving the two states will remain.

The remainder of this section is devoted to the proof of Theorem 3. The proof is similar to that of the analogous theorem in the state-based case [27], but some changes are necessary and we include the proof for completeness.

Let θ be an accepting path in R. An infinite sequence of accepting paths $\pi_0, \pi_1, \ldots$ will be constructed, where $\pi_0 = \theta$. For each $i \geq 0$, π_i will be decomposed as $\eta_i \circ \theta_i$, where η_i is a finite path of length i in R', θ_i is an infinite path, and η_i is a prefix of η_{i+1}. For $i = 0$, η_0 is empty and $\theta_0 = \theta$.

Assume $i \geq 0$ and we have defined η_j and θ_j for $j \leq i$. Write

$$\theta_i \;=\; \langle q_0, s_0 \rangle \xrightarrow{a_1} \langle q_1, s_1 \rangle \xrightarrow{a_2} \cdots \tag{1}$$

Then η_{i+1} and θ_{i+1} are defined as follows. Let $E = \mathsf{amp}(q_0, s_0)$. There are two cases:

Case 1: $a_1 \in E$. Let η_{i+1} be the path obtained by appending the first transition of θ_i to η_i, and θ_{i+1} the path obtained by removing the first transition from θ_i.

Case 2: $a_1 \notin E$. Then there are two sub-cases:

Case 2a: Some operation in E occurs in θ_i. Let n be the index of the first such occurrence. By **C1**, a_j and a_n are independent for $1 \leq j < n$. By repeated application of the independence property, there is a path in M of the form

$$q_0 \xrightarrow{a_n} q_1' \xrightarrow{a_1} q_2' \xrightarrow{a_2} \cdots \xrightarrow{a_{n-2}} q_{n-1}' \xrightarrow{a_{n-1}} q_n \xrightarrow{a_{n+1}} q_{n+1} \xrightarrow{a_{n+2}} \cdots.$$

By **C2**, a_n is invisible. By Definition 11, B has an accepting path of the form

$$s_0 \xrightarrow{a_n} s_0' \xrightarrow{a_1} s_1 \xrightarrow{a_2} \cdots \xrightarrow{a_{n-2}} s_{n-2} \xrightarrow{a_{n-1}} s_{n-1} \xrightarrow{a_{n+1}} s_{n+1} \xrightarrow{a_{n+2}} \cdots.$$

Composing these two paths yields a path in R. Removing the first transition (labeled a_n) yields θ_{i+1}. Appending that transition to η_i yields η_{i+1}.

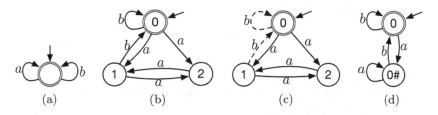

Fig. 1. Counterexample to Theorem 3 if B is not in interrupt normal form: (a) the LTS M, (b) the BA B representing **GF**b, (c) the product space—dashed edges are in the full, but not reduced, space, and (d) the result of normalizing B and removing unreachable states, which also depicts the resulting full product space.

Case 2b: No operation in E occurs in θ_i. By **C0**, E is nonempty. Let $b \in E$. By **C2**, every action in θ_i is independent of b. As in the case above, we obtain a path in R

$$\langle q_0, s_0 \rangle \xrightarrow{b} \langle q_1', s_0' \rangle \xrightarrow{a_1} \langle q_2', s_1 \rangle \xrightarrow{a_2} \langle q_3', s_2 \rangle \xrightarrow{a_3} \cdots .$$

and define θ_{i+1} and η_{i+1} as above.

Let η be the limit of the η_i, i.e., $\eta(i) = \eta_{i+1}(i)$. It is clear that η is an infinite path in R', but we must show it passes through an accepting state infinitely often. To see this, define integers d_i for $i \geq 0$ as follows. Let $\xi_i = s_0 s_1 \cdots$ be the sequence of BA states traced by θ_i. Let d_i be the minimum $j \geq 0$ such that s_j is accepting. Note that $d_i = 0$ iff $\mathsf{last}(\eta_i)$ is accepting.

Suppose $i \geq 0$ and $d_i > 0$. If Case 1 holds, then $d_{i+1} = d_i - 1$, since $\xi_{i+1} = \xi_i^1$. It is not hard to see that if Case 2 holds, $d_{i+1} \leq d_i$. Note that in Case 2a, if $d_i = n$, the accepting state s_n is removed, but Definition 11(2) guarantees that at least one of s_{n-1} and s_{n+1} is accepting. In the worst case (s_{n-1} is not accepting), we still have $d_{i+1} = n$.

We claim there are an infinite number of $i \geq 0$ such that Case 1 holds. Otherwise, there is some $i > 0$ such that Case 2 holds for all $j \geq i$. Let a be the first action in θ_i. Then for all $j \geq i$, a is the first action of θ_j and a is not in the ample set of $\mathsf{last}(\eta_j)$. Since the number of states of R is finite, there is some $k > i$ such that $\mathsf{last}(\eta_k) = \mathsf{last}(\eta_i)$. Hence there is a cycle in R' for which a is always enabled but never in the ample set, contradicting **C3**.

If η does not pass through an accepting state infinitely often, there is some $i \geq 0$ such that for all $j \geq i$, $\mathsf{first}(\theta_j)$ is not accepting. But then $(d_j)_{j \geq i}$ is a nondecreasing sequence of positive integers which strictly decreases infinitely often, a contradiction.

4.2 Ample Sets for a Parallel Composition of LTSs

We now describe the specific method used by McRERS to select ample sets. Since this method is similar to existing approaches, such as [32, Algorithm 4.3], we just outline the main ideas.

Let $n \geq 1$, $P = \{1, \ldots, n\}$, and let $M_1, \ldots, M_n$ be LTSs over Act. Write $M_i = (Q_i, A_i, \rightarrow_i, q_i^0)$ and

$$M = M_1 \parallel \cdots \parallel M_n = (Q, A, \rightarrow, q^0).$$

For $a \in A$, let $\mathsf{procs}(a) = \{i \in P \mid a \in A_i\}$. It can be shown that if a and b are dependent actions, then $\mathsf{procs}(a) \cap \mathsf{procs}(b) \neq \emptyset$.

Let $q = (q_1, \ldots, q_n) \in Q$ and $E_i = \mathsf{enabled}(M_i, q_i)$ for $i \in P$. Let

$$R_q = \{(i, j) \in P \times P \mid E_i \cap A_j \neq \emptyset\}.$$

Suppose $C \subseteq P$ is closed under R_q, i.e., for all $i \in C$ and $j \in P$, $(i, j) \in R_q \Rightarrow j \in C$. This implies that if $a \in E_i$ for some $i \in C$ then $\mathsf{procs}(a) \subseteq C$. Define

$$\mathsf{enabled}(C, q) = \mathsf{enabled}(M, q) \cap \bigcup_{i \in C} A_i.$$

Let $E = \mathsf{enabled}(C, q)$. Note $E \subseteq \bigcup_{i \in C} E_i$. Hence for any $a \in E$, $\mathsf{procs}(a) \subseteq C$.

Lemma 3. *On any trace in M starting from q, no action outside of E but dependent on an action in E can occur without an action in E occurring first.*

Proof. Let ζ be a trace in M starting from q, such that no element of E occurs in ζ. We claim no action involving C (i.e., an action a for which $\mathsf{procs}(a) \cap C \neq \emptyset$) can occur in ζ. Otherwise, let x be the first such action. Then $x \in E_i$, for some $i \in C$, so $\mathsf{procs}(x) \subseteq C$. As $x \notin E$, $x \notin \mathsf{enabled}(M, q)$. So some earlier action y in ζ caused x to become enabled, and therefore $\mathsf{procs}(x) \cap \mathsf{procs}(y) \neq \emptyset$, hence $\mathsf{procs}(y) \cap C \neq \emptyset$, contradicting the assumption that x was the first action involving C in ζ.

Now any action b dependent on an action $a \in E$ must satisfy $\mathsf{procs}(a) \cap \mathsf{procs}(b)$ is nonempty. Since $\mathsf{procs}(a) \subseteq C$, $\mathsf{procs}(b) \cap C$ is nonempty. Hence no action dependent on an action in E can occur in ζ.   □

We now describe how to find an ample set in the context of NDFS. Let (q, s) be a new product state that has just been pushed onto the outer DFS stack. The relation R_q defined above gives P the structure of a directed graph. Suppose that graph has a strongly connected component C_0 such that all of the following hold for $E = \mathsf{enabled}(C_0, q)$:

1. $E \neq \emptyset$,
2. $E \cap V = \emptyset$,
3. $\mathsf{enabled}(C', q) = \emptyset$ for all SCCs C' reachable from C_0 other than C_0, and
4. E does not contain a "back edge", i.e., if $(q, s) \xrightarrow{a} \sigma$ for some $a \in E$ and $\sigma \in Q \times S$, then σ is not on the outer DFS stack.

Then set $\mathsf{amp}(q, s) = E$. If no such SCC exists, set $\mathsf{amp}(q, s) = \mathsf{enabled}(M, q)$. It follows that **C0–C4** hold. Note that the union C of all SCCs reachable from C_0 is closed under R_q, and $\mathsf{enabled}(C, q) = E$, so Lemma 3 guarantees **C1**. For **C3**, we actually have the stronger condition that in any cycle in the reduced space, at least one state is fully enabled. In our implementation, the SCCs are computed using Tarjan's algorithm. Among all SCCs C_0 satisfying the conditions above, we choose one for which $|\mathsf{enabled}(C_0, q)|$ is minimal.

One known issue when combining NDFS with on-the-fly POR is that the inner DFS must explore the same subspace as the outer DFS, i.e., amp must be a deterministic function of its input (q, s) [18]. To accomplish this, McRERS stores one additional integer j in the state: j is the root node of the SCC C_0, or -1 if the state is fully enabled. The outer search saves j in the state, and the inner search uses j to reconstruct the SCC C_0 and the ample set E.

5   Related Work

There has been significant earlier research on the use of partial order reduction to model check LTSs (or the closely related concept of process algebras); see, e.g., [14,16,30–33,35]. To understand how this previous work relates to this paper, we must explain a subtle, but important, distinction concerning how a property is specified. In much of this literature, a property of an LTS with alphabet A is essentially a pair $\pi = (V, T)$, where $V \subseteq A$ is a set of visible actions and T is a set of (finite and infinite) words over V. A property in this sense specifies acceptable behaviors *after invisible actions have been removed*. (See, e.g., Def. 2.4 and preceding comments in [32].) We can translate π to a property P in our sense by taking its inverse image under the projection map:

$$P = \{\zeta \in A^\omega \mid \zeta|_V \in T\}.$$

Note that P *is V-interruptible by definition*. Hence the need to distinguish interruptible properties does not arise in this context.

Much of the earlier work on POR for LTSs deals with the "offline" case, i.e., the construction of a subspace of M that preserves certain classes of properties. In contrast, Theorem 3 deals with an on-the-fly algorithm, i.e., the construction of a subspace of $M \parallel B$. The on-the-fly approach is an essential optimization in model checking, but recent work in the state-based formalism has shown that offline POR schemes do not always generalize easily to on-the-fly algorithms [27].

One work that does describe an on-the-fly model checking algorithm for LTSs is [32] (see also [17], which deals with the same ideas in a state formalism). The property is specified by a *tester process* B. Consistent with the notion of *property* described above, the alphabet of B does not include the invisible actions. Hence, in the parallel composition $M \parallel B$, the tester does not move when M executes an invisible action. In order to specify both finite and infinite words of visible actions, the tester has two kinds of accepting states: "livelock monitor states" and "infinite trace monitor states." (Two additional classes of states for detecting other kinds of violations are not relevant to the discussion here.) A version of the stubborn set theory is used to define the reduced space, and a special condition is used to solve the "ignoring problem" (instead of our **C3**). It would be interesting to compare this algorithm with the one described here.

There are many algorithms for reducing or even minimizing the size of an LTS while preserving various properties, e.g., *bisimulation equivalence* [8] or *divergence preserving bisimilarity* [6]. These algorithms could be applied to the individual components of a parallel composition (taking all visible and communication actions to be "visible"), as a preprocessing step before beginning the model checking search. An exploration of these algorithms, and how they impact POR, is beyond the scope of this paper, but we hope to explore that avenue in future work.

The RERS Challenge [9,19–21] is an annual event involving a number of different categories of large model checking problems. The "parallel LTL category," offered from 2016 on, is directly relevant to this paper. Each problem in that category consists of a Graphviz "dot" file specifying an LTS as a parallel composition, and a text file containing 20 LTL formulas. The goal is to identify the formulas satisfied by the LTS. The solutions are initially known only to the organizers, and are published after the event. The RERS semantics for LTSs, LTL, and satisfiability are exactly the same as in this paper.

The methods for generating the LTS and the properties are complicated, and have varied over the years, but are designed to satisfy certain hardness guarantees. The approach described in [29] is "...based on the weak refinement ...of convergent systems which preserves an interesting class of temporal properties." It can be seen that the properties preserved by weak refinement are exactly the interruptible properties. While [29] does not describe a method for determining whether a property is interruptible, the authors have informed us that they developed a sufficient condition for an LTL formula to be interruptible, and used this in combination with a random method to generate the formulas for 2016 and 2019. Our analysis (Sect. 6) confirms that all formulas from 2016 and 2019 are interruptible, while 2017 and 2018 contain some non-interruptible formulas.

There is a well-known way to translate a system and property expressed in an action-based formalism to a state-based formalism. The idea is to add a shared variable *last* which records the last action executed. An LTL formula over actions can be transformed to one over states by replacing each action a with the predicate $last = a$. This is the approach taken in the Promela representations of the parallel problems provided with the RERS challenges.

This translation is semantics-preserving but performance-destroying. Every transition writes to the shared variable *last*, so any state-based POR scheme will assume that no two transitions commute. Furthermore, since the property references *last*, all transitions are visible. This effectively disables POR, even when the property is stutter-invariant, as can be seen in the poor performance of SPIN on the RERS Promela models (Sect. 6). It is possible that there are more effective SPIN translations; [34, §2.2], for example, suggests not updating *last* on invisible actions, and adding a global boolean variable that is flipped on every visible action (in addition to updating *last*). We note that this would also require modifying the LTL formula, or specifying the property in some other way. In any case, it suggests another interesting avenue for future work.

6 Experimental Results and Conclusions

We implemented a model checker named MCRERS based on the algorithms described in this paper. MCRERS is a library and set of command line tools. It is written in sequential C and uses the Spot library [4] for several tasks: (1) determining equivalence of LTL formulas, (2) determining language equivalence of BAs, and (3) converting an LTL formula to a BA. The source code for MCRERS as well as all artifacts related to the experiments discussed in this section, are available at https://vsl.cis.udel.edu/cav2020. The experiments were run on an 8-core 3.7GHz Intel Xeon W-2145 Linux machine with 256 GB RAM, though MCRERS is a sequential program and most experiments required much less memory.

As described in Sect. 5, each edition of RERS includes a number of problems, each of which comes with 20 LTL formulas. The numbers of problems for years 2016–2019 are, in order, 20, 15, 3, and 9, for a total of 47 problems, or $47 * 20 = 940$ distinct model checking tasks. (Some formulas become identical after renaming propositions.) We used the MCRERS *property analyzer* to analyze these formulas to determine which are interruptible; the algorithm used is based on Theorem 1. The results show that all formulas from 2016 and 2019 are interruptible, which agrees with the expectations of the RERS organizers. In 2017, 22 of the 300 formulas are not interruptible; these include

- **GF¬a111_SIGTRAP**,
- **G**[a71_SIGVTALRM → **X**¬a71_SIGVTALRM], and
- **G**[(a59_SIGUSR1 ∧ **X**[(¬a112_SIGHUP)**U**a59_SIGUSR1]) → **FG**a104_SIGPIPE].

In 2018, 3 of the 60 formulas are not interruptible. In summary, only 25 of the 940 tasks involve non-interruptible formulas. The total runtime for the analysis of all 940 formulas was 6 s.

We next used the MCRERS *automaton analyzer* to create BAs from each of the interruptible formulas, and then to determine which of these Spot-generated BAs was not in interrupt normal form. This uses a straightforward algorithm that iterates over all states and checks the conditions of Definition 11. For each BA not in normal form, the analyzer transforms it to normal form using function norm of Sect. 3.4. Interestingly, all of the Spot-generated BAs in 2016 and 2019 were already in normal form. Four of the BAs from interruptible formulas in 2017 were not in normal form; all of these formulas had the form $\mathbf{F}[a \vee ((\neg b)\mathbf{W}c)]$. In 2018, 6 interruptible formulas have non-normal BAs; these formulas have several different non-isomorphic forms, some of which are quite complex. The details can be seen on the online archive. The total runtime for this analysis (including writing all BAs to a file) was 11 s.

The MCRERS model checker parses RERS "dot" and property files to construct an internal representation of a parallel composition $M = M_1 \parallel \cdots \parallel M_n$ of LTSs and a list of LTL formulas. Each formula f is converted to a BA B; if f is interruptible and B is not already in normal form, B is transformed to normal form. The NDFS algorithm is used to determine language emptiness, and if f is interruptible, the POR scheme described in Sect. 4 is also used. States are saved in a hash table.

One other simple optimization is used regardless of whether f is interruptible. Let αM denote the set of actions labeling at least one transition in M, and define αB similarly. If $\alpha M \neq \alpha B$, then all transitions labeled by an action in $(\alpha M \setminus \alpha B) \cup (\alpha B \setminus \alpha M)$ are removed from the M_i and B; all unreachable states and transitions in the M_i and B are also removed. This is repeated until $\alpha M = \alpha B$.

We applied the model checker to all problems in the 2019 benchmarks. Interestingly, all 180 tasks completed, with the correct results, using at most 8 GB RAM; the times are given in Fig. 2.

We also ran these problems with POR turned off, to measure the impact of that optimization. As is often the case with POR schemes, the difference is dramatic. The non-POR tests ran out of memory on our 256 GB machine after problem 106. We show the resources consumed for a representative task in Fig. 3; this property holds, so a complete search is required. In terms of number of states or time, the performance differs by about 5 orders of magnitude.

Problem	101	102	103	104	105	106	107	108	109
Components	8	10	12	15	20	25	50	60	70
Time (s)	1	1	1	1	1	1	14	54	432

Fig. 2. Time to solve RERS 2019 parallel LTL problems using McRERS. Each problem comprises 20 LTL formulas. Memory limited to 8 GB. Rows: problem number, number of components in the LTS, and total McRERS wall time rounded up to nearest second.

POR?	States saved	Transitions	Memory (MB)	Time (s)
YES	1.55×10^4	1.55×10^4	1.26×10^2	< 0.1
NO	1.89×10^9	1.35×10^{10}	2.61×10^5	7865.0

Fig. 3. Performance impact of POR on solving RERS 2019 problem 106, formula 1, $(\mathsf{a}6 \rightarrow \mathbf{F}\mathsf{a}7)\mathbf{W}(\mathsf{a}7 \lor \mathsf{a}88)$.

Tool	States	Transitions	Memory(MB)	Time(s)
SPIN	8.16×10^7	2.01×10^8	1.09×10^4	292.0
McRERS	1.80×10^2	1.93×10^2	5.06×10^1	< 0.1

Fig. 4. Performance of SPIN v6.5.1 and McRERS on RERS 2019 problem 101, property 1. Both tools used POR. SPIN used `-DCOLLAPSE` for state compression and `-m100000000` for search depth bound.

As explained in Sect. 5, the RERS SPIN models can not be expected to perform well. We ran the latest version of SPIN on these using `-DCOLLAPSE` compression. We show the result for just the first task in Fig. 4. There is at least a 4 order of magnitude performance difference (measured in states or time) between the tools. An examination of SPIN's output in verbose mode reveals the problem to be as described in Sect. 5: the full set of enabled transitions is explored at each transition due to the update of the shared variable.

The 2016 RERS problems are more challenging for McRERS. The problems are numbered from 101 to 120. To scale beyond problem 111, with a memory bound of 256 GB, additional reduction techniques, such as the component minimization methods discussed in Sect. 5, must be used. We plan to carry out a thorough study of those methods and how they interact with POR.

Acknowledgements. We are grateful to Marc Jasper of TU Dortmund for answering many of our questions about the RERS benchmarks, and for coining the term "interruptible" to describe the class of properties that are the topic of this paper. This material is based upon work by the RAPIDS Institute, supported by the U.S. Department of Energy, Office of Science, Office of Advanced Scientific Computing Research, Scientific Discovery through Advanced Computing (SciDAC) program. Funding was also provided by DoE award DE-SC0012566, and by the U.S. National Science Foundation award CCF-1319571.

References

1. Clarke Jr., E.M., Grumberg, O., Kroening, D., Peled, D., Veith, H.: Model Checking, 2nd edn. MIT press, Cambridge (2018). https://mitpress.mit.edu/books/model-checking-second-edition
2. Courcoubetis, C., Vardi, M., Wolper, P., Yannakakis, M.: Memory-efficient algorithms for the verification of temporal properties. Formal Methods Syst. Des. **1**(2), 275–288 (1992). https://doi.org/10.1007/BF00121128
3. De Nicola, R., Vaandrager, F.: Action versus state based logics for transition systems. In: Guessarian, I. (ed.) LITP 1990. LNCS, vol. 469, pp. 407–419. Springer, Heidelberg (1990). https://doi.org/10.1007/3-540-53479-2_17
4. Duret-Lutz, A., Lewkowicz, A., Fauchille, A., Michaud, T., Renault, É., Xu, L.: Spot 2.0 — a framework for LTL and ω-automata manipulation. In: Artho, C., Legay, A., Peled, D. (eds.) ATVA 2016. LNCS, vol. 9938, pp. 122–129. Springer, Cham (2016). https://doi.org/10.1007/978-3-319-46520-3_8
5. Dwyer, M.B., Avrunin, G.S., Corbett, J.C.: Property specification patterns for finite-state verification. In: Proceedings of the Second Workshop on Formal Methods in Software Practice, FMSP 1998, pp. 7–15. ACM, New York (1998). https://doi.org/10.1145/298595.298598
6. Eloranta, J., Tienari, M., Valmari, A.: Essential transitions to bisimulation equivalences. Theor. Comput. Sci. **179**(1–2), 397–419 (1997). https://doi.org/10.1016/S0304-3975(96)00281-2
7. Fantechi, A., Gnesi, S., Ristori, G.: Model checking for action-based logics. Formal Methods Syst. Des. **4**(2), 187–203 (1994). https://doi.org/10.1007/BF01384084
8. Fernandez, J.C.: An implementation of an efficient algorithm for bisimulation equivalence. Sci. Comput. Programm. **13**(2), 219–236 (1990). https://doi.org/10.1016/0167-6423(90)90071-K
9. Geske, M., Jasper, M., Steffen, B., Howar, F., Schordan, M., van de Pol, J.: RERS 2016: parallel and sequential benchmarks with focus on LTL verification. In: Margaria, T., Steffen, B. (eds.) ISoLA 2016. LNCS, vol. 9953, pp. 787–803. Springer, Cham (2016). https://doi.org/10.1007/978-3-319-47169-3_59
10. Gheorghiu Bobaru, M., Păsăreanu, C.S., Giannakopoulou, D.: Automated assume-guarantee reasoning by abstraction refinement. In: Gupta, A., Malik, S. (eds.) CAV 2008. LNCS, vol. 5123, pp. 135–148. Springer, Heidelberg (2008). https://doi.org/10.1007/978-3-540-70545-1_14
11. Giannakopoulou, D.: Model checking for concurrent software architectures. Ph.D. thesis, Imperial College of Science, Technology and Medicine, University of London (1999). https://pdfs.semanticscholar.org/0215/b74b21112520569f6e6b930312e228c90e0b.pdf
12. Giannakopoulou, D., Magee, J.: Fluent model checking for event-based systems. In: Proceedings of the 9th European Software Engineering Conference Held Jointly with 11th ACM SIGSOFT International Symposium on Foundations of Software Engineering, pp. 257–266. ESEC/FSE-11, Association for Computing Machinery, New York (2003). https://doi.org/10.1145/940071.940106
13. Gibson-Robinson, T., et al.: FDR: from theory to industrial application. In: Gibson-Robinson, T., Hopcroft, P., Lazić, R. (eds.) Concurrency, Security, and Puzzles. LNCS, vol. 10160, pp. 65–87. Springer, Cham (2017). https://doi.org/10.1007/978-3-319-51046-0_4

14. Gibson-Robinson, T., Hansen, H., Roscoe, A.W., Wang, X.: Practical partial order reduction for CSP. In: Havelund, K., Holzmann, G., Joshi, R. (eds.) NFM 2015. LNCS, vol. 9058, pp. 188–203. Springer, Cham (2015). https://doi.org/10.1007/978-3-319-17524-9_14

15. Godefroid, P. (ed.): Partial-Order Methods for the Verification of Concurrent Systems - An Approach to the State-Explosion Problem. LNCS, vol. 1032. Springer, Heidelberg (1996). https://doi.org/10.1007/3-540-60761-7

16. Groote, J.F., Mathijssen, A., Reniers, M., Usenko, Y., van Weerdenburg, M.: The formal specification language mCRL2. In: Brinksma, E., Harel, D., Mader, A., Stevens, P., Wieringa, R. (eds.) Methods for Modelling Software Systems (MMOSS). No. 06351 in Dagstuhl Seminar Proceedings, Internationales Begegnungs- und Forschungszentrum für Informatik (IBFI), Schloss Dagstuhl, Germany, Dagstuhl, Germany (2007). http://drops.dagstuhl.de/opus/volltexte/2007/862

17. Hansen, H., Penczek, W., Valmari, A.: Stuttering-insensitive automata for on-the-fly detection of livelock properties. Electron. Notes Theor. Comput. Sci. **66**(2), 178–193 (2002). https://doi.org/10.1016/S1571-0661(04)80411-0. FMICS 2002, 7th International ERCIM Workshop in Formal Methods for Industrial Critical Systems (ICALP 2002 Satellite Workshop)

18. Holzmann, G., Peled, D., Yannakakis, M.: On nested depth first search. In: The Spin Verification System, DIMACS - Series in Discrete Mathematics and Theoretical Computer Science, vol. 32, pp. 23–31. AMS and DIMACS (1997). https://bookstore.ams.org/dimacs-32/

19. Jasper, M., et al.: The RERS 2017 challenge and workshop (invited paper). In: SPIN 2017, pp. 11–20. ACM (2017). https://doi.org/10.1145/3092282.3098206

20. Jasper, M., et al.: RERS 2019: combining synthesis with real-world models. In: Beyer, D., Huisman, M., Kordon, F., Steffen, B. (eds.) TACAS 2019. LNCS, vol. 11429, pp. 101–115. Springer, Cham (2019). https://doi.org/10.1007/978-3-030-17502-3_7

21. Jasper, M., Mues, M., Schlüter, M., Steffen, B., Howar, F.: RERS 2018: CTL, LTL, and reachability. In: Margaria, T., Steffen, B. (eds.) ISoLA 2018. LNCS, vol. 11245, pp. 433–447. Springer, Cham (2018). https://doi.org/10.1007/978-3-030-03421-4_27

22. Michaud, T., Duret-Lutz, A.: Practical stutter-invariance checks for ω-regular languages. In: Fischer, B., Geldenhuys, J. (eds.) SPIN 2015. LNCS, vol. 9232, pp. 84–101. Springer, Cham (2015). https://doi.org/10.1007/978-3-319-23404-5_7

23. Peled, D.: Combining partial order reductions with on-the-fly model-checking. Formal Methods Syst. Des. **8**(1), 39–64 (1996). https://doi.org/10.1007/BF00121262

24. Peled, D., Wilke, T.: Stutter-invariant temporal properties are expressible without the next-time operator. Inf. Process. Lett. **63**(5), 243–246 (1997). https://doi.org/10.1016/S0020-0190(97)00133-6

25. Peled, D.: All from one, one for all: on model checking using representatives. In: Courcoubetis, C. (ed.) CAV 1993. LNCS, vol. 697, pp. 409–423. Springer, Heidelberg (1993). https://doi.org/10.1007/3-540-56922-7_34

26. Pnueli, A.: The temporal logic of programs. In: Proceedings of the 18th Annual Symposium on Foundations of Computer Science, SFCS 1977, pp. 46–57. IEEE Computer Society (1977). https://doi.org/10.1109/SFCS.1977.32

27. Siegel, S.F.: What's wrong with on-the-fly partial order reduction. In: Dillig, I., Tasiran, S. (eds.) CAV 2019. LNCS, vol. 11562, pp. 478–495. Springer, Cham (2019). https://doi.org/10.1007/978-3-030-25543-5_27

28. Siegel, S.F., Yan, Y.: Action-based model checking: Logic, automata, and reduction (extended version). Technical report UD-CIS-2020-0515, University of Delaware (2020). http://vsl.cis.udel.edu/pubs/action.html

29. Steffen, B., Jasper, M.: Property-preserving parallel decomposition. In: Aceto, L., et al. (eds.) Models, Algorithms, Logics and Tools. LNCS, vol. 10460, pp. 125–145. Springer, Cham (2017). https://doi.org/10.1007/978-3-319-63121-9_7

30. Sun, J., Liu, Y., Dong, J.S.: Model checking CSP revisited: introducing a process analysis toolkit. In: Margaria, T., Steffen, B. (eds.) ISoLA 2008. CCIS, vol. 17, pp. 307–322. Springer, Heidelberg (2008). https://doi.org/10.1007/978-3-540-88479-8_22

31. Valmari, A.: Stubborn sets for reduced state space generation. In: Rozenberg, G. (ed.) ICATPN 1989. LNCS, vol. 483, pp. 491–515. Springer, Heidelberg (1991). https://doi.org/10.1007/3-540-53863-1_36

32. Valmari, A.: On-the-fly verification with stubborn sets. In: Courcoubetis, C. (ed.) CAV 1993. LNCS, vol. 697, pp. 397–408. Springer, Heidelberg (1993). https://doi.org/10.1007/3-540-56922-7_33

33. Valmari, A.: Stubborn set methods for process algebras. In: Proceedings of the DIMACS Workshop on Partial Order Methods in Verification, POMIV 1996, pp. 213–231. American Math. Soc., New York (1997). http://dl.acm.org/citation.cfm?id=266557.266608

34. Valmari, A.: The state explosion problem. In: Reisig, W., Rozenberg, G. (eds.) ACPN 1996. LNCS, vol. 1491, pp. 429–528. Springer, Heidelberg (1998). https://doi.org/10.1007/3-540-65306-6_21

35. Valmari, A.: More stubborn set methods for process algebras. In: Gibson-Robinson, T., Hopcroft, P., Lazić, R. (eds.) Concurrency, Security, and Puzzles. LNCS, vol. 10160, pp. 246–271. Springer, Cham (2017). https://doi.org/10.1007/978-3-319-51046-0_13

36. Vardi, M.Y.: An automata-theoretic approach to linear temporal logic. In: Moller, F., Birtwistle, G. (eds.) Logics for Concurrency: Structure versus Automata. LNCS, vol. 1043, pp. 238–266. Springer, Heidelberg (1996). https://doi.org/10.1007/3-540-60915-6_6

37. Vardi, M.Y.: Automata-theoretic model checking revisited. In: Cook, B., Podelski, A. (eds.) VMCAI 2007. LNCS, vol. 4349, pp. 137–150. Springer, Heidelberg (2007). https://doi.org/10.1007/978-3-540-69738-1_10

Global Guidance for Local Generalization in Model Checking

Hari Govind Vediramana Krishnan[1](✉), YuTing Chen[2], Sharon Shoham[3], and Arie Gurfinkel[1]

[1] University of Waterloo, Waterloo, Canada
hgvk94@gmail.com
[2] Chalmers University of Technology, Gothenburg, Sweden
[3] Tel Aviv University, Tel Aviv, Israel

Abstract. SMT-based model checkers, especially IC3-style ones, are currently the most effective techniques for verification of infinite state systems. They infer *global* inductive invariants via *local* reasoning about a single step of the transition relation of a system, while employing SMT-based procedures, such as interpolation, to mitigate the limitations of local reasoning and allow for better generalization. Unfortunately, these mitigations intertwine model checking with heuristics of the underlying SMT-solver, negatively affecting stability of model checking.

In this paper, we propose to tackle the limitations of locality in a systematic manner. We introduce explicit *global guidance* into the local reasoning performed by IC3-style algorithms. To this end, we extend the SMT-IC3 paradigm with three novel rules, designed to mitigate fundamental sources of failure that stem from locality. We instantiate these rules for the theory of Linear Integer Arithmetic and implement them on top of SPACER solver in Z3. Our empirical results show that GSPACER, SPACER extended with global guidance, is significantly more effective than both SPACER and sole global reasoning, and, furthermore, is insensitive to interpolation.

1 Introduction

SMT-based Model Checking algorithms that combine SMT-based search for bounded counterexamples with interpolation-based search for inductive invariants are currently the most effective techniques for verification of infinite state systems. They are widely applicable, including for verification of synchronous systems, protocols, parameterized systems, and software.

The Achilles heel of these approaches is the mismatch between the *local* reasoning used to establish absence of bounded counterexamples and a *global* reason for absence of unbounded counterexamples (i.e., existence of an inductive invariant). This is particularly apparent in IC3-style algorithms [7], such as SPACER [18]. IC3-style algorithms establish bounded safety by repeatedly computing predecessors of error (or bad) states, blocking them by local reasoning

© The Author(s) 2020
S. K. Lahiri and C. Wang (Eds.): CAV 2020, LNCS 12225, pp. 101–125, 2020.
https://doi.org/10.1007/978-3-030-53291-8_7

about a single step of the transition relation of the system, and, later, using the resulting *lemmas* to construct a candidate inductive invariant for the global safety proof. The whole process is driven by the choice of local lemmas. Good lemmas lead to quick convergence, bad lemmas make even simple-looking problems difficult to solve.

The effect of local reasoning is somewhat mitigated by the use of interpolation in lemma construction. In addition to the usual inductive generalization by dropping literals from a blocked bad state, interpolation is used to further generalize the blocked state using theory-aware reasoning. For example, when blocking a bad state $x = 1 \land y = 1$, inductive generalization would infer a subclause of $x \neq 1 \lor y \neq 1$ as a lemma, while interpolation might infer $x \neq y$ – a predicate that might be required for the inductive invariant. SPACER, that is based on this idea, is extremely effective, as demonstrated by its performance in recent CHC-COMP competitions [10]. The downside, however, is that the approach leads to a highly unstable procedure that is extremely sensitive to syntactic changes in the system description, changes in interpolation algorithms, and any algorithmic changes in the underlying SMT-solver.

An alternative approach, often called *invariant inference*, is to focus on the global safety proof, i.e., an inductive invariant. This has long been advocated by such approaches as Houdini [15], and, more recently, by a variety of machine-learning inspired techniques, e.g., FreqHorn [14], LinearArbitrary [28], and ICE-DT [16]. The key idea is to iteratively generate positive (i.e., reachable states) and negative (i.e., states that reach an error) examples and to compute a candidate invariant that separates these two sets. The reasoning is more focused towards the invariant, and, the search is restricted by either predicates, templates, grammars, or some combination. Invariant inference approaches are particularly good at finding simple inductive invariants. However, they do not generalize well to a wide variety of problems. In practice, they are often used to complement other SMT-based techniques.

In this paper, we present a novel approach that extends, what we call, *local reasoning* of IC3-style algorithms with *global guidance* inspired by the invariant inference algorithms described above. Our main insight is that the set of lemmas maintained by IC3-style algorithms hint towards a potential global proof. However, these hints are lost in existing approaches. We observe that letting the current set of lemmas, that represent candidate global invariants, guide local reasoning by introducing new lemmas and states to be blocked is often sufficient to direct IC3 towards a better global proof.

We present and implement our results in the context of SPACER—a solver for Constrained Horn Clauses (CHC)—implemented in the Z3 SMT-solver [13]. SPACER is used by multiple software model checking tools, performed remarkably well in CHC-COMP competitions [10], and is open-sourced. However, our results are fundamental and apply to any other IC3-style algorithm. While our implementation works with arbitrary CHC instances, we simplify the presentation by focusing on infinite state model checking of transition systems.

We illustrate the pitfalls of local reasoning using three examples shown in Fig. 1. All three examples are small, simple, and have simple inductive invariants.

All three are challenging for SPACER. Where these examples are based on SPACER-specific design choices, each exhibits a fundamental deficiency that stems from local reasoning. We believe they can be adapted for any other IC3-style verification algorithm. The examples assume basic familiarity with the IC3 paradigm. Readers who are not familiar with it may find it useful to read the examples after reading Sect. 2.

```
 1  a, c := 0, 0;           a, b := 0, 0;              a, b, c := 0, 0, 0;
 2  // b, d := a, c;        while(nd())                while(nd())
 3  b, d := 0, 0;           // inv: a ≥ 0 ∧ b ≥ 0;     // inv: b = c;
 4  while(nd())             {                          {
 5  // inv: a - c = b - d;    a := a + b;                a++; b++; c++;
 6  {                         b++;                      }
 7    if(nd()) { a++; b++; } }                          assert(a ≥ 100 ⇒ b = c);
 8    else { c++; d++; }    assert(a ≥ 0);
 9  }
10  assert(a ≤ c ⇒ b ≤ d);
```

| (a) myopic generalization | (b) excessive generalization | (c) stuck in a rut |

Fig. 1. Verification tasks to illustrate sources of divergence for SPACER. The call $nd()$ non-deterministically returns a Boolean value.

Myopic Generalization. SPACER diverges on the example in Fig. 1(a) by iteratively learning lemmas of the form $(a - c \le k) \Rightarrow (b - d \le k)$ for different values of k, where a, b, c, d are the program variables. These lemmas establish that there are no counterexamples of longer and longer lengths. However, the process never converges to the desired lemma $(a - c) \le (b - d)$, which excludes counterexamples of any length. The lemmas are discovered using interpolation, based on proofs found by the SMT-solver. A close examination of the corresponding proofs shows that the relationship between $(a - c)$ and $(b - d)$ does not appear in the proofs, making it impossible to find the desired lemma by tweaking local interpolation reasoning. On the other hand, looking at the global proof (i.e., the set of lemmas discovered to refute a bounded counterexample), it is almost obvious that $(a - c) \le (b - d)$ is an interesting generalization to try. Amusingly, a small, syntactic, but semantic preserving change of swapping line 2 for line 3 in Fig. 1(a) changes the SMT-solver proofs, affects local interpolation, and makes the instance trivial for SPACER.

Excessive (Predecessor) Generalization. SPACER diverges on the example in Fig. 1(b) by computing an infinite sequence of lemmas of the form $a + k_1 \times b \ge k_2$, where a and b are program variables, and k_1 and k_2 are integers. The root cause is excessive generalization in predecessor computation. The *Bad* states are $a < 0$, and their predecessors are states such as $(a = 1 \land b = -10)$, $(a = 2 \land b = -10)$, etc., or, more generally, regions $(a + b < 0)$, $(a + 2b < -1)$, etc. SPACER always attempts to compute the most general predecessor states.

This is the best local strategy, but blocking these regions by learning their negation leads to the aforementioned lemmas. According to the global proof these lemmas do not converge to a linear invariant. An alternative strategy that under-approximates the problematic regions by (numerically) simpler regions and, as a result, learns simpler lemmas is desired (and is effective on this example). For example, region $a + 3b \leq -4$ can be under-approximated by $a \leq 32 \wedge b \leq -12$, eventually leading to a lemma $b \geq 0$, that is a part of the final invariant: $(a \geq 0 \wedge b \geq 0)$.

Stuck in a Rut. Finally, SPACER converges on the example in Fig. 1(c), but only after unrolling the system for 100 iterations. During the first 100 iterations, SPACER learns that program states with $(a \geq 100 \wedge b \neq c)$ are not reachable because a is bounded by 1 in the first iteration, by 2 in the second, and so on. In each iteration, the global proof is updated by replacing a lemma of the form $a < k$ by lemma of the form $a < (k + 1)$ for different values of k. Again, the strategy is good locally – total number of lemmas does not grow and the bounded proof is improved. Yet, globally, it is clear that no progress is made since the same set of bad states are blocked again and again in slightly different ways. An alternative strategy is to abstract the literal $a \geq 100$ from the formula that represents the bad states, and, instead, conjecture that no states in $b \neq c$ are reachable.

Our Approach: Global Guidance. As shown in the examples above, in all the cases that SPACER diverges, the missteps are not obvious locally, but are clear when the overall proof is considered. We propose three new rules, Subsume, Concretize, and, Conjecture, that provide global guidance, by considering existing lemmas, to mitigate the problems illustrated above. Subsume introduces a lemma that generalizes existing ones, Concretize under-approximates partially-blocked predecessors to focus on repeatedly unblocked regions, and Conjecture over-approximates a predecessor by abstracting away regions that are repeatedly blocked. The rules are generic, and apply to arbitrary SMT theories. Furthermore, we propose an efficient instantiation of the rules for the theory Linear Integer Arithmetic.

We have implemented the new strategy, called GSPACER, in SPACER and compared it to the original implementation of SPACER. We show that GSPACER outperforms SPACER in benchmarks from CHC-COMP 2018 and 2019. More significantly, we show that the performance is independent of interpolation. While SPACER is highly dependent on interpolation parameters, and performs poorly when interpolation is disabled, the results of GSPACER are virtually unaffected by interpolation. We also compare GSPACER to LinearArbitrary [28], a tool that *infers invariants* using global reasoning. GSPACER outperforms LinearArbitrary on the benchmarks from [28]. These results indicate that global guidance mitigates the shortcomings of local reasoning.

The rest of the paper is structured as follows. Sect. 2 presents the necessary background. Sect. 3 introduces our *global guidance* as a set of abstract inference rules. Sect. 4 describes an instantiation of the rules to Linear Integer Arithmetic

(LIA). Sect. 5 presents our empirical evaluation. Finally, Sect. 7 describes related work and concludes the paper.

2 Background

Logic. We consider first order logic modulo theories, and adopt the standard notation and terminology. A first-order language modulo theory $\mathcal{T}$ is defined over a signature Σ that consists of constant, function and predicate symbols, some of which may be *interpreted* by $\mathcal{T}$. As always, *terms* are constant symbols, variables, or function symbols applied to terms; *atoms* are predicate symbols applied to terms; *literals* are atoms or their negations; *cubes* are conjunctions of literals; and *clauses* are disjunctions of literals. Unless otherwise stated, we only consider *closed* formulas (i.e., formulas without any free variables). As usual, we use sets of formulas and their conjunctions interchangeably.

MBP. Given a set of constants $\boldsymbol{v}$, a formula φ and a model $M \models \varphi$, Model Based Projection (MBP) of φ over the constants $\boldsymbol{v}$, denoted $\mathrm{MBP}(\boldsymbol{v}, \varphi, M)$, computes a model-preserving under-approximation of φ projected onto $\Sigma \setminus \boldsymbol{v}$. That is, $\mathrm{MBP}(\boldsymbol{v}, \varphi, M)$ is a formula over $\Sigma \setminus \boldsymbol{v}$ such that $M \models \mathrm{MBP}(\boldsymbol{v}, \varphi, M)$ and any model $M' \models \mathrm{MBP}(\boldsymbol{v}, \varphi, M)$ can be extended to a model $M'' \models \varphi$ by providing an interpretation for $\boldsymbol{v}$. There are polynomial time algorithms for computing MBP in Linear Arithmetic [5,18].

Interpolation. Given an unsatisfiable formula $A \wedge B$, an interpolant, denoted $\mathrm{ITP}(A, B)$, is a formula I over the shared signature of A and B such that $A \Rightarrow I$ and $I \Rightarrow \neg B$.

Safety Problem. A *transition system* is a pair $\langle Init, Tr \rangle$, where $Init$ is a formula over Σ and Tr is a formula over $\Sigma \cup \Sigma'$, where $\Sigma' = \{s' \mid s \in \Sigma\}$.[1] The states of the system correspond to structures over Σ, $Init$ represents the initial states and Tr represents the transition relation, where Σ is used to represent the pre-state of a transition, and Σ' is used to represent the post-state. For a formula φ over Σ, we denote by φ' the formula obtained by substituting each $s \in \Sigma$ by $s' \in \Sigma'$. A *safety problem* is a triple $\langle Init, Tr, Bad \rangle$, where $\langle Init, Tr \rangle$ is a transition system and Bad is a formula over Σ representing a set of bad states.

The safety problem $\langle Init, Tr, Bad \rangle$ has a *counterexample of length* k if the following formula is satisfiable: $Init^0 \wedge \bigwedge_{i=0}^{k-1} Tr^i \wedge Bad^k$, where φ^i is defined over $\Sigma^i = \{s^i \mid s \in \Sigma\}$ (a copy of the signature used to represent the state of the system after the execution of i steps) and is obtained from φ by substituting each $s \in \Sigma$ by $s^i \in \Sigma^i$, and Tr^i is obtained from Tr by substituting $s \in \Sigma$ by $s^i \in \Sigma^i$ and $s' \in \Sigma'$ by $s^{i+1} \in \Sigma^{i+1}$. The transition system is *safe* if the safety problem has no counterexample, of any length.

---

[1] In fact, a primed copy is introduced in Σ' only for the uninterpreted symbols in Σ. Interpreted symbols remain the same in Σ'.

Algorithm 1: SPACER algorithm as a set of guarded commands. We use the shorthand $\mathcal{F}(\varphi) = \mathcal{U}' \vee (\varphi \wedge Tr)$.

---

function SPACER:
In: $\langle Init, Tr, Bad \rangle$
Out: $\langle$ SAFE, $Inv \rangle$ or UNSAFE
$Q := \emptyset$ // pob queue
$N := 0$ // maximum safe level
$\mathcal{O}_0 := Init, \mathcal{O}_i := \top$ **for all** $i > 0$ // lemma trace
$\mathcal{U} := Init$ // reachable states
forever do
  Candidate ⟦ ISSAT($\mathcal{O}_N \wedge Bad$) ⟧ $Q := Q \cup \langle Bad, N \rangle$
  Predecessor ⟦ $\langle \varphi, i+1 \rangle \in Q,\ M \models \mathcal{O}_i \wedge Tr \wedge \varphi'$ ⟧ $Q := Q \cup \langle \text{MBP}(x', Tr \wedge \varphi', M), i \rangle$
  Successor ⟦ $\langle \varphi, i+1 \rangle \in Q,\ M \models \mathcal{F}(\mathcal{U}) \wedge \varphi'$ ⟧ $\mathcal{U} := \mathcal{U} \vee \text{MBP}(x, \mathcal{F}(\mathcal{U}), M)[x' \mapsto x]$
  Conflict ⟦ $\langle \varphi, i+1 \rangle \in Q,\ \mathcal{F}(\mathcal{O}_i) \Rightarrow \neg\varphi'$ ⟧ $\mathcal{O}_j := (\mathcal{O}_j \wedge \text{ITP}(\mathcal{F}(\mathcal{O}_i), \varphi')[x' \mapsto x])$ **for all** $j \leq i+1$
  Induction ⟦ $\ell \in \mathcal{O}_{i+1}, \ell = (\varphi \vee \psi), \mathcal{F}(\varphi \wedge \mathcal{O}_i) \Rightarrow \varphi'$ ⟧ $\mathcal{O}_j := \mathcal{O}_j \wedge \varphi$ **for all** $j \leq i+1$
  Propagate ⟦ $\ell \in \mathcal{O}_i, \mathcal{O}_i \wedge Tr \Rightarrow \ell'$ ⟧ $\mathcal{O}_{i+1} := (\mathcal{O}_{i+1} \wedge \ell)$
  Unfold ⟦ $\mathcal{O}_N \Rightarrow \neg Bad$ ⟧ $N := N + 1$
  Safe ⟦ $\mathcal{O}_{i+1} \Rightarrow \mathcal{O}_i$ **for some** $i < N$ ⟧ **return** $\langle$ SAFE, $\mathcal{O}_i \rangle$
  Unsafe ⟦ ISSAT($Bad \wedge \mathcal{U}$) ⟧ **return** UNSAFE

Algorithm 2: Global guidance rules for SPACER.

Subsume ⟦ $\mathcal{L} \subseteq \mathcal{O}_i, k \geq i, \mathcal{F}(\mathcal{O}_k) \Rightarrow \psi', \forall \ell \in \mathcal{L}. \psi \Rightarrow \ell$ ⟧
  $\mathcal{O}_j := (\mathcal{O}_j \wedge \psi)$ **for all** $j \leq k+1$

Concretize ⟦ $\mathcal{L} \subseteq \mathcal{O}_i, \langle \varphi, j \rangle \in Q, \forall \ell \in \mathcal{L}. \text{ISSAT}(\varphi \wedge \neg \ell), \text{ISSAT}(\varphi \wedge \bigwedge \mathcal{L}), \gamma \Rightarrow \varphi, \text{ISSAT}(\gamma \wedge \bigwedge \mathcal{L})$ ⟧
  $Q := Q \cup \langle \gamma, k+1 \rangle$ **where** $k = \max\{j \mid \mathcal{O}_j \Rightarrow \neg \gamma\}$

Conjecture ⟦ $\mathcal{L} \subseteq \mathcal{O}_i, \langle \varphi, j \rangle \in Q, \varphi \equiv \alpha \wedge \beta, \forall \ell \in \mathcal{L}. \ell \Rightarrow \neg \beta \wedge \text{ISSAT}(\ell \wedge \alpha), \mathcal{U} \Rightarrow \neg \alpha$ ⟧
  $Q := Q \cup \langle \alpha, k+1 \rangle$ **where** $k = \max\{j \mid \mathcal{O}_j \Rightarrow \neg \alpha\}$

Inductive Invariants. An *inductive invariant* is a formula *Inv* over Σ such that (i) $Init \Rightarrow Inv$, (ii) $Inv \wedge Tr \Rightarrow Inv'$, and (iii) $Inv \Rightarrow \neg Bad$. If such an inductive invariant exists, then the transition system is safe.

Spacer. The safety problem defined above is an instance of a more general problem, CHC-SAT, of satisfiability of Constrained Horn Clauses (CHC). SPACER is a semi-decision procedure for CHC-SAT. However, to simplify the presentation, we describe the algorithm only for the particular case of the safety problem. We stress that SPACER, as well as the developments of this paper, apply to the more general setting of CHCs (both linear and non-linear). We assume that the only uninterpreted symbols in Σ are constant symbols, which we denote x. Typically, these represent program variables. Without loss of generality, we assume that *Bad* is a cube.

Algorithm 1 presents the key ingredients of SPACER as a set of guarded commands (or rules). It maintains the following. Current unrolling depth N at which a counterexample is searched (there are no counterexamples with depth less than N). A *trace* $\mathcal{O} = (\mathcal{O}_0, \mathcal{O}_1, \ldots)$ of *frames*, such that each frame $\mathcal{O}_i$ is a set of *lemmas*, and each lemma $\ell \in \mathcal{O}_i$ is a clause. A queue of *proof obligations* Q, where each proof obligation (POB) in Q is a pair $\langle \varphi, i \rangle$ of a cube φ and a level number i, $0 \leq i \leq N$. An under-approximation $\mathcal{U}$ of reachable states. Intuitively, each frame $\mathcal{O}_i$ is a candidate inductive invariant s.t. $\mathcal{O}_i$ over-approximates states reachable up to i steps from $Init$. The latter is ensured since $\mathcal{O}_0 = Init$, the trace is monotone, i.e., $\mathcal{O}_{i+1} \subseteq \mathcal{O}_i$, and each frame is inductive *relative* to its previous one, i.e., $\mathcal{O}_i \wedge \mathit{Tr} \Rightarrow \mathcal{O}'_{i+1}$. Each POB $\langle \varphi, i \rangle$ in Q corresponds to a suffix of a potential counterexample that has to be blocked in $\mathcal{O}_i$, i.e., has to be proven unreachable in i steps.

The Candidate rule adds an initial POB $\langle Bad, N \rangle$ to the queue. If a POB $\langle \varphi, i \rangle$ cannot be blocked because φ is reachable from frame $(i-1)$, the Predecessor rule generates a predecessor ψ of φ using MBP and adds $\langle \psi, i-1 \rangle$ to Q. The Successor rule updates the set of reachable states if the POB is reachable. If the POB is blocked, the Conflict rule strengthens the trace $\mathcal{O}$ by using interpolation to learn a new lemma ℓ that blocks the POB, i.e., ℓ implies $\neg\varphi$. The Induction rule strengthens a lemma by inductive generalization and the Propagate rule pushes a lemma to a higher frame. If the Bad state has been blocked at N, the Unfold rule increments the depth of unrolling N. In practice, the rules are scheduled to ensure progress towards finding a counterexample.

3   Global Guidance of Local Proofs

As illustrated by the examples in Fig. 1, while SPACER is generally effective, its local reasoning is easily confused. The effectiveness is very dependent on the local computation of predecessors using model-based projection, and lemmas using interpolation. In this section, we extend SPACER with three additional *global* reasoning rules. The rules are inspired by the deficiencies illustrated by the motivating examples in Fig. 1. In this section, we present the rules abstractly, independent of any underlying theory, focusing on pre- and post-conditions. In Sect. 4, we specialize the rules for Linear Integer Arithmetic, and show how they are scheduled with the other rules of SPACER in an efficient verification algorithm. The new global rules are summarized in Algorithm 2. We use the same guarded command notation as in description of SPACER in Algorithm 1. Note that the rules supplement, and not replace, the ones in Algorithm 1.

Subsume is the most natural rule to explain. It says that if there is a set of lemmas $\mathcal{L}$ at level i, and there exists a formula ψ such that (a) ψ is stronger than every lemma in $\mathcal{L}$, and (b) ψ over-approximates states reachable in at most k steps, where $k \geq i$, then ψ can be added to the trace to subsume $\mathcal{L}$. This rule reduces the size of the global proof – that is, the number of total not-subsumed lemmas. Note that the rule allows ψ to be at a level k that is higher than i. The choice of ψ is left open. The details are likely to be specific to the theory involved. For example, when instantiated for LIA, Subsume is sufficient to solve example in Fig. 1(a). Interestingly, Subsume is not likely to be effective for propositional IC3. In that case, ψ is a clause and the only way for it to be stronger than $\mathcal{L}$ is for ψ to be a syntactic sub-sequence of every lemma in $\mathcal{L}$, but such ψ is already explored by local inductive generalization (rule Induction in Algorithm 1).

Concretize applies to a POB, unlike Subsume. It is motivated by example in Fig. 1(b) that highlights the problem of excessive local generalization. SPACER always computes as general predecessors as possible. This is necessary for refutational completeness since in an infinite state system there are infinitely many potential predecessors. Computing the most general predecessor ensures that SPACER finds a counterexample, if it exists. However, this also forces SPACER to discover more general, and sometimes more complex, lemmas than might be necessary for an inductive invariant. Without a global view of the overall proof, it is hard to determine when the algorithm generalizes too much. The intuition for Concretize is that generalization is excessive when there is a single POB $\langle \varphi, j \rangle$ that is not blocked, yet, there is a set of lemmas $\mathcal{L}$ such that every lemma $\ell \in \mathcal{L}$ partially blocks φ. That is, for any $\ell \in \mathcal{L}$, there is a sub-region φ_ℓ of POB φ that is blocked by ℓ (i.e., $\ell \Rightarrow \neg\varphi_\ell$), and there is at least one state $s \in \varphi$ that is not blocked by any existing lemma in $\mathcal{L}$ (i.e., $s \models \varphi \wedge \bigwedge \mathcal{L}$). In this case, Concretize computes an under-approximation γ of φ that includes some not-yet-blocked state s. The new POB is added to the lowest level at which γ is not yet blocked. Concretize is useful to solve the example in Fig. 1(b).

Conjecture guides the algorithm away from being stuck in the same part of the search space. A single POB φ might be blocked by a different lemma at each level that φ appears in. This indicates that the lemmas are too strong, and cannot be propagated successfully to a higher level. The goal of the Conjecture rule is to identify such a case to guide the algorithm to explore alternative proofs with a better potential for generalization. This is done by abstracting away the part of the POB that has been blocked in the past. The pre-condition for Conjecture is the existence of a POB $\langle \varphi, j \rangle$ such that φ is split into two (not necessarily disjoint) sets of literals, α and β. Second, there must be a set of lemmas $\mathcal{L}$, at a (typically much lower) level $i < j$ such that every lemma $\ell \in \mathcal{L}$ blocks φ, and, moreover, blocks φ by blocking β. Intuitively, this implies that while there are many different lemmas (i.e., all lemmas in $\mathcal{L}$) that block φ at different levels, all of them correspond to a *local* generalization of $\neg\beta$ that could not be propagated to block φ at higher levels. In this case, Conjecture abstracts the POB φ into α, hoping to generate an alternative way to block φ. Of course, α is conjectured only if it is not already blocked and does not contain any known reachable states. Conjecture is necessary for a quick convergence on the example in Fig. 1(c). In some respect, Conjecture is akin to widening in Abstract Interpretation [12] – it abstracts a set of states by dropping constraints that appear to prevent further exploration. Of course, it is also quite different since it does not guarantee termination. While Conjecture is applicable to propositional IC3 as well, it is much more significant in SMT-based setting since in many FOL theories a single literal in a POB might result in infinitely many distinct lemmas.

Each of the rules can be applied by itself, but they are most effective in combination. For example, Concretize creates less general predecessors, that, in the worst case, lead to many simple lemmas. At the same time, Subsume combines lemmas together into more complex ones. The interaction of the two produces lemmas that neither one can produce in isolation. At the same time, Conjecture helps unstuck the algorithm from a single unproductive POB, allowing the other rules to take effect.

4 Global Guidance for Linear Integer Arithmetic

In this section, we present a specialization of our general rules, shown in Algorithm 2, to the theory of Linear Integer Arithmetic (LIA). This requires solving two problems: identifying subsets of lemmas for pre-conditions of the rules (clearly using all possible subsets is too expensive), and applying the rule once its pre-condition is met. For lemma selection, we introduce a notion of syntactic clustering based on anti-unification. For rule application, we exploit basic properties of LIA for an effective algorithm. Our presentation is focused on LIA exclusively. However, the rules extend to combinations of LIA with other theories, such as the combined theory of LIA and Arrays.

The rest of this section is structured as follows. We begin with a brief background on LIA in Sect. 4.1. We then present our lemma selection scheme, which is common to all the rules, in Sect. 4.2, followed by a description of how the rules Subsume (in Sect. 4.3), Concretize (in Sect. 4.4), and Conjecture (in Sect. 4.5) are instantiated for LIA. We conclude in Sect. 4.6 with an algorithm that integrates all the rules together.

4.1 Linear Integer Arithmetic: Background

In the theory of Linear Integer Arithmetic (LIA), formulas are defined over a signature that includes interpreted function symbols $+, -, \times$, interpreted predicate symbols $<, \leq, |$, interpreted constant symbols $0, 1, 2, \ldots$, and uninterpreted constant symbols $a, b, \ldots, x, y, \ldots$. We write $\mathbb{Z}$ for the set interpreted constant symbols, and call them *integers*. We use *constants* to refer exclusively to the uninterpreted constants (these are often called *variables* in LIA literature). Terms (and accordingly formulas) in LIA are restricted to be *linear*, that is, multiplication is never applied to two constants.

We write $\mathrm{LIA}^{-\mathrm{div}}$ for the fragment of LIA that excludes divisiblity $(d|h)$ predicates. A literal in $\mathrm{LIA}^{-\mathrm{div}}$ is a linear inequality; a cube is a conjunction of such inequalities, that is, a polytope. We find it convenient to use matrix-based notation for representing cubes in $\mathrm{LIA}^{-\mathrm{div}}$. A ground cube $c \in \mathrm{LIA}^{-\mathrm{div}}$ with p inequalities (literals) over k (uninterpreted) constants is written as $A \cdot \boldsymbol{x} \leq \boldsymbol{n}$, where A is a $p \times k$ matrix of coefficients in $\mathbb{Z}^{p \times k}$, $\boldsymbol{x} = (x_1 \cdots x_k)^T$ is a column vector that consists of the (uninterpreted) constants, and $\boldsymbol{n} = (n_1 \cdots n_p)^T$ is a column vector in $\mathbb{Z}^p$. For example, the cube $x \geq 2 \wedge 2x + y \leq 3$ is written as $\left[\begin{smallmatrix} -1 & 0 \\ 2 & 1 \end{smallmatrix}\right] \cdot \left[\begin{smallmatrix} x \\ y \end{smallmatrix}\right] \leq \left[\begin{smallmatrix} -2 \\ 3 \end{smallmatrix}\right]$. In the sequel, all vectors are column vectors, super-script T denotes transpose, dot is used for a dot product and $[\boldsymbol{n}_1; \boldsymbol{n}_2]$ stands for a matrix of column vectors $\boldsymbol{n}_1$ and $\boldsymbol{n}_2$.

4.2 Lemma Selection

A common pre-condition for all of our global rules in Algorithm 2 is the existence of a subset of lemmas $\mathcal{L}$ of some frame $\mathcal{O}_i$. Attempting to apply the rules for every subset of $\mathcal{O}_i$ is infeasible. In practice, we use syntactic similarity between lemmas as a predictor that one of the global rules is applicable, and restrict $\mathcal{L}$ to subsets of syntactically similar lemmas. In the rest of this section, we formally define what we mean by *syntactic similarity*, and how syntactically similar subsets of lemmas, called *clusters*, are maintained efficiently throughout the algorithm.

Syntactic Similarity. A formula π with free variables is called a *pattern*. Note that we do not require π to be in LIA. Let σ be a substitution, i.e., a mapping from variables to terms. We write $\pi\sigma$ for the result of replacing all occurrences of free variables in π with their mapping under σ. A substitution σ is called *numeric* if it maps every variable to an integer, i.e., the range of σ is $\mathbb{Z}$. We say that a formula φ *numerically matches* a pattern π iff there exists a numeric substitution σ such that $\varphi = \pi\sigma$. Note that, as usual, the equality is syntactic. For example, consider the pattern $\pi = v_0 a + v_1 b \leq 0$ with free variables v_0 and v_1 and uninterpreted constants a and b. The formula $\varphi_1 = 3a + 4b \leq 0$ matches π via a numeric substitution $\sigma_1 = \{v_0 \mapsto 3, v_1 \mapsto 4\}$. However, $\varphi_2 = 4b + 3a \leq 0$, while semantically equivalent to φ_1, does not match π. Similarly $\varphi_3 = a + b \leq 0$ does not match π as well.

Matching is extended to patterns in the usual way by allowing a substitution σ to map variables to variables. We say that a pattern π_1 is more general than a pattern π_2 if π_2 matches π_1. A pattern π is a *numeric anti-unifier* for a pair of formulas φ_1 and φ_2 if both φ_1 and φ_2 match π numerically. We write $anti(\varphi_1, \varphi_2)$ for a most general numeric anti-unifier of φ_1 and φ_2. We say that two formulas φ_1 and φ_2 are *syntactically similar* if there exists a numeric anti-unifier between them (i.e., $anti(\varphi_1, \varphi_2)$ is defined). Anti-unification is extended to sets of formulas in the usual way.

Clusters. We use anti-unification to define *clusters* of syntactically similar formulas. Let Φ be a fixed set of formulas, and π a pattern. A *cluster*, $\mathcal{C}_\Phi(\pi)$, is a subset of Φ such that every formula $\varphi \in \mathcal{C}_\Phi(\pi)$ numerically matches π. That is, π is a numeric anti-unifier for $\mathcal{C}_\Phi(\pi)$. In the implementation, we restrict the pre-conditions of the global rules so that a subset of lemmas $\mathcal{L} \subseteq \mathcal{O}_i$ is a cluster for some pattern π, i.e., $\mathcal{L} = \mathcal{C}_{\mathcal{O}_i}(\pi)$.

Clustering Lemmas. We use the following strategy to efficiently keep track of available clusters. Let ℓ_{new} be a new lemma to be added to $\mathcal{O}_i$. Assume there is at least one lemma $\ell \in \mathcal{O}_i$ that numerically anti-unifies with ℓ_{new} via some pattern π. If such an ℓ does not belong to any cluster, a new cluster $\mathcal{C}_{\mathcal{O}_i}(\pi) = \{\ell_{new}, \ell\}$ is formed, where $\pi = anti(\ell_{new}, \ell)$. Otherwise, for every lemma $\ell \in \mathcal{O}_i$ that numerically matches ℓ_{new} and every cluster $\mathcal{C}_{\mathcal{O}_i}(\hat{\pi})$ containing ℓ, ℓ_{new} is added to $\mathcal{C}_{\mathcal{O}_i}(\hat{\pi})$ if ℓ_{new} matches $\hat{\pi}$, or a new cluster is formed using ℓ, ℓ_{new}, and any other lemmas in $\mathcal{C}_{\mathcal{O}_i}(\hat{\pi})$ that anti-unify with them. Note that a new lemma ℓ_{new} might belong to multiple clusters.

For example, suppose $\ell_{\text{new}} = (a \leq 6 \vee b \leq 6)$, and there is already a cluster $\mathcal{C}_{\mathcal{O}_i}(a \leq v_0 \vee b \leq 5) = \{(a \leq 5 \vee b \leq 5), (a \leq 8 \vee b \leq 5)\}$. Since ℓ_{new} anti-unifies with each of the lemmas in the cluster, but does not match the pattern $a \leq v_0 \vee b \leq 5$, a new cluster that includes all of them is formed w.r.t. a more general pattern: $\mathcal{C}_{\mathcal{O}_i}(a \leq v_0 \vee b \leq v_1) = \{(a \leq 6 \vee b \leq 6), (a \leq 5 \vee b \leq 5), (a \leq 8 \vee b \leq 5)\}$.

In the presentation above, we assumed that anti-unification is completely syntactic. This is problematic in practice since it significantly limits the applicability of the global rules. Recall, for example, that $a+b \leq 0$ and $2a+2b \leq 0$ do not anti-unify numerically according to our definitions, and, therefore, do not cluster together. In practice, we augment syntactic anti-unification with simple rewrite rules that are applied greedily. For example, we normalize all LIA terms, take care of implicit multiplication by 1, and of associativity and commutativity of addition. In the future, it is interesting to explore how advanced anti-unification algorithms, such as [8,27], can be adapted for our purpose.

4.3   Subsume Rule for LIA

Recall that the Subsume rule (Algorithm 2) takes a cluster of lemmas $\mathcal{L} = \mathcal{C}_{\mathcal{O}_i}(\pi)$ and computes a new lemma ψ that subsumes all the lemmas in $\mathcal{L}$, that is $\psi \Rightarrow \bigwedge \mathcal{L}$. We find it convenient to dualize the problem. Let $\mathcal{S} = \{\neg \ell \mid \ell \in \mathcal{L}\}$ be the dual of $\mathcal{L}$, clearly $\psi \Rightarrow \bigwedge \mathcal{L}$ iff $(\bigvee \mathcal{S}) \Rightarrow \neg \psi$. Note that $\mathcal{L}$ is a set of clauses, $\mathcal{S}$ is a set of cubes, ψ is a clause, and $\neg \psi$ is a cube. In the case of $\text{LIA}^{-\text{div}}$, this means that $\bigvee \mathcal{S}$ represents a union of convex sets, and $\neg \psi$ represents a convex set that the Subsume rule must find. The strongest such $\neg \psi$ in $\text{LIA}^{-\text{div}}$ exists, and is the convex closure of $\mathcal{S}$. Thus, applying Subsume in the context of $\text{LIA}^{-\text{div}}$ is reduced to computing a convex closure of a set of (negated) lemmas in a cluster. Full LIA extends $\text{LIA}^{-\text{div}}$ with divisibility constraints. Therefore, Subsume obtains a stronger $\neg \psi$ by adding such constraints.

Example 1. For example, consider the following cluster:

$$\mathcal{L} = \{(x > 2 \vee x < 2 \vee y > 3), (x > 4 \vee x < 4 \vee y > 5), (x > 8 \vee x < 8 \vee y > 9)\}$$
$$\mathcal{S} = \{(x \leq 2 \wedge x \geq 2 \wedge y \leq 3), (x \geq 4 \wedge x \leq 4 \wedge y \leq 5), (x \geq 8 \wedge x \leq 8 \wedge y \leq 9)\}$$

The convex closure of $\mathcal{S}$ in $\text{LIA}^{-\text{div}}$ is $2 \leq x \leq 8 \wedge y \leq x+1$. However, a stronger over-approximation exists in LIA: $2 \leq x \leq 8 \wedge y \leq x + 1 \wedge (2 \mid x)$.   □

In the sequel, we describe SUBSUMECUBE (Algorithm 3) which computes a cube φ that over-approximates $(\bigvee \mathcal{S})$. Subsume is then implemented by removing from $\mathcal{L}$ lemmas that are already subsumed by existing lemmas in $\mathcal{L}$, dualizing the result into $\mathcal{S}$, invoking SUBSUMECUBE on $\mathcal{S}$ and returning $\neg \varphi$ as a lemma that subsumes $\mathcal{L}$.

Recall that Subsume is tried only in the case $\mathcal{L} = \mathcal{C}_{\mathcal{O}_i}(\pi)$. We further require that the negated pattern, $\neg \pi$, is of the form $A \cdot \boldsymbol{x} \leq \boldsymbol{v}$, where A is a coefficients matrix, $\boldsymbol{x}$ is a vector of constants and $\boldsymbol{v} = (v_1 \cdots v_p)^T$ is a vector of p free variables. Under this assumption, $\mathcal{S}$ (the dual of $\mathcal{L}$) is of the form $\{(A \cdot \boldsymbol{x} \leq \boldsymbol{n}_i) \mid$

$1 \leq i \leq q\}$, where $q = |\mathcal{S}|$, and for each $1 \leq i \leq q$, n_i is a numeric substitution to v from which one of the negated lemmas in $\mathcal{S}$ is obtained. That is, $|n_i| = |v|$. In Example 1, $\neg\pi = x \leq v_1 \wedge -x \leq v_2 \wedge y \leq v_3$ and

$$A = \begin{bmatrix} 1 & 0 \\ -1 & 0 \\ 0 & 1 \end{bmatrix} \quad x = \begin{bmatrix} x \\ y \end{bmatrix} \quad v = \begin{bmatrix} v_1 \\ v_2 \\ v_3 \end{bmatrix} \quad n_1 = \begin{bmatrix} 2 \\ -2 \\ 3 \end{bmatrix} \quad n_2 = \begin{bmatrix} 4 \\ -4 \\ 5 \end{bmatrix} \quad n_3 = \begin{bmatrix} 8 \\ -8 \\ 9 \end{bmatrix}$$

Each cube $(A \cdot x \leq n_i) \in \mathcal{S}$ is equivalent to $\exists v. A \cdot x \leq v \wedge (v = n_i)$. Finally, $(\bigvee \mathcal{S}) \equiv \exists v. (A \cdot x \leq v) \wedge (\bigvee(v = n_i))$. Thus, computing the over-approximation of $\mathcal{S}$ is reduced to (a) computing the convex hull H of a set of points $\{n_i \mid 1 \leq i \leq q\}$, (b) computing divisibility constraints D that are satisfied by all the points, (c) substituting $H \wedge D$ for the disjunction in the equation above, and (c) eliminating variables v. Both the computation of $H \wedge D$ and the elimination of v may be prohibitively expensive. We, therefore, over-approximate them. Our approach for doing so is presented in Algorithm 3, and explained in detail below.

Computing the convex hull of $\{n_i \mid 1 \leq i \leq q\}$. lines 3 to 8 compute the convex hull of $\{n_i \mid 1 \leq i \leq q\}$ as a formula over v, where variable v_j, for $1 \leq j \leq p$, represents the jth coordinates in the vectors (points) n_i. Some of the coordinates, v_j, in these vectors may be linearly dependent upon others. To simplify the problem, we first identify such dependencies and compute a set of linear equalities that expresses them (L in line 4). To do so, we consider a matrix $N_{q \times p}$, where the ith row consists of n_i^T. The jth column in N, denoted N_{*j}, corresponds to the jth coordinate, v_j. The rank of N is the number of linearly independent columns (and rows). The other columns (coordinates) can be expressed by linear combinations of the linearly independent ones. To compute these linear combinations we use the kernel of $[N; \mathbf{1}]$ (N appended with a column vector of 1's), which is the set of all vectors y such that $[N; \mathbf{1}] \cdot y = \mathbf{0}$, where $\mathbf{0}$ is the zero vector. Let $B = \text{kernel}([N; \mathbf{1}])$ be a basis for the kernel of $[N; \mathbf{1}]$. Then $|B| = p - \text{rank}(N)$, and for each vector $y \in B$, the linear equality $[v_1 \cdots v_p \ 1] \cdot y = 0$ holds in all the rows of N (i.e., all the given vectors satisfy it). We accumulate these equalities, which capture the linear dependencies between the coordinates, in L. Further, the equalities are used to compute $\text{rank}(N)$ coordinates (columns in N) that are linearly independent and, modulo L, uniquely determine the remaining coordinates. We denote by $v^{L_\downarrow}$ the subset of v that consists of the linearly independent coordinates. We further denote by $n_i^{L_\downarrow}$ the projection of n_i to these coordinates and by $N^{L_\downarrow}$ the projection of N to the corresponding columns. We have that $(\bigvee(v = n_i)) \equiv L \wedge (\bigvee(v^{L_\downarrow} = n_i^{L_\downarrow}))$.

In Example 1, the numeral matrix is $N = \begin{bmatrix} 2 & -2 & 3 \\ 4 & -4 & 5 \\ 8 & -8 & 9 \end{bmatrix}$, for which $\text{kernel}([N; \mathbf{1}]) = \{(1\,1\,0\,0)^T, (1\,0\,-1\,1)^T\}$. Therefore, L is the conjunction of equalities $v_1 + v_2 = 0 \wedge v_1 - v_3 + 1 = 0$, or, equivalently $v_3 = v_1 + 1 \wedge v_2 = -v_1$, $v^{L_\downarrow} = (v_1)^T$, and

$$\boldsymbol{n}_1^{L_\downarrow} = [2] \qquad \boldsymbol{n}_2^{L_\downarrow} = [4] \qquad \boldsymbol{n}_3^{L_\downarrow} = [8] \qquad N^{L_\downarrow} = \begin{bmatrix} 2 \\ 4 \\ 8 \end{bmatrix}$$

Next, we compute the convex closure of $\bigvee(\boldsymbol{v}^{L_\downarrow} = \boldsymbol{n}_i^{L_\downarrow})$, and conjoin it with L to obtain H, the convex closure of $(\bigvee(\boldsymbol{v} = \boldsymbol{n}_i))$.

If the dimension of $\boldsymbol{v}^{L_\downarrow}$ is one, as is the case in the example above, convex closure, C, of $\bigvee(\boldsymbol{v}^{L_\downarrow} = \boldsymbol{n}_i^{L_\downarrow})$ is obtained by bounding the sole element of $\boldsymbol{v}^{L_\downarrow}$ based on its values in $N^{L_\downarrow}$ (line 6). In Example 1, we obtain $C = 2 \leq v_1 \leq 8$.

If the dimension of $\boldsymbol{v}^{L_\downarrow}$ is greater than one, just computing the bounds of one of the constants is not sufficient. Instead, we use the concept of syntactic convex closure from [2] to compute the convex closure of $\bigvee(\boldsymbol{v}^{L_\downarrow} = \boldsymbol{n}_i^{L_\downarrow})$ as $\exists \boldsymbol{\alpha}. C$ where $\boldsymbol{\alpha}$ is a vector that consists of q fresh *rational* variables and C is defined as follows (line 8): $C = \boldsymbol{\alpha} \geq 0 \wedge \Sigma\boldsymbol{\alpha} = 1 \wedge \boldsymbol{\alpha}^T \cdot N^{L_\downarrow} = (\boldsymbol{v}^{L_\downarrow})^T$. C states that $(\boldsymbol{v}^{L_\downarrow})^T$ is a convex combination of the rows of $N^{L_\downarrow}$, or, in other words, $\boldsymbol{v}^{L_\downarrow}$ is a convex combination of $\{\boldsymbol{n}_i^{L_\downarrow} \mid 1 \leq i \leq q\}$.

To illustrate the syntactic convex closure, consider a second example with a set of cubes: $\mathcal{S} = \{(x \leq 0 \wedge y \leq 6), (x \leq 6 \wedge y \leq 0), (x \leq 5 \wedge y \leq 5)\}$. The coefficient matrix A, and the numeral matrix N are then: $A = \begin{bmatrix} 1 & 0 \\ 0 & 1 \end{bmatrix}$ and $N = \begin{bmatrix} 0 & 6 \\ 6 & 0 \\ 5 & 5 \end{bmatrix}$. Here, kernel$([N; 1])$ is empty – all the columns are linearly independent, hence, $L = true$ and $\boldsymbol{v}^{L_\downarrow} = \boldsymbol{v}$. Therefore, syntactic convex closure is applied to the full matrix N, resulting in

$$C = (\alpha_1 \geq 0) \wedge (\alpha_2 \geq 0) \wedge (\alpha_3 \geq 0) \wedge (\alpha_1 + \alpha_2 + \alpha_3 = 1) \wedge$$
$$(6\alpha_2 + 5\alpha_3 = v_1) \wedge (6\alpha_1 + 5\alpha_3 = v_2)$$

The convex closure of $\bigvee(\boldsymbol{v} = \boldsymbol{n}_i)$ is then $L \wedge \exists \boldsymbol{\alpha}. C$, which is $\exists \boldsymbol{\alpha}. C$ here.

Divisibility Constraints. Inductive invariants for verification problems often require divisibility constraints. We, therefore, use such constraints, denoted D, to obtain a stronger over-approximation of $\bigvee(\boldsymbol{v} = \boldsymbol{n}_i)$ than the convex closure. To add a divisibility constraint for $v_j \in \boldsymbol{v}^{L_\downarrow}$, we consider the column $N_{*j}^{L_\downarrow}$ that corresponds to v_j in $N^{L_\downarrow}$. We find the largest positive integer d such that each integer in $N_{*j}^{L_\downarrow}$ leaves the same remainder when divided by d; namely, there exists $0 \leq r < d$ such that $n \bmod d = r$ for every $n \in N_{*j}^{L_\downarrow}$. This means that $d \mid (v_j - r)$ is satisfied by all the points $\boldsymbol{n}_i$. Note that such r always exists for $d = 1$. To avoid this trivial case, we add the constraint $d \mid (v_j - r)$ only if $d \neq 1$ (line 12). We repeat this process for each $v_j \in \boldsymbol{v}^{L_\downarrow}$.

In Example 1, all the elements in the (only) column of the matrix $N^{L_\downarrow}$, which corresponds to v_1, are divisible by 2, and no larger d has a corresponding r. Thus, line 12 of Algorithm 3 adds the divisibility condition $(2 \mid v_1)$ to D.

Eliminating Existentially Quantified Variables Using MBP. By combining the linear equalities exhibited by N, the convex closure of $N^{L_\downarrow}$ and the divisibility constraints on $\boldsymbol{v}$, we obtain $\exists \boldsymbol{\alpha}.\, L \wedge C \wedge D$ as an over-approximation of $\bigvee (\boldsymbol{v} = \boldsymbol{n}_i)$. Accordingly, $\exists \boldsymbol{v}.\, \exists \boldsymbol{\alpha}.\, \psi$, where $\psi = (A \cdot \boldsymbol{x} \leq \boldsymbol{v}) \wedge L \wedge C \wedge D$, is an over-approximation of $(\bigvee \mathcal{S}) \equiv \exists \boldsymbol{v}.\, (A \cdot \boldsymbol{x} \leq \boldsymbol{v}) \wedge (\bigvee (\boldsymbol{v} = \boldsymbol{n}_i))$ (line 13). In order to get a LIA cube that overapproximates $\bigvee \mathcal{S}$, it remains to eliminate the existential quantifiers. Since quantifier elimination is expensive, and does not necessarily generate convex formulas (cubes), we approximate it using MBP. Namely, we obtain a cube φ that under-approximates $\exists \boldsymbol{v}.\, \exists \boldsymbol{\alpha}.\, \psi$ by applying MBP on ψ and a model $M_0 \models \psi$. We then use an SMT solver to drop literals from φ until it over-approximates $\exists \boldsymbol{v}.\, \exists \boldsymbol{\alpha}.\, \psi$, and hence also $\bigvee \mathcal{S}$ (lines 16 to 19). The result is returned by Subsume as an over-approximation of $\bigvee \mathcal{S}$.

Models M_0 that satisfy ψ and do not satisfy any of the cubes in $\mathcal{S}$ are preferred when computing MBP (line 14) as they ensure that the result of MBP is not subsumed by any of the cubes in $\mathcal{S}$.

Note that the $\boldsymbol{\alpha}$ are rational variables and $\boldsymbol{v}$ are integer variables, which means we require MBP to support a mixture of integer and rational variables. To achieve this, we first relax all constants to be rationals and apply MBP over LRA to eliminate $\boldsymbol{\alpha}$. We then adjust the resulting formula back to integer arithmetic by multiplying each atom by the least common multiple of the denominators of the coefficients in it. Finally, we apply MBP over the integers to eliminate $\boldsymbol{v}$.

Considering Example 1 again, we get that $\psi = (x \leq v_1) \wedge (-x \leq v_2) \wedge (y \leq v_3) \wedge (v_3 = 1 + v_1) \wedge (v_2 = -v_1) \wedge (2 \leq v_1 \leq 8) \wedge (2 \mid v_1)$ (the first three conjuncts correspond to $(A \cdot (x\ y)^T \leq (v_1\ v_2\ v_3)^T)$). Note that in this case we do not have rational variables $\boldsymbol{\alpha}$ since $|\boldsymbol{v}^{L_\downarrow}| = 1$. Depending on the model, the result of MBP can be one of

$$y \leq x + 1 \wedge 2 \leq x \leq 8 \wedge (2 \mid y - 1) \wedge (2 \mid x) \qquad x \geq 2 \wedge x \leq 2 \wedge y \leq 3$$
$$y \leq x + 1 \wedge 2 \leq x \leq 8 \wedge (2 \mid x) \qquad x \geq 8 \wedge x \leq 8 \wedge y \leq 9$$
$$y \geq x + 1 \wedge y \leq x + 1 \wedge 3 \leq y \leq 9 \wedge (2 \mid y - 1)$$

However, we prefer a model that does not satisfy any cube in $\mathcal{S} = \{(x \geq 2 \wedge x \leq 2 \wedge y \leq 3), (x \leq 4 \wedge x \geq 4 \wedge y \leq 5), (x \leq 8 \wedge x \geq 8 \wedge y \leq 9)\}$, rules off the two possibilities on the right. None of these cubes cover ψ, hence generalization is used.

If the first cube is obtained by MBP, it is generalized into $y \leq x + 1 \wedge x \geq 2 \wedge x \leq 8 \wedge (2|x)$; the second cube is already an over-approximation; the third cube is generalized into $y \leq x + 1 \wedge y \leq 9$. Indeed, each of these cubes over-approximates $\bigvee \mathcal{S}$.

4.4   Concretize Rule for LIA

The Concretize rule (Algorithm 2) takes a cluster of lemmas $\mathcal{L} = \mathcal{C}_{\mathcal{O}_i}(\pi)$ and a POB $\langle \varphi, j \rangle$ such that each lemma in $\mathcal{L}$ partially blocks φ, and creates a new POB γ that is still not blocked by $\mathcal{L}$, but γ is more concrete, i.e., $\gamma \Rightarrow \varphi$. In our implementation, this rule is applied when φ is in LIA$^{-\mathrm{div}}$. We further require that the pattern, π, of $\mathcal{L}$ is non-linear, i.e., some of the constants appear in π with free variables

Algorithm 3: An implementation of the Subsume rule for the dual of a cluster $S = \{A \cdot x \leq n_i \mid 1 \leq i \leq q\}$.

```
1 function SUBSUMECUBE:
   In: S = {(A · x ≤ nᵢ) | 1 ≤ i ≤ q},
   Out: An over-approximation of (⋁ S).
   /* v are integer variables such that:
      (⋁ S) ⟺ ∃v.(A · x ≤ v) ∧ (⋁ v = nᵢ)   */
2  N := [n₁; · · · ; n_q]ᵀ
   /* Compute the set of linear dependencies
      implied by N                           */
3  B := kernel([N; 1])
4  L := ⋀_{y ∈ B}(v₁ · · · v_p 1) · y = 0
5  if |v^{L↓}| = 1 then
      // Convex closure over a single constant vᵢ ∈ v^{L↓}

6     C := min(N_{*i}) ≤ vᵢ ≤ max(N_{*i})
7  else
      // Syntactic convex closure
8     C := (αᵀ · N^{L↓} = (v^{L↓})ᵀ) ∧ (Σα = 1) ∧ (α ≥ 0)
      /* Compute divisibility constraints      */
9     D := T
10    for v_j ∈ v^{L↓} do
11    if

         ∃d, r. d ≠ 1 ∧ (∀n ∈ N_{*j}^{L↓}. (n mod d = r)) then
12       D := D ∧ d | (v_j − r)
13 ψ := (A · x ≤ v) ∧ L ∧ C ∧ D
   /* Under-approximate quantifier elimination */
14 find M₀ s.t. M₀ ⊨ ψ and, if possible, M₀ ⊭ (⋁ S)
15 φ := MBP((α v), ψ, M₀)
   /* Over-approximate quantifier elimination  */
16 while ISSAT(¬φ ∧ ψ) do
17    find M₁ s.t. M₁ ⊨ (¬φ ∧ ψ)
18    φ := ⋀{ℓ ∈ φ | ¬(M₁ ⊨ ¬ℓ)}
19 return φ
```

Algorithm 4: An implementation of the Concretize rule in LIA.

```
1 function CONCRETIZE:
   In: A POB ⟨φ, j⟩ in LIA⁻ᵈⁱᵛ, a cluster of
       LIA⁻ᵈⁱᵛ lemmas L = C_{O_j}(π) s.t. π is
       non-linear, ISSAT(φ ∧ ⋀ L)
   Out: A cube γ such that γ ⇒ φ and
        ∀ℓ ∈ L. ISSAT(γ ∧ ℓ)
2  U := {x | COEFF(x, π) ∈ VARS(π)}
3  find M s.t. M ⊨ φ ∧ ⋀ L
4  γ := T
5  foreach lit ∈ φ do
6     if CONSTS(lit) ∩ U ≠ ∅ then
         γ := γ ∧ CONCRETIZE_LIT(lit, M, U)
7     else γ := γ ∧ lit
8  γ := RM_SUBSUME(γ)
9  return γ

10 function CONCRETIZE_LIT:
   In: A literal lit = Σᵢ nᵢxᵢ ≤ b_j in LIA⁻ᵈⁱᵛ,
       model M ⊨ lit, and a set of constants U
   Out: A cube γ^{lit} that concretizes lit
   /* Construct a single literal using all the
      constants in CONSTS(lit) \ U             */
11 γ^{lit} := ∅
12 s := 0
13 foreach xᵢ ∈ CONSTS(lit) \ U do
14    s := s + nᵢxᵢ
15 γ^{lit} := (s ≤ M[s])
   /* Generate one dimensional literals for each
      constant in U                            */
16 foreach xᵢ ∈ CONSTS(lit) ∩ U do
17    γ^{lit} := γ^{lit} ∧ (nᵢxᵢ ≤ M[nᵢxᵢ])
18 return γ^{lit}
```

as their coefficients. We denote these constants by U. An example is the pattern $\pi = v_0 x + v_1 y + z \leq 0$, where $U = \{x, y\}$. Having such a cluster is an indication that attempting to block φ in full with a single lemma may require to track non-linear correlations between the constants, which is impossible to do in LIA. In such cases, we identify the coupling of the constants in U in POBs (and hence in lemmas) as the potential source of non-linearity. Hence, we concretize (strengthen) φ into a POB γ where the constants in U are no longer coupled to any other constant.

Coupling. Formally, constants u and v are *coupled* in a cube c, denoted $u \bowtie_c v$, if there exists a literal lit in c such that both u and v appear in lit (i.e., their coefficients in lit are non-zero). For example, x and y are coupled in $x + y \leq 0 \wedge z \leq 0$ whereas neither of them are coupled with z. A constant u is said to be *isolated* in a cube c, denoted $\text{ISO}(u, c)$, if it appears in c but it is not coupled with any other constant in c. In the above cube, z is isolated.

Concretization by Decoupling. Given a POB φ (a cube) and a cluster L, Algorithm 4 presents our approach for concretizing φ by decoupling the constants in U—those that have variables as coefficients in the pattern of L (line 2). Concretization is guided by a model $M \models \varphi \wedge \bigwedge L$, representing a part of φ that is not yet blocked by the lemmas in L (line 3). Given such M, we concretize φ

into a *model-preserving* under-approximation that isolates all the constants in U and preserves all other couplings. That is, we find a cube γ, such that

$$\gamma \Rightarrow \varphi \quad M \models \gamma \quad \forall u \in U. \, \mathrm{Iso}(u, \gamma) \quad \forall u, v \notin U. \, (u \bowtie_\varphi v) \Rightarrow (u \bowtie_\gamma v) \quad (1)$$

Note that γ is not blocked by $\mathcal{L}$ since M satisfies both $\bigwedge \mathcal{L}$ and γ. For example, if $\varphi = (x + y \leq 0) \wedge (x - y \leq 0) \wedge (x + z \geq 0)$ and $M = [x = 0, y = 0, z = 1]$, then $\gamma = 0 \leq y \leq 0 \wedge x \leq 0 \wedge x + z \geq 1$ is a model preserving under-approximation that isolates $U = \{y\}$.

Algorithm 4 computes such a cube γ by a point-wise concretization of the literals of φ followed by the removal of subsumed literals. Literals that do not contain constants from U remain unchanged. A literal of the form $lit = t \leq b$, where $t = \sum_i n_i x_i$ (recall that every literal in $\mathrm{LIA}^{-\mathrm{div}}$ can be normalized to this form), that includes constants from U is concretized into a *cube* by (1) isolating each of the summands $n_i x_i$ in t that include U from the rest, and (2) for each of the resulting sub-expressions creating a literal that uses its value in M as a bound. Formally, t is decomposed to $s + \sum_{x_i \in U} n_i x_i$, where $s = \sum_{x_i \notin U} n_i x_i$. The concretization of lit is the cube $\gamma^{lit} = s \leq M[s] \wedge \bigwedge_{x_i \in U} n_i x_i \leq M[n_i x_i]$, where $M[t']$ denotes the interpretation of t' in M. Note that $\gamma^{lit} \Rightarrow lit$ since the bounds are stronger than the original bound on t: $M[s] + \sum_{x_i \in U} M[n_i x_i] = M[t] \leq b$. This ensures that γ, obtained by the conjunction of literal concretizations, implies φ. It trivially satisfies the other conditions of Eq. (1).

For example, the concretization of the literal $(x + y \leq 0)$ with respect to $U = \{y\}$ and $M = [x = 0, y = 0, z = 1]$ is the cube $x \leq 0 \wedge y \leq 0$. Applying concretization in a similar manner to all the literals of the cube $\varphi = (x + y \leq 0) \wedge (x - y \leq 0) \wedge (x + z \geq 0)$ from the previous example, we obtain the concretization $x \leq 0 \wedge 0 \leq y \leq 0 \wedge x + z \geq 0$. Note that the last literal is not concretized as it does not include y.

4.5   Conjecture Rule for LIA

The `Conjecture` rule (see Algorithm 2) takes a set of lemmas $\mathcal{L}$ and a POB $\varphi \equiv \alpha \wedge \beta$ such that all lemmas in $\mathcal{L}$ block β, but none of them blocks α, where α does not include any known reachable states. It returns α as a new POB.

For LIA, `Conjecture` is applied when the following conditions are met: (1) the POB φ is of the form $\varphi_1 \wedge \varphi_2 \wedge \varphi_3$, where $\varphi_3 = (n^T \cdot x \leq b)$, and φ_1 and φ_2 are any cubes. The sub-cube $\varphi_1 \wedge \varphi_2$ acts as α, while the sub-cube $\varphi_2 \wedge \varphi_3$ acts as β. (2) The cluster $\mathcal{L}$ consists of $\{bg \vee (n^T \cdot x \geq b_i) \mid 1 \leq i \leq q\}$, where $b_i > b$ and $bg \Rightarrow \neg \varphi_2$. This means that each of the lemmas in $\mathcal{L}$ blocks $\beta = \varphi_2 \wedge \varphi_3$, and they may be ordered as a sequence of increasingly stronger lemmas, indicating that they were created by trying to block the POB at different levels, leading to too strong lemmas that failed to propagate to higher levels. (3) The formula $(bg \vee (n^T \cdot x \geq b_i)) \wedge \varphi_1 \wedge \varphi_2$ is satisfiable, that is, none of the lemmas in $\mathcal{L}$ block $\alpha = \varphi_1 \wedge \varphi_2$, and (4) $\mathcal{U} \Rightarrow \neg(\varphi_1 \wedge \varphi_2)$, that is, no state in $\varphi_1 \wedge \varphi_2$ is known to be reachable. If all four conditions are met, we conjecture $\alpha = \varphi_1 \wedge \varphi_2$. This is implemented by CONJECTURE, that returns α (or $\bot$ when the pre-conditions are not met).

Algorithm 5: GSPACER for LIA.

1 **function** GSPACER:	24 **function** CONCRETIZEPOB:
In: $\langle Init, Tr, Bad \rangle$	25 $\langle \pi_1, \mathcal{L}_1 \rangle := \mathcal{C}_{pob}(\langle \varphi, i \rangle)$
Out: An Inductive invariant or UNSAFE	26 $\mathcal{L}_2 := \{\ell \mid \ell \in \mathcal{L}_1 \wedge \text{ISSAT}(\ell \wedge \varphi) \wedge \text{ISSAT}(\neg \ell \wedge \varphi)\}$
/* Initialize state of the solver */	27 **if** $(\mathcal{L}_2 \neq \emptyset \wedge \text{NONLIN}(\pi_1) \wedge \text{ISSAT}(\bigwedge \mathcal{L}_2 \wedge \varphi))$ **then**
2 $Q := \emptyset; N := 0; \mathcal{U} := Init;$	28 $\gamma := \text{CONCRETIZE}(\varphi, \langle \pi_1, \mathcal{L}_2 \rangle)$
3 $\mathcal{O}_0 := Init; \mathcal{O}_i := \top, \forall i > 0$	29 $k := \max\{j \mid \mathcal{O}_j \Rightarrow \neg\gamma\}$
4 ENQUEUE$(Q, \langle Bad, 0 \rangle)$	30 PUSH$(Q, \langle \gamma, k \rangle)$ // Concretize
5 **while** $\top$ **do**	31 PUSH$(Q, \langle \varphi, i \rangle)$
6 $\langle \varphi, i \rangle := \text{POP}(Q)$	32 **return** $\top$
7 **if** CONCRETIZEPOB$(\langle \varphi, i \rangle) = \top$ **then**	33 **else return** $\bot$
8 **continue**	
9 **if** ISSAT$(\mathcal{F}(\mathcal{O}_{i-1}) \wedge \varphi')$ **then**	34 **function** ADDPREDECESSOR:
// The pob φ cannot be blocked at i	35 **if** ISSAT$(\mathcal{F}(\mathcal{U}) \wedge \varphi')$ **then**
10 ADDPREDECESSOR$(\langle \varphi, i \rangle)$	36 find M_1 s.t $M_1 \models \mathcal{F}(\mathcal{U}) \wedge \varphi'$
11 **if** ISSAT$(\mathcal{U} \wedge Bad)$ **then**	37 $s := (\text{MBP}(x, \mathcal{F}(\mathcal{U}), M_1)[x' \mapsto x])$
12 **return** UNSAFE // Unsafe	38 $\mathcal{U} := \mathcal{U} \vee s$ // Successor
13 **else**	39 **return**
// The pob φ can be blocked at i	40 find M_2 s.t $M_2 \models \Theta$
14 BLOCK$(\langle \varphi, i \rangle)$	41 $p := \text{MBP}(x', Tr \wedge \varphi', M_2)$
15 **for** $0 \leq j \leq N$ **do**	42 PUSH$(Q, \langle p, i-1 \rangle)$ // Predecessor
16 **for** $\ell \in \mathcal{O}_j \setminus \mathcal{O}_{j+1}$ **do**	43 PUSH$(Q, \langle \varphi, i \rangle)$
17 **if** $\mathcal{O}_j \wedge Tr \Rightarrow \ell'$ **then**	
18 $\mathcal{O}_{j+1} := \mathcal{O}_{j+1} \wedge \ell$ // Propagate	44 **function** BLOCK:
19 **if** $\exists 0 \leq j < N \cdot \mathcal{O}_j \Rightarrow \mathcal{O}_{j-1}$ **then**	45 $\ell := \text{GEN}(\mathcal{F}(\mathcal{O}_{i-1}), \varphi')$ // Conflict
20 **return** $\langle \text{SAFE}, \mathcal{O}_j \rangle$ // Safe	46 **for** $0 \leq j \leq i$ **do** $\mathcal{O}_j := \mathcal{O}_j \wedge \ell$
21 **if** $\mathcal{O}_N \Rightarrow \neg Bad$ **then**	47 $\langle \pi_3, \mathcal{L}_3 \rangle = \mathcal{C}_{lemma}(\ell)$
22 $N := N + 1$ // Unfold	48 $\alpha := \text{CONJECTURE}(\varphi, \mathcal{L}_3, \mathcal{U})$
23 PUSH$(Q, \langle Bad, N \rangle)$	49 **if** $\alpha \neq \bot$ **then**
	50 $k := \max\{j \mid \mathcal{O}_j \Rightarrow \neg\alpha\}$
	51 PUSH$(Q, \langle \alpha, k \rangle)$ // Conjecture
	52 **if** $\neg\pi_3 = A \cdot x \leq v$ **then**
	53 $\psi := \text{SUBSUME}(\langle \pi_3, \mathcal{L}_3 \rangle)$
	54 $k := \max\{j \mid \mathcal{F}(\mathcal{O}_j) \Rightarrow \psi'\}$
	55 $\mathcal{O}_j := \mathcal{O}_j \wedge \psi$ **for all** $j \leq k+1$ // Subsume

---

For example, consider the POB $\varphi = x \geq 10 \wedge (x + y \geq 10) \wedge y \leq 10$ and a cluster of lemmas $\mathcal{L} = \{(x + y \leq 0 \vee y \geq 101), (x + y \leq 0 \vee y \geq 102)\}$. In this case, $\varphi_1 = x \geq 10$, $\varphi_2 = (x + y \geq 10)$, $\varphi_3 = y \leq 10$, and $bg = x + y \leq 0$. Each of the lemmas in $\mathcal{L}$ block $\varphi_2 \wedge \varphi_3$ but none of them block $\varphi_1 \wedge \varphi_2$. Therefore, we conjecture $\varphi_1 \wedge \varphi_2$: $x \geq 10 \wedge (x + y \geq 10)$.

4.6 Putting It All Together

Having explained the implementation of the new rules for LIA, we now put all the ingredients together into an algorithm, GSPACER. In particular, we present our choices as to when to apply the new rules, and on which clusters of lemmas and POBs. As can be seen in Sect. 5, this implementation works very well on a wide range of benchmarks.

Algorithm 5 presents GSPACER. The comments to the right side of a line refer to the abstract rules in Algorithm 1 and 2. Just like SPACER, GSPACER iteratively computes predecessors (line 10) and blocks them (line 14) in an infinite loop. Whenever a POB is proven to be reachable, the reachable states are updated (line 38). If *Bad* intersects with a reachable state, GSPACER terminates and returns UNSAFE (line 12). If one of the frames is an inductive invariant, GSPACER terminates with SAFE (line 20).

When a POB $\langle \varphi, i \rangle$ is handled, we first apply the Concretize rule, if possible (line 7). Recall that CONCRETIZE (Algorithm 4) takes as input a cluster that partially blocks φ and has a non-linear pattern. To obtain such a cluster, we first find, using $\mathcal{C}_{pob}(\langle \varphi, i \rangle)$, a cluster $\langle \pi_1, \mathcal{L}_1 \rangle = \mathcal{C}_{\mathcal{O}_k}(\pi_1)$, where $k \leq i$, that includes *some* lemma (from frame k) that blocks φ; if none exists, $\mathcal{L}_1 = \emptyset$. We then filter out from $\mathcal{L}_1$ lemmas that completely block φ as well as lemmas that are irrelevant to φ, i.e., we obtain $\mathcal{L}_2$ by keeping only lemmas that partially block φ. We apply CONCRETIZE on $\langle \pi_1, \mathcal{L}_2 \rangle$ to obtain a new POB that under-approximates φ if (1) the remaining sub-cluster, $\mathcal{L}_2$, is non-empty, (2) the pattern, π_1, is non-linear, and (3) $\bigwedge \mathcal{L}_2 \wedge \varphi$ is satisfiable, i.e., a part of φ is not blocked by any lemma in $\mathcal{L}_2$.

Once a POB is blocked, and a new lemma that blocks it, ℓ, is added to the frames, an attempt is made to apply the Subsume and Conjecture rules on a cluster that includes ℓ. To that end, the function $\mathcal{C}_{lemma}(\ell)$ finds *a* cluster $\langle \pi_3, \mathcal{L}_3 \rangle = \mathcal{C}_{\mathcal{O}_i}(\pi_3)$ to which ℓ belongs (Sect. 4.2). Note that the choice of cluster is arbitrary. The rules are applied on $\langle \pi_3, \mathcal{L}_3 \rangle$ if the required pre-conditions are met (line 49 and line 53, respectively). When applicable, SUBSUME returns a new lemma that is added to the frames, while CONJECTURE returns a new POB that is added to the queue. Note that the latter is a *may* POB, in the sense that some of the states it represents *may not* lead to safety violation.

Ensuring Progress. SPACER always makes progress: as its search continues, it establishes absence of counterexamples of deeper and deeper depths. However, GSPACER does not ensure progress. Specifically, unrestricted application of the Concretize and Conjecture rules can make GSPACER diverge even on executions of a fixed bound. In our implementation, we ensure progress by allotting a fixed amount of *gas* to each pattern, π, that forms a cluster. Each time Concretize or Conjecture is applied to a cluster with π as the pattern, π loses some gas. Whenever π runs out of gas, the rules are no longer applied to any cluster with π as the pattern. There are finitely many patterns (assuming LIA terms are normalized). Thus, in each bounded execution of GSPACER, the Concretize and Conjecture rules are applied only a finite number of times, thereby, ensuring progress. Since the Subsume rule does not hinder progress, it is applied without any restriction on gas.

5   Evaluation

We have implemented[2] GSPACER (Algorithm 5) as an extension to SPACER. To reduce the dimension of a matrix (in SUBSUME, Sect. 4.3), we compute pairwise linear dependencies between all pairs of columns instead of computing the full kernel. This does not necessarily reduce the dimension of the matrix to its rank, but, is sufficient for our benchmarks. We have experimented with computing the full kernel using SageMath [25], but the overall performance did not improve. Clustering is implemented by anti-unification. LIA terms are normalized using

---

[2] https://github.com/hgvk94/z3/tree/gspacer-cav-ae.

default Z3 simplifications. Our implementation also supports global generalization for non-linear CHCs. We have also extended our work to the theory of LRA. We defer the details of this extension to an extended version of the paper.

To evaluate our implementation, we have conducted two sets of experiments[3]. All experiments were run on Intel E5-2690 V2 CPU at 3 GHz with 128 GB memory with a timeout of 10 min. First, to evaluate the performance of local reasoning with global guidance against pure local reasoning, we have compared GSPACER with the latest SPACER, to which we refer as the *baseline*. We took the benchmarks from CHC-COMP 2018 and 2019 [10]. We compare to SPACER because it dominated the competition by solving 85% of the benchmarks in CHC-COMP 2019 (20% more than the runner up) and 60% of the benchmarks in CHC-COMP 2018 (10% more than runner up). Our evaluation shows that GSPACER outperforms SPACER both in terms of number of solved instances and, more importantly, in overall robustness.

Second, to examine the performance of local reasoning with global guidance compared to solely global reasoning, we have compared GSPACER with an ML-based data-driven invariant inference tool LINEARARBITRARY [28]. Compared to other similar approaches, LINEARARBITRARY stands out by supporting invariants with arbitrary Boolean structure over arbitrary linear predicates. It is completely automated and does not require user-provided predicates, grammars, or any other guidance. For the comparison with LINEARARBITRARY, we have used both the CHC-COMP benchmarks, as well as the benchmarks from the artifact evaluation of [28]. The machine and timeout remain the same. Our evaluation shows that GSPACER is superior in this case as well.

Comparison with SPACER. Table 1 summarizes the comparison between SPACER and GSPACER on CHC-COMP instances. Since both tools can use a variety of interpolation strategies during lemma generalization (Line 45 in Algorithm 5), we compare three different configurations of each: *bw* and *fw* stand for two interpolation strategies, *backward* and *forward*, respectively, already implemented in SPACER, and *sc* stands for turning interpolation off and generalizing lemmas only by *subset clauses* computed by inductive generalization.

Any configuration of GSPACER solves significantly more instances than even the best configuration of SPACER. Figure 2 provides a more detailed comparison between the best configurations of both tools in terms of running time and depth of convergence. There is no clear trend in terms of running time on instances solved by both tools. This is not surprising—SMT-solving run time is highly non-deterministic and any change in strategy has a significant impact on performance of SMT queries involved. In terms of depth, it is clear that GSPACER converges at the same or lower depth. The depth is significantly lower for instances solved only by GSPACER.

Moreover, the performance of GSPACER is not significantly affected by the interpolation strategy used. In fact, the configuration *sc* in which interpolation is

---

[3] Detailed experimental results including the effectiveness of each rule, and the extensions to non-linear CHCs and LRA can be found at https://hgvk94.github.io/gspacer/.

disabled performs the best in CHC-COMP 2018, and only slightly worse in CHC-COMP 2019! In comparison, disabling interpolation hurts SPACER significantly.

Figure 3 provides a detailed comparison of GSPACER with and without interpolation. Interpolation makes no difference to the depth of convergence. This implies that lemmas that are discovered by interpolation are discovered as efficiently by the global rules of GSPACER. On the other hand, interpolation significantly increases the running time. Interestingly, the time spent in interpolation itself is insignificant. However, the lemmas produced by interpolation tend to slow down other aspects of the algorithm. Most of the slow down is in increased time for inductive generalization and in computation of predecessors. The comparison between the other interpolation-enabled strategy and GSPACER (*sc*) shows a similar trend.

Table 1. Comparison between SPACER and GSPACER on CHC-COMP.

Bench	SPACER						GSPACER						VBS	
	fw		bw		sc		fw		bw		sc			
	safe	unsafe	safe	unsafe	safe	unsafe	safe	unsafe	safe	unsafe	safe	unsafe	safe	unsafe
CHC-18	159	66	163	69	123	68	**214**	67	**214**	63	**214**	69	229	74
CHC-19	193	84	186	84	125	84	**202**	84	196	**85**	200	84	207	85

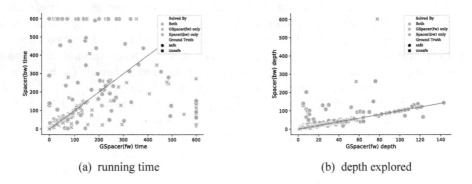

(a) running time   (b) depth explored

Fig. 2. Best configurations: GSPACER versus SPACER.

Comparison with LINEARARBITRARY. In [28], the authors show that LINEARARBITRARY, to which we refer as LARB for short, significantly outperforms SPACER on a curated subset of benchmarks from SV-COMP [24] competition.

At first, we attempted to compare LARB against GSPACER on the CHC-COMP benchmarks. However, LARB did not perform well on them. Even the

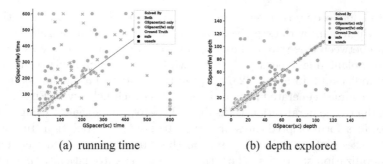

(a) running time   (b) depth explored

Fig. 3. Comparing GSPACER with different interpolation tactics.

baseline SPACER has outperformed LARB significantly. Therefore, for a more meaningful comparison, we have also compared SPACER, LARB and GSPACER on the benchmarks from the artifact evaluation of [28]. The results are summarized in Table 2. As expected, LARB outperforms the baseline SPACER on the safe benchmarks. On unsafe benchmarks, SPACER is significantly better than LARB. In both categories, GSPACER dominates solving more safe benchmarks than either SPACER or LARB, while matching performance of SPACER on unsafe instances. Furthermore, GSPACER remains orders of magnitude faster than LARB on benchmarks that are solved by both. This comparison shows that incorporating local reasoning with global guidance not only mitigates its shortcomings but also surpasses global data-driven reasoning.

Table 2. Comparison with LARB.

Bench	SPACER		LARB		GSPACER		VB	
	safe	unsafe	safe	unsafe	safe	unsafe	safe	unsafe
PLDI18	216	**68**	270	65	**279**	**68**	284	68

6   Related Work

The limitations of local reasoning in SMT-based infinite state model checking are well known. Most commonly, they are addressed with either (a) different strategies for local generalization in interpolation (e.g., [1,6,19,23]), or (b) shifting the focus to *global* invariant inference by learning an invariant of a restricted shape (e.g., [9,14–16,28]).

Interpolation Strategies. Albarghouthi and McMillan [1] suggest to minimize the number of literals in an interpolant, arguing that simpler (i.e., fewer half-spaces) interpolants are more likely to generalize. This helps with myopic generalizations (Fig. 1(a)), but not with excessive generalizations (Fig. 1(b)). On the contrary,

Blicha et al. [6] decompose interpolants to be numerically simpler (but with more literals), which helps with excessive, but not with myopic, generalizations. Deciding *locally* between these two techniques or on their combination (i.e., some parts of an interpolant might need to be split while others combined) seems impossible. Schindler and Jovanovic [23] propose local interpolation that bounds the number of lemmas generated from a single POB (which helps with Fig. 1(c)), but only if inductive generalization is disabled. Finally, [19] suggests using external guidance, in a form of predicates or terms, to guide interpolation. In contrast, GSPACER uses global guidance, based on the current proof, to direct different local generalization strategies. Thus, the guidance is automatically tuned to the specific instance at hand rather than to a domain of problems.

Global Invariant Inference. An alternative to inferring lemmas for the inductive invariant by blocking counterexamples is to enumerate the space of potential candidate invariants [9,14–16,28]. This does not suffer from the pitfall of local reasoning. However, it is only effective when the search space is constrained. While these approaches perform well on their target domain, they do not generalize well to a diverse set of benchmarks, as illustrated by results of CHC-COMP and our empirical evaluation in Sect. 5.

Locality in SMT and IMC. Local reasoning is also a known issue in SMT, and, in particular, in DPLL(T) (e.g., [22]). However, we are not aware of global guidance techniques for SMT solvers. Interpolation-based Model Checking (IMC) [20,21] that uses interpolants from proofs, inherits the problem. Compared to IMC, the propagation phase and inductive generalization of IC3 [7], can be seen as providing global guidance using lemmas found in other parts of the search-space. In contrast, GSPACER magnifies such global guidance by exploiting patterns within the lemmas themselves.

IC3-SMT-based Model Checkers. There are a number of IC3-style SMT-based infinite state model checkers, including [11,17,18]. To our knowledge, none extend the IC3-SMT framework with a global guidance. A rule similar to Subsume is suggested in [26] for the theory of bit-vectors and in [4] for LRA, but in both cases without global guidance. In [4], it is implemented via a combination of syntactic closure with interpolation, whereas we use MBP instead of interpolation. Refinement State Mining in [3] uses similar insights to our Subsume rule to refine predicate abstraction.

7   Conclusion and Future Work

This paper introduces *global guidance* to mitigate the limitations of the local reasoning performed by SMT-based IC3-style model checking algorithms. Global guidance is necessary to redirect such algorithms from divergence due to persistent local reasoning. To this end, we present three general rules that introduce new lemmas and POBs by taking a global view of the lemmas learned so far. The new rules are not theory-specific, and, as demonstrated by Algorithm 5, can be incorporated to IC3-style solvers without modifying existing architecture. We instantiate, and implement, the rules for LIA in GSPACER, which extends SPACER.

Our evaluation shows that global guidance brings significant improvements to local reasoning, and surpasses invariant inference based solely on global reasoning. More importantly, global guidance decouples SPACER's dependency on interpolation strategy and performs almost equally well under all three interpolation schemes we consider. As such, using global guidance in the context of theories for which no good interpolation procedure exists, with bit-vectors being a primary example, arises as a promising direction for future research.

Acknowledgements. We thank Xujie Si for running the LARB experiments and collecting results. We thank the ERC starting Grant SYMCAR 639270 and the Wallenberg Academy Fellowship TheProSE for supporting the research visit. This research was partially supported by the United States-Israel Binational Science Foundation (BSF) grant No. 2016260, and the Israeli Science Foundation (ISF) grant No. 1810/18. This research was partially supported by grants from Natural Sciences and Engineering Research Council Canada.

References

1. Albarghouthi, A., McMillan, K.L.: Beautiful interpolants. In: Sharygina, N., Veith, H. (eds.) CAV 2013. LNCS, vol. 8044, pp. 313–329. Springer, Heidelberg (2013). https://doi.org/10.1007/978-3-642-39799-8_22
2. Benoy, F., King, A., Mesnard, F.: Computing convex hulls with a linear solver. TPLP $5(1-2)$, 259–271 (2005)
3. Birgmeier, J., Bradley, A.R., Weissenbacher, G.: Counterexample to induction-guided abstraction-refinement (CTIGAR). In: Biere, A., Bloem, R. (eds.) CAV 2014. LNCS, vol. 8559, pp. 831–848. Springer, Cham (2014). https://doi.org/10.1007/978-3-319-08867-9_55
4. Bjørner, N., Gurfinkel, A.: Property directed polyhedral abstraction. In: D'Souza, D., Lal, A., Larsen, K.G. (eds.) VMCAI 2015. LNCS, vol. 8931, pp. 263–281. Springer, Heidelberg (2015). https://doi.org/10.1007/978-3-662-46081-8_15
5. Bjørner, N., Janota, M.: Playing with quantified satisfaction. In: 20th International Conferences on Logic for Programming, Artificial Intelligence and Reasoning - Short Presentations, LPAR 2015, Suva, Fiji, 24–28 November 2015, pp. 15–27 (2015)
6. Blicha, M., Hyvärinen, A.E.J., Kofroň, J., Sharygina, N.: Decomposing farkas interpolants. In: Vojnar, T., Zhang, L. (eds.) TACAS 2019. LNCS, vol. 11427, pp. 3–20. Springer, Cham (2019). https://doi.org/10.1007/978-3-030-17462-0_1
7. Bradley, A.R.: SAT-based model checking without unrolling. In: Jhala, R., Schmidt, D. (eds.) VMCAI 2011. LNCS, vol. 6538, pp. 70–87. Springer, Heidelberg (2011). https://doi.org/10.1007/978-3-642-18275-4_7
8. Bulychev, P.E., Kostylev, E.V., Zakharov, V.A.: Anti-unification algorithms and their applications in program analysis. In: Pnueli, A., Virbitskaite, I., Voronkov, A. (eds.) PSI 2009. LNCS, vol. 5947, pp. 413–423. Springer, Heidelberg (2010). https://doi.org/10.1007/978-3-642-11486-1_35
9. Champion, A., Chiba, T., Kobayashi, N., Sato, R.: ICE-based refinement type discovery for higher-order functional programs. In: Beyer, D., Huisman, M. (eds.) TACAS 2018. LNCS, vol. 10805, pp. 365–384. Springer, Cham (2018). https://doi.org/10.1007/978-3-319-89960-2_20

10. CHC-COMP. CHC-COMP. https://chc-comp.github.io
11. Cimatti, A., Griggio, A., Mover, S., Tonetta, S.: Infinite-state invariant checking with IC3 and predicate abstraction. Formal Methods Syst. Des. **49**(3), 190–218 (2016). https://doi.org/10.1007/s10703-016-0257-4
12. Cousot, P., Cousot, R.: Abstract interpretation: a unified lattice model for static analysis of programs by construction or approximation of fixpoints. In: Conference Record of the Fourth ACM Symposium on Principles of Programming Languages, Los Angeles, California, USA, January 1977, pp. 238–252 (1977)
13. de Moura, L., Bjørner, N.: Z3: an efficient SMT solver. In: Ramakrishnan, C.R., Rehof, J. (eds.) TACAS 2008. LNCS, vol. 4963, pp. 337–340. Springer, Heidelberg (2008). https://doi.org/10.1007/978-3-540-78800-3_24
14. Fedyukovich, G., Kaufman, S.J., Bodík, R.: Sampling invariants from frequency distributions. In: 2017 Formal Methods in Computer Aided Design, FMCAD 2017, Vienna, Austria, 2–6 October 2017, pp. 100–107 (2017)
15. Flanagan, C., Leino, K.R.M.: Houdini, an annotation assistant for ESC/Java. In: Oliveira, J.N., Zave, P. (eds.) FME 2001. LNCS, vol. 2021, pp. 500–517. Springer, Heidelberg (2001). https://doi.org/10.1007/3-540-45251-6_29
16. Garg, P., Neider, D., Madhusudan, P., Roth, D.: Learning invariants using decision trees and implication counterexamples. In: Proceedings of the 43rd Annual ACM SIGPLAN-SIGACT Symposium on Principles of Programming Languages, POPL 2016, St. Petersburg, FL, USA, 20–22 January 2016, pp. 499–512 (2016)
17. Jovanovic, D., Dutertre, B.: Property-directed k-induction. In: 2016 Formal Methods in Computer-Aided Design, FMCAD 2016, Mountain View, CA, USA, 3–6 October 2016, pp. 85–92 (2016)
18. Komuravelli, A., Gurfinkel, A., Chaki, S.: SMT-based model checking for recursive programs. In: Biere, A., Bloem, R. (eds.) CAV 2014. LNCS, vol. 8559, pp. 17–34. Springer, Cham (2014). https://doi.org/10.1007/978-3-319-08867-9_2
19. Leroux, J., Rümmer, P., Subotić, P.: Guiding Craig interpolation with domain-specific abstractions. Acta Informatica **53**(4), 387–424 (2015). https://doi.org/10.1007/s00236-015-0236-z
20. McMillan, K.L.: Interpolation and SAT-based model checking. In: Hunt, W.A., Somenzi, F. (eds.) CAV 2003. LNCS, vol. 2725, pp. 1–13. Springer, Heidelberg (2003). https://doi.org/10.1007/978-3-540-45069-6_1
21. McMillan, K.L.: Lazy abstraction with interpolants. In: Ball, T., Jones, R.B. (eds.) CAV 2006. LNCS, vol. 4144, pp. 123–136. Springer, Heidelberg (2006). https://doi.org/10.1007/11817963_14
22. McMillan, K.L., Kuehlmann, A., Sagiv, M.: Generalizing DPLL to richer logics. In: Bouajjani, A., Maler, O. (eds.) CAV 2009. LNCS, vol. 5643, pp. 462–476. Springer, Heidelberg (2009). https://doi.org/10.1007/978-3-642-02658-4_35
23. Schindler, T., Jovanović, D.: Selfless interpolation for infinite-state model checking. VMCAI 2018. LNCS, vol. 10747, pp. 495–515. Springer, Cham (2018). https://doi.org/10.1007/978-3-319-73721-8_23
24. SV-COMP. SV-COMP. https://sv-comp.sosy-lab.org/
25. The Sage Developers. SageMath, the Sage Mathematics Software System (Version 8.1.0) (2017). https://www.sagemath.org
26. Welp, T., Kuehlmann, A.: QF_BV model checking with property directed reachability. In: Design, Automation and Test in Europe, DATE 13, Grenoble, France, 18–22 March 2013, pp. 791–796 (2013)
27. Yernaux, G., Vanhoof, W.: Anti-unification in constraint logic programming. TPLP **19**(5–6), 773–789 (2019)

28. Zhu, H., Magill, S., Jagannathan, S.: A data-driven CHC solver. In: Proceedings of the 39th ACM SIGPLAN Conference on Programming Language Design and Implementation, PLDI 2018, Philadelphia, PA, USA, 18–22 June 2018, pp. 707–721 (2018)

Towards Model Checking Real-World Software-Defined Networks

Vasileios Klimis$^{(\boxtimes)}$ (ID), George Parisis (ID), and Bernhard Reus (ID)

University of Sussex, Brighton, UK
{v.klimis,g.parisis,bernhard}@sussex.ac.uk

Abstract. In software-defined networks (SDN), a controller program is in charge of deploying diverse network functionality across a large number of switches, but this comes at a great risk: deploying buggy controller code could result in network and service disruption and security loopholes. The automatic detection of bugs or, even better, verification of their absence is thus most desirable, yet the size of the network and the complexity of the controller makes this a challenging undertaking. In this paper, we propose MOCS, a highly expressive, optimised SDN model that allows capturing subtle real-world bugs, in a reasonable amount of time. This is achieved by (1) analysing the model for possible partial order reductions, (2) statically pre-computing packet equivalence classes and (3) indexing packets and rules that exist in the model. We demonstrate its superiority compared to the state of the art in terms of expressivity, by providing examples of realistic bugs that a prototype implementation of MOCS in UPPAAL caught, and performance/scalability, by running examples on various sizes of network topologies, highlighting the importance of our abstractions and optimisations.

1 Introduction

Software-Defined Networking (SDN) [16] has brought about a paradigm shift in designing and operating computer networks. A logically centralised controller implements the control logic and 'programs' the data plane, which is defined by flow tables installed in network switches. SDN enables the rapid development of advanced and diverse network functionality; e.g. in designing next-generation inter-data centre traffic engineering [10], load balancing [19], firewalls [24], and Internet exchange points (IXPs) [15]. SDN has gained noticeable ground in the industry, with major vendors integrating OpenFlow [37], the de-facto SDN standard maintained by the Open Networking Forum, in their products. Operators deploy it at scale [27,38]. SDN presents a unique opportunity for innovation and rapid development of complex network services by enabling all players, not just vendors, to develop and deploy control and data plane functionality in networks. This comes at a great risk; deploying buggy code at the controller could result in problematic flow entries at the data plane and, potentially, service disruption [13,18,47,49] and security loopholes [7,26]. Understanding and fixing such

© The Author(s) 2020
S. K. Lahiri and C. Wang (Eds.): CAV 2020, LNCS 12225, pp. 126–148, 2020.
https://doi.org/10.1007/978-3-030-53291-8_8

bugs is far from trivial, given the distributed and concurrent nature of computer networks and the complexity of the control plane [44].

With the advent of SDN, a large body of research on verifying network properties has emerged [33]. Static network analysis approaches [2,11,30,34,45,51] can only verify network properties on a given fixed network configuration but this may be changing very quickly (e.g. as in [1]). Another key limitation is the fact that they cannot reason about the controller program, which, itself, is responsible for the changes in the network configuration. Dynamic approaches, such as [23,29,31,40,48,50], are able to reason about network properties as changes happen (i.e. as flow entries in switches' flow tables are being added and deleted), but they cannot reason about the controller program either. As a result, when a property violation is detected, there is no straightforward way to fix the bug in the controller code, as these systems are oblivious of the running code. Identifying bugs in large and complex deployments can be extremely challenging.

Formal verification methods that include the controller code in the model of the network can solve this important problem. Symbolic execution methods, such as [5,8,11,12,14,28,46], evaluate programs using symbolic variables accumulating path-conditions along the way that then can be solved logically. However, they suffer from the path explosion problem caused by loops and function calls which means verification does not scale to larger controller programs (bug finding still works but is limited). Model checking SDNs is a promising area even though only few studies have been undertaken [3,8,28,35,36,43]. Networks and controller can be naturally modelled as transition systems. State explosion is always a problem but can be mitigated by using abstraction and optimisation techniques (i.e. partial order reductions). At the same time, modern model checkers [6,9,20,21,25] are very efficient.

NetSMC [28] uses a bespoke *symbolic* model checking algorithm for checking properties given a subset of computation tree logic that allows quantification only over all paths. As a result, this approach scales relatively well, but the requirement that only one packet can travel through the network at any time is very restrictive and ignores race conditions. NICE [8] employs model checking but only looks at a limited amount of input packets that are extracted through symbolically executing the controller code. As a result, it is a bug-finding tool only. The authors in [43] propose a model checking approach that can deal with dynamic controller updates and an arbitrary number of packets but require manually inserted non-interference lemmas that constrain the set of packets that can appear in the network. This significantly limits its applicability in realistic network deployments. Kuai [35] overcomes this limitation by introducing model-specific partial order reductions (PORs) that result in pruning the state space by avoiding redundant explorations. However, it has limitations explained at the end of this section.

In this paper, we take a step further towards the full realisation of model checking real-world SDNs by introducing MOCS (MOdel Checking for Software defined networks)[1], a highly expressive, optimised SDN model which we

---

[1] A release of MOCS is publicly available at https://tinyurl.com/y95qtv5k.

implemented in UPPAAL[2] [6]. MOCS, compared to the state of the art in model checking SDNs, can model network behaviour more realistically and verify larger deployments using fewer resources. The main contributions of this paper are:

Model Generality. The proposed network model is closer to the Open-Flow standard than previous models (e.g. [35]) to reflect commonly exhibited behaviour between the controller and network switches. More specifically, it allows for race conditions between control messages and includes a significant number of OpenFlow interactions, including barrier response messages. In our experimentation section, we present families of elusive bugs that can be efficiently captured by MOCS.

Model Checking Optimisations. To tackle the state explosion problem we propose context-dependent *partial order reductions* by considering the concrete control program and specification in question. We establish the soundness of the proposed optimisations. Moreover, we propose *state representation optimisations*, namely packet and rule indexing, identification of packet equivalence classes and bit packing, to improve performance. We evaluate the benefits from all proposed optimisations in Sect. 4.

Our model has been inspired by Kuai [35]. According to the contributions above, however, we consider MOCS to be a considerable improvement. We model more OpenFlow messages and interactions, enabling us to check for bugs that [35] cannot even express (see discussion in Sect. 4.2). Our context-dependent PORs systematically explore possibilities for optimisation. Our optimisation techniques still allow MOCS to run at least as efficiently as Kuai, often with even better performance.

2   Software-Defined Network Model

A key objective of our work is to enable the verification of network-wide properties in real-world SDNs. In order to fulfill this ambition, we present an extended network model to capture complex interactions between the SDN controller and the network. Below we describe the adopted network model, its state and transitions.

2.1   Formal Model Definition

The formal definition of the proposed SDN model is by means of an action-deterministic transition system. We parameterise the model by the underlying network topology λ and the controller program CP in use, as explained further below (Sect. 2.2).

Definition 1. *An SDN model is a 6-tuple* $\mathcal{M}_{(\lambda,\text{CP})} = (S, s_0, A, \hookrightarrow, AP, L)$, *where* S *is the set of all states the SDN may enter,* s_0 *the initial state,* A *the set of*

---

[2] UPPAAL has been chosen as future plans include extending the model to timed actions like e.g. timeouts. Note that the model can be implemented in any model checker.

actions which encode the events the network may engage in, $\hookrightarrow\, \subseteq\, S \times A \times S$ the transition relation describing which execution steps the system undergoes as it perform actions, AP a set of atomic propositions describing relevant state properties, and $L : S \rightarrow 2^{AP}$ is a labelling function, which relates to any state $s \in S$ a set $L(s) \in 2^{AP}$ of those atomic propositions that are true for s. Such an SDN model is composed of several smaller systems, which model network components (hosts, switches and the controller) that communicate via queues and, combined, give rise to the definition of $\hookrightarrow$. The states of an SDN transition system are 3-tuples (π, δ, γ), where π represents the state of each host, δ the state of each switch, and γ the controller state. The components are explained in Sect. 2.2 and the transitions $\hookrightarrow$ in Sect. 2.3.

Figure 1 illustrates a high-level view of OpenFlow interactions (left side), modelled actions and queues (right side).

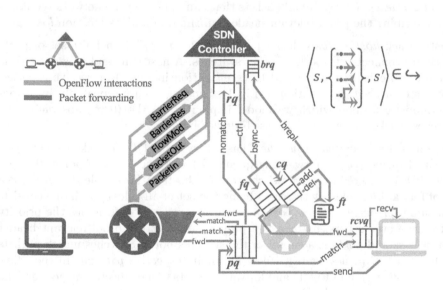

Fig. 1. A high-level view of OpenFlow interactions using OpenFlow specification terminology (left half) and the modelled actions (right half). A red solid-line arrow depicts an action which, when fired, (1) dequeues an item from the queue the arrow begins at, and (2) adds an item in the queue the arrowhead points to (or multiple items if the arrow is double-headed). Deleting an item from the target queue is denoted by a reverse arrowhead. A forked arrow denotes multiple targeted queues. (Color figure online)

2.2 SDN Model Components

Throughout we will use the common "dot-notation" (_._) to refer to components of composite gadgets (tuples), e.g. queues of switches, or parts of the state. We use obvious names for the projections functions like $s.\delta.sw.pq$ for the packet queue of the switch sw in state s. At times we will also use t_1 and t_2 for the first and second projection of tuple t.

Network Topology. A location (n, pt) is a pair of a node (host or switch) n and a port pt. We describe the network topology as a bijective function $\lambda : (Switches \cup Hosts) \times Ports \rightarrow (Switches \cup Hosts) \times Ports$ consisting of a set of directed edges $\langle (n, pt), (n', pt') \rangle$, where pt' is the input port of the switch or host n' that is connected to port pt at host or switch n. *Hosts*, *Switches* and *Ports* are the (finite) sets of all hosts, switches and ports in the network, respectively. The topology function is used when a packet needs to be forwarded in the network. The location of the next hop node is decided when a *send*, *match* or *fwd* action (all defined further below) is fired. Every SDN model is w.r.t. a fixed topology λ that does not change.

Packets. Packets are modelled as finite bit vectors and transferred in the network by being stored to the queues of the various network components. A *packet* $\in$ *Packets* (the set of all packets that can appear in the network) contains bits describing the proof-relevant header information and its location *loc*.

Hosts. Each *host* $\in$ *Hosts*, has a packet queue (*rcvq*) and a finite set of ports which are connected to ports of other switches. A host can send a packet to one or more switches it is connected to (*send* action in Fig. 1) or receive a packet from its own *rcvq* (*recv* action in Fig. 1). Sending occurs repeatedly in a non-deterministic fashion which we model implicitly via the $(0, \infty)$ abstraction at switches' packet queues, as discussed further below.

Switches. Each *switch* $\in$ *Switches*, has a flow table (*ft*), a packet queue (*pq*), a control queue (*cq*), a forwarding queue (*fq*) and one or more ports, through which it is connected to other switches and/or hosts. A flow table $ft \subseteq Rules$ is a set of forwarding rules (with *Rules* being the set of all rules). Each one consists of a tuple $(priority, pattern, ports)$, where $priority \in \mathbb{N}$ determines the priority of the rule over others, *pattern* is a proposition over the proof-relevant header of a packet, and *ports* is a subset of the switch's ports. Switches match packets in their packet queues against rules (i.e. their respective *pattern*) in their flow table (*match* action in Fig. 1) and forward packets to a connected device (or final destination), accordingly. Packets that cannot be matched to any rule are sent to the controller's request queue (*rq*) (*nomatch* action in Fig. 1); in OpenFlow, this is done by sending a *PacketIn* message. The forwarding queue *fq* stores packets forwarded by the controller in *PacketOut* messages. The control queue stores messages sent by the controller in *FlowMod* and *BarrierReq* messages. *FlowMod* messages contain instructions to add or delete rules from the flow table (that trigger *add* and *del* actions in Fig. 1). *BarrierReq* messages contain barriers to synchronise the addition and removal of rules. MOCS conforms to the OpenFlow specifications and always execute instructions in an interleaved fashion obeying the ordering constraints imposed by barriers.

OpenFlow Controller. The controller is modelled as a finite state automaton embedded into the overall transition system. A controller program CP, as used to parametrise an SDN model, consists of $(CS, pktIn, barrierIn)$. It uses its own local state $cs \in CS$, where CS is the finite set of control program states. Incoming

PacketIn and *BarrierRes* messages from the SDN model are stored in separate queues (*rq* and *brq*, respectively) and trigger *ctrl* or *bsync* actions (see Fig. 1) which are then processed by the controller program in its current state. The controller's corresponding handler, *pktIn* for *PacketIn* messages and *barrierIn* for *BarrierRes* messages, responds by potentially changing its local state and sending messages to a subset of *Switches*, as follows. A number of *PacketOut* messages (pairs of *pkt, ports*) can be sent to a subset of *Switches*. Such a message is stored in a switch's forward queue and instructs it to forward packet *pkt* along the ports *ports*. The controller may also send any number of *FlowMod* and *BarrierReq* messages to the control queue of any subset of *Switches*. A *FlowMod* message may contain an *add* or *delete* rule modification instruction. These are executed in an arbitrary order by switches, and *barriers* are used to synchronise their execution. Barriers are sent by the controller in *BarrierReq* messages. OpenFlow requires that a response message (*BarrierRes*) is sent to the controller by a switch when a barrier is consumed from its control queue so that the controller can synchronise subsequent actions. Our model includes a *brepl* action that models the sending of a *BarrierRes* message from a switch to the controller's barrier reply queue (*brq*), and a *bsync* action that enables the controller program to react to barrier responses.

Queues. All queues in the network are modelled as *finite* state. Packet queues *pq* for switches are modelled as multisets, and we adopt $(0, \infty)$ abstraction [41]; i.e. a packet is assumed to appear either zero or an arbitrary (unbounded) amount of times in the respective multiset. This means that once a packet has arrived at a switch or host, (infinitely) many other packets of the same kind repeatedly arrive at this switch or host. Switches' forwarding queues *fq* are, by contrast, modelled as sets, therefore if multiple identical packets are sent by the controller to a switch, only one will be stored in the queue and eventually forwarded by the switch. The controller's request *rq* and barrier reply queues *brq* are modelled as sets as well. Hosts' receive queues *rcvq* are also modelled as sets. Controller queues *cq* at switches are modelled as a finite sequence of sets of control messages (representing add and remove rule instructions), interleaved by any number of barriers. As the number of barriers that can appear at any execution is finite, this sequence is finite.

2.3   Guarded Transitions

Here we provide a detailed breakdown of the transition relation $s \xrightarrow{\alpha(\vec{a})} s'$ for each action $\alpha(\vec{a}) \in A(s)$, where $A(s)$ the set of all enabled actions in s in the proposed model (see Fig. 1). Transitions are labelled by action names α with arguments $\vec{a}$. The transitions are only enabled in state s if s satisfies certain conditions called *guards* that can refer to the arguments $\vec{a}$. In guards, we make use of predicate *bestmatch*(sw, r, pkt) that expresses that r is the highest priority rule in $sw.ft$ that matches pkt's header. Below we list all possible actions with their respective guards.

***send*(h, pt, pkt).** Guard: *true*. This transition models packets arriving in the network in a non-deterministic fashion. When it is executed, *pkt* is added to the packet queue of the network switch connected to the port pt of host h (or, formally, to $\lambda(h, pt)_1.pq$, where λ is the topology function described above). As described in Sect. 3.2, only relevant representatives of packets are actually sent by end-hosts. This transition is unguarded, therefore it is always enabled.

$recv(h, pkt)$. Guard: $pkt \in h.rcvq$. This transition models hosts receiving (and removing) packets from the network and is enabled if pkt is in h's receive queue.

$match(sw, pkt, r)$. Guard: $pkt \in sw.pq \wedge r \in sw.ft \wedge bestmatch(sw, r, pkt)$. This transition models matching and forwarding packet pkt to zero or more next hop nodes (hosts and switches), as a result of highest priority matching of rule r with pkt. The packet is then copied to the packet queues of the connected hosts and/or switches, by applying the topology function to the port numbers in the matched rule; i.e. $\lambda(sw, pt)_1.pq, \forall pt \in r.ports$. Dropping packets is modelled by having a special 'drop' port that can be included in rules. The location of the forwarded packet(s) is updated with the respective destination (switch/host, port) pair; i.e. $\lambda(sw, pt)$. Due to the $(0, \infty)$ abstraction, the packet is not removed from $sw.pq$.

$nomatch(sw, pkt)$. Guard: $pkt \in sw.pq \wedge \nexists r \in sw.ft \ . \ bestmatch(sw, r, pkt)$. This transition models forwarding a packet to the OpenFlow controller when a switch does not have a rule in its forwarding table that can be matched against the packet header. In this case, pkt is added to rq for processing. pkt is not removed from $sw.pq$ due to the supported $(0, \infty)$ abstraction.

$ctrl(sw, pkt, cs)$. Guard: $pkt \in controller.rq$. This transition models the execution of the packet handler by the controller when packet pkt that was previously sent by sw is available in rq. The controller's packet handler function $pktIn(sw, pkt, cs)$ is executed which, in turn (i) reads the current controller state cs and changes it according to the controller program, (ii) adds a number of rules, interleaved with any number of barriers, into the cq of zero or more switches, and (iii) adds zero or more forwarding messages, each one including a packet along with a set of ports, to the fq of zero or more switches.

$fwd(sw, pkt, ports)$. Guard: $(pkt, ports) \in sw.fq$. This transition models forwarding packet pkt that was previously sent by the controller to sw's forwarding queue $sw.fq$. In this case, pkt is removed from $sw.fq$ (which is modelled as a set), and added to the pq of a number of network nodes (switches and/or hosts), as defined by the topology function $\lambda(sw, pt)_1.pq, \forall pt \in ports$. The location of the forwarded packet(s) is updated with the respective destination (switch/host, port) pair; i.e. $\lambda(n, pt)$.

$FM(sw, r)$, where $FM \in \{add, del\}$. Guard: $(FM, r) \in head(sw.cq)$. These transitions model the addition and deletion, respectively, of a rule in the flow table of switch sw. They are enabled when one or more add and del control messages are in the set at the head of the switch's control queue. In this case, r is added to – or deleted from, respectively – $sw.ft$ and the control message is deleted from the set at the head of cq. If the set at the head of cq becomes empty it is removed. If then the next item in cq is a barrier, a $brepl$ transition becomes enabled (see below).

brepl(sw, xid). Guard: $b(xid) = head(sw.cq)$. This transition models a switch sending a barrier response message, upon consuming a barrier from the head of its control queue; i.e. if $b(xid)$ is the head of $sw.cq$, where $xid \in \mathbb{N}$ is an identifier for the barrier set by the controller, $b(xid)$ is removed and the barrier reply message $br(sw, xid)$ is added to the controller's brq.

bsync(sw, xid, cs). Guard: $br(sw, xid) \in controller.brq$. This transition models the execution of the barrier response handler by the controller when a barrier response sent by switch sw is available in brq. In this case, $br(sw, xid)$ is removed from the brq, and the controller's barrier handler $barrierIn(sw, xid, cs)$ is executed which, in turn (i) reads the current controller state cs and changes it according to the controller program, (ii) adds a number of rules, interleaved with any number of barriers, into the cq of zero or more switches, and (iii) adds zero or more forwarding messages, each one including a packet along with a set of ports, to the fq of zero or more switches.

An Example Run. In Fig. 2, we illustrate a sequence of MOCS transitions through a simple packet forwarding example. The run starts with a *send* transition; packet p is copied to the packet queue of the switch in black. Initially, switches' flow tables are empty, therefore p is copied to the controller's request queue (*nomatch* transition); note that p remains in the packet queue of the switch in black due to the $(0, \infty)$ abstraction. The controller's packet handler is then called (*ctrl* transition) and, as a result, (1) p is copied to the forwarding queue of the switch in black, (2) rule r_1 is copied to the control queue of the switch in black, and (3) rule r_2 is copied to the control queue of the switch in white. Then, the switch in black forwards p to the packet queue of the switch in white (*fwd* transition). The switch in white installs r_2 in its flow table (*add* transition) and then matches p with the newly installed rule and forwards it to the receive queue of the host in white (*match* transition), which removes it from the network (*recv* transition).

2.4   Specification Language

In order to specify properties of packet flow in the network, we use LTL formulas without "next-step" operator $\bigcirc$[3], where atomic formulae denoting properties of states of the transition system, i.e. SDN network. In the case of safety properties, i.e. an invariant w.r.t. states, the $LTL_{\backslash\{\bigcirc\}}$ formula is of the form $\square\varphi$, i.e. has only an outermost $\square$ temporal connective.

Let P denote unary predicates on packets which encode a property of a packet based on its fields. An atomic *state condition* (proposition) in AP is either of the following: (i) existence of a packet pkt located in a packet queue (pq) of a switch or in a receive queue ($rcvq$) of a host that satisfies P (we denote this by $\exists pkt \in n.pq . P(pkt)$ with $n \in Switches$, and $\exists pkt \in h.rcvq . P(pkt)$

---

[3] This is the largest set of formulae supporting the partial order reductions used in Sect. 3, as stutter equivalence does not preserve the truth value of formulae with the $\bigcirc$.

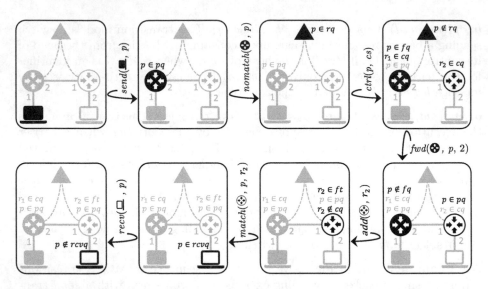

Fig. 2. Forwarding p from 🖳 to 💻. Non greyed-out icons are the ones whose state changes in the current transition.

with $h \in Hosts)^4$; (ii) the controller is in a specific *controller* state $q \in CS$, denoted by a unary predicate symbol $Q(q)$ which holds in system state $s \in S$ if $q = s.\gamma.cs$. The specification logic comprises first-order formula with equality on the finite domains of switches, hosts, rule priorities, and ports which are *state-independent* (and decidable).

For example, $\exists pkt \in sw.pq . P(pkt)$ represents the fact that the packet predicate $P(\_)$ is true for at least one packet pkt in the pq of switch sw. For every atomic packet proposition $P(pkt)$, also its negation $\neg P(pkt)$ is an atomic proposition for the reason of simplifying syntactic checks of formulae in Table 1 in the next section. Note that universal quantification over packets in a queue is a derived notion. For instance, $\forall pkt \in n.pq . P(pkt)$ can be expressed as $\nexists pk \in n.pq . \neg P(pkt)$. Universal and existential quantification over switches or hosts can be expressed by finite iterations of $\wedge$ and $\vee$, respectively.

In order to be able to express that a condition holds when a certain event happened, we add to our propositions instances of *propositional dynamic logic* [17,42]. Given an action $\alpha(\cdot) \in A$ and a proposition P that may refer to any variables in $\vec{x}$, $[\alpha(\vec{x})]P$ is also a proposition and $[\alpha(\vec{x})]P$ is true if, and only if, after firing transition $\alpha(\vec{a})$ (to get to the current state), P holds with the variables in $\vec{x}$ bound to the corresponding values in the actual arguments $\vec{a}$. With the help of those basic modalities one can then also specify that more complex events occurred. For instance, dropping of a packet due to a *match* or *fwd* action can be expressed by $[match(sw, pkt, r)](r.fwd\_port = \mathbf{drop}) \wedge [fwd(sw, pkt, pt)](pt = \mathbf{drop})$. Such predicates derived from modalities are used in [32] (extended version of this paper, with proofs and controller programs), Appendix B-CP5.

---

[4] Note that these are *atomic* propositions despite the use of the existential quantifier notation.

The meaning of temporal LTL operators is standard depending on the trace of a transition sequence $s_0 \overset{\alpha_1}{\hookrightarrow} s_1 \overset{\alpha_2}{\hookrightarrow} \ldots$. The trace $L(s_0)L(s_1)\ldots L(s_i)\ldots$ is defined as usual. For instance, trace $L(s_0)L(s_1)L(s_2)\ldots$ satisfies invariant $\Box\varphi$ if each $L(s_i)$ implies φ.

3 Model Checking

In order to verify desired properties of an SDN, we use its model as described in Definition 1 and apply model checking. In the following we propose optimisations that significantly improve the performance of model checking.

3.1 Contextual Partial-Order Reduction

Partial order reduction (POR) [39] reduces the number of interleavings (traces) one has to check. Here is a reminder of the main result (see [4]) where we use a stronger condition than the regular (*C4*) to deal with cycles:

Theorem 1 (Correctness of POR). *Given a finite transition system $\mathcal{M} = (S, A, \hookrightarrow, s_0, AP, L)$ that is action-deterministic and without terminal states, let $A(s)$ denote the set of actions in A enabled in state $s \in S$. Let $ample(s) \subseteq A(s)$ be a set of actions for a state $s \in S$ that satisfies the following conditions:*

C1 (Non)emptiness condition: $\varnothing \neq ample(s) \subseteq A(s)$.

C2 Dependency condition: Let $s \overset{\alpha_1}{\hookrightarrow} s_1 \ldots \overset{\alpha_n}{\hookrightarrow} s_n \overset{\beta}{\hookrightarrow} t$ be a run in $\mathcal{M}$. If $\beta \in A \setminus ample(s)$ depends on $ample(s)$, then $\alpha_i \in ample(s)$ for some $0 < i \leqslant n$, which means that in every path fragment of $\mathcal{M}$, β cannot appear before some transition from $ample(s)$ is executed.

C3 Invisibility condition: If $ample(s) \neq A(s)$ (i.e., state s is not fully expanded), then every $\alpha \in ample(s)$ is invisible.

C4 Every cycle in $\mathcal{M}^{ample}$ contains a state s such that $ample(s) = A(s)$.

where $\mathcal{M}^{ample} = (S_a, A, \hookrightarrow\!\!\!\!\twoheadrightarrow, s_0, AP, L_a)$ is the new, optimised, model defined as follows: let $S_a \subseteq S$ be the set of states reachable from the initial state s_0 under $\hookrightarrow\!\!\!\!\twoheadrightarrow$, let $L_a(s) = L(s)$ for all $s \in S_a$, and define $\hookrightarrow\!\!\!\!\twoheadrightarrow \subseteq S_a \times A \times S_a$ inductively by the rule

$$\frac{s \overset{\alpha}{\hookrightarrow} s'}{s \overset{\alpha}{\hookrightarrow\!\!\!\!\twoheadrightarrow} s'} \qquad \text{if } \alpha \in ample(s)$$

If $ample(s)$ satisfies conditions (C1)–(C4) as outlined above, then for each path in $\mathcal{M}$ there exists a stutter-trace equivalent path in $\mathcal{M}^{ample}$, and vice-versa, denoted $\mathcal{M} \overset{st}{\equiv} \mathcal{M}^{ample}$.

The intuitive reason for this theorem to hold is the following: Assume an action sequence $\alpha_i\ldots\alpha_{i+n}\beta$ that reaches the state s, and β is *independent* of $\{\alpha_i, \ldots \alpha_{i+n}\}$. Then, one can permute β with α_{i+n} through α_i successively n times. One can therefore construct the sequence $\beta\alpha_i...\alpha_{i+n}$ that also reaches the state s. If this shift of β does not affect the labelling of the states with atomic propositions (β is called *invisible* in this case), then it is not detectable by the property to be shown and the permuted and the original sequence are equivalent w.r.t. the property and thus don't have to be checked both. One must, however, ensure, that in case of loops (infinite execution traces) the ample sets do not *preclude* some actions to be fired altogether, which is why one needs ($C4$).

The more actions that are both stutter and provably independent (also referred to as *safe actions* [22]) there are, the smaller the transition system, and the more efficient the model checking. One of our contributions is that we attempt to identify *as many safe actions as possible* to make PORs more widely applicable to our model.

The PORs in [35] consider only dependency and invisibility of *recv* and *barrier* actions, whereas we explore systematically all possibilities for applications of Theorem 1 to reduce the search space. When identifying safe actions, we consider (1) the actual controller program CP, (2) the topology λ and (3) the state formula φ to be shown invariant, which we call the *context* CTX of actions. It turns out that two actions may be dependent in a given context of abstraction while independent in another context, and similarly for invisibility, and we exploit this fact. The argument of the action thus becomes relevant as well.

Definition 2 (Safe Actions). *Given a context* CTX $= (\text{CP}, \lambda, \varphi)$, *and SDN model* $\mathcal{M}_{(\lambda, \text{CP})} = (S, A, \hookrightarrow, s_0, AP, L)$, *an action* $\alpha(\cdot) \in A(s)$ *is called 'safe' if it is independent of any other action in A and invisible for φ. We write safe actions* $\breve{\alpha}(\cdot)$.

Definition 3 (Order-sensitive Controller Program). *A controller program* CP *is order-sensitive if there exists a state $s \in S$ and two actions α, β in $\{ctrl(\cdot), bsync(\cdot)\}$ such that $\alpha, \beta \in A(s)$ and $s \overset{\alpha}{\hookrightarrow} s_1 \overset{\beta}{\hookrightarrow} s_2$ and $s \overset{\beta}{\hookrightarrow} s_3 \overset{\alpha}{\hookrightarrow} s_4$ with $s_2 \neq s_4$.*

Definition 4. *Let φ be a state formula. An action $\alpha \in A$ is called 'φ-invariant' if $s \models \varphi$ iff $\alpha(s) \models \varphi$ for all $s \in S$ with $\alpha \in A(s)$.*

Lemma 1. *For transition system $\mathcal{M}_{(\lambda, \text{CP})} = (S, A, \hookrightarrow, s_0, AP, L)$ and a formula $\varphi \in LTL_{\backslash\{\bigcirc\}}$, $\alpha \in A$ is safe iff $\bigwedge_{i=1}^{3} Safe_i(\alpha)$, where $Safe_i$, given in Table 1, are per-row.*

Proof. See [32] Appendix A.

Theorem 2 (POR instance for SDN). *Let $(\text{CP}, \lambda, \varphi)$ be a context such that $\mathcal{M}_{(\lambda, \text{CP})} = (S, A, \hookrightarrow, s_0, AP, L)$ is an SDN network model from Definition 1; and let safe actions be as in Definition 2. Further, let ample(s) be defined by:*

$$ample(s) = \begin{cases} \{\alpha \in A(s) \mid \alpha \text{ safe }\} & \text{if } \{\alpha \in A(s) \mid \alpha \text{ safe }\} \neq \varnothing \\ A(s) & \text{otherwise} \end{cases}$$

Table 1. Safeness predicates

Action $Safe_1(\alpha)$	Independence $Safe_2(\alpha)$	Invisibility $Safe_3(\alpha)$
$\alpha = ctrl(sw, pk, cs)$	CP is not order-sensitive	if $Q(q)$ occurs in φ, where $q \in CS$, then α is φ-invariant
$\alpha = bsync(sw, xid, cs)$	CP is not order-sensitive	if $Q(q)$ occurs in φ, where $q \in CS$, then α is φ-invariant
$\alpha = fwd(sw, pk, ports)$	$\top$	if $\exists pk \in b.q \,.\, P(pk)$ occurs in φ, for any $b \in \{sw\} \cup \{\lambda(sw,p)_1 \mid p \in ports\}$ and $q \in \{pq, recvq\}$, then α is φ-invariant
$\alpha = brepl(sw, xid)$	$\top$	$\top$
$\alpha = recv(h, pk)$	$\top$	if $\exists pk \in h.rcvq \,.\, P(pk)$ occurs in φ, then α is φ-invariant

Then, ample satisfies the criteria of Theorem 1 and thus $\mathcal{M}_{(\lambda,\mathrm{CP})} \overset{st}{\equiv} \mathcal{M}^{ample}_{(\lambda,\mathrm{CP})}$ [5]

Proof.

C1 The (non)emptiness condition is trivial since by definition of $ample(s)$ it follows that $ample(s) = \varnothing$ iff $A(s) = \varnothing$.

C2 By assumption $\beta \in A \backslash ample(s)$ depends on $ample(s)$. But with our definition of $ample(s)$ this is impossible as all actions in $ample(s)$ are safe and by definition independent of all other actions.

C3 The validity of the invisibility condition is by definition of $ample$ and safe actions.

C4 We now show that every cycle in $\mathcal{M}^{ample}_{(\lambda,\mathrm{CP})}$ contains a fully expanded state s, i.e. a state s such that $ample(s) = A(s)$. By definition of $ample(s)$ in Theorem 2 it is equivalent to show that there is no cycle in $\mathcal{M}^{ample}_{(\lambda,\mathrm{CP})}$ consisting of safe actions only. We show this by contradiction, assuming such a cycle of only safe actions exists. There are five safe action types to consider: *ctrl*, *fwd*, *brepl*, *bsync* and *recv*. Distinguish two cases.

Case 1. A sequence of safe actions of same type. Let us consider the different safe actions:

- Let ρ an execution of $\mathcal{M}^{ample}_{(\lambda,\mathrm{CP})}$ which consists of only one type of *ctrl*-actions:

$$\rho = s_1 \xrightarrow{ctrl(pkt_1, cs_1)} s_2 \xrightarrow{ctrl(pkt_2, cs_2)} ...s_{i-1} \xrightarrow{ctrl(pkt_{i-1}, cs_{i-1})} s_i$$

  Suppose ρ is a cycle. According to the *ctrl* semantics, for each transition $s \xrightarrow{ctrl(pkt, cs)} s'$, where $s = (\pi, \delta, \gamma)$, $s' = (\pi', \delta', \gamma')$, it holds that $\gamma'.rq = \gamma.rq \backslash \{pkt\}$ as we use sets to represent rq buffers. Hence, for the execution ρ it holds $\gamma_i.rq = \gamma_1.rq \backslash \{pkt_1, pkt_2, ...pkt_{i-1}\}$ which implies that $s_1 \neq s_i$. Contradiction.

---

[5] Stutter equivalence here implicitly is defined w.r.t. the atomic propositions appearing in φ, but this suffices as we are just interested in the validity of φ.

- Let ρ an execution which consists of only one type of *fwd*-actions: similar argument as above since *fq*-s are represented by sets and thus forward messages are removed from *fq*.
- Let ρ an execution which consists of only one type of *brepl*-actions: similar argument as above since control messages are removed from *cq*.
- Let ρ an execution which consists of only one type of *bsync*-actions: similar argument as above, as barrier reply messages are removed from *brq*-s that are represented by sets.
- Let ρ an execution which consists of only one type of *recv*-actions: similar argument as above, as packets are removed from *rcvq* buffers that are represented by sets.

Case 2. A sequence of different safe actions. Suppose there exists a cycle with mixed safe actions starting in s_1 and ending in s_i. Distinguish the following cases.

i) There exists at least a *ctrl* and/or a *bsync* action in the cycle. According to the effects of safe transitions, the *ctrl* action will change to a state with smaller *rq* and the *bsync* will always switch to a state with smaller *brq*. It is important here that *ctrl* does not interfere with *bsync* regarding *rq*, *brq*, and no safe action of other type than *ctrl* and *bsync* accesses *rq* or *brq*. This implies that $s_1 \neq s_i$. Contradiction.

ii) Neither *ctrl*, nor *bsync* actions in the cycle.
   a) There is a *fwd* and/or *brepl* in the cycle: *fwd* will always switch to a state with smaller *fq* and *brepl* will always switch to a state with smaller *cq* (*brepl* and *recv* do not interfere with *fwd*). This implies that $s_1 \neq s_i$. Contradiction.
   b) There is neither *fwd* nor *brepl* in the cycle. This means that only *recv* is in the cycle which is already covered by the first case.

$\square$

Due to the definition of the transition system via ample sets, each safe action is immediately executed after its enabling one. Therefore, one can merge every transition of a safe action with its precursory enabling one. Intuitively, the semantics of the merged action is defined as the successive execution of its constituent actions. This process can be repeated if there is a chain of safe actions; for instance, in the case of $s \xrightarrow{nomatch(sw,pkt)} s' \xrightarrow{ctrl(sw,pkt,cs)} s'' \xrightarrow{fwd(sw,pkt,ports)} s'''$ where each transition enables the next and the last two are assumed to be safe. These transitions can be merged into one, yielding a stutter equivalent trace as the intermediate states are invisible (w.r.t. the context and thus the property to be shown) by definition of safe actions.

3.2   State Representation

Efficient state representation is crucial for minimising MOCS's memory footprint and enabling it to scale up to relatively large network setups.

Packet and Rule Indexing. In MOCS, only a single instance of each packet and rule that can appear in the modelled network is kept in memory. An index is then used to associate queues and flow tables with packets and rules, with a single bit indicating their presence (or absence). This data structure is illustrated in Fig. 3. For a data packet, a value of 1 in the *pq* section of the entry indicates that infinite copies of it are stored in the packet queue of the respective switch. A value of 1 in the *fq* section indicates that a single copy of the packet is stored in the forward queue of the respective switch. A value of 1 in the *rq* section indicates that a copy of the packet sent by the respective switch (when a *nomatch* transition is fired) is stored in the controller's request queue. For a rule, a value of 1 in the *ft* section indicates that the rule is installed in the respective switch's flow table. A value of 1 in the *cq* section indicates that the rule is part of a *FlowMod* message in the respective switch's control queue.

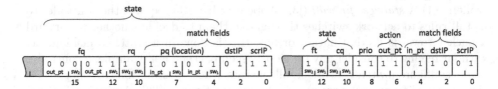

Fig. 3. Packet (left) and rule (right) indices

The proposed optimisation enables scaling up the network topology by minimising the required memory footprint. For every switch, MOCS only requires a few bits in each packet and rule entry in the index.

Discovering Equivalence Classes of Packets. Model checking with all possible packets, including all specified fields in the OpenFlow standard, would entail a huge state space that would render any approach unusable. Here, we propose the discovery of equivalence classes of packets that are then used for model checking. We first remove all fields that are not referenced in a statement or rule creation or deletion in the controller program. Then, we identify packet classes that would result in the same controller behaviour. Currently, as with the rest of literature, we focus on simple controller programs where such equivalence classes can be easily identified by analysing static constraints and rule manipulation in the controller program. We then generate one representative packet from each class and assign it to all network switches that are directly connected to end-hosts; i.e. modelling clients that can send an arbitrarily large number of packets in a non-deterministic fashion. We use the minimum possible number of bits to represent the identified equivalence classes. For example, if the controller program exerts different behaviour if the destination TCP port of a packet is 23 (i.e. destined to an SSH server) or not, we only use a 1-bit field to model this behaviour.

Bit Packing. We reduce the size of each recorded state by employing bit packing using the *int* type supported by UPPAAL, and bit-level operations for the entries in the packet and rule indices as well as for the packets and rules themselves.

4   Experimental Evaluation

In this section, we experimentally evaluate MOCS by comparing it with the state of the art, in terms of performance (verification throughput and memory footprint) and model expressivity. We have implemented MOCS in UPPAAL [6] as a network of parallel automata for the controller and network switches, which communicate asynchronously by writing/reading packets to/from queues that are part of the model discussed in Sect. 2. As discussed in Sect. 3, this is implemented by directly manipulating the packet and rule indices.

Throughout this section we will be using three examples of network controllers: (1) A *stateless firewall* ([32] Appendix B-CP1) requires the controller to install rules to network switches that enable them to decide whether to forward a packet towards its destination or not; this is done in a stateless fashion, i.e. without having to consider any previously seen packets. For example, a controller could configure switches to block all packets whose destination TCP port is 22 (i.e. destined to an SSH server). (2) A *stateful firewall* ([32] Appendix B-CP2) is similar to the stateless one but decisions can take into account previously seen packets. A classic example of this is to allow bi-directional communication between two end-hosts, when one host opens a TCP connection to the other. Then, traffic flowing from the other host back to the connection initiator should be allowed to go through the switches on the reverse path. (3) A *MAC learning application* ([32] Appendix B-CP3) enables the controller and switches to learn how to forward packets to their destinations (identified with respective MAC addresses). A switch sends a *PacketIn* message to the controller when it receives a packet that it does not know how to forward. By looking at this packet, the controller learns a mapping of a source switch (or host) to a port of the requesting switch. It then installs a rule (by sending a *FlowMod* message) that will allow that switch to forward packets back to the source switch (or host), and asks the requesting switch (by sending a *PacketOut* message) to flood the packet to all its ports except the one it received the packet from. This way, the controller eventually learns all mappings, and network switches receive rules that enable them to forward traffic to their neighbours for all destinations in the network.

4.1   Performance Comparison

We measure MOCS's performance, and also compare it against Kuai [35][6] using the examples described above, and we investigate the behaviour of MOCS as we scale up the network (switches and clients/servers). We report three metrics:

---

[6] Note that parts of Kuai's source code are not publicly available, therefore we implemented it's model in UPPAAL.

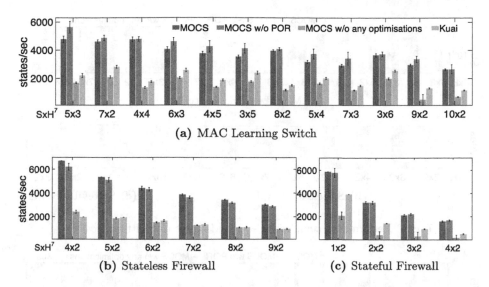

(a) MAC Learning Switch

(b) Stateless Firewall   (c) Stateful Firewall

Fig. 4. Performance comparison – verification throughput

(1) *verification throughput* in visited states per second, (2) number of visited states, and (3) required memory. We have run all verification experiments on an 18-Core iMac pro, 2.3 GHz Intel Xeon W with 128 GB DDR4 memory.

Verification Throughput. We measure the verification throughput when running a single experiment at a time on one CPU core and report the average and standard deviation for the first 30 min of each run. In order to assess how MOCS's different optimisations affect its performance, we report results for the following system variants: (1) MOCS, (2) MOCS without POR, (3) MOCS without any optimisations (neither POR, state representation), and (4) Kuai. Figure 4 shows the measured throughput (with error bars denoting standard deviation).

For the MAC learning and stateless firewall applications, we observe that MOCS performs significantly better than Kuai for all different network setups and sizes[7], achieving at least double the throughput Kuai does. The throughput performance is much better for the stateful firewall, too. This is despite the fact that, for this application, Kuai employs the unrealistic optimisation where the *barrier* transition forces the immediate update of the forwarding state. In other words, MOCS is able to explore significantly more states and identify bugs that Kuai cannot (see Sect. 4.2).

The computational overhead induced by our proposed PORs is minimal. This overhead occurs when PORs require dynamic checks through the safety predicates described in Table 1. This is shown in Fig. 4a, where, in order to decide about the (in)visibility of *fwd(sw,pk,pt)* actions, a lookup is performed in the history-array of packet *pk*, checking whether the bit which corresponds to switch *sw'*, which is connected with port *pt* of *sw*, is set. On the other hand, if a POR does not require any dynamic checks, no penalty is induced, as shown in Figs. 4b

---

[7] S × H in Figs. 4 to 6 indicates the number of switches S and hosts H.

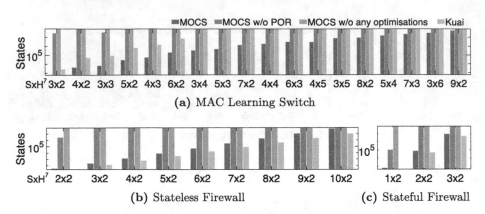

Fig. 5. Performance comparison – visited states (logarithmic scale)

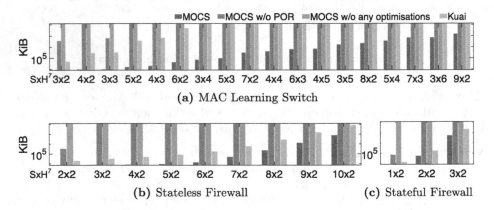

Fig. 6. Performance comparison – memory footprint (logarithmic scale)

and 4c, where the throughput when the PORs are disabled is almost identical to the case where PORs are enabled. This is because it has been statically established at a pre-analysis stage that all actions of a particular type are always safe for any argument/state. It is important to note that even when computational overhead is induced, PORs enable MOCS to scale up to larger networks because the number of visited states can be significantly reduced, as discussed below.

In order to assess the contribution of the state representation optimisation in MOCS's performance, we measure the throughput when both PORs and state representation optimisations are disabled. It is clear that they contribute significantly to the overall throughput; without these the measured throughput was at least less than half the throughput when they were enabled.

Number of Visited States and Required Memory. Minimising the number of visited states and required memory is crucial for scaling up verification to larger networks. The proposed partial order reductions (Sect. 3.1) and identification of packet equivalent classes aim at the former, while packet/rule indexing and bit packing aim at the latter (§3.2). In Fig. 5, we present the results for the various setups and network deployments discussed above. We stopped scaling up the network deployment for each setup when the verification process required more than 24 h or started swapping memory to disk. For these cases we killed the process and report a topped-up bar in Figs. 5 and 6.

For the MAC learning application, MOCS can scale up to larger network deployments compared to Kuai, which could not verify networks consisting of more than 2 hosts and 6 switches. For that network deployment, Kuai visited ~7 m states, whereas MOCS visited only ~193 k states. At the same time, Kuai required around 48 GBs of memory (7061 bytes/state) whereas MOCS needed ~43 MBs (228 bytes/state). Without the partial order reductions, MOCS can only verify tiny networks. The contribution of the proposed state representation optimisations is also crucial; in our experiments (results not shown due to lack of space), for the 6×2 network setups (the largest we could do without these optimisations), we observed a reduction in state space (due to the identification of packet equivalence classes) and memory footprint (due to packet/rule indexing and bit packing) from ~7 m to ~200k states and from ~6 KB per state to ~230 B per state. For the stateless and stateful firewall applications, resp., MOCS performs equally well to Kuai with respect to scaling up.

4.2   Model Expressivity

The proposed model is significantly more expressive compared to Kuai as it allows for more asynchronous concurrency. To begin with, in MOCS, controller messages sent before a barrier request message can be interleaved with all other enabled actions, other than the control messages sent after the barrier. By contrast, Kuai always flushes all control messages until the last barrier in one go, masking a large number of interleavings and, potentially, buggy behaviour. Next, in MOCS *nomatch, ctrl* and *fwd* can be interleaved with other actions. In Kuai, it is enforced a mutual exclusion concurrency control policy through the *wait*-semaphore: whenever a *nomatch* occurs the mutex is locked and it is unlocked by the *fwd* action of the thread *nomatch-ctrl-fwd* which refers to the same packet; all other threads are forced to wait. Moreover, MOCS does not impose any limit on the size of the *rq* queue, in contrast to Kuai where only one packet can exist in it. In addition, Kuai does not support notifications from the data plane to the controller for completed operations as it does not support reply messages and as a result any bug related to the fact that the controller is not synced to data-plane state changes is hidden.[8] Also, our specification language for states is more expressive than Kuai's, as we can use any property in LTL without "next", whereas Kuai only uses invariants with a single outermost □.

The MOCS extensions, however, are conservative with respect to Kuai, that is we have the following theorem (without proof, which is straightforward):

---

[8] There are further small extensions; for instance, in MOCS the controller can send multiple *PacketOut* messages (as OpenFlow prescribes).

Theorem 3 (MOCS Conservativity). *Let* $\mathcal{M}_{(\lambda,\mathrm{CP})} = (S, A, \hookrightarrow, s_0, AP, L)$ *and* $\mathcal{M}_{(\lambda,\mathrm{CP})}^K = (S_K, A_K, \hookrightarrow_K, s_0, AP, L)$ *the original SDN models of MOCS and Kuai, respectively, using the same topology and controller. Furthermore, let* $Traces(\mathcal{M}_{(\lambda,\mathrm{CP})})$ *and* $Traces(\mathcal{M}_{(\lambda,\mathrm{CP})}^K)$ *denote the set of all initial traces in these models, respectively. Then,* $Traces(\mathcal{M}_{(\lambda,\mathrm{CP})}^K) \subseteq Traces(\mathcal{M}_{(\lambda,\mathrm{CP})})$.

For each of the extensions mentioned above, we briefly describe an example (controller program and safety property) that expresses a bug that is impossible to occur in Kuai.

Control Message Reordering Bug. Let us consider a stateless firewall in Fig. 7a (controller is not shown), which is supposed to block incoming SSH packets from reaching the server (see [32] Appendix B-CP1). Formally, the safety property to be checked here is $\square(\forall pkt \in S.rcvq \,.\, \neg pkt.\mathrm{SSH})$. Initially, flow tables are empty. Switch A sends a *PacketIn* message to the controller when it receives the first packet from the client (as a result of a *nomatch* transition). The controller, in response to this request (and as a result of a *ctrl* transition), sends the following *FlowMod* messages to switch A; rule r1 has the highest priority and drops all SSH packets, rule r2 sends all packets from port 1 to port 2, and rule r3 sends all packets from port 2 to port 1. If the packet that triggered the transition above is an SSH one, the controller drops it, otherwise, it instructs (through a *PacketOut* message) A to forward the packet to S. A bug-free controller should ensure that r1 is installed before any other rule, therefore it must send a barrier request after the *FlowMod* message that contains r1. If, by mistake, the *FlowMod* message for r2 is sent before the barrier request, A may install r2 before r1, which will result in violating the given property. MOCS is able to capture this buggy behaviour as its semantics allows control messages prior to the barrier to be processed in a interleaved manner.

(a)   (b)

Fig. 7. Two networks with (a) two switches, and (b) n stateful firewall replicas

Wrong Nesting Level Bug. Consider a correct controller program that enforces that server S (Fig. 7a) is not accessible through SSH. Formally, the safety property to be checked here is $\square(\forall pkt \in S.rcvq \,.\, \neg pkt.\mathrm{SSH})$. For each incoming *PacketIn* message from switch A, it checks if the enclosed packet is an SSH one and destined to S. If not, it sends a *PacketOut* message instructing A to forward the packet to S. It also sends a *FlowMod* message to A with a rule that allows packets of the same protocol (not SSH) to reach S. In the opposite case (SSH), it checks (a Boolean flag) whether it had previously sent drop rules for SSH packets to the switches. If not, it sets flag to true, sends a *FlowMod* message with a rule that drops SSH packets to A and drops the packet. Note that this inner block does not have an **else** statement.

A fairly common error is to write a statement at the wrong nesting level ([32] Appendix B-CP4). Such a mistake can be built into the above program by nesting the outer **else** branch in the inner **if** block, such that it is executed any time an SSH-packet is encountered but the SSH drop-rule has already been installed (i.e. flag **f** is true). Now, the SSH drop rule, once installed in switch A, disables immediately a potential $nomatch(A, p)$ with $p.SSH = true$ that would have sent packet p to the controller, but if it has not yet been installed, a second incoming SSH packet would lead to the execution of the **else** statement of the inner branch. This would violate the property defined above, as p will be forwarded to S^9.

MOCS can uncover this bug because of the correct modelling of the controller request queue and the asynchrony between the concurrent executions of control messages sent before a barrier. Otherwise, the second packet that triggers the execution of the wrong branch would not have appeared in the buffer before the first one had been dealt with by the controller. Furthermore, if all rules in messages up to a barrier were installed synchronously, the second packet would be dealt with correctly, so no bug could occur.

Inconsistent Update Bug. OpenFlow's barrier and barrier reply mechanisms allow for updating multiple network switches in a way that enables *consistent packet processing*, i.e., a packet cannot see a partially updated network where only a subset of switches have changed their forwarding policy in response to this packet (or any other event), while others have not done so. MOCS is expressive enough to capture this behaviour and related bugs. In the topology shown in Fig. 7a, let us assume that, by default, switch B drops all packets destined to S. Any attempt to reach S through A are examined separately by the controller and, when granted access, a relevant rule is installed at both switches (e.g. allowing all packets from C destined to S for given source and destination ports). Updates must be consistent, therefore the packet cannot be forwarded by A and dropped by B. Both switches must have the new rules in place, before the packet is forwarded. To do so, the controller, ([32] Appendix B-CP5), upon receiving a *PacketIn* message from the client's switch, sends the relevant rule to switch B (*FlowMod*) along with respective barrier (*BarrierReq*) and temporarily stores the packet that triggered this update. Only after receiving *BarrierRes* message from B, the controller will forward the previously stored packet back to A along with the relevant rule. This update is consistent and the packet is guaranteed to reach S. A (rather common) bug would be one where the controller installs the rules to both switches and at the same time forwards the packet to A. In this case, the packet may end up being dropped by B, if it arrives and gets processed before the relevant rule is installed, and therefore the invariant $\Box([drop(pkt, sw)] . \neg(pkt.dest = S))$, where $[drop(pkt, sw)]$ is a quantifier that binds dropped packets (see definition in [32] Appendix B-CP5), would

---

9 Here, we assume that the controller looks up a static forwarding table before sending *PacketOut* messages to switches.

be violated. For this example, it is crucial that MOCS supports barrier response messages.

5   Conclusion

We have shown that an OpenFlow compliant SDN model, with the right optimisations, can be model checked to discover subtle real-world bugs. We proved that MOCS can capture real-world bugs in a more complicated semantics without sacrificing performance.

But this is not the end of the line. One could automatically compute equivalence classes of packets that cover all behaviours (where we still computed manually). To what extent the size of the topology can be restricted to find bugs in a given controller is another interesting research question, as is the analysis of the number and length of interleavings necessary to detect certain bugs. In our examples, all bugs were found in less than a second.

References

1. Al-Fares, M., Radhakrishnan, S., Raghavan, B.: Hedera: dynamic flow scheduling for data center networks. In: NSDI (2010)
2. Al-Shaer, E., Al-Haj, S.: FlowChecker: configuration analysis and verification of federated OpenFlow infrastructures. In: SafeConfig (2010)
3. Albert, E., Gómez-Zamalloa, M., Rubio, A., Sammartino, M., Silva, A.: SDN-Actors: modeling and verification of SDN programs. In: Havelund, K., Peleska, J., Roscoe, B., de Vink, E. (eds.) FM 2018. LNCS, vol. 10951, pp. 550–567. Springer, Cham (2018)
4. Baier, C., Katoen, J.P.: Principles of Model Checking. The MIT Press, Cambridge (2008)
5. Ball, T., Bjørner, N., Gember, A., et al.: VeriCon: towards verifying controller programs in software-defined networks. In: PLDI (2014)
6. Behrmann, G., David, A., Larsen, K.G., et al.: Developing UPPAAL over 15 years. In: Practice and Experience, Software (2011)
7. Braga, R., Mota, E., Passito, A.: Lightweight DDoS flooding attack detection using NOX/OpenFlow. In: LCN (2010)
8. Canini, M., Venzano, D., Perešíni, P., et al.: A NICE way to test OpenFlow applications. In: NSDI (2012)
9. Cimatti, A., et al.: NuSMV 2: an OpenSource tool for symbolic model checking. In: Brinksma, E., Larsen, K.G. (eds.) CAV 2002. LNCS, vol. 2404, pp. 359–364. Springer, Heidelberg (2002)
10. Curtis, A.R., Mogul, J.C., Tourrilhes, J., et al.: DevoFlow: scaling flow management for high-performance networks. In: SIGCOMM (2011)
11. Dobrescu, M., Argyraki, K.: Software dataplane verification. In: Communications of the ACM (2015)
12. El-Hassany, A., Tsankov, P., Vanbever, L., Vechev, M.: Network-wide configuration synthesis. In: Majumdar, R., Kunčak, V. (eds.) CAV 2017. LNCS, vol. 10427, pp. 261–281. Springer, Cham (2017)

13. Fayaz, S.K., Sharma, T., Fogel, A., et al.: Efficient network reachability analysis using a succinct control plane representation. In: OSDI (2016)
14. Fayaz, S.K., Yu, T., Tobioka, Y., et al.: BUZZ: testing context-dependent policies in stateful networks. In: NSDI (2016)
15. Feamster, N., Rexford, J., Shenker, S., et al.: SDX: A Software-defined Internet Exchange. Open Networking Summit (2013)
16. Feamster, N., Rexford, J., Zegura, E.: The road to SDN. SIGCOMM Comput. Commun. Rev. (2014)
17. Fischer, M.J., Ladner, R.E.: Propositional dynamic logic of regular programs. J. Comput. Syst. Sci. **18**, 194–211 (1979)
18. Fogel, A., Fung, S., Angeles, L., et al.: A general approach to network configuration analysis. In: NSDI (2015)
19. Handigol, N., Seetharaman, S., Flajslik, M., et al.: Plug-n-Serve: load-balancing web traffic using OpenFlow. In: SIGCOMM (2009)
20. Havelund, K., Pressburger, T.: Model checking JAVA programs using JAVA PathFinder. STTT **2**, 366–381 (2000)
21. Holzmann, G.J.: The model checker SPIN. IEEE Trans. Softw. Eng. **23**, 279–295 (1997)
22. Holzmann, G.J., Peled, D.: An improvement in formal verification. In: Hogrefe D., Leue S. (eds) Formal Description Techniques VII. IAICT, pp. 197–211. Springer, Boston, MA (1995)
23. Horn, A., Kheradmand, A., Prasad, M.R.: Delta-net: real-time network verification using atoms. In: NSDI (2017)
24. Hu, H., Ahn, G.J., Han, W., et al.: Towards a reliable SDN firewall. In: ONS (2014)
25. Jackson, D.: Alloy: a lightweight object modelling notation. ACM Trans. Softw. Eng. Methodol. **11**, 256–290 (2002)
26. Jafarian, J.H., Al-Shaer, E., Duan, Q.: OpenFlow random host mutation: transparent moving target defense using software defined networking. In: HotSDN (2012)
27. Jain, S., Zhu, M., Zolla, J., et al.: B4: experience with a globally-deployed software defined WAN. In: SIGCOMM (2013)
28. Jia, Y.: NetSMC: a symbolic model checker for stateful network verification. In: NSDI (2020)
29. Kazemian, P., Chang, M., Zeng, H., et al.: Real time network policy checking using header space analysis. In: NSDI (2013)
30. Kazemian, P., Varghese, G., McKeown, N.: Header space analysis: static checking for networks. In: NSDI (2012)
31. Khurshid, A., Zou, X., Zhou, W., et al.: VeriFlow: verifying network-wide invariants in real time. In: NSDI (2013)
32. Klimis, V., Parisis, G., Reus, B.: Towards model checking real-world software-defined networks (version with appendix). preprint arXiv:2004.11988 (2020)
33. Li, Y., Yin, X., Wang, Z., et al.: A survey on network verification and testing with formal methods: approaches and challenges. IEEE Surv. Tutorials **21**, 940–969 (2019)
34. Mai, H., Khurshid, A., Agarwal, R., et al.: Debugging the data plane with anteater. In: SIGCOMM (2011)
35. Majumdar, R., Deep Tetali, S., Wang, Z.: Kuai: a model checker for software-defined networks. In: FMCAD (2014)
36. McClurg, J., Hojjat, H., Černý, P., et al.: Efficient synthesis of network updates. In: PLDI (2015)
37. McKeown, N., Anderson, T., Balakrishnan, H., et al.: OpenFlow: enabling innovation in campus networks. SIGCOMM Comput. Commun. Rev. **38**, 69–74 (2008)

38. Patel, P., Bansal, D., Yuan, L., et al.: Ananta: cloud scale load balancing. SIG-COMM **43**, 207–218 (2013)
39. Peled, D.: All from one, one for all: on model checking using representatives. In: Courcoubetis, C. (ed.) CAV 1993. LNCS, vol. 697, pp. 409–423. Springer, Heidelberg (1993)
40. Plotkin, G.D., Bjørner, N., Lopes, N.P., et al.: Scaling network verification using symmetry and surgery. In: POPL (2016)
41. Pnueli, A., Xu, J., Zuck, L.: Liveness with $(0,1, \infty)$- counter abstraction. In: Brinksma, E., Larsen, K.G. (eds.) CAV 2002. LNCS, vol. 2404, pp. 107–122. Springer, Heidelberg (2002)
42. Pratt, V.R.: Semantical considerations on Floyd-Hoare logic. In: FOCS (1976)
43. Sethi, D., Narayana, S., Malik, S.: Abstractions for model checking SDN controllers. In: FMCAD (2013)
44. Shenker, S., Casado, M., Koponen, T., et al.: The future of networking, and the past of protocols. In: ONS (2011). https://tinyurl.com/yxnuxobt
45. Son, S., Shin, S., Yegneswaran, V., et al.: Model checking invariant security properties in OpenFlow. In: IEEE (2013)
46. Stoenescu, R., Popovici, M., Negreanu, L., et al.: SymNet: scalable symbolic execution for modern networks. In: SIGCOMM (2016)
47. Varghese, G.: Vision for network design automation and network verification. In: NetPL (Talk) (2018). https://tinyurl.com/y2cnhvhf
48. Yang, H., Lam, S.S.: Real-time verification of network properties using atomic predicates. IEEE/ACM Trans. Network. **24**, 887–900 (2016)
49. Zeng, H., Kazemian, P., Varghese, G., et al.: A survey on network troubleshooting. Technical report TR12-HPNG-061012, Stanford University (2012)
50. Zeng, H., Zhang, S., Ye, F., et al.: Libra: divide and conquer to verify forwarding tables in huge networks. In: NSDI (2014)
51. Zhang, S., Malik, S.: SAT based verification of network data planes. In: Van Hung, D., Ogawa, M. (eds.) ATVA 2013. LNCS, vol. 8172, pp. 496–505. Springer, Cham (2013)

Software Verification

Code2Inv: A Deep Learning Framework for Program Verification

Xujie Si[1]($\boxtimes$), Aaditya Naik[1], Hanjun Dai[2], Mayur Naik[1], and Le Song[3]

[1] University of Pennsylvania, Philadelphia, USA
xsi@cis.upenn.edu
[2] Google Brain, Mountain View, USA
[3] Georgia Institute of Technology, Atlanta, USA

Abstract. We propose a general end-to-end deep learning framework Code2Inv, which takes a verification task and a proof checker as input, and automatically learns a valid proof for the verification task by interacting with the given checker. Code2Inv is parameterized with an embedding module and a grammar: the former encodes the verification task into numeric vectors while the latter describes the format of solutions Code2Inv should produce. We demonstrate the flexibility of Code2Inv by means of two small-scale yet expressive instances: a loop invariant synthesizer for C programs, and a Constrained Horn Clause (CHC) solver.

1 Introduction

A central challenge in automating program verification lies in effective proof search. Counterexample-guided Inductive Synthesis (CEGIS) [3,4,17,31,32] has emerged as a promising paradigm for solving this problem. In this paradigm, a *generator* proposes a candidate solution, and a *checker* determines whether the solution is correct or not; in the latter case, the checker provides a counterexample to the generator, and the process repeats.

Finding loop invariants is arguably the most crucial part of proof search in program verification. Recent works [2,9,10,26,29,38] have instantiated the CEGIS paradigm for synthesizing loop invariants. Since *checking* loop invariants is a relatively standard process, these works target *generating* loop invariants using various approaches, such as stochastic sampling [29], syntax-guided enumeration [2,26], and decision trees with templates [9,10] or linear classifiers [38]. Despite having greatly advanced the state-of-the-art in program verification, however, there remains significant room for improvement in practice.

We set out to build a CEGIS-based program verification framework and identified five key objectives that it must address to be useful:

- The proof search should automatically evolve according to a given verification task as opposed to using exhaustive enumeration or a fixed set of search heuristics common in existing approaches.

X. Si, A. Naik—Both authors contributed equally to the paper.

© The Author(s) 2020
S. K. Lahiri and C. Wang (Eds.): CAV 2020, LNCS 12225, pp. 151–164, 2020.
https://doi.org/10.1007/978-3-030-53291-8_9

- The framework should be able to transfer knowledge across programs, that is, past runs should boost performance on similar programs in the future, which is especially relevant for CI/CD settings [15, 20, 25].
- The framework should be able to adapt to generate different kinds of invariants (e.g. non-linear or with quantifiers) beyond linear invariants predominantly targeted by existing approaches.
- The framework should be extensible to a new domain (e.g. constraint solving-based) by simply switching the underlying checker.
- The generated invariants should be natural, e.g. avoid overfitting due to human-induced biases in the proof search heuristic or invariant structure commonly imposed through templates.

We present Code2Inv, an end-to-end deep learning framework which aims to realize the above objectives. Code2Inv has two key differences compared to existing CEGIS-based approaches. First, instead of simply focusing on counterexamples but ignoring program structure, Code2Inv learns a neural representation of program structure by leveraging graph neural networks [8, 11, 19, 28], which enable to capture structural information and thereby generalize to different but structurally similar programs. Secondly, Code2Inv reduces loop invariant generation into a deep reinforcement learning problem [22, 34]. No search heuristics or training labels are needed from human experts; instead, a neural policy for loop invariant generation can be automatically learned by interacting with the given proof checker on the fly. The learnable neural policy generates a loop invariant by taking a sequence of actions, which can be flexibly controlled by a grammar that defines the structure of loop invariants. This decoupling of the action definition from policy learning enables Code2Inv to adapt to different loop invariants or other reasoning tasks in a new domain with almost no changes except for adjusting the grammar or the underlying checker.

We summarize our contributions as follows:

- We present a framework for program verification, Code2Inv, which leverages deep learning and reinforcement learning through the use of graph neural network, tree-structured long short-term memory network, attention mechanism, and policy gradient.
- We show two small-scale yet expressive instances of Code2Inv: a loop invariant synthesizer for C programs and a Constrained Horn Clause (CHC) solver.
- We evaluate Code2Inv on a suite of 133 C programs from SyGuS [2] by comparing its performance with three state-of-the-art approaches and showing that the learned neural policy can be transferred to similar programs.
- We perform two case studies showing the flexibility of Code2Inv on different classes of loop invariants. We also perform a case study on the naturalness of the loop invariants generated by various approaches.

2   Background

In this section, we introduce artificial neural network concepts used by Code2Inv. A multilayer perceptron (MLP) is a basic neural network model which can approximate an arbitrary continuous function $\mathbf{y} = f^*(\mathbf{x})$, where $\mathbf{x}$ and $\mathbf{y}$ are numeric vectors. An MLP defines a mapping $\mathbf{y} = f(\mathbf{x}; \theta)$, where θ denotes weights of connections, which are usually trained using gradient descent methods.

Recurrent neural networks (RNNs) approximate the mapping from a sequence of inputs $\mathbf{x}^{(1)}, ..., \mathbf{x}^{(t)}$ to either a single output $\mathbf{y}$ or a sequence of outputs $\mathbf{y}^{(1)}, ..., \mathbf{y}^{(t)}$. An RNN defines a mapping $\mathbf{h}^{(t)} = f(\mathbf{h}^{(t-1)}, \mathbf{x}^{(t)}; \theta)$, where $\mathbf{h}^{(t)}$ is the hidden state, from which the final output $\mathbf{y}^{(t)}$ can be computed (e.g. by a non-linear transformation or an MLP). A common RNN model is the long short-term memory network (LSTM) [16] which is used to learn long-term dependencies. Two common variants of LSTM are gated recurrent units (GRUs) [7] and tree-structured LSTM (Tree-LSTM) [35]. The former simplifies the LSTM for efficiency while the latter extends the modeling ability to tree structures.

In many domains, graphs are used to represent data with rich structure, such as programs, molecules, social networks, and knowledge bases. Graph neural networks (GNNs) [1,8,11,19,36] are commonly used to learn over graph-structured data. A GNN learns an embedding (i.e. real-valued vector) for each node of the given graph using a recursive neighborhood aggregation (or neural message passing) procedure. After training, a node embedding captures the structural information within the node's K-hop neighborhood, where K is a hyper-parameter. A simple aggregation of all node embeddings or pooling [37] according to the graph structure summarizes the entire graph into an embedding. GNNs are parametrized with other models such as MLPs, which are the learnable non-linear transformations used in message passing, and GRUs, which are used to update the node embedding.

Lastly, the generalization ability of neural networks can be improved by an external memory [12,13,33] which can be accessed using a differentiable *attention mechanism* [5]. Given a set of neural embeddings, which form the external memory, an attention mechanism assigns a likelihood to each embedding, under a given neural context. These likelihoods guide the selection of decisions that are represented by the chosen embeddings.

3   Framework

We first describe the general framework, Code2Inv, and then illustrate two instances, namely, a loop invariant synthesizer for C programs and a CHC solver.

Figure 1 defines the domains of program structures and neural structures used in Code2Inv. The framework is parameterized by graph constructors $\mathcal{G}$ that produce graph representations of verification instance T and invariant grammar A, denoted G_{inst} and G_{inv}, respectively. The invariant grammar uses placeholder symbols H, which represent *abstract* values of entities such as variables, constants, and operators, and will be replaced by *concrete* values from the verification instance during invariant generation. The framework requires a black-box function *check* that takes a verification instance T and a candidate invariant *inv*, and returns success (denoted $\perp$) or a counterexample *cex*.

Domains of Program Structures:

$$\mathcal{G}(T) = G_{\text{inst}} \qquad (G_{\text{inst}} \text{ is graph representation of } \textit{verification instance } T)$$
$$\mathcal{G}(A) = G_{\text{inv}} \qquad (G_{\text{inv}} \text{ is graph representation of } \textit{invariant grammar } A)$$

$$A = \langle \Sigma \uplus H, N, P, S \rangle \qquad \text{(invariant grammar)}$$
$$x \in H \uplus N \qquad \text{(set of placeholder symbols and non-terminals)}$$
$$v \in \Sigma \qquad \text{(set of terminals)}$$
$$n \in N \qquad \text{(set of non-terminals)}$$
$$p \in P \qquad \text{(production rule)}$$
$$S \qquad \text{(start symbol)}$$
$$inv \in \mathcal{L}(A) \qquad \text{(invariant candidate)}$$
$$cex \in \mathbb{C} \qquad \text{(counterexample)}$$
$$C \in \mathcal{P}(\mathbb{C}) \qquad \text{(set of counterexamples)}$$
$$check(T, inv) \in \{\bot\} \uplus \mathbb{C} \qquad \text{(invariant validation)}$$

Domains of Neural Structures:

$$\pi = \langle \nu_T, \nu_A, \eta_T, \eta_A, \alpha_{\text{ctx}}, \epsilon_{\text{inv}} \rangle \quad \text{(neural policy)}$$
$$d \qquad \text{(positive integer size of embedding)}$$
$$\nu_T, \eta_T(G_{\text{inst}}) \in \mathbb{R}^{|G_{\text{inst}}| \times d} \quad \text{(graph embedding of verification instance)}$$
$$\nu_A, \eta_A(G_{\text{inv}}) \in \mathbb{R}^{|G_{\text{inv}}| \times d} \quad \text{(graph embedding of invariant grammar)}$$
$$ctx \in \mathbb{R}^d \quad \text{(neural context)}$$
$$state \in \mathbb{R}^d \quad \text{(partially generated invariant state)}$$
$$\alpha_{\text{ctx}} \in \mathbb{R}^d \times \mathbb{R}^d \to \mathbb{R}^d \quad \text{(attention context)}$$
$$\epsilon_{\text{inv}} \in \mathcal{L}(A) \to \mathbb{R}^d \quad \text{(invariant encoder)}$$
$$aggregate \in \mathbb{R}^{k \times d} \to \mathbb{R}^d \quad \text{(aggregation of embeddings)}$$
$$\nu_A[n] \in \mathbb{R}^{k \times d} \quad \text{(embedding of production rules for non-terminal } n,$$
$$\text{where k is number of production rules of } n \text{ in } G_{\text{inv}})$$
$$\nu_T[h] \in \mathbb{R}^{k \times d} \quad \text{(embedding of nodes annotated by placeholder } h,$$
$$\text{where k is number of nodes annotated by } h \text{ in } G_{\text{inst}})$$

Fig. 1. Semantic domains. $\mathcal{L}(A)$ denotes the set of all sentential forms of A.

The key component of the framework is a neural policy π which comprises four neural networks. Two graph neural networks, η_T and η_A, are used to compute neural embeddings, ν_T and ν_A, for graph representations G_{inst} and G_{inv}, respectively. The neural network α_{ctx}, implemented as a GRU, maintains the attention context ctx which controls the selection of the production rule to apply or the concrete value to replace a placeholder symbol at each step of invariant generation. The neural network ϵ_{inv}, implemented as a Tree-LSTM, encodes the partially generated invariant into a numeric vector denoted $state$, which captures the state of the generation that is used to update the attention context ctx.

Algorithm 1 depicts the main algorithm underlying Code2Inv. It takes a verification instance and a proof checker as input and produces an invariant that suffices to verify the given instance[1]. At a high level, Code2Inv learns a neural policy, in lines 1–5. The algorithm first initializes the neural policy and the set of counterexamples (line 1–2). The algorithm then iteratively samples a candidate invariant (line 4) and improves the policy using a reward for the new

---

[1] Fuzzers may be applied first so that the confidence of existence of a proof is high.

Algorithm 1. Code2Inv Framework

Input: a verification instance T and a proof checker *check*
Output: a invariant *inv* satisfying $check(T, inv) = \bot$
Parameter: graph constructor $\mathcal{G}$ and invariant grammar A

1 $\pi \leftarrow$ initPolicy(T, A)
2 $C \leftarrow \emptyset$
3 **while** *true* **do**
4      $inv \leftarrow$ sample(π, T, A)
5      $\langle \pi, C \rangle \leftarrow$ improve(π, inv, C)

6 **Function** initPolicy(T, A)
7   Initialize weights of $\eta_T, \eta_A, \alpha_{ctx}, \epsilon_{inv}$ with random values
8      $\nu_T \leftarrow \eta_T(\mathcal{G}(T))$
9      $\nu_A \leftarrow \eta_A(\mathcal{G}(A))$
10   **return** $\langle \nu_T, \nu_A, \eta_T, \eta_A, \alpha_{ctx}, \epsilon_{inv} \rangle$

11 **Function** sample(π, T, A)
12    $inv \leftarrow A.S$
13    $ctx \leftarrow aggregate(\pi.\nu_T)$
14   **while** *inv* is partially derived **do**
15      $x \leftarrow$ leftmost non-terminal or placeholder symbol in *inv*
16      $state \leftarrow \pi.\epsilon_{inv}(inv)$
17      $ctx \leftarrow \pi.\alpha_{ctx}(ctx, state)$
18   **if** x is non-terminal **then**
19          $p \leftarrow$ attention$(ctx, \pi.\nu_A[x], \mathcal{G}(A))$
20   expand *inv* according to p
21   **else**
22          $v \leftarrow$ attention$(ctx, \pi.\nu_T[x], \mathcal{G}(T))$
23   replace x in *inv* with v

24   **return** *inv*

25 **Function** improve(π, inv, C)
26    $n \leftarrow$ number of counter-examples C that *inv* can satisfy
27   **if** $n = |C|$ **then**
28      $cex \leftarrow check(T, inv)$
29   **if** $cex = \bot$ **then**
30   save *inv* and weights of π
31   **exit**   `// a sufficient invariant is found`
32   **else**
33          $C \leftarrow C \cup \{cex\}$

34    $r \leftarrow n/|C|$
35    $\pi \leftarrow$ updatePolicy(π, r)
36   **return** $\langle \pi, C \rangle$

37 **Function** updatePolicy(π, r)
38   Update weights of $\pi.\eta_T, \pi.\eta_A, \pi.\alpha_{ctx}, \pi.\epsilon_{inv}, \pi.\nu_T, \pi.\nu_A$ by
39   standard policy gradient [34] using reward r

40 **Function** attention(ctx, ν, G)
41   Return node t in G such that dot product of ctx and $\nu[t]$
42   is maximum over all nodes of G

---

candidate based on the accumulated counterexamples (line 5). We next elucidate upon the initialization, policy sampling, and policy improvement procedures.

Initialization. The `initPolicy` procedure (line 6–10) initializes the neural policy. All four neural networks are initialized with random weights (line 7), and graph embeddings ν_T, ν_A for verification task T and invariant grammar A are computed by applying corresponding graph neural networks η_T, η_A to their graph representations $\mathcal{G}(T), \mathcal{G}(A)$ respectively. Alternatively, the neural networks can be initialized with pre-trained weights, which can boost overall performance.

Neural Policy Sampling. The `sample` procedure (lines 11–24) generates a candidate invariant by executing the current neural policy. The candidate is first initialized to the start symbol of the given grammar (line 12), and then updated iteratively (lines 14–23) until it is complete (i.e. there are no non-terminals). Specifically, the candidate is updated by either expanding its leftmost non-terminal according to one of its production rules (lines 19–20) or by replacing its leftmost placeholder symbol with some concrete value from the verification instance (lines 22–23). The selection of a production rule or concrete value is done through an *attention mechanism*, which picks the most likely one according to the current context and corresponding region of external memory. The neural context is initialized to the aggregation of embeddings of the given verification instance (line 13), and then maintained by α_{ctx} (line 17) which, at each step, incorporates the neural state of the partially generated candidate invariant (line 16), where the neural state is encoded by ϵ_{inv}.

Neural Policy Improvement. The `improve` procedure (lines 25–36) improves the current policy by means of a *continuous* reward. Simply checking whether the current candidate invariant is sufficient or not yields a discrete reward of 1 (yes) or 0 (no). This reward is too sparse to improve the policy, since most candidate invariants generated are insufficient, thereby almost always yielding a zero reward. Code2Inv addresses this problem by accumulating counterexamples provided by the checker. Whenever a new candidate invariant is generated, Code2Inv tests the number of counterexamples it can satisfy (line 26), and uses the fraction of satisfied counterexamples as the reward (line 34). If all counterexamples are satisfied, Code2Inv queries the checker to validate the candidate (line 28). If the candidate is accepted by the checker, then a sufficient invariant was found, and the learned weights of the neural networks are saved for speeding up similar verification instances in the future (lines 29–31). Otherwise, a new counterexample is accumulated (line 33). Finally, the neural policy (including the neural embeddings) is updated based on the reward.

Framework Instantiations. We next show two instantiations of Code2Inv by customizing the graph constructor $\mathcal{G}$. Specifically, we demonstrate two scenarios of graph construction: 1) by carefully exploiting task specific knowledge, and 2) with minimum information of the given task.

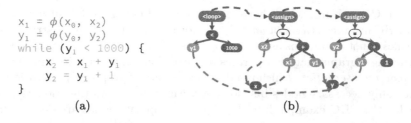

$$x_1 = \phi(x_0, x_2)$$
$$y_1 = \phi(y_0, y_2)$$
while $(y_1 < 1000)$ {
$$\quad x_2 = x_1 + y_1$$
$$\quad y_2 = y_1 + 1$$
}

(a)   (b)

Fig. 2. (a) C program snippet in SSA form; (b) its graph representation.

Instantiation to Synthesize Loop Invariants for C Programs. An effective graph representation for a C program should reflect its control-flow and data-flow information. We leverage the static single assignment (SSA) transformation for this purpose. Figure 2 illustrates the graph construction process. Given a C program, we first apply SSA transformation as shown in Fig. 2a, from which a graph is constructed as shown in Fig. 2b. The graph is essentially abstract syntax trees (ASTs) augmented with control-flow (black dashed) edges and data-flow (blue dashed) edges. Different types of edges will be modeled as different message passing channels used in graph neural networks so that rich structural information can be captured more effectively by the neural embeddings. Furthermore, certain nodes (marked black) are annotated with placeholder symbols and will be used to fill corresponding placeholders during invariant generation. For instance, variables x and y are annotated with VAR, integer values 1000 and 1 are annotated with CONST, and the operator < is annotated with OP.

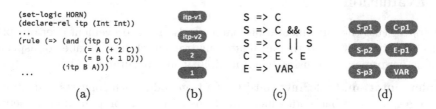

(a)   (b)   (c)   (d)

Fig. 3. (a) CHC instance snippet; (b) node representation for the CHC example; (c) example of invariant grammar; (d) node representation for the grammar.

Instantiation to Solve Constrained Horn Clauses (CHC). CHC are a uniform way to represent recursive, inter-procedural, and multi-threaded programs, and serve as a suitable basis for automatic program verification [6] and refinement type inference [21]. Solving a CHC instance involves determining unknown predicates that satisfy a set of logical constraints. Figure 3a shows a simple example of a CHC instance where *itp* is the unknown predicate. It is easy to see that *itp* in fact represents an invariant of a loop. Thus, CHC solving can be viewed as a generalization of finding loop invariants [6].

Unlike C programs, which have explicit control-flow and data-flow information, a CHC instance is a set of *un-ordered* Horn rules. The graph construction for Horn rules is not as obvious as for C programs. Therefore, instead of deliberately constructing a graph that incorporates detailed domain-specific information, we use a *node representation*, which is a degenerate case of graph representation and requires only necessary nodes but no edges. Figure 3b shows the node representation for the CHC example from Fig. 3a. The top two nodes are derived from the signature of unknown predicate *itp* and represent the first and the second arguments of *itp*. The bottom two nodes are constants extracted from the Horn rule. We empirically show that node representation works reasonably well. The downside of node representation is that no structural information is captured by the neural embeddings which in turn prevents the learned neural policy from generalizing to other structurally similar instances.

Embedding Invariant Grammar. Lastly, both instantiations must define the embedding of the invariant grammar. The grammar can be arbitrarily defined, and similar to CHCs, there is no obvious information such as control- or data-flow to leverage. Thus, we use node representation for the invariant grammar as well. Figure 3c and Fig. 3d shows an example of invariant grammar and its node representation, respectively. Each node in the graph represents either a terminal or a production rule for a non-terminal. Note that this representation does not prevent the neural policy from generalizing to similar instances as long as they share the same invariant grammar. This is feasible because the invariant grammar does not contain instance specific details, which are abstracted away by placeholder symbols like VAR, CONST, and OP.

4   Evaluation

We first discuss the implementation, particularly the improvement over our previous prototype [30], and then evaluate our framework in a number of aspects, such as performance, transferability, flexibility, and naturalness.

Implementation. Code2Inv[2] consists of a frontend, which converts an instance into a graph, and a backend, which maintains all neural components (i.e. neural embeddings and policy) and interacts with a checker. Our previous prototype has a very limited frontend based on CIL [24] and no notion of invariant grammar in the backend. We made significant improvements in both the frontend and the backend. We re-implemented the frontend for C programs based on Clang and implemented a new frontend for CHCs. We also re-implemented the backend to accept a configurable invariant grammar. Furthermore, we developed a standard graph format, which decouples the frontend and backend, and a clean interface between the backend and the checker. No changes are needed in the backend to support new instantiations.

Evaluation Setup. We evaluate both instantiations of Code2Inv by comparing each instantiation with corresponding state-of-the-art solvers. For the task of

---

[2] Our artifacts are available on GitHub: https://github.com/PL-ML/code2inv.

synthesizing loop invariants for C programs, we use the same suite of benchmarks from our previous work [30], which consists of 133 C programs from SyGuS [2]. We compare Code2Inv with our previous specialized prototype and three other state-of-the-art verification tools: C2I [29], LoopInvGen [26] and ICE-DT [10]. For the CHC solving task, we collect 120 CHC instances using SeaHorn [14] to reduce the C benchmark programs into CHCs.[3] We compare Code2Inv with two state-of-the-art CHC solvers: Spacer [18], which is the default fixedpoint engine of Z3, and LinearyArbitrary [38]. We run all solvers on a single 2.4 GHz AMD CPU core up to 12 h and using up to 4 GB memory. Unless specified otherwise, Code2Inv is always initialized randomly, that is, untrained.

Performance. Given that both the hardware and the software environments could affect the absolute running time and that all solvers for loop invariant generation for C programs rely on the same underlying SMT engine, Z3 [23], we compare the performance in terms of number of Z3 queries. We note that this is an imperfect metric but a relatively objective one that also highlights salient features of Code2Inv. Figure 4a shows the plot of verification cost (i.e. number of Z3 queries) by each solver and the number of C programs success-fully verified within the corresponding cost. Code2Inv significantly outperforms other state-of-the-art solvers in terms of verification cost and the general frame-work Code2Inv-G achieves performance comparable to (slightly better than) the previous specialized prototype Code2Inv-S.

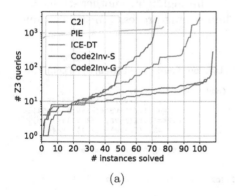

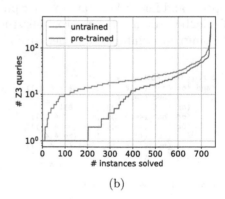

(a)   (b)

Fig. 4. (a) Comparison of Code2Inv with state-of-the-art solvers; (b) comparison between untrained model and pre-trained model.

Transferability. Another hallmark of Code2Inv is that, along with the desired loop invariant, it also learns a neural policy. To evaluate the performance ben-efits of the learned policy, we randomly perturb the C benchmark programs by various edits (e.g. renaming existing variables and injecting new variables and

---

[3] SeaHorn produces empty Horn rules on 13 (out of 133) C programs due to optimiza-tions during VC generation that result in proving the assertions of interest.

statements). For each program, we obtain 100 variants, and use 90 for training and 10 for testing. Figure 4b shows the performance difference between the untrained model (i.e. initialized with random weights) and the pre-trained model (i.e. initialized with pre-trained weights). Our results indicate that the learned neural policy can be transferred to accelerate the search for loop invariants for similar programs. This is especially useful in the CI/CD setting [25] where programs evolve incrementally and quick turnaround time is indispensable.

Flexibility. Code2Inv can be instantiated or extended in a very flexible manner. For one instance, with a simple frontend (e.g. node representation as discussed above), Code2Inv can be customized as a CHC solver. Our evaluation shows that, without any prior knowledge about Horn rules, Code2Inv can solve 94 (out of 120) CHC instances. Although it is not on a par with state-of-the-art CHC solvers Spacer and LinearArbitrary, which solve 112 and 118 instances, respectively, Code2Inv provides new insights for solving CHCs and could be further improved by better embeddings and reward design.

As another example, by simply adjusting the invariant grammar, Code2Inv is immediately ready for solving CHC tasks involving *non-linear* arithmetic. Our case study shows that Code2Inv successfully solves 5 (out of 7) non-linear instances we created[4], while both Spacer and LinearArbitrary failed to solve any of them. Tasks involving non-linear arithmetic are particularly challenging because the underlying checker is more likely to get stuck, and no feedback (e.g. counterexample) can be provided, which is critical for existing solvers like Spacer and LinearArbitrary to make progress. This highlights another strength of Code2Inv—even if the checker gets stuck, the learning process can still continue by simply assigning zero or negative reward.

```
Solution found by Spacer:                    Solution found by LinearArbitrary:
(and (or (not (<= B 16)) (not (>= A 8)))     (or
         (not (<= B 0))                         (and true !(V0<=-50)
    (or (not (<= B 2)) (<= A 0))                     V1<=5  ((1*V0)+(-1*V1))<=-45
    (or (not (<= B 4)) (not (>= A 2)))              V1<=4  !(((1*V0)+(-1*V1))<=-51)
    (or (not (<= B 6)) (not (>= A 3)))              !(V1<=2)!(((1*V0)+(-1*V1))<=-50)
    (or (not (<= B 8)) (not (>= A 4)))              !(V1<=3) ((1*V0)+(1*V1))<=-40
    (or (not (<= B 10)) (not (>= A 5)))        )
    (or (not (<= B 12)) (not (>= A 6)))        ... // omitting other 4 similar (and ...)
    (or (not (<= B 14)) (not (>= A 7)))))))))  )

Code2Inv: (<= v0 (- v1 v0))                   Code2Inv: (or (< V0 (+ 0 0)) (> V1 V0))
```

(a) Spacer on add2.smt   (b) LinearArbitrary on 84.c.smt

Fig. 5. Comparison of solution naturalness.

Naturalness. Our final case study concerns the naturalness of solutions. As illustrated in Fig. 5, solutions discovered by Code2Inv tend to be more natural, whereas Spacer and LinearArbitrary tend to find solutions that unnecessarily depend on constants from the given verification instance. Such *overfitted* solutions may become invalid when these constants change. Note that

---

[4] The non-linear instances we created are available in the artifact.

expressions such as (+ 0 0) in Code2Inv's solutions can be eliminated by post-processing simplification akin to peephole optimization in compilers. Alternatively, the reward mechanism in Code2Inv could incorporate a regularizer on the naturalness.

Limitations. Code2Inv does not support finding loop invariants for programs with multiple loops, function calls, or recursion. Code2Inv generally runs slower compared to other contemporary approaches. Specifically, 90% of the solved C instances took 2 h or less, and the rest could take up to 12 hours to solve. This could be improved upon by leveraging GPUs, developing more efficient training algorithms, or leveraging templates [27].

5 Conclusion

We presented a framework Code2Inv which automatically learns invariants (or more generally unknown predicates) by interacting with a proof checker. Code2Inv is a general and learnable tool for solving many different verification tasks and can be flexibly configured with a grammar and a graph constructor. We compared its performance with state-of-the-art solvers for both C programs and CHC formulae, and showed that it can adapt to different types of inputs with minor changes. We also showed, by simply varying the input grammar, how it can tackle non-linear invariant problems which other solvers are not equipped to work with, while still giving results that are relatively natural to read.

Acknowledgements. We thank the reviewers for insightful comments. We thank Elizabeth Dinella, Pardis Pashakhanloo, and Halley Young for feedback on improving the paper. This research was supported by grants from NSF (#1836936 and #1836822), ONR (#N00014-18-1-2021), AFRL (#FA8750-20-2-0501), and Facebook.

References

1. Allamanis, M., Brockschmidt, M., Khademi, M.: Learning to represent programs with graphs. In: Proceedings of the International Conference on Learning Representations (ICLR) (2018)
2. Alur, R., et al.: Syntax-guided synthesis. In: Proceedings of Formal Methods in Computer-Aided Design (FMCAD) (2013)
3. Alur, R., Radhakrishna, A., Udupa, A.: Scaling enumerative program synthesis via divide and conquer. In: Legay, A., Margaria, T. (eds.) TACAS 2017. LNCS, vol. 10205, pp. 319–336. Springer, Heidelberg (2017). https://doi.org/10.1007/978-3-662-54577-5_18
4. Alur, R., Singh, R., Fisman, D., Solar-Lezama, A.: Search-based program synthesis. Commun. ACM **61**(12), 84–93 (2018)
5. Bahdanau, D., Cho, K., Bengio, Y.: Neural machine translation by jointly learning to align and translate. In: Proceedings of the International Conference on Learning Representations (ICLR) (2015)

6. Bjørner, N., Gurfinkel, A., McMillan, K., Rybalchenko, A.: Horn clause solvers for program verification. In: Beklemishev, L.D., Blass, A., Dershowitz, N., Finkbeiner, B., Schulte, W. (eds.) Fields of Logic and Computation II. LNCS, vol. 9300, pp. 24–51. Springer, Cham (2015). https://doi.org/10.1007/978-3-319-23534-9_2
7. Chung, J., Gülçehre, Ç., Cho, K., Bengio, Y.: Empirical evaluation of gated recurrent neural networks on sequence modeling. CoRR abs/1412.3555 (2014)
8. Dai, H., Dai, B., Song, L.: Discriminative embeddings of latent variable models for structured data. In: Proceedings of the International Conference on Machine Learning (ICML) (2016)
9. Garg, P., Löding, C., Madhusudan, P., Neider, D.: ICE: a robust framework for learning invariants. In: Biere, A., Bloem, R. (eds.) CAV 2014. LNCS, vol. 8559, pp. 69–87. Springer, Cham (2014). https://doi.org/10.1007/978-3-319-08867-9_5
10. Garg, P., Neider, D., Madhusudan, P., Roth, D.: Learning invariants using decision trees and implication counterexamples. In: Proceedings of the ACM Symposium on Principles of Programming Languages (POPL) (2016)
11. Gilmer, J., Schoenholz, S.S., Riley, P.F., Vinyals, O., Dahl, G.E.: Neural message passing for quantum chemistry. In: Proceedings of the International Conference on Machine Learning (ICML), pp. 1263–1272 (2017)
12. Graves, A., Wayne, G., Danihelka, I.: Neural turing machines. CoRR abs/1410.5401 (2014)
13. Grefenstette, E., Hermann, K.M., Suleyman, M., Blunsom, P.: Learning to transduce with unbounded memory. In: Proceedings of the Conference on Neural Information Processing Systems (NIPS), pp. 1828–1836 (2015)
14. Gurfinkel, A., Kahsai, T., Komuravelli, A., Navas, J.A.: The SeaHorn verification framework. In: Kroening, D., Păsăreanu, C.S. (eds.) CAV 2015. LNCS, vol. 9206, pp. 343–361. Springer, Cham (2015). https://doi.org/10.1007/978-3-319-21690-4_20
15. Heo, K., Raghothaman, M., Si, X., Naik, M.: Continuously reasoning about programs using differential Bayesian inference. In: Proceedings of the ACM Conference on Programming Language Design and Implementation (PLDI) (2019)
16. Hochreiter, S., Schmidhuber, J.: Long short-term memory. Neural Comput. **9**(8), 1735–1780 (1997)
17. Jha, S., Gulwani, S., Seshia, S.A., Tiwari, A.: Oracle-guided component-based program synthesis. In: Proceedings of the 32nd ACM/IEEE International Conference on Software Engineering (2010)
18. Komuravelli, A., Gurfinkel, A., Chaki, S.: SMT-based model checking for recursive programs. Formal Methods Syst. Des. **48**(3), 175–205 (2016)
19. Li, Y., Tarlow, D., Brockschmidt, M., Zemel, R.: Gated graph sequence neural networks. arXiv preprint arXiv:1511.05493 (2015)
20. Logozzo, F., Lahiri, S.K., Fähndrich, M., Blackshear, S.: Verification modulo versions: towards usable verification. In: Proceedings of the ACM Conference on Programming Language Design and Implementation (PLDI) (2014)
21. McMillan, K.L., Rybalchenko, A.: Solving constrained horn clauses using interpolation. Technical report MSR-TR-2013-6 (2013)
22. Mnih, V., et al.: Human-level control through deep reinforcement learning. Nature **518**(7540), 529–533 (2015)
23. de Moura, L., Bjørner, N.: Z3: an efficient SMT solver. In: Ramakrishnan, C.R., Rehof, J. (eds.) TACAS 2008. LNCS, vol. 4963, pp. 337–340. Springer, Heidelberg (2008). https://doi.org/10.1007/978-3-540-78800-3_24

24. Necula, G.C., McPeak, S., Rahul, S.P., Weimer, W.: CIL: intermediate language and tools for analysis and transformation of C programs. In: Horspool, R.N. (ed.) CC 2002. LNCS, vol. 2304, pp. 213–228. Springer, Heidelberg (2002). https://doi.org/10.1007/3-540-45937-5_16

25. O'Hearn, P.: Continuous reasoning: scaling the impact of formal methods. In: Proceedings of the Annual ACM/IEEE Symposium on Logic in Computer Science (LICS) (2018)

26. Padhi, S., Sharma, R., Millstein, T.: Data-driven precondition inference with learned features. In: Proceedings of the ACM Conference on Programming Language Design and Implementation (PLDI) (2016)

27. Ryan, G., Wong, J., Yao, J., Gu, R., Jana, S.: CLN2INV: learning loop invariants with continuous logic networks. In: Proceedings of the International Conference on Learning Representations (ICLR) (2020)

28. Scarselli, F., Gori, M., Tsoi, A.C., Hagenbuchner, M., Monfardini, G.: The graph neural network model. IEEE Trans. Neural Networks **20**(1), 61–80 (2009)

29. Sharma, R., Aiken, A.: From invariant checking to invariant inference using randomized search. In: Biere, A., Bloem, R. (eds.) CAV 2014. LNCS, vol. 8559, pp. 88–105. Springer, Cham (2014). https://doi.org/10.1007/978-3-319-08867-9_6

30. Si, X., Dai, H., Raghothaman, M., Naik, M., Song, L.: Learning loop invariants for program verification. In: Proceedings of the Conference on Neural Information Processing Systems (NIPS) (2018)

31. Solar-Lezama, A., Tancau, L., Bodik, R., Saraswat, V., Seshia, S.: Combinatorial sketching for finite programs. In: Proceedings of Architectural Support for Programming Languages and Operating Systems (ASPLOS) (2006)

32. Srivastava, S., Gulwani, S., Foster, J.S.: From program verification to program synthesis. In: Proceedings of the ACM Symposium on Principles of Programming Languages (POPL) (2010)

33. Sukhbaatar, S., Weston, J., Fergus, R., et al.: End-to-end memory networks. In: Proceedings of the Conference on Neural Information Processing Systems (NIPS) (2015)

34. Sutton, R.S., Barto, A.G.: Reinforcement Learning - An Introduction. MIT Press, Adaptive computation and machine learning (1998)

35. Tai, K.S., Socher, R., Manning, C.D.: Improved semantic representations from tree-structured long short-term memory networks. In: Proceedings of the Association for Computational Linguistics (ACL) (2015)

36. Xu, K., Hu, W., Leskovec, J., Jegelka, S.: How powerful are graph neural networks? In: Proceedings of the International Conference on Learning Representations (ICLR) (2019)

37. Ying, R., et al.: Hierarchical graph representation learning with differentiable pooling. In: Proceedings of the Conference on Neural Information Processing Systems (NIPS) (2018)

38. Zhu, H., Magill, S., Jagannathan, S.: A data-driven CHC solver. In: Proceedings of the ACM Conference on Programming Language Design and Implementation (PLDI) (2018)

MetaVal: Witness Validation via Verification

Dirk Beyer and Martin Spiessl

LMU Munich, Munich, Germany

Abstract. Witness validation is an important technique to increase trust in verification results, by making descriptions of error paths (violation witnesses) and important parts of the correctness proof (correctness witnesses) available in an exchangeable format. This way, the verification result can be validated independently from the verification in a second step. The problem is that there are unfortunately not many tools available for witness-based validation of verification results. We contribute to closing this gap with the approach of *validation via verification*, which is a way to automatically construct a set of validators from a set of existing verification engines. The idea is to take as input a specification, a program, and a verification witness, and produce a new specification and a transformed version of the original program such that the transformed program satisfies the new specification if the witness is useful to confirm the result of the verification. Then, an 'off-the-shelf' verifier can be used to validate the previously computed result (as witnessed by the verification witness) via an ordinary verification task. We have implemented our approach in the validator METAVAL, and it was successfully used in SV-COMP 2020 and confirmed 3 653 violation witnesses and 16 376 correctness witnesses. The results show that METAVAL improves the effectiveness (167 uniquely confirmed violation witnesses and 833 uniquely confirmed correctness witnesses) of the overall validation process, on a large benchmark set. All components and experimental data are publicly available.

Keywords: Computer-aided verification · Software verification · Program analysis · Software model checking · Certification · Verification witnesses · Validation of verification results · Reducer

1 Introduction

Formal software verification becomes more and more important in the development process for software systems of all types. There are many verification tools available to perform verification [4]. One of the open problems that was addressed only recently is the topic of results validation [10–12,37]: The verification work is often done by untrusted verification engines, on untrusted computing infrastructure, or even on approximating computation systems, and static-analysis tools suffer from false positives that engineers in practice hate because they are tedious to refute [20]. Therefore, it is necessary to validate verification results,

This work was funded by the Deutsche Forschungsgemeinschaft (DFG) – 378803395.

S. K. Lahiri and C. Wang (Eds.): CAV 2020, LNCS 12225, pp. 165–177, 2020.
https://doi.org/10.1007/978-3-030-53291-8_10

ideally by an independent verification engine that likely does not have the same weaknesses as the original verifier. Witnesses also help serving as an interface to the verification engine, in order to overcome integration problems [1].

The idea to witness the correctness of a program by annotating it with assertions is as old as programming [38], and from the beginning of model checking it was felt necessary to witness counterexamples [21]. Certifying algorithms [30] are not only computing a solution but also produce a witness that can be used by a computationally much less expensive checker to (re-)establish the correctness of the solution. In software verification, witnesses became standardized[1] and exchangeable about five years ago [10,11]. In the meanwhile, the exchangeable witnesses can be used also for deriving tests from witnesses [12], such that an engineer can study an error report additionally with a debugger. The ultimate goal of this direction of research is to obtain witnesses that are certificates and can be checked by a fully trusted validator based on trusted theorem provers, such as Coq and Isabelle, as done already for computational models that are 'easier' than C programs [40].

Yet, although considered very useful, there are not many witness validators available. For example, the most recent competition on software verification (SV-COMP 2020)[2] showcases 28 software verifiers but only 6 witness validators. Two were published in 2015 [11], two more in 2018 [12], the fifth in 2020 [37], and the sixth is METAVAL, which we describe here. Witness validation is an interesting problem to work on, and there is a large, yet unexplored field of opportunities. It involves many different techniques from program analysis and model checking. However, it seems that this also requires a lot of engineering effort.

Our solution *validation via verification* is a construction that takes as input an off-the-shelf software verifier and a new program transformer, and composes a witness validator in the following way (see Fig. 1): First, the transformer takes the original input program and transforms it into a new program. In case of a violation witness, which describes a path through the program to a specific program location, we transform the program such that all parts that are marked as unnecessary for the path by the witness are pruned. This is similar to the reducer for a condition in reducer-based conditional model checking [14]. In case of a correctness witness, which describes invariants that can be used in a correctness proof, we transform the program such that the invariants are asserted (to check that they really hold) and assumed (to use them in a re-constructed correctness proof). A standard verification engine is then asked to verify that (1) the transformed program contains a feasible path that violates the original specification (violation witness) or (2) the transformed program satisfies the original specification and all assertions added to the program hold (correctness witness).

METAVAL is an implementation of this concept. It performs the transformation according to the witness type and specification, and can be configured to use any of the available software verifiers[3] as verification backend.

---

[1] Latest version of standardized witness format: https://github.com/sosy-lab/sv-witnesses

[2] https://sv-comp.sosy-lab.org/2020/systems.php

[3] https://gitlab.com/sosy-lab/sv-comp/archives-2020/tree/master/2020

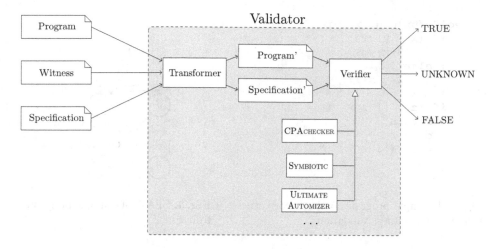

Fig. 1. Validator construction using readily available verifiers

Contributions. METAVAL contributes several important benefits:

- The program transformer was a one-time effort and is available from now on.
- Any existing standard verifier can be used as verification backend.
- Once a new verification technology becomes available in a verification tool, it can immediately be turned into a validator using our new construction.
- Technology bias can be avoided by complementing the verifier by a validator that is based on a different technology.
- Selecting the strongest verifiers (e.g., by looking at competition results) can lead to strong validators.
- All data and software that we describe are publicly available (see Sect. 6).

2 Preliminaries

For the theoretical part, we will have to set a common ground for the concepts of verification witnesses [10, 11] as well as reducers [14]. In both cases, programs are represented as control-flow automata (CFAs). A *control-flow automaton* $C = (L, l_0, G)$ consists of a set L of control locations, an initial location $l_0 \in L$, and a set $G \subseteq L \times Ops \times L$ of control-flow edges that are labeled with the operations in the program. In the mentioned literature on witnesses and reducers, a simple programming language is used in which operations are either assignments or assumptions over integer variables. Operations $op \in Ops$ in such a language can be represented by formulas in first order logic over the sets V, V' of program variables before and after the transition, which we denote by $op(V, V')$. In order to simplify our construction later on, we will also allow mixed operations of the form $f(V) \wedge (x' = g(V))$ that combine assumptions with an assignment, which would otherwise be represented as an assumption followed by an assignment operation.

```
1    void fun(uint x, uint y, uint z) {
2      if (x > y) {
3        z = 2*x-y;
4      } else {
5        z = 2*y-x+1;
6      }
7      if (z>y || z>x) {
8        return;
9      } else {
10       error();
11     }
12   }
```

Fig. 2. Example program for both correctness and violation witness validation

Fig. 3. CFA C of example program from Fig. 2

The conversion from the source code into a CFA and vice versa is straight forward, provided that the CFA is deterministic. A CFA is called *deterministic* if in case there are multiple outgoing CFA edges from a location l, the assumptions in those edges are mutually exclusive (but not necessarily exhaustive).

Since our goal is to validate (i.e., prove or falsify) the statement that a program fulfills a certain specification, we need to additionally model the property to be verified. For properties that can be translated into non-reachability, this can be done by defining a set $T \subseteq L$ of target locations that shall not be reached. For the example program in Fig. 2 we want to verify that the call in line 10 is not reachable. In the corresponding CFA in Fig. 3 this is represented by the reachability of the location labeled with 10. Depending on whether or not a verifier accounts for the overflow in this example program, it will either consider the program safe or unsafe, which makes it a perfect example that can be used to illustrate both correctness and violation witnesses.

In order to reason about the soundness of our approach, we need to also formalize the program semantics. This is done using the concept of concrete data states. A *concrete data state* is a mapping from the set V of program variables to their domain $\mathbb{Z}$, and a *concrete state* is a pair of control location and concrete data state. A *concrete program path* is then defined as a sequence $\pi = (c_0, l_0) \xrightarrow{g_1} \ldots \xrightarrow{g_n} (c_n, l_n)$ where c_0 is the initial concrete data state, $g_i = (l_{i-1}, op_i, l_i) \in G$, and $c_{i-1}(V), c_i(V') \vDash op_i$. A *concrete execution* $ex(\pi)$ is then derived from a path π by only looking at the sequence $(c_0, l_0) \ldots (c_n, l_n)$ of concrete states from the path. Note the we deviate here from the definition given in [14], where concrete executions do not contain information about the program locations. This is necessary here since we want to reason about the concrete executions that fulfill a given non-reachability specification, i.e., that never reach certain locations in the original program.

Witnesses are formalized using the concept of protocol automata [11]. A *protocol automaton* $W = (Q, \Sigma, \delta, q_0, F)$ consists of a set Q of states, a set of transition labels $\Sigma = 2^G \times \Phi$, a transition relation $\delta \subseteq Q \times \Sigma \times Q$, an initial state q_0, and a set $F \subseteq Q$ of final states. A state is a pair that consists of a name to identify the state and a predicate over the program variables V to represent the state invariant.[4] A transition label is a pair that consists of a subset of control-flow edges and a predicate over the program variables V to represent the guard condition for the transition to be taken. An *observer automaton* [11,13,32,34,36] is a protocol automaton that does not restrict the state space, i.e., if for each state $q \in Q$ the disjunction of the guard conditions of all outgoing transitions is a tautology. Violation witnesses are represented by protocol automata in which all state invariants are *true*. Correctness witnesses are represented by observer automata in which the set of final states is empty.

3   Approach

3.1   From Witnesses to Programs

When given a CFA $C = (L, l_0, G)$, a specification $T \subseteq L$, and a witness automaton $W = (Q, \Sigma, \delta, q_0, F)$, we can construct a product automaton $A_{C \times W} = (L \times Q, (l_0, q_0), \Gamma, T \times F)$ where $\Gamma \subseteq (L \times Q) \times (Ops \times \Phi) \times (L \times Q)$. The new transition relation Γ is defined by allowing for each transition g in the CFA only those transitions (S, φ) from the witness where $g \in S$ holds:

$$\Gamma = \left\{ ((l_i, q_i), (op, \varphi), (l_j, q_j)) \mid \exists S : (q_i, (S, \varphi), q_j) \in \delta, (l_i, op, l_j) \in S \right\}$$

We can now define the semantics of a witness by looking at the paths in the product automaton and mapping them to concrete executions in the original program. A path of the product automaton $A_{C,W}$ is a sequence $(l_0, q_0) \xrightarrow{\alpha_0} \ldots \xrightarrow{\alpha_{n-1}} (l_n, q_n)$ such that $((l_i, q_i), \alpha_i, (l_{i+1}, q_{i+1})) \in \Gamma$ and $\alpha_i = (op_i, \phi_i)$.

It is evident that the automaton $A_{C \times W}$ can easily be mapped to a new program $C_{C \times W}$ by reducing the pair (op, φ) in its transition relation to an operation $\overline{op}$. In case op is a pure assumption of the form $f(V)$ then $\overline{op}$ will simply be $f(V) \land \varphi(V)$. If op is an assignment of the form $f(V) \land (x' = g(V))$, then $\overline{op}$ will be $(f(V) \land \varphi(V)) \land (x' = g(V))$. This construction has the drawback that the resulting CFA might be non-deterministic, but this is actually not a problem when the corresponding program is only used for verification. The non-determinism can be expressed in the source code by using non-deterministic values, which are already formalized by the community and established in the SV-COMP rules, and therefore also supported by all participating verifiers. The concrete executions of $C_{C \times W}$ can be identified with concrete executions of C by projecting their pairs (l, q) on their first element. Let $proj_C(ex(C_{C \times W}))$ denote the set of concrete executions that is derived this way. Due to how the relation Γ of $A_{C \times W}$ is constructed, it is guaranteed that this is a subset of the executions of C, i.e., $proj_C(ex(C_{C \times W})) \subseteq ex(C)$. In this respect the witness acts in very much the same way as a reducer [14], and the reduction of the search space is also one of the desired properties of a validator for violation witnesses.

---

[4] These invariants are the central piece of information in correctness witnesses. While invariants that proof a program correct can be hard to come up with, they are usually easier to check.

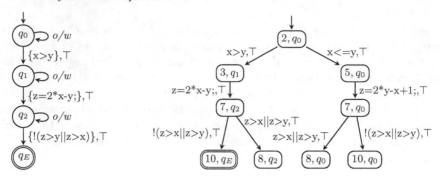

Fig. 4. Violation witness W_V **Fig. 5.** Product automaton $A_{C \times W_V}$

3.2 Programs from Violation Witnesses

For explaining the validation of results based on a violation witness, we consider the witness in Fig. 4 for our example C program in Fig. 2. The program $C_{C \times W_V}$ resulting from product automaton $A_{C \times W_V}$ in Fig. 5 can be passed to a verifier. If this verification finds an execution that reaches a specification violation, then this violation is guaranteed to be also present in the original program. There is however one caveat: In the example in Fig. 5, a reachable state $(10, q_0)$ at program location 10 (i.e., a state that violates the specification) can be found that is not marked as accepting state in the witness automaton W_V. For a strict version of witness validation, we can remove all states that are in $T \times Q$ but not in $T \times F$ from the product automaton, and thus, from the generated program. This will ensure that if the verifier finds a violation in the generated program, the witness automaton also accepts the found error path. The version of METAVAL that was used in SV-COMP 2020 did not yet support strict witness validation.

3.3 Programs from Correctness Witnesses

Correctness witnesses are represented by observer automata. Figure 6 shows a potential correctness witness W_C for our example program C in Fig. 2, where the invariants are annotated in bold font next to the corresponding state. The construction of the product automaton $A_{C \times W_C}$ in Fig. 7 is a first step towards reestablishing the proof of correctness: the product states tell us to which control locations of the CFA for the program the invariants from the witness belong.

The idea of a result validator for correctness witnesses is to

1. check the invariants in the witness and
2. use the invariants to establish that the original specification holds.

We can achieve the second goal by extracting the invariants from each state in the product automaton $A_{C \times W_C}$ and adding them as conditions to all edges by which the state can be reached. This will then be semantically equivalent to assuming that the invariants hold at the state and potentially make the consecutive proof easier. For soundness we need to also ensure the first goal. To achieve that, we add transitions into a (new) accepting state from $T \times F$ whenever we transition

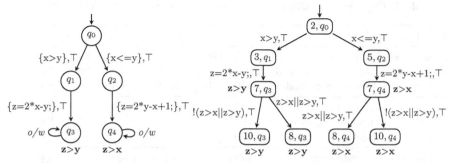

Fig. 6. Correctness witness W_C **Fig. 7.** Product automaton $A_{C \times W_C}$

into a state q and the invariant of q does not hold, and we add self-loops such that the automaton stays in the new accepting state forever. In sum, for each invariant, there are two transitions, one with the invariant as guard (to assume that the invariant holds) and one with the negation of the invariant as guard (to assert that the invariant holds, going to an accepting (error) state if it does not hold). This transformation ensures that the resulting automaton after the transformation is still a proper observer automaton.

4 Evaluation

This section describes the results that were obtained in the 9th Competition on Software Verification (SV-COMP 2020), in which METAVAL participated as validator. We did not perform a separate evaluation because the results of SV-COMP are complete, accurate, and reproducible; all data and tools are publicly available for inspection and replication studies (see data availability in Sect. 6).

4.1 Experimental Setup

Execution Environment. In SV-COMP 2020, the validators were executed in a benchmark environment that makes use of a cluster with 168 machines, each of them having an Intel Xeon E3-1230 v5 CPU with 8 processing units, 33 GB of RAM, and the GNU/Linux operating system Ubuntu 18.04. Each validation run was limited to 2 processing units and 7 GB of RAM, in order to allow up to 4 validation runs to be executed on the same machine at the same time. The time limit for a validation run was set to 15 min for correctness witnesses and to 90 s for violation witnesses. The benchmarking framework BENCHEXEC 2.5.1 was used to ensure that the different runs do not influence each other and that the resource limits are measured and enforced reliably [15]. The exact information to replicate the runs of SV-COMP 2020 can be found in Sect. 3 of the competition report [4].

Benchmark Tasks. The verification tasks[5] of SV-COMP can be partitioned wrt. their specification into ReachSafety, MemSafety, NoOverflows, and Termination. Validators can be configured using different options for each specification.

---

[5] https://github.com/sosy-lab/sv-benchmarks/tree/svcomp20

Table 1. Overview of validation for violation witnesses in SV-COMP 2020

Specification	Measure	CPACHECKER	CPA-WTT	FSHELL-WTT	METAVAL	NITWIT	UAUTOMIZER
ReachSafety (35 652 witnesses)	executed on	35 652	25 812	25 812	35 652	21 636	25 812
	uniquely confirmed	3 043	42	175	44	398	547
	jointly confirmed	8 019	6 010	6 740	1 566	8 055	3 802
Termination (9 720 witnesses)	executed on	3 043			9 720		9 720
	uniquely confirmed	566			9		235
	jointly confirmed	1 539			256		1 493
NoOverflow (3 149 witnesses)	executed on	3 149	3 149	3 149	3 149		3 149
	uniquely confirmed	6	1	31	1		89
	jointly confirmed	1 668	1 067	1 267	1 186		1 590
MemSafety (2 681 witnesses)	executed on	2 681	2 213	2 681	2 681		2 681
	uniquely confirmed	278	0	21	113		44
	jointly confirmed	737	250	364	478		372

Table 2. Overview of validation for correctness witnesses in SV-COMP 2020

Specification	Measure	CPACHECKER	METAVAL	UAUTOMIZER
ReachSafety (66 435 witnesses)	executed on	66 435	66 435	66 435
	uniquely confirmed	1 750	391	708
	jointly confirmed	17 592	13 862	16 834
NoOverflow (3 179 witnesses)	executed on		3 179	3 179
	uniquely confirmed		44	74
	jointly confirmed		870	870
MemSafety (4 426 witnesses)	executed on		4 426	4 426
	uniquely confirmed		398	173
	jointly confirmed		811	811

Validator Configuration. Since our architecture (cf. Fig. 1) allows for a wide range of verifiers to be used for validation, there are many interesting configurations for constructing a validator. Exploring all of these in order to find the best configuration, however, would require significant computational resources, and also be susceptible to over-fitting. Instead, we chose a heuristic based on the results of the competition from the previous year, i.e., SV-COMP 2019 [3]. The idea is that a verifier which performed well at *verifying* tasks for a specific specification is also a promising candidate to be used in *validating* results for that specification. Therefore the configuration of our validator METAVAL uses CPA-SEQ as verifier for tasks with specification ReachSafety, ULTIMATE AUTOMIZER for NoOverflow and Termination, and SYMBIOTIC for MemSafety.

4.2 Results

The results of the validation phase in SV-COMP 2020 [5] are summarized in Table 1 (for violation witnesses) and Table 2 (for correctness witnesses). For each specification, METAVAL was able to not only confirm a large number of results that were also validated by other tools, but also to confirm results that were not previously validated by any of the other tools.[6]

For violation witnesses, we can observe that METAVAL confirms significantly less witnesses than the other validators. This can be explained partially by the restrictive time limit of 90 s. Our approach not only adds overhead when generating the program from the witness, but this new program can also be harder to parse and analyze for the verifier we use in the backend. It is also the case that the verifiers that we use in METAVAL are not tuned for such a short time limit, as a verifier in the competition will always get the full 15 min. For specification ReachSafety, for example, we use CPA-SEQ, which starts with a very simply analysis and switches verification strategies after a fixed time that happens to be also 90 s. So in this case we will never benefit from the more sophisticated strategies that CPA-SEQ offers.

For validation of correctness witnesses, where the time limit is higher, this effect is less noticeable such that the number of results confirmed by METAVAL is more in line with the numbers achieved by the other validators. For specification MemSafety, METAVAL even confirms more correctness witnesses than ULTIMATE AUTOMIZER. This indicates that SYMBIOTIC was a good choice in our configuration for that specification. SYMBIOTIC generally performs much better in verification of MemSafety tasks than ULTIMATE AUTOMIZER, so this result was expected.

Before the introduction of METAVAL, there was only one validator for correctness witnesses in the categories NoOverflow and MemSafety, while constructing a validator for those categories with our approach did not require any additional development effort.

5   Related Work

Programs from Proofs. Our approach for generating programs can be seen as a variant of the Programs from Proofs (PfP) framework [27,41]. Both generate programs from an abstract reachability graph of the original program. The difference is that PfP tries to remove all specification violations from the graph, while we just encode them into the generated program as violation of the standard reachability property. We do this for the original specification and the invariants in the witness, which we treat as additional specifications.

Automata-Based Software Model Checking. Our approach is also similar to that of the validator ULTIMATE AUTOMIZER [10]. For violation witnesses, it also constructs the product of CFA and witness. For correctness witnesses, it instruments the invariants directly into the CFA of the program (see [10], Sect. 4.2) and passes the result to its verification engine, while METAVAL constructs the product of CFA and witness, and applies a similar instrumentation. In both cases, METAVAL's transformer produces a C program, which can be passed to an independent verifier.

Reducer-Based Conditional Model Checking. The concept of generating programs from an ARG has also been used to successfully construct conditional verifiers [14].

---

[6] In the statistics, a witness is only counted as confirmed if the verifier correctly stated whether the input program satisfies the respective specification.

Our approach for correctness witnesses can be seen as a special case of this technique, where METAVAL acts as initial verifier that does not try to reduce the search space and instead just instruments the invariants from the correctness witness as additional specification into the program.

Verification Artifacts and Interfacing. The problem that verification results are not treated well enough by the developers of verification tools is known [1] and there are also other works that address the same problem, for example, the work on execution reports [19] or on cooperative verification [17].

Test-Case Generation. The idea to generate test cases from verification counterexamples is more than ten years old [8,39], has since been used to create debuggable executables [31,33], and was extended and combined to various successful automatic test-case generation approaches [24,25,29,35].

Execution. Other approaches [18,22,28] focus on creating tests from concrete and tool-specific counterexamples. In contrast, witness validation does not require full counterexamples, but works on more flexible, possibly abstract, violation witnesses from a wide range of verification tools.

Debugging and Visualization. Besides executing a test, it is important to understand the cause of the error path [23], and there are tools and methods to debug and visualize program paths [2,9,26].

6   Conclusion

We address the problem of constructing a tool for witness validation in a systematic and generic way: We developed the concept of *validation via verification*, which is a two-step approach that first applies a program transformation and then applies an off-the-shelf verification tool, without development effort.

The concept is implemented in the witness validator METAVAL, which has already been successfully used in SV-COMP 2020. The validation results are impressive: the new validator enriches the competition's validation capabilities by 164 uniquely confirmed violation results and 834 uniquely confirmed correctness results, based on the witnesses provided by the verifiers. This paper does not contain an own evaluation, but refers to results from the recent competition in the field.

The major benefit of our concept is that it is now possible to configure a spectrum of validators with different strengths, based on different verification engines. The 'time to market' of new verification technology into validators is negligibly small because there is no development effort necessary to construct new validators from new verifiers. A potential technology bias is also reduced.

Data Availability Statement. All data from SV-COMP 2020 are publicly available: witnesses [7], verification and validation results as well as log files [5], and benchmark programs and specifications [6][7]. The validation statistics in Tables 1 and 2 are available in the archive [5] and on the SV-COMP website[8]. METAVAL 1.0 is available on GitLab[9] and in our AEC-approved virtual machine [16].

---

[7] https://github.com/sosy-lab/sv-benchmarks/tree/svcomp20
[8] https://sv-comp.sosy-lab.org/2020/results/results-verified/validatorStatistics.html
[9] https://gitlab.com/sosy-lab/software/metaval/-/tree/1.0

References

1. Alglave, J., Donaldson, A.F., Kröning, D., Tautschnig, M.: Making software verification tools really work. In: Proc. ATVA, LNCS, vol. 6996, pp. 28–42. Springer, Heidelberg (2011). https://doi.org/10.1007/978-3-642-24372-1_3
2. Artho, C., Havelund, K., Honiden, S.: Visualization of concurrent program executions. In: Proc. COMPSAC, pp. 541–546. IEEE (2007). https://doi.org/10.1109/COMPSAC.2007.236
3. Beyer, D.: Automatic verification of C and Java programs: SV-COMP 2019. In: Proc. TACAS (3), LNCS, vol. 11429, pp. 133–155. Springer, Cham (2019). https://doi.org/10.1007/978-3-030-17502-3_9
4. Beyer, D.: Advances in automatic software verification: SV-COMP 2020. In: Proc. TACAS (2), LNCS, vol. 12079, pp. 347–367. Springer, Cham (2020). https://doi.org/10.1007/978-3-030-45237-7_21
5. Beyer, D.: Results of the 9th International Competition on Software Verification (SV-COMP 2020). Zenodo (2020). https://doi.org/10.5281/zenodo.3630205
6. Beyer, D.: SV-Benchmarks: Benchmark set of 9th Intl. Competition on Software Verification (SV-COMP 2020). Zenodo (2020). https://doi.org/10.5281/zenodo.3633334
7. Beyer, D.: Verification witnesses from SV-COMP 2020 verification tools. Zenodo (2020). https://doi.org/10.5281/zenodo.3630188
8. Beyer, D., Chlipala, A.J., Henzinger, T.A., Jhala, R., Majumdar, R.: Generating tests from counterexamples. In: Proc. ICSE, pp. 326–335. IEEE (2004). https://doi.org/10.1109/ICSE.2004.1317455
9. Beyer, D., Dangl, M.: Verification-aided debugging: An interactive web-service for exploring error witnesses. In: Proc. CAV (2), LNCS, vol. 9780, pp. 502–509. Springer, Cham (2016). https://doi.org/10.1007/978-3-319-41540-6_28
10. Beyer, D., Dangl, M., Dietsch, D., Heizmann, M.: Correctness witnesses: Exchanging verification results between verifiers. In: Proc. FSE, pp. 326–337. ACM (2016). https://doi.org/10.1145/2950290.2950351
11. Beyer, D., Dangl, M., Dietsch, D., Heizmann, M., Stahlbauer, A.: Witness validation and stepwise testification across software verifiers. In: Proc. FSE, pp. 721–733. ACM (2015). https://doi.org/10.1145/2786805.2786867
12. Beyer, D., Dangl, M., Lemberger, T., Tautschnig, M.: Tests from witnesses: Execution-based validation of verification results. In: Proc. TAP, LNCS, vol. 10889, pp. 3–23. Springer, Cham (2018). https://doi.org/10.1007/978-3-319-92994-1_1
13. Beyer, D., Gulwani, S., Schmidt, D.: Combining model checking and data-flow analysis. In: Handbook of Model Checking, pp. 493–540. Springer, Cham (2018). https://doi.org/10.1007/978-3-319-10575-8_16
14. Beyer, D., Jakobs, M.C., Lemberger, T., Wehrheim, H.: Reducer-based construction of conditional verifiers. In: Proc. ICSE, pp. 1182–1193. ACM (2018). https://doi.org/10.1145/3180155.3180259
15. Beyer, D., Löwe, S., Wendler, P.: Reliable benchmarking: Requirements and solutions. Int. J. Softw. Tools Technol. Transfer 21(1), 1–29 (2017). https://doi.org/10.1007/s10009-017-0469-y
16. Beyer, D., Spiessl, M.: Replication package (virtual machine) for article 'METAVAL: Witness validation via verification' in Proc. CAV 2020. Zenodo (2020). https://doi.org/10.5281/zenodo.3831417
17. Beyer, D., Wehrheim, H.: Verification artifacts in cooperative verification: Survey and unifying component framework. arXiv/CoRR 1905(08505), May 2019. https://arxiv.org/abs/1905.08505

18. Cadar, C., Ganesh, V., Pawlowski, P.M., Dill, D.L., Engler, D.R.: EXE: Automatically generating inputs of death. In: Proc. CCS, pp. 322–335. ACM (2006). https://doi.org/10.1145/1180405.1180445
19. Castaño, R., Braberman, V.A., Garbervetsky, D., Uchitel, S.: Model checker execution reports. In: Proc. ASE, pp. 200–205. IEEE (2017). https://doi.org/10.1109/ASE.2017.8115633
20. Christakis, M., Bird, C.: What developers want and need from program analysis: An empirical study. In: Proc. ASE, pp. 332–343. ACM (2016). https://doi.org/10.1145/2970276.2970347
21. Clarke, E.M., Grumberg, O., McMillan, K.L., Zhao, X.: Efficient generation of counterexamples and witnesses in symbolic model checking. In: Proc. DAC, pp. 427–432. ACM (1995). https://doi.org/10.1145/217474.217565
22. Csallner, C., Smaragdakis, Y.: Check 'n' crash: Combining static checking and testing. In: Proc. ICSE, pp. 422–431. ACM (2005). https://doi.org/10.1145/1062455.1062533
23. Ermis, E., Schäf, M., Wies, T.: Error invariants. In: Proc. FM, LNCS, vol. 7436, pp. 187–201. Springer, Heidelberg (2012). https://doi.org/10.1007/978-3-642-32759-9_17
24. Godefroid, P., Klarlund, N., Sen, K.: DART: Directed automated random testing. In: Proc. PLDI, pp. 213–223. ACM (2005). https://doi.org/10.1145/1065010.1065036
25. Gulavani, B.S., Henzinger, T.A., Kannan, Y., Nori, A.V., Rajamani, S.K.: SYNERGY: A new algorithm for property checking. In: Proc. FSE, pp. 117–127. ACM (2006). https://doi.org/10.1145/1181775.1181790
26. Gunter, E.L., Peled, D.A.: Path exploration tool. In: Proc. TACAS, LNCS, vol. 1579, pp. 405–419. Springer, Heidelberg (1999). https://doi.org/10.1007/3-540-49059-0_28
27. Jakobs, M.C., Wehrheim, H.: Programs from proofs: A framework for the safe execution of untrusted software. ACM Trans. Program. Lang. Syst. **39**(2), 7:1–7:56 (2017). https://doi.org/10.1145/3014427
28. Li, K., Reichenbach, C., Csallner, C., Smaragdakis, Y.: Residual investigation: Predictive and precise bug detection. In: Proc. ISSTA, pp. 298–308. ACM (2012). https://doi.org/10.1145/2338965.2336789
29. Majumdar, R., Sen, K.: Hybrid concolic testing. In: Proc. ICSE, pp. 416–426. IEEE (2007). https://doi.org/10.1109/ICSE.2007.41
30. McConnell, R.M., Mehlhorn, K., Näher, S., Schweitzer, P.: Certifying algorithms. Comput. Sci. Rev. **5**(2), 119–161 (2011). https://doi.org/10.1016/j.cosrev.2010.09.009
31. Müller, P., Ruskiewicz, J.N.: Using debuggers to understand failed verification attempts. In: Proc. FM, LNCS, vol. 6664, pp. 73–87. Springer, Heidelberg (2011). https://doi.org/10.1007/978-3-642-21437-0_8
32. Plasil, F., Visnovsky, S.: Behavior protocols for software components. IEEE Trans. Software Eng. **28**(11), 1056–1076 (2002). https://doi.org/10.1109/TSE.2002.1049404
33. Rocha, H., Barreto, R.S., Cordeiro, L.C., Neto, A.D.: Understanding programming bugs in ANSI-C software using bounded model checking counter-examples. In: Proc. IFM, LNCS, vol. 7321, pp. 128–142. Springer, Heidelberg (2012). https://doi.org/10.1007/978-3-642-30729-4_10
34. Schneider, F.B.: Enforceable security policies. ACM Trans. Inf. Syst. Secur. **3**(1), 30–50 (2000). https://doi.org/10.1145/353323.353382

35. Sen, K., Marinov, D., Agha, G.: CUTE: A concolic unit testing engine for C. In: Proc. FSE, pp. 263–272. ACM (2005). https://doi.org/10.1145/1081706.1081750
36. Šerý, O.: Enhanced property specification and verification in BLAST. In: Proc. FASE, LNCS, vol. 5503, pp. 456–469. Springer, Heidelberg (2009). https://doi.org/10.1007/978-3-642-00593-0_32
37. Svejda, J., Berger, P., Katoen, J.P.: Interpretation-based violation witness validation for C: NITWIT. In: Proc. TACAS, LNCS, vol. 12078, pp. 40–57. Springer, Cham (2020). https://doi.org/10.1007/978-3-030-45190-5_3
38. Turing, A.: Checking a large routine. In: Report on a Conference on High Speed Automatic Calculating Machines, pp. 67–69. Cambridge Univ. Math. Lab. (1949)
39. Visser, W., Păsăreanu, C.S., Khurshid, S.: Test-input generation with Java PATHFINDER. In: Proc. ISSTA, pp. 97–107. ACM (2004). https://doi.org/10.1145/1007512.1007526
40. Wimmer, S., von Mutius, J.: Verified certification of reachability checking for timed automata. In: Proc. TACAS, LNCS, vol. 12078, pp. 425–443. Springer, Cham (2020). https://doi.org/10.1007/978-3-030-45190-5_24
41. Wonisch, D., Schremmer, A., Wehrheim, H.: Programs from proofs: A PCC alternative. In: Proc. CAV, LNCS, vol. 8044, pp. 912–927. Springer, Heidelberg (2013). https://doi.org/10.1007/978-3-642-39799-8_65

Recursive Data Structures in SPARK

Claire Dross[(✉)] and Johannes Kanig

AdaCore, 75009 Paris, France
{dross,kanig}@adacore.com

Abstract. SPARK is both a deductive verification tool for the Ada language and the subset of Ada on which it operates. In this paper, we present a recent extension of the SPARK language and toolset to support pointers. This extension is based on an ownership policy inspired by Rust to enforce non-aliasing through a move semantics of assignment. In particular, we consider pointer-based recursive data structures, and discuss how they are supported in SPARK. We explain how iteration over these structures can be handled using a restricted form of aliasing called local borrowing. To avoid introducing a memory model and to stay in the first-order logic background of SPARK, the relation between the iterator and the underlying structure is encoded as a predicate which is maintained throughout the program control flow. Special first-order contracts, called pledges, can be used to describe this relation. Finally, we give examples of programs that can be verified using this framework.

Keywords: Deductive verification · Recursive structures · Ownership

1 Introduction

The programming language SPARK [8] has been designed to be amenable to formal verification, and one of the most impactful design choices was the exclusion of aliasing. While this choice vastly simplified the tool design and improved the expected proof performance, it also meant that pointers, as a major source of aliasing, were excluded from the language. While SPARK over the years had seen the addition of many language features, adding pointers just seemed impossible without violating the non-aliasing property. Then came Rust [11] democratizing a type system based on ownership [5]. Taking inspiration from it, it was possible to add pointers to the language in a way that still excludes aliasing. We will give an overview of the rules in this paper.

However, it was unclear if programs traversing recursive data structures such as lists and trees could be supported in this setting. In particular, iteration using a loop requires an alias between the traversed structure and the iterator. In this paper, we detail an approach, inspired by recent work by Astrauskas et al. [1], that enables proofs about recursive pointer-based data structures in SPARK. We have implemented this approach in the industrial formal verification tool SPARK, and, using this tool, developed a number of examples. Some important restrictions remain - we will also discuss them in this paper.

S. K. Lahiri and C. Wang (Eds.): CAV 2020, LNCS 12225, pp. 178–189, 2020.
https://doi.org/10.1007/978-3-030-53291-8_11

Ada [2] is a general-purpose procedural programming language. The design of the Ada language puts great emphasis on the safety and correctness of the program. This objective is realized by using a readable syntax that uses keywords instead of symbols where reasonable. The type system is strong and strict and many potential violations of type constraints can be detected statically by the compiler. If not, a run-time check is inserted into the program, to guarantee the detection of incorrect situations.

```
declare                  -- Block introducing new declarations
  type My_Int is range -100 .. 100;
  -- User-defined integer type ranging from -100 to 100
  subtype My_Nat is My_Int range 0 .. My_Int'Last;
  -- Subtype of My_Int with additional constraints

  X : My_Int := 50; -- Static check that 50 is in the bounds of My_Int
  Y : My_Nat;
begin                    -- Part of the block containing statements
  ...
  Y := X;                -- Dynamic check that X is in the bounds of My_Nat
end;                     -- End of scope of the entities declared in the block
```

Ada 2012 introduced contract based programming to Ada. In particular, it is possible to attach pre- and postconditions to subprograms[1]. These conditions can be checked during the execution of the program, just like assertions.

SPARK is the name of a tool that provides formal verification for Ada. It uses the user-provided contracts and attempts to prove that the runtime checks cannot fail and that postconditions are established by the corresponding subprograms. As formal verification for the whole Ada language would be intractable, SPARK is also the name of the subset of the Ada language that is supported by the SPARK tool[2]. This subset contains almost all features of Ada, though sometimes in a restricted form. In particular, expressions should be free from side effects, and aliasing is forbidden (no two variables should share the same memory location or overlap in memory). This restriction greatly simplifies the memory model used in the SPARK tool: any program variables can be reasoned about independently from other variables.

The SPARK tool uses the Why3 platform to generate verification conditions for SMT solvers via a weakest-precondition calculus [4].

2   Support for Pointers

Pointers in Ada are called *access types*. It is possible to declare an access type using the access keyword. Objects of an access type are null if no initial values are supplied. It is possible to allocate an object on the heap using the keyword new. An initial value can be supplied for the allocated object. A dereference of a pointer is written as a record component access, but using the keyword all.

---

[1] In Ada, a distinction is made between functions that return a value, and procedures, which do not. *Subprogram* is the term that designates both.

[2] http://docs.adacore.com/spark2014-docs/html/ug/.

```
declare
  type Int_Acc is access Integer;  -- Declare a new access type
  X : Int_Acc;                      -- Declare an object of this type
  pragma Assert (X = null);         -- No initial values provided, X is null
  Y : Integer;
begin
  X := new Integer;                 -- Allocation of uninitialized data
  X := new Integer'(3);             -- Allocation of initialized data
  Y := X.all;                       -- Dereference the access
end;
```

When a pointer is dereferenced, a runtime check is introduced to make sure that it is not null. Ada does not mandate garbage collection. Memory allocated on the heap can be reclaimed manually by the user using a generic function named Unchecked_Deallocation, which also sets its argument pointer to null. There are several kinds of access types. The basic access types, like Int_Acc defined above, are called pool specific access types. They can only designate objects allocated on the heap. General access types, introduced by the keyword all, can also be used to designate objects allocated on the stack or global data.

Pointers were excluded from the SPARK subset until recently. Indeed, allowing pointers in a straightforward way would break the absence of aliasing in SPARK. In addition, pointers are associated with a list of classes of bugs such as memory leaks, use-after-free and dereferencing a null-pointer.

To support pointers in SPARK, we designed a subset of Ada's access types which does not introduce aliasing and avoids some pointer-specific issues, while retaining as much expressivity as possible. The first restriction we selected is the exclusion of general access types. This means that SPARK can only create pointers designating memory allocated on the heap, and not on the stack. As a result, pointers can only be made invalid by explicit deallocation, and deallocation of a valid pointer is always legal. To eliminate aliasing between (heap) pointers, ownership rules inspired by Rust have been added on top of Ada's legality rules. These rules enforce a single writer/multiple readers policy. They ensure that, when a value designated by a pointer is modified, all other objects can be considered to be preserved.

The basis of the ownership policy of SPARK is the move semantics of assignments. When a pointer is assigned to a variable, both the source and the target of the assignment designate the same memory region: assigning an object containing a pointer creates an alias. To alleviate this problem, when an object containing a pointer is assigned, the memory region designated by the pointer is said to be *moved*. The source of the assignment loses the ownership of the designated data while the target of the assignment gains it. The ownership system makes sure that the designated data is not accessed again through the source of the assignment.

```
Y : Int_Acc := X;     -- Ownership of the data designated by X is moved to Y
Y.all := Y.all + 1;   -- The data can be read and modified through Y
Z := X.all;           -- Illegal: Reading or modifying X.all is not allowed
```

As the ownership policy ensures that no aliasing can occur between access objects, it is possible to reason about the program almost as if the pointer was replaced by the data it points to. When an object containing a pointer is assigned to another variable, it is safe to consider that the designated data is copied by the assignment. Indeed, any effects that could occur because variables are sharing a substructure cannot be observed because of the ownership rules.

Pointers are handled in the verification model of the SPARK proof tool as *maybe*, or *option* types: access objects are either null, or they contain a value. In addition, access objects also contain an address, which can be used to handle comparison (two pointers may not be equal even if the values they designate are equal). When a pointer is dereferenced, a verification condition is generated to make sure that the pointer is not null, so that its value can be accessed.

```
X : Int_Acc;                --  X is null
X := new Integer'(3);       --  X has a value which is 3
Y := X;                     --  Y has a value which is 3
Z := Y.all;                 --  Check that Y is not null, Z is 3
```

Note that the ownership policy is key for this translation to be correct, as it prevents the program from observing side-effects caused by the modification of a shared reference, which would not be accounted for in the verification model.

3   Recursive Data Structures

In Ada, recursivity can only be introduced through pointers. The idea is to first declare a type, but without giving its definition. This declaration, called an *incomplete declaration*, introduces a place-holder for the type, which can only be used in restricted circumstances. In particular, this place-holder can be used to declare an access type designating pointers to values of this type. Using this mechanism, it is possible to declare a recursive data structure, since the access type can be used in the type definition as it comes afterward.

```
type List_Cell;
type List is access List_Cell;
type List_Cell is record
  Data : Integer;
  Next : List;
end record;
```

There are no specific restrictions concerning recursive types in SPARK. However, the ownership policy of SPARK implies that it will not be possible to create a structure which has either cycles (e.g. doubly linked lists) or shared substructures (e.g. DAGs) in it. The ownership policy may also impact how recursive structures can be manipulated. In general, working with such structures involves a traversal, which can be done either recursively, or iteratively using a loop. Algorithms working in a recursive way are generally compliant with the ownership policy of SPARK. Indeed, the recursive calls will allow reading or modifying the structure in depth without having to deconstruct it[3].

```
function Length (L : access constant List_Cell) return My_Nat is
  (if L = null then 0 else Length (L.Next) + 1);
function Nth (L : access constant List_Cell; N : My_Pos) return Integer is
  (if N = 1 then L.Data else Nth (L.Next, N - 1))
with Pre ⇒ N ≤ Length (L);
```

---

[3] In Length and Nth, addition on My_Nat and My_Pos has been redefined to saturate so as to avoid the overflow checking mandated by Ada.

Algorithms involving loops are trickier. The declaration of the iterator used for the loop creates an alias of the traversed data structure. As per SPARK's ownership policy, this is considered to be a move, so it makes it illegal to access the initial structure. Further assignments to the iterator during the traversal contribute to losing definitively one by one the ownership of every node in the structure, making it impossible to restore the ownership at the end.

```
procedure Set_All_To_Zero (X : in out List) is
   Y : List := X;      -- The ownership of X is transferred to Y
begin
   while Y ≠ null loop
      Y.Data := 0;
      Y := Y.Next;      -- Ownership of the first cell of Y is lost for good
   end loop;            -- The ownership of X cannot be restored
end Set_All_To_Zero;
```

To traverse recursive data structures, a move is not what we want. Here we need a way to lend the ownership of a memory region for a period of time and automatically restore it at the end. A similar mechanism, called *borrowing*, is available in the Rust language. We have adapted it to SPARK.

4   Borrowing Ownership

As Ada is an imperative language, losing the possibility to traverse a linked data structure using a loop was deemed too restrictive. To alleviate this problem, a notion of ownership borrowing was introduced in SPARK. It allows the users to declare a variable, called a borrower, which is initialized with a reference to a part of an existing data structure. To state that this initialization should not be considered a move, an *anonymous access type* is used for the borrower[4]. During the scope of the borrower, the borrowed part of the underlying structure is frozen, meaning that it is illegal to read or modify it. Once the borrower has gone out of scope, the ownership automatically returns to the borrowed object, so that it is again fully accessible.

```
X := ...;                        -- X is initialized to the list {1,2,3,4}
declare
   Y : access List_Cell := X;   -- Y has an anonymous access type.
   -- Ownership of X is transferred to Y for the duration of its lifetime.
begin
   Y.Data := Y.Data + 1;        -- Y can be used to read or modify X
   pragma Assert (X.Data = 2);  -- Illegal, during the lifetime of Y, X
                                -- cannot be read or modified directly
end;
pragma Assert (X.Data = 2);     -- Afterwards, the ownership returns to X
```

A borrower can be used to modify the underlying structure. This makes it effectively an alias of the borrowed object. To allow the tool to statically determine the cases of aliasing, SPARK restricts the initial value of a local borrower to be the name of a part of an existing object. This forbids for example borrowing one of two structures depending on a condition.

---

[4] A type is said to be anonymous if it does not have a previous declaration. Here access List_Cell is anonymous while List is named.

It is possible to update a borrower to change the part of the object it designates (as opposed to modifying the designated object). This is called a reborrow. In SPARK, the value assigned to the borrower in a reborrow should be rooted at the borrower. This means that reborrows only go deeper into the structure.

```
declare
  Y : access List_Cell := X;   --  Y is X
begin
  Y := Y.Next;                 --  This is a reborrow, Y is now X.Next
end;
```

Borrowing can be used to allow simple iterative traversals of a recursive data structure like the loop of Set_All_To_Zero. More complex traversals, involving stacks for example, cannot be written iteratively in SPARK.

```
procedure Set_All_To_Zero (X : in out List) is
  Y : access List_Cell := X;
  -- The ownership of X is transferred to Y for the duration of its lifetime
begin
  while Y ≠ null loop
    Y.Data := 0;
    Y := Y.Next;  --  Reborrow: Y designates something deeper
  end loop;
end Set_All_To_Zero; --  The ownership of X is restored
```

Using reborrows, local borrowers allow one to indirectly modify a data structure at an arbitrarily-deep position, which may not be statically-known. While in the scope of the borrower, these indirect modifications can be ignored by the analysis, as the ownership policy makes them impossible to observe. However, after the end of the borrow, ownership is transferred back to the borrowed object, and SPARK needs to take into account whatever modifications may have occurred through the borrower.

```
X := ...; --  X is initialized to the list {1,2,3,4}
declare
  Y : access List_Cell := X;              --  Y is X
begin
  Y := Y.Next.Next;
  --  Through reborrows, Y designates an arbitrarily-deep part of X
  Y.Data := 42;                --  Y is used to indirectly modify X
end;
pragma Assert (X.Next.Next.Data = 42);  --  The assertion should hold
```

To be able to reconstruct the borrowed object from the value of the borrower, we must track the relation between them. As this relation cannot be statically determined because of reborrows, SPARK handles it as an additional object in the program. This allows us to take advantage of the normal mechanism for handling value dependent control-flow in SPARK (the weakest-precondition calculus of Why3). The idea is the following. When a borrower is declared in Ada, we create two objects: the borrower itself, which is considered as a stand-alone structure, independent of the borrowed object, and a predicate. The predicate, which we call the borrow relation, encodes the most precise relation between the borrower and the borrowed object which does not depend on the actual value designated by the borrower. The value of the *borrow relation* is computed by the tool from the definition of the borrower, and is updated at each reborrow. Modifications of the underlying data structure don't impact this relation. At the end of the borrow, the borrowed object is reconstructed using both the borrow relation and the current value of the borrower.

```
X := ...; -- X is initialized to the list {1,2,3,4}
declare
   Y : access List_Cell := X; -- Create borrow relation to relate X and Y
   -- b_rel := λ new_x, new_y. new_x ≠ null ∧ new_x = new_y
begin
   Y := Y.Next.Next; -- Update the predicate to model the new relation
   -- b_rel := λ new_x, new_y. new_x ≠ null ∧ new_x.data = 1 ∧
   --    new_x.next ≠ null ∧ new_x.next.data = 2 ∧ new_x.next.next ≠ null
   --    ∧ new_x.next.next = new_y
   Y.Data := 42; -- The borrow relation is not modified
end;
pragma Assert (X.Next.Next.Data = 42);
-- Follows from the fact that X.Next.Next = Y and Y.Data = 42
```

5   Describing the Borrow Relation

SPARK performs deductive verification, which relies on user-specified invariants to handle loops. When traversing a linked data structure, the loop body contains a reborrow, which means that the borrow relation is modified in the loop. As a general rule, if a variable is modified in a loop, it should be described in the loop invariant, lest nothing is known about its value afterward. Thus, we need a way to describe the borrow relation in the loop invariant.

As part of their work on the Prusti proof tool for Rust, Astrauskas et al. found the need for a similar annotation that they call *pledges* [1]. In Rust, a pledge is an assertion associated with a borrower which is guaranteed to hold at the time when the borrow expires, no matter what may happen in between. In SPARK, a property guaranteed to hold at the end of the borrow must be a consequence of the borrow relation, since the borrow relation is the most precise relation which does not depend on the actual value of the borrower. Therefore, the user-visible notion of a pledge is suitable to approximate the internally computed borrow relation. Similar to user-provided postconditions, which must be implied by the strongest postcondition computed by a verifying tool, the user-provided pledge should follow from the borrow relation.

Since the Ada syntax has no support for pledges, we have resorted in SPARK to introducing special functions (dedicated to each access type) called pledge functions, which mark expressions which should be considered as pledge expressions by the tool. A pledge function is a *ghost* function (meaning that it is not allowed to have any effect on the output of the program) which has two parameters. The first one is used to identify the borrower on which the pledge should apply, while the second holds the assertion. Note that a call to a pledge function isn't really a call for the SPARK analyzer. It is simply a marker that the expression in argument is a pledge.

```
function Pledge
   (L : access constant Cell; -- The borrower to which the pledge applies
    P : Boolean)              -- The property we want to assert in the pledge
      return Boolean
is (P)   -- For execution, the function evaluates the property
with Ghost,
   Annotate ⇒ (GNATprove, Pledge); -- Identifies a pledge function for SPARK
```

When a pledge function is called in an assertion, SPARK recognizes it and identifies its parameter as a pledge. It therefore attempts to show that the property is implied by the borrow relation (as opposed to implied by the current value of the borrower).

```
X := ...; -- X is initialized to the list {1,2,3,4}
declare
  Y : access List_Cell := X;
begin
  Y := Y.Next.Next;
  pragma Assert (Pledge (Y, Y = X.Next.Next));
  -- True as this is implied by borrow relation
  pragma Assert (Pledge (Y, X.Data = 1 and X.Next.Data = 2));
  -- True again as the first 2 elements of X are frozen
  pragma Assert (Pledge (Y, X.Next.Next.Data = 3));
  -- False, though this is true at the current program point, as it is not
  -- guaranteed to hold at the end of the borrow.
  ...
end;
```

Using pledges, we can formally verify the Set_All_To_Zero procedure. Its postcondition states that all elements of the list have been set to 0 using the Nth function. To be able to express the loop invariant in a similar way, we have introduced a ghost variable C to count the number of iterations. Its value is maintained by the first loop invariant. The second and third invariants are pledges, describing how the value of X can be reconstructed from the value of the iterator Y. The second invariant gives the length of the list, while the third describes the value of its elements using the Nth function. Elements which have already been processed are frozen by the borrow. Their value is known to be 0. Other elements can be linked to the corresponding position in the iterator Y.

```
procedure Set_All_To_Zero (X : List) with
  Pre  => Length (X) < My_Nat'Last,
  Post => Length (X) = Length (X)'Old
    and (for all I in 1 .. Length (X) => Nth (X, I) = 0);
  -- All elements of X are 0 after the call

procedure Set_All_To_Zero (X : List) is
  C : My_Nat := 0 with Ghost;
  Y : access List_Cell := X;
begin
  while Y /= null loop
    pragma Loop_Invariant (C = Length (Y)'Loop_Entry - Length (Y));
    -- C elements have been traversed
    pragma Loop_Invariant
      (Pledge (Y, Length (X) = Length (Y) + C));
    pragma Loop_Invariant
      (Pledge (Y, (for all I in 1 .. Length (X) =>
        Nth (X, I) = (if I <= C then 0 else Nth (Y, I - C)))));
    -- All elements are 0 up to C, others are elements of Y
    Y.Data := 0;
    Y := Y.Next;
    C := C + 1;
  end loop;
end Set_All_To_Zero;
```

Note that, in general, it is not necessary to write a pledge to verify a program using a local borrower. Indeed, the analysis tool is able to precisely track the borrow relation through successive reborrows. Pledges need only be provided when the borrow relation itself cannot be tracked by the tool, for example because of a loop, like in our example.

6   Evaluation

We could not try the tool on any pre-existing benchmark since SPARK codebases do not have pointers, and Ada codebases usually violate some SPARK rules. In particular, Ada codebases have no reason to abide by the ownership policy of SPARK. So instead, we mostly had to write new tests to assess the correctness and performance of our implementation. The public testsuite of SPARK contains more than 150 tests mentioning access types, be they supported cases or not.

To assess expressivity and provability on programs dealing with recursive data structures, we have written 6 examples, none of them very big, but ranging over various levels of complexity[5]. On all of these examples, we have shown that the runtime checks imposed by the Ada language are guaranteed to pass and that no uninitialized value can be read. In addition, we have manually supplied functional properties.

Figure 1 gives some metrics over these examples. Under the tab Loc are listed the total number of lines of code in the example, the number of lines of specification (including contracts and specification functions), and the number of additional ghost annotations (assertions, loop invariants, ghost variables. . .). The #Checks column gives the number of checks generated by the tool (contracts, assertions, invariants, language defined checks...). In the last three columns, we can see the total running time of SPARK, both from scratch using its default strategy and only replaying the proofs through the replay facility, as well as the maximal time needed to prove a single verification condition.

Example	#Subp	LOC			#Checks	Analysis time (s)		
		All	Spec	Ghost		Default	Replay	Max VC
set all to zero	5	57	19 (33%)	8 (14%)	25	4	3	< 1
linear search	7	136	67 (49%)	24 (17%)	109	10	9	< 1
pointer-based maps	7	130	38 (29%)	12 (9%)	64	6	5	< 1
route shift	8	99	50 (50%)	3 (3%)	64	9	6	< 1
binary search	13	239	99 (41%)	42 (17%)	129	24	17	4
red black trees	37	611	107 (17%)	384 (63%)	920	258	152	16

Fig. 1. Overview of the examples involving recursive data structures

Though these examples are small, we think they demonstrate that it is possible to define recursive data structures in SPARK, and to verify iterative programs using them. When writing the algorithms, we found that the limitations mostly come from the ownership policy of SPARK. Some data structures are not supported, requiring either to switch to full Ada for their implementations, or to change the algorithm to work around the missing links. In general, we found

---

[5] https://github.com/AdaCore/spark2014/tree/master/papers/Pledge2020/examples.

that the annotation effort required to describe the borrow relations, though non-negligible, was acceptable. In particular, it uses the standard SPARK expressions, with no mentions of memory separation or permission.

7 Related Work

Program verification tools for mainstream languages such as C or Java generally support aliasing, because the concept of pointer or reference is more central. They deal with it by modeling the heap. The WP plugin of Frama-C uses by default a *typed memory model* where different arrays are used for the basic types of C [6]. The VerCors [3] toolset handles high-level programming languages, such as Java, by extending the annotation language with separation logic with permission [10]. In SPARK we have chosen a different approach, as we avoid modeling the heap completely by using ownership rules to enforce non-aliasing.

The ownership rules introduced in SPARK are largely inspired by the Rust language [11]. The differences are mostly motivated by the need to comply with the preexisting Ada semantics of pointers. In addition, SPARK was aiming at coming up with a subset as easy to verify as possible. The resulting model is simpler because it does not make lifetime of borrowers explicit, and aliases created through borrows are always statically known.

The Prusti verification tool for Rust [1] allows users to verify that a program complies with its specification. Both tools provide similar guarantees and require similar annotations. However, they differ in their implementation. Indeed, Prusti works by translating separation constraints enforced by the Rust type system to the intermediate verification language of the Viper tool [9]. Our work differs here, as we use the ownership system to abstract away memory related concerns, so that the verification process does not need to be aware of them.

In a recent work [7], Matsushita et al. propose a translation to CHCs for Rust programs. Like in our approach, the restrictions imposed by the ownership policy are key for the soundness of their method. However, while we introduce the notion of borrow relation to be able to use a standard WP calculus, they present a new calculus specifically tailored to Rust references.

8 Conclusion

We have presented a recent extension of the SPARK language and toolset to support pointers. It is based on an ownership policy enforcing non-aliasing. To support pointer-based recursive data structures, a restricted form of aliasing is introduced in SPARK through local borrowers, which can be used to iterate through a linked data structure in an imperative way. We have described how local borrowers can be supported by the verification tool, without introducing a memory model, by using a mutable predicate named the borrow relation. This borrow relation can be described when necessary using special annotations named pledges, which solely consist of SPARK standard expressions, and do not expose the underlying verification technique. Our work is available in the 20.1 release of SPARK Pro and will be part of the next community release.

As for future work, we would like to extend the subset of Ada pointers supported in SPARK. In particular, we would like to introduce function pointers to model callbacks, pointers to constants with a more permissive ownership policy, and local borrowing of objects allocated on the stack.

References

1. Astrauskas, V., Müller, P., Poli, F., Summers, A.J.: Leveraging rust types for modular specification and verification. Proc. ACM Program. Lang. **3**(OOPSLA), 147:1–147:30 (2019)
2. Barnes, J.: Programming in Ada 2012. Cambridge University Press, Cambridge (2014)
3. Blom, S., Darabi, S., Huisman, M., Oortwijn, W.: The VerCors tool set: verification of parallel and concurrent software. In: Polikarpova, N., Schneider, S. (eds.) IFM 2017. LNCS, vol. 10510, pp. 102–110. Springer, Cham (2017). https://doi.org/10.1007/978-3-319-66845-1_7
4. Bobot, F., Filliâtre, J.-C., Marché, C., Paskevich, A.: Why3: shepherd your herd of provers (2011)
5. Clarke, D.G., Potter, J.M., Noble, J.: Ownership types for flexible alias protection. In: ACM SIGPLAN Notices, vol. 33, no. 10, pp. 48–64 (1998)
6. Kirchner, F., Kosmatov, N., Prevosto, V., Signoles, J., Yakobowski, B.: Frama-C: a software analysis perspective. In: Formal Aspects of Computing, pp. 573–609 (2015)
7. Matsushita, Y., Tsukada, T., Kobayashi, N.: RustHorn: CHC-based verification for rust programs. In: 29th European Symposium on Programming (2020)
8. McCormick, J.W., Chapin, P.C.: Building High Integrity Applications with SPARK. Cambridge University Press, Cambridge (2015)
9. Müller, P., Schwerhoff, M., Summers, A.J.: Viper: a verification infrastructure for permission-based reasoning. In: Jobstmann, B., Leino, K.R.M. (eds.) VMCAI 2016. LNCS, vol. 9583, pp. 41–62. Springer, Heidelberg (2016). https://doi.org/10.1007/978-3-662-49122-5_2
10. Reynolds, J.C.: Separation logic: a logic for shared mutable data structures. In: 17h Annual IEEE Symposium on Logic in Computer Science (2002)
11. The Rust Programming Language: References and Borrowing (2019). https://doc.rust-lang.org/1.8.0/book/references-and-borrowing.html

Ivy: A Multi-modal Verification Tool for Distributed Algorithms

Kenneth L. McMillan[1(✉)] and Oded Padon[2]

[1] Microsoft Research, Redmond, USA
kenmcmil@microsoft.com
[2] Stanford University, Stanford, USA
padon@cs.stanford.edu

Abstract. Ivy is a multi-modal verification tool for correct design and implementation of distributed protocols and algorithms, supporting modular specification, implementation and proof. Ivy supports proving safety and liveness properties of parameterized and infinite-state systems via three modes: deductive verification using an SMT solver, abstraction and model checking, and manual proofs using natural deduction. It supports light-weight formal methods via compositional specification-based testing and bounded model checking. Ivy can extract executable distributed programs by translation to efficient C++ code. It is designed to support decidable automated reasoning, to improve proof stability and to provide transparency in the case of proof failures. For this purpose, it presents concrete finite counterexamples, automatically audits proofs for decidability of verification conditions, and provides modular hiding of theories.

1 Introduction

Ivy is an open-source [16] multi-modal verification tool for correct design and implementation of distributed algorithms, supporting modular specification, implementation and proof. The motivating principles of Ivy are *predictability*, *stability* and *transparency*. That is, automated proof steps should provide complexity bounds, should be insensitive to small perturbations, and when they fail should provide actionable feedback. To the extent consistent with these principles, Ivy aims to maximize expressiveness and proof automation, and thus to achieve a high level of user productivity in designing, implementing and proving programs. A major goal of Ivy is to support *decidable reasoning*. That is, automated proof should be restricted to logical fragments for which the tool is a decision procedure. This greatly improves the stability of automated provers, which otherwise rely on fragile heuristics to avoid divergence [28]. This is important for the maintenance of large proofs, to prevent small changes from creating unpredictable proof failures. Moreover, on decidable problems, provers fail transparently by providing true counterexamples, which greatly simplifies the iterative development of proofs. Ivy supports the decomposition of proofs to decidable theories by the use of modular abstraction.

© The Author(s) 2020
S. K. Lahiri and C. Wang (Eds.): CAV 2020, LNCS 12225, pp. 190–202, 2020.
https://doi.org/10.1007/978-3-030-53291-8_12

The architecture of Ivy is depicted in Fig. 1. The figure shows the major components of the tool and the information flow between them. Ivy provides a language (also called "Ivy") for the modular description of distributed programs, along with their specifications and proofs (see Sect. 2). Ivy is a synchronous, reactive programming language [3], meaning that the program only executes actions in response to input from its environment, and these actions appear to execute atomically. From an Ivy program, the tool can extract an asynchronous, distributed implementation. A program is made up of reactive modules [1], each having a temporal assume/guarantee-style specification. After parsing of this description and elaboration of templates, the program is decomposed into its component modules, each with associated assumptions and proof obligations, according to a system of proof rules for circular assume/guarantee reasoning (see Sect. 2.1).

These proof obligations are passed on to the tactics engine (see Sect. 3). This engine orchestrates the use of various built-in proof tactics, including decidable invariant checking with an SMT solver (Sect. 3.1), model checking with eager abstraction [19] (Sect. 3.2), liveness proof by translation to safety (Sect. 3.3) and logical deduction rules (Sect. 3.4). Each tactic works by reducing a given proof goal to a (possibly empty) set of sub-goals, from which the original goal can be proved. Combined with modular reasoning, the tactics engine makes it possible to use a variety of proof approaches and proof automation tools in constructing a proof.

Ivy extracts executable distributed programs by translation to C++ (see Sect. 5). From the specifications of a module, Ivy can also generate a modular randomized specification-based tester [7] (see Sect. 4.1). This also makes it possible to test infrastructure not written in Ivy (including hardware) against Ivy specifications.

1.1 Related Work

Ivy can be thought of as a hybrid between program verification tools such as ESC-Java [11] and Dafny [14], based on the Floyd/Hoare approach, compositional model checking tools, such as Mocha [2] and Cadence SMV [17] and proof assistants based on the LCF model, such as Isabelle [26] or Coq [4]. Compared to program verification tools that support only procedure modularity, Ivy provides a richer form of specification that allows complete hiding of internal state, and provides architectural support for decidable reasoning (see Sect. 2.1). Compared to compositional tools, Ivy integrates a richer variety of reasoning techniques (see Sect. 3). Compared to proof assistants, Ivy provides domain-specific support for decidable proof automation, supporting a greater degree of proof automation [28]. On the other hand, Ivy relies on a vastly larger trusted computing base than typical proof assistants. Moreover, Ivy has no mechanism of reflection, and thus cannot be used for meta-reasoning about programs and program transformations. In principle, all the techniques in Ivy could be integrated into a tool such as Isabelle or Coq but the effort would be large. A less foundational tool such as

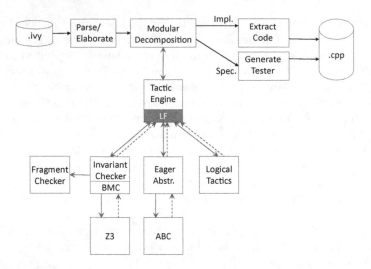

Fig. 1. Ivy architecture, showing flow between major components. Red, solid arrows represent flow of proof goals and assumptions. Green, dashed arrows represent flow of proofs and/or counterexamples. Not shown is VC generator, shared between Invariant Checking/BMC and Eager Abstraction components. (Color figure online)

Ivy makes it possible to rapidly experiment with new proof and proof automation strategies. Compared to all of these tools, Ivy differs in providing native support for extracting distributed programs, and specification-based testing. A related tool, mypyvy, focuses on more powerful invariant inference techniques, but lacks the other features of Ivy [10, 29].

2   A Modular Language for Decidable Reasoning

The primary design goal of Ivy's language is to support decidable reasoning while maximizing expressiveness and performance. Figure 2 is an example of the basic unit of verification in Ivy, called an *isolate*. An isolate is a reactive module that hides internal state and provides a temporal (that is, stateful) specification of its interface. An isolate has named traits that include types, properties, variables and actions. It is divided into a *specification* part and an *implementation* part. The figure shows an example of a simple module that inputs a sequence of numbers and outputs an upper bound on the numbers received thus far.

Types, Variables and Actions. The native datatypes in Ivy include just the Boolean type, uninterpreted types, records (structs) over datatypes, and pure first-order functions. In the figure, line 2 declares an uninterpreted type t. Line 6 declares a state variable 'seen' holding a predicate over t. This variable is initialized at line 9. This assigns 'seen(X)' to be the function that returns false for all values of X.

Procedures in Ivy are called *actions* and may have side effects on variables. Parameters are passed by value and there are no references. This greatly simplifies modular reasoning (see Sect. 2.1) and also allows for aggressive compiler optimizations due to the absence of aliasing (see Sect. 5).

In the figure, line 3 declares an action 'ub' that takes an input x of type t and outputs y of type t. Its implementation is given at lines 24 to 27. It updates a state variable 'max' holding the maximum value received thus far, and returns this value by assigning it to the output variable y.

2.1 Modularity and Decidability

The specification part of the isolate (lines 5 to 18) consists of *ghost* variables and code that are *visible* outside the isolate. The implementation part (lines 19 to 30) consists of *real* variables and code that are *invisible* outside the module. At line 15 the ghost predicate 'seen' is updated to reflect the fact that value x has been seen as an input. Specification code contains assume/guarantee specifications in terms of **require** and **ensure** statements. For example, line 12 represents an assumption that input values are non-negative. Line 16 represents a guarantee that output values will be an upper bound on all seen values.

Ghost and real code are kept syntactically separate in Ivy. The specification code is interleaved with the implementation code using the directives 'before' (line 11) and 'after' (line 14). Thus, in the figure, the 'require' statement acts as a precondition, while the 'ensure' statement acts as a postcondition. The implementation code is not allowed to side effect any externally visible state, so it is sound to erase (or 'slice') this code when verifying other modules. Other modules see only the ghost code, which provides an abstract model of the isolate. Similarly, when extracting executable code, it is safe to erase the ghost code (which must be proven to be terminating). This makes it possible, for example, to provide a pure, functional specification of a module interface, even though internally it has state.

Theories can also be hidden inside modules. For example, the implementation of our example interprets the type t as the integers (line 28). For verification purposes, this instantiates the theory of Peano arithmetic for type t. This theory is used *only* to prove correctness of the isolate, and is invisible to other isolates. The theory can be used to prove properties (such as the irreflexivity property at line 7) that provide an abstraction of the type externally. The ability to hide theories behind abstractions provides an important strategy for keeping proof obligations decidable.

An isolate with no implementation part (that is, a "ghost" module) can act as an abstract model of a protocol. Using Ivy's modular rules, an abstract model can be *refined* to an implementation, using properties of the abstract model as lemmas. In addition to simplifying the proof, abstract models provide another useful strategy to hide functions, properties or theories that break decidability. This approach, in combination with theory hiding, was used to verify implementations of distributed consensus protocols [28]. Modularity provides the primary means in Ivy of keeping the automated reasoning decidable.

```
 1  isolate foo = {
 2      type t
 3      action ub(x:t) returns (y:t)
 4
 5      specification {
 6          relation seen(X:t)
 7          property ∀X : t.¬(X < X)
 8          after init {
 9              seen(X) := false;
10          }
11          before ub {
12              require x ≥ 0;
13          }
14          after ub {
15              seen(x) := true;
16              ensure seen(X) → X ≤ y;
17          }
18      }
19      implementation {
20          var max : t
21          after init {
22              max := 0;
23          }
24          implement ub {
25              max := x if x > max else max;
26              y := max;
27          }
28          interpret t → int
29          invariant seen(X) → X ≤ max
30      }
31  }
```

Fig. 2. Example of an Ivy isolate.

3 Verification Tactics

Ivy provides a range of automated tactics for discharging proof goals that are selected for their relatively predictable and stable performance, and for the ability to fail transparently.

3.1 Invariant Checking with SMT

The default tactic for proving safety properties is proof by inductive invariant, using the SMT solver Z3 [21]. For example, in Fig. 2, the guarantee at line 16 is proved using the auxiliary inductive invariant at line 29. The invariant relates the hidden implementation state variable 'max' with the visible specification state variable 'seen'. An invariant is a property that is required to hold only between executions of actions of the isolate. That is, actions may temporarily violate an invariant, but must re-establish it before terminating. The VC (verification condition) for the isolate holds if all invariants are established by the initializers and preserved by the interface actions, and if the invariant implies that no assertion in the code fails. These conditions are verified modulo the visible theories.

Before attempting to prove the VC, the invariance tactic sends it to the *fragment checker*, which determines whether the VC is in a logical fragment called FAU [12] for which Z3 is a decision procedure. If the VC is not in FAU, Ivy provides an explanation to the user, by pointing to formulas that create a *function cycle* or that violate rules for the use of quantifiers and interpreted operators of the visible theories. A function cycle is a cycle in a graph whose vertices are types and whose edges are functions (including Skolem functions). This transparent mode of failure helps the user to reorganize the proof to keep the VC's in the decidable fragment.

If a VC in the decidable fragment is false, Z3 fails transparently, producing a true finite counter-model, which is in turn translated into an execution trace that violates an invariant or guarantee. Ivy provides a graphical interactive tool to help the user in strengthening invariants [25] based on counterexamples. If the VC is valid, the tactic discharges the proof goal, returning the empty set of subgoals.

3.2 Eager Abstraction and Model Checking

An alternative tactic to prove safety properties is model checking with eager abstraction [19]. This technique allows parameterized and infinite-state systems to be verified with a finite-state model checker. The tactic first propositionally strengthens the symbolic transition relation by adding instances of axioms of the logic and theories, or of proved properties. It then propositionally abstracts the transition relation by converting the atomic predicates to Boolean variables. The resulting finite-state abstraction is verified by the ABC model checker [8]. If the property is false, the user is presented with an abstract counterexample expressed in terms of the truth values of the atomic propositions. The user may refine the abstraction by adding instantiation terms or auxiliary invariants. In [19] it was shown that this technique can reduce the burden of constructing auxiliary invariants, simplifying the overall proof of distributed protocols. As an example, the isolate of Fig. 2 can be proved without the auxiliary invariant. With eager abstraction, one need not be concerned with function cycles, but on the other hand, diagnosing abstract counterexamples can be challenging.

This approach is consistent with Ivy's philosophy of using stable and transparent automation, since the finite-state model checker has a single-exponential upper complexity bound and terminates with a proof or a counterexample. This is in contrast to more powerful proof engines such as Horn solvers [6] that suffer from unpredictable divergence. In practice, although eager abstraction is not fully automated, it can handle problems that are substantially beyond the capabilities of current Horn solvers.

3.3 Liveness-to-Safety Transformation

Ivy supports proofs of temporal properties, e.g., liveness properties, via a liveness-to-safety transformation. Temporal properties are specified in first-order linear temporal logic (FO-LTL). The liveness-to-safety tactic reduces a temporal proof goal into a safety proof goal, which can then be proven using an inductive invariant. For finite-state or parameterized systems, any temporal property can be proven by showing the absence of fair cycles, which is a safety property [27]. For infinite-state systems such an argument is not sound, and Ivy implements *dynamic abstraction* which generalizes the notion of fair cycles to infinite-state systems in a sound and powerful way [23,24]. With dynamic abstraction, Ivy's liveness-to-safety tactic supports temporal proofs of infinite-state systems, including both distributed systems with infinite-state per process and systems with *unbounded parallelism*, where new processes can be dynamically created so an infinite trace may involve infinite set of processes.

```
 1  isolate bar = {
 2      finite type t
 3      action step(x:t)                16     temporal property (□◊ enter.now) →
 4      specification {                 17         ◊ ∀X. ¬pending(X)
 5          relation pending(X:t)       18     proof {
 6          instance enter : signal     19         tactic l2s with
 7                                       20         invariant ◊ enter.now
 8          after init {                21         invariant ($was$ ¬pending(X)) → ¬pending(X)
 9              pending(X) := true;     22         invariant ($happened$ enter.now) →
10          }                           23             ∃X. ($was$ pending(X)) ∧ ¬pending(X)
11          before step {               24     }
12              require pending(x);     25     }
13              call enter.raise;       26  }
14              pending(x) := false;
15          }
```

Fig. 3. Example of an Ivy isolate with a temporal property.

The liveness-to-safety tactic fits within Ivy's philosophy of using decidable reasoning. The more standard way of proving liveness properties is to use ranking functions, but for distributed systems, the required rankings often involve cardinalities of sets defined via first-order formulas, resulting in verification conditions that fall outside FAU and other decidable fragments. In contrast, the transformation to safety based on fair cycles and dynamic abstraction results in verification conditions which are often in the FAU fragment. Furthermore, since the temporal proof is transformed to a safety verification problem, it is possible to leverage for liveness proofs all the tactics and mechanisms that Ivy contains for safety verification.

When the liveness-to-safety tactic is applied, Ivy constructs a symbolic *cycle detection transition system*, which tracks fairness constraints and includes a *shadow* or *saved copy* of the state variables, similar to [5]. For finite-state or parameterized systems, it is enough to show that it is not possible to revisit the saved state while satisfying all fairness constraints. This can be shown by an inductive invariant, and Ivy contains special syntax for writing the invariant of the cycle detection system (e.g., to access the saved copy of state variables). For infinite-state systems, Ivy's cycle detection system includes dynamic abstraction, and invariants may also refer to the state of the abstraction [23].

Figure 3 shows an example of a simple liveness proof of an abstract model in Ivy. The type t (line 2) is declared as finite, which means it is sound to use a fair cycle argument without dynamic abstraction. The specification state of the system consists of a single unary relation, pending, which is initialized to true for all values of type t. The step action (line 11) removes a single value from the pending relation. This can model, e.g., execution of tasks from a finite pool of pending tasks. The temporal property that we prove (line 16) is that if step is called infinitely often, then eventually nothing is pending. At line 13, we detect the call by raising a flag enter.now. The proof applies the liveness-to-safety (l2s) tactic (line 19), and supplies inductive invariants for the cycle detection system. The special operators was and $happened$ are used to refer to the saved state, and the fairness constraints, respectively. The crux of the invariant is that after

```
1  axiom eid(X) = eid(Y) → X = Y
2  axiom mgr(X, Y) ∧ mgr(X, Z) → Y = Z
3  explicit axiom [mgr_total] ∃Y. mgr(X, Y)
4  axiom mgr(X, X) → X = ceo
5
6  invariant mgr(X, Y) ∧ scanned(Y) → mid(X) = eid(Y)
7
8  action get_mid(x:emp) returns (res:id) = {
9      require ∀Y.scanned(Y);
10     res := mid(x);
11     ensure x ≠ ceo → res ≠ eid(x);
12     proof {
13         assume mgr_total with X = x
14     }
15 }
```

Fig. 4. Example of manual quantifier instantiation with a tactic

enter.now has happened, there is some element which was pending in the saved state and is not pending anymore, showing that the system has no fair cycle.

3.4 Logical Tactics

Though most of a proof in Ivy is done with the above automated proof tactics, there are occasional situations in which a small amount of detailed manually-guided proof is needed, or is preferable to restructuring the proof. For this purpose, Ivy provides logical proof tactics that can be applied to properties, invariants or code assertions, either to complete the proof or to reduce it to subgoals that can be discharged by the automated tactics. A simple example is shown in Fig. 4. Here, $mgr(X, Y)$ indicates that the manager of employee X is Y and $eid(X)$ is the employee id of X. We assume that employee ids are unique, each employee has exactly one manager and that only the CEO is her own manager (lines 1 to 4). Action $get\_mid(x)$ returns the id of the manager of employee x. For this purpose, a procedure (not shown) scans the employees m and sets $mid(x) = eid(m)$ for each x managed by m, establishing the invariant at line 6. Action $get\_mid(x)$ requires that all employees have been scanned and ensures that the return value is not the id of x, unless x is the CEO.

Axiom mgr_total states that for all employees there exists a manager (the universal quantifier on X is implicit). Ivy complains that this quantifier alternation puts the VC outside the decidable fragment. We can solve this with a manual quantifier instantiation. We first tag the axiom *explicit*, meaning that it is not used by the default tactic. We then apply the tactic 'assume' (line 13) to instantiate this axiom for $X = x$. The resulting assumption $∃Y.mgr(x, Y)$ has no alternation. The modified proof goal is discharged by the default tactic using Z3. Ivy's proof engine is based on the $\lambda\Pi$ calculus [13] and a deterministic second-order matching algorithm [30]. The Ivy standard library uses this framework to define proof rules for natural deduction, similarly to Isabelle/FOL [26]. Logical tactics also make it possible to perform theory reasoning outside the decidable fragment, for example, applying the Peano induction axiom.

4 Light-Weight Formal Methods

4.1 Compositional Specification-Based Testing

Before attempting a formal proof that an isolate satisfies its specification, it is useful to debug it using testing. For this purpose, Ivy provides compositional specification-based testing. The testers that Ivy produces generate randomized input sequences for an isolate that satisfy its assumptions and check the outputs against the isolate's guarantees. This is similar in principle to specification-based testing tools such as QuickCheck [9], but is reactive and compositional. Compositionality provides a kind of completeness for unit testing. That is, if a system fails its specification, then there is a local test of some component that fails. Unlike QuickCheck, Ivy does not require the user to provide generators for datatypes, instead relying on SMT solving for this purpose. Ivy can also be used to generate specification-based tests for hardware or software systems not written in Ivy. For example, it has been used to find bugs in memory hierarchy components for RISC-V processors [18], and the QUIC secure Internet transport protocol [20].

4.2 Bounded and Finite-State Model Checking

For debugging, Ivy supports bounded model checking. This is decidable if the VC's are in the decidable fragment. It also allows uninterpreted types to be finitely instantiated, allowing under-approximate model checking in the style of TLC [31].

5 Extracting Efficient Executable Code

Compilation. The implementation part of an Ivy program can be extracted as executable code in C++. To be extractable, the implementation must satisfy certain computability conditions, for example that all quantifiers in conditionals be bounded. For functions, the compiler can choose among several representations: a closure, a dense representation as an array, or a sparse representation as a hash table. The dense representation is unboxed, allowing a cache-efficient contiguous representation of an array of structures and reducing allocation overhead.

Because there are no references in Ivy, there is a risk of copying large structures passed as arguments. However, the lack of aliasing makes it relatively easy for the compiler to detect linear use of data, allowing call and return by reference in the extracted code, and in-place update of structures. Subtype polymorphism in Ivy is implemented by the compiler using smart pointers, allowing structure sharing (and potentially copy-on-write, though this is not yet implemented). In addition, the compiler borrows a technique from the Rust language [22] to introduce references. Consider the Ivy code on the left of Fig. 5 that looks up a value in a map, operates on it, then writes it back into the map. The compiler recognizes this as an instance of the "borrowing" pattern and renders it as the C++ code on the right, which operates on the value in the map by reference.

```
1  b := m(x);                      1  auto &b = m[x];
2  b := f(b);                      2  f(b);
3  m(x) := b;
```

Fig. 5. Updating a map in place using the borrow pattern.

This is possible because the of lack of aliasing and the fact that the compiler understands the underlying data structures. A C++ compiler cannot accomplish this optimization because of the difficulty of pointer analysis in the map implementation and the called operator f. Benchmarks of an older Ivy compiler [28] on distributed protocols showed comparable performance to implementation in OCaml and Go, though Ivy is purely value-based, while these languages support references.

Concurrency. Although Ivy is a synchronous reactive language, the compiler can extract parameterized distributed programs from Ivy programs in a sound way. In a parameterized module, each action and state variable has a first parameter representing a *location*. The compiler verifies that different locations do not interfere with each-other, and then extracts an executable process that takes its location as a parameter. Ivy guarantees that executing the locations concurrently is observably equivalent sequential execution, based on a left-mover/right-mover argument [15,28].

Run-Time Support. Ivy provide a standard library that includes useful abstractions, such ordered datatypes and arrays, as well as formally specified interfaces to networking services provided by operating systems. In addition, the compiler automatically generates marshaling and unmarshaling code for user-defined datatypes. These facilities make it relatively straightforward to implement verified networked protocols in Ivy.

6 Conclusion

Ivy has been designed to provide predictability, stability and transparency in the process of developing verified systems. For this purpose, it integrates a collection of verification techniques that provide these properties, while attempting to maximize the expressiveness of the language, the degree of proof automation, and the efficiency of extracted code. By setting the division of labor between the human and automated provers appropriately, it aims to increase the productivity of the overall process of formal development.

References

1. Alur, R., Henzinger, T.A.: Reactive modules. In: Proceedings, 11th Annual IEEE Symposium on Logic in Computer Science, New Brunswick, New Jersey, USA, 27–30 July 1996, pp. 207–218. IEEE Computer Society (1996)

2. Alur, R., Henzinger, T.A., Mang, F.Y.C., Qadeer, S., Rajamani, S.K., Tasiran, S.: MOCHA: modularity in model checking. In: Hu, A.J., Vardi, M.Y. (eds.) CAV 1998. LNCS, vol. 1427, pp. 521–525. Springer, Heidelberg (1998). https://doi.org/10.1007/BFb0028774

3. Berry, G., Gonthier, G.: The Esterel synchronous programming language: design, semantics, implementation. Sci. Comput. Program. **19**(2), 87–152 (1992)

4. Bertot, Y., Castéran, P.: Interactive Theorem Proving and Program Development - Coq'Art: The Calculus of Inductive Constructions. Texts in Theoretical Computer Science. An EATCS Series. Springer, Heidelberg (2004). https://doi.org/10.1007/978-3-662-07964-5

5. Biere, A., Artho, C., Schuppan, V.: Liveness checking as safety checking. Electr. Notes Theor. Comput. Sci. **66**(2), 160–177 (2002)

6. Bjørner, N., Gurfinkel, A., McMillan, K., Rybalchenko, A.: Horn clause solvers for program verification. In: Beklemishev, L.D., Blass, A., Dershowitz, N., Finkbeiner, B., Schulte, W. (eds.) Fields of Logic and Computation II. LNCS, vol. 9300, pp. 24–51. Springer, Cham (2015). https://doi.org/10.1007/978-3-319-23534-9_2

7. Blundell, C., Giannakopoulou, D., Pasareanu, C.S.: Assume-guarantee testing. ACM SIGSOFT Softw. Eng. Notes **31**(2), 1–8 (2006)

8. Brayton, R., Mishchenko, A.: ABC: an academic industrial-strength verification tool. In: Touili, T., Cook, B., Jackson, P. (eds.) CAV 2010. LNCS, vol. 6174, pp. 24–40. Springer, Heidelberg (2010). https://doi.org/10.1007/978-3-642-14295-6_5

9. Claessen, K., Hughes, J.: Quickcheck: a lightweight tool for random testing of Haskell programs. SIGPLAN Not. **35**(9), 268–279 (2000)

10. Feldman, Y.M.Y., Wilcox, J.R., Shoham, S., Sagiv, M.: Inferring inductive invariants from phase structures. In: Dillig, I., Tasiran, S. (eds.) CAV 2019. LNCS, vol. 11562, pp. 405–425. Springer, Cham (2019). https://doi.org/10.1007/978-3-030-25543-5_23

11. Flanagan, C., Leino, K.R.M., Lillibridge, M., Nelson, G., Saxe, J.B., Stata, R.: Extended static checking for java. In: Proceedings of the ACM SIGPLAN 2002 Conference on Programming Language Design and Implementation, PLDI 2002, pp. 234–245. ACM (2002)

12. Ge, Y., de Moura, L.: Complete instantiation for quantified formulas in satisfiabiliby modulo theories. In: Bouajjani, A., Maler, O. (eds.) CAV 2009. LNCS, vol. 5643, pp. 306–320. Springer, Heidelberg (2009). https://doi.org/10.1007/978-3-642-02658-4_25

13. Harper, R., Honsell, F., Plotkin, G.D.: A framework for defining logics. J. ACM **40**(1), 143–184 (1993)

14. Leino, K.R.M.: Dafny: an automatic program verifier for functional correctness. In: Clarke, E.M., Voronkov, A. (eds.) LPAR 2010. LNCS (LNAI), vol. 6355, pp. 348–370. Springer, Heidelberg (2010). https://doi.org/10.1007/978-3-642-17511-4_20

15. Lipton, R.J.: Reduction: a method of proving properties of parallel programs. Commun. ACM **18**(12), 717–721 (1975)

16. McMillan, K.L.: Ivy. http://microsoft.github.io/ivy/. Accessed 28 Jan 2020

17. McMillan, K.L.: A methodology for hardware verification using compositional model checking. Sci. Comput. Program. **37**(1–3), 279–309 (2000)

18. McMillan, K.L.: Modular specification and verification of a cache-coherent interface. In: 2016 Formal Methods in Computer-Aided Design, FMCAD 2016, Mountain View, CA, USA, 3–6 October 2016, pp. 109–116. IEEE (2016)

19. McMillan, K.L.: Eager abstraction for symbolic model checking. In: Chockler, H., Weissenbacher, G. (eds.) CAV 2018. LNCS, vol. 10981, pp. 191–208. Springer, Cham (2018). https://doi.org/10.1007/978-3-319-96145-3_11
20. McMillan, K.L., Zuck, L.D.: Formal specification and testing of QUIC. In: Wu, J., Hall, W. (eds.) Proceedings of the ACM Special Interest Group on Data Communication, SIGCOMM 2019, Beijing, China, 19–23 August 2019, pp. 227–240. ACM (2019)
21. de Moura, L.M., Bjørner, N.: Z3: an efficient SMT solver. In: TACAS, pp. 337–340 (2008)
22. Nichols, C., Klabnik, S.: The Rust Programming Language. No Starch Press, San Francisco (2018)
23. Padon, O., Hoenicke, J., Losa, G., Podelski, A., Sagiv, M., Shoham, S.: Reducing liveness to safety in first-order logic. PACMPL 2(POPL), 26:1–26:33 (2018)
24. Padon, O., Hoenicke, J., McMillan, K.L., Podelski, A., Sagiv, M., Shoham, S.: Temporal prophecy for proving temporal properties of infinite-state systems. In: 2018 Formal Methods in Computer-Aided Design, FMCAD 2018, Austin, Texas, USA, 30 October–2 November 2018, pp. 74–84 (2018)
25. Padon, O., McMillan, K.L., Panda, A., Sagiv, M., Shoham, S.: Ivy: safety verification by interactive generalization. In: Krintz, C., Berger, E. (eds.) Proceedings of the 37th ACM SIGPLAN Conference on Programming Language Design and Implementation, PLDI 2016, Santa Barbara, CA, USA, 13–17 June 2016, pp. 614–630. ACM (2016)
26. Paulson, L.C. (ed.): Isabelle. LNCS, vol. 828. Springer, Heidelberg (1994). https://doi.org/10.1007/BFb0030541
27. Pnueli, A., Shahar, E.: Liveness and acceleration in parameterized verification. In: Emerson, E.A., Sistla, A.P. (eds.) CAV 2000. LNCS, vol. 1855, pp. 328–343. Springer, Heidelberg (2000). https://doi.org/10.1007/10722167_26
28. Taube, M., et al.: Modularity for decidability of deductive verification with applications to distributed systems. In: Foster, J.S., Grossman, D. (eds.) Proceedings of the 39th ACM SIGPLAN Conference on Programming Language Design and Implementation, PLDI 2018, Philadelphia, PA, USA, 18–22 June 2018, pp. 662–677. ACM (2018)
29. Wilcox, J.: mypyvy. https://github.com/wilcoxjay/mypyvy. Accessed 15 May 2020
30. Yokoyama, T., Hu, Z., Takeichi, M.: Deterministic second-order patterns. Inf. Process. Lett. 89(6), 309–314 (2004)
31. Yu, Y., Manolios, P., Lamport, L.: Model checking TLA$^+$ specifications. In: Pierre, L., Kropf, T. (eds.) CHARME 1999. LNCS, vol. 1703, pp. 54–66. Springer, Heidelberg (1999). https://doi.org/10.1007/3-540-48153-2_6

Reasoning over Permissions Regions in Concurrent Separation Logic

James Brotherston[1]($\boxtimes$), Diana Costa[1], Aquinas Hobor[2], and John Wickerson[3]

[1] University College London, London, UK
J.Brotherston@ucl.ac.uk
[2] National University of Singapore, Singapore, Singapore
[3] Imperial College London, London, UK

Abstract. We propose an extension of separation logic with fractional permissions, aimed at reasoning about concurrent programs that share arbitrary *regions* or data structures in memory. In existing formalisms, such reasoning typically either fails or is subject to stringent side conditions on formulas (notably *precision*) that significantly impair automation. We suggest two formal syntactic additions that collectively remove the need for such side conditions: first, the use of both "weak" and "strong" forms of separating conjunction, and second, the use of nominal labels from hybrid logic. We contend that our suggested alterations bring formal reasoning with fractional permissions in separation logic considerably closer to common pen-and-paper intuition, while imposing only a modest bureaucratic overhead.

Keywords: Separation logic · Permissions · Concurrency · Verification

1 Introduction

Concurrent separation logic (CSL) is a version of separation logic designed to enable compositional reasoning about concurrent programs that manipulate memory possibly shared between threads [6,26]. Like standard separation logic [28], CSL is based on *Hoare triples* $\{A\} C \{B\}$, where C is a program and A and B are formulas (called the *precondition* and *postcondition* of the code respectively). The heart of the formalism is the following *concurrency rule*:

$$\frac{\{A_1\} C_1 \{B_1\} \quad \{A_2\} C_2 \{B_2\}}{\{A_1 \circledast A_2\} C_1 \,\|\, C_2 \{B_1 \circledast B_2\}}$$

where $\circledast$ is a so-called *separating conjunction*. This rule says that if two threads C_1 and C_2 are run on spatially separated resources $A_1 \circledast A_2$ then the result will be the spatially separated result, $B_1 \circledast B_2$, of running the two threads individually.

However, since many or perhaps even most interesting concurrent programs do share some resources, $\circledast$ typically does not denote strict disjoint separation of memories, as it does in standard separation logic (where it is usually written as $*$).

© The Author(s) 2020
S. K. Lahiri and C. Wang (Eds.): CAV 2020, LNCS 12225, pp. 203–224, 2020.
https://doi.org/10.1007/978-3-030-53291-8_13

Instead, it usually denotes a weaker sort of "separation" designed to ensure that the two threads at least cannot interfere with each others' data. This gives rise to the idea of *fractional permissions*, which allow us to divide writeable memory into multiple read-only copies by adding a permission value to each location in heap memory. In the usual model, due to Boyland [5], permissions are rational numbers in the half-open interval $(0, 1]$, with 1 denoting the write permission, and values in $(0, 1)$ denoting read-only permissions. We write the formula A^π, where π is a permission, to denote a "π share" of the formula A. For example, $(x \mapsto a)^{0.5}$ (typically written as $x \overset{0.5}{\mapsto} a$ for convenience) denotes a "half share" of a single heap cell, with address x and value a. The separating conjunction $A \circledast B$ then denotes heaps realising A and B that are "compatible", rather than disjoint: where the heaps overlap, they must agree on the data value, and one adds the permissions at the overlapping locations [4]. E.g., at the logical level, we have the entailment:

$$x \overset{0.5}{\mapsto} a \circledast x \overset{0.5}{\mapsto} b \models a = b \wedge x \mapsto a. \tag{1}$$

Happily, the concurrency rule of CSL is still sound in this setting (see e.g. [29]).

However, the use of this weaker notion of separation $\circledast$ causes complications for formal reasoning in separation logic, especially if one wishes to reason over arbitrary regions of memory rather than individual pointers. There are two particular difficulties, as identified by Le and Hobor [24]. The first is that, since $\circledast$ denotes possibly-overlapping memories, one loses the main useful feature of separation logic: its nonambiguity about separation, which means that desirable entailments such as $A^{0.5} \circledast B^{0.5} \models (A \circledast B)^{0.5}$ turn out to be false. E.g.:

$$x \overset{0.5}{\mapsto} a \circledast y \overset{0.5}{\mapsto} b \not\models (x \mapsto a \circledast y \mapsto b)^{0.5}.$$

Here, the two "half-pointers" on the LHS might be aliased ($x = y$ and $a = b$), meaning they are two halves of the same pointer, whereas on the RHS they must be non-aliased (because we cannot combine two "whole" pointers). This ambiguity becomes quite annoying when one adds arbitrary predicate symbols to the logic, e.g. to support inductively defined data structures.

The second difficulty is that although recombining single pointers is straightforward, as indicated by Eq. (1), recombining the shares of arbitrary formulae is challenging. E.g., $A^{0.5} \circledast A^{0.5} \not\models A$, as shown by the counterexample

$$(x \mapsto 1 \vee y \mapsto 2)^{0.5} \circledast (x \mapsto 1 \vee y \mapsto 2)^{0.5} \not\models x \mapsto 1 \vee y \mapsto 2.$$

The LHS can be satisfied by a heap with a 0.5-share of x and a 0.5-share of y, whereas the RHS requires a full (1) share of either x or y.

Le et al. [24] address these problems by a combination of the use of *tree shares* (essentially Boolean binary trees) rather than rational numbers as permissions, and semantic restrictions on when the above sorts of permissions reasoning can be applied. For example, recombining permissions ($A^{0.5} \circledast A^{0.5} \models A$) is permitted only when the formula is *precise* in the usual separation logic sense (cf. [28]). The chief drawback with this approach is the need to repeatedly check these side conditions on formulas when reasoning, as well as that said reasoning cannot be performed on imprecise formulas.

Instead, we propose to resolve these difficulties by a different, two-pronged extension to the syntax of the logic. First, we propose that the usual "strong" separating conjunction $*$, which enforces the strict disjointness of memory, *should be retained* in the formalism in addition to the weaker $\circledast$. The stronger $*$ supports entailments such as $A^{0.5} * B^{0.5} \models (A * B)^{0.5}$, which does not hold when $\circledast$ is used instead. Second, we introduce *nominal labels* from hybrid logic (cf. [3,10]) to remember that two copies of a formula have the same origin. We write a nominal α to denote a unique heap, in which case entailments such as $(\alpha \wedge A)^{0.5} \circledast (\alpha \wedge A)^{0.5} \models \alpha \wedge A$ become valid. We remark that labels have been adopted for similar "tracking" purposes in several other separation logic proof systems [10,21,23,25].

The remainder of this paper aims to demonstrate that our proposed extensions are (i) weakly *necessary*, in that expected reasoning patterns fail under the usual formalism, (ii) *correct*, in that they recover the desired logical principles, and (iii) *sufficient* to verify typical concurrent programming patterns that use sharing. Section 2 gives some simple examples that motivate our extensions. Section 3 then formally introduces the syntax and semantics of our extended formalism. In Sect. 4 we show that our logic obeys the logical principles that enable us to reason smoothly with fractional permissions over arbitrary formulas, and in Sect. 5 we give some longer worked examples. Finally, in Sect. 6 we conclude and discuss directions for future work.

2 Motivating Examples

In this section, we aim to motivate our extensions to separation logic with permissions by showing, firstly, how the failures of the logical principles described in the introduction actually arise in program verification examples and, secondly, how these failures are remedied by our proposed changes.

The overall context of our work is reasoning about concurrent programs that share some data structure or region in memory, which can be described as a formula in the assertion language. If A is such a formula then we write A^π to denote a "π share" of the formula A, meaning informally that all of the pointers in the heap memory satisfying A are owned with share π. The main question then becomes how this notion interacts with the separating conjunction $\circledast$. There are two key desirable logical equivalences:

$$(A \circledast B)^\pi \equiv A^\pi \circledast B^\pi \tag{I}$$
$$A^{\pi \oplus \sigma} \equiv A^\pi \circledast A^\sigma \tag{II}$$

Equivalence (I) describes distributing a fractional share over a separating conjunction, whereas equivalence (II) describes combining two pieces of a previously split resource. Both equivalences are true in the $\models$ direction but, as we have seen in the Introduction, false in the $\dashv$ one. Generally speaking, $\circledast$ is like Humpty Dumpty: easy to break apart, but not so easy to put back together again.

The key to understanding the difficulty is the following equivalence:

$$x \stackrel{\pi}{\mapsto} a \circledast y \stackrel{\sigma}{\mapsto} b \equiv (x \stackrel{\pi}{\mapsto} a * y \stackrel{\sigma}{\mapsto} b) \vee (x = y \wedge a = b \wedge x \stackrel{\pi \oplus \sigma}{\mapsto} a)$$

In other words, either x and y are not aliased, or they *are* aliased and the permissions combine (the additive operation $\oplus$ on rational shares is simply normal addition when the sum is ≤ 1 and undefined otherwise). This disjunction undermines the notational economies that have led to separation logic's great successes in scalable verification [11]; in particular, (I) fails because the left disjunct might be true, and (II) fails because the right disjunct might be. At a high level, $\circledast$ is a bit too easy to introduce, and therefore also a bit too hard to eliminate.

2.1   Weak vs. Strong Separation and the Distribution Principle

One of the challenges of the weak separating conjunction $\circledast$ is that it interacts poorly with inductively defined predicates. Consider porting the usual separation logic definition of a possibly-cyclic linked list segment from x to y from a sequential setting to a concurrent one by a simple substitution of $\circledast$ for $*$:

$$\mathsf{ls}\,x\,y \ =_{\mathrm{def}} \ (x = y \wedge \mathsf{emp}) \vee (\exists z.\ x \mapsto z \circledast \mathsf{ls}\,z\,y).$$

Now consider a simple recursive procedure `foo(x,y)` that traverses a linked list segment from `x` to `y`:

```
foo(x,y) { if x=y then return; else foo([x],y); }
```

It is easy to see that `foo` leaves the list segment unchanged, and therefore satisfies the following Hoare triple:

$$\{(\mathsf{ls}\,x\,y)^{0.5}\}\,\texttt{foo(x,y)}\,;\{(\mathsf{ls}\,x\,y)^{0.5}\}.$$

The intuitive proof of this fact would run approximately as follows:

$\{(\mathsf{ls}\,x\,y)^{0.5}\}\,\texttt{foo(x,y)}\,\{$

$\qquad$ if x=y then return; $\quad \{(\mathsf{ls}\,x\,y)^{0.5}\}$

$\qquad$ else $\qquad\qquad\qquad\quad \{x \neq y \wedge (x \mapsto z \circledast \mathsf{ls}\,z\,y)^{0.5}\}$

$\qquad\qquad\qquad\qquad\qquad\quad \{x \stackrel{0.5}{\mapsto} z \circledast (\mathsf{ls}\,z\,y)^{0.5}\}$

$\qquad$ foo([x],y); $\qquad\qquad \{x \stackrel{0.5}{\mapsto} z \circledast (\mathsf{ls}\,z\,y)^{0.5}\}$

$\qquad\qquad\qquad\qquad\qquad\quad \{(x \mapsto z \circledast \mathsf{ls}\,z\,y)^{0.5}\}$

$\qquad\qquad\qquad\qquad\qquad\quad \{(\mathsf{ls}\,x\,y)^{0.5}\}$

$\qquad$ } $\quad \{(\mathsf{ls}\,x\,y)^{0.5}\}$

However, because of the use of $\circledast$, the highlighted inference step is not sound:

$$x \stackrel{0.5}{\mapsto} z \circledast (\mathsf{ls}\,z\,y)^{0.5} \not\models (x \mapsto z \circledast \mathsf{ls}\,z\,y)^{0.5}. \tag{2}$$

To see this, consider a heap with the following structure, viewed in two ways:

$$x \overset{0.5}{\mapsto} z \circledast z \overset{0.5}{\mapsto} x \circledast x \overset{0.5}{\mapsto} z \;=\; x \mapsto z \circledast z \overset{0.5}{\mapsto} x$$

This heap satisfies the LHS of the entailment in (2), as it is the $\circledast$-composition of a 0.5-share of $x \mapsto z$ and a 0.5-share of $\mathsf{ls}\, z\, z$, a cyclic list segment from z back to itself (note that here $z = y$). However, it does not satisfy the RHS, since it is not a 0.5-share of the $\circledast$-composition of $x \mapsto z$ with $\mathsf{ls}\, z\, z$, which would require the pointer to be disjoint from the list segment.

The underlying reason for the failure of this example is that, in going from $(x \mapsto z \circledast \mathsf{ls}\, z\, z)^{0.5}$ to $x \overset{0.5}{\mapsto} z \circledast (\mathsf{ls}\, z\, z)^{0.5}$, we have lost the information that the pointer and the list segment are actually disjoint. This is reflected in the general failure of the distribution principle $A^\pi \circledast B^\pi \models (A \circledast B)^\pi$, of which the above is just one instance. Accordingly, our proposal is that the "strong" separating conjunction $*$ from standard separation logic, which forces disjointness of the heaps satisfying its conjuncts, should *also* be retained in the logic alongside $\circledast$, on the grounds that (II) *is* true for the stronger connective:

$$(A * B)^\pi \equiv A^\pi * B^\pi. \tag{3}$$

If we then define our list segments using $*$ in the traditional way, namely

$$\mathsf{ls}\, x\, y \;=_{\mathrm{def}}\; (x = y \wedge \mathsf{emp}) \vee (\exists z.\; x \mapsto z * \mathsf{ls}\, z\, y),$$

then we can observe that this second definition of ls is identical to the first on permission-free formulas, since $\circledast$ and $*$ coincide in that case. However, when we replay the verification proof above with the new definition of ls, every $\circledast$ in the proof above becomes a $*$, and the proof then becomes sound. Nevertheless, we can still use $\circledast$ to describe permission-decomposition of list segments at a higher level; e.g., $\mathsf{ls}\, x\, y$ can still be decomposed as $(\mathsf{ls}\, x\, y)^{0.5} \circledast (\mathsf{ls}\, x\, y)^{0.5}$.

2.2 Nominal Labelling and the Combination Principle

Unfortunately, even when we use the strong separating conjunction $*$ to define list segments ls, a further difficulty still remains. Consider a simple concurrent program that runs two copies of `foo` in parallel on the same list segment:

```
foo(x,y);  ||  foo(x,y);
```

Since `foo` only reads from its input list segment, and satisfies the specification $\{(\mathsf{ls}\, x\, y)^{0.5}\}\, \mathtt{foo(x,y)};\, \{(\mathsf{ls}\, x\, y)^{0.5}\}$, this program satisfies the specification

$$\{\mathsf{ls}\, x\, y\}\, \mathtt{foo(x,y)};\; ||\; \mathtt{foo(x,y)};\, \{\mathsf{ls}\, x\, y\}.$$

Now consider constructing a proof of this specification in CSL. First we view the list segment $\mathsf{ls}\, x\, y$ as the $\circledast$-composition of two read-only copies, with permission 0.5 each; then we use CSL's concurrency rule (see Sect. 1) to compose the specifications of the two threads; last we recombine the two read-only copies to obtain the original list segment. The proof diagram is as follows:

$$\{\mathsf{ls}\,x\,y\}$$

$$\{(\mathsf{ls}\,x\,y)^{0.5} \circledast (\mathsf{ls}\,x\,y)^{0.5}\}$$

$$\{(\mathsf{ls}\,x\,y)^{0.5}\} \quad \Big\| \quad \{(\mathsf{ls}\,x\,y)^{0.5}\}$$

$$\texttt{foo(x,y);} \quad \Big\| \quad \texttt{foo(x,y);}$$

$$\{(\mathsf{ls}\,x\,y)^{0.5}\} \quad \Big\| \quad \{(\mathsf{ls}\,x\,y)^{0.5}\}$$

$$\{(\mathsf{ls}\,x\,y)^{0.5} \circledast (\mathsf{ls}\,x\,y)^{0.5}\}$$

$$\rightsquigarrow \{\mathsf{ls}\,x\,y\}$$

However, again, the highlighted inference step in this proof is not correct:

$$(\mathsf{ls}\,x\,y)^{0.5} \circledast (\mathsf{ls}\,x\,y)^{0.5} \not\models \mathsf{ls}\,x\,y. \tag{4}$$

A countermodel is a heap with the following structure, again viewed in two ways:

$$(x \overset{0.5}{\mapsto} y \circledast y \overset{0.5}{\mapsto} y) \circledast x \overset{0.5}{\mapsto} y \; = \; x \mapsto y \circledast y \overset{0.5}{\mapsto} y$$

According to the first view of such a heap, it satisfies the LHS of (4), as it is the $\circledast$-composition of two 0.5-shares of $\mathsf{ls}\,x\,y$ (one of two cells, and one of a single cell). However, it does not satisfy $\mathsf{ls}\,x\,y$, since that would require every cell in the heap to be owned with permission 1.

Like in our previous example, the reason for the failure of this example is that we have lost information. In going from $\mathsf{ls}\,x\,y$ to $(\mathsf{ls}\,x\,y)^{0.5} \circledast (\mathsf{ls}\,x\,y)^{0.5}$, we have forgotten that the two formulas $(\mathsf{ls}\,x\,y)^{0.5}$ are in fact *copies of the same region*. For formulas A that are *precise* in that they uniquely describe part of any given heap [12], e.g. formulas $x \mapsto a$, this loss of information does not happen and we do have $A^{0.5} \circledast A^{0.5} \models A$; but for non-precise formulas such as $\mathsf{ls}\,x\,y$, this principle fails.

However, we regard this primarily as a technical shortcoming of the formalism, rather than a failure of our intuition. It *ought* to be true that we can take any region of memory, split it into two read-only copies, and then later merge the two copies to re-obtain the original region. Were we conducting the above proof on pen and paper, we would very likely explain the difficulty away by adopting some kind of labelling convention, allowing us to remember that two formulas have been obtained from the same memory region by dividing permissions.

In fact, that is almost exactly our proposed remedy to the situation. We introduce *nominals*, or *labels*, from hybrid logic, where a nominal α is interpreted as denoting a unique heap. Any formula of the form $\alpha \wedge A$ is then precise (in the above sense), and so obeys the combination principle

$$(\alpha \wedge A)^{\pi} \circledast (\alpha \wedge A)^{\sigma} \models (\alpha \wedge A)^{\sigma \oplus \pi}, \tag{5}$$

where $\oplus$ is addition on permissions. Thus we can repair the faulty CSL proof above by replacing every instance of the formula $\mathsf{ls}\,x\,y$ by the "labelled" formula $\alpha \wedge \mathsf{ls}\,x\,y$ (and adding an initial step in which we introduce the fresh label α).

2.3   The Jump Modality

However, this is not quite the end of the story. Readers may have noticed that replacing $\mathsf{ls}\,x\,y$ by the "labelled" version $\alpha \wedge \mathsf{ls}\,x\,y$ also entails establishing a slightly stronger specification for the function foo, namely:

$$\{(\alpha \wedge \mathsf{ls}\,x\,y)^{0.5}\}\,\texttt{foo(x,y)}\,;\,\{(\alpha \wedge \mathsf{ls}\,x\,y)^{0.5}\}.$$

This introduces an extra difficulty in the proof (cf. Sect. 2.1); at the recursive call to foo([x],y), the precondition now becomes $\alpha^{0.5} \wedge (x \overset{0.5}{\mapsto} z * (\mathsf{ls}\,z\,y)^{0.5}))$, which means that we cannot apply separation logic's *frame rule* [32] to the pointer formula without first weakening away the label-share $\alpha^{0.5}$.

For this reason, we shall also employ hybrid logic's "jump" modality $@\_$, where the formula $@_\alpha A$ means that A is true of the heap denoted by the label α. In the above, we can introduce labels β and γ for the list components $x \mapsto z$ and $\mathsf{ls}\,z\,y$ respectively, whereby we can represent the decomposition of the list by the assertion $@_\alpha(\beta * \gamma)$. Since this is a *pure* assertion that does not depend on the heap, it can be safely maintained when applying the frame rule, and used after the function call to restore the label α, using the easily verifiable fact that

$$@_\alpha(\beta * \gamma) \wedge (\beta * \gamma) \models \alpha.$$

Similar reasoning over labelled decompositions of data structures is seemingly necessary whenever treating recursion; we return to it in more detail in Sect. 5.

3   Separation Logic with Labels and Permissions ($\mathsf{SL_{LP}}$)

Following the motivation given in the previous section, here we give the syntax and semantics of a separation logic, $\mathsf{SL_{LP}}$, with permissions over arbitrary formulas, making use of both strong *and* weak separating conjunctions, and nominal labels (from hybrid logic [3,10]). First, we define a suitable notion of permissions and associated operations.

Definition 3.1. *A* permissions algebra *is a tuple* $\langle \mathsf{Perm}, \oplus, \otimes, 1 \rangle$, *where* Perm *is a set (of "permissions"),* $1 \in \mathsf{Perm}$ *is called the* write permission, *and* $\oplus$ *and* $\otimes$ *are respectively partial and total binary functions on* Perm, *satisfying associativity, commutativity, cancellativity and the following additional axioms:*

$$\begin{array}{ll}
\pi_1 \oplus \pi_2 \neq \pi_2 & \textit{(non-zero)} \\
\forall \pi.\ \pi \oplus 1 \textit{ is undefined} & \textit{(top)} \\
\forall \pi.\ \exists \pi_1, \pi_2.\ \pi = \pi_1 \oplus \pi_2 & \textit{(divisibility)} \\
(\pi_1 \oplus \pi_2) \otimes \pi = (\pi_1 \otimes \pi) \oplus (\pi_2 \otimes \pi) & \textit{(left-dist)}
\end{array}$$

The most common example of a permissions algebra is the Boyland fractional permission model $\langle (0,1] \cap \mathbb{Q}, \oplus, \times, 1 \rangle$, where permissions are rational numbers in $(0,1]$, $\times$ is standard multiplication, and $\oplus$ is standard addition but undefined if $p + p' > 1$. From now on, we assume a fixed but arbitrary permissions algebra.

With the permissions structure in place, we can now define the syntax of our logic. We assume disjoint, countably infinite sets Var of variables, Pred of predicate symbols (with associated arities) and Label of labels.

Definition 3.2. *We define* formulas *of* $\mathsf{SL_{LP}}$ *by the grammar:*

$$
\begin{array}{lll}
A ::= & x = y \mid \neg A \mid A \wedge A \mid A \vee A \mid A \to A & \textit{(pure)} \\
& \mid \mathsf{emp} \mid x \mapsto y \mid P(\mathbf{x}) \mid A * A \mid A \circledast A \mid A \mathbin{-\!\!*} A \mid A \mathbin{-\!\!\circledast} A & \textit{(spatial)} \\
& \mid A^\pi \mid \alpha \mid @_\alpha A & \textit{(perms/labels)}
\end{array}
$$

where x, y *range over* Var, π *ranges over* Perm, P *ranges over* Pred, α *ranges over* Label *and* $\mathbf{x}$ *ranges over tuples of variables of length matching the arity of the predicate symbol* P. *We write* $x \xmapsto{\pi} y$ *for* $(x \mapsto y)^\pi$, *and* $x \neq y$ *for* $\neg(x = y)$.

The "magic wands" $-\!\!*$ and $-\!\!\circledast$ are the implications adjoint to $*$ and $\circledast$, as usual in separation logic. We include them for completeness, but we use $-\!\!*$ only for fairly complex examples (see Sect. 5.3) and in fact do not use $-\!\!\circledast$ at all.

Semantics. We interpret formulas in a standard model of stacks and heaps-with-permissions (cf. [4]), except that our models also incorporate a valuation of nominal labels. We assume an infinite set Val of *values* of which an infinite subset Loc $\subset$ Val are considered addressable *locations*. A *stack* is as usual a map $s : \mathsf{Var} \to \mathsf{Val}$. A *heap-with-permissions*, which we call a *p-heap* for short, is a finite partial function $h : \mathsf{Loc} \to_{\mathrm{fin}} \mathsf{Val} \times \mathsf{Perm}$ from locations to value-permission pairs. We write dom (h) for the *domain* of h, i.e. the set of locations on which h is defined. Two p-heaps h_1 and h_2 are called *disjoint* if dom $(h_1) \cap$ dom $(h_2) = \emptyset$, and *compatible* if, for all $\ell \in$ dom $(h_1) \cap$ dom (h_2), we have $h_1(\ell) = (v, \pi_1)$ and $h_2(v, \pi_2)$ and $\pi_1 \oplus \pi_2$ is defined. (Thus, trivially, disjoint heaps are also compatible.) We define the multiplication $\pi \cdot h$ of a p-heap h by permission π by extending $\otimes$ pointwise:

$$
(\pi \cdot h)(\ell) = (v, \pi \otimes \pi') \quad \Leftrightarrow \quad h(\ell) = (v, \pi').
$$

We also assume that each predicate symbol P of arity k is given a fixed interpretation $\llbracket P \rrbracket \in (\mathsf{Val}^k \times \mathsf{PHeaps})$, where PHeaps is the set of all p-heaps. Here we allow an essentially free interpretation of predicate symbols, but they could also be given by a suitable inductive definition schema, as is done in many papers on separation logic (e.g. [7,8]). Finally, a *valuation* is a function $\rho : \mathsf{Label} \to \mathsf{PHeaps}$ assigning a single p-heap $\rho(\alpha)$ to each label α.

Definition 3.3 (Strong and weak heap composition). *The* strong composition $h_1 \circ h_2$ *of two disjoint p-heaps* h_1 *and* h_2 *is defined as their union:*

$$
(h_1 \circ h_2)(\ell) = \begin{cases} h_1(\ell) & \textit{if } \ell \notin \mathrm{dom}\,(h_2) \\ h_2(\ell) & \textit{if } \ell \notin \mathrm{dom}\,(h_1) \end{cases}
$$

$$\begin{array}{lll}
s, h, \rho \models x = y & \Leftrightarrow & s(x) = s(y) \\
s, h, \rho \models \neg A & \Leftrightarrow & s, h, \rho \not\models A \\
s, h, \rho \models A \wedge B & \Leftrightarrow & s, h, \rho \models A \text{ and } s, h, \rho \models B \\
s, h, \rho \models A \vee B & \Leftrightarrow & s, h, \rho \models A \text{ or } s, h, \rho \models B \\
s, h, \rho \models A \rightarrow B & \Leftrightarrow & s, h, \rho \models A \text{ implies } s, h, \rho \models B \\
s, h, \rho \models \mathsf{emp} & \Leftrightarrow & \mathrm{dom}\,(h) = \emptyset \\
s, h, \rho \models x \mapsto y & \Leftrightarrow & \mathrm{dom}\,(h) = \{s(x)\} \text{ and } h(s(x)) = (s(y), 1) \\
s, h, \rho \models P(\mathbf{x}) & \Leftrightarrow & (s(\mathbf{x}), h) \in \llbracket P \rrbracket \\
s, h, \rho \models A * B & \Leftrightarrow & \exists h_1, h_2.\ h = h_1 \circ h_2 \text{ and } s, h_1, \rho \models A \text{ and } s, h_2, \rho \models B \\
s, h, \rho \models A \circledast B & \Leftrightarrow & \exists h_1, h_2.\ h = h_1 \,\bar{\circ}\, h_2 \text{ and } s, h_1, \rho \models A \text{ and } s, h_2, \rho \models B \\
s, h, \rho \models A \mathbin{-\!*} B & \Leftrightarrow & \forall h'.\ \text{if } h \circ h' \text{ defined and } s, h', \rho \models A \text{ then } s, h \circ h', \rho \models B \\
s, h, \rho \models A \mathbin{-\!\circledast} B & \Leftrightarrow & \forall h'.\ \text{if } h \,\bar{\circ}\, h' \text{ defined and } s, h', \rho \models A \text{ then } s, h \,\bar{\circ}\, h', \rho \models B \\
s, h, \rho \models A^\pi & \Leftrightarrow & \exists h'.\ h = \pi \cdot h' \text{ and } s, h', \rho \models A \\
s, h, \rho \models \alpha & \Leftrightarrow & h = \rho(\alpha) \\
s, h, \rho \models @_\alpha A & \Leftrightarrow & s, \rho(\alpha), \rho \models A
\end{array}$$

Fig. 1. Definition of the satisfaction relation $s, h, \rho \models A$ for $\mathsf{SL_{LP}}$.

If h_1 and h_2 are not disjoint then $h_1 \circ h_2$ is undefined.

The weak composition *$h_1 \,\bar{\circ}\, h_2$ of two compatible p-heaps h_1 and h_2 is defined as their union, adding permissions at overlapping locations:*

$$(h_1 \,\bar{\circ}\, h_2)(\ell) = \begin{cases} (v, \pi_1 \oplus \pi_2) & \text{if } h_1(\ell) = (v, \pi_1) \text{ and } h_2(\ell) = (v, \pi_2) \\ h_1(\ell) & \text{if } \ell \notin \mathrm{dom}\,(h_2) \\ h_2(\ell) & \text{if } \ell \notin \mathrm{dom}\,(h_1) \end{cases}$$

If h_1 and h_2 are not compatible then $h_1 \,\bar{\circ}\, h_2$ is undefined.

Definition 3.4. *The satisfaction relation $s, h, \rho \models A$, where s is a stack, h a p-heap, ρ a valuation and A a formula, is defined by structural induction on A in Fig. 1. We write the entailment $A \models B$, where A and B are formulas, to mean that if $s, h, \rho \models A$ then $s, h, \rho \models B$. We write the equivalence $A \equiv B$ to mean that $A \models B$ and $B \models A$.*

4   Logical Principles of $\mathsf{SL_{LP}}$

In this section, we establish the main logical entailments and equivalences of $\mathsf{SL_{LP}}$ that capture the various interactions between the separating conjunctions $\circledast$ and $*$, permissions and labels. As well as being of interest in their own right, many of these principles will be essential in treating the practical verification examples in Sect. 5. In particular, the permission distribution principle for $*$ (cf. (3), Sect. 2) is given in Lemma 4.3, and the permission combination principle for labelled formulas (cf. (5), Sect. 2) is given in Lemma 4.4.

Proposition 4.1. *The following equivalences all hold in* $\mathsf{SL_{LP}}$:

$$A \circledast B \equiv B \circledast A \qquad\qquad A * B \equiv B * A$$
$$A \circledast (B \circledast C) \equiv (A \circledast B) \circledast C \qquad A * (B * C) \equiv (A * B) * C$$
$$A \circledast \mathsf{emp} \equiv A \qquad\qquad A * \mathsf{emp} \equiv A$$

Additionally, the following residuation laws hold:

$$A \models B \mathbin{-\!\circledast} C \iff A \circledast B \models C \quad and \quad A \models B \mathbin{-\!*} C \iff A * B \models C.$$

In addition, we can always weaken $*$ *to* $\circledast$: $A * B \models A \circledast B$.

Next, we establish an additional connection between the two separating conjunctions $\circledast$ and $*$.

Lemma 4.2 ($\circledast/*$ distribution). *For all formulas* A, B, C *and* D,

$$(A \circledast B) * (C \circledast D) \models (A * C) \circledast (B * D). \qquad (\circledast/*)$$

Proof. First we show a corresponding model-theoretic property: for any p-heaps h_1, h_2, h_3 and h_4 such that $(h_1 \mathbin{\bar{\circ}} h_2) \circ (h_3 \mathbin{\bar{\circ}} h_4)$ is defined,

$$(h_1 \mathbin{\bar{\circ}} h_2) \circ (h_3 \mathbin{\bar{\circ}} h_4) = (h_1 \circ h_3) \mathbin{\bar{\circ}} (h_2 \circ h_4) \qquad (6)$$

Since $(h_1 \mathbin{\bar{\circ}} h_2) \circ (h_3 \mathbin{\bar{\circ}} h_4)$ is defined by assumption, we have that $h_1 \mathbin{\bar{\circ}} h_2$ and $h_3 \mathbin{\bar{\circ}} h_4$ are disjoint and that h_1 and h_2, as well as h_3 and h_4 are compatible. In particular, h_1 and h_3 are disjoint, so $h_1 \circ h_3$ is defined; the same reasoning applies to h_2 and h_4. Moreover, since h_1 and h_2 are compatible, $h_1 \circ h_3$ and $h_2 \circ h_4$ must be compatible and so $(h_1 \circ h_3) \mathbin{\bar{\circ}} (h_2 \circ h_4)$ is defined. Now, writing h for $(h_1 \mathbin{\bar{\circ}} h_2) \circ (h_3 \mathbin{\bar{\circ}} h_4)$, and letting $\ell \in \mathrm{dom}\,(h)$, we have

$$h(\ell) = \begin{cases} h_1(\ell) & \text{if } \ell \notin \mathrm{dom}\,(h_3),\ell \notin \mathrm{dom}\,(h_4) \text{ and } \ell \notin \mathrm{dom}\,(h_2) \\ h_2(\ell) & \text{if } \ell \notin \mathrm{dom}\,(h_3),\ell \notin \mathrm{dom}\,(h_4) \text{ and } \ell \notin \mathrm{dom}\,(h_1) \\ (v, \pi_1 \oplus \pi_2) & \text{if } \ell \notin \mathrm{dom}\,(h_3),\ell \notin \mathrm{dom}\,(h_4) \text{ and } h_1(\ell) = (v, \pi_1) \\ & \quad \text{and } h_2(\ell) = (v, \pi_2) \\ h_3(\ell) & \text{if } \ell \notin \mathrm{dom}\,(h_1),\ell \notin \mathrm{dom}\,(h_2) \text{ and } \ell \notin \mathrm{dom}\,(h_4) \\ h_4(\ell) & \text{if } \ell \notin \mathrm{dom}\,(h_1),\ell \notin \mathrm{dom}\,(h_2) \text{ and } \ell \notin \mathrm{dom}\,(h_3) \\ (u, \pi_3 \oplus \pi_4) & \text{if } \ell \notin \mathrm{dom}\,(h_1),\ell \notin \mathrm{dom}\,(h_2) \text{ and } h_3(\ell) = (u, \pi_3) \\ & \quad \text{and } h_4(\ell) = (u, \pi_4) \end{cases}$$

We can merge the first and fourth cases by noting that $h(\ell) = (h_1 \circ h_3)(\ell)$ if $\ell \notin \mathrm{dom}\,(h_2 \circ h_4)$, and similarly for the second and fifth cases. We can also rewrite the last two cases by observing that $\ell \notin \mathrm{dom}\,(h_3)$ implies $h_1(\ell) = (h_1 \circ h_3)(\ell)$, and so on, resulting in

$$h(\ell) = \begin{cases} (h_1 \circ h_3)(\ell) & \text{if } \ell \notin \mathrm{dom}\,(h_2 \circ h_4) \\ (h_2 \circ h_4)(\ell) & \text{if } \ell \notin \mathrm{dom}\,(h_1 \circ h_3) \\ (w, \sigma_1 \oplus \sigma_2) & \text{if } (h_1 \circ h_3)(\ell) = (w, \sigma_1) \text{ and } (h_2 \circ h_4)(\ell) = (w, \sigma_2) \end{cases}$$

$$= ((h_1 \circ h_3) \mathbin{\bar{\circ}} (h_2 \circ h_4))(\ell).$$

Now we show the main result. Suppose $s, h, \rho \models (A \circledast B) * (C \circledast D)$. This gives us $h = (h_1 \bar{\circ} h_2) \circ (h_3 \bar{\circ} h_4)$, where $s, h_1, \rho \models A$ and $s, h_2, \rho \models B$ and $s, h_3, \rho \models C$ and $s, h_4, \rho \models D$. By Eq. (6), we have $h = (h_1 \circ h_3) \bar{\circ} (h_2 \circ h_4)$, which gives us exactly that $s, h, \rho \models (A * C) \circledast (B * D)$, as required. $\square$

Next, we establish principles for distributing permissions over various connectives, in particular over the strong $*$, stated earlier as (3) in Sect. 2.

Lemma 4.3 (Permission distribution). *The following equivalences hold for all formulas A and B, and permissions π and σ:*

$$(A^\sigma)^\pi \equiv A^{\sigma \otimes \pi} \tag{$\otimes$}$$

$$(A \vee B)^\pi \equiv A^\pi \vee B^\pi \tag{$\vee^\pi$}$$

$$(A \wedge B)^\pi \equiv A^\pi \wedge B^\pi \tag{$\wedge^\pi$}$$

$$(A * B)^\pi \equiv A^\pi * B^\pi \tag{$*^\pi$}$$

Proof. We just show the most interesting case, $(*^\pi)$. First of all, we establish a corresponding model-theoretic property: for any permission π and disjoint p-heaps h_1 and h_2, meaning $h_1 \circ h_2$ is defined,

$$\pi \cdot (h_1 \circ h_2) = (\pi \cdot h_1) \circ (\pi \cdot h_2). \tag{7}$$

To see this, we first observe that for any $\ell \in \mathrm{dom}\,(h_1 \circ h_2)$, we have that either $\ell \in \mathrm{dom}\,(h_1)$ or $\ell \in \mathrm{dom}\,(h_2)$. We just show the case $\ell \in \mathrm{dom}\,(h_1)$, since the other is symmetric. Writing $h_1(\ell) = (v_1, \pi_1)$, and using the fact that $\ell \notin \mathrm{dom}\,(h_2)$,

$$\pi \cdot (h_1 \circ h_2)(\ell) = (v_1, \pi \otimes \pi_1) = (\pi \cdot h_1)(\ell) = ((\pi \cdot h_1) \circ (\pi \cdot h_2))(\ell).$$

Now for the main result, let s, h and ρ be given. We have

$$
\begin{aligned}
& s, h, \rho \models (A * B)^\pi \\
\Leftrightarrow\quad & h = \pi \cdot h' \text{ and } s, h', \rho \models A * B \\
\Leftrightarrow\quad & h = \pi \cdot h' \text{ and } h' = h_1 \circ h_2 \text{ and } s, h_1, \rho \models A \text{ and } s, h_2, \rho \models B \\
\Leftrightarrow\quad & h = \pi \cdot (h_1 \circ h_2) \text{ and } s, h_1, \rho \models A \text{ and } s, h_2, \rho \models B \\
\Leftrightarrow\quad & h = (\pi \cdot h_1) \circ (\pi \cdot h_2) \text{ and } s, h_1, \rho \models A \text{ and } s, h_2, \rho \models B \qquad \text{by (7)} \\
\Leftrightarrow\quad & h = h_1' \circ h_2' \text{ and } s, h_1', \rho \models A^\pi \text{ and } s, h_2', \rho \models B^\pi \\
\Leftrightarrow\quad & s, h, \rho \models A^\pi * B^\pi. \qquad\qquad\qquad\qquad\qquad\qquad\qquad\qquad\quad \square
\end{aligned}
$$

We now establish the main principles for dividing and combining permissions formulas using $\circledast$. As foreshadowed in Sect. 2, the combination principle holds only for formulas that are conjoined with a nominal label (cf. Eq. (5)).

Lemma 4.4 (Permission division and combination). *For all formulas A, nominals α, and permissions π_1, π_2 such that $\pi_1 \oplus \pi_2$ is defined:*

$$A^{\pi_1 \oplus \pi_2} \models A^{\pi_1} \circledast A^{\pi_2} \tag{Split $\circledast$}$$

$$(\alpha \wedge A)^{\pi_1} \circledast (\alpha \wedge A)^{\pi_2} \models (\alpha \wedge A)^{\pi_1 \oplus \pi_2} \tag{Join $\circledast$}$$

Proof. **Case** (Split $\circledast$)**:** Suppose that $s, h, \rho \models A^{\pi_1 \oplus \pi_2}$. We have $h = (\pi_1 \oplus \pi_2) \cdot h'$, where $s, h', \rho \models A$. That is, for any $\ell \in \text{dom}\,(h)$, we have $h'(\ell) = (v, \pi)$ say and, using the permissions algebra axiom (left-dist) from Definition 3.1,

$$h(\ell) = (v, (\pi_1 \oplus \pi_2) \otimes \pi) = (v, (\pi_1 \otimes \pi) \oplus (\pi_2 \otimes \pi)).$$

Now we define p-heaps h_1 and h_2, both with domain exactly $\text{dom}\,(h)$, by

$$h_i(\ell) = (v, \pi_i \otimes \pi) \iff h'(\ell) = (v, \pi) \qquad \text{for } i \in \{1, 2\}.$$

By construction, $h_1 = \pi_1 \cdot h'$ and $h_2 = \pi_2 \cdot h'$. Since $s, h', \rho \models A$, this gives us $s, h_1, \rho \models A^{\pi_1}$ and $s, h_2, \rho \models A^{\pi_2}$. Furthermore, also by construction, h_1 and h_2 are compatible, with $h = h_1 \,\overline{\circ}\, h_2$. Thus $s, h, \rho \models A^{\pi_1} \circledast A^{\pi_2}$, as required.

Case (Join $\circledast$)**:** First of all, we show that for any p-heap h,

$$(\pi_1 \cdot h) \,\overline{\circ}\, (\pi_2 \cdot h) = (\pi_1 \oplus \pi_2) \cdot h. \tag{8}$$

To see this, we observe that for any $\ell \in \text{dom}\,(h)$, writing $h(\ell) = (v, \pi)$ say,

$$
\begin{aligned}
&((\pi_1 \oplus \pi_2) \cdot h)(\ell) \\
&= (v, (\pi_1 \oplus \pi_2) \otimes \pi) \\
&= (v, (\pi_1 \otimes \pi) \oplus (\pi_2 \otimes \pi)) \qquad \text{by (left-dist)} \\
&= (h_1 \oplus h_2)(\ell) \text{ where } h_1(\ell) = (v, \pi_1 \otimes \pi) \text{ and } h_2 = (v, \pi_2 \otimes \pi) \\
&= ((\pi_1 \cdot h) \,\overline{\circ}\, (\pi_2 \cdot h))(\ell).
\end{aligned}
$$

Now, for the main result, suppose $s, h, \rho \models (\alpha \wedge A)^{\pi_1} \circledast (\alpha \wedge A)^{\pi_2}$. We have $h = h_1 \,\overline{\circ}\, h_2$ where $s, h_1, \rho \models (\alpha \wedge A)^{\pi_1}$ and $s, h_2, \rho \models (\alpha \wedge A)^{\pi_2}$. That is, $h = (\pi_1 \cdot h'_1) \,\overline{\circ}\, (\pi_2 \cdot h'_2)$, where $s, h'_1, \rho \models \alpha \wedge A$ and $s, h'_2, \rho \models \alpha \wedge A$. Thus $h'_1 = h'_2 = \rho(\alpha)$ and so, by (8), we have $h = (\pi_1 \oplus \pi_2) \cdot h'_1$, where $s, h'_1, \rho \models \alpha \wedge A$. This gives us $s, h, \rho \models (\alpha \wedge A)^{\pi_1 \oplus \pi_2}$, as required.

Lastly, we state some useful principles for labels and the "jump" modality.

Lemma 4.5 (Labelling and jump). *For all formulas A and labels α,*

$$@_\alpha A \wedge \alpha^\pi \models A^\pi \tag{@ Elim}$$

$$(\alpha \wedge A)^\pi \models @_\alpha A \tag{@ Intro}$$

$$@_\alpha(\beta_1{}^\pi * \beta_2{}^\sigma) \wedge (\beta_1{}^\pi \circledast \beta_2{}^\sigma) \models \alpha \wedge (\beta_1{}^\pi * \beta_2{}^\sigma) \tag{@/ $*$ /$\circledast$}$$

Proof. We just show the case (@/ $*$ /$\circledast$), the others being easy. Suppose $s, h, \rho \models @_\alpha(\beta_1{}^\pi * \beta_2{}^\sigma) \wedge (\beta_1{}^\pi \circledast \beta_2{}^\sigma)$, meaning that $s, \rho(\alpha), \rho \models \beta_1{}^\pi * \beta_2{}^\sigma$ and $s, h, \rho \models \beta_1{}^\pi \circledast \beta_2{}^\sigma$. Then we have $\rho(\alpha) = (\pi \cdot \rho(\beta_1)) \circ (\sigma \cdot \rho(\beta_2))$, while $h = (\pi \cdot \rho(\beta_1)) \,\overline{\circ}\, (\sigma \cdot \rho(\beta_2))$. Since $\circ$ is defined only when its arguments are disjoint p-heaps, we obtain that $h = \rho(\alpha) = (\pi \cdot \rho(\beta_1)) \circ (\sigma \cdot \rho(\beta_2))$. Thus $s, h, \rho \models \alpha \wedge (\beta_1{}^\pi * \beta_2{}^\sigma)$. $\square$

$$\frac{\{A_1\}\,C_1\,\{B_1\} \quad \{A_2\}\,C_2\,\{B_2\}}{\{A_1 \circledast A_2\}\,C_1 \,\|\, C_2\,\{B_1 \circledast B_2\}}\ (\boxplus)\ \text{(Par)} \qquad \frac{\{\alpha \wedge A\}\,C\,\{B\}}{\{A\}\,C\,\{B\}}\ (\boxtimes)\ \text{(Label)}$$

$$\frac{\{A\}\,C\,\{B\}}{\{A * F\}\,C\,\{B * F\}}\ (\dagger, \ddagger)\ \text{(Frame *)} \qquad \frac{\{A\}\,C\,\{B\}}{\{A \circledast F\}\,C\,\{B \circledast F\}}\ (\dagger)\ \text{(Frame } \circledast)$$

$(\boxplus)$ ModVars$(C_2) \cap$ FreeVars$(A_1, B_1) =$ ModVars$(C_1) \cap$ FreeVars$(A_2, B_2) = \emptyset$

$(\boxtimes)\ \alpha$ fresh $\quad$ $(\dagger)$ ModVars$(C) \cap$ FreeVars$(F) = \emptyset$ $\quad$ $(\ddagger)$ see §5.3

Fig. 2. The key CSL proof rules used in our examples; not shown are standard rules for consequence, conditionals, load/store, etc. The fresh-labelling rule (Label) and combination of both weak (Frame $\circledast$) and strong (Frame *) frame rules are novel to our approach. We require weak conjunction $\circledast$ for the parallel rule (Par).

5 Concurrent Program Verification Examples

In this section, we demonstrate how SL$_{\text{LP}}$ can be used in conjunction with the usual principles of CSL to construct verification proofs of concurrent programs, taking three examples of increasing complexity.

Our examples all operate on *binary trees* in memory, defined as usual in separation logic (again note the use of * rather than $\circledast$):

$$\text{tree}(x) \ =_{\text{def}}\ (x = null \wedge \text{emp}) \vee (\exists d, l, r.\ x \mapsto (d, l, r) * \text{tree}(l) * \text{tree}(r)).$$

Our proofs employ (a subset of) the standard rules of CSL—with the most important being the concurrency rule from the Introduction, the separation logic *frame rules* for both * and $\circledast$, and a new rule enabling us to introduce fresh labels into the precondition of a triple (similar to the way Hoare logic usually handles existential quantifiers). These key rules are shown in Fig. 2. We simplify our Hoare triple to remove elements to handle function call/return and furthermore omit the presentation of the standard collection of rules for consequence, load, store, if-then-else, assignment, etc.; readers interested in such aspects can consult [1]. Both of our frame rules have the usual side condition on modified program variables. The strong frame rule (Frame *) has an additional side condition that will be discussed in Sect. 5.3; until then it is trivially satisfied.

5.1 Parallel Read

Consider the following program:

```
check(x) {
    if (x == null) { return; }
    read(x);   ||   read(x);
}
```

This is intended to be a straightforward example where we take a tree rooted at x and, if x is non-null, split into parallel threads that run the program read on x, and whose specification is $\{\alpha^\pi \wedge \mathsf{tree}(x)^\sigma\}\,\mathtt{read(x)}\,\{\alpha^\pi \wedge \mathsf{tree}(x)^\sigma\}$. We prove that check satisfies the specification $\{\mathsf{tree}(x)^\pi\}\,\mathtt{check(x)}\,\{\mathsf{tree}(x)^\pi\}$; the verification proof is in Fig. 3. The proof makes use of the basic operations of our theory: labelling, splitting and joining. The example follows precisely these steps, starting by labelling the formula $\mathsf{tree}(x)^\pi \wedge x \neq null$ with α. The concurrency rule (Par) allows us to put formulas back together after the parallel call, and the two copies $(\alpha \wedge \mathsf{tree}(x)^\pi)^{0.5}$ that were obtained are glued back together to yield $\mathsf{tree}(x)^\pi$, since they have the same label.

```
{tree(x)^π}
check(x) {
{(tree(x)^π ∧ x = null) ∨ (tree(x)^π ∧ x ≠ null)}
if (x == null) { {x = null ∧ tree(x)^π}
return;
{tree(x)^π}
}
```

$\{\alpha \wedge \mathsf{tree}(x)^\pi \wedge x \neq null\}$ by (Label)

$\{(\alpha \wedge \mathsf{tree}(x)^\pi)^{0.5} \circledast (\alpha \wedge \mathsf{tree}(x)^\pi)^{0.5}\}$ by (Split $\circledast$)

$\{(\alpha \wedge \mathsf{tree}(x)^\pi)^{0.5}\}$

$\{\alpha^{0.5} \wedge \mathsf{tree}(x)^{\pi \otimes 0.5}\}$ $\|$ by $(\wedge^\pi),(\otimes)$

```
read(x);
```
    $\|$ ...

$\{\alpha^{0.5} \wedge \mathsf{tree}(x)^{\pi \otimes 0.5}\}$ $\|$

$\{(\alpha \wedge \mathsf{tree}(x)^\pi)^{0.5}\}$ $\|$ by $(\wedge^\pi),(\otimes)$

$\{(\alpha \wedge \mathsf{tree}(x)^\pi)^{0.5} \circledast (\alpha \wedge \mathsf{tree}(x)^\pi)^{0.5}\}$ by (Par)

$\{\alpha \wedge \mathsf{tree}(x)^\pi\}$ by (Join $\circledast$)

```
}
```
$\{\mathsf{tree}(x)^\pi\}$

Fig. 3. Verification proof of program check in Example 5.1.

5.2 Parallel Tree Processing (Le and Hobor [24])

Consider the following program, which was also employed as an example in [24]:

```
proc(x) {
    if (x == null) { return; }
    print(x->d);     ‖  print(x->d);
    proc(x->l);      ‖  proc(x->l);
    proc(x->r);      ‖  proc(x->r);
}
```

This code takes a tree rooted at x and, if x is non-null, splits into parallel threads that call proc recursively on its left and right branches. We prove, in Fig. 4, that `proc` satisfies the specification $\{\alpha \wedge \mathsf{tree}(x)^\pi\}\,\mathtt{proc(x)}\,\{\alpha \wedge \mathsf{tree}(x)^\pi\}$. First we unroll the definition of $\mathsf{tree}(x)$ and distribute the permission over Boolean connectives and $*$. If the tree is empty the process stops. Otherwise, we label each component with a new label and introduce the "jump" statement $@_\alpha(\beta_1 * \beta_2 * \beta_3)$, recording the decomposition of the tree into its three components. Since such statements are *pure*, i.e. independent of the heap, we can "carry" this formula along our computation without interfering with the frame rule(s). Now that every subregion is labelled, we split the formula into two copies, each with half share, but after distributing 0.5 over $*$ and $\wedge$ we end up with half shares in the labels as well. We relabel each subregion with new "whole" labels, and again introduce pure @-formulas that record the relation between the old and the new labels. At this moment we enter the parallel threads and recursively apply `proc` to the left and right subtrees of x. Assuming the specification of `proc` for subtrees of x, we then retrieve the original label α from the trail of crumbs left by the @-formulas. We can then recombine the α-labelled threads using (Join $\circledast$) to arrive at the desired postcondition.

5.3   Cross-thread Data Transfer

Our previous examples involve only "isolated tank" concurrency: a program has some resources and splits them into parallel threads that do not communicate with each other before—remembering Humpty Dumpty!—ultimately re-merging. For our last example, we will show that our technique is expressive enough to handle more sophisticated kinds of sharing, in particular inter-thread coarse-grained communication. We will show that we can not only share read-only data, but in fact prove that one thread has acquired the full ownership of a structure, even when the associated root pointers are not easily exposed.

To do so, we add some communication primitives to our language, together with their associated Hoare rules. Coarse-grained concurrency such as locks, channels, and barriers have been well-investigated in various flavours of concurrent separation logic [19,26,31]. We will use a channel for our example in this section but with simplified rules: the Hoare rule for a channel c to send message number i whose message invariant is R_i^c is $\{R_i^c(x)\}\,\mathtt{send}(c, x)\,\{\mathsf{emp}\}$, while the corresponding rule to receive is $\{\mathsf{emp}\}\,\mathtt{receive}(c)\,\{\lambda ret.\ R_i^c(ret)\}$. We ignore details such as identifying which party is allowed to send/receive at a given time [14] or the resource ownership of the channel itself [18].

These rules interact poorly with the strong frame rule from Fig. 2:

$$\frac{\{A\}\,C\,\{B\}}{\{A * F\}\,C\,\{B * F\}}\,(\dagger, \ddagger)\ (\text{Frame } *) \qquad \begin{array}{l}(\dagger)\ \mathrm{ModVars}(C) \cap \mathrm{FreeVars}(F) = \emptyset \\ (\ddagger)\ C \text{ does not receive resources}\end{array}$$

The revealed side condition ($\ddagger$) means that C does not contain any subcommands that "transfer in" resources, such as `unlock`, `receive`, etc.; this side condition is a bit stronger than necessary but has a simple definition and can be checked syntactically. Without ($\ddagger$), we can reach a contradiction. Assume that the current

$\{\alpha \wedge \mathsf{tree}(x)^\pi\}$
```
proc(x) {
```
$\quad\{(\alpha \wedge (x = null \wedge \mathsf{emp})^\pi) \vee (\alpha \wedge (x \mapsto (d,l,r) * \mathsf{tree}(l) * \mathsf{tree}(r))^\pi)\}$ by $(\wedge^\pi),(\vee^\pi)$
$\quad\{(\alpha \wedge x = null \wedge \mathsf{emp}) \vee (\alpha \wedge (x \mapsto (d,l,r) * \mathsf{tree}(l) * \mathsf{tree}(r))^\pi)\}$
```
  if (x == null) { {α ∧ x = null ∧ emp}
  return;
```
$\quad\{\alpha \wedge (x = null \wedge \mathsf{emp})^\pi\}$
$\quad\{\alpha \wedge \mathsf{tree}(x)^\pi\}$
```
  }
```

$\quad\{\alpha \wedge (x \overset{\pi}{\mapsto} (d,l,r) * \mathsf{tree}(l)^\pi * \mathsf{tree}(r)^\pi)\}$ by $(*^\pi)$

$\quad\{((\beta_1 \wedge x \overset{\pi}{\mapsto} (d,l,r)) * (\beta_2 \wedge \mathsf{tree}(l)^\pi) * (\beta_3 \wedge \mathsf{tree}(r)^\pi)) \wedge$ by (Label),
$\quad\quad @_\alpha(\beta_1 * \beta_2 * \beta_3)\}$ (@ Intro)

$\quad\{(((\beta_1^{0.5} \wedge x \overset{\pi \otimes 0.5}{\mapsto} (d,l,r)) * (\beta_2^{0.5} \wedge \mathsf{tree}(l)^{\pi \otimes 0.5})*$
$\quad\quad(\beta_3^{0.5} \wedge \mathsf{tree}(r)^{\pi \otimes 0.5})) \wedge (@_\alpha(\beta_1 * \beta_2 * \beta_3))^{0.5})\circledast$
$\quad\quad(((\beta_1^{0.5} \wedge x \overset{\pi \otimes 0.5}{\mapsto} (d,l,r)) * (\beta_2^{0.5} \wedge \mathsf{tree}(l)^{\pi \otimes 0.5})*$ by (Split $\circledast$),
$\quad\quad(\beta_3^{0.5} \wedge \mathsf{tree}(r)^{\pi \otimes 0.5})) \wedge (@_\alpha(\beta_1 * \beta_2 * \beta_3))^{0.5})\}$ $(*^\pi),(\wedge^\pi)$

$\quad\{(((\gamma_1 \wedge x \overset{\pi \otimes 0.5}{\mapsto} (d,l,r) \wedge @_{\gamma_1}\beta_1^{0.5}) * (\gamma_2 \wedge \mathsf{tree}(l)^{\pi \otimes 0.5} \wedge @_{\gamma_2}\beta_2^{0.5})*$
$\quad\quad(\gamma_3 \wedge \mathsf{tree}(r)^{\pi \otimes 0.5} \wedge @_{\gamma_3}\beta_3^{0.5})) \wedge @_\alpha(\beta_1 * \beta_2 * \beta_3))\circledast$
$\quad\quad(((\gamma_4 \wedge x \overset{\pi \otimes 0.5}{\mapsto} (d,l,r) \wedge @_{\gamma_4}\beta_1^{0.5}) * (\gamma_5 \wedge \mathsf{tree}(l)^{\pi \otimes 0.5} \wedge @_{\gamma_5}\beta_2^{0.5})*$ by (Label),
$\quad\quad(\gamma_6 \wedge \mathsf{tree}(r)^{\pi \otimes 0.5} \wedge @_{\gamma_6}\beta_3^{0.5})) \wedge @_\alpha(\beta_1 * \beta_2 * \beta_3))\}$ (@ Intro)

$\quad\{((\gamma_1 \wedge x \overset{\pi \otimes 0.5}{\mapsto} (d,l,r) \wedge @_{\gamma_1}\beta_1^{0.5})*$
$\quad\quad(\gamma_2 \wedge \mathsf{tree}(l)^{\pi \otimes 0.5} \wedge @_{\gamma_2}\beta_2^{0.5})*$
$\quad\quad(\gamma_3 \wedge \mathsf{tree}(r)^{\pi \otimes 0.5} \wedge @_{\gamma_3}\beta_3^{0.5})) \wedge @_\alpha(\beta_1 * \beta_2 * \beta_3)\}$
```
  print(x->d);
```
$\quad\{((\gamma_1 \wedge x \overset{\pi \otimes 0.5}{\mapsto} (d,l,r) \wedge @_{\gamma_1}\beta_1^{0.5})*$
$\quad\quad(\gamma_2 \wedge \mathsf{tree}(l)^{\pi \otimes 0.5} \wedge @_{\gamma_2}\beta_2^{0.5})*$
$\quad\quad(\gamma_3 \wedge \mathsf{tree}(r)^{\pi \otimes 0.5} \wedge @_{\gamma_3}\beta_3^{0.5})) \wedge @_\alpha(\beta_1 * \beta_2 * \beta_3)\}$
```
  proc(x->l);                                            ...
```
$\quad\{((\gamma_1 \wedge x \overset{\pi \otimes 0.5}{\mapsto} (d,l,r) \wedge @_{\gamma_1}\beta_1^{0.5})*$
$\quad\quad(\gamma_2 \wedge \mathsf{tree}(l)^{\pi \otimes 0.5} \wedge @_{\gamma_2}\beta_2^{0.5})*$
$\quad\quad(\gamma_3 \wedge \mathsf{tree}(r)^{\pi \otimes 0.5} \wedge @_{\gamma_3}\beta_3^{0.5})) \wedge @_\alpha(\beta_1 * \beta_2 * \beta_3)\}$
```
  proc(x->r);
```
$\quad\{((\gamma_1 \wedge x \overset{\pi \otimes 0.5}{\mapsto} (d,l,r) \wedge @_{\gamma_1}\beta_1^{0.5})*$
$\quad\quad(\gamma_2 \wedge \mathsf{tree}(l)^{\pi \otimes 0.5} \wedge @_{\gamma_2}\beta_2^{0.5})*$
$\quad\quad(\gamma_3 \wedge \mathsf{tree}(r)^{\pi \otimes 0.5} \wedge @_{\gamma_3}\beta_3^{0.5})) \wedge @_\alpha(\beta_1 * \beta_2 * \beta_3)\}$

$\quad\{((\beta_1^{0.5} \wedge x \overset{\pi \otimes 0.5}{\mapsto} (d,l,r)) * (\beta_2^{0.5} \wedge \mathsf{tree}(l)^{\pi \otimes 0.5})*$
$\quad\quad(\beta_3^{0.5} \wedge \mathsf{tree}(r)^{\pi \otimes 0.5})) \wedge (@_\alpha(\beta_1 * \beta_2 * \beta_3))^{0.5}\}$

$\quad\{(((\beta_1 \wedge x \overset{\pi}{\mapsto} (d,l,r)) * (\beta_2 \wedge \mathsf{tree}(l)^\pi)*$
$\quad\quad(\beta_3 \wedge \mathsf{tree}(r)^\pi)) \wedge @_\alpha(\beta_1 * \beta_2 * \beta_3))^{0.5}\}$ by $(\wedge^\pi),(*^\pi)$
$\quad\{(\alpha \wedge (x \overset{\pi}{\mapsto} (d,l,r) * \mathsf{tree}(l)^\pi * \mathsf{tree}(r)^\pi))^{0.5}\}$ by (@/*/$\circledast$)
$\quad\{(\alpha \wedge (x \overset{\pi}{\mapsto} (d,l,r) * \mathsf{tree}(l)^\pi * \mathsf{tree}(r)^\pi))^{0.5}\circledast$
$\quad\quad(\alpha \wedge (x \overset{\pi}{\mapsto} (d,l,r) * \mathsf{tree}(l)^\pi * \mathsf{tree}(r)^\pi))^{0.5}\}$ by (Par)
$\quad\{\alpha \wedge (x \overset{\pi}{\mapsto} (d,l,r) * \mathsf{tree}(l)^\pi * \mathsf{tree}(r)^\pi)\}$ by (Join $\circledast$)
```
}
```
$\{\alpha \wedge \mathsf{tree}(x)^\pi\}$

Fig. 4. Verification proof of Le and Hobor's program from [24] in Example 5.2.

```
100  void transfer(int key) {    { emp }
101                    rt* = make_tree();
102                    { tree(rt) }
```

$$\{ (\alpha \wedge \mathsf{tree}(rt))^{0.5} \} \qquad\qquad || \{ (\alpha \wedge \mathsf{tree}(rt))^{0.5} \}$$

```
   tree* sub = find(rt, key)  ||  ...                              ;
   send(ch, sub)              ||  tree* sub = receive(ch)  ;
   ...                        ||  modify(sub)                      ;
   receive(ch)                ||  send(ch, ())                     ;
```

$$\{ (\epsilon \wedge \mathsf{tree}(rt))^{0.5} \} \qquad\qquad || \{ (\epsilon \wedge \mathsf{tree}(rt))^{0.5} \}$$

```
400                    { tree(rt) }
401                    delete_tree(rt);   { emp } }
```

Fig. 5. Verification proof of the top and bottom of **transfer** in Example 5.3.

message invariant R_i^c is $x \overset{0.5}{\mapsto} a$, which has been sent by thread B. Now thread A, which had the other half of $x \overset{0.5}{\mapsto} a$, can reason as follows:

$$\frac{\{\mathsf{emp}\}\,\mathtt{receive(c)}\,\{x \overset{0.5}{\mapsto} a\}}{\{\mathsf{emp} * x \overset{0.5}{\mapsto} a\}\,\mathtt{receive(c)}\,\{x \overset{0.5}{\mapsto} a * x \overset{0.5}{\mapsto} a\}} \; (\text{Frame} *), \text{ without } (\ddagger)$$

The postcondition is a contradiction as no location strongly separates from itself. However, given (‡) the strong frame rule can be proven by induction.

The consequence of (‡), from a verification point of view, is that when resources are transferred in they arrive *weakly separated*, by ⊛, since we must use the weak frame rule around the receiving command. The troublesome issue is that this newly "arriving" state can thus ⊛-overlap awkwardly with the existing state. Fortunately, judicious use of labels can sort things out.

Consider the code in Fig. 5. The basic idea is simple: we create some data at the top (line 101) and then split its ownership 50-50 to two threads. The left thread finds a subtree, and passes its half of that subtree to the right via a channel. The right thread receives the root of that subtree, and thus has full ownership of that subtree along with half-ownership of the rest of the tree. Accordingly, the right thread can modify that subtree before notifying the left subtree and passing half of the modified subtree back. After merging, full ownership of the entire tree is restored and so on line 401 the program can delete it. Figure 5 only contains the proof and line numbers for the top and bottom shared portions. The left and the right thread's proofs appear in Fig. 6.

By this point the top and bottom portions of the verification are straightforward. After creating the tree $\mathsf{tree}(rt)$ at line 102, we introduce the label α, split the formula using (Split ⊛), and then pass $(\alpha \wedge \mathsf{tree}(rt))^{0.5}$ to both threads. After the parallel execution, due to the call to modify(sub) in the right thread, the tree has changed in memory. Accordingly, the label for the tree must also change as indicated by the $(\epsilon \wedge \mathsf{tree}(rt))^{0.5}$ in both threads after parallel processing. These are then recombined on line 400 using the re-combination principle (Join ⊛), before the tree is deallocated via standard sequential techniques.

```
200 { (α ∧ tree(rt))^{0.5} }
201 tree* sub = find(rt, key);
```

202 $\{ (\alpha^{0.5} \wedge \text{tree}(\text{sub}) * (\text{tree}(\text{sub}) \twoheadrightarrow \text{tree}(\text{rt})))^{0.5} \}$

203 $\{ (\alpha^{0.5} \wedge (\beta \wedge \text{tree}(\text{sub})) * (\gamma \wedge (\text{tree}(\text{sub}) \twoheadrightarrow \text{tree}(\text{rt}))))^{0.5} \}$

204 $\left\{ \begin{array}{l} \alpha^{0.5} \wedge ((\beta \wedge \text{tree}(\text{sub})) * (\gamma \wedge (\text{tree}(\text{sub}) \twoheadrightarrow \text{tree}(\text{rt}))))^{0.5} \wedge \\ (@_\alpha^{0.5}((\beta \wedge \text{tree}(\text{sub})) * (\gamma \wedge (\text{tree}(\text{sub}) \twoheadrightarrow \text{tree}(\text{rt})))))^{0.5}) \end{array} \right\}$

205 $\left\{ \begin{array}{l} (\beta \wedge \text{tree}(\text{sub}))^{0.5} * (\gamma \wedge (\text{tree}(\text{sub}) \twoheadrightarrow \text{tree}(\text{rt})))^{0.5} \wedge \\ (@_\alpha^{0.5}((\beta \wedge \text{tree}(\text{sub})) * (\gamma \wedge (\text{tree}(\text{sub}) \twoheadrightarrow \text{tree}(\text{rt})))))^{0.5}) \end{array} \right\}$

206 $\left\{ \begin{array}{l} (\gamma \wedge (\text{tree}(\text{sub}) \twoheadrightarrow \text{tree}(\text{rt})))^{0.5} \circledast (\beta \wedge \text{tree}(\text{sub}))^{0.5} \wedge \\ (@_\alpha^{0.5}((\beta \wedge \text{tree}(\text{sub})) * (\gamma \wedge (\text{tree}(\text{sub}) \twoheadrightarrow \text{tree}(\text{rt})))))^{0.5}) \end{array} \right\}$

```
207 send(ch, sub);
```

208 $\{ (\gamma \wedge (\text{tree}(\text{sub}) \twoheadrightarrow \text{tree}(\text{rt})))^{0.5} \}$

209 ...

210 $\{ (\gamma \wedge (\text{tree}(\text{sub}) \twoheadrightarrow \text{tree}(\text{rt})))^{0.5} \}$

```
211 receive(ch);
```

212 $\left\{ \begin{array}{l} (\gamma \wedge (\text{tree}(\text{sub}) \twoheadrightarrow \text{tree}(\text{rt})))^{0.5} \circledast ((@_\gamma^{0.5}(\delta \wedge \text{tree}(\text{sub}) \twoheadrightarrow \epsilon \wedge \text{tree}(\text{rt}))^{0.5}) \wedge \\ \gamma \perp \delta \wedge \delta \wedge \text{tree}(\text{sub})^{0.5}) \end{array} \right\}$

213 $\{ \gamma \wedge (\delta \wedge \text{tree}(\text{sub}) \twoheadrightarrow \epsilon \wedge \text{tree}(\text{rt}))^{0.5} \circledast \delta \wedge \text{tree}(\text{sub})^{0.5} \wedge \gamma \perp \delta \}$

214 $\{ (\delta \wedge \text{tree}(\text{sub}) \twoheadrightarrow \epsilon \wedge \text{tree}(\text{rt}))^{0.5} * \delta \wedge \text{tree}(\text{sub})^{0.5} \}$

215 $\{ (\epsilon \wedge \text{tree}(\text{rt}))^{0.5} \}$

---

300 $\{ (\alpha \wedge \text{tree}(\text{rt}))^{0.5} \}$

301 ...

302 $\{ (\alpha \wedge \text{tree}(\text{rt}))^{0.5} \}$

```
303 tree* sub = receive(ch);
```

304 $\left\{ \begin{array}{l} (\alpha \wedge \text{tree}(\text{rt}))^{0.5} \circledast (\beta \wedge \text{tree}(\text{sub}))^{0.5} \wedge \\ (@_\alpha^{0.5}((\beta \wedge \text{tree}(\text{sub})) * (\gamma \wedge (\text{tree}(\text{sub}) \twoheadrightarrow \text{tree}(\text{rt})))))^{0.5}) \end{array} \right\}$

305 $\{ ((\beta \wedge \text{tree}(\text{sub})) * (\gamma \wedge (\text{tree}(\text{sub}) \twoheadrightarrow \text{tree}(\text{rt}))))^{0.5} \circledast (\beta \wedge \text{tree}(\text{sub}))^{0.5} \}$

306 $\{ ((\beta \wedge \text{tree}(\text{sub}))^{0.5} \circledast (\beta \wedge \text{tree}(\text{sub}))^{0.5}) * (\gamma \wedge (\text{tree}(\text{sub}) \twoheadrightarrow \text{tree}(\text{rt})))^{0.5} \}$

307 $\{ \text{tree}(\text{sub}) * (\gamma \wedge (\text{tree}(\text{sub}) \twoheadrightarrow \text{tree}(\text{rt})))^{0.5} \}$

```
308 modify(sub);
```

309 $\{ \text{tree}(\text{sub}) * (\gamma \wedge (\text{tree}(\text{sub}) \twoheadrightarrow \text{tree}(\text{rt})))^{0.5} \}$

310 $\{ (\delta \wedge \text{tree}(\text{sub})) * (\gamma \wedge ((\delta \wedge \text{tree}(\text{sub})) \twoheadrightarrow (\epsilon \wedge \text{tree}(\text{rt}))))^{0.5} \wedge \gamma \perp \delta \}$

311 $\left\{ \begin{array}{l} ((\delta \wedge \text{tree}(\text{sub}))^{0.5} \circledast (\delta \wedge \text{tree}(\text{sub}))^{0.5}) * (\gamma \wedge ((\delta \wedge \text{tree}(\text{sub})) \twoheadrightarrow (\epsilon \wedge \text{tree}(\text{rt}))))^{0.5} \wedge \\ \gamma \perp \delta \wedge (@_\gamma^{0.5}((\delta \wedge \text{tree}(\text{sub})) \twoheadrightarrow (\epsilon \wedge \text{tree}(\text{rt})))^{0.5}) \end{array} \right\}$

312 $\left\{ \begin{array}{l} ((\delta \wedge \text{tree}(\text{sub}))^{0.5} * (\gamma \wedge ((\delta \wedge \text{tree}(\text{sub})) \twoheadrightarrow (\epsilon \wedge \text{tree}(\text{rt}))))^{0.5}) \circledast \\ (\delta \wedge \text{tree}(\text{sub}))^{0.5} \wedge \gamma \perp \delta \wedge (@_\gamma^{0.5}((\delta \wedge \text{tree}(\text{sub})) \twoheadrightarrow (\epsilon \wedge \text{tree}(\text{rt})))^{0.5}) \end{array} \right\}$

313 $\left\{ \begin{array}{l} (\epsilon \wedge \text{tree}(\text{rt}))^{0.5} \circledast \\ (\delta \wedge \text{tree}(\text{sub}))^{0.5} \wedge \gamma \perp \delta \wedge (@_\gamma^{0.5}((\delta \wedge \text{tree}(\text{sub})) \twoheadrightarrow (\epsilon \wedge \text{tree}(\text{rt})))^{0.5}) \end{array} \right\}$

```
314 send(ch, ());
```

315 $\{ (\epsilon \wedge \text{tree}(\text{rt}))^{0.5} \}$

Fig. 6. Verifications of the left (top) and right (bottom) threads of `transfer`.

Let us now examine the more interesting proofs of the individual threads in Fig. 6. Line 201 calls the `find` function, which searches a binary tree for a subtree rooted with key `key`. Following Cao *et al.* [13] we specify `find` as follows:

$$\{ \text{tree}(x)^\pi \} \ \text{find}(x) \ \{ \lambda ret. \ (\text{tree}(ret) * (\text{tree}(ret) \twoheadrightarrow \text{tree}(x)))^\pi \}$$

Here *ret* is bound to the return value of find, and the postcondition can be considered to represent the returned subtree tree(ret) separately from the tree-with-a-hole tree(ret) $-\!\!*$ tree(x), using a $*/-\!\!*$ style to represent replacement as per Hobor and Villard [20]. This is the invariant on line 202.

Line 203 then attaches the fresh labels β and γ to the $*$-separated subparts, and line 204 snapshots the formula current at label α using the @ operator; $@_\alpha^\pi P$ should be read as "when one has a π-fraction of α, P holds"; it is definable using @ and an existential quantifier over labels. On line 205 we forget (in the left thread) the label α for the current heap for housekeeping purposes, and then on line 206 we weaken the strong separating conjunction $*$ to the weak one $\circledast$ before sending the root of the subtree sub on line 207.

In the transfer program, the invariant for the first channel message is

$$(\beta \wedge \mathsf{tree}(\mathsf{sub}))^{0.5} \wedge \left(@_\alpha^{0.5}((\beta \wedge \mathsf{tree}(\mathsf{sub})) * (\gamma \wedge (\mathsf{tree}(\mathsf{sub}) -\!\!* \mathsf{tree}(\mathsf{rt}))))\right)^{0.5})$$

In other words, half of the ownership of the tree rooted at sub plus the (pure) @-fact about the shape of the heap labeled by α. Comparing lines 206 and 208 we can see that this information has been shipped over the wire (the @-information has been dropped since no longer needed). The left thread then continues to process until synchronizing again with the receive in line 211.

Before we consider the second synchronization, however, let us instead jump to the corresponding receive in the right thread at line 303. After the receive, the invariant on line 304 has the (weakly separated) resources sent from the left thread on line 206. We then "jump" label α using the @-information to reach line 305. We can redistribute the β inside the $*$ on line 306 since we already know that β and γ are disjoint. On line 307 we reach the payoff by combining both halves of the subtree sub, enabling the modification of the subtree in line 308.

On line 310 we label the two subheaps, and specialize the magic wand so that given the specific heap δ it will yield the specific heap ϵ; we also record the pure fact that γ and δ are disjoint, written $\gamma \perp \delta$. On line 311 we snapshot γ and split the tree sub 50-50; then on line 312 we push half of sub out of the strong $*$. On line 313 we combine the subtree and the tree-with-hole to reach the final tree ϵ. We then send on line 314 with the channel's second resource invariant:

$$(\delta \wedge \mathsf{tree}(\mathsf{sub}))^{0.5} \wedge \gamma \perp \delta \wedge \left(@_\gamma^{0.5}((\delta \wedge \mathsf{tree}(\mathsf{sub})) -\!\!* (\epsilon \wedge \mathsf{tree}(\mathsf{rt})))\right)^{0.5})$$

After the send, on line 315 we have reached the final fractional tree ϵ.

Back in the left-hand thread, the second send is received in line 211, leading to the weakly-separated postcondition in line 212. In line 213 we "jump" label γ, and then in line 214 we use the known disjointness of γ and δ to change the $\circledast$ to $*$. Finally in line 215 we apply the magic wand to reach the postcondition.

6   Conclusions and Future Work

We propose an extension of separation logic with fractional permissions [4] in order to reason about sharing over arbitrary regions of memory. We identify two fundamental logical principles that fail when the "weak" separating conjunction $\circledast$ is used in place of the usual "strong" $*$, the first being distribution of permissions—$A^\pi \circledast B^\pi \not\models (A \circledast B)^\pi$—and the second being the re-combination of permission-divided formulas, $A^\pi \circledast A^\sigma \not\models A^{\pi \oplus \sigma}$. We avoid the former difficulty by *retaining* the strong $*$ in the formalism alongside $\circledast$, and the latter by using nominal *labels*, from hybrid logic, to record exact aliasing between read-only copies of a formula.

The main previous work addressing these issues, by Le and Hobor [24], uses a combination of permissions based on *tree shares* [17] and semantic side conditions on formulas to overcome the aforementioned problems. The *rely-guarantee* separation logic in [30] similarly restricts concurrent reasoning to structures described by precise formulas only. In contrast, our logic is a little more complex, but we can use permissions of any kind, and do not require side conditions. In addition, our use of labelling enables us to handle examples involving the transfer of data structures between concurrent threads.

On the other hand, we think it probable that the kind of examples we consider in this paper could also be proven by hand in at least some of the verification formalisms derived from CSL (e.g. [16,22,27]). For example, using the "concurrent abstract predicates" in [16], one can explicitly declare shared regions of memory in a fairly ad-hoc way. However, such program logics are typically very complicated and, we believe, quite unlikely to be amenable to automation.

We feel that the main appeal of the present work lies in its relative simplicity—we build on standard CSL with permissions and invoke only a modest amount of extra syntax—which bodes well for its potential automation (at least for simpler examples). In practical terms, an obvious way to proceed would be to develop a prototype verifier for concurrent programs based on our logic SL_{LP}. An important challenge in this area is to develop heuristics—e.g., for splitting, labelling and combining formulas—that work acceptably well in practice.

An even greater challenge is to move from *verifying* user-provided specifications to *inferring* them automatically, as is done e.g. by Facebook INFER. In separation logic, this crucially depends on solving the *biabduction* problem, which aims to discover "best fit" solutions for applications of the frame rule [9,11]. In the CSL setting, a further problem seems to lie in deciding how applications of the concurrency rule should divide resources between threads.

Finally, automating the verification approach set out in this paper will likely necessitate restricting our full logic to some suitably tractable fragment, e.g. one analogous to the well-known *symbolic heaps* in standard separation logic (cf. [2,15]). The identification of such tractable fragments is another important theoretical problem in this area. It is our hope that this paper will serve to stimulate interest in the automation of concurrent separation logic in particular, and permission-sensitive reasoning in general.

References

1. Appel, A.W., et al.: Program Logics for Certified Compilers. Cambridge University Press, New York (2014)

2. Berdine, J., Calcagno, C., O'Hearn, P.W.: A decidable fragment of separation logic. In: Lodaya, K., Mahajan, M. (eds.) FSTTCS 2004. LNCS, vol. 3328, pp. 97–109. Springer, Heidelberg (2004). https://doi.org/10.1007/978-3-540-30538-5_9
3. Blackburn, P., de Rijke, M., Venema, Y.: Modal Logic. Cambridge University Press, Cambridge (2001)
4. Bornat, R., Calcagno, C., O'Hearn, P., Parkinson, M.: Permission accounting in separation logic. In: Proceedings of POPL-32, pp. 59–70. ACM (2005)
5. Boyland, J.: Checking interference with fractional permissions. In: Cousot, R. (ed.) SAS 2003. LNCS, vol. 2694, pp. 55–72. Springer, Heidelberg (2003). https://doi.org/10.1007/3-540-44898-5_4
6. Brookes, S.: A semantics for concurrent separation logic. Theoret. Comput. Sci. **375**(1–3), 227–270 (2007)
7. Brotherston, J.: Formalised inductive reasoning in the logic of bunched implications. In: Nielson, H.R., Filé, G. (eds.) SAS 2007. LNCS, vol. 4634, pp. 87–103. Springer, Heidelberg (2007). https://doi.org/10.1007/978-3-540-74061-2_6
8. Brotherston, J., Fuhs, C., Gorogiannis, N., Navarro Pérez, J.: A decision procedure for satisfiability in separation logic with inductive predicates. In: Proceedings of CSL-LICS, pp. 25:1–25:10. ACM (2014)
9. Brotherston, J., Gorogiannis, N., Kanovich, M.: Biabduction (and related problems) in array separation logic. In: de Moura, L. (ed.) CADE 2017. LNCS (LNAI), vol. 10395, pp. 472–490. Springer, Cham (2017). https://doi.org/10.1007/978-3-319-63046-5_29
10. Brotherston, J., Villard, J.: Parametric completeness for separation theories. In: Proceedings of POPL-41, pp. 453–464. ACM (2014)
11. Calcagno, C., Distefano, D., O'Hearn, P., Yang, H.: Compositional shape analysis by means of bi-abduction. J. ACM **58**(6), 1–66 (2011)
12. Calcagno, C., O'Hearn, P., Yang, H.: Local action and abstract separation logic. In: Proceedings of LICS-22, pp. 366–378. IEEE Computer Society (2007)
13. Cao, Q., Wang, S., Hobor, A., Appel, A.W.: Proof pearl: magic wand as frame (2019)
14. Costea, A., Chin, W.-N., Qin, S., Craciun, F.: Automated modular verification for relaxed communication protocols. In: Ryu, S. (ed.) APLAS 2018. LNCS, vol. 11275, pp. 284–305. Springer, Cham (2018). https://doi.org/10.1007/978-3-030-02768-1_16
15. Demri, S., Lozes, E., Lugiez, D.: On symbolic heaps modulo permission theories. In: Proceedings of FSTTCS-37, pp. 25:1–25:13. Dagstuhl (2017)
16. Dinsdale-Young, T., Dodds, M., Gardner, P., Parkinson, M.J., Vafeiadis, V.: Concurrent abstract predicates. In: D'Hondt, T. (ed.) ECOOP 2010. LNCS, vol. 6183, pp. 504–528. Springer, Heidelberg (2010). https://doi.org/10.1007/978-3-642-14107-2_24
17. Dockins, R., Hobor, A., Appel, A.W.: A fresh look at separation algebras and share accounting. In: Hu, Z. (ed.) APLAS 2009. LNCS, vol. 5904, pp. 161–177. Springer, Heidelberg (2009). https://doi.org/10.1007/978-3-642-10672-9_13
18. Hobor, A., Appel, A.W., Nardelli, F.Z.: Oracle semantics for concurrent separation logic. In: Drossopoulou, S. (ed.) ESOP 2008. LNCS, vol. 4960, pp. 353–367. Springer, Heidelberg (2008). https://doi.org/10.1007/978-3-540-78739-6_27
19. Hobor, A., Gherghina, C.: Barriers in concurrent separation logic: now with tool support!. Logical Methods Comput. Sci. **8**, 1–36 (2012)
20. Hobor, A., Villard, J.: The ramifications of sharing in data structures. In: Proceedings of POPL-40, pp. 523–536. ACM (2013)

21. Hóu, Z., Clouston, R., Goré, R., Tiu, A.: Proof search for propositional abstract separation logics via labelled sequents. In: Proceedings of POPL-41, pp. 465–476. ACM (2014)

22. Krebbers, R., Jung, R., Bizjak, A., Jourdan, J.-H., Dreyer, D., Birkedal, L.: The essence of higher-order concurrent separation logic. In: Yang, H. (ed.) ESOP 2017. LNCS, vol. 10201, pp. 696–723. Springer, Heidelberg (2017). https://doi.org/10.1007/978-3-662-54434-1_26

23. Larchey-Wendling, D., Galmiche, D.: Exploring the relation between intuitionistic BI and Boolean BI: an unexpected embedding. Math. Struct. Comput. Sci. **19**, 1–66 (2009)

24. Le, X.-B., Hobor, A.: Logical reasoning for disjoint permissions. In: Ahmed, A. (ed.) ESOP 2018. LNCS, vol. 10801, pp. 385–414. Springer, Cham (2018). https://doi.org/10.1007/978-3-319-89884-1_14

25. Lee, W., Park, S.: A proof system for separation logic with magic wand. In: Proceedings of POPL-41, pp. 477–490. ACM (2014)

26. O'Hearn, P.W.: Resources, concurrency and local reasoning. Theoret. Comput. Sci. **375**(1–3), 271–307 (2007)

27. Raad, A., Villard, J., Gardner, P.: CoLoSL: concurrent local subjective logic. In: Vitek, J. (ed.) ESOP 2015. LNCS, vol. 9032, pp. 710–735. Springer, Heidelberg (2015). https://doi.org/10.1007/978-3-662-46669-8_29

28. Reynolds, J.C.: Separation logic: a logic for shared mutable data structures. In: Proceedings of LICS-17, pp. 55–74. IEEE Computer Society (2002)

29. Vafeiadis, V.: Concurrent separation logic and operational semantics. In: Proceedings of MFPS-27, pp. 335–351. Elsevier (2011)

30. Vafeiadis, V., Parkinson, M.: A marriage of rely/guarantee and separation logic. In: Caires, L., Vasconcelos, V.T. (eds.) CONCUR 2007. LNCS, vol. 4703, pp. 256–271. Springer, Heidelberg (2007). https://doi.org/10.1007/978-3-540-74407-8_18

31. Villard, J., Lozes, É., Calcagno, C.: Tracking heaps that hop with heap-hop. In: Esparza, J., Majumdar, R. (eds.) TACAS 2010. LNCS, vol. 6015, pp. 275–279. Springer, Heidelberg (2010). https://doi.org/10.1007/978-3-642-12002-2_23

32. Yang, H., O'Hearn, P.: A semantic basis for local reasoning. In: Nielsen, M., Engberg, U. (eds.) FoSSaCS 2002. LNCS, vol. 2303, pp. 402–416. Springer, Heidelberg (2002). https://doi.org/10.1007/3-540-45931-6_28

Local Reasoning About the Presence of Bugs: Incorrectness Separation Logic

Azalea Raad[1]([✉]), Josh Berdine[2], Hoang-Hai Dang[1], Derek Dreyer[1],
Peter O'Hearn[2,3], and Jules Villard[2]

[1] Max Planck Institute for Software Systems (MPI-SWS),
Kaiserslautern and Saarbrücken, Germany
{azalea,haidang,dreyer}@mpi-sws.org
[2] Facebook, London, UK
{jjb,peteroh,jul}@fb.com
[3] University College London, London, UK

Abstract. There has been a large body of work on local reasoning for proving the *absence* of bugs, but none for proving their *presence*. We present a new formal framework for local reasoning about the presence of bugs, building on two complementary foundations: 1) separation logic and 2) incorrectness logic. We explore the theory of this new *incorrectness separation logic* (ISL), and use it to derive a begin-anywhere, intra-procedural symbolic execution analysis that has no false positives *by construction*. In so doing, we take a step towards transferring modular, scalable techniques from the world of program verification to bug catching.

Keywords: Program logics · Separation logic · Bug catching

1 Introduction

There has been significant research on sound, local reasoning about the state for proving the absence of bugs (e.g., [2,13,26,29,30,41]). Locality leads to techniques that are compositional *both* in code (concentrating on a program component) and in the resources accessed (spatial locality), without tracking the entire global state or the global program within which a component sits. Compositionality enables reasoning to scale to large teams and codebases: reasoning can be done even when a global program is not present (e.g., a library, or during program construction), without having to write the analogue of a test or verification harness, and the results of reasoning about components can be composed efficiently [11].

Meanwhile, many of the practical applications of symbolic reasoning have aimed at proving the *presence* of bugs (i.e., bug catching), rather than proving their absence (i.e., correctness). Logical bug catching methods include symbolic model checking [7,12] and symbolic execution for testing [9]. These methods are usually formulated as global analyses; but, the rationale of local reasoning holds just as well for bug catching as it does for correctness: it has the potential to

© The Author(s) 2020
S. K. Lahiri and C. Wang (Eds.): CAV 2020, LNCS 12225, pp. 225–252, 2020.
https://doi.org/10.1007/978-3-030-53291-8_14

benefit scalability, reasoning about incomplete code, and continuous incremental reasoning about a changing codebase within a continuous integration (CI) system [34]. Moreover, local evidence of a bug without usually-irrelevant contextual information can be more convincing and easier to understand and correct.

There do exist symbolic bug catchers that, at least partly, address scalability and continuous reasoning. Tools such as Coverity [5,32] and Infer [18] hunt for bugs in large codebases with tens of millions of LOC, and they can even run incrementally (within minutes for small code changes), which is compatible with deployment in CI to detect regressions. However, although such tools intuitively share ideas with correctness-based compositional analyses [16], the existing foundations of correctness-based analyses do not adequately explain what these bug-catchers do, why they work, or the extent to which they work in practice.

A notable such example is the relation between *separation logic* (SL) and Infer. SL provides novel techniques for local reasoning [28], with concise specifications that focus only on the memory accessed [36]. Using SL, symbolic execution need not begin from a "main" program, but rather can "begin anywhere" in a codebase, with constraints on the environment synthesized along the way. When analyzing a component, SL's frame rule is used in concert with abductive inference to isolate a description of the memory utilized by the component [11]. Infer was closely inspired by SL, and demonstrates the power of SL's local reasoning: the ability to begin anywhere supports incremental analysis in CI, and compositionality leads to highly scalable methods. These features have led to non-trivial impact: a recent paper quotes over 100,000 Infer-reported bugs fixed in Facebook's codebases, and thousands of security bugs found by a compositional taint analyzer, Zoncolan [18]. However, Infer reports bugs using *heuristics based on failed proofs*, whereas the SL theory behind Infer is based on *over-approximation* [11]. Thus, a critical aspect of Infer's successful deployment is not supported by the theory that inspired it. This is unfortunate, especially given that the begin-anywhere and scalable aspects of Infer's algorithms do not appear to be fundamentally tied to over-approximation.

In this paper, we take a step towards transferring the local reasoning techniques from the world of program verification to that of bug catching. To approach the problem from first principles, we do not try to understand tools such as Coverity and Infer as they are. Instead, we take their existence and reported impact as motivation for revisiting the foundations of SL, this time re-casting it as a formalism for proving the *presence* of bugs rather than their absence.

Our new logic, *incorrectness separation logic* (ISL), marries local reasoning based on SL's frame rule with the recently-advanced incorrectness logic [35], a formalism for reasoning about errors based on an *under-approximate* analogue of Hoare triples [43]. We observe that the original SL model, based on partial heaps, is incompatible with local, under-approximate reasoning. The problem is that the original model does not distinguish a pointer known to be dangling from one about which we have no knowledge; this in turn contradicts the frame rule for under-approximate reasoning. However, we recover the frame rule for a refined model with negative heap assertions of the form $x \not\mapsto$, read "invalidated x", stating that the location at x has been deallocated (and not re-allocated). Negative heaps were present informally in the original Infer, unsupported by theory but added for reporting use-after-free bugs (i.e., not for proving correctness). Interestingly, this semantic feature is needed in ISL for logical (and not merely pragmatic) reasons, in that it yields a *sound* logic for proving the presence of bugs: when ISL identifies a bug, then there is indeed a bug (no false positives), given the assumptions of the underlying ISL model. (That is, as usual, soundness is a relationship between assumptions and conclusions, and whether those assumptions match reality (i.e., running code) is a separate concern, outside the purview of logic.)

As well as being superior for bug reporting, our new model has a pleasant fundamental property in that it meshes better with intuitions originally expressed of SL. Specifically, our model admits a *footprint theorem*, stating that the meaning of a command is solely determined by its transitions on input-output heaplets of minimal size (including only the locations accessed), a theorem that was not true in full generality for the original SL model. Interestingly, ISL supports local reasoning for technically simpler reasons than the original SL (see Sect. 4.2).

We validate part of the ISL promise using an illustrative program analysis, Pulse, and use it to detect *memory safety bugs*, namely null-pointer-dereference and use-after-free bugs. Pulse is written inside Infer [18] and deployed at Facebook where it is used to report issues to C++ developers. Pulse is currently under active development. In this paper, we explore the *intra-procedural* analysis, i.e., how it provides purely local reasoning about one procedure at a time without using results from other procedures; we defer formalising its *inter-procedural* (between procedures) analysis to future work. While leaving out the inter-procedural capabilities of Pulse only partly validates the promise of the ISL theory, it already demonstrates how ISL can scale to large codebases, and run incrementally in a way compatible with CI. Pulse thus has the capability to begin anywhere, and it achieves scalability while embracing under- rather than over-approximation.

Outline. In Sect. 2 we present an intuitive account of ISL. In Sect. 3 we present the ISL proof system. In Sect. 4 we present the semantic model of ISL. In Sect. 5 we present our ISL-based Pulse analysis. In Sect. 6 we discuss related work and conclude. The full proofs of all stated theorems are given in the technical appendix [38].

2   Proof of a Bug

We proceed with an intuitive description of ISL for detecting memory safety bugs. To do this, in Fig. 1 we present an example of C++ use-after-lifetime bug, abstracted from real occurrences we have observed at Facebook, where use-after-lifetime bugs were one of the leading developer requests for C++ analysis. Given a vector v, a call to `push_back(v)` in the `std::vector` library may cause the internal array backing v to be (deallocated and subsequently) reallocated when v

```
void deref_after_pb(std::vector<int> *v) {
  int *x = &v->at(1);
  v->push_back(42);
  std::cout << *x << "\n"; }
```
push_back.cpp:7: error: VECTOR_INVALIDATION. accessing memory that was
potentially invalidated by 'std::vector::push_back()' on line 6.
```
  5.     int *x = &(v->at(1));
  6.     v->push_back(42);
  7. >   std::cout << *x << "\n"; }
```

Fig. 1. The C++ use-after-lifetime bug (above); the Pulse error message (below).

needs to grow to accommodate new elements. If the internal array is reallocated during the v->push_back(42) call, a use-after-lifetime bug occurs on the next line as x points into the previous array. Note how the Pulse error message (at the bottom of Fig. 1) refers to memory that has been invalidated. As we describe shortly, this information is tracked in Pulse with an invalidated heap assertion.

For the theory in this paper, we do not want to descend into the details of C++, vectors, and so forth. Thus, for illustrative purposes, in Fig. 2 we present an adaptation of such use-after-lifetime bugs in C rather than C++, alongside its representation in the ISL language used in this paper. In this adaptation, the array at v is of size 1, and is reallocated in push_back non-deterministically to model its dynamic reallocation when growing. We next demonstrate how we can use ISL to detect the use-after-lifetime bug in the client procedure in Fig. 2.

ISL Triples. The ISL theory uses *under-approximate triples* [35] of the form [presumption] $\mathbb{C}$ [ϵ : result], interpreted as: the result assertion describes a *subset* of the states that can be reached from the presumption assertion by executing $\mathbb{C}$, where ϵ denotes an *exit condition* indicating either normal or exceptional (erroneous) termination. The under-approximate triples can be equivalently interpreted as: every state in result can be obtained by executing $\mathbb{C}$ on a starting state in presumption. By contrast, given a Hoare triple {pre} $\mathbb{C}$ {post}, the postcondition post describes a *superset* of states that are reachable from the precondition pre, and may include states unreachable from pre. Hoare logic is about over-approximation, allowing false positives but not negatives, whereas ISL is about under-approximation, allowing false negatives but not positives.

Bug Specification of client(v). Using ISL, we can specify the use-after-lifetime bug in client(v) as follows:

$$[v \mapsto a * a \mapsto -] \ \texttt{client}(v) \ [er(\mathrm{L}_{rx}) : \exists a'. \ v \mapsto a' * a' \mapsto - * a \not\mapsto] \qquad (\text{PB-Client})$$

We make several remarks to illustrate the crucial features of ISL:

- As in standard SL, $*$ denotes the separating conjunction, read "and separately". It implies, e.g., that v, a' and a are distinct in the result assertion.
- The exit condition $er(\mathrm{L}_{rx})$ denotes an erroneous termination: an error state is reached at line L_{rx}, where a is dangling (invalidated).

```
                                    push_back(v) ≜
    void push_back(int **v)             local z, y in
    {                                       z := *;
        if (nondet()) {                     (assume(z ≠ 0); L_rv: y := [v];
            free(*v);                       L_f: free(y);
            *v = malloc(sizeof(int));       y := malloc(); [v] := y)
        }                                 + (assume(z = 0); skip)
    }
                                    client(v) ≜
    void client(v) {                    local x in
        int* x = *v;                    x := [v];
        push_back(v);                   push_back(v);
        *x = 88; }                      L_rx: [x] := 88
```

Fig. 2. The push_back example in C (left); and in the ISL language (right).

- The result is under-approximate: any state satisfying the result assertion can be reached from some state satisfying the presumption.
- The specification is local: it focuses only on memory locations in the client(v) footprint (i.e., those touched by client(v)), and ignores other locations.

Let us next consider how we reason symbolically about this bug. Note that for the client(v) execution to reach an error at line L_{rx}, the push_back(v) call within it must not cause an error. That is, in contrast to PB-CLIENT, we need a specification for push_back(v) that describes normal, non-erroneous termination. We specify this normal execution with the ok exit condition as follows:

$$[v \mapsto a * a \mapsto -] \, \text{push\_back}(v) \, [ok: \exists a'. \, v \mapsto a' * a' \mapsto - * a \not\mapsto] \quad \text{(PB-OK)}$$

PB-OK describes the case when push_back(v) frees the internal array of v at a (denoted by $a \not\mapsto$ in the result), and subsequently reallocates it at a'. Consequently, as a is invalidated after the push_back(v) call, the instruction following the call in client(v) dereferences invalidated memory at L_{rx}, causing an error.

Note that the result assertion in PB-OK is strictly under-approximate in that it is smaller (stronger) than the exact "strongest post". Given the assertion in the presumption, the strongest post must also consider the else clause of the conditional, when nondet() returns zero and push_back(v) does nothing. That is, the strongest post is the disjunction of the given result and the presumption. The ability to go below the strongest post soundly is a hallmark of under-approximate reasoning: it allows for compromise in an analyzer, where we might choose, e.g., to limit the number of paths explored for efficiency reasons, or to concretize an assertion partially when symbolic reasoning becomes difficult [35].

We present proof outlines for PB-OK and PB-CLIENT in Fig. 3, where we annotate each step with a proof rule to connect to the ISL theory in Sect. 3. For legibility, uses of the FRAME rule are omitted as it is used in almost every step, and the consequence rule CONS is usually omitted when rewriting a formula to an equivalent one. For the moment, we encourage the reader to attempt to follow, prior to formalization, by mentally executing the program instructions on the assertions and asking: does the assertion at each program point under-approximate the states that can be obtained from the prior state? Note that each step updates assertions in-place, just as concrete execution does on concrete memory. For example, L_f: free(y) replaces $a \mapsto -$ with $a \nmapsto$. In-place reasoning is a capability that the separating conjunction brings to symbolic execution; formally, this in-place aspect is achieved in the logic by applying the frame rule.

3   Incorrectness Separation Logic (ISL)

As a first attempt, it is tempting to obtain ISL straightforwardly by composing the standard semantics of SL [41] and the semantics of incorrectness logic [35]. Interestingly, this simplistic approach does not work. To see this, consider the following axiom for freeing memory, adapted from the corresponding SL axiom:

$$[x \mapsto -] \, \texttt{free}(x) \, [ok : \texttt{emp} \wedge \texttt{loc}(x)]$$

Here, emp describes the empty heap and $\texttt{loc}(x)$ states that x is an addressable location; e.g., x cannot be null. Note that this ISL triple is valid in that any state satisfying the result assertion can be obtained from one satisfying the presumption assertion, and thus we do have a true under-approximate triple.

However, in SL one can arbitrarily extend the state using the frame rule:

$$\frac{\vdash [p] \, \mathbb{C} \, [\epsilon : q] \qquad \mathsf{mod}(\mathbb{C}) \cap \mathsf{fv}(r) = \emptyset}{\vdash [p * r] \, \mathbb{C} \, [\epsilon : q * r]} \, (\text{FRAME})$$

Intuitively, the state described by the *frame* assertion r lies outside the footprint of $\mathbb{C}$ and thus remains unchanged when executing $\mathbb{C}$. However, if we do this with the $\texttt{free}(x)$ axiom above, choosing $x \mapsto -$ as our frame, we run into a problem:

$$[x \mapsto - * x \mapsto -] \, \texttt{free}(x) \, [ok : (\texttt{emp} \wedge \texttt{loc}(x)) * x \mapsto -]$$

Here, the presumption is inconsistent but the result is not, and thus there is no way to get back to the presumption from the result; i.e., the triple is invalid. In over-approximate reasoning this does not cause a problem since an inconsistent precondition renders an over-approximate triple vacuously valid. By contrast, an inconsistent presumption does not validate under-approximate reasoning.

Our way out of this conundrum is to consider a modified model in which the knowledge that a location was previously freed is a resource-oriented fact, using negative heap assertions. The negative heap assertion $x \nmapsto$ conveys more knowledge than the $\texttt{loc}(x)$ assertion. Specifically, $x \nmapsto$ conveys: 1) the *knowledge* that x is an addressable location; 2) the knowledge that x has been deallocated; and 3) the *ownership* of location x. In other words, $x \nmapsto$ is analogous to the

$[v \mapsto a * a \mapsto -]$

```
local y, z in
  z := *; // Havoc
```
$[ok\!:\! z{=}1 * v \mapsto a * a \mapsto -]$
```
  ( assume(z ≠ 0); // Assume
```
$[ok\!:\! z{=}1 * z{\neq}0 * v \mapsto a * a \mapsto -]$

$\mathrm{L}_{rv}\!: y := [v]; // $ Load

$[ok\!:\! z{=}1 * y{=}a * v \mapsto a * a \mapsto -]$

$\mathrm{L}_{f}\!:$ free$(y); // $ Free

$[ok\!:\! z{=}1 * y{=}a * v \mapsto a * a \not\mapsto\ ]$
```
  y := malloc(); // Alloc1, Choice
```
$[ok\!:\! z{=}1 * v \mapsto a * a \not\mapsto\ * y \mapsto -]$
```
  [v] := y; // Store
```
$[ok\!:\! z{=}1 * v \mapsto y * a \not\mapsto\ * y \mapsto -]$
```
  ) + (...) // Choice
```
$[ok\!:\! z{=}1 * v \mapsto y * a \not\mapsto\ * y \mapsto -]$

// Local

$[ok\!:\! \exists a'.\ v \mapsto a' * a' \mapsto - * a \not\mapsto\ ]$

$[v \mapsto a * a \mapsto -]$

```
local x in
  x := [v]; // Load
```
$[ok\!:\! x{=}a * v \mapsto a * a \mapsto -]$
```
  push_back(v); // PB-Ok
```
$[ok\!:\! \exists a'.\ x{=}a * v \mapsto a' * a' \mapsto - * a \not\mapsto\ ] //$ Cons

$[ok\!:\! \exists a'.\ x{=}a * v \mapsto a' * a' \mapsto - * x \not\mapsto\ ]$

$\mathrm{L}_{rx}\!: [x] := 88; // $ StoreEr

$[er(\mathrm{L}_{rx})\!:\! \exists a'.\ x{=}a * v \mapsto a' * a' \mapsto - * x \not\mapsto\ ]$

// Local

$[er(\mathrm{L}_{rx})\!:\! \exists a'.\ v \mapsto a' * a' \mapsto - * a \not\mapsto\ ]$

Fig. 3. The proof sketches of PB-Ok (left) and PB-Client (right).

points-to assertion $x \mapsto -$ and is thus manipulated similarly, taking up space in
$*$-conjuncts. That is, we cannot consistently $*$-conjoin $x \not\mapsto$ either with $x \mapsto -$
or with itself: $x \mapsto - * x \not\mapsto\ \Leftrightarrow$ false and $x \not\mapsto\ * x \not\mapsto\ \Leftrightarrow$ false.

With such negative assertions, we can specify free() as the Free axiom in
Fig. 5. Note that this allows us to recover the frame rule: when we frame $x \mapsto -$
on both sides, we obtain the inconsistent assertion $x \mapsto - * x \not\mapsto$ (i.e., false) in
the result, which always makes an under-approximate triple vacuously valid.

We demonstrated how we arrived at negative heaps as a theoretical solution
to recover the frame rule. However, negative heaps are more than a technical
curiosity. In particular, a similar idea was informally present in Infer and has
been used formally to reason about JavaScript [21]. Moreover, as we show in
Sect. 4, negative heaps give rise to a *footprint theorem* (see Theorem 2).

Negative heap assertions were previously used informally in Infer. They
were also independently and formally introduced in a separation logic for
JavaScript [21] to state that a field is not present in a JavaScript object, which
is a natural property to express when reasoning about JavaScript.

$$\text{COMM} \ni \mathbb{C} ::= \texttt{skip} \mid x := e \mid x := * \mid \texttt{assume}(B) \mid \texttt{local } x \texttt{ in } \mathbb{C} \mid \mathbb{C}_1 ; \mathbb{C}_2 \mid \mathbb{C}_1 + \mathbb{C}_2 \mid \mathbb{C}^\star$$
$$\mid x := \texttt{alloc}() \mid \texttt{L}: \texttt{free}(x) \mid \texttt{L}: x := [y] \mid \texttt{L}: [x] := y \mid \texttt{L}: \texttt{error}$$

$$\texttt{if } B \texttt{ then } \mathbb{C}_1 \texttt{ else } \mathbb{C}_2 \triangleq (\texttt{assume}(B); \mathbb{C}_1) + (\texttt{assume}(!B); \mathbb{C}_2)$$
$$\texttt{while}(B) \ \mathbb{C} \triangleq (\texttt{assume}(B); \mathbb{C})^\star ; \texttt{assume}(!B)$$
$$\texttt{assert}(B) \triangleq (\texttt{assume}(!B); \texttt{error}) + \texttt{assume}(B)$$
$$x := \texttt{malloc}() \triangleq x := \texttt{alloc}() \ + \ x := \texttt{null}$$

Fig. 4. The ISL Language (above); encoding standard constructs in ISL (below).

Programming Language. To keep our presentation concise, we employ a simple heap-manipulating language as shown in Fig. 4. We assume an infinite set VAL of *values*; a finite set VAR of (program) *variables*; a standard interpreted language for *expressions*, EXP, containing variables and values; and a standard interpreted language for *Boolean expressions*, BEXP. We use v as a metavariable for values; x, y, z for program variables; e for expressions; and B for Boolean expressions.

Our language is given by the $\mathbb{C}$ grammar and includes the standard constructs of skip, assignment ($x := e$), non-deterministic assignment ($x := *$, where $*$ denotes a non-deterministically picked value), assume statements ($\texttt{assume}(B)$), scoped variable declaration ($\texttt{local } x \texttt{ in } \mathbb{C}$), sequential composition ($\mathbb{C}_1 ; \mathbb{C}_2$), non-deterministic choice ($\mathbb{C}_1 + \mathbb{C}_2$) and loops ($\mathbb{C}^\star$), as well as error statements (error) and heap-manipulating instructions. Note that deterministic choice and loops (e.g.,if and while statements) can be encoded using their non-deterministic counterparts and assume statements, as shown in Fig. 4.

To better track errors, we annotate instructions that may cause an error with a label $\texttt{L} \in \text{LABEL}$. When an error is encountered (e.g., in $\texttt{L}: \texttt{error}$), we report the label of the offending instruction (e.g., L). As such, we only consider *well-formed* programs: those with unique labels across their constituent instructions. For brevity, we drop the instruction labels when they are immaterial to the discussion.

As is standard practice, we use error statements as test oracles to detect violations. In particular, error statements can be used to encode *assert* statements as shown in Fig. 4. Heap-manipulating instructions include allocation, deallocation, lookup and mutation. The $x := \texttt{alloc}()$ instruction allocates a new (unused) location on the heap and returns it in x, and can be used to represent the standard, possibly null-returning $\texttt{malloc}()$ from C as shown in Fig. 4. Dually, $\texttt{free}(x)$ deallocates the location denoted by x. Heap lookup $x := [y]$ reads the contents of the location denoted by y and returns it in x; heap mutation $[x] := y$ overwrites the contents of the location denoted by x with y.

Assertions. The *ISL assertion language* is given by the grammar below, where $\oplus \in \{=, \neq, <, \leq, \ldots\}$. We use p, q, r as metavariables for assertions.

$$\text{AST} \ni p, q, r ::= \texttt{false} \mid p \Rightarrow q \mid \exists x. \ p \mid e \oplus e' \qquad \text{classical and Boolean assertions}$$
$$\mid \texttt{emp} \mid e \mapsto e' \mid e \not\mapsto \mid p * q \qquad\qquad \text{structural assertions}$$

As we describe formally in Sect. 4, assertions describe sets of *states*, where each state comprises a (variable) store and a heap. The classical (first-order logic) and Boolean assertions are standard. Other classical connectives can be encoded using existing ones (e.g., $\neg p \triangleq p \Rightarrow \mathsf{false}$). Aside from the highlighted $x \not\mapsto$, structural assertions are as defined in SL [28], and describe a set of states by constraining the shape of the underlying heap. More concretely, emp describes states in which the heap is empty; $e \mapsto e'$ describes states in which the heap comprises a single location denoted by e containing the value denoted by e'; and $p * q$ describes states in which the heap can be split into two disjoint sub-heaps, one satisfying p and the other q. We often write $e \mapsto -$ as a shorthand for $\exists v.\ e \mapsto v$.

As described above, we extend our structural assertions with the *negative* heap assertion $e \not\mapsto$ (read "e is invalidated"). As with its positive counterpart $e \mapsto e'$, the negative assertion $e \not\mapsto$ describes states in which the heap comprises a single location at e. However, whilst $e \mapsto e'$ states that the location at e is allocated (and contains the value e'), $e \not\mapsto$ states that the location at e is *deallocated*.

ISL Proof Rules (Syntactic ISL Triples). We present the ISL proof rules in Fig. 5. As in incorrectness logic [35], the ISL triples are of the form $\vdash [p]\ \mathbb{C}\ [\epsilon : q]$, denoting that *every* state in the *result* assertion q is reachable from *some* state in the *presumption* assertion p with *exit condition* ϵ. That is, for each state σ_q in q, there exists σ_p in p such that executing $\mathbb{C}$ on σ_p terminates with ϵ and yields σ_q. As such, since false describes an empty state set, $[p]\ \mathbb{C}\ [\epsilon : \mathsf{false}]$ is vacuously valid for all p, $\mathbb{C}$, ϵ. Dually, $[\mathsf{false}]\ \mathbb{C}\ [\epsilon : q]$ is always invalid when $q \not\Leftrightarrow \mathsf{false}$.

An exit condition, $\epsilon \in \mathrm{EXIT}$, may be: 1) *ok*, denoting a successful execution; or 2) *er*(L), denoting an erroneous execution with the error encountered at the L-labeled instruction. Compared to [35], we further annotate our error conditions to track the offending instructions. Moreover, whilst [35] rules only detect explicit errors caused by error statements, ISL rules additionally allow us to track errors caused by *memory safety violations*, namely "use-after-free" violations, where a previously deallocated location is subsequently accessed in the program, and "null-pointer-dereference" violations. Although it is straightforward to distinguish between explicit and memory safety errors, for brevity we use *er*(L) for both.

Thanks to the separation afforded by ISL assertions, compared to incorrectness triples in [35], ISL triples are *local* in that the states described by their presumptions only contain the resources needed by the program. For instance, as skip requires no resource for successful execution, the presumption of SKIP is simply given by emp, which remains unchanged in the result. Similarly, $\mathsf{assume}(B)$ requires no resource and results in a state satisfying B. The ASSIGN rule is analogous to its SL counterpart. Similarly, $x := *$ in HAVOC assigns a non-deterministic value to x. Although these axioms (and ALLOC1, ALLOC2) ask for a single equality $x = x'$ in their presumption, one can derive more general triples starting from any presumption p by picking a fresh x' and applying the axiom, and the FRAME and CONS rules on the equivalent presumption $x = x' * p[x'/x]$.

SKIP
$\vdash [emp]\, \texttt{skip}\, [ok\!:\!emp]$

ASSIGN
$\vdash [x\!=\!x']\; x := e\; [ok\!:\!x\!=\!e[x'/x]]$

HAVOC
$\vdash [x\!=\!x']\; x := *\; [ok\!:\!x\!=\!v]$

ASSUME
$\vdash [emp]\, \texttt{assume}(B)\, [ok\!:\!B]$

ERROR
$\vdash [emp]\, \texttt{L:\,error}\; [er(\textsc{l})\!:\!emp]$

SEQ1
$$\frac{\vdash [p]\; \mathbb{C}_1\; [er(\textsc{l})\!:\!q]}{\vdash [p]\; \mathbb{C}_1; \mathbb{C}_2\; [er(\textsc{l})\!:\!q]}$$

SEQ2
$$\frac{\vdash [p]\; \mathbb{C}_1\; [ok\!:\!r] \qquad \vdash [r]\; \mathbb{C}_2\; [\epsilon\!:\!q]}{\vdash [p]\; \mathbb{C}_1; \mathbb{C}_2\; [\epsilon\!:\!q]}$$

LOOP1
$\vdash [p]\; \mathbb{C}^*\; [ok\!:\!p]$

CHOICE
$$\frac{\vdash [p]\; \mathbb{C}_i\; [\epsilon\!:\!q] \qquad \text{for some } i \in \{1,2\}}{\vdash [p]\; \mathbb{C}_1 + \mathbb{C}_2\; [\epsilon\!:\!q]}$$

EXIST
$$\frac{\vdash [p]\; \mathbb{C}\; [\epsilon\!:\!q] \qquad x \notin \mathsf{fv}(\mathbb{C})}{\vdash [\exists x.p]\; \mathbb{C}\; [\epsilon\!:\!\exists x.q]}$$

LOOP2
$$\frac{\vdash [p]\; \mathbb{C}^*; \mathbb{C}\; [\epsilon\!:\!q]}{\vdash [p]\; \mathbb{C}^*\; [\epsilon\!:\!q]}$$

CONS
$$\frac{p' \Rightarrow p \qquad \vdash [p']\; \mathbb{C}\; [\epsilon\!:\!q'] \qquad q \Rightarrow q'}{\vdash [p]\; \mathbb{C}\; [\epsilon\!:\!q]}$$

DISJ
$$\frac{\vdash [p_1]\; \mathbb{C}\; [\epsilon\!:\!q_1] \qquad \vdash [p_2]\; \mathbb{C}\; [\epsilon\!:\!q_2]}{\vdash [p_1 \vee p_2]\; \mathbb{C}\; [\epsilon\!:\!q_1 \vee q_2]}$$

SUBST
$$\frac{\vdash [p]\; \mathbb{C}\; [\epsilon\!:\!q] \qquad y \notin \mathsf{fv}(p, \mathbb{C}, q)}{\vdash [p[y/x]]\; \mathbb{C}[y/x]\; [\epsilon\!:\!q[y/x]]}$$

LOCAL
$$\frac{\vdash [p]\; \mathbb{C}\; [\epsilon\!:\!q]}{\vdash [\exists x.\, p]\, \texttt{local}\; x\; \texttt{in}\; \mathbb{C}\; [\epsilon\!:\!\exists x.\, q]}$$

FRAME
$$\frac{\vdash [p]\; \mathbb{C}\; [\epsilon\!:\!q] \qquad \mathsf{mod}(\mathbb{C}) \cap \mathsf{fv}(r) = \emptyset}{\vdash [p * r]\; \mathbb{C}\; [\epsilon\!:\!q * r]}$$

ALLOC1
$\vdash [x\!=\!x']\; x := \texttt{alloc()}\; [ok\!:\!x \mapsto -]$

FREE
$\vdash [x \mapsto e]\, \texttt{L:\,free}(x)\; [ok\!:\!x \not\mapsto\,]$

ALLOC2
$\vdash [x\!=\!x' * y \not\mapsto\,]\; x := \texttt{alloc()}\; [ok\!:\!x\!=\!y * y \mapsto -]$

FREEER
$\vdash [x \not\mapsto\,]\, \texttt{L:\,free}(x)\; [er(\textsc{l})\!:\!x \not\mapsto\,]$

FREENULL
$\vdash [x\!=\!null]\, \texttt{L:\,free}(x)\; [er(\textsc{l})\!:\!x\!=\!null]$

LOAD
$\vdash [x\!=\!x' * y \mapsto e]\, \texttt{L:}\, x := [y]\; [ok\!:\!x\!=\!e[x'/x] * y \mapsto e[x'/x]]$

STORE
$\vdash [x \mapsto e]\, \texttt{L:}\, [x] := y\; [ok\!:\!x \mapsto y]$

LOADER
$\vdash [y \not\mapsto\,]\, \texttt{L:}\, x := [y]\; [er(\textsc{l})\!:\!y \not\mapsto\,]$

STOREER
$\vdash [x \not\mapsto\,]\, \texttt{L:}\, [x] := y\; [er(\textsc{l})\!:\!x \not\mapsto\,]$

LOADNULL
$\vdash [y\!=\!null]\, \texttt{L:}\, x := [y]\; [er(\textsc{l})\!:\!y\!=\!null]$

STORENULL
$\vdash [x\!=\!null]\, \texttt{L:}\, [x] := y\; [er(\textsc{l})\!:\!x\!=\!null]$

Fig. 5. The ISL proof rules where x and x' are distinct variables.

Note that $\texttt{skip}$, assignments and assume statements always terminate successfully (with ok). By contrast, $\texttt{L:\,error}$ always terminates erroneously (with $er(\textsc{l})$) and requires no resource. The ISL rules SEQ1, SEQ2, CHOICE, LOOP1, LOOP2, CONS, DISJ and SUBST are as in [35]. The SEQ1 rule captures short-circuiting when the first statement ($\mathbb{C}_1$) encounters an error and thus the program terminates erroneously. Analogously, SEQ2 states that when $\mathbb{C}_1$ executes successfully, the program terminates with ϵ when the subsequent $\mathbb{C}_2$ statement terminates with ϵ. The CHOICE rule states that the states in q are reachable from p when executing $\mathbb{C}_1 + \mathbb{C}_2$ if they are reachable from p when executing either branch. LOOP1 captures immediate exit from the loop; LOOP2 states that q is reachable from p when executing $\mathbb{C}^\star$ if it is reachable after a non-zero number of $\mathbb{C}$ iterations.

The CONS rule allows us to strengthen the result and weaken the presumption: if q' is reachable from p', then the smaller q is reachable from the bigger p. Note that compared to SL, the direction of implications in the CONS premise are flipped. Using CONS, we can rewrite the premises of DISJ as $[p_1 \vee p_2] \; \mathbb{C} \; [\epsilon : q_1]$ and $[p_1 \vee p_2] \; \mathbb{C} \; [\epsilon : q_2]$. As such, if both q_1 and q_2 are reachable from $p_1 \vee p_2$, then $q_1 \vee q_2$ is also reachable from $p_1 \vee p_2$, as shown in DISJ. The EXIST rule is derived from DISJ; SUBST is standard and allows us to substitute x with a fresh variable y; LOCAL is equivalent to that in [35] but uses the Barendregt variable convention, renaming variables in formulas instead of in commands to avoid clashes.

As in SL, the crux of ISL reasoning lies in the FRAME rule, allowing one to extend the presumption and the result of a triple with disjoint resources in r. The $\mathsf{fv}(r)$ function returns the set of free variables in r, and $\mathsf{mod}(\mathbb{C})$ returns the set of (program) variables modified by $\mathbb{C}$ (i.e., those on the left-hand of ':=' in assignment, lookup and allocation). These definitions are standard and elided.

Negative assertions allow us to detect memory safety violations when accessing deallocated locations. For instance, FREEER states that attempting to deallocate x causes an error when x is already deallocated; *mutatis mutandis* for LOADER and STOREER. As shown in ALLOC2, we can use negative assertions to allocate a previously-deallocated location: if y is deallocated ($y \not\mapsto$ holds in the presumption), then it may be reallocated. The FREENULL, LOADNULL and STORENULL rules state that accessing x causes an error when x is null. Finally, LOAD and STORE describe the successful execution of heap lookup and mutation, respectively.

Remark 1. Note that mutation and deallocation rules in SL are given as $\{x \mapsto -\}$ $[x] := y \; \{x \mapsto y\}$ and $\{x \mapsto -\} \; \mathtt{free}(x) \; \{\mathtt{emp}\}$; i.e., the value of x is existentially quantified in the precondition. We can similarly rewrite the ISL rules as:

STOREWEAK
$$\vdash [x \mapsto -] \, [x] := y \, [ok : x \mapsto y]$$

FREEWEAK
$$\vdash [x \mapsto -] \, \mathtt{free}(x) \, [ok : x \not\mapsto \,]$$

However, these rules are too weak. For instance, we cannot use STOREWEAK to prove $[x \mapsto 7] \, [x] := y \, [ok : x \mapsto y]$. This is because the implications in the premise of the CONS rule are flipped from those in their SL counterpart, and thus to use STOREWEAK we must show $x \mapsto - \Rightarrow x \mapsto 7$ which we cannot. Put differently, STOREWEAK states that for *some* value v, executing $[x] := y$ on a state satisfying $x \mapsto v$ yields a state satisfying $x \mapsto y$. However, this statement is valid for *all* values of v. As such, we strengthen the presumption of STORE to $x \mapsto e$, allowing for an arbitrary (universally quantified) expression e at x.

In general, in over-approximate logics (e.g., SL) the aim is to *weaken* the preconditions and *strengthen* the postconditions of specifications as much as possible. This is to ensure that we can optimally apply the CONS rule to adapt the specifications to broader contexts. Conversely, in under-approximate logics (e.g., ISL) we should strengthen the presumptions and weaken the results as much as possible, since the implication directions in the premise of CONS are flipped.

Remark 2. The backward reasoning rules of SL [28] are generally unsound for ISL, just as the backward reasoning rules of Hoare logic are unsound for incorrectness logic [35]. For instance, the backward axiom for store is $\{x \mapsto - * (x \mapsto y \twoheadrightarrow p)\}\ [x] := y\ \{p\}$. However, taking $p = \mathsf{emp}$ yields an inconsistent precondition, resulting in the triple $\{\mathsf{false}\}\ [x] := y\ \{\mathsf{emp}\}$, which is valid in SL but not ISL.

Proving. PB-OK **and** PB-CLIENT. We next return to the proof sketch of PB-OK in Fig. 3. For brevity, rather than giving full derivations, we follow the classical Hoare logic proof outline, annotating each line of the code with its presumption and result. We further commentate each proof step and write e.g., //CHOICE to denote an application of CHOICE. Note that when applying CHOICE, we *pick* a branch (e.g., the left branch in PB-OK) to execute. Observe that unlike in SL where one needs to reason about *all* branches, in ISL it suffices to pick and reason about a *single* branch, and the remaining branches are ignored.

As in Hoare logic proof outlines, we assume that SEQ2 is applied at every step; i.e., later instructions are executed only if the earlier ones execute successfully. In most steps, we apply FRAME to frame off the unused resource r, carry out the instruction effect, and subsequently frame on r. For instance, when verifying $z := *$ in the proof sketch of PB-OK, we apply HAVOC to pick a non-zero value for z (in this case 1) after the assignment. As such, since the presumption of HAVOC is emp, we use FRAME to frame off the resource $v \mapsto a * a \mapsto -$ in the presumption, apply HAVOC to obtain $z = 1$, and subsequently frame on $v \mapsto a * a \mapsto -$, yielding $z = 1 * v \mapsto a * a \mapsto -$. For brevity, we keep the applications of FRAME and SEQ2 implicit and omit them in our annotations. The proof of PB-CLIENT in Fig. 3 is then straightforward and applies the PB-OK specification when calling push_back(v). We refer the reader to the technical appendix [38] where we apply ISL to a further example to detect a null-pointer-dereference bug in OpenSSL.

4   The ISL Model

Denotational Semantics. We present the ISL semantics in Fig. 6. The semantics of a statement $\mathbb{C} \in$ Comm under an exit condition $\epsilon \in$ EXIT, written $[\![\mathbb{C}]\!]\epsilon$, is described as a relation on *program states*. A program state, $\sigma \in$ STATE, is a pair of the form (s, h), comprising a (variable) *store* $s \in$ STORE and a *heap* $h \in$ HEAP.

$$[.] : \text{COMM} \to \text{EXIT} \to \mathcal{P}(\text{STATE} \times \text{STATE}) \qquad \sigma \in \text{STATE} \triangleq \text{STORE} \times \text{HEAP}$$

$$s \in \text{STORE} \triangleq \text{VAR} \xrightarrow{\text{fin}} \text{VAL} \qquad h \in \text{HEAP} \triangleq \text{LOC} \xrightarrow{\text{fin}} \text{VAL} \uplus \{\bot\} \qquad l \in \text{LOC} \subseteq \text{VAL}$$

$$[\![\text{skip}]\!] ok \triangleq \{(\sigma, \sigma) \mid \sigma \in \text{STATE}\} \qquad\qquad [\![\text{skip}]\!] er(-) \triangleq \emptyset$$

$$[\![x := e]\!] ok \triangleq \{((s, h), (s[x \mapsto s(e)], h))\} \qquad [\![x := e]\!] er(-) \triangleq \emptyset$$

$$[\![x := *]\!] ok \triangleq \{((s, h), (s[x \mapsto v], h)) \mid v \in \text{VAL}\} \qquad [\![x := *]\!] er(-) \triangleq \emptyset$$

$$[\![\text{assume}(B)]\!] ok \triangleq \{(\sigma, \sigma) \mid \sigma = (s, h) \wedge s(B) \neq 0\} \qquad [\![\text{assume}(B)]\!] er(-) \triangleq \emptyset$$

$$[\![\text{L: error}]\!] ok \triangleq \emptyset \qquad\qquad [\![\text{L: error}]\!] er(\text{L}') \triangleq \{(\sigma, \sigma) \mid \text{L} = \text{L}'\}$$

$$[\![\mathbb{C}_1; \mathbb{C}_2]\!]\epsilon \triangleq \left\{ (\sigma, \sigma') \;\middle|\; \begin{array}{l} \epsilon \neq ok \wedge (\sigma, \sigma') \in [\![\mathbb{C}_1]\!]\epsilon \\ \vee \, \exists \sigma''. \, (\sigma, \sigma'') \in [\![\mathbb{C}_1]\!] ok \wedge (\sigma'', \sigma') \in [\![\mathbb{C}_2]\!]\epsilon \end{array} \right\}$$

$$[\![\text{local } x \text{ in } \mathbb{C}]\!]\epsilon \triangleq \{((s[x \mapsto v], h), (s'[x \mapsto v], h')) \mid ((s, h), (s', h')) \in [\![\mathbb{C}]\!]\epsilon\}$$

$$[\![\mathbb{C}_1 + \mathbb{C}_2]\!]\epsilon \triangleq [\![\mathbb{C}_1]\!]\epsilon \cup [\![\mathbb{C}_2]\!]\epsilon$$

$$[\![\mathbb{C}^*]\!]\epsilon \triangleq \bigcup_{i \in \mathbb{N}} [\![\mathbb{C}^i]\!]\epsilon \quad \text{with} \quad \mathbb{C}^0 \triangleq \text{skip} \quad \text{and} \quad \mathbb{C}^{i+1} \triangleq \mathbb{C}; \mathbb{C}^i$$

$$[\![x := \text{alloc}()]\!] ok \triangleq \left\{ (\sigma, (s[x \mapsto l], h[l \mapsto v])) \;\middle|\; \begin{array}{l} \sigma = (s, h) \wedge v \in \text{VAL} \\ \wedge \, (l \notin dom(h) \vee h(l) = \bot) \end{array} \right\}$$

$$[\![x := \text{alloc}()]\!] er(-) \triangleq \emptyset$$

$$[\![\text{L: free}(x)]\!] ok \triangleq \{(\sigma, (s, h[s(x) \mapsto \bot])) \mid \sigma = (s, h) \wedge h(s(x)) \in \text{VAL}\}$$

$$[\![\text{L: free}(x)]\!] er(\text{L}') \triangleq \{(\sigma, \sigma) \mid \text{L} = \text{L}' \wedge \sigma = (s, h) \wedge (s(x) = \text{null} \vee h(s(x)) = \bot)\}$$

$$[\![\text{L: } x := [y]]\!] ok \triangleq \{(\sigma, (s[x \mapsto v], h)) \mid \sigma = (s, h) \wedge h(s(y)) = v \in \text{VAL}\}$$

$$[\![\text{L: } x := [y]]\!] er(\text{L}') \triangleq \{(\sigma, \sigma) \mid \text{L} = \text{L}' \wedge \sigma = (s, h) \wedge (s(y) = \text{null} \vee h(s(y)) = \bot)\}$$

$$[\![\text{L: } [x] := y]\!] ok \triangleq \{(\sigma, (s, h[s(x) \mapsto s(y)])) \mid \sigma = (s, h) \wedge h(s(x)) \in \text{VAL}\}$$

$$[\![\text{L: } [x] := y]\!] er(\text{L}') \triangleq \{(\sigma, \sigma) \mid \text{L} = \text{L}' \wedge \sigma = (s, h) \wedge (s(x) = \text{null} \vee h(s(x)) = \bot)\}$$

$$(\!|\text{emp}|\!) \triangleq \{(s, h) \mid dom(h) = \emptyset\} \qquad (\!|e \mapsto e'|\!) \triangleq \{(s, h) \mid dom(h) = \{s(e)\} \wedge h(s(e)) = s(e') \neq \bot\}$$

$$(\!|e \not\mapsto |\!) \triangleq \{(s, h) \mid dom(h) = \{s(e)\} \wedge h(s(e)) = \bot\} \qquad (\!|p * q|\!) \triangleq \{\sigma_p \bullet \sigma_q \mid \sigma_p \in (\!|p|\!) \wedge \sigma_q \in (\!|q|\!)\}$$

$$\text{where} \qquad (s_1, h_1) \bullet (s_2, h_2) \triangleq \begin{cases} (s_1, h_1 \uplus h_2) & \text{if } s_1 = s_2 \wedge dom(h_1) \cap dom(h_2) = \emptyset \\ \text{undefined} & \text{otherwise} \end{cases}$$

Fig. 6. The ISL denotational semantics (top); the ISL assertion semantics (bottom).

A store is a function from variables to values. Given a store s, expression e and Boolean expression B, we write $s(e)$ and $s(B)$ for the values to which e and B evaluate under s, respectively. These definitions are standard and omitted.

A heap is a partial function from *locations*, LOC, to VAL $\uplus \{\bot\}$. We model heaps as partial functions as they may grow gradually by allocating additional locations. We use the designated value $\bot \notin$ VAL to track those locations that have been deallocated. That is, given $l \in$ LOC, if $h(l) \in$ VAL then l is allocated in h and holds value $h(l)$; and if $h(l) = \bot$ then l has been deallocated. As we demonstrate shortly, we use $\bot$ to model invalidated assertions such as $x \not\mapsto$.

The semantics in Fig. 6 closely corresponds to ISL rules in Fig. 5. For instance, $[\![x := [y]]\!]ok$ underpins LOAD, while $[\![x := [y]]\!]er(-)$ underpins LOADER and LOADNULL; e.g., if the location at y is deallocated ($h(s(y))=\bot$), then executing $x := [y]$ terminates erroneously as captured by $[\![x := [y]]\!]er(-)$. The semantics of mutation, allocation and deallocation are defined analogously. As shown, skip, assignment and assume(B) never terminate erroneously (e.g., $[\![\text{skip}]\!]er(-)=\emptyset$), and the semantics of their successful execution is standard. The two disjuncts in $[\![\mathbb{C}_1; \mathbb{C}_2]\!]\epsilon$ capture SEQ1 and SEQ2, respectively. The semantics of $\mathbb{C}_1 + \mathbb{C}_2$ is defined as the union of those of its two branches. The semantics of $\mathbb{C}^\star$ is defined as the union of the semantics of zero or more $\mathbb{C}$ iterations.

Heap Monotonicity. Note that for all $\mathbb{C}$, ϵ and $(\sigma_p, \sigma_q) \in [\![\mathbb{C}]\!]\epsilon$, the (domain of the) underlying heap in σ_p *monotonically grows* from σ_p to σ_q and *never shrinks*. In particular, whilst the heap domain grows via allocation, all other base cases (including deallocation) leave the domain of the heap (i.e., the heap size) unchanged – deallocation merely updates the value of the given location in the heap to $\bot$ and thus does not alter the heap domain. This is in contrast to the original SL model [28], where deallocation *removes* the given location from the heap, and thus the underlying heap may grow or shrink. As we discuss shortly, this monotonicity is the key reason why our model supports a footprint theorem.

ISL Assertion Semantics. The *semantics of ISL assertions* is given at the bottom of Fig. 6 via the function $(\!|.|\!) : \text{AST} \rightarrow \mathcal{P}(\text{STATE})$, interpreting each assertion as a set of states. The semantics of classical and Boolean assertions are standard and omitted. As described in Sect. 3, emp describes states in which the heap is empty; and $e \mapsto e'$ describes states of the form (s, h) in which h contains a single location at $s(e)$ with value $s(e')$. Analogously, $e \not\mapsto$ describes states of the form (s, h) in which h contains a single deallocated location at $s(e)$. Finally, the interpretation of $p * q$ contains a state σ iff it can be split into two parts, $\sigma = \sigma_p \bullet \sigma_q$, such that σ_p and σ_q are included in the interpretations of p and q, respectively. The function $\bullet : \text{STATE} \times \text{STATE} \rightharpoonup \text{STATE}$ given at the bottom of Fig. 6 denotes *state composition*, and is defined when the constituent stores agree and the heaps are disjoint. For brevity, we often write $\sigma \in p$ for $\sigma \in (\!|p|\!)$.

Semantic Incorrectness Triples. We next present the formal interpretation of ISL triples. Recall from Sect. 3 that an ISL triple $[p]\,\mathbb{C}\,[\epsilon : q]$ states that every state in q is reachable from some state in p under ϵ. Put formally:

$$\models [p]\,\mathbb{C}\,[\epsilon : q] \overset{\text{def}}{\iff} \forall \sigma_q \in q.\ \exists \sigma_p \in p.\ (\sigma_p, \sigma_q) \in [\![\mathbb{C}]\!]\epsilon$$

Finally, in the following theorem we show that the ISL proof rules are *sound*: if a triple $\vdash [p]\,\mathbb{C}\,[\epsilon : q]$ is derivable using the rules in Fig. 5, then $\models [p]\,\mathbb{C}\,[\epsilon : q]$ holds.

Theorem 1 (Soundness). *For all $p, \mathbb{C}, \epsilon, q$, if $\vdash [p]\,\mathbb{C}\,[\epsilon : q]$, then $\models [p]\,\mathbb{C}\,[\epsilon : q]$.*

4.1   The Footprint Theorem

The frame rule of SL enables *local* reasoning about a command $\mathbb{C}$ by concentrating only on the parts of the memory that are accessed by $\mathbb{C}$, i.e., the $\mathbb{C}$ *footprint*:

> 'To understand how a program works, it should be possible for reasoning and specification to be confined to the cells that the program actually accesses. The value of any other cell will automatically remain unchanged.' [36]

Local reasoning is then enabled by semantic observations about the local effect of heap accesses. In what follows we describe some of the semantic structure underpinning under-approximate local reasoning, including how it differs from the classic over-approximate theory. Our main result is a footprint theorem, stating that the meaning of a command $\mathbb{C}$ is determined by its action on the "small" part of the memory accessed by $\mathbb{C}$ (i.e., the $\mathbb{C}$ footprint). The overall meaning of $\mathbb{C}$ can then be obtained by "fleshing out" its footprint.

To see this, consider the following example:

$$
\begin{aligned}
&1.\ \texttt{free}(y); \\
&2.\ \text{L}_2\text{:}\texttt{free}(y)\ +\ \texttt{free}(x); \qquad\qquad\qquad\qquad (\text{FOOT}) \\
&3.\ \text{L}_3\text{:}\texttt{free}(x)\ +\ \texttt{skip}
\end{aligned}
$$

For simplicity, let us ignore variable stores for the moment and consider the executions of FOOT from an initial heap $h \triangleq [l_x \mapsto 1, l_y \mapsto 2, l_z \mapsto 3]$, containing locations l_x, l_y and l_z, corresponding to variables x, y and z, respectively. Note that starting from h, FOOT gives rise to four executions depending on the $+$ branches taken at lines 2 and 3. Let us consider the successful execution from h that first frees y, then frees x (the right branch of $+$ on line 2), and finally executes $\texttt{skip}$ (the right branch of $+$ on line 3). The footprint of this execution from h is then given by $(ok : [l_x \mapsto 1, l_y \mapsto 2], [l_x \mapsto \bot, l_y \mapsto \bot])$, denoting an ok execution from the initial sub-heap $[l_x \mapsto 1, l_y \mapsto 2]$, yielding the final sub-heap $[l_x \mapsto \bot, l_y \mapsto \bot]$ upon termination. That is, the initial and final sub-heaps in the footprint do not include the untouched location l_z as it remains unchanged, and the overall effect of FOOT is obtained from its footprint by adding $l_z \mapsto 3$ to both the initial and final sub-heaps; i.e., by "fleshing out" the footprint.

Next, consider the execution in which the left branch of $+$ on line 2 is taken, resulting in a use-after free error. The footprint of this second execution from h is given by $(er(\text{L}_2) : [l_y \mapsto 2], [l_y \mapsto \bot])$, denoting an error at L_2. Note that as this execution terminates erroneously at L_2, unlike in the first execution, location l_x remains untouched by FOOT and is thus not included in the footprint.

Put formally, let $\texttt{foot}\,(.) : \text{Comm} \to \text{EXIT} \to \mathcal{P}(\text{STATE} \times \text{STATE})$ denote a *footprint function* such that $\texttt{foot}\,(\mathbb{C})\,\epsilon$ describes the *minimal* state needed for *some* $\mathbb{C}$ execution under ϵ: if $((s, h), (s', h')) \in \texttt{foot}\,(\mathbb{C})\,\epsilon$, then h contains only the locations accessed by some $\mathbb{C}$ execution, yielding h' on termination. In Fig. 7 we present an excerpt of $\texttt{foot}\,(.)$, with its full definition given in [38].

$$\texttt{foot}\,(\mathbb{C}_1 + \mathbb{C}_2)\,\epsilon \triangleq \texttt{foot}\,(\mathbb{C}_1)\,\epsilon \cup \texttt{foot}\,(\mathbb{C}_2)\,\epsilon$$

$$\texttt{foot}\,(\text{L: } \texttt{free}(x))\,ok \triangleq \big\{\,((s, [l \mapsto v]), (s, [l \mapsto \bot]))\,\big|\,s(x){=}l \land v \in \textsc{Val}\big\}$$

$$\texttt{foot}\,(\text{L: } \texttt{free}(x))\,er(\text{L}') \triangleq \big\{\,((s, [l \mapsto \bot]), (s, [l \mapsto \bot]))\,\big|\,\text{L}{=}\text{L}' \land s(x){=}l\big\}$$

$$\cup\,\big\{\,((s, h_0), (s, h_0))\,\big|\,\text{L}{=}\text{L}' \land s(x){=}\texttt{null}\big\}$$

Fig. 7. The `foot` (.) function (excerpt), where h_0 denotes an empty heap $(dom(h_0) = \emptyset)$.

Our footprint theorem (Theorem 2) then states that any pair (σ_p, σ_q) resulting from executing $\mathbb{C}$ (i.e., $(\sigma_p, \sigma_q) \in [\![\mathbb{C}]\!]\epsilon$) can be obtained by fleshing out a pair (σ'_p, σ'_q) in the $\mathbb{C}$ footprint (i.e., $(\sigma'_p, \sigma'_q) \in \texttt{foot}\,(\mathbb{C})\,\epsilon$): $(\sigma_p, \sigma_q) = (\sigma'_p \bullet \sigma_r, \sigma'_q \bullet \sigma_r)$ for some σ_r.

Theorem 2 (Footprints). *For all* $\mathbb{C}$ *and* ϵ: $[\![\mathbb{C}]\!]\epsilon = \texttt{frame}\,(\texttt{foot}\,(\mathbb{C})\,\epsilon)$, *where* $\texttt{frame}\,(R) \triangleq \big\{(\sigma_p \bullet \sigma_r, \sigma_q \bullet \sigma_r)\,\big|\,(\sigma_p, \sigma_q) \in R\big\}$.

We note that our footprint theorem is a positive by-product of the ISL *model* and *not* the ISL logic. That is, the footprint theorem is an added bonus of the heap monotonicity in the ISL model, brought about by negative heap resources, and is orthogonal to the notion of under-approximation. As such, the footprint theorem would be analogously valid in the original SL model, were we to alter its model to achieve heap monotonicity through negative heaps. That said, there are important differences with the classic SL theory, which we discuss next.

4.2 Differences with the Classic (Over-Approximate) Theory

Existing work [14,40] presents footprint theorems for classical SL based on the notion of *safe states*; i.e., those that do not lead to erroneous executions. This is understandable as the informal reasoning which led to the frame rule for SL was based on safety [36,45]. According to the *fault-avoiding interpretation* of an SL triple $\{p\}\,\mathbb{C}\,\{q\}$, deemed invalid when a state in p leads to an error, if $\mathbb{C}$ accesses a location outside p, then this leads to a safety violation. As such, any location not guaranteed to exist in p must remain unchanged, thereby yielding the frame rule. The existing footprint theorems were for safe states only.

By contrast, our theorem considers footprints involving both unsafe and safe states. For instance, given the FOOT program and an initial state (e.g., h in Sect. 4.1), we distinguished a footprint leading to an erroneous execution (e.g., $(er(\text{L}_2) : [l_y \mapsto 2], [l_y \mapsto \bot]))$ from one leading to a safe execution (e.g., $(ok : [l_x \mapsto 1, l_y \mapsto 2], [l_x \mapsto \bot, l_y \mapsto \bot]))$. This distinction is important, as otherwise we could not distinguish further bugs that follow a safe execution. To see this, consider a second error in FOOT, namely the possible use-after-free of x on line 3, following a successful execution of lines 1 and 2.

For reasoning about incorrectness, it is essential that we consider unsafe states when accounting for why things work; this is a technical difference with the classic footprint results. But it also points to a deeper conceptual difference between the correctness and incorrectness theories. Above, we explained how safety, and its violation, played a crucial role in justifying the frame rule of over-approximate SL. However, as we describe below, ISL and its frame rule do not rely on safety.

As shown in [35], an under-approximate triple can be equivalently defined as: $[p] \mathbb{C} [\epsilon : q] \stackrel{\text{def}}{\Longleftrightarrow} \text{post}(\mathbb{C}, p) \supseteq q$, where $\text{post}(\mathbb{C}, p)$ describes the states obtained by executing $\mathbb{C}$ on p. While this under-approximate definition equivalently justifies the frame rule, the analogous over-approximate (Hoare) triple obtained by flipping $\supseteq$ (i.e., $\{p\} \mathbb{C} \{q\} \stackrel{\text{def}}{\Longleftrightarrow} \text{post}(\mathbb{C}, p) \subseteq q$) invalidates the frame rule:

$$\frac{\{\text{true}\}[x] := 23\{\text{true}\}}{\{x \mapsto 17 * \text{true}\}[x] := 23\{x \mapsto 17 * \text{true}\}} \text{ (FRAME)}$$

The premise of this derivation is valid according to the standard interpretation of over-approximate triples, but its conclusion (obtained by framing on $x \mapsto 17$) certainly is not, as it states that the value of x remains unchanged after mutation.

The frame rule is then recovered by strengthening the $\{p\} \mathbb{C} \{q\}$ interpretation, *either* by requiring that executing $\mathbb{C}$ on p not fault (fault avoidance), *or* by "baking in" frame preservation: $\forall r. \text{post}(\mathbb{C}, p * r) \subseteq q * r$. Both solutions then invalidate the premise of the above derivation. We found it remarkable that our ISL theory is consistent with the technically simpler interpretation of triples – namely as $\text{post}(\mathbb{C}, p) \supseteq q$, the dual of Hoare's interpretation – and that it supports a simple footprint theorem at once, again in contrast to the over-approximate theory.

5   Begin-Anywhere, Intra-procedural Symbolic Execution

ISL lends itself naturally to the definition of forward symbolic execution analyses. We demonstrate that using the ISL rules, it is straightforward to derive a *begin-anywhere, intra-procedural* analysis that allows us to infer valid ISL triples *automatically* for a given piece of code, with the goal of finding only true bugs reachable from an initial state. This is implemented in the intra-procedural-only mode of the Pulse analysis inside Infer [18] (accessible by passing `--pulse --pulse-intraprocedural-only` to `infer`). The analysis follows principles from bi-abduction [11], but takes its most successful application – bug catching [18] – as the sole objective. This allows us to make a number of adjustments and to obtain an analysis that is a much closer fit to the ISL theory of under-approximation than the original bi-abduction analysis was to the SL theory of over-approximation.

The original bi-abduction analysis in Abductor [11] and Infer [18] aimed at discovering fault-avoiding specifications for procedures. Ideally, one would find specifications for *all* procedures in the codebase, all the way to an entry-point (e.g., the `main()` function), thus proving the program safe. In practice, however, virtually all sizable codebases have bugs, and known abstract domains are imprecise when proving memory safety for large codebases. As such, specifications were

$$p, q ::= \mathsf{emp} \mid e \oplus e' \mid e \mapsto e' \mid e \not\mapsto \mid p * q \qquad\qquad \text{Symbolic Heaps}$$

SE-SEQ
$$\frac{[p_0]\,\mathbb{C}_0\,[ok\colon q_0]\ \mathbb{C}_1 \rightsquigarrow [p_1]\,\mathbb{C}_0;\mathbb{C}_1\,[\epsilon_1\colon q_1]}{[p_1]\,\mathbb{C}_0;\mathbb{C}_1\,[\epsilon_1\colon q_1]\ \mathbb{C}_2 \rightsquigarrow [p_2]\,\mathbb{C}_0;\mathbb{C}_1;\mathbb{C}_2\,[\epsilon_2\colon q_2]}{[p_0]\,\mathbb{C}_0\,[ok\colon q_0]\ \mathbb{C}_1;\mathbb{C}_2 \rightsquigarrow [p_2]\,\mathbb{C}_0;\mathbb{C}_1;\mathbb{C}_2\,[\epsilon_2\colon q_2]}$$

SE-CHOICE
$$\frac{[p_0]\,\mathbb{C}_0\,[ok\colon q_0]\ \mathbb{C}_i \rightsquigarrow [p_i]\,\mathbb{C}_0;\mathbb{C}_i\,[\epsilon_i\colon q_i]}{[p_0]\,\mathbb{C}_0\,[ok\colon q_0]\ \mathbb{C}_1 + \mathbb{C}_2 \rightsquigarrow [p_i]\,\mathbb{C}_0;\mathbb{C}_1 + \mathbb{C}_2\,[\epsilon_i\colon q_i]}$$

SE-STORE
$$\frac{q * M \dashv x \mapsto e * F \qquad \mathsf{mod}(\mathbb{C}) \cap \mathsf{fv}(M) = \emptyset}{[p]\,\mathbb{C}\,[ok\colon q]\ [x] := y \rightsquigarrow [p * M]\,\mathbb{C};[x] := y\,[ok\colon x \mapsto y * F]}$$

SE-STOREER
$$\frac{q \vdash x \not\mapsto * \mathsf{true} \ \text{or}\ q \vdash x = \mathsf{null} * \mathsf{true}}{[p]\,\mathbb{C}\,[ok\colon q]\ \mathsf{L}\colon [x] := y \rightsquigarrow [p]\,\mathbb{C};\mathsf{L}\colon [x] := y\,[er(\mathsf{L})\colon q]}$$

Fig. 8. Symbolic heaps (above) and selected symbolic execution rules (below).

found for only 40–70% of the procedures in the experiments of [11]. Nonetheless, proof failures, a by-product of proof search, became practically more valuable than proofs, as they can indicate errors. Complex heuristics came into play to classify proof failures and to report to the programmer those more likely to be errors. These heuristics have not been given a formal footing, contributing to the gap between the theory of proofs and the practice of bug catching.

Pulse approaches bug reporting more directly: by looking for them. It infers under-approximate specifications, while recording invalidated addresses. If such an address is later accessed, a bug is reported soundly, in line with the theory.

Symbolic Execution. In Fig. 8 we present our symbolic execution as big-step, syntax-directed inference rules of the form $[p_0]\,\mathbb{C}_0\,[\epsilon_0\colon q_0]\ \mathbb{C} \rightsquigarrow [p]\,\mathbb{C}_0;\mathbb{C}\,[\epsilon\colon q]$, which can be read as: "having already executed $\mathbb{C}_0$ yielding (discovering) the presumption p_0 and the result q_0, then executing $\mathbb{C}$ yields the presumption p and result q". As is standard in SL-based tools [4,11], our abstract states consist of *-conjoined predicates, with the notable addition of the invalidated assertion and omission of inductive predicates. The latter are not needed because we never perform the over-approximation steps that would introduce them.

SE-SEQ describes how the symbolic execution goes forward step by step. SE-CHOICE describes how the analysis computes one specification per path taken in the program. To ensure termination, loops are unrolled up to a fixed bound N_{loops}, borrowing from symbolic bounded model checking [12]. These two ideas avoid the arduous task of inventing join and widen operators [15]. For added efficiency, in practice we also limit the maximum number of paths leading to the same program point to a fixed bound $N_{\mathrm{disjuncts}}$. The N_{loops} and $N_{\mathrm{disjuncts}}$ bounds give us easy "knobs" to tune the precision of the analysis. Note that pruning paths by limiting disjuncts is also sound for under-approximate reasoning [35].

To analyze a program $\mathbb{C}$, we start from $\mathbb{C}_0 = \texttt{skip}$ and produce $[\texttt{emp}]\,\texttt{skip}$ $[ok:\texttt{emp}]\;\mathbb{C} \rightsquigarrow [p]\,\texttt{skip};\mathbb{C}\;[\epsilon:q]$. As $\models [\texttt{emp}]\,\texttt{skip}\,[ok:\texttt{emp}]$ holds and symbolic execution rules preserve validity, we then obtain valid triples for $\mathbb{C}$ by Theorem 3.

Theorem 3 (Soundness of Symbolic Execution). *If* $\models [p_0]\,\mathbb{C}_0\,[\epsilon:q_0]$ *and* $[p_0]\,\mathbb{C}_0\,[\epsilon_0:q_0]\;\mathbb{C} \rightsquigarrow [p]\,\mathbb{C}_0;\mathbb{C}\,[\epsilon:q]$, *then* $\models [p]\,\mathbb{C}_0;\mathbb{C}\,[\epsilon:q]$.

Symbolic execution of individual commands follows the derived SYMBEXEC rule below, with the side-condition that $\text{mod}(\mathbb{C}_0)\cap\text{fv}(M) = \text{mod}(\mathbb{C})\cap\text{fv}(F) = \emptyset$:

SYMBEXEC

$$\frac{[p_0]\,\mathbb{C}_0\,[ok{:}q_0] \qquad q_0 * M \dashv p * F \qquad \dfrac{[p]\,\mathbb{C}\,[\epsilon{:}q]}{[p*F]\,\mathbb{C}\,[\epsilon q*F]}}{[p_0 * M]\;\mathbb{C}_0;\mathbb{C}\,[\epsilon:q*F]}$$

If executing $\mathbb{C}_0$ yields the presumption p_0 and the current state q_0, then SYMBEXEC allows us to execute the next command $\mathbb{C}$ with specification $[p]\,\mathbb{C}$ $[\epsilon:q]$. This may 1) materialize a state M that is *missing* from q_0 (and is needed to execute $\mathbb{C}$); and 2) carry over an unchanged *frame* F. The unknowns M and F in the *bi-abduction question* $p * F \vdash q_0 * M$ have analogous counterparts in over-approximate bi-abduction; but, as in the CONS rule, their roles have flipped: the *frame* F is *abduced*, while the missing M is *framed* (or *anti-abduced*).

Bi-abduction and ISL. Bi-abduction is arguably a better fit for ISL than SL: in SL adding the missing M to the overall precondition p_0 is only valid for straight-line code, and not across control flow branches. Intuitively, there is no guarantee that a safe precondition for one path is safe for the other. This is especially the case in the presence of non-determinism or over-approximation of Boolean conditions, where one cannot find definitive predicates to force the analysis down one path. It is thus necessary to *re-execute* the whole procedure on the inferred preconditions, eliminating those that are not safe for all paths. By contrast, in our setting SE-CHOICE is *sound*, and this re-execution is not needed!

We allow the analysis to abduce information only for *successful* execution; *erroneous* executions have to be *manifest* and realizable using only the information at hand. We do this by requiring M to be $\texttt{emp}$ in SYMBEXEC when applied to error triples. We go even further and require that the implication be in both directions, i.e., that the current state *force* the error – note that if $q \vdash x \not\mapsto *\texttt{true}$ then there exists F such that $x \not\mapsto * F \vdash q$, and similarly for $q \vdash x = \texttt{null} *\texttt{true}$. This is a practical choice and only one of many ways to decide *where* to report, trying to avoid blaming the code for issues it did not itself cause. For instance, thanks to this restriction, we do not report on $[x] := 10$ (which has error specifications through STOREER and STORENULL) unless a previous instruction actively invalidated x. This choice also chimes well with the fact that the analysis can *start anywhere* in a program and give results relevant to the code analyzed.

Solving the bi-abduction entailment in SYMBEXEC can be done using the techniques developed for SL [11, §3]. We do not detail them here as they are straightforwardly adapted to our simpler setting without inductive predicates.

Finding a Bug in client, Automatically. We now describe how Pulse automatically finds a proof of the bug in the unnanotated code of client from Fig. 3, by automatically applying the only possible symbolic execution rule at each step. Starting from emp and going past the first instruction $x := [v]$ requires solving $v \mapsto u * F \vdash \mathsf{emp} * M$. The bi-abduction entailment solver then answers with $F = \mathsf{emp}$ and $M = v \mapsto u$, yielding the inferred presumption $v \mapsto u$ and the next current state $v \mapsto u * x = u$. The next instruction is the call to push_back(v). For ease of presentation, let us consider this library call as an axiomatized instruction that has been given the specification in Fig. 3. This corresponds to writing a model for it in the analyzer, which is actually the case in the implementation, although the analysis would work equally well if we were to inline the code inside client. Applying SYMBEXEC requires solving the entailment $v \mapsto a * a \mapsto w * F \vdash v \mapsto u * x = u * M$. The solver then answers with the solution $F = (x = u * a = u)$ and $M = u \mapsto w$. Finally, the following instance of SE-StoreEr is used to report an error, where $\mathbb{C} = \mathsf{skip}; x := [v]; \mathsf{push\_back}(v)$ and $q_{rx} = v \mapsto a' * a' \mapsto w * a \not\mapsto * x = u * a = u$:

$$[v \mapsto u * u \mapsto w] \, \mathbb{C} \, [ok : q_{rx}] \, \mathrm{L}_{rx} : [x] := 88$$
$$\rightsquigarrow [v \mapsto u * u \mapsto w] \, \mathbb{C}; \mathrm{L}_{rx} : [x] := 88 \, [er(\mathrm{L}_{rx}) : q_{rx}]$$

Preliminary Results. Our analysis handles the examples in this paper, modulo function inlining. While our analysis shows how to derive a sound static analysis from first principles, it does not yet fully exploit the theory, as it does not handle function calls, and in particular *summarization*. Under-approximate triples pave the way towards succinct summaries. However, this is a subtle problem, requiring significant theoretical and empirical work out of the scope of this initial paper.

Pragmatically, we can make Pulse scale by skipping over procedure calls instead of inlining them, in effect assuming that the call has no effect beyond assigning fresh (non-deterministic) values to the return address and the parameters passed by reference – note that such fresh values are treated optimistically by Pulse as we do not know them to be invalid. In theory, this may cause false positives and false negatives, but in practice we observed that such an analysis reports very few issues. For instance, it reports no issues on OpenSSL 1.0.2d (with 8681 C functions) at the time of writing, and only 17 issues on our proprietary C++ codebase of hundreds of thousands of procedures. As expected, the analysis is very fast and scales well (6 s for OpenSSL, running on a Linux machine with 24 cores). Moreover, 30 disjuncts suffice to detect all 17 issues (in comparison, using 20 disjuncts misses 1 issue, while using 100 disjuncts detects no more issues than using 30 disjuncts), and varying loop unrollings between 1–10 has no effect.

We also ran Pulse in production at Facebook and reported issues to developers as they submit code changes, where bugs are more likely than in mature codebases. Over the course of 4 months, Pulse reported 20 issues to developers, of which 15 were fixed. This deployment relies crucially on the begin-anywhere capability: though the codebase in question has 10s of MLOC, analysing a code change starts from the changed files and usually visits only a small fraction of the codebase.

Under-Approximation in Pulse. Pulse achieves under-approximate reasoning in several ways. First, Pulse uses the under-approximate CHOICE, LOOP1 and LOOP2 rules in Fig. 5 which prune paths by considering one execution branch (CHOICE) or finite loop unrollings (LOOP1 and LOOP2). Second, Pulse does not use ALLOC2, and thus prunes further paths. Third, Pulse uses under-approximate models of certain library procedures; e.g., the vector::push_back() model assumes the internal array is always deallocated. Finally, our bi-abduction implementation assumes that memory locations are distinct unless known otherwise, thus leading to further path pruning. These choices are all sound thanks to the under-approximate theory of ISL; it is nevertheless possible to make different pragmatic choices.

Although our implementation does not do it, we can use ISL to derive strongest posts for primitive statements, using a combination of their axioms and the FRAME, DISJ and EXIST rules. Given the logic fragment we use (which excludes inductive predicates) and a programming language with Boolean conditions restricted to a decidable fragment, there is likely a bounded decidability result obtained by unrolling loops up to a given bound and then checking the strongest post on each path. However, the ability to under-approximate (by forgetting paths/disjuncts) gives us the leeway to tune a deployment for optimizing the bugs/minute rate: in one experiment, we found that running Pulse on a codebase with 100s kLOC and a limit of 20 disjuncts was ~3.1x user-time faster than running it with a limit of 50 disjuncts, and yet found 97% of the issues found in the 50-disjuncts case.

Remark 3. Note that although the underlying heaps in ISL grow monotonically, the impact on the size of the manipulated states in our analysis is comparable to that of the original bi-abductive analysis for SL [11]. This is in part thanks to the compositionality afforded by ISL and its footprint property (Theorem 2), especially when individual procedures analyzed are not too big. In particular, the original bi-abduction work for SL already tracks the allocated memory; in ISL we additionally track deallocated memory which is of the same order of magnitude.

6   Context, Related Work and Conclusions

Although the foundations of program verification have been mostly developed with correctness in mind, industrial uses of symbolic reasoning often derive value from their deployment as *bug catchers* rather than *provers* of bug absence. There is a fundamental tension in correctness-based techniques, most thoroughly explored in the model checking field, between compact representations versus strength and utility of counter-examples. Abstraction techniques are typically used to increase compactness. This has the undesired side-effect that counter-examples become "abstract": they may be infeasible, in that they may not actually witness a concrete execution that violates a given property. Using proofs of bugs, this paper aims to provide a symbolic mechanism to express the *definite* existence of a concrete counter-example, without committing to a particular one, while simultaneously enabling sound, compositional, local reasoning. Our working hypothesis is that bugs are a fundamental enough phenomenon to warrant a fundamental compositional theory for reasoning positively about their existence, rather than only being about failed proofs. We hope that future work will explore the practical ramifications of these foundational ideas more thoroughly.

Amongst static bug-catching techniques, there is a dichotomy between the highly scalable, compositional static tools such as Coverity [5], Facebook Infer [18] and those deployed at Google [42], which suffer from false positives as well as negatives, and the under-approximating global bug hunters such as fuzzers [23] and symbolic executors [9], which suffer from scalability limitations but not false positives (at least, ideally). In a recent survey, Godefroid remarks "How to engineer exhaustive symbolic testing (that is, a form of verification) in a cost-effective manner is still an open problem for large applications" [23]. The ability to apply compositional analyses incrementally to large codebases has led to considerable impact that is complementary to that of the global analyses. But, compositional techniques can have less precision compared to global ones: examining all call sites of a procedure can naturally lead to more precise results.

Our illustrative analysis, Pulse, starts from the scalable end of the spectrum and moves towards the under-approximate end. An equally valid research direction would be to start from existing under-approximate analyses and make them more scalable and with lower start-up-cost. There has indeed been valuable research in this direction. For example, SMART [22] tries to make symbolic execution more scalable by using summaries as in inter-procedural static analysis, and UC-KLEE [39] allows symbolic execution to begin anywhere, and thus does not need a complete program. UC-KLEE uses a "lazy initialization" mechanism to synthesize assumptions about data structures; this is not unlike the bi-abductive approach here and in [10]. An interesting research question is whether this similarity can be made rigorous. There are many papers on marrying under- and over-approximation e.g., [1], but they often lack the scalability that is crucial to the impact of modular bug catchers. In general, there is a large unexplored territory, relevant to Godefroid's open problem stated above, between the existing modular but not-quite-under-approximate bug catchers such as Infer and Coverity, and the existing global and under-approximate tools such as KLEE [8], CBMC [12] and DART [24]. This paper provides not a solution, but a step in the exploration.

Gillian [20] is a platform for developing symbolic analysis tools using a symbolic execution engine based on separation logic. Gillian has C and JavaScript instantiations for precise reasoning about a finite unwinding of a program, similar to symbolic bounded model checking. Gillian's execution engine is currently exact for primitive commands (it is both over- and under-approximate); however, it uses over-approximate bi-abduction for function calls, and is thus open to false positives (Petar Maksimović, personal communication). We believe Gillian can be modified to embrace under-approximation more strongly, serving as a general engine for proving ISL specifications. Aiming for under-approximate results rather than exact ones gives additional flexibility to the analysis designer, just as aiming for over-approximate rather than exact results does for correctness tools.

Many assertion languages for heap reasoning have been developed, including ones not based on SL (e.g., [3,27,31,46]). We do not claim that, compared to these alternatives, the ISL assertion language in this paper is particularly advantageous for reasoning along individual paths, or exhaustive (but bounded) reasoning about complete programs. Rather, the key point is that our analysis solves abduction and anti-abduction problems, which in turn facilitates its application to large codebases. In particular, as our analysis synthesizes contextual heap assumptions (using anti-abduction), it can begin anywhere in a codebase instead of starting from `main()`. For example, it can start on a modified function that is part of a larger program: this capability enables continuous deployment in codebases with millions of LOC [18,34]. To our knowledge, the cited assertion languages have only ever been applied in a whole-program fashion on small codebases (with low thousands of LOC). We speculate that this is not because of the assertion languages *per se*: if methods to solve analogues of abduction and anti-abduction queries were developed, perhaps they too could be applied to large codebases.

It is natural to consider how the ideas of ISL extend to concurrency. The RacerD analyzer [25] provided a static analysis for data races in concurrent programs; this analysis was provably under-approximate under certain assumptions. RacerD was intuitively inspired by concurrent separation logic (CSL [6]), but did not match the over-approximate CSL theory (just as Infer did not match SL). We speculate that RacerD and other concurrency analyses might be seen as constructing proofs in a yet-to-be-defined incorrectness version of CSL, a logic which would aim at finding bugs in concurrent programs via modular reasoning.

Our approach supports reasoning that is local not only in code, but also in state (spatial locality). Spatially local symbolic heap update has led to advances in scalability of global shape analyses of mutable data structures, where heap predicates are modified in-place in a way reminiscent of operational in-place update, and where transfer functions need not track global heap information [44]. Mutable data structures have been suggested as one area where classic symbolic execution has scaling challenges, and SL has been employed with human-directed proof on heap-intensive components to aid the overall scalability of symbolic execution [37]. An interesting question is whether spatial locality in the analysis can benefit scalability of fully automatic, global, under-approximate analyses.

We probed the semantic fundamentals underpinning local reasoning in Sect. 4, including a footprint theorem (Theorem 2) that is independent of the logic. The semantic principles are more deeply fundamental than the surface syntax of the logic. Indeed, in the early days of work on SL, it was remarked that local reasoning flows from locality properties of the semantics, and that separation logic is but one convenient syntax to exploit these [45]. Since then, a number of correctness logics with non-SL syntax have been proposed for local reasoning (e.g., [33] and its references) that exploit the semantic locality of heap update, and it stands to reason that the same will be possible for incorrectness logics.

Relating this paper to the timeline of SL for correctness, we have developed the basic logic (like [36] but under-approximate) and a simple local intra-procedural analysis (like [19] but under-approximate). We have not yet made the next steps to relatively-scalable global analyses [44] or extremely-scalable inter-procedural, compositional ones [11]. These future directions are challenging for theory and especially practice, and are the subject of ongoing and future work.

Conclusions. Long ago, Dijkstra (in)famously remarked that "testing can be quite effective for showing the presence of bugs, but is hopelessly inadequate for showing their absence" [17], and he advocated the use of logic for the latter. As noted by others, many of the benefits of logic hold for both bug catching and verification, particularly the ability to cover many states and paths succinctly, even if not the alluring all. But there remains a frustrating division between testing and verification, where e.g., distinct tools are used for each. With more research on the fundamentals of symbolic bug catching and correctness, division may be replaced by unified foundations and toolsets in the future. For under-approximate reasoning in particular, we hope that bug catching eventually becomes more modular, scalable, easier to deploy and with elegant foundations similar to those of verification. This paper presents but one modest step towards that goal.

Acknowledgments. We thank Petar Maksimović, Philippa Gardner, and the CAV reviewers for their feedback, and Ralf Jung for fruitful discussions in early stages of this work. This work was supported in part by a European Research Council (ERC) Consolidator Grant for the project "RustBelt", funded under the European Union's Horizon 2020 Framework Programme (grant no. 683289).

References

1. Albarghouthi, A., Gurfinkel, A., Chechik, M.: From under-approximations to over-approximations and back. In: Flanagan, C., König, B. (eds.) TACAS 2012. LNCS, vol. 7214, pp. 157–172. Springer, Heidelberg (2012). https://doi.org/10.1007/978-3-642-28756-5_12
2. Banerjee, A., Naumann, D.A., Rosenberg, S.: Local reasoning for global invariants, part I: region logic. J. ACM **60**(3), 18:1–18:56 (2013). https://doi.org/10.1145/2485982
3. Bansal, K., Reynolds, A., King, T., Barrett, C., Wies, T.: Deciding local theory extensions via E-matching. In: Kroening, D., Păsăreanu, C.S. (eds.) CAV 2015, Part II. LNCS, vol. 9207, pp. 87–105. Springer, Cham (2015). https://doi.org/10.1007/978-3-319-21668-3_6

4. Berdine, J., Calcagno, C., O'Hearn, P.W.: Smallfoot: modular automatic assertion checking with separation logic. In: de Boer, F.S., Bonsangue, M.M., Graf, S., de Roever, W.-P. (eds.) FMCO 2005. LNCS, vol. 4111, pp. 115–137. Springer, Heidelberg (2006). https://doi.org/10.1007/11804192_6
5. Bessey, A., et al.: A few billion lines of code later: using static analysis to find bugs in the real world. Commun. ACM **53**(2), 66–75 (2010). https://doi.org/10.1145/1646353.1646374
6. Brookes, S., O'Hearn, P.W.: Concurrent separation logic. SIGLOG News **3**(3), 47–65 (2016). https://dl.acm.org/citation.cfm?id=2984457
7. Burch, J.R., Clarke, E.M., McMillan, K.L., Dill, D.L., Hwang, L.J.: Symbolic model checking: $10^{\wedge}20$ states and beyond. In: Proceedings of the Fifth Annual Symposium on Logic in Computer Science (LICS 1990), Philadelphia, Pennsylvania, USA, 4–7 June 1990, pp. 428–439 (1990). https://doi.org/10.1109/LICS.1990.113767
8. Cadar, C., Dunbar, D., Engler, D.R.: KLEE: unassisted and automatic generation of high-coverage tests for complex systems programs. In: 8th USENIX Symposium on Operating Systems Design and Implementation, OSDI 2008, San Diego, California, USA, 8–10 December 2008, Proceedings, pp. 209–224 (2008). http://www.usenix.org/events/osdi08/tech/full_papers/cadar/cadar.pdf
9. Cadar, C., Sen, K.: Symbolic execution for software testing: three decades later. Commun. ACM **56**(2), 82–90 (2013). https://doi.org/10.1145/2408776.2408795
10. Calcagno, C., Distefano, D., O'Hearn, P.W., Yang, H.: Footprint analysis: a shape analysis that discovers preconditions. In: Nielson, H.R., Filé, G. (eds.) SAS 2007. LNCS, vol. 4634, pp. 402–418. Springer, Heidelberg (2007). https://doi.org/10.1007/978-3-540-74061-2_25
11. Calcagno, C., Distefano, D., O'Hearn, P.W., Yang, H.: Compositional shape analysis by means of bi-abduction. J. ACM **58**(6), 26:1–26:66 (2011). https://doi.org/10.1145/2049697.2049700
12. Clarke, E., Kroening, D., Lerda, F.: A tool for checking ANSI-C programs. In: Jensen, K., Podelski, A. (eds.) TACAS 2004. LNCS, vol. 2988, pp. 168–176. Springer, Heidelberg (2004). https://doi.org/10.1007/978-3-540-24730-2_15
13. Cohen, E., Moskal, M., Schulte, W., Tobies, S.: Local verification of global invariants in concurrent programs. In: Touili, T., Cook, B., Jackson, P. (eds.) CAV 2010. LNCS, vol. 6174, pp. 480–494. Springer, Heidelberg (2010). https://doi.org/10.1007/978-3-642-14295-6_42
14. Costanzo, D., Shao, Z.: A case for behavior-preserving actions in separation logic. In: Jhala, R., Igarashi, A. (eds.) APLAS 2012. LNCS, vol. 7705, pp. 332–349. Springer, Heidelberg (2012). https://doi.org/10.1007/978-3-642-35182-2_24
15. Cousot, P., Cousot, R.: Abstract interpretation: a unified lattice model for static analysis of programs by construction or approximation of fixpoints. In: POPL, pp. 238–252 (1977). https://doi.org/10.1145/512950.512973
16. Cousot, P., Cousot, R.: Modular static program analysis. In: Horspool, R.N. (ed.) CC 2002. LNCS, vol. 2304, pp. 159–179. Springer, Heidelberg (2002). https://doi.org/10.1007/3-540-45937-5_13
17. Dijkstra, E.W.: A Discipline of Programming. Prentice-Hall, Upper Saddle River (1976)
18. Distefano, D., Fähndrich, M., Logozzo, F., O'Hearn, P.W.: Scaling static analyses at Facebook. Commun. ACM **62**(8), 62–70 (2019). https://doi.org/10.1145/3338112
19. Distefano, D., O'Hearn, P.W., Yang, H.: A local shape analysis based on separation logic. In: Hermanns, H., Palsberg, J. (eds.) TACAS 2006. LNCS, vol. 3920, pp. 287–302. Springer, Heidelberg (2006). https://doi.org/10.1007/11691372_19

20. Fragoso Santos, J., Maksimović, P., Ayoun, S., Gardner, P.: Gillian, part i: a multi-language platform for symbolic execution. In: Proceedings of the 41st ACM SIG-PLAN International Conference on Programming Language Design and Implementation (PLDI 2020), London, UK, 15–20 June 2020 (2020). https://doi.org/10.1145/3385412.3386014
21. Gardner, P.A., Maffeis, S., Smith, G.D.: Towards a program logic for javascript. SIGPLAN Not. **47**(1), 31–44 (2012). https://doi.org/10.1145/2103621.2103663
22. Godefroid, P.: Compositional dynamic test generation. In: Proceedings of the 34th ACM SIGPLAN-SIGACT Symposium on Principles of Programming Languages, POPL 2007, Nice, France, 17–19 January 2007, pp. 47–54 (2007). https://doi.org/10.1145/1190216.1190226
23. Godefroid, P.: Fuzzing: hack, art, and science. Commun. ACM **63**(2), 70–76 (2020). https://doi.org/10.1145/3363824
24. Godefroid, P., Klarlund, N., Sen, K.: DART: directed automated random testing. In: Proceedings of the ACM SIGPLAN 2005 Conference on Programming Language Design and Implementation, Chicago, IL, USA, 12–15 June 2005, pp. 213–223 (2005). https://doi.org/10.1145/1065010.1065036
25. Gorogiannis, N., O'Hearn, P.W., Sergey, I.: A true positives theorem for a static race detector. PACMPL **3**(POPL), 57:1–57:29 (2019). https://doi.org/10.1145/3290370
26. Hoare, C.A.R.: An axiomatic basis for computer programming. Commun. ACM **12**(10), 576–580 (1969). https://doi.org/10.1145/363235.363259
27. Holík, L., Hruška, M., Lengál, O., Rogalewicz, A., Vojnar, T.: Counterexample validation and interpolation-based refinement for forest automata. In: Bouajjani, A., Monniaux, D. (eds.) VMCAI 2017. LNCS, vol. 10145, pp. 288–309. Springer, Cham (2017). https://doi.org/10.1007/978-3-319-52234-0_16
28. Ishtiaq, S.S., O'Hearn, P.W.: BI as an assertion language for mutable data structures. In: Proceedings of the 28th ACM SIGPLAN-SIGACT Symposium on Principles of Programming Languages, POPL, pp. 14–26. Association for Computing Machinery, New York (2001). https://doi.org/10.1145/360204.375719
29. Kassios, I.T.: The dynamic frames theory. Formal Asp. Comput. **23**(3), 267–288 (2011). https://doi.org/10.1007/s00165-010-0152-5
30. Leino, K.R.M.: Dafny: an automatic program verifier for functional correctness. In: Clarke, E.M., Voronkov, A. (eds.) LPAR 2010. LNCS (LNAI), vol. 6355, pp. 348–370. Springer, Heidelberg (2010). https://doi.org/10.1007/978-3-642-17511-4_20
31. Mathur, U., Murali, A., Krogmeier, P., Madhusudan, P., Viswanathan, M.: Deciding memory safety for single-pass heap-manipulating programs. Proc. ACM Program. Lang. **4**(POPL), 35:1–35:29 (2020). https://doi.org/10.1145/3371103
32. McPeak, S., Gros, C., Ramanathan, M.K.: Scalable and incremental software bug detection. In: Joint Meeting of the European Software Engineering Conference and the ACM SIGSOFT Symposium on the Foundations of Software Engineering, ESEC/FSE 2013, Saint Petersburg, Russian Federation, 18–26 August 2013, pp. 554–564 (2013). https://doi.org/10.1145/2491411.2501854
33. Murali, A., Peña, L., Löding, C., Madhusudan, P.: A first-order logic with frames. ESOP 2020. LNCS, vol. 12075, pp. 515–543. Springer, Cham (2020). https://doi.org/10.1007/978-3-030-44914-8_19
34. O'Hearn, P.W.: Continuous reasoning: scaling the impact of formal methods. In: Proceedings of the 33rd Annual ACM/IEEE Symposium on Logic in Computer Science, LICS 2018, Oxford, UK, 09–12 July 2018, pp. 13–25 (2018). https://doi.org/10.1145/3209108.3209109

35. O'Hearn, P.W.: Incorrectness logic. Proc. ACM Program. Lang. 4(POPL), 10:1–10:32 (2019). https://doi.org/10.1145/3371078
36. O'Hearn, P., Reynolds, J., Yang, H.: Local reasoning about programs that alter data structures. In: Fribourg, L. (ed.) CSL 2001. LNCS, vol. 2142, pp. 1–19. Springer, Heidelberg (2001). https://doi.org/10.1007/3-540-44802-0_1
37. Pirelli, S., Zaostrovnykh, A., Candea, G.: A formally verified NAT stack. In: Proceedings of the 2018 Afternoon Workshop on Kernel Bypassing Networks, KBNets@SIGCOMM 2018, Budapest, Hungary, 20 August 2018, pp. 8–14 (2018). https://doi.org/10.1145/3229538.3229540
38. Raad, A., Berdine, J., Dang, H.H., Dreyer, D., O'Hearn, P., Villard, J.: Technical appendix (2020). http://plv.mpi-sws.org/ISL/
39. Ramos, D.A., Engler, D.R.: Under-constrained symbolic execution: correctness checking for real code. In: 2016 USENIX Annual Technical Conference, USENIX ATC 2016, Denver, CO, USA, 22–24 June 2016 (2016). https://www.usenix.org/conference/atc16/technical-sessions/presentation/ramos
40. Raza, M., Gardner, P.: Footprints in local reasoning. Logical Methods Comput. Sci. 5(2) (2009). https://doi.org/10.2168/LMCS-5(2:4)2009
41. Reynolds, J.C.: Separation logic: a logic for shared mutable data structures. In: Proceedings of the 17th Annual IEEE Symposium on Logic in Computer Science. LICS 2002, pp. 55–74. IEEE Computer Society, Washington, DC (2002). http://dl.acm.org/citation.cfm?id=645683.664578
42. Sadowski, C., Aftandilian, E., Eagle, A., Miller-Cushon, L., Jaspan, C.: Lessons from building static analysis tools at Google. Commun. ACM 61(4), 58–66 (2018). https://doi.org/10.1145/3188720
43. de Vries, E., Koutavas, V.: Reverse hoare logic. In: Barthe, G., Pardo, A., Schneider, G. (eds.) SEFM 2011. LNCS, vol. 7041, pp. 155–171. Springer, Heidelberg (2011). https://doi.org/10.1007/978-3-642-24690-6_12
44. Yang, H., et al.: Scalable shape analysis for systems code. In: Gupta, A., Malik, S. (eds.) CAV 2008. LNCS, vol. 5123, pp. 385–398. Springer, Heidelberg (2008). https://doi.org/10.1007/978-3-540-70545-1_36
45. Yang, H., O'Hearn, P.: A semantic basis for local reasoning. In: Nielsen, M., Engberg, U. (eds.) FoSSaCS 2002. LNCS, vol. 2303, pp. 402–416. Springer, Heidelberg (2002). https://doi.org/10.1007/3-540-45931-6_28
46. Yorsh, G., Rabinovich, A.M., Sagiv, M., Meyer, A., Bouajjani, A.: A logic of reachable patterns in linked data-structures. J. Log. Algebr. Program. 73(1–2), 111–142 (2007). https://doi.org/10.1016/j.jlap.2006.12.001

Stochastic Systems

Maximum Causal Entropy Specification Inference from Demonstrations

Marcell Vazquez-Chanlatte$^{(\boxtimes)}$ and Sanjit A. Seshia

University of California, Berkeley, USA
marcell.vc@eecs.berkeley.edu

Abstract. In many settings, such as robotics, demonstrations provide a natural way to specify tasks. However, most methods for learning from demonstrations either do not provide guarantees that the learned artifacts can be safely composed or do not explicitly capture temporal properties. Motivated by this deficit, recent works have proposed learning Boolean *task specifications*, a class of Boolean non-Markovian rewards which admit well-defined composition and explicitly handle historical dependencies. This work continues this line of research by adapting maximum *causal* entropy inverse reinforcement learning to estimate the posteriori probability of a specification given a multi-set of demonstrations. The key algorithmic insight is to leverage the extensive literature and tooling on reduced ordered binary decision diagrams to efficiently encode a time unrolled Markov Decision Process. This enables transforming a naïve algorithm with running time exponential in the episode length, into a polynomial time algorithm.

1 Introduction

In many settings, episodic demonstrations provide a natural and robust mechanism to partially specify a task, even in the presence of errors. For example, consider the agent operating in the gridworld illustrated in Fig. 1. Blue arrows denote intended actions and the solid black arrow shows the agent's actual path. This path can stochastically differ from the blue arrows due to a downward wind. One might naturally ask: "What task was this agent attempting to perform?" Even without knowing if this was a positive or negative example, based on the agent's state/action sequence, one can reasonably infer the agent's intent, namely, "reach the yellow tile while avoiding the red tiles." Compared with traditional learning from positive and negative examples, this is somewhat surprising, particularly given that the task is never actually demonstrated in Fig. 1.

S. K. Lahiri and C. Wang (Eds.): CAV 2020, LNCS 12225, pp. 255–278, 2020.
https://doi.org/10.1007/978-3-030-53291-8_15

This problem, inferring intent from demonstrations, has received a fair amount of attention over the past two decades particularly within the robotics community [5,22,30,33]. In this literature, one traditionally models the demonstrator as operating within a dynamical system whose transition relation only depends on the current state and action (called the Markov condition). However, even if the dynamics are Markovian, many tasks are naturally modeled in history

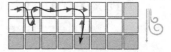

Fig. 1. Example of an agent unsuccessfully demonstrating the task "reach a yellow tile while avoiding red tiles". (Color figure online)

dependent (non-Markovian) terms, e.g., "if the robot enters a blue tile, then it must touch a brown tile *before* touching a yellow tile". Unfortunately, most methods for learning from demonstrations either do not provide guarantees that the learned artifacts (e.g. rewards) can be safely composed or do not explicitly capture history dependencies [30].

Motivated by this deficit, recent works have proposed specializing to **task specifications**, a class of Boolean non-Markovian rewards induced by formal languages. This additional structure admits well-defined compositions and explicitly captures temporal dependencies [15,30]. A particularly promising direction has been to adapt maximum entropy inverse reinforcement learning [33] to task specifications, enabling a form of robust specification inference, even in the presence unlabeled demonstration errors [30].

However, while powerful, the principle of maximum entropy is limited to settings where the dynamics are deterministic or agents that use open-loop policies [33]. This is because the principle of maximum entropy incorrectly allows the agent's predicted policy to depend on future state values resulting in an overly optimistic agent [19]. For instance, in our gridworld example (Fig. 1), the principle of maximum entropy would discount the possibility of slipping, and thus we would not forecast the agent to correct its trajectory after slipping once.

This work continues this line of research by instead using the principle of maximum *causal* entropy, which generalizes the principle of maximum entropy to general stochastic decision processes [32]. While a conceptually straightforward extension, a naïve application of maximum *causal* entropy inverse reinforcement learning to non-Markovian rewards results in an algorithm with run-time exponential in the episode length, a phenomenon sometimes known as the **curse of history** [24]. The key algorithmic insight in this paper is to leverage the extensive literature and tooling on Reduced Ordered Binary Decision Diagrams (BDDs) [3] to efficiently encode the time unrolled composition of the dynamics and task specification. This allows us to translate a naïve exponential time algorithm into a polynomial time algorithm. In particular, we shall show that this BDD has size at most linear in the episode length making inference comparatively efficient.

1.1 Related Work

Our work is intimately related to the fields of Inverse Reinforcement Learning and Grammatical Inference. **Grammatical inference** [8] refers to the well-developed literature on learning a formal grammar (often an automaton) from data. Examples include learning the smallest automata that in consistent with a set of positive and negative strings [7,8] or learning an automaton using membership and equivalence queries [1]. This and related work can be seen as extending these methods to unlabeled and potentially noisy demonstrations, where demonstrations differ from examples due to the existence of a dynamics model. This notion of demonstration derives from the Inverse Reinforcement Learning literature.

In **Inverse Reinforcement Learning** (IRL) [22] the demonstrator, operating in a stochastic environment, is assumed to attempt to (approximately) optimize some unknown reward function over the trajectories. In particular, one traditionally assumes a trajectory's reward is the sum of state rewards of the trajectory. This formalism offers a succinct mechanism to encode and generalize the goals of the demonstrator to new and unseen environments.

In the IRL framework, the problem of learning from demonstrations can then be cast as a Bayesian inference problem [25] to predict the most probable reward function. To make this inference procedure well-defined and robust to demonstration/modeling noise, Maximum Entropy [33] and Maximum Causal Entropy [32] IRL appeal to the principles of maximum entropy [13] and maximum causal entropy respectively [32]. This results in a likelihood over the demonstrations which is no more committed to any particular behavior than what is required to match observed statistical features, e.g., average distance to an obstacle. While this approach was initially limited to rewards represented as linear combinations of scalar features, IRL has been successfully adapted to arbitrary function approximators such as Gaussian processes [20] and neural networks [5]. As stated in the introduction, while powerful, traditional IRL provides no principled mechanism for composing the resulting rewards.

Compositional RL: To address this deficit, composition using soft optimality has recently received a fair amount of attention; however, the compositions are limited to either strict disjunction (do X *or* Y) [26,27] or conjunction (do X *and* Y) [6]. Further, this soft optimality only bounds the deviation from simultaneously optimizing both rewards. Thus, optimizing the composition does not preclude violating safety constraints embedded in the rewards (e.g., do not enter the red tiles).

Logic Based IRL: Another promising approach for introducing compositionality has been the recent research on automata and logic based encodings of rewards [11,14] which admit well defined compositions. To this end, work has been done on inferring Linear Temporal Logic (LTL) formulas by finding the specification that minimizes the expected number of violations by an optimal agent compared to the expected number of violations by an agent applying actions uniformly at random [15]. The computation of the optimal agent's expected violations is done via dynamic programming on the explicit product of the deterministic Rabin automaton [4] of the specification and the state dynamics. A fundamental drawback of this procedure is that due to the curse of history, it incurs a heavy run-time cost, even on simple two state and two action Markov Decision Processes. Additionally, as with early work on grammatical inference and IRL, these techniques do not produce likelihood estimates amenable to Bayesian inference.

Maximum Entropy Specification Inference: In our previous work [30], we adapted maximum entropy IRL to learn task specifications. Similar to standard maximum entropy IRL, this technique produces robust likelihood estimates. However, due to the use of the principle of maximum entropy, rather than maximum *causal* entropy, this model is limited to settings where the dynamics are deterministic or agents with open-loop policies [33].

Inference Using BDDs: This work makes heavy use of Binary Decision Diagrams (BDDs) [3] which are frequently used in symbolic value iteration for Markov Decision Processes [9] and reachability analysis for probabilistic systems [18]. However, the literature has largely relied on Multi-Terminal BDDs to encode the transition probabilities for a **single** time step. In contrast, this work introduces a two-terminal encoding based on the finite unrolling of a probabilistic circuit. To the best of our knowledge, the most similar usage of BDDs for inference appears in the independently discovered literal weight based encoding of [10] - although their encoding does not directly support non-determinism or state-indexed random variables.

Contributions: The primary contributions of this work are two fold. First, we leverage the principle of maximum causal entropy to provide the likelihood of a specification given a set of demonstrations. This formulation removes the deterministic and/or open-loop restriction imposed by prior work based on the principle of maximum entropy. Second, to mitigate the curse of history, we propose using a BDD to encode the time unrolled Markov Decision Process that the maximum causal entropy forecaster is defined over. We prove that this BDD has size that grows linearly with the horizon and quasi-linearly with the number of actions. Furthermore, we prove that our derived likelihood estimates are robust to the particular reward associated with satisfying the specification. Finally, we provide an initial experimental validation of our method. An overview of this pipeline is provided in Fig. 8.

2   Problem Setup

We seek to learn task specifications from demonstrations provided by a teacher who executes a sequence of actions that probabilistically change the system state. For simplicity, we assume that the set of actions and states are finite and fully observed. Further, until Sect. 5.3, we shall assume that all demonstrations are a fixed length, $\tau \in \mathbb{N}$. Formally, we begin by modeling the underlying dynamics as a probabilistic automaton.

Definition 1 *A **probabilistic automaton** (PA) is a tuple (S, s_0, A, δ), where S is the finite set of states, $s_0 \in S$ is the initial state, A is a finite set of actions, and δ specifies the transition probability of going from state s to state s' given action a, i.e. $\delta(s, a, s') = \Pr(s' \mid s, a)$.*
*A **trace**[a], ξ, is a sequence of (action, state) pairs implicitly starting from s_0. A trace of length $\tau \in \mathbb{N}$ is an element of $(A \times S)^\tau$.*

---

[a] *sometimes referred to as a trajectory or behavior.*

Note that probabilistic automata are equivalently characterized as $1^1/2$ *player games* where each round has the agent choose an action and then the environment samples a state transition outcome. In fact, this alternative characterization is implicitly encoded in the directed bipartite graph used to visualize probabilistic automata (see Fig. 2b). In this language, we refer to the nodes where the agent makes a decision as a **decision node** and the nodes where the environment samples an outcome as a **chance node**.

Next, we develop machinery to distinguish between desirable and undesirable traces. For simplicity, we focus on finite trace properties, referred to as specifications, that are decidable within some fixed $\tau \in \mathbb{N}$ time steps, e.g., "Recharge before t = 20."

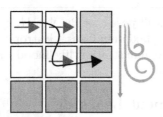 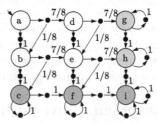

(a) Example trajectory in a gridworld where the agent can attempt to move right and down, although with a small probability the wind will move the agent down, independent of the action.

(b) PA describing the dynamics of Fig 2a as a $1^1/2$ player game. The large circles indicate states (agent decisions) and the small black circles denote the environment response probabilities.

Fig. 2. Example of gridworld probabilistic automata (PA).

Definition 2 *A **task specification**, φ, (or simply **specification**) is a subset of traces. For simplicity, we shall assume that each trace is of a fixed length $\tau \in \mathbb{N}$, e.g.,*

$$\varphi \subseteq (A \times S)^\tau \tag{1}$$

*A collection of specifications, Φ, is called a **concept class**. Further, we define $true \overset{\text{def}}{=} (A \times S)^\tau$, $\neg\varphi \overset{\text{def}}{=} true \setminus \varphi$, and $false \overset{\text{def}}{=} \neg true$.*

Often specifications are not directly given as sets, but induced by abstract descriptions of a task. For example, the task "avoid lava" induces a concrete set of traces that never enter lava tiles. If the workspace/world/dynamics change, this abstract specification would map to a different set of traces.

2.1   Specification Inference from Demonstrations

The primary task in this paper is to find the specification that best explains/-forecasts the behavior of an agent. As in our prior work [30], we formalize our problem statement as:

Definition 3 *The **specification inference from demonstrations** problem is a tuple (M, X, Φ, D) where $M = (S, s_0, A, \delta)$ is a probabilistic automaton, X is a (multi-)set of τ-length traces drawn from an unknown distribution induced by a teacher attempting to demonstrate (satisfy) some unknown task specification within M, Φ is a concept class of specifications, and D is a prior distribution over Φ. A solution to (M, X, Φ, D) is:*

$$\varphi^* \in \arg\max_{\varphi \in \Phi} \Pr(X \mid M, \varphi) \cdot \Pr_{\varphi \sim D}(\varphi) \tag{2}$$

where $\Pr(X \mid M, \varphi)$ denotes the likelihood that the teacher would have demonstrated X given the task φ.

Of course, by itself, the above formulation is ill-posed as $\Pr(X \mid M, \varphi)$ is left undefined. Below, we shall propose leveraging Maximum Causal Entropy Inverse Reinforcement Learning (IRL) to select the demonstration likelihood distribution in a regret minimizing manner.

3   Leveraging Inverse Reinforcement Learning

The key idea of Inverse Reinforcement Learning (IRL), or perhaps more accurately Inverse Optimal Control, is to find the reward structure that best explains the actions of a reward optimizing agent operating in a Markov Decision Process. We formalize below.

Definition 4 *A **Markov Decision Process (MDP)** is a probabilistic automaton endowed with a **reward map** from states to reals, $r : S \to \mathbb{R}$. This reward mapping is lifted to traces via,*

$$R(\xi) \overset{\text{def}}{=} \sum_{s \in \xi} r(s). \tag{3}$$

Remark 1. Note that a temporal discount factor, $\gamma \in [0, 1]$ can be added into (3) by introducing a sink state, \$, to the MDP, where $r(\$) = 0$ and

$$\Pr(s' = \$ \mid s, a) = \begin{cases} \gamma & \text{if } s \neq \$ \\ 1 & \text{otherwise} \end{cases}. \tag{4}$$

Given a MDP, the goal of an agent is to maximize the expected trace reward. In this work, we shall restrict ourselves to rewards that are given as a linear combination of **state features**, $\mathbf{f} : S \to \mathbb{R}^n_{\geq 0}$, e.g.,

$$r(s) = \theta \cdot \mathbf{f}(s) \tag{5}$$

for some $\theta \in \mathbb{R}^n$. Note that since state features can themselves be rewards, such a restriction does not actually restrict the space of possible rewards.

Example 1. Let the components of $\mathbf{f}(s)$ be distances to various locations on a map. Then the choice of θ characterizes the relative preferences in avoiding/reaching the respective locations.

Formally, we model an agent as acting according to a **policy**.

Definition 5 *A policy, π, is a state indexed distribution over actions,*

$$\Pr(a \mid s) = \pi(a \mid s). \tag{6}$$

In this language, the agent's goal is equivalent to finding a policy which maximizes the expected trace reward. We shall refer to a trace generated by such an agent as a **demonstration**. Due to the Markov requirement, the likelihood of a demonstration, ξ, given a particular policy, π, and probabilistic automaton, M, is easily stated as:

$$\Pr(\xi \mid M, \pi) = \prod_{s',a,s \in \xi} \Pr(s' \mid s, a) \cdot \Pr(a \mid s). \tag{7}$$

Thus, the likelihood of multi-set of i.i.d demonstrations, X, is given by:

$$\Pr(X \mid M, \pi) = \prod_{\xi \in X} \Pr(\xi \mid M, \pi). \tag{8}$$

3.1   Inverse Reinforcement Learning (IRL)

As previously stated, the main motivation in introducing the MDP formalism has been to discuss the inverse problem. Namely, given a set of demonstrations, find the reward that best "explains" the agent's behavior, where by "explain" one typically means that under the conjectured reward, the agent's behavior was approximately optimal. Notice however, that many undesirable rewards satisfy this property. For example, consider the following reward in which every demonstration is optimal,

$$r : s \mapsto 0. \tag{9}$$

Furthermore, observe that given a fixed reward, many policies are approximately optimal! For instance, using (9), an optimal agent could pick actions uniformly at random or select a single action to always apply.

3.2 Maximum Causal Entropy IRL

A popular, and in practice effective, solution to the lack of unique policy conundrum is to appeal to the **principle of maximum causal entropy** [32]. To formalize this principle, we recall the definitions of causally conditioned probability [17] and causal entropy [17,23].

Definition 6 *Let $X_{1:\tau} \overset{\text{def}}{=} X_1, \ldots, X_\tau$ denote a temporal sequence of $\tau \in \mathbb{N}$ random variables. The probability of a sequence $Y_{1:\tau}$ **causally conditioned** on sequence $X_{1:\tau}$ is:*

$$\Pr(Y_{1:\tau} \parallel X_{1:\tau}) \overset{\text{def}}{=} \prod_{t=1}^{\tau} \Pr(Y_t \mid X_{1:t}, Y_{1:t-1}) \tag{10}$$

*The **causal entropy** of $Y_{1:\tau}$ given $X_{1:\tau}$ is defined as,*

$$H(Y_{1:\tau} \parallel X_{1:\tau}) \overset{\text{def}}{=} \underset{Y_{1:\tau}, X_{1:\tau}}{\mathbb{E}} [-\log(\Pr(Y_{1:\tau} \parallel X_{1:\tau}))] \tag{11}$$

In the case of inverse reinforcement learning, the principle of maximum causal entropy suggests forecasting using the policy whose action sequence, $A_{1:\tau}$, has the highest causal entropy, conditioned on the state sequence, $S_{1:\tau}$. That is, find the policy that maximizes

$$H(A_{1:\tau} \parallel S_{1:\tau}), \tag{12}$$

subject to feature matching constraints, $\mathbb{E}[\mathbf{f}]$, e.g., does the resulting policy, π^*, complete the task as seen in the data. Compared to all other policies, this policy (i) minimizes regret with respect to model/reward uncertainty, (ii) ensures that the agent's predicted policy does not depend on the future, (iii) is consistent with observed feature statistics [32].

Concretely, as proved in [32], when an agent is attempting to maximize the sum of feature state rewards, $\sum_{t=1}^{T} \theta \cdot \mathbf{f}(s_t)$, the principle of maximum causal entropy prescribes the following policy:

Maximum Causal Entropy Policy:

$$\log\left(\pi_\theta(a_t \mid s_t)\right) \overset{\text{def}}{=} Q_\theta(a_t, s_t) - V_\theta(s_t) \tag{13}$$

where

$$Q_\theta(a_t, s_t) \overset{\text{def}}{=} \underset{s_{t+1}}{\mathbb{E}} [V_\theta(s_{t+1}) \mid s_t, a_t] + \theta \cdot \mathbf{f}(s_t)$$

$$V_\theta(s_t) \overset{\text{def}}{=} \ln \sum_{a_t} e^{Q_\theta(a_t, s_t)} \overset{\text{def}}{=} \text{softmax}_{a_t} Q_\theta(a_t, s_t). \tag{14}$$

---

where, θ is such that (14) results in a policy which matches feature demonstrations.

Remark 2. Note that replacing softmax with max in (14) yields the standard Bellman Backup [2] used to compute the optimal policy in tabular reinforcement learning. Further, it can be shown that maximizing causal entropy corresponds to believing that the agent is exponentially biased towards high reward policies [32]:

$$\Pr(\pi_\theta \mid M) \propto \exp\left(\underset{\xi}{\mathbb{E}}[R_\theta(\xi) \mid \pi_\theta, M] \right), \tag{15}$$

where (14) is the most likely policy under (15).

Remark 3. In the special case of scalar state features, $\mathbf{f} : S \to \mathbb{R}_{\geq 0}$, the maximum causal entropy policy (14) becomes increasingly optimal as $\theta \in \mathbb{R}$ increases (since softmax monotonically approaches max). In this setting, we shall refer to θ as the agent's **rationality coefficient**.

3.3 Non-Markovian Rewards

The MDP formalism traditionally requires that the reward map be Markovian (i.e., state based); however, in practice, many tasks are history dependent, e.g. touch a red tile and then a blue tile.

A common trick within the reinforcement learning literature is to simply change the MDP and add the necessary history to the state so that the reward is Markovian, e.g. a flag for touching a red tile. However, in the case of inverse reinforcement learning, by definition, one does not know what the reward is. Therefore, one cannot assume to a priori know what history suffices.

Further exacerbating the situation is the fact that naïvely including the entire history into the state results in exponential increase in the number of states. Nevertheless, as we shall soon see, by restricting the class of rewards to represent task specifications, this curse can be mitigated to only result in a blow-up that is at most **linear** in the state space size and in the trace length!

To this end, we shall find it fruitful to develop machinery for embedding the full trace history into the state space. Explicitly, we shall refer to the process of adding all history to a probabilistic automaton's (or MDP's) state as **unrolling**.

Definition 7 *Let $M = (S, s_0, A, \delta)$ be a PA. The **unrolling** of M is a PA, $M' = (S', s_0, A, \delta')$, where*

$$S' = \{s_0\} \times \bigcup_{i=0}^{\infty} (A \times S)^i \qquad\qquad \delta'(\xi_{n+1}, a, \xi_n) = \delta(s_{n+1}, a, s_n)$$

$$\xi_n = \Big(s_0, \ldots, (a_{n-1}, s_n)\Big) \qquad\qquad \xi_{n+1} = \Big(s_0, \ldots, (a_n, s_{n+1})\Big) \tag{16}$$

If $R : S^\tau \to \mathbb{R}$ is a non-Markovian reward over τ-length traces, then we endow the corresponding unrolled PA with the now Markovian Reward,

$$r'\Big(s_0, \ldots, (a_{n-1}, s_n)\Big) \stackrel{\text{def}}{=} \begin{cases} R(s_0, \ldots, s_n) & \text{if } n = \tau \\ 0 & \text{otherwise} \end{cases}. \tag{17}$$

Further, by construction the reward is Markovian in S' and only depends only τ-length state sequences,

$$\sum_{t=0}^{\infty} r'((s_0, a_0), \ldots s_\tau) = R(s_0, \ldots, s_\tau). \tag{18}$$

Next, observe that for τ-length traces, the $1^{1}/_{2}$ player game formulation's bipartite graph forms a tree of depth τ (see Fig. 3). Further, observe that each leaf corresponds to unique τ-length trace. Thus, to each leaf, we associate the corresponding trace's reward, $R(\xi)$. We shall refer to this tree as a **decision tree**, denoted $\mathbb{T}$.

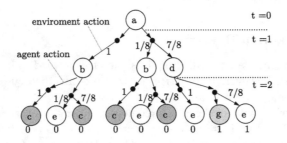

Fig. 3. Decision tree generated by the PA shown in Fig. 2 and specification "By $\tau = 2$, reach a yellow tile while avoiding red tiles.". Here a binary reward is given depending on whether or not the agent satisfies the specification. (Color figure online)

Finally, observe that the trace reward depends only on the sequence of agent actions, A, and environment actions, A_e. That is, $\mathbb{T}$ can be interpreted as a function:

$$\mathbb{T} : (A \times A_e)^\tau \to \mathbb{R}. \tag{19}$$

3.4 Specifications as Non-Markovian Rewards

Next, with the intent to frame our specification inference problem as an inverse reinforcement learning problem, we shall overload notation and denote by φ the following non-Markovian reward corresponding to a specification $\varphi \in (A \times S)^\tau$,

$$\varphi(\xi) \stackrel{\text{def}}{=} \begin{cases} 1 & \text{if } \xi \in \varphi \\ 0 & \text{otherwise} \end{cases}. \tag{20}$$

Note that the corresponding decision tree is then a Boolean predicate:

$$\mathbb{T}_\varphi : (A \times A_e)^\tau \to \{0, 1\}. \tag{21}$$

3.5   Computing Maximum Causal Entropy Specification Policies

Now let us return to the problem of computing the policy prescribed by (14). In particular, note that viewing the unrolled reward (17) as a scalar state feature results in the following soft-Bellman Backup:

$$Q_\theta(a_t, \xi_t) = \mathbb{E}\left[V_\theta(s_{t+1}) \mid \xi_t, a_t\right]$$

$$V_\theta(\xi_t) = \begin{cases} \theta \cdot \varphi(\xi_t) & \text{if } t = \tau \\ \text{softmax}_{a_t} Q_\theta(a_t, \xi_t) & \text{otherwise} \end{cases}, \qquad (22)$$

where $\xi_i \in \{s_0\} \times (A \times S)^i$ denotes a state in the unrolled MDP.

Equation (22) thus suggests a naïve dynamic programming scheme over $\mathbb{T}$ starting at the $t = \tau$ leaves to compute Q_θ and V_θ (and thus π_θ).

Namely, in $\mathbb{T}$, the chance nodes, which correspond to action/state pairs, are responsible for computing Q values and the decision nodes, which correspond to states waiting for an action to be applied, are responsible for computing V values. For chance nodes this is done by taking the softmax of the values of the child nodes. Similarly, for decision nodes, this is done by taking a weighted average of the child nodes, where the weights correspond to the probability of a given transition. This,

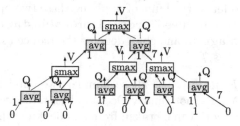

Fig. 4. Computation graph generated from applying (14) to the decision tree shown in Fig. 3. Here smax and avg denote the softmax and weighted average respectively.

at least conceptually, corresponds to transforming $\mathbb{T}$ into a bipartite computation graph (see Fig. 4).

Next, note that (i) the above dynamic programming scheme can be trivially modified to compute the expected trace reward of the maximum causal entropy policy and (ii) the expected reward increases[1] with the rationality coefficient θ.

Observe then that, due to monotonicity, bisection (binary search) approximates θ to tolerance ϵ in $O(\log(1/\epsilon))$ time. Additionally, notice that the likelihood of each demonstration can be computed by traversing the path of length τ in $\mathbb{T}$ corresponding to the trace and multiplying the corresponding policy and transition probabilities (8). Therefore, if $|A_e| \in \mathbb{N}$ denotes the maximum number of outcomes the environment can choose from (i.e, the branching factor for chance nodes), it follows that the run-time of this naïve scheme is:

$$O\left(\underbrace{\overbrace{\left(|A| \cdot |A_e|\right)^\tau}^{\text{compute policy}} \cdot \underbrace{\log(1/\epsilon)}_{\text{Feature Matching}} + \underbrace{\tau|X|}_{\text{evaluate demos}} \right). \qquad (23)$$
$$\underbrace{}_{|\mathbb{T}|}$$

---

[1] Formally, this is due to (a) softmax and average being monotonic (b) trajectory rewards only increasing with θ, and (c) π exponentially biasing towards high Q-values.

3.6   Task Specification Rewards

Of course, the problem with this naïve approach is that explicitly encoding the unrolled tree, $\mathbb{T}$, results in an exponential blow-up in the space and time complexity. The key insight in this paper is that the additional structure of task specifications enables avoiding such costs while still being expressive. In particular, as is exemplified in Fig. 4, the computation graphs for task specifications are often highly redundant and apt for compression.

In particular, we shall apply the following two semantic preserving transformations: (i) Eliminate nodes whose children are isomorphic sub-graphs, i.e., inconsequential decisions (ii) Combine all isomorphic sub-graphs i.e., equivalent decisions. We refer to the limit of applying these two operations as a **reduced ordered probabilistic decision diagram** and shall denote[2] the reduced variant of $\mathbb{T}$ as $\mathcal{T}$.

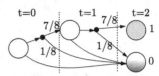

Fig. 5. Reduction of the decision tree shown in Fig. 3.

Remark 4. For those familiar, we emphasize that these decision diagrams are MDPs, not Binary Decision Diagrams (see Sect. 4). Importantly, more than two actions can be taken from a node if $\max(|A|, |A_e|) \geq 2$ and A_e has a state dependent probability distribution attached to it. That said, the above transformations are **exactly** the reduction rules for BDDs [3].

As Fig. 5 illustrates, reduced decision diagrams can be much smaller than their corresponding decision tree. Nevertheless, we shall briefly postpone characterizing $|\mathcal{T}|$ until developing some additional machinery in Sect. 4. Computationally, three problems remain.

1. How can our naïve dynamic programming scheme be adapted to this compressed structure. In particular, because many interior nodes have been eliminated, one must take care when applying (22).
2. How do concrete demonstrations map to paths in the compressed structure when evaluating likelihoods (8).
3. How can one construct $\mathcal{T}$ without first constructing $\mathbb{T}$, since failing to do so would negate any complexity savings.

We shall postpone discussing solutions to the second and third problems until Sect. 4. The first problem however, can readily be addressed with the tools at hand. Recall that in the variable ordering, nodes alternate between decision and chance nodes (i.e., agent and environment decisions), and thus alternate between taking a softmax and expectations of child values in (22). Next, by definition, if a node is skipped in $\mathcal{T}$, then it must have been inconsequential. Thus the trace reward must have been independent of the decision made at that node. Therefore, the softmax/expectation's corresponding to eliminated nodes must have been over a constant value - otherwise the eliminated sequences would

---

[2] Mnemonic: $\mathcal{T}$ is a (typographically) slimmed down variant of $\mathbb{T}$.

be distinguishable w.r.t φ. The result is summarized in the following identities, where α denotes the value of an eliminated node's children.

$$\text{softmax}(\overbrace{\alpha, \dots, \alpha}^{|A|}) = \log(e^\alpha + \dots + e^\alpha) = \ln(|A|) + \alpha \tag{24}$$

$$\mathbb{E}_x[\alpha] = \sum_x p(x)\alpha = \alpha \tag{25}$$

Of course, it could also be the case that a sequence of nodes is skipped in $\mathcal{T}$. Using (24), one can compute the change in value, Δ, that the eliminated sequence of n decision nodes and any number of chance nodes would have applied in $\mathbb{T}$:

$$\Delta(n, \alpha) = \ln(|A|^n) + \alpha = n\ln(|A|) + \alpha \tag{26}$$

Crucially, evaluation of this compressed computation graph is linear in $|\mathcal{T}|$ which as shall later prove, is often much smaller than $|\mathbb{T}|$.

4 Constructing and Characterizing $\mathcal{T}$

Let us now consider how to avoid the construction of $\mathbb{T}$ and characterize the size of the reduced ordered decision diagram, $\mathcal{T}$. We begin by assuming that the underlying dynamics is well-approximated in the random-bit model.

Definition 8 *For $q \in \mathbb{N}$, let $\mathbf{c} \sim \{0,1\}^q$ denote the random variable representing the result of flipping $q \in \mathbb{N}$ fair coins. We say a probabilistic automata $M = (S, s_0, A, \delta)$ is (ϵ, q) approximated in the random bit model if there exists a mapping,*

$$\hat{\delta} : S \times A \times \{0,1\}^q \to S \tag{27}$$

such that for all $s, a, s' \in S \times A \times S$:

$$\left| \delta(s, a, s') - \Pr_{\mathbf{c} \sim \{0,1\}^q} \left(\hat{\delta}(s, a, \mathbf{c}) = s' \right) \right| \le \epsilon. \tag{28}$$

For example, in our gridworld example (Fig. 2a), if $\mathbf{c} \in \{0,1\}^3$, elements of s are interpreted as pairs in $\mathbb{R}^2$, and the right/down actions are interpreted as the addition of the unit vectors $(1, 0)$ and $(0, 1)$ then,

$$\hat{\delta}(s, a, \mathbf{c}) = \begin{cases} s & \text{if } \max_i[(s + a)_i] > 1 \\ s + (0, 1) & \text{else if } \mathbf{c} = 0 \\ s + a & \text{otherwise} \end{cases}, \tag{29}$$

As can be easily confirmed, (29) satisfies (28) with $\epsilon = 0$. In the sequel, we shall take access to $\hat{\delta}$ as given[3]. Further, to simplify exposition, until Sect. 5.1, we

---

[3] See [31] for an explanation on systematically deriving such encodings.

shall additionally require that the number of actions, $|A|$, be a power of 2. This assumption implies that A can be encoded using exactly $\log_2(|A|)$ bits.

Under the above two assumptions, the key observation is to recognize that $\mathbb{T}$ (and thus $\mathcal{T}$) can be viewed as a Boolean predicate over an alternating sequence of action bit strings and coin flip outcomes determining if the task specification is satisfied, i.e.,

$$\mathbb{T} : \{0,1\}^n \to \{0,1\}, \tag{30}$$

where $n \overset{\text{def}}{=} \tau \cdot \log_2(|A \times A_e|) = \tau \cdot (q + \log_2(|A|))$. That is to say, the resulting decision diagram can be re-encoded as a reduced ordered **binary** decision diagram [3].

Definition 9 *A reduced ordered binary decision diagram (BDD), is a representation of a Boolean predicate $h(x_1, x_2, \ldots, x_n)$ as a reduced ordered (deterministic) decision diagram, where each decision corresponds to testing a bit $x_i \in \{0,1\}$. We denote the BDD encoding of $\mathcal{T}$ as $\mathcal{B}$.*

Binary decision diagrams are well developed both in a theoretical and practical sense. Before exploring these benefits, we first note that this change has introduced an additional problem. First, note that in $\mathcal{B}$, decision and chance nodes from $\mathbb{T}$ are now encoded as sequences of decision and chance nodes. For example, if $a \in A$ is encoded by the 4-length bit sequence $b_1 b_2 b_3 b_4$, then four decisions are made by the agent before selecting an action. Notice however that the original semantics are preserved due to associativity of the softmax and $\mathbb{E}$ operators. In particular, recall that by definition,

$$\text{softmax}(\alpha_1, \ldots, \alpha_4) = \ln(\sum_{i=1}^{4} e^{\alpha_i}) = \ln(e^{\ln(e^{\alpha_1} + e^{\alpha_2})} + e^{\ln(e^{\alpha_3} + e^{\alpha_4})})$$
$$\overset{\text{def}}{=} \text{softmax}(\text{softmax}(\alpha_1, \alpha_2), \text{softmax}(\alpha_3, \alpha_4)) \tag{31}$$

and thus the semantics of the sequence decision nodes is equivalent to the decision node in $\mathbb{T}$. Similarly, recall that the coin flips are fair, and thus expectations are computed via $\text{avg}(\alpha_1, \ldots, \alpha_n) = 1/n(\sum_{i=1}^{n} \alpha_i)$. Therefore, averaging over two sequential coin flips yields,

$$\text{avg}(\alpha_1, \ldots, \alpha_4) \overset{\text{def}}{=} \frac{1}{4} \sum_{i=1}^{4} \alpha_i = \frac{1}{2}(\frac{1}{2}(\alpha_1 + \alpha_2) + \frac{1}{2}(\alpha_3 + \alpha_4))$$
$$\overset{\text{def}}{=} \text{avg}(\text{avg}(\alpha_1, \alpha_2), \text{avg}(\alpha_3, \alpha_4)) \tag{32}$$

which by assumption (28), is the same as applying $\mathbb{E}$ on the original chance node. Finally, note that skipping over decisions needs to be adjusted slightly to account for sequences of decisions. Recall that via (26), the corresponding change in value, Δ, is a function of initial value, α, and the number of agent actions skipped, i.e., $|A|^n$ for n skipped decision nodes. Thus, in the BDD, since each decision node has two actions, skipping k decision bits corresponds to skipping

2^k actions. Thus, if k decision bits are skipped over in the BDD, the change in value, Δ, becomes,

$$\Delta(k,\alpha) = \alpha + k\ln(2). \tag{33}$$

Further, note that Δ can be computed in constant time while traversing the BDD. Thus, the dynamic programming scheme is linear in the size of $\mathcal{B}$.

4.1 Size of $\mathcal{B}$

Next we return to the question of how big the compressed decision diagram can actually be. To this aim, we cite the following (conservative) bound on the size of an BDD given an encoding of the corresponding Boolean predicate in the linear model computation illustrated in Fig. 6 (for more details, we refer the reader to [16]).

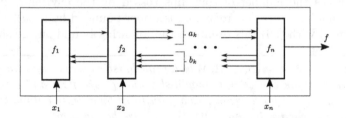

Fig. 6. Generic network of Boolean modules for which Theorem 1 holds.

In particular, consider an arbitrary Boolean predicate

$$f : \{0,1\}^n \to \{0,1\} \tag{34}$$

and a sequential arrangement of n Boolean modules, $f_1, f_2, \ldots, f_n$ where each f_i has shape:

$$f_i : \{0,1\} \times \{0,1\}^{a_{i-1}} \times \{0,1\}^{b_i} \to \{0,1\}^{a_i} \times \{0,1\}^{b_{i-1}}, \tag{35}$$

and takes as input x_i as well as a_{i-1} outputs of its left neighbor and b_i outputs of the right neighbor ($b_0 = 0, a_n = 1$). Further, assume that this arrangement is well defined, e.g. for each assignment to $x_1, \ldots, x_n$ there exists a unique way to set each of the inter-module wires. We say these modules compute f if the final output is equal to $f(x_1, \ldots, x_n)$.

Theorem 1 *If f can be computed by a linear arrangement of such modules, ordered $x_1, x_2, \ldots, x_n$, then the size, $S \in \mathbb{N}$, of its BDD (in the same order), is upper bounded [3] by:*

$$S \leq \sum_{k=1}^{n} 2^{a_k \cdot \left(2^{b_k}\right)}. \tag{36}$$

To apply this bound to our problem, recall that $\mathcal{B}$ computes a Boolean function where the decisions are temporally ordered and alternate between sequences of agent and environment decisions. Next, observe that because the traces are bounded (and all finite sets are regular), there exists a finite state machine which can monitor the satisfaction of the specification.

Remark 5. In the worst case, the monitor could be the unrolled decision tree, $\mathbb{T}$. This monitor would have exponential number of states. In practice, the composition of the dynamics and the monitor is expected to be much smaller.

Further, note that because this composed system is causal, no backward wires are needed, e.g., $\forall k . b_k = 0$. In particular, observe that because the composition of the dynamics and the monitor is Markovian, the entire system can be uniquely described using the monitor/dynamics state and agent/environment action (see Fig. 7). This description can be encoded in $\log_2(2^q|A \times S \times S_\varphi|)$ bits, where q denotes the number of coin flips tossed by the environment and S_φ denotes the monitor state. Therefore, a_k is upper bounded by $\log_2(2^q|A \times S \times S_\varphi|)$. Combined with (36) this results in the following bound on the size of $\mathcal{B}$.

Corollary 1 *Let $M = (S, s_0, A, \delta)$ be a probabilistic automaton whose probabilistic transitions can be approximated using q coin flips and let φ be a specification defined for horizon τ and monitored by a finite automaton with states S_φ. The corresponding BDD, $\mathcal{B}$, has size bounded by:*

$$|\mathcal{B}| \leq \tau \cdot \overbrace{\big(\log(|A|) + q\big)}^{\text{\# inputs}} \cdot \overbrace{\big(2^q|A \times S \times S_\varphi|\big)}^{\text{bound on } 2^{a_k}} \tag{37}$$

Notice that the above argument implies that as the episode length grows, $|\mathcal{B}|$ grows linearly in the horizon/states and quasilinearly in the agent/environment actions!

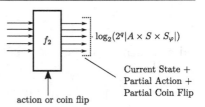

Remark 6. Note that this bound actually holds for the minimal representation of the composed dynamics/monitor (even if it's unknown a-prori!). For example, if the property is *true*, the BDD requires only one state (always evaluate true). This also illustrates that the above bound is often very conserva-

Fig. 7. Generic module in linear model of computation for $\mathcal{B}$. Note that backward edges are not required.

tive. In particular, note that for $\varphi = true$, $|\mathcal{B}| = 1$, independent of the horizon or dynamics. However, the above bound will always be linear in τ. In general, the size of the BDD will depend on the particular symmetries compressed.

Remark 7. With hindsight, Corollary 1 is not too surprising. In particular, if the monitor is known, then one could explicitly compose the dynamics MDP with the monitor, with the resulting MDP having at most $|S \times S_\varphi|$ states. If one then includes the time step in the state, one could perform the soft-Bellman

Backup directly on this automaton. In this composed automaton each (action, state) pair would need to be recorded. Thus, one would expect $O(|S \times S_\varphi \times A|)$ space to be used. In practice, this explicit representation is much bigger than $\mathcal{B}$ due to the BDDs ability to skip over time steps and automatically compress symmetries.

4.2   Constructing $\mathcal{B}$

One of the biggest benefits of the BDD representation of a Boolean function is the ability to build BDDs from a Boolean combinations of other BDDs. Namely, given two BDDs with n and m nodes respectively, it is well known that the conjunction or disjunction of the BDDs has at most $n \cdot m$ nodes. Thus, in practice, if the combined BDD's remain relatively small, Boolean combinations remain efficient to compute and one does not construct the full binary decision tree! Further, note that BDDs support function composition. Namely, given predicates $f(x_1, \ldots, x_n)$ and n predicates $g_i(y_1, \ldots, y_k)$ the function

$$f\Big(g_1(y_1, \ldots, y_k), \ldots, g_n(y_1, \ldots, y_k)\Big) \tag{38}$$

can be computed in time [16]:

$$O(n \cdot |B_f|^2 \cdot \max_i |B_{g_i}|), \tag{39}$$

where B_f is the BDD for f and B_{g_i} are the BDDs for g_i. Now, suppose $\hat{\delta}_1, \ldots \hat{\delta}_{\log(|S|)}$ are Boolean predicates such that:

$$\hat{\delta}(\mathbf{s}, \mathbf{a}, \mathbf{c}) = (\hat{\delta}_1(\mathbf{s}, \mathbf{a}, \mathbf{c}), \ldots, \hat{\delta}_{\log(|S|)}(\mathbf{s}, \mathbf{a}, \mathbf{c})). \tag{40}$$

Theorem 1 and an argument similar to that for Corollary 1 imply then that constructing $\mathcal{B}$, using repeated composition, takes time bounded by a low degree polynomial in $|A \times S \times S_\varphi|$ and the horizon. Moreover, the space complexity before and after composition are bounded by Corollary 1.

4.3   Evaluating Demonstrations

Next let us return to the question of how to evaluate the likelihood of a concrete demonstration in our compressed BDD. The key problem is that the BDD can only evaluate (binary) sequences of actions/coin flips, where as demonstrations are given as sequences of action/state pairs. That is, we need to algorithmically perform the following transformation.

$$s_0 \mathbf{a}_0 s_1 \ldots \mathbf{a}_n s_{n+1} \mapsto \mathbf{a}_1 \mathbf{c}_1 \ldots \mathbf{a}_n \mathbf{c}_n \tag{41}$$

Given the random bit model assumption, this transformation can be rewritten as a series of Boolean Satisfiability problems:

$$\exists \, \mathbf{c}_i \, . \, \hat{\delta}(\mathbf{s}_i, \mathbf{a}_i, \mathbf{c}_i) = \mathbf{s}_{i+1} \tag{42}$$

While potentially intimidating, in practice such problems are quite simple for modern SAT solvers, particularly if the number of coin flips used is small. Furthermore, many systems are translation invariant. In such systems, the results of a single query (42), can be reused on other queries. For example, in (29), $\mathbf{c} = \mathbf{0}$ always results in the agent moving to the right. Nevertheless, in general, if q coin flips are used, encoding all the demonstrations takes at most $O(|X| \cdot \tau \cdot 2^q)$, in the worst case.

4.4   Run-Time Analysis

We are finally ready to provide a run-time analysis for our new inference algorithm. The high-level likelihood estimation procedure is described in Fig. 8. First, the user specifies a dynamical system and a (multi-) set of demonstrations. Then, using a user-defined mechanism, a candidate task specification is selected. The system then creates a compressed representation of the composition of the dynamical system with the task specification. Then, in parallel, the maximum causal entropy policy is estimated and the demonstrations are themselves encoded as bit-vectors. Finally, the likelihood of generating the encoded demonstrations is computed.

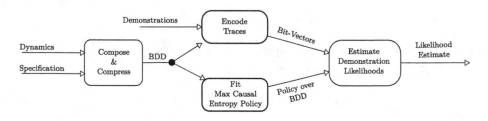

Fig. 8. High level likelihood estimation procedure described in this paper.

There are three computational bottlenecks in the compressed scheme. First, given a candidate specification, φ, one needs to construct $\mathcal{B}$. As argued in Sect. 4.2, this takes time at most polynomial in the horizon, monitoring automata size, and MDP size (in the random-bit model). Second is the process of computing Q and V values by tuning the rationality coefficient to match a particular satisfaction probability. Just as with the naïve run-time (23), this process takes time linear in the size of $|\mathcal{B}|$ and logarithmic in the inverse tolerance $1/\epsilon$. Further, using Corollary 1, we know that $|\mathcal{B}|$ is at most linear in horizon and quasi-linear in the MDP size. Thus, the policy computation takes time polynomial in the MDP size and logarithmic in the inverse tolerance. Finally, as before, evaluating the likelihoods takes time linear in the number of demonstrations and the horizon. However, we now require an additional step of finding coin-flips which are consistent with the demonstrations. Thus, the compressed run-time is bounded by:

$$O\left(\left(\overbrace{|X|\cdot\underbrace{\log\left(\epsilon^{-1}\right)}}\right)\cdot\text{POLY}\left(\overbrace{\tau,}^{\text{Horizon}}\underbrace{|S|,|S_{|\varphi|}|,|A|,\overbrace{2^q}^{\#\text{Coin Flip Outcomes}}}\right)\right) \tag{43}$$

Feature Matching   #Demos   Composed MDP size

Remark 8. In practice, this analysis is fairly conservative since BDD composition is often fast, the bound given by Corollary 1 is loose, and the SAT queries under-consideration are often trivial.

5 Additional Model Refinements

5.1 Conditioning on Valid Actions

So far, we have assumed that the number of actions is a power of 2. Functionally, this assumption makes it so each assignment to the action decision bits corresponds to a valid action. Of course, general MDPs have non-power of 2 action sets, and so it behooves us to adapt our method for such settings. The simplest way to do so is to use a 3-terminal Binary Decision Diagram. In particular, while each decision is still Boolean, there has now three possible types of leaves, 0, 1, and $\perp$. In the adapted algorithm, edges leading to $\perp$ are simply ignored, as they semantically correspond to invalid assignments to action or coin flip bits. A similar analysis can be done using these three valued decision diagrams, and as with BDDs, there exist efficient implementations of multi-terminal BDDs.

Remark 9. This generalization also opens up the possibility of state dependent action sets, where A is now the union of all possible actions, e.g, disable the action for moving to the right when the agent is on the right edge of the grid.

5.2 Choice of Binary Co-Domain

One might wonder how sensitive this formulation is to the choice of $R(\xi) = \theta \cdot \varphi(\xi)$. In particular, how does changing the co-domain of φ from $\{0,1\}$ to any other real values, i.e.,

$$\varphi' : (A \times S)^\tau \rightarrow \{a, b\},$$

change the likelihood estimates in our maximum causal entropy model. We briefly remark that, subject to some mild technical assumptions, almost any two real values could be used for φ's co-domain. Namely, observe that unless both a and b are zero, the expected satisfaction probability, p, is in one-to-one correspondence with the expected value of φ', i.e.,

$$\mathbb{E}[\varphi'] = a \cdot p + b \cdot (1 - p).$$

Thus, if a policy is feature matching for φ, it must be feature matching for φ' (and vice-versa). Therefore, the space of consistent policies is invariant under such transformations. Finally, because the space of policies is unchanged, the maximum causal entropy policies must remain unchanged. In practice, we prefer the use of $\{0,1\}$ as the co-domain for φ since it often simplifies many calculations.

5.3   Variable Episode Lengths (with Discounting)

As earlier promised, we shall now discuss how to extend our model to include variable length episodes. For simplicity, we shall limit our discussion to the setting where at each time step, the probability that the episode will end is $\gamma \in (0, 1]$. As we previously discussed, this can be modeled by introducing a sink state, \$, representing the end of an episode (4). In the random bit model, this simply adds a few additional environment coin flips, corresponding to the environments new transitions to the sink state.

Remark 10. Note that when unrolled, once the end of episode transition happens, all decisions are assumed inconsequential w.r.t φ. Thus, all subsequent decisions will be compressed by in the BDD, $\mathcal{B}$.

Finally, observe that the probability that the episode ending increases exponentially, implying that the planning horizon need not be too big, i.e., the probability that the episode has not ended by timestep, $\tau \in \mathbb{N}$, is: $(1 - \gamma)^{\tau}$. Thus, letting $\tau = \lceil \ln(\epsilon/1-\gamma) \rceil$ ensures that with probability at least $1 - \epsilon$ the episode has ended.

6   Experiment

Below we report empirical results that provide evidence that our proposed technique is robust to demonstration errors and that the produced BDDs are smaller than a naïve dynamic programming scheme. To this end, we created a reference implementation [29] in Python. BDD and SAT solving capabilities are provided via dd [21] and pySAT [12] respectively. To encode the task specifications and the random-bit model MDP, we leveraged the py-aiger ecosystem [28] which includes libraries for modeling Markov Decision Processes and encoding Past Tense Temporal Logic as sequential circuits.

Problem: Consider a gridworld where an agent can attempt to move up, down, left, or right; however, with probability 1/32, the agent slips and moves left. Further, suppose a demonstrator has provided the six unlabeled demonstrations shown in Fig. 9 for the task: "Within 10 time steps, touch a yellow (recharge) tile while avoiding red (lava) tiles. Additionally, if a blue (water) tile is stepped on, the agent must step on a brown (drying) tile before going to a yellow (recharge) tile." All of the solid paths satisfy the task. The dotted path fails because

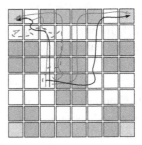

Fig. 9. Example Gridworld (Color figure online)

the agent keeps slipping left and thus cannot dry off by $t = 10$. Note that due to slipping, all the demonstrations that did not enter the water are sub-optimal.

Spec	Policy size (#nodes)	ROBDD build time	Relative log likelihood (compared to true)
True	1	0.48s	0
$\varphi_1 = $ Avoid lava	1797	1.5s	−22
$\varphi_2 = $ Eventually Recharge	1628	1.2s	5
$\varphi_3 = $ Don't recharge while wet	850	1.6s	−10
$\varphi_4 \overset{\text{def}}{=} \varphi_1 \wedge \varphi_2$	523	1.9s	4
$\varphi_5 \overset{\text{def}}{=} \varphi_1 \wedge \varphi_3$	1913	1.5s	−2
$\varphi_6 \overset{\text{def}}{=} \varphi_2 \wedge \varphi_3$	1842	2s	15
$\varphi^* \overset{\text{def}}{=} \varphi_1 \wedge \varphi_2 \wedge \varphi_3$	577	1.6s	27

Results: For a small collection of specifications, we have computed the size of the BDD, the time it took to construct the BDD, and the *relative* log likelihoods of the demonstrations[4],

$$\text{RelativeLogLikelihood}(\varphi) \overset{\text{def}}{=} \ln \left(\frac{\Pr(\text{demos} \mid \varphi)}{\Pr(\text{demos} \mid \text{true})} \right), \qquad (44)$$

where each maximum entropy policy was fit to match the corresponding specification's empirical satisfaction probability. We remark that the computed BDDs are small compared to other straw-man approaches. For example, an explicit construction of the product of the monitor, dynamics, and the current time step would require space given by:

$$\tau \cdot |S| \cdot |A| \cdot |S_\varphi| = (10 \cdot 8 \cdot 8 \cdot 4) \cdot |S_\varphi| = 2560 \cdot |S_\varphi| \qquad (45)$$

The resulting BDDs are much smaller than (45) and the naïve unrolled decision tree. We note that the likelihoods appear to (qualitatively) match expectations. For example, **despite** an unlabeled negative example, the demonstrated task, φ^*, is the most likely specification. Moreover, under the second most likely specification, which omits the avoid lava constraint, the sub-optimal traces that do not enter the water appear more attractive.

Finally, to emphasize the need for our causal extension, we compute the likelihoods of $\varphi^*, \varphi_1, \varphi_2$ for our opening example (Fig. 1) using both our causal model and the prior non-causal model [30]. Concretely, we take $\tau = 15$, a slip probability of $1/32$, and fix the expected satisfaction probability to 0.9. The trace shown in Fig. 1 acts as the sole (failed) demonstration for φ^*. As desired, our causal extension assigned more than 3 times the relative likelihood to φ^* compared to φ_1, φ_2, and *true*. By contrast, the non-causal model assigns relative log likelihoods $(-2.83, -3.16, -3.17)$ for $(\varphi_1, \varphi_2, \varphi^*)$. This implies that (i) φ^* is the least likely specification and (ii) each specification is less likely than *true*!

---

[4] The maximum entropy policy for $\varphi = $ true applies actions uniformly at random.

7   Conclusion and Future Work

Motivated by the problem of learning specifications from demonstrations, we have adapted the principle of maximum causal entropy to provide a posterior probability to a candidate task specification given a multi-set of demonstrations. Further, to exploit the structure of task specifications, we proposed an algorithm that computes this likelihood by first encoding the unrolled Markov Decision Process as a reduced ordered binary decision diagram (BDD). As illustrated on a few toy examples, BDDs are often much smaller than the unrolled Markov Decision Process and thus could enable efficient computation of maximum causal entropy likelihoods, at least for well behaved dynamics and specifications.

Nevertheless, two major questions remain unaddressed by this work. First is the question of how to select which specifications to compute likelihoods for. For example, is there a way to systematically mutate a specification to make it more likely and/or is it possible to systematically reuse computations for previously evaluated specifications to propose new specifications.

Second is how to set prior probabilities. Although we have largely ignored this question, we view the problem of setting good prior probabilities as essential to avoid over fitting and/or making this technique require only one or two demonstrations. However, we note that prior probabilities can make inference arbitrarily more difficult since any structure useful for optimization imposed by our likelihood estimate can be overpowered.

Finally, additional future work includes extending the formalism to infinite horizon specifications, continuous dynamics, and characterizing the optimal set of teacher demonstrations.

Acknowledgments. We would like to thank the anonymous referees as well as Daniel Fremont, Ben Caulfield, Marissa Ramirez de Chanlatte, Gil Lederman, Dexter Scobee, and Hazem Torfah for their useful suggestions and feedback. This work was supported in part by NSF grants 1545126 (VeHICaL) and 1837132, the DARPA BRASS program under agreement number FA8750-16-C0043, the DARPA Assured Autonomy program, Toyota under the iCyPhy center, and Berkeley Deep Drive.

References

1. Angluin, D.: Learning regular sets from queries and counterexamples. Inf. Comput. **75**(2), 87–106 (1987)
2. Bellman, R.E., et al.: Dynamic programming, ser. Rand Corporation research study. Princeton University Press, Princeton (1957)
3. Bryant, R.E.: Symbolic boolean manipulation with orderedbinary-decisiondiagrams. ACM Comput. Surv. (CSUR) **24**, 293–318 (1992)
4. Farwer, B.: ω-automata. In: Grädel, E., Thomas, W., Wilke, T. (eds.) Automata Logics, and Infinite Games. LNCS, vol. 2500, pp. 3–21. Springer, Heidelberg (2002). https://doi.org/10.1007/3-540-36387-4_1
5. Finn, C., Levine, S., Abbeel, P.: Guided cost learning: deep inverse optimal control via policy optimization. In: International Conference on Machine Learning, pp. 49–58 (2016)

6. Haarnoja, T., Pong, V., Zhou, A., Dalal, M., Abbeel, P., Levine, S.: Composable deep reinforcement learning for robotic manipulation. arXiv preprint arXiv:1803.06773 (2018)
7. Heule, M.J.H., Verwer, S.: Exact DFA identification using SAT solvers. In: Sempere, J.M., García, P. (eds.) ICGI 2010. LNCS (LNAI), vol. 6339, pp. 66–79. Springer, Heidelberg (2010). https://doi.org/10.1007/978-3-642-15488-1_7
8. De la Higuera, C.: Grammatical Inference: Learning Automata and Grammars. Cambridge University Press, Cambridge (2010)
9. Hoey, J., St-Aubin, R., Hu, A., Boutilier, C.: SPUDD: stochastic planning using decision diagrams. In: Proceedings of the Fifteenth Conference on Uncertainty in Artificial Intelligence, pp. 279–288. Morgan Kaufmann Publishers Inc. (1999)
10. Holtzen, S., Millstein, T.D., den Broeck, G.V.: Symbolic exact inference for discrete probabilistic programs. CoRR abs/1904.02079 (2019). http://arxiv.org/abs/1904.02079
11. Icarte, R.T., Klassen, T., Valenzano, R., McIlraith, S.: Using reward machines for high-level task specification and decomposition in reinforcement learning. In: International Conference on Machine Learning, pp. 2112–2121 (2018)
12. Ignatiev, A., Morgado, A., Marques-Silva, J.: PySAT: a python toolkit for prototyping with SAT oracles. In: Beyersdorff, O., Wintersteiger, C.M. (eds.) SAT 2018. LNCS, vol. 10929, pp. 428–437. Springer, Cham (2018). https://doi.org/10.1007/978-3-319-94144-8_26
13. Jaynes, E.T.: Information theory and statistical mechanics. Phys. Rev. **106**(4), 620 (1957)
14. Jothimurugan, K., Alur, R., Bastani, O.: A composable specification language for reinforcement learning tasks. In: Advances in Neural Information Processing Systems, pp. 13021–13030 (2019)
15. Kasenberg, D., Scheutz, M.: Interpretable apprenticeship learning with temporal logic specifications. arXiv preprint arXiv:1710.10532 (2017)
16. Knuth, D.E.: The Art of Computer Programming: Vol. 4, No. 1: Bitwise Tricks and Techniques-Binary Decision Diagrams. Addison Wesley Professional (2009)
17. Kramer, G.: Directed Information for Channels with Feedback. Hartung-Gorre (1998)
18. Kwiatkowska, M., Norman, G., Parker, D.: PRISM 4.0: verification of probabilistic real-time systems. In: Gopalakrishnan, G., Qadeer, S. (eds.) CAV 2011. LNCS, vol. 6806, pp. 585–591. Springer, Heidelberg (2011). https://doi.org/10.1007/978-3-642-22110-1_47
19. Levine, S.: Reinforcement learning and control as probabilistic inference: tutorial and review. CoRR abs/1805.00909 (2018). http://arxiv.org/abs/1805.00909
20. Levine, S., Popovic, Z., Koltun, V.: Nonlinear inverse reinforcement learning with gaussian processes. In: Advances in Neural Information Processing Systems 24 (2011)
21. Livingston, S.C.: Binary Decision Diagrams (BDDs) in pure Python and Cython wrappers of CUDD, Sylvan, and BuDDy (2019)
22. Ng, A.Y., Russell, S.J., et al.: Algorithms for inverse reinforcement learning. In: ICML, pp. 663–670 (2000)
23. Permuter, H.H., Kim, Y.H., Weissman, T.: On directed information and gambling. In: 2008 IEEE International Symposium on Information Theory, pp. 1403–1407. IEEE (2008)
24. Pineau, J., Gordon, G., Thrun, S., et al.: Point-based value iteration: an anytime algorithm for POMDPs. In: IJCAI, vol. 3, pp. 1025–1032 (2003)

25. Ramachandran, D., Amir, E.: Bayesian inverse reinforcement learning. In: IJCAI (2007)
26. Todorov, E.: Linearly-solvable Markov decision problems. In: Advances in Neural Information Processing Systems, pp. 1369–1376 (2007)
27. Todorov, E.: General duality between optimal control and estimation. In: 47th IEEE Conference on Decision and Control, 2008, CDC 2008, pp. 4286–4292. IEEE (2008)
28. Vazquez-Chanlatte, M.: mvcisback/py-aiger, August 2018. https://doi.org/10.5281/zenodo.1326224
29. Vazquez-Chanlatte, M.: mce-spec-inference (2020). https://github.com/mvcisback/mce-spec-inference/
30. Vazquez-Chanlatte, M., Jha, S., Tiwari, A., Ho, M.K., Seshia, S.: Learning task specifications from demonstrations. In: Advances in Neural Information Processing Systems, vol. 31, pp. 5368–5378 (2018)
31. Vazquez-Chanlatte, M., Rabe, M.N., Seshia, S.A.: A model counter's guide to probabilistic systems. arXiv preprint arXiv:1903.09354 (2019)
32. Ziebart, B.D., Bagnell, J.A., Dey, A.K.: Modeling interaction via the principle of maximum causal entropy (2010)
33. Ziebart, B.D., Maas, A.L., Bagnell, J.A., Dey, A.K.: Maximum entropy inverse reinforcement learning. In: AAAI, Chicago, IL, USA, vol. 8, pp. 1433–1438 (2008)

Certifying Certainty and Uncertainty in Approximate Membership Query Structures

Kiran Gopinathan[1]([✉]) [iD] and Ilya Sergey[1,2] [iD]

[1] School of Computing,
National University of Singapore,
Singapore, Singapore
{kirang,ilya}@comp.nus.edu.sg
[2] Yale-NUS College, Singapore, Singapore

Abstract. Approximate Membership Query structures (AMQs) rely on randomisation for time- and space-efficiency, while introducing a possibility of false positive and false negative answers. Correctness proofs of such structures involve subtle reasoning about bounds on probabilities of getting certain outcomes. Because of these subtleties, a number of unsound arguments in such proofs have been made over the years.

In this work, we address the challenge of building rigorous and reusable computer-assisted proofs about probabilistic specifications of AMQs. We describe the framework for systematic decomposition of AMQs and their properties into a series of interfaces and reusable components. We implement our framework as a library in the Coq proof assistant and showcase it by encoding in it a number of non-trivial AMQs, such as Bloom filters, counting filters, quotient filters and blocked constructions, and mechanising the proofs of their probabilistic specifications.

We demonstrate how AMQs encoded in our framework guarantee the absence of false negatives *by construction*. We also show how the proofs about probabilities of false positives for complex AMQs can be obtained by means of *verified reduction* to the implementations of their simpler counterparts. Finally, we provide a library of domain-specific theorems and tactics that allow a high degree of automation in probabilistic proofs.

1 Introduction

Approximate Membership Query structures (AMQs) are probabilistic data structures that compactly implement (multi-)sets via hashing. They are a popular alternative to traditional collections in algorithms whose utility is not affected by some fraction of wrong answers to membership queries. Typical examples of such data structures are Bloom filters [6], quotient filters [5,38], and count-min sketches [12]. In particular, versions of Bloom filters find many applications in security and privacy [16,18,36], static program analysis [37], databases [17], web search [22], suggestion systems [45], and blockchain protocols [19,43].

Hashing-based AMQs achieve efficiency by means of losing precision when answering queries about membership of certain elements. Luckily, most of the

© The Author(s) 2020
S. K. Lahiri and C. Wang (Eds.): CAV 2020, LNCS 12225, pp. 279–303, 2020.
https://doi.org/10.1007/978-3-030-53291-8_16

applications listed above can tolerate *some* loss of precision. For instance, a static points-to analysis may consider two memory locations as aliases even if they are not (a *false positive*), still remaining sound. However, it would be unsound for such an analysis to claim that two locations do not alias in the case they do (a *false negative*). Even if it increases the number of false positives, a randomised data structure can be used to answer aliasing queries in a sound way—as long as it does not have false negatives [37]. But *how much* precision would be lost if, *e.g.*, a Bloom filter with certain parameters is chosen to answer these queries? Another example, in which quantitative properties of false positives are critical, is the security of Bitcoin's Nakamoto consensus [35] that depends on the counts of block production per unit time [19].

In the light of the described above applications, of particular interest are two kinds of properties specifying the behaviour of AMQs:

- *No-False-Negatives* properties, stating that a set-membership query for an element x always returns true if x is, in fact, in the set represented by the AMQ.
- Properties quantifying the rate of *False Positives* by providing a probabilistic bound on getting a wrong "yes"-answer to a membership query, given certain parameters of the data structure and the past history of its usage.

Given the importance of such claims for practical applications, it is desirable to have machine-checked formal proofs of their validity. And, since many of the existing AMQs share a common design structure, one may expect that a large portion of those validity proofs can be reused across different implementations.

Computer-assisted reasoning about the absence of *false negatives* in a particular AMQ (Bloom filter) has been addressed to some extent in the past [7]. However, to the best of our knowledge, mechanised proofs of probabilistic bounds on the *rates of false positives* did not extend to such structures. Furthermore, to the best of our knowledge, no other existing AMQs have been formally verified to date, and no attempts were made towards characterising the commonalities in their implementations in order to allow efficient proof reuse.

In this work, we aim to advance the state of the art in machine-checked proofs of probabilistic theorems about false positives in randomised hash-based data structures. As recent history demonstrates, when done in a "paper-and-pencil" way, such proofs may contain subtle mistakes [8,10] due to misinterpreted assumptions about relations between certain kinds of events. These mistakes are not surprising, as the proofs often need to perform a number complicated manipulations with expressions that capture probabilities of certain events. Our goal is to factor out these reasoning patterns into a standalone library of *reusable* program- and specification-level definitions and theorems, implemented in a proof assistant enabling computer-aided verification of a variety of AMQs.

Our Contributions. The key novel observation we make in this work is the decomposition of the common AMQ implementations into the following components: (a) a hashing strategy and (b) a state component that operates over hash outcomes, together capturing most AMQs that provide fixed constant-time insertion and query operations. Any AMQ that is implemented as an instance of those components enjoys the *no-false-negatives* property *by construction*. Furthermore, such a decomposition streamlines the proofs of structure-specific bounds on false positive rates, while allowing for proof reuse for complex AMQ implementations, which are built on top of simpler AMQs [40]. Powered by those insights, this work makes the following technical contributions:

- A Coq-based mechanised framework Ceramist, specialised for reasoning about AMQs.[1] Implemented as a Coq library, it provides a systematic decomposition of AMQs and their properties in terms of Coq modules and uses these interfaces to to derive certain properties "for free", as well as supporting proof-by-reduction arguments between classes of similar AMQs.
- A library of non-trivial theorems for expressing closed-form probabilities on false positive rates in AMQs. In particular, we provide the first mechanised proof of the closed form for Stirling numbers of the second kind [26, Chap. 6].
- A collection of proven facts and tactics for effective construction of proofs of probabilistic properties. Our approach adopts the style of Ssreflect reasoning [21,31], and expresses its core lemmas in terms of rewrites and evaluation.
- A number of case study AMQs mechanised via Ceramist: ordinary [6] and counting [46] Bloom filters, quotient filters [5,38], and Blocked AMQs [40].

For ordinary Bloom filters, we provide the first mechanised proof that the probability of a false positive in a Bloom filter can be written as a closed form expression in terms of the input parameters; a bound that has often been mischaracterised in the past due to oversight of subtle dependencies between the components of the structure [6,34]. For Counting Bloom filters, we provide the first mechanised proofs of several of their properties: that they have no false negatives, its false positive rate, that an element can be removed without affecting queries for other elements, and the fact that Counting Bloom filters preserve the number of inserted elements irrespective of the randomness of the hash outputs. For quotient filters, we provide a mechanised proof of the false positive rate and of the absence of false negatives. Finally, alongside the standard Blocked Bloom filter [40], we derive two novel AMQ data structures: *Counting Blocked Bloom filters* and *Blocked Quotient filters*, and prove corresponding no-false-negatives and false positive rates for all of them. Our case studies illustrate that Ceramist can be repurposed to verify hash-based AMQ structures, including entirely new ones that have not been described in the literature, but rather have been obtained by composing existing AMQs via the "blocked" construction.

Our mechanised development [24] is entirely *axiom-free*, and is compatible with Coq 8.11.0 [11] and MathComp 1.10 [31]. It relies on the infotheo library [2] for encoding discrete probabilities.

Paper Outline. We start by providing the intuition on Bloom filters, our main motivating example, in Sect. 2. We proceed by explaining the encoding of their semantics, auxiliary hash-based structures, and key properties in Coq in Sect. 3.

---

[1] Ceramist stands for **Cer**tified **A**pproximate **M**embership **St**ructures.

Section 4 generalises that encoding to a general AMQ interface, and provides an overview of Ceramist, its embedding into Coq, showcasing it by another example instance—Counting Bloom filters. Section 5 describes the specific techniques that help to structure our mechanised proofs. In Sect. 6, we report on the evaluation of Ceramist on various case studies, explaining in detail our compositional treatment of blocked AMQs and their properties. Section 7 provides a discussion on the state of the art in reasoning about probabilistic data structures.

2   Motivating Example

Ceramist is a library specialised for reasoning about AMQ data structures in which the underlying randomness arises from the interaction of one or more hashing operations. To motivate this development, we thus consider applying it to the classical example of such an algorithm—a Bloom filter [6].

2.1   The Basics of Bloom Filters

Bloom filters are probabilistic data structures that provide compact encodings of mathematical sets, trading increased space efficiency for a weaker membership test [6]. Specifically, when testing membership for a value *not* in the Bloom filter, there is a possibility that the query may be answered as positive. Thus a property of direct practical importance is the exact probability of this event, and how it is influenced by the other parameters of the implementation.

A Bloom filter *bf* is implemented as a binary vector of m bits (all initially zeros), paired with a sequence of k hash functions $f_1, \ldots, f_k$, collectively mapping each input value to a vector of k indices from $\{1 \ldots m\}$, the indices determine the bits set to true in the m-bit array Assuming an ideal selection of hash functions, we can treat the output of $f_1, \ldots, f_k$ on new values as a uniformly-drawn random vector.

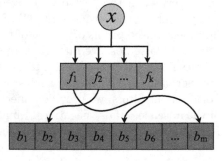

To insert a value x into the Bloom filter, we can treat each element of the "hash vector" produced from $f_1, \ldots, f_k$ as an index into *bf* and set the corresponding bits to ones. Similarly, to test membership for an element x, we can check that all k bits specified by the hash-vector are raised.

2.2   Properties of Bloom Filters

Given this model, there are two obvious properties of practical importance: that of false positives and of false negatives.

False Negatives. It turns out that these definitions are sufficient to guarantee the lack of false-negatives with complete certainty, *i.e.*, irrespective of the random outcome of the hash functions. This follows from the fact that once a bit is raised, there are no permitted operations that will unset it.

Theorem 1 (No False Negatives). *If* $x \in bf$, *then* $\Pr[x \in_? bf] = 1$, *where* $x \in_? bf$ *stands for the approximate membership test, while the relation* $x \in bf$ *means that* x *has been previously inserted into* bf.

False Positives. This property is more complex as the occurrence of a false positive is entirely dependent on the particular outcomes of the hash functions $f_1, \ldots, f_k$ and one needs to consider situations in which the hash functions happen to map some values to *overlapping* sets of indices. That is, after inserting a series of values xs, subsequent queries for $y \notin xs$ might incorrectly return true.

This leads to subtle dependencies that can invalidate the analysis, and have lead to a number of incorrect probabilistic bounds on the event, including in the analysis by Bloom in his original paper [6]. Specifically, Bloom first considered the probability that inserting l distinct items into the Bloom filter will set a particular bit b_i. From the independence of the hash functions, he was able to show that the probability of this event has a simple closed-form representation:

Lemma 1 (Probability of a single bit being set). *If the only values previously inserted into* bf *are* $x_1, \ldots, x_l$, *then the probability of a particular single bit at the position* i *being set is* $\Pr\left[i^{\mathrm{th}} \text{ bit in } bf \text{ is set}\right] = 1 - \left(1 - \frac{1}{m}\right)^{kl}$.

Bloom then claimed that the probability of a false positive was simply the probability of a single bit being set, raised to the power of k, reasoning that a false positive for an element $y \notin bf$ only occurs when all the k bits corresponding to the hash outputs are set.

Unfortunately, as was later pointed out by Bose *et al.* [8], as the bits specified by $f_1(x), \ldots, f_{k-1}(x)$ may overlap, we cannot guarantee the independence that is required for any simple relation between the probabilities. Bose *et al.* rectified the analysis by instead interpreting the bits within a Bloom filter as maintaining a set $\mathrm{bits}(bf) \subseteq \mathbb{N}_{[0,\ldots,m-1]}$, corresponding to the indices of raised bits. With this interpretation, an element y only tests positive if the random set of indices produced by the hash functions on y is such that $\mathrm{inds}(y) \subseteq \mathrm{bits}(bf)$. Therefore, the chance of a positive result for $y \notin bf$ resolves to the chance that the random set of indices from hashing y is a subset of the union of $\mathrm{inds}(x)$ for each $x \in bf$. The probability of this reduced event is described by the following theorem:

Theorem 2 (Probability of False Positives). *If the only values inserted into* bf *are* $x_1, \ldots, x_l$, *then for any* $y \notin bf$, $\Pr[y \in_? bf] = \frac{1}{m^{k(l+1)}} \sum_{i=1}^m i^k i!$ $\binom{m}{i} \left\{ \begin{matrix} kl \\ i \end{matrix} \right\}$, *where* $\left\{ \begin{matrix} s \\ t \end{matrix} \right\}$ *stands for the* Stirling number of the second kind, *capturing the number of surjections from a set of size* s *to a set of size* t.

The key step in capturing these program properties is in treating the outcomes of hashes as *random variables* and then propagating this randomness to the results of the other operations. A formal treatment of program outcomes requires a suitable semantics, representing programs as distributions of such random variables. In moving to mechanised proofs, we must first fully characterise this semantics, formally defining a notion of a probabilistic computation in Coq.

3   Encoding AMQs in Coq

To introduce our encoding of AMQs and their probabilistic behaviours in Coq, we continue with our running example, transitioning from mathematical notation to Gallina, Coq's language. The rest of this section will introduce each of the key components of this encoding through the lens of Bloom filters.

3.1   Probability Monad

Our formalisation represents probabilistic computations using an embedding following the style of the FCF library [39]. We do not use FCF directly, due to its primary focus on cryptographic proofs, wherein it provides little support for proving probabilistic bounds directly, instead prioritising a reduction-based approach of expressing arbitrary computations as compositions of known distributions.

Following the adopted FCF notation, a term of type Comp A represents a probabilistic computation returning a value of type A, and is constructed using the standard monadic operators, with an additional primitive rand n that allows sampling from a uniform distribution over the range $\mathbb{Z}_n$:

$$\text{ret} : A \to \text{Comp } A$$
$$\text{bind} : \text{Comp } A \to (A \to \text{Comp } B) \to \text{Comp } B$$
$$\text{rand} : (n : \mathbb{N}) \to \text{Comp } (\mathbb{Z}_n)$$

We implement a Haskell-style do-notation over this monad to allow descriptions of probabilistic computations within Gallina. For example, the following code is used to implement the query operation for the Bloom filter:

```
hash_res <-$ hash_vec_int x hashes;  (* hash x using the hash functions *)
let (new_hashes, hash_vec) := hash_res in
(* check if all the corresponding bits are set *)
let qres := bf_query_int hash_vec bf in
(* return the query result and the new hashes *)
    ret (new_hashes, qres).
```

In the above listing, we pass the queried value x along with the hash functions hashes to a probabilistic hashing operation hash_vec_int to hash x over each function in hashes. The result of this random operation is then bound to hash_res and split into its constituent components—a sequence of hash outputs hash_vec and an updated copy `new_hashes` of the hash functions, now incorporating the mapping for `x`. Then, having mapped our input into a sequence of indices, we can query the Bloom filter for membership using a corresponding deterministic operation `bf_query_int` to check that all the bits specified by `hash_vec` are set. Finally, we complete the computation by returning the query outcome `qres` and the updated hash functions `new_hashes` using the `ret` operation to lift our result to a probabilistic outcome.

Using the code snippet above, we can define the query operation `bf_query` as a function that maps a Bloom filter, a value to query, and a collection of hash functions to a probabilistic computation returning the query result and an updated set of hash functions. However, because our computation type does not impose any particular semantics, this result only encodes the *syntax* of the probabilistic query and has no actual meaning without a separate interpretation.

Thus, given a Gallina term of type `Comp` A, we must first evaluate it into a distribution over possible results to state properties on the probabilities of its outcomes. We interpret our monadic encoding in terms of Ramsey's probability monad [42], which decomposes a complex distribution into composition of primitive ones bound together via conditional distributions. To capture this interpretation within Coq, we then use the encoding of this monad from the infotheo library [1,2], and provide a function `eval_dist` : `Comp` $A \to$ `dist` A that evaluates computations into distributions by recursively mapping them to the probability monad. Here, `dist A` represents infotheo's encoding of distributions over a finite support `A`, defined as being composed of a measure function `pmf` : $A \to \mathbb{R}^+$, and a proof that the sum of the measure over the support A produces 1.

This mapping from computations to distributions must be done to a program e (involving, *e.g.*, Bloom filter) before stating its probability bound. Therefore, we hide this evaluation process behind a notation that allows stating probabilistic properties in a form closer to their mathematical counterparts:

$$\Pr[e = v] \triangleq (\texttt{eval\_dist } e) \; v$$
$$\Pr[e] \triangleq (\texttt{eval\_dist } e) \; \texttt{true}$$

Above, v is an arbitrary element in the support of the distribution induced by e. Finally, we introduce a binding operator $\rhd$ to allow concise representation of dependent distributions: $e \rhd f \triangleq \texttt{bind } e \; f$.

3.2 Representing Properties of Bloom Filters

We define the state of a Bloom filter (`BF`) in Coq as a binary vector of a fixed length m, using Ssreflect's `m.-tuple` data type:

```
Record BF := mkBF { bloomfilter_state: m.-tuple bool }.
Definition bf_new : BF := (* construct a BF with all bits cleared *).
Definition bf_get_int i : BF → bool := (* retrieve BF's ith bit *).
```

We define the deterministic components of the Bloom filter implementation as pure functions taking an instance of `BF` and a series of indices assumed to be obtained from earlier calls to the associated hash functions:

$$\texttt{bf\_add\_int} : \text{BF} \to \text{seq } \mathbb{Z}_m \to \text{BF}$$
$$\texttt{bf\_query\_int} : \text{BF} \to \text{seq } \mathbb{Z}_m \to \text{bool}$$

That is, `bf_add_int` takes the Bloom filter state and a sequence of indices to insert and returns a new state with the requested bits also set. Conversely, `bf_query_int` returns true *iff* all the queried indices are set. These pure operations are then called within a probabilistic wrapper that handles hashing the input and the book-keeping associated with hashing to provide the standard interface for AMQs:

$$\texttt{bf\_add} : B \to (\text{HashVec } B * \text{BF}) \to \text{Comp } (\text{HashVec } B * \text{BF})$$
$$\texttt{bf\_query} : B \to (\text{HashVec } B * \text{BF}) \to \text{Comp } (\text{HashVec } B * \text{bool})$$

The component `HashVec` B (to be defined in Sect. 3.3), parameterised over an input type B, keeps track of *known results* of the involved hash functions and is provided as an external parameter to the function rather than being a part of the data structure to reflect typical uses of AMQs, wherein the hash operation is pre-determined and shared by *all* instances.

With these definitions and notation, we can now state the main theorems of interest about Bloom filters directly within Coq:[2]

Theorem 3 (No False Negatives). *For any Bloom filter state bf, a vector of hash functions hs, after having inserted an element x into bf, followed by a series xs of other inserted elements, the result of query x* $\in_?$ *bf is always* true. *That is, in terms of probabilities:* $\Pr\left[\texttt{bf\_add } x \ (hs, bf) \triangleright \texttt{bf\_addm } xs \triangleright \texttt{bf\_query } x\right] = 1.$

Lemma 2 (Probability of Flipping a Single Bit). *For a vector of hash functions hs of length k, after inserting a series of l distinct values xs, all unseen in hs, into an empty Bloom filter bf, represented by a vector of m bits, the probability of its any index i being set is* $\Pr\left[\texttt{bf\_addm } xs \ (hs, \texttt{bf\_new}) \triangleright \texttt{bf\_get } i\right] = 1 - \left(1 - \frac{1}{m}\right)^{kl}$. *Here,* `bf_get` *is a simple embedding of the pure function* `bf_get_int` *into a probabilistic computation.*

Theorem 4 (Probability of a False Positive). *After having inserted a series of l distinct values xs, all unseen in hs, into an empty Bloom filter bf, for any unseen y* $\notin$ *xs, the probability of a subsequent query y* $\in_?$ *bf for y returning* true *is given as* $\Pr\left[\texttt{bf\_addm } xs \ (hs, \texttt{bf\_new}) \triangleright \texttt{bf\_query } y\right] = \frac{1}{m^{k(l+1)}} \sum_{i=1}^{m} i^k i! \binom{m}{i} \left\{ \begin{matrix} kl \\ i \end{matrix} \right\}.$

The proof of this theorem required us to provide *the first axiom-free mechanised proof* for the closed form for Stirling numbers of the second kind [26].

In the definitions above, we used the output of the hashing operation as the bound between the deterministic and probabilistic components of the Bloom filter. For instance, in our earlier description of the Bloom filter query operation

---

[2] `bf_addm` is a trivial generalisation of the insertion to multiple elements.

in Sect. 3.1, we were able to implement the entire operation with the only probabilistic operation being the call `hash_vec_int x hashes`. In general, structuring AMQ operations as manipulations with hash outputs via *pure* deterministic functions allows us to decompose reasoning about the data structure into a series of specialised properties about its deterministic primitives and a separate set of reusable properties on its hash operations.

3.3   Reasoning About Hash Operations

We encode hash operations within our development using a random oracle-based implementation. In particular, in order to keep track of *seen* hashes learnt by hashing previously observed values, we represent a *state* of a hash function from elements of type `B` to a range $\mathbb{Z}_m$ using a finite map to ensure that previously hashed values produce the same hash output:

```
Definition HashState B := FixedMap B 'I_m.
```

The state is paired with a hash function generating uniformly random outputs for unseen values, and otherwise returns the value as from its prior invocations:

```
Definition hash value state : Comp (HashState B * B) :=
  match find value state with
  | Some(output) ⇒ ret (state, output)
  | None ⇒ rnd <-$ rand m;
           new_state <- put value rnd state;
           ret (new_state, rnd)
  end.
```

A *hash vector* is a generalisation of this structure to represent a vector of states of k independent hash functions:

```
Definition HashVec B := k.-tuple HashState B.
```

The corresponding hash operation over the hash vector, `hash_vec_int`, is then defined as a function taking a value and the current hash vector and then returning a pair of the updated hash vector and associated random vector, internally calling out to `hash` to compute individual hash outputs.

This random oracle-based implementation allows us to formulate several helper theorems for simplifying probabilistic computations using hashes by considering whether the hashed values *have been seen before or not*. For example, if we knew that a value x had not been seen before, we would know that the possibility of obtaining any particular choice of a vector of indices would be equivalent to obtaining the same vector by a draw from a corresponding uniform distribution. We can formalise this intuition in the form of the following theorem:

Theorem 5 (Uniform Hash Output). *For any two hash vectors hs, hs' of length k, a value x that has not been hashed before, and an output vector ιs of length m obtained by hashing x via hs, if the state of hs' has the same mappings* *as hs and also maps x to ιs, the probability of obtaining the pair $(hs', \iota s)$ is uniform:* $\Pr\left[\texttt{hash\_vec\_int } x \; hs = (hs', \iota s)\right] = \left(\frac{1}{m}\right)^k$.

Similarly, there are also often cases where we are hashing a value that we *have already seen*. In these cases, if we know the exact indices a value hashes to, we can prove a certainty on the value of the outcome:

Theorem 6 (Hash Consistency). *For any hash vector hs, a value x, if hs maps x to outputs ιs, then hashing x again will certainly produce ιs and not change hs, that is,* $\Pr\left[\texttt{hash\_vec\_int } x \; hs = (hs, \iota s)\right] = 1$.

By combining these types of probabilistic properties about hashes with the earlier Bloom filter operations, we are able to prove the prior theorems about Bloom filters by reasoning primarily about the core logical interactions of the *deterministic components* of the data structure. This decomposition is not just applicable to the case of Bloom filters, but can be extended into a general framework for obtaining modular proofs of AMQs, as we will show in the next section.

4 Ceramist at Large

Zooming out from the previous discussion of Bloom filters, we now present Ceramist in its full generality, describing the high-level design in terms of the various interfaces it requires to instantiate to obtain verified AMQ implementations.

The core of our framework revolves around the decomposition of an AMQ data structure into separate interfaces for hashing (AMQHash) and state (AMQ), generalising the specific decomposition used for Bloom filters (hash vectors and bit vectors respectively). More specifically, the AMQHash interface captures the probabilistic properties of the hashing operation, while the AMQ interface captures the deterministic interactions of the state with the hash outcomes.

4.1 AMQHash Interface

The AMQHash interface generalises the behaviours of hash vectors (Sect. 3.3) to provide a generic description of the hashing operation used in AMQs.

The interface first abstracts over the specific types used in the prior hashing operations (such as, *e.g.*, `HashVec B`) by treating them as opaque parameters: using a parameter `AMQHashState` to represent the state of the hash operation; types `Key` and `Value` encoding the hash inputs and outputs respectively, and finally, a deterministic operation `AMQHash_add_internal : AMQHashState →` `Key → Value → AMQHashState` to encode the interaction of the state with the outputs and inputs. For example, in the case of a single hash, the state parameter `AMQHashState` would be `HashState B`, while for a hash vector this would instead be `HashVec B`.

To use this hash state in probabilistic computations, the interface assumes a separate probabilistic operation that will take the hash state and randomly generate an output (*e.g.*, `hash` for single hashes and `hash_vec_int` for hash vectors):

```
Parameter AMQHash_hash: Key → AMQHashState → Comp (AMQHash * Value).
```

Then, to abstractly capture the kinds of reasoning about the outcomes of hash operations done with Bloom filters in Sect. 3.3, the interface assumes a few predicates on the hash state to provide information about its contents:

```
Parameter AMQHash_hashstate_contains: AMQHashState → Key → Value → bool.
Parameter AMQHash_hashstate_unseen: AMQHashState → Key → bool.
```

These components are then combined together to produce more abstract formulations of the previous Theorems 5 and 6 on hash operations.

Property 1 (Generalised Uniform Hash Output). *There exists a probability p_{hash}, such that for any two AMQ hash states hs, hs', a value x that is unseen, and an output $\imath s$ obtained by hashing x via hs, if the state of hs' has the same mappings as hs and also maps x to $\imath s$, the probability of obtaining the pair $(hs', \imath s)$ is given by:* $\Pr\left[\texttt{AMQHash\_hash } x \ hs = (hs', \imath s)\right] = p_{hash}$.

Property 2 (Generalised Hash Consistency). *For any AMQ hash state hs, a value x, if hs maps x to an output $\imath s$, then hashing x again will certainly produce $\imath s$ and not change hs:* $\Pr\left[\texttt{AMQhash\_hash } x \ hs = (hs, \imath s)\right] = 1$

Proofs of these corresponding properties must also be provided to instantiate the AMQHash interface. Conversely, components operating over this interface can assume their existence, and use them to abstractly perform the same kinds of simplifications as done with Bloom filters, resolving many probabilistic proofs to dealing with deterministic properties on the AMQ states.

4.2   The **AMQ** Interface

Building on top of an abstract AMQHash component, the AMQ interface then provides a unified view of the state of an AMQ and how it deterministically interacts with the output type `Value` of a particular hashing operation.

As before, the interface begins by abstracting the specific types and operations of the previous analysis of Bloom filters, first introducing a type `AMQState` to capture the state of the AMQ, and then assuming deterministic implementations of the typical *add* and *query* operations of an AMQ:

```
Parameter AMQ_add_internal: AMQState → Value → AMQState.
Parameter AMQ_query_internal: AMQState → Value → bool.
```

In the case of Bloom filters, these would be instantiated with the `BF`, `bf_add_int` and `bf_query_int` operations respectively (*cf.* Sect. 3.2), thereby setting the associated hashing operation to the hash vector (Sect. 3.3).

As we move on to reason about the behaviours of these operations, the interface diverges slightly from that of the Bloom filter by conditioning the behaviours on the assumption that the state has sufficient capacity:

```
Parameter AMQ_available_capacity: AMQState → nat → bool.
```

While the Bloom filter has no real deterministic notion of a capacity, this cannot be said of all AMQs in general, such as the Counting Bloom filter or Quotient filter, as we will discuss later.

With these definitions in hand, the behaviours of the AMQ operations are characterised using a series of associated assumptions:

Property 3 (AMQ insertion validity). *For a state s with sufficient capacity, inserting any hash output ıs into s via* `AMQ_add_internal` *will produce a new state s' for which any subsequent queries for ıs via* `AMQ_query_internal` *will return* true.

Property 4 (AMQ query preservation). *For any AMQ state s with sufficient remaining capacity, if queries for a particular hash output ıs in s via* `AMQ_query_internal` *happen to return* true, *then inserting any further outputs ıs' into s will return a state for which queries for ıs will still return* true.

Even though these assumptions seemingly place strict restrictions on the permitted operations, we found that these properties are satisfied by most common AMQ structures. One potential reason for this might be because they are in fact *sufficient* to ensure the No-False-Negatives property standard of most AMQs:

Theorem 7 (Generalised No False Negatives). *For any AMQ state s, a corresponding hash state hs, after having inserted an element x into s, followed by a series xs of other inserted elements, the result of query for x is always* true. *That is,* $\Pr[\texttt{AMQ\_add } x \ (hs, s) \ \triangleright \ \texttt{AMQ\_addm } xs \ \triangleright \ \texttt{AMQ\_query } x] = 1.$

Here, `AMQ_add`, `AMQ_addm`, and `AMQ_query` are generalisations of the probabilistic wrappers of Bloom filters (*cf.* Sect. 3.1) for doing the bookkeeping associated with hashing and delegating to the internal deterministic operations.

The generalised Theorem 7 illustrates one of the key facilities of our framework, wherein by simply providing components satisfying the AMQHash and AMQ interfaces, it is possible to obtain proofs of certain standard probabilistic properties or simplifications *for free*.

The diagram in Fig. 1 provides a high-level overview of the interfaces of Ceramist, their specific instances, and dependencies between them, demonstrating Ceramist's take on compositional reasoning and proof reuse. For instance Bloom filter implementation instantiates the AMQ interface implementation and uses, as a component, hash vectors, which themselves instantiate AMQHash used by AMQ. Bloom filter itself is also used as a proof reduction target by Counting Bloom filter. We will elaborate on this and the other noteworthy dependencies between interfaces and instances of Ceramist in the following sections.

4.3 Counting Bloom Filters Through Ceramist

To provide a concrete demonstration of the use of the AMQ interface, we now switch over to a new running example—Counting Bloom filters [46]. A Counting Bloom filter is a variant of the Bloom filter in which individual bits are replaced

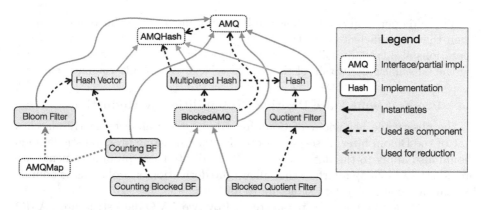

Fig. 1. Overview of Ceramist and dependencies the between its components.

with counters, thereby allowing the removal of elements. The implementation of the structure closely follows the Bloom filter, generalising the logic from bits to counters: insertion increments the counters specified by the hash outputs, while queries treat counters as set if greater than 0. In the remainder of this section, we will show how to encode and verify the Counting Bloom filter for the standard AMQ properties. We have also proven two novel domain-specific properties of Counting Bloom filters (*cf.* Appendix A of the extended paper version [25]).

First, as the Counting Bloom filter uses the same hashing strategy as the Bloom filter, the hash interface can be instantiated with the Hash Vector structure used for the Bloom filter, entirely reusing the earlier proofs on hash vectors. Next, in order to instantiate the AMQ interface, the state parameter can be defined as a vector of bounded integers, all initially set to 0:

```
Record CF := mkCF { countingbloomfilter_state: m.-tuple Z_p }.
Definition cf_new : CF := (* a new CF with all counters set to 0 *).
```

As mentioned before, the *add* operation increments counters rather than setting bits, and the *query* operation treats counters greater than 0 as raised.

$$\texttt{cf\_add\_int} : \texttt{CF} \to \texttt{seq}\ \mathbb{Z}_m \to \texttt{CF}$$
$$\texttt{cf\_query\_int} : \texttt{CF} \to \texttt{seq}\ \mathbb{Z}_m \to \texttt{bool}$$

To prevent integer overflows, the counters in the Counting Bloom filter are bounded to some range $\mathbb{Z}_p$, so the overall data structure too has a maximum capacity. It would not be possible to insert any values if doing such would raise any of the counters above their maximum. To account for this, the capacity parameter of the AMQ interface is instantiated with a simple predicate `cf_available_capacity` that verifies that the structure can support l further inserts by ensuring that each counter has at least $k * l$ spaces free (where k is the number of hash functions used by the data structure).

The add operation can be shown to be monotone on the value of any counter when there is sufficient capacity (Property 3). The remaining properties of the operations also trivially follow, thereby completing the instantiation, and allowing the automatic derivation of the No-False-Negatives result via Theorem 7.

4.4 Proofs About False Positive Probabilities by Reduction

As the observable behaviour of Counting Bloom filter almost exactly matches that of the Bloom filter, it seems reasonable that the same probabilistic bounds should also apply to the data structure. To facilitate these proof arguments, we provide the AMQMap interface that allows the derivation of probabilistic bounds by reducing one AMQ data structure to another.

The AMQMap interface is parameterised by two AMQ data structures, AMQ A and B, using the same hashing operation. It is assumed that corresponding bounds on False Positive rates have already been proven for AMQ B, while have not for AMQ A. The interface first assumes the existence of some mapping from the state of AMQ A to AMQ B, which satisfies a number of properties:

`Parameter AMQ_state_map: A.AMQState → B.AMQState.`

In the case of our Counting Bloom filter example, this mapping would convert the Counting Bloom filter state to a bit vector by mapping each counter to a raised bit if its value is greater than 0. To provide the of the false positive rate boundary, the AMQMap interface then requires the behaviour of this mapping to satisfy a number of additional assumptions:

Property 5 (AMQ Mapping Add Commutativity). *Adding a hash output to the AMQ B obtained by applying the mapping to an instance of AMQ A produces the same result as first adding a hash output to AMQ A and then applying the mapping to the result.*

Property 6 (AMQ Mapping Query Preservation). *Applying B's query operation to the result of mapping an instance of AMQ A produces the same result as applying A's query operation directly.*

In the case of reducing Counting Bloom filters (A) to Bloom filters (B), both results follow from the fact that after incrementing the some counters, all of them will have values greater than 0 and thus be mapped to raised bits.

Having instantiated the AMQMap interface with the corresponding function and proofs about it, it is now possible to derive the false positive rate of Bloom filters for Counting Bloom filters for free through the following generalised lemma:

Theorem 8 (AMQ False Positive Reduction). *For any two AMQs A, B, related by the AMQMap interface, if the false positive rate for B after inserting l items is given by the function f on l, then the false positive rate for A is also given by f on l. That is, in terms of probabilities:*

$$\Pr\left[\texttt{B.AMQ\_addm } xs \ (hs, \texttt{B.AMQ\_new}) \rhd \texttt{B.AMQ\_query } y\right] = f(\texttt{length } xs) \implies$$
$$\Pr\left[\texttt{A.AMQ\_addm } xs \ (hs, \texttt{A.AMQ\_new}) \rhd \texttt{A.AMQ\_query } y\right] = f(\texttt{length } xs).$$

5   Proof Automation for Probabilistic Sums

We have, until now, avoided discussing details of how facts about the probabilistic computations can be composed, and thereby also the specifics of how our proofs are structured. As it turns out, most of this process resolves to reasoning about summations over real values as encoded by Ssreflect's bigop library. Our development also relies on the tactic library by Martin-Dorel and Soloviev [32].

In this section, we outline some of the most essential proof principles facilitating the proofs-by-rewriting about probabilistic sums. While most of the provided rewriting primitives are standalone general equality facts, some of our proof techniques are better understood as combining a series of rewritings into a more general rewriting pattern. To delineate these two cases, will use the terminology **Pattern** to refer to a general pattern our library supports by means of a dedicated Coq tactic, while **Lemma** will refer to standalone proven equalities.

5.1   The Normal Form for Composed Probabilistic Computations

When stating properties on outcomes of a probabilistic computation (*cf.* Sect. 3.1), the computation must first be recursively evaluated into a distribution, where the intermediate results are combined using the probabilistic bind operator. Therefore, when decomposing a probabilistic property into smaller subproofs, we must rely on its semantics that is defined for discrete distributions as follows:

$$\texttt{bind\_dist}\ (P : \texttt{dist}\ A)\ (f : A \to \texttt{dist}\ B) \triangleq \sum_{a:\ A} \sum_{b:\ B} P\ a\ \times\ (f\ a)\ b$$

Expanding this definition, one can represent any statement on the outcome of a probabilistic computation in a *normal form* composed of only nested summations over a product of the probabilities of each intermediate computational step. This paramount transformation is captured as the following pattern:

Pattern 1 (Bind normalisation)

$$\Pr\left[(c_1 \rhd \ldots \rhd c_m) = v\right] = \sum_{v_1} \cdots \sum_{v_{m-1}} \Pr\left[c_1 = v_1\right] \times \cdots \times \Pr\left[c_m\ v_{m-1} = v\right]$$

Here, by $c_i\ v_{i-1} = v_i$, we denote the event in which the result of evaluating the command $c_i\ v_{i-1}$ is v_i, where v_{i-1} is the result of evaluating the previous command in the chain. This transformation then allows us to resolve the proof of a given probabilistic property into proving simpler statements on its substeps. For instance, consider the implementation of Bloom filter's query operation from Sect. 3.1. When proving properties of the result of a particular query (as in Theorem 3), we use this rule to decompose the program into its component parts, namely as being the product of a hash invocation $\Pr\left[\texttt{hash\_vec\_int}\ x\ hs\right]$ and the deterministic query operation $\texttt{bf\_query\_int}$. This allows dealing with the hash operation and the deterministic component *separately* by applying subsequent rewritings to each factor on the right-hand side of the above equality.

5.2   Probabilistic Summation Patterns

Having resolved a property into our normal form via a tactic implementing Pattern 1, the subsequent reductions rely on the following patterns and lemmas.

Sequential Composition. When reasoning about the properties of composite programs, it is common for some subprogram e to return a probabilistic result that is then used as the arguments for a probabilistic function f. This composition is encapsulated by the operation $e \triangleright f$, as used by Theorems 3, 2, and 4. The corresponding programs, once converted to the normal form, are characterised by having factors within its internal product that simply evaluate the probability of the final statement $\mathtt{ret}\ v'$ to produce a particular value v_k:

$$
\sum_{v_1} \cdots \sum_{v_{m-1}} \underbrace{\Pr\left[c_1 = v_1\right] \times \cdots \Pr\left[\mathtt{ret}\ v' = v_k\right]}_{e} \underbrace{\cdots \times \Pr\left[c_m\ v_{m-1} = v\right]}_{f}
$$

Since the return operation is defined as a delta distribution with a peak at the return value v', we can simplify the statement by removing the summation over v_k, and replacing all occurrences of v_k with v', via the following pattern:

Pattern 2 (Probability of a Sequential Composition).

$$
\sum_{v_1} \cdots \sum_{v_{m-1}} \Pr\left[\mathtt{ret}\ v' = v_1\right] \cdots \times \Pr\left[c_m\ v_{m-1} = v\right]]
$$

$$
= \sum_{v_2} \cdots \sum_{v_{m-1}} \Pr\left[[v'/v_1](c_2\ v_1) = v_2\right] \times \cdots \times \Pr\left[[v'/v_1]c_m\ v_{m-1} = v\right]
$$

Notice that, without loss of generality, Pattern 2 assumes that the v'-containing factor is in the head. Our tactic implicitly rewrites the statement to this form.

Plausible Statement Sequencing. One common issue with the normal form, is that, as each statement is evaluated over the entirety of its support, some of the dependencies between statements are obscured. That is, the outputs of one statement may in fact be constrained to *some subset* of the complete support. To recover these dependencies, we provide the following theorem, that allows reducing computations under the assumption that their inputs are plausible:

Lemma 3 (Plausible Sequencing). *For any computation sequence $c_1 \triangleright c_2$, if it is possible to reduce the computation $c_2\ x$ to a simpler form $c_3\ x$ when x is amongst plausible outcomes of c_1, (i.e., $\Pr\left[c_1 = x\right] \neq 0$ holds) then it is possible to rewrite c_2 to c_3 without changing the resulting distribution:*

$$
\sum_{x} \sum_{y} \Pr\left[c_1 = x\right] \times \Pr\left[c_2\ x = y\right] = \sum_{x} \sum_{y} \Pr\left[c_1 = x\right] \times \Pr\left[c_3\ x = y\right]
$$

Plausible Outcomes. As was demonstrated in the previous paragraph, it is sometimes possible to gain knowledge that a particular value v is a plausible outcome for a composite probabilistic computation $c_1 \triangleright \ldots \triangleright c_m$:

$$\sum_{v_1} \cdots \sum_{v_{m-1}} \Pr\left[c_1 = v_1\right] \times \cdots \times \Pr\left[c_m \ v_{m-1} = v\right] \neq 0$$

This fact in itself is not particularly helpful as it does not immediately provide any usable constraints on the value v. However, we can now turn this inequality into a conjunction of inequalities for individual probabilities, thus getting more information about the intermediate steps of the computation:

Pattern 3. If $\sum_{v_1} \cdots \sum_{v_{m-1}} \Pr\left[c_1 = v_1\right] \times \cdots \times \Pr\left[c_m \ v_{m-1} = v\right] \neq 0$, then there exist $v_1, \ldots, v_{m-1}$ such that $\Pr\left[c_1 = v_1\right] \neq 0 \wedge \cdots \wedge \Pr\left[c_m = v\right] \neq 0$.

This transformation is possible due to the fact that probabilities are always nonnegative, thus if a summation is positive, there must exist at least one element in the summation that is also positive.

Summary of the Development. By composing these components together, we obtain a comprehensive toolbox for effectively reasoning about probabilistic computations. We find that our summation patterns end up encapsulating most of the book-keeping associated with our encoding of probabilistic computations, which, combined with the AMQ/AMQHash decomposition from Sect. 4, allows for a fairly straightforward approach for verifying properties of AMQs.

5.3 A Simple Proof of Generalised No False Negatives Theorem

To showcase the fluid interaction of our proof principles in action, let us consider the proof of the generalised No-False-Negatives Theorem 7, stating the following:

$$\Pr\left[\underbrace{\texttt{AMQ\_add}\ x\ (hs, s)}_{(a),(b)} \ \triangleright\ \underbrace{\texttt{AMQ\_addm}\ xs}_{(c)} \ \triangleright\ \underbrace{\texttt{AMQ\_query}\ x}_{(d),(e)} \right] = 1 \qquad (1)$$

As with most of our probabilistic proofs, we begin by applying normalisation Pattern 1 to reduce the computation into our normal form:

$$\sum_{\iota s_0, hs_0} \sum_{s_0} \sum_{s_1, hs_1} \sum_{\iota s_2, hs_2} \left(\begin{array}{ll} (a)\ \Pr\left[\texttt{AMQHash\_hash}\ x\ hs = (\iota s_0, hs_0)\right] & \times \\ (b)\ \Pr\left[\texttt{ret}\ (\texttt{AMQ\_add\_internal}\ s\ \iota s_0) = s_0\right] \times \\ (c)\ \Pr\left[\texttt{AMQ\_addm}\ xs\ (s_0, hs_0) = (s_1, hs_1)\right] & \times \\ (d)\ \Pr\left[\texttt{AMQHash\_hash}\ x\ hs_1 = (\iota s_2, hs_2)\right] & \times \\ (e)\ \Pr\left[\texttt{ret}\ (\texttt{AMQ\_query\_internal}\ s_1\ \iota s_2)\right] \end{array} \right)$$

We label the factors to be rewritten as (a)–(e) for the convenience of the presentation, indicating the correspondence to the components of the statement (1). From here, as all values are assumed to be unseen, we can use Property 1 in conjunction with the sequencing Pattern 2 to reduce factors (a) and (b) as follows:

$$\sum_{\iota s_0} \sum_{s_1,hs_1} \sum_{\iota s_2,hs_2} \begin{pmatrix} (a) \; p_{\text{hash}} & \times \\ (c) \; \Pr\left[\texttt{AMQ\_addm} \; xs \; ((s \leftarrow_{\text{add}} \iota s_0),(hs \leftarrow_{\text{hash}} (x:\iota s_0))) = (s_1,hs_1)\right] & \times \\ (d) \; \Pr\left[\texttt{AMQHash\_hash} \; x \; hs_1 = (\iota s_2, hs_2)\right] & \times \\ (e) \; \Pr\left[\texttt{AMQ\_query\_internal} \; s_1 \; \iota s_2\right] & \end{pmatrix}$$

Here, p_{hash} is the probability from the statement of Property 1. We also introduce the notations $s \leftarrow_{\text{add}} \iota s_0$ and $hs \leftarrow_{\text{hash}} (x:\iota s_0)$ to denote the deterministic operations $\texttt{AMQ\_add\_internal}$ and $\texttt{AMQHash\_add\_internal}$ respectively. Then, using Pattern 3 for decomposing plausible outcomes, it is possible to separately show that any plausible hs_1 from $\texttt{AMQ\_addm}$ must map x to ιs_0, as hash operations preserve mappings. Combining this fact with Lemma 3 (plausible sequencing) and Hash Consistency (Property 2), we can derive that the execution of $\texttt{AMQHash\_hash}$ on x in (d) must return ιs_0, simplifying the summation even further:

$$\sum_{\iota s_0} \sum_{s_1,hs_1} \begin{pmatrix} (a) \; p_{\text{hash}} & \times \\ (c) \; \Pr\left[\texttt{AMQ\_addm} \; xs \; ((s \leftarrow_{\text{add}} \iota s_0),(hs \leftarrow_{\text{hash}} (x:\iota s_0))) = (s_1,hs_1)\right] & \times \\ (e) \; \Pr\left[\texttt{AMQ\_query\_internal} \; s_1 \; \iota s_0\right] & \end{pmatrix}$$

Finally, as s_1 is a plausible outcome from $\texttt{AMQ\_addm}$ called on $s \leftarrow_{\text{add}} \iota s_0$, we can then show, using Property 4 (query preservation), that querying for ιs_0 on s_1 must succeed. Therefore, the entire summation reduces to the summation of distributions over their support, which can be trivially shown to be 1.

6 Overview of the Development and More Case Studies

The Ceramist mechanised framework is implemented as library in Coq proof assistant [24]. It consists of three main sub-parts, each handling a different aspect of constructing and reasoning about AMQs: (*i*) a library of *bounded-length data structures*, enhancing MathComp's [31] support for reasoning about finite sequences with varying lengths; (*ii*) a library of *probabilistic computations*, extending the infotheo probability theory library [2] with definitions of deeply embedded probabilistic computations and a collection of tactics and lemmas on summations described in Sect. 5; and (*iii*) the *AMQ interfaces and instances* representing the core of our framework described in Sect. 4.

Alongside these core components, we also include four specific case studies to provide concrete examples of how the library can be used for practical verification. Our first two case studies are the mechanisation of the Bloom filter [6] and the Counting Bloom filter [46], as discussed earlier. In proving the false-positive rate for Bloom

Section	Size (LOC)	
	Specifications	Proofs
Bounded containers	286	1051
Notation (Sect. 3.1)	77	0
Summations (Sect. 5)	742	2122
Hash operations (Sect. 4.1)	201	568
AMQ framework (Sect. 4.2)	594	695
Bloom filter (Sect. 3.2)	322	1088
Counting BF (Sect. 4.4, [25, Sect. A])	312	674
Quotient filter (Sect. 6.1)	197	633
Blocked AMQ (Sect. 6.2)	269	522

filters, we follow the proof by Bose *et al.* [8], also providing the first mechanised proof of the closed expression for Stirling numbers of the second kind. Our third case study provides mechanised verification of the quotient filter [5]. Our final case study is a mechanisation of the Blocked AMQ—a family of AMQs with a common aggregation strategy. We instantiate this abstract structure with each of the prior AMQs, obtaining, among others, a mechanisation of Blocked Bloom filters [40]. The sizes of each library component, along with the references to the sections that describe them, are given in the table above.

Of particular note, in effect due to the extensive proof reuse supported by Ceramist, the proof size for each of our case-studies *progressively decreases*, with around a 50% reduction in the size from our initial proofs of Bloom filters to the final case-studies of different Blocked AMQs instances.

6.1 Quotient Filter

A quotient filter [5] is a type of AMQ data structure optimised to be more cache-friendly than other typical AMQs. In contrast to the relatively simple internal vector-based states of the Bloom filters, a quotient filter works by internally maintaining a hash table to track its elements.

The internal operations of a quotient filter build upon a fundamental notion of *quotienting*, whereby a single p-bit hash outcome is split into two by treating the upper q-bits (the quotient) and the lower r-bits (the remainder) separately. Whenever an element is inserted or queried, the item is first hashed over a single hash function and then the output quotiented. The operations of the quotient filter then work by using the q-bit quotient to specify a bucket of the hash table, and the r-bit remainder as a proxy for the element, such that a query for an element will succeed if its remainder can be found in the corresponding bucket.

A false positive can occur if the outputs of the hash function happen to exactly collide for two particular values (collisions in just the quotient or remainder are not sufficient to produce an incorrect result). Therefore, it is then possible to reduce the event of a false positive in a quotient filter to the event that at least one in several draws from a uniform distribution produces a particular value. We encode quotient filters by instantiating the AMQHash interface from Sect. 4.1 with a *single* hash function, rather than a vector of hash functions, which is used by the Bloom filter variants (Sect. 2). The size of the output of this hashing operation is defined to be $2^q * 2^r$, and a corresponding quotienting operation is defined by taking the quotient and remainder from dividing the hash output by 2^q. With this encoding, we are able to provide a mechanised proof of the false positive rate for the quotient filter implemented using p-bit hash as being:

Theorem 9 (Quotient filter False Positive Rate). *For a hash-function hs, after inserting a series of l unseen distinct values xs into an empty quotient filter qf, for any unseen $y \notin xs$, the probability of a query $y \in_? qf$ for y returning true is given by:* $\Pr\left[\mathtt{qf\_addm}\ xs\ (hs, \mathtt{qf\_new}) \triangleright \mathtt{qf\_query}\ y\right] = 1 - \left(1 - \frac{1}{2^p}\right)^l$.

6.2   Blocked AMQ

Blocked Bloom filters [40] are a cache-efficient variant of Bloom filters where a single instance of the structure is composed of a vector of m independent Bloom filters, using an additional "meta"-hash operation to distribute values between the elements. When querying for a particular element, the meta-hash operation would first be consulted to select a particular instance to delegate the query to.

While prior research has only focused on applying this blocking design to Bloom filters, we found that this strategy is in fact generic over the choice of AMQ, allowing us to formalise an abstract Blocked AMQ structure, and later instantiate it for particular choices of "basic" AMQs. As such, this data structure highlights the scalability of Ceramist *wrt.* composition of programs and proofs.

Our encoding of Blocked AMQs within Ceramist is done via means of two higher-order modules as in Fig. 1: (i) a *multiplexed-hash* component, parameterised over an arbitrary hashing operation, and (ii) a *blocked-state* component, parameterised over some instantiation of the AMQ interface. The multiplexed hash captures the relation between the meta-hash and the hashing operations of the basic AMQ, randomly multiplexing hashes to particular hashing operations of the sub-components. We construct a multiplexed-hash as a composition of the hashing operation H used by the AMQ in each of the m blocks, and a meta-hash function to distribute queries between the m blocks. The state of this structure is defined as pairing of m states of the hashing operation H, one for each of the m blocks of the AMQ, with the state of the meta-hash function. As such, hashing a value v with this operation produces a *pair* of type $(\mathbb{Z}_m, \mathtt{Value})$, where the first element is obtained by hashing v over the meta-hash to select a particular block, and the second element is produced by hashing v again over the hash operation H for this selected block. With this custom hashing operation, the state component of the Blocked AMQ is defined as sequence of m states of the AMQ, one for each block. The insertion and query operations work on the output of the multiplexed hash by using the first element to select a particular element of the sequence, and then use the second element as the value to be inserted into or queried on this selected state.

Having instantiated the data structure as described above, we proved the following abstract result about the false positive rate for blocked AMQs:

Theorem 10 (Blocked AMQ False Positive Rate). *For any AMQ A with a false positive rate after inserting l elements estimated as $f(l)$, for a multiplexed hash-function hs, after having inserted l distinct values xs, all unseen in hs, into an empty Blocked AMQ filter bf composed of m instances of A, for any unseen $y \notin xs$, the probability of a subsequent query $y \in_? bf$ for y returning* true *is given by:* $\Pr\left[\mathtt{BA\_addm}\ xs\ (hs, \mathtt{BA\_new}) \rhd \mathtt{BA\_query}\ y\right] = \sum_{i=0}^{l} \binom{l}{i}(\frac{1}{m})^i(1 - \frac{1}{m})^{l-i} f(i).$

We instantiated this interface with each of the previously defined AMQ structures, obtaining the Blocked Bloom filters, Counting Blocked Bloom filters and Blocked Quotient filter along with proofs of similar properties for them, for free.

7   Discussion and Related Work

Proofs About AMQs. While there has been a wealth of prior research into approximate membership query structures and their probabilistic bounds, the prevalence of paper-and-pencil proofs has meant that errors in analysis have gone unnoticed and propagated throughout the literature.

The most notable example is in Bloom's original paper [6], wherein dependencies between setting bits lead to an incorrect formulation of the bound (equation (17)), which has since been repeated in several papers [9,14,15,33] and even textbooks [34]. While this error was later identified by Bose *et al.* [8], their own analysis was also marred by an error in their definition of Stirling numbers of the second kind, resulting in yet another incorrect bound, corrected two years later by Christensen *et al.* [10], who avoided the error by eliding Stirling numbers altogether, and deriving the bound directly. Furthermore, despite these corrections, many subsequent papers [13,28–30,40,41,46] still use Bloom's original incorrect bounds. For example, in Putze *et al.* [40]'s analysis of a Blocked Bloom filter, they derive an incorrect bound on the false positive rate by assuming that the false positive of the constituent Bloom filters are given by Bloom's bound. While the Ceramist is the first development that, to the best of our knowledge, provides a mechanised proof of the probabilistic properties of Bloom filters, prior research has considered their deterministic properties. In particular, Blot *et al.* [7] provided a mechanised proof of the absence of false negatives for their implementation of a Bloom filter.

Mechanically Verified Probabilistic Algorithms. Past research has also focused on the verification of probabilistic algorithms, and our work builds on the results and ideas from several of these developments. The ALEA library tackles the task of proving properties of probabilistic algorithms [3], however in contrast to our deep embedding of computations, ALEA uses a shallow embedding through a Giry monad [20], representing probabilistic programs as measures over their outcomes. ALEA also axiomatises a custom type to represent reals between 0 and 1, which means they must independently prove any properties on reals they use, increasing the proof effort. The Foundational Cryptography Framework (FCF) [39] was developed for proving the security properties of cryptographic programs and provides an encoding of probabilistic algorithms. Rather than developing tooling for solving probabilistic obligations, their library proves probabilistic properties by reducing them to standard programs with known distributions. While this strategy follows the structure of cryptographic proofs, the simple tooling makes directly proving probabilistic bounds challenging. Tassarotti *et al.*'s Polaris [47] library for reasoning about probabilistic concurrent algorithms, also uses the same reduction strategy, and thereby inherits the same issues with proving standalone bounds. Hölzl considers mechanised verification of probabilistic programs in Isabelle/HOL [27], using a similar composition of probability and computation monads to encode probabilistic programs. However, his construction defines the semantics of programs as infinite Markov chains represented as a co-inductive streams, making it unsuitable for capturing terminating programs. Our previous effort on mechanising the probabilistic properties of blockchains also considered the encoding of probabilistic computations in Coq [23]. While that work also relied on infotheo's probability monad, it only considered a restricted form of probabilistic properties, and did not deliver reusable tooling for the task.

Proofs of Differential Privacy. A popular motivation for reasoning about probabilistic computations is for the purposes of demonstrating differential privacy. Barthe *et al.*'s CertiPriv framework [4] extends ALEA to support reasoning using a Probabilistic Relational Hoare logic, and uses this fragment to prove probabilistic non-interference arguments. More recently, Barthe *et al.* [44] have developed a mechanisation that supports a more general coupling between distributions. Given the focus on relational properties, these developments are not suited for proving explicit numerical bounds as Ceramist is.

8   Conclusion

The key properties of Approximate Membership Query structures are inherently probabilistic. Formalisations of those properties are frequently stated incorrectly, due to the complexity of the underlying proofs. We have demonstrated the feasibility of conducting such proofs in a machine-assisted framework. The main ingredients of our approach are a principled decomposition of structure definitions and proof automation for manipulating probabilistic sums. Together, they enable scalable and reusable mechanised proofs about a wide range of AMQs.

Acknowledgements. We thank Georges Gonthier, Karl Palmskog, George Pîrlea, Prateek Saxena, and Anton Trunov for their comments on the prelimiary versions of the paper. We thank the CPP'20 referees (especially Reviewer D) for pointing out that the formulation of the closed form for Stirling numbers of the second kind, which we adopted as an axiom from the work by Bose *et al.* [8] who used it in the proof of Theorem 4, implied False. This discovery has forced us to prove the closed form statement in Coq from the first principles, thus getting rid of the corresponding axiom and eliminating all potentially erroneous assumptions. Finally, we are grateful to the CAV'20 reviewers for their feedback.

Ilya Sergey's work has been supported by the grant of Singapore NRF National Satellite of Excellence in Trustworthy Software Systems (NSoE-TSS) and by Crystal Centre at NUS School of Computing.

References

1. Affeldt, R., Hagiwara, M.: Formalization of Shannon's theorems in SSReflect-Coq. In: Beringer, L., Felty, A. (eds.) ITP 2012. LNCS, vol. 7406, pp. 233–249. Springer, Heidelberg (2012). https://doi.org/10.1007/978-3-642-32347-8_16

2. Affeldt, R., Hagiwara, M., Sénizergues, J.: Formalization of Shannon's theorems. J. Autom. Reason. **53**(1), 63–103 (2014)

3. Audebaud, P., Paulin-Mohring, C.: Proofs of randomized algorithms in Coq. Sci. Comput. Program. **74**(8), 568–589 (2009)

4. Barthe, G., Köpf, B., Olmedo, F., Béguelin, S.Z.: Probabilistic relational reasoning for differential privacy. In: POPL, pp. 97–110. ACM (2012)
5. Bender, M.A., et al.: Don't thrash: how to cache your hash on flash. PVLDB **5**(11), 1627–1637 (2012)
6. Bloom, B.H.: Space/time trade-offs in hash coding with allowable errors. Commun. ACM **13**(7), 422–426 (1970)
7. Blot, A., Dagand, P.É., Lawall, J.: From sets to bits in Coq. In: Kiselyov, O., King, A. (eds.) FLOPS 2016. LNCS, vol. 9613, pp. 12–28. Springer, Cham (2016). https://doi.org/10.1007/978-3-319-29604-3_2
8. Bose, P., et al.: On the false-positive rate of bloom filters. Inf. Process. Lett. **108**(4), 210–213 (2008)
9. Broder, A.Z., Mitzenmacher, M.: Survey: network applications of bloom filters: a survey. Internet Math. **1**(4), 485–509 (2003)
10. Christensen, K., Roginsky, A., Jimeno, M.: A new analysis of the false positive rate of a bloom filter. Inf. Process. Lett. **110**(21), 944–949 (2010)
11. Coq Development Team. The Coq Proof Assistant Reference Manual - Version 8.10, January 2020. http://coq.inria.fr/
12. Cormode, G., Muthukrishnan, S.: An improved data stream summary: the count-min sketch and its applications. J. Algorithms **55**(1), 58–75 (2005)
13. Debnath, B., Sengupta, S., Li, J., Lilja, D.J., Du, D.H.C.: BloomFlash: bloom filter on flash-based storage. In: 2011 31st International Conference on Distributed Computing Systems, pp. 635–644. IEEE (2011)
14. Dharmapurikar, S., Krishnamurthy, P., Sproull, T.S., Lockwood, J.W.: Deep packet inspection using parallel bloom filters. IEEE Micro **24**(1), 52–61 (2004)
15. Dharmapurikar, S., Krishnamurthy, P., Taylor, D.E.: Longest prefix matching using Bloom filters. IEEE/ACM Trans. Netw. **14**(2), 397–409 (2006)
16. Erlingsson, Ú., Pihur, V., Korolova, A.: RAPPOR: randomized aggregatable privacy-preserving ordinal response. In: CCS, pp. 1054–1067. ACM (2014)
17. Apache Software Foundation. Apache cassandra documentation: bloom filters (2016). http://cassandra.apache.org/doc/4.0/operating/bloom_filters.html
18. Gerbet, T., Kumar, A., Lauradoux, C.: The power of evil choices in bloom filters. In: DSN, pp. 101–112. IEEE Computer Society (2015)
19. Gervais, A., Capkun, S., Karame, G.O., Gruber,D.: On the privacy provisions of Bloom filters in lightweight bitcoin clients. In: ACSAC, pp. 326–335. ACM (2014)
20. Giry, M.: A categorical approach to probability theory. In: Banaschewski, B. (ed.) Categorical Aspects of Topology and Analysis. LNM, vol. 915, pp. 68–85. Springer, Heidelberg (1982). https://doi.org/10.1007/BFb0092872
21. Gonthier, G., Mahboubi, A., Tassi, E.: A small scale reflection extension for the Coq system. Technical report 6455, Microsoft Research - Inria Joint Centre (2009)
22. Goodwin, B., et al.: BitFunnel: revisiting signatures for search. In: SIGIR, pp. 605–614. ACM (2017)
23. Gopinathan, K., Sergey, I.: Towards mechanising probabilistic properties of a blockchain. In: CoqPL 2019: The Fifth International Workshop on Coq for Programming Languages (2019)
24. Gopinathan, K., Sergey, I.: Ceramist: verified hash-based approximate membership structures, 2020. CAV 2020 Artefact. https://doi.org/10.5281/zenodo.3749474. https://github.com/certichain/ceramist
25. Gopinathan, K., Sergey, I.: Certifying certainty and uncertainty in approximate membership query structures - extended version. CoRR, abs/2004.13312 (2020). http://arxiv.org/abs/2004.13312

26. Graham, R.L., Knuth, D.E., Patashnik, O.: Concrete Mathematics: A Foundation for Computer Science, 2nd edn. Addison-Wesley, Boston (1994)
27. Hölzl, J.: Markov processes in Isabelle/HOL. In: CPP, pp. 100–111. ACM (2017)
28. Jing, C.: Application and research on weighted bloom filter and bloom filter in web cache. In: 2009 Second Pacific-Asia Conference on Web Mining and Web-based Application, pp. 187–191 (2009)
29. Li, Y.-Z.: Memory efficient parallel bloom filters for string matching. In: 2009 International Conference on Networks Security, Wireless Communications and Trusted Computing, vol. 1, pp. 485–488 (2009)
30. Lim, H., Lee, J., Yim, C.: Complement bloom filter for identifying true positiveness of a bloom filter. IEEE Commun. Lett. **19**(11), 1905–1908 (2015)
31. Assia Mahboubi and Enrico Tassi. Mathematical Components (2017). https://math-comp.github.io/mcb
32. Martin-Dorel, É., Soloviev, S.: A formal study of boolean games with random formulas as payoff functions. In: TYPES 2016. LIPIcs, vol. 97, pp. 14:1–14:22. Schloss Dagstuhl - Leibniz-Zentrum fuer Informatik (2018)
33. Mitzenmacher, M.: Compressed bloom filters. IEEE/ACM Trans. Netw. **10**(5), 604–612 (2002)
34. Mitzenmacher, M., Upfal, E.: Probability and Computing: Randomized Algorithms and Probabilistic Analysis, 2nd edn. Cambridge University Press, Cambridge (2017). ISBN 978-1-107-15488-9
35. Nakamoto, S.: Bitcoin: a peer-to-peer electronic cash system (2008). http://bitcoin.org/bitcoin.pdf
36. Naor, M., Yogev, E.: Bloom filters in adversarial environments. ACM Trans. Algorithms **15**(3), 35:1–35:30 (2019)
37. Nasre, R., Rajan, K., Govindarajan, R., Khedker, U.P.: Scalable context-sensitive points-to analysis using multi-dimensional bloom filters. In: Hu, Z. (ed.) APLAS 2009. LNCS, vol. 5904, pp. 47–62. Springer, Heidelberg (2009). https://doi.org/10.1007/978-3-642-10672-9_6
38. Pagh, A., Pagh, R., Rao, S.S.: An optimal bloom filter replacement. In: SODA, pp. 823–829. SIAM (2005)
39. Petcher, A., Morrisett, G.: The foundational cryptography framework. In: Focardi, R., Myers, A. (eds.) POST 2015. LNCS, vol. 9036, pp. 53–72. Springer, Heidelberg (2015). https://doi.org/10.1007/978-3-662-46666-7_4
40. Putze, F., Sanders, P., Singler, J.: Cache-, hash-, and space-efficient bloom filters. ACM J. Exp. Algorithmics **14**, 108–121 (2009)
41. Qiao, Y., Li, T., Chen, S.: One memory access Bloom filters and their generalization. In: INFOCOM, pp. 1745–1753. IEEE (2011)
42. Ramsey, N., Pfeffer, A.: Stochastic lambda calculus and monads of probability distributions. In: POPL, pp. 154–165. ACM (2002)
43. Rush, N.: ETH goes bloom: filling up Ethereum's bloom filters (2018). https://medium.com/@naterush1997/eth-goes-bloom-filling-up-ethereums-bloom-filters-68d4ce237009
44. Strub, P.-Y., Sato, T., Hsu, J., Espitau, T., Barthe, G.: Relational ⋆-liftings for differential privacy. Log. Methods Comput. Sci. **15**(4), 18:1–18:32 (2019)
45. Talbot, J.: What are Bloom filters? (2015). https://blog.medium.com/what-are-bloom-filters-1ec2a50c68ff
46. Tarkoma, S., Rothenberg, C.E., Lagerspetz, E.: Theory and practice of bloom filters for distributed systems. IEEE Commun. Surv. Tutor. **14**(1), 131–155 (2012)
47. Tassarotti, J., Harper, R.: A separation logic for concurrent randomized programs. PACMPL **3**(POPL), 64:1–64:30 (2019)

Global PAC Bounds for Learning Discrete Time Markov Chains

Hugo Bazille[1], Blaise Genest[1], Cyrille Jegourel[2(✉)], and Jun Sun[3]

[1] Univ Rennes, CNRS & Rennes 1, Rennes, France
{hbazille,bgenest}@irisa.fr
[2] Singapore University of Technology and Design, Singapore, Singapore
cyrille.jegourel@gmail.com
[3] Singapore Management University, Singapore, Singapore
junsun@smu.edu.sg

Abstract. Learning models from observations of a system is a powerful tool with many applications. In this paper, we consider learning Discrete Time Markov Chains (DTMC), with different methods such as *frequency estimation* or *Laplace smoothing*. While models learnt with such methods converge asymptotically towards the exact system, a more practical question in the realm of trusted machine learning is how accurate a model learnt with a limited time budget is. Existing approaches provide bounds on how close the model is to the original system, in terms of bounds on *local* (transition) probabilities, which has unclear implication on the *global* behavior.

In this work, we provide *global bounds on the error* made by such a learning process, in terms of global behaviors formalized using *temporal logic*. More precisely, we propose a learning process ensuring a bound on the error in the probabilities of these properties. While such learning process cannot exist for the full LTL logic, we provide one ensuring a bound that is uniform over all the formulas of CTL. Further, given one time-to-failure property, we provide an improved learning algorithm. Interestingly, frequency estimation is sufficient for the latter, while Laplace smoothing is needed to ensure non-trivial uniform bounds for the full CTL logic.

1 Introduction

Discrete-Time Markov Chains (DTMC) are commonly used in model checking to model the behavior of stochastic systems [3,4,7,26]. A DTMC is described by a set of states and transition probabilities between these states. The main issue with modeling stochastic systems using DTMCs is to obtain the transition probabilities. One appealing approach to overcome this issue is to observe the system and to *learn automatically* these transition probabilities [8,30], e.g., using frequency estimation or Laplace (or additive) smoothing [12]. Frequency

---

All authors have contributed equally.

S. K. Lahiri and C. Wang (Eds.): CAV 2020, LNCS 12225, pp. 304–326, 2020.
https://doi.org/10.1007/978-3-030-53291-8_17

estimation works by observing a long run of the system and estimating each individual transition by its empirical frequency. However, in this case, the unseen transitions are estimated as zeros. Once the probability of a transition is set to zero, the probability to reach a state could be tremendously changed, e.g., from 1 to 0 if the probability of this transition in the system is small but non-zero. To overcome this problem, when the set of transitions with non-zero probability is known (but not their probabilities), Laplace smoothing assigns a positive probability to the unseen transitions, i.e., by adding a small quantity both to the numerator and the denominator of the estimate used in frequency estimation. Other smoothing methods exist, such as Good-Turing [15] and Kneser-Sey estimations [7], notably used in natural language processing. Notwithstanding smoothing generates estimation biases, all these methods converge asymptotically to the exact transition probabilities.

In practice, however, there is often limited budget in observing and learning from the system, and the validity of the learned model is in question. In trusted machine learning, it is thus crucial to measure how the learned model differs from the original system and to provide practical guidelines (e.g., on the number of observations) to guarantee some control of their divergence.

Comparing two Markov processes is a common problem that relies on a notion of divergence. Most existing approaches focus on deviations between the probabilities of local transitions (e.g., [5,10,27]). However, a single deviation in a transition probability between the original system and the learned model may lead to large differences in their global behaviors, even when no transitions are overlooked, as shown in our example 1. For instance, the probability of reaching certain state may be magnified by paths which go through the same deviated transition many times. It is thus important to use a measure that quantifies the differences over global behaviors, rather than simply checking whether the differences between the individual transition probabilities are low enough.

Technically, the knowledge of a lower bound on the transition probabilities is often assumed [1,14]. While it is a soft assumption in many cases, such as when all transition probabilities are large enough, it is less clear how to obtain such a lower bound in other cases, such as when a very unlikely transition exists (e.g., a very small error probability). We show how to handle this in several cases: learning a Markov chain accurate w.r.t. this error rate, or learning a Markov chain accurate over all its global behaviors, which is possible if we know the underlying structure of the system (e.g., because we designed it, although we do not know the precise transition probabilities which are governed by uncertain forces). For the latter, we define a new concept, namely *conditioning* of a DTMC.

In this work, we model global behaviors using temporal logics. We consider Linear Temporal Logic (LTL) [24] and Computational Tree Logic (CTL) [11]. Agreeing on all formulas of LTL means that the first order behaviors of the system and the model are the same, while agreeing on CTL means that the system and the model are bisimilar [2]. Our goal is to provide stopping rules in the learning process of DTMCs that provides Probably Approximately Correct (PAC) bounds on the error in probabilities of every property in the logic between the model and the system. In Sect. 2, we recall useful notions on DTMCs and PAC-learning. We point out related works in Sect. 3. Our main contributions are as follows:

- In Sect. 4, we show that it is impossible to learn a DTMC accurate for all LTL formulas, by adapting a result from [13].
- We provide in Sect. 6 a learning process bounding the difference in probability *uniformly over all CTL properties*. To do so, we use Laplace smoothing, and we provide rationale on choosing the smoothing parameter.
- For the particular case of a time-to-failure property, notably used to compute the mean time between failures of critical systems (see e.g., [25]), we provide tighter bounds in Sect. 5, based on frequency estimation.

In Sect. 4, we formally state the problem and the specification that the learning process must fulfill. We also show our first contribution: the impossibility of learning a DTMC, accurate for all LTL formulas. Nevertheless, we prove in Sect. 5 our second contribution: the existence of a global bound for the time-to-failure properties, notably used to compute the mean time between failures of critical systems (see e.g., [25]) and provide an improved learning process, based on frequency estimation. In Sect. 6, we present our main contribution: a global bound guaranteeing that the original system and a model learned by Laplace smoothing have similar behaviors for all the formulas in CTL. We show that the error bound that we provide on the probabilities of properties is close to optimal. We evaluate our approach in Sect. 7 and conclude in Sect. 8.

2 Background

In this section, we introduce the notions and notations used throughout the paper. A stochastic system $\mathcal{S}$ is interpreted as a set of interacting components in which the state is determined randomly with respect to a global probability measure described below.

Definition 1 (Discrete-Time Markov Chains). *A Discrete-Time Markov Chain is a triple* $\mathcal{M} = (S, \mu, A)$ *where:*

- *S is a finite set of states;*
- *$\mu : S \to [0, 1]$ is an initial probability distribution over S;*
- *$A : S \times S \to [0, 1]$ is a transition probability matrix, such that for every $s \in S$,* $\sum_{s' \in S} A(s, s') = 1$.

We denote by m the cardinal of S and $A = (a_{ij})_{1 \le i,j \le m} = (A(i, j))_{1 \le i,j \le m}$ the probability matrix. Figures 1 and 2 show the graph of two DTMCs over 3 states $\{s_1, s_2, s_3\}$ (with $\mu(s_1) = 1$). A run is an infinite sequence $\omega = s_0 s_1 \cdots$ and a path is a finite sequence $\omega = s_0 \cdots s_l$ such that $\mu(s_0) > 0$ and $A(s_i, s_{i+1}) > 0$ for all i, $0 \le i \le l$. The length $|\omega|$ of a path ω is its number of transitions.

The cylinder set of ω, denoted $C(\omega)$, consists of all the runs starting by a path ω. Markov chain $\mathcal{M}$ underlies a probability space $(\Omega, \mathcal{F}, \mathbb{P})$, where Ω is the

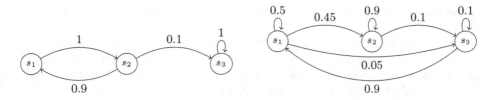

Fig. 1. An example of DTMC $\mathcal{M}_1$ **Fig. 2.** DTMC $\mathcal{M}_2$

set of all runs from $\mathcal{M}$; $\mathcal{F}$ is the sigma-algebra generated by all the cylinders $C(\omega)$ and $\mathbb{P}$ is the unique probability measure [32] such that $\mathbb{P}(C(s_0 \cdots s_l)) = \mu(s_0) \prod_{i=1}^{l} A(s_{i-1}, s_i)$. For simplicity, we assume a unique initial state s_0 and denote $\mathbb{P}(\omega) = \mathbb{P}(C(\omega))$. Finally, we sometimes use the notation $\mathbb{P}_i^A$ to emphasize that the probability distribution is parameterized by the probability matrix A, and the starting state is i.

2.1 PAC-Learning for Properties

To analyze the behavior of a system, properties are specified in temporal logic (e.g., LTL or CTL, respectively introduced in [24] and [11]). Given a logic $\mathcal{L}$ and φ a property of $\mathcal{L}$, decidable in finite time, we denote $\omega \models \varphi$ if a path ω satisfies φ. Let $z : \Omega \times \mathcal{L} \rightarrow \{0, 1\}$ be the function that assigns 1 to a path ω if $\omega \models \varphi$ and 0 otherwise. In what follows, we assume that we have a procedure that draws path ω with respect to $\mathbb{P}^A$ and outputs $z(\omega, \varphi)$. Further, we denote $\gamma(A, \varphi)$ the probability that a path drawn with respect to $\mathbb{P}^A$ satisfies φ. We omit the property or the matrix in the notation when it is clear from the context. Finally, note that the behavior of $z(., \varphi)$ can be modeled as a Bernoulli random variable Z_φ parameterized by the mean value $\gamma(A, \varphi)$.

Probably Approximately Correct (PAC) learning [28] is a framework for mathematical analysis of machine learning. Given $\varepsilon > 0$ and $0 < \delta < 1$, we say that a property φ of $\mathcal{L}$ is PAC-learnable if there is an algorithm $\mathcal{A}$ such that, given a sample of n paths drawn according to the procedure, with probability of at least $1-\delta$, $\mathcal{A}$ outputs in polynomial time (in $1/\varepsilon$ and $1/\delta$) an approximation of the average value for Z_φ close to its exact value, up to an error less than or equal to ε. Formally, φ is PAC-learnable if and only if $\mathcal{A}$ outputs an approximation $\hat{\gamma}$ such that:

$$\mathbb{P}(|\gamma - \hat{\gamma}| > \varepsilon) \leq \delta \tag{1}$$

Moreover, if the above statement for algorithm $\mathcal{A}$ is true for every property in $\mathcal{L}$, we say that $\mathcal{A}$ is a PAC-learning algorithm for $\mathcal{L}$.

2.2 Monte-Carlo Estimation and Algorithm of Chen

Given a sample W of n paths drawn according to $\mathbb{P}^A$ until φ is satisfied or violated (for φ such that with probability 1, φ is eventually satisfied or violated), the crude Monte-Carlo estimator, denoted $\hat{\gamma}_W(A, \varphi)$, of the mean value for the random variable Z_φ is given by the empirical frequency: $\hat{\gamma}_W(A, \varphi) = \frac{1}{n}\sum_{i=1}^{n} z(\omega_i) \approx \gamma(A, \varphi)$.

The Okamoto inequality [23] (also called the Chernoff bound in the literature) is often used to guarantee that the deviation between a Monte-Carlo estimator $\hat{\gamma}_W$ and the exact value γ by more than $\varepsilon > 0$ is bounded by a predefined confidence parameter δ. However, several sequential algorithms have been recently proposed to guarantee the same confidence and accuracy with fewer samples[1]. In what follows, we use the Massart bound [22], implemented in the algorithm of Chen [6].

Theorem 1 (Chen bound). *Let $\varepsilon > 0$, δ such that $0 < \delta < 1$ and $\hat{\gamma}_W$ be the crude Monte-Carlo estimator, based on n samples, of probability γ.*
If $n \geq \frac{2}{\varepsilon^2} \log\left(\frac{2}{\delta}\right) \left[\frac{1}{4} - (|\frac{1}{2} - \hat{\gamma}_W| - \frac{2}{3}\varepsilon)^2\right]$,

$$\mathbb{P}(|\gamma - \hat{\gamma}_W| > \varepsilon) \leq \delta.$$

To ease the readability, we write $n_{\text{succ}} = \sum_{i=1}^{n} z(\omega_i)$ and $H(n, n_{\text{succ}}, \epsilon, \delta) = \frac{2}{\varepsilon^2} \log\left(\frac{2}{\delta}\right) \left[\frac{1}{4} - (|\frac{1}{2} - \hat{\gamma}_W| - \frac{2}{3}\varepsilon)^2\right]$. When it is clear from the context, we only write $H(n)$. Then, the algorithm $\mathcal{A}$ that stops sampling as soon as $n \geq H(n)$ and outputs a crude Monte-Carlo estimator for $\gamma(A, \varphi)$ is a PAC-learning algorithm for φ. The condition over n is called the stopping criteria of the algorithm. As far as we know, this algorithm requires fewer samples than the other sequential algorithms (see e.g., [18]). Note that the estimation of a probability close to $1/2$ likely requires more samples since $H(n)$ is maximized in $\hat{\gamma}_W = 1/2$.

3   Related Work

Our work shares similar statistical results (see Sect. 2.3) with Statistical Model Checking (SMC) [32]. However, the context and the outputs are different. SMC is a simulation-based approach that aims to estimate one probability for a given property [9,29], within acceptable margins of error and confidence [17,18,33]. A challenge in SMC is posed by unbounded properties (e.g., fairness) since the sampled executions are finite. Some algorithms have been proposed to handle unbounded properties but they require the knowledge of the minimal probability transition of the system [1,14], which we avoid. While this restriction is light in many contexts, such as when every state and transition appears with a sufficiently high probability, contexts where probabilities are unknown and some are very small seems much harder to handle. In the following, we propose 2 solutions not requiring this assumption. The first one is the closest to SMC: we learn a Markov chain accurate for a given time-to-error property, and it does not require knowledge on the Markov chain. The second one is much more ambitious than SMC as it learns a Markov chain accurate for *all* its global behaviors, formalized as all properties of a temporal logic; it needs the assumption that the set

---

[1] We recall the Okamoto-Chernoff bound in the extended version (as well as the Massart bound), but we do not use it in this work.

of transitions is known, but not their probabilities nor a lower bound on them. This assumption may seem heavy, but it is reasonable for designers of systems, for which (a lower bound on) transition probabilities are not known (e.g. some error rate of components, etc).

For comparison with SMC, our final output is the (approximated) transition matrix of a DTMC rather than one (approximated) probability of a given property. This learned DTMC can be used for different purposes, e.g. as a component in a bigger model or as a simulation tool. In terms of performances, we will show that we can learn a DTMC w.r.t. a given property with the same number of samples as we need to estimate this property using SMC (see Sect. 5). That is, there is no penalty to estimate a DTMC rather than estimate one probability, and we can scale as well as SMC. In terms of expressivity, we can handle unbounded properties (e.g. fairness properties). Even better, we can learn a DTMC accurate uniformly over a possibly infinite set of properties, e.g. all formulas of CTL. This is something SMC is not designed to achieve.

Other related work can be cited: In [13], the authors investigate several distances for the estimation of the difference between DTMCs. But they do not propose algorithms for learning. In [16], the authors propose to analyze the learned model a posteriori to test whether it has some good properties. If not, then they tweak the model in order to enforce these properties. Also, several PAC-learning algorithms have been proposed for the estimation of stochastic systems [5,10] but these works focus on local transitions instead of global properties.

4   Problem Statement

In this work, we are interested to learn a DTMC model from a stochastic system S such that the behaviors of the system and the model are similar. We assume that the original system is a DTMC parameterized by a matrix A of transition probabilities. The transition probabilities are unknown, but the set of states of the DTMC is assumed to be known.

Our goal is to provide a learning algorithm $\mathcal{A}$ that guarantees an accurate estimation of S with respect to certain global properties. For that, a sampling process is defined as follows. A path (i.e., a sequence of states from s_0) of S is observed, and at steps specified by the sampling process, a reset action is performed, setting S back to its initial state s_0. Then another path is generated. This process generates a set W of paths, called traces, used to learn a matrix $\hat{A}_W$. Formally, we want to provide a learning algorithm that guarantees the following specification:

$$\mathbb{P}(\mathcal{D}(A, \hat{A}_W) > \varepsilon) \leq \delta \tag{2}$$

where $\varepsilon > 0$ and $\delta > 0$ are respectively *accuracy* and *confidence* parameters and $\mathcal{D}(A, \hat{A}_W)$ is a measure of the divergence between A and $\hat{A}_W$.

There exist several ways to specify the divergence between two transition matrices, e.g., the Kullback-Leibler divergence [19] or a distance based on a matrix norm. However, the existing notions remain heuristic because they are based on the difference between the individual probabilistic transitions of the matrix. We argue that what matters in practice is often to quantify the similarity between the global behaviors of the systems and the learned model.

In order to specify the behaviors of interest, we use a property φ or a set of properties Ψ on the set of states visited. We are interested in the difference between the probabilities of φ (i.e., the measure of the set of runs satisfying φ) with respect to A and $\hat{A}_W$. We want to ensure that this difference is less than some predefined ε with (high) probability $1 - \delta$. Hence, we define:

$$\mathcal{D}_\varphi(A, \hat{A}_W) = |\gamma(A, \varphi) - \gamma(\hat{A}_W, \varphi)| \tag{3}$$

$$\mathcal{D}_\Psi(A, \hat{A}_W) = \max_{\varphi \in \Psi}(\mathcal{D}_\varphi(A, \hat{A}_W)) \tag{4}$$

Our problem is to construct an algorithm which takes the following as inputs:

- confidence δ, $0 < \delta < 1$,
- absolute error $\varepsilon > 0$, and
- a property φ (or a set of properties Ψ),

and provides a learning procedure sampling a set W of paths, outputs $\hat{A}_W$, and terminates the sampling procedure while fulfilling Specification (2), with $\mathcal{D} = \mathcal{D}_\varphi (= \mathcal{D}_\Psi)$.

In what follows, we assume that the confidence level δ and absolute error ε are fixed. We first start with a negative result: if Ψ is the set of LTL formulas [2], such a learning process is impossible.

Theorem 2. *Given $\varepsilon > 0$, $0 < \delta < 1$, and a finite set W of paths randomly drawn with respect to a DTMC A, there is no learning strategy such that, for every LTL formula φ,*

$$\mathbb{P}(|\gamma(A, \varphi) - \gamma(\hat{A}_W, \varphi)| > \varepsilon) \leq \delta \tag{5}$$

Note that contrary to Theorem 1, the deviation in Theorem 2 is a difference between two exact probabilities (of the original system and of a learned model). The theorem holds as long as $\hat{A}_W$ and A are not strictly equal, no matter how $\hat{A}_W$ is learned. To prove this theorem, we show that, for any number of observations, we can always define a sequence of LTL properties that violates the specification above. It only exploits a single deviation in one transition. The proof, inspired by a result from [13], is given in the extended version.

Example 1. We show in this example that in general, one needs to have some knowledge on the system in order to perform PAC learning - either a positive lower bound $\ell > 0$ on the lowest probability transition, as in [1,14], or the support of transitions (but no knowledge on their probabilities), as we use in Sect. 6. Further, we show that the latter assumption does not imply the former, as even if no transitions are overlooked, the error in some reachability property can be arbitrarily close to 0.5 even with arbitrarily small error on the transition probabilities.

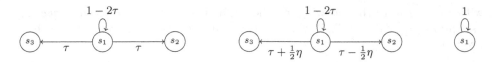

Fig. 3. Three DTMCs $A, \hat{A}, \hat{B}$ (from left to right), with $0 < \eta < 2\tau < 1$

Let us consider DTMCs $A, \hat{A}, \hat{B}$ in Fig. 3, and formula $\mathbf{F}\, s_2$ stating that s_2 is eventually reached. The probabilities to satisfy this formula in $A, \hat{A}, \hat{B}$ are respectively $\mathbb{P}^A(\mathbf{F}\, s_2) = \frac{1}{2}$, $\mathbb{P}^{\hat{A}}(\mathbf{F}\, s_2) = \frac{2\tau-\eta}{4\tau} = \frac{1}{2} - \frac{\eta}{4\tau}$ and $\mathbb{P}^{\hat{B}}(\mathbf{F}\, s_2) = 0$.

Assume that A is the real system and that $\hat{A}$ and $\hat{B}$ are DTMCs we learned from A. Obviously, one wants to avoid learning $\hat{B}$ from A, as the probability of $\mathbf{F}\, s_2$ is very different in $\hat{B}$ and in $\hat{A}$ (0 instead of 0.5). If one knows that $\tau > \ell$ for some lower bound $\ell > 0$, then one can generate enough samples from s_1 to evaluate τ with an arbitrarily small error $\frac{\eta}{2} << \ell$ on probability transitions with an arbitrarily high confidence, and in particular learn a DTMC similar to $\hat{A}$.

On the other hand, if one knows there are transitions from s_1 to s_2 and to s_3, then immediately, one does not learn DTMC $\hat{B}$, but a DTMC similar to DTMC $\hat{A}$ (using e.g. Laplace smoothing [12]). While this part is straightforward with this assumption, evaluating τ is much harder when one does not know a priori a lower bound $\ell > 0$ such that $\tau > \ell$. That is very important: while one can make sure that the error $\frac{\eta}{2}$ on probability transitions is arbitrarily small, if τ is unknown, then it could be the case that τ is as small as $\frac{\eta}{2(1-\varepsilon)} > \frac{\eta}{2}$, for a small $\varepsilon > 0$. This gives us $\mathbb{P}^{\hat{A}}(\mathbf{F}\, s_2) = \frac{1}{2} - \frac{1-\varepsilon}{2} = \frac{\varepsilon}{2}$, which is arbitrarily small, whereas $\mathbb{P}^A(\mathbf{F}\, s_2) = 0.5$, leading to a huge error in the probability to reach s_2. We work around that problem in Sect. 6 by defining and computing the *conditioning* of DTMC $\hat{A}$. In some particular cases, as the one discussed in the next section, one can avoid that altogether (actually, the conditioning in these cases is perfect (=1), and it needs not be computed explicitly).

5   Learning for a Time-to-failure Property

In this section, we focus on property φ of reaching a failure state s_F from an initial state s_0 without re-passing by the initial state, which is often used for assessing the failure rate of a system and the mean time between failures (see e.g., [25]). We assume that with probability 1, the runs eventually re-pass by s_0 or reach s_F. Also, without loss of generality, we assume that there is a unique failure state s_F in A. We denote $\gamma(A, \varphi)$ the probability, given DTMC A, of satisfying property φ, i.e., the probability of a failure between two visits of s_0.

Assume that the stochastic system $\mathcal{S}$ is observed from state s_0. Between two visits of s_0, property φ can be monitored. If s_F is observed between two instances of s_0, we say that the path $\omega = s_0 \cdot \rho \cdot s_F$ satisfies φ, with $s_0, s_F \notin \rho$. Otherwise, if s_0 is visited again from s_0, then we say that the path $\omega = s_0 \cdot \rho \cdot s_0$ violates φ, with $s_0, s_F \notin \rho$. We call *traces* paths of the form $\omega = s_0 \cdot \rho \cdot (s_0 \vee s_F)$

with $s_0, s_F \notin \rho$. In the following, we show that it is sufficient to use a *frequency estimator* to learn a DTMC which provides a good approximation for such a property.

5.1 Frequency Estimation of a DTMC

Given a set W of n traces, we denote n_{ij}^W the number of times a transition from state i to state j has occurred and n_i^W the number of times a transition has been taken from state i.

The *frequency estimator* of A is the DTMC $\hat{A}_W = (\hat{a}_{ij})_{1 \leq i,j \leq m}$ given by $\hat{a}_{ij} = \frac{n_{ij}^W}{n_i^W}$ for all i,j, with $\sum_{i=1}^m n_i^W = \sum_{i=1}^m \sum_{j=1}^m n_{ij}^W = |W|$. In other words, to learn $\hat{A}_W$, it suffices to count the number of times a transition from i to j occurred, and divide by the number of times state i has been observed. The matrix $\hat{A}_W$ is trivially a DTMC, except for states i which have not been visited. In this case, one can set $\hat{a}_{ij} = \frac{1}{m}$ for all states j and obtain a DTMC. This has no impact on the behavior of $\hat{A}_W$ as i is not reachable from s_0 in $\hat{A}_W$.

Let $\hat{A}_W$ be the matrix learned using the frequency estimator from the set W of traces, and let A be the real probabilistic matrix of the original system $\mathcal{S}$. We show that, in the case of time-to-failure properties, $\gamma(\hat{A}_W, \varphi)$ is equal to the crude Monte Carlo estimator $\hat{\gamma}_W(A, \varphi)$ induced by W.

5.2 PAC Bounds for a Time-to-failure Property

We start by stating the main result of this section, bounding the error between $\gamma(A, \varphi)$ and $\gamma(\hat{A}_W, \varphi)$:

Theorem 3. *Given a set W of n traces such that $n = \lceil H(n) \rceil$, we have:*

$$\mathbb{P}\left(|\gamma(A, \varphi) - \gamma(\hat{A}_W, \varphi)| > \varepsilon\right) \leq \delta \tag{6}$$

where $\hat{A}_W$ is the frequency estimator of A.

To prove Theorem (3), we first invoke Theorem 1 to establish:

$$\mathbb{P}\left(|\gamma(A, \varphi) - \hat{\gamma}_W(A, \varphi)| > \varepsilon\right) \leq \delta \tag{7}$$

It remains to show that $\hat{\gamma}_W(A, \varphi) = \gamma(\hat{A}_W, \varphi)$:

Proposition 1. *Given a set W of traces, $\gamma(\hat{A}_W, \varphi) = \hat{\gamma}_W(A, \varphi)$.*

It might be appealing to think that this result can be proved by induction on the size of the traces, mimicking the proof of computation of reachability probabilities by linear programming [2]. This is actually not the case. The remaining of this section is devoted to proving Proposition (1).

We first define $q_W(u)$ the number of occurrences of sequence u in the traces of W. Note that u can be a state, an individual transition or even a path. We also use the following definitions in the proof.

Definition 2 (Equivalence). *Two sets of traces W and W' are equivalent if for all $s, t \in S$, $\frac{q_W(s \cdot t)}{q_W(s)} = \frac{q_{W'}(s \cdot t)}{q_{W'}(s)}$.*

We define a set of traces W' equivalent with W, implying that $\hat{A}_W = \hat{A}_{W'}$. This set W' of traces satisfies the following:

Lemma 1. *For any set of traces W, there exists a set of traces W' such that:*

(i) W and W' are equivalent,

(ii) for all $r, s, t \in S$, $q_{W'}(r \cdot s \cdot t) = \dfrac{q_{W'}(r \cdot s) \times q_{W'}(s \cdot t)}{q_{W'}(s)}$.

The proof of Lemma 1 is provided in the extended version. In Lemma 1, (i) ensures that $\hat{A}_{W'} = \hat{A}_W$ and (ii) ensures the equality between the proportion of runs of W' passing by s and satisfying γ, denoted $\hat{\gamma}^s_{W'}$, and the probability of reaching s_F before s_0 starting from s with respect to $\hat{A}_{W'}$. Formally,

Lemma 2. *For all $s \in S$, $\mathbb{P}^{\hat{A}_{W'}}_s(\text{reach } s_f \text{ before } s_0) = \hat{\gamma}^s_{W'}$.*

Proof. Let S_0 be the set of states s with no path in $\hat{A}_{W'}$ from s to s_f without passing through s_0. For all $s \in S_0$, let $p_s = 0$. Also, let $p_{s_f} = 1$. Let $S_1 = S \setminus (S_0 \cup \{s_f\})$. Consider the system of Eq. (8) with variables $(p_s)_{s \in S_1} \in [0, 1]^{|S_1|}$:

$$\forall s \in S_1, \quad p_s = \sum_{t=1}^{m} \hat{A}_{W'}(s, t) p_t \tag{8}$$

The system of Eq. (8) admits a unique solution according to [2] (Theorem 10.19. page 766). Then, $(\mathbb{P}^{\hat{A}_{W'}}_s(\text{reach } s_f \text{ before } s_0))_{s \in S_1}$ is trivially a solution of (8). But, since W' satisfies the conditions of Lemma 1, we also have that $(\hat{\gamma}^s_{W'})_{s \in S_1}$ is a solution of (8), and thus we have the desired equality.   □

Notice that Lemma 2 does not hold in general with the set W. We have:

$$\begin{aligned}
\hat{\gamma}_W(A, \varphi) &= \hat{\gamma}^{s_0}_W \quad \text{(by definition)} \\
&= \hat{\gamma}^{s_0}_{W'} \quad \text{(by Lemma 1)} \\
&= \mathbb{P}^{\hat{A}_{W'}}_{s_0}(\text{reach } s_f \text{ before } s_0) \quad \text{(by Lemma 2)} \\
&= \mathbb{P}^{\hat{A}_W}_{s_0}(\text{reach } s_f \text{ before } s_0) \quad \text{(by Lemma 1)} \\
&= \gamma(\hat{A}_W, \varphi) \quad \text{(by definition)}.
\end{aligned}$$

That concludes the proof of Proposition 1. It shows that learning can be as efficient as statistical model-checking on comparable properties.

6   Learning for the Full CTL Logic

In this section, we learn a DTMC $\hat{A}_W$ such that $\hat{A}_W$ and A have similar behaviors over all CTL formulas. This provides a much stronger result than on time-to-failure property, e.g., properties can involve liveness and fairness, and more importantly they are not known before the learning. Notice that PCTL [2] cannot be used, since an infinitesimal error on one >0 probability can change the probability of a PCTL formula from 0 to 1. (State)-CTL is defined as follows:

Definition 3. *Let Prop be the set of state names. (State)-CTL is defined by the following grammar* $\varphi ::= \bot \mid \top \mid p \mid \neg\varphi \mid \varphi \wedge \varphi \mid \varphi \vee \varphi \mid \varphi \wedge \varphi \mid \mathbf{AX}\varphi \mid$ $\mathbf{EX}\varphi \mid \mathbf{AF}\varphi \mid \mathbf{EF}\varphi \mid \mathbf{AF}\varphi \mid \mathbf{EG}\varphi \mid \mathbf{AG}\varphi \mid \mathbf{E}(\varphi\mathbf{U}\varphi) \mid \mathbf{A}(\varphi\mathbf{U}\varphi)$, *with* $p \in Prop.$ $\mathbf{E}$*(xists) and* $\mathbf{A}$*(ll) are quantifiers on paths, ne***X***t,* **G***lobally,* **F***inally and* **U***ntil are path-specific quantifiers. Notice that some operators are redundant. A minimal set of operators is* $\{\top, \vee, \neg, \mathbf{EG}, \mathbf{EU}, \mathbf{EX}\}$.

As we want to compute the probability of *paths* satisfying a CTL formula, we consider the set Ψ of *path-CTL* properties, that is formulas φ of the form $\varphi = \mathbf{X}\varphi_1$, $\varphi = \varphi_1\mathbf{U}\varphi_2$, $\varphi = \mathbf{F}\varphi_1$ or $\varphi = \mathbf{G}\varphi_1$, with φ_1, φ_2 (state)-CTL formulas. For instance, the property considered in the previous section is $(\neg s_0)\mathbf{U}s_F$.

In this section, for the sake of simplicity, the finite set W of traces is obtained by observing paths till a state is seen twice on the path. Then, the reset action is used and another trace is obtained from another path. That is, a trace ω from W is of the form $\omega = \rho \cdot s \cdot \rho' \cdot s$, with $\rho \cdot s \cdot \rho'$ a loop-free path.

As explained in example 1, some additional knowledge on the system is necessary. In this section, we assume that the support of transition probabilities is known, i.e., for any state i, we know the set of states j such that $a_{ij} \neq 0$. This assumption is needed both for Theorem 5 and to apply Laplace smoothing.

6.1   Learning DTMCs with Laplace Smoothing

Let $\alpha > 0$. For any state s, let k_s be the number of successors of s, that we know by hypothesis, and $T = \sum_{s \in S} k_s$ be the number of non-zero transitions. Let W be a set of traces, n_{ij}^W the number of transitions from state i to state j, and $n_i^W = \sum_j n_{ij}^W$. The *estimator for W with Laplace smoothing α* is the DTMC $\hat{A}_W^\alpha = (\hat{a}_{ij})_{1 \leq i,j \leq m}$ given for all i, j by:

$$\hat{a}_{ij} = \frac{n_{ij}^W + \alpha}{n_i^W + k_i\alpha} \text{ if } a_{ij} \neq 0 \quad \text{and} \quad \hat{a}_{ij} = 0 \text{ otherwise}$$

In comparison with the frequency estimator, the Laplace smoothing adds for each state s a term α to the numerator and k_s times α to the denominator. This preserves the fact that $\hat{A}_W^\alpha$ is a Markov chain, and it ensures that $\hat{a}_{ij} \neq 0$ iff $a_{ij} \neq 0$. In particular, compared with the frequency estimator, it avoids creating zeros in the probability tables.

6.2   Conditioning and Probability Bounds

Using Laplace smoothing slightly changes the probability of each transition by an additive offset η. We now explain how this small error η impacts the error on the probability of a CTL property.

Let A be a DTMC, and A_η be a DTMC such that $A_\eta(i,j) \neq 0$ iff $A(i,j) \neq 0$ for all states i,j, and such that $\sum_j |A_\eta(i,j) - A(i,j)| \leq \eta$ for all states i. For all states $s \in S$, let $R(s)$ be the set of states i such that there exists a path from i to s. Let $R_*(s) = R(s) \setminus \{s\}$. Since both DTMCs have the same support, R (and also R_*) is equal for A and A_η. Given m the number of states, the conditioning of A for $s \in S$ and $\ell \leq m$ is:

$$\mathrm{Cond}_s^\ell(A) = \min_{i \in R_*(s)} \mathbb{P}_i^A(\mathbf{F}_{\leq \ell} \neg R_*(s))$$

i.e., the minimal probability from state $i \in R_*(s)$ to move away from $R_*(s)$ in at most ℓ steps. Let ℓ_s be the minimal value such that $\mathrm{Cond}_s^{\ell_s}(A) > 0$. This minimal ℓ_s exists as $\mathrm{Cond}_s^m(A) > 0$ since, for all $s \in S$ and $i \in R_*(s)$, there is at least one path reaching s from i (this path leaves $R_*(s)$), and taking a cycle-free path, we obtain a path of length at most m. Thus, the probability $\mathbb{P}_i^A(\mathbf{F}_{\leq m} \neg R_*(s))$ is at least the positive probability of the cylinder defined by this finite path. Formally,

Theorem 4. *Denoting φ the property of reaching state s in DTMC A, we have:*

$$|\gamma(A,\varphi) - \gamma(A_\eta,\varphi)| < \frac{\ell_s \cdot \eta}{\mathrm{Cond}_s^{\ell_s}(A)}$$

Proof. Let v_s be the stochastic vector with $v_s(s) = 1$. We denote $v_0 = v_{s_0}$. Let $s \in S$. We assume that $s_0 \in R_*(s)$ (else $\gamma(A,\varphi) = \gamma(A_\eta,\varphi)$ and the result is trivial). Without loss of generality, we can also assume that $A(s,s) = A_\eta(s,s) = 1$ (as we are interested in reaching s at any step). With this assumption:

$$|\gamma(A,\varphi) - \gamma(A_\eta,\varphi)| = \lim_{t \to \infty} |v_0 \cdot (A^t - A_\eta^t) \cdot v_s|$$

We bound this error, through bounding by induction on t:

$$E(t) = \max_{i \in R_*(s)} |v_i \cdot (A^t - A_\eta^t) \cdot v_s|$$

We then have trivially:

$$|\gamma(A,\varphi) - \gamma(A_\eta,\varphi)| \leq \lim_{t \to \infty} E(t)$$

Note that for $i = s$, $\lim_{t \to \infty} v_i \cdot (A^t) \cdot v_s = 1 = \lim_{t \to \infty} v_i \cdot A_\eta^t \cdot v_s$, and thus their difference is null.

Let $t \in \mathbb{N}$. We let $j \in R_*(s)$ such that $E(t) = |v_j \cdot (A^t - A_\eta^t) \cdot v_s|$.

By the triangular inequality, introducing the term $v_j \cdot A^{\ell_s} A_\eta^{t-k} \cdot v_s - v_j \cdot A^{\ell_s} A_\eta^{t-k} \cdot v_s = 0$, we have:

$$E(t) \leq |v_j \cdot (A_\eta^t - A^{\ell_s} A_\eta^{t-\ell_s}) \cdot v_s| + |(v_j \cdot A^{\ell_s}) \cdot (A_\eta^{t-\ell_s} - A^{t-\ell_s}) \cdot v_s|$$

We separate vector $(v_j \cdot A^{\ell_s}) = w_1 + w_2 + w_3$ in three sub-stochastic vectors w_1, w_2, w_3: vector w_1 is over $\{s\}$, and thus we have $w_1 \cdot A_\eta^{t-\ell_s} = w_1 = w_1 \cdot A^{t-\ell_s}$, and the term cancels out. Vector w_2 is over states of $R_*(s)$, with $\sum_{i \in R_*} w_2[i] \leq (1 - \mathrm{Cond}_s^{\ell_s}(A))$, and we obtain an inductive term $\leq (1 - \mathrm{Cond}_s^{\ell_s}(A)) E(t - \ell_s)$. Last, vector w_3 is over states not in $R(s)$, and we have $w_3 \cdot A_\eta^{t-\ell_s} \cdot v_s = 0 = w_3 \cdot A^{t-\ell_s} \cdot v_s$, and the term cancels out.

We also obtain that $|v_j \cdot (A_\eta^t - A^{\ell_s} A_\eta^{t-\ell_s}) \cdot v_s| \leq \ell_s \cdot \eta$. Thus, we have the inductive formula $E(t) \leq (1 - \mathrm{Cond}_s^{\ell_s}(A)) E(t - \ell_s) + \ell_s \cdot \eta$. It yields for all $t \in \mathbb{N}$:

$$E(t) \leq (\ell_s \cdot \eta) \sum_{i=1}^{\infty} (1 - \mathrm{Cond}_s^{\ell_s}(A))^i$$

$$E(t) \leq \frac{\ell_s \cdot \eta}{\mathrm{Cond}_s^{\ell_s}(A)} \qquad \qquad \square$$

We can extend this result from reachability to formulas of the form $S_0 \mathsf{U} S_F$, where S_0, S_F are subsets of states. This formula means that we reach the set of states S_F through only states in S_0 on the way.

We define $R(S_0, S_F)$ to be the set of states which can reach S_F using only states of S_0, and $R_*(S_0, S_F) = R(S_0, S_F) \setminus S_F$. For $\ell \in \mathbb{N}$, we let:

$$\mathrm{Cond}_{S_0, S_F}^{\ell}(A) = \min_{i \in R_*(S_0, S_F)} \mathbb{P}_i^A(\mathbf{F}_{\leq \ell} \neg R_*(S_0, S_F) \vee \neg S_0).$$

Now, one can remark that $\mathrm{Cond}_{S_0, S_F}(A) \geq \mathrm{Cond}_{S, S_F}(A) > 0$. Let $\mathrm{Cond}_{S_F}^{\ell}(A) = \mathrm{Cond}_{S, S_F}^{\ell}(A)$. We have $\mathrm{Cond}_{S_0, S_F}^{\ell}(A) \geq \mathrm{Cond}_{S_F}^{\ell}(A)$. As before, we let $\ell_{S_F} \leq m$ be the minimal ℓ such that $\mathrm{Cond}_{S_F}^{\ell}(A) > 0$, and obtain:

Theorem 5. *Denoting φ the property $S_0 \mathsf{U} S_F$, we have, given DTMC A:*

$$|\gamma(A, \varphi) - \gamma(A_\eta, \varphi)| < \frac{\ell_{S_F} \cdot \eta}{\mathrm{Cond}_{S_F}^{\ell_{S_F}}(A)}$$

We can actually improve this conditioning: we defined it as the probability to reach S_F or $S \setminus R(S, S_F)$. At the price of a more technical proof, we can obtain a better bound by replacing S_F by the set of states $R_1(S_F)$ that have probability 1 to reach S_F. We let $\overline{R}_*(S_F) = R(S, S_F) \setminus R_1(S_F)$ the set of states that can reach S_F with < 1 probability, and define the *refined conditioning* as follows:

$$\overline{\mathrm{Cond}}_{S_F}^{\ell}(A) = \min_{i \in \overline{R}_*(S_F)} \mathbb{P}_i^A(\mathbf{F}_{\leq \ell} \neg \overline{R}_*(S_F))$$

6.3   Optimality of the Conditioning

We show now that the bound we provide in Theorem 4 is close to optimal.

Consider again DTMCs $A, \hat{A}$ in Fig. 3 from example 1, and formula $\mathbf{F}\, s_2$ stating that s_2 is eventually reached. The probabilities to satisfy this formula in $A, \hat{A}$ are respectively $\mathbb{P}^A(\mathbf{F}\, s_2) = \frac{1}{2}$ and $\mathbb{P}^{\hat{A}}(\mathbf{F}\, s_2) = \frac{1}{2} - \frac{\eta}{4\tau}$. Assume that A is the real system and that $\hat{A}$ is the DTMC we learned from A.

As we do not know precisely the transition probabilities in A, we can only compute the conditioning on $\hat{A}$ and not on A (it suffices to swap A and A_η in Theorem 4 and 5 to have the same formula using $\mathrm{Cond}(A_\eta) = \mathrm{Cond}(\hat{A})$). We have $R(s_2) = \{s_1, s_2\}$ and $R_*(s_2) = \overline{R}_*(s_2) = \{s_1\}$. The probability to stay in $R_*(s_2)$ after $\ell_{s_2} = 1$ step is $(1 - 2\tau)$, and thus $\mathrm{Cond}^1_{\{s_2\}}(\hat{A}) = \overline{\mathrm{Cond}}^1_{\{s_2\}}(\hat{A}) = 1 - (1 - 2\tau) = 2\tau$. Taking $A_\eta = \hat{A}$, Theorem 5 tells us that $|\mathbb{P}^A(\mathbf{F}\, s_2) - \mathbb{P}^{\hat{A}}(\mathbf{F}\, s_2)| \leq \frac{\eta}{2\tau}$. Notice that on that example, using $\ell_{s_2} = m = 3$, we obtain $\mathrm{Cond}^3_{\{s_2\}}(\hat{A}) = 1 - (1 - 2\tau)^3 \approx 6\tau$, and we find a similar bound $\approx \frac{3\eta}{6\tau} = \frac{\eta}{2\tau}$.

Compare our bound with the exact difference $|\mathbb{P}^A(\mathbf{F}\, s_2) - \mathbb{P}^{\hat{A}}(\mathbf{F}\, s_2)| = \frac{1}{2} - (\frac{1}{2} - \frac{\eta}{4\tau}) = \frac{\eta}{4\tau}$. Our upper bound only has an overhead factor of 2, even while the conditioning is particularly bad (small) in this example.

6.4   PAC Bounds for $\sum_j |\hat{A}_W(i, j) - A(i, j)| \leq \eta$

We use Theorem 1 in order to obtain PAC bounds. We use it to estimate individual transition probabilities, rather than the probability of a property.

Let W be a set of traces drawn with respect to A such that every $\omega \in W$ is of the form $\omega = \rho \cdot s \cdot \rho' \cdot s$. Recall for each state i, j of S, n_i^W is the number of transitions originating from i in W and n_{ij}^W is the number of transitions ss' in W. Let $\delta' = \frac{\delta}{m_{\text{stoch}}}$, where m_{stoch} is the number of $stochastic$ states, i.e., with at least two outgoing transitions.

We want to sample traces until the empirical transition probabilities $\frac{n_{ij}^W}{n_i^W}$ are relatively close to the exact transition probabilities a_{ij}, for all $i, j \in S$. For that, we need to determine a stopping criteria over the number of state occurrences $(n_i)_{1 \leq i \leq m}$ such that:

$$\mathbb{P}\left(\exists i \in S, \sum_j \left| a_{ij} - \frac{n_{ij}^W}{n_i^W} \right| > \varepsilon \right) \leq \delta$$

First, note that for any observed state $i \in S$, if $a_{ij} = 0$ (or $a_{ij} = 1$), then with probability 1, $\frac{n_{ij}^W}{n_i^W} = 0$ (respectively $\frac{n_{ij}^W}{n_i^W} = 1$). Thus, for all $\varepsilon > 0$, $|a_{ij} - \frac{n_{ij}^W}{n_i^W}| < \varepsilon$ with probability 1. Second, for two distinct states i and i', the transition probabilities $\frac{n_{ij}^W}{n_i^W}$ and $\frac{n_{i'j'}^W}{n_{i'}^W}$ are independent for all j, j'.

Let $i \in S$ be a stochastic state. If we observe n_i^W transitions from i such that $n_i^W \geq \frac{2}{\varepsilon^2} \log\left(\frac{2}{\delta'}\right) \left[\frac{1}{4} - \left(\max_j |\frac{1}{2} - \frac{n_{ij}^W}{n_i^W}| - \frac{2}{3}\varepsilon \right)^2 \right]$, then, according to Theorem 1,

$\mathbb{P}\left(\bigvee_{j=1}^m |a_{ij} - \frac{n_{ij}^W}{n_i^W}| > \varepsilon\right) \le \delta'$. In particular, $\mathbb{P}\left(\max_{j \in S} |a_{ij} - \frac{n_{ij}^W}{n_i^W}| > \varepsilon\right) \le \delta'$.
Moreover, we have:

$$\mathbb{P}\left(\bigvee_{j=1}^m \max_{j \in S} |a_{ij} - \frac{n_{ij}^W}{n_i^W}| > \varepsilon\right) \le \sum_{j=1}^m \mathbb{P}\left(\max_{j \in S} |a_{ij} - \frac{n_{ij}^W}{n_i^W}| > \varepsilon\right)$$
$$\le m_{\text{stoch}}\delta'$$
$$\le \delta$$

In other words, the probability that "there exists a state $i \in S$ such that the deviation between the exact and empirical outgoing transitions from i exceeds ε" is bounded by δ as soon as for each state $i \in S$, n_i^W satisfies the stopping rule of the algorithm of Chen using ε and the corresponding δ'. This gives the hypothesis $\sum_j |A_\eta(i,j) - A(i,j)| \le \epsilon$ for all states i of Sect. 6.2.

6.5   A Matrix $\hat{A}_W$ Accurate for all CTL properties

We now use Laplace smoothing in order to ensure the other hypothesis $A_\eta(i,j) \ne 0$ iff $A(i,j) \ne 0$ for all states i,j. For all $i \in S$, we define the Laplace offset depending on the state i as $\alpha_i = \frac{(n_i^W)^2 \varepsilon}{10 \cdot k_i^2 \max_j n_{ij}^W}$, where k_i is the number of transitions from state i. This ensures that the error from Laplace smoothing is at most one tenth of the statistical error. Let $\alpha = (\alpha_i)_{1 \le i \le m}$. From the sample set W, we output the matrix $\hat{A}_W^\alpha = (\hat{a}_{ij})_{1 \le i,j \le m}$ with Laplace smoothing α_i for state i, i.e.:

$$\hat{a}_{ij} = \frac{n_{ij}^W + \alpha_i}{n_i^W + k_i \alpha_i} \text{ if } a_{ij} \ne 0 \quad \text{and} \quad \hat{a}_{ij} = 0 \text{ otherwise}$$

It is easy to check that we have for all $i, j \in S$: $\left|\hat{a}_{ij} - \frac{n_{ij}^W}{n_i^W}\right| \le \frac{\varepsilon}{10 \cdot k_i}$

That is, for all states i, $\sum_j \left|\hat{a}_{ij} - \frac{n_{ij}^W}{n_i^W}\right| \le \frac{\varepsilon}{10}$. Using the triangular inequality:

$$\mathbb{P}\left(\exists i \in S, \sum_j |a_{ij} - \hat{a}_{ij}| > \frac{11}{10}\varepsilon\right) \le \delta$$

For all $i \in S$, let $H^*(n_i^W, \epsilon, \delta') = \max_{j \in S} H(n_i^W, n_{ij}^W, \epsilon, \delta')$ be the maximal Chen bound over all the transitions from state i. Let $B(\hat{A}_W^\alpha) = \max_{S_F} \frac{\ell_{S_F}}{\text{Cond}_{S_F}^{\ell_{S_F}}(\hat{A}_W^\alpha)}$. Since in Theorem 5, the original model and the learned one have symmetric roles, by applying this theorem on $\hat{A}_W^\alpha$, we obtain that:

Theorem 6. *Given a set W of traces, for $0 < \epsilon < 1$ and $0 < \delta < 1$, if for all $i \in S$, $n_i^W \geq \left(\frac{11}{10} B(\hat{A}_W^\alpha)\right)^2 H^*(n_i^W, \epsilon, \delta')$, we have for any CTL property φ:*

$$\mathbb{P}(|\gamma(A, \varphi) - \gamma(\hat{A}_W^\alpha, \varphi)|) > \varepsilon) \leq \delta \tag{9}$$

Proof. First, $\hat{a}_{ij} \neq 0$ iff $a_{ij} \neq 0$, by definition of $\hat{A}_W^\alpha$. Second, $\mathbb{P}(\exists i, \sum_j |a_{ij} - \hat{a}_{ij}| > \frac{11}{10}\varepsilon) \leq \delta$. We can thus apply Theorem 5 on $\hat{A}_W^\alpha, A$ and obtain (9) for φ any formula of the form $S_1 \mathbf{U} S_2$. It remains to show that for any formula $\varphi \in \Psi$, we can define $S_1, S_2 \subseteq S$ such that φ can be expressed as $S_1 \mathbf{U} S_2$.

Consider the different cases: If φ is of the form $\varphi = \varphi_1 \mathbf{U} \varphi_2$ (it subsumes the case $\varphi = \mathbf{F}\varphi_1 = \top \mathbf{U}\varphi_1$) with φ_1, φ_2 CTL formulas, we define S_1, S_2 as the sets of states satisfying φ_1 and φ_2, and we have the equivalence (see [2] for more details). If $\varphi = X\varphi_2$, define $S_1 = \emptyset$ and S_2 as the set of states satisfying φ_2.

The last case is $\varphi = \mathbf{G}\varphi_1$, with φ_1 a CTL formula. Again, we define S_1 the set of states satisfying φ_1, and S_2 the set of states satisfying the CTL formula $\mathbf{AG}\varphi_1$. The probability of the set of paths satisfying $\varphi = \mathbf{G}\varphi_1$ is exactly the same as the probability of the set of paths satisfying $S_1 \mathbf{U} S_2$. $\qquad\square$

6.6   Algorithm

We give more details about the learning process of a Markov Chain, accurate for every CTL formula. For completeness, we also provide in the extended version a similar algorithm for a time-to-failure property.

A path ω is observed from s_0 till a state is observed twice. Then ω is added to W and the reset operation is performed. We use Laplace smoothing to compute

---

Algorithm 1: Learning a matrix accurate for CTL

Data:
$\mathcal{S}, s_0, \delta, \varepsilon$
1 $W := \emptyset$
2 $m = |S|$
3 for all $s \in S$, $n_s^W := 0$
4 Compute $\hat{A} := \hat{\Lambda}_W^\alpha$
5 Compute $B := B(\hat{A})$
6 **while** $\exists s \in S, n_s^W < \left(\frac{11}{10} B(\hat{A})\right)^2 H^*(n_s^W, \epsilon, \frac{\delta}{m})$ **do**
7 $\quad$ Generate a new trace $\omega := s_0 \rho s_1 \rho' s_1$, and reset $\mathcal{S}$
8 $\quad$ for all $s \in S$, $n_s^W := n_s^W + n_s^{\{\omega\}}$
9 $\quad$ add ω to W
10 $\quad$ Compute $\hat{A} := \hat{A}_W^\alpha$
11 $\quad$ Compute $B := B(\hat{A})$

Output: $\hat{A}_W^\alpha$

---

the corresponding matrix $\hat{A}_W^\alpha$. The error bound is computed on W, and a new path ω' is then being generated if the error bound is not as small as desired.

This algorithm is guaranteed to terminate since, as traces are generated, with probability 1, n_s^W tends towards ∞, $\hat{A}_W^\alpha$ tends towards A, and $B(\hat{A}_W^\alpha)$ tends towards $B(A)$.

7   Evaluation and Discussion

In this section, we first evaluate Algorithm 1 on 5 systems which are crafted to evaluate the algorithm under different conditions (e.g., rare states). The objective of the evaluation is to provide some idea on how many samples would be sufficient for learning accurate DTMC estimations, and compare learning for all properties of CTL and learning for one time-to-failure property.

Then, we evaluate our algorithm on very large PRISM systems (millions or billions of states). Because of the number of states, we cannot learn a DTMC accurate for all properties of CTL there: it would ask to visit every single state a number of times. However, we can learn a DTMC for one specific (unbounded) property. We compare with an hypothesis testing algorithm from [31] which can handle the same unbounded property through a reachability analysis using the topology of the system.

Table 1. Average number of observed events N (and relative standard deviation in parenthesis) given $\varepsilon = 0.1$ and $\delta = 0.05$ for a time-to-failure property and for the full CTL logic using the refined conditioning $\overline{\text{Cond}}$.

	System 1	System 2	System 3	System 4	System 5
# states	3	3	30	64	200
# transitions	4	7	900	204	40,000
# events for time-to-failure	191 (16%)	991 (10%)	2,753 (7.4%)	1,386 (17.9%)	18,335 (7.2%)
# events for full CTL	1,463 (12.9%)	4,159 (11.7%)	8,404 (3.8%)	1,872,863	79,823 (1.7%)

7.1   Evaluation on Crafted Models

We first describe the 5 systems: Systems 1 and 2 are three-state models described in Fig. 1 and Fig. 2. Systems 3 (resp. 5) is a 30-state (resp. 200-states) clique in which every individual transition probability is 1/30 (resp. 1/200). System 4 is a 64-state system modeling failure and repair of 3 types of components (3 components each, 9 components in total), see the extended version for a full description of the system, including a PRISM [20] model for the readers interested to investigate this system in details.

We tested time-to-failure properties by choosing as failure states s_3 for Systems 1, 2, 3, 5, and the state where all 9 components fail for System 4.

We also tested Algorithm 1 (for full CTL logic) using the refined conditioning $\overline{\text{Cond}}$. We performed our algorithms 100 times for each model, except for full CTL on System 4, for which we only tested once since it is very time-consuming. We report our results in Table 1 for $\varepsilon = 0.1$ and $\delta = 0.05$. In particular, we output for each model its number of states and transitions. For each (set of) property, we provide the average number of observations (i.e. the number of samples times their average length) and the relative standard deviation (in parenthesis, that is the standard deviation divided by the average number of observed events).

The results show that we can learn a DTMC with more than 40000 stochastic transitions, such that the DTMC is accurate for all CTL formulas. Notice that for some particular systems such as System 4, it can take a lot of events to be observed before Algorithm 1 terminates. The reason is the presence of rare states, such as the state where all 9 components fail, which are observed with an extremely small probability. In order to evaluate the probabilities of CTL properties of the form: "if all 9 components fail, then CTL property φ is satisfied", this state needs to be explored many times, explaining the high number of events observed before the algorithm terminates. On the other hand, for properties that do not involve the 9 components failing as prior, such as time-to-failure, one does not need to observe this state even once to conclude that it has an extremely small probability to happen. This suggests that efficient algorithms could be developed for subsets of CTL formulas, e.g., in defining a subset of important events to consider. We believe that Theorem 4 and 5 could be extended to handle such cases. Over different runs, the results stay similar (notice the rather small relative standard deviation).

Comparing results for time-to-failure (or equivalently SMC) and for the full CTL logic is interesting. Excluding System 4 which involves rare states, the number of events that needs to be observed for the full CTL logic is 4.3 to 7 times more. Surprisingly, the highest difference is obtained on the smallest System 1. It is because every run of System 1 generated for time-to-failure is short ($s_1 s_2 s_1$ and $s_1 s_2 s_3$). However, in Systems 2,3 and 5, samples for time-to-failure can be much longer, and the performances for time-to-failure (or equivalently SMC) is not so much better than for learning a DTMC accurate for all CTL properties.

For the systems we tested, the unoptimized Cond was particularly large (more than 20) because for many states s, there was probability 0 to leave $R(s)$, and hence $\ell(s)$ was quite large. These are the cases where $\overline{\text{Cond}}$ is much more efficient, as then we can choose $\ell_s = 1$ as the probability to reach s from states in $R(s)$ is 1 ($R_1(s) = R(s)$ and $\overline{R_*(s)} = \emptyset$). We used $\overline{\text{Cond}}$ in our algorithm.

Finally, we evaluate experimental confidence by comparing the time-to-failure probabilities in the learned DTMC and the original system. We repeat our algorithms 1000 times on System 1 and 2 (with $\varepsilon = 0.1$ and $\delta = 0.05$). These probabilities differ by less than ε, respectively 999 and 995 times out of 1000. Specification (2) is thus largely fulfilled (the specification should be ensured 950 out of 1000 times), that empirically endorses our approach. Hence, while our PAC bound over-approximates the confidence in the learned system (which is unavoidable), it is not that far from experimental values.

7.2   Evaluation on Large Models

We also evaluated our algorithm on large PRISM models, ranging from hundreds of thousands to billions of states. With these numbers of states, we cannot use the more ambitious learning over all the properties of CTL, which would need to visit every states a number of times. However, we can use our algorithm for learning a DTMC which is accurate given a particular (unbounded) property: it will visit only a fraction of the states, which is enough to give a model accurate for that property, with a well-learned kernel of states and some other states representatives for the remaining of the runs. We consider three test-cases from PRISM, satisfying the property that the sample stops with a conclusion (yes or no) with probability 1. Namely, *herman, leader* and *egl*.

Table 2. Results for $\varepsilon = 0.01$ and $\delta = 0.001$ of our algorithm compared with sampling with reachability analysis [31], as reported in [14], page 20. Numbers of samples needed by our method are given by the Massart bound (resp. by the Okamoto-Chernoff bound in parenthesis). TO and MO means time out (> 15 minutes on an Opteron 6134) and memory out (> 5GB) respectively.

Model name	Size	Our learning method		Sampling with reachability analysis [31]	
		Samples	Path length	Samples	Path length
herman(17)	129M	506 (38K)	27	219	30
herman(19)	1162M	506 (38K)	40	219	38
herman(21)	10G	506 (38K)	43	219	48
leader(6, 6)	280K	506 (38K)	7.4	219	7
leader(6, 8)	>280K	506 (38K)	7.4	(MO)	(MO)
leader(6, 11)	>280K	506 (38K)	7.3	(MO)	(MO)
egl(15, 10)	616G	38K (38K)	470	1100	201
egl(20, 15)	1279T	38K (38K)	930	999	347
egl(20, 20)	1719T	38K (38K)	1200	(TO)	(TO)

Our prototype tool used in the previous subsection is implemented in Scilab: it cannot simulate very large systems of PRISM. Instead, we use PRISM to generate the samples needed for the learning. Hence, we report the usual Okamoto-Chernoff bound on the number of samples, which is what is implemented in PRISM. We also compare with the Massart bound used by the Chen algorithm (see Sect. 2.2), which is implemented in our tool and is more efficient as it takes into account the probability of the property.

For each model, we report its parameters, its *size*, i.e. its number of states, the number of *samples* needed using the Massart bound (the conservative Okamoto-Chernoff bound is in parenthesis), and the average *path length*. For comparison, we consider an hypothesis testing algorithm from [31] which can also handle unbounded properties. It uses the knowledge of the topology to do reachability analysis to stop the sampling if the property cannot be reached anymore. Hypothesis testing is used to decide with high confidence whether a probability exceeds a threshold or not. This requires less samples than SMC algorithms which estimate probabilities, but it is also less precise. We chose to compare with this algorithm because as in our work, it does not require knowledge on the probabilities, such as a lower bound on the transition probabilities needed by e.g. [14]. We do not report runtime as they cannot be compared (different platforms, different nature of result, etc.).

There are several conclusions we can draw from the experimental results (shown in Table 2). First, the number of samples from our algorithm (Chen algorithm implementing the Massart bound) are larger than in the algorithm from [31]. This is because they do hypothesis testing, which requires less samples than even estimating the probability of a property, while we learn a DTMC accurate for this property. For *herman* and *leader*, the difference is small (2.5x), because it is a case where the Massart bound is very efficient (80 times better than Okamoto-Chernoff implemented in PRISM). The *egl* system is the worst-case for the Massart bound (the probability of the property is $\frac{1}{2}$), and it coincides with Okamoto-Chernoff. The difference with [31] is 40x in that case. Also, as shown in *egl*, paths in our algorithm can be a bit larger than in the algorithm from [31], where they can be stopped early by the reachability analysis. However, the differences are never larger than 3x. On the other hand, we learn a model representative of the original system for a given property, while [31] only provide a yes/no answer to hypothesis testing (performing SMC evaluating the probability of a property with the Massart bound would give exactly the same number of samples as we report for our learning algorithm). Last, the reachability analysis from [31] does time out or memory out on some complex systems, which is not the case with our algorithm.

8 Conclusion

In this paper, we provided theoretical grounds for obtaining global PAC bounds when learning a DTMC: we bound the error made between the behaviors of the model and of the system, formalized using temporal logics. While it is not possible to obtain a learning framework for LTL properties, we provide it for the whole CTL logic. For subsets of CTL, e.g. for a fixed timed-to-failure property, we obtain better bounds, as efficient as Statistical MC. Overall, this work should help in the recent trends of establishing trusted machine learning [16].

Our techniques are useful for designers of systems for which probabilities are governed by uncertain forces (e.g. error rates): in this case, it is not easy to have a lower bound on the minimal transition probability, but we can assume that the set of transitions is known. Technically, our techniques provides rationale to set the constant in Laplace smoothing, otherwise left to an expert to set.

Some cases remain problematic, such as systems where states are visited very rarely. Nevertheless, we foresee potential solutions involving rare event simulation [21]. This goes beyond the scope of this work and it is left to future work.

Acknowledgment. Jun Sun's research is supported by the National Research Foundation Singapore under its AI Singapore Programme (Award Number: AISG-RP-2019-012).

References

1. Ashok, P., Křetínský, J., Weininger, M.: PAC statistical model checking for Markov decision processes and stochastic games. In: Dillig, I., Tasiran, S. (eds.) CAV 2019. LNCS, vol. 11561, pp. 497–519. Springer, Cham (2019). https://doi.org/10.1007/978-3-030-25540-4_29
2. Baier, C., Katoen, J.-P.: Principles of Model Checking. MIT Press, Cambridge (2008)
3. Bortolussi, L., Sanguinetti, G.: Learning and designing stochastic processes from logical constraints. In: Joshi, K., Siegle, M., Stoelinga, M., D'Argenio, P.R. (eds.) QEST 2013. LNCS, vol. 8054, pp. 89–105. Springer, Heidelberg (2013). https://doi.org/10.1007/978-3-642-40196-1_7
4. Brambilla, M., Pinciroli, C., Birattari, M., Dorigo, M.: Property-driven design for swarm robotics. In: International Conference on Autonomous Agents and Multiagent Systems, AAMAS, Valencia, Spain, pp. 139–146 (2012)
5. Castro, J., Gavaldà, R.: Towards feasible PAC-learning of probabilistic deterministic finite automata. In: Clark, A., Coste, F., Miclet, L. (eds.) ICGI 2008. LNCS (LNAI), vol. 5278, pp. 163–174. Springer, Heidelberg (2008). https://doi.org/10.1007/978-3-540-88009-7_13
6. Chen, J.: Properties of a new adaptive sampling method with applications to scalable learning. In: Web Intelligence, Atlanta, pp. 9–15 (2013)
7. Chen, S.F., Goodman, J.: An empirical study of smoothing techniques for language modeling. Comput. Speech Lang. **13**(4), 359–394 (1999)
8. Chen, Y., Mao, H., Jaeger, M., Nielsen, T.D., Guldstrand Larsen, K., Nielsen, B.: Learning Markov models for stationary system behaviors. In: Goodloe, A.E., Person, S. (eds.) NFM 2012. LNCS, vol. 7226, pp. 216–230. Springer, Heidelberg (2012). https://doi.org/10.1007/978-3-642-28891-3_22
9. Chernoff, H.: A measure of asymptotic efficiency for tests of a hypothesis based on the sum of observations. Ann. Math. Statist. **23**(4), 493–507 (1952)
10. Clark, A., Thollard, F.: PAC-learnability of probabilistic deterministic finite state automata. J. Mach. Learn. Res. **5**, 473–497 (2004)
11. Clarke, E.M., Emerson, E.A.: Design and synthesis of synchronization skeletons using branching time temporal logic. In: Kozen, D. (ed.) Logic of Programs 1981. LNCS, vol. 131, pp. 52–71. Springer, Heidelberg (1982). https://doi.org/10.1007/BFb0025774
12. Cochran, W.G.: Contributions to survey sampling and applied statistics, chapter Laplace's ratio estimator, pp. 3–10. Academic Press, New York (1978)
13. Daca, P., Henzinger, T.A., Kretínský, J., Petrov, T.: Linear distances between Markov chains. In: 27th International Conference on Concurrency Theory, CONCUR 2016, 23–26 August 2016, Québec City, Canada, pp. 20:1–20:15 (2016)
14. Daca, P., Henzinger, T.A., Kretínský, J., Petrov, T.: Faster statistical model checking for unbounded temporal properties. ACM Trans. Comput. Log. **18**(2), 12:1–12:25 (2017)
15. Gale, W.A., Sampson, G.: Good-turing frequency estimation without tears. J. Quantit. Linguist. **2**, 217–237 (1995)
16. Ghosh, S., Lincoln, P., Tiwari, A., Zhu, X.: Trusted machine learning: model repair and data repair for probabilistic models. In: AAAI-17 Workshop on Symbolic Inference and Optimization (2017)
17. Hérault, T., Lassaigne, R., Magniette, F., Peyronnet, S.: Approximate probabilistic model checking. In: Steffen, B., Levi, G. (eds.) VMCAI 2004. LNCS, vol. 2937, pp. 73–84. Springer, Heidelberg (2004). https://doi.org/10.1007/978-3-540-24622-0_8

18. Jegourel, C., Sun, J., Dong, J.S.: Sequential schemes for frequentist estimation of properties in statistical model checking. In: Bertrand, N., Bortolussi, L. (eds.) QEST 2017. LNCS, vol. 10503, pp. 333–350. Springer, Cham (2017). https://doi.org/10.1007/978-3-319-66335-7_23

19. Kullback, S., Leibler, R.A.: On information and sufficiency. Ann. Math. Stat. **22**(1), 79–86 (1951)

20. Kwiatkowska, M., Norman, G., Parker, D.: PRISM 4.0: verification of probabilistic real-time systems. In: Gopalakrishnan, G., Qadeer, S. (eds.) CAV 2011. LNCS, vol. 6806, pp. 585–591. Springer, Heidelberg (2011). https://doi.org/10.1007/978-3-642-22110-1_47

21. Legay, A., Sedwards, S., Traonouez, L.-M.: Rare events for statistical model checking an overview. In: Larsen, K.G., Potapov, I., Srba, J. (eds.) RP 2016. LNCS, vol. 9899, pp. 23–35. Springer, Cham (2016). https://doi.org/10.1007/978-3-319-45994-3_2

22. Massart, P.: The tight constant in the Dvoretzky-Kiefer-Wolfowitz inequality. Ann. Probab. **18**, 1269–1283 (1990)

23. Okamoto, M.: Some inequalities relating to the partial sum of binomial probabilities. Ann. Inst. Stat. Math. **10**, 29–35 (1958)

24. Pnueli, A.: The temporal logic of programs. In: 18th Annual Symposium on Foundations of Computer Science, Providence, Rhode Island, USA, pp. 46–57 (1977)

25. Ridder, A.: Importance sampling simulations of Markovian reliability systems using cross-entropy. Ann. OR **134**(1), 119–136 (2005)

26. Dorsa Sadigh, K. et al.: Data-driven probabilistic modeling and verification of human driver behavior. In: Formal Verification and Modeling in Human-Machine Systems - AAAI Spring Symposium (2014)

27. Sherlaw-Johnson, C., Gallivan, S., Burridge, J.: Estimating a Markov transition matrix from observational data. J. Oper. Res. Soc. **46**(3), 405–410 (1995)

28. Valiant, L.G.: A theory of the learnable. Commun. ACM **27**(11), 1134–1142 (1984)

29. Wald, A.: Sequential tests of statistical hypotheses. Ann. Math. Stat. **16**(2), 117–186 (1945)

30. Wang, J., Sun, J., Yuan, Q., Pang, J.: Should we learn probabilistic models for model checking? A new approach and an empirical study. In: Huisman, M., Rubin, J. (eds.) FASE 2017. LNCS, vol. 10202, pp. 3–21. Springer, Heidelberg (2017). https://doi.org/10.1007/978-3-662-54494-5_1

31. Younes, H.L.S., Clarke, E.M., Zuliani, P.: Statistical verification of probabilistic properties with unbounded until. In: Davies, J., Silva, L., Simao, A. (eds.) SBMF 2010. LNCS, vol. 6527, pp. 144–160. Springer, Heidelberg (2011). https://doi.org/10.1007/978-3-642-19829-8_10

32. Younes, H.L.S., Simmons, R.G.: Probabilistic verification of discrete event systems using acceptance sampling. In: Brinksma, E., Larsen, K.G. (eds.) CAV 2002. LNCS, vol. 2404, pp. 223–235. Springer, Heidelberg (2002). https://doi.org/10.1007/3-540-45657-0_17

33. Zuliani, P., Platzer, A., Clarke, E.M.: Bayesian statistical model checking with application to stateflow/simulink verification. FMSD **43**(2), 338–367 (2013)

Unbounded-Time Safety Verification of Stochastic Differential Dynamics

Shenghua Feng[1,2(✉)] , Mingshuai Chen[3(✉)], Bai Xue[1,2(✉)],
Sriram Sankaranarayanan[4(✉)], and Naijun Zhan[1,2(✉)]

[1] SKLCS, Institute of Software, CAS, Beijing, China
{fengsh,xuebai,znj}@ios.ac.cn
[2] University of Chinese Academy of Sciences,
Beijing, China
[3] Lehrstuhl für Informatik 2, RWTH Aachen
University, Aachen, Germany
chenms@cs.rwth-aachen.de
[4] University of Colorado, Boulder, USA
sriram.sankaranarayanan@colorado.edu

Abstract. In this paper, we propose a method for bounding the probability that a stochastic differential equation (SDE) system violates a safety specification over the infinite time horizon. SDEs are mathematical models of stochastic processes that capture how states evolve continuously in time. They are widely used in numerous applications such as engineered systems (e.g., modeling how pedestrians move in an intersection), computational finance (e.g., modeling stock option prices), and ecological processes (e.g., population change over time). Previously the safety verification problem has been tackled over finite and infinite time horizons using a diverse set of approaches. The approach in this paper attempts to connect the two views by first identifying a finite time bound, beyond which the probability of a safety violation can be bounded by a negligibly small number. This is achieved by discovering an exponential barrier certificate that proves exponentially converging bounds on the probability of safety violations over time. Once the finite time interval is found, a finite-time verification approach is used to bound the probability of violation over this interval. We demonstrate our approach over a collection of interesting examples from the literature, wherein our approach can be used to find tight bounds on the violation probability of safety properties over the infinite time horizon.

Keywords: Stochastic differential equations (SDEs) · Unbounded safety verification · Failure probability bound · Barrier certificates

This work was partially funded by NSFC under grant No. 61625206, 61732001 and 61872341, by the ERC Advanced Project FRAPPANT under grant No. 787914, by the US NSF under grant No. CCF 1815983 and by the CAS Pioneer Hundred Talents Program under grant No. Y8YC235015.

S. K. Lahiri and C. Wang (Eds.): CAV 2020, LNCS 12225, pp. 327–348, 2020.
https://doi.org/10.1007/978-3-030-53291-8_18

1   Introduction

In this paper, we investigate the problem of verifying probabilistic safety properties for continuous stochastic dynamics modeled by stochastic differential equations (SDEs). The study of SDEs dates back to the 1900s when, e.g., Einstein used SDEs to model the phenomenon of Brownian motion [10]. Since then, SDEs have witnessed numerous applications including models of disturbances in engineered systems ranging from wind forces [37] to pedestrian motion [14]; models of financial instruments such as options [5]; and models of biological/ecological processes for instance predator-prey models [25]. In the meantime, SDEs are hard to reason about: they are defined using ideas from stochastic calculus that reimagine basic concepts such as integration in order to conform to the basic laws of probability and stochastic processes [24].

There are many important verification problems for SDEs. Prominent topics include the safety verification problem which seeks to know the probability that a given SDE with specified initial conditions will enter an unsafe region (or leave a safe region) over a given time horizon. Generally, safety verification can be performed over a finite-time horizon setting, wherein the probability is sought over a finite time interval $[0, T]$. On the other hand, the infinite-time horizon problem seeks a bound on the probability of satisfying a safety property over the unbounded time horizon $[0, \infty)$. A handful of methods have been proposed for verifying SDE systems, such as the barrier certificate-based methods over both the infinite time horizon [27] and finite time horizons [35], the moment optimization-based method over finite time horizons [33] and the Hamilton-Jacobi-based method over the infinite time horizon [16]. The novelty of our work lies in the reduction of infinite-time horizon verification problems to finite time problems.

In this paper, we propose a novel reduction-based method to verify unbounded-time safety properties of stochastic systems modeled as nonlinear polynomial SDEs. We employ a similar idea as in [11] (for verifying delay differential equations) that reduces the safety verification problem over the infinite time horizon to the one over a finite time interval. This is achieved by computing an *exponential stochastic barrier certificate* which witnesses an exponentially decreasing upper bound on the probability that a target system violates a given safety specification. Consequently, for any $\epsilon > 0$, we can identify a time instant T beyond which the violation (a.k.a. failure) probability is smaller than the negligibly small cutoff ϵ. The reduced bounded-time safety verification problem over $[0, T]$ can hence be tackled by any of the available methods. We furthermore present an alternative method to address the reduced finite-time horizon verification problem based on the discovery of a *time-dependent stochastic barrier certificate*. We show that both the exponential and the time-dependent stochastic barrier certificate can be synthesized by respectively solving a pertinent *semidefinite programming* (SDP) [38] optimization problem. Experimental results on some interesting examples taken from the literature demonstrated the effectiveness of the reduction and that our method often produces tighter bounds on the failure probability. Our approach has some broad similarities to related approaches in symbolic execution of probabilistic programs that conclude facts about infinitely many behaviors by analyzing finitely many paths in the program that account for a sufficient probability among all the behaviors [31].

Contributions. The main contributions of this work can be summarized as follows: (1) We reduce the unbounded-time safety verification of stochastic systems to a bounded one, based on an exponentially decreasing bound on the failure probability which guarantees the dominance of the overall failure probability by the truncated finite time horizon. (2) We show how the obtained bound on the overall failure probability is tighter than that produced by existing methods for some interesting SDEs.

Related Work. The use of mathematical models of processes–ranging from finite state machines to various types of differential equations–has allowed us to reason about rich behaviors of Cyber-Physical Systems produced by the interaction between digital computers and physical plants [29]. In this regard, many modeling formalisms have been studied including finite state machines, ordinary differential equations (ODEs), timed automata, hybrid automata, etc. [8], on top of which a large variety of verification problems have been extensively investigated, e.g., safety verification through reachability analysis and temporal logic verification [3].

In the existing literature on formal verification, ODEs are often used to describe the behavior of deterministic continuous-time systems. However, these models have been shown over-simplistic in many applications that involve time delays, nondeterministic inputs and stochastic noises. SDEs hence arose as an important class of models that have been employed in practical domains covering, among others [24], financial models such as the famous Black-Scholes model used extensively in the theory of options pricing [5], wind disturbances [37], human pedestrian motion [14] and ecological models [25].

In what follows, we place our work in the context of formal verification techniques tailored for stochastic differential dynamics modeled as SDEs, and discuss contributions thereof that are highly related to our approach. Unbounded-time stochastic safety verification of SDE systems was first studied by Prajna et al. in [27,28], where a typical supermartingale was employed as a stochastic barrier certificate followed by computational conditions derived from Doob's martingale inequality [15]. Thereafter, the stochastic barrier certificate-based method was extended to cater for bounded-time safety verification by Steinhardt and Tedrake [35] by leveraging a relaxed formulation called c-martingale for locally stable systems. The barrier certificate-based method by Prajna et al. (ibid.) for unbounded-time safety verification often leads to conservative bound on the failure probability. On the other hand, Steinhardt and Tedrake (ibid.) established impressive probability bounds but only for finite time horizons. In order to reduce the conservativeness, we propose a method of reducing the unbounded safety verification to a bounded one. Although our method in this paper is also based on the construction of stochastic barrier certificates, the gain of stochastic barrier certificates only helps to identify a finite time interval such that the violation probability of interest beyond this time interval is arbitrarily negligibly small. A time-dependent barrier certificate is further proposed to solve the resulting bounded-time safety verification. The Unbounded-time safety verification problem has also been studied by Koutsoukos and Riley [16], who linked the reachability probability to the viscosity solution of certain Hamilton-Jacobi partial differential equations, under restrictions on bounded state space and non-degenerate diffusion. Grid-based numerical approaches, e.g., the finite difference method in [16] and the level set method in [22], are traditionally used to solve these equations, leading to the fact that the Hamilton-Jacobi reachability method only scales well to systems of special structures. More recently, a novel constraint solving-based method has been proposed in [20] for algebraically over- and under-approximating the reachability probability, which is nevertheless limited to bounded-time safety verification. In addition to the abovementioned methods, we refer the readers to [7] for a Dirichlet form-based method for stochastic hybrid systems featuring "nice" Markov properties, while to [6,18,39] and [1,17] respectively for related contributions in statistical and discrete/numerical methods for stochastic verification and control.

Finally, we mention a relation between the ideas in this paper and previously proposed ideas for (non-stochastic) ODEs due to Sogokon et al. [34]. The key similarity lies in the use of a non-negative matrix through which a vector of functions whose derivatives are related to their current value. Whereas Sogokon et al. explored this idea for ODEs, we do so for SDEs. Another significant difference, in our work, is that we use the super-martingale functions to identify a time horizon $[0, T]$ and bound the probability of safety violation beyond T.

The reminder of this paper is structured as follows. Section 2 introduces stochastic differential dynamics modeled by SDEs and the unbounded-time safety verification problem of interest. Section 3 elucidates the reduction of unbounded safety verification to bounded ones based on the witness of stochastic barrier certificates. Section 4 presents the SDP formulation for discovering such barrier certificates over the reduced bounded time interval. After demonstrating our method on several examples in Sect. 5, we conclude the paper in Sect. 6.

2   Problem Formulation

Notations. Let $\mathbb{R}$ be the set of real numbers. For a vector $x \in \mathbb{R}^n$, x_i refers to its i-th component and $|x|$ denotes the ℓ^2-norm. Particularly, $\mathbf{0}$ and $\mathbf{1}$ denote respectively the vector of zeros and ones of appropriate dimension, and the comparison between vectors, e.g., $x \leq \mathbf{0}$, is component-wise. We define for $\delta > 0$, $\mathfrak{B}(x, \delta) \hat{=} \{x' \in \mathbb{R}^n \mid |x' - x| \leq \delta\}$ as the δ-closed ball centered at x. We abuse the notation $|\cdot|$ for an $m \times n$ matrix M as $|M| \hat{=} \sqrt{\sum_{i=1}^m \sum_{j=1}^n |M_{ij}|^2}$. The exponential of a square matrix $M \in \mathbb{R}^{n \times n}$, denoted by e^M, is the $n \times n$ matrix given by the power series $e^M \hat{=} \sum_{k=0}^\infty \frac{1}{k!} M^k$. For a set $\mathcal{X} \subseteq \mathbb{R}^n$, $\partial \mathcal{X}$, $\overline{\mathcal{X}}$ and $\mathcal{X}^\circ$ denote respectively the boundary, the closure and the interior of $\mathcal{X}$. Let C^k be the space of functions on $\mathbb{R}$ with continuous derivatives up to order k; a function $f(t, x) \colon \mathbb{R} \times \mathbb{R}^n \to \mathbb{R}$ is in $C^{1,2}(\mathbb{R} \times \mathbb{R}^n)$ if $f \in C^1$ w.r.t. $t \in R$ and $f \in C^2$ w.r.t. $x \in \mathbb{R}^n$.

Let $(\Omega, \mathcal{F}, P)$ be a probability space, where Ω is a sample space, $\mathcal{F} \subseteq 2^{\Omega}$ is a σ-algebra on Ω, and $P \colon \mathcal{F} \to [0, 1]$ is a probability measure on the measurable space $(\Omega, \mathcal{F})$. A *random variable* X defined on the probability space $(\Omega, \mathcal{F}, P)$ is an $\mathcal{F}$-measurable function $X \colon \Omega \to \mathbb{R}^n$; its *expectation* (w.r.t. P) is denoted by $E[X]$. Every random variable X induces a probability measure $\mu_X \colon \mathcal{B} \to [0, 1]$ on $\mathbb{R}^n$, defined as $\mu_X(B) \triangleq P(X^{-1}(B))$ for Borel sets B in the Borel σ-algebra $\mathcal{B}$ on $\mathbb{R}^n$. μ_X is called the *distribution of X*; its *support set* is $\mathsf{supp}(\mu_X) \triangleq \overline{\bigcup_{\mu_X(B)>0} B}$, which will also be referred to as the support of X.

A (continuous-time) *stochastic process* is a parametrized collection of random variables $\{X_t\}_{t \in T}$ where the parameter space T is interpreted as, unless explicitly notated in this paper, the halfline $[0, \infty)$. We sometimes further drop the brackets in $\{X_t\}$ when it is clear from the context. A collection $\{\mathcal{F}_t \mid t \geq 0\}$ of σ-algebras of sets in $\mathcal{F}$ is a *filtration* if $\mathcal{F}_t \subseteq \mathcal{F}_{t+s}$ for $t, s \in [0, \infty)$. Intuitively, $\mathcal{F}_t$ carries the information known to an observer at time t. A random variable $\tau \colon \Omega \to [0, \infty)$ is called a *stopping time* w.r.t. some filtration $\{\mathcal{F}_t \mid t \geq 0\}$ of $\mathcal{F}$ if $\{\tau \leq t\} \in \mathcal{F}_t$ for all $t \geq 0$. A stochastic process $\{X_t\}$ adapted to a filtration $\{\mathcal{F}_t \mid t \geq 0\}$ is called a *supermartingale* if $E[X_t] < \infty$ for any $t \geq 0$ and $E[X_t \mid \mathcal{F}_s] \leq X_s$ for all $0 \leq s \leq t$. That is, the conditional expected value of any future observation, given all the past observations, is no larger than the most recent observation.

Stochastic Differential Dynamics. We consider a class of dynamical systems featuring stochastic differential dynamics governed by time-homogeneous SDEs of the form[1]

$$\mathrm{d}X_t = b(X_t)\,\mathrm{d}t + \sigma(X_t)\,\mathrm{d}W_t, \quad t \geq 0 \tag{1}$$

where $\{X_t\}$ is an n-dimensional continuous-time stochastic process, $\{W_t\}$ denotes an m-dimensional Wiener process (standard Brownian motion), $b \colon \mathbb{R}^n \to \mathbb{R}^n$ is a vector-valued polynomial flow field (called the *drift coefficient*) modeling deterministic evolution of the system, and $\sigma \colon \mathbb{R}^n \to \mathbb{R}^{n \times m}$ is a matrix-valued polynomial flow field (called the *diffusion coefficient*) that encodes the coupling of the system to Gaussian white noise $\mathrm{d}W_t$.

Suppose there exists a Lipschitz constant D s.t. $|b(x) - b(y)| + |\sigma(x) - \sigma(y)| \leq D\,|x - y|$ holds for all $x, y \in \mathbb{R}^n$. Then, given an initial state (a random variable) X_0, an SDE of the form (1) has a unique *solution* which is a stochastic process $X_t(\omega) = X(t, \omega) \colon [0, \infty) \times \Omega \to \mathbb{R}^n$ satisfying the stochastic integral equation (à la Itô's interpretation)

$$X_t = X_0 + \int_0^t b(X_s)\,\mathrm{d}s + \int_0^t \sigma(X_s)\,\mathrm{d}W_s. \tag{2}$$

The solution $\{X_t\}$ in Eq. (2) is also referred to as an *(Itô) diffusion process*, and will be denoted by X_t^{0, X_0} (or simply $X_t^{X_0}$), if necessary, to indicate the initial condition X_0 at $t = 0$.

A great deal of information about a diffusion process can be encoded in a partial differential operator termed the *infinitesimal generator*, which generalizes

---

[1] The general time-inhomogeneous case with time-dependent b and σ can be reduced to this form (cf. [24, Chap. 10]).

the Lie derivative that captures the evolution of a function along the diffusion process:

Definition 1 (Infinitesimal generator [24]**).** *Let* $\{X_t\}$ *be a (time-homogeneous) diffusion process in* $\mathbb{R}^n$. *The* infinitesimal generator $\mathcal{A}$ *of* X_t *is defined by*

$$\mathcal{A}f(s,x) = \lim_{t\downarrow 0} \frac{E^{s,x}\left[f(s+t,X_t)\right] - f(s,x)}{t}, \quad x \in \mathbb{R}^n.$$

The set of functions $f\colon \mathbb{R} \times \mathbb{R}^n \to \mathbb{R}$ *s.t. the limit exists at* (s,x) *is denoted by* $\mathcal{D}_\mathcal{A}(s,x)$, *while* $\mathcal{D}_\mathcal{A}$ *denotes the set of functions for which the limit exists for all* $(s,x) \in \mathbb{R} \times \mathbb{R}^n$.

In subsequent sections, the readers may find applications of the operator $\mathcal{A}$ to a vector-valued function in a component-wise manner. The relation between $\mathcal{A}$ and the coefficients b, σ in SDE (1) is captured by the following result:

Lemma 1 [24]. *Let* $\{X_t\}$ *be a diffusion process defined by Eq.* (1). *If* $f \in C^{1,2}(\mathbb{R} \times \mathbb{R}^n)$ *with compact support, then* $f \in \mathcal{D}_\mathcal{A}$ *and*

$$\mathcal{A}f(t,x) = \frac{\partial f}{\partial t} + \sum_{i=1}^{n} b_i(x)\frac{\partial f}{\partial x_i} + \frac{1}{2}\sum_{i,j}(\sigma\sigma^\mathsf{T})_{ij}\frac{\partial^2 f}{\partial x_i \partial x_j}.$$

As a stochastic generalization of the Newton-Leibniz axiom, Dynkin's formula gives the expected value of any adequately smooth function of an Itô diffusion at a stopping time:

Theorem 1 (Dynkin's formula [9]**).** *Let* $\{X_t\}$ *be a diffusion process in* $\mathbb{R}^n$. *Suppose* τ *is a stopping time with* $E[\tau] < \infty$, *and* $f \in C^{1,2}(\mathbb{R} \times \mathbb{R}^n)$ *with compact support. Then*

$$E^{h,x}\left[f(\tau, X_\tau)\right] = f(h,x) + E^{h,x}\left[\int_0^\tau \mathcal{A}f(s, X_s)\, \mathrm{d}s\right].$$

In order to specify the behavior of an Itô diffusion across the domain boundary, we introduce the concept of *stopped process*, which is a stochastic process that is forced to have the same value after a prescribed (possibly random) time.

Definition 2 (Stopped process [12]**).** *Given a stopping time* τ *and a stochastic process* $\{X_t\}$, *the* stopped process $\{X_t^\tau\}$ *is defined by*

$$X^\tau(t,\omega) \triangleq X_{t\wedge\tau}(\omega) = \begin{cases} X(t,\omega) & \text{if } t \leq \tau(\omega), \\ X(\tau(\omega),\omega) & \text{otherwise.} \end{cases}$$

Remark 1. By definition, a stopped process preserves, among others, continuity and the Markov property, and hence the aforementioned results on a stochastic process apply also to a stopped process.

Now consider a stochastic system modeled by an SDE of the form (1) that evolves "within" a not necessarily bounded set $\mathcal{X} \subseteq \mathbb{R}^n$. Since the solution $\{X_t\}$ of Eq. (1) may escape from $\mathcal{X}$ at any time instant $t > 0$, due to the unbounded nature of Gaussian, we define a stopped process $\tilde{X}_t \triangleq X_{t \wedge \tau_\mathcal{X}}$ with $\tau_\mathcal{X} \triangleq \inf\{t \mid X_t \notin \mathcal{X}\}$. $\tilde{X}_t$ hence represents the process that will stop at the boundary of $\mathcal{X}$. Denote the infinitesimal generator of the stopped process as $\tilde{\mathcal{A}}$. One plausible property here is that, for all compactly-supported $f \in C^{1,2}(\mathbb{R} \times \mathbb{R}^n)$,

$$\tilde{\mathcal{A}}f(t,x) = \begin{cases} \mathcal{A}f(t,x) & \text{for } x \in \mathcal{X}^\circ, \\ \frac{\partial f}{\partial t}(t,x) & \text{for } x \in \partial\mathcal{X}. \end{cases} \tag{3}$$

The ∞-Safety Problem. Given an SDE of the form (1), a (not necessarily bounded[2]) domain set $\mathcal{X} \subseteq \mathbb{R}^n$, an initial set $\mathcal{X}_0 \subset \mathcal{X}$, and an unsafe set $\mathcal{X}_u \subset \mathcal{X}$. We aim to bound the failure probability

$$P\left(\exists t \in [0, \infty) \colon \tilde{X}_t \in \mathcal{X}_u\right),$$

for any initial state X_0 whose support lies within $\mathcal{X}_0$. Accordingly, the *T-safety problem*, with $T < \infty$, refers to the problem where one aims to bound the failure probability within the finite time horizon $[0, T]$.

Remark 2. Roughly speaking, if we denote by ϕ the proposition "$\tilde{X}_t$ evolves within $\mathcal{X}$" and by ψ the proposition "$\tilde{X}_t$ evolves into $\mathcal{X}_u$", then the above ∞-safety problem asks for a bound on the probability that the LTL formula $\phi \mathcal{U} \psi$ holds.

3 Reducing ∞-Safety to T-Safety

We dedicate this section to the reduction of the ∞-safety problem to its bounded counterpart. Observe that for any $0 \le T < \infty$,

$$P(\exists t \ge 0 \colon \tilde{X}_t \in \mathcal{X}_u) \le P(\exists t \in [0, T] \colon \tilde{X}_t \in \mathcal{X}_u) + P(\exists t \ge T \colon \tilde{X}_t \in \mathcal{X}_u).$$

The key idea behind our approach is to first compute an exponentially decreasing bound on the *tail failure probability* over $[T^*, \infty)$ (the computation of $T^* \ge 0$ will be shown later), and then for any constant $\epsilon > 0$, we can identify (out of the exponentially decreasing bound) a time instant $\tilde{T} \ge T^*$ such that $P(\exists t \ge \tilde{T} \colon \tilde{X}_t \in \mathcal{X}_u) \le \epsilon$. The overall bound on the failure probability over $[0, \infty)$ can consequently be obtained by solving the truncated $\tilde{T}$-safety problem.

---

[2] In practice, if we can specify $\mathcal{X}$ based on prior knowledge when modeling a physical system, then the larger $\mathcal{X}$ we choose, the greater (bound on) failure probability we will obtain.

3.1   Exponentially Decreasing Bound on the Tail Failure Probability

We first state a result that gives conditions when a linear map keeps vector inequality:

Lemma 2 [4, Chap. 4]. *For a matrix* $M \in \mathbb{R}^{n \times n}$,

- $\forall x, y \in \mathbb{R}^n : x \leq y \implies Mx \leq My$ *iff* M *is non-negative, i.e.,* $M_{ij} \geq 0$ *for all* $1 \leq i, j \leq n$.
- *The matrix* e^{Mt} *is non-negative for all* $t \geq 0$ *iff* M *is essentially non-negative, i.e.,* $M_{ij} \geq 0$ *for* $i \neq j$.

The existence of an exponentially decreasing bound on the tail failure probability relies on a witness of a supermartingale of the exponential type:

Theorem 2. *Suppose there exists an essentially non-negative matrix* $\Lambda \in \mathbb{R}^{m \times m}$, *together with an* m-*dimensional polynomial function (termed* exponential stochastic barrier certificate) $V(x) = (V_1(x), V_2(x), \ldots, V_m(x))^\mathsf{T}$, *with* $V_i \colon \mathbb{R}^n \to \mathbb{R}$ *for* $1 \leq i \leq m$, *satisfying*[3],[4]

$$V(x) \geq \mathbf{0} \quad \text{for } x \in \mathcal{X}, \tag{4}$$

$$\mathcal{A}V(x) \leq -\Lambda V(x) \quad \text{for } x \in \mathcal{X}, \tag{5}$$

$$\Lambda V(x) \leq \mathbf{0} \quad \text{for } x \in \partial\mathcal{X}. \tag{6}$$

Define a function

$$F(t, x) \triangleq e^{\Lambda t} V(x),$$

then every component of $F(t, \tilde{X}_t)$ *is a supermartingale.*

Proof. For cases with a bounded domain $\mathcal{X}$, one can trivially extend the domain of $F(t, x)$ s.t. F is compactly-supported, and thus Dynkin's formula in Theorem 1 applies immediately. For cases where $\mathcal{X}$ is unbounded, we introduce a stopping time

$$\tau_\delta \triangleq \inf \left\{ t \mid F\left(t, \tilde{X}_t\right) \geq \mathfrak{B}(\mathbf{0}, \delta) \right\},$$

and denote by $X_t^{(\delta)} \triangleq (t \wedge \tau_\delta, \tilde{X}_{t \wedge \tau_\delta})$ the corresponding stopped process involving the timeline, and by $\mathcal{A}^{(\delta)}$ the corresponding infinitesimal generator. Then $X_t^{(\delta)}$ evolves within the δ-closed ball $\mathfrak{B}(\mathbf{0}, \delta)$ and hence boils down to the case with a bounded domain. Moreover, by Eq. (3), we have

$$\mathcal{A}^{(\delta)} F\left(X_t^{(\delta)}\right) = \mathcal{A}^{(\delta)} F\left(t \wedge \tau_\delta, \tilde{X}_{t \wedge \tau_\delta}\right)$$

$$= \begin{cases} 0 & \text{if } \tau_\delta(\omega) \leq t, \\ \frac{\partial F}{\partial t}(t, X_t) + e^{\Lambda t} \mathcal{A}V(X_t) \leq 0 & \text{if } \tau_\delta(\omega) > t \wedge \tau_\mathcal{X}(\omega) > t, \\ \frac{\partial F}{\partial t}(t, X_t) \leq 0 & \text{if } \tau_\delta(\omega) > t \wedge \tau_\mathcal{X}(\omega) \leq t, \end{cases}$$

---

[3] Condition (5) is slightly stronger than the corresponding one used in [27, 28], yet will lead to an exponentially decreasing bound on the tail failure probability in return.

[4] Condition (6) is to ensure that when $\tilde{X}_t$ stops at the boundary of $\mathcal{X}$, we still have $\tilde{\mathcal{A}}V(x) \leq -\Lambda V(x)$ for $x \in \partial\mathcal{X}$. If $\mathcal{X} = \mathbb{R}^n$, however, this condition can be omitted.

where $\tau_{\mathcal{X}}$ represents the time instant when escaping from the state space $\mathcal{X}$. Note that the second and the third case hold due to the non-negativity of $e^{\Lambda t}$ (as Λ is essentially non-negative), which implies that $e^{\Lambda t}$ preserves vector inequalities (5) and (6). Hence by Dynkin's formula (in a component-wise manner), for fixed $t, h \in [0, \infty)$, we have

$$
\begin{aligned}
E\left[F\left((t+h) \wedge \tau_\delta, \tilde{X}_{(t+h)\wedge\tau_\delta}\right) \mid \mathcal{F}_h\right] &= E^{X_h^{(\delta)}}\left[F\left(X_{t+h}^{(\delta)}\right)\right] \\
&= F\left(X_h^{(\delta)}\right) + E^{X_h^{(\delta)}}\left[\int_0^t \mathcal{A}^{(\delta)} F\left(X_s^{(\delta)}\right) \, \mathrm{d}s\right] \\
&\leq F\left(X_h^{(\delta)}\right) \\
&= F\left(h \wedge \tau_\delta, \tilde{X}_{h\wedge\tau_\delta}\right).
\end{aligned}
$$

Since $F(t, x) > \mathbf{0}$, by Fatou's lemma, we have

$$
\begin{aligned}
E\left[F\left(t+h, \tilde{X}_{t+h}\right) \mid \mathcal{F}_h\right] &= E\left[\liminf_{\delta\to\infty} F\left((t+h) \wedge \tau_\delta, \tilde{X}_{(t+h)\wedge\tau_\delta}\right) \mid \mathcal{F}_h\right] \\
&\leq \liminf_{\delta\to\infty} E\left[F\left((t+h) \wedge \tau_\delta, \tilde{X}_{(t+h)\wedge\tau_\delta}\right) \mid \mathcal{F}_h\right] \\
&\leq \liminf_{\delta\to\infty} F\left(h \wedge \tau_\delta, \tilde{X}_{h\wedge\tau_\delta}\right) \\
&\leq F\left(h, \tilde{X}_h\right).
\end{aligned}
$$

It follows consequently that every component of $F(t, \tilde{X}_t)$ is a supermartingale. $\square$

We will show in Sect. 4 that the synthesis of the exponential stochastic barrier certificate $V(x)$ (and thereby the function $F(t, x)$) boils down to solving a pertinent SDP optimization problem.

In order to further establish the relation between the exponential supermartingale $F(t, \tilde{X}_t)$ (and thereby $V(x)$) and the bound on tail failure probability, we recall Doob's maximal inequality for supermartingales, which gives a bound on the probability that a non-negative supermartingale exceeds some given value over a given time interval:

Lemma 3 (Doob's supermartingale inequality [15]). *Let $\{X_t\}_{t>0}$ be a right continuous non-negative supermartingale adapted to a filtration $\{\mathcal{F}_t \mid t > 0\}$. Then for any $\lambda > 0$,*

$$
\lambda P\left(\sup_{t\geq 0} X_t \geq \lambda\right) \leq E[X_0].
$$

The following theorem claims an intermediate fact that will later reveal the exponentially decreasing bound on the tail failure probability.

Theorem 3. *Suppose the conditions in Theorem 2 are satisfied. Then for any $T \geq 0$ and any positive vector $\gamma \in \mathbb{R}^m$,*

$$
P\left(\sup_{t\geq T} V\left(\tilde{X}_t\right) \geq \sup_{t\geq T} \left(e^{-\Lambda t}\gamma\right)\right) \leq E\left[V_i(X_0)\right]/\gamma_i \tag{7}
$$

holds for all $i \in \{1, \ldots, m\}$.

Proof. Observe the following chain of (in-)equalities:

$$P\left(\sup_{t \geq T} V\left(\tilde{X}_t\right) \geq \sup_{t \geq T}\left(\mathrm{e}^{-\Lambda t}\gamma\right)\right) \leq P\left(\exists t \geq T: V\left(\tilde{X}_t\right) \geq \mathrm{e}^{-\Lambda t}\gamma\right)$$

$$\leq P\left(\exists t \geq T: \mathrm{e}^{\Lambda t}V\left(\tilde{X}_t\right) \geq \gamma\right) \qquad \text{[non-negative } \mathrm{e}^{\Lambda t}\text{]}$$

$$= P\left(\sup_{t \geq T} F\left(t, \tilde{X}_t\right) \geq \gamma\right)$$

$$\leq P\left(\sup_{t \geq T} F_i\left(t, \tilde{X}_t\right) \geq \gamma_i\right)$$

$$\leq E\left[F_i\left(T, \tilde{X}_T\right)\right]/\gamma_i \qquad \text{[Lemma 3]}$$

$$\leq E\left[V_i\left(X_0\right)\right]/\gamma_i \qquad \text{[Theorem 2]}$$

which holds for any $i \in \{1, 2, \cdots, m\}$. This completes the proof. □

Now, we are ready to give the exponentially decreasing bound on the tail failure probability derived from Theorem 3. We start by considering the simple case where the barrier certificate $V(x)$ is a scalar function, i.e., with $m = 1$.

Proposition 1. *Suppose there exists a positive constant $\Lambda \in \mathbb{R}$ and a scalar function $V: \mathbb{R}^n \to \mathbb{R}$ satisfying Theorem 2. Then,*

$$P\left(\sup_{t \geq T} V\left(\tilde{X}_t\right) \geq \gamma\right) \leq \frac{E\left[V(X_0)\right]}{\mathrm{e}^{\Lambda T}\gamma} \qquad (8)$$

holds for any $\gamma > 0$ and $T \geq 0$. Moreover, if there exists $l > 0$ such that

$$V(x) \geq l \quad \text{for all } x \in \mathcal{X}_u,$$

then

$$P\left(\exists t \geq T: \tilde{X}_t \in \mathcal{X}_u\right) \leq \frac{E\left[V(X_0)\right]}{\mathrm{e}^{\Lambda T}l} \qquad (9)$$

holds for any $T \geq 0$.

Proof. Equation (8) holds since

$$P\left(\sup_{t \geq T} V\left(\tilde{X}_t\right) \geq \gamma\right) = P\left(\sup_{t \geq T} V\left(\tilde{X}_t\right) \geq \mathrm{e}^{-\Lambda T}\left(\mathrm{e}^{\Lambda T}\gamma\right)\right)$$

$$\leq P\left(\sup_{t \geq T} V\left(\tilde{X}_t\right) \geq \sup_{t \geq T}\left(\mathrm{e}^{-\Lambda t}\left(\mathrm{e}^{\Lambda T}\gamma\right)\right)\right)$$

$$\text{[monotonicity on } t\text{]}$$

$$\leq \frac{E[V(X_0)]}{\mathrm{e}^{\Lambda T}\gamma}. \qquad \text{[Theorem 3]}$$

For Eq. (9), it is immediately obvious that

$$P\left(\exists t \geq T \colon \tilde{X}_t \in \mathscr{X}_u\right) \leq P\left(\sup_{t \geq T} V\left(\tilde{X}_t\right) \geq l\right) \leq \frac{E[V(X_0)]}{e^{\Lambda T} l}.$$

This completes the proof. □

Now we lift the results to the slightly more involved case with $m > 1$.

Proposition 2. *Suppose there exists an essentially non-negative matrix $\Lambda \in \mathbb{R}^{m \times m}$ and an m-dimensional polynomial function $V \colon \mathbb{R}^n \to \mathbb{R}^m$ satisfying Theorem 2. If all of the eigenvalues of Λ have positive real parts, i.e.,*

$$\min_{1 \leq i \leq m} \{\Re(\lambda_i) \mid \lambda_i \text{ is an eigenvalue of } \Lambda\} > 0,$$

then for any positive vector $\gamma \in \mathbb{R}^m$, there exists $T^* = T^*(\gamma, M, \Lambda) \in \mathbb{R}$ such that for any $T \geq T^*$,

$$P\left(\sup_{t \geq T} V\left(\tilde{X}_t\right) \geq \gamma\right) \leq \frac{E[V_i(X_0)]}{(e^{MT}\gamma)_i} \tag{10}$$

holds for all $i \in \{1, \dots, m\}$. Here, M is an essentially non-negative matrix s.t. all of the eigenvalues of $\Lambda - M$ have positive real parts[5]. Moreover, if there exists a positive vector $l \in \mathbb{R}^m$ such that

$$V(x) \geq l \quad \text{for all } x \in \mathscr{X}_u,$$

then for any $T \geq T^*$,

$$P\left(\exists t \geq T \colon \tilde{X}_t \in \mathscr{X}_u\right) \leq \frac{E[V_i(X_0)]}{(e^{MT}l)_i} \tag{11}$$

holds for all $i \in \{1, \dots, m\}$.

Proof. By substituting γ in Eq. (7) with $e^{MT}\gamma$, we have that for all $T \geq 0$,

$$\begin{aligned}\frac{E[V_i(X_0)]}{(e^{MT}\gamma)_i} &\geq P\left(\sup_{t \geq T} V\left(\tilde{X}_t\right) \geq \sup_{t \geq T}\left(e^{-\Lambda t}e^{MT}\gamma\right)\right) \\ &= P\left(\sup_{t \geq T} V\left(\tilde{X}_t\right) \geq \sup_{t \geq T}\left(e^{-\Lambda(t-T)}e^{-(\Lambda-M)T}\gamma\right)\right)\end{aligned} \tag{12}$$

holds for any $\gamma \in \mathbb{R}^m$ with $\gamma > \mathbf{0}$. Observe that

$$\begin{aligned}\left|\sup_{t \geq T}\left(e^{-\Lambda(t-T)}e^{-(\Lambda-M)T}\gamma\right)\right|_\infty &= \left|\sup_{t \geq 0}\left(e^{-\Lambda t}e^{-(\Lambda-M)T}\gamma\right)\right|_\infty \\ &\leq \left|\sup_{t \geq 0}\left(e^{-\Lambda t}\right)\right|_\infty \left|e^{-(\Lambda-M)T}\gamma\right|_\infty,\end{aligned}$$

---

[5] Such matrix M always exists, for instance, $M \cong \Lambda/2$.

where $|\cdot|_\infty$ denotes the infinity norm. Moreover, since all of the eigenvalues of $\Lambda - M$ have positive real parts, then by the Lyapunov stability established in the theory of ODEs, we have

$$\lim_{T \to \infty} \mathrm{e}^{-(\Lambda-M)T}\gamma = \mathbf{0}.$$

There hence exists T^* s.t. for all $T \geq T^*$,

$$\sup_{t \geq T} \left(\mathrm{e}^{-\Lambda(t-T)}\mathrm{e}^{-(\Lambda-M)T}\gamma \right) \leq \gamma. \tag{13}$$

By Combining Eq. (13) and Eq. (12), we obtain Eq. (10). For Eq. (11), it follows immediately that

$$P\left(\exists t \geq T \colon \tilde{X}_t \in \mathcal{X}_u \right) \leq P\left(\sup_{t \geq T} V\left(\tilde{X}_t \right) \geq l \right) \leq \frac{E[V_i(X_0)]}{(\mathrm{e}^{MT}l)_i}.$$

This completes the proof.   □

Remark 3. Proposition 2 argues the existence of T^* that suffices to "split off" the tail failure probability. From a computational perspective, this is algorithmically tractable as the matrix exponential involved in Eq. (13) is symbolically computable (cf., e.g., [23]).

The following theorem states the main result of this section, that is, for any given constant ϵ, there exists $\tilde{T} \geq 0$ such that the truncated $\tilde{T}$-tail failure probability is bounded by ϵ:

Theorem 4. *Suppose the conditions in Proposition 1 and 2 are satisfied. If there exists $\alpha > 0$, s.t. $\forall x \in \mathcal{X}_0 \colon V_i(x) \leq \alpha$ holds for some $i \in \{1, \ldots, m\}$. Then for any $\epsilon > 0$, there exists $\tilde{T} \geq 0$ such that*

$$P\left(\exists t \geq \tilde{T} \colon \tilde{X}_t \in \mathcal{X}_u \right) \leq \epsilon.$$

Proof. Observe that for Eq. (11) in Proposition 2, the assumption $\forall x \in \mathcal{X}_0 \colon V_i(x) \leq \alpha$ guarantees an upper bound on the numerator $E[V_i(X_0)]$, while the essential non-negativity of M (with all its eigenvalues having positive real parts) ensures that the denominator $(\mathrm{e}^{MT}l)_i \to +\infty$ as $T \to \infty$. An analogous argument applies to Eq. (9) in Proposition 1. The claim in this theorem then follows immediately.   □

3.2   Bounding the Failure Probability over $[0, T]$

The reduced T-safety problem can be solved by existing methods tailored for bounded verification of SDEs, e.g., [32,35]. In what follows, we propose an alternative method leveraging time-dependent polynomial stochastic barrier certificates. Our method requires constraints (on the barrier certificates) of simpler form compared to [35]; meanwhile, it yields strictly more expressive form of barrier certificates, against the approach on unbounded verification as in [27, 28], thus leading to theoretically non-looser (usually tighter) failure bound. A detailed argument will be given at the end of this section.

The following theorem states a sufficient condition, i.e., a collection of constraints on the time-dependent polynomial stochastic barrier certificates $H(t, x)$, under which the failure probability of a stochastic system over a finite time horizon can be explicitly bounded from above.

Theorem 5. *Suppose there exists a constant $\eta > 0$ and a polynomial function (termed* time-dependent stochastic barrier certificate*) $H(t, x) \colon \mathbb{R} \times \mathbb{R}^n \to \mathbb{R}$, satisfying[6]*

$$H(t, x) \geq 0 \quad \text{for } (t, x) \in [0, T] \times \mathcal{X}, \tag{14}$$

$$AH(t, x) \leq 0 \quad \text{for } (t, x) \in [0, T] \times (\mathcal{X} \setminus \mathcal{X}_u), \tag{15}$$

$$\frac{\partial H}{\partial t} \leq 0 \quad \text{for } (t, x) \in [0, T] \times \partial \mathcal{X}, \tag{16}$$

$$H(t, x) \geq \eta \quad \text{for } (t, x) \in [0, T] \times \mathcal{X}_u. \tag{17}$$

Then,

$$P\left(\exists t \in [0, T] \colon \tilde{X}_t \in \mathcal{X}_u\right) \leq \frac{E[H(0, X_0)]}{\eta}. \tag{18}$$

Proof. Assume in the following that the system evolves within a bounded domain $\mathcal{X}$[7]. Define a stopping time

$$\tau_u \triangleq \inf\left\{t \mid \tilde{X}_t \notin \mathcal{X} \setminus \mathcal{X}_u\right\},$$

and denote by $X_t^{(u)} \triangleq (t \wedge \tau_u \wedge T, \tilde{X}_{t \wedge \tau_u \wedge T})$ the corresponding stopped process, and by $\mathcal{A}^{(u)}$ the corresponding infinitesimal generator. By Eq. (3), we have

$$\mathcal{A}^{(u)} H\left(X_t^{(u)}\right) = \mathcal{A}^{(u)} H\left(t \wedge \tau_u \wedge T, \tilde{X}_{t \wedge \tau_u \wedge T}\right)$$

$$= \begin{cases} 0 & \text{if } t \geq T \vee t \geq \tau_u(\omega), \\ AH(t, X_t) \leq 0 & \text{if } t < \min\{T, \tau_u(\omega), \tau_{\mathcal{X}}(\omega)\}, \\ \frac{\partial H}{\partial t}(t, X_t) \leq 0 & \text{if } t < \min\{T, \tau_u(\omega)\} \wedge t \geq \tau_{\mathcal{X}}(\omega). \end{cases}$$

By Dynkin's formula, for fixed $t, h \in [0, T]$, we have

$$E\left[H\left(X_{t+h}^{(u)}\right) \mid \mathcal{F}_h\right] = E^{X_h^{(u)}}\left[H\left(X_{t+h}^{(u)}\right)\right]$$

$$= E\left[H\left(X_h^{(u)}\right)\right] + E^{X_h^{(u)}}\left[\int_0^t \mathcal{A}^{(u)} H\left(X_s^{(u)}\right) \, \mathrm{d}s\right]$$

$$\leq E\left[H\left(X_h^{(u)}\right)\right].$$

---

[6] Condition (16) is to ensure that when $\tilde{X}_t$ stops at the boundary of $\mathcal{X}$, we still have $\tilde{A}H(t, x) \leq 0$ for $x \in \partial \mathcal{X}$. If $\mathcal{X} = \mathbb{R}^n$, however, this condition can be dropped.

[7] For cases with an unbounded $\mathcal{X}$, the same proof technique of introducing a δ-closed ball as in the proof of Theorem 2 applies.

Thus $H(X_t^{(u)})$ is a non-negative supermartingale. Then by Doob's maximal inequality in Lemma 3, we have

$$P\left(\exists t \in [0,T]\colon \tilde{X}_t \in \mathcal{X}_u\right) = P\left(\exists t \geq 0\colon \tilde{X}_{t \wedge \tau_u \wedge T} \in \mathcal{X}_u\right)$$
$$\leq P\left(\exists t \geq 0\colon H\left(X_t^{(u)}\right) \geq \eta\right)$$
$$\leq \frac{E[H(0, X_0)]}{\eta}.$$

This completes the proof.   □

The following fact is then immediately obvious:

Corollary 1. *Suppose the conditions in Theorem 5 hold, and there exists $\beta > 0$, s.t. $H(0, x) \leq \beta$ for $x \in \mathcal{X}_0$. Then,*

$$P\left(\exists t \in [0,T]\colon \tilde{X}_t \in \mathcal{X}_u\right) \leq \frac{\beta}{\eta}.$$

Proof. This is a direct consequence of Theorem 5.   □

Remarks on Potentially Tighter Bound. There exists already in the literature a barrier certificate-based method proposed in [27,28] that can deal with the ∞-safety problem. It is worth highlighting, however, that our bound on the overall failure probability derived from Proposition 1, 2 and Theorem 5 (with appropriate $\tilde{T}$ chosen) is at least as tight as (and usually tighter than, as can be seen later in the experiments) that in [27,28]. The reasons are twofold: (1) the reduction to a finite-time horizon $\tilde{T}$-safety problem substantially "trims off" verification efforts pertaining to $t > \tilde{T}$; (2) our method for the reduced $\tilde{T}$-safety problem admits time-dependent barrier certificates, which are strictly more expressive than those time-independent ones exploited in [27,28], in the sense that any feasible solution thereof shall also be a feasible solution satisfying Theorem 5.

Remark 4. Roughly speaking, by setting the diffusion coefficients σ in SDEs to zero, our method applies trivially to ODE dynamics with either a known or an unknown probability distribution over the initial set of states. For the former, we can even obtain a tighter bound on the failure probability, since in this case we do not need to compute a bound on the barrier certificate over all possible initial distributions.

4   Synthesizing Stochastic Barrier Certificates Using SDP

In this section, we encode the synthesis of the aforementioned exponential and time-dependent stochastic barrier certificates into semidefinite programming [38] optimizations, and thus a solution thereof yields an upper bound on the failure probability over the infinite-time horizon. Specifically, an SDP problem is formulated, for each of the two barrier certificates, to encode the constraints for "being an exponential/time-dependent stochastic barrier certificate", while in the meantime optimizing the tightness of the failure probability bound.

It is worth noting that SDP is a generalization of the standard linear programming in which the element-wise non-negativity constraints are replaced by a generalized inequality w.r.t. the cone of positive semidefinite matrices. The generalization preserves *convexity*, leading to the fact that SDP admits polynomial-time algorithms, say the well-known *interior-point methods*, that can efficiently solve the synthesis problem, albeit numerically. We remark that the numerical computation employed in off-the-shelf SDP solvers and the use of interior-point algorithms may potentially lead to erroneous results and thereby unsoundness in the verification/synthesis results. There have been numerous attempts to validate the results from the solver through a-posteriori numerical verification of the solution. For more details, we refer the readers to [30] and the references therein.

Exponential Stochastic Barrier Certificate $V(x)$. To encode the synthesis problem into an SDP optimization, we first fix the dimension m together with Λ satisfying Proposition 1 or 2 (depending on m), and then assume a polynomial template $V^a(x)$ of certain degree k with unknown parameters a, as the barrier certificate to be discovered. It then suffices to solve the following SDP problem[8]:

$$\underset{a,\alpha}{\text{minimize}} \quad \alpha \tag{19}$$

$$\text{subject to} \quad V^a(x) \geq \mathbf{0} \quad \text{for } x \in \mathcal{X} \tag{20}$$

$$\mathcal{A}V^a(x) \leq -\Lambda V^a(x) \quad \text{for } x \in \mathcal{X} \tag{21}$$

$$\Lambda V^a(x) \leq \mathbf{0} \quad \text{for } x \in \partial\mathcal{X} \tag{22}$$

$$V^a(x) \geq \mathbf{1} \quad \text{for } x \in \mathcal{X}_u \tag{23}$$

$$V^a(x) \leq \alpha\mathbf{1} \quad \text{for } x \in \mathcal{X}_0 \tag{24}$$

Here, the constraints (20)–(22) encode the definition of an exponential stochastic barrier certificate (cf. Theorem 2), while constraint (23) (resp., (24)) corresponds to the lower (resp., upper) bound of $V(x)$ as in Proposition 1 and 2 (resp., Theorem 4)[9]. Hence, minimizing the upper bound α of (each component of) $V^a(x)$ gives a tight exponentially decreasing bound on the tail failure probability, as claimed in Proposition 1 and 2.

Remark 5. If Λ is chosen as a non-negative matrix, the combination of condition (20) and (22) will force $V^a(x) = \mathbf{0}$ for $x \in \partial\mathcal{X}$, whereof the strict equality

---

[8] SDP problems in this paper refer to those that can be readily translated into the standard form of SDP, through, e.g., Stengle's Positivstellensatz [36] and sum-of-squares decomposition [26].

[9] The lower bound l of $V(x)$ in Proposition 1 and 2 is normalized to a vector with all its components no less than 1, based on the observation that, for any $c > 0$, $V^a(x)$ is a feasible solution implies $cV^a(x)$ is also a feasible solution.

may be violated due to numerical computations in SDP. In practice, however, this issue can be well addressed by looking for a barrier certificate of the form $g(x)V(x)$, where $g(x)$ satisfies $\partial \mathcal{X} \subseteq \{x \mid g(x) = 0\}$, namely, an overapproximation of the boundary of $\mathcal{X}$.

Remark 6. The choice of m is arbitrary, while the choices of Λ and k can be heuristic: If Λ_1 admits no feasible solution, neither will $\Lambda_2 \geq \Lambda_1$ (point-wise, with all the rest parameters fixed); similarly, if k_1 admits no feasible solution, neither will $k_2 \leq k_1$ (with all the rest parameters fixed). Therefore, one may decrease Λ (say, by a half) or increase k (say, by one) whenever a valid barrier certificate was not found.

Time-Dependent Stochastic Barrier Certificate $H(t, x)$. Given the results established in Sect. 3, the corresponding synthesis problem can be analogously encoded as the following SDP problem:

$$\underset{b,\beta}{\text{minimize}} \quad \beta \tag{25}$$

$$\text{subject to} \quad H^b(t, x) \geq 0 \quad \text{for } (t, x) \in [0, T] \times \mathcal{X} \tag{26}$$

$$\mathcal{A}H^b(t, x) \leq 0 \quad \text{for } (t, x) \in [0, T] \times (\mathcal{X} \setminus \mathcal{X}_u) \tag{27}$$

$$\frac{\partial H^b}{\partial t} \leq 0 \quad \text{for } (t, x) \in [0, T] \times \partial \mathcal{X} \tag{28}$$

$$H^b(t, x) \geq 1 \quad \text{for } (t, x) \in [0, T] \times \mathcal{X}_u \tag{29}$$

$$H^b(0, x) \leq \beta \quad \text{for } x \in \mathcal{X}_0 \tag{30}$$

Similarly, the constraints (26)–(29) encode the definition of a time-dependent stochastic barrier certificate (cf. Theorem 5), while constraint (30) corresponds to the upper bound of $H(t, x)$ as in Corollary 1 (with η being normalized to 1, as in constraint (29)). Consequently, minimizing the upper bound β of $H^b(t, x)$ produces a tight bound on the failure probability over the reduced finite-time horizon, as stated in Corollary 1.

Remark 7. The state-of-the-art interior-point methods solve an SDP problem up to an error ε in time that is polynomial in the program description size (number of variables) and $\log(1/\varepsilon)$. The former is exponential in the degree of V^a and H^b, as it corresponds to the number of monomials in the template polynomials.

5   Implementation and Experimental Results

To further demonstrate the practical performance of our approach, we have carried out a prototypical implementation in MATLAB R2019b, with the toolbox YALMIP [21] and MOSEK [2] equipped for formulating and solving the underlying SDP problems. Given an ∞-safety problem as input, our implementation works toward an upper bound on the failure probability over the infinite time horizon, leveraging the reduction to a T-safety problem based on a computed exponentially decreasing bound on the tail failure probability. A collection of benchmark examples from the literature has been evaluated on a 1.8 GHz Intel Core-i7 processor with 8 GB RAM running 64-bit Windows 10. Each of the examples has been successfully tackled within 30 s. In what follows, we demonstrate the applicability of our techniques to SDEs featuring different dimensionalities and nonlinear dynamics, and show particularly that our approach usually produces tighter bounds compared to existing methods.

Example 1 (Population growth [25]). Consider the stochastic system

$$dX_t = b(X_t) \, dt + \sigma(X_t) \, dW_t,$$

which is a stochastic model of population dynamics subject to random fluctuations that, possibly, can be attributed to extraneous or chance factors such as the weather, location, and the general environment. Suppose that the state space is restricted within $\mathcal{X} = \{x \mid x \geq 0\}$ with $b(X_t) = -X_t$ and $\sigma(X_t) = \sqrt{2}/2X_t$. We instantiate the ∞-safety problem as $\mathcal{X}_0 = \{x \mid x = 1\}$ and $\mathcal{X}_u = \{x \mid x \geq 2\}$, namely, we expect that the population does not diverge beyond 2.

Let $\Lambda = 1$ (with $m = 1$) and set the polynomial template degree of the exponential stochastic barrier certificate $V^a(x)$ to 4, the SDP solver gives

$$V^a(x) = 0.000001474596322 - 0.000044643990040x$$
$$+ 0.125023372121222x^2 + 0.000000001430428x^3,$$

which satisfies

$$V^a(x) \geq 1 \quad \text{for } x \in \mathcal{X}_u \quad \text{and} \quad V^a(x) \leq 0.12498 \quad \text{for } x \in \mathcal{X}_0.$$

Thus by Proposition 1, we obtain the exponentially decreasing bound

$$P\left(\exists t \geq T \colon \tilde{X}_t \in \mathcal{X}_u\right) \leq \frac{0.12498}{e^T} \quad \text{for all } T > 0.$$

The user then may choose any $T > 0$ and solve the reduced T-safety problem. As depicted in the left of Fig. 1, different choices lead to different bounds on the failure probability. Nevertheless, one may surely select an appropriate T that yields a way tighter overall bound on the failure probability than that produced by the method in [27,28].

Example 2 (Harmonic oscillator [13]). Consider a two-dimensional harmonic oscillator with noisy damping:

$$dX_t = \begin{pmatrix} 0 & \omega \\ -\omega & -k \end{pmatrix} X_t \, dt + \begin{pmatrix} 0 & 0 \\ 0 & -\sigma \end{pmatrix} X_t \, dW_t,$$

with constants $\omega = 1, k = 7$ and $\sigma = 2$. We instantiate the ∞-safety problem as $\mathcal{X} = \mathbb{R}^n$, $\mathcal{X}_0 = \{(x_1, x_2) \mid -1.2 \leq x_1 \leq 0.8, -0.6 \leq x_2 \leq 0.4\}$ and $\mathcal{X}_u = \{(x_1, x_2) \mid |x_1| \geq 2\}$.

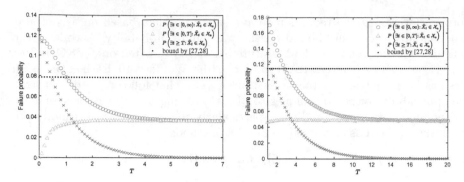

Fig. 1. Different choices of T lead to different bounds on the failure probability (with the time-dependent stochastic barrier certificates of degree 4). Note that '∘' = '×' + '△' and '•' depicts the overall bound on the failure probability produced by the method in [27,28].

Let $\varLambda = \begin{pmatrix} 0.45 & 0.1 \\ 0.1 & 0.45 \end{pmatrix}$ and set the polynomial template degree of the exponential stochastic barrier certificate $V^a(x)$ to 4, the SDP solver produces a two-dimensional $V^a(x)$ (abbreviated for clear presentation) satisfying

$$V^a(x) \leq \begin{pmatrix} 0.19946 \\ 0.19946 \end{pmatrix} \quad \text{for } x \in \mathcal{X}_0 \quad \text{and} \quad V^a(x) \geq l = \begin{pmatrix} 1.000237 \\ 1.000236 \end{pmatrix} \quad \text{for } x \in \mathcal{X}_u.$$

According to the proof of Proposition 2, we set $M = \begin{pmatrix} 0.3 & 0.1 \\ 0.1 & 0.3 \end{pmatrix}$ and aim to find $T^* \geq 0$ such that for all $T \geq T^*$,

$$\sup_{t \geq 0} \left(e^{-\varLambda t} e^{-(\varLambda - M)T} \begin{pmatrix} 1.000237 \\ 1.000236 \end{pmatrix} \right) \leq \begin{pmatrix} 1.000237 \\ 1.000236 \end{pmatrix}. \tag{31}$$

Symbolic computation on the matrix exponential gives

$$\sup_{t \geq 0} \left(e^{-\varLambda t} e^{-(\varLambda - M)T} \begin{pmatrix} 1.000237 \\ 1.000236 \end{pmatrix} \right) = \sup_{t \geq 0} \begin{pmatrix} e^{-0.15T}(1.0002365 e^{-0.55t} + 0.0000005 e^{-0.35t}) \\ e^{-0.15T}(1.0002365 e^{-0.55t} - 0.0000005 e^{-0.35t}) \end{pmatrix}$$

$$\leq \begin{pmatrix} 1.0002365 e^{-0.15T} \\ 1.0002365 e^{-0.15T} \end{pmatrix}.$$

Therefore, $T^* = 1$ satisfies condition (31). Further by Corollary 2, for any $T \geq T^* = 1$, we have

$$P\left(\exists t \geq T \colon \tilde{X}_t \in \mathcal{X}_u \right) \leq \frac{E[V_1(X_0)]}{(e^{MT}l)_1} \leq \frac{0.19946}{0.0000005 e^{0.2T} + 1.00024 e^{0.4T}}.$$

Analogously, a comparison with existing methods concerning the tightness of the synthesized failure probability bound (under different choices of T) is shown in the right of Fig. 1.

Example 3 (Nonlinear drift [27]). We consider in this example a stochastic system involving nonlinear dynamics in its drift coefficient:

$$dx_1(t) = x_2(t)\ dt$$
$$dx_2(t) = -x_1(t) - x_2(t) - 0.5x_1^3(t)\ dt + 0.1\ dW_t.$$

As in [27], let $\mathcal{X} = \{(x_1, x_2) \mid |x_1| \leq 3, |x_2| \leq 3, x_1^2 + x_2^2 \geq 0.5^2\}$, $\mathcal{X}_0 = \{(x_1, x_2) \mid (x_1 + 2)^2 + x_2^2 \leq 0.1^2\}$ and $\mathcal{X}_u = \{(x_1, x_2) \in \mathcal{X} \mid x_2 \geq 2.25\}$. With $\Lambda = 1.5$ ($m = 1$), we obtain an exponential stochastic barrier certificate $V^a(x)$ of degree 8 satisfying

$$V^a(x) \leq 4.00014 \text{ for } x \in \mathcal{X}_0 \quad \text{and} \quad V^a(x) \geq 1.05248 \text{ for } x \in \mathcal{X}_u.$$

Thus by Corollary 1, we have for any $T \geq 0$,

$$P\left(\exists t \geq T \colon \tilde{X}_t \in \mathcal{X}_u\right) \leq \frac{3.80070}{e^{1.5T}}.$$

Setting, for instance, $T = 6$, we have

$$P\left(\exists t \geq 0 \colon \tilde{X}_t \in \mathcal{X}_u\right) \leq P\left(\exists t \in [0, 6] \colon \tilde{X}_t \in \mathcal{X}_u\right) + \frac{3.80070}{e^9}.$$

For the reduced T-safety problem with $T = 6$, a time-dependent stochastic barrier certificate of degree 8 is synthesized, thereby yielding $P\left(\exists t \in [0, 6] \colon \tilde{X}_t \in \mathcal{X}_u\right) \leq 0.196124$, thus together we get

$$P\left(\exists t \geq 0 \colon \tilde{X}_t \in \mathcal{X}_u\right) \leq 0.196593,$$

which is tighter than 0.265388 produced (on the same machine) by the method in [27] under the same template degree.

6   Conclusion

We proposed a constructive method, based on the synthesis of stochastic barrier certificates, for computing an exponentially decreasing upper bound, if existent, on the tail probability that an SDE system violates a given safety specification. We showed that such an upper bound facilitates a reduction of the verification problem over an unbounded temporal horizon to that over a bounded one. Preliminary experimental results on a set of interesting examples from the literature demonstrated the effectiveness of the reduction and that our method often produces tighter bounds on the failure probability.

For future work, we plan to investigate a possible convergence result in the sense that the derived failure probability bound may converge to the exact one as increasing the degree of the barrier certificates. Extending our technique to tackle SDEs with control inputs will also be of interest. Moreover, checking whether a given parametric (polynomial) formula keeps probabilistic invariance plays a central in the verification of SDEs. Several kinds of sufficient conditions on probabilistic barrier certificates were proposed, including the ones given in this paper. It consequently deserves to investigate a necessary and sufficient condition for checking the probabilistic invariance of a given template, like for ODEs in [19]. Apart from that, we are interested in carrying our results to the verification of probabilistic programs without conditioning, which can be viewed as discrete-time stochastic dynamics.

References

1. Abate, A., Prandini, M., Lygeros, J., Sastry, S.: Probabilistic reachability and safety for controlled discrete time stochastic hybrid systems. Automatica **44**(11), 2724–2734 (2008)
2. Andersen, E.D., Roos, C., Terlaky, T.: On implementing a primal-dual interior-point method for conic quadratic optimization. Math. Program. **95**(2), 249–277 (2003)
3. Baier, C., Katoen, J.-P.: Principles of Model Checking. MIT Press, Cambridge (2008)
4. Beckenbach, E.F., Bellman, R.E.: Inequalities. Ergeb. Math. Grenzgeb., vol. 30. Springer, Heidelberg (1961). https://doi.org/10.1007/978-3-642-64971-4
5. Black, F., Scholes, M.: The pricing of options and corporate liabilities. J. Polit. Econ. **81**(3), 637–654 (1973)
6. Blom, H., Bakker, G., Krystul, J.: Probabilistic reachability analysis for large scale stochastic hybrid systems. In: CDC 2007, pp. 3182–3189 (2007)
7. Bujorianu, M.L.: Extended stochastic hybrid systems and their reachability problem. In: Alur, R., Pappas, G.J. (eds.) HSCC 2004. LNCS, vol. 2993, pp. 234–249. Springer, Heidelberg (2004). https://doi.org/10.1007/978-3-540-24743-2_16
8. Deshmukh, J.V., Sankaranarayanan, S.: Formal techniques for verification and testing of cyber-physical systems. In: Al Faruque, M.A., Canedo, A. (eds.) Design Automation of Cyber-Physical Systems, pp. 69–105. Springer, Cham (2019). https://doi.org/10.1007/978-3-030-13050-3_4
9. Dynkin, E.B.: Markov Processes, vol. 2. Springer, Heidelberg (1965). https://doi.org/10.1007/978-3-662-00031-1
10. Einstein, A.: On the theory of Brownian motion. Ann. Phys. **19**, 371–381 (1906)
11. Feng, S., Chen, M., Zhan, N., Fränzle, M., Xue, B.: Taming delays in dynamical systems. In: Dillig, I., Tasiran, S. (eds.) CAV 2019. LNCS, vol. 11561, pp. 650–669. Springer, Cham (2019). https://doi.org/10.1007/978-3-030-25540-4_37
12. Gallager, R.G.: Stochastic Processes: Theory for Applications. Cambridge University Press, Cambridge (2013)
13. Hafstein, S., Gudmundsson, S., Giesl, P., Scalas, E.: Lyapunov function computation for autonomous linear stochastic differential equations using sum-of-squares programming. Discrete Contin. Dyn. Syst. Series B **23**(2), 939–956 (2018)
14. Hoogendoorn, S., Bovy, P.: Pedestrian route-choice and activity scheduling theory and models. Transp. Res. Part B Methodol. **38**(2), 169–190 (2004)
15. Karatzas, I., Shreve, S.: Brownian Motion and Stochastic Calculus. Graduate Texts in Mathematics. Springer, New York (2014). https://doi.org/10.1007/978-1-4684-0302-2

16. Koutsoukos, X.D., Riley, D.: Computational methods for verification of stochastic hybrid systems. IEEE Trans. Syst. Man Cybern. Part A Syst. Hum. **38**(2), 385–396 (2008)
17. Kushner, H., Dupuis, P.: Numerical Methods for Stochastic Control Problems in Continuous Time. Springer, New York (2001). https://doi.org/10.1007/978-1-4613-0007-6
18. Lecchini-Visintini, A., Lygeros, J., Maciejowski, J.: Stochastic optimization on continuous domains with finite-time guarantees by Markov chain Monte Carlo methods. IEEE Trans. Automat. Control **55**(12), 2858–2863 (2010)
19. Liu, J., Zhan, N., Zhao, H.: Computing semi-algebraic invariants for polynomial dynamical systems. In: EMSOFT 2011, pp. 97–106. ACM (2011)
20. Liu, K., Li, M, She, Z.: Reachability estimation of stochastic dynamical systems by semi-definite programming. In: CDC 2019, pp. 7727–7732. IEEE (2019)
21. Löfberg, J.: YALMIP: a toolbox for modeling and optimization in MATLAB. In: CACSD 2004, pp. 284–289 (2004)
22. Mitchell, I.M., Templeton, J.A.: A toolbox of Hamilton-Jacobi solvers for analysis of nondeterministic continuous and hybrid systems. In: Morari, M., Thiele, L. (eds.) HSCC 2005. LNCS, vol. 3414, pp. 480–494. Springer, Heidelberg (2005). https://doi.org/10.1007/978-3-540-31954-2_31
23. Moler, C., Van Loan, C.: Nineteen dubious ways to compute the exponential of a matrix, twenty-five years later. SIAM Rev. **45**(1), 3–49 (2003)
24. Øksendal, B.: Stochastic differential equation. In: Dubitzky, W., Wolkenhauer, O., Cho, K.H., Yokota, H. (eds.) Encyclopedia of Systems Biology. Springer, New York (2013). https://doi.org/10.1007/978-1-4419-9863-7_101409
25. Panik, M.: Stochastic Differential Equations: An Introduction with Applications in Population Dynamics Modeling. Wiley, Hoboken (2017)
26. Parillo, P.A.: Semidefinite programming relaxation for semialgebraic problems. Math. Program. Ser. B **96**(2), 293–320 (2003)
27. Prajna, S., Jadbabaie, A., Pappas, G.J.: Stochastic safety verification using barrier certificates. In: CDC 2004, vol. 1, pp. 929–934. IEEE (2004)
28. Prajna, S., Jadbabaie, A., Pappas, G.J.: A framework for worst-case and stochastic safety verification using barrier certificates. IEEE Trans. Automat. Control **52**(8), 1415–1428 (2007)
29. Rajkumar, R., Lee, I., Sha, L., Stankovic, J.: Cyber-physical systems: the next computing revolution. In: DAC 2010, pp. 731–736. ACM (2010)
30. Roux, P., Voronin, Y.-L., Sankaranarayanan, S.: Validating numerical semidefinite programming solvers for polynomial invariants. Formal Methods Syst. Des. **53**(2), 286–312 (2017). https://doi.org/10.1007/s10703-017-0302-y
31. Sankaranarayanan, S., Chakarov, A., Gulwani, S.: Static analysis for probabilistic programs: inferring whole program properties from finitely many paths. In: PLDI 2013, pp. 447–458 (2013)
32. Santoyo, C., Dutreix, M., Coogan, S.: Verification and control for finite-time safety of stochastic systems via barrier functions. In: CCTA 2019, pp. 712–717. IEEE (2019)
33. Sloth, C., Wisniewski, R.: Safety analysis of stochastic dynamical systems. In: ADHS 2015, pp. 62–67 (2015)
34. Sogokon, A., Ghorbal, K., Tan, Y.K., Platzer, A.: Vector barrier certificates and comparison systems. In: Havelund, K., Peleska, J., Roscoe, B., de Vink, E. (eds.) FM 2018. LNCS, vol. 10951, pp. 418–437. Springer, Cham (2018). https://doi.org/10.1007/978-3-319-95582-7_25

35. Steinhardt, J., Tedrake, R.: Finite-time regional verification of stochastic non-linear systems. Int. J. Robot. Res. **31**(7), 901–923 (2012)
36. Stengle, G.: A nullstellensatz and a positivstellensatz in semialgebraic geometry. Math. Ann. **207**(2), 87–97 (1974)
37. Wang, X., Chiang, H., Wang, J., Liu, H., Wang, T.: Long-term stability analysis of power systems with wind power based on stochastic differential equations: model development and foundations. IEEE Trans. Sustain. Energy **6**(4), 1534–1542 (2015)
38. Wolkowicz, H., Saigal, R., Vandenberghe, L.: Handbook of Semidefinite Programming: Theory, Algorithms, and Applications. International Series in Operations Research & Management Science, vol. 27. Springer, Boston (2012). https://doi.org/10.1007/978-1-4615-4381-7
39. Younes, H.L.S., Simmons, R.G.: Probabilistic Verification of Discrete Event Systems Using Acceptance Sampling. In: Brinksma, E., Larsen, K.G. (eds.) CAV 2002. LNCS, vol. 2404, pp. 223–235. Springer, Heidelberg (2002). https://doi.org/10.1007/3-540-45657-0_17

Widest Paths and Global Propagation in Bounded Value Iteration for Stochastic Games

Kittiphon Phalakarn[1], Toru Takisaka[2(✉)], Thomas Haas[3], and Ichiro Hasuo[2,4]

[1] University of Waterloo, Waterloo, Canada
kphalakarn@uwaterloo.ca
[2] National Institute of Informatics, Tokyo, Japan
{takisaka,hasuo}@nii.ac.jp
[3] Technical University of Braunschweig, Braunschweig, Germany
thohaas@tu-bs.de
[4] The Graduate University for Advanced Studies (SOKENDAI), Tokyo, Japan

Abstract. Solving *stochastic games* with the reachability objective is a fundamental problem, especially in quantitative verification and synthesis. For this purpose, *bounded value iteration (BVI)* attracts attention as an efficient iterative method. However, BVI's performance is often impeded by costly *end component (EC) computation* that is needed to ensure convergence. Our contribution is a novel BVI algorithm that conducts, in addition to local propagation by the Bellman update that is typical of BVI, *global* propagation of upper bounds that is not hindered by ECs. To conduct global propagation in a computationally tractable manner, we construct a weighted graph and solve the *widest path problem* in it. Our experiments show the algorithm's performance advantage over the previous BVI algorithms that rely on EC computation.

1 Introduction

1.1 Stochastic Game (SG)

A *stochastic game* [13] is a two-player game played on a graph. In an SG, an action a of a player causes a transition from the current state s to a successor s', with the latter chosen from a prescribed probability distribution $\delta(s, a, s')$. Under the reachability objective, the two players (called *Maximizer* and *Minimizer*) aim to maximize and minimize, respectively, the reachability probability to a designated target state.

Stochastic games are a fundamental construct in theoretical computer science, especially in the analysis of probabilistic systems. Its complexity is interesting in its own: the problem of threshold reachability—whether Maximizer has a strategy that ensures the reachability probability to be at least given p—is known

---

K. Phalakarn—The work was done during K.P.'s internship at National Institute of Informatics, Japan, while he was a student at Chulalongkorn University, Thailand.

S. K. Lahiri and C. Wang (Eds.): CAV 2020, LNCS 12225, pp. 349–371, 2020.
https://doi.org/10.1007/978-3-030-53291-8_19

to be in UP ∩ coUP [19], but no polynomial algorithm is known. The practical significance of SGs comes from the number of problems that can be encoded to SGs and then solved. Examples include the following: solving deterministic parity games [8], solving stochastic games with the parity or mean-payoff objective [1], and a variety of probabilistic verification and reactive synthesis problems in different application domains such as cyber-physical systems. See e.g. [25].

SGs are often called 2.5-player games, where probabilistic branching is counted as 0.5 players. They generalize deterministic automata (0-player), Markov chains (MCs, 0.5-player), nondeterministic automata (1-player), Markov decision processes (MDPs, 1.5-player) and (deterministic) games (2-player). Many theoretical considerations on these special cases carry over smoothly to SGs. However, SGs have their peculiarities, too. One example is the treatment of end components in bounded value iteration, as we describe later.

1.2   Value Iteration (VI)

In an SG, we are interested in the *optimal* reachability probability, that is, the reachability probability when both Maximizer and Minimizer take their optimal strategies. The function that returns these optimal reachability probabilities is called the *value function* $V(\mathcal{G})$ of the SG $\mathcal{G}$; our interest is in computing this value function, desirably constructing optimal strategies for the two players at the same time. For this purpose, two principal families of solution methods are *strategy iteration (SI)* [19] and *value iteration (VI)* [10,13]—the latter is commonly preferred for performance reasons.

The mathematical principle that underpins VI is the characterization of the value function $V(\mathcal{G})$ as the *least fixed point (lfp)* of an function update operator $\mathbb{X}$ called the *Bellman operator*. The Bellman operator $\mathbb{X}$ back-propagates function values by one step, using the average. For the simple case of Markov chains shown on the right, it is defined by $(\mathbb{X}f)(s) = \sum_i p_i \cdot f(s_i)$, turning a function $f\colon S \to [0,1]$ (i.e., assignment of "scores" to states) to $\mathbb{X}f\colon S \to [0,1]$.

Since $V(\mathcal{G})$ is the lfp $\mu\mathbb{X}$, Kleene's fixed point theorem tells us the sequence

$$\bot \leq \mathbb{X}\bot \leq \mathbb{X}^2\bot \leq \cdots, \tag{1}$$

where $\bot$ is the least element of the function space $S \to [0,1]$, converges to $V(\mathcal{G}) = \mu\mathbb{X}$. VI consists of the iterative approximation of $V(\mathcal{G})$ via the sequence (1).

An issue from the practical point of view, however, is that $\mathbb{X}^i\bot$ never becomes equal to $V(\mathcal{G})$ in general. Even worse, one cannot know how close the current approximant $\mathbb{X}^i\bot$ is to the desired function $V(\mathcal{G})$ [18]. In summary, VI as an iterative approximation method does not give any precision guarantee.

1.3   Bounded Value Iteration (BVI) and End Components

Bounded value iteration (BVI) has been actively studied as an extension of VI that comes with a precision guarantee [2,3,5,16,18,20,23]. Its core ideas are the following two.

Firstly, BVI computes not only iterative lower bounds $L_i = \mathbb{X}^i \bot$ for $V(\mathcal{G})$, but also iterative *upper bounds* U_i, as shown on the right in (2). This gives us a precision guarantee—$V(\mathcal{G})$ must lie between the approximants L_i and U_i.

$$
\begin{aligned}
L_0 \leq L_1 \leq \cdots \\
U_0 \geq U_1 \geq \cdots
\end{aligned} \searrow \nearrow V(\mathcal{G}) \qquad (2)
$$

Secondly, for computing upper bounds U_i, BVI uses the Bellman operator again: $U_i = \mathbb{X}^i \top$ where $\top$ is the greatest element of the function space $S \to [0,1]$. This leads to the following approximation sequence that is dual to (1):

$$\top \geq \mathbb{X}\top \geq \mathbb{X}^2\top \geq \cdots. \qquad (3)$$

The sequence (3) converges to the *greatest fixed point (gfp)* $\nu\mathbb{X}$ of $\mathbb{X}$, which must be above the lfp $V(\mathcal{G}) = \mu\mathbb{X}$. Therefore the elements in (3) are all above $V(\mathcal{G})$.

The problem, however, is that the gfp $\nu\mathbb{X}$ is not necessarily the same as $\mu\mathbb{X}$. Therefore the upper bounds $U_0 \geq U_1 \geq \cdots$ given by (3) may not converge to $V(\mathcal{G})$. In other words, for a given threshold $\varepsilon > 0$, the bounds in (2) may fail to achieve $U_i - L_i \leq \varepsilon$, no matter how large i is.

In the literature, the source of this convergence issue has been identified to be *end components (ECs)* in MCs/MDPs/SGs. ECs are much like loops without exits—an example is in Fig. 1, where we use a Markov chain (MC) for simplicity. Any function f that assigns the same value to the states s_I and s can be a fixed point of the Bellman operator $\mathbb{X}$ (that back-propagates f by averages); therefore, the gfp

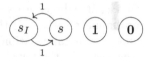

Fig. 1. A Markov chain (MC) for which the naive BVI fails to converge

$\nu\mathbb{X}$ assigns 1 to both s_I and s. In contrast, $(\mu\mathbb{X})(s_I) = (\mu\mathbb{X})(s) = 0$, which says one never reaches the target **1** from s_I or s (which is obvious).

Most previous works on BVI have focused on the problem of how to deal with ECs. Their solutions are to get somehow rid of ECs. For example, ECs in MDPs are discovered and *collapsed* in [5,18]; ECs in SGs cannot simply be collapsed, and an elaborate method is proposed in the recent work [20] that *deflates* them. This is the context of the current work, and we aim to enhance BVI for SGs.

1.4 Contribution: Global Propagation in BVI with Widest Paths

The algorithms in [20] seem to be the only BVI algorithms known for SGs. In their performance, however, EC computation often becomes a bottleneck. Our contribution in this paper is a new BVI algorithm for SGs that is *free from the need for EC computation*.

The key idea of our algorithm is *global propagation* for upper bounds, as sketched below. In each iteration for upper bounds $U_0 \geq U_1 \geq \cdots$, we conduct *global* propagation, in addition to the *local* propagation in the usual BVI. The latter means the application of $\mathbb{X}$ to $\mathbb{X}^i\top$, leading to $\mathbb{X}^{i+1}\top$; this local propagation, as we previously discussed, gets trapped in end components. In contrast, our global propagation looks at paths from each state s to the target **1**, ignoring end components. For example, in Fig. 1, our global propagation sees that there is no path from s_I to the target $\mathbf{1}$, and consequently assigns 0 as an upper bound for the value function $V(\mathcal{G})(s_I)$.

Such global propagation is easier said than done—in fact, the very advantage of VI is that the *global* quantities (namely reachability probabilities) get computed by iterations of *local* propagation. Conducting global propagation in a computationally tractable manner requires a careful choice of its venue. The solution in this paper is to compute *widest paths* in a suitable (directed) weighted graph.

More specifically, in each iteration where we compute an upper bound U_i, we conduct the following operations.

- (Player reduction) We turn the given SG $\mathcal{G}$ into an MDP $\mathcal{M}_i$, by restricting Minimizer's actions to the *empirically optimal* ones. The latter means they are optimal with respect to the current under-approximation L_i of $V(\mathcal{G})$.
- (Local propagation) The MDP $\mathcal{M}_i$ is then turned into a weighted graph (WG) $\mathcal{W}_i$. The construction of $\mathcal{W}_i$ consists of the application of $\mathbb{X}$ to the previous bound U_{i-1} (i.e. local propagation), and forgetting the information that cannot be expressed in a weighted graph (such as the precise transition probabilities $\delta(s, a, s')$ that depend on the action a).

  Due to this information loss, our analysis in $\mathcal{W}_i$ is necessarily approximate. Nevertheless, the benefit of $\mathcal{W}_i$'s simplicity is significant, as in the following step.
- (Global propagation) In the WG $\mathcal{W}_i$, we solve the *widest path problem*. This classic graph-theoretic problem can be solved efficiently, e.g., by the Dijkstra algorithm. The widest path width gives a new upper bound U_i.

We prove the correctness of our algorithm: soundness ($V(\mathcal{G}) \leq U_i$), and convergence ($U_i \to V(\mathcal{G})$ as $i \to \infty$). That the upper bounds decrease ($U_0 \geq U_1 \geq \cdots$) will be obvious by construction. These correctness proofs are technically nontrivial, combining combinatorial, graph-theoretic, and analytic arguments.

We have also implemented our algorithm. Our experiments compare its performance to the algorithms from [20] (the original one and its learning-based variation). The results show our consistent performance advantage: depending on SGs, our performance is from comparable to dozens of times faster. The advantage is especially eminent in SGs with many ECs.

1.5   Related Works

VI and BVI have been pursued principally for MDPs. The only work we know that deals with SGs is [20]—with the exception of [26] that works in a restricted setting where every end component belongs exclusively to either player. The work closest to ours is therefore [20], in that we solve the same problem.

For MDPs, the idea of BVI is first introduced in [23]; they worked in a limited setting where ECs do not cause the convergence issue. Its extension to general MDPs with the reachability objective is presented in [5,18], where ECs are computed and then collapsed. BVI is studied under different names in these works: *bounded real time dynamic programming* [5,23] and *interval iteration* [18]. The work [20] is an extension of this line of work from MDPs to SGs.

The work [20] has seen a few extensions to more advanced settings: black-box settings [3], concurrent reachability [16], and generalized reachability games [2].

Most BVI algorithms involve EC computation (although ours does not). The EC algorithm in [14,15] is used in [18,20]; more recent algorithms include [7,9].

1.6 Organization

In Sect. 2 we present some preliminaries. In Sect. 3 we review VI and BVI with an emphasis on the role of Kleene's fixed point theorem. This paves the way to Sect. 4 where we present our algorithm. We do so in three steps, and prove the correctness—soundness and convergence—in the end. Experiment results are shown in Sect. 5.

2 Preliminaries

We fix some basic notations. Let X be a set. We let X^* denote the set of finite sequences over X, that is, $X^* = \bigcup_{i \in \mathbb{N}} X^i$. We let $X^+ = X^* \setminus \{\varepsilon\}$, where ε denotes the empty sequence (of length 0). The set of infinite sequences over X is denoted by X^ω. The set of functions from X to Y is denoted by $X \to Y$.

2.1 Stochastic Games

In a stochastic game, two players (*Maximizer* $\square$ and *Minimizer* $\bigcirc$) play against each other. The goals of the two players are to maximize and minimize the *value function*, respectively. Many different definitions are possible for value functions. In this paper (as well as all the works on (bounded) value iteration), we focus on the *reachability objective*, in which case a value function is defined by the reachability probability to a designated target state **1**.

Definition 2.1 (stochastic game (SG)). A stochastic game (SG) is a tuple $\mathcal{G} = (S, S_\square, S_\bigcirc, s_I, \mathbf{1}, \mathbf{0}, A, \mathrm{Av}, \delta)$ where

- S is a finite set of *states*, partitioned into $S_\square$ and $S_\bigcirc$ (i.e., $S = S_\square \cup S_\bigcirc$, $S_\square \cap S_\bigcirc = \emptyset$). $s \in S_\square$ is *Maximizer's* state; $s \in S_\bigcirc$ is *Minimizer's* state.
- $s_I \in S$ is an *initial* state, $\mathbf{1} \in S_\square$ is a *target*, and $\mathbf{0} \in S_\bigcirc$ is a *sink*.
- A is a finite set of *actions*.
- $\mathrm{Av} : S \to 2^A$ defines the set of actions that are *available* at each state $s \in S$.
- $\delta : S \times A \times S \to [0,1]$ is a *transition function*, where $\delta(s, a, s')$ gives a probability with which to reach the state s' when the action a is taken at the state s. The value $\delta(s, a, s')$ is non-zero only if $a \in \mathrm{Av}(s)$; it must satisfy $\sum_{s' \in S} \delta(s, a, s') = 1$ for all $s \in S$ and $a \in \mathrm{Av}(s)$.

We assume that each of **1** and **0** allows only one action that leads to a self-loop with probability 1. Moreover, for theoretical convenience, we assume that all SGs are non-blocking. That is, $\mathrm{Av}(s) \neq \emptyset$ for each $s \in S$.

We introduce some notations: $\mathrm{post}(s,a) = \{s' \mid \delta(s,a,s') > 0\}$, and for $S' \subseteq S$, we let $S'_\square = S' \cap S_\square$ and $S'_\bigcirc = S' \cap S_\bigcirc$.

Definition 2.2 (Markov decision process (MDP), Markov chain (MC)). An SG such that $S_\square = S \setminus \{\mathbf{0}\}$ (i.e. Minimizer is absent) is called a *Markov decision process (MDP)*. We often omit the second and third components for MDPs, writing $\mathcal{M} = (S, s_I, \mathbf{1}, \mathbf{0}, A, \mathrm{Av}, \delta)$.

An SG such that $|\mathrm{Av}(s)| = 1$ for each $s \in S$—both Maximizer and Minimizer are absent—is called a *Markov chain (MC)*. It is also denoted simply by a tuple $\mathcal{G} = (S, s_I, \mathbf{1}, \mathbf{0}, \delta)$ where its transition function is of the type $\delta : S \times S \to [0,1]$.

Every notion for SGs that appears below applies to MDPs and MCs, too.

Example 2.3. Figure 2 presents an example of an SG. At the state s_1 of Minimizer, two actions α and β are in $\mathrm{Av}(s_1)$. If Minimizer chooses α, the next state is s_2 with probability $\delta(s_1, \alpha, s_2) = 1$. If Minimizer instead chooses β, the next state is **1** with probability $\delta(s_1, \beta, \mathbf{1}) = 0.8$ or **0** with probability $\delta(s_1, \beta, \mathbf{0}) = 0.2$.

Maximizer's goal is to reach **1** as often as possible by choosing suitable actions. Minimizer's goal is to avoid reaching **1**—this can be achieved, for example but not exclusively, by reaching **0**.

Both players choose their actions according to their *strategies*. It is well-known [13] that *positional* (also called *memoryless*) and *deterministic* (also called *pure*) strategies are complete for finite SGs with the reachability objective.

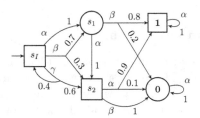

Fig. 2. A stochastic game (SG), an example

Definition 2.4 (strategy, path). Let $\mathcal{G}$ be the SG in Definition 2.1. A *strategy* for Maximizer in $\mathcal{G}$ is a function $\sigma : S_\square \to A$ such that $\sigma(s) \in \mathrm{Av}(s)$ for each $s \in S_\square$. A *strategy* for Minimizer is defined similarly. The set of Maximizer's strategies in $\mathcal{G}$ is denoted by $\mathrm{str}^{\mathcal{G}}_\square$; that of Minimizer's is denoted by $\mathrm{str}^{\mathcal{G}}_\bigcirc$.

Strategies $\tau \in \mathrm{str}^{\mathcal{G}}_\square$ and $\sigma \in \mathrm{str}^{\mathcal{G}}_\bigcirc$ in $\mathcal{G}$ turn the game $\mathcal{G}$ into a Markov chain, which is denoted by $\mathcal{G}^{\tau,\sigma}$. Similarly, a strategy τ for Maximizer (who is the only player) in an MDP $\mathcal{M}$ induces an MC, denoted by $\mathcal{M}^\tau$.

An *infinite path* in $\mathcal{G}$ is a sequence $s_0 a_0 s_1 a_1 s_2 a_2 \ldots \in (S \times A)^\omega$ such that for all $i \in \mathbb{N}$, $a_i \in \mathrm{Av}(s_i)$ and $s_{i+1} \in \mathrm{post}(s_i, a_i)$. A prefix $s_0 a_0 s_1 \ldots s_k$ of an infinite path ending with a state is called a *finite path*. If $\mathcal{G}$ is an MC, then we omit actions in a path and write $s_0 s_1 s_2 \ldots$ or $s_0 s_1 \ldots s_k$.

Given a game $\mathcal{G}$ and strategies τ, σ for the two players, the induced MC $\mathcal{G}^{\tau,\sigma}$ assigns to each state $s \in S$ a probability distribution $\mathbb{P}^{\tau,\sigma}_s$. The distribution is with respect to the standard measurable structure of S^ω; see, e.g., [4, Chap. 10].

For each measurable subset $X \subseteq S^\omega$, $\mathbb{P}_s^{\tau,\sigma}(X)$ is the probability with which $\mathcal{G}^{\tau,\sigma}$, starting from the state s, produces an infinite path π that belongs to X.

It is well-known that all the LTL properties are measurable in S^ω. In the current setting with the reachability objective, we are interested in the probability of eventually reaching $\mathbf{1}$, denoted by $\mathbb{P}_s^{\tau,\sigma}(\Diamond\mathbf{1})$.

Definition 2.5 (value function $V(\mathcal{G})$). Let $\mathcal{G}$ be the SG in Definition 2.1. The *value function* $V(\mathcal{G})$ of $\mathcal{G}$ is defined by

$$V(\mathcal{G})(s) = \max_{\tau \in \mathrm{str}_{\square}^{\mathcal{G}}} \min_{\sigma \in \mathrm{str}_{\bigcirc}^{\mathcal{G}}} \mathbb{P}_s^{\tau,\sigma}(\Diamond\mathbf{1}) = \min_{\sigma \in \mathrm{str}_{\bigcirc}^{\mathcal{G}}} \max_{\tau \in \mathrm{str}_{\square}^{\mathcal{G}}} \mathbb{P}_s^{\tau,\sigma}(\Diamond\mathbf{1}),$$

where the last equality is shown in [13].

We say a strategy τ of Maximizer's is *optimal* if $V(\mathcal{G})(s) = \min_\sigma \mathbb{P}_s^{\tau,\sigma}(\Diamond\mathbf{1})$ for each $s \in S$; similarly, we say a strategy σ of Minimizer's is *optimal* if $V(\mathcal{G})(s) = \max_\sigma \mathbb{P}_s^{\sigma,\tau}(\Diamond\mathbf{1})$ for each $s \in S$.

We write V for $V(\mathcal{G})$ when the dependence on $\mathcal{G}$ is clear from the context.

The set of states with a non-zero value is denoted by $S_{\Diamond\mathbf{1}}$. That is, $S_{\Diamond\mathbf{1}} = \{s \in S \mid V(\mathcal{G})(s) > 0\}$.

Example 2.6. Consider the SG $\mathcal{G}$ from Fig. 2. At s_2, Maximizer's action should be α. Hence, $V(\mathcal{G})(s_2) = 0.9$. At s_1, if Minimizer chooses α, then the probability of reaching $\mathbf{1}$ will be 0.9 by $V(\mathcal{G})(s_2)$. Thus, Minimizer should choose β at s_1, which yields $V(\mathcal{G})(s_1) = 0.8$. Finally, at s_I, γ is the best choice, since Maximizer can choose this action infinitely often until it gets to s_2. We have $V(\mathcal{G})(s_I) = 0.9$.

2.2   The Widest Path Problem

Definition 2.7 (weighted graph (WG)). A (directed) *weighted graph* is a triple $\mathcal{W} = (V, E, w)$ of a finite set V of *vertices*, a set $E \subseteq V \times V$ of *edges*, and a *weight function* $w \colon E \to [0,1]$ where $[0,1]$ is the unit interval.

A (finite) *path* in a WG is defined in the usual graph-theoretic way.

In the widest path problem, an edge weight $w(v, v')$ is thought of as its *capacity*, and the capacity of a path is determined by its bottleneck. The problem asks for a path with the greatest capacity. In this paper, we use the following *all-source single-destination* version of the problem.

Definition 2.8 (the widest path problem (WPP)). A (finite) *path* in $\mathcal{W} = (V, E, w)$ is a sequence $v_0 v_1 \dots v_n$ of vertices such that $(v_i, v_{i+1}) \in E$ for each $i \in [0, n-1]$. The *width* of a path $v_0 v_1 \dots v_n$ is given by $\min_{i \in [0,n-1]} w(v_i, v_{i+1})$. The *widest path problem* is the following problem.

Given: a WG $\mathcal{W} = (V, E, w)$ and a target vertex $v_t \in V$.
Answer: for each $v \in V$, the widest width of the paths from v to v_t, that is,

$$\max_{n \in \mathbb{N}, v = v_0, v_1, \dots, v_n = v_t} \min_{i \in [0, n-1]} w(v_i, v_{i+1}),$$

We let $\mathrm{WPW}(\mathcal{W}, v_t)$ denote a function that solves this problem, and let $\mathrm{WPath}(\mathcal{W}, v_t)$ denote a function that assigns to each $v \in V$ a widest path to v_t. Furthermore, we assume the following property of WPath: if $\mathrm{WPath}(\mathcal{W}, v_t)(v_0) = v_0 v_1 \ldots v_k v_t$, then $\mathrm{WPath}(\mathcal{W}, v_t)(v_i) = v_i v_{i+1} \ldots v_k v_t$ for each $i \in [0, k]$.

Efficient algorithms are known for $\mathrm{WPW}(\mathcal{W}, v_t)$. An example is the Dijkstra search algorithm with Fibonacci heaps [17]; it is originally for the single-source all-destination version but its adaptation is easy. The algorithm runs in time $O(|E| + |V| \log |V|)$. It returns a widest path in addition to its width, too, computing the function $\mathrm{WPath}(\mathcal{W}, v_t)$ with the property required in the above.

3   (Bounded) Value Iteration

3.1   Bellman Operator and Value Iteration

The following construct—used for "local propagation" in computing the value function—is central to formal analysis of probabilistic systems and games.

Definition 3.1 (Bellman Operator). Let $\mathcal{G} = (S, S_\square, S_\bigcirc, s_I, \mathbf{1}, \mathbf{0}, A, \mathrm{Av}, \delta)$ be a stochastic game. For each state $s \in S$, an available action $a \in \mathrm{Av}(s)$, and $f : S \to [0, 1]$, we define a function $\mathbb{X}_a f : S \to [0, 1]$ by the following.

$$(\mathbb{X}_a f)(s) = \begin{cases} 1 & \text{if } s = \mathbf{1}, \\ 0 & \text{if } s = \mathbf{0}, \\ \sum_{s' \in S} \delta(s, a, s') \cdot f(s') & \text{if } s \neq \mathbf{0}, \mathbf{1}. \end{cases}$$

These functions are used in the following definition of the *Bellman operator* $\mathbb{X} \colon (S \to [0, 1]) \to (S \to [0, 1])$ over $\mathcal{G}$:

$$(\mathbb{X}f)(s) = \begin{cases} \max_{a \in \mathrm{Av}(s)} (\mathbb{X}_a f)(s) & \text{if } s \in S_\square \text{ is a Maximizer state,} \\ \min_{a \in \mathrm{Av}(s)} (\mathbb{X}_a f)(s) & \text{if } s \in S_\bigcirc \text{ is a Minimizer state.} \end{cases}$$

The function space $S \to [0, 1]$ inherits the usual order $\leq$ between real numbers in the unit interval $[0, 1]$, that is, $f \leq g$ if $f(s) \leq g(s)$ for each $s \in S$. The Bellman operator $\mathbb{X}$ over $S \to [0, 1]$ is clearly monotone; it is easily seen to preserve max and min, using the fact that the state space S of an SG is finite. Therefore we obtain the following, as consequences of Kleene's fixed point theorem.

Lemma 3.2. *Assume the setting of Definition 3.1.*

1. *The Bellman operator $\mathbb{X}$ has the greatest fixed point (gfp) $\nu\mathbb{X} \colon S \to [0, 1]$. It is obtained as the limit of the descending ω-chain*

$$\top \geq \mathbb{X}\top \geq \mathbb{X}^2\top \geq \cdots,$$

where $\top$ is the greatest element of $S \to [0, 1]$ (i.e., $\top(s) = 1$ for each $s \in S$). In other words, we have $(\nu\mathbb{X})(s) = \inf_{i \in \mathbb{N}} ((\mathbb{X}^i \top)(s))$ for each $s \in S$.

Algorithm 1: Value iteration (VI) for a stochastic game $\mathcal{G} =$ $(S, S_\square, S_\bigcirc, s_I, \mathbf{1}, \mathbf{0}, A, \mathrm{Av}, \delta)$ and a stopping threshold $\Delta > 0$

```
1  procedure VI(G, Δ)
2  │   L₀ ← ⊥                                    // Initialize lower bound
3  │   while Lᵢ(sᵢ) − Lᵢ₋₁(sᵢ) < Δ do           // Typical stopping criterion
4  │   │   i++
5  │   │   Lᵢ ← XLᵢ₋₁                             // Bellman update
6  │   return Lᵢ(sᵢ)
```

---

2. *Symmetrically, $\mathbb{X}$ has the least fixed point (lfp) $\mu\mathbb{X} \colon S \to [0,1]$, obtained as the limit of the ascending chain*

$$\bot \leq \mathbb{X}\bot \leq \mathbb{X}^2\bot \leq \cdots, \tag{4}$$

where $\bot(s) = 0$ for each $s \in S$. That is, we have $(\mu\mathbb{X})(s) = \sup_{i \in \mathbb{N}}\big((\mathbb{X}^i\bot)(s)\big)$ for each $s \in S$. □

The following characterization is fundamental. See, e.g., [10].

Theorem 3.3. *Let $\mathcal{G}$ be a stochastic game. The value function $V = V(\mathcal{G})$ (Definition 2.5) coincides with the least fixed point $\mu\mathbb{X}$.* □

The fact that $V(\mathcal{G})$ is the least fixed point of $\mathbb{X}$ implies the following: a strategy τ of Maximizer is optimal if and only if $\big(\mathbb{X}_{\tau(s)}(V(\mathcal{G}))\big)(s) = V(\mathcal{G})(s)$ holds for each $s \in S_\square$; similarly for Minimizer. We say $a \in \mathrm{Av}(s)$ is *optimal* at s if $\mathbb{X}_a V(\mathcal{G})(s) = V(\mathcal{G})(s)$ holds; otherwise a is *suboptimal*.

Lemma 3.2.2 & Theorem 3.3 suggest iterative *under*-approximation of $V(\mathcal{G})$ by $\bot \leq \mathbb{X}\bot \leq \mathbb{X}^2\bot \leq \cdots$. This is the principle of *value iteration* (VI); see Algorithm 1.

Example 3.4. The values L_i computed by Algorithm 1, for the SG in Fig. 2, are shown in the following table. The values at $\mathbf{0}$ and $\mathbf{1}$ are omitted.

s	L_0	L_1	L_2	L_3	L_4	L_5	...	$V(\mathcal{G})$
s_I	0	0	0.54	0.83	0.872	0.8888		0.9
s_1	0	0	0.8	0.8	0.8	0.8	...	0.8
s_2	0	0.9	0.9	0.9	0.9	0.9		0.9

$L_i(s_I)$ converges to, but is never equal to, $V(\mathcal{G})(s_I)$. The converges rate can be arbitrarily slow: for any $\varepsilon \in (0,1)$ and $k \in \mathbb{N}$ there is an SG $\mathcal{G}$ and a state s such that $V(\mathcal{G})(s) - L_k(s) > \varepsilon$. One sees this by modifying Fig. 2 with $\delta(s_I, \gamma, s_2) = \varepsilon'$ and $\delta(s_I, \gamma, s_I) = 1 - \varepsilon'$, where $\varepsilon' > 0$ is an arbitrary small positive constant.

Algorithm 2: Bounded value iteration (BVI) for a stochastic game $\mathcal{G} = (S, S_\square, S_\bigcirc, s_I, \mathbf{1}, \mathbf{0}, A, \mathrm{Av}, \delta)$ and a stopping threshold $\varepsilon > 0$—a naive prototype that suffers from end components

---

1 **procedure** $\mathrm{VI}(\mathcal{G}, \varepsilon)$
2     $L_0 \leftarrow \bot$, $U_0 \leftarrow \top$ // Initialize lower and upper bound
3   **while** $U_i(s_I) - L_i(s_I) > \varepsilon$ **do**   // Check the gap at the initial state
4        $i{+}{+}$
5        $L_i \leftarrow \mathbb{X} L_{i-1}$, $U_i \leftarrow \mathbb{X} U_{i-1}$ // Bellman update
6   **return** $L_i(s_I)$

There is no known stopping criterion for VI (Algorithm 1) with a precision guarantee, besides the one in [10] that is too pessimistic to be practical. The one shown in Line 3 ("little progress") is a commonly used heuristic, but it is known to lead to arbitrarily wrong results [18].

3.2 Bounded Value Iteration

When we turn back to Lemma 3.2, Lemma 3.2.1 suggests another iterative approximation, namely *over*-approximation of the value function V by $\top \geq \mathbb{X}\top \geq \mathbb{X}^2\top \geq \cdots$. The chain converges to the gfp $\nu\mathbb{X}$ that is necessarily above the lfp $\mu\mathbb{X}$. This is the principle that underlies *bounded value iteration* (BVI); see Algorithm 2 for its naive prototype. BVI has been actively studied in the literature [2,3,5,16,18,20,23], sometimes under different names (such as *bounded real time dynamic programming* [5,23] or *interval iteration* [18]).

BVI comes with a precision guarantee: since $V(\mathcal{G})$ lies between L_i and U_i (whose gap is at most ε), the approximation L_i is at most ε apart from $V(\mathcal{G})$.

The catch, however, is that $\mu\mathbb{X}$ and $\nu\mathbb{X}$ may not coincide, and therefore the overapproximation might not converge to the desired $\mu\mathbb{X}$. This means Algorithm 2 might not terminate. This is the main technical challenge addressed in the previous works on BVI, including [5,20].

In those works, the source of the failure of convergence is identified to be *end components*. See the (very simple) Markov chain in Fig. 1, where the reachability probability from s_I to $\mathbf{1}$ is clearly 0. However, due to the loop between s_I and s, the values $U_i(s_I)$ and $U_i(s)$—these get updated to the average of U_{i-1} at successors—are easily seen to remain 1. Roughly speaking, end components generalize such loops defined in MDPs and SGs (the definitions are graph-theoretic, in terms of strongly connected components). End components cause non-convergence of naive BVI, essentially for the reason we just described.

The solutions previously proposed to this challenge have been to "get rid of end components." For MDPs (1.5 players), the *collapsing* technique detects end components and collapses each of them into a single state [5,18]. After doing so, the Bellman operator $\mathbb{X}$ has a unique fixed point (therefore $\mu\mathbb{X} = \nu\mathbb{X}$), assuring convergence of BVI (Algorithm 2). In the case of SGs (2.5 players), end components cannot simply be collapsed into single states—they must be handled carefully, taking the "best exits" into account. This is the key idea of the *deflating* technique proposed for SGs in [20].

4   Our Algorithm: Bounded Value Iteration with Upper Bounds Given by Widest Paths

In our algorithm, like in other BVI algorithm, we iteratively construct upper and lower bounds U_i, L_i of the value function $V(\mathcal{G})$ at the same time. See (2). In updating U_i, however, we go beyond the *local* propagation by the Bellman update and conduct *global* propagation, too. This frees us from the curse of end components. The outline of our algorithm is as follows.

- The lower bound L_i is given by $L_i = \mathbb{X}^i \perp$, following Lemma 3.2.2 and Theorem 3.3. This is the same as the other VI algorithms.
- The upper bounds U_i is constructed in the following three steps, using a *global* propagation that takes advantage of fast widest path algorithms.
  - **(Player reduction)** Firstly, we turn the SG $\mathcal{G}$ into an MDP $\mathcal{M}_i$ by fixing Minimizer's strategy to a specific one σ_i.
    Any choice of σ_i would do for the sake of *soundness* (that is, $V(\mathcal{G}) \leq U_i$). However, for *convergence* (that is, $U_i \to V(\mathcal{G})$ as $i \to \infty$), it is important to have $\sigma_0, \sigma_1, \dots$ eventually converge to Minimizer's optimal strategy $\sigma_{\bigcirc}$. Therefore we let L_i—the current lower estimate of $V(\mathcal{G})$—induce σ_i. Recall that L_i converges to $V(\mathcal{G})$ (Lemma 3.2.2, Theorem 3.3).
  - **(Preprocessing by local propagation)** Secondly, we turn the MDP $\mathcal{M}_i$ into a weighted graph (WG) W_i.
    The construction here is *local* propagation of the previous upper bound U_{i-1}, from each state s to its predecessors in $\mathcal{M}_i$. This is much like an application of the Bellman operator $\mathbb{X}$.
  - **(Global propagation by widest paths)** Finally, we solve the widest path problem in the WG W_i, from each state s to the target state $\mathbf{1}$. The maximum path width from s to $\mathbf{1}$ is used as the value of the upper bound $U_i(s)$.
    This way, we conduct *global* propagation of upper bounds, for which end components pose no threats. Our global propagation is still computationally feasible, thanks to the preprocessing in the previous step that turns a problem on an MDP into one on a WG (modulo some sound approximation).

The use of *global* propagation for upper bounds is a distinguishing feature of our algorithm. This is unlike other BVI algorithms (such as [5,20]) where upper-bound propagation is only local and stepwise. The latter gets trapped when it encounters an EC—therefore some trick such as collapsing [5] and deflating [20] is needed—while our global propagation looks directly at the target state $\mathbf{1}$.

The above outline is presented as pseudocode in Algorithm 3. We describe the three steps in the rest of the section. In particular, we exhibit the definitions of $\mathcal{M}_{\mathrm{PlRd}}$ and $\mathcal{W}_{\mathrm{LcPg}}$ (WPW has been defined and discussed in Definition 2.8), providing some of their properties towards the correctness proof of the algorithm (Sect. 4.3).

Algorithm 3: Our BVI algorithm via widest paths. Here $\mathcal{G} = (S, S_\square, S_\bigcirc, s_I, \mathbf{1}, \mathbf{0}, A, \mathrm{Av}, \delta)$ is an SG; $\varepsilon > 0$ is a stopping threshold.

```
1  procedure BVI_WP(G, ε)
2  │   L₀ ← ⊥, U₀ ← ⊤, i ← 0
3  │   while Uᵢ(sᵢ) − Lᵢ(sᵢ) > ε do
4  │   │   i++
5  │   │   Lᵢ ← 𝕏Lᵢ₋₁                      // value iteration for lower bounds
6  │   │   Mᵢ ← M_PIRd(G, Lᵢ)                          // player reduction
7  │   │   Wᵢ ← W_LcPg(Mᵢ, Uᵢ₋₁)                     // local propagation
8  │   │   Uᵢ ← min{Uᵢ₋₁, WPW(Wᵢ)}          // widest path computation
9  │   return Uᵢ(sᵢ)
```

4.1 Player Reduction: From SGs to MDPs

The following general definition is not directly used in Algorithm 3. It is used in our theoretical development below, towards the algorithm's correctness.

Definition 4.1 (the MDP $\mathcal{M}(\mathcal{G}, \mathrm{Av}')$). Let $\mathcal{G}$ be the game in Algorithm 3, and $\mathrm{Av}' \colon S \to 2^A$ be such that $\emptyset \neq \mathrm{Av}'(s) \subseteq \mathrm{Av}(s)$ for each $s \in S$.

Then the MDP given by the tuple $(S, S \setminus \{\mathbf{0}\}, \{\mathbf{0}\}, s_I, \mathbf{1}, \mathbf{0}, A, \mathrm{Av}', \delta)$ shall be denoted by $\mathcal{M}(\mathcal{G}, \mathrm{Av}')$, and we say it is induced from $\mathcal{G}$ by restricting Av to Av'.

The above construction consists of 1) restricting actions (from Av to Av'), and 2) turning Minimizer's states into Maximizer's.

The following class of action restrictions will be heavily used.

Definition 4.2 (Minimizer restriction). Let $\mathcal{G}$ be as in Algorithm 3. A *Minimizer restriction* of Av is a function $\mathrm{Av}' \colon S \to 2^A$ such that 1) $\emptyset \neq \mathrm{Av}'(s) \subseteq \mathrm{Av}(s)$ for each $s \in S$, and 2) $\mathrm{Av}'(s) = \mathrm{Av}(s)$ for each state $s \in S_\square$ of Maximizer's.

In Algorithm 3, we will be using the MDP induced by the following specific Minimizer restriction induced by a function f.

Definition 4.3 (the MDP $\mathcal{M}_{\mathrm{PIRd}}(\mathcal{G}, f)$). Let $\mathcal{G}$ be the game in Algorithm 3, and $f \colon S \to [0, 1]$ be a function. The MDP $\mathcal{M}_{\mathrm{PIRd}}(\mathcal{G}, f)$ is defined to be $\mathcal{M}(\mathcal{G}, \mathrm{Av}_f)$ (Definition 4.1), where the function $\mathrm{Av}_f \colon S \to 2^A$ is defined as follows.

$$\mathrm{Av}_f(s) = \mathrm{Av}(s) \qquad\qquad\qquad\qquad \text{for } s \in S_\square,$$
$$\mathrm{Av}_f(s) = \{a \in \mathrm{Av}(s) \mid \forall b \in \mathrm{Av}(s). (\mathbb{X}_a f)(s) \leq (\mathbb{X}_b f)(s)\} \quad \text{for } s \in S_\bigcirc. \tag{5}$$

The function Av_f is a Minimizer restriction in $\mathcal{G}$ (Definition 4.2).

The intuition of (5) is that $a = \arg\min_{b \in \mathrm{Av}(s)} (\mathbb{X}_b f)(s)$. In the use of this construction in Algorithm 3, the function f will be our "best guess" L_i of the value function $V(\mathcal{G})$. In this situation, $\arg\min_{b \in \mathrm{Av}(s)} (\mathbb{X}_b f)(s)$ is the best action for Minimizer based on the guess $f = L_i$.

Definition 4.4 (the MDP $\mathcal{M}_i$, and Av_i). In Algorithm 3, the MDP $\mathcal{M}_i$ is given by $\mathcal{M}_{\mathrm{PIRd}}(\mathcal{G}, L_i) = \mathcal{M}(\mathcal{G}, \mathrm{Av}_{L_i})$. We write Av_i for available actions in $\mathcal{M}_i$, that is, $\mathcal{M}_i = (S, \mathbf{1}, \mathbf{0}, A, \mathrm{Av}_i, \delta)$.

In the case of Algorithm 3, the MDPs $\mathcal{M}_0, \mathcal{M}_1, \ldots$ do not only "converge" to $\mathcal{G}$, but also "reach $\mathcal{G}$ in finitely many steps," in the following sense. The proof is deferred to [24]. The proof relies crucially on the fact that the set $\mathrm{Av}(s)$ of available actions is finite—there is uniform $\varepsilon > 0$ such that every suboptimal action is suboptimal by a gap at least ε.

Lemma 4.5. *In Algorithm 3, there exists $i_\mathrm{M} \in \mathbb{N}$ such that, for each $i \geq i_\mathrm{M}$, we have $V(\mathcal{G}) = V(\mathcal{M}_i)$.* □

4.2 Local Propagation: From MDPs to WGs

Here is a technical observation that motivates the function $\mathcal{W}_{\mathrm{LcPg}}$.

Lemma 4.6. *Let $\mathcal{G}$ be the game in Algorithm 3, and $\mathrm{Av}' \colon S \to 2^A$ be a Minimizer restriction (Definition 4.2).*

1. *For each state $s \in S$, we have $V(\mathcal{G})(s) \leq \max_{a \in \mathrm{Av}'(s)}\big(\mathbb{X}_a\big(V(\mathcal{G})\big)\big)(s)$.*
2. *For each $k \in \mathbb{N}$, we have*

$$V(\mathcal{G})(s_0) \leq \max_{s_0 \xrightarrow{a_0} s_1 \xrightarrow{a_1} \cdots \xrightarrow{a_k} \text{ in } \mathrm{Av}'} \big(\mathbb{X}_{a_k}\big(V(\mathcal{G})\big)\big)(s_k), \tag{6}$$

where the maximum is taken over $a_0, s_1, a_1, \ldots, s_k, a_k$ such that $a_0 \in \mathrm{Av}'(s_0), s_1 \in \mathrm{post}(s_0, a_0), a_1 \in \mathrm{Av}'(s_1), \ldots, s_k \in \mathrm{post}(s_{k-1}, a_{k-1}), a_k \in \mathrm{Av}'(s_k)$.

Proof. For the item 1, recall that $V(\mathcal{G})$ is the least fixed point of the Bellman operator (Theorem 3.3). For each Minimizer state $s \in S_\bigcirc$, we have

$$V(\mathcal{G})(s) = \min_{a \in \mathrm{Av}(s)}\big(\mathbb{X}_a\big(V(\mathcal{G})\big)\big)(s) \leq \min_{a \in \mathrm{Av}'(s)}\big(\mathbb{X}_a\big(V(\mathcal{G})\big)\big)(s) \leq \max_{a \in \mathrm{Av}'(s)}\big(\mathbb{X}_a\big(V(\mathcal{G})\big)\big)(s).$$

For each Maximizer state $s \in S_\square$, we have

$$V(\mathcal{G})(s) = \max_{a \in \mathrm{Av}(s)}\big(\mathbb{X}_a\big(V(\mathcal{G})\big)\big)(s) = \max_{a \in \mathrm{Av}'(s)}\big(\mathbb{X}_a\big(V(\mathcal{G})\big)\big)(s).$$

The latter equality is because Av' does not restrict Maximizer's actions. This proves the item 1.

The item 2 is proved by induction as follows, using the item 1 in its course.

$$V(\mathcal{G})(s_0)$$

$$\le \max_{a_0 \in \mathrm{Av}'(s_0)} \big(\mathbb{X}_{a_0}(V(\mathcal{G})) \big)(s_0) \qquad \text{by the item 1.}$$

$$= \max_{a_0 \in \mathrm{Av}'(s_0)} \sum_{s_1 \in \mathrm{post}(s_0, a_0)} \delta(s_0, a_0, s_1) \cdot V(\mathcal{G})(s_1)$$

$$\le \max_{a_0 \in \mathrm{Av}'(s_0)} \sum_{s_1 \in \mathrm{post}(s_0, a_0)} \delta(s_0, a_0, s_1) \cdot \Big(\max_{s_1 \xrightarrow{a_1} \cdots \xrightarrow{a_k} \text{ in } \mathrm{Av}'} \big(\mathbb{X}_{a_k}(V(\mathcal{G})) \big)(s_k) \Big)$$

$$\text{by the induction hypothesis (for } k-1) \tag{7}$$

$$\le \max_{a_0 \in \mathrm{Av}'(s_0)} \max_{s_1 \in \mathrm{post}(s_0, a_0)} \Big(\max_{s_1 \xrightarrow{a_1} \cdots \xrightarrow{a_k} \text{ in } \mathrm{Av}'} \big(\mathbb{X}_{a_k}(V(\mathcal{G})) \big)(s_k) \Big)$$

$$= \max_{s_0 \xrightarrow{a_0} s_1 \xrightarrow{a_1} \cdots \xrightarrow{a_k} \text{ in } \mathrm{Av}'} \big(\mathbb{X}_{a_k}(V(\mathcal{G})) \big)(s_k). \tag{8}$$

The inequality in (8) holds since an average over s_1 on the left-hand side is replaced by the corresponding maximum on the right-hand side. Note that the value $\max_{s_1 \xrightarrow{a_1} \cdots \xrightarrow{a_k} \text{ in } \mathrm{Av}'} \min_{i \in [1,k]} \big(\mathbb{X}_{a_i}(V(\mathcal{G})) \big)(s_i)$ that occurs on both sides is determined once s_1 is determined. This concludes the proof. $\qquad\square$

Lemma 4.6.2, although not itself used in the following technical development, suggests the idea of global propagation for upper bounds. Note that a bound is given in (6) for each k; it is possible that a bound for some $k > 1$ is tighter than that for $k = 1$, motivating us to take a "look-ahead" further than one step.

However, the bound in (6) is not particularly tuned for tractability: computation of the maximum involves words whose number is exponential in k, and moreover, we want to do so for many k's.

In the end, our main technical contribution is that a similar "look-ahead" can be done by solving the widest path problem in the following weighted graph. The soundness of this method is not so easy as for Lemma 4.6.2—see Sect. 4.3.

Definition 4.7 (the WG $\mathcal{W}_{\mathrm{LcPg}}(\mathcal{M}, f)$). Let $\mathcal{M} = (S, \mathbf{1}, \mathbf{0}, A, \mathrm{Av}', \delta)$ be an MDP, and $f \colon S \to [0, 1]$. The WG $\mathcal{W}_{\mathrm{LcPg}}(\mathcal{M}, f)$ is the following triple (S, E, w).

- Its set of vertices is S.
- We have $(s, s') \in E$ if and only if, for some $a \in \mathrm{Av}'(s)$, we have $s' \in \mathrm{post}(s, a)$ (i.e., $\delta(s, a, s') > 0$).
- The weight function $w \colon E \to [0, 1]$ is given by

$$w(s, s') = \max\{\, \mathbb{X}_a f(s) \mid a \in \mathrm{Av}'(s), s' \in \mathrm{post}(s, a) \,\}. \tag{9}$$

In (9), the function f—that is, the previous upper bound U_{i-1} in Algorithm 3—is propagated one step by the application of $\mathbb{X}_a$. This way of encoding these propagated values as weights in a WG seems pretty rough. For example, in case both s' and s'' are in $\mathrm{post}(s, a)$ for each $a \in \mathrm{Av}'(s)$, we have $w(s, s') = w(s, s'')$, no matter what the transition probabilities from s to s', s'' are. The return

---

Algorithm 4: A construction of $\mathsf{PATH} : S_{\Diamond 1} \to S^+$ for Lemma 4.8

---

1   $S_{\mathrm{v}} \leftarrow \{1\}$, $\mathsf{PATH}(1) \leftarrow 1$

2   **while** $S_{\Diamond 1} \setminus S_{\mathrm{v}} \neq \emptyset$ **do**

3   Choose a pair of states $(s_{\mathrm{c}}, s_{\mathrm{p}})$ that satisfies the following:
      $s_{\mathrm{c}} \in S \setminus S_{\mathrm{v}}$, $s_{\mathrm{p}} \in S_{\mathrm{v}}$, $V(\mathcal{G})(s_{\mathrm{c}}) = \max_{s \in S \setminus S_{\mathrm{v}}} V(\mathcal{G})(s)$, and
      for an optimal action a at s_{c} in $\mathcal{M}$, $s_{\mathrm{p}} \in \mathrm{post}(s_{\mathrm{c}}, a)$

4      $\mathsf{PATH}(s_{\mathrm{c}}) \leftarrow s_{\mathrm{c}} \cdot \mathsf{PATH}(s_{\mathrm{p}})$, $S_{\mathrm{v}} \leftarrow S_{\mathrm{v}} \cup \{s_{\mathrm{c}}\}$

5   **return** PATH

---

for this paid price (namely the information lost in the rough encoding) is that the resulting data structure (WG) allows fast *global* analysis via the widest path problem. Our experiment results in Sect. 5 demonstrate that this rough yet global approximation can make upper bounds quickly converge.

4.3 Soundness and Convergence

In Algorithm 3, an SG $\mathcal{G}$ is turned into an MDP $\mathcal{M}_i$ and then to a WG $\mathcal{W}_i$. Our claim is that computing a widest path in $\mathcal{W}_i$ gives the next upper bound U_i in the iteration. Here we prove the following correctness properties: soundness ($V(\mathcal{G}) \leq U_i$) and convergence ($U_i \to V(\mathcal{G})$ as $i \to \infty$).

We start with a technical lemma. The choice of the MDP $\mathcal{M}(\mathcal{G}, \mathrm{Av}')$ and the value function $V(\mathcal{G})$ (for $\mathcal{G}$, not for $\mathcal{M}(\mathcal{G}, \mathrm{Av}')$) in the statement is subtle; it turns out to be just what we need.

Lemma 4.8. *Let $\mathcal{G}$ be as in Algorithm 3, and $\mathrm{Av}' \colon S \to 2^A$ be a Minimizer restriction (Definition 4.2). Let $s_0 \in S_{\Diamond 1}$ be a state with a non-zero value (Definition 2.5). Consider the MDP $\mathcal{M}(\mathcal{G}, \mathrm{Av}')$ (Definition 4.1), for which we write simply $\mathcal{M}$. Then there is a finite path $\pi = s_0 a_0 s_1 a_1 \ldots a_{n-1} s_n$ in $\mathcal{M}$ that satisfies the following.*

- *The path π reaches 1, that is, $s_n = 1$.*
- *Each action is optimal in $\mathcal{M}$ with respect to $V(\mathcal{G})$, that is, $\big(\mathbb{X}_{a_i}\big(V(\mathcal{G})\big)\big)(s_i) = max_{a \in \mathrm{Av}'(s_i)} \big(\mathbb{X}_a\big(V(\mathcal{G})\big)\big)(s_i)$ for each $i \in [0, n-1]$.*
- *The value function $V(\mathcal{G})$ does not decrease along the path, that is, $V(\mathcal{G})(s_i) \leq V(\mathcal{G})(s_{i+1})$ for each $i \in [0, n-1]$.*

Proof. We construct a function $\mathsf{PATH} : S_{\Diamond 1} \to S^+$ by Algorithm 4. It is clear that PATH assigns a desired path to each $s_0 \in S_{\Diamond 1}$. In particular, $V(\mathcal{G})$ does not decrease along $\mathsf{PATH}(s_0)$ since always a state with a smaller value of $V(\mathcal{G})$ is prepended.

It remains to be shown that, in Line 3, a required pair $(s_{\mathrm{c}}, s_{\mathrm{p}})$ is always found. Let $S_{\mathrm{v}} \subsetneq S_{\Diamond 1}$ be a subset with $1 \in S_{\mathrm{v}}$; here S_{v} is a proper subset of $S_{\Diamond 1}$ since otherwise we should be already out of the while loop (Line 2).

Let $S_{\max} = \{s \in S \setminus S_v \mid V(\mathcal{G})(s) = \max_{s' \in S \setminus S_v} V(\mathcal{G})(s')\}$. Since $S_v \subsetneq S_{\Diamond 1}$, we have $\emptyset \neq S_{\max} \subseteq S_{\Diamond 1}$ and thus $V(\mathcal{G})(s) > 0$ for each $s \in S_{\max}$. We also have $\mathbf{1} \notin S_{\max}$ since $\mathbf{1} \in S_v$.

We argue by contradiction: assume that for any $s \in S \setminus S_v$, $s' \in S_v$, we have $s' \notin \mathrm{post}(s, a_s)$, where a_s is any optimal action at s in $\mathcal{M}$ with respect to $V(\mathcal{G})$. Now let $s \in S_{\max}$ be an arbitrary element. It follows that $V(\mathcal{G})(s) > 0$.

$V(\mathcal{G})(s) \leq (\mathbb{X}_{a_s}(V(\mathcal{G})))(s)$

> using Lemma 4.6; here a_s is an optimal action at s in $\mathcal{M}$ with respect to $V(\mathcal{G})$,

$= \sum_{s' \in S \setminus S_v} \delta(s, a_s, s') \cdot V(\mathcal{G})(s')$

> by the assumption that $s' \notin \mathrm{post}(s, a_s)$ for each $s' \in S_v$

$\leq \sum_{s' \in S \setminus S_v} \delta(s, a_s, s') \cdot V(\mathcal{G})(s)$

> since $s \in S_{\max}$ and hence $V(\mathcal{G})(s') \leq V(\mathcal{G})(s)$

$= V(\mathcal{G})(s) \qquad$ since $\sum_{s' \in S \setminus S_v} \delta(s_c, a, s') = 1$. $\qquad$ (10)

Therefore both inequalities in the above must be equalities. In particular, for the second inequality (in (10)) to be an equality, we must have the weight for each suboptimal s' to be 0. That is, $\delta(s, a_s, s') = 0$ for each $s' \in (S \setminus S_v) \setminus S_{\max}$.

The above holds for arbitrary $s \in S_{\max}$. Therefore, for any strategy that is optimal in $\mathcal{M}$ with respect to $V(\mathcal{G})$, once a play is in $S_{\max}$, it never comes out of $S_{\max}$, hence the play never reaches $\mathbf{1}$. Moreover, an optimal strategy in $\mathcal{M}$ with respect to $V(\mathcal{G})$ is at least as good as an optimal strategy for Maximizer in $\mathcal{G}$ (with respect to $V(\mathcal{G})$), that is, the latter reaches $\mathbf{1}$ no more often than the former. This follows from Lemma 4.6. Altogether, we conclude that a Maximizer optimal strategy in $\mathcal{G}$ does not lead any $s \in S_{\max}$ to $\mathbf{1}$, i.e., $V(\mathcal{M})(s) = 0$ for each $s \in S_{\max}$. Now we come to a contradiction. $\qquad \square$

In the following lemma, we use the value function $V(\mathcal{G})$ in the position of f in Definition 4.7. This cannot be done in actual execution of Algorithm 4: unlike U_{i-1} in Algorithm 3, the value function $V(\mathcal{G})$ is not known to us. Nevertheless, the lemma is an important theoretical vehicle towards soundness of Algorithm 3.

Lemma 4.9. *Let $\mathcal{G}$ be the game in Algorithm 3, and $\mathrm{Av}': S \to 2^A$ be a Minimizer restriction (Definition 4.2). Let $\mathcal{M} = \mathcal{M}(\mathcal{G}, \mathrm{Av}')$, and $\mathcal{W} = \mathcal{W}_{\mathrm{LcPg}}(\mathcal{M}, V(\mathcal{G}))$. Then, for each state $s \in S$, we have $\mathrm{WPW}(\mathcal{W})(s, \mathbf{1}) \geq V(\mathcal{G})(s)$.*

Proof. In what follows, we let the WG $\mathcal{W} = \mathcal{W}_{\mathrm{LcPg}}(\mathcal{M}, V(\mathcal{G}))$ be denoted by $\mathcal{W} = (S, E, w)$. Let $\pi = s_0 a_0 s_1 a_1 \ldots a_{n-1} s_n$ be a path of the MDP $\mathcal{M}$ such that $s_n = \mathbf{1}$, each action is optimal in $\mathcal{M}$ with respect to $V(\mathcal{G})$, and $V(\mathcal{G})(s_i) \leq V(\mathcal{G})(s_{i+1})$ for each $i \in [0, n-1]$. Existence of such a path π is shown by Lemma 4.8. Let $\pi' = s_0 s_1 \ldots s_{n-1} \mathbf{1}$ be the path in the WG $\mathcal{W}$ induced by π—we simply omit actions.

The path π' satisfies the following, for each $i \in [0, n-1]$.

$$w(s_i, s_{i+1}) = \max\{ (\mathbb{X}_a(V(\mathcal{G})))(s_i) \mid a \in \mathrm{Av}'(s_i), s_{i+1} \in \mathrm{post}(s_i, a) \} \quad \text{by Definition 4.7}$$
$$= (\mathbb{X}_{a_i}(V(\mathcal{G})))(s_i) \quad \text{since } a_i \text{ is optimal wrt. } V(\mathcal{G});$$
$$\text{note that } a_i \in \mathrm{Av}'(s_i), s_{i+1} \in \mathrm{post}(s_i, a_i) \text{ hold since } \pi \text{ is a path in } \mathcal{M}$$
$$= \max_{a \in \mathrm{Av}'(s)} (\mathbb{X}_a(V(\mathcal{G})))(s_i) \quad \text{since } a_i \text{ is optimal wrt. } V(\mathcal{G})$$
$$\geq V(\mathcal{G})(s_i) \quad \text{by Lemma 4.6.}$$

This observation, combined with $V(\mathcal{G})(s_0) \leq V(\mathcal{G})(s_1) \leq \cdots \leq V(\mathcal{G})(s_n)$ (by the definition of π), implies that the width of the path π' is at least $V(\mathcal{G})(s_0)$. The widest path width is no smaller than that. $\qquad \square$

Theorem 4.10 (soundness). *In Algorithm 3, $V(\mathcal{G}) \leq U_i$ holds for each $i \in \mathbb{N}$.*

Proof. We let the function

$$\min\{ U, \mathrm{WPW}(\mathcal{W}_{\mathrm{LcPg}}(\mathcal{M}(\mathcal{G}, \mathrm{Av}'), U))(\_, 1) \} \quad : \quad S \longrightarrow [0, 1]$$
$$\text{denoted by} \quad T(\mathrm{Av}', U) : \quad S \longrightarrow [0, 1],$$

clarifying its dependence on Av' and $U : S \to [0, 1]$. Clearly, for each $i \in \mathbb{N}$, we have $U_i = T(\mathrm{Av}_{L_i}, U_{i-1})$.

The rest of the proof is by induction. It is trivial if $i = 0$ ($U_0 = \top$).

$$U_{i+1} = T(\mathrm{Av}_{L_i}, U_i)$$
$$\geq T(\mathrm{Av}_{L_i}, V(\mathcal{G})) \quad \text{by ind. hyp., and } T(\mathrm{Av}_{L_i}, \_) \text{ is monotone}$$
$$= \min\{ V(\mathcal{G}), \mathrm{WPW}(\mathcal{W}_{\mathrm{LcPg}}(\mathcal{M}(\mathcal{G}, \mathrm{Av}_{L_i}), V(\mathcal{G})))(\_, 1) \}$$
$$= V(\mathcal{G}) \quad \text{by Lemma 4.9.}$$

$\qquad \square$

It is clear that U_i decreases with respect to i ($U_0 \geq U_1 \geq \cdots$), by the presence of min in Line 8. It remains to show the following.

Theorem 4.11 (convergence). *In Algorithm 3, let the while loop iterate forever. Then $U_i \to V(\mathcal{G})$ as $i \to \infty$.*

Proof. We give a proof using the infinitary pigeonhole principle. The proof is nonconstructive—it is not suited for analyzing the speed of convergence, for example—but the proof becomes simpler.

In what follows, we let $\mathbb{X}_\sigma : (S \to [0, 1]) \to (S \to [0, 1])$ denote the Bellman operator on an MDP $\mathcal{M}$ induced by a strategy σ, i.e., $(\mathbb{X}_\sigma f)(s) := (\mathbb{X}_{\sigma(s)} f)(s)$. The MC obtained from an MDP $\mathcal{M}$ by fixing a strategy σ is denoted by $\mathcal{M}^\sigma$.

Towards the statement of the theorem, for each $i \in \mathbb{N}$, we choose a (positional) strategy σ_i in the MDP $\mathcal{M}_i$ as follows.

- For each $s \in S_{\Diamond 1}$, take the widest path $\mathrm{WPath}(\mathcal{W}_i, \mathbf{1})(s) = s s_1 \ldots \mathbf{1}$ in $\mathcal{W}_i$ from s to $\mathbf{1}$ (Definition 2.8). Such a path from s to $\mathbf{1}$ exists—otherwise we have $U_i(s) = 0$, hence $V(\mathcal{G})(s) = 0$ by Theorem 4.10.
  Let $\sigma_i(s)$ be an action that justifies the first edge in the chosen widest path, that is, $a \in \mathrm{Av}_i(s)$ such that $s_1 \in \mathrm{post}(s, a)$.
- For each $s \in S \setminus S_{\Diamond 1}$, $\sigma_i(s)$ is freely chosen from $\mathrm{Av}_i(s)$.

It is then easy to see that

$$\mathrm{WPW}(\mathcal{W}_i)(s) \le (\mathbb{X}_{\sigma_i} U_{i-1})(s) \qquad \text{for each } i \in \mathbb{N} \text{ and } s \in S_{\Diamond 1}. \qquad (11)$$

Indeed, by the definition of σ_i, the right-hand side is the weight of the first edge in the chosen widest path. This must be no smaller than the widest path width, that is, the width of the chosen path.

Now, since there are only finitely many strategies for the SG $\mathcal{G}$, the same is true for the MDPs $\mathcal{M}_0, \mathcal{M}_1, \ldots$ that are obtained from $\mathcal{G}$ by restricting Minimizer's actions. Therefore, by the infinitary pigeonhole principle, there are infinitely many $i_0 < i_1 < \cdots$ such that $\sigma_{i_0} = \sigma_{i_1} = \cdots =: \sigma^{\dagger}$. Moreover, we can choose them so that they are all beyond i_{M} in Lemma 4.5, in which case we have

$$V(\mathcal{M}_{i_m}^{\sigma^{\dagger}}) \le V(\mathcal{G}) \quad \text{for each } m \in \mathbb{N}. \qquad (12)$$

Indeed, Minimizer's actions are already optimized in $\mathcal{M}_i$ (Lemma 4.5), and thus the only freedom left for $\sigma^{\dagger}$ is to choose suboptimal actions of Maximizer's.

In what follows, we cut down the domain of discourse from $S \to [0, 1]$ to $S_{\Diamond 1} \to [0, 1]$, i.e., 1) every function of the type $f : S \to [0, 1]$ is now seen as the restriction over $S_{\Diamond 1}$, and 2) the Bellman operator only adds up the value of the input function over $S_{\Diamond 1}$, namely it is now defined by $\hat{\mathbb{X}}_a f(s) = \sum_{s' \in S_{\Diamond 1}} \delta(s, a, s') \cdot f(s')$. The operator $\hat{\mathbb{X}}_\sigma$ is also defined in a similar way to $\mathbb{X}_\sigma$.

Now proving convergence in $S_{\Diamond 1} \to [0, 1]$ suffices for the theorem. Indeed, for each $i \ge i_{\mathrm{M}}$, we have $V(\mathcal{M}_i)(s) = V(\mathcal{G})(s) = 0$ for each $s \in S \setminus S_{\Diamond 1}$. This implies that there is no path from s to $\mathbf{1}$ in $\mathcal{M}_i$, thus neither in the WG $\mathcal{W}_i$. Therefore $U_i \le \mathrm{WPW}(\mathcal{W}_i) = 0$.

A benefit of this domain restriction is that the Bellman operator $\hat{\mathbb{X}}_\sigma$ has a unique fixed point in $S_{\Diamond 1} \to [0, 1]$ if the set of non-sink states in $\mathcal{M}^\sigma$ is exactly $S_{\Diamond 1}$, i.e., $V(\mathcal{M}^\sigma)(s) > 0$ holds if and only if $s \in S_{\Diamond 1}$. Furthermore, this unique fixed point is the value function $V(\mathcal{M}^\sigma)$ restricted to $S_{\Diamond 1} \subseteq S$ [4, Theorem 10.19]. Therefore $V(\mathcal{M}^\sigma)$ is computed by the gfp Kleene iteration, too:

$$\top \ge \hat{\mathbb{X}}_\sigma \top \ge (\hat{\mathbb{X}}_\sigma)^2 \top \ge \cdots \longrightarrow V(\mathcal{M}^\sigma) \quad \text{in the space } S_{\Diamond 1} \to [0, 1]. \qquad (13)$$

We show the following by induction on m.

$$U_{i_m} \le (\hat{\mathbb{X}}_{\sigma^{\dagger}})^m \top \quad \text{for each } m \in \mathbb{N}. \qquad (14)$$

It is obvious for $m = 0$. For the step case, we have the following. Notice that the inequality (11) holds in the restricted domain for $i \geq i_M$.

$$U_{i_{m+1}} \leq \text{WPW}(\mathcal{W}_{i_{m+1}}) \quad \text{by Line 8 of Algorithm 3}$$
$$\leq \hat{\mathbb{X}}_{\sigma^\dagger} U_{i_{m+1}-1} \quad \text{by (11)}$$
$$\leq \hat{\mathbb{X}}_{\sigma^\dagger} U_{i_m} \quad \text{by monotonicity of } \hat{\mathbb{X}}_{\sigma^\dagger}, \text{ decrease of } U_i \text{ and } i_m < i_{m+1}$$
$$\leq (\hat{\mathbb{X}}_{\sigma^\dagger})^{m+1} \top \quad \text{by the induction hypothesis.}$$

We have proved (14) which proves $\inf_i U_i \leq \inf_m (\hat{\mathbb{X}}_{\sigma^\dagger})^m \top$.

Lastly, we prove that $V(\mathcal{M}_{i_m}^{\sigma^\dagger})(s) > 0$ holds if and only if $s \in S_{\Diamond 1}$ for each $m \in \mathbb{N}$, and thus $\sigma^\dagger$ follows the characterization in (13). This proves

$$\inf_i U_i \leq V(\mathcal{M}_{i_m}^{\sigma^\dagger}) \quad \text{for each } m \in \mathbb{N}. \tag{15}$$

Implication to the right is clear as Minimizer restriction is done optimally in $\mathcal{M}_{i_m}$. Conversely, if $s \in S_{\Diamond 1}$, then there is a path from s to $\mathbf{1}$ in $\mathcal{W}_{i_m}$. Let $\text{WPath}(\mathcal{W}_{i_m}, \mathbf{1})(s) = s_0 s_1 \ldots s_k$, where $s_0 = s$, $k \in \mathbb{N}$ and $s_k = \mathbf{1}$. Then by the property of WPath and $\sigma^\dagger$, we have $\delta(s_j, \sigma^\dagger(s_j), s_{j+1}) > 0$ for each $j < k$. Thus, the probability that the finite path $\text{WPath}(\mathcal{W}_{i_m}, \mathbf{1})(s)$ is obtained by running $\mathcal{M}_{i_m}^{\sigma^\dagger}$ starting from s, which is apparently at most $V(\mathcal{M}_{i_m}^{\sigma^\dagger})(s)$, is nonzero. Hence we have implication to the left.

Combining (12), (15) and Theorem 4.10, we obtain the claim. $\qquad\square$

5   Experiment Results

Experiment Settings. We compare the following four algorithms.

- *WP* is our BVI algorithm via widest paths. It avoids end component (EC) computation by global propagation of upper bounds.
- *DFL* is the implementation of the main algorithm in [20]. It relies on EC computation for deflating.
- *DFL_m* is our modification of DFL, where some unnecessary repetition of EC computation is removed.
- *DFL_BRTDP* is the learning-based variant of DFL. It restricts bound update to those states which are visited by simulations. See [20] for details.

The latter three—coming from [20]—are the only existing BVI algorithms for SGs with a convergence guarantee, to the best of our knowledge. The implementation of DFL and DFL_BRTDP is provided by the authors of [20].

The four algorithms are implemented on top of PRISM-games [21] version 2.0. We used the stopping threshold $\varepsilon = 10^{-6}$. The experiments were conducted on Dell Inspiron 3421 Laptop with 4.00 GB RAM and Intel(R) Core(TM) i5-3337U 1.80 GHz processor.

In the implementations of DFL and DFL_BRTDP, the deflating operation is applied only once every five iterations [20, Sect. B.3]. Following this, our WP also solves the widest path problem (Line 8) only once every five iterations, while other operations are applied in each iteration.

For input SGs, we took four models from the literature: *mdsm* [11], *cloud* [6], *teamform* [12] and *investor* [22]. In addition, we used our model *manyECs*—an artificial model with many ECs—to assess the effect of ECs on performance. The model manyECs is presented in the appendix in [24]. Each of these five models comes with a model parameter N.

There is another model called *cdmsn* in [20]. We do not discuss cdmsn since all the algorithms (ours and those from [20]) terminated within 0.001 seconds.

Results. The number i of iterations and the running time for each algorithm and each input SG is shown in Table 1. For DFL_BRTDP, the ratio of states visited by the algorithm is shown in percentage; the smaller it is, the more efficient the algorithm is in reducing the state space. Each number for DFL_BRTDP (a probabilistic algorithm) is the average over 5 runs.

Table 1. Experimental results, comparing WP (our algorithm) with those in [20]. N is a model parameter (the bigger the more complex). #states, #trans, #EC show the numbers of states, transitions and ECs in the SG, respectively. itr is the number i of iterations at termination; time is the execution time in seconds. For each SG, the fastest algorithm is shaded in green. The settings that did not terminate are shaded in gray; TO is time out (6 h), OOM is out of memory, and SO is stack overflow.

model	N	#states	#trans	#EC	DFL		DFL_m		DFL_BRTDP			WP	
					itr	time	itr	time	itr	visit%	time	itr	time
mdsm	3	62245	151143	1	121	3	121	4	17339	49.3	15	120	5
	4	335211	882765	1	125	15	125	47	91301	42.1	86	124	38
cloud	5	8842	60437	4421	7	7	7	1	167	6.9	14	7	<1
	6	34954	274965	17477	11	177	11	5	41	0.6	3	11	1
	7	139402	1237525	69701	11	19721	11	62	41	0.2	4	11	5
teamform	3	12475	15228	2754	2	<1	2	<1	972	49.0	137	2	<1
	4	96665	116464	19800	2	<1	2	<1	4154	34.6	9603	2	<1
	5	907993	1084752	176760	2	<1	2	<1			TO	2	<1
investor	50	211321	673810	29690	441	184	441	249			TO	364	48
	100	807521	2587510	114390	801	3318		OOM			TO	688	736
manyECs	500	1004	3007	502	6	7	6	7			TO	5	<1
	1000	2004	6007	1002	6	51	6	51			TO	5	<1
	5000	10004	30007	5002		SO		SO			TO	5	<1

Discussion. We observe consistent performance advantage of our algorithm (WP). Even in the mdsm model where the DFL algorithms do not suffer from EC computation (#EC is just 1), WP's performance is comparable to DFL. The cloud model is where the learning-based approach in [20] works well—see visit% that are very small. Our WP performs comparably against DFL_BRTDP, too.

The performance advantage of our WP algorithm is eminent, not only in the artificial model of manyECs (where WP is faster by magnitudes), but also in the realistic model investor that comes from a financial application scenario [22]. The results for these two models suggest that WP is indeed advantageous when EC computation poses a bottleneck for other algorithms.

Overall, we observe that our WP algorithm can be the first choice when it comes to solving SGs: for some models, it runs much faster than other algorithms; for other models, even if the performances of other algorithms differs a lot, WP's performance is comparable with the best algorithm.

6   Conclusions and Future Work

In this paper, we presented a new BVI algorithm for solving stochastic games. It features global propagation of upper bounds by widest paths, via a novel encoding of the problem to a suitable weighted graph. This way we avoid computation of end components that often penalizes the performance of the other BVI-based algorithms. Our experimental comparison with known BVI algorithms for SGs demonstrates the efficiency of our algorithm. For correctness of the algorithm, we presented proofs for soundness and convergence.

Extending the current algorithm for more advanced settings is future work—this is much like the results in [20] are extended and used in [2,3,16]. In doing so, we hope to make essential use of structures that are unique to those advanced problem settings. Another important direction is to push forward the idea of global propagation in verification and synthesis, seeking further instances of the idea. Finally, pursuing the global propagation idea in the context of reinforcement learning—where problems are often formalized using MDPs and the Bellman operator is heavily utilized—may open up another fruitful collaboration between formal methods and statistical machine learning.

Acknowledgment. The authors are supported by ERATO HASUO Metamathematics for Systems Design Project (No. JPMJER1603), JST; I.H. is supported by Grant-in-Aid No. 15KT0012, JSPS. Thanks are due to Maximilian Weininger and Edon Kelmendi for sharing their implementation, and to Pranav Ashok and David Sprunger for useful discussions and comments.

References

1. Andersson, D., Miltersen, P.B.: The complexity of solving stochastic games on graphs. In: Dong, Y., Du, D.-Z., Ibarra, O. (eds.) ISAAC 2009. LNCS, vol. 5878, pp. 112–121. Springer, Heidelberg (2009). https://doi.org/10.1007/978-3-642-10631-6_13
2. Ashok, P., Kretinsky, J., Weininger, M.: Approximating values of generalized-reachability stochastic games. CoRR abs/1908.05106 (2019). http://arxiv.org/abs/1908.05106
3. Ashok, P., Křetínský, J., Weininger, M.: PAC statistical model checking for Markov decision processes and stochastic games. In: Dillig, I., Tasiran, S. (eds.) CAV 2019. LNCS, vol. 11561, pp. 497–519. Springer, Cham (2019). https://doi.org/10.1007/978-3-030-25540-4_29

4. Baier, C., Katoen, J.P.: Principles of Model Checking. MIT Press, Cambridge (2008)
5. Brázdil, T., et al.: Verification of Markov decision processes using learning algorithms. In: Cassez, F., Raskin, J.-F. (eds.) ATVA 2014. LNCS, vol. 8837, pp. 98–114. Springer, Cham (2014). https://doi.org/10.1007/978-3-319-11936-6_8
6. Calinescu, R., Kikuchi, S., Johnson, K.: Compositional reverification of probabilistic safety properties for large-scale complex IT systems. In: Calinescu, R., Garlan, D. (eds.) Monterey Workshop 2012. LNCS, vol. 7539, pp. 303–329. Springer, Heidelberg (2012). https://doi.org/10.1007/978-3-642-34059-8_16
7. Chatterjee, K., Dvorák, W., Henzinger, M., Svozil, A.: Near-linear time algorithms for streett objectives in graphs and MDPS. In: Fokkink, W., van Glabbeek, R. (eds.) 30th International Conference on Concurrency Theory CONCUR 2019, 27–30 August 2019, Amsterdam, the Netherlands. LIPIcs, vol. 140, pp. 7:1–7:16. Schloss Dagstuhl - Leibniz-Zentrum für Informatik (2019). https://doi.org/10.4230/LIPIcs.CONCUR.2019.7
8. Chatterjee, K., Fijalkow, N.: A reduction from parity games to simple stochastic games. In: D'Agostino, G., La Torre, S. (eds.) Proceedings of Second International Symposium on Games, Automata, Logics and Formal Verification, GandALF 2011, Minori, Italy, 15–17 June 2011. EPTCS, vol. 54, pp. 74–86 (2011). https://doi.org/10.4204/EPTCS.54.6
9. Chatterjee, K., Henzinger, M.: Efficient and dynamic algorithms for alternating büchi games and maximal end-component decomposition. J. ACM (JACM) **61**(3), 15 (2014)
10. Chatterjee, K., Henzinger, T.A.: Value iteration. In: Grumberg, O., Veith, H. (eds.) 25 Years of Model Checking. LNCS, vol. 5000, pp. 107–138. Springer, Heidelberg (2008). https://doi.org/10.1007/978-3-540-69850-0_7
11. Chen, T., Forejt, V., Kwiatkowska, M.Z., Parker, D., Simaitis, A.: Automatic verification of competitive stochastic systems. Formal Methods Syst. Design **43**(1), 61–92 (2013). https://doi.org/10.1007/s10703-013-0183-7
12. Chen, T., Kwiatkowska, M., Parker, D., Simaitis, A.: Verifying team formation protocols with probabilistic model checking. In: Leite, J., Torroni, P., Ågotnes, T., Boella, G., van der Torre, L. (eds.) CLIMA 2011. LNCS (LNAI), vol. 6814, pp. 190–207. Springer, Heidelberg (2011). https://doi.org/10.1007/978-3-642-22359-4_14
13. Condon, A.: The complexity of stochastic games. Inf. Comput. **96**(2), 203–224 (1992). https://doi.org/10.1016/0890-5401(92)90048-K
14. Courcoubetis, C., Yannakakis, M.: The complexity of probabilistic verification. J. ACM **42**(4), 857–907 (1995). https://doi.org/10.1145/210332.210339
15. De Alfaro, L.: Formal verification of probabilistic systems. Citeseer (1997)
16. Eisentraut, J., Kretinsky, J., Rotar, A.: Stopping criteria for value and strategy iteration on concurrent stochastic reachability games. CoRR abs/1909.08348 (2019). http://arxiv.org/abs/1909.08348
17. Fredman, M.L., Tarjan, R.E.: Fibonacci heaps and their uses in improved network optimization algorithms. J. ACM **34**(3), 596–615 (1987). https://doi.org/10.1145/28869.28874
18. Haddad, S., Monmege, B.: Interval iteration algorithm for MDPs and IMDPs. Theoret. Comput. Sci. **735**, 111–131 (2018)
19. Hoffman, A.J., Karp, R.M.: On nonterminating stochastic games. Manage. Sci. **12**(5), 359–370 (1966). https://doi.org/10.1287/mnsc.12.5.359

20. Kelmendi, E., Krämer, J., Křetínský, J., Weininger, M.: Value iteration for simple stochastic games: stopping criterion and learning algorithm. In: Chockler, H., Weissenbacher, G. (eds.) CAV 2018. LNCS, vol. 10981, pp. 623–642. Springer, Cham (2018). https://doi.org/10.1007/978-3-319-96145-3_36
21. Kwiatkowska, M., Parker, D., Wiltsche, C.: PRISM-games: verification and strategy synthesis for stochastic multi-player games with multiple objectives. Int. J. Softw. Tools Technol. Transf. **20**(2), 195–210 (2017)
22. McIver, A., Morgan, C.: Results on the quantitative μ-calculus qmμ. ACM Trans. Comput. Log. **8**(1), 3 (2007). https://doi.org/10.1145/1182613.1182616
23. McMahan, H.B., Likhachev, M., Gordon, G.J.: Bounded real-time dynamic programming: RTDP with monotone upper bounds and performance guarantees. In: Raedt, L.D., Wrobel, S. (eds.) Machine Learning, Proceedings of the Twenty-Second International Conference (ICML 2005), Bonn, Germany, 7–11 August 2005. ACM International Conference Proceeding Series, vol. 119, pp. 569–576. ACM (2005). https://doi.org/10.1145/1102351.1102423
24. Phalakarn, K., Takisaka, T., Haas, T., Hasuo, I.: Widest paths and global propagation in bounded value iteration for stochastic games. arXiv preprint (2020)
25. Svorenová, M., Kwiatkowska, M.: Quantitative verification and strategy synthesis for stochastic games. Eur. J. Control **30**, 15–30 (2016). https://doi.org/10.1016/j.ejcon.2016.04.009
26. Ujma, M.: On Verication and Controller Synthesis for Probabilistic Systems at Runtime. Ph.D. thesis, Wolfson College, University of Oxford (2015)

Checking Qualitative Liveness Properties of Replicated Systems with Stochastic Scheduling

Michael Blondin[1] , Javier Esparza[2], Martin Helfrich[2],
Antonín Kučera[3], and Philipp J. Meyer[2(✉)]

[1] Université de Sherbrooke, Sherbrooke, Canada
`michael.blondin@usherbrooke.ca`
[2] Technical University of Munich, Munich, Germany
`{esparza,helfrich,meyerphi}@in.tum.de`
[3] Masaryk University, Brno, Czechia
`tony@fi.muni.cz`

Abstract. We present a sound and complete method for the verification of qualitative liveness properties of replicated systems under stochastic scheduling. These are systems consisting of a finite-state program, executed by an unknown number of indistinguishable agents, where the next agent to make a move is determined by the result of a random experiment. We show that if a property of such a system holds, then there is always a witness in the shape of a *Presburger stage graph*: a finite graph whose nodes are Presburger-definable sets of configurations. Due to the high complexity of the verification problem (non-elementary), we introduce an incomplete procedure for the construction of Presburger stage graphs, and implement it on top of an SMT solver. The procedure makes extensive use of the theory of well-quasi-orders, and of the structural theory of Petri nets and vector addition systems. We apply our results to a set of benchmarks, in particular to a large collection of population protocols, a model of distributed computation extensively studied by the distributed computing community.

Keywords: Parameterized verification · Liveness · Stochastic systems

1 Introduction

Replicated systems consist of a fully symmetric finite-state program executed by an unknown number of indistinguishable agents, communicating by rendez-vous

Michael Blondin is supported by a Discovery Grant from the Natural Sciences and Engineering Research Council of Canada (NSERC) and by the Fonds de recherche du Québec – Nature et technologies (FRQNT). Javier Esparza, Martin Helfrich and Philipp J. Meyer have received funding from the European Research Council (ERC) under the European Union's Horizon 2020 research and innovation programme under grant agreement No 787367 (PaVeS). Antonín Kučera is supported by the Czech Science Foundation, grant No. 18-11193S.

S. K. Lahiri and C. Wang (Eds.): CAV 2020, LNCS 12225, pp. 372–397, 2020.
https://doi.org/10.1007/978-3-030-53291-8_20

or via shared variables [14, 16, 41, 46]. Examples include distributed protocols and multithreaded programs, or abstractions thereof. The communication graph of replicated systems is a clique. They are a special class of *parameterized systems*, i.e., infinite families of systems that admit a finite description in some suitable modeling language. In the case of replicated systems, the (only) parameter is the number of agents executing the program.

Verifying a replicated system amounts to proving that an infinite family of systems satisfies a given property. This is already a formidable challenge, made even harder by the fact that we want to verify liveness (more difficult than safety) against stochastic schedulers. Loosely speaking, stochastic schedulers select the set of agents that should execute the next action as the result of a random experiment. Stochastic scheduling often appears in distributed protocols, and in particular also in population protocols—a model much studied in distributed computing with applications in computational biology[1]—that supplies many of our case studies [9, 58]. Under stochastic scheduling, the semantics of a replicated system is an infinite family of finite-state Markov chains. In this work, we study *qualitative* liveness properties, stating that the infinite runs starting at configurations of the system satisfying a precondition almost surely reach and stay in configurations satisfying a postcondition. In this case, whether the property holds or not depends only on the topology of the Markov chains, and not on the concrete probabilities.

We introduce a formal model of replicated systems, based on multiset rewriting, where processes can communicate by shared variables or multiway synchronization. We present a sound and complete verification method called *Presburger stage graphs*. A Presburger stage graphs is a directed acyclic graphs with Presburger formulas as nodes. A formula represents a possibly infinite inductive set of configurations, i.e., a set of configurations closed under reachability. A node S (which we identify with the set of configurations it represents) has the following property: A run starting at any configuration of S almost surely reaches some configuration of some successor S' of S, and, since S' is inductive, get trapped in S'. A stage graph labels the node S with a witness of this property in the form of a *Presburger certificate*, a sort of ranking function expressible in Presburger arithmetic. The completeness of the technique, i.e., the fact that for every property of the replicated system that holds there exists a stage graph proving it, follows from deep results of the theory of vector addition systems (VASs) [52–54].

Unfortunately, the theory of VASs also shows that, while the verification problems we consider are decidable, they have non-elementary computational complexity [33]. As a consequence, verification techniques that systematically explore the space of possible stage graphs for a given property are bound to be very inefficient. For this reason, we design an incomplete but efficient algorithm for the computation of stage graphs. Inspired by theoretical results, the algorithm combines a solver for linear constraints with some elements of the theory of well-structured systems [2, 39]. We report on the performance of this algorithm for a large number of case studies. In particular, the algorithm automatically verifies

---

[1] Under the name of *chemical reaction networks*.

many standard population protocols described in the literature [5, 8, 20, 22, 23, 28, 31], as well as liveness properties of distributed algorithms for leader election and mutual exclusion [3, 40, 42, 44, 50, 59, 61, 64].

Related Work. The parameterized verification of replicated systems was first studied in [41], where they were modeled as counter systems. This allows one to apply many efficient techniques [11, 24, 37, 47]. Most of these works are inherently designed for safety properties, and some can also handle fair termination [38], but none of them handles stochastic scheduling. To the best of our knowledge, the only works studying parameterized verification of liveness properties under our notion of stochastic scheduling are those on verification of population protocols. For *fixed* populations, protocols can be verified with standard probabilistic model checking [13, 65], and early works follow this approach [28, 31, 60, 63]. Subsequently, an algorithm and a tool for the *parameterized* verification of population protocols were described in [21, 22], and a first version of stage graphs was introduced in [23] for analyzing the expected termination time of population protocols. In this paper we overhaul the framework of [23] for liveness verification, drawing inspiration from the safety verification technology of [21, 22]. Compared to [21, 22], our approach is not limited to a specific subclass of protocols, and captures models beyond population protocols. Furthermore, our new techniques for computing Presburger certificates subsume the procedure of [22]. In comparison to [23], we provide the first completeness and complexity results for stage graphs. Further, our stage graphs can prove correctness of population protocols and even more general liveness properties, while those of [23] can only prove termination. We also introduce novel techniques for computing stage graphs, which compared to [23] can greatly reduce their size and allows us to prove more examples correct.

There is also a large body of work on parameterized verification via cutoff techniques: one shows that a specification holds for any number of agents iff it holds for any number of agents below some threshold called the cutoff (see [6, 26, 30, 34, 46], and [16] for a comprehensive survey). Cut-off techniques can be applied to systems with an array or ring communication structure, but they require the existence and effectiveness of a cutoff, which is not the case in our setting. Further parameterized verification techniques are regular model checking [1, 25] and automata learning [7]. The classes of communication structures they can handle are orthogonal to ours: arrays and rings for regular model checking and automata learning, and cliques in our work. Regular model checking and learning have recently been employed to verify safety properties [29], liveness properties under arbitrary schedulers [55] and termination under finitary fairness [51]. The classes of schedulers considered in [51, 55] are incomparable to ours: arbitrary schedulers in [55], and finitary-fair schedulers in [51]. Further, these works are based on symbolic state-space exploration, while our techniques are based on automatic construction of invariants and ranking functions [16].

2   Preliminaries

Let $\mathbb{N}$ denote $\{0, 1, \ldots\}$ and let E be a finite set. A *unordered vector* over E is a mapping $V \colon E \to \mathbb{Z}$. In particular, a *multiset* over E is an unordered vector $M \colon E \to \mathbb{N}$ where $M(e)$ denotes the number of occurrences of e in M. The sets of all unordered vectors and multisets over E are respectively denoted $\mathbb{Z}^E$ and $\mathbb{N}^E$. Vector addition, subtraction and comparison are defined componentwise. The *size* of a multiset M is denoted $|M| = \sum_{e \in E} M(e)$. We let $E^{\langle k \rangle}$ denote the set of all multisets over E of size k. We sometimes describe multisets using a set-like notation, e.g. $M = \{f, g, g\}$ or equivalently $M = \{f, 2 \cdot g\}$ is such that $M(f) = 1$, $M(g) = 2$ and $M(e) = 0$ for all $e \notin \{f, g\}$.

Presburger Arithmetic. Let X be a set of variables. The set of formulas of *Presburger arithmetic* over X is the result of closing atomic formulas, as defined in the next sentence, under Boolean operations and first-order existential quantification. Atomic formulas are of the form $\sum_{i=1}^{k} a_i x_i \sim b$, where a_i and b are integers, x_i are variables and $\sim$ is either $<$ or $\equiv_m$, the latter denoting the congruence modulo m for any $m \geq 2$. Formulas over X are interpreted on $\mathbb{N}^X$. Given a formula ϕ of Presburger arithmetic, we let $[\![\phi]\!]$ denote the set of all multisets satisfying ϕ. A set $E \subseteq \mathbb{N}^X$ is a *Presburger set* if $E = [\![\phi]\!]$ for some formula ϕ.

2.1   Replicated Systems

A *replicated system* over Q of arity n is a tuple $\mathcal{P} = (Q, T)$, where $T \subseteq \bigcup_{k=0}^{n} Q^{\langle k \rangle} \times Q^{\langle k \rangle}$ is a *transition relation* containing the set of *silent* transitions $\bigcup_{k=0}^{n} \{(\boldsymbol{x}, \boldsymbol{x}) \mid \boldsymbol{x} \in Q^{\langle k \rangle}\}^2$. A *configuration* is a multiset C of states, which we interpret as a global state with $C(q)$ agents in each state $q \in Q$.

For every $t = (\boldsymbol{x}, \boldsymbol{y}) \in T$ with $\boldsymbol{x} = \{X_1, X_2, \ldots, X_k\}$ and $\boldsymbol{y} = \{Y_1, Y_2, \ldots, Y_k\}$, we write $X_1 X_2 \cdots X_k \mapsto Y_1 Y_2 \cdots Y_k$ and let $\,^\bullet t \overset{\text{def}}{=} \boldsymbol{x}$, $t^\bullet \overset{\text{def}}{=} \boldsymbol{y}$ and $\Delta(t) \overset{\text{def}}{=} t^\bullet - \,^\bullet t$. A transition t is *enabled* at a configuration C if $C \geq \,^\bullet t$ and, if so, can *occur*, leading to the configuration $C' = C + \Delta(t)$. If t is not enabled at C, then we say that it is *disabled*. We use the following reachability notation:

$$C \xrightarrow{t} C' \iff t \text{ is enabled at } C \text{ and its occurrence leads to } C',$$

$$C \to C' \iff C \xrightarrow{t} C' \text{ for some } t \in T,$$

$$C \xrightarrow{w} C' \iff C = C_0 \xrightarrow{w_1} C_1 \cdots \xrightarrow{w_n} C_n = C' \text{ for some } C_0, C_1, \ldots, C_n \in \mathbb{N}^Q,$$

$$C \xrightarrow{*} C' \iff C \xrightarrow{w} C' \text{ for some } w \in T^*.$$

Observe that, by definition of transitions, $C \to C'$ implies $|C| = |C'|$, and likewise for $C \xrightarrow{*} C'$. Intuitively, transitions cannot create or destroy agents.

A *run* is an infinite sequence $C_0 t_1 C_1 t_2 C_2 \cdots$ such that $C_i \xrightarrow{t_{i+1}} C_{i+1}$ for every $i \geq 0$. Given $L \subseteq T^*$ and a set of configurations $\mathcal{C}$, we let

$$post_L(\mathcal{C}) \overset{\text{def}}{=} \{C' : C \in \mathcal{C}, w \in L, C \xrightarrow{w} C'\}, \qquad post^*(\mathcal{C}) \overset{\text{def}}{=} post_{T^*}(\mathcal{C}),$$

$$pre_L(\mathcal{C}) \overset{\text{def}}{=} \{C : C' \in \mathcal{C}, w \in L, C \xrightarrow{w} C'\}, \qquad pre^*(\mathcal{C}) \overset{\text{def}}{=} pre_{T^*}(\mathcal{C}).$$

---

[2]   In the paper, we will omit the silent transitions when giving replicated systems.

Stochastic Scheduling. We assume that, given a configuration C, a probabilistic scheduler picks one of the transitions enabled at C. We only make the following two assumptions about the random experiment determining the transition: first, the probability of a transition depends only on C, and, second, every transition enabled at C has a nonzero probability of occurring. Since $C \xrightarrow{*} C'$ implies $|C| = |C'|$, the number of configurations reachable from any configuration C is finite. Thus, for every configuration C, the semantics of $\mathcal{P}$ from C is a finite-state Markov chain rooted at C.

Example 1. Consider the replicated system $\mathcal{P} = (Q, T)$ of arity 2 with states $Q = \{A_Y, A_N, P_Y, P_N\}$ and transitions $T = \{t_1, t_2, t_3, t_4\}$, where

$$t_1 \colon A_Y A_N \mapsto P_Y P_N, \qquad t_2 \colon A_Y P_N \mapsto A_Y P_Y,$$
$$t_3 \colon A_N P_Y \mapsto A_N P_N, \qquad t_4 \colon P_Y P_N \mapsto P_N P_N.$$

Intuitively, at every moment in time, agents are either *Active* or *Passive*, and have output *Yes* or *No*, which corresponds to the four states of Q. This system is designed to satisfy the following property: for every configuration C in which all agents are initially active, i.e., C satisfies $C(P_Y) = C(P_N) = 0$, if $C(A_Y) > C(A_N)$, then eventually all agents stay forever in the "yes" states $\{A_Y, P_Y\}$, and otherwise all agents eventually stay forever in the "no" states $\{A_N, P_N\}$.   ◁

2.2   Qualitative Model Checking

Let us fix a replicated system $\mathcal{P} = (Q, T)$. Formulas of *linear temporal logic (LTL)* on $\mathcal{P}$ are defined by the following grammar:

$$\varphi ::= \phi \mid \neg\varphi \mid \varphi \vee \varphi \mid \varphi \wedge \varphi \mid \mathbf{X}\varphi \mid \varphi \, \mathbf{U} \, \varphi$$

where ϕ is a Presburger formula over Q. We look at ϕ as an atomic proposition over the set $\mathbb{N}^Q$ of configurations. Formulas of LTL are interpreted over runs of $\mathcal{P}$ in the standard way. We abbreviate $\Diamond\varphi \equiv \mathit{true} \, \mathbf{U} \, \varphi$ and $\Box\varphi \equiv \neg\Diamond\neg\varphi$.

Let us now introduce the probabilistic interpretation of LTL. A configuration C of $\mathcal{P}$ satisfies an LTL formula φ *with probability* p if $\Pr[C, \varphi] = p$, where $\Pr[C, \varphi]$ denotes the probability of the set of runs of $\mathcal{P}$ starting at C that satisfy φ in the finite-state Markov chain rooted at C. The measurability of this set of runs for every C and φ follows from well-known results [65]. The *qualitative model checking problem* consists of, given an LTL formula φ and a set of configurations $\mathcal{I}$, deciding whether $\Pr[C, \varphi] = 1$ for every $C \in \mathcal{I}$. We will often work with the complement problem, i.e., deciding whether $\Pr[C, \neg\varphi] > 0$ for some $C \in \mathcal{I}$.

In contrast to the action-based qualitative model checking problem of [35], our version of the problem is undecidable due to adding atomic propositions over configurations (see the full version of the paper [19] for a proof):

Theorem 1. *The qualitative model checking problem is not semi-decidable.*

It is known that qualitative model checking problems of finite-state probabilistic systems reduces to model checking of non-probabilistic systems under an adequate notion of fairness.

Definition 1. *A* run *of a replicated system* $\mathcal{P}$ *is* fair *if for every possible step* $C \xrightarrow{t} C'$ *of* $\mathcal{P}$ *the following holds: if the run contains infinitely many occurrences of* C, *then it also contains infinitely many occurrences of* $C \, t \, C'$.

So, intuitively, if a run can execute a step infinitely often, it eventually will. It is readily seen that a fair run of a finite-state transition system eventually gets "trapped" in one of its bottom strongly connected components, and visits each of its states infinitely often. Hence, fair runs of a finite-state Markov chain have probability one. The following proposition was proved in [35] for a model slightly less general than replicated systems; the proof can be generalized without effort:

Proposition 1 ([35, Prop. 7]). *Let* $\mathcal{P}$ *be a replicated system, let* C *be a configuration of* $\mathcal{P}$, *and let* φ *be an LTL formula. It is the case that* $\Pr[C, \varphi] = 1$ *iff every fair run of* $\mathcal{P}$ *starting at* C *satisfies* φ.

We implicitly use this proposition from now on. In particular, we define:

Definition 2. *A configuration* C satisfies φ *with probability 1, or just* satisfies φ, *if every fair run starting at* C *satisfies* φ, *denoted by* $C \models \varphi$. *We let* $[\![\varphi]\!]$ *denote the set of configurations satisfying* φ. *A set* $\mathcal{C}$ *of configurations* satisfies φ *if* $\mathcal{C} \subseteq [\![\varphi]\!]$, *i.e., if* $C \models \varphi$ *for every* $C \in \mathcal{C}$.

Liveness Specifications for Replicated Systems. We focus on a specific class of temporal properties for which the qualitative model checking problem is decidable and which is large enough to formalize many important specifications. Using well-known automata-theoretic technology, this class can also be used to verify all properties describable in action-based LTL, see e.g. [35].

A *stable termination property* is given by a pair $\Pi = (\varphi_{\text{pre}}, \Phi_{post})$, where $\Phi_{post} = \{\varphi_{\text{post}}^1, \dots, \varphi_{\text{post}}^k\}$ and $\varphi_{\text{pre}}, \varphi_{\text{post}}^1, \dots, \varphi_{\text{post}}^k$ are Presburger formulas over Q describing sets of configurations. Whenever $k = 1$, we sometimes simply write $\Pi = (\varphi_{\text{pre}}, \varphi_{\text{post}})$. The pair Π induces the LTL property

$$\varphi_\Pi \overset{\text{def}}{=} \Diamond \bigvee_{i=1}^{k} \Box \varphi_{\text{post}}^i.$$

Abusing language, we say that a replicated system $\mathcal{P}$ *satisfies* Π if $[\![\varphi_{\text{pre}}]\!] \subseteq [\![\varphi_\Pi]\!]$, that is, if every configuration C satisfying φ_{pre} satisfies φ_Π with probability 1. The *stable termination problem* is the qualitative model checking problem for $\mathcal{I} = [\![\varphi_{\text{pre}}]\!]$ and $\varphi = \varphi_\Pi$ given by a stable termination property $\Pi = (\varphi_{\text{pre}}, \Phi_{post})$.

Example 2. Let us reconsider the system from Example 1. We can formally specify that all agents will eventually agree on the majority output *Yes* or *No*. Let $\Pi^{\text{Y}} = (\varphi_{\text{pre}}^{\text{Y}}, \varphi_{\text{post}}^{\text{Y}})$ and $\Pi^{\text{N}} = (\varphi_{\text{pre}}^{\text{N}}, \varphi_{\text{post}}^{\text{N}})$ be defined by:

$$\varphi_{\text{pre}}^{\text{Y}} = (A_{\text{Y}} > A_{\text{N}} \wedge P_{\text{Y}} + P_{\text{N}} = 0), \qquad \varphi_{\text{post}}^{\text{Y}} = (A_{\text{N}} + P_{\text{N}} = 0),$$
$$\varphi_{\text{pre}}^{\text{N}} = (A_{\text{Y}} \leq A_{\text{N}} \wedge P_{\text{Y}} + P_{\text{N}} = 0), \qquad \varphi_{\text{post}}^{\text{N}} = (A_{\text{Y}} + P_{\text{Y}} = 0).$$

The system satisfies the property specified in Example 1 iff it satisfies Π^{Y} and Π^{N}. As an alternative (weaker) property, we could specify that the system always stabilizes to either output by $\Pi = (\varphi_{\text{pre}}^{\text{Y}} \vee \varphi_{\text{pre}}^{\text{N}}, \{\varphi_{\text{post}}^{\text{Y}}, \varphi_{\text{post}}^{\text{N}}\})$.   ◁

3   Stage Graphs

In the rest of the paper, we fix a replicated system $\mathcal{P} = (Q, T)$ and a stable termination property $\Pi = (\varphi_{\mathrm{pre}}, \Phi_{post})$, where $\Phi_{post} = \{\varphi_{\mathrm{post}}^1, \ldots, \varphi_{\mathrm{post}}^k\}$, and address the problem of checking whether $\mathcal{P}$ satisfies Π. We start with some basic definitions on sets of configurations.

Definition 3 (inductive sets, leads to, certificates)

- A set of configurations $\mathcal{C}$ is inductive if $C \in \mathcal{C}$ and $C \to C'$ implies $C' \in \mathcal{C}$.
- Let $\mathcal{C}, \mathcal{C}'$ be sets of configurations. We say that $\mathcal{C}$ leads to $\mathcal{C}'$, denoted $\mathcal{C} \rightsquigarrow \mathcal{C}'$, if for all $C \in \mathcal{C}$, every fair run from C eventually visits a configuration of $\mathcal{C}'$.
- A certificate for $\mathcal{C} \rightsquigarrow \mathcal{C}'$ is a function $f \colon \mathcal{C} \to \mathbb{N}$ satisfying that for every $C \in \mathcal{C} \setminus \mathcal{C}'$, there exists an execution $C \xrightarrow{*} C'$ such that $f(C) > f(C')$.

Note that certificates only require the existence of some executions decreasing f, not for all of them to to decrease it. Despite this, we have:

Proposition 2. *For all inductive sets $\mathcal{C}, \mathcal{C}'$ of configurations, it is the case that: $\mathcal{C}$ leads to $\mathcal{C}'$ iff there exists a certificate for $\mathcal{C} \rightsquigarrow \mathcal{C}'$.*

The proof, which can be found in the full version [19], depends on two properties of replicated systems with stochastic scheduling. First, every configuration has only finitely many descendants. Second, for every fair run and for every finite execution $C \xrightarrow{w} C'$, if C appears infinitely often in the run, then the run contains infinitely many occurrences of $C \xrightarrow{w} C'$. We can now introduce stage graphs:

Definition 4 (stage graph). *A stage graph of $\mathcal{P}$ for the property Π is a directed acyclic graph whose nodes, called stages, are sets of configurations satisfying the following conditions:*

1. *every stage is an inductive set;*
2. *every configuration of $[\![\varphi_{\mathrm{pre}}]\!]$ belongs to some stage;*
3. *if $\mathcal{C}$ is a non-terminal stage with successors $\mathcal{C}_1, \ldots, \mathcal{C}_n$, then there exists a certificate for $\mathcal{C} \rightsquigarrow (\mathcal{C}_1 \cup \cdots \cup \mathcal{C}_n)$;*
4. *if $\mathcal{C}$ is a terminal stage, then $\mathcal{C} \models \varphi_{\mathrm{post}}^i$ for some i.*

The existence of a stage graph implies that $\mathcal{P}$ satisfies Π. Indeed, by conditions 2–3 and repeated application of Proposition 2, every run starting at a configuration of $[\![\varphi_{\mathrm{pre}}]\!]$ eventually reaches a terminal stage, say $\mathcal{C}$, and, by condition 1, stays in $\mathcal{C}$ forever. Since, by condition 4, all configurations of $\mathcal{C}$ satisfy some $\varphi_{\mathrm{post}}^i$, after its first visit to $\mathcal{C}$ every configuration satisfies $\varphi_{\mathrm{post}}^i$.

Example 3. Figure 1 depicts stage graphs for the system of Example 1 and the properties defined in Example 2. The reader can easily show that every stage $\mathcal{C}$ is inductive by checking that for every $C \in \mathcal{C}$ and every transition $t \in \{t_1, \ldots, t_4\}$ enabled at C, the step $C \xrightarrow{t_i} C'$ satisfies $C' \in \mathcal{C}$. For example, if a configuration satisfies $A_Y > A_N$, so does any successor configuration.   ◁

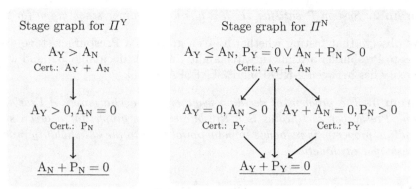

Fig. 1. Stage graphs for the system of Example 1.

The following proposition shows that stage graphs are a sound and complete technique for proving stable termination properties.

Proposition 3. *System $\mathcal{P}$ satisfies Π iff it has a stage graph for Π.*

Proposition 3 does not tell us anything about the decidability of the stable termination problem. To prove that the problem is decidable, we introduce Presburger stage graphs. Intuitively these are stage graphs whose stages and certificates can be expressed by formulas of Presburger arithmetic.

Definition 5 (Presburger stage graphs)

- *A stage $\mathcal{C}$ is Presburger if $\mathcal{C} = \llbracket \phi \rrbracket$ for some Presburger formula ϕ.*
- *A bounded certificate for $\mathcal{C} \rightsquigarrow \mathcal{C}'$ is a pair (f, k), where $f \colon \mathcal{C} \to \mathbb{N}$ and $k \in \mathbb{N}$, satisfying that for every $C \in \mathcal{C} \setminus \mathcal{C}'$, there exists an execution $C \xrightarrow{w} C'$ such that $f(C) > f(C')$ and $|w| \leq k$.*
- *A Presburger certificate is a bounded certificate (f, k) satisfying $f(C) = n \iff \varphi(C, n)$ for some Presburger formula $\varphi(\boldsymbol{x}, y)$.*
- *A Presburger stage graph is a stage graph whose stages and certificates are all Presburger.*

Using a powerful result from [36], we show that: (1) $\mathcal{P}$ satisfies Π iff it has a Presburger stage graph for Π (Theorem 2); (2) there exists a denumerable set of candidates for a Presburger stage graph for Π; and (3) there is an algorithm that decides whether a given candidate is a Presburger stage graph for Π (Theorem 3). Together, (1–3) show that the stable termination problem is semi-decidable. To obtain decidability, we observe that the complement of the stable termination problem is also semi-decidable. Indeed, it suffices to enumerate all initial configurations $C \models \varphi_{\text{pre}}$, build for each such C the (finite) graph G_C of configurations reachable from C, and check if some bottom strongly connected component $\mathcal{B}$ of G_C satisfies $\mathcal{B} \not\models \varphi_{\text{post}}^i$ for all i. This is the case iff some fair run starting at C visits and stays in $\mathcal{B}$, which in turn is the case iff $\mathcal{P}$ violates Π.

Theorem 2. *System $\mathcal{P}$ satisfies Π iff it has a Presburger stage graph for Π.*

We observe that testing whether a given graph is a Presburger stage graph reduces to Presburger arithmetic satisfiability, which is decidable [62] and whose complexity lies between 2-NEXP and 2-EXPSPACE [15]:

Theorem 3. *The problem of deciding whether an acyclic graph of Presburger sets and Presburger certificates is a Presburger stage graph, for a given stable termination property, is reducible in polynomial time to the satisfiability problem for Presburger arithmetic.*

4   Algorithmic Construction of Stage Graphs

At the current state of our knowledge, the decision procedure derived from Theorem 3 has little practical relevance. From a theoretical point of view, the TOWER-hardness result of [33] implies that the stage graph may have non-elementary size in the system size. In practice, systems have relatively small stage graphs, but, even so, the enumeration of all candidates immediately leads to a prohibitive combinatorial explosion.

For this reason, we present a procedure to automatically *construct* (not guess) a Presburger stage graph G for a given replicated system $\mathcal{P}$ and a stable termination property $\Pi = (\varphi_{\mathrm{pre}}, \Phi_{post})$. The procedure may *fail*, but, as shown in the experimental section, it succeeds for many systems from the literature.

The procedure is designed to be implemented on top of a solver for the existential fragment of Presburger arithmetic. While every formula of Presburger arithmetic has an equivalent formula within the existential fragment [32,62], quantifier-elimination may lead to a doubly-exponential blow-up in the size of the formula. Thus, it is important to emphasize that our procedure *never requires to eliminate quantifiers*: If the pre- and postconditions of Π are supplied as quantifier-free formulas, then all constraints of the procedure remain in the existential fragment.

We give a high-level view of the procedure (see Algorithm 1), which uses several functions, described in detail in the rest of the paper. The procedure maintains a workset WS of Presburger stages, represented by existential Presburger formulas. Initially, the only stage is an inductive Presburger overapproximation $PotReach(\llbracket\varphi_{\mathrm{pre}}\rrbracket)$ of the configurations reachable from $\llbracket\varphi_{\mathrm{pre}}\rrbracket$ (*PotReach* is an abbreviation for "potentially reachable"). Notice that we must necessarily use an overapproximation, since $post^*(\llbracket\varphi_{\mathrm{pre}}\rrbracket)$ is not always expressible in Presburger arithmetic[3]. We use a refinement of the overapproximation introduced in [22,37], equivalent to the overapproximation of [24].

In its main loop (lines 2–9), Algorithm 1 picks a Presburger stage $\mathcal{S}$ from the workset, and processes it. First, it calls Terminal($\mathcal{S}, \Phi_{post}$) to check if $\mathcal{S}$ is terminal, i.e., whether $\mathcal{S} \models \varphi_{\mathrm{post}}^i$ for some $\varphi_{\mathrm{post}}^i \in \Phi_{post}$. This reduces to checking

---

[3] This follows easily from the fact that $post^*(\psi)$ is not always expressible in Presburger arithmetic for vector addition systems, even if ψ denotes a single configuration [43].

Algorithm 1: procedure for the construction of stage graphs.

Input: replicated system $\mathcal{P} = (Q, T)$, stable term. property $\Pi = (\varphi_{\mathrm{pre}}, \Phi_{post})$
Result: a stage graph of $\mathcal{P}$ for Π

1 $WS \leftarrow \{PotReach(\llbracket \varphi_{\mathrm{pre}} \rrbracket)\}$
2 **while** $WS \neq \emptyset$ **do**
3 $\quad$ remove $\mathcal{S}$ from WS
4 $\quad$ **if** $\neg Terminal(\mathcal{S}, \Phi_{post})$ **then**
5 $\quad\quad$ $U \leftarrow AsDead(\mathcal{S})$
6 $\quad\quad$ **if** $U \neq \emptyset$ **then**
7 $\quad\quad\quad$ $WS \leftarrow WS \cup \{IndOverapprox(\mathcal{S}, U)\}$
8 $\quad\quad$ **else**
9 $\quad\quad\quad$ $WS \leftarrow WS \cup Split(\mathcal{S})$

---

the unsatisfiability of the existential Presburger formula $\phi \wedge \neg \varphi_{post}^i$, where ϕ is the formula characterizing $\mathcal{S}$. If $\mathcal{S}$ is not terminal, then the procedure attempts to construct successor stages in lines 5–9, with the help of three further functions: *AsDead*, *IndOverapprox*, and *Split*. In the rest of this section, we present the intuition behind lines 5–9, and the specification of the three functions. Sections 5, 6 and 7 present the implementations we use for these functions.

$\quad$Lines 5–9 are inspired by the behavior of most replicated systems designed by humans, and are based on the notion of *dead* transitions, which can never occur again (to be formally defined below). Replicated systems are usually designed to run in *phases*. Initially, all transitions are alive, and the end of a phase is marked by the "death" of one or more transitions, i.e., by reaching a configuration at which these transitions are dead. The system keeps "killing transitions" until no transition that is still alive can lead to a configuration violating the postcondition. The procedure mimics this pattern. It constructs stage graphs in which if $\mathcal{S}'$ is a successor of $\mathcal{S}$, then the set of transitions dead at $\mathcal{S}'$ is a *proper superset* of the transitions dead at $\mathcal{S}$. For this, $AsDead(\mathcal{S})$ computes a set of transitions that are alive at some configuration of $\mathcal{S}$, but which will become dead in every fair run starting at $\mathcal{S}$ (line 5). Formally, $AsDead(\mathcal{S})$ returns a set $U \subseteq \overline{Dead(\mathcal{S})}$ such that $\mathcal{S} \models \Diamond \mathrm{dead}(U)$, defined as follows.

Definition 6. *A transition of a replicated system $\mathcal{P}$ is* dead *at a configuration C if it is disabled at every configuration reachable from C (including C itself). A transition is* dead *at a stage $\mathcal{S}$ if it is dead at every configuration of $\mathcal{S}$. Given a stage $\mathcal{S}$ and a set U of transitions, we use the following notations:*

- *$Dead(\mathcal{S})$: the set of transitions dead at $\mathcal{S}$;*
- *$\llbracket dis(U) \rrbracket$: the set of configurations at which all transitions of U are disabled;*
- *$\llbracket dead(U) \rrbracket$: the set of configurations at which all transitions of U are dead.*

Observe that we can compute $Dead(\mathcal{S})$ by checking unsatisfiability of a sequence of existential Presburger formulas: as $\mathcal{S}$ is inductive, we have $Dead(\mathcal{S}) =$

$\{t \mid \mathcal{S} \models \text{dis}(t)\}$, and $\mathcal{S} \models \text{dis}(t)$ holds iff the existential Presburger formula $\exists C \colon \phi(C) \wedge C \geq {}^\bullet t$ is unsatisfiable, where ϕ is the formula characterizing $\mathcal{S}$.

The following proposition, whose proof appears in the full version [19], shows that determining whether a given transition will eventually become dead, while decidable, is PSPACE-hard. Therefore, Sect. 7 describes two implementations of this function, and a way to combine them, which exhibit a good trade-off between precision and computation time.

Proposition 4. *Given a replicated system $\mathcal{P}$, a stage $\mathcal{S}$ represented by an existential Presburger formula ϕ and a set of transitions U, determining whether $\mathcal{S} \models \Diamond dead(U)$ holds is decidable and PSPACE-hard.*

If the set U returned by $AsDead(\mathcal{S})$ is nonempty, then we know that every fair run starting at a configuration of $\mathcal{S}$ will eventually reach a configuration of $\mathcal{S} \cap [\![\text{dead}(U)]\!]$. So, this set, or any inductive overapproximation of it, can be a legal successor of $\mathcal{S}$ in the stage graph. Function $IndOverapprox(\mathcal{S}, U)$ returns such an inductive overapproximation (line 7). To be precise, we show in Sect. 5 that $[\![\text{dead}(U)]\!]$ is a Presburger set that can be computed exactly, albeit in doubly-exponential time in the worst case. The section also shows how to compute overapproximations more efficiently. If the set U returned by $AsDead(\mathcal{S})$ is empty, then we cannot yet construct any successor of $\mathcal{S}$. Indeed, recall that we want to construct stage graphs in which if $\mathcal{S}'$ is a successor of $\mathcal{S}$, then $Dead(\mathcal{S}')$ is a *proper superset* of $Dead(\mathcal{S})$. In this case, we proceed differently and try to split $\mathcal{S}$:

Definition 7. *A split of some stage $\mathcal{S}$ is a set $\{\mathcal{S}_1, \ldots, \mathcal{S}_k\}$ of (not necessarily disjoint) stages such that the following holds:*

- *$Dead(\mathcal{S}_i) \supset Dead(\mathcal{S})$ for every $1 \leq i \leq k$, and*
- *$\mathcal{S} = \bigcup_{i=1}^{k} \mathcal{S}_i$.*

If there exists a split $\{\mathcal{S}_1, \ldots, \mathcal{S}_k\}$ of $\mathcal{S}$, then we can let $\mathcal{S}_1, \ldots, \mathcal{S}_k$ be the successors of $\mathcal{S}$ in the stage graph. Observe that a stage may indeed have a split. We have $Dead(\mathcal{C}_1 \cup \mathcal{C}_2) = Dead(\mathcal{C}_1) \cap Dead(\mathcal{C}_2)$, and hence $Dead(\mathcal{C}_1 \cup \mathcal{C}_2)$ may be a proper subset of both $Dead(\mathcal{C}_1)$ and $Dead(\mathcal{C}_2)$:

Example 4. Consider the system with states $\{q_1, q_2\}$ and transitions $t_i \colon q_i \mapsto q_i$ for $i \in \{1, 2\}$. Let $\mathcal{S} = \{C \mid C(q_1) = 0 \vee C(q_2) = 0\}$, i.e., $\mathcal{S}$ is the (inductive) stage of configurations disabling either t_1 or t_2. The set $\{\mathcal{S}_1, \mathcal{S}_2\}$, where $\mathcal{S}_i = \{C \in \mathcal{S} \mid C(q_i) = 0\}$, is a split of $\mathcal{S}$ satisfying $Dead(\mathcal{S}_i) = \{t_i\} \supset \emptyset = Dead(\mathcal{S})$. ◁

The canonical split of $\mathcal{S}$, if it exists, is the set $\{\mathcal{S} \cap [\![\text{dead}(t)]\!] \mid t \notin Dead(\mathcal{S})\}$. As mentioned above, Sect. 5 shows that $[\![\text{dead}(U)]\!]$ can be computed exactly for every U, but the computation can be expensive. Hence, the canonical split can be computed exactly at potentially high cost. Our implementation uses an underapproximation of $[\![\text{dead}(t)]\!]$, described in Sect. 6.

5   Computing and Approximating $[\![\mathrm{dead}(U)]\!]$

We show that, given a set U of transitions,

- we can effectively compute an existential Presburger formula describing the set $[\![\mathrm{dead}(U)]\!]$, with high computational cost in the worst case, and
- we can effectively compute constraints that overapproximate or underapproximate $[\![\mathrm{dead}(U)]\!]$, at a reduced computational cost.

Downward and Upward Closed Sets. We enrich $\mathbb{N}$ with the limit element ω in the usual way. In particular, $n < \omega$ holds for every $n \in \mathbb{N}$. An ω-*configuration* is a mapping $C^\omega\colon Q \to \mathbb{N} \cup \{\omega\}$. The *upward closure* and *downward closure* of a set $\mathcal{C}^\omega$ of ω-configurations are the sets of configurations $\uparrow\mathcal{C}^\omega$ and $\downarrow\mathcal{C}^\omega$, respectively defined as:

$$\uparrow\mathcal{C}^\omega \overset{\mathrm{def}}{=} \{C \in \mathbb{N}^Q \mid C \geq C^\omega \text{ for some } C^\omega \in \mathcal{C}^\omega\},$$

$$\downarrow\mathcal{C}^\omega \overset{\mathrm{def}}{=} \{C \in \mathbb{N}^Q \mid C \leq C^\omega \text{ for some } C^\omega \in \mathcal{C}^\omega\}.$$

A set $\mathcal{C}$ of configurations is *upward closed* if $\mathcal{C} = \uparrow\mathcal{C}$, and *downward closed* if $\mathcal{C} = \downarrow\mathcal{C}$. These facts are well-known from the theory of well-quasi orderings:

Lemma 1. *For every set $\mathcal{C}$ of configurations, the following holds:*

1. *$\mathcal{C}$ is upward closed iff $\overline{\mathcal{C}}$ is downward closed (and vice versa);*
2. *if $\mathcal{C}$ is upward closed, then there is a unique minimal finite set of configurations $\inf(\mathcal{C})$, called its* basis, *such that $\mathcal{C} = \uparrow\inf(\mathcal{C})$;*
3. *if $\mathcal{C}$ is downward closed, then there is a unique minimal finite set of ω-configurations $\sup(\mathcal{C})$, called its* decomposition, *such that $\mathcal{C} = \downarrow\sup(\mathcal{C})$.*

Computing $[\![\mathrm{dead}(U)]\!]$ Exactly. It follows immediately from Definition 6 that both $[\![\mathrm{dis}(U)]\!]$ and $[\![\mathrm{dead}(U)]\!]$ are downward closed. Indeed, if all transitions of U are disabled at C, and $C' \leq C$, then they are also disabled at C', and clearly the same holds for transitions dead at C. Furthermore:

Proposition 5. *For every set U of transitions, the (downward) decomposition of both $\sup([\![\mathrm{dis}(U)]\!])$ and $\sup([\![\mathrm{dead}(U)]\!])$ is effectively computable.*

Proof. For every $t \in U$ and $q \in {}^\bullet t$, let $C^\omega_{t,q}$ be the ω-configuration such that $C^\omega_{t,q}(q) = {}^\bullet t(q) - 1$ and $C^\omega_{t,q}(p) = \omega$ for every $p \in Q \setminus \{q\}$. In other words, $C^\omega_{t,q}$ is the ω-configuration made only of ω's except for state q which falls short from ${}^\bullet t(q)$ by one. This ω-configurations captures all configurations disabled in t due to an insufficient amount of agents in state q. We have:

$$\sup([\![\mathrm{dis}(U)]\!]) = \{C^\omega_{t,q} : t \in U, q \in {}^\bullet t\}.$$

The latter can be made minimal by removing superfluous ω-configurations.

For the case of $\sup([\![\mathrm{dead}(U)]\!])$, we invoke [45, Prop. 2] which gives a proof for the more general setting of (possibly unbounded) Petri nets. Their procedure is based on the well-known backwards reachability algorithm (see, e.g., [2,39]). $\square$

Since $\sup(\llbracket \text{dead}(U) \rrbracket)$ is finite, its computation allows to describe $\llbracket \text{dead}(U) \rrbracket$ by the following linear constraint[4]:

$$\bigvee_{C^\omega \in \sup(\llbracket \text{dead}(U) \rrbracket)} \bigwedge_{q \in Q} [C(q) \leq C^\omega(q)] .$$

However, the cardinality of $\sup(\llbracket \text{dead}(U) \rrbracket)$ can be exponential [45, Remark for Prop. 2] in the system size. For this reason, we are interested in constructing both under- and over-approximations.

Overapproximations of $\llbracket \text{dead}(U) \rrbracket$. For every $i \in \mathbb{N}$, define $\llbracket \text{dead}(U) \rrbracket^i$ as:

$$\llbracket \text{dead}(U) \rrbracket^0 \overset{\text{def}}{=} \llbracket \text{dis}(U) \rrbracket \quad \text{and} \quad \llbracket \text{dead}(U) \rrbracket^{i+1} \overset{\text{def}}{=} \overline{pre_T(\overline{\llbracket \text{dead}(U) \rrbracket^i})} \cap \llbracket \text{dis}(U) \rrbracket .$$

Loosely speaking, $\llbracket \text{dead}(U) \rrbracket^i$ is the set of configurations C such that every configuration reachable in at most i steps from C disables U. We immediately have:

$$\llbracket \text{dead}(U) \rrbracket = \bigcap_{i=0}^{\infty} \llbracket \text{dead}(U) \rrbracket^i .$$

Using Proposition 5 and the following proposition, we obtain that $\llbracket \text{dead}(U) \rrbracket^i$ is an effectively computable overapproximation of $\llbracket \text{dead}(U) \rrbracket$.

Proposition 6. *For every Presburger set C and every set of transitions U, the sets $pre_U(C)$ and $post_U(C)$ are effectively Presburger.*

Recall that function *IndOverapprox*(S, U) of Algorithm 1 must return an *inductive* overapproximation of $\llbracket \text{dead}(U) \rrbracket$. Since $\llbracket \text{dead}(U) \rrbracket^i$ might not be inductive in general, our implementation uses either the inductive overapproximations *IndOverapprox*$^i(S, U) \overset{\text{def}}{=} PotReach(S \cap \llbracket \text{dead}(U) \rrbracket^i)$, or the exact value *IndOverapprox*$^\infty(S, U) \overset{\text{def}}{=} S \cap \llbracket \text{dead}(U) \rrbracket$. The table of results in the experimental section describes for each benchmark which overapproximation was used.

Underapproximations of $\llbracket \text{dead}(U) \rrbracket$: Death Certificates. A *death certificate* for U in $\mathcal{P}$ is a finite set C^ω of ω-configurations such that:

1. $\downarrow C^\omega \models \text{dis}(U)$, i.e., every configuration of $\downarrow C^\omega$ disables U, and
2. $\downarrow C^\omega$ is inductive, i.e., $post_T(\downarrow C^\omega) \subseteq \downarrow C^\omega$.

If U is dead at a set C of configurations, then there is always a certificate that proves it, namely $\sup(\llbracket \text{dead}(U) \rrbracket)$. In particular, if C^ω is a death certificate for U then $\downarrow C^\omega \subseteq \llbracket \text{dead}(U) \rrbracket$, that is, $\downarrow C^\omega$ is an underapproximation of $\llbracket \text{dead}(U) \rrbracket$

Using Proposition 6, it is straightforward to express in Presburger arithmetic that a finite set C^ω of ω-configurations is a death certificate for U:

Proposition 7. *For every $k \geq 1$ there is an existential Presburger formula DeathCert$_k(U, C^\omega)$ that holds iff C^ω is a death certificate of size k for U.*

---

[4] Observe that if $C^\omega(q) = \omega$, then the term "$C(q) \leq \omega$" is equivalent to "**true**".

6   Splitting a Stage

Given a stage $\mathcal{S}$, we try to find a set $\mathcal{C}_1^\omega, \ldots, \mathcal{C}_\ell^\omega$ of death certificates for transitions $t_1, \ldots, t_\ell \in T \setminus Dead(\mathcal{S})$ such that $\mathcal{S} \subseteq \downarrow\mathcal{C}_1^\omega \cup \cdots \cup \downarrow\mathcal{C}_\ell^\omega$. This allows us to split $\mathcal{S}$ into $\mathcal{S}_1, \ldots, \mathcal{S}_\ell$, where $\mathcal{S}_i \stackrel{\text{def}}{=} \mathcal{S} \cap \downarrow\mathcal{C}_i^\omega$.

For any fixed size $k \geq 1$ and any fixed ℓ, we can find death certificates $\mathcal{C}_1^\omega, \ldots, \mathcal{C}_\ell^\omega$ of size at most k by solving a Presburger formula. However, the formula does not belong to the existential fragment, because the inclusion check $\mathcal{S} \subseteq \downarrow\mathcal{C}_1^\omega \cup \cdots \cup \downarrow\mathcal{C}_\ell^\omega$ requires universal quantification. For this reason, we proceed iteratively. For every $i \geq 0$, after having found $\mathcal{C}_1^\omega, \ldots, \mathcal{C}_i^\omega$ we search for a pair $(C_{i+1}, \mathcal{C}_{i+1}^\omega)$ such that

(i) $\mathcal{C}_{i+1}^\omega$ is a death certificate for some $t_{i+1} \in T \setminus Dead(\mathcal{S})$;
(ii) $C_{i+1} \in \mathcal{S} \cap \downarrow\mathcal{C}_{i+1}^\omega \setminus (\downarrow\mathcal{C}_1^\omega \cup \cdots \cup \downarrow\mathcal{C}_i^\omega)$.

An efficient implementation requires to guide the search for $(C_{i+1}, \mathcal{C}_{i+1}^\omega)$, because otherwise the search procedure might not even terminate, or might split $\mathcal{S}$ into too many parts, blowing up the size of the stage graph. Our search procedure employs the following heuristic, which works well in practice. We only consider the case $k = 1$, and search for a pair $(C_{i+1}, \mathcal{C}_{i+1}^\omega)$ satisfying (i) and (ii) above, and additionally:

(iii) all components of $\mathcal{C}_{i+1}^\omega$ are either ω or between 0 and $\max_{t \in T, q \in Q} {}^\bullet t(q) - 1$;
(iv) for every ω-configuration C^ω, if (C_{i+1}, C^ω) satisfies (i)–(iii), then $\mathcal{C}_{i+1}^\omega \leq C^\omega$;
(v)   for every pair (C, C^ω), if (C, C^ω) satisfies (i)–(iv), then $C^\omega \leq \mathcal{C}_{i+1}^\omega$.

Condition (iii) guarantees termination. Intuitively, condition (iv) leads to certificates valid for sets $U \subseteq T \setminus Dead(\mathcal{S})$ as large as possible. So it allows us to avoid splits that, loosely speaking, do not make as much progress as they could. Condition (v) allows us to avoid splits with many elements because each element of the split has a small intersection with $\mathcal{S}$.

An example illustrating these conditions is given in the full version [19].

7   Computing Eventually Dead Transitions

Recall that the function $AsDead(\mathcal{S})$ takes an inductive Presburger set $\mathcal{S}$ as input, and returns a (possibly empty) set $U \subseteq \overline{Dead(\mathcal{S})}$ of transitions such that $\mathcal{S} \models \Diamond dead(U)$. This guarantees $\mathcal{S} \rightsquigarrow [\![dead(U)]\!]$ and, since $\mathcal{S}$ is inductive, also $\mathcal{S} \rightsquigarrow \mathcal{S} \cap [\![dead(U)]\!]$.

By Proposition 4, deciding if there exists a non-empty set U of transitions such that $\mathcal{S} \models \Diamond dead(U)$ holds is PSPACE-hard, which makes a polynomial reduction to satisfiability of existential Presburger formulas unlikely. So we design incomplete implementations of $AsDead(\mathcal{S})$ with lower complexity. Combining these implementations, the lack of completeness essentially vanishes in practice.

The implementations are inspired by Proposition 2, which shows that $\mathcal{S} \rightsquigarrow [\![dead(U)]\!]$ holds iff there exists a certificate f such that:

$$\forall C \in \mathcal{S} \setminus [\![dead(U)]\!] \, : \, \exists C \stackrel{*}{\rightarrow} C' : f(C) > f(C'). \tag{Cert}$$

To find such certificates efficiently, we only search for *linear* functions $f(C) = \sum_{q \in Q} \boldsymbol{a}(q) \cdot C(q)$ with coefficients $\boldsymbol{a}(q) \in \mathbb{N}$ for each $q \in Q$.

7.1 First Implementation: Linear Ranking Functions

Our first procedure computes the existence of a linear *ranking function*.

Definition 8. *A function* $r \colon \mathcal{S} \to \mathbb{N}$ *is a ranking function for* $\mathcal{S}$ *and* U *if for every* $C \in \mathcal{S}$ *and every step* $C \xrightarrow{t} C'$ *the following holds:*

1. *if* $t \in U$, *then* $r(C) > r(C')$; *and*
2. *if* $t \notin U$, *then* $r(C) \geq r(C')$.

Proposition 8. *If* $r \colon \mathcal{S} \to \mathbb{N}$ *is a ranking function for* $\mathcal{S}$ *and* U, *then there exists* $k \in \mathbb{N}$ *such that* (r, k) *is a bounded certificate for* $\mathcal{S} \rightsquigarrow [\![dead(U)]\!]$.

Proof. Let M be the minimal finite basis of the upward closed set $\overline{[\![dead(U)]\!]}$. For every configuration $D \in M$, let σ_D be a shortest sequence that enables some transition of $t_D \in U$ from D, i.e., such that $D \xrightarrow{\sigma_D} D' \xrightarrow{t_D} D''$ for some D', D''. Let $k \stackrel{\text{def}}{=} \max\{|\sigma_D t_D| : D \in M\}$.

Let $C \in \mathcal{S} \setminus [\![dead(U)]\!]$. Since $C \in \overline{[\![dead(U)]\!]}$, we have $C \geq D$ for some $D \in M$. By monotonicity, we have $C \xrightarrow{\sigma_D} C' \xrightarrow{t_D} C''$ for some configurations C' and C''. By Definition 8, we have $r(C) \geq r(C') > r(C'')$, and so condition (Cert) holds. As $|\sigma_D t_D| \leq k$, we have that (r, k) is a bounded certificate. $\qquad\square$

It follows immediately from Definition 8 that if r_1 and r_2 are ranking functions for sets U_1 and U_2 respectively, then r defined as $r(C) \stackrel{\text{def}}{=} r_1(C) + r_2(C)$ is a ranking function for $U_1 \cup U_2$. Therefore, there exists a unique maximal set of transitions U such that $\mathcal{S} \rightsquigarrow [\![dead(U)]\!]$ can be proved by means of a ranking function. Further, U can be computed by collecting all transitions $t \in \overline{Dead(\mathcal{S})}$ such that there exists a ranking function r_t for $\{t\}$. The existence of a *linear* ranking function r_t can be decided in polynomial time via linear programming, as follows. Recall that for every step $C \xrightarrow{u} C'$, we have $C' = C + \Delta(u)$. So, by linearity, we have $r_t(C) \geq r_t(C') \iff r_t(C' - C) \leq 0 \iff r_t(\Delta(u)) \leq 0$. Thus, the constraints of Definition 8 can be specified as:

$$\boldsymbol{a} \cdot \Delta(t) < 0 \quad \wedge \bigwedge_{u \in \overline{Dead(\mathcal{S})}} \boldsymbol{a} \cdot \Delta(u) \leq 0,$$

where $\boldsymbol{a} \colon Q \to \mathbb{Q}_{\geq 0}$ gives the coefficients of r_t, that is, $r_t(C) = \boldsymbol{a} \cdot C$, and $\boldsymbol{a} \cdot \boldsymbol{x} \stackrel{\text{def}}{=} \sum_{q \in Q} \boldsymbol{a}(q) \cdot \boldsymbol{x}(q)$ for $\boldsymbol{x} \in \mathbb{N}^Q$. Observe that a solution may yield a function whose codomain differs from $\mathbb{N}$. However, this is not an issue since we can scale it with the least common denominator of each $\boldsymbol{a}(q)$.

7.2   Second Implementation: Layers

Transitions layers were introduced in [22] as a technique to find transitions that will eventually become dead. Intuitively, a set U of transitions is a layer if (1) no run can contain only transitions of U, and (2) U becomes dead once disabled; the first condition guarantees that U eventually becomes disabled, and the second that it eventually becomes dead. We formalize layers in terms of *layer functions*.

Definition 9. *A function* $\ell \colon S \to \mathbb{N}$ *is a* layer function *for* S *and* U *if:*

C1. $\ell(C) > \ell(C')$ *for every* $C \in S$ *and every step* $C \xrightarrow{t} C'$ *with* $t \in U$; *and*
C2. $[\![dis(U)]\!] = [\![dead(U)]\!]$.

Proposition 9. *If* $\ell \colon S \to \mathbb{N}$ *is a layer function for* S *and* U, *then* $(\ell, 1)$ *is a bounded certificate for* $S \rightsquigarrow [\![dead(U)]\!]$.

Proof. Let $C \in S \setminus [\![dead(U)]\!]$. By condition **C2**, we have $C \notin [\![dis(U)]\!]$. So there exists a step $C \xrightarrow{u} C'$ where $u \in U$. By condition **C1**, we have $\ell(C) > \ell(C')$, so condition (Cert) holds and $(\ell, 1)$ is a bounded certificate.

Let S be a stage. For every set of transitions $U \subseteq \overline{Dead(S)}$ we can construct a Presburger formula *lin-layer*$(U, \boldsymbol{a})$ that holds iff there there exists a *linear* layer function for U, i.e., a layer function of the form $\ell(C) = \boldsymbol{a} \cdot C$ for a vector of coefficients $\boldsymbol{a} \colon Q \to \mathbb{Q}_{\geq 0}$. Condition **C1**, for a linear function $\ell(C)$, is expressed by the existential Presburger formula

$$lin\text{-}layer\text{-}fun(U, \boldsymbol{a}) \overset{\text{def}}{=} \bigwedge_{u \in U} \boldsymbol{a} \cdot \Delta(u) < 0.$$

Condition **C2** is expressible in Presburger arithmetic because of Proposition 5. However, instead of computing $[\![dead(U)]\!]$ explicitly, there is a more efficient way to express this constraint. Intuitively, $[\![dis(U)]\!] = [\![dead(U)]\!]$ is the case if enabling a transition $u \in U$ requires to have previously enabled some transition $u' \in U$. This observation leads to:

Proposition 10. *A set* U *of transitions satisfies* $[\![dis(U)]\!] = [\![dead(U)]\!]$ *iff it satisfies the existential Presburger formula*

$$dis\text{-}eq\text{-}dead(U) \overset{\text{def}}{=} \bigwedge_{t \in T} \bigwedge_{u \in U} \bigvee_{u' \in U} {}^{\bullet}t + ({}^{\bullet}u \ominus t^{\bullet}) \geq {}^{\bullet}u'$$

where $\boldsymbol{x} \ominus \boldsymbol{y} \in \mathbb{N}^Q$ *is defined by* $(\boldsymbol{x} \ominus \boldsymbol{y})(q) \overset{\text{def}}{=} \max(\boldsymbol{x}(q) - \boldsymbol{y}(q), 0)$ *for* $\boldsymbol{x}, \boldsymbol{y} \in \mathbb{N}^Q$.

This allows us to give the constraint *lin-layer*$(U, \boldsymbol{a})$, which is of polynomial size:

$$lin\text{-}layer(U, \boldsymbol{a}) \overset{\text{def}}{=} lin\text{-}layer\text{-}fun(U, \boldsymbol{a}) \wedge dis\text{-}eq\text{-}dead(U).$$

7.3   Comparing Ranking and Layer Functions

The ranking and layer functions of Sects. 7.1 and 7.2 are incomparable in power, that is, there are sets of transitions for which a ranking function but no layer function exists, and vice versa. This is shown by the following two systems:

$$\mathcal{P}_1 = (\{A, B, C\}, \{t_1 : A\,B \mapsto C\,C, \; t_2 : A \mapsto B, \; t_3 : B \mapsto A\}),$$
$$\mathcal{P}_2 = (\{A, B\}, \quad \{t_4 : A\,B \mapsto A\,A, \; t_5 : A \mapsto B\}).$$

Consider the system $\mathcal{P}_1$, and let $\mathcal{S} = \mathbb{N}^Q$, i.e., $\mathcal{S}$ contains all configurations. Transitions t_2 and t_3 never become dead at $\langle A \rangle$ and can thus never be included in any U. Transition t_1 eventually becomes dead, as shown by the linear ranking function $r(C) = C(A) + C(B)$ for $U = \{t_1\}$. But for this U, the condition **C2** for layer functions is not satisfied, as $[\![\text{dis}(U)]\!] \ni \langle A, A \rangle \xrightarrow{t_2} \langle A, B \rangle \notin [\![\text{dis}(U)]\!]$, so $[\![\text{dis}(U)]\!] \neq [\![\text{dead}(U)]\!]$. Therefore no layer function exists for this U.

Consider now the system $\mathcal{P}_2$, again with $\mathcal{S} = \mathbb{N}^Q$, and let $U = \{t_5\}$. Once t_5 is disabled, there is no agent in A, so both t_4 and t_5 are dead. So $[\![\text{dis}(U)]\!] = [\![\text{dead}(U)]\!]$. The linear layer function $\ell(C) = C(A)$ satisfies *lin-layer-fun*$(U, \boldsymbol{a})$, showing that U eventually becomes dead. As $C \xrightarrow{t_4 t_5} C$ for $C = \langle A, B \rangle$, there is no ranking function r for this U, which would need to satisfy $r(C) < r(C)$.

For our implementation of $AsDead(\mathcal{S})$, we therefore combine both approaches. We first compute (in polynomial time) the unique maximal set U for which there is a linear ranking function. If this U is non-empty, we return it, and otherwise compute a set U of maximal size for which there is a linear layer function.

8   Experimental Results

We implemented the procedure of Sect. 4 on top of the SMT solver *Z3* [57], and use the Owl [48] and HOA [12] libraries for translating LTL formulas. The resulting tool automatically constructs stage graphs that verify stable termination properties for replicated systems. We evaluated it on two sets of benchmarks, described below. The first set contains population protocols, and the second leader election and mutual exclusion algorithms. All tests where performed on a machine with an Intel Xeon CPU E5-2630 v4 @ 2.20 GHz and 8GB of RAM. The results are depicted in Fig. 2 and can be reproduced by the certified artifact [18]. For parametric families of replicated systems, we always report the largest instance that we were able to verify with a timeout of one hour. For *IndOverapprox*, from the approaches in Sect. 5, we use *IndOverapprox*^{0} in the examples marked with $*$ and *IndOverapprox*$^\infty$ otherwise. Almost all constructed stage graphs are a chain with at most 3 stages. The only exceptions are the stage graphs for the approximate majority protocols that contained a binary split and 5 stages. The size of the Presburger formulas increases with increasing size of the replicated system. In the worst case, this growth can be exponential. However, the growth is linear in all examples marked with $*$.

Population protocols (correctness) Parameters	$\|Q\|$	$\|T\|$	Time
Broadcast [31,22] *			
	2	1	$< 1s$
Majority (Example 1)[22] *			
	4	4	$< 1s$
Majority [23, Ex. 3] *			
	5	6	$< 1s$
Majority [5] ("fast & exact")			
$m=13, d=1$	16	136	$4s$
$m=21, d=1$ (TO: 23,1)	24	300	$466s$
$m=21, d=20$ (TO: 23,22)	62	1953	$3301s$
Flock-of-birds [28,22] *: $x \geq c$			
$c = 20$	21	210	$5s$
$c = 40$	41	820	$45s$
$c = 60$	61	1830	$341s$
$c = 80$ (TO: $c = 90$)	81	3240	$1217s$
Flock-of-birds [20, Sect. 3]: $x \geq c$			
$c = 60$	8	18	$15s$
$c = 90$	9	21	$271s$
$c = 120$ (TO: $c = 127$)	9	21	$2551s$
Flock-of-birds [31,22, *threshold-n*] *: $x \geq c$			
$c = 10$	11	19	$< 1s$
$c = 15$	16	29	$1s$
$c = 20$ (TO: $c = 25$)	21	39	$18s$
Threshold [8][22, $v_{max}=c + 1$] *: $a \cdot x \geq c$			
$c = 2$	28	288	$7s$
$c = 4$	44	716	$26s$
$c = 6$	60	1336	$107s$
$c = 8$ (TO: $c = 10$)	76	2148	$1089s$
Threshold [20] ("succinct"): $a \cdot x \geq c$			
$c = 7$	13	37	$2s$
$c = 31$	17	55	$11s$
$c = 127$	21	73	$158s$
$c = 511$ (TO: $c = 1023$)	25	91	$2659s$
Remainder [22] *: $a \cdot x \equiv_m c$			
$m = 5$	7	20	$< 1s$
$m = 15$	17	135	$34s$
$m = 20$ (TO: $m = 25$)	22	230	$1646s$

Population protocols (stable cons.) Parameters	$\|Q\|$	$\|T\|$	Time
Approx. majority [27] (Cell cycle sw.) *			
	3	4	$< 1s$
Approx. majority [51] (Coin game) *			
$k = 3$	2	4	$< 1s$
Approx. majority [56] (Moran proc.) *			
	2	2	$< 1s$

Leader election/Mutex algorithms Processes	$\|Q\|$	$\|T\|$	Time
Leader election [44] (Israeli-Jalfon)			
20	40	80	$7s$
60	120	240	$1493s$
70 (TO: 80)	140	280	$3295s$
Leader election [42] (Herman)			
21	42	42	$9s$
51	102	102	$300s$
81 (TO: 91)	162	162	$2800s$
Mutex [40] (Array)			
2	15	95	$2s$
5	33	239	$5s$
10 (TO: 11)	63	479	$938s$
Mutex [59] (Burns)			
2	11	75	$1s$
4	19	199	$119s$
5 (TO: 6)	23	279	$2232s$
Mutex [3] (Dijkstra)			
2	19	196	$66s$
3 (TO: 4)	27	488	$3468s$
Mutex [50] (Lehmann Rabin)			
2	19	135	$3s$
5	43	339	$115s$
9 (TO: 10)	75	611	$2470s$
Mutex [61] (Peterson)			
2	13	86	$2s$
Mutex [64] (Szymanski)			
2	17	211	$10s$
3 (TO: 4)	24	895	$667s$

Fig. 2. Columns $\|Q\|$, $\|T\|$, and **Time** give the number of states and non-silent transitions, and the time for verification. Population protocols are verified for an infinite set of configurations. For parametric families, the smallest instance that could not be verified within one hour is shown in brackets, e.g. (TO: $c = 90$). Leader election and mutex algorithms are verified for one configuration. The number of processes leading to a timeout is given in brackets, e.g. (TO: 10).

Population Protocols. Population protocols [8,9] are replicated systems that compute Presburger predicates following the computation-as-consensus paradigm [10]. Depending on whether the initial configuration of agents satisfies the predicate or not, the agents of a correct protocol eventually agree on the output "yes" or "no", almost surely. Example 1 can be interpreted as a population protocol for the majority predicate $A_Y > A_N$, and the two stable termination properties that verify its correctness are described in Example 2. To show that a population protocol correctly computes a given predicate, we thus construct two Presburger stage graphs for the two corresponding stable termination properties. In all these examples, correctness is proved for an infinite set of initial configurations.

Our set of benchmarks contains a broadcast protocol [31], three majority protocols (Example 1, [23, Ex. 3], [5]), and multiple instances of parameterized families of protocols, where each protocol computes a different instance of a parameterized family of predicates[5]. These include various *flock-of-birds* protocol families ([28], [20, Sect. 3], [31, *threshold-n*]) for the family of predicates $x \geq c$ for some constant $c \geq 0$; two families for threshold predicates of the form $\boldsymbol{a} \cdot \boldsymbol{x} \geq c$ [8,20]; and one family for remainder protocols of the form $\boldsymbol{a} \cdot \boldsymbol{x} \equiv_m c$ [22]. Further, we check approximate majority protocols ([27,56], [51, *coin game*]). As these protocols only compute the predicate with large probability but not almost surely, we only verify that they always converge to a stable consensus.

Comparison with [22]. The approach of [22] can only be applied to so-called *strongly-silent* protocols. However, this class does not contain many fast and succinct protocols recently developed for different tasks [4,17,20].

We are able to verify all six protocols reported in [22]. Further, we are also able to verify the fast Majority [5] protocol as well as the succinct protocols Flock-of-birds [20, Sect. 3] and Threshold [20]. All three protocols are not strongly-silent. Although our approach is more general and complete, the time to verify many strongly-silent protocol does not differ significantly between the two approaches. Exceptions are the Flock-of-birds [28] protocols where we are faster ([22] reaches the timeout at $c = 55$) as well as the Remainder and the Flock-of-birds-threshold-n protocols where we are substantially slower ([22] reaches the timeout at $m = 80$ and $c = 350$, respectively). Loosely speaking, the approach of [22] can be faster because they compute inductive overapproximations using an iterative procedure instead of *PotReach*. In some instances already a very weak overapproximation, much less precise than *PotReach*, suffices to verify the result. Our procedure can be adapted to accommodate this (it essentially amounts to first running the procedure of [22], and if it is inconclusive then run ours).

Other Distributed Algorithms. We have also used our approach to verify arbitrary LTL liveness properties of non-parameterized systems with arbitrary communication structure. For this we apply standard automata-theoretic techniques and

---

[5] Notice that for each protocol we check correctness for all inputs; we cannot yet automatically verify that infinitely many protocols are correct, each of them for all possible inputs.

construct a product of the system and a *limit-deterministic Büchi automaton* for the negation of the property. Checking that no fair runs of the product are accepted by the automaton reduces to checking a stable termination property.

Since we only check correctness of one single finite-state system, we can also apply a probabilistic model checker based on state-space exploration. However, our technique delivers a stage graph, which plays two roles. First, it gives an explanation of why the property holds in terms of invariants and ranking functions, and second, it is a certificate of correctness that can be efficiently checked by independent means.

We verify liveness properties for several leader election and mutex algorithms from the literature [3,40,42,44,50,59,61,64] under the assumption of a probabilistic scheduler. For the leader election algorithms, we check that a leader is eventually chosen; for the mutex algorithms, we check that the first process enters its critical section infinitely often.

Comparison with PRISM [49]. We compared execution times for verification by our technique and by PRISM on the same models. While PRISM only needs a few seconds to verify instances of the mutex algorithms [3,40,50,59,61,64] where we reach the time limit, it reaches the memory limit for the two leader election algorithms [42,44] already for 70 and 71 processes, which we can still verify.

9   Conclusion and Further Work

We have presented stage graphs, a sound and complete technique for the verification of stable termination properties of replicated systems, an important class of parameterized systems. Using deep results of the theory of Petri nets, we have shown that Presburger stage graphs, a class of stage graphs whose correctness can be reduced to the satisfiability problem of Presburger arithmetic, are also sound and complete. This provides a decision procedure for the verification of termination properties, which is of theoretical nature since it involves a blind enumeration of candidates for Presburger stage graphs. For this reason, we have presented a technique for the algorithmic construction of Presburger stage graphs, designed to exploit the strengths of SMT-solvers for existential Presburger formulas, i.e., integer linear constraints. Loosely speaking, the technique searches for *linear* functions certifying the progress between stages, even though only the much larger class of Presburger functions guarantees completeness.

We have conducted extensive experiments on a large set of benchmarks. In particular, our approach is able to prove correctness of nearly all the standard protocols described in the literature, including several protocols that could not be proved by the technique of [22], which only worked for so-called strongly-silent protocols. We have also successfully applied the technique to some self-stabilization algorithms, leader election and mutual exclusion algorithms.

Our technique is based on the mechanized search for invariants and ranking functions. It avoids the use of state-space exploration as much as possible. For this reason, it also makes sense as a technique for the verification of liveness properties of non-parameterized systems with a finite but very large state space.

References

1. Abdulla, P.A.: Regular model checking. Int. J. Softw. Tools Technol. Transf. **14**(2), 109–118 (2012). https://doi.org/10.1007/s10009-011-0216-8
2. Abdulla, P.A., Cerans, K., Jonsson, B., Tsay, Y.: General decidability theorems for infinite-state systems. In: Proceedings of the 11th Annual IEEE Symposium on Logic in Computer Science, LICS 1996, New Brunswick, New Jersey, USA, 27–30 July 1996, pp. 313–321. IEEE Computer Society (1996). https://doi.org/10.1109/LICS.1996.561359
3. Abdulla, P.A., Delzanno, G., Henda, N.B., Rezine, A.: Regular model checking without transducers (on efficient verification of parameterized systems). In: Grumberg, O., Huth, M. (eds.) TACAS 2007. LNCS, vol. 4424, pp. 721–736. Springer, Heidelberg (2007). https://doi.org/10.1007/978-3-540-71209-1_56
4. Alistarh, D., Gelashvili, R.: Recent algorithmic advances in population protocols. SIGACT News **49**(3), 63–73 (2018). https://doi.org/10.1145/3289137.3289150
5. Alistarh, D., Gelashvili, R., Vojnovic, M.: Fast and exact majority in population protocols. In: Georgiou, C., Spirakis, P.G. (eds.) Proceedings of the 34th ACM Symposium on Principles of Distributed Computing, PODC 2015, Donostia-San Sebastián, Spain, 21–23 July 2015, pp. 47–56. ACM (2015). https://doi.org/10.1145/2767386.2767429
6. Aminof, B., Rubin, S., Zuleger, F., Spegni, F.: Liveness of parameterized timed networks. In: Halldórsson, M.M., Iwama, K., Kobayashi, N., Speckmann, B. (eds.) ICALP 2015, Part II. LNCS, vol. 9135, pp. 375–387. Springer, Heidelberg (2015). https://doi.org/10.1007/978-3-662-47666-6_30
7. Angluin, D.: Learning regular sets from queries and counterexamples. Inf. Comput. **75**(2), 87–106 (1987). https://doi.org/10.1016/0890-5401(87)90052-6
8. Angluin, D., Aspnes, J., Diamadi, Z., Fischer, M.J., Peralta, R.: Computation in networks of passively mobile finite-state sensors. In: Chaudhuri, S., Kutten, S. (eds.) Proceedings of the 23rd Annual ACM Symposium on Principles of Distributed Computing, PODC 2004, St. John's, Newfoundland, Canada, 25–28 July 2004, pp. 290–299. ACM (2004). https://doi.org/10.1145/1011767.1011810
9. Angluin, D., Aspnes, J., Diamadi, Z., Fischer, M.J., Peralta, R.: Computation in networks of passively mobile finite-state sensors. Distrib. Comput. **18**(4), 235–253 (2006). https://doi.org/10.1007/s00446-005-0138-3
10. Angluin, D., Aspnes, J., Eisenstat, D., Ruppert, E.: The computational power of population protocols. Distrib. Comput. **20**(4), 279–304 (2007). https://doi.org/10.1007/s00446-007-0040-2
11. Athanasiou, K., Liu, P., Wahl, T.: Unbounded-thread program verification using thread-state equations. In: Olivetti, N., Tiwari, A. (eds.) IJCAR 2016. LNCS (LNAI), vol. 9706, pp. 516–531. Springer, Cham (2016). https://doi.org/10.1007/978-3-319-40229-1_35
12. Babiak, T., et al.: The Hanoi omega-automata format. In: Kroening, D., Păsăreanu, C.S. (eds.) CAV 2015, Part I. LNCS, vol. 9206, pp. 479–486. Springer, Cham (2015). https://doi.org/10.1007/978-3-319-21690-4_31
13. Baier, C., Katoen, J.: Principles of Model Checking. MIT Press, Cambridge (2008)
14. Basler, G., Mazzucchi, M., Wahl, T., Kroening, D.: Symbolic counter abstraction for concurrent software. In: Bouajjani, A., Maler, O. (eds.) CAV 2009. LNCS, vol. 5643, pp. 64–78. Springer, Heidelberg (2009). https://doi.org/10.1007/978-3-642-02658-4_9

15. Berman, L.: The complexitiy of logical theories. Theoret. Comput. Sci. **11**, 71–77 (1980). https://doi.org/10.1016/0304-3975(80)90037-7

16. Bloem, R., Jacobs, S., Khalimov, A., Konnov, I., Rubin, S., Veith, H., Widder, J.: Decidability of Parameterized Verification. Synthesis Lectures on Distributed Computing Theory. Morgan & Claypool Publishers (2015). https://doi.org/10.2200/S00658ED1V01Y201508DCT013

17. Blondin, M., Esparza, J., Genest, B., Helfrich, M., Jaax, S.: Succinct population protocols for presburger arithmetic. In: Proceedings of 37th International Symposium on Theoretical Aspects of Computer Science, STACS 2020, 10–13 March 2020, Montpellier, France. LIPIcs, vol. 154, pp. 40:1–40:15. Schloss Dagstuhl - Leibniz-Zentrum für Informatik (2020). https://doi.org/10.4230/LIPIcs.STACS.2020.40

18. Blondin, M., Esparza, J., Helfrich, M., Kučera, A., Meyer, P.J.: Artifact evaluation VM and instructions to generate experimental results for the CAV20 paper: checking Qualitative Liveness Properties of Replicated Systems with Stochastic Scheduling. figshare:12295982 (2020). https://doi.org/10.6084/m9.figshare.12295982.v2

19. Blondin, M., Esparza, J., Helfrich, M., Kučera, A., Meyer, P.J.: Checking qualitative liveness properties of replicated systems with stochastic scheduling. arXiv:2005.03555 [cs.LO] (2020). https://arxiv.org/abs/2005.03555

20. Blondin, M., Esparza, J., Jaax, S.: Large flocks of small birds: on the minimal size of population protocols. In: Proceedings of 35th Symposium on Theoretical Aspects of Computer Science, STACS 2018, 28 February - 3 March 2018, Caen, France. LIPIcs, vol. 96, pp. 16:1–16:14. Schloss Dagstuhl - Leibniz-Zentrum für Informatik (2018). https://doi.org/10.4230/LIPIcs.STACS.2018.16

21. Blondin, M., Esparza, J., Jaax, S.: Peregrine: a tool for the analysis of population protocols. In: Chockler, H., Weissenbacher, G. (eds.) CAV 2018, Part I. LNCS, vol. 10981, pp. 604–611. Springer, Cham (2018). https://doi.org/10.1007/978-3-319-96145-3_34

22. Blondin, M., Esparza, J., Jaax, S., Meyer, P.J.: Towards efficient verification of population protocols. In: Schiller, E.M., Schwarzmann, A.A. (eds.) Proceedings of 36th ACM Symposium on Principles of Distributed Computing, PODC 2017, Washington, DC, USA, 25–27 July 2017, pp. 423–430. ACM (2017). https://doi.org/10.1145/3087801.3087816

23. Blondin, M., Esparza, J., Kučera, A.: Automatic analysis of expected termination time for population protocols. In: Schewe, S., Zhang, L. (eds.) Proceedings of 29th International Conference on Concurrency Theory, CONCUR 2018, 4–7 September 2018, Beijing, China. LIPIcs, vol. 118, pp. 33:1–33:16. Schloss Dagstuhl - Leibniz-Zentrum für Informatik (2018). https://doi.org/10.4230/LIPIcs.CONCUR.2018.33

24. Blondin, M., Finkel, A., Haase, C., Haddad, S.: The logical view on continuous petri nets. ACM Trans. Comput. Log. (TOCL) **18**(3), 24:1–24:28 (2017). https://doi.org/10.1145/3105908

25. Bouajjani, A., Jonsson, B., Nilsson, M., Touili, T.: Regular model checking. In: Emerson, E.A., Sistla, A.P. (eds.) CAV 2000. LNCS, vol. 1855, pp. 403–418. Springer, Heidelberg (2000). https://doi.org/10.1007/10722167_31

26. Browne, M.C., Clarke, E.M., Grumberg, O.: Reasoning about networks with many identical finite state processes. Inf. Comput. **81**(1), 13–31 (1989). https://doi.org/10.1016/0890-5401(89)90026-6

27. Cardelli, L., Csikász-Nagy, A.: The cell cycle switch computes approximate majority. Sci. Rep. **2**(1), 656 (2012). https://doi.org/10.1038/srep00656
pagebreak

28. Chatzigiannakis, I., Michail, O., Spirakis, P.G.: Algorithmic verification of population protocols. In: Dolev, S., Cobb, J., Fischer, M., Yung, M. (eds.) SSS 2010. LNCS, vol. 6366, pp. 221–235. Springer, Heidelberg (2010). https://doi.org/10.1007/978-3-642-16023-3_19

29. Chen, Y., Hong, C., Lin, A.W., Rümmer, P.: Learning to prove safety over parameterised concurrent systems. In: Stewart, D., Weissenbacher, G. (eds.) Proceedings of 17th International Conference on Formal Methods in Computer Aided Design, FMCAD 2017, Vienna, Austria, 2–6 October 2017, pp. 76–83. IEEE (2017). https://doi.org/10.23919/FMCAD.2017.8102244

30. Clarke, E., Talupur, M., Touili, T., Veith, H.: Verification by network decomposition. In: Gardner, P., Yoshida, N. (eds.) CONCUR 2004. LNCS, vol. 3170, pp. 276–291. Springer, Heidelberg (2004). https://doi.org/10.1007/978-3-540-28644-8_18

31. Clément, J., Delporte-Gallet, C., Fauconnier, H., Sighireanu, M.: Guidelines for the verification of population protocols. In: Proceedings of 31st International Conference on Distributed Computing Systems, ICDCS 2011, Minneapolis, Minnesota, USA, 20–24 June 2011, pp. 215–224. IEEE Computer Society (2011). https://doi.org/10.1109/ICDCS.2011.36

32. Cooper, D.C.: Theorem proving in arithmetic without multiplication. Mach. Intell. **7**, 91–99 (1972)

33. Czerwinski, W., Lasota, S., Lazic, R., Leroux, J., Mazowiecki, F.: The reachability problem for petri nets is not elementary. In: Charikar, M., Cohen, E. (eds.) Proceedings of 51st Annual ACM SIGACT Symposium on Theory of Computing, STOC 2019, Phoenix, AZ, USA, 23–26 June 2019, pp. 24–33. ACM (2019). https://doi.org/10.1145/3313276.3316369

34. Emerson, E.A., Namjoshi, K.S.: On reasoning about rings. Int. J. Found. Comput. Sci. **14**(4), 527–550 (2003). https://doi.org/10.1142/S0129054103001881

35. Esparza, J., Ganty, P., Leroux, J., Majumdar, R.: Model checking population protocols. In: Lal, A., Akshay, S., Saurabh, S., Sen, S. (eds.) Proceedings of 36th IARCS Annual Conference on Foundations of Software Technology and Theoretical Computer Science, FSTTCS 2016, Chennai, India, 13–15 December 2016. LIPIcs, vol. 65, pp. 27:1–27:14. Schloss Dagstuhl - Leibniz-Zentrum für Informatik (2016). https://doi.org/10.4230/LIPIcs.FSTTCS.2016.27

36. Esparza, J., Ganty, P., Leroux, J., Majumdar, R.: Verification of population protocols. Acta Inf. **54**(2), 191–215 (2017). https://doi.org/10.1007/s00236-016-0272-3

37. Esparza, J., Ledesma-Garza, R., Majumdar, R., Meyer, P., Niksic, F.: An SMT-based approach to coverability analysis. In: Biere, A., Bloem, R. (eds.) CAV 2014. LNCS, vol. 8559, pp. 603–619. Springer, Cham (2014). https://doi.org/10.1007/978-3-319-08867-9_40

38. Esparza, J., Meyer, P.J.: An SMT-based approach to fair termination analysis. In: Kaivola, R., Wahl, T. (eds.) Proceedings of 15th International Conference on Formal Methods in Computer-Aided Design, FMCAD 2015, Austin, Texas, USA, 27–30 September 2015, pp. 49–56. IEEE (2015)

39. Finkel, A., Schnoebelen, P.: Well-structured transition systems everywhere!. Theoret. Comput. Sci. **256**(1–2), 63–92 (2001). https://doi.org/10.1016/S0304-3975(00)00102-X

40. Fribourg, L., Olsén, H.: Reachability sets of parameterized rings as regular languages. In: Moller, F. (ed.) Proceedings of 2nd International Workshop on Verification of Infinite State Systems, Infinity 1997, Bologna, Italy, 11–12 July 1997. Electronic Notes in Theoretical Computer Science, vol. 9, p. 40. Elsevier (1997). https://doi.org/10.1016/S1571-0661(05)80427-X
41. German, S.M., Sistla, A.P.: Reasoning about systems with many processes. J. ACM **39**(3), 675–735 (1992). https://doi.org/10.1145/146637.146681
42. Herman, T.: Probabilistic self-stabilization. Inf. Process. Lett. **35**(2), 63–67 (1990). https://doi.org/10.1016/0020-0190(90)90107-9
43. Hopcroft, J.E., Pansiot, J.: On the reachability problem for 5-dimensional vector addition systems. Theoret. Comput. Sci. **8**, 135–159 (1979). https://doi.org/10.1016/0304-3975(79)90041-0
44. Israeli, A., Jalfon, M.: Token management schemes and random walks yield self-stabilizing mutual exclusion. In: Dwork, C. (ed.) Proceedings of 9th Annual ACM Symposium on Principles of Distributed Computing, PODC 1990, Quebec City, Quebec, Canada, 22–24 August 1990, pp. 119–131. ACM (1990). https://doi.org/10.1145/93385.93409
45. Jancar, P., Purser, D.: Structural liveness of petri nets is expspace-hard and decidable. Acta Inf. **56**(6), 537–552 (2019). https://doi.org/10.1007/s00236-019-00338-6
46. Kaiser, A., Kroening, D., Wahl, T.: Dynamic cutoff detection in parameterized concurrent programs. In: Touili, T., Cook, B., Jackson, P. (eds.) CAV 2010. LNCS, vol. 6174, pp. 645–659. Springer, Heidelberg (2010). https://doi.org/10.1007/978-3-642-14295-6_55
47. Kaiser, A., Kroening, D., Wahl, T.: A widening approach to multithreaded program verification. ACM Trans. Program. Lang. Syst. **36**(4), 14:1–14:29 (2014). https://doi.org/10.1145/2629608
48. Křetínský, J., Meggendorfer, T., Sickert, S.: Owl: a library for ω-words, automata, and LTL. In: Lahiri, S.K., Wang, C. (eds.) ATVA 2018. LNCS, vol. 11138, pp. 543–550. Springer, Cham (2018). https://doi.org/10.1007/978-3-030-01090-4_34
49. Kwiatkowska, M., Norman, G., Parker, D.: PRISM 4.0: verification of probabilistic real-time systems. In: Gopalakrishnan, G., Qadeer, S. (eds.) CAV 2011. LNCS, vol. 6806, pp. 585–591. Springer, Heidelberg (2011). https://doi.org/10.1007/978-3-642-22110-1_47
50. Lehmann, D., Rabin, M.O.: On the advantages of free choice: a symmetric and fully distributed solution to the dining philosophers problem. In: White, J., Lipton, R.J., Goldberg, P.C. (eds.) Proceedings of 8th Annual ACM Symposium on Principles of Programming Languages, POPL 1981, Williamsburg, Virginia, USA, January 1981, pp. 133–138. ACM Press (1981). https://doi.org/10.1145/567532.567547
51. Lengál, O., Lin, A.W., Majumdar, R., Rümmer, P.: Fair termination for parameterized probabilistic concurrent systems. In: Legay, A., Margaria, T. (eds.) TACAS 2017, Part I. LNCS, vol. 10205, pp. 499–517. Springer, Heidelberg (2017). https://doi.org/10.1007/978-3-662-54577-5_29
52. Leroux, J.: Vector addition systems reachability problem (a simpler solution). In: Voronkov, A. (ed.) Proceedings of the Alan Turing Centenary Conference, Turing 100, Manchester, UK, 22–25 June 2012. EPiC Series in Computing, vol. 10, pp. 214–228. EasyChair (2012). https://doi.org/10.29007/bnx2
53. Leroux, J.: Presburger vector addition systems. In: Proceedings of 28th Annual ACM/IEEE Symposium on Logic in Computer Science, LICS 2013, New Orleans, LA, USA, 25–28 June 2013. pp. 23–32. IEEE Computer Society (2013). https://doi.org/10.1109/LICS.2013.7

54. Leroux, J.: Vector addition system reversible reachability problem. Log. Methods Comput. Sci. **9**(1) (2013). https://doi.org/10.2168/LMCS-9(1:5)2013
55. Lin, A.W., Rümmer, P.: Liveness of randomised parameterised systems under arbitrary schedulers. In: Chaudhuri, S., Farzan, A. (eds.) CAV 2016, Part II. LNCS, vol. 9780, pp. 112–133. Springer, Cham (2016). https://doi.org/10.1007/978-3-319-41540-6_7
56. Moran, P.A.P.: Random processes in genetics. Math. Proc. Cambridge Philos. Soc. **54**(1), 60–71 (1958). https://doi.org/10.1017/S0305004100033193
57. de Moura, L., Bjørner, N.: Z3: an efficient SMT solver. In: Ramakrishnan, C.R., Rehof, J. (eds.) TACAS 2008. LNCS, vol. 4963, pp. 337–340. Springer, Heidelberg (2008). https://doi.org/10.1007/978-3-540-78800-3_24
58. Navlakha, S., Bar-Joseph, Z.: Distributed information processing in biological and computational systems. Commun. ACM **58**(1), 94–102 (2015). https://doi.org/10.1145/2678280
59. Nilsson, M.: Regular model checking. Ph.D. thesis, Uppsala University (2000)
60. Pang, J., Luo, Z., Deng, Y.: On automatic verification of self-stabilizing population protocols. In: Proceedings of 2nd IEEE/IFIP International Symposium on Theoretical Aspects of Software Engineering, TASE 2008, 17–19 June 2008, Nanjing, China, pp. 185–192. IEEE Computer Society (2008). https://doi.org/10.1109/TASE.2008.8
61. Peterson, G.L.: Myths about the mutual exclusion problem. Inf. Process. Lett. **12**(3), 115–116 (1981). https://doi.org/10.1016/0020-0190(81)90106-X
62. Presburger, M.: Über die Vollständigkeit eines gewissen Systems der Arithmetik ganzer Zahlen, in welchem die Addition als einzige Operation hervortritt. Comptes Rendus du Ier Congrès des mathématiciens des pays slaves, pp. 192–201 (1929)
63. Sun, J., Liu, Y., Dong, J.S., Pang, J.: PAT: towards flexible verification under fairness. In: Bouajjani, A., Maler, O. (eds.) CAV 2009. LNCS, vol. 5643, pp. 709–714. Springer, Heidelberg (2009). https://doi.org/10.1007/978-3-642-02658-4_59
64. Szymanski, B.K.: A simple solution to Lamport's concurrent programming problem with linear wait. In: Lenfant, J. (ed.) Proceedings of 2nd International Conference on Supercomputing, ICS 1988, Saint Malo, France, 4–8 July 1988, pp. 621–626. ACM (1988). https://doi.org/10.1145/55364.55425
65. Vardi, M.Y.: Automatic verification of probabilistic concurrent finite-state programs. In: Proceedings of 26th Annual Symposium on Foundations of Computer Science, FOCS 1985, Portland, Oregon, USA, 21–23 October 1985, pp. 327–338. IEEE Computer Society (1985). https://doi.org/10.1109/SFCS.1985.12

Stochastic Games with Lexicographic Reachability-Safety Objectives

Krishnendu Chatterjee[1] , Joost-Pieter Katoen[3] , Maximilian Weininger[2] ,
and Tobias Winkler[3](✉)

[1] IST Austria, Klosterneuburg, Austria
[2] Technical University of Munich,
Munich, Germany
[3] RWTH Aachen University, Aachen, Germany
tobias.winkler@cs.rwth-aachen.de

Abstract. We study turn-based stochastic zero-sum games with lexicographic preferences over reachability and safety objectives. Stochastic games are standard models in control, verification, and synthesis of stochastic reactive systems that exhibit both randomness as well as angelic and demonic non-determinism. Lexicographic order allows to consider multiple objectives with a strict preference order over the satisfaction of the objectives. To the best of our knowledge, stochastic games with lexicographic objectives have not been studied before. We establish determinacy of such games and present strategy and computational complexity results. For strategy complexity, we show that lexicographically optimal strategies exist that are deterministic and memory is only required to remember the already satisfied and violated objectives. For a constant number of objectives, we show that the relevant decision problem is in NP ∩ coNP, matching the current known bound for single objectives; and in general the decision problem is PSPACE-hard and can be solved in NEXPTIME ∩ coNEXPTIME. We present an algorithm that computes the lexicographically optimal strategies via a reduction to computation of optimal strategies in a sequence of single-objectives games. We have implemented our algorithm and report experimental results on various case studies.

1 Introduction

Simple stochastic games (SGs) [26] are zero-sum turn-based stochastic games played over a finite state space by two adversarial players, the Maximizer and Minimizer, along with randomness in the transition function. These games allow the interaction of angelic and demonic non-determinism as well as stochastic uncertainty. They generalize classical models such as Markov decision processes (MDPs) [39] which have only one player and stochastic uncertainty. An objective

This research was funded in part by the TUM IGSSE Grant 10.06 (PARSEC), the German Research Foundation (DFG) project KR 4890/2-1 "Statistical Unbounded Verification", the ERC CoG 863818 (ForM-SMArt), the Vienna Science and Technology Fund (WWTF) Project ICT15-003, and the RTG 2236 UnRAVeL.

S. K. Lahiri and C. Wang (Eds.): CAV 2020, LNCS 12225, pp. 398–420, 2020.
https://doi.org/10.1007/978-3-030-53291-8_21

specifies a desired set of trajectories of the game, and the goal of the Maximizer is to maximize the probability of satisfying the objective against all choices of the Minimizer. The basic decision problem is to determine whether the Maximizer can ensure satisfaction of the objective with a given probability threshold. This problem is among the rare and intriguing combinatorial problems that are NP ∩ coNP, and whether it belongs to P is a major and long-standing open problem. Besides the theoretical interest, SGs are a standard model in control and verification of stochastic reactive systems [4,18,31,39], as well as they provide robust versions of MDPs when precise transition probabilities are not known [22,45].

The multi-objective optimization problem is relevant in the analysis of systems with multiple, potentially conflicting goals, and a trade-off must be considered for the objectives. While the multi-objective optimization has been extensively studied for MDPs with various classes of objectives [1,28,39], the problem is notoriously hard for SGs. Even for multiple reachability objectives, such games are not determined [23] and their decidability is still open.

This work considers SGs with multiple reachability and safety objectives with lexicographic preference order over the objectives. That is, we consider SGs with several objectives where each objective is either reachability or safety, and there is a total preference order over the objectives. The motivation to study such lexicographic objectives is twofold. First, they provide an important special case of general multiple objectives. Second, lexicographic objectives are useful in many scenarios. For example, (i) an autonomus vehicle might have a primary objective to avoid clashes and a secondary objective to optimize performance; and (b) a robot saving lives during fire in a building might have a primary objective to save as many lives as possible, and a secondary objective to minimize energy consumption. Thus studying reactive systems with lexicographic objectives is a very relevant problem which has been considered in many different contexts [7,33]. In particular non-stochastic games with lexicographic objectives [6,25] and MDPs with lexicographic objectives [47] have been considered, but to the best of our knowledge SGs with lexicographic objectives have not been studied.

In this work we present several contributions for SGs with lexicographic reachability and safety objectives. The main contributions are as follows.

- *Determinacy.* In contrast to SGs with multiple objectives that are not determined, we establish determinacy of SGs with lexicographic combination of reachability and safety objectives.
- *Computational complexity.* For the associated decision problem we establish the following: (a) if the number of objectives is constant, then the decision problem lies in NP ∩ coNP, matching the current known bound for SGs with a single objective; (b) in general the decision problem is PSPACE-hard and can be solved in NEXPTIME ∩ coNEXPTIME.
- *Strategy complexity.* We show that lexicographically optimal strategies exist that are deterministic but require finite memory. We also show that memory is only needed in order to remember the already satisfied and violated objectives.

- *Algorithm.* We present an algorithm that computes the unique lexicographic value and the witness lexicographically optimal strategies via a reduction to computation of optimal strategies in a sequence of single-objectives games.
- *Experimental results.* We have implemented the algorithm and present experimental results on several case studies.

Technical Contribution. The key idea is that, given the lexicographic order of the objectives, we can consider them sequentially. After every objective, we remove all actions that are not optimal, thereby forcing all following computation to consider only locally optimal actions. The main complication is that local optimality of actions does not imply global optimality when interleaving reachability and safety, as the latter objective can use locally optimal actions to stay in the safe region without reaching the more important target. We introduce quantified reachability objectives as a means to solve this problem.

Related Work. We present related works on: (a) MDPs with multiple objectives; (b) SGs with multiple objectives; (c) lexicographic objectives in related models; and (d) existing tool support.

(a) MDPs with multiple objectives have been widely studied over a long time [1,39]. In the context of verifying MDPs with multiple objectives, both qualitative objectives such as reachability and LTL [29], as well as quantitative objectives, such as mean payoff [8,13], discounted sum [17], or total reward [34] have been considered. Besides multiple objectives with expectation criterion, other criteria have also been considered, such as, combination with variance [9], or multiple percentile (threshold) queries [8,20,32,41]. Practical applications of MDPs with multiple objectives are described in [2,3,42].

(b) More recently, SGs with multiple objectives have been considered, but the results are more limited [43]. Multiple mean-payoff objectives were first examined in [5] and the qualitative problems are coNP-complete [16]. Some special classes of SGs (namely stopping SGs) have been solved for total-reward objectives [23] and applied to autonomous driving [24]. However, even for the most basic question of solving SGs with multiple reachability objectives, decidability remains open.

(c) The study of lexicographic objectives has been considered in many different contexts [7,33]. Non-stochastic games with lexicographic mean-payoff objectives and parity conditions have been studied in [6] for the synthesis of reactive systems with performance guarantees. Non-stochastic games with multiple ω-regular objectives equipped with a monotonic preorder, which subsumes lexicographic order, have been studied in [12]. Moreover, the beyond worst-case analysis problems studied in [11] also considers primary and secondary objectives, which has a lexicographic flavor. MDPs with lexicographic discounted-sum objectives have been studied in [47], and have been extended with partial-observability in [46]. However, SGs with lexicographic reachability and safety objectives have not been considered so far.

(d) PRISM-Games [37] provides tool support for several multi-player multi-objective settings. MultiGain [10] is limited to generalized mean-payoff MDPs. STORM [27] can, among numerous single-objective problems, solve Markov automata with multiple timed reachability or expected cost objectives [40], multi-cost bounded reachability MDPs [35], and it can provide simple strategies for multiple expected reward objectives in MDPs [28].

Structure of this Paper. After recalling preliminaries and defining the problem in Sect. 2, we first consider games where all target sets are absorbing in Sect. 3. Then, in Sect. 4 we extend our insights to general games, yielding the full algorithm and the theoretical results. Finally, Sect. 5 describes the implementation and experimental evaluation. Section 6 concludes.

2   Preliminaries

Notation. A probability distribution on a finite set A is a function $f : A \to [0, 1]$ such that $\sum_{x \in A} f(x) = 1$. We denote the set of all probability distributions on A by $\mathcal{D}(A)$. Vector-like objects $\boldsymbol{x}$ are denoted in a bold font and we use the notation $\boldsymbol{x}_i$ for the i-th component of $\boldsymbol{x}$. We use $\boldsymbol{x}_{<n}$ as a shorthand for $(\boldsymbol{x}_1, \ldots, \boldsymbol{x}_{n-1})$.

2.1   Basic Definitions

Probabilistic Models. In this paper, we consider *(simple) stochastic games* [26], which are defined as follows. Let $L = \{a, b, \ldots\}$ be a finite set of actions labels.

Definition 1 (SG). *A stochastic game (SG) is a tuple* $\mathcal{G} = (S_\square, S_\diamond, \mathsf{Act}, P)$ *with* $S := S_\square \uplus S_\diamond \neq \emptyset$ *a finite set of states,* $\mathsf{Act} : S \to 2^L \setminus \{\emptyset\}$ *defines finitely many actions available at every state, and* $P : S \times L \to \mathcal{D}(S)$ *is the transition probability function.* $P(s, a)$ *is undefined if* $a \notin \mathsf{Act}(s)$.

We abbreviate $P(s, a)(s')$ to $P(s, a, s')$. We refer to the two players of the game as Max and Min and the sets $S_\square$ and $S_\diamond$ are the Max- and Min-states, respectively. As the game is *turn based*, these sets partition the state space S such that in each state it is either Max's or Min's turn. The intuitive semantics of an SG is as follows: In every turn, the corresponding player picks one of the finitely many available actions $a \in \mathsf{Act}(s)$ in the current state s. The game then transitions to the next state according to the probability distribution $P(s, a)$. The winning conditions are not part of the game itself and need to be further specified.

Sinks, Markov Decision Processes and Markov Chains. A state $s \in S$ is called *absorbing* (or sink) if $P(s, a, s) = 1$ for all $a \in \mathsf{Act}(s)$ and $\mathsf{Sinks}(\mathcal{G})$ denotes the set of all absorbing states of SG $\mathcal{G}$. A *Markov Decision Process* (MDP) is an SG where either $S_\diamond = \emptyset$ or $S_\square = \emptyset$, i.e. a one-player game. A *Markov Chain* (MC) is an SG where $|\mathsf{Act}(s)| = 1$ for all $s \in S$. For technical reasons, we allow countably infinite state spaces S for both MDPs and MCs.

Strategies. We define the formal semantics of games by means of *paths* and *strategies*. An *infinite path* π is an infinite sequence $\pi = s_0 a_0 s_1 a_1 \cdots \in (S \times L)^\omega$, such that for every $i \in \mathbb{N}$, $a_i \in \mathsf{Act}(s_i)$ and $s_{i+1} \in \{s' \mid P(s_i, a_i, s') > 0\}$. *Finite paths* are defined analogously as elements of $(S \times L)^* \times S$. Note that when considering MCs, every state just has a single action, so an infinite path can be identified with an element of S^ω.

A strategy of player Max is a function $\sigma \colon (S \times L)^* \times S_\square \to \mathcal{D}(L)$ where $\sigma(\pi s)(s') > 0$ only if $s \in \mathsf{Act}(s)$. It is *memoryless* if $\sigma(\pi s) = \sigma(\pi' s)$ for all $\pi, \pi' \in (S \times L)^*$. More generally, σ has memory of class-size at most m if the set $(S \times L)^*$ can be partitioned in m classes $M_1, \ldots, M_m \subseteq (S \times L)^*$ such that $\sigma(\pi s) = \sigma(\pi' s)$ for all $1 \leq i \leq m$, $\pi, \pi' \in M_i$ and $s \in S_\square$. A memory of class-size m can be represented with $\lceil \log(m) \rceil$ bits.

A strategy is *deterministic* if $\sigma(\pi s)$ is Dirac for all πs. Strategies that are both memoryless and deterministic are called *MD* and can be identified as functions $\sigma \colon S_\square \to L$. Notice that there are at most $|L|^{S_\square}$ different MD strategies, that is, exponentially many in $S_\square$; in general, there can be uncountably many strategies.

Strategies τ of player Min are defined analogously, with $S_\square$ replaced by $S_\lozenge$. The set of all strategies of player Max is denoted with Σ_{Max}, the set of all MD strategies with $\Sigma_{\mathsf{Max}}^{\mathsf{MD}}$, and similarly Σ_{Min} and $\Sigma_{\mathsf{Min}}^{\mathsf{MD}}$ for player Min.

Fixing a strategy σ of one player in a game $\mathcal{G}$ yields the *induced MDP* $\mathcal{G}^\sigma$. Fixing a strategy τ of the second player too, yields the *induced MC* $\mathcal{G}^{\sigma,\tau}$. Notice that the induced models are finite if and only if the respective strategies use finite memory.

Given an (induced) MC $\mathcal{G}^{\sigma,\tau}$, we let $\mathbb{P}_s^{\sigma,\tau}$ be its associated probability measure on the Borel-measurable sets of infinite paths obtained from the standard cylinder construction where s is the initial state [39].

Reachability and Safety. In our setting, a *property* is a Borel-measurable set $\Omega \subseteq S^\omega$ of infinite paths in an SG. The *reachability* property Reach (T) where $T \subseteq S$ is the set Reach $(T) = \{s_0 s_1 \ldots \in S^\omega \mid \exists i \geq 0 \colon s_i \in T\}$. The set Safe $(T) = S^\omega \setminus$ Reach (T) is called a *safety property*. Further, for sets $T_1, T_2 \subseteq S$ we define the *until property* $T_1 \sqcup T_2 = \{s_0 s_1 \ldots \in S^\omega \mid \exists i \geq 0 \colon s_i \in T_2 \wedge \forall j < i \colon s_j \in T_1\}$. These properties are measurable (e.g. [4]). A reachability or safety property where the set T satisfies $T \subseteq \mathsf{Sinks}(\mathcal{G})$ is called *absorbing*. For the safety probabilities in an (induced) MC, it holds that $\mathbb{P}_s(\mathsf{Safe}\ (T)) = 1 - \mathbb{P}_s(\mathsf{Reach}\ (T))$. We highlight that an objective Safe (T) is specified by the set of paths to avoid, i.e. paths satisfying the objective remain forever in $S \setminus T$.

2.2 Stochastic Lexicographic Reachability-Safety Games

SGs with lexicographic preferences are a straightforward adaptation of the ideas of e.g. [46] to the game setting. The *lexicographic* order on $\mathbb{R}^n$ is defined as $\boldsymbol{x} \leq_{\mathsf{lex}} \boldsymbol{y}$ iff $\boldsymbol{x}_i \leq \boldsymbol{y}_i$ where $i \leq n$ is the greatest position such that for all $j < i$ it holds that $\boldsymbol{x}_j = \boldsymbol{y}_j$. The position i thus acts like a *tiebreaker*. Notice that for arbitrary sets $X \subseteq [0, 1]^n$, suprema and infima exist in the lexicographic order.

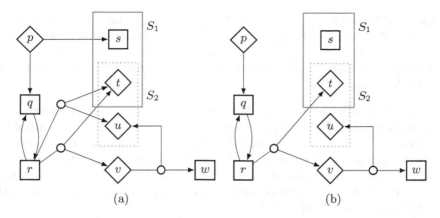

(a)   (b)

Fig. 1. (a) An example of a stochastic game. Max-states are rendered as squares □ and Min-states as rhombs ◊. Probabilistic choices are indicated with small circles. In this example, all probabilities equal $1/2$. The absorbing lex-objective $\Omega =$ {Reach (S_1), Safe (S_2)} is indicated by the thick green line around $S_1 = \{s,t\}$ and the dotted red line around $S_2 = \{t,u\}$. Self-loops in sinks are omitted. (b) Restriction of the game to lex-optimal actions only.

Definition 2 (Lex-Objective and Lex-Value). *A lexicographic reachability-safety objective (*lex-objective, for short*) is a vector* $\Omega = (\Omega_1, \ldots, \Omega_n)$ *such that* $\Omega_i \in$ {Reach (S_i), Safe (S_i)} *with* $S_i \subseteq S$ *for all* $1 \leq i \leq n$. *We call* Ω *absorbing if all the* Ω_i *are absorbing, i.e., if* $S_i \subseteq \mathsf{Sinks}(\mathcal{G})$ *for all* $1 \leq i \leq n$. *The lex-(icographic)value of* Ω *at state* $s \in S$ *is defined as:*

$$^{\Omega}\mathbf{v}^{\mathsf{lex}}(s) = \sup_{\sigma \in \Sigma_{\mathsf{Max}}} \inf_{\tau \in \Sigma_{\mathsf{Min}}} \mathbb{P}_s^{\sigma,\tau}(\Omega) \tag{1}$$

where $\mathbb{P}_s^{\sigma,\tau}(\Omega)$ *denotes the vector* $(\mathbb{P}_s^{\sigma,\tau}(\Omega_1), \ldots, \mathbb{P}_s^{\sigma,\tau}(\Omega_n))$ *and the suprema and infima are taken with respect to the order* $\leq_{\mathsf{lex}}$ *on* $[0,1]^n$.

Thus the lex-value at state s is the lexicographically supremal vector of probabilities that Max can ensure against all possible behaviors of Min. We will prove in Sect. 4.3 that the supremum and infimum in (1) can be exchanged; this property is called *determinacy*. We omit the superscript Ω in $^{\Omega}\mathbf{v}^{\mathsf{lex}}$ if it is clear from the context. We also omit the sets Σ_{Max} and Σ_{Min} in the suprema in (1), e.g. we will just write $\sup_{\sigma}$.

Example 1 (SGs and lex-values). Consider the SG sketched in Fig. 1a with the lex-objective $\Omega =$ {Reach (S_1), Safe (S_2)}. Player Max must thus maximize the probability to reach S_1 and, moreover, among all possible strategies that do so, it must choose one that maximizes the probability to avoid S_2 forever. △

Lex-Value of Actions and Lex-Optimal Actions. We extend the notion of value to actions. Let $s \in S$ be a state. The *lex-value of an action* $a \in \mathsf{Act}(s)$ is defined as $\mathbf{v}^{\mathsf{lex}}(s,a) = \sum_{s'} P(s,a,s')\mathbf{v}^{\mathsf{lex}}(s')$. If $s \in S_\square$, then action a is called *lex-optimal* if $\mathbf{v}^{\mathsf{lex}}(s,a) = \max_{b \in \mathsf{Act}(s)} \mathbf{v}^{\mathsf{lex}}(s,b)$. Lex-optimal actions are defined analogously for states $s \in S_\Diamond$ by considering the minimum instead of the maximum. Notice that there is always at least one optimal action because $\mathsf{Act}(s)$ is finite by definition.

Example 2 (Lex-value of actions). We now intuitively explain the lex-values of all states in Fig. 1a. The lex-value of sink states s, t, u and w is determined by their membership in the sets S_1 and S_2. E.g., $\mathbf{v}^{\mathsf{lex}}(s) = (1,1)$, as it is part of the set S_1 that should be reached and not part of the set S_2 that should be avoided. Similarly we get the lex-values of t, u and w as $(1,0)$, $(0,0)$ and $(0,1)$ respectively. State v has a single action that yields $(0,0)$ or $(0,1)$ each with probability $1/2$, thus $\mathbf{v}^{\mathsf{lex}}(v) = (0,1/2)$.

State p has one action going to s, which would yield $(1,1)$. However, as p is a Min-state, its best strategy is to avoid giving such a high value. Thus, it uses the action going downwards and $\mathbf{v}^{\mathsf{lex}}(p) = \mathbf{v}^{\mathsf{lex}}(q)$. State q only has a single action going to r, so $\mathbf{v}^{\mathsf{lex}}(q) = \mathbf{v}^{\mathsf{lex}}(r)$.

State r has three choices: (i) Going back to q, which results in an infinite loop between q and r, and thus never reaches S_1. So a strategy that commits to this action will not achieve the optimal value. (ii) Going to t or u each with probability $1/2$. In this case, the safety objective is definitely violated, but the reachability objective achieved with $1/2$. (iii) Going to t or v each with probability $1/2$. Similarly to (ii), the probability to reach S_1 is $1/2$, but additionally, there is a $1/2 \cdot 1/2$ chance to avoid S_2. Thus, since r is a Max-state, its lex-optimal choice is the action leading to t or v and we get $\mathbf{v}^{\mathsf{lex}}(r) = (1/2, 1/4)$. $\triangle$

Notice that with the kind of objectives considered, we can easily swap the roles of Max and Min by exchanging safety objectives with reachability and vice versa. It is thus no loss of generality to consider subsequently introduced notions such as optimal strategies only from the perspective of Max.

Definition 3 (Lex-Optimal Strategies). *A strategy $\sigma \in \Sigma_{\mathsf{Max}}$ is* lex-optimal *for Ω if for all $s \in S$, $\mathbf{v}^{\mathsf{lex}}(s) = \inf_{\tau'} \mathbb{P}_s^{\sigma,\tau'}(\Omega)$. A strategy τ of Min is a* lex-optimal counter-strategy *against σ if $\mathbb{P}_s^{\sigma,\tau}(\Omega) = \inf_{\tau'} \mathbb{P}_s^{\sigma,\tau'}(\Omega)$.*

We stress that counter-strategies of Min depend on the strategy chosen by Max.

Locally Lex-Optimal Strategies. An MD strategy σ of Max (Min, resp.) is called *locally lex-optimal* if for all $s \in S_\square$ ($s \in S_\Diamond$, resp.) and $a \in \mathsf{Act}(s)$, we have $\sigma(s)(a) > 0$ implies that action a is lex-optimal. Thus, locally lex-optimal strategies only assign positive probability to lex-optimal actions.

Convention. For the rest of the paper, unless stated otherwise, we use $\mathcal{G} = (S_\square, S_\Diamond, \mathsf{Act}, P)$ to denote an SG and $\Omega = (\Omega_1, \ldots, \Omega_n)$ is a suitable (not necessarily absorbing) lex-objective, that is $\Omega_i \in \{\mathsf{Reach}\,(S_i), \mathsf{Safe}\,(S_i)\}$ with $S_i \subseteq S$ for all $1 \leq i \leq n$.

3 Lexicographic SGs with Absorbing Targets

In this section, we show how to compute the lexicographic value for SGs where *all target sets are absorbing*. We first show various theoretical results in Sect. 3.1 upon which the algorithm for computing the values and optimal strategies presented in Sect. 3.2 is then built. The main technical difficulty arises from interleaving reachability and safety objectives. In Sect. 4, we will reduce solving general (not necessarily absorbing) SGs to the case with absorbing targets.

3.1 Characterizing Optimal Strategies

This first subsection derives a characterization of lex-optimal strategies in terms of local optimality and an additional reachability condition (Lemma 2 further below). It is one of the key ingredients for the correctness of the algorithm presented later and also gives rise to a (non-constructive) proof of existence of MD lex-optimal strategies in the absorbing case.

We begin with the following lemma that summarizes some straightforward facts we will frequently use. Recall that a strategy is *locally lex-optimal* if it only selects actions with optimal lex-value.

Lemma 1. *The following statements hold for any absorbing lex-objective Ω:*

(a) If $\sigma \in \Sigma_{\mathrm{Max}}^{\mathrm{MD}}$ is lex-optimal and $\tau \in \Sigma_{\mathrm{Min}}^{\mathrm{MD}}$ is a lex-optimal counter strategy against σ, then σ and τ are both locally lex-optimal. (We do not yet claim that such strategies σ, τ always exist.)

(b) Let $\widetilde{\mathcal{G}}$ be obtained from $\mathcal{G}$ by removing all actions (of both players) that are not locally lex-optimal. Let $\widetilde{\mathbf{v}}^{\mathrm{lex}}$ be the lex-values in $\widetilde{\mathcal{G}}$. Then $\widetilde{\mathbf{v}}^{\mathrm{lex}} = \mathbf{v}^{\mathrm{lex}}$.

Proof (Sketch). Both claims follow from the definitions of lex-value and lex-optimal strategy. For (b) in particular, we show that a strategy using actions which are not lex-optimal can be transformed into a strategy that achieves a greater (lower, resp.) value. Thus removing the non lex-optimal actions does not affect the lex-value. See [19, Appendix A.1] for more technical details.   □

Example 3 (Modified game $\widetilde{\mathcal{G}}$). Consider again the SG from Fig. 1a. Recall the lex-values from Example 1. Now we remove the actions that are not locally lex-optimal. This means we drop the action that leads from p to s and the action that leads from r to t or u (Fig. 1b). Since these actions were not used by the lex-optimal strategies, the value in the modified SG is the same as that of the original game.   △

Example 4 (Locally lex-optimal does not imply globally lex-optimal). Note that we do not drop the action that leads from r to q, because $\mathbf{v}^{\mathrm{lex}}(r) = \mathbf{v}^{\mathrm{lex}}(q)$, so this action is locally lex-optimal. In fact, a lex-optimal strategy can use it arbitrarily many times without reducing the lex-value, as long as eventually it picks the action leading to t or v. However, if we only played the action leading to q, the lex-value would be reduced to $(0, 1)$ as we would not reach S_1, but would also avoid S_2.

We stress the following consequence of this: Playing a locally lex-optimal strategy is not necessarily globally lex-optimal. It is not sufficient to just restrict the game to locally lex-optimal actions of the previous objectives and then solve the current one. Note that in fact the optimal strategy for the second objective Safe (S_2) would be to remain in $\{p, q\}$; however, we must not pick this safety strategy, before we have not "tried everything" for all previous reachability objectives, in this case reaching S_1.   △

This idea of "trying everything" for an objective Reach (S_i) is equivalent to the following: either reach the target set S_i, or reach a set of states from which S_i cannot be reached anymore. Formally, let $\mathsf{Zero}_i = \{s \in S \mid \mathbf{v}_i^{\mathsf{lex}}(s) = 0\}$ be the set of states that cannot reach the target set S_i anymore. Note that it depends on the lex-value, not the single-objective value. This is important, as the single-objective value could be greater than 0, but a more important objective has to be sacrificed to achieve it.

We define the set of states where we have "tried everything" for all reachability objectives as follows:

Definition 4 (Final Set). *For absorbing Ω, let $R_{<i} = \{j < i \mid \Omega_j = \mathsf{Reach}\ (S_j)\}$. We define the* final set *$F_{<i} = \bigcup_{k \in R_{<i}} S_k\ \cup\ \bigcap_{k \in R_{<i}} \mathsf{Zero}_k$ with the convention that $F_{<i} = S$ if $R_{<i} = \emptyset$. We also let $F = F_{<n+1}$.*

The final set contains all target states as well as the states that have lex-value 0 for all reachability objectives; we need the intersection of the sets Zero_k, because as long as a state still has a positive probability to reach any target set, its optimal behaviour is to try that.

Example 5 (Final set). For the game in Fig. 1, we have $\mathsf{Zero}_1 = \{u, v, w\}$ and thus $F = \mathsf{Zero}_1 \cup S_1 = \{s, t, u, v, w\}$. An MD lex-optimal strategy of Max must almost-surely reach this set against any strategy of Min; only then it has "tried everything".   △

The following lemma characterizes MD lex-optimal strategies in terms of local lex-optimality and the final set.

Lemma 2. *Let Ω be an absorbing lex-objective and $\sigma \in \Sigma_{\mathsf{Max}}^{\mathsf{MD}}$. Then σ is lex-optimal for Ω if and only if σ is locally lex-optimal and for all $s \in S$ we have*

$$\forall \tau \in \Sigma_{\mathsf{Min}}^{\mathsf{MD}} : \mathbb{P}_s^{\sigma, \tau}(\mathsf{Reach}\ (F)) = 1. \qquad (\star)$$

Proof (Sketch). The "*if*"-direction is shown by induction on the number n of targets. We make a case distinction according to the type of Ω_n: If it is safety, then we prove that local lex-optimality is already sufficient for global lex-optimality. Else if Ω_n is reachability, then intuitively, the additional condition $(\star)$ ensures that the strategy σ indeed "tries everything" and either reaches the target S_n or eventually a state in Zero_n where the opponent Min can make sure that Max cannot escape. The technical details of these assertions rely on a fixpoint characterization of the reachability probabilities combined with the classic Knaster-Tarski Fixpoint Theorem [44] and are given in [19, Appendix A.2].

For the *"only if"*-direction recall that lex-optimal strategies are necessarily locally lex-optimal by Lemma 1 (a). Further let i be such that $\Omega_i = \mathsf{Reach}\ (S_i)$ and assume for contradiction that σ remains forever within $S \setminus (S_i \cup \mathsf{Zero}_i)$ with positive probability against some strategy of Min. But then σ visits states with positive lex-value for Ω_i infinitely often without ever reaching S_i. Thus σ is not lex-optimal, contradiction.   □

Finally, this characterization allows us to prove that MD lex-optimal strategies exist for absorbing objectives.

Theorem 1. *For an absorbing lex-objective Ω, there exist MD lex-optimal strategies for both players.*

Proof (Sketch). We consider the subgame $\widetilde{\mathcal{G}}$ obtained by removing lex-suboptimal actions for both players and then show that the (single-objective) value of $\mathsf{Reach}\ (F)$ in $\widetilde{\mathcal{G}}$ equals 1. An optimal MD strategy for $\mathsf{Reach}\ (F)$ exists [26]; further, it is locally lex-optimal, because we are in $\widetilde{\mathcal{G}}$, and it reaches F almost surely. Thus, it is lex-optimal for Ω by the *"if"*-direction of Lemma 2. See [19, Appendix A.3] for more details on the proof.   □

3.2   Algorithm for SGs with Absorbing Targets

Theorem 1 is not constructive because it relies on the values $\mathbf{v}^{\mathsf{lex}}$ without showing how to compute them. Computing the values and constructing an optimal strategy for Max in the case of an absorbing lex-objective is the topic of this subsection.

Definition 5 (QRO). *A quantified reachability objective (QRO) is determined by a function $q \colon S' \to [0, 1]$ where $S' \subseteq S$. For all strategies σ and τ, we define:*

$$\mathbb{P}_s^{\sigma, \tau}(\mathsf{Reach}\ (q)) = \sum_{t \in S'} \mathbb{P}_s^{\sigma, \tau}((S \setminus S')\ \mathsf{U}\ t) \cdot q(t).$$

Intuitively, a QRO generalizes its standard Boolean counterpart by additionally assigning a weight to the states in the target set S'. Thus the probability of a QRO is obtained by computing the sum of the $q(t)$, $t \in S'$, weighted by the probability to avoid S' until reaching t. Note that this probability does not depend on what happens after reaching S'; so it is unaffected by making all states in S' absorbing.

In Sect. 4, we need the dual notion of a quantified safety property, defined as $\mathbb{P}_s^{\sigma, \tau}(\mathsf{Safe}\ (q)) = 1 - \mathbb{P}_s^{\sigma, \tau}(\mathsf{Reach}\ (q))$; intuitively, this amounts to minimizing the reachability probability.

Remark 1. A usual reachability property Reach (S') is a special case of a quantified one with $q(s) = 1$ for all $s \in S'$. Vice versa, quantified properties can be easily reduced to usual ones defined only by the set S': Convert all states $t \in S'$ into sinks, then for each such t prepend a new state t' with a single action a and $P(t', a, t) = q(t)$ and $P(t', a, \perp) = 1 - q(t)$ where $\perp$ is a sink state. Finally, redirect all transitions leading into t to t'. Despite this equivalence, it turns out to be convenient and natural to use QROs.

Example 6 (QRO). Example 4 illustrated that solving a safety objective after a reachability objective can lead to problems, as the optimal strategy for Safe (S_2) did not use the action that actually reached S_1. In Example 5 we indicated that the final set $F = \{s, t, u, v, w\}$ has to be reached almost surely, and among those states the ones with the highest safety values should be preferred. This can be encoded in a QRO as follows: Compute the values for the Safe (S_2) objective for the states in F. Then construct the function $q_2 \colon F \to [0, 1]$ that maps all states in F to their safety value, i.e., $q_2 : \{s \mapsto 1, t \mapsto 0, u \mapsto 0, v \mapsto 1/2, w \mapsto 1\}$.   △

Thus using QROs, we can effectively reduce (interleaved) safety objectives to quantified *reachability* objectives:

Lemma 3 (Reduction Safe → Reach). *Let Ω be an absorbing lex-objective with $\Omega_n = $ Safe (S_n), $q_n \colon F \to [0, 1]$ with $q_n(t) = \mathbf{v}_n^{\mathsf{lex}}(t)$ for all $t \in F$ where F is the final set (Definition 4), and $\Omega' = (\Omega_1, \ldots, \Omega_{n-1}, $ Reach $(q_n))$. Then: $\Omega \mathbf{v}^{\mathsf{lex}} = \Omega' \mathbf{v}^{\mathsf{lex}}$.*

Proof (Sketch). By definition, $\Omega \mathbf{v}^{\mathsf{lex}}(s) = \Omega' \mathbf{v}^{\mathsf{lex}}(s)$ for all $s \in F$, so we only need to consider the states in $S \setminus F$. Since any lex-optimal strategy for Ω or Ω' must also be lex-optimal for $\Omega_{<n}$, we know by Lemma 2 that such a strategy reaches $F_{<n}$ almost-surely. Note that we have $F_{<n} = F$, as the n-th objective, either the QRO or the safety objective, does not add any new states to F. The reachability objective Reach (q_n) weighs the states in F with their lexicographic safety values $\mathbf{v}_n^{\mathsf{lex}}$. Thus we additionally ensure that in order to reach F, we use those actions that give us the best safety probability afterwards. In this way we obtain the correct lex-values $\mathbf{v}_n^{\mathsf{lex}}$ even for states in $S \setminus F$. See [19, Appendix A.4] for the full technical proof.   □

Example 7 (Reduction Safe → Reach). Recall Example 6. By the preceding Lemma 3, computing $\sup_\sigma \inf_\tau \mathbb{P}_s^{\sigma, \tau}($Reach $(S_1),$ Reach $(q_2))$ yields the correct lex-value $\mathbf{v}^{\mathsf{lex}}(s)$ for all $s \in S$. Consider for instance state r in the running example: The action leading to q is clearly suboptimal for Reach (q_2) as it does not reach F. Both other actions surely reach F. However, since $q_2(t) = q_2(u) = 0$ while $q_2(v) = 1/2$, the action leading to u and v is preferred over that leading to t and u, as it ensures the higher safety probability after reaching F.   △

We now explain the basic structure of Algorithm 1. More technical details are explained in the proof sketch of Theorem 2 and the full proof is in [19, Appendix A.5]. The idea of Algorithm 1 is, as sketched in Sect. 3.1, to consider the objectives sequentially in the order of importance, i.e., starting with Ω_1.

Algorithm 1. Solve absorbing lex-objective

Input: SG $\mathcal{G}$, absorbing lex-objective $\Omega = (\Omega_1, \ldots, \Omega_n)$
Output: Vector of lex-values $\mathbf{v}^{\text{lex}}$, MD lex-optimal strategy σ for Max
1: **procedure** SolveAbsorbing($\mathcal{G}, \Omega$)
2:     initialize $\mathbf{v}^{\text{lex}}$ and σ arbitrarily
3:     $\widetilde{\mathcal{G}} \leftarrow \mathcal{G}$ ▷ Consider whole game in the beginning.

4:     **for** $1 \leq i \leq n$ **do**
5:         $(v, \widetilde{\sigma}) \leftarrow$ SolveSingleObj($\widetilde{\mathcal{G}}, \Omega_i$)
6:         **if** $\Omega_i = \text{Safe}(S_i)$ **then**
7:             $F_{<i} \leftarrow$ final set with respect to $\widetilde{\mathcal{G}}$ and $\Omega_{<i}$ ▷ see Def. 4
8:             $q_i(s) \leftarrow v(s)$ for all $s \in F_{<i}$ ▷ see Def. 5
9:             $(v, \sigma_Q) \leftarrow$ SolveSingleObj($\widetilde{\mathcal{G}}$, Reach (q_i))
10:        **end if**

11:        $\widetilde{\mathcal{G}} \leftarrow$ restriction of $\widetilde{\mathcal{G}}$ to optimal actions w.r.t. v

12:        $\mathbf{v}_i^{\text{lex}} \leftarrow v$
13:        **for** $s \in S$ **do**
14:            **if** ($\Omega_i = \text{Reach}(S_i)$ and $v(s) > 0$) or ($\Omega_i = \text{Safe}(S_i)$ and $s \in F_{<i}$) **then**
15:                $\sigma(s) \leftarrow \widetilde{\sigma}(s)$ ▷ Strategy improvement
16:            **else if** $\Omega_i = \text{Safe}(S_i)$ and $s \notin F_{<i}$
17:                $\sigma(s) \leftarrow \sigma_Q(s)$
18:            **end if**
19:        **end for**
20:    **end for**
        return ($\mathbf{v}^{\text{lex}}, \sigma$)
21: **end procedure**

The i-th objective is solved (Lines 5–10) and the game is restricted to only the locally optimal actions (Line 11). This way, in the i-th iteration of the main loop, only actions that are locally lex-optimal for objectives 1 through $(i-1)$ are considered. Finally, we construct the optimal strategy and update the result variables (Lines 12–19).

Theorem 2. *Given an SG $\mathcal{G}$ and an absorbing lex-objective $\Omega = (\Omega_1, \ldots, \Omega_n)$, Algorithm 1 correctly computes the vector of lex-values $\mathbf{v}^{\text{lex}}$ and an MD lex-optimal strategy σ for player Max. It needs n calls to a single objective solver.*

Proof (Sketch).

- $\widetilde{\mathcal{G}}$**-invariant:** For $i > 1$, in the i-th iteration of the loop, $\widetilde{\mathcal{G}}$ is the original SG restricted to only those actions that are locally lex-optimal for the targets 1 to $(i-1)$; this is the case because Line 11 was executed for all previous targets.
- **Single-objective case:** The single-objective that is solved in Line 5 can be either reachability or safety. We can use any (precise) single-objective solver as a black box, e.g. strategy iteration [36]. Recall that by Remark 1, it is no problem to call a single-objective solver with a QRO since there is a trivial reduction.
- **QRO for safety:** If an objective is of type reachability, no further steps need to be taken; if on the other hand it is safety, we need to ensure that the problem explained in Example 4 does not occur. Thus we compute the final set $F_{<i}$ for the i-th target and then construct and solve the QRO as in Lemma 3.

- **Resulting strategy:** When storing the resulting strategy, we again need to avoid errors induced by the fact that locally lex-optimal actions need not be globally lex-optimal. This is why for a reachability objective, we only update the strategy in states that have a positive value for the current objective; if the value is 0, the current strategy does not have any preference, and we need to keep the old strategy. For safety objectives, we need to update the strategy in two ways: for all states in the final set $F_{<i}$, we set it to the safety strategy $\tilde{\sigma}$ (from Line 5) as within $F_{<i}$ we do not have to consider the previous reachability objectives and therefore must follow an optimal safety strategy. For all states in $S \setminus F_{<i}$, we set it to the reachability strategy from the QRO σ_Q (from Line 9). This is correct, as σ_Q ensures almost-sure reachability of $F_{<i}$ which is necessary to satisfy all preceding reachability objectives; moreover σ_Q prefers those states in $F_{<i}$ that have a higher safety value (cf. Lemma 3).
- **Termination:** The main loop of the algorithm invokes SolveSingleObj for each of the n objectives. $\qquad\square$

4   General Lexicographic SGs

We now consider Ω where $S_i \subseteq \mathsf{Sinks}(\mathcal{G})$ does *not* necessarily hold. Section 4.1 describes how we can reduce these general lex-objectives to the absorbing case. The resulting algorithm is given in Sect. 4.2 and the theoretical implications in Sect. 4.3.

4.1   Reducing General Lexicographic SGs to SGs with Absorbing Targets

In general lexicographic SG, strategies need memory, because they need to remember which of the S_i have already been visited and behave accordingly. We formalize the solution of such games by means of *stages*. Intuitively, one can think of a stage as a copy of the game with less objectives, or as the sub-game that is played after visiting some previously unseen set S_i.

Definition 6 (Stage). *Given an arbitrary lex-objective $\Omega = (\Omega_1, \dots, \Omega_n)$ and a set $I \subseteq \{i \le n\}$, a stage $\Omega(I)$ is the objective vector where the objectives Ω_i are removed for all $i \in I$.*

For state $s \in S$, let $\Omega(s) = \Omega(\{i \mid s \in S_i\})$. If a stage contains only one objective, we call it simple.

Example 8 (Stages). Consider the SG in Fig. 2a. As there are two objectives, there are four possible stages: The one where we consider both objectives (the region denoted with Ω in Fig. 2b), the *simple* ones where we consider only one of the objectives (regions $\Omega(\{1\})$ and $\Omega(\{2\})$), and the one where both objectives have been visited. The last stage is trivial since there are no more objectives, hence we do not depict it and do not have to consider it. The actions of q and r are omitted in the Ω-stage, as upon visiting these states, a new stage begins.

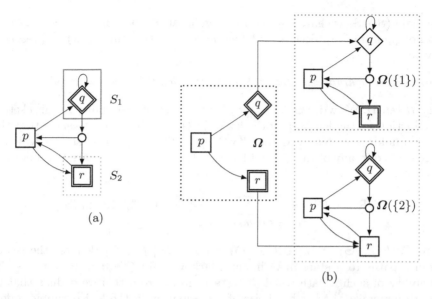

Fig. 2. (a) SG with non-absorbing lex-objective $\Omega = (\text{Reach }(S_1), \text{Reach }(S_2))$. (b) The three stages identified by the sub-objectives Ω, $\Omega(\{1\}) = (\text{Reach }(S_2))$ and $\Omega(\{2\}) = (\text{Reach }(S_1))$. The two stages on the right are both *simple*.

Consider the simple stages: in stage $\Omega(\{1\})$, q has value 0, as it is a Min-state and will use the self-loop to avoid reaching $r \in S_2$. In stage $\Omega(\{2\})$, both p and r have value 1, as they can just go to the target state $q \in S_1$. Combining this knowledge, we can get an optimal strategy for every state. In particular, note that an optimal strategy for state p needs memory: First go to r and thereby reach stage $\Omega(\{2\})$. Afterwards, go from r to p and now, on the second visit in a different stage, use the other action in p to reach q. In this example, we observe another interesting fact about lexicographic games: it can be optimal to first satisfy less important objectives.   △

In the example, we combined our knowledge of the sub-stages to find the lex-values for the whole lex-objective. In general, the values for the stages are numbers in $[0, 1]$. Thus we reuse the idea of *quantified* reachability and safety objectives, see Definition 5.

For all $1 \le i \le n$, let $q_i \colon \bigcup_{j \le n} S_j \to [0, 1]$ by defined by:

$$q_i(s) = \begin{cases} 1 & \text{if } s \in S_i \text{ and else:} \\ {}^{\Omega(s)}\mathbf{v}_i^{\text{lex}}(s) & \text{if } \Omega_i \text{ is reachability} \\ 1 - {}^{\Omega(s)}\mathbf{v}_i^{\text{lex}}(s) & \text{if } \Omega_i \text{ is safety.} \end{cases}$$

To keep the correct type of every objective, we let $\mathsf{q}\Omega = (\text{type}_1(q_1), \dots, \text{type}_n(q_n))$ where for all $1 \le i \le n$, $\text{type}_i = \text{Reach}$ if $\Omega_i = \text{Reach }(S_i)$ and else $\text{type}_i = \text{Safe}$ if

$\Omega_i = \mathsf{Safe}\ (S_i)$. So we have now reduced a general lexicographic objective Ω to a vector of quantitative objectives $\mathsf{q}\Omega$. Lemma 4 shows that this reduction preserves the values.

Lemma 4. *For arbitrary lex-objectives Ω it holds that $^{\Omega}\mathbf{v}^{\mathsf{lex}} = {}^{\mathsf{q}\Omega}\mathbf{v}^{\mathsf{lex}}$.*

Proof (Sketch). We write $\mathfrak{S} = \bigcup_{j \leq n} S_j$ for the sake of readability in this sketch. By induction on the length n of the lex-objective Ω, it is easy to show that the equation holds in states $s \in \mathfrak{S}$, i.e., $^{\Omega}\mathbf{v}^{\mathsf{lex}}(s) = {}^{\mathsf{q}\Omega}\mathbf{v}^{\mathsf{lex}}(s)$. For a state s which is not contained in any of the S_j, and for any strategies σ, τ we have the following equation

$$\mathbb{P}_s^{\sigma,\tau}(\mathsf{Reach}\ (S_i)) = \sum_{\pi t \in Paths_{fin}(\mathfrak{S})} \mathbb{P}_s^{\sigma,\tau}(\pi t) \cdot \mathbb{P}_{\pi t}^{\sigma,\tau}(\mathsf{Reach}\ (S_i))$$

where $Paths_{fin}(\mathfrak{S}) = \{\pi t \in ((S \setminus \mathfrak{S}) \times L)^* \times S \mid t \in \mathfrak{S}\}$ denotes the set of all finite paths to a state in $\mathfrak{S}$ in the Markov chain $\mathcal{G}^{\sigma,\tau}$ and $\mathbb{P}_s^{\sigma,\tau}(\pi t)$ is the probability of such a path when $\mathcal{G}^{\sigma,\tau}$ starts in s. From this we deduce that in order to maximize the left hand size of the equation in the lexicographic order, we should play such that we prefer reaching states in $\mathfrak{S}$ where q_i has a higher value; that is, we should maximize the QRO Reach (q_i). The argument for safety is similar and detailed in [19, Appendix A.6]. □

The functions q_i involved in $\mathsf{q}\Omega$ *all have the same domain* $\bigcup_{j \leq n} S_j$. Hence we can, as mentioned below Definition 5, consider $\mathsf{q}\Omega$ on the game where all states in $\bigcup_{j \leq n} S_j$ are sinks without changing the lex-value. This is precisely the definition of an absorbing game, and hence we can compute $^{\mathsf{q}\Omega}\mathbf{v}^{\mathsf{lex}}$ using Algorithm 1 from Sect. 3.2.

4.2   Algorithm for General SG

Algorithm 2 computes the lex-value $^{\Omega}\mathbf{v}^{\mathsf{lex}}$ for a given lexicographic objective Ω and an arbitrary SG $\mathcal{G}$. We highlight the following technical details:

- **Reduction to absorbing case:** We just have seen, that once we have the quantitative objective vector $\mathsf{q}\Omega$, we can use the algorithm for absorbing SG (Line 12).
- **Computing the quantitative objective vector:** To compute $\mathsf{q}\Omega$, the algorithm calls itself recursively on all states in the union of all target sets (Line 5–7). We annotated this recursive call "With dynamic programming", as we can reuse the results of the computations. In the worst case, we have to solve all $2^n - 1$ possible non-empty stages. Finally, given the values $^{\Omega(s)}\mathbf{v}^{\mathsf{lex}}$ for all $s \in \bigcup_{j \leq n} S_j$, we can construct the quantitative objective (Line 9 and 11) that is used for the call to `SolveAbsorbing`.
- **Termination:** Since there are finitely many objectives in Ω and in every recursive call at least one objective is removed from consideration, eventually we have a *simple* objective that can be solved by `SolveSingleObj` (Line 3).

Algorithm 2. Solve general lex-objective

Input: SG $\mathcal{G}$, lex-objective $\Omega = (\Omega_1, \ldots, \Omega_n)$
Output: Lex-values ${}^{\Omega}\mathbf{v}^{\mathsf{lex}}$, lex-optimal $\sigma \in \Sigma_{\mathsf{Max}}$ with memory of class-size $\leq 2^n - 1$

1: **procedure** SolveLex($\mathcal{G}, \Omega$)
2:     **if** Ω is *simple* **then**
3:         **return** SolveSingleObj($\mathcal{G}, \Omega_1$)
4:     **end if**

5:     **for** $s \in \bigcup_{j \leq n} S_j$ **do**
6:         $\left({}^{\Omega(s)}\mathbf{v}^{\mathsf{lex}}, {}^{\Omega(s)}\sigma\right) \leftarrow$ SolveLex($\mathcal{G}, \Omega(s)$)   ▷ With dynamic programming
7:     **end for**
8:     **for** $1 \leq i \leq n$ **do**

9:         Let $q_i \colon \bigcup_{j \leq n} S_j \to [0,1]$, $q_i(s) \leftarrow \begin{cases} 1 & \text{if } s \in S_i \text{ and else:} \\ {}^{\Omega(s)}\mathbf{v}_i^{\mathsf{lex}}(s) & \text{if type}(\Omega_i) = \mathsf{Reach} \\ 1 - {}^{\Omega(s)}\mathbf{v}_i^{\mathsf{lex}}(s) & \text{if type}(\Omega_i) = \mathsf{Safe} \end{cases}$

10:     **end for**
11:     ${}^{\mathsf{q}}\Omega \leftarrow (\mathsf{type}_1(q_1), \ldots, \mathsf{type}_n(q_n))$

12:     $\left({}^{\mathsf{q}\Omega}\mathbf{v}^{\mathsf{lex}}, {}^{\mathsf{q}\Omega}\sigma\right) \leftarrow$ SolveAbsorbing($\mathcal{G}, {}^{\mathsf{q}}\Omega$)
13:     $\sigma \leftarrow$ adhere to ${}^{\mathsf{q}\Omega}\sigma$ until some $s \in \bigcup_{j \leq n} S_j$ is reached. Then adhere to ${}^{\Omega(s)}\sigma$.
14:     **return** $\left({}^{\mathsf{q}\Omega}\mathbf{v}^{\mathsf{lex}}, \sigma\right)$
15: **end procedure**

- **Resulting strategy:** The resulting strategy is composed in Line 13: It adheres to the strategy for the quantitative query ${}^{\mathsf{q}\Omega}\sigma$ until some $s \in \bigcup_{j \leq n} S_j$ is reached. Then, to achieve the values promised by $q_i(s)$ for all i with $s \notin S_i$, it adheres to ${}^{\Omega(s)}\sigma$, the optimal strategy for stage $\Omega(s)$ obtained by the recursive call.

Corollary 1. *Given an SG $\mathcal{G}$ and an arbitrary lex-objective $\Omega = (\Omega_1, \ldots, \Omega_n)$, Algorithm 2 correctly computes the vector of lex-values $\mathbf{v}^{\mathsf{lex}}$ and a deterministic lex-optimal strategy σ of player Max which uses memory of class-size $\leq 2^n - 1$. The algorithm needs at most $2^n - 1$ calls to* SolveAbsorbing *or* SolveSingleObj.

Proof. Correctness of the algorithm and termination follows from the discussion of the algorithm, Lemma 4 and Theorem 2.   □

4.3   Theoretical Implications: Determinacy and Complexity

Theorem 3 below states that lexicographic games are *determined* for arbitrary lex-objectives Ω. Intuitively, this means that the lex-value is independent from the player who fixes their strategy first. Recall that this property does not hold for non-lexicographic multi-reachability/safety objectives [23].

Theorem 3 (Determinacy). *For general SG $\mathcal{G}$ and lex-objective Ω, it holds for all $s \in S$ that:*

$$\mathbf{v}^{\mathsf{lex}}(s) = \sup_{\sigma} \inf_{\tau} \mathbb{P}_s^{\sigma,\tau}(\Omega) = \inf_{\tau} \sup_{\sigma} \mathbb{P}_s^{\sigma,\tau}(\Omega).$$

Proof. This statement follows because single-objective games are determined [26] and Algorithm 2 obtains all values by either solving single-objective instances directly (Line 3) or calling Algorithm 1, which also reduces everything to the single-objective case (Line 5 of Algorithm 1). Thus the sup-inf values $\mathbf{v}^{\text{lex}}$ returned by the algorithm are in fact equal to the inf-sup values.   □

By analyzing Algorithm 2, we also get the following complexity results:

Theorem 4 (Complexity). *For any SG $\mathcal{G}$ and lex-objective $\Omega = (\Omega_1, \ldots, \Omega_n)$:*

1. Strategy complexity: *Deterministic strategies with $2^n - 1$ memory-classes (i.e., bit-size n) are sufficient and necessary for lex-optimal strategies.*
2. Computational complexity: *The lex-game decision problem ($\mathbf{v}^{\text{lex}}(s_0) \geq_{\text{lex}} \boldsymbol{x}$?) is* PSPACE-*hard and can be solved in* NEXPTIME ∩ coNEXPTIME. *If n is a constant or Ω is absorbing, then it is contained in* NP ∩ coNP.

Proof. 1. For each stage, Algorithm 2 computes an MD strategy for the quantitative objective. These strategies are then concatenated whenever a new stage is entered. Equivalently, every stage has an MD strategy for every state, so as there are at most $2^n - 1$ stages (since there are n objectives), the strategy needs at most $2^n - 1$ states of memory; these can be represented with n bits. Intuitively, we save for every target set whether it has been visited. The memory lower bound already holds in non-stochastic reachability games where all n targets have to be visited with certainty [30].

2. The work of [41] shows that in MDPs, it is PSPACE-hard to decide if n targets can be visited almost-surely. This problem trivially reduces to ours. For the NP upper bound, observe that there are at most $2^n - 1$ stages, i.e., a constant amount if n is assumed to be constant (or even just one stage if Ω is absorbing). Thus we can guess an MD strategy for player Max in every stage. The guessed overall strategy can then be checked by analyzing the induced MDP in polynomial time [29]. The same procedure works for player Min and since the game is determined, we have membership in coNP. In the same way we obtain the NEXPTIME ∩ coNEXPTIME upper bound in the general case where n is arbitrary.   □

We leave the question whether PSPACE is also an upper bound open. The main obstacle towards proving PSPACE-membership is that it is unclear if the lex-value – being dependent on the value of *exponentially* many stages in the worst-case – may actually have exponential bit-complexity.

5 Experimental Evaluation

In this section, we report the results of a series of experiments made with a prototypical implementation of our algorithm.

Case Studies. We have considered the following case studies for our experiments:

Dice. This example is shipped with PRISM-games [37] and models a simple dice game between two players. The number of throws in this game is a configurable parameter, which we instantiate with 10, 20 and 50. The game has three possible outcomes: Player Max wins, Player Min wins or draw. A natural lex-objective is thus to maximize the winning probability and then the probability of a draw.

Charlton. This case study [24] is also included in PRISM-games. It models an autonomous car navigating through a road network. A natural lex-objective is to minimize the probability of an accident (possibly damaging human life) and then maximize the probability to reach the destination.

Hallway (HW). This instance is based on the Hallway example standard in the AI literature [15,38]. A robot can move north, east, south or west in a known environment, but each move only succeeds with a certain probability and otherwise rotates or moves the robot in an undesired direction. We extend the example by a target wandering around based on a mixture of probabilistic and demonic non-deterministic behavior, thereby obtaining a stochastic game modeling for instance a panicking human in a building on fire. Moreover, we assume a 0.01 probability of damaging the robot when executing certain movements; the damaged robot's actions succeed with even smaller probability. The primary objective is to save the human and the secondary objective is to avoid damaging the robot. We use square grid-worlds of sizes 5×5, 8×8 and 10×10.

Avoid the Observer (AV). This case study is inspired by a similar example in [14]. It models a game between an intruder and an observer in a grid-world. The grid can have different sizes as in HW, and we use 10×10, 15×15 and 20×20. The most important objective of the intruder is to avoid the observer, its secondary objective is to exit the grid. We assume that the observer can only detect the intruder within a certain distance and otherwise makes random moves. At every position, the intruder moreover has the option to stay and search to find a precious item. In our example, this occurs with probability 0.1 and is assumed to be the third objective.

Implementation and Experimental Results. We have implemented our algorithm within PRISM-games [37]. Since PRISM-games does not provide an *exact* algorithm to solve SGs, we used the available value iteration to implement our single-objective blackbox. Note that since this value iteration is not exact for single-objective SGs, we cannot compute the exact lex-values. Nevertheless, we can still measure the overhead introduced by our algorithm compared to a single-objective solver.

In our implementation, value iteration stops if the values do not change by more than 10^{-8} per iteration, which is PRISM's default configuration. The experiments were conducted on a 2.4 GHz Quad-Core Intel© Core™ i5 processor, with 4 GB of RAM available to the Java VM. The results are reported in Table 1. We only recorded the run time of the actual algorithms; the time needed to parse and build the model is excluded. All numbers are rounded to full seconds. All instances (even those with state spaces of order 10^6) could be solved within a few minutes.

Table 1. Experimental Results. The two leftmost columns of the table show the type of the lex-objective, the name of the case studies, possibly with scaling parameters, and the number of states in the model. The next three columns give the verification times (excluding time to parse and build the model), rounded to full seconds. The final three columns provide the average number of actions for the original SG as well as all considered subgames $\widetilde{\mathcal{G}}$ in the main stage, and lastly the fraction of stages considered, i.e. the stages solved by the algorithm compared to the theoretically maximal possible number of stages $(2^n - 1)$.

Model	$|S|$	Time			Avg. actions		Stages
		Lex.	First	All	$\mathcal{G}$	$\widetilde{\mathcal{G}}$	
R − R							
Dice[10]	4,855	<1	<1	<1	1.42	1.41	1/3
Dice[20]	16,915	<1	<1	<1	1.45	1.45	1/3
Dice[50]	96,295	3	2	2	1.48	1.48	1/3
S − R							
Charlton	502	<1	<1	<1	1.56	1.07	3/3
R − S							
HW[5 × 5]	25,000	10	7.15	7	2.44	1.02	3/3
HW[8 × 8]	163,840	152	117	117	2.50	1.01	3/3
HW[10 × 10]	400,000	548	435	435	2.52	1.01	3/3
S–R–R							
AV[10 × 10]	106,524	15	<1	10	2.17	1.55, 1.36	4/7
AV[15 × 15]	480,464	85	<1	50	2.14	1.52, 1.36	4/7
AV[20 × 20]	1,436,404	281	3	172	2.13	1.51, 1.37	4/7

The case studies are grouped by the type of lex-objective, where R indicates reachability, S safety. For each combination of case study and scaling parameters, we report the state size in column $|S|$, three different model checking runtimes, the average number of actions in the original and all considered restricted games, and the fraction of stages considered, i.e. the stages solved by the algorithm compared to the theoretically maximal possible number of stages $(2^n - 1)$.

We compare the time of our algorithm on the lexicographic objective (Lex.) to the time for checking the first single objective (First) and the sum of checking all single objectives (All). We see that the runtimes of our algorithm and checking all single objectives are always in the same order of magnitude. This shows that our algorithm works well in practice and that the overhead is often small. Even on SGs of non-trivial size (HW[10 × 10] and AV[20 × 20]), our algorithm returns the result within a few minutes.

Regarding the average number of actions, we see that the decrease in the number of actions in the sub-games $\widetilde{\mathcal{G}}$ obtained by restricting the input game to optimal actions varies: For example, very few actions are removed in the Dice instances, in AV we have a moderate decrease and in HW a significant decrease, almost eliminating all non-determinism after the first objective. It is our intuition that the less actions are removed, the higher is the overhead compared to the individual single-objective solutions. Consider the AV and HW examples: While for AV$[20 \times 20]$, computing the lexicographic solution takes 1.7 times as long as all the single-objective solutions, it took only about 25% longer for HW$[10 \times 10]$; this could be because in HW, after the first objective only little nondeterminism remains, while in AV also for the second and third objectives lots of choices have to be considered. Note that the first objective sometimes (HW), but not always (AV) needs the majority of the runtime.

We also see that the algorithm does not have to explore all possible stages. For example, for Dice we always just need a single stage, because the SG is absorbing. For charlton and HW all stages are relevant for the lex-objective, while for AV 4 of 7 need to be considered.

6 Conclusion and Future Work

In this work we considered simple stochastic games with lexicographic reachability and safety objectives. Simple stochastic games are a standard model in reactive synthesis of stochastic systems, and lexicographic objectives let one consider multiple objectives with an order of preference. We focused on the most basic objectives: safety and reachability. While simple stochastic games with lexicographic objectives have not been studied before, we have presented (a) determinacy; (b) strategy complexity; (c) computational complexity; and (d) algorithms; for these games. Moreover, we showed how these games can model many different case studies and we present experimental results for them.

There are several directions for future work. First, for the general case closing the complexity gap (NEXPTIME∩coNEXPTIME upper bound and PSPACE lower bound) is an open question. Second, the study of lexicographic simple stochastic games with more general objectives, e.g., quantitative or parity objectives poses interesting questions. In particular, in the case of parity objectives, there are some indications that the problem is significantly harder: Consider the case of a reachability-safety lex-objective. If the lex-value is $(1, 1)$ then both objectives can be guaranteed almost surely. Since almost-sure safety is sure safety, our results imply that sure safety and almost-sure reachability can be achieved with constant memory. In contrast, for parity objectives the combination of sure and almost-sure requires infinite-memory (e.g, see [21, Appendix A.1]).

References

1. Altman, E.: Constrained Markov Decision Processes. CRC Presss, Boca Raton (1999)

2. Baier, C., Dubslaff, C., Klüppelholz, S.: Trade-off analysis meets probabilistic model checking. In: CSL-LICS, pp. 1:1–1:10 (2014)
3. Baier, C., et al.: Probabilistic model checking and non-standard multi-objective reasoning. In: Gnesi, S., Rensink, A. (eds.) FASE 2014. LNCS, vol. 8411, pp. 1–16. Springer, Heidelberg (2014). https://doi.org/10.1007/978-3-642-54804-8_1
4. Baier, C., Katoen, J.P.: Principles of Model Checking. MIT Press, Cambridge (2008)
5. Basset, N., Kwiatkowska, M., Topcu, U., Wiltsche, C.: Strategy synthesis for stochastic games with multiple long-run objectives. In: Baier, C., Tinelli, C. (eds.) TACAS 2015. LNCS, vol. 9035, pp. 256–271. Springer, Heidelberg (2015). https://doi.org/10.1007/978-3-662-46681-0_22
6. Bloem, R., Chatterjee, K., Henzinger, T.A., Jobstmann, B.: Better quality in synthesis through quantitative objectives. In: Bouajjani, A., Maler, O. (eds.) CAV 2009. LNCS, vol. 5643, pp. 140–156. Springer, Heidelberg (2009). https://doi.org/10.1007/978-3-642-02658-4_14
7. Blume, L., Brandenburger, A., Dekel, E.: Lexicographic probabilities and choice under uncertainty. Econometrica J. Econ. Soc. **59**(1), 61–79 (1991)
8. Brázdil, T., Brozek, V., Chatterjee, K., Forejt, V., Kucera, A.: Two views on multiple mean-payoff objectives in Markov decision processes. LMCS **10**(1) (2014). https://doi.org/10.2168/LMCS-10(1:13)2014
9. Brázdil, T., Chatterjee, K., Forejt, V., Kucera, A.: Trading performance for stability in Markov decision processes. In: LICS, pp. 331–340 (2013)
10. Brázdil, T., Chatterjee, K., Forejt, V., Kučera, A.: MultiGain: a controller synthesis tool for MDPs with multiple mean-payoff objectives. In: Baier, C., Tinelli, C. (eds.) TACAS 2015. LNCS, vol. 9035, pp. 181–187. Springer, Heidelberg (2015). https://doi.org/10.1007/978-3-662-46681-0_12
11. Bruyère, V., Filiot, E., Randour, M., Raskin, J.: Meet your expectations with guarantees: beyond worst-case synthesis in quantitative games. Inf. Comput. **254**, 259–295 (2017)
12. Bruyère, V., Hautem, Q., Raskin, J.: Parameterized complexity of games with monotonically ordered omega-regular objectives. CoRR abs/1707.05968 (2017)
13. Chatterjee, K.: Markov decision processes with multiple long-run average objectives. In: Arvind, V., Prasad, S. (eds.) FSTTCS 2007. LNCS, vol. 4855, pp. 473–484. Springer, Heidelberg (2007). https://doi.org/10.1007/978-3-540-77050-3_39
14. Chatterjee, K., Chmelík, M.: POMDPs under probabilistic semantics. Artif. Intell. **221**, 46–72 (2015). https://doi.org/10.1016/j.artint.2014.12.009
15. Chatterjee, K., Chmelik, M., Gupta, R., Kanodia, A.: Optimal cost almost-sure reachability in POMDPs. Artif. Intell. **234**, 26–48 (2016). https://doi.org/10.1016/j.artint.2016.01.007
16. Chatterjee, K., Doyen, L.: Perfect-information stochastic games with generalized mean-payoff objectives. In: LICS. pp. 247–256. ACM (2016)
17. Chatterjee, K., Forejt, V., Wojtczak, D.: Multi-objective discounted reward verification in graphs and MDPs. In: McMillan, K., Middeldorp, A., Voronkov, A. (eds.) LPAR 2013. LNCS, vol. 8312, pp. 228–242. Springer, Heidelberg (2013). https://doi.org/10.1007/978-3-642-45221-5_17
18. Chatterjee, K., Henzinger, T.A.: A survey of stochastic ω-regular games. J. Comput. Syst. Sci. **78**(2), 394–413 (2012)
19. Chatterjee, K., Katoen, J.P., Weininger, M., Winkler, T.: Stochastic games with lexicographic reachability-safety objectives. CoRR abs/2005.04018 (2020). http://arxiv.org/abs/2005.04018

20. Chatterjee, K., Kretínská, Z., Kretínský, J.: Unifying two views on multiple mean-payoff objectives in Markov decision processes. LMCS **13**(2) (2017). https://doi.org/10.23638/LMCS-13(2:15)2017

21. Chatterjee, K., Piterman, N.: Combinations of qualitative winning for stochastic parity games. CoRR abs/1804.03453 (2018). http://arxiv.org/abs/1804.03453

22. Chatterjee, K., Sen, K., Henzinger, T.A.: Model-checking ω-regular properties of interval Markov chains. In: Amadio, R. (ed.) FoSSaCS 2008. LNCS, vol. 4962, pp. 302–317. Springer, Heidelberg (2008). https://doi.org/10.1007/978-3-540-78499-9_22

23. Chen, T., Forejt, V., Kwiatkowska, M., Simaitis, A., Wiltsche, C.: On stochastic games with multiple objectives. In: Chatterjee, K., Sgall, J. (eds.) MFCS 2013. LNCS, vol. 8087, pp. 266–277. Springer, Heidelberg (2013). https://doi.org/10.1007/978-3-642-40313-2_25

24. Chen, T., Kwiatkowska, M., Simaitis, A., Wiltsche, C.: Synthesis for multi-objective stochastic games: an application to autonomous urban driving. In: Joshi, K., Siegle, M., Stoelinga, M., D'Argenio, P.R. (eds.) QEST 2013. LNCS, vol. 8054, pp. 322–337. Springer, Heidelberg (2013). https://doi.org/10.1007/978-3-642-40196-1_28

25. Colcombet, T., Jurdzinski, M., Lazic, R., Schmitz, S.: Perfect half space games. In: Logic in Computer Science, LICS 2017, pp. 1–11 (2017)

26. Condon, A.: The complexity of stochastic games. Inf. Comput. **96**(2), 203–224 (1992). https://doi.org/10.1016/0890-5401(92)90048-K

27. Dehnert, C., Junges, S., Katoen, J.-P., Volk, M.: A STORM is coming: a modern probabilistic model checker. In: Majumdar, R., Kunčak, V. (eds.) CAV 2017, Part II. LNCS, vol. 10427, pp. 592–600. Springer, Cham (2017). https://doi.org/10.1007/978-3-319-63390-9_31

28. Delgrange, F., Katoen, J.-P., Quatmann, T., Randour, M.: Simple strategies in multi-objective MDPs. In: Biere, A., Parker, D. (eds.) TACAS 2020. LNCS, vol. 12078, pp. 346–364. Springer, Cham (2020). https://doi.org/10.1007/978-3-030-45190-5_19

29. Etessami, K., Kwiatkowska, M.Z., Vardi, M.Y., Yannakakis, M.: Multi-objective model checking of Markov decision processes. LMCS **4**(4) (2008). https://doi.org/10.2168/LMCS-4(4:8)2008

30. Fijalkow, N., Horn, F.: The surprizing complexity of generalized reachability games. arXiv:1010.2420 [cs], October 2010

31. Filar, J., Vrieze, K.: Competitive Markov Decision Processes. Springer, New York (1997). https://doi.org/10.1007/978-1-4612-4054-9

32. Filar, J., Krass, D., Ross, K.: Percentile performance criteria for limiting average Markov decision processes. IEEE Trans. Autom. Control. **40**(1), 2–10 (1995)

33. Fishburn, P.C.: Exceptional paper – lexicographic orders, utilities and decision rules: a survey. Manag. Sci. **20**(11), 1442–1471 (1974)

34. Forejt, V., Kwiatkowska, M., Norman, G., Parker, D., Qu, H.: Quantitative multi-objective verification for probabilistic systems. In: Abdulla, P.A., Leino, K.R.M. (eds.) TACAS 2011. LNCS, vol. 6605, pp. 112–127. Springer, Heidelberg (2011). https://doi.org/10.1007/978-3-642-19835-9_11

35. Hartmanns, A., Junges, S., Katoen, J.-P., Quatmann, T.: Multi-cost bounded reachability in MDP. In: Beyer, D., Huisman, M. (eds.) TACAS 2018, Part II. LNCS, vol. 10806, pp. 320–339. Springer, Cham (2018). https://doi.org/10.1007/978-3-319-89963-3_19

36. Hoffman, A.J., Karp, R.M.: On nonterminating stochastic games. Manag. Sci. **12**(5), 359–370 (1966). https://doi.org/10.1287/mnsc.12.5.359

37. Kwiatkowska, M., Parker, D., Wiltsche, C.: PRISM-games: verification and strategy synthesis for stochastic multi-player games with multiple objectives. STTT **20**(2), 195–210 (2018). https://doi.org/10.1007/s10009-017-0476-z
38. Littman, M.L., Cassandra, A.R., Kaelbling, L.P.: Learning policies for partially observable environments: scaling up. In: ICML, pp. 362–370. Morgan Kaufmann (1995)
39. Puterman, M.L.: Markov Decision Processes: Discrete Stochastic Dynamic Programming. Wiley, Hoboken (2014)
40. Quatmann, T., Junges, S., Katoen, J.-P.: Markov automata with multiple objectives. In: Majumdar, R., Kunčak, V. (eds.) CAV 2017, Part I. LNCS, vol. 10426, pp. 140–159. Springer, Cham (2017). https://doi.org/10.1007/978-3-319-63387-9_7
41. Randour, M., Raskin, J.-F., Sankur, O.: Percentile queries in multi-dimensional Markov decision processes. Form. Methods Syst. Des. **50**(2–3), 207–248 (2017). https://doi.org/10.1007/s10703-016-0262-7
42. Roijers, D.M., Whiteson, S.: Multi-objective decision making. Synth. Lect. Artif. Intell. Mach. Learn. **11**(1), 1–129 (2017)
43. Svorenová, M., Kwiatkowska, M.: Quantitative verification and strategy synthesis for stochastic games. Eur. J. Control **30**, 15–30 (2016). https://doi.org/10.1016/j.ejcon.2016.04.009
44. Tarski, A.: A lattice-theoretical fixpoint theorem and its applications. Pacific J. Math. **5**(2), 285–309 (1955). https://doi.org/10.2140/pjm.1955.5.285
45. Weininger, M., Meggendorfer, T., Křetínský, J.: Satisfiability bounds for ω-regular properties in bounded-parameter Markov decision processes. In: CDC (2019, to appear)
46. Wray, K.H., Zilberstein, S.: Multi-objective POMDPs with lexicographic reward preferences. In: IJCAI, pp. 1719–1725. AAAI Press (2015)
47. Wray, K.H., Zilberstein, S., Mouaddib, A.: Multi-objective MDPs with conditional lexicographic reward preferences. In: AAAI, pp. 3418–3424. AAAI Press (2015)

Qualitative Controller Synthesis for Consumption Markov Decision Processes

František Blahoudek[1], Tomáš Brázdil[2], Petr Novotný[2], Melkior Ornik[3],
Pranay Thangeda[3(✉)], and Ufuk Topcu[1]

[1] The University of Texas at Austin, Austin, USA
frantisek.blahoudek@gmail.com,
utopcu@utexas.edu
[2] Masaryk University, Brno, Czech Republic
{xbrazdil,petr.novotny}@fi.muni.cz
[3] University of Illinois at Urbana-Champaign, Urbana, USA
{mornik,pranayt2}@illinois.edu

Abstract. Consumption Markov Decision Processes (CMDPs) are probabilistic decision-making models of resource-constrained systems. In a CMDP, the controller possesses a certain amount of a critical resource, such as electric power. Each action of the controller can consume some amount of the resource. Resource replenishment is only possible in special *reload states,* in which the resource level can be reloaded up to the full capacity of the system. The task of the controller is to prevent resource exhaustion, i.e. ensure that the available amount of the resource stays non-negative, while ensuring an additional linear-time property. We study the complexity of strategy synthesis in consumption MDPs with almost-sure Büchi objectives. We show that the problem can be solved in polynomial time. We implement our algorithm and show that it can efficiently solve CMDPs modelling real-world scenarios.

1 Introduction

In the context of formal methods, controller synthesis typically boils down to computing a strategy in an *agent-environment* model, a nondeterministic state-transition model where some of the nondeterministic choices are resolved by the controller and some by an uncontrollable environment. Such models are typically either two-player graph games with an adversarial environment or Markov decision process (MDPs); the latter case being apt for modelling statistically predictable environments. In this paper, we consider controller synthesis for *resource-constrained MDPs*, where the computed controller must ensure, in addition to satisfying some linear-time property, that the system's operation is not compromised by a lack of necessary resources.

This work was partially supported by NASA under Early Stage Innovations grant No. 80NSSC19K0209, and by DARPA under grant No. HR001120C0065. Petr Novotný is supported by the Czech Science Foundation grant No. GJ19-15134Y.

S. K. Lahiri and C. Wang (Eds.): CAV 2020, LNCS 12225, pp. 421–447, 2020.
https://doi.org/10.1007/978-3-030-53291-8_22

Resource-Constrained Probabilistic Systems. Resource-constrained systems need a supply of some resource (e.g. power) for steady operation: the interruption of the supply can lead to undesirable consequences and has to be avoided. For instance, an autonomous system, e.g. an autonomous electric vehicle (*AEV*), is not able to draw power directly from an endless source. Instead, it has to rely on an internal storage of the resource, e.g. a battery, which has to be replenished in regular intervals to prevent resource exhaustion. Practical examples of AEVs include driverless cars, drones, or planetary rovers [8]. In these domains, resource failures may cause a costly mission failure and even safety risks. Moreover, the operation of autonomous systems is subject to probabilistic uncertainty [54]. Hence, in this paper, we study the resource-constrained strategy synthesis problem for MDPs.

Models of Resource-Constrained Systems & Limitations of Current Approaches. There is a substantial body of work in the area of verification of resource-constrained systems [3,5,7,9,11,23,38,39,53,58]. The typical approach is to model them as finite-state systems augmented with an integer-valued counter representing the current *resource level,* i.e. the amount of the resource present in the internal storage. The resource constraint requires that the resource level never drops below zero.[1] In the well-known *energy* model [11,23], each transition is labelled by an integer, and performing an ℓ-labelled transition results in ℓ being added to the counter. Thus, negative numbers stand for resource consumption while positive ones represent re-charging by the respective amount. Many variants of both MDP and game-based energy models were studied, as detailed in the related work. In particular, [26] considers controller synthesis for energy MDPs with qualitative Büchi and parity objectives. The main limitation of energy-based agent-environment models is that in general, they are not known to admit polynomial-time controller synthesis algorithms. Indeed, already the simplest problem, deciding whether a non-negative energy can be maintained in a two-player energy game, is at least as hard as solving mean-payoff graph games [11]; the complexity of the latter being a well-known open problem [45]. This hardness translates also to MDPs [26], making polynomial-time controller synthesis for energy MDPs impossible without a theoretical breakthrough.

   Consumption models, introduced in [14], offer an alternative to energy models. In a consumption model, a non-negative integer, *cap,* represents the maximal amount of the resource the system can hold, e.g. the battery capacity. Each transition is labelled by a non-negative number representing the amount of the resource *consumed* when taking the transition (i.e., taking an ℓ-labelled transition decreases the resource level by ℓ). The resource replenishment is different from the energy approach. The consumption approach relies on the fact that reloads are often *atomic events,* e.g. an AEV plugging into a charging station and waiting to finish the charging cycle. Hence, some states in the consumption model are designated as *reload states,* and whenever the system visits a

---

[1] In some literature, the level is required to stay positive as opposed to non-negative, but this is only a matter of definition: both approaches are equivalent.

reload state, the resource level is replenished to the full capacity *cap*. Modelling reloads as atomic events is natural and even advantageous: consumption models typically admit more efficient analysis than energy models [14,47]. However, consumption models have not yet been considered in the probabilistic setting.

Our Contribution. We study strategy synthesis in consumption MDPs with Büchi objectives. Our main theoretical result is stated in the following theorem.

Theorem 1. *Given a consumption MDP $\mathcal{M}$ with a capacity cap, an initial resource level $0 \leq d \leq cap$, and a set T of accepting states, we can decide, in polynomial time, whether there exists a strategy σ such that when playing according to σ, the following* consumption-Büchi objectives *are satisfied:*

- *Starting with resource level d, the resource level never[2] drops below 0.*
- *With probability 1, the system visits some state in T infinitely often.*

Moreover, if such a strategy exists then we can compute, in polynomial time, its polynomial-size representation.

For the sake of clarity, we restrict to proving Theorem 1 for a natural sub-class of MDPs called *decreasing consumption MDPs,* where there are no cycles of zero consumption. The restriction is natural (since in typical resource-constrained systems, each action – even idling – consumes some energy, so zero cycles are unlikely) and greatly simplifies presentation. In addition to the theoretical analysis, we implemented the algorithm behind Theorem 1 and evaluated it on several benchmarks, including a realistic model of an AEV navigating the streets of Manhattan. The experiments show that our algorithm is able to efficiently solve large CMDPs, offering a good scalability.

Significance. Some comments on Theorem 1 are in order. First, all the numbers in the MDP, and in particular the capacity *cap*, are encoded in binary. Hence, "polynomial time" means time polynomial in the encoding size of the MDP itself and in $\log(cap)$. In particular, a naive "unfolding" of the MDP, i.e. encoding the resource levels between 0 and *cap* into the states, does not yield a polynomial-time algorithm, but an exponential-time one, since the unfolded MDP has size proportional to *cap*. We employ a value-iteration-like algorithm to compute minimal energy levels with which one can achieve the consumption-Büchi objectives.

A similar concern applies to the "polynomial-size representation" of the strategy σ. To satisfy a consumption-Büchi objective, σ generally needs to keep track of the current resource level. Hence, under the standard notion of a finite-memory (FM) strategy (which views FM strategies as transducers), σ would require memory proportional to *cap*, i.e. a memory exponentially large w.r.t. size of the input. However, we show that for each state s we can partition the integer interval $[0, \ldots, cap]$ into polynomially many sub-intervals $I_1^s, \ldots, I_k^s$ such that, for each $1 \leq j \leq k$, the strategy σ picks the same action whenever the current state is

---

[2] In our model, this is equivalent to requiring that with probability 1, the resource level never drops below 0.

s and the current resource level is in I_j^s. As such, the endpoints of the intervals are the only extra knowledge required to represent σ, a representation which we call a *counter selector*. We instrument our main algorithm so as to compute, in polynomial time, a polynomial-size counter selector representing the witness strategy σ.

Finally, we consider linear-time properties encoded by Büchi objectives over the states of the MDP. In essence, we assume that the translation of the specification to the Büchi automaton and its product with the original MDP model of the system were already performed. Probabilistic analysis typically requires the use of deterministic Büchi automata, which cannot express all linear-time properties. However, in this paper we consider qualitative analysis, which can be performed using restricted versions of non-deterministic Büchi automata that are still powerful enough to express all ω-regular languages. Examples of such automata are limit-deterministic Büchi automata [51] or good-for-MDPs automata [41]. Alternatively, consumption MDPs with parity objectives could be reduced to consumption-Büchi MPDs using the standard parity-to-Büchi MDP construction [25, 30, 32, 33]. We abstract from these aspects and focus on the technical core of our problem, solving consumption-Büchi MDPs.

Consequently, to our best knowledge, we present the first polynomial-time algorithm for controller synthesis in resource-constrained MDPs with ω-regular objectives.

Related Work. There is an enormous body of work on energy models. Stemming from the models introduced in [11, 23], the subsequent work covered energy games with various combinations of objectives [10, 12, 13, 18, 20, 21, 27, 48], energy games with multiple resource types [15, 24, 28, 31, 37, 43, 44, 57] or the variants of the above in the MDP [17, 49], infinite-state [1], or partially observable [34] settings. As argued previously, the controller synthesis within these models is at least as hard as solving mean-payoff games. The paper [29] presents polynomial-time algorithms for non-stochastic energy games with special weight structures. Recently, an abstract algebraic perspective on energy models was presented in [22, 35, 36].

Consumption systems were introduced in [14] in the form of consumption games with multiple resource types. Minimizing mean-payoff in automata with consumption constraints was studied in [16].

Our main result requires, as a technical sub-component, solving the *resource-safety* (or just *safety*) problem in consumption MDPs, i.e. computing a strategy which prevents resource exhaustion. The solution to this problem consists (in principle) of a Turing reduction to the problem of minimum cost reachability in two-player games with non-negative costs. The latter problem was studied in [46], with an extension to arbitrary costs considered in [19] (see also [40]). We present our own, conceptually simple, value-iteration-like algorithm for the problem, which is also used in our implementation.

Elements of resource-constrained optimization and minimum-cost reachability are also present in the line of work concerning *energy-utility quantiles* in MDPs [4–7, 42]. In this setting, there is no reloading in the consumption- or energy-model sense, and the task is typically to minimize the total amount of the resource consumed while maximizing the probability that some other objective is satisfied.

Paper Organization & Outline of Techniques. After the preliminaries (Sect. 2), we present counter selectors in Sect. 3. The next three sections contain the three main steps of our analysis. In Sect. 4, we solve the safety problem in consumption MDPs. The technical core of our approach is presented in Sect. 5, where we solve the problem of *safe positive reachability*: finding a resource-safe strategy which ensures that the set T of accepting states is visited with positive probability. Solving consumption-Büchi MDPs then, in principle, consists of repeatedly applying a strategy for safe positive reachability of T, ensuring that the strategy is "re-started" whenever the attempt to reach T fails. Details are given in Sect. 6. Finally, Sect. 7 presents our experiments. Due to space constraints, most technical proofs were moved to the full version.

2   Preliminaries

We denote by $\mathbb{N}$ the set of all non-negative integers and by $\overline{\mathbb{N}}$ the set $\mathbb{N} \cup \{\infty\}$. Given a set I and a vector $\mathbf{v} \in \overline{\mathbb{N}}^I$ of integers indexed by I, we use $\mathbf{v}(i)$ to denote the i-component of $\mathbf{v}$. We assume familiarity with basic notions of probability theory. In particular, a *probability distribution* on an at most countable set X is a function $f: X \to [0,1]$ s.t. $\sum_{x \in X} f(x) = 1$. We use $\mathcal{D}(X)$ to denote the set of all probability distributions on X.

Definition 1 (CMDP). *A consumption Markov decision process (CMDP) is a tuple $M = (S, A, \Delta, C, R, cap)$ where S is a finite set of states, A is a finite set of actions, $\Delta: S \times A \to \mathcal{D}(S)$ is a total transition function, $C: S \times A \to \mathbb{N}$ is a total consumption function, $R \subseteq S$ is a set of reload states where the resource can be reloaded, and cap is a resource capacity.*

Figure 1 shows a visual representation of an CMDP. We denote by $M(R')$ for $R' \subseteq S$ the CMDP obtained from M by changing the set of reloads to R'. For

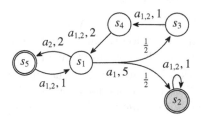

Distributions in Δ are indicated by gray numbers (we leave out 1 when an action has only one successor), and the cost of an action follows its name in the edge labels. Actions labeled by $a_{1,2}$ represent that Δ and C are defined identically for both actions a_1 and a_2. The blue background indicates a target set $T = \{s_2\}$, while the double circles represent the reload states.

Fig. 1. CMDP $M = (\{s_1, s_2, s_3, s_4, s_5\}, \{a_1, a_2\}, \Delta, C, \{s_2, s_5\}, 20)$. Details are given on the right.

$s \in S$ and $a \in A$, we denote by $Succ(s,a)$ the set $\{t \mid \Delta(s,a)(t) > 0\}$. A *path* is a (finite or infinite) state-action sequence $\alpha = s_1 a_1 s_2 a_2 s_3 \cdots \in (S \times A)^\omega \cup (S \cdot A)^* \cdot S$ such that $s_{i+1} \in Succ(s_i, a_i)$ for all i. We define $\alpha_i = s_i$ and $Act^i(\alpha) = a_i$. We use $\alpha_{..i}$ for the finite prefix $s_1 a_1 \ldots s_i$ of α, $\alpha_{i..}$ for the suffix $s_i a_i \ldots$, and $\alpha_{i..j}$ for the infix $s_i a_i \ldots s_j$. A finite path is a *cycle* if it starts and ends in the same state and is *simple* if none of its infixes forms a cycle. The *length* of a path α is the number $len(\alpha)$ of actions on α and $len(\alpha) = \infty$ if α is infinite.

A CMDP is *decreasing* if for every cycle $s_1 a_1 s_2 \ldots a_{k-1} s_k$ there exists $1 \leq i < k$ such that $C(s_i, a_i) > 0$. Throughout this paper we consider only decreasing CMDPs. The only place where this assumption is used are the proofs of Theorem 4 and Theorem 8.

An infinite path is called a *run*. We typically name runs by variants of the symbol ϱ. The set of all runs in $\mathcal{M}$ is denoted $\mathsf{Runs}_{\mathcal{M}}$. A finite path is called *history*. The set of all possible histories of $\mathcal{M}$ is $hist_{\mathcal{M}}$ or simply $hist$. We use $last(\alpha)$ for the last state of α. Let α be a history with $last(\alpha) = s_1$ and $\beta = s_1 a_1 s_2 a_2 \ldots$; we define a *joint path* as $\alpha \odot \beta = \alpha a_1 s_2 a_2 \ldots$.

A *strategy* for $\mathcal{M}$ is a function $\sigma \colon hist_{\mathcal{M}} \to A$ assigning to each history an action to play. A strategy is *memoryless* if $\sigma(\alpha) = \sigma(\beta)$ whenever $last(\alpha) = last(\beta)$. We do not consider randomized strategies in this paper, as they are non-necessary for qualitative ω-regular objectives on finite MDPs [30,32,33].

A computation of $\mathcal{M}$ under the control of a given strategy σ from some initial state $s \in S$ creates a path. The path starts with $s_1 = s$. Assume that the current path is α and let $s_i = last(\alpha)$ (we say that $\mathcal{M}$ is currently in s_i). Then the next action on the path is $a_i = \sigma(\alpha)$ and the next state s_{i+1} is chosen randomly according to $\Delta(s_i, a_i)$. Repeating this process *ad infinitum* yields an infinite sample run ϱ. We say that ϱ is σ-*compatible* if it can be produced using this process, and s-*initiated* if it starts in s. We denote the set of all σ-compatible, s-initiated runs by $\mathsf{Comp}_{\mathcal{M}}(\sigma, s)$.

We denote by $\mathbb{P}^\sigma_{\mathcal{M},s}(\mathsf{A})$ the probability that a sample run from $\mathsf{Comp}_{\mathcal{M}}(\sigma, s)$ belongs to a given measurable set of runs A. For details on the formal construction of measurable sets of runs as well as the probability measure $\mathbb{P}^\sigma_{\mathcal{M},s}$ see [2]. Throughout the paper, we drop the $\mathcal{M}$ subscripts in symbols whenever $\mathcal{M}$ is known from the context.

2.1 Resource: Consumption, Levels, and Objectives

We denote by $cap(\mathcal{M})$ the battery capacity in the MDP $\mathcal{M}$. A resource is consumed along paths and can be reloaded in the reload states up to the full capacity. For a path $\alpha = s_1 a_1 s_2 \ldots$ we define the consumption of α as $cons(\alpha) = \sum_{i=1}^{len(\alpha)} C(s_i, a_i)$ (since the consumption is non-negative, the sum is always well defined, though possibly diverging). Note that $cons$ does not consider reload states at all. To accurately track the remaining amount of the resource, we use the concept of a *resource level*.

Definition 2 (Resource level). *Let $\mathcal{M}$ be a CMDP with a set of reload states R, let α be a history, and let $0 \leq d \leq cap(\mathcal{M})$ be an integer called* initial load.

Then the energy level after α initialized by d, denoted by $RL_d^{\mathcal{M}}(\alpha)$ *or simply as* $RL_d(\alpha)$, *is defined inductively as follows: for a zero-length history s we have* $RL_d^{\mathcal{M}}(s) = d$. *For a non-zero-length history* $\alpha = \beta at$ *we denote* $c = C(last(\beta), a)$, *and put*

$$
RL_d^{\mathcal{M}}(\alpha) = \begin{cases} RL_d^{\mathcal{M}}(\beta) - c & \text{if } last(\beta) \notin R \text{ and } c \leq RL_d^{\mathcal{M}}(\beta) \neq \bot \\ cap(\mathcal{M}) - c & \text{if } last(\beta) \in R \text{ and } c \leq cap(\mathcal{M}) \text{ and } RL_d^{\mathcal{M}}(\beta) \neq \bot \\ \bot & \text{otherwise} \end{cases}
$$

Consider $\mathcal{M}$ from Fig. 1 and the history $\alpha(i) = (s_1 a_2 s_5 a_2)^i s_1$ with i as a parameter. We have $cons(\alpha(i)) = 3i$ and at the same time, following the inductive definition of $RL_d(\alpha(i))$ we have $RL_2(\alpha(i)) = 19$ for all $i \geq 1$ as the resource is reloaded every time in s_5. This generalizes into the following. Let α be a history and let $f, l \geq 0$ be the minimal and maximal indices i such that $\alpha_i \in R$, respectively. For $RL_d(\alpha) \neq \bot$, it holds $RL_d(\alpha_{..i}) = d - cons(\alpha_{..i})$ for all $i \leq f$ and $RL_d(\alpha) = cap(\mathcal{M}) - cons(\alpha_{l..})$. Further, for each history α and d such that $e = RL_d(\alpha) \neq \bot$, and each history β suitable for joining with α it holds that $RL_d(\alpha \odot \beta) = RL_e(\beta)$.

A run ϱ is *d-safe* if and only if the energy level initialized by d is a non-negative number for each finite prefix of ρ, i.e. if for all $i > 0$ we have $RL_d(\varrho_{..i}) \neq \bot$. We say that a run is safe if it is $cap(\mathcal{M})$-safe. The next lemma follows immediately from the definition of an energy level.

Lemma 1. *Let* $\varrho = s_1 a_1 s_2 \ldots$ *be a d-safe run for some d and let α be a history such that $last(\alpha) = s_1$. Then the run $\alpha \odot \varrho$ is e-safe if $RL_e(\alpha) \geq d$.*

Example 1. Recall the CMDP and the parameterized history $\alpha(i)$ from above. We know that $RL_2(\alpha(i)) = 19$ for all i. Therefore, a strategy that always picks a_2 in s_1 is d-safe in s_1 for all $d \geq 2$. On the other hand, a strategy that always picks a_1 in s_1 is *not* d-safe in s_1 for any $0 \leq d \leq 20 = cap(\mathcal{M})$ because for all runs ϱ that visit s_3 at least three times before s_2 we have $RL_d(\varrho) = \bot$.

Objectives. An *objective* is a set of runs. The objective $\mathsf{SafeRuns}(d)$ contains exactly d-safe runs. Given a *target set* $T \subseteq S$ and $i \in \mathbb{N}$, we define $\mathsf{Reach}_T^i = \{\varrho \in \mathsf{Runs} \mid \varrho_j \in T \text{ for some } 1 \leq j \leq i + 1\}$ to be the set of all runs that reach some state from T within the first i steps. We put $\mathsf{Reach}_T = \bigcup_{i \in \mathbb{N}} \mathsf{Reach}_T^i$. Finally, the set $\mathsf{Büchi}_T = \{\varrho \in \mathsf{Runs} \mid \varrho_i \in T \text{ for infinitely many } i \in \mathbb{N}\}$.

Problems. We solve three main qualitative problems for CMDPs, namely *safety*, *positive reachability*, and *Büchi*.

Let us fix a state s and a target set of states T. We say that a strategy σ is *d-safe in s* if $\mathsf{Comp}(\sigma, s) \subseteq \mathsf{SafeRuns}(d)$. We say that σ is *T-positive d-safe in s* if it is d-safe in s and $\mathbb{P}_s^\sigma(\mathsf{Reach}_T) > 0$, which means that there exists a run in $\mathsf{Comp}(\sigma, s)$ that visits T. Finally, we say that σ is *T-Büchi d-safe in a state s* if it is d-safe in s and $\mathbb{P}_s^\sigma(\mathsf{Büchi}_T) = 1$.

The vectors *Safe*, *SafePR$_T$* (PR for "positive reachability"), and *SafeBüchi$_T$* of type $\overline{\mathbb{N}}^S$ contain, for each $s \in S$, the minimal d such that there exists a strategy that is d-safe in s, T-positive d-safe in s, and T-Büchi d-safe in s, respectively, and ∞ if no such strategy exists.

The problems we consider for a given CMDP are:

- *Safety:* compute the vector *Safe* and a strategy that is $Safe(s)$-safe in every $s \in S$.
- *Positive reachability:* compute the vector $SafePR_T$ and a strategy that is T-positive $SafePR_T(s)$-safe in every state s.
- *Büchi:* compute $SafeBüchi_T$ and a strategy that is T-Büchi $SafeBüchi_T(s)$-safe in every state s.

Example 2. Now consider again the d-safe strategy from Example 1 that always picks a_2; such a strategy is 2-safe in s_1, but is not useful if we attempt to eventually reach T. Hence memoryless strategies are not sufficient in our setting. Consider, instead, a strategy σ that picks a_1 in s_1 whenever the current resource level is at least 10 and picks a_2 otherwise. Such a strategy is 2-safe in s_1 and guarantees reaching s_2 with a positive probability: we need at least 10 units of energy to return to s_5 in the case we are unlucky and picking a_1 leads us to s_3. If we are lucky, a_1 leads us to s_2 by consuming just 5 units of the resource, witnessing that σ is T-positive. As a matter of fact, during *every* revisit of s_5 there is a $\frac{1}{2}$ chance of hitting s_2 during the next try, so σ actually ensures that s_2 is visited with probability 1.

Solving a CMDP is substantially different from solving a consumption 2-player game [14]. Indeed, imagine that in M from Fig. 1, the outcome of the action a_1 from state s_1 is resolved by an adversarial player. In such a game, the strategy σ does not produce any run that reaches s_2. In fact, there would be no strategy that guarantees reaching T in a 2-player game like this at all.

The strategy σ from our example uses finite memory to track the resource level exactly. We describe an efficient representation of such strategies in the next section.

3   Counter Strategies

In this section, we define a succinct representation of finite-memory strategies via so called counter selectors. Under the standard definition, a strategy σ is a *finite memory* strategy, if σ can be encoded by a *memory structure*, a type of finite transducer. Formally, a memory structure is a tuple $\mu = (M, nxt, up, m_0)$ where M is a finite set of *memory elements*, $nxt: M \times S \to A$ is a *next action* function, $up: M \times S \times A \times S \to M$ is a *memory update* function, and $m_0: S \to M$ is the *memory initialization function*. The function up can be lifted to a function $up^*: M \times hist \to M$ as follows.

$$up^*(m, \alpha) = \begin{cases} m & \text{if } \alpha = s \text{ has length } 0 \\ up\big(up^*(m, \beta), last(\beta), a, t\big) & \text{if } \alpha = \beta at \text{ for some } a \in A \text{ and } t \in S \end{cases}$$

The structure μ encodes a strategy σ_μ such that for each history $\alpha = s_1 a_1 s_2 \ldots s_n$ we have $\sigma_\mu(\alpha) = nxt\big(up^*(m_0(s_1), \alpha), s_n\big)$.

In our setting, strategies need to track energy levels of histories. Let us fix an CMDP $\mathcal{M} = (S, A, \Delta, C, R, cap)$. A non-exhausted energy level is always a number between 0 and $cap(\mathcal{M})$, which can be represented with a binary-encoded bounded counter. We call strategies with such counters *finite counter (FC) strategies*. An FC strategy selects actions to play according to *selection rules*.

Definition 3 (Selection rule). *A selection rule φ for $\mathcal{M}$ is a partial function from the set $\{0, \ldots, cap(\mathcal{M})\}$ to A. Undefined value for some n is indicated by $\varphi(n) = \bot$.*

We use $dom(\varphi) = \{n \in \{0, \ldots, cap(\mathcal{M})\} \mid \varphi(n) \neq \bot\}$ to denote the domain of φ and we use $Rules_{\mathcal{M}}$ or simply $Rules$ for the set of all selection rules for $\mathcal{M}$. Intuitively, a selection according to rule φ selects the action that corresponds to the largest value from $dom(\varphi)$ that is not larger than the current energy level. To be more precise, if $dom(\varphi)$ consists of numbers $n_1 < n_2 < \cdots < n_k$, then the action to be selected in a given moment is $\varphi(n_i)$, where n_i is the largest element of $dom(\varphi)$ which is less then or equal to the current amount of the resource. In other words, $\varphi(n_i)$ is to be selected if the current resource level is in $[n_i, n_{i+1})$ (putting $n_{k+1} = \infty$).

Definition 4 (Counter selector). *A counter selector for $\mathcal{M}$ is a function $\Sigma \colon S \to Rules$.*

A counter selector itself is not enough to describe a strategy. A strategy needs to keep track of the energy level throughout the path. With a vector $\mathbf{r} \in \{0, \ldots, cap(\mathcal{M})\}^S$ of initial resource levels, each counter selector Σ defines a strategy $\Sigma^{\mathbf{r}}$ that is encoded by the following memory structure (M, nxt, up, m_0) with $a \in A$ being a globally fixed action (for uniqueness). We stipulate that $\bot < n$ for all $n \in \mathbb{N}$.

- $M = \{\bot\} \cup \{0, \ldots, cap(\mathcal{M})\}$.
- Let $m \in M$ be a memory element, let $s \in S$ be a state, let $n \in dom(\Sigma(s))$ be the largest element of $dom(\Sigma(s))$ such that $n \leq m$. Then $nxt(m, s) = \Sigma(s)(n)$ if n exists, and $nxt = a$ otherwise.
- The function up is defined for each $m \in M, a \in A, s, t \in S$ as follows.

$$up(m, s, a, t) = \begin{cases} m - C(s, a) & \text{if } s \notin R \text{ and } C(s, a) \leq m \neq \bot \\ cap(\mathcal{M}) - C(s, a) & \text{if } s \in R \text{ and } C(s, a) \leq cap(\mathcal{M}) \text{ and } m \neq \bot \\ \bot & \text{otherwise.} \end{cases}$$

- The function m_0 is $m_0(s) = \mathbf{r}(s)$.

A strategy σ is a finite counter (FC) strategy if there is a counter selector Σ and a vector $\mathbf{r}$ such that $\sigma = \Sigma^{\mathbf{r}}$. The counter selector can be imagined as a finite-state device that implements σ using $O(\log(cap(\mathcal{M})))$ bits of additional memory (counter) used to represent numbers $0, 1, \ldots, cap(\mathcal{M})$. The device uses the counter to keep track of the current resource level, the element $\bot$ representing energy exhaustion. Note that a counter selector can be exponentially more succinct than the corresponding memory structure.

Example 3. Consider again the CMDP $\mathcal{M}$ in Fig. 1 and a counter selector Σ defined as follows: Let φ be a selection rule with $dom(\varphi) = \{0, 10\}$ such that $\varphi(0) = a_2$ and $\varphi(10) = a_1$. Then let φ' be a selection rule such that $dom(\varphi') = \{0\}$ and $\varphi(0) = a_1$. Finally, let Σ be a counter selector such that $\Sigma(s_1) = \varphi$ and $\Sigma(s_i) = \varphi'$ for all $i \neq 1$. Then, for a vector of initial resource levels $\mathbf{r}$, the strategy σ informally described in Example 2 can be formally represented by putting $\sigma = \Sigma^{\mathbf{r}}$. Note that for any $\mathbf{r}$ with $\mathbf{r}(s_1) \geq 2$, $\mathbf{r}(s_2) \geq 0$, $\mathbf{r}(s_3) \geq 5$, $\mathbf{r}(s_4) \geq 4$, and $\mathbf{r}(s_5) \geq 0$ and for any state s of $\mathcal{M}$ the strategy $\Sigma^{\mathbf{r}}$ is $\mathbf{r}(s)$-safe in s.

4   Safety

In this section, we present an algorithm that computes, for each state, the minimal value d (if it exists) such that there exists a d-safe strategy from that state. We also provide the corresponding strategy. In the remainder of the section we fix an MDP $\mathcal{M}$.

A d-safe run has the following two properties: (i) It consumes at most d units of the resource (energy) before it reaches the first reload state, and (ii) it never consumes more than $cap(\mathcal{M})$ units of the resource between 2 visits of reload states. To ensure (ii), we need to identify a maximal subset $R' \subseteq R$ of reload states for which there is a strategy σ that, starting in some $r \in R'$, can always reach R' again (within at least one step) using at most $cap(\mathcal{M})$ resource units. The d-safe strategy we seek can be then assembled from σ and from a strategy that suitably navigates towards R', which is needed for (i).

In the core of both properties (i) and (ii) lies the problem of *minimum cost reachability*. Hence, in the next subsection, we start with presenting necessary results on this problem.

4.1   Minimum Cost Reachability

The problem of minimum cost reachability with non-negative costs was studied before [46]. Here we present a simple approach to the problem used in our implementation and most of the technical details are available in the full version.

Definition 5. *Let $T \subseteq S$ be a set of* target *states, let $\alpha = s_1 a_1 s_2 \ldots$ be a finite or infinite path, and let $1 \leq f$ be the smallest index such that $s_f \in T$. We define* consumption of α to T *as $ReachCons_{\mathcal{M},T}(\alpha) = cons(\alpha_{..f})$ if f exists and we set $ReachCons_{\mathcal{M},T}(\alpha) = \infty$ otherwise. For a strategy σ and a state $s \in S$ we define $ReachCons_{\mathcal{M},T}(\sigma, s) = \sup_{\varrho \in Comp(\sigma,s)} ReachCons_{\mathcal{M},T}(\varrho)$.*
A minimum cost reachability *of T from s is a vector defined as*

$$MinReach_{\mathcal{M},T}(s) = \inf \{ ReachCons_{\mathcal{M},T}(\sigma, s) \mid \sigma \text{ is a strategy for } \mathcal{M} \}.$$

Intuitively, $d = MinReach_T(s)$ is the minimal initial load with which some strategy can ensure reaching T with consumption at most d, when starting in s. We say that a strategy σ is optimal for $MinReach_T$ if we have that $MinReach_T(s) = ReachCons_T(\sigma, s)$ for all states $s \in S$.

We also define functions $ReachCons^+_{M,T}$ and the vector $MinReach^+_{M,T}$ in a similar fashion with one exception: we require the index f from definition of $ReachCons_{M,T}(\alpha)$ to be strictly larger than 1, which enforces to take at least one step to reach T.

For the rest of this section, fix a target set T and consider the following functional $\mathcal{F}$:

$$\mathcal{F}(\mathbf{v})(s) = \begin{cases} \min_{a \in A} \left(C(s,a) + \max_{t \in Succ(s,a)} \mathbf{v}(t) \right) & s \notin T \\ 0 & s \in T \end{cases}$$

$\mathcal{F}$ is a simple generalization of the standard Bellman functional used for computing shortest paths in graphs. The proof of the following Theorem is rather standard and moved to the full version of the paper.

Theorem 2. *Denote by n the length of the longest simple path in M. Let $\mathbf{x}_T$ be a vector such that $\mathbf{x}_T(s) = 0$ if $s \in T$ and $\mathbf{x}_T(s) = \infty$ otherwise. Then iterating $\mathcal{F}$ on $\mathbf{x}_T$ yields a fixpoint in at most n steps and this fixpoint equals $MinReach_T$.*

To compute $MinReach^+_{M,T}$, we construct a new CMDP $\widetilde{M}$ from M by adding a copy $\tilde{s}$ of each state $s \in S$ such that dynamics in $\tilde{s}$ is the same as in s; i.e. for each $a \in A$, $\Delta(\tilde{s}, a) = \Delta(s, a)$ and $C(\tilde{s}, a) = C(s, a)$. We denote the new state set as $\widetilde{S}$. We don't change the set of reload states, so $\tilde{s}$ is *never* in T, even if s is. Given the new CMDP $\widetilde{M}$ and the new state set as $\widetilde{S}$, the following lemma is straightforward.

Lemma 2. *Let M be a CMDP and let $\widetilde{M}$ be the CMDP constructed as above. Then for each state s of M it holds $MinReach^+_{M,T}(s) = MinReach_{\widetilde{M},T}(\tilde{s})$.*

4.2 Safely Reaching Reload States

In the following, we use $MinInitCons_M$ (read *minimal initial consumption*) for the vector $MinReach^+_{M,R}$ – minimal resource level that ensures we can surely reach a reload state in at least one step. By Lemma 2 and Theorem 2 we can construct $\widetilde{M}$ and iterate the operator $\mathcal{F}$ for $|S|$ steps to compute $MinInitCons_M$. Note that S is the state space of M since introducing the new states into $\widetilde{M}$ did not increase the length of the maximal simple path. However, we can avoid the construction of $\widetilde{M}$ and still compute $MinInitCons_M$ using a *truncated* version of the functional $\mathcal{F}$, which is the approach used in our implementation. We first introduce the following truncation operator:

$$\lVert \mathbf{x} \rVert_M(s) = \begin{cases} \mathbf{x}(s) & \text{if } s \notin R, \\ 0 & \text{if } s \in R. \end{cases}$$

Algorithm 1: Algorithm for computing $MinInitCons_{\mathcal{M}}$.

Input: CMDP $\mathcal{M} = (S, A, \Delta, C, R, cap)$
Output: The vector $MinInitCons_{\mathcal{M}}$

1 initialize $\mathbf{x} \in \overline{\mathbb{N}}^S$ to be ∞ in every component;
2 **repeat**
3 $\quad$ $\mathbf{x}_{old} \leftarrow \mathbf{x}$;
4 $\quad$ **foreach** $s \in S$ **do**
5 $\quad\quad$ $c \leftarrow \min_{a \in A} \left\{ C(s, a) + \max_{s' \in Succ(s,a)} \| \mathbf{x}_{old} \|_{\mathcal{M}}(s') \right\}$;
6 $\quad\quad$ **if** $c < \mathbf{x}(s)$ **then**
7 $\quad\quad\quad$ $\mathbf{x}(s) \leftarrow c$;

8 **until** $\mathbf{x}_{old} = \mathbf{x}$;
9 **return** $\mathbf{x}$

Then, we define a truncated functional $\mathcal{G}$ as follows:

$$\mathcal{G}(\mathbf{v})(s) = \min_{a \in A} \left(C(s, a) + \max_{s' \in Succ(s,a)} \| \mathbf{v} \|_{\mathcal{M}}(s') \right).$$

The following lemma connects the iteration of $\mathcal{G}$ on $\mathcal{M}$ with the iteration of $\mathcal{F}$ on $\widetilde{\mathcal{M}}$.

Lemma 3. *Let $\infty \in \overline{\mathbb{N}}^S$ be a vectors with all components equal to ∞. Consider iterating $\mathcal{G}$ on ∞ in $\mathcal{M}$ and $\mathcal{F}$ on $\mathbf{x}_R$ in $\widetilde{\mathcal{M}}$. Then for each $i \geq 0$ and each $s \in R$ we have $\mathcal{G}^i(\infty)(s) = \mathcal{F}^i(\mathbf{x}_R)(\tilde{s})$ and for every $s \in S \setminus R$ we have $\mathcal{G}^i(\infty)(s) = \mathcal{F}^i(\mathbf{x}_R)(s)$.*

Algorithm 1 uses $\mathcal{G}$ to compute the vector $MinInitCons_{\mathcal{M}}$.

Theorem 3. *Algorithm 1 correctly computes the vector $MinInitCons_{\mathcal{M}}$. Moreover, the repeat-loop terminates after at most $|S|$ iterations.*

4.3 Solving the Safety Problem

We want to identify a set $R' \subseteq R$ such that we can reach R' in at least 1 step and with consumption at most $cap = cap(\mathcal{M})$, from each $r \in R'$. This entails identifying the maximal $R' \subseteq R$ such that $MinInitCons_{\mathcal{M}(R')} \leq cap$ for each $r \in R'$. This can be done by initially setting $R' = R$ and iteratively removing states that have $MinInitCons_{\mathcal{M}(R')} > cap$, from R', as in Algorithm 2.

Theorem 4. *Algorithm 2 computes the vector $Safe_{\mathcal{M}}$ in polynomial time.*

Proof. The algorithm clearly terminates. Computing $MinInitCons_{\mathcal{M}(Rel)}$ on line 5 takes a polynomial number of steps per call due to Theorem 3 and since $\mathcal{M}(Rel)$ has asymptotically the same size as $\mathcal{M}$. Since the repeat loop performs at most $|R|$ iterations, the complexity follows.

Algorithm 2: Computing the vector $Safe_{\mathcal{M}}$.

Input: CMDP $\mathcal{M}$
Output: The vector $Safe_{\mathcal{M}}$
1 $cap \leftarrow cap(\mathcal{M})$;
2 $Rel \leftarrow R$; $ToRemove \leftarrow \emptyset$;
3 **repeat**
4 | $Rel \leftarrow Rel \setminus ToRemove$;
5 | $\mathbf{mic} \leftarrow MinInitCons_{M(Rel)}$;
6 | $ToRemove \leftarrow \{r \in Rel \mid \mathbf{mic}(r) > cap\}$;
7 **until** $ToRemove = \emptyset$;
8 **foreach** $s \in S$ **do**
9 | **if** $\mathbf{mic}(s) > cap$ **then** $\mathbf{out}(s) = \infty$;
10 | **else** $\mathbf{out}(s) = \mathbf{mic}(s)$;
11 **return** out

As for correctness, we first prove that $\mathbf{out} \leq Safe_{\mathcal{M}}$. It suffices to prove for each $s \in S$ that upon termination, $\mathbf{mic}(s) \leq Safe_{\mathcal{M}}(s)$ whenever the latter value is finite. Since $MinInitCons_{M'}(s) \leq Safe_{M'}(s)$ for each MDP M' and each its state such that $Safe_{M'}(s) < \infty$, it suffices to show that $Safe_{M(Rel)} \leq Safe_{\mathcal{M}}$ is an invariant of the algorithm (as a matter of fact, we prove that $Safe_{M(Rel)} = Safe_{\mathcal{M}}$). To this end, it suffices to show that at every point of execution $Safe_{\mathcal{M}}(t) = \infty$ for each $t \in R \setminus Rel$: indeed, if this holds, no strategy that is safe for some state $s \neq t$ can play an action a from s such that $t \in Succ(s, a)$, so declaring such states non-reloading does not influence the $Safe_{\mathcal{M}}$-values. So denote by Rel_i the contents of Rel after the i-th iteration. We prove, by induction on i, that $Safe_{\mathcal{M}}(s) = \infty$ for all $s \in R \setminus Rel$. For $i = 0$ we have $R = Rel$, so the statement holds. For $i > 0$, let $s \in R \setminus Rel_i$, and let σ be any strategy. If some run from $\mathsf{Comp}(\sigma, s)$ visits a state from $R \setminus Rel_{i-1}$, then σ is not cap-safe, by induction hypothesis. Now assume that all such runs only visit reload states from Rel_{i-1}. Then, since $MinInitCons_{M(Rel_{i-1})}(s) > cap$, there must be a run $\varrho \in \mathsf{Comp}(\sigma, s)$ with $ReachCons_{Rel_{i-1}}^{+}(\varrho) > cap$. Assume that ϱ is cap-safe in s. Since we consider only decreasing CMDPs, ϱ must infinitely often visit a reload state (as it cannot get stuck in a zero cycle). Hence, there exists an index $f > 1$ such that $\varrho_f \in Rel_{i-1}$, and for this f we have $RL_{cap}(\varrho_{..f}) = \bot$, a contradiction. So again, σ is not safe in s. Since there is no safe strategy from s, we have $Safe_{\mathcal{M}}(s) = \infty$.

Finally, we need to prove that upon termination, $\mathbf{out} \geq Safe_{\mathcal{M}}$. Informally, per the definition of $\mathbf{out}$, from every state s we can ensure reaching a state of Rel by consuming at most $\mathbf{out}(s)$ units of the resource. Once in Rel, we can ensure that we can again return to Rel without consuming more than cap units of the resource. Hence, when starting with $\mathbf{out}(s)$ units, we can surely prevent resource exhaustion.   □

Definition 6. *We call an action a safe in a state s if one of the following conditions holds:*

- $s \notin R$ and $C(s,a) + \max_{t \in Succ(s,a)} Safe_M(t) \leq Safe_M(s)$; or
- $s \in R$ and $C(s,a) + \max_{t \in Succ(s,a)} Safe_M(t) \leq cap(M)$.

Note that by the definition of $Safe_M$, for each state s with $Safe_M(s) < \infty$ there is always at least one action safe in s. For states s s.t. $Safe_M(s) = \infty$, we stipulate all actions to be safe in s.

Theorem 5. *Any strategy which always selects an action that is safe in the current state is $Safe_M(s)$-safe in every state s. In particular, in each consumption MDP M there is a memoryless strategy σ that is $Safe_M(s)$-safe in every state s. Moreover, σ can be computed in polynomial time.*

Proof. The first part of the theorem follows directly from Definition 6, Definition 2 (resource levels), and from definition of d-safe runs. The second part is a corollary of Theorem 4 and the fact that in each state, the safe strategy from Definition 6 can fix one such action in each state and thus is memoryless. The complexity follows from Theorem 4. □

Example 4. Consider again the M from Fig. 1. *Algorithm* 1 returns, for input M, the vector **mic** $= (2, 1, 5, 4, 3)$. Algorithm 2 reuses **mic** on line 5 and returns it unchanged. Hence, the vector **mic** equals $Safe_M$. The strategies described in Example 1 witness that $Safe(s_1) \leq 2$. Here we see that there is no strategy that would be 1-safe in s_1.

5   Positive Reachability

In this section, we focus on strategies that are safe and such that at least one run they produce visits a given set $T \subseteq S$ of *targets*. The main contribution of this section is Algorithm 3 used to compute such strategies as well as the vector $SafePR_{M,T}$ of minimal initial resource levels for which such a strategy exist. As before, for the rest of this section we fix a CMDP M.

We define a function $SPR\text{-}Val_M \colon S \times A \times \overline{\mathbb{N}}^S \to \overline{\mathbb{N}}$ (SPR for safe positive reachability) s.t. for all $s \in S, a \in A$, and $\mathbf{x} \in \overline{\mathbb{N}}^S$ we have

$$SPR\text{-}Val_M(s, a, \mathbf{x}) = C(s,a) + \min_{t \in Succ(s,a)} \left\{ \max \left\{ \mathbf{x}(t), Safe_M(t') \mid t' \in Succ(s,a), t' \neq t \right\} \right\}$$

The max operator considers, for given t, the value $\mathbf{x}(t)$ and the values needed to survive from all possible outcomes of a other than t. Let $v = SPR\text{-}Val_M(s, a, \mathbf{x})$ and t the outcome selected by min. Intuitively, v is the minimal amount of resource needed to reach t with at least $\mathbf{x}(t)$ resource units, or survive if the outcome of a is different from t.

We now define a functional whose fixed point characterizes $SPR\text{-}Val_{M,T}$. We first define a two-sided version of the truncation operator from the previous section: the operator $[\![\cdot]\!]_M$ such that

$$[\![\mathbf{x}]\!]_M(s) = \begin{cases} \infty & \text{if } \mathbf{x}(s) > cap(M) \\ \mathbf{x}(s) & \text{if } \mathbf{x}(s) \leq cap(M) \text{ and } s \notin R \\ 0 & \text{if } \mathbf{x}(s) \leq cap(M) \text{ and } s \in R \end{cases}$$

Using the functions $SPR\text{-}Val$ and $[\![\cdot]\!]_M$, we now define an auxiliary operator $\mathcal{A}$ and the main operator $\mathcal{B}$ as follows.

$$\mathcal{A}_M(\mathbf{r})(s) = \begin{cases} Safe_M(s) & \text{if } s \in T \\ \min_{a \in A}(SPR\text{-}Val_M(s, a, \mathbf{r})) & \text{otherwise;} \end{cases}$$

$$\mathcal{B}_M(\mathbf{r}) = [\![\mathcal{A}_M(\mathbf{r})]\!]_M$$

Let $SafePR_T^i$ be the vector such that for a state $s \in S$ the number $d = SafePR_T^i(s)$ is the minimal number ℓ such that there exists a strategy that is ℓ-safe in s and produces at least one run that visits T within first i steps. Further, we denote by $\mathbf{y}_T$ a vector such that

$$\mathbf{y}_T(s) = \begin{cases} Safe_M(s) & \text{if } s \in T \\ \infty & \text{if } s \notin T \end{cases}$$

The following lemma can proved by a rather straightforward but technical induction.

Lemma 4. *Consider the iteration of $\mathcal{B}_M$ on the initial vector $\mathbf{y}_T$. Then for each $i \geq 0$ it holds that $\mathcal{B}_M^i(\mathbf{y}_T) = SafePR_{M,T}^i$.*

The following lemma says that iterating $\mathcal{B}_M$ reaches a fixed point in a polynomial number of iterations. Intuitively, this is because when trying to reach T, it doesn't make sense to perform a cycle between two visits of a reload state (as this can only increase the resource consumption) and at the same time it doesn't make sense to visit the same reload state twice (since the resource is reloaded to the full capacity upon each visit). The proof is straightforward and is omitted in the interest of brevity. Detailed proofs for Lemma 4 and Lemma 5 are available in the full version of the paper.

Lemma 5. *Let $K = |R| + (|R| + 1) \cdot (|S| - |R| + 1)$. Taking the same initial vector $\mathbf{y}_T$ as in Lemma 4, we have $\mathcal{B}_M^K(\mathbf{y}_T) = SafePR_{M,T}$.*

The computation of $SafePR_{M,T}$ and of the associated witness strategy is presented in Algorithm 3.

Example 5. Consider again the CMDP M from Fig. 1. After one iteration of the loop on line 5, we have $\mathbf{r} = (10, 0, \infty, \infty, \infty)$, as $\mathbf{r}$ is only finite for s_2 before this iteration. In the next iteration, we have $\mathbf{r} = (10, 0, \infty, 12, 0)$. Thus, the next iteration changes the value for s_1 to 2 and in the end, we end up with $\mathbf{r} = (2, 0, 4, 5, 0)$. The iteration with $\mathbf{r}(s_1) = 10$ influences the selector Σ. Note that the computed $\mathbf{r}$ and Σ match those mentioned in Example 3.

Theorem 6. *The Algorithm 3 always terminates after a polynomial number of steps, and upon termination, $\mathbf{r} = SafePR_{M,T}$.*

Algorithm 3: Positive reachability of T in $\mathcal{M}$

Input: CMDP $\mathcal{M}$ with states S, set of target states $T \subseteq S$
Output: The vector $SafePR_{\mathcal{M},T}$, corerresponding rule selector Σ

1   $\mathbf{r} \leftarrow \{\infty\}^S$;
2   **foreach** $s \in S$ *s.t.* $Safe_{\mathcal{M}}(s) < \infty$ **do**
3     $\bigl\lfloor \; \Sigma(s)(Safe_{\mathcal{M}}(s)) \leftarrow$ arbitrary action safe in s
4   **foreach** $t \in T$ **do** $\mathbf{r}(t) \leftarrow Safe_{\mathcal{M}}(t)$;
5   **repeat**
6     $\mathbf{r}_{old} \leftarrow \mathbf{r}$;
7   **foreach** $s \in S \setminus T$ **do**
8       $\mathbf{a}(s) \leftarrow \arg\min_{a \in A} SPR\text{-}Val(s, a, \mathbf{r}_{old})$;
9       $\mathbf{r}(s) \leftarrow \min_{a \in A} SPR\text{-}Val(s, a, \mathbf{r}_{old})$;
10    $\mathbf{r} \leftarrow [\![\mathbf{r}]\!]_{\mathcal{M}}$;
11   **foreach** $s \in S \setminus T$ **do**
12   **if** $\mathbf{r}(s) < \mathbf{r}_{old}(s)$ **then**
13       $\bigl\lfloor \; \Sigma(s)(\mathbf{r}(s)) \leftarrow \mathbf{a}(s)$;
14 **until** $\mathbf{r}_{old} = \mathbf{r}$;
15 **return** $\mathbf{r}, \Sigma$

Proof. The repeat loop on lines 1–4 initialize $\mathbf{r}$ to $\mathbf{y}_T$. The repeat loop on lines 5–14 then iterates the operator $\mathcal{B}$. By Lemma 5, the iteration reaches a fixed point in at most K steps, and this fixed point equals $SafePR_{\mathcal{M},T}$. The complexity bound follows easily, since K is of polynomial magnitude.

The most intricate part of our analysis is extracting a strategy that is T-positive $SafePR_{\mathcal{M},T}(s)$-safe in every state s.

Theorem 7. *Let $\mathbf{v} = SafePR_{\mathcal{M},T}$. Upon termination of Algorithm 3, the computed selector Σ has the property that the finite counter strategy $\Sigma^{\mathbf{v}}$ is, for each state $s \in S$, T-positive $\mathbf{v}(s)$-safe in s. That is, a polynomial-size finite counter strategy for the positive reachability problem can be computed in polynomial time.*

The rest of this section is devoted to the proof of Theorem 7. The complexity follows from Theorem 6. Indeed, since the algorithm has a polynomial complexity, also the size of Σ is polynomial. The correctness proof is based on the following invariant of the main repeat loop: the finite counter strategy $\pi = \Sigma^{\mathbf{r}}$ has these properties:

(a) Strategy π is $Safe_{\mathcal{M}}(s)$-safe in every state $s \in S$; in particular, we have for $l = \min\{\mathbf{r}(s), cap(\mathcal{M})\}$ that $RL_l(\alpha) \neq \perp$ for every finite path α produced by π from s.
(b) For each state $s \in S$ such that $\mathbf{r}(s) \leq cap(\mathcal{M})$ there exists a π-compatible finite path $\alpha = s_1 a_1 s_2 \ldots s_n$ such that $s_1 = s$ and $s_n \in T$ and such that "the resource level with initial load $\mathbf{r}(s)$ never decreases below $\mathbf{r}$ along α", which means that for each prefix $\alpha_{..i}$ of α it holds $RL_{\mathbf{r}(s)}(\alpha_{..i}) \geq \mathbf{r}(s_i)$.

The theorem then follows from this invariant (parts (a) and the first half of (b)) and from Theorem 6. We start with the following support invariant, which is easy to prove.

Lemma 6. *The inequality* $\mathbf{r} \geq Safe_{\mathcal{M}}$ *is an invariant of the main repeat-loop.*

Proving Part (a) of the Main Invariant. We use the following auxiliary lemma.

Lemma 7. *Assume that* Σ *is a counter selector such that for all* $s \in S$ *such that* $Safe(s) < \infty$:

(1.) $Safe(s) \in dom(\Sigma(s))$.
(2.) *For all* $x \in dom(\Sigma(s))$, *for* $a = \Sigma(s)(x)$ *and for all* $t \in Succ(s,a)$ *we have* $RL_x(sat) = d - C(s,a) \geq Safe(t)$ *where* $d = x$ *for* $s \notin R$ *and* $d = cap(\mathcal{M})$ *otherwise.*

Then for each vector $\mathbf{y} \geq Safe$ *the strategy* $\pi = \Sigma^{\mathbf{y}}$ *is* $Safe(s)$-*safe in every state* s.

Proof. Let s be a state such that $\mathbf{y}(s) < \infty$. It suffices to prove that for every π-compatible finite path α started in s it holds $\perp \neq RL_{\mathbf{y}(s)}(\alpha)$. We actually prove a stronger statement: $\perp \neq RL_{\mathbf{y}(s)}(\alpha) \geq Safe(last(\alpha))$. We proceed by induction on the length of α. If $len(\alpha) = 0$ we have $RL_{\mathbf{y}(s)}(\alpha) = \mathbf{y}(s) \geq Safe_{\mathcal{M}}(s) \geq 0$. Now let $\alpha = \beta \odot t_1 a t_2$ for some shorter path β with $last(\beta) = t_1$ and $a \in A$, $t_1, t_2 \in S$. By induction hypothesis, $l = RL_{\mathbf{y}(s)}(\beta) \geq Safe_{\mathcal{M}}(t_1)$, from which it follows that $Safe_{\mathcal{M}}(t_1) < \infty$. Due to (1.), it follows that there exists at least one $x \in dom(\Sigma(t_1))$ such that $x \leq l$. We select maximal x satisfying the inequality so that $a = \Sigma(t_1)(x)$. We have that $RL_{\mathbf{y}(s)}(\alpha) = RL_l(t_1 a t_2)$ by definition and from (2.) it follows that $\perp \neq RL_x(t_1 a t_2) \geq Safe(t_2) \geq 0$. All together, as $l \geq x$ we have that $RL_{\mathbf{y}(s)}(\alpha) \geq RL_x(t_1 a t_2) \geq Safe(t_2) \geq 0$. $\square$

Now we prove the part (a) of the main invariant. We show that throughout the execution of Algorithm 3, Σ satisfies the assumptions of Lemma 7. Property (1.) is ensured by the initialization on line 3. The property (2.) holds upon first entry to the main loop by the definition of a safe action (Definition 6). Now assume that $\Sigma(s)(\mathbf{r}(s))$ is redefined on line 13, and let a be the action $\mathbf{a}(s)$.

We first handle the case when $s \notin R$. Since a was selected on line 8, from the definition of *SPR-Val* we have that there is $t \in Succ(s,a)$ such that after the loop iteration,

$$\mathbf{r}(s) = C(s,a) + \max\{\mathbf{r}_{old}(t), Safe(t') \mid t \neq t' \in Succ(s,a)\} \geq C(s,a) + \max_{t' \in Succ(s,a)} Safe_{\mathcal{M}}(t'),$$

$$(1)$$

the latter inequality following from Lemma 6. Satisfaction of property (2.) in s then follows immediately from the Eq. (1).

If $s \in R$, then (1) holds before the truncation on line 10, at which point $\mathbf{r}(s) < cap(\mathcal{M})$. Hence, $cap(\mathcal{M}) - C(s,a) \geq \max_{t \in Succ(s,a)} Safe_{\mathcal{M}}(t)$ as required by (2.). From Lemmas 6 and 7 it follows that $\Sigma^{\mathbf{r}}$ is $Safe_{\mathcal{M}}(s)$-safe in every state s. This finishes the proof of part (a) of the invariant.

Proving Part (b) of the Main Invariant. Clearly, (b) holds after initialization. Now assume that an iteration of the main repeat loop was performed. Denote by π_{old} the strategy $\Sigma^{\mathbf{r}_{old}}$ and by π the strategy $\Sigma^{\mathbf{r}}$. Let s be any state such that $\mathbf{r}(s) \leq cap(\mathcal{M})$. If $\mathbf{r}(s) = \mathbf{r}_{old}(s)$, then we claim that (b) follows directly from the induction hypothesis: indeed, we have that there is an s-initiated π_{old}-compatible path α ending in a target state s.t. the $\mathbf{r}_{old}(s)$-initiated resource level along α never drops $\mathbf{r}_{old}$, i.e. for each prefix β of α it holds $RL_{\mathbf{r}_{old}(s)}(\beta) \geq \mathbf{r}_{old}(last(\beta))$. But then β is also π-compatible, since for each state q, $\Sigma(q)$ was only redefined for values smaller than $\mathbf{r}_{old}(q)$.

The case when $\mathbf{r}(s) < \mathbf{r}_{old}(s)$ is treated similarly. As in the proof of part (a), denote by a the action $\mathbf{a}(s)$ assigned on line 13. There must be a state $t \in Succ(s,a)$ s.t. (1) holds before the truncation on line 10. In particular, for this t it holds $RL_{\mathbf{r}(s)}(sat) \geq \mathbf{r}_{old}(t)$. By induction hypothesis, there is a t-initiated π_{old}-compatible path β ending in T satisfying the conditions in (b). We put $\alpha = sat \odot \beta$. Clearly α is s-initiated and reaches T. Moreover, it is π-compatible. To see this, note that $\Sigma^{\mathbf{r}}(s)(\mathbf{r}(s)) = a$; moreover, the resource level after the first transition is $e(t) = RL_{\mathbf{r}(s)}(sat) \geq \mathbf{r}_{old}(t)$, and due to the assumed properties of β, the $\mathbf{r}_{old}(t)$-initiated resource level (with initial load $e(t)$) never decreases below $\mathbf{r}_{old}$ along β. Since Σ was only re-defined for values smaller than those given by the vector $\mathbf{r}_{old}$, π mimics π_{old} along β. Since $\mathbf{r} \leq \mathbf{r}_{old}$, we have that along α, the $\mathbf{r}(s)$-initiated resource level never decreases below $\mathbf{r}$. This finishes the proof of part (b) of the invariant and thus also the proof of Theorem 7. □

6   Büchi

This section proofs Theorem 1 which is the main theoretical result of the paper. The proof is broken down into the following steps.

(1.) We identify a largest set $R' \subseteq R$ of reload states such that from each $r \in R'$ we can reach R' again (in at least one step) while consuming at most cap resource units and restricting ourselves only to strategies that (i) avoid $R \backslash R'$ and (ii) guarantee positive reachability of T in $\mathcal{M}(R')$.

(2.) We show that $SafeBüchi_{M,T} = SafePR_{M(R'),T}$ and that the corresponding strategy (computed by Algorithm 3) is also T-Büchi $SafeBüchi_{M,T}(s)$-safe for each $s \in S$.

Algorithm 4: Almost-sure Büchi reachability of T in $\mathcal{M}$.

Input: CMDP $\mathcal{M} = (S, A, \Delta, C, R, cap)$, target states $T \subseteq S$
Output: The largest set $Rel \subseteq R$ such that $SafePR_{\mathcal{M}(Rel),T}(r) \leq cap$ for all
  $\qquad r \in Rel$.

1 $Rel \leftarrow R;\ ToRemove \leftarrow \emptyset$;
2 **repeat**
3 $\quad$ | $Rel \leftarrow Rel \smallsetminus ToRemove$;
4 $\quad$ | $(\textbf{reach}, \Sigma) \leftarrow SafePR_{\mathcal{M}(Rel),\, T}$;
5 $\quad$ | $ToRemove \leftarrow \{r \in Rel \mid \textbf{reach}(r) > cap\}$;
6 **until** $ToRemove = \emptyset$;
7 **return reach**, Σ

Algorithm 4 solves (1.) in a similar fashion as Algorithm 2 handled safety. In each iteration, we declare as non-reloading all states from which positive reachability of T and safety within $\mathcal{M}(Rel)$ cannot be guaranteed. This is repeated until we reach a fixed point. The number of iterations is clearly bounded by $|R|$.

Theorem 8. *Let $\mathcal{M} = (S, A, \Delta, C, R, cap)$ be a CMDP and $T \subseteq S$ be a target set. Moreover, let R' be the contents of Rel upon termination of Algorithm 4 for the input $\mathcal{M}$ and T. Finally let $\mathbf{r}$ and Σ be the vector and the selector returned by Algorithm 3 for the input $\mathcal{M}$ and T. Then for every state s, the finite counter strategy $\sigma = \Sigma^{\mathbf{r}}$ is T-Büchi $\mathbf{r}(s)$-safe in s in both $\mathcal{M}(R')$ and $\mathcal{M}$. Moreover, the vector $\mathbf{r}$ is equal to $SafeBüchi_{\mathcal{M},T}$.*

Proof. We first show that σ is T-Büchi $\mathbf{r}(s)$-safe in $\mathcal{M}(R')$ for all $s \in S$ with $\mathbf{r}(s) \leq cap$. Clearly it is $\mathbf{r}(s)$-safe, so it remains to prove that T is visited infinitely often with probability 1. We know that upon every visit of a state $r \in R'$, σ guarantees a future visit to T with positive probability. As a matter of fact, since σ is a finite memory strategy, there is $\delta > 0$ such that upon every visit of some $r \in R'$, the probability of a future visit to T is at least δ. As $\mathcal{M}(R')$ is decreasing, every s-initiated σ-compatible run must visit the set R' infinitely many times. Hence, with probability 1 we reach T at least once. The argument can then be repeated from the first point of visit to T to show that with probability 1 ve visit T at least twice, three times, etc. *ad infinitum*. By the monotonicity of probability, $\mathbb{P}^{\sigma}_{\mathcal{M},s}(\mathsf{Büchi}_T) = 1$.

It remains to show that $\mathbf{r} \leq SafeBüchi_{\mathcal{M},T}$. Assume that there is a state $s \in S$ and a strategy σ' such that σ' is d-safe in s for some $d < \mathbf{r}(s) = SafePR_{\mathcal{M}(R'),T}(s)$. We show that this strategy is not T-Büchi d-safe in $\mathcal{M}$. If all σ'-compatible runs reach T, then there must be at least one history α produced by σ' that visits $r \in R \setminus R'$ before reaching T (otherwise $d \geq \mathbf{r}(s)$).

Then either (a) $SafePR_{\mathcal{M},T}(r) = \infty$, in which case any σ'-compatible extension of α avoids T; or (b) since $SafePR_{\mathcal{M}(R'),T}(r) > cap$, there must be an extension of α that visits, between the visit of r and T, another $r' \in R \setminus R'$ such that $r' \neq r$. We can then repeat the argument, eventually reaching the case (a) or running out of the resource, a contradiction with σ' being d-safe.   □

We can finally proceed to prove Theorem 1.

Proof (of Theorem 1). The theorem follows immediately from Theorem 8 since we can (a) compute $SafeB\ddot{u}chi_{\mathcal{M},T}$ and the corresponding strategy σ_T in polynomial time (see Theorem 7 and Algorithm 4); (b) we can easily check whether $d \geq SafeB\ddot{u}chi_{\mathcal{M},T}(s)$, if yes, than σ_T is the desired strategy σ; and (c) represent σ_T in polynomial space as it is a finite counter strategy represented by a polynomial-size counter selector.   □

7   Implementation and Case Studies

We implemented the presented algorithms in Python and released it as an open-source tool called *FiMDP (Fuel in MDP)* available at https://github.com/ xblahoud/FiMDP. The docker artifact is available at https://hub.docker.com/r/ xblahoud/fimdp and can be run without installation via the Binder project [50]. We investigate the practical behavior of our algorithms using two case studies: (1) An autonomous electric vehicle (AEV) routing problem in the streets of Manhattan modeled using realistic traffic and electric car energy consumption data, and (2) a multi-agent grid world model inspired by the Mars Helicopter Scout [8] to be deployed from the planned Mars 2020 rover. The first scenario demonstrates the utility of our algorithm for solving real-world problems [59], while the second scenario studies the algorithm's scalability limits.

The consumption-Büchi objective can be also solved by a naive approach that encodes the energy constraints in the state space of the MDP, and solves it using techniques for standard MDPs [33]. States of such an MDP are tuples (s, e) where s is a state of the input CMDP and e is the current level of energy. Naturally, all actions that would lead to states with $e < 0$ lead to a special sink state. The standard techniques rely on decomposition of the MDP into maximal end-components (MEC). We implemented the explicit encoding of CMDP into MDP, and the MEC-decomposition algorithm.

All computations presented in the following were performed on a PC with Intel Core i7-8700 3.20 GHz 12 core processor and a RAM of 16 GB running Ubuntu 18.04 LTS. All running times are means from at least 5 runs and the standard deviation was always below 5% among these runs.

7.1 Electric Vehicle Routing

We consider the area in the middle of Manhattan, from 42nd to 116th Street, see Fig. 2. Street intersections and directions of feasible movement form the state and action spaces of the MDP. Intersections in the proximity of real-world fast charging stations [56] represent the set of reload states.

After the AEV picks a direction, it reaches the next intersection in that direction deterministically with a stochastic energy consumption. We base our model of consumption on distributions of vehicle travel times from the area [55] and conversion of velocity and travel times to energy consumption [52]. We discretize the consumption distribution into three possible values (c_1, c_2, c_3) reached with corresponding probabilities (p_1, p_2, p_3). We then model the transition from one intersection (I_1) to another (I_2) using additional dummy states as explained in Fig. 2.

The corresponding CMDP has 7378 states and 8473 actions. For a fixed set of 100 randomly selected target states, Fig. 3 shows influence of requested capacity on running times for (a) strategy for Büchi objective using CMDP (our approach), and (b) MEC-decomposition for the corresponding explicit MDP. With constant number of states, our algorithm runs rea-

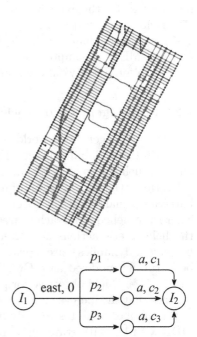

Fig. 2. (Top:) Street network in the considered area. Charging stations are red, one way roads green, and two-way roads blue. (Bottom:) Transition from intersection I_1 to I_2 with stochastic consumption. The small circles are dummy states. (Color figure online)

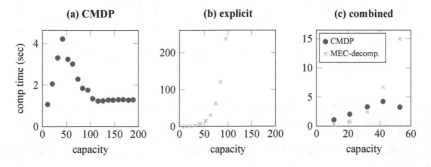

Fig. 3. Mean computation times for a fixed target set of size 100 and varying capacity: (a) **CMDP** – computating Büchi objective via CMDP, (b) **explicit** – computating MEC decomposition of the explicit MDP, (c) **combined** – (a) and (b) combined for small capacity values.

sonably fast for all capacities and the running time stabilizes for $cap > 95$; this is not the case for the explicit approach where the number of states keeps growing (52747 for $cap = 95$) as well as the running time. The decomposition to MECs is slightly faster than solving Büchi using CMDP for the small capacities (Fig. 3 (c)), but MECs decomposition is only a part of the solution and running the full algorithm for Büchi would most likely diminish this advantage.

7.2   Multi-agent Grid World

We use multi-agent grid world to generate CMDP with huge number of states to study the scalability limits of the proposed algorithms. We model the rover and the helicopter of the Mars 2020 mission with the following realistic considerations: the rover enjoys infinite energy while the helicopter is restricted by batteries recharged at the rover. These two vehicle jointly operate on a mission where the helicopter reaches areas inaccessible to the rover. The outcomes of the helicopter's actions are deterministic while those of the rover—influenced by terrain dynamics—are stochastic. For a grid world of size n, this system can be naturally modeled as a CMDP with n^4 states. Figure 4 shows the running times of the Büchi objective for growing grid sizes and capacities in CMDP. We observe that the increase in the computational time of CMDP follows the growth in the number of states roughly linearly, and our implementation deals with an MDP with 1.6×10^5 states in no more than seven minutes. The figure also shows the running time for the MEC decomposition of the corresponding explicit MDP when the capacity is 10 and, for certain smaller, computationally feasible grid sizes, when the capacity is 20.

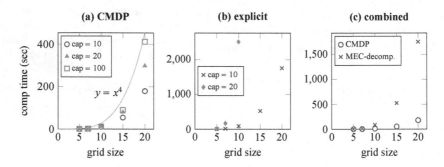

Fig. 4. Mean computation times for varying grid sizes and of size capacities: **(a) CMDP** – computing Büchi objective via CMDP, the gray line shows the corresponding growth in the number of states on separate scale, **(b) explicit** – computing MEC decomposition of the explicit MDP, **(c) combined** – combined computation time for a capacity of 10.

8 Conclusion and Future Work

We presented a first study of consumption Markov decision processes (CMDPs) with qualitative ω-regular objectives. We developed and implemented a polynomial-time algorithm for CMDPs with an objective of probability-1 satisfaction of a given Büchi condition. Possible directions for the future work are extensions to quantitative analysis (e.g. minimizing the expected resource consumption), stochastic games, or partially observable setting.

Acknowledgements. We acknowledge the kind help of Vojtěch Forejt, David Klaška, and Martin Kučera in the discussions leading to this paper.

References

1. Abdulla, P.A., Atig, M.F., Hofman, P., Mayr, R., Kumar, K.N., Totzke, P.: Infinite-state energy games. In: Joint Meeting of the 23rd EACSL Annual Conference on Computer Science Logic and the 29th Annual ACM/IEEE Symposium on Logic in Computer Science, pp. 7:1–7:10 (2014)
2. Ash, R., Doléans-Dade, C.: Probability and Measure Theory. Harcourt/Academic Press, San Diego (2000)
3. Bacci, G., Bouyer, P., Fahrenberg, U., Larsen, K.G., Markey, N., Reynier, P.-A.: Optimal and robust controller synthesis. In: Havelund, K., Peleska, J., Roscoe, B., de Vink, E. (eds.) FM 2018. LNCS, vol. 10951, pp. 203–221. Springer, Cham (2018). https://doi.org/10.1007/978-3-319-95582-7_12
4. Baier, C., Chrszon, P., Dubslaff, C., Klein, J., Klüppelholz, S.: Energy-utility analysis of probabilistic systems with exogenous coordination. In: de Boer, F., Bonsangue, M., Rutten, J. (eds.) It's All About Coordination. LNCS, vol. 10865, pp. 38–56. Springer, Cham (2018). https://doi.org/10.1007/978-3-319-90089-6_3
5. Baier, C., Daum, M., Dubslaff, C., Klein, J., Klüppelholz, S.: Energy-utility quantiles. In: Badger, J.M., Rozier, K.Y. (eds.) NFM 2014. LNCS, vol. 8430, pp. 285–299. Springer, Cham (2014). https://doi.org/10.1007/978-3-319-06200-6_24
6. Baier, C., Dubslaff, C., Klein, J., Klüppelholz, S., Wunderlich, S.: Probabilistic model checking for energy-utility analysis. In: van Breugel, F., Kashefi, E., Palamidessi, C., Rutten, J. (eds.) Horizons of the Mind. A Tribute to Prakash Panangaden. LNCS, vol. 8464, pp. 96–123. Springer, Cham (2014). https://doi.org/10.1007/978-3-319-06880-0_5
7. Baier, C., Dubslaff, C., Klüppelholz, S., Leuschner, L.: Energy-utility analysis for resilient systems using probabilistic model checking. In: Ciardo, G., Kindler, E. (eds.) PETRI NETS 2014. LNCS, vol. 8489, pp. 20–39. Springer, Cham (2014). https://doi.org/10.1007/978-3-319-07734-5_2
8. Balaram, B., et al.: Mars helicopter technology demonstrator. In: AIAA Atmospheric Flight Mechanics Conference (2018)
9. Boker, U., Henzinger, T.A., Radhakrishna, A.: Battery transition systems. In: 41st ACM SIGPLAN-SIGACT Symposium on Principles of Programming Languages, pp. 595–606 (2014)
10. Bouyer, P., Fahrenberg, U., Larsen, K.G., Markey, N.: Timed automata with observers under energy constraints. In: 13th ACM International Conference on Hybrid Systems: Computation and Control, pp. 61–70. ACM (2010)

11. Bouyer, P., Fahrenberg, U., Larsen, K.G., Markey, N., Srba, J.: Infinite runs in weighted timed automata with energy constraints. In: Cassez, F., Jard, C. (eds.) FORMATS 2008. LNCS, vol. 5215, pp. 33–47. Springer, Heidelberg (2008). https://doi.org/10.1007/978-3-540-85778-5_4

12. Bouyer, P., Hofman, P., Markey, N., Randour, M., Zimmermann, M.: Bounding average-energy games. In: Esparza, J., Murawski, A.S. (eds.) FoSSaCS 2017. LNCS, vol. 10203, pp. 179–195. Springer, Heidelberg (2017). https://doi.org/10.1007/978-3-662-54458-7_11

13. Bouyer, P., Markey, N., Randour, M., Larsen, K.G., Laursen, S.: Average-energy games. Acta Informatica $55(2)$, 91–127 (2018)

14. Brázdil, T., Chatterjee, K., Kučera, A., Novotný, P.: Efficient controller synthesis for consumption games with multiple resource types. In: Madhusudan, P., Seshia, S.A. (eds.) CAV 2012. LNCS, vol. 7358, pp. 23–38. Springer, Heidelberg (2012). https://doi.org/10.1007/978-3-642-31424-7_8

15. Brázdil, T., Jančar, P., Kučera, A.: Reachability games on extended vector addition systems with states. In: Abramsky, S., Gavoille, C., Kirchner, C., Meyer auf der Heide, F., Spirakis, P.G. (eds.) ICALP 2010. LNCS, vol. 6199, pp. 478–489. Springer, Heidelberg (2010). https://doi.org/10.1007/978-3-642-14162-1_40

16. Brázdil, T., Klaška, D., Kučera, A., Novotný, P.: Minimizing running costs in consumption systems. In: Biere, A., Bloem, R. (eds.) CAV 2014. LNCS, vol. 8559, pp. 457–472. Springer, Cham (2014). https://doi.org/10.1007/978-3-319-08867-9_30

17. Brázdil, T., Kučera, A., Novotný, P.: Optimizing the expected mean payoff in energy Markov decision processes. In: Artho, C., Legay, A., Peled, D. (eds.) ATVA 2016. LNCS, vol. 9938, pp. 32–49. Springer, Cham (2016). https://doi.org/10.1007/978-3-319-46520-3_3

18. Brenguier, R., Cassez, F., Raskin, J.-F.: Energy and mean-payoff timed games. In: 17th International Conference on Hybrid Systems: Computation and Control, pp. 283–292 (2014)

19. Brihaye, T., Geeraerts, G., Haddad, A., Monmege, B.: Pseudopolynomial iterative algorithm to solve total-payoff games and min-cost reachability games. Acta Informatica $54(1)$, 85–125 (2017)

20. Brim, L., Chaloupka, J., Doyen, L., Gentilini, R., Raskin, J.: Faster algorithms for mean-payoff games. Form. Methods Syst. Des. $38(2)$, 97–118 (2011)

21. Bruyère, V., Hautem, Q., Randour, M., Raskin, J.-F.: Energy mean-payoff games. In: 30th International Conference on Concurrency Theory, pp. 21:1–21:17 (2019)

22. Cachera, D., Fahrenberg, U., Legay, A.: An ω-algebra for real-time energy problems. Log. Methods Comput. Sci. $15(2)$ (2019)

23. Chakrabarti, A., de Alfaro, L., Henzinger, T.A., Stoelinga, M.: Resource interfaces. In: Alur, R., Lee, I. (eds.) EMSOFT 2003. LNCS, vol. 2855, pp. 117–133. Springer, Heidelberg (2003). https://doi.org/10.1007/978-3-540-45212-6_9

24. Chaloupka, J.: Z-reachability problem for games on 2-dimensional vector addition systems with states is in P. Fundamenta Informaticae $123(1)$, 15–42 (2013)

25. Chatterjee, K.: Stochastic ω-regular games. Ph.D. thesis, University of California, Berkeley (2007)

26. Chatterjee, K., Doyen, L.: Energy and mean-payoff parity Markov decision processes. In: Murlak, F., Sankowski, P. (eds.) MFCS 2011. LNCS, vol. 6907, pp. 206–218. Springer, Heidelberg (2011). https://doi.org/10.1007/978-3-642-22993-0_21

27. Chatterjee, K., Doyen, L.: Energy parity games. Theor. Comput. Sci. 458, 49–60 (2012)

28. Chatterjee, K., Doyen, L., Henzinger, T., Raskin, J.-F.: Generalized mean-payoff and energy games. In: 30th Annual Conference on Foundations of Software Technology and Theoretical Computer Science, pp. 505–516 (2010)
29. Chatterjee, K., Henzinger, M., Krinninger, S., Nanongkai, D.: Polynomial-time algorithms for energy games with special weight structures. In: 20th Annual European Symposium on Algorithms, pp. 301–312 (2012)
30. Chatterjee, K., Jurdziński, M., Henzinger, T.: Quantitative stochastic parity games. In: 15th Annual ACM-SIAM Symposium on Discrete Algorithms, pp. 121–130 (2004)
31. Chatterjee, K., Randour, M., Raskin, J.-F.: Strategy synthesis for multidimensional quantitative objectives. Acta informatica $51(3$–$4)$, 129–163 (2014)
32. Courcoubetis, C., Yannakakis, M.: The complexity of probabilistic verification. J. ACM $42(4)$, 857–907 (1995)
33. de Alfaro, L.: Formal verification of probabilistic systems. Ph.D. thesis, Stanford University (1998)
34. Degorre, A., Doyen, L., Gentilini, R., Raskin, J.-F., Toruńczyk, S.: Energy and mean-payoff games with imperfect information. In: Dawar, A., Veith, H. (eds.) CSL 2010. LNCS, vol. 6247, pp. 260–274. Springer, Heidelberg (2010). https://doi.org/10.1007/978-3-642-15205-4_22
35. Ésik, Z., Fahrenberg, U., Legay, A., Quaas, K.: An algebraic approach to energy problems I - continuous Kleene ω-algebras. Acta Cybernetica $23(1)$, 203–228 (2017)
36. Ésik, Z., Fahrenberg, U., Legay, A., Quaas, K.: An algebraic approach to energy problems II - the algebra of energy functions. Acta Cybernetica $23(1)$, 229–268 (2017)
37. Fahrenberg, U., Juhl, L., Larsen, K.G., Srba, J.: Energy games in multiweighted automata. In: Cerone, A., Pihlajasaari, P. (eds.) ICTAC 2011. LNCS, vol. 6916, pp. 95–115. Springer, Heidelberg (2011). https://doi.org/10.1007/978-3-642-23283-1_9
38. Fahrenberg, U., Legay, A.: Featured weighted automata. In: 5th International FME Workshop on Formal Methods in Software Engineering, pp. 51–57 (2017)
39. Fijalkow, N., Zimmermann, M.: Cost-parity and cost-Streett games. In: 32nd Annual Conference on Foundations of Software Technology and Theoretical Computer Science, pp. 124–135 (2012)
40. Filiot, E., Gentilini, R., Raskin, J.-F.: Quantitative languages defined by functional automata. In: Koutny, M., Ulidowski, I. (eds.) CONCUR 2012. LNCS, vol. 7454, pp. 132–146. Springer, Heidelberg (2012). https://doi.org/10.1007/978-3-642-32940-1_11
41. Hahn, E.M., Perez, M., Schewe, S., Somenzi, F., Trivedi, A., Wojtczak, D.: Good-for-MDPs automata for probabilistic analysis and reinforcement learning. TACAS 2020. LNCS, vol. 12078, pp. 306–323. Springer, Cham (2020). https://doi.org/10.1007/978-3-030-45190-5_17
42. Herrmann, L., Baier, C., Fetzer, C., Klüppelholz, S., Napierkowski, M.: Formal parameter synthesis for energy-utility-optimal fault tolerance. In: Bakhshi, R., Ballarini, P., Barbot, B., Castel-Taleb, H., Remke, A. (eds.) EPEW 2018. LNCS, vol. 11178, pp. 78–93. Springer, Cham (2018). https://doi.org/10.1007/978-3-030-02227-3_6
43. Juhl, L., Guldstrand Larsen, K., Raskin, J.-F.: Optimal bounds for multiweighted and parametrised energy games. In: Liu, Z., Woodcock, J., Zhu, H. (eds.) Theories of Programming and Formal Methods. LNCS, vol. 8051, pp. 244–255. Springer, Heidelberg (2013). https://doi.org/10.1007/978-3-642-39698-4_15

44. Jurdziński, M., Lazić, R., Schmitz, S.: Fixed-dimensional energy games are in pseudo-polynomial time. In: Halldórsson, M.M., Iwama, K., Kobayashi, N., Speckmann, B. (eds.) ICALP 2015. LNCS, vol. 9135, pp. 260–272. Springer, Heidelberg (2015). https://doi.org/10.1007/978-3-662-47666-6_21
45. Jurdziński, M.: Deciding the winner in parity games is in UP ∩ co-UP. Inf. Process. Lett. **68**(3), 119–124 (1998)
46. Khachiyan, L., et al.: On short paths interdiction problems: total and node-wise limited interdiction. Theory Comput. Syst. **43**(2), 204–233 (2008)
47. Klaška, D.: Complexity of Consumption Games. Bachelor's thesis, Masaryk University (2014)
48. Larsen, K.G., Laursen, S., Zimmermann, M.: Limit your consumption! Finding bounds in average-energy games. In: 14th International Workshop Quantitative Aspects of Programming Languages and Systems, pp. 1–14 (2016)
49. Mayr, R., Schewe, S., Totzke, P., Wojtczak, D.: MDPs with energy-parity objectives. In: 32nd Annual ACM/IEEE Symposium on Logic in Computer Science, pp. 1–12 (2017)
50. Jupyter, P., et al.: Binder 2.0 - reproducible, interactive, sharable environments for science at scale. In: 17th Python in Science Conference, pp. 113–120 (2018)
51. Sickert, S., Esparza, J., Jaax, S., Křetínský, J.: Limit-deterministic Büchi automata for linear temporal logic. In: Chaudhuri, S., Farzan, A. (eds.) CAV 2016. LNCS, vol. 9780, pp. 312–332. Springer, Cham (2016). https://doi.org/10.1007/978-3-319-41540-6_17
52. Straubel, J.B.: Roadster efficiency and range (2008). https://www.tesla.com/blog/roadster-efficiency-and-range
53. Sugumar, G., Selvamuthukumaran, R., Dragicevic, T., Nyman, U., Larsen, K.G., Blaabjerg, F.: Formal validation of supervisory energy management systems for microgrids. In: 43rd Annual Conference of the IEEE Industrial Electronics Society, pp. 1154–1159 (2017)
54. Sutton, R.S., Barto, A.G.: Reinforcement Learning: An Introduction. MIT Press, Cambridge (2018)
55. Uber Movement: Traffic speed data for New York City (2019). https://movement.uber.com/
56. United States Department of Energy. Alternative fuels data center (2019). https://afdc.energy.gov/stations/
57. Velner, Y., Chatterjee, K., Doyen, L., Henzinger, T.A., Rabinovich, A.M., Raskin, J.: The complexity of multi-mean-payoff and multi-energy games. Inf. Comput. **241**, 177–196 (2015)
58. Wognsen, E.R., Hansen, R.R., Larsen, K.G., Koch, P.: Energy-aware scheduling of FIR filter structures using a timed automata model. In: 19th International Symposium on Design and Diagnostics of Electronic Circuits and Systems, pp. 1–6 (2016)
59. Zhang, H., Sheppard, C.J.R., Lipman, T.E., Moura, S.J.: Joint fleet sizing and charging system planning for autonomous electric vehicles. IEEE Trans. Intell. Transp. Syst. (2019)

STMC: Statistical Model Checker with Stratified and Antithetic Sampling

Nima Roohi[1][(✉)] , Yu Wang[2] , Matthew West[3], Geir E. Dullerud[3], and Mahesh Viswanathan[3]

[1] University of California, San Diego, USA
nroohi@ucsd.edu
[2] Duke University, Durham, USA
yw354@duke.edu
[3] University of Illinois at Urbana-Champaign,
Urbana, USA
{mwest,dullerud,vmahesh}@illinois.edu

Abstract. STMC is a statistical model checker that uses antithetic and stratified sampling techniques to reduce the number of samples and, hence, the amount of time required before making a decision. The tool is capable of statistically verifying any *black-box* probabilistic system that PRISM can simulate, against probabilistic bounds on any property that PRISM can evaluate over individual executions of the system. We have evaluated our tool on many examples and compared it with both symbolic and statistical algorithms. When the number of strata is large, our algorithms reduced the number of samples more than 3 times on average. Furthermore, being a statistical model checker makes STMC able to verify models that are well beyond the reach of current symbolic model checkers. On large systems (up to 10^{14} states) STMC was able to check 100% of benchmark systems, compared to existing symbolic methods in PRISM, which only succeeded on 13% of systems. The tool, installation instructions, benchmarks, and scripts for running the benchmarks are all available online as open source.

1 Introduction

Statistical model checking (SMC) plays an important role in verifying probabilistic temporal logics on cyber-physical systems [1,14,15]. In SMC, we treat the objective bounded temporal specifications as statistical hypothesis, and infer their correctness with high confidence from samples of the systems. Compared to analytic approaches, statistical model checkers rely only on samples from the systems, and hence are more scalable to large real-world problems with complicated stochastic behavior [3,6,18].

To our knowledge, all existing SMC tools use independent samples. Admittedly, independent sampling is easy to implement, and it is the only option when the model is completely unknown. However, as shown recently in [24,25], if the model is partially known, then we can exploit this knowledge to generate

© The Author(s) 2020
S. K. Lahiri and C. Wang (Eds.): CAV 2020, LNCS 12225, pp. 448–460, 2020.
https://doi.org/10.1007/978-3-030-53291-8_23

semantically negatively correlated samples to increase the sample efficiency in SMC. In [24,25], we present the *stratified and antithetic sampling* techniques for discrete-time Markov chains (DTMC). In this work, we extend the technique to continuous-time Markov chains (CTMC), and implement the corresponding SMC algorithms in the tool STMC. The tool is evaluated on several case studies under hundreds of different scenarios, some of which are well beyond the capabilities of current symbolic model checkers. The results show that the sample efficiency can be significantly improved by using semantically negatively correlated sampling, instead of independent sampling.

This work also provides experimental comparisons between our SMC method and common symbolic model checking methods. Since we use large values for parameters in our case studies, it is no surprise that symbolic engines fail on many of them. However, without our results, the meaning of the word "large" is unclear. Our results give a good understanding of what is currently beyond the capabilities of symbolic engines in a popular tool like PRISM. Next, restricting our attention to the cases in which symbolic engines successfully terminate, our results give us a helpful comparison between symbolic and statistical verification times. It is well-known that symbolic algorithms do not scale well, while statistical ones do. However, that knowledge alone does not give us any insight into how much more or less time a symbolic method requires compared to a statistical one. Finally, when a symbolic method terminates, one might argue that its result is far more valuable than the result of a statistical approach since statistical methods can produce incorrect results. Unfortunately, that is not entirely true. Since the complexity of solving a problem is too high in practice, many symbolic algorithms, including those in PRISM, employ an iterative method to approximate probabilities. This approximation can be far from the actual probability, leading to incorrect model checking results (*e.g.,* [5]).

Related Work. Among the existing statistical model checkers, PRISM [4,12], MRMC [10], VESTA [19], YMER [27], and COSMOS [2] only support independent sampling on DTMC, CTMC, or other more general probabilistic models. PLASMA [9] also supports importance sampling. In importance sampling, although samples may have different weights, they are still generated independently. To our knowledge, our tool STMC is the only existing statistical model checker that employs semantically negatively related sampling on DTMC and CTMC.

2 Stratified and Antithetic Sampling

Stratified and antithetic samplings are two approaches for generating negatively correlated random samples. When using stratified sampling to draw n samples from a distribution, we divide the support into sets with equal measure, and then draw one sample from each partition. When using antithetic sampling, a random seed is first drawn from $x \in [0,1]$, and then two correlated samples are generated using x and $1-x$, respectively. Figures 1 and 2 compare independent and stratified sampling for 625 samples that we drew from the joint distribution of two random variables. In Fig. 1, each variable is uniformly distributed in $[0, 1]$, and in Fig. 2, each variable is exponentially distributed with rate 3 (we only show samples that are within the unit square). It is clear that the stratified samples are (visually) better distributed in both figures.

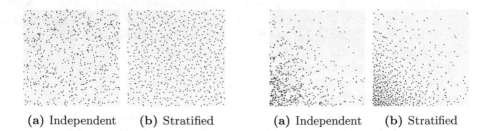

(a) Independent   (b) Stratified   (a) Independent   (b) Stratified

Fig. 1. Uniform distribution   **Fig. 2.** Exponential distribution

We have shown in [24] that by choosing a proper representation of a Markov chain, the stratified sampling technique can be applied to generate semantically negatively correlated sample paths. This technique reduces the sampling cost for statistically verifying temporal formulas. In the rest of this section, we list two algorithms: Stratified sampling of a CTMC, and stratified sequential probability ratio test for a CTMC. The antithetic variants are simpler and we do not present them here for the lack of space. Compared to our algorithms in [24], there are two main differences. First, we present these algorithms for CTMCs instead of DTMCs, as they are slightly more involved. Second, for the stratified sampling of a CTMC, our algorithm supports stratification over multiple steps directly.

Algorithm 1 shows the pseudo-code for stratified sampling of a CTMC; to obtain a stratified sampling algorithm for DTMC, we only need to remove π_2, index$_2$, offset$_2$, rate, r_2, and r_3. It takes two inputs: ψ, a temporal formula that we want to evaluate on every sampled path, and strata_sizes, the number of strata at every step. This is a non-empty list of positive integers. Let K be the length of this list, and N be the product of its elements. If the i_{th} item of the list is n then the number of strata at steps $i, i + K, i + 2K, i + 3K, \ldots$ must be n.[1] The algorithm simultaneously simulates N paths and terminates after the value of ψ on all these paths are known. Inside the main loop, simulation is performed incrementally, K steps at a time. Random permutations π_1, π_2, and variables index$_1$, index$_2$ are used to make simulations of every K steps and random numbers r_1 and r_2 (defined later in the code) independent of each other. The number of strata at every step is an input to this algorithm. Using that number, variables offset$_1$ and offset$_2$ determine which strata we should use at step s. Finally, r_2 is a uniformly distributed stratified sample in $[0, 1)$. However,

---

[1] The current version of **PRISM** only handles one initial state for simulation. Therefore, there will be no stratification for initializing paths.

we need an exponentially distributed stratified sample, which is precisely what $-\ln(1-r_2)/\text{rate}$ gives us.

Algorithm 2 shows pseudo-code for statistical verification of CTMC and DTMC using stratified samples. The algorithm is quite simple. It keeps sampling using Algorithm 1 and computes the average and variance of the values it receives until a termination condition is satisfied. Checking the termination conditions after every step suggests using an online algorithm for computing the mean and variance of samples. We use Welford's online algorithm [26] in our implementation.

Algorithm 1 Stratified Sampling for CTMC

```
1  // Take stratified samples and return fraction of samples that satisfy ψ.
2  // Param ψ is an LTL formula.
3  // Param strata_sizes is a non−empty list of positive integers.
4  function stratified_sampling(ψ, strata_sizes)
5      val K     = strata_sizes.length    // Length of the list
6      val N     = strata_sizes.product   // Product of elements in the list
7      val paths = initialize N paths     // index starts at 0
8      val evals = initialize N evaluators // incrementally evaluate ψ on paths
9      // Evaluation in the condition of the while loop is performed by PRISM
10     while(∃ j∈{0,...,N−1}, evals[j](path[j])='unknown')
11         val π₁ = random permutation of 0,1,...,N−1
12         val π₂ = random permutation of 0,1,...,N−1
13         for(i ← 0,...,N−1)
14             vars index₁, index₂ = π₁[i], π₂[i]
15             for(s ← 0,...,K−1)
16                 val  size = strata_sizes[s] // number of strata at step s
17                 vals offset₁, offset₂ = index₁%size, index₂%size
18                 index₁, index₂ /= size
19                 val rate = rate of last state in path[i]    // by PRISM
20                 val r₁   = rnd(0,1) / size + offset₁ / size // rnd(0,1) ∈ [0,1)
21                 val r₂   = rnd(0,1) / size + offset₂ / size
22                 val r₃   = −ln(1−r₂) / rate // stratified exponentially distributed
23                 Simulate one step in path[i] using r₁ and r₃ // by PRISM
24     return number of paths that satisfy ψ / N
```

Finally, one can extend the following results from [24] to include CTMC.

Theorem 1. *Let ψ be a bounded LTL formula.*

1. *The output of Algorithm 1 has the same expected value as the probability of a random path satisfying ψ.*
2. *If ψ is of the form $\psi_1 \mathcal{U}_I \psi_2$, such that the set of states satisfying ψ_2 is a subset of the same set for ψ_1, then the satisfaction values of different paths simulated by Algorithm 1 are non-positively correlated.*

Theorem 2. *The sampling cost of Algorithm 2 is asymptotically no more than the sampling cost of SPRT [20] using i.i.d. samples.*

3   Tool Architecture

We have implemented our algorithms in `Scala` and published it under the GNU General Public License v3.0. The tool can be downloaded from https://github.com/nima-roohi/STMC/, where installation instructions, benchmarks, and scripts for running the benchmarks are located. We use `PRISM` to load models from files, simulate them, and evaluate simulated paths against non-probabilistic bounded temporal properties. Therefore, `STMC` is capable of statistically verifying any model, as long as it can be simulated by `PRISM`, and bounded temporal properties can be evaluated on single executions of that model. Figure 3 shows `STMC` at a very high level. Boxes marked with 'P' are where we directly use `PRISM`.

Algorithm 2 Stratified Sequential Probability Ratio Test

1 // Verify $\mathcal{P}_{\leq t}\psi$ using stratified sampling.
2 // Param t is the input threshold
3 // Param ψ is an LTL formula (non−probabilistic).
4 // Param strata_sizes is a non−empty list of positive integers.
5 // Param min_iter is the minimum number of iters. the algorithm should take.
6 // Param α is Type−I error probability (must satisfy $0 < \alpha < \frac{1}{2}$).
7 // Param β is Type−II error probability (must satisfy $0 < \beta < \frac{1}{2}$).
8 // Param δ is half of the size of indifference region.
9 **function** stratified_SPRT($\mathbb{P}_{\leq t}\psi$, strata_sizes, min_iter, α, β, δ)
10   **var** iter = 1
11   **var** μ = 0 // average of stratified_sampling return values
12   **var** σ = 0 // standard deviation of stratified_sampling return values
13   **while(true)**
14   iter ++
15   **val** x = stratified_sampling (ψ,strata_sizes)
16   update μ and σ using x // e.g. Welford's online algorithm [27]
17   **if** iter > min_iter **then**
18   **if** $\mu - t < -\frac{\sigma^2}{2\delta\,\text{iter}} \ln \frac{1-\alpha}{\beta}$ **then return true** // accept $\mathcal{P}_{\leq t}\psi$
19   **if** $\mu - t > \frac{\sigma^2}{2\delta\,\text{iter}} \ln \frac{1-\beta}{\alpha}$ **then return false** // reject $\mathcal{P}_{\leq t}\psi$

Executions of `STMC` are configured through different options/switches. The most basic options are `help`, which prints out a list of switches for both `STMC` and `PRISM`, and `stmc`, which enables the tool (without `stmc`, everything will be passed to `PRISM`, pretty much like `STMC` was not there in the first place). Statistical verification is enabled using option `sim`; it is always required when `stmc` is used. The sampling method is specified using option `smp_method` or `sm`. Possible values for the sampling method are **independent**, **antithetic**, and **stratified**. Using option `hyp_test_method` or `hm`, users also have to specify a hypothesis testing method that they would like to use. Supported values for this option are currently `SPRT`, `TSPRT`, `GLRT`, and `SSPRT`. `SPRT` is used for the sequential probability ratio test [20]. This algorithm has already been implemented in `PRISM` and in our experience it has a very similar performance to our implementation (`SPRT` in Sect. 4 refers to the implementation from `PRISM`). We use our implementation for the next option, `TSPRT`. Sequential probability ratio test assumes that the actual probability is not within the δ-neighborhood of the input

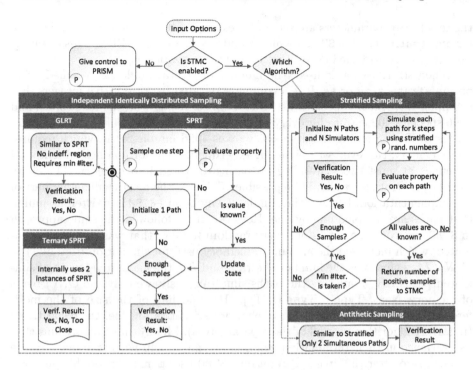

Fig. 3. Architecture of STMC. Boxes marked with letter 'P' use PRISM directly. N is the number of strata, K is the length of strata-size list (see option strata_size below).

threshold. If this assumption is not satisfied, then the algorithm does not guarantee any error probability. TSPRT, which stands for Ternary SPRT, solves this problem by introducing a third possible answer: TOO_CLOSE. The algorithm was introduced in [28]. *Without* assuming that the actual probability is not within the δ-neighborhood of the input threshold, TSPRT guarantees Type-I and Type-II error probabilities are bounded by the input parameters α and β, respectively. Furthermore, it guarantees that if the actual probability and the input threshold are not δ-close, then the probability of returning TOO_CLOSE is less than another input parameter γ; we call this Type-III error probability. The sequential probability ratio test was originally developed for simple hypotheses, and the test is not necessarily optimal when composite hypotheses are used [13]. To overcome this problem, the generalized likelihood ratio test (GLRT) was designed in [7]. The algorithm does not require an indifference region as an input parameter and provides guarantees on Type-I and Type-II error probabilities *asymptotically*. The main issue with this test is that since probabilistic error guarantees are asymptotic, for the test to perform reasonably well in practice (*i.e.*, respect the input error parameters), a correct minimum number of samples must be given as an extra input parameter. If this parameter is too large then the number of samples will be unnecessarily high, and if the parameter is too small then the actual error probability of the algorithm could be close to 0.5, even though the input error parameters are set to, for example, 10^{-7}. The last possible value for `hyp_test_method` is `SSPRT`, which stands for Stratified SPRT. This option is used whenever stratified or antithetic samplings are desired.

When stratification is used, the number of strata should be specified using option `strata_size` or `ss`. It is a comma-separated list of positive integers. For example, 4, 4, 4, 4, 4, 4 specifies 4 strata for six consecutive steps (4096 total), and 4096 specifies 4096 strata for every single step. Note that in both of these examples, stratified sampling simultaneously takes 4096 sample paths, which requires more memory. However, we saw in our experiments that for non-nested temporal formulas, at most two states of each path are stored into memory. Therefore, even larger strata sizes should be possible. This was the most challenging part of the implementation, because the simulator engine in PRISM is written assuming that paths are sampled one by one. However, if we followed the same approach in STMC, we would have to store every random number that was previously generated, which increased the amount of memory used for simulation from $\mathcal{O}(1)$ to $\mathcal{O}(N \times L)$, where N is the number of strata and L is the maximum length of simulated paths. By simulating the paths simultaneously, we only use $\mathcal{O}(N)$ bytes of memory. Next, Type-I, Type-II, Type-III, and half of the size of the indifference region are specified using `alpha`, `beta`,[2] `gamma` and `delta`, respectively (not every algorithm uses all of these parameters). Finally, most algorithms that use variance in their termination condition, require help when sample variance remains zero after the first few iterations. STMC uses `min_iter` for this purpose, and PRISM uses `simvar`.

4   Experimental Results

We evaluated our algorithms on 10 different sets of examples. Each set contains four variations of the same problem with varying parameters and, hence, various sizes, and each of those variations includes four symbolic tests as well as 16 statistical ones. Furthermore, we repeat each of the statistical tests 20 times, to compute 95% confidence intervals for time and number of samples taken by the statistical algorithms. This gives us a total of 800 tests and 12 960 runs to obtain results for those tests. Regarding the stratified sampling, for each variation, we consider 13 settings in 4 groups. Each group uses a different number of strata: 2, 16, 256, and 4096. When the number of strata is more than 2, we also consider different possibilities for how to divide strata among different steps. For example, when 256 strata are used, 256^1 means every step has 256 strata, but different steps are independent of each other. On the other hand, 2^8 means every step has only two strata, but stratification is performed over every 8 consecutive steps.

For the sake of space, we only present 15% of our results in this paper. Full experimental results are available at https://nima-roohi.github.io/STMC/#/benchmarks. Also, all the benchmark source files, along with scripts for running them, can be obtained from the tool's repository page https://github.com/nima-roohi/STMC/. The parameters we chose resulted in large systems, and

---

[2] To the best of our knowledge, PRISM always assumes $\alpha = \beta$.

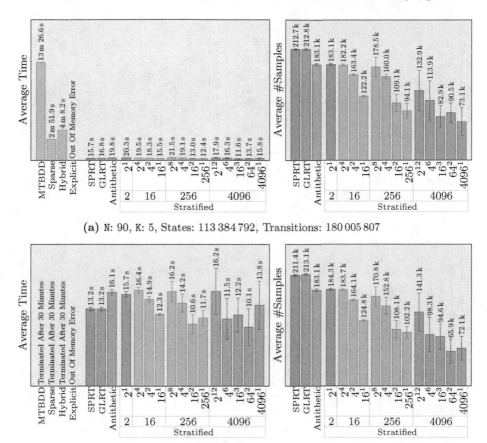

(a) N: 90, K: 5, States: 113 384 792, Transitions: 180 005 807

(b) N: 150, K: 11, States: 1 849 234 352, Transitions: 2 944 935 077

Fig. 4. NAND multiplexing (DTMC - macOS) [17]

significant time has been spent to run and collect the results. To perform our experiments faster, we ran all of our tests using four processes (using option '`-mt 4`'). We also divided out our 10 sets of examples into two groups and ran each set on one of two machines. One of them is running Ubuntu 18.04 with an i7-8700 CPU 3.2 GHz and 16 GB memory, and the other one is running macOS Mojave with an i7 CPU 3.5 GHz and 32 GB memory. STMC's webpage contains a short description for each example and a link to another page for the full explanation. We end this section with a few notes regarding our results.

1. Like any statistical test that is run in a black-box setting, we need to assume simulation of every path will eventually terminate. In fact, PRISM uses the parameter `simpathlen`, with 10 000 as its default value, to restrict the maximum number of simulation steps in each path. Currently, `simpathlen` can be as large as $2^{63} - 1$, which is more than enough in most practical applications.

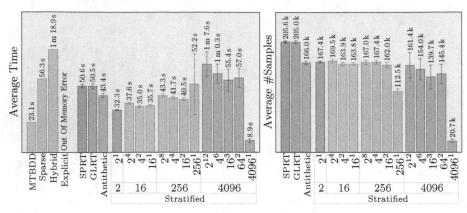

(a) `MAX_COUNT`: 10 000, States: 8 451 788, Transitions: 35 677 505

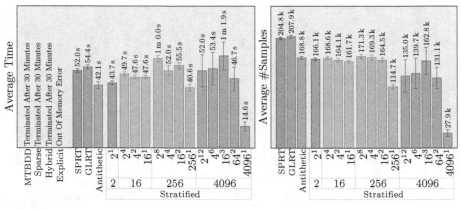

(b) `MAX_COUNT`: 1 000 000, States: about 845 017 880, Transitions: about 3 567 075 050

Fig. 5. Embedded control system (CTMC - Ubuntu) [11,16]

2. To make the configurations less in favor of statistical algorithms, we used small values for α, β, and δ in our benchmarks (between 0.0001 and 0.001). Also, we have estimated the actual probabilities using a symbolic model checker or using a statistical algorithm in `PRISM` and set the threshold close to the actual probability. These settings cause the statistical algorithms to take more samples, which indeed makes it possible for us to observe the effect of antithetic and stratification on the number of samples. As a side effect, we did not observe any performance benefits of GLRT over SPRT.

3. In many of our examples, the variance is particularly high when strata size is 4096. This is because in our benchmarks, whenever 4096 strata are used, we set the minimum number of iterations to 2 (*i.e.*, 8192 samples). This means that when the average number of samples in our results is, for example, around 20 000, only 5 iterations have been taken on average, and every iteration adds or removes about 20% of the samples from the test.

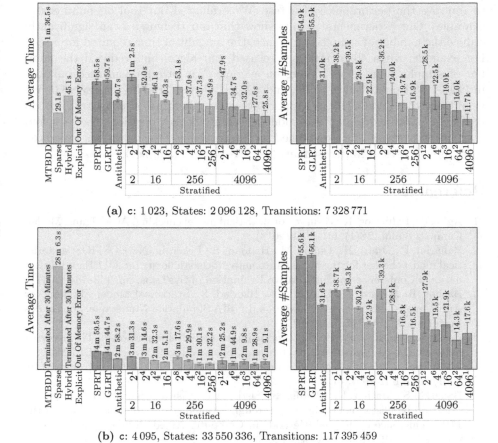

(a) c: 1 023, States: 2 096 128, Transitions: 7 328 771

(b) c: 4 095, States: 33 550 336, Transitions: 117 395 459

Fig. 6. Tandem queueing network (CTMC - macOS) [8]

4. In general, the more strata we use, the greater reduction in the number of samples we observe. Also, the performance of antithetic sampling is similar to the case of using only two strata. Our best results are obtained when 4096^1 is used for the number of strata. For example, in Fig. 5a, comparing SPRT and 4096^1 strata shows almost ten times reduction in the average number of samples. The tool's webpage contains an example in which stratification reduces variance to 0. This results in the termination of the algorithm immediately after a minimum number of samples have been taken, giving us 3 orders of magnitude reduction in the number of samples.

5 Conclusion

We presented our new tool called STMC for statistical model checking of discrete and continuous Markov chains. It uses antithetic and stratified sampling to improve the performance of a test. We evaluated our tool on hundreds of examples. Our experimental results show that our techniques can significantly reduce the number of samples and hence, the amount of time required for a test. For example, when 4096[1] strata were used, our algorithms reduced the number of samples more than 3 times on average. We have implemented our tool in PRISM, and published it online under GNU General Public License v3.0. We would like to extend STMC to support other stratification-based algorithms. In particular, stratified sampling in model checking Markov decision processes, and temporal properties that are defined on the sequence of distributions generated by different types of Markov chains (see [21–23] for examples).

References

1. Agha, G., Palmskog, K.: A survey of statistical model checking. ACM Trans. Model. Comput. Simul. **28**(1), 6:1–6:39 (2018)
2. Ballarini, P., Djafri, H., Duflot, M., Haddad, S., Pekergin, N.: COSMOS: a statistical model checker for the hybrid automata stochastic logic. In: 2011 Eighth International Conference on Quantitative Evaluation of SysTems, pp. 143–144 (2011)
3. Barbot, B., Bérard, B., Duplouy, Y., Haddad, S.: Statistical Model-Checking for Autonomous Vehicle Safety Validation. In: SIA Simulation Numérique. Société des Ingénieurs de l'Automobile (2017)
4. Basu, S., Ghosh, A.P., He, R.: Approximate model checking of PCTL involving unbounded path properties. In: Breitman, K., Cavalcanti, A. (eds.) ICFEM 2009. LNCS, vol. 5885, pp. 326–346. Springer, Heidelberg (2009). https://doi.org/10.1007/978-3-642-10373-5_17
5. Bauer, M.S., Mathur, U., Chadha, R., Sistla, A.P., Viswanathan, M.: Exact quantitative probabilistic model checking through rational search. In: Proceedings of the 17th Conference on Formal Methods in Computer-Aided Design, FMCAD 2017, pp. 92–99. FMCAD Inc., Austin (2017)
6. David, A., Larsen, K.G., Legay, A., Mikučionis, M., Poulsen, D.B., Sedwards, S.: Runtime verification of biological systems. In: Margaria, T., Steffen, B. (eds.) ISoLA 2012. LNCS, vol. 7609, pp. 388–404. Springer, Heidelberg (2012). https://doi.org/10.1007/978-3-642-34026-0_29
7. Fan, J., Zhang, C., Zhang, J.: Generalized likelihood ratio statistics and Wilks phenomenon. Ann. Stat. **29**(1), 153–193 (2001)
8. Hermanns, H., Meyer-Kayser, J., Siegle, M.: Multi terminal binary decision diagrams to represent and analyse continuous time Markov chains. In: Plateau, B., Stewart, W., Silva, M. (eds.) Proceedings of the 3rd International Workshop on Numerical Solution of Markov Chains (NSMC 1999), pp. 188–207. Prensas Universitarias de Zaragoza (1999)
9. Jegourel, C., Legay, A., Sedwards, S.: A platform for high performance statistical model checking – PLASMA. In: Flanagan, C., König, B. (eds.) TACAS 2012. LNCS, vol. 7214, pp. 498–503. Springer, Heidelberg (2012). https://doi.org/10.1007/978-3-642-28756-5_37
10. Katoen, J., Khattri, M., Zapreevt, I.S.: A Markov reward model checker. In: Second International Conference on the Quantitative Evaluation of Systems (QEST 2005), pp. 243–244 (2005)
11. Kwiatkowska, M., Norman, G., Parker, D.: Controller dependability analysis by probabilistic model checking. Control. Eng. Pract. **15**(11), 1427–1434 (2006)

12. Kwiatkowska, M., Norman, G., Parker, D.: PRISM 4.0: verification of probabilistic real-time systems. In: Gopalakrishnan, G., Qadeer, S. (eds.) CAV 2011. LNCS, vol. 6806, pp. 585–591. Springer, Heidelberg (2011). https://doi.org/10.1007/978-3-642-22110-1_47
13. Lai, T.L.: Sequential Analysis: Some Classical Problems and New Challenges. Statistica Sinica 11(2), 303–351 (2001)
14. Larsen, K.G., Legay, A.: Statistical model checking: past, present, and future. In: Margaria, T., Steffen, B. (eds.) ISoLA 2016. LNCS, vol. 9952, pp. 3–15. Springer, Cham (2016). https://doi.org/10.1007/978-3-319-47166-2_1
15. Legay, A., Delahaye, B., Bensalem, S.: Statistical model checking: an overview. In: Barringer, H., Falcone, Y., Finkbeiner, B., Havelund, K., Lee, I., Pace, G., Roşu, G., Sokolsky, O., Tillmann, N. (eds.) RV 2010. LNCS, vol. 6418, pp. 122–135. Springer, Heidelberg (2010). https://doi.org/10.1007/978-3-642-16612-9_11
16. Muppala, J., Ciardo, G., Trivedi, K.: Stochastic reward nets for reliability prediction. Commun. Reliab. Maint. Serv. 1(2), 9–20 (1994)
17. Norman, G., Parker, D., Kwiatkowska, M., Shukla, S.: Evaluating the reliability of NAND multiplexing with PRISM. IEEE Trans. Comput. Aided Des. Integr. Circuits Syst. 24(10), 1629–1637 (2005)
18. Roohi, N., Wang, Y., West, M., Dullerud, G.E., Viswanathan, M.: Statistical verification of the Toyota powertrain control verification benchmark. In: 20th ACM International Conference on Hybrid Systems: Computation and Control (HSCC), pp. 65–70. ACM (2017)
19. Sen, K., Viswanathan, M., Agha, G.: VESTA: A statistical model-checker and analyzer for probabilistic systems. In: Second International Conference on the Quantitative Evaluation of Systems, pp. 251–252 (2005)
20. Wald, A.: Sequential tests of statistical hypotheses. Ann. Math. Stat. 16(2), 117–186 (1945)
21. Wang, Y., Roohi, N., West, M., Viswanathan, M., Dullerud, G.: A Mori-Zwanzig and MITL based approach to statistical verification of continuous-time dynamical systems. In: International Federation of Automatic Control (IFAC PapersOnLine), vol. 48, no. 27, pp. 267–273 (2015)
22. Wang, Y., Roohi, N., West, M., Viswanathan, M., Dullerud, G.: Statistical verification of dynamical systems using set oriented methods. In: Hybrid Systems: Computation and Control (HSCC), pp. 169–178 (2015)
23. Wang, Y., Roohi, N., West, M., Viswanathan, M., Dullerud, G.: Verifying continuous-time stochastic hybrid systems via Mori-Zwanzig model reduction. In: 2016 IEEE 55th Conference on Decision and Control (CDC), pp. 3012–3017 (2016)
24. Wang, Y., Roohi, N., West, M., Viswanathan, M., Dullerud, G.E.: Statistical Verification of PCTL Using Antithetic and Stratified Samples. Form. Methods Syst. Des. 54, 145–163 (2019). https://doi.org/10.1007/s10703-019-00339-8
25. Wang, Y., Roohi, N., West, M., Viswanathan, M., Dullerud, G.E.: Statistical verification of PCTL using stratified samples. In: 6th IFAC Conference on Analysis and Design of Hybrid Systems (ADHS), IFAC-PapersOnLine, vol. 51, pp. 85–90 (2018)
26. Welford, B.P.: Note on a method for calculating corrected sums of squares and products. Technometrics 4(3), 419–420 (1962)

27. Younes, H.L.S.: Ymer: a statistical model checker. In: Etessami, K., Rajamani, S.K. (eds.) CAV 2005. LNCS, vol. 3576, pp. 429–433. Springer, Heidelberg (2005). https://doi.org/10.1007/11513988_43
28. Younes, H.L.S.: Error control for probabilistic model checking. In: Emerson, E.A., Namjoshi, K.S. (eds.) VMCAI 2006. LNCS, vol. 3855, pp. 142–156. Springer, Heidelberg (2005). https://doi.org/10.1007/11609773_10

AMYTISS: Parallelized Automated Controller Synthesis for Large-Scale Stochastic Systems

Abolfazl Lavaei[1]([✉]), Mahmoud Khaled[2],
Sadegh Soudjani[3], and Majid Zamani[1,4]

[1] Department of Computer Science,
LMU Munich, Munich, Germany
lavaei@lmu.de

[2] Department of Electrical Engineering, TU Munich, Munich, Germany
[3] School of Computing, Newcastle University, Newcastle upon Tyne, UK
[4] Department of Computer Science, University of Colorado Boulder, Boulder, USA

Abstract. In this paper, we propose a software tool, called AMYTISS, implemented in C++/OpenCL, for designing correct-by-construction controllers for large-scale discrete-time stochastic systems. This tool is employed to (i) build finite Markov decision processes (MDPs) as finite abstractions of given original systems, and (ii) synthesize controllers for the constructed finite MDPs satisfying bounded-time high-level properties including safety, reachability and reach-avoid specifications. In AMYTISS, scalable parallel algorithms are designed such that they support the parallel execution within CPUs, GPUs and hardware accelerators (HWAs). Unlike all existing tools for stochastic systems, AMYTISS can utilize high-performance computing (HPC) platforms and cloud-computing services to mitigate the effects of the state-explosion problem, which is always present in analyzing large-scale stochastic systems. We benchmark AMYTISS against the most recent tools in the literature using several physical case studies including robot examples, room temperature and road traffic networks. We also apply our algorithms to a 3-dimensional autonomous vehicle and 7-dimensional nonlinear model of a BMW 320i car by synthesizing an autonomous parking controller.

Keywords: Parallel algorithms · Finite MDPs · Automated controller synthesis · Discrete-time stochastic systems · High performance computing platform

1 Introduction

1.1 Motivations

Large-scale stochastic systems are an important modeling framework to describe many real-life safety-critical systems such as power grids, traffic networks, self-driving cars, and many other applications. For this type of complex systems,

A. Lavaei and M. Khaled—Authors have contributed equally.
This work was supported in part by the H2020 ERC Starting Grant AutoCPS (grant agreement No. 804639).

S. K. Lahiri and C. Wang (Eds.): CAV 2020, LNCS 12225, pp. 461–474, 2020.
https://doi.org/10.1007/978-3-030-53291-8_24

automating the controller synthesis procedure to achieve high-level specifications, *e.g.,* those expressed as linear temporal logic (LTL) formulae [24], is inherently very challenging mainly due to their computational complexity arising from uncountable sets of states and actions. To mitigate the encountered difficulty, finite abstractions, *i.e.,* systems with finite state sets, are usually employed as replacements of original continuous-space systems in the controller synthesis procedure. More precisely, one can first abstract a given continuous-space system by a simpler one, *e.g.,* a finite Markov decision process (MDP), and then perform analysis and synthesis over the abstract model (using algorithmic techniques from computer science [3]). Finally, the results are carried back to the original system, while providing a guaranteed error bound [5, 13–21, 23].

Unfortunately, construction of finite MDPs for large-scale complex systems suffers severely from the so-called *curse of dimensionality*: the computational complexity grows exponentially as the number of state variables increases. To alleviate this issue, one promising solution is to employ high-performance computing (HPC) platforms together with cloud-computing services to mitigate the state-explosion problem. In particular, HPC platforms have a large number of processing elements (PEs) and this significantly affects the time complexity when serial algorithms are parallelized [7].

1.2   Contributions

The main contributions and merits of this work are:

(1) We propose a novel data-parallel algorithm for constructing finite MDPs from discrete-time stochastic systems and storing them in efficient distributed data containers. The proposed algorithm handles large-scale systems.

(2) We propose a parallel algorithm for synthesizing discrete controllers using the constructed MDPs to satisfy safety, reachability, or reach-avoid specifications. More specifically, we introduce a parallel algorithm for the iterative computation of Bellman equation in standard dynamic programming [26, 27].

(3) Unlike the existing tools in the literature, AMYTISS accepts bounded disturbances and natively supports both additive and multiplicative noises with different practical distributions including normal, uniform, exponential, and beta.

We apply the proposed implementations to real-world applications including robot examples, room temperature and road traffic networks, and autonomous vehicles. This extends the applicability of formal methods to some safety-critical real-world applications with high dimensions. The results show remarkable reductions in the memory usage and computation time outperforming all existing tools in the literature.

We provide AMYTISS as an *open-source* tool. After compilation, AMYTISS is loaded via pFaces [10] and launched for parallel execution within available parallel computing resources. The source of AMYTISS and detailed instructions on its building and running can be found in: https://github.com/mkhaled87/pFaces-AMYTISS

Due to lack of space, we provide details of traditional serial and proposed parallel algorithms, case studies, etc. in an arXiv version of the paper [12].

1.3 Related Literature

There exist several software tools on verification and synthesis of stochastic systems with different classes of models. SReachTools [30] performs stochastic reachability analysis for linear, potentially time-varying, discrete-time stochastic systems. ProbReach [25] is a tool for verifying the probabilistic reachability for stochastic hybrid systems. SReach [31] solves probabilistic bounded reachability problems for two classes of models: (i) nonlinear hybrid automata with parametric uncertainty, and (ii) probabilistic hybrid automata with additional randomness for both transition probabilities and variable resets. Modest Toolset [6] performs modeling and analysis for hybrid, real-time, distributed and stochastic systems. Two competitions on tools for formal verification and policy synthesis of stochastic models are organized with reports in [1,2].

FAUST^2 [29] generates formal abstractions for continuous-space discrete-time stochastic processes, and performs verification and synthesis for safety and reachability specifications. However, FAUST^2 is originally implemented in MATLAB and suffers from the curse of dimensionality due to its lack of scalability for large-scale models. StocHy [4] provides the quantitative analysis of discrete-time stochastic hybrid systems such that it constructs finite abstractions, and performs verification and synthesis for safety and reachability specifications.

AMYTISS differs from FAUST^2 and StocHy in two main directions. First, AMYTISS implements novel parallel algorithms and data structures targeting HPC platforms to reduce the undesirable effects of the state-explosion problem. Accordingly, it is able to perform parallel execution in different heterogeneous computing platforms including CPUs, GPUs and HWAs. Whereas, FAUST^2 and StocHy can only run serially on one CPU, and consequently, it is limited to small systems. Additionally, AMYTISS can handle the abstraction construction and controller synthesis for two and a half player games (*e.g.*, stochastic systems with bounded disturbances), whereas FAUST^2 and StocHy only handle one and a half player games (*e.g.*, disturbance-free systems).

Unlike all existing tools, AMYTISS offers highly scalable, distributed execution of parallel algorithms utilizing all available processing elements (PEs) in any heterogeneous computing platform. To the best of our knowledge, AMYTISS is the only tool of its kind for continuous-space stochastic systems that is able to utilize all types of compute units (CUs), simultaneously.

We compare AMYTISS with FAUST^2 and StocHy in Table 1 in detail in terms of different technical aspects. Although there have been some efforts in FAUST^2 and StocHy for parallel implementations, these are not compatible with HPC platforms. Specifically, FAUST^2 employs some parallelization techniques using parallel

Table 1. Comparison between AMYTISS, FAUST^2 and StocHy based on native features.

Aspect	FAUST^2	StocHy	AMYTISS
Platform	CPU	CPU	All platforms
Algorithms	Serial on HPC	Serial on HPC	Parallel on HPC
Model	Stochastic control systems: linear, bilinear	Stochastic hybrid systems: linear, bilinear	Stochastic control systems: nonlinear
Specification	Safety, reachability	Safety, reachability	Safety, reachability, reach-avoid
Stochasticity	Additive noise	Additive noise	Additive & multiplicative noises
Distribution	Normal, user-defined	Normal, user-defined	Normal, uniform, exponential, beta, user-defined
Disturbance	Not supported	Not supported	Supported

for-loops and sparse matrices inside Matlab, and StocHy uses Armadillo, a multi-threaded library for scientific computing. However, these tools are not designed for the parallel computation on HPC platforms. Consequently, they can only utilize CPUs and cannot run on GPUs or HWAs. In comparison, AMYTISS is developed in OpenCL, a language specially designed for data-parallel tasks, and supports heterogeneous computing platforms combining CPUs, GPUs and HWAs.

Note that FAUST^2 and StocHy do not natively support reach-avoid specifications in the sense that users can explicitly provide some avoid sets. Implementing this type of properties requires some modifications inside those tools. In addition, we do not make a comparison here with SReachTools since it is mainly for stochastic reachability analysis of linear, potentially time-varying, discrete-time stochastic systems, while AMYTISS is not limited to reachability analysis and can handle nonlinear systems as well.

Note that we also provide a script in the tool repository[1] that converts the MDPs constructed by AMYTISS into PRISM-input-files [11]. In particular, AMYTISS can natively construct finite MDPs from continuous-space stochastic control systems. PRISM can then be employed to perform the controller synthesis for those classes of complex specifications that AMYTISS does not support.

2   Discrete-Time Stochastic Control Systems

We formally introduce discrete-time stochastic control systems (dt-SCS) below.

Definition 1. *A discrete-time stochastic control system (dt-SCS) is a tuple*

$$\Sigma = (X, U, W, \varsigma, f),\tag{1}$$

---
[1] https://github.com/mkhaled87/pFaces-AMYTISS/blob/master/interface/export PrismMDP.m.

where,

- $X \subseteq \mathbb{R}^n$ *is a Borel space as the state set and* $(X, \mathcal{B}(X))$ *is its measurable space;*
- $U \subseteq \mathbb{R}^m$ *is a Borel space as the input set;*
- $W \subseteq \mathbb{R}^p$ *is a Borel space as the disturbance set;*
- ς *is a sequence of independent and identically distributed (i.i.d.) random variables from a sample space* Ω *to a measurable set* $\mathcal{V}_\varsigma$

$$\varsigma := \{\varsigma(k) : \Omega \to \mathcal{V}_\varsigma, \ k \in \mathbb{N}\};$$

- $f : X \times U \times W \to X$ *is a measurable function characterizing the state evolution of the system.*

The state evolution of Σ, for a given initial state $x(0) \in X$, an input sequence $\nu(\cdot) : \mathbb{N} \to U$, and a disturbance sequence $w(\cdot) : \mathbb{N} \to W$, is characterized by the difference equations

$$\Sigma : x(k+1) = f(x(k), \nu(k), w(k)) + \Upsilon(k), \qquad k \in \mathbb{N}, \tag{2}$$

where $\Upsilon(k) := \varsigma(k)$ with $\mathcal{V}_\varsigma = \mathbb{R}^n$ for the case of the additive noise, and $\Upsilon(k) := \varsigma(k) x(k)$ with $\mathcal{V}_\varsigma$ equals to the set of diagonal matrices of the dimension n for the case of the multiplicative noise [22]. We keep the notation Σ to indicate both cases and use respectively Σ_{a} and Σ_{m} when discussing these cases individually.

We should mention that our parallel algorithms are independent of the noise distribution. For an easier presentation of the contribution, we present our algorithms and case studies based on normal distributions but our tool natively supports other practical distributions including uniform, exponential, and beta. In addition, we provide a subroutine in our software tool so that the user can still employ the parallel algorithms by providing the density function of the desired class of distributions.

Remark 1. Our synthesis is based on a max-min optimization problem for two and a half player games by considering the disturbance and input of the system as players [9]. Particularly, we consider the disturbance affecting the system as an adversary and maximize the probability of satisfaction under the worst-case strategy of a rational adversary. Hence, we minimize the probability of satisfaction with respect to disturbances, and maximize it over control inputs.

One may be interested in analyzing dt-SCSs without disturbances (cf. case studies). In this case, the tuple (1) reduces to $\Sigma = (X, U, \varsigma, f)$, where $f : X \times U \to X$, and the Eq. (2) can be re-written as

$$\Sigma : x(k+1) = f(x(k), \nu(k)) + \Upsilon(k), \qquad k \in \mathbb{N}. \tag{3}$$

Note that input models in this tool paper are given inside configuration text files. Systems are described by stochastic difference equations as (2)–(3), and the user should provide the right-hand-side of equations[2]. In the next section, we formally define MDPs and discuss how to build finite MDPs from given dt-SCSs.

---

[2] An example of such a configuration file is provided at: https://github.com/mkhaled 87/pFaces-AMYTISS/blob/master/examples/ex-toy-safety/toy2d.cfg.

3   Finite Markov Decision Processes (MDPs)

A dt-SCS Σ in (1) is *equivalently* represented by the following MDP [8, Proposition 7.6]:

$$\Sigma = (X, U, W, T_{\mathsf{x}}),$$

where the map $T_{\mathsf{x}} : \mathcal{B}(X) \times X \times U \times W \to [0, 1]$, is a conditional stochastic kernel that assigns to any $x \in X$, $\nu \in U$, and $w \in W$, a probability measure $T_{\mathsf{x}}(\cdot | x, \nu, w)$. The alternative representation as the MDP is utilized in [28] to approximate a dt-SCS Σ with a *finite* MDP $\widehat{\Sigma}$ using an abstraction algorithm. This algorithm first constructs a finite partition of the state set $X = \cup_i \mathsf{X}_i$, the input set $U = \cup_i \mathsf{U}_i$, and the disturbance set $W = \cup_i \mathsf{W}_i$. Then representative points $\bar{x}_i \in \mathsf{X}_i$, $\bar{\nu}_i \in \mathsf{U}_i$, and $\bar{w}_i \in \mathsf{W}_i$ are selected as abstract states, inputs, and disturbances. The transition probability matrix for the finite MDP $\widehat{\Sigma}$ is also computed as

$$\hat{T}_{\mathsf{x}}(x' | x, \nu, w) = T_{\mathsf{x}}(\Xi(x') | x, \nu, w), \quad \forall x, x' \in \hat{X}, \forall \nu \in \hat{U}, \forall w \in \hat{W}, \qquad (4)$$

where the map $\Xi : X \to 2^X$ assigns to any $x \in X$, the corresponding partition element it belongs to, *i.e.*, $\Xi(x) = \mathsf{X}_i$ if $x \in \mathsf{X}_i$. Since $\hat{X}$, $\hat{U}$ and $\hat{W}$ are finite sets, $\hat{T}_{\mathsf{x}}$ is a static map. It can be represented with a matrix and we refer to it, from now on, as the transition probability matrix.

For a given logic specification φ and accuracy level ϵ, the discretization parameter δ can be selected a priori such that

$$|\mathbb{P}(\Sigma \vDash \varphi) - \mathbb{P}(\widehat{\Sigma} \vDash \varphi)| \leq \epsilon, \qquad (5)$$

where ϵ depends on the horizon of formula φ, the Lipschitz constant of the stochastic kernel, and the *state* discretization parameter δ (cf. [28, Theorem 9]). We refer the interested reader to the arXiv version [12] for more details.

In the next sections, we propose novel parallel algorithms for the construction of finite MDPs and the synthesis of their controllers.

4   Parallel Construction of Finite MDPs

In this section, we propose an approach to efficiently compute the transition probability matrix $\hat{T}_{\mathsf{x}}$ of the finite MDP $\widehat{\Sigma}$, which is essential for any controller synthesis procedure, as we discuss later in Sect. 5.

4.1   Data-Parallel Threads for Computing $\hat{T}_{\mathsf{x}}$

The serial algorithm for computing $\hat{T}_{\mathsf{x}}$ is presented in Algorithm 1 in the arXiv version [12]. Computations of mean $\mu = f(\bar{x}_i, \bar{\nu}_j, \bar{w}_k, 0)$, $\text{PDF}(x \mid \mu, \Sigma)$, where PDF stands for probability density functions and Σ is a noise covariance matrix, and of $\hat{T}_{\mathsf{x}}$ all do not share data from one inner-loop to another. Hence, this is an embarrassingly data-parallel section of the algorithm. pFaces [10] can be utilized to launch necessary number of parallel threads on the employed hardware configuration (HWC) to improve the computation time of the algorithm. Each thread will eventually compute and store, independently, its corresponding values within $\hat{T}_{\mathsf{x}}$.

4.2   Less Memory for Post States in $\hat{T}_\mathsf{x}$

$\hat{T}_\mathsf{x}$ is a matrix with the dimension of $(n_x \times n_\nu \times n_w, n_x)$. The number of columns is n_x as we need to compute and store the probability for each reachable partition element $\Xi(x'_l)$, corresponding to the representing post state x'_l. Here, we consider the Gaussian PDFs for the sake of a simpler presentation. For simplicity, we now focus on the computation of tuple $(\bar{x}_i, \bar{\nu}_j, \bar{w}_k)$. In many cases, when the PDF is decaying fast, only partition elements near μ have high probabilities of being reached, starting from $\bar{x}_i$ and applying an input $\bar{\nu}_j$.

We set a cutting probability threshold $\gamma \in [0, 1]$ to control how many partition elements around μ should be stored. For a given mean value μ, a covariance matrix Σ and a cutting probability threshold γ, $x \in X$ is called a PDF cutting point if $\gamma = \mathrm{PDF}(x|\mu, \Sigma)$. Since Gaussian PDFs are symmetric, by repeating this cutting process dimension-wise, we end up with a set of points forming a hyper-rectangle in X, which we call it the cutting region and denote it by $\hat{X}^\Sigma_\gamma$. This is visualized in Fig. 1 in the arXiv version [12] for a 2-dimensional system. Any partition element $\Xi(x'_l)$ with x'_l outside the cutting region is considered to have zero probability of being reached. Such approximation allows controlling the sparsity of the columns of $\hat{T}_\mathsf{x}$. The closer the value of γ to zero, the more accurate $\hat{T}_\mathsf{x}$ in representing transitions of $\hat{\Sigma}$. On the other hand, the closer the value of γ to one, less post state values need to be stored as columns in $\hat{T}_\mathsf{x}$. The number of probabilities to be stored for each $(\bar{x}_i, \bar{\nu}_j, \bar{w}_k)$ is then $|\hat{X}^\Sigma_\gamma|$.

Note that since Σ is fixed prior to running the algorithm, number of columns needed for a fixed γ can be identified before launching the computation. We can then accurately allocate a uniform fixed number of memory locations for any tuple $(\bar{x}_i, \bar{\nu}_j, \bar{w}_k)$ in $\hat{T}_\mathsf{x}$. Hence, there is no need for a dynamic sparse matrix data structure and $\hat{T}_\mathsf{x}$ is now a matrix with a dimension of $(n_x \times n_\nu \times n_w, |\hat{X}^\Sigma_\gamma|)$.

4.3   A Parallel Algorithm for Constructing Finite MDP $\hat{\Sigma}$

We present a novel parallel algorithm (Algorithm 2 in the arXiv version [12]) to efficiently construct and store $\hat{T}_\mathsf{x}$ as a successor. We employ the discussed enhancements in Subsect. 4.1 and 4.2 within the proposed algorithm. We do not parallelize the for-loop in Algorithm 2, Step 2, to avoid excessive parallelism (*i.e.,* we parallelize loops only over X and U, but not over W). Note that, practically, for large-scale systems, $|\hat{X} \times \hat{U}|$ can reach up to billions. We are interested in the number of parallel threads that can be scheduled reasonably by available HW computing units.

5   Parallel Synthesis of Controllers

In this section, we employ dynamic programming to synthesize controllers for constructed finite MDPs $\hat{\Sigma}$ satisfying safety, reachability, and reach-avoid properties [26, 27]. The classical serial algorithm and its proposed parallelized version are respectively presented as Algorithms 3 and 4 in the arXiv version [12]. We should highlight that the parallelism here mainly comes from the parallelization of matrix multiplication and the loop over time-steps cannot be parallelized due to the data dependency. More details can be found in the arXiv version.

5.1 On-the-Fly Construction of $\hat{T}_{\mathsf{x}}$

In AMYTISS, we also use another technique that further reduces the required memory for computing $\hat{T}_{\mathsf{x}}$. We refer to this approach as *on-the-fly abstractions* (OFA). In OFA version of Algorithm 4 [12], we skip computing and storing the MDP $\hat{T}_{\mathsf{x}}$ and the matrix $\hat{T}_{0\mathsf{x}}$ (*i.e.*, Steps 1 and 5). We instead compute the required entries of $\hat{T}_{\mathsf{x}}$ and $\hat{T}_{0\mathsf{x}}$ on-the-fly as they are needed (*i.e.*, Steps 13 and 15). This significantly reduces the required memory for $\hat{T}_{\mathsf{x}}$ and $\hat{T}_{0\mathsf{x}}$ but at the cost of repeated computation of their entries in each time step from 1 to T_d. This gives the user an additional control over the trade-off between the computation time and memory.

5.2 Supporting Multiplicative Noises and Practical Distributions

AMYTISS natively supports multiplicative noises and practical distributions such as uniform, exponential, and beta distributions. The technique introduced in Subsect. 4.2 for reducing the memory usage is also tuned for other distributions based on the support of their PDFs. Since AMYTISS is designed for extensibility, it allows also for customized distributions. Users need to specify their desired PDFs and hyper-rectangles enclosing their supports so that AMYTISS can include them in the parallel computation of $\hat{T}_{\mathsf{x}}$. Further details on specifying customized distributions are provided in the README file.

AMYTISS also supports multiplicative noises as introduced in (2). Currently, the memory reduction technique of Subsect. 4.2 is disabled for systems with multiplicative noises. This means users should expect larger memory requirements for systems with multiplicative noises. However, users can still benefit from the proposed OFA version to compensate for the increase in memory requirement. We plan to include this feature for multiplicative noises in a future update of AMYTISS. Note that for a better demonstration, previous sections were presented by the additive noise and Gaussian normal PDF to introduce the concepts.

6 Benchmarking and Case Studies

AMYTISS is self-contained and requires only a modern C++ compiler. It supports all major operating systems: Windows, Linux and Mac OS. Once compiled, utilizing AMYTISS is a matter of providing text configuration files and launching the tool. AMYTISS implements scalable parallel algorithms that run on top of pFaces [10]. Hence, users can utilize computing power in HPC platforms and cloud computing to scale the computation and control the computational complexities of their problems. Table 2 lists the HW configuration we use to benchmark AMYTISS. The devices range from local devices in desktop computers to advanced compute devices in Amazon AWS cloud computing services.

Table 2. HW configurations for benchmarking AMYTISS.

Id	Description	PEs	Frequency
CPU_1	Local machine: Intel Xeon E5-1620	8	3.6 GHz
CPU_2	Macbook Pro 15: Intel i9-8950HK	12	2.9 GHz
CPU_3	AWS instance `c5.18xlarge`: Intel Xeon Platinum 8000	72	3.6 GHz
GPU_1	Macbook Pro 15 laptop laptop: Intel UHD Graphics 630	23	0.35 GHz
GPU_2	Macbook Pro 15 laptop: AMD Radeon Pro Vega 20	1280	1.2 GHz
GPU_3	AWS p3.2xlarge instance: NVIDIA Tesla V100	5120	0.8 GHz

Table 3 shows the benchmarking results running AMYTISS with these HWCs for several case studies and makes comparisons between AMYTISS, FAUST[2], and StocHy. We employ a machine with Windows operating system (Intel i7@3.6 GHz CPU and 16 GB of RAM) for FAUST[2], and StocHy. It should be mentioned that FAUST[2] predefines a minimum number of representative points based on the desired abstraction error, and accordingly the computation time and memory usage reported in Table 3 are based on the minimum number of representative points. In addition, to have a fair comparison, we run all the case studies with additive noises since neither FAUST[2] nor StocHy supports multiplicative noises.

To show the applicability of our results to large-scale systems, we apply our techniques to several physical case studies. We synthesize controllers for 3- and 5-dimensional *room temperature networks* to keep temperatures in a comfort zone. Furthermore, we synthesize controllers for *road traffic networks* with 3 and 5 dimensions to keep the density of the traffic below some desired level. In addition, we apply our algorithms to a 2-dimensional nonlinear robot and synthesize controllers satisfying safety and reach-avoid specifications. Finally, we consider 3- and 7-dimensional *nonlinear* models of an autonomous vehicle and synthesize reach-avoid controllers to automatically park the vehicles. For details of case studies, see the arXiv version [12].

Table 3 presents a comparison between AMYTISS, FAUST[2] and StocHy w.r.t the computation time and required memory. For each HWC, we show the time in seconds to solve the problem. Clearly, employing HWCs with more PEs reduces the time to solve the problem. This is a strong indication for the scalability of the proposed algorithms. Since AMYTISS is the only tool for stochastic systems that can utilize the reported HWCs, we do not compare it with other similar tools.

In Table 3, first 13 rows, we also include the benchmark provided in StocHy [4, Case study 3]. Table 4 in the arXiv version [12] shows an additional comparison between StocHy and AMYTISS on a machine with the same configuration as the one employed in [4] (a laptop having an Intel Core i7 − 8550U CPU at 1.80GHz with 8 GB of RAM). StocHy suffers significantly from the state-explosion problem as seen from its exponentially growing computation time. AMYTISS, on the other hand, outperforms StocHy and can handle bigger systems using the same hardware.

Table 3. Comparison between AMYTISS, FAUST² and StocHy based on their native features for several (physical) case studies. CSB refers to the continuous-space benchmark provided in [4]. † refers to cases when we run AMYTISS with the OFA algorithm. N/M refers to the situation when there is not enough memory to run the case study. N/S refers to the lack of native support for nonlinear systems. (Kx) refers to an 1000-times speedup. The presented speedup is the maximum speedup value across all reported devices. The required memory usage and computation time for FAUST² and StocHy are reported for just constructing finite MDPs. The reported times and memories are respectively in seconds and MB, unless other units are denoted.

Problem	Spec.	$|\hat{X} \times \hat{U}|$	T_d	AMYTISS (time)							FAUST²		fStocHy		Speedup w.r.t	
				Mem.	CPU₁	CPU₂	CPU₃	GPU₁	GPU₂	GPU₃	Mem.	Time	Mem.	Time	FAUST	StocHy
2-d StocHy CSB	Safety	4	6	≤1.0	≤1.0	≤1.0	≤1.0	≤1.0	≤1.0	0.0001	≤1.0	0.002	8.5	0.015	20 x	150 x
3-d StocHy CSB	Safety	8	6	≤1.0	≤1.0	≤1.0	≤1.0	≤1.0	≤1.0	0.0001	≤1.0	0.002	8.5	0.08	20 x	800 x
4-d StocHy CSB	Safety	16	6	≤1.0	≤1.0	≤1.0	≤1.0	≤1.0	≤1.0	0.0002	≤1.0	0.01	8.5	0.17	50 x	850 Kx
5-d StocHy CSB	Safety	32	6	≤1.0	≤1.0	≤1.0	≤1.0	≤1.0	≤1.0	0.0003	≤1.0	0.01	8.7	0.54	33 x	1.8 Kx
6-d StocHy CSB	Safety	64	6	≤1.0	≤1.0	≤1.0	≤1.0	≤1.0	≤1.0	0.0006	4.251	1.2	9.6	2.17	2.0 Kx	3.6 Kx
7-d StocHy CSB	Safety	128	6	≤1.0	≤1.0	≤1.0	≤1.0	≤1.0	≤1.0	0.0012	38.26	6	12.9	9.57	5 Kx	7.9 Kx
8-d StocHy CSB	Safety	256	6	≤1.0	≤1.0	≤1.0	≤1.0	≤1.0	≤1.0	0.0026	344.3	37	26.6	40.5	14.2 Kx	15.6 Kx
9-d StocHy CSB	Safety	512	6	1.0	≤1.0	≤1.0	≤1.0	≤1.0	≤1.0	0.0057	3 GB	501	80.7	171.6	87.8 Kx	30.1 Kx
10-d StocHy CSB	Safety	1024	6	4.0	≤1.0	≤1.0	≤1.0	≤1.0	≤1.0	0.0122	N/M	N/M	297.5	385.5	N/A	32 Kx
11-d StocHy CSB	Safety	2048	6	16.0	1.0912	≤1.0	≤1.0	≤1.0	≤1.0	0.0284	N/M	N/M	1 GB	1708.2	N/A	60 Kx
12-d StocHy CSB	Safety	4096	6	64.0	4.3029	4.1969	≤1.0	≤1.0	≤1.0	0.0624	N/M	N/M	4 GB	11216	N/A	179 Kx
13-d StocHy CSB	Safety	8192	6	256.0	18.681	19.374	1.8515	1.6802	≤1.0	0.1277	N/M	N/M	N/A	≥24h	N/A	≥676 Kx
14-d StocHy CSB	Safety	16384	6	1024.0	81.647	94.750	7.9987	7.3489	6.1632	0.2739	N/M	N/M	N/A	≥24h	N/A	≥320 Kx
2-d Robot†	Safety	203401	8	≤1.0	8.5299	5.0991	0.7572	≤1.0	≤1.0	0.0154	N/A	N/A	N/A	N/A	N/A	N/A
2-d Robot	R.Avoid	741321	16	482.16	48.593	18.554	4.5127	2.5311	3.4353	0.3083	N/S	N/S	N/S	N/S	N/A	N/A
2-d Robot†	R.Avoid	741321	16	4.2484	132.10	41.865	11.745	5.3161	3.6264	0.1301	N/A	N/A	N/A	N/A	N/A	N/A
3-d Room Temp.	Safety	7776	8	6.4451	0.1072	0.0915	0.0120	≤1.0	≤1.0	0.0018	3.12	1247	N/M	N/M	692 Kx	N/A

(continued)

Table 3. (*continued*)

Problem	Spec.	$|\hat{X} \times \hat{U}|$	T_d	AMYTISS (time)							FAUST^2		fStocHy		Speedup w.r.t	
				Mem.	CPU$_1$	CPU$_2$	CPU$_3$	GPU$_1$	GPU$_2$	GPU$_3$	Mem.	Time	Mem.	Time	FAUST	StocHy
3-d Room Temp.†	Safety	7776	8	≤1.0	0.5701	0.3422	0.0627	≤1.0	≤1.0	0.0028	N/A	N/A	N/A	N/A	N/A	N/A
5-d Room Temp.	Safety	279936	8	3338.4	200.00	107.93	19.376	10.084	N/M	1.8663	2 GB	3248	N/M	N/M	1740 x	N/A
5-d Room Temp.†	Safety	279936	8	1.36	716.84	358.23	63.758	30.131	22.334	0.5639	N/A	N/A	N/A	N/M	N/A	N/A
3-d Road Traffic	Safety	2125764	16	1765.7	29.200	131.30	3.0508	5.7345	10.234	1.2895	N/M	N/M	N/M	N/M	N/A	N/A
3-d Road Traffic†	Safety	2125764	16	14.19	160.45	412.79	13.632	12.707	11.657	0.3062	N/A	N/A	N/A	N/M	N/A	N/A
5-d Road Traffic	Safety	68841472	7	8797.4	N/M	537.91	38.635	N/M	N/M	4.3935	N/M	N/M	N/M	N/M	N/A	N/A
5-d Road Traffic†	Safety	68841472	7	393.9	1148.5	1525.1	95.767	44.285	36.487	0.7397	N/A	N/A	N/A	N/A	N/A	N/A
3-d Vehicle	R.Avoid	1528065	32	1614.7	2.5 h	1.1 h	871.89	898.38	271.41	10.235	N/S	N/S	N/S	N/S	N/A	N/A
3-d Vehicle†	R.Avoid	1528065	32	11.17	2.8 h	1.9 h	879.78	903.2	613.55	107.68	N/A	N/A	N/A	N/A	N/A	N/A
7-d BMW 320i	R.Avoid	3937500	32	10169.4	N/M	≥24 h	21.5 h	N/M	N/M	825.62	N/S	N/S	N/S	N/S	N/A	N/A
7-d BMW 320i†	R.Avoid	3937500	32	30.64	≥24 h	≥24 h	≥24 h	≥24 h	≥24 h	1251.7	N/A	N/A	N/A	N/A	N/A	N/A

As seen in Table 3, AMYTISS outperforms FAUST^2 and StocHy in all the case studies (maximum speedups up to 692000 times). Moreover, AMYTISS is the only tool that can utilize the available HW resources. The OFA feature in AMYTISS reduces dramatically the required memory, while still solves the problems in a reasonable time. FAUST^2 and StocHy fail to solve many of the problems since they lack the native support for nonlinear systems, they require large amounts of memory, or they do not finish computing within 24 hours.

Note that considering only dimensions of systems can be sometimes misleading. In fact, number of transitions in MDPs ($|\hat{X} \times \hat{U}|$) can give a better judgment on the size of systems since it directly affects the memory/time needed for solving the problem. For instance in Table 3, the number of transitions for the 14-dimensional case study is 16384, while for the 5-dimensional room temperature example is 279936 transitions (*i.e.*, almost 17 times bigger). This means AMYTISS can clearly handle much larger systems than existing tools.

Acknowledgment. The authors would like to thank Thomas Gabler for his help in implementing traditional serial algorithms for the purpose of analysis and then comparing with the parallel ones.

References

1. Abate, A., et al.: ARCH-COMP19 category report: stochastic modelling. EPiC Ser. Comput. **61**, 62–102 (2019)
2. Abate, A., et al.: ARCH-COMP18 category report: Stochastic modelling. In: ARCH@ ADHS, pp. 71–103 (2018)
3. Baier, C., Katoen, J.P.: Principles of Model Checking. MIT Press, Cambridge (2008)
4. Cauchi, N., Abate, A.: StocHy: automated verification and synthesis of stochastic processes. In: Vojnar, T., Zhang, L. (eds.) TACAS 2019. LNCS, vol. 11428, pp. 247–264. Springer, Cham (2019). https://doi.org/10.1007/978-3-030-17465-1_14
5. Haesaert, S., Soudjani, S.: Robust dynamic programming for temporal logic control of stochastic systems. CoRR abs/1811.11445 (2018). http://arxiv.org/abs/1811.11445
6. Hartmanns, A., Hermanns, H.: The modest toolset: an integrated environment for quantitative modelling and verification. In: Ábrahám, E., Havelund, K. (eds.) TACAS 2014. LNCS, vol. 8413, pp. 593–598. Springer, Heidelberg (2014). https://doi.org/10.1007/978-3-642-54862-8_51
7. Jaja, J.: An Introduction to Parallel Algorithms. Addison-Wesley, Boston (1992)
8. Kallenberg, O.: Foundations of Modern Probability. Springer, New York (1997). https://doi.org/10.1007/b98838
9. Kamgarpour, M., Ding, J., Summers, S., Abate, A., Lygeros, J., Tomlin, C.: Discrete time stochastic hybrid dynamical games: Verification & controller synthesis. In: Proceedings of the 50th IEEE Conference on Decision and Control and European Control Conference, pp. 6122–6127 (2011)
10. Khaled, M., Zamani, M.: pFaces: an acceleration ecosystem for symbolic control. In: Proceedings of the 22nd ACM International Conference on Hybrid Systems: Computation and Control, pp. 252–257 (2019)

11. Kwiatkowska, M., Norman, G., Parker, D.: PRISM: probabilistic symbolic model checker. In: Field, T., Harrison, P.G., Bradley, J., Harder, U. (eds.) TOOLS 2002. LNCS, vol. 2324, pp. 200–204. Springer, Heidelberg (2002). https://doi.org/10.1007/3-540-46029-2_13

12. Lavaei, A., Khaled, M., Soudjani, S., Zamani, M.: AMYTISS: parallelized automated controller synthesis for large-scale stochastic system. arXiv:2005.06191, May 2020

13. Lavaei, A., Soudjani, S., Majumdar, R., Zamani, M.: Compositional abstractions of interconnected discrete-time stochastic control systems. In: Proceedings of the 56th IEEE Conference on Decision and Control, pp. 3551–3556 (2017)

14. Lavaei, A., Soudjani, S., Zamani, M.: Compositional synthesis of finite abstractions for continuous-space stochastic control systems: a small-gain approach. In: Proceedings of the 6th IFAC Conference on Analysis and Design of Hybrid Systems, vol. 51, pp. 265–270 (2018)

15. Lavaei, A., Soudjani, S., Zamani, M.: From dissipativity theory to compositional construction of finite Markov decision processes. In: Proceedings of the 21st ACM International Conference on Hybrid Systems: Computation and Control, pp. 21–30 (2018)

16. Lavaei, A., Soudjani, S., Zamani, M.: Compositional abstraction-based synthesis of general MDPs via approximate probabilistic relations. arXiv: 1906.02930 (2019)

17. Lavaei, A., Soudjani, S., Zamani, M.: Compositional construction of infinite abstractions for networks of stochastic control systems. Automatica **107**, 125–137 (2019)

18. Lavaei, A., Soudjani, S., Zamani, M.: Compositional abstraction-based synthesis for networks of stochastic switched systems. Automatica **114**, 108827 (2020)

19. Lavaei, A., Soudjani, S., Zamani, M.: Compositional abstraction of large-scale stochastic systems: a relaxed dissipativity approach. Nonlinear Anal. Hybrid Syst. **36**, 100880 (2020)

20. Lavaei, A., Soudjani, S., Zamani, M.: Compositional (in)finite abstractions for large-scale interconnected stochastic systems. IEEE Trans. Autom. Control. (2020). https://doi.org/10.1109/TAC.2020.2975812

21. Lavaei, A., Zamani, M.: Compositional construction of finite MDPs for large-scale stochastic switched systems: a dissipativity approach. In: Proceedings of the 15th IFAC Symposium on Large Scale Complex Systems: Theory and Applications 52(3), 31–36 (2019)

22. Li, W., Todorov, E., Skelton, R.E.: Estimation and control of systems with multiplicative noise via linear matrix inequalities. In: Proceedings of the American Control Conference, pp. 1811–1816 (2005)

23. Mallik, K., Schmuck, A., Soudjani, S., Majumdar, R.: Compositional synthesis of finite-state abstractions. IEEE Trans. Autom. Control. **64**(6), 2629–2636 (2019)

24. Pnueli, A.: The temporal logic of programs. In: Proceedings of the 18th Annual Symposium on Foundations of Computer Science, pp. 46–57 (1977)

25. Shmarov, F., Zuliani, P.: ProbReach: verified probabilistic delta-reachability for stochastic hybrid systems. In: Proceedings of the 18th International Conference on Hybrid Systems: Computation and Control, pp. 134–139 (2015)

26. Soudjani, S.: Formal abstractions for automated verification and synthesis of stochastic systems. Ph.D. thesis, Technische Universiteit Delft, The Netherlands (2014)

27. Soudjani, S., Abate, A.: Adaptive and sequential gridding procedures for the abstraction and verification of stochastic processes. SIAM J. Appl. Dyn. Syst. **12**(2), 921–956 (2013)

28. Soudjani, S., Abate, A., Majumdar, R.: Dynamic Bayesian networks as formal abstractions of structured stochastic processes. In: Proceedings of the 26th International Conference on Concurrency Theory, pp. 1–14 (2015)

29. Soudjani, S.E.Z., Gevaerts, C., Abate, A.: FAUST^2: Formal Abstractions of Uncountable-STate STochastic Processes. In: Baier, C., Tinelli, C. (eds.) TACAS 2015. LNCS, vol. 9035, pp. 272–286. Springer, Heidelberg (2015). https://doi.org/10.1007/978-3-662-46681-0_23

30. Vinod, A.P., Gleason, J.D., Oishi, M.M.: SReachTools: a MATLAB stochastic reachability toolbox. In: Proceedings of the 22nd ACM International Conference on Hybrid Systems: Computation and Control, pp. 33–38 (2019)

31. Wang, Q., Zuliani, P., Kong, S., Gao, S., Clarke, E.M.: SReach: a probabilistic bounded delta-reachability analyzer for stochastic hybrid systems. In: Roux, O., Bourdon, J. (eds.) CMSB 2015. LNCS, vol. 9308, pp. 15–27. Springer, Cham (2015). https://doi.org/10.1007/978-3-319-23401-4_3

PRISM-games 3.0: Stochastic Game Verification with Concurrency, Equilibria and Time

Marta Kwiatkowska[1], Gethin Norman[2],
David Parker[3(✉)], and Gabriel Santos[1]

[1] Department of Computing Science,
University of Oxford, Oxford, UK
[2] School of Computing Science,
University of Glasgow, Glasgow, UK
[3] School of Computer Science,
University of Birmingham, Birmingham, UK
d.a.parker@cs.bham.ac.uk

Abstract. We present a major new release of the PRISM-games model checker, featuring multiple significant advances in its support for verification and strategy synthesis of stochastic games. Firstly, *concurrent* stochastic games bring more realistic modelling of agents interacting in a concurrent fashion. Secondly, *equilibria*-based properties provide a means to analyse games in which competing or collaborating players are driven by distinct objectives. Thirdly, a *real-time* extension of (turn-based) stochastic games facilitates verification and strategy synthesis for systems where timing is a crucial aspect. This paper describes the advances made in the tool's modelling language, property specification language and model checking engines in order to implement this new functionality. We also summarise the performance and scalability of the tool, and describe a selection of case studies, ranging from security protocols to robot coordination, which highlight the benefits of the new features.

1 Introduction

Quantitative verification and strategy synthesis are powerful techniques for the modelling and analysis of computerised systems which require reasoning about *quantitative* aspects such as probability, time or resource usage. They can be used either to produce formal *guarantees* about a system's behaviour, for example relating to its safety, reliability or efficiency, or to synthesise controllers which ensure that such guarantees will be met at runtime. Examples of applications where these techniques have been used include power controllers, unmanned aerial vehicles, autonomous driving and communication protocols.

As computing systems increasingly involve concurrently acting autonomous agents, *game-theoretic* approaches are becoming widespread in computer science as a faithful modelling abstraction. These techniques can be used to reason

© The Author(s) 2020
S. K. Lahiri and C. Wang (Eds.): CAV 2020, LNCS 12225, pp. 475–487, 2020.
https://doi.org/10.1007/978-3-030-53291-8_25

about the *competitive* or *collaborative* behaviour of multiple rational agents or entities with distinct goals or objectives. Applications include designing a defence strategy against attackers in a cybersecurity context or building controllers for autonomous robots operating in an unknown or potentially malicious environment. More broadly, game theory techniques such as mechanism design can be used to design protocols that are robust in the context of selfish participants, for example by incorporating *incentive/reward* schemes. They have been successfully deployed in diverse contexts such as network routing [29], auction design [10], public good provisioning [15] and ranking or recommender systems [30].

However, designing game-theoretic systems correctly is a challenge, in view of the complexity of behaviours arising from the interactions between autonomy, concurrency and quantitative rewards. This motivates the development of formal verification techniques to check their correctness and synthesise correct-by-construction strategies for them. Furthermore, many of these applications require reasoning about *stochasticity*: protocols may employ randomisation, e.g., for reliable dissemination across a network, or to minimise the impact of information leakage to an observer; autonomous robots operate in uncertain environments and may use unreliable hardware components or noisy sensors; and data-driven systems such as ranking or navigation systems rely on learnt probabilistic models for their execution.

These challenges have inspired the development of PRISM-games [22], a model checking tool for *stochastic games*. To date, it supports verification and strategy synthesis for *turn-based* stochastic multi-player games (TSGs) using a variety of objectives, expressed in the temporal logic rPATL (probabilistic alternating-time temporal logic with rewards) [8]. This allows specification of *zero-sum* objectives relating to one coalition of players trying to maximise a probabilistic or reward-based objective, while the remaining players form a second coalition trying to minimise the objective. It has also been extended to include (zero-sum) *multi-objective* properties and additional reward measures such as *long-run average* and *ratio reward* [22]. These methods have been successfully applied to several case studies such as autonomous vehicles, user-centric networks, temperature control and an aircraft electric power system [21,23,32].

In this paper, we present PRISM-games 3.0, which significantly extends its predecessor's functionality in several ways [18–20]. First, it supports the modelling and analysis of *concurrent stochastic multi-player games* (CSGs). Previous versions of the tool supported TSGs, in which it is assumed that each state of the game is controlled by a specific player. CSGs allow players to make decisions simultaneously, without knowledge of each other's choices, providing a more realistic model of concurrent execution and decision making. For this, we extend the PRISM-games modelling language, allowing the user to specify concurrency and synchronisation among agents, as well as to associate rewards to either joint or single actions.

In the first instance, PRISM-games now supports verification and strategy synthesis for CSGs using zero-sum specifications in rPATL [19], which we extend to accommodate *instantaneous rewards*. The second major addition to the tool is the possibility of reasoning about *equilibria-based* properties, which allow players to have distinct, not necessarily conflicting objectives. We extend rPATL to express properties relating to (subgame perfect) *social-welfare optimal Nash equilibria (SWNE)* [20]. This provides synthesis of strategies for all players (or coalitions) from which there is no incentive for any of them to unilaterally deviate in any state of the game, and where the combined probabilities or rewards are maximised (or minimised).

Thirdly, PRISM-games now adds support for *probabilistic timed multi-player games* (TPTGs) [18] (currently just the turn-based variant of the model). These extend stochastic multi-player games with real-valued clocks, in the style of (probabilistic) timed automata. This allows real-time aspects of a system to be more accurately modelled. Using the *digital clocks* approach [18], timed models are automatically translated to discrete-time models in order to be verified.

In this paper, we describe the key enhancements made to the tool, notably to its modelling and property specification languages. We also summarise the results, algorithms and implementation of the verification and strategy synthesis techniques developed [18–20] to support the new functionality. We then describe a selection of case studies which showcase the advantages of the new features, and summarise the performance and scalability of the tool.

PRISM-games is open source and runs on all major operating systems. It is available from the tool's website [34]. Supporting material for the paper, including a virtual machine that allows easy running of the tool and reproduction of the results presented in Sect. 4, can be found at [33].

Related Tools. Other model checking tools have been developed to provide support for games. For non-stochastic games, model checking tools such as PRALINE [5], EAGLE [31] and EVE [16] support Nash equilibria [27], as does MCMAS-SLK [6] via strategy logic. UPPAAL STRATEGO [11] is a tool that uses machine learning, model checking and simulation for the synthesis of strategies for stochastic priced timed games. GAVS+ [9] is a general-purpose tool for algorithmic game solving, supporting TSGs and (non-stochastic) concurrent games, but not CSGs. GIST [7] allows the analysis of ω-regular properties on probabilistic games, but again focuses on turn-based, not concurrent, games. General purpose tools such as Gambit [26] can compute a variety of equilibria but not for stochastic games.

2   Modelling and Property Specification Languages

2.1   Modelling Concurrent and Timed Games

The new features in PRISM-games 3.0 have required some significant enhancements to the language used to specify models. For the addition of real-time aspects (i.e., TPTGs), the changes are a straightforward combination of the existing language features for specifying TSGs in PRISM-games (player specifications and mapping of model states to them) and for probabilistic timed automata in PRISM (clock variables, module invariants, guards and clock resets).

We therefore focus in this paper on the specification of CSGs, where the language changes are more fundamental.

PRISM-games has an existing language for specifying TSGs, which is an extension of the native PRISM modelling language [22]. Components of the system to be modelled are encapsulated as *modules*, whose states are defined by a set of finite-range *variables* and whose behaviour is specified using action-labelled *guarded commands*. In a state, one or more modules can execute a command to make a transition: if the guard (a predicate over state variables) is satisfied, the state can be modified (probabilistically) by applying the *updates* of the command. Multiple modules can execute simultaneously if their commands are labelled with the same action.

```
1  csg
2  // Player specification
3  player p1 mac1 endplayer
4  player p2 mac2 endplayer
5  // Max energy per user
6  const int emax;
7  // User 1
8  module mac1
9          s1 : [0..1] init 0; // Has user 1 sent?
10         e1 : [0..emax] init emax; // Energy level of user 1
11         [w1] true -> (s1'=0); // Wait
12         [t1] e1>0 -> (s1'=c'?0:1) & (e1'=e1-1); // Transmit
13 endmodule
14 // Define second user using module renaming
15 module mac2 = mac1 [ s1=s2, e1=e2, w1=w2, t1=t2 ] endmodule
```

```
1  // Probability qi for transmission success when i users send
2  const double q1;
3  const double q2;
4  // Channel (computes joint transmission probabilities)
5  module channel
6          c : bool init false; // Did a collision occur during transmission?
7          [t1,w2] true -> q1:(c'=false) + (1-q1):(c'=true); // User 1 transmits
8          [w1,t2] true -> q1:(c'=false) + (1-q1):(c'=true); // User 2 transmits
9          [t1,t2] true -> q2:(c'=false) + (1-q2):(c'=true); // Both transmit
10 endmodule
```

```
1  // Reward structures
2  rewards "mess1" // Number of messages sent by user 1
3          s1=1 : 1;
4  endrewards
5  rewards "mess2" // Number of messages sent by user 2
6          s2=1 : 1;
7  endrewards
8  rewards "send2" // Number of times users 1 and 2 transmit simultaneously
9          [t1,t2] true : 1;
10 endrewards
```

Fig. 1. An example PRISM-games 3.0 CSG model of medium access control.

CSGs cannot naturally be modelled with this approach for several reasons: (i) players need to be able to concurrently choose between multiple commands with different action labels; (ii) the update performed by one player may be different depending on the action chosen by another player; (iii) when multiple players execute, variables may need to be updated according to an arbitrary probability distribution, rather than being limited to the product of separate distributions specified locally by individual modules.

Figure 1 shows an example of the PRISM-games 3.0 modelling language, which we use to illustrate some of its new features. It models a probabilistic version of the *medium access control* problem, previously described in [5]. Two users share a communication channel. At each time step, user maci ($i = 1, 2$) can choose between transmitting a message (ti) or waiting (wi). Variable si tracks whether a user successfully sent its message in the last time step and ei represents its energy level: transmissions can only occur when energy is positive. A third component is the channel channel, modelled by Boolean variable c denoting whether a collision occurred on the last transmission attempt.

The first difference (with respect to modelling of TSGs) is the player specification: players are associated with modules (rather than states). In the example, module maci constitutes player i. Modules with no nondeterministic choice (like channel) do not need to be tied to a player.

In each state of the CSG, each player chooses between enabled commands of the corresponding modules; if no command is enabled, the player idles. The players move simultaneously so transitions are labelled with *lists* of action labels $[a_1, \ldots, a_n]$. So the guarded command notation is extended accordingly: note how the channel's behaviour depends on which actions the two users take (the same principle applies when specifying reward structures; see send2). Furthermore, variable updates within a command can now be dependent on the updated values of other variables, provided there are no cyclic dependencies. See for example (s1'=c'?0:1), which updates s1 depending on whether there was a channel collision (reflected in c', the updated value of c). We use this mechanism to model interference on the channel: module channel specifies a joint probability distribution which is used to update variables s1 and s2 simultaneously.

2.2 Property Specification

PRISM-games 3.0 also extends the language used to specify properties for verification and strategy synthesis. The previous version already supported *zero-sum* queries for TSGs using the logic rPATL, which combines the game logic ATL with reward-based extensions of the probabilistic logic PCTL. Again, for the new real-time models, it is relatively easy to combine the existing rPATL notation with real-valued time bounds. So, we focus here on the case of CSGs, and in particular *equilibria-based* properties.

We compute values or synthesise strategies which are *social-welfare optimal Nash equilibria (SWNE)*, i.e., which maximise (or minimise) the sum of the values associated to the objectives for each player, but from which there is no incentive for any of them to unilaterally deviate in any state of the game. We express such properties by adding to rPATL the $+$ operator, which is then used to denote the sum of the values associated to both *bounded* and *unbounded* objectives.

When using the rewards operator in equilibria-based properties, we can reason about *cumulative* ($C^{\leq k}$), *instantaneous* ($I^{=k}$) and *expected reachability* (F)

objectives. For properties with the probability operator, we support bounded and unbounded reachability using the temporal operators *next* (X), *eventually* (F) and *until* (U). In order to express zero-sum properties for CSGs, we have implemented all the previous temporal operators for probabilistic queries and a subset of the rPATL operators reported in [8] for reward-based queries, adding to that the instantaneous reward operator.

Finally, following the style of rPATL we separate players into *coalitions* with the syntax $\langle\langle coalition \rangle\rangle$, in order to specify the player or association of players for which we seek to maximise or minimise the values for a given zero-sum property. For equilibria-based properties, given that we maximise/minimise the sum, we use the same operator to separate players in different coalitions using a colon, while players in the same coalition are separated by a comma.

The following are examples of both zero-sum and equilibria-based properties for the medium access CSG model described in Fig. 1.

- $\langle\langle p1 \rangle\rangle P_{max=?}[\,s2{=}0\;U\;s1{=}1\,]$ – what is the maximum probability user 1 can ensure of being the first to transmit, regardless of the behaviour of user 2?
- $\langle\langle p2 \rangle\rangle R^{mess2}_{\geq 2.0}[\,F\;e2{=}0\,]$ – can user 2 ensure the expected number of messages it sends before running out of energy is at least 2, whatever user does?
- $\langle\langle p1{:}p2 \rangle\rangle_{max\geq 2}(P[\,F\;s1{=}1\,] + P[\,F\;s2{=}1\,])$ – if each user's objective is to send their packet with the maximum probability, is it possible for them to collaborate and both transmit their packets with probability 1?
- $\langle\langle p1{:}p2 \rangle\rangle_{max=?}(P[\,s2{=}0\;U\;s1{=}1\,] + P[\,s1{=}0\;U\;s2{=}1\,])$ – what is the sum of SWNE values if each user tries to maximise the probability of being the first to successfully transmit?
- $\langle\langle p1{:}p2 \rangle\rangle_{max=?}(R^{mess1}[\,F\;e1{=}0\,] + R^{mess2}[\,C^{\leq k}\,])$ – what is the sum of SWNE values if user 1 tries to maximise the expected number of packets before running out of energy and user 2 maximises the expected number of packets in the first k steps?

3   Verification and Strategy Synthesis Algorithms

3.1   Zero-Sum Properties for CSGs

When verifying zero-sum properties of CSGs, PRISM-games makes use of the model checking algorithms described in [19], which were based on the methods formulated in [2,3]. We rely on *value iteration* and classical convergence criteria to approximate/compute the values for all states of the game under study, and on solving a *linear program* to compute a *minimax* strategy at each state. This corresponds to solving a *matrix game*, which represents a *one-shot zero-sum* game for the actions of each player in a state. For unbounded properties, the solutions of the matrix games are used to synthesise an optimal (memoryless and randomised) strategy for each player. Prior to this numerical solution phase, we find and remove the states for which the optimal expected reward values are infinite by using the qualitative algorithms developed in [1].

Our current implementation uses the LPsolve [24] library to solve the matrix games at each state. CSGs are built and stored in a explicit-state fashion using an extension of PRISM's Java-implemented *explicit* (sparse-matrix based) engine.

3.2 Equilibria-Based Properties for CSGs

For equilibria-based properties of CSGs, PRISM-games implements the methods described in [20]. We rely on value iteration and *backwards induction* to approximate/compute values and synthesise strategies that are SWNE. For unbounded properties, we can only compute values that are ε-Nash equilibria, since Nash equilibria are not guaranteed to exist. At each state, we solve a *bimatrix game*, which is a representation of a *one-shot nonzero-sum* game and is a linear complementarity problem. We solve these games via *labelled polytopes*, finding all equilibria values through an SMT-based implementation, for which we use third-party SMT solvers Z3 [12] and Yices [13]. We make use of a precomputation step of finding and removing *dominated strategies* in order to minimise the number of calls to the solver.

Unlike zero-sum properties, the synthesised strategies for bounded and unbounded equilibria-based properties require (finite) memory. This is needed due to the fact that a player's choices may change once their objectives have been satisfied. We synthesise strategies by combining the strategy vectors computed for each bimatrix game and the strategy generated by computing optimal values for the MDP resulting from playing the game after either goal has been met. As we use value iteration to approximate values for infinite-horizon properties, we can only synthesise ε-Nash strategy profiles.

3.3 Turn-Based Probabilistic Timed Games

Verification and strategy synthesis of TPTGs relies on the algorithms from [18], which use the *digital clocks* approach that has been a developed for a variety of real-time models. A translation, at the level of the PRISM-games modelling languages, automatically converts the problem of analysing a TPTG into one of solving a (discrete-time) TSG, for which PRISM-games's existing engines can be used. Time-bounded properties are handled by automatically integrating a timing clock into the model prior to translation. As in the rest of PRISM-games, TSGs are also built and solved using the Java-based *explicit* engine.

4   Case Studies and Experimental Results

The features added in PRISM-games 3.0 have been used for over 10 new case studies across a wide range of application domains, including computer security (intrusion detection, radio jamming, non-repudiation), communication protocols (medium access control, Aloha), incentive schemes for cooperative networking, multi-robot navigation problems and processor task scheduling. Details can be found in [18–20] and on the case studies section of the PRISM-games website [35].

Supporting material is at [33]. In this section, we showcase four selected case studies that demonstrate the benefits of the tool's new functionality. We also include a discussion of the scalability and performance of the tool.

Future Markets Investor. This example models two investors playing against the stock market. Investors choose when to invest or to cash in, and the stock market can decide to bar investments at certain points; fluctuations in share values are modelled stochastically. PRISM-games can, for example, synthesise optimal strategies for the two investors to maximise their expected joint profit over time, acting against the stock market which aims to minimise it.

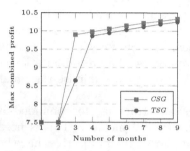

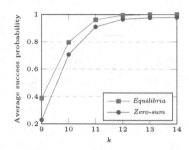

(a) **Future markets investor:** avoiding unrealistic strategy choices using CSGs

(b) **Robot coordination:** using equilibria for mutually beneficial navigation plans

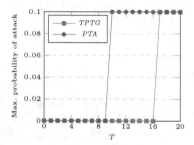

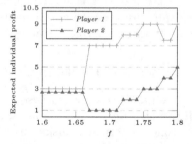

(c) **Non-repudiation:** Attack & defence strategies in a timed, randomised protocol

(d) **Public good game:** Tuning incentive parameter f by synthesising equilibria

Fig. 2. Results illustrating the benefits of the new verification and strategy synthesis techniques implemented in PRISM-games 3.0; see Sect. 4 for details. (Color figure online)

Figure 2(a) shows the results obtained for this property using both a *turn-based* stochastic game (TSG) and a *concurrent* stochastic game (CSG). The former leads to unrealistic modelling as the market can see the choices made by the investors and gain an unfair advantage: the values in the blue plot in Fig. 2(a) are artificially low. In the CSG model, using PRISM 3.0, decisions are taken simultaneously, yielding the correct strategies and values (red plot).

Robot Coordination. Our next example models two robots navigating in opposite directions across a 10-by-10 grid as a CSG. Obstacles which hinder the robots as they move from location to location are modelled stochastically; and if the robots collide, both of them fail in their attempt to reach their goal. We use PRISM-games to find navigation strategies for the two robots, where each robot does not know the choice being made by the other at each step.

The objective for each robot is to navigate successfully, so we maximise the average probability (across the two robots) of success. Figure 2(b) shows the best value that can be achieved within a fixed period of k moves across the grid. One robot aiming single-handedly to achieve this goal performs reasonably well (blue plot), but we can achieve better collective performance by using PRISM-games to synthesise a (social welfare Nash) *equilibrium* strategy (red plot).

Non-repudiation. Next we consider a non-repudiation protocol [25], which permits an originator O to transfer information to a recipient R while guaranteeing non-repudiation, i.e., that neither O nor R can deny that they participated in the transfer. Here, both *probability* (the protocol is randomised) and *time* (the protocol relies on acknowledgement time-outs) are essential ingredients for checking correctness. Furthermore, we model the two participants of the protocol as opposing players, resulting in a TPTG model.

To verify the protocol, we check the worst-case probability that a malicious recipient R can obtain the information being transferred within time T. This can be done with a PTA model (as in [28]) but, with a timed game model, we can also analyse counter-strategies of the honest participant. The results (see Fig. 2(c)) show that, while it is not possible to prevent the information being received, it *is* possible to delay it (the red plot shows lower probabilities for higher times). Note that the bound T is an actual time bound, unlike the examples above, where step-bounded properties measure the number of steps or rounds.

Public Good Game. Lastly, we show a new case study modelling a *public good game*, a well studied model of social choice in economics where participants repeatedly decide how much of an endowment to keep for themselves or to share it with the other players. The total shared by the players is boosted by a factor f in order to incentivise sharing and then divided equally between the players.

Figure 2(d) shows results from a 2-player game, modelled as a CSG. Player choices are necessarily *concurrent*, to avoid cheating. We also need to use *equilibria* since the players have distinct individual goals (maximising personal expected profit). Figure 2(d) shows the values for each player in a synthesised optimal (social welfare Nash) equilibrium for varying f. Changes in f affect both the resulting profit *and* potential inequalities between players in equilibria, indicating the subtleties involved when tuning parameters in an incentive mechanism and the usefulness of analysing this with PRISM-games.

Scalability and Performance. Finally, we show some experimental results for a representative selection of larger examples, to give an indication of the scalability and performance of PRISM-games 3.0. Table 1 shows a range of models (the first 4 are CSGs; the last is a TPTG), the statistics for each one (number of

Table 1. Model statistics for some of the case studies.

Case study	Players	States transitions	Constr. time(s)	Property	Verif. time(s)
Robot coordination	2	159,202 10,765,010	30.94	$\langle\langle p_1 \rangle\rangle P_{max=?}[\,\neg c \cup^{\leqslant k} g_1\,]$	114.5
	2	159,202 10,765,010	39.00	$\langle\langle p_1{:}p_2 \rangle\rangle_{max=?}(P[\,\neg c \cup^{\leqslant k} g_1\,]+P[\,\neg c \cup^{\leqslant k} g_2\,])$	1,080
Future markets investors	3	1,398,441 7,374,616	51.2	$\langle\langle i_1 \rangle\rangle R_{max=?}[\,F^c \text{ cashed}_1\,]$	1,030
	3	478,761 2,265,560	13.47	$\langle\langle i_1{:}i_2 \rangle\rangle_{max=?}(R[\,F\ c_1\,]+R[\,F\ c_2\,])$	13,110
User-centric networks	7	2,993,308 11,392,196	198.6	$\langle\langle user \rangle\rangle R_{max=?}[\,F^c \text{ services}=K\,]$	1,061
Aloha	3	556,168 2,401,113	15.7	$\langle\langle p_2, p_3 \rangle\rangle R_{min=?}[\,F \text{ sent}_{2,3}\,]$	317.8
	3	3,334,681 17,834,254	146.1	$\langle\langle p_1{:}p_2,p_3 \rangle\rangle_{min=?}(R[\,F\ s_1\,]+R[\,F\ s_{2,3}\,])$	3,129
Task graph scheduling	2	659,948 1,798,198	11.16	$\langle\langle sched \rangle\rangle R_{max=?}[\,F \text{ done}\,]$	89.7

players, states, transitions) and the time taken to build and verify the model for some example properties on a 2.10 GHz Intel Xeon with 8 GB of JVM memory.

Verification of CSGs is more computationally expensive than for TSGs supported in earlier versions of the tool, but PRISM-games 3.0 is able to build and analyse CSGs with more than 3 million states on relatively modest hardware. The majority of the time is spent solving (bi)matrix games, which is done repeatedly for all states of the model. Hence, the number of choices per state, which dictates the size of these games, has a greater impact on performance than for TSGs. Unsurprisingly, equilibria properties are slower than zero-sum ones. For both types of property, the number of players in the game does not have a major impact since they are grouped into coalitions yielding a 2-player game to solve. For TPTGs, the digital clocks translation is fast since it is done syntactically, and then a TSG is solved whose size depends on several factors, primarily the number of locations and the magnitude of any time bound in the property.

5   Conclusions

We have presented PRISM-games 3.0, which adds three major new features: (i) concurrent stochastic games; (ii) synthesis of equilibria; and (iii) timed probabilistic games. The usefulness of these has been illustrated on several newly created or extended applications.

CSGs are considerably more expensive to solve than their turn-based counterparts and a key challenge is efficiently solving the matrix game at each state, which is itself a non-trivial optimisation problem. For equilibria, the main difficulty is finding an optimal equilibrium, which currently relies on iteratively restricting the solution search space. Both problems are sensitive to the limitations and issues of floating-point arithmetic, particularly equilibria computation, and might benefit from arbitrary precision representations. Recent research has also pointed out the shortcomings of only using a lower bound approximation as a stopping criterion for value iteration, as it can lead to inaccuracies [4,14,17]. The impact of similar issues on model checking for games is still to be studied.

A range of further challenges exist for future work. These include providing support for *multi-coalitional* properties and implementing other techniques for equilibria computation. For timed games, we plan to investigate concurrent variants, and also zone-based solution techniques. More broadly speaking, partial information variants of games would be a useful addition.

Acknowledgements. This project has received funding from the European Research Council (ERC) under the European Union's Horizon 2020 research and innovation programme (grant agreement No. 834115) and the EPSRC Programme Grant on Mobile Autonomy (EP/M019918/1).

References

1. de Alfaro, L., Henzinger, T.: Concurrent omega-regular games. In: LICS 2000, pp. 141–154 (2000)
2. de Alfaro, L., Henzinger, T., Kupferman, O.: Concurrent reachability games. Theor. Comput. Sci. **386**(3), 188–217 (2007)
3. de Alfaro, L., Majumdar, R.: Quantitative solution of omega-regular games. J. Comput. Syst. Sci. **68**(2), 374–397 (2004)
4. Baier, C., Klein, J., Leuschner, L., Parker, D., Wunderlich, S.: Ensuring the reliability of your model checker: interval iteration for Markov decision processes. In: Majumdar, R., Kunčak, V. (eds.) CAV 2017. LNCS, vol. 10426, pp. 160–180. Springer, Cham (2017). https://doi.org/10.1007/978-3-319-63387-9_8
5. Brenguier, R.: PRALINE: a tool for computing nash equilibria in concurrent games. In: Sharygina, N., Veith, H. (eds.) CAV 2013. LNCS, vol. 8044, pp. 890–895. Springer, Heidelberg (2013). https://doi.org/10.1007/978-3-642-39799-8_63
6. Čermák, P., Lomuscio, A., Mogavero, F., Murano, A.: MCMAS-SLK: a model checker for the verification of strategy logic specifications. In: Biere, A., Bloem, R. (eds.) CAV 2014. LNCS, vol. 8559, pp. 525–532. Springer, Cham (2014). https://doi.org/10.1007/978-3-319-08867-9_34
7. Chatterjee, K., Henzinger, T.A., Jobstmann, B., Radhakrishna, A.: GIST: a solver for probabilistic games. In: Touili, T., Cook, B., Jackson, P. (eds.) CAV 2010. LNCS, vol. 6174, pp. 665–669. Springer, Heidelberg (2010). https://doi.org/10.1007/978-3-642-14295-6_57. pub.ist.ac.at/gist/
8. Chen, T., Forejt, V., Kwiatkowska, M., Parker, D., Simaitis, A.: Automatic verification of competitive stochastic systems. Form. Methods Syst. Des. **43**(1), 61–92 (2013)
9. Cheng, C.-H., Knoll, A., Luttenberger, M., Buckl, C.: GAVS+: an open platform for the research of algorithmic game solving. In: Abdulla, P.A., Leino, K.R.M. (eds.) TACAS 2011. LNCS, vol. 6605, pp. 258–261. Springer, Heidelberg (2011). https://doi.org/10.1007/978-3-642-19835-9_22. sourceforge.net/projects/gavsplus/
10. Cramton, P., Shoham, Y., Steinberg, R.: An overview of combinatorial auctions. SIGecom Exch. **7**, 3–14 (2007)

11. David, A., Jensen, P.G., Larsen, K.G., Mikučionis, M., Taankvist, J.H.: UPPAAL STRATEGO. In: Baier, C., Tinelli, C. (eds.) TACAS 2015. LNCS, vol. 9035, pp. 206–211. Springer, Heidelberg (2015). https://doi.org/10.1007/978-3-662-46681-0_16. people.cs.aau.dk/marius/stratego/
12. de Moura, L., Bjørner, N.: Z3: an efficient SMT solver. In: Ramakrishnan, C.R., Rehof, J. (eds.) TACAS 2008. LNCS, vol. 4963, pp. 337–340. Springer, Heidelberg (2008). https://doi.org/10.1007/978-3-540-78800-3_24. github.com/Z3Prover/z3
13. Dutertre, B.: Yices 2.2. In: Biere, A., Bloem, R. (eds.) CAV 2014. LNCS, vol. 8559, pp. 737–744. Springer, Cham (2014). https://doi.org/10.1007/978-3-319-08867-9_49. yices.csl.sri.com
14. Haddad, S., Monmege, B.: Interval iteration algorithm for MDPs and IMDPs. Theor. Comput. Sci. **735**, 111–131 (2018)
15. Hauser, O., Hilbe, C., Chatterjee, K., Nowak, M.: Social dilemmas among unequals. Nature **572**, 524–527 (2019)
16. Gutierrez, J., Najib, M., Perelli, G., Wooldridge, M.: EVE: a tool for temporal equilibrium analysis. In: Lahiri, S.K., Wang, C. (eds.) ATVA 2018. LNCS, vol. 11138, pp. 551–557. Springer, Cham (2018). https://doi.org/10.1007/978-3-030-01090-4_35. github.com/eve-mas/eve-parity
17. Kelmendi, E., Krämer, J., Křetínský, J., Weininger, M.: Value iteration for simple stochastic games: stopping criterion and learning algorithm. In: Chockler, H., Weissenbacher, G. (eds.) CAV 2018. LNCS, vol. 10981, pp. 623–642. Springer, Cham (2018). https://doi.org/10.1007/978-3-319-96145-3_36
18. Kwiatkowska, M., Norman, G., Parker, D.: Verification and control of turn-based probabilistic real-time games. In: Alvim, M.S., Chatzikokolakis, K., Olarte, C., Valencia, F. (eds.) The Art of Modelling Computational Systems: A Journey from Logic and Concurrency to Security and Privacy. LNCS, vol. 11760, pp. 379–396. Springer, Cham (2019). https://doi.org/10.1007/978-3-030-31175-9_22
19. Kwiatkowska, M., Norman, G., Parker, D., Santos, G.: Automated verification of concurrent stochastic games. In: McIver, A., Horvath, A. (eds.) QEST 2018. LNCS, vol. 11024, pp. 223–239. Springer, Cham (2018). https://doi.org/10.1007/978-3-319-99154-2_14
20. Kwiatkowska, M., Norman, G., Parker, D., Santos, G.: Equilibria-based probabilistic model checking for concurrent stochastic games. In: ter Beek, M.H., McIver, A., Oliveira, J.N. (eds.) FM 2019. LNCS, vol. 11800, pp. 298–315. Springer, Cham (2019). https://doi.org/10.1007/978-3-030-30942-8_19
21. Kwiatkowska, M., Parker, D., Simaitis, A.: Strategic analysis of trust models for user-centric networks. In: Proceedings of the SR'13, EPTCS, vol. 112, pp. 53–60. Open Publishing Association (2013)
22. Kwiatkowska, M., Parker, D., Wiltsche, C.: PRISM-games 2.0: a tool for multi-objective strategy synthesis for stochastic games. In: Chechik, M., Raskin, J.-F. (eds.) TACAS 2016. LNCS, vol. 9636, pp. 560–566. Springer, Heidelberg (2016). https://doi.org/10.1007/978-3-662-49674-9_35
23. Kwiatkowska, M., Parker, D., Wiltsche, C.: PRISM-games: verification and strategy synthesis for stochastic multi-player games with multiple objectives. Softw. Tools Technol. Transf. **20**(2), 195–210 (2018)
24. LPSolve (version 5.5). lpsolve.sourceforge.net/5.5/
25. Markowitch, O., Roggeman, Y.: Probabilistic non-repudiation without trusted third party. In: Proceedings of the 2nd Workshop on Security in Communication Networks (1999)
26. McKelvey, R., McLennan, A., Turocy, T.: Gambit: Software tools for game theory, version 16.0.1 (2016). gambit-project.org

27. Nash, J.: Equilibrium points in n-person games. Proc. Natl. Acad. Sci **36**, 48–49 (1950)
28. Norman, G., Parker, D., Sproston, J.: Model checking for probabilistic timed automata. Form. Methods Syst. Des. **43**(2), 164–190 (2013). https://doi.org/10.1007/s10703-012-0177-x
29. Roughgarden, T., Tardos, E.: How bad is selfish routing? J. ACM **49**, 236–259 (2002)
30. Tennenholtz, M., Kurland, O.: Rethinking search engines and recommendation systems: a game theoretic perspective. Commun. ACM **62**, 66–75 (2019)
31. Toumi, A., Gutierrez, J., Wooldridge, M.: A tool for the automated verification of nash equilibria in concurrent games. In: Leucker, M., Rueda, C., Valencia, F.D. (eds.) ICTAC 2015. LNCS, vol. 9399, pp. 583–594. Springer, Cham (2015). https://doi.org/10.1007/978-3-319-25150-9_34
32. Wiltsche, C.: Assume-guarantee strategy synthesis for stochastic games. Ph.D. thesis, University of Oxford (2015)
33. Supporting materials and artifact. prismmodelchecker.org/files/cav20pg3/
34. PRISM-games website. prismmodelchecker.org/games/
35. PRISM-games case studies. prismmodelchecker.org/games/casestudies.php

Optimistic Value Iteration

Arnd Hartmanns[1]([✉]) [iD] and Benjamin Lucien Kaminski[2] [iD]

[1] University of Twente,
Enschede, The Netherlands
arnd.hartmanns@utwente.nl
[2] University College London, London, UK
b.kaminski@ucl.ac.uk

Abstract. Markov decision processes are widely used for planning and verification in settings that combine controllable or adversarial choices with probabilistic behaviour. The standard analysis algorithm, value iteration, only provides *lower bounds* on infinite-horizon probabilities and rewards. Two "sound" variations, which also deliver an *upper bound*, have recently appeared. In this paper, we present a new sound approach that leverages value iteration's ability to *usually* deliver good lower bounds: we obtain a lower bound via standard value iteration, use the result to "guess" an upper bound, and prove the latter's correctness. We present this *optimistic value iteration* approach for computing reachability probabilities as well as expected rewards. It is easy to implement and performs well, as we show via an extensive experimental evaluation using our implementation within the mcsta model checker of the MODEST TOOLSET.

1 Introduction

Markov decision processes (MDP, [30]) are a widely-used formalism to represent discrete-state and -time systems in which *probabilistic* effects meet controllable *nondeterministic* decisions. The former may arise from an environment or agent whose behaviour is only known statistically (e.g. message loss in wireless communication or statistical user profiles), or it may be intentional as part of a randomised algorithm (such as exponential backoff in Ethernet). The latter may be under the control of the system—then we are in a planning setting and typically look for a *scheduler* (or strategy, policy) that minimises the probability of unsafe behaviour or maximises a reward—or it may be considered adversarial, which is the standard assumption in verification: we want to establish that the maximum probability of unsafe behaviour is below, or that the minimum reward is above, a specified threshold. Extensions of MDP cover continuous time [11,26],

The authors are listed alphabetically. This work was partly performed while author B. L. Kaminski was at RWTH Aachen University, Aachen, Germany. This work was supported by ERC Advanced Grant 787914 (FRAPPANT), DFG Research Training Group 2236 (UnRAVeL), and NWO VENI grant no. 639.021.754.

S. K. Lahiri and C. Wang (Eds.): CAV 2020, LNCS 12225, pp. 488–511, 2020.
https://doi.org/10.1007/978-3-030-53291-8_26

and the analysis of complex formalisms such as stochastic hybrid automata [13] can be reduced to the analysis of MDP abstractions.

The standard algorithm to compute optimal (maximum or minimum) probabilities or reward values on MDP is *value iteration* (VI). It implicitly computes the corresponding optimal scheduler, too. It keeps track of a value for every state of the MDP, locally improves the values iteratively until a "convergence" criterion is met, and then reports the final value for the initial state as the overall result. The initial values are chosen to be an underapproximation of the true values (e.g. 0 for all states in case of probabilities or non-negative rewards). The final values are then an improved underapproximation of the true values. For unbounded (infinite-horizon) properties, there is unfortunately no (known and practical) convergence criterion that could guarantee a predefined error on the final result. Still, probabilistic model checkers such as PRISM [24] report the final result obtained via simple relative or absolute global error criteria as the definitive probability. This is because, on *most* case studies considered so far, value iteration in fact converges fast enough that the (relative or absolute) difference between the reported and the true value approximately meets the error ϵ specified for the convergence criterion. Only relatively recently has this problem of soundness come to the attention of the probabilistic verification and planning communities [7,14,28]. First highlighted on hand-crafted counterexamples, it has by now been found to affect benchmarks and real-life case studies, too [3].

The first proposal to compute sound reachability probabilities was to use *interval iteration* (II [15], first presented in [14]). The idea is to perform two iterations concurrently, one starting from 0 as before, and one starting from 1. The latter improves an overapproximation of the true values, and the process can be stopped once the (relative or absolute) difference between the two values for the initial state is below the specified ϵ, or at any earlier time with a correspondingly larger but known error. Baier et al. extended interval iteration to expected accumulated reward values [3]; here, the complication is to find initial values that are guaranteed to be an overapproximation. The proposed graph-based (i.e. not numerical) algorithm in practice tends to compute conservative initial values from which many iterations are needed until convergence. More recently, *sound value iteration* (SVI) [31] improved upon interval iteration by computing upper bounds on-the-fly and performing larger value improvements per iteration, for both probabilities and expected rewards. However, we found SVI tricky to implement correctly; some edge cases not considered by the algorithm as presented in [31] initially caused our implementation to deliver incorrect results or diverge on very few benchmarks. Both II and SVI fundamentally depend on the MDP being *contracting*; this must be ensured by appropriate structural transformations, e.g. by collapsing end components, a priori. These transformations additionally complicate implementations, and increase memory requirements.

Our Contribution. We present (in Sect. 4) a new algorithm to compute sound reachability probabilities and expected rewards that is both simple and practically efficient. We first (1) perform standard value iteration until "convergence", resulting in a lower bound on the value for every state. To this we (2) apply specific heuristics to "guess", for every state, a candidate upper bound value.

Further value iterations (3) then confirm (if all values decrease) or disprove (if all values increase, or lower and upper bounds cross) the soundness of the upper bounds. In the latter case, we perform more lower bound iterations with reduced ϵ before retrying from step 2. We combine classic results from domain theory with specific properties of value iteration to show that our algorithm terminates. In problematic cases, many retries may be needed before termination, and performance may be worse than interval or sound value iteration. However, on many existing case studies, value iteration already worked well, and our approach attaches a soundness proof to its result with moderate overhead. We thus refer to it as *optimistic value iteration* (OVI). In contrast to II and SVI, it also works well for non-contracting MDP, albeit without a general termination guarantee. Our experimental evaluation in Sect. 5 uses all applicable models from the Quantitative Verification Benchmark Set [21] to confirm that OVI indeed performs as expected. It uses our publicly available implementations of II, SVI, and now OVI in the mcsta model checker of the MODEST TOOLSET [20].

Related Work. In parallel to [15], the core idea behind II was also presented in [7] (later improved in [2]), embedded in a learning-based framework that manages to alleviate the state space explosion problem in models with a particular structure. In this approach, end components are statistically detected and collapsed on-the-fly. II has recently been extended to stochastic games in [23], offering *deflating* as a new alternative to collapsing end components in MDP. Deflating does not require a structural transformation, but rather extra computation steps in each iteration applied to the states of all (a priori identified) end components.

The only known convergence criterion for pure VI was presented in [9, Sect. 3.5]: if we run VI until the absolute error between two iterations is less than a certain value α, then the computed values at that point are within α of the true values, and can in fact be rounded to the exact true values (as implemented in the *rational search* approach [5]). However, α cannot be freely chosen; it is a fixed number that depends on the size of the MDP and the largest denominator of the (rational) transition probabilities. The number of iterations needed is exponential in the size and the denominators. While not very useful in practice, this establishes an exponential upper bound on the number of iterations needed in unbounded-horizon VI. Additionally, Balaji et al. [4] recently showed the computations in finite-horizon value iteration to be EXPTIME-complete.

As an alternative to the iterative numeric road, guaranteed correct results (modulo implementation errors) can be obtained by using precise rational arithmetic. It does not combine too well with iterative methods like II or SVI due to the increasingly small differences between the values and the actual solution. The probabilistic model checker STORM [10] thus combines topological decomposition, policy iteration, and exact solvers for linear equation systems based on Gaussian elimination when asked to use rational arithmetic [22, Section 7.4.8]. The disadvantage is the significant runtime cost for performing the unlimited-precision calculations, limiting such methods to relatively smaller MDP.

The only experimental evaluations using large sets of benchmarks that we are aware of compared VI with II to study the overhead needed to obtain sound

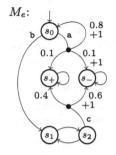

M_e:

Fig. 1. Example MDP

Table 1. VI and OVI example on M_e

i	$v(s_0)$	$u(s_0)$	$v(s_1)$	$u(s_1)$	$v(s_2)$	$u(s_2)$	error	α
0	0		0		0			0.05
1	0.1		0		0.4		0.4	0.05
2	0.18		0.4		0.4		0.4	0.05
3	0.4		0.4		0.4		0.22	0.05
4	0.42	0.47	0.4	0.45	0.4	0.45	0.02	0.05
5	0.436	0.47	0.4	0.45	0.4	0.45	0.016	
6	0.4488		0.4		0.4		0.0128	0.008
7	0.45904		0.4		0.4		0.01024	0.008
8	0.467232		0.4		0.4		0.008192	0.008
9	0.4737856	0.5237856	0.4	0.45	0.4	0.45	0.0065536	0.008
10	0.47902848	0.51902848	0.4	0.45	0.4	0.45	0.00524288	

results via II [3], and II with SVI to show the performance improvements of SVI [31]. The learning-based method with deflation of [2] does not compete against II and SVI; its aim is rather in dealing with state space explosion (i.e. memory usage). Its performance was evaluated on 16 selected small ($<400\,\mathrm{k}$ states) benchmark instances in [2], showing absolute errors on the order of 10^{-4} on many benchmarks with a 30-min timeout. SVI thus appears the most competitive technique in runtime and precision so far. Consequently, in our evaluation in Sect. 5, we compare OVI with SVI, and II for reference, using the default relative error of 10^{-6}, including large and excluding clearly acyclic benchmarks (since they are trivial even for VI), with a 10-min timeout which is rarely hit.

2   Preliminaries

$\mathbb{R}_0^+$ is the set of all non-negative real numbers. We write $\{x_1 \mapsto y_1, \dots\}$ to denote the function that maps all x_i to y_i, and if necessary in the respective context, implicitly maps to 0 all x for which no explicit mapping is specified. Given a set S, its powerset is 2^S. A (discrete) *probability distribution* over S is a function $\mu \in S \to [0,1]$ with countable *support* $spt(\mu) \stackrel{\text{def}}{=} \{s \in S \mid \mu(s) > 0\}$ and $\sum_{s \in spt(\mu)} \mu(s) = 1$. $Dist(S)$ is the set of all probability distributions over S.

Markov Decision Processes (MDP) combine nondeterministic choices as in labelled transition systems with discrete probabilistic decisions as in discrete-time Markov chains (DTMC). We define them formally and describe their semantics.

Definition 1. *A* Markov decision process *(MDP) is a triple* $M = \langle S, s_I, T \rangle$ *where S is a finite set of* states *with* initial state *$s_I \in S$ and $T \colon S \to 2^{Dist(\mathbb{R}_0^+ \times S)}$ is the* transition function. *$T(s)$ must be finite and non-empty for all $s \in S$.*

For $s \in S$, an element of $T(s)$ is a *transition*, and a pair $\langle r, s' \rangle \in spt(T(s))$ is a *branch* to successor state s' with *reward* r and probability $T(s)(\langle r, s' \rangle)$. Let $M^{(s'_I)}$ be M but with initial state s'_I, and M^0 be M with all rewards set to zero.

Example 1. Figure 1 shows our example MDP M_e. We draw transitions as lines to an intermediate node from which branches labelled with probability and reward (if not zero) lead to successor states. We omit the intermediate node and probability 1 for transitions with a single branch, and label some transitions to refer to them in the text. M^e has 5 states, 7 transitions, and 10 branches.

In practice, higher-level modelling languages like MODEST [17] are used to specify MDP. The semantics of an MDP is captured by its *paths*. A path represents a concrete resolution of all nondeterministic and probabilistic choices. Formally:

Definition 2. *A finite path is a sequence* $\pi_{\text{fin}} = s_0\,\mu_0\,r_0\,s_1\,\mu_1\,r_1\ldots\mu_{n-1}r_{n-1}s_n$ *where* $s_i \in S$ *for all* $i \in \{0,\ldots,n\}$ *and* $\exists\,\mu_i \in T(s_i)\colon \langle r_i, s_{i+1}\rangle \in spt(\mu_i)$ *for all* $i \in \{0,\ldots,n-1\}$. *Let* $|\pi_{\text{fin}}| \overset{\text{def}}{=} n$, $\text{last}(\pi_{\text{fin}}) \overset{\text{def}}{=} s_n$, *and* $\text{rew}(\pi_{\text{fin}}) \overset{\text{def}}{=} \sum_{i=0}^{n-1} r_i$. Π_{fin} *is the set of all finite paths starting in* s_I. *A path is an analogous infinite sequence* π, *and* Π *is the set of all paths starting in* s_I. *We write* $s \in \pi$ *if* $\exists i\colon s = s_i$, *and* $\pi_{\to G}$ *for the shortest prefix of* π *that contains a state in* $G \subseteq S$, *or* $\bot$ *if* π *contains no such state. Let* $\text{rew}(\bot) \overset{\text{def}}{=} \infty$.

A scheduler (or *adversary*, *policy* or *strategy*) only resolves the nondeterministic choices of M. For this paper, memoryless deterministic schedulers suffice [6].

Definition 3. *A function* $\mathfrak{s}\colon S \to Dist(\mathbb{R}_0^+ \times S)$ *is a scheduler if, for all* $s \in S$, *we have* $\mathfrak{s}(s) \in T(s)$. *The set of all schedulers of* M *is* $\mathfrak{S}(M)$.

Given an MDP M as above, let $M|_{\mathfrak{s}} = \langle S, s_I, T|_{\mathfrak{s}}\rangle$ with $T|_{\mathfrak{s}}(s) = \{\,\mathfrak{s}(s)\,\}$ be the DTMC induced by $\mathfrak{s}$. Via the standard cylinder set construction [12, Sect. 2.2] on $M|_{\mathfrak{s}}$, a scheduler induces a probability measure $\mathbb{P}_{\mathfrak{s}}^M$ on measurable sets of paths starting in s_I. For goal state $g \in S$, the maximum and minimum **probability of reaching** g is defined as $\mathrm{P}_{\max}^M(\diamond\, g) = \sup_{\mathfrak{s}\in\mathfrak{S}} \mathbb{P}_{\mathfrak{s}}^M(\{\,\pi \in \Pi \mid g \in \pi\,\})$ and $\mathrm{P}_{\min}^M(\diamond\, g) = \inf_{\mathfrak{s}\in\mathfrak{S}} \mathbb{P}_{\mathfrak{s}}^M(\{\,\pi \in \Pi \mid g \in \pi\,\})$, respectively. The definition extends to sets G of goal states. Let $R_G^M\colon \Pi \to \mathbb{R}_0^+$ be the random variable defined by $R_G^M(\pi) = \text{rew}(\pi_{\to G})$ and let $\mathbb{E}_{\mathfrak{s}}^M(G)$ be the expected value of R_G^M under $\mathbb{P}_{\mathfrak{s}}^M$. Then the maximum and minimum **expected reward to reach** G is defined as $\mathrm{E}_{\max}^M(G) = \sup_{\mathfrak{s}} \mathbb{E}_{\mathfrak{s}}^M(G)$ and $\mathrm{E}_{\min}^M(G) = \inf_{\mathfrak{s}} \mathbb{E}_{\mathfrak{s}}^M(G)$, respectively. We omit the superscripts for M when they are clear from the context. From now on, whenever we have an MDP with a set of goal states G, we assume that they have been made absorbing, i.e. for all $g \in G$ we only have a self-loop: $T(g) = \{\,\{\,\langle 0, g\rangle \mapsto 1\,\}\,\}$.

Definition 4. *An* end component *of* M *as above is a (sub-)MDP* $\langle S', T', s_I'\rangle$ *where* $S' \subseteq S$, $T'(s) \subseteq T(s)$ *for all* $s \in S'$, *if* $\mu \in T'(s)$ *for some* $s \in S'$ *and* $\langle r, s'\rangle \in spt(\mu)$ *then* $r = 0$, *and the directed graph with vertex set* S' *and edge set* $\{\,\langle s, s'\rangle \mid \exists\,\mu \in T'(s)\colon \langle 0, s'\rangle \in spt(\mu)\,\}$ *is strongly connected.*

3   Value Iteration

The standard algorithm to compute reachability probabilities and expected rewards is *value iteration* (VI) [30]. In this section, we recall its theoretical foundations and its limitations regarding convergence.

```
1  function GSVI(M = ⟨S, s_I, T⟩, S_?, v, α, diff)
2      repeat
3          error := 0
4          foreach s ∈ S_? do
5              v_new := Φ(v)(s)                              // iterate lower bound
6              if v_new > 0 then error := max(error, diff(v(s), v_new))
7              v(s) := v_new
8      until error ≤ α
```

Algorithm 1. Gauss-Seidel value iteration

3.1 Theoretical Foundations

Let $\mathbb{V} = \{ v \mid v\colon S \to \mathbb{R}_0^+ \cup \{\infty\} \}$ be a space of vectors of values. It can easily be shown that $\langle \mathbb{V}, \preceq \rangle$ with

$$v \preceq w \qquad \text{if and only if} \qquad \forall s \in S\colon v(s) \le w(s)$$

forms a complete lattice, i.e. every subset $V \subseteq \mathbb{V}$ has a supremum (and an infimum) in $\mathbb{V}$ with respect to $\preceq$. We write $v \prec w$ for $v \preceq w \wedge v \neq w$ and $v \not\prec w$ for $\neg(v \preceq w \vee w \preceq v)$.

Minimum and maximum reachability probabilities and expected rewards can be expressed as the *least fixed point* of the *Bellman operator* $\Phi\colon \mathbb{V} \to \mathbb{V}$ given by

$$\Phi(v) \stackrel{\text{def}}{=} \lambda\, s. \begin{cases} opt_{\mu \in T(s)} \sum_{\langle r, s' \rangle \in spt(\mu)} \mu(s') \cdot (r + v(s')) & \text{if } s \in S_? \\ d & \text{if } s \notin S_? \end{cases}$$

where $opt \in \{\max, \min\}$ and the choice of both $S_? \subseteq S$ and d depends on whether we wish to compute reachability probabilities or expected rewards. In any case, the Bellman operator Φ can be shown to be Scott-continuous [1], i.e. in our case: for any subset $V \subseteq \mathbb{V}$, we have $\Phi(\sup V) = \sup \Phi(V)$.

The Kleene fixed point theorem for Scott-continuous self-maps on complete lattices [1,27] guarantees that $\mathsf{lfp}\,\Phi$, the least fixed point of Φ, indeed exists. Note that Φ can still have more than one fixed point. In addition to mere existence of $\mathsf{lfp}\,\Phi$, the Kleene fixed point theorem states that $\mathsf{lfp}\,\Phi$ can be expressed by

$$\mathsf{lfp}\,\Phi = \lim_{n \to \infty} \Phi^n(\bar{0}) \tag{1}$$

where $\bar{0} \in \mathbb{V}$ is the zero vector and $\Phi^n(v)$ denotes n-fold application of Φ to v. Equation 1 is the basis of VI: the algorithm iteratively constructs a sequence of vectors

$$v_0 = \bar{0} \qquad \text{and} \qquad v_{i+1} = \Phi(v_i),$$

which converges to the sought-after least fixed point. This convergence is *monotonic*: for every $n \in \mathbb{N}$, we have $\Phi^n(\bar{0}) \preceq \Phi^{n+1}(\bar{0})$ and hence $\Phi^n(\bar{0}) \preceq \mathsf{lfp}\,\Phi$. In particular, $\Phi^n(\bar{0})(s_I)$ is an *under*approximation of the sought-after quantity for every n. Note that iterating Φ on *any* underapproximation $v \preceq \mathsf{lfp}\,\Phi$ (instead of $\bar{0}$) will still converge to $\mathsf{lfp}\,\Phi$ and $\Phi^n(v) \preceq \mathsf{lfp}\,\Phi$ will hold for any n.

Gauss-Seidel Value Iteration. Algorithm 1 shows the pseudocode of a VI implementation that uses the so-called *Gauss-Seidel optimisation*: Whereas standard VI needs to store two vectors v_i and v_{i+1}, Gauss-Seidel VI stores only a single vector v and performs updates in place. This does not affect the correctness of VI, but may speed up convergence depending on the order in which the loop in line 4 considers the states in $S_?$. The error metric *diff* is used to check for convergence.

VI for Probabilities. For determining reachability probabilities, we operate on M^0 and set $S_? = S \setminus G$ and $d = 1$. Then the corresponding Bellman operator satisfies

$$(\mathsf{lfp}\, \Phi)(s) = \mathrm{P}_{opt}^{M^{(s)}}(\diamond G),$$

and VI will iteratively approximate this quantity *from below*. The corresponding call to Algorithm 1 is $\mathtt{GSVI}(M^0, S \setminus G, \{ s \mapsto 0 \mid s \in S \setminus G \} \cup \{ s \mapsto 1 \mid s \in G \}, \alpha,\, \textit{diff})$.

VI for Expected Rewards. For determining the expected reward $\mathrm{E}_{opt}^{M^{(s)}}(G)$, we operate on M and first have to determine the set S_∞ of states from which the minimum (if $opt = \max$) or maximum (if $opt = \min$) probability to reach G is less than 1.[1] If $s_I \in S_\infty$, then the result is ∞ due to the definition of $\mathrm{rew}(\bot)$. Otherwise, we choose $S_? = S \setminus S_\infty$ and $d = \infty$. Then, for $opt = \max$, the least fixed point of the corresponding Bellman operator satisfies

$$(\mathsf{lfp}\, \Phi)(s) = \mathrm{E}_{opt}^{M^{(s)}}(G).$$

Again, VI underapproximates this quantity. The same holds for $opt = \min$ if M does not have end components containing states other than those in G and S_∞. The corresponding call to Algorithm 1 is $\mathtt{GSVI}(M, S \setminus S_\infty, \{ s \mapsto 0 \mid s \in S \setminus S_\infty \} \cup \{ s \mapsto \infty \mid s \in S_\infty \}, \alpha,\, \textit{diff})$.

3.2   Uniqueness of Fixed Points

$\mathsf{lfp}\, \Phi$ may not be unique for two reasons: states that cannot reach G under the optimal scheduler may take any value (causing fixed points greater than $\mathsf{lfp}\, \Phi$ for $\mathrm{P}_{\min}$ and $\mathrm{P}_{\max}$), and states in end components may take values higher than $\mathsf{lfp}\, \Phi$. The latter affects $\mathrm{P}_{\max}$ (higher fixed points) and $\mathrm{E}_{\min}$ (lower fixed points).

Example 2. In M_e of Fig. 1, s_1 and s_2 and the two transitions in-between form an end component. For $\mathrm{P}_{\max}^{M_e}(\diamond \{ s_+ \})$, $v = \{ s \mapsto 1 \}$ is a non-least fixed point for the corresponding Bellman operator; with appropriate values for s_1 and s_2, we can obtain fixed points with any $v(s_0) > 0.5$ of our choice. Similarly, we have $\mathrm{E}_{\min}^{M}(\{ s_+, s_- \}) = 0.6$ (by scheduling b in s_0), but due to the end component (with only zero-reward transitions by definition), the fixed point is s.t. $v(s_0) = 0$.

---

[1] This can be done via Algs. 2 (for $S_{\min}^1$) and 4 (for $S_{\max}^1$) of [12], respectively. These algorithms do not consider the probabilities, but only whether there is a transition and branch (with positive probability) from one state to another or not. We thus call them *graph-based* algorithms, as opposed to *numeric* algorithms like VI itself.

VI works for $P_{\min}$, $P_{\max}$, and $E_{\max}$ with multiple fixed points: we anyway seek lfp Φ and start from a (trivial) underapproximation. For $E_{\min}$, (zero-reward) end components need to be collapsed: we determine the maximal end components using algorithms similar to [15, Alg. 1], then replace each of them by a single state, keeping all transitions leading out of the end component. We refer to this as the *ECC* transformation. However, such end components rarely occur in case studies for $E_{\min}$ since they indicate Zeno behaviour w.r.t. to the reward. As rewards are often associated to time progress, such behaviour would be unrealistic.

To make the fixed points unique, for $E_{\max}$ and $E_{\min}$ we fix the values of all states in G to 0. For $P_{\min}$, we precompute the set $S_{\min}^0$ of states that reach G with minimum probability 0 using Alg. 1 of [12], then fix their values to 0. For $P_{\max}$, we analogously use $S_{\max}^0$ via Alg. 3 of [12]. For $P_{\max}$ and $E_{\min}$, we additionally need to remove end components via ECC. In contrast to the precomputations, ECC changes the structure of the MDP and is thus more memory-intensive.

3.3 Convergence

VI and GSVI will not *reach* a fixed point in general, except for special cases such as acyclic MDP. It is thus standard to use a convergence criterion based on the difference between two consecutive iterations (lines 6 and 8) to make GSVI terminate: we either check the *absolute error*, i.e.

$$ diff = diff_{abs} \stackrel{\text{def}}{=} \lambda \langle v_{old}, v_{new} \rangle.\ v_{new} - v_{old}, $$

or the *relative error*, i.e.

$$ diff = diff_{rel} \stackrel{\text{def}}{=} \lambda \langle v_{old}, v_{new} \rangle.\ (v_{new} - v_{old})/v_{new}. $$

By default, probabilistic model checkers like PRISM and STORM use $diff_{rel}$ and $\alpha = 10^{-6}$. Upon termination of GSVI, v is then closer to the least fixed point, but remains an underapproximation. In particular, α has, in general, no relation to the final difference between $v(s_I)$ and $P_{opt}(\diamond G)$ or $E_{opt}(G)$, respectively.

Example 3. Consider MDP M_e of Fig. 1 again with $G = \{ s_+ \}$. The first four rows in the body of Table 1 show the values for v after the i-th iteration of the outer loop of a call to GSVI(M_e^0, $\{ s_0, s_1, s_2 \}$, max, $\{ s_+ \mapsto 1 \} \cup \{ s \mapsto 0 \mid s \neq s_+ \}$, 0.05, $diff_{abs}$). After the fourth iteration, GSVI terminates since the error is less than $\alpha = 0.05$; at this point, we have $P_{\max}(\diamond s_+) - v(s_0) = 0.08 > \alpha$.

To obtain a value within a prescribed error ϵ of the true value, we can compute an upper bound in addition to the lower bound provided by VI. Interval iteration (II) [3,15] does so by performing, in parallel, a second value iteration on a second vector u that starts from a known overapproximation. For probabilities, the vector $\bar{1} = \{ s \mapsto 1 \}$ is a trivial overapproximation; for rewards, more involved graph-based algorithms need to be used to precompute (a very conservative) one [3]. II terminates when $diff(v(s_I), u(s_I)) \leq 2\epsilon$

Table 2. Preprocessing requirements of value iteration variants

Type	VI	II and SVI	OVI
P_{min}	–	S^0_{min}	–
P_{max}	–	$S^0_{max} + ECC$	ECC^a
E_{min}	$S^1_{max} + ECC$	$S^1_{max} + ECC$	$S^1_{max} + ECC$
E_{max}	S^1_{min}	S^1_{min}	S^1_{min}

[a] ECC preprocessing for OVI is needed to guarantee termination in theory, however we have not yet found a case study where OVI diverges without ECC.

and returns $v_{II} = \frac{1}{2}(u(s_I) + v(s_I))$. With $v_{true} = P_{opt}(\diamond\, G)$, II thus guarantees that $v_{II} \in [v_{true} - \epsilon \cdot v_{true}, v_{true} + \epsilon \cdot v_{true}]$ and analogously for expected rewards. However, to ensure termination, II requires a unique fixed point: u converges from above to the greatest fixed point $\mathsf{gfp}\,\Phi$, thus for every MDP where $\mathit{diff}((\mathsf{lfp}\,\Phi)(s_I), (\mathsf{gfp}\,\Phi)(s_I)) > 2\epsilon$, II diverges. For P_{max}, we have $\mathsf{gfp}\,\Phi(s_{ec}) = 1$ for all s_{ec} in end components, thus II tends to diverge when there is an end component. Sound value iteration (SVI) [31] is similar, but uses a different approach to derive upper bounds that makes it perform better overall, and that eliminates the need to precompute an initial overapproximation for expected rewards. However, SVI still requires unique fixed points.

We summarise the preprocessing requirements of VI, II, and SVI in Table 2. With unique fixed points, we can transform P_{min} into P_{max} by making S^0_{min} states absorbing and setting G to S^0_{min}, and P_{max} into E_{max} by a similar transformation adding reward 1 to entering G. Most of the literature on VI variants works in such a setting and describes the P_{max} or E_{max} case only. Since OVI also works with multiple fixed points, we have to consider all four cases individually.

4   Optimistic Value Iteration

We now present a new, practical solution to the convergence problem for unbounded reachability and expected rewards. It exploits the empirical observation that on many case studies VI delivers results which are roughly α-close to the true value—it only lacks the ability to prove it. Our approach, *optimistic value iteration* (OVI), extends standard VI with the ability to deliver such a proof.

The key idea is to exploit a property of the Bellman operator Φ and its Gauss-Seidel variant as in Algorithm 1 to determine whether a candidate vector is a lower bound, an upper bound, or neither. The foundation is basic domain theory: by Scott-continuity of Φ it follows that Φ is monotonic, meaning $v \preceq w$ implies $\Phi(v) \preceq \Phi(w)$. A principle called *Park induction* [29] for monotonic self-maps on complete lattices yields the following induction rules: For any $u \in \mathbb{V}$,

```
 1  function OVI(M = ⟨S, s_I, T⟩, S_?, v, ε, α, diff)
 2      GSVI(M, S_?, v, α, diff)                              // perform standard value iteration
 3      u := { s ↦ diff⁺(s) | s ∈ S_? }, viters := 0         // guess candidate upper bound
 4      while viters < 1/α do                                 // start verification phase
 5          up_∀ := true, down_∀ := true, viters := viters + 1, error := 0
 6          foreach s ∈ S_? do
 7              v_new := Φ(v)(s), u_new := Φ(u)(s)           // iterate both bounds
 8              if v_new > 0 then  error := max { error, diff(v(s), v_new) }
 9              if u_new < u(s) then                         // upper value decreased:
10                  u(s) := u_new, up_∀ := false             // update u with new lower u_new
11              else if u_new > u(s) then                    // upper value increased:
12                  down_∀ := false                          // discard new higher u_new
13              v(s) := v_new                                // update v with new value v_new
14              if v(s) > u(s) then goto line 17             // lower bound crossed u
15          if down_∀ then return ½(u(s_I) + v(s_I))        // u is inductive upper bound
16          else if up_∀ then goto line 17                   // u is inductive lower bound
17      return OVI(M, S_?, v, ε, error/2, diff)              // retry with reduced α
```

Algorithm 2. Optimistic value iteration

$$\Phi(u) \preceq u \quad\quad \text{implies} \quad\quad \mathsf{lfp}\,\Phi \preceq u. \tag{2}$$

$$\text{and} \quad u \preceq \Phi(u) \quad\quad \text{implies} \quad\quad u \preceq \mathsf{gfp}\,\Phi. \tag{3}$$

Thus, if we can construct a candidate vector u s.t. $\Phi(u) \preceq u$, then u is in fact an upper bound on the sought-after $\mathsf{lfp}\,\Phi$. We call such a u an *inductive upper bound*. Optimistic value iteration uses this insight and can be summarised as follows:

---

1. Perform value iteration on v until "convergence" w.r.t. α.
2. Heuristically determine a candidate upper bound u.
3. If $\Phi(u) \preceq u$, then $v \preceq \mathsf{lfp}\,\Phi \preceq u$.
   - If $diff(v(s_I), u(s_I)) \leq 2\epsilon$, terminate and return $\frac{1}{2}\big(u(s_I) + v(s_I)\big)$.
4. If $u \preceq \Phi(u)$ or $u \not\succ v$, then reduce α and go to step 1.
5. Set v to $\Phi(v)$, u to $\Phi(u)$, and go to step 3.

The resulting procedure in more detail is shown as Algorithm 2. Starting from the same initial vectors v as for VI, we first perform standard Gauss-Seidel value iteration (in line 2). We refer to this as the *iteration phase* of OVI. After that, vector v is an improved underapproximation of the actual probabilities or reward values. We then "guess" a vector u of *upper values* from the *lower values* in v (line 3). The guessing heuristics depends on *diff*: if $diff = diff_{abs}$, then we use

$$diff^{+}(s) = \begin{cases} 0 & \text{if } v(s) = 0 \\ v(s) + \epsilon & \text{otherwise;} \end{cases}$$

if $diff = diff_{rel}$, then

$$diff^+(s) = v(s) \cdot (1 + \epsilon).$$

We cap the result at 1 for P_{min} and P_{max}. These heuristics have three important properties: (**H1**) $v(s) = 0$ implies $diff^+(s) = 0$, (**H2**) $diff(v(s), diff^+(s)) \le 2\epsilon$, and (**H3**) $diff(v(s), diff^+(s)) > 0$ unless $v(s) = 0$ or $v(s) = 1$ for P_{min} and P_{max}.

Then the *verification phase* starts in line 4: we perform value iteration on the lower values v and upper values u at the same time, keeping track of the direction in which the upper values move. For u, line 7 and the conditions around line 10 mean that we actually use operator $\Phi_{min}(u) = \lambda s. \min(\Phi(u)(s), u(s))$. This may shorten the verification phases, and is crucial for our termination argument. A state s is *blocked* if $\Phi(u)(s) > \Phi_{min}(u)(s)$ and *unblocked* if $\Phi(u)(s) < u(s)$ here.

If, in some iteration, no state was blocked (line 15), then we had $\Phi(u) \preceq u$ before the start of the iteration. We thus know by Eq. 2 that the current u is an inductive upper bound for the values of all states, and the true value must be in the interval $[v(s_I), u(s_I)]$. By property H2, our use of Φ_{min} for u, and the monotonicity of Φ as used on v, we also know that $diff(v(s_I), u(s_I)) \le 2\epsilon$, so we immediately terminate and return the interval's centre $v_I = \frac{1}{2}(u(s_I) + v(s_I))$. The true value $v_{true} = (\mathsf{lfp}\,\Phi)(s_I)$ must then be in $[v_I - \epsilon \cdot v_{true}, v_I + \epsilon \cdot v_{true}]$.

If, in some iteration, no state was unblocked (line 16), then again by Park induction we know that $u \preceq \mathsf{gfp}\,\Phi$. If we are in a situation of unique fixed points, this also means $u \preceq \mathsf{lfp}\,\Phi$, thus the current u is no upper bound: we cancel verification and go back to the iteration phase to further improve v before trying again. We do the same if v crosses u: then $u(s) < v(s) \le (\mathsf{lfp}\,\Phi)(s)$ for some s, so this u was just another bad guess, too.

Otherwise, we do not yet know the relationship between u and $\mathsf{lfp}\,\Phi$, so we remain in the verification phase until we encounter one of the cases above, or until we exceed the verification budget of $\frac{1}{\alpha}$ iterations (as checked by the loop condition in line 4). This budget is a technical measure to ensure termination.

Optimisation. In case the fixed point of Φ is *unique*, by Park induction (via Eq. 3) we know that $u \preceq \Phi(u)$ implies that u is a lower bound on $\mathsf{lfp}\,\Phi$. In such situations of single fixed points, we can—as an optimisation—additionally replace v by u before the *goto* in line 16.

Heuristics. OVI relies on heuristics to gain an advantage over alternative methods such as II or SVI; it cannot be better on *all* MDP. Concretely, we can choose

1. a stopping criterion for the iteration phase,
2. how to guess candidate upper values from the result of the iteration phase, and
3. how much to reduce α when going back from verification to iteration.

Algorithm 2 shows the choices made by our implementation. We employ the standard stopping criteria used by probabilistic model checkers for VI, and the "weakest" guessing heuristics that satisfies properties H1, H2, and H3 (i.e. guessing any higher values would violate one of these properties). The only arbitrary choice is how to reduce α, which we at least halve on every retry. We experimentally found this to be a good compromise on benchmarks that we consider in Sect. 5, where

(a) reducing α further causes more and potentially unnecessary iterations in GSVI (continuing to iterate when switching to the verification phase would already result in upper values sufficient for termination), and
(b) reducing α less results in more verification phases (whose iterations are computationally more expensive than those of GSVI) being started before the values in v are high enough such that we manage to guess a u with lfp $\Phi \preceq u$.

Example 4. We now use the version of Φ to compute $\mathrm{P}_{\max}$ and call

$$\mathtt{OVI}(M_e^0, \{\, s_0, s_1, s_2 \,\}, \{\, s_+ \mapsto 1 \,\} \cup \{\, s \mapsto 0 \mid s \neq s_+ \,\}, 0.05, 0.05, \mathit{diff}_{abs}).$$

Table 1 shows the values in v and u during this run, assuming that we use non-Gauss-Seidel iterations. The first iteration phase lasts from $i = 0$ to 4. At this point, u is initialised with the values shown in italics. The first verification phase needs only one iteration to realise that u is actually a lower bound (to a fixed point which is not the least fixed point, due to the uncollapsed end component). Blocked states are marked with a $\overline{\text{bar}}$; unblocked states have a lower u-value than in the previous iteration. We resume GSVI from $i = 6$. The error in GSVI is again below α, which had been reduced to 0.008, during iteration $i = 9$. We thus start another verification phase, which immediately (in one iteration) finds the newly guessed vector u to be an upper bound, with $\mathit{diff}(v(s_0), u(s_0)) < 2\epsilon$.

4.1   Termination of OVI

We showed above that OVI returns an ϵ-correct result when it terminates. We now show that it terminates in all cases except for $\mathrm{P}_{\max}$ with multiple fixed points. Note that this is a stronger result than what II and SVI can achieve.

Let us first consider the situations where lfp Φ is the unique fixed point of Φ. First, GSVI terminates by Eq. 1. Let us now write v_i and u_i for the vectors u and v as they are at the beginning of verification phase iteration i. We know that $v_0 \preceq u_0$. We distinguish three cases relating the initial guess u_0 to lfp Φ.

1. $u_0 \not\succ$ lfp Φ or $u_0 \prec$ lfp Φ, i.e. there is a state s with $u_0(s) < (\text{lfp }\Phi)(s)$. Since we use $\Phi_{\min}$ on the upper values, it follows $u_i(s) \leq u_0(s) < (\text{lfp }\Phi)(s)$ for all i. By Eq. 1, there must thus be a j such that $v_j(s) > u_j(s)$, triggering a retry with reduced α in line 14. Such a retry could also be triggered earlier in line 16. Due to the reduction of α and Eq. 1, every call to GSVI will further increase some values in v or reach $v = \text{lfp }\Phi$ (in special cases), and for some subsequent guess u we must have $u_0(s) < u(s)$. Consequently, after some repetitions of this case 1, we must eventually guess a u with lfp $\Phi \preceq u$.

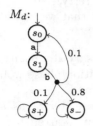

Fig. 2. DTMC M_d

Table 3. Nontermination of OVI on M'_e without ECC

i	$v(s_0)$	$u(s_0)$	$v(s_1)$	$u(s_1)$	$v(s_2)$	$u(s_2)$	error	α
0	0		0		0			0.05
1	0.1		0		0.25		0.25	0.05
2	0.18		0.25		0.375		0.25	0.05
3	0.25		0.375		0.4375		0.125	0.05
4	0.375		0.4375		0.46875		0.125	0.05
5	0.4375	0.5375	0.46875	0.56875	0.484375	0.584375	0.0625	0.05
6	0.46875	$\overline{0.5375}$	0.484375	$\overline{0.56875}$	0.4921875	0.56875	0.03125	
7	0.484375	$\overline{0.5375}$	0.4921875	0.56875	0.49609375	0.56875	0.015625	

2. lfp $\Phi \prec u_0$. Observe that operators Φ and $\Phi_{\min}$ are *local* [9], i.e. a state's value can only change if a direct successor's value changes. In particular, a state's value can only decrease (increase) if a direct successor's value decreases (increases). If $u_i(s) < u_{i-1}(s)$, then s cannot be blocked again in any later iteration $j > i$: for it to become blocked, a successor's upper value would have to increase, but $\Phi_{\min}$ ensures non-increasing upper values for all states. Analogously to Eq. 1, we know that [3, Lemma 3.3 (c)]

$$\text{lfp } \Phi \preceq u \quad \text{implies} \quad \lim_{n \to \infty} \Phi^n_{\min}(u) = \text{lfp } \Phi$$

(for the unique fixpoint case, since [3] assumes contracting MDP as usual). Thus, for all states s, there must be an i such that $u_i(s) < u_{i-1}(s)$; in consequence, there is also an iteration j where no state is blocked any more. Then the condition in line 15 will be true and OVI terminates.

3. lfp $\Phi \preceq u_0$ but not lfp $\Phi \prec u_0$, i.e. there is a state s with $u_0(s) = (\text{lfp } \Phi)(s)$. If there is an i where no state, including s, is blocked, then OVI terminates as above. For $P_{\min}$ and $P_{\max}$, if $u_0(s) = 1$, s cannot be blocked, so we can w.l.o.g. exclude such s. For other s not to be blocked in iteration i, we must have $u_i(s') = (\text{lfp } \Phi)(s')$ for all states s' reachable from s under the optimal scheduler, i.e. all of those states must *reach* the fixed point. This cannot be guaranteed on general MDP. Since this case is a very particular situation unlikely to be encountered in practice with our heuristics, OVI adopts a pragmatic solution: it bounds the number of iterations in every verification phase (cf. line 4). Due to property H3 of our heuristics, $u_0(s) = (\text{lfp } \Phi)(s)$ requires $v_0(s) < (\text{lfp } \Phi)(s)$, thus some subsequent guess u will have $u(s) > u_0(s)$, and eventually we must get a u with lfp $\Phi \prec u$, which is case 2. Since we strictly increase the iteration bound on every retry, we will eventually encounter case 2 with a sufficiently high bound for termination.

Three of the four situations with multiple fixed points reduce to the corresponding unique fixed point situation due to property H1 of our guessing heuristics:

1. For $P_{\min}$, recall from Sect. 3.2 that the fixed point is unique if we fix the values of all $S^0_{\min}$ states to 0. In OVI without preprocessing, such states are

in $S_?$, thus they initially have value 0. Φ will not increase their values, neither will guessing due to H1, and neither will $\Phi_{\min}$. Thus OVI here operates on a sublattice of $\langle \mathbb{V}, \preceq \rangle$ where the fixed point of Φ is unique.

2. For $\mathrm{E}_{\min}$, after the preprocessing steps of Table 2, we only need to fix the values of all goal states to 0. Then the argument is the same as for $\mathrm{P}_{\min}$.

3. For $\mathrm{E}_{\max}$, we reduce to a unique fixed point sublattice in the same way, too.

The only case where OVI may not terminate is for $\mathrm{P}_{\max}$ without ECC. Here, end components may cause states to be permanently blocked. However, we did not encounter this on any benchmark used in Sect. 5, so in contrast to e.g. II, OVI is still *practically* useful in this case despite the lack of a termination guarantee.

Example 5. We turn M_e of Fig. 1 into M'_e by replacing the c-labelled transition from s_2 by transition $\{\langle 0, s_2 \rangle \mapsto \frac{1}{2}, \langle 0, s_+ \rangle \mapsto \frac{1}{4}, \langle 1, s_- \rangle \mapsto \frac{1}{4}\}$, i.e. we can now go from s_2 back to s_2 with probability $\frac{1}{2}$ and to each of s_+, s_- with probability $\frac{1}{4}$. The probability-1 transition from s_2 to s_1 remains. Then Table 3 shows a run of OVI for $\mathrm{P}_{\max}$ with diff_{abs} and $\alpha = 0.1$. s_0 is forever blocked from iteration 6 on.

4.2   Variants of OVI

While the core idea of OVI rests on classic results from domain theory, Algorithm 2 includes several particular choices that work together to achieve good performance and ensure termination. We sketch two variants to motivate these choices.

First, let us use Φ instead of $\Phi_{\min}$ for the upper values, i.e. move the assignment $u(s) := u_{new}$ down into line 13. Then we cannot prove termination because the arguments of case 2 for $\mathsf{lfp}\,\Phi \prec u_0$ no longer hold. Consider DTMC M_d of Fig. 2 and $\mathrm{P}_{\max}(\diamond\, s_+) = \mathrm{P}_{\min}(\diamond\, s_+)$. Let

$$u = \{\, s_0 \mapsto 0.2, s_1 \mapsto 1, s_+ \mapsto 1, s_- \mapsto 0 \,\} \succ \{\, s_0 \mapsto \tfrac{1}{9}, s_1 \mapsto \tfrac{1}{9}, \ldots \,\} = \mathsf{lfp}\,\Phi.$$

Iterating Φ, we then get the following sequence of pairs $\langle u(s_0), u(s_1) \rangle$:

$$\langle 0.2, 1 \rangle, \langle 1, 0.12 \rangle, \langle 0.12, 0.2 \rangle, \langle 0.2, 0.112 \rangle, \langle 0.112, 0.12 \rangle, \langle 0.12, 0.1112 \rangle, \ldots$$

Observe how the value of s_0 increases iff s_1 decreases and vice-versa. Thus we never encounter an inductive upper or lower bound. In Algorithm 2, we use Gauss-Seidel VI, which would not show the same effect on this model; however, if we insert another state between s_0 and s_1 that is updated last, Algorithm 2 would behave in the same alternating way. This particular u is contrived, but we could have guessed one with a similar relationship of the values leading to similar behaviour.

An alternative that allows us to use Φ instead of $\Phi_{\min}$ is to change the conditions that lead to retrying and termination: We separately store the initial guess of a verification phase as u_0, and then compare each newly calculated u with u_0. If $u \preceq u_0$, then we know that there is an i such that $u = \Phi^i(u) \preceq u_0$.

Φ^i retains all properties of Φ needed for Park induction, so this would also be a proof of $\mathsf{lfp}\,\Phi \preceq u$. The other conditions and the termination proofs can be adapted analogously. However, this variant needs $\approx 50\,\%$ more memory (to store an additional vector of values), and we found it to be significantly slower than Algorthm 2 and the first variant on almost all benchmark instances of Sect. 5.

5 Experimental Evaluation

We have implemented interval iteration (II) (using the "variant 2" approach of [3] to compute initial overapproximations for expected rewards), sound value iteration (SVI), and now optimistic value iteration (OVI) precisely as described in the previous section, in the mcsta model checker of the MODEST TOOLSET [20], which is publicly available at modestchecker.net. It is cross-platform, implemented in C#, and built around the MODEST [17] high-level modelling language. Via support for the JANI format [8], mcsta can exchange models with other tools like EPMC [18] and STORM [10]. Its performance is competitive with STORM and PRISM [16]. We tried to spend equal effort performance-tuning our VI, II, SVI, and OVI implementations to avoid unfairly comparing highly-optimised OVI code with naïve implementations of the competing algorithms.

In the following, we report on our experimental evaluation of OVI using mcsta on all applicable models of the Quantitative Verification Benchmark Set (QVBS) [21]. All models in the QVBS are available in JANI and can thus be used by mcsta. Most are parameterised, and come with multiple properties of different types. Aside from MDP models, the QVBS also includes DTMCs (which are a special case of MDP), continuous-time Markov chains (CTMC, for which the analysis of unbounded properties reduces to checking the embedded DTMC), Markov automata (MA [11], on which the embedded MDP suffices for unbounded properties), and probabilistic timed automata (PTA [26], some of which can be converted into MDP via the digital clocks semantics [25]). We use all of these model types. The QVBS thus gives rise to a large number of benchmark *instances*: combinations of a model, a parameter valuation, and a property to check. For every model, we chose one instance per probabilistic reachability and expected-reward property such that state space exploration did not run out of memory and VI took at least 10 s where possible. We only excluded

- 2 models with multiple initial states (which mcsta does not yet support),
- 4 PTA with open clock constraints (they cannot be converted to MDP),
- 29 probabilistic reachability properties for which the result is 0 or 1 (they are easily solved by the graph-based precomputations and do not challenge VI),
- 16 instances for which VI very quickly *reaches* the fixed point, which indicates that (the relevant part of) the MDP is acyclic and thus trivial to solve,
- 3 models for which no parameter valuation allowed state space exploration to complete without running out of memory or taking more than 600 s,
- 7 instances where, on the largest state space we could explore, no iterative algorithm took more than 1 s (which does not allow reliable comparisons), and
- the *oscillators* model due to its very large model files,

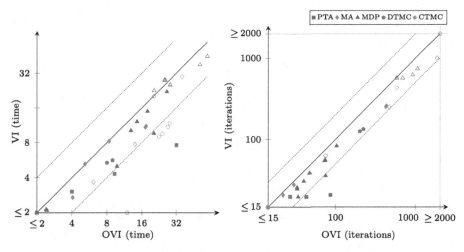

Fig. 3. OVI runtime and iteration count compared to VI (probabilistic reachability)

As a result, we considered 38 instances with probabilistic reachability and 41 instances with expected-reward properties, many comprising several million states.

We ran all experiments on an Intel Core i7-4790 workstation (3.6–4.0 GHz) with 8 GB of memory and 64-bit Ubuntu Linux 18.04. By default, we request a relative half-width of $\epsilon = 10^{-6}$ for the result probability or reward value, and configure OVI to use the relative-error criterion with $\alpha = 10^{-6}$ in the iteration phase. We use a 600 s timeout ("TO"). Due to the number of instances, we show most results as scatter plots like in Fig. 3. Each such plot compares two methods in terms of runtime or number of iterations. Every point $\langle x, y \rangle$ corresponds to an instance and indicates that the method noted on the x-axis took x seconds or iterations to solve this instance while the method noted on the y-axis took y seconds or iterations. Thus points above the solid diagonal line correspond to instances where the x-axis method was faster (or needed fewer iterations); points above (below) the upper (lower) dotted diagonal line are where the x-axis method took less than half (more than twice) as long or as many iterations.

5.1 Comparison with VI

All methods except VI delivered correct results up to ϵ. VI offers low runtime at the cost of occasional incorrect results, and in general the absence of any guarantee about the result. We thus compare with VI separately to judge the overhead caused by performing additional verification, and possibly iteration, phases. This is similar to the comparison done for II in [3]. Figures 3 and 4 show the results. The unfilled shapes indicate instances where VI produced an incorrect result. In terms of runtime, we see that OVI does not often take more than twice as long as VI, and frequently requires less than 50% extra time. On several instances where OVI incurs most overhead, VI produces an incorrect result, indicating

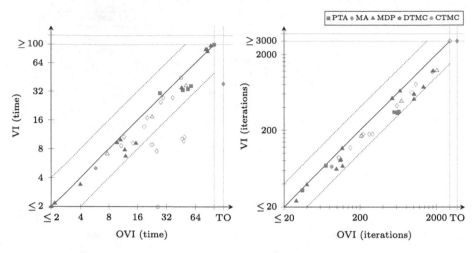

Fig. 4. OVI runtime and iteration count compared to VI (expected rewards)

that they are "hard" instances for value iteration. The unfilled CTMCs where OVI takes much longer to compute probabilities are all instances of the *embedded* model; the DTMC on the x-axis is *haddad-monmege*, an adversarial model built to highlight the convergence problem of VI in [14]. The problematic cases for expected rewards include most MA instances, the two expected-reward instances of the *embedded* CTMC, and again *haddad-monmege*. In terms of iterations, the overhead of OVI is even less than in runtime.

5.2 Comparison with II and SVI

We compare the runtime of OVI with the runtime of II and that of SVI separately for reachability probabilities (shown in Fig. 5) and expected rewards (shown in Fig. 6). As shown in Table 2, OVI has almost the same requirements on precomputations as VI, while II and SVI require extra precomputations and ECC for reachability probabilities. The precomputations and ECC need extra runtime (which turned out to be negligible in some cases but significant enough to cause a timeout in others) prior to the numeric iterations. However, doing the precomputations can reduce the size of the set $S_?$, and ECC can reduce the size of the MDP itself. Both can thus reduce the runtime needed for the numeric iterations. For the overall runtime, we found that none of these effects dominates the other over all models. Thus sometimes it may be better to perform only the required precomputations and transformations, while on other models performing all applicable ones may lead to lower total runtime. For reachability probabilities, we thus compare OVI, II, and SVI in two scenarios: once in the default ("std") setting of mcsta that uses only required preprocessing steps

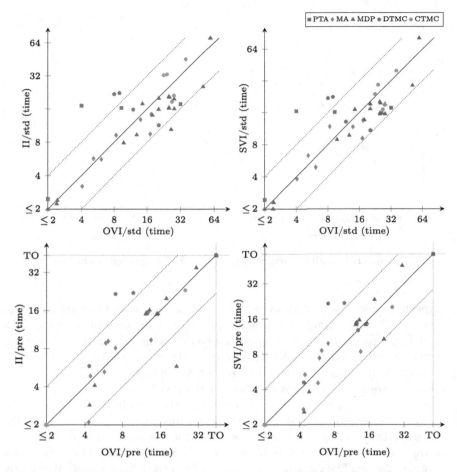

Fig. 5. OVI runtime compared to II and SVI (probabilities)

(without ECC for OVI; we report the total runtime for preprocessing and iterations), and once with all of them enabled ("pre", where we report only the runtime for numeric iterations, plus the computation of initial upper bounds in case of II).

For probabilistic reachability, we see in Fig. 5 that there is no clear winner among the three methods in the "std" setting (top plots). In some cases, the extra precomputations take long enough to give an advantage to OVI, while in others they speed up II and SVI significantly, compensating for their overhead. The "pre" setting (bottom), in which all three algorithms operate on exactly the same input w.r.t. to MDP M and set $S_?$, however, shows a clearer picture: now OVI is faster, sometimes significantly so, than II and SVI on most instances.

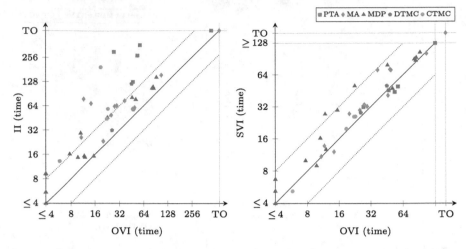

Fig. 6. OVI runtime compared to II and SVI (expected rewards)

Expected-reward properties were more challenging for all three methods (as well as for VI, which produced more errors here than for probabilities). The plots in Fig. 6 paint a very clear picture of OVI being significantly faster for expected rewards than II (which suffers from the need to precompute initial upper bounds that then turn out to be rather conservative), and faster (though by a lesser margin and with few exceptions) than SVI.

In Fig. 7, we give a summary view combining the data from Figs. 3 to 6. For each algorithm, we plot the instances sorted by runtime, i.e. a point $\langle x, y \rangle$ on the line for algorithm z means that some instance took y seconds to solve via z, and there are x instances that z solves in less time. Note in particular that the times are *not* cumulative. The right-hand plot zooms into the left-hand one. We clearly see the speedup offered by OVI over SVI and especially II. Where the scatter plots merely show that OVI often does not obtain more than a 2× speedup compared to SVI, these plots provide an explanation: the VI line is a rough

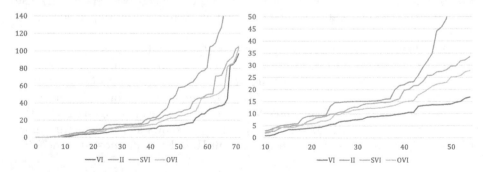

Fig. 7. Summary comparison to VI, II, and SVI, instances ordered by runtime

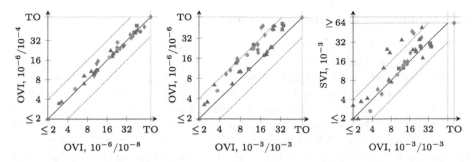

Fig. 8. Influence of ϵ/α on runtime (expected rewards, relative error)

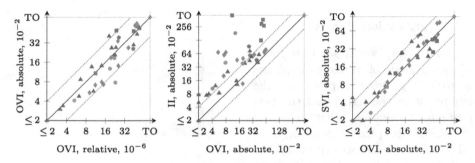

Fig. 9. Runtime comparison with absolute error (expected rewards)

bound on the performance that any *extension* of VI can deliver. Comparing the SVI and VI lines, over much of the plot's range, OVI thus cannot take less than half the runtime of SVI without outperforming VI itself.

5.3 On the Effect of ϵ and α

We also compared the four algorithms for different values of ϵ and, where applicable, α. We show a selection of the results in Fig. 8. The axis labels are of the form "algorithm, ϵ/α". On the left, we see that the runtime of OVI changes if we set α to values different from ϵ, however there is no clear trend: some instances are checked faster, some slower. We obtained similar plots for other combinations of α values, with only a slight tendency towards longer runtimes as $\alpha > \epsilon$. mcsta thus uses $\alpha = \epsilon$ as a default that can be changed by the user.

In the middle, we study the impact of reducing the desired precision by setting ϵ to 10^{-3}. This allows OVI to speed up by factors mostly between 1 and 2; the same comparison for SVI and II resulted in similar plots, however VI was able to more consistently achieve higher speedups. When we compare the right plot with the right-hand plot of Fig. 6, we consequently see that the overall result of our comparison between OVI and SVI does not change significantly with the lower precision, although OVI does gain slightly more than SVI.

5.4 Comparing Relative and Absolute Error

In Fig. 9, we show comparison plots for the runtime when using $diff_{abs}$ instead of $diff_{rel}$. Requiring absolute-error-correct results may make instances with low result values much easier and instances with high results much harder. We chose $\epsilon = 10^{-2}$ as a compromise, and the leftmost plot confirms that we indeed chose an ϵ that keeps the expected-reward benchmarks on average roughly as hard as with 10^{-6} relative error. In the middle and right plots, we again see OVI compared with II and SVI. Compared to Fig. 6, both II and SVI gain a little, but there are no significant differences overall. Our experiments thus confirm that the relative performance of OVI is stable under varying precision requirements.

5.5 Verification Phases

On the right, we show histograms of the number of verification phases started (top, from 1 phase on the left to 20 on the right) and the percentage of iterations that are done in verification phases (bottom) over all benchmark instances (probabilities and rewards). We see that, in the vast majority of cases, we need few verification attempts, with many succeeding in the first attempt, and most iterations are performed in the iteration phases.

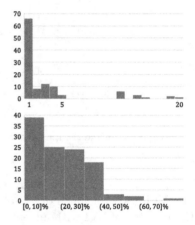

6   Conclusion

We have presented *optimistic value iteration* (OVI), a new approach to making non-exact probabilistic model checking via iterative numeric algorithms sound in the sense of delivering results within a prescribed interval around the true value (modulo floating-point and implementation errors). Compared to interval (II) and sound value iteration (SVI), OVI has slightly stronger termination guarantees in presence of multiple fixed points, and works in practice for max. probabilities without collapsing end components despite the lack of a guarantee. Like II, it can be combined with alternative methods for dealing with end components such as the new *deflating* technique of [23]. OVI is a *simple* algorithm that is *easy* to add to any tool that already implements value iteration, and it is *fast*, further closing the performance gap between VI and sound methods.

Acknowledgments. The authors thank Tim Quatmann (RWTH Aachen) for fruitful discussions when the idea of OVI initially came up in late 2018, and for his help in implementing and optimising the SVI implementation in mcsta.

Data Availability. A dataset to replicate our experimental evaluation is archived and available at DOI 10.4121/uuid:3df859e6-edc6-4e2d-92f3-93e478bbe8dc [19].

References

1. Abramsky, S., Jung, A.: Domain theory. In: Handbook of Logic in Computer Science, vol. 3, pp. 1–168. Oxford University Press (1994). http://www.cs.bham.ac.uk/~axj/pub/papers/handy1.pdf (corrected and expanded version)
2. Ashok, P., Křetínský, J., Weininger, M.: PAC statistical model checking for Markov decision processes and stochastic games. In: Dillig, I., Tasiran, S. (eds.) CAV 2019. LNCS, vol. 11561, pp. 497–519. Springer, Cham (2019). https://doi.org/10.1007/978-3-030-25540-4_29
3. Baier, C., Klein, J., Leuschner, L., Parker, D., Wunderlich, S.: Ensuring the reliability of your model checker: interval iteration for Markov decision processes. In: Majumdar, R., Kunčak, V. (eds.) CAV 2017. LNCS, vol. 10426, pp. 160–180. Springer, Cham (2017). https://doi.org/10.1007/978-3-319-63387-9_8
4. Balaji, N., Kiefer, S., Novotný, P., Pérez, G.A., Shirmohammadi, M.: On the complexity of value iteration. In: 46th International Colloquium on Automata, Languages, and Programming (ICALP). LIPIcs, vol. 132, pp. 102:1–102:15. Schloss Dagstuhl - Leibniz-Zentrum für Informatik (2019). https://doi.org/10.4230/LIPIcs.ICALP.2019.102
5. Bauer, M.S., Mathur, U., Chadha, R., Sistla, A.P., Viswanathan, M.: Exact quantitative probabilistic model checking through rational search. In: FMCAD, pp. 92–99. IEEE (2017). https://doi.org/10.23919/FMCAD.2017.8102246
6. Bianco, A., de Alfaro, L.: Model checking of probabilistic and nondeterministic systems. In: Thiagarajan, P.S. (ed.) FSTTCS 1995. LNCS, vol. 1026, pp. 499–513. Springer, Heidelberg (1995). https://doi.org/10.1007/3-540-60692-0_70
7. Brázdil, T., et al.: Verification of Markov decision processes using learning algorithms. In: Cassez, F., Raskin, J.-F. (eds.) ATVA 2014. LNCS, vol. 8837, pp. 98–114. Springer, Cham (2014). https://doi.org/10.1007/978-3-319-11936-6_8
8. Budde, C.E., Dehnert, C., Hahn, E.M., Hartmanns, A., Junges, S., Turrini, A.: JANI: quantitative model and tool interaction. TACAS. LNCS **10206**, 151–168 (2017). https://doi.org/10.1007/978-3-662-54580-5_9
9. Chatterjee, K., Henzinger, T.A.: Value iteration. In: Grumberg, O., Veith, H. (eds.) 25 Years of Model Checking. LNCS, vol. 5000, pp. 107–138. Springer, Heidelberg (2008). https://doi.org/10.1007/978-3-540-69850-0_7
10. Dehnert, C., Junges, S., Katoen, J.-P., Volk, M.: A STORM is coming: a modern probabilistic model checker. In: Majumdar, R., Kunčak, V. (eds.) CAV 2017. LNCS, vol. 10427, pp. 592–600. Springer, Cham (2017). https://doi.org/10.1007/978-3-319-63390-9_31
11. Eisentraut, C., Hermanns, H., Zhang, L.: On probabilistic automata in continuous time. In: LICS, pp. 342–351. IEEE Computer Society (2010). https://doi.org/10.1109/LICS.2010.41
12. Forejt, V., Kwiatkowska, M., Norman, G., Parker, D.: Automated verification techniques for probabilistic systems. In: Bernardo, M., Issarny, V. (eds.) SFM 2011. LNCS, vol. 6659, pp. 53–113. Springer, Heidelberg (2011). https://doi.org/10.1007/978-3-642-21455-4_3
13. Fränzle, M., Hahn, E.M., Hermanns, H., Wolovick, N., Zhang, L.: Measurability and safety verification for stochastic hybrid systems. In: HSCC, pp. 43–52. ACM (2011). https://doi.org/10.1145/1967701.1967710

14. Haddad, S., Monmege, B.: Reachability in MDPs: refining convergence of value iteration. In: Ouaknine, J., Potapov, I., Worrell, J. (eds.) RP 2014. LNCS, vol. 8762, pp. 125–137. Springer, Cham (2014). https://doi.org/10.1007/978-3-319-11439-2_10

15. Haddad, S., Monmege, B.: Interval iteration algorithm for MDPs and IMDPs. Theor. Comput. Sci. **735**, 111–131 (2018). https://doi.org/10.1016/j.tcs.2016.12.003

16. Hahn, E.M., et al.: The 2019 comparison of tools for the analysis of quantitative formal models. In: Beyer, D., Huisman, M., Kordon, F., Steffen, B. (eds.) TACAS 2019. LNCS, vol. 11429, pp. 69–92. Springer, Cham (2019). https://doi.org/10.1007/978-3-030-17502-3_5

17. Hahn, E.M., Hartmanns, A., Hermanns, H., Katoen, J.P.: A compositional modelling and analysis framework for stochastic hybrid systems. Formal Methods Syst. Des. **43**(2), 191–232 (2013). https://doi.org/10.1007/s10703-012-0167-z

18. Hahn, E.M., Li, Y., Schewe, S., Turrini, A., Zhang, L.: iscasMc: a web-based probabilistic model checker. In: Jones, C., Pihlajasaari, P., Sun, J. (eds.) FM 2014. LNCS, vol. 8442, pp. 312–317. Springer, Cham (2014). https://doi.org/10.1007/978-3-319-06410-9_22

19. Hartmanns, A.: Optimistic value iteration (artifact). 4TU.Centre for Research Data (2019). https://doi.org/10.4121/uuid:3df859e6-edc6-4e2d-92f3-93e478bbe8dc

20. Hartmanns, A., Hermanns, H.: The Modest Toolset: an integrated environment for quantitative modelling and verification. In: Ábrahám, E., Havelund, K. (eds.) TACAS 2014. LNCS, vol. 8413, pp. 593–598. Springer, Heidelberg (2014). https://doi.org/10.1007/978-3-642-54862-8_51

21. Hartmanns, A., Klauck, M., Parker, D., Quatmann, T., Ruijters, E.: The quantitative verification benchmark set. In: Vojnar, T., Zhang, L. (eds.) TACAS 2019. LNCS, vol. 11427, pp. 344–350. Springer, Cham (2019). https://doi.org/10.1007/978-3-030-17462-0_20

22. Hensel, C.: The probabilistic model checker Storm: symbolic methods for probabilistic model checking. Ph.D. thesis, RWTH Aachen University, Germany (2018)

23. Kelmendi, E., Krämer, J., Křetínský, J., Weininger, M.: Value iteration for simple stochastic games: stopping criterion and learning algorithm. In: Chockler, H., Weissenbacher, G. (eds.) CAV 2018. LNCS, vol. 10981, pp. 623–642. Springer, Cham (2018). https://doi.org/10.1007/978-3-319-96145-3_36

24. Kwiatkowska, M., Norman, G., Parker, D.: PRISM 4.0: verification of probabilistic real-time systems. In: Gopalakrishnan, G., Qadeer, S. (eds.) CAV 2011. LNCS, vol. 6806, pp. 585–591. Springer, Heidelberg (2011). https://doi.org/10.1007/978-3-642-22110-1_47

25. Kwiatkowska, M.Z., Norman, G., Parker, D., Sproston, J.: Performance analysis of probabilistic timed automata using digital clocks. Formal Methods Syst. Des. **29**(1), 33–78 (2006). https://doi.org/10.1007/s10703-006-0005-2

26. Kwiatkowska, M.Z., Norman, G., Segala, R., Sproston, J.: Automatic verification of real-time systems with discrete probability distributions. Theor. Comput. Sci. **282**(1), 101–150 (2002). https://doi.org/10.1016/S0304-3975(01)00046-9

27. Lassez, J.L., Nguyen, V.L., Sonenberg, L.: Fixed point theorems and semantics: a folk tale. Inf. Process. Lett. **14**(3), 112–116 (1982)

28. McMahan, H.B., Likhachev, M., Gordon, G.J.: Bounded real-time dynamic programming: RTDP with monotone upper bounds and performance guarantees. In: ICML, ACM International Conference Proceeding Series, vol. 119, pp. 569–576. ACM (2005). https://doi.org/10.1145/1102351.1102423

29. Park, D.: Fixpoint induction and proofs of program properties. Mach. Intell. **5** (1969)
30. Puterman, M.L.: Markov Decision Processes: Discrete Stochastic Dynamic Programming. Wiley Series in Probability and Mathematical Statistics: Applied Probability and Statistics. Wiley, New York (1994)
31. Quatmann, T., Katoen, J.-P.: Sound value iteration. In: Chockler, H., Weissenbacher, G. (eds.) CAV 2018. LNCS, vol. 10981, pp. 643–661. Springer, Cham (2018). https://doi.org/10.1007/978-3-319-96145-3_37

PrIC3: Property Directed Reachability for MDPs

Kevin Batz[1]([envelope]) [iD], Sebastian Junges[2] [iD], Benjamin Lucien Kaminski[3] [iD],
Joost-Pieter Katoen[1] [iD], Christoph Matheja[4] [iD], and Philipp Schröer[1] [iD]

[1] RWTH Aachen University, Aachen, Germany
kevin.batz@cs.rwth-aachen.de
[2] University of California, Berkeley, USA
[3] University College London, London, UK
[4] ETH Zürich, Zürich, Switzerland

Abstract. IC3 has been a leap forward in symbolic model checking. This
paper proposes PrIC3 (pronounced pricy-three), a conservative extension of IC3 to symbolic model checking of MDPs. Our main focus is
to develop the theory underlying PrIC3. Alongside, we present a first
implementation of PrIC3 including the key ingredients from IC3 such as
generalization, repushing, and propagation.

1 Introduction

IC3. Also known as property-directed reachability (PDR) [23], IC3 [13] is a symbolic approach for verifying finite transition systems (TSs) against safety properties like *"bad states are unreachable"*. It combines bounded model checking
(BMC) [12] and inductive invariant generation. Put shortly, IC3 either proves that
a set B of bad states is *unreachable* by finding a set of non-B states closed under
reachability—called an *inductive invariant*—or refutes reachability of B by a *counterexample* path reaching B. Rather than unrolling the transition relation (as in
BMC), IC3 attempts to incrementally strengthen the invariant "no state in B is
reachable" into an inductive one. In addition, it applies aggressive abstraction to
the explored state space, so-called generalization [36]. These aspects together with
the enormous advances in modern SAT solvers have led to IC3's success. IC3 has
been extended [27,38] and adapted to software verification [19,44]. This paper
develops a *quantitative* IC3 framework for probabilistic models.

MDPs. Markov decision processes (MDPs) extend TSs with discrete probabilistic
choices. They are central in planning, AI as well as in modeling randomized distributed algorithms. A key question in verifying MDPs is *quantitative* reachability:
"is the (maximal) probability to reach B at most λ?". Quantitative reachability [5,6]

This work has been supported by the ERC Advanced Grant 787914 (FRAPPANT),
NSF grants 1545126 (VeHICaL) and 1646208, the DARPA Assured Autonomy program, Berkeley Deep Drive, and by Toyota under the iCyPhy center.

S. K. Lahiri and C. Wang (Eds.): CAV 2020, LNCS 12225, pp. 512–538, 2020.
https://doi.org/10.1007/978-3-030-53291-8_27

reduces to solving linear programs (LPs). Various tools support MDP model check-ing, e.g., Prism [43], Storm [22], modest [34], and EPMC [31]. The LPs are mostly solved using (variants of) value iteration [8,28,35,51]. Symbolic BDD-based MDP model checking originated two decades ago [4] and is rather successful.

Towards IC3 *for MDPs.* Despite the success of BDD-based symbolic methods in tools like Prism, IC3 has not penetrated probabilistic model checking yet. The success of IC3 and the importance of quantitative reachability in probabilistic model checking raises the question *whether and how* IC3 *can be adapted—not just utilized—to reason about quantitative reachability in MDPs.* This paper addresses the challenges of answering this question. It extends IC3 in several dimensions to overcome these hurdles, making PrIC3—to our knowledge—*the first* IC3 *frame-work for quantitative reachability in MDPs*[1]. Notably, PrIC3 is conservative: For a threshold $\lambda = 0$, PrIC3 solves the same qualitative problem *and behaves (almost) the same as standard* IC3. Our main contribution is developing the theory under-lying PrIC3, which is accompanied by a proof-of-concept implementation.

Challenge 1 (Leaving the Boolean domain). IC3 iteratively computes *frames*, which are over-approximations of sets of states that can reach B in a bounded number of steps. For MDPs, Boolean reachability becomes a *quantitative reach-ability probability.* This requires a shift: frames become real-valued functions rather than sets of states. Thus, there are infinitely many possible frames—even for finite-state MDPs—just as for infinite-state software [19,44] and hybrid sys-tems [54]. Additionally, whereas in TSs a state reachable within k steps remains reachable on increasing k, the reachability probability in MDPs may increase. This complicates ensuring termination of an IC3 algorithm for MDPs.   △

Challenge 2 (Counterexamples ≠ single paths). For TSs, a single cycle-free path[2] to B suffices to refute that *"B is not reachable"*. This is not true in the proba-bilistic setting [32]. Instead, proving that the probability of reaching B exceeds the threshold λ requires *a set of possibly cyclic paths*—e.g., represented as a sub-MDP [15]—whose probability mass exceeds λ. Handling sets of paths as counterexamples in the context of IC3 is new.   △

Challenge 3 (Strengthening). This key IC3 technique intuitively turns a proof obligation of type (I) "state s is unreachable from the initial state s_I" into type (II) "s's *predecessors* are unreachable from s_I". A first issue is that in the quantitative setting, the standard characterization of reachability probabilities in MDPs (the Bellman equations) inherently *reverses* the direction of reasoning (cf. "reverse" IC3 [53]): Hence, strengthening turns (I) "s cannot reach B" into (II) "s's *successors* cannot reach B".

A much more challenging issue, however, is that in the quantitative setting obligations of type (I) read "s is reachable *with at most probability* δ". However,

---

[1] Recently, (standard) IC3 for TSs was *utilized* in model checking Markov chains [49] to on-the-fly compute the states that cannot reach B.

[2] In [38], tree-like counterexamples are used for non-linear predicate transformers in IC3.

the strengthened type (II) obligation must then read: "*the weighted sum over the reachability probabilities of the successors of* s is at most δ". In general, there are infinitely many possible choices of subobligations for the successors of s in order to satisfy the original obligation, because—grossly simplified—there are infinitely many possibilities for a and b to satisfy weighted sums such as $\frac{1}{3}a + \frac{2}{3}b \leq \delta$. While we only need one choice of subobligations, picking a *good* one is approximately as hard as solving the entire problem altogether. We hence require a heuristic, which is guided by a *user-provided oracle*.   △

Challenge 4 (Generalization). "One of the key components of IC3 is [inductive] generalization" [13]. Generalization [36] abstracts single states. It makes IC3 scale, but is *not* essential for correctness. To facilitate generalization, systems should be encoded symbolically, i.e., integer-valued program variables describe states. Frames thus map variables to probabilities. A first aspect is how to effectively present them to an SMT-solver. Conceptually, we use uninterpreted functions and universal quantifiers (encoding program behavior) together with linear real arithmetic to encode the weighted sums occurring when reasoning about probabilities. A second aspect is more fundamental: Abstractly, IC3's generalization guesses an unreachable set of states. We, however, need to guess this set *and* a probability for each state. To be effective, these guesses should moreover eventually yield an inductive frame, which is often highly nonlinear. We propose three SMT-guided interpolation variants for guessing these maps.   △

Structure of this Paper. We develop PrIC3 gradually: We explain the underlying rationale in Sect. 3. We also describe the core of PrIC3—called PrIC3$_\mathcal{H}$—which resembles closely the main loop of standard IC3, but uses adapted frames and termination criteria (Challenge 1). In line with Challenge 3, PrIC3$_\mathcal{H}$ is parameterized by a heuristic $\mathcal{H}$ which is applied whenever we need to select one out of infinitely many probabilities. No requirements on the quality of $\mathcal{H}$ are imposed. PrIC3$_\mathcal{H}$ is *sound* and always terminates: If it returns `true`, then the maximal reachability probability is bounded by λ. Without additional assumptions about $\mathcal{H}$, PrIC3$_\mathcal{H}$ is *incomplete*: on returning `false`, it is unknown whether the returned sub-MDP is indeed a counterexample (Challenge 2). Section 4 details strengthening (Challenge 3). Section 5 presents a sound *and* complete algorithm PrIC3 on top of PrIC3$_\mathcal{H}$. Section 6 presents a prototype, discusses our chosen heuristics, and addresses Challenge 4. Section 7 shows some encouraging experiments, but also illustrates need for further progress.

Related Work. Just like IC3 has been a symbiosis of different approaches, PrIC3 has been inspired by several existing techniques from the verification of probabilistic systems.

BMC. Adaptions of BMC to Markov chains (MCs) with a dedicated treatment of cycles have been pursued in [57]. The encoding in [24] annotates sub-formulae with probabilities. The integrated SAT solving process implicitly unrolls all paths leading to an exponential blow-up. In [52], this is circumvented by grouping paths, discretizing them, and using an encoding with quantifiers and bit-vectors, but without numerical values. Recently, [56] extends this idea to a PAC algorithm by purely propositional encodings and (approximate) model counting [17]. These approaches focus on MCs and are not mature yet.

Invariant Synthesis. Quantitative loop invariants are key in analyzing *probabilistic programs* whose operational semantics are (possibly infinite) MDPs [26]. A quantitative invariant I maps states to probabilities. I is shown to be an invariant by comparing I to the result of applying the MDP's Bellman operator to I. Existing approaches for invariant synthesis are, e.g., based on weakest pre-expectations [33,39,40,42,46], template-based constraint solving [25], notions of martingales [3,9,16,55], and solving recurrence relations [10]. All but the last technique require user guidance.

Abstraction. To combat state-space explosion, abstraction is often employed. CEGAR for MDPs [37] deals with explicit sets of paths as counterexamples. Game-based abstraction [30,41] and partial exploration [14] exploit that not all paths have to be explored to prove bounds on reachability probabilities.

Statistical Methods and (deep) Reinforcement Learning. Finally, an avenue that avoids storing a (complete) model are simulation-based approaches (statistical model checking [2]) and variants of reinforcement learning, possibly with neural networks. For MDPs, these approaches yield weak statistical guarantees [20], but may provide good oracles.

2   Problem Statement

Our aim is to prove that the *maximal probability* of *reaching* a *set B of bad states* from the initial state s_I of a *Markov decision process* $\mathfrak{M}$ is at most some *threshold* λ. Below, we give a formal description of our problem. We refer to [7,50] for a thorough introduction.

Definition 1 (MDPs). *A Markov decision process (MDP) is a tuple $\mathfrak{M} = (S, s_I, \text{Act}, P)$, where S is a finite set of states, $s_I \in S$ is the initial state, Act is a finite set of actions, and $P \colon S \times \text{Act} \times S \to [0,1]$ is a transition probability function. For state s, let $\text{Act}(s) = \{a \in \text{Act} \mid \exists s' \in S \colon P(s,a,s') > 0\}$ be the enabled actions at s. For all states $s \in S$, we require $|\text{Act}(s)| \geq 1$ and $\sum_{s' \in S} P(s,a,s') = 1$.* △

For this paper, we fix an MDP $\mathfrak{M} = (S, s_I, \text{Act}, P)$, a set of *bad states* $B \subseteq S$, and a threshold $\lambda \in [0,1]$. The *maximal*[3] *(unbounded) reachability probability* to eventually reach a state in B from a state s is denoted by $\text{Pr}^{\max}(s \models \Diamond B)$. We characterize $\text{Pr}^{\max}(s \models \Diamond B)$ using the so-called *Bellman operator*. Let M^N denote the set of functions from N to M. Anticipating IC3 terminology, we call a function $F \in [0,1]^S$ a *frame*. We denote by $F[s]$ the evaluation of frame F for state s.

---

[3] Maximal with respect to all possible resolutions of nondeterminism in the MDP.

Definition 2 (Bellman Operator). *For a set of actions $A \subseteq$ Act, we define the Bellman operator for A as a frame transformer $\Phi_A \colon [0,1]^S \to [0,1]^S$ with*

$$\Phi_A(F)[s] = \begin{cases} 1, & \text{if } s \in B \\ \max\limits_{a \in A} \sum\limits_{s' \in S} P(s,a,s') \cdot F[s'], & \text{if } s \notin B. \end{cases}$$

We write Φ_a for $\Phi_{\{a\}}$, Φ for Φ_{Act}, and call Φ simply the Bellman operator. △

For every state s, the maximal reachability probability $\mathrm{Pr}^{\max}(s \models \Diamond B)$ is then given by the least fixed point of the Bellman operator Φ. That is,

$$\forall s: \quad \mathrm{Pr}^{\max}(s \models \Diamond B) = \left(\mathrm{lfp}\ \Phi\right)[s],$$

where the underlying partial order on frames is a complete lattice with ordering

$$F_1 \leq F_2 \quad \text{iff} \quad \forall s \in S: \quad F_1[s] \leq F_2[s].$$

In terms of the Bellman operator, our formal problem statement reads as follows:

Given an MDP $\mathfrak{M}$ with initial state s_I, a set B of bad states, and a *threshold* $\lambda \in [0,1]$,

prove or refute that $\mathrm{Pr}^{\max}(s_I \models \Diamond B) = \left(\mathrm{lfp}\ \Phi\right)[s_I] \leq \lambda$.

Whenever $\mathrm{Pr}^{\max}(s_I \models \Diamond B) \leq \lambda$ indeed holds, we say that the MDP $\mathfrak{M}$ is *safe* (with respect to the set of bad states B and threshold λ); otherwise, we call it *unsafe*.

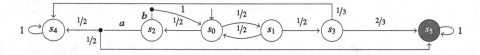

Fig. 1. The MDP $\mathfrak{M}$ serving as a running example.

Recovery Statement 1. *For $\lambda = 0$, our problem statement is equivalent to the* qualitative reachability *problem solved by (reverse) standard* IC3, *i.e, prove or refute that all bad states in B are* unreachable *from the initial state s_I.*

Example 1. The MDP $\mathfrak{M}$ in Fig. 1 consists of 6 states with initial state s_0 and bad states $B = \{s_5\}$. In s_2, actions a and b are enabled; in all other states, one unlabeled action is enabled. We have $\mathrm{Pr}^{\max}(s_0 \models \Diamond B) = 2/3$. Hence, $\mathfrak{M}$ is safe for all thresholds $\lambda \geq 2/3$ and unsafe for $\lambda < 2/3$. In particular, $\mathfrak{M}$ is unsafe for $\lambda = 0$ as s_5 is *reachable* from s_0. △

3   The Core PrIC3 Algorithm

The purpose of PrIC3 is to prove or refute that the maximal probability to reach a bad state in B from the initial state s_I of the MDP $\mathfrak{M}$ is at most λ. In this section, we explain the rationale underlying PrIC3. Moreover, we describe the core of PrIC3—called PrIC3$_{\mathcal{H}}$—which bears close resemblance to the main loop of standard IC3 for TSs.

Because of the inherent direction of the Bellman operator, we build PrIC3 on *reverse* IC3 [53], cf. Challenge 3. Reversing constitutes a shift from reasoning along the direction *initial-to-bad* to *bad-to-initial*. While this shift is mostly *inessential* to the fundamentals underlying IC3, the reverse direction is unswayable in the probabilistic setting. Whenever we draw a connection to standard IC3, we thus generally mean *reverse* IC3.

3.1   Inductive Frames

IC3 for TSs operates on (*qualitative*) frames representing sets of states of the TS at hand. A frame F can hence be thought of as a mapping[4] from states to $\{0, 1\}$. In PrIC3 for MDPs, we need to move from a Boolean to a quantitative regime. Hence, a (*quantitative*) frame is a mapping from states to probabilities in $[0, 1]$.

For a given TS, consider the frame transformer T that adds to a given input frame F' all bad states in B and all predecessors of the states contained in F'. The rationale of standard (reverse) IC3 is to find a frame $F \in \{0, 1\}^S$ such that (I) the initial state s_I does not belong to F and (II) applying T takes us down in the partial order on frames, i.e.,

$$(\text{I}) \quad F[s_I] = 0 \qquad \text{and} \qquad (\text{II}) \quad T(F) \leq F .$$

Intuitively, (I) postulates the *hypothesis* that s_I cannot reach B and (II) expresses that F is closed under adding bad states and taking predecessors, thus affirming the hypothesis.

Analogously, the rationale of PrIC3 is to find a frame $F \in [0, 1]^S$ such that (I) F postulates that the probability of s_I to reach B is at most the threshold λ and (II) applying the Bellman operator Φ to F takes us down in the partial order on frames, i.e.,

$$(\text{I}) \quad F[s_I] \leq \lambda \qquad \text{and} \qquad (\text{II}) \quad \Phi(F) \leq F .$$

Frames satisfying the above conditions are called *inductive invariants* in IC3. We adopt this terminology. By *Park's Lemma* [48], which in our setting reads

$$\Phi(F) \leq F \quad \text{implies} \quad \text{lfp } \Phi \leq F ,$$

---

[4] In IC3, frames are typically characterized by logical formulae. To understand IC3's fundamental principle, however, we prefer to think of frames as functions in $\{0, 1\}^S$ partially ordered by $\leq$.

an inductive invariant F would indeed *witness* that $\mathrm{Pr}^{\max}\left(s_I \models \Diamond B\right) \leq \lambda$, because

$$\mathrm{Pr}^{\max}\left(s_I \models \Diamond B\right) = (\mathrm{lfp}\ \Phi)[s_I] \leq F[s_I] \leq \lambda\,.$$

If no inductive invariant exists, then standard IC3 will find a counterexample: a *path* from the initial state s_I to a bad state in B, which serves as a witness to refute. Analogously, PrIC3 will find a counterexample, but of a different kind: Since single paths are insufficient as counterexamples in the probabilistic realm (Challenge 2), PrIC3 will instead find a *subsystem* of states of the MDP witnessing $\mathrm{Pr}^{\max}\left(s_I \models \Diamond B\right) > \lambda$.

3.2 The PrIC3 Invariants

Analogously to standard IC3, PrIC3 aims to find the inductive invariant by maintaining a *sequence of frames* $F_0 \leq F_1 \leq F_2 \leq \ldots$ such that $F_i[s]$ overapproximates the maximal probability of reaching B from s within *at most i steps*. This *i-step-bounded reachability probability* $\mathrm{Pr}^{\max}\left(s \models \Diamond^{\leq i} B\right)$ can be characterized using the Bellman operator: $\Phi\left(\mathbf{0}\right)$ is the 0-step probability; it is 1 for every $s \in B$ and 0 otherwise. For any $i \geq 0$, we have

$$\mathrm{Pr}^{\max}\left(s \models \Diamond^{\leq i} B\right) = \left(\Phi^i\left(\Phi\left(\mathbf{0}\right)\right)\right)[s] = \left(\Phi^{i+1}\left(\mathbf{0}\right)\right)[s]\,,$$

where $\mathbf{0}$, the frame that maps every state to 0, is the least frame of the underlying complete lattice. For a finite MDP, the *unbounded* reachability probability is then given by the limit

$$\mathrm{Pr}^{\max}\left(s \models \Diamond B\right) = (\mathrm{lfp}\ \Phi)[s] \overset{(*)}{=} \left(\lim_{n \to \infty} \Phi^n\left(\mathbf{0}\right)\right)[s] = \lim_{n \to \infty} \mathrm{Pr}^{\max}\left(s \models \Diamond^{\leq n} B\right)\,,$$

where $(*)$ is a consequence of the well-known Kleene fixed point theorem [45].

The sequence $F_0 \leq F_1 \leq F_2 \leq \ldots$ maintained by PrIC3 should frame-wise overapproximate the increasing sequence $\Phi\left(\mathbf{0}\right) \leq \Phi^2\left(\mathbf{0}\right) \leq \Phi^3\left(\mathbf{0}\right)\ldots$. Pictorially:

$$
\begin{array}{ccccccccc}
F_0 & \leq & F_1 & \leq & F_2 & \leq & \cdots & \leq & F_k \\[4pt]
\text{VI} & & \text{VI} & & \text{VI} & & & & \text{VI} \\[4pt]
\mathbf{0} \leq & \Phi\left(\mathbf{0}\right) & \leq & \Phi^2\left(\mathbf{0}\right) & \leq & \Phi^3\left(\mathbf{0}\right) & \leq & \cdots & \leq & \Phi^{k+1}\left(\mathbf{0}\right)
\end{array}
$$

However, the sequence $\Phi\left(\mathbf{0}\right),\ \Phi^2\left(\mathbf{0}\right),\ \Phi^3\left(\mathbf{0}\right),\ \ldots$ will never explicitly be known to PrIC3. Instead, PrIC3 will ensure the above frame-wise overapproximation property implicitly by enforcing the so-called PrIC3 *invariants* on the frame sequence $F_0,\ F_1,\ F_2,\ \ldots$. Apart from allowing for a threshold $0 \leq \lambda \leq 1$ on the maximal reachability probability, these invariants coincide with the standard IC3 invariants (where $\lambda = 0$ is fixed). Formally:

Definition 3 (PrIC3 Invariants). *Frames $F_0, \ldots, F_k$, for $k \geq 0$, satisfy the PrIC3 invariants, a fact we will denote by $\mathsf{PrIC3Inv}(F_0, \ldots, F_k)$, if all of the following hold:*

1. **Initiality :** $F_0 = \Phi(0)$
2. **Chain Property :** $\forall 0 \leq i < k: \quad F_i \leq F_{i+1}$
3. **Frame-safety :** $\forall 0 \leq i \leq k: \quad F_i[s_I] \leq \lambda$
4. **Relative Inductivity :** $\forall 0 \leq i < k: \quad \Phi(F_i) \leq F_{i+1}$ $\triangle$

The PrIC3 invariants enforce the above picture: The *chain property* ensures $F_0 \leq F_1 \leq \ldots \leq F_k$. We have $\Phi(0) = F_0 \leq F_0$ by *initiality*. Assuming $\Phi^{i+1}(0) \leq F_i$ as induction hypothesis, monotonicity of Φ and *relative inductivity* imply $\Phi^{i+2}(0) \leq \Phi(F_i) \leq F_{i+1}$.

By overapproximating $\Phi(0), \Phi^2(0), \ldots, \Phi^{k+1}(0)$, the frames $F_0, \ldots, F_k$ in effect bound the maximal step-bounded reachability probability of every state:

Lemma 1. *Let frames $F_0, \ldots, F_k$ satisfy the PrIC3 invariants. Then*

$$\forall s \ \forall i \leq k: \quad Pr^{max}\left(s \models \Diamond^{\leq i} B\right) \leq F_i[s].$$

In particular, Lemma 1 together with *frame-safety* ensures that the maximal step-bounded reachability probability of the *initial state* s_I to reach B is at most the threshold λ.

As for proving that the *unbounded* reachability probability is also at most λ, it suffices to find two consecutive frames, say F_i and F_{i+1}, that coincide:

Lemma 2. *Let frames $F_0, \ldots, F_k$ satisfy the PrIC3 invariants. Then*

$$\exists i < k: \quad F_i = F_{i+1} \qquad implies \qquad Pr^{max}(s_I \models \Diamond B) \leq \lambda.$$

Proof. $F_i = F_{i+1}$ and *relative inductivity* yield $\Phi(F_i) \leq F_{i+1} = F_i$, rendering F_i *inductive*. By Park's lemma (cf. Sect. 3.1), we obtain lfp $\Phi \leq F_i$ and—by *frame-safety*—conclude

$$Pr^{max}(s_I \models \Diamond B) = (\text{lfp } \Phi)[s_I] \leq F_i[s_I] \leq \lambda. \qquad \square$$

3.3   Operationalizing the PrIC3 Invariants for Proving Safety

Lemma 2 gives us a clear angle of attack for *proving* an MDP safe: Repeatedly add and refine frames approximating step-bounded reachability probabilities for more and more steps while enforcing the PrIC3 invariants (cf. Definition 3.2) until two consecutive frames coincide.

Analogously to standard IC3, this approach is taken by the core loop $\mathsf{PrIC3}_{\mathcal{H}}$ depicted in Algorithm 1; differences to the main loop of IC3 (cf. [23, Fig. 5]) are highlighted in red. A particular difference is that $\mathsf{PrIC3}_{\mathcal{H}}$ is parameterized by a heuristic $\mathcal{H}$ for finding suitable probabilities (see Challenge 3). Since the precise choice of $\mathcal{H}$ is irrelevant for the soundness of $\mathsf{PrIC3}_{\mathcal{H}}$, we defer a detailed discussion of suitable heuristics to Sect. 4.

Data: MDP $\mathfrak{M}$,   set of bad states B,   threshold λ
Result: true or false and a subset of the states of $\mathfrak{M}$

```
1  F₀ ← Φ(0);  F₁ ← 1;  k ← 1;   oldSubsystem ← ∅;
2  while true do
3  │   success, F₀, ..., Fₖ, subsystem ← Strengthen_H (F₀, ..., Fₖ);
4  │   if ¬success then returnfalse, subsystem;
5  │   Fₖ₊₁ ← 1;
6  │   F₀, ..., Fₖ₊₁ ← Propagate (F₀, ..., Fₖ₊₁);
7  │   if ∃ 1 ≤ i ≤ k: Fᵢ = Fᵢ₊₁ then returntrue, __;
8  │   if oldSubsystem = subsystem then returnfalse, subsystem;
9  │   k ← k + 1;   oldSubsystem ← subsystem;
10 end
```

$$\text{\textbf{Algorithm 1:} PrIC3}_{\mathcal{H}}\,(\mathfrak{M},\,B,\,\lambda)$$

As input, $\text{PrIC3}_{\mathcal{H}}$ takes an MDP $\mathfrak{M} = (S, s_I, \text{Act}, P)$, a set $B \subseteq S$ of bad states, and a threshold $\lambda \in [0,1]$. Since the input is never changed, we assume it to be *globally available*, also to subroutines. As output, $\text{PrIC3}_{\mathcal{H}}$ returns true if two consecutive frames become equal. We hence say that $\text{PrIC3}_{\mathcal{H}}$ is *sound* if it only returns true if $\mathfrak{M}$ is safe.

We will formalize soundness using Hoare triples. For precondition ϕ, postcondition ψ, and program P, the triple $\{\,\phi\,\}\,P\,\{\,\psi\,\}$ is *valid* (for partial correctness) if, whenever program P starts in a state satisfying precondition ϕ and terminates in some state s', then s' satisfies postcondition ψ. Soundness of $\text{PrIC3}_{\mathcal{H}}$ then means validity of the triple

$$\{\,\text{true}\,\}\,safe,\_\_ \;\leftarrow\; \text{PrIC3}_{\mathcal{H}}\,(\mathfrak{M},\,B,\,\lambda)\,\{\,safe \;\Rightarrow\; \text{Pr}^{\max}\,(s_I \models \Diamond B) \leq \lambda\,\}\,.$$

Let us briefly go through the individual steps of $\text{PrIC3}_{\mathcal{H}}$ in Algorithm 1 and convince ourselves that it is indeed sound. After that, we discuss why $\text{PrIC3}_{\mathcal{H}}$ terminates and what happens if it is unable to prove safety by finding two equal consecutive frames.

How $\text{PrIC3}_{\mathcal{H}}$ works. Recall that $\text{PrIC3}_{\mathcal{H}}$ maintains a sequence of frames $F_0, \ldots, F_k$ which is initialized in l. 1 with $k = 1$, $F_0 = \Phi(0)$, and $F_1 = 1$, where the frame 1 maps every state to 1. Every time upon entering the **while**-loop in terms l. 2, the initial segment $F_0, \ldots, F_{k-1}$ satisfies all PrIC3 invariants (cf. Definition 3), whereas the full sequence $F_0, \ldots, F_k$ potentially violates frame-safety as it is possible that $F_k[s_I] > \lambda$.

In l. 3, procedure $\text{Strengthen}_{\mathcal{H}}$—detailed in Sect. 4—is called to restore *all* PrIC3 invariants on the *entire* frame sequence: It either returns true if successful or returns false and a counterexample (in our case a subsystem of the MDP) if it was unable to do so. To ensure soundness of $\text{PrIC3}_{\mathcal{H}}$, it suffices that $\text{Strengthen}_{\mathcal{H}}$ restores the PrIC3 invariants whenever it returns true. Formally, $\text{Strengthen}_{\mathcal{H}}$ must meet the following specification:

Definition 4. *Procedure* Strengthen$_\mathcal{H}$ *is sound if the following Hoare triple is valid:*

$$\{ \text{PrIC3Inv}(F_0, \ldots, F_{k-1}) \ \wedge \ F_{k-1} \leq F_k \ \wedge \ \Phi(F_{k-1}) \leq F_k \}$$
$$success, F_0, \ldots, F_k, \_\_ \ \leftarrow \ \text{Strengthen}_\mathcal{H}(F_0, \ldots, F_k)$$
$$\{ success \ \Rightarrow \ \text{PrIC3Inv}(F_0, \ldots, F_k) \}.$$

If Strengthen$_\mathcal{H}$ returns `true`, then a new frame $F_{k+1} = 1$ is created in l. 5. After that, the (now initial) segment $F_0, \ldots, F_k$ again satisfies all PrIC3 invariants, whereas the full sequence $F_0, \ldots, F_{k+1}$ potentially violates frame-safety at F_{k+1}. *Propagation* (l. 6) aims to speed up termination by updating $F_{i+1}[s]$ by $F_i[s]$ iff this does not violate relative inductivity. Consequently, the previously mentioned properties remain unchanged.

If Strengthen$_\mathcal{H}$ returns `false`, the PrIC3 invariants—premises to Lemma 2 for witnessing safety—cannot be restored and PrIC3$_\mathcal{H}$ terminates returning `false` (l. 4). Returning `false` (also possible in l. 8) has by specification no affect on soundness of PrIC3$_\mathcal{H}$.

In l. 7, we check whether there exist two identical consecutive frames. If so, Lemma 2 yields that the MDP is safe; consequently, PrIC3$_\mathcal{H}$ returns `true`. Otherwise, we increment k and are in the same setting as upon entering the loop, now with an increased frame sequence; PrIC3$_\mathcal{H}$ then performs another iteration. In summary, we obtain:

Theorem 1 (Soundness of PrIC3$_\mathcal{H}$). *If* Strengthen$_\mathcal{H}$ *is sound and* Propagate *does not affect the* PrIC3 *invariants, then* PrIC3$_\mathcal{H}$ *is sound, i.e., the following triple is valid:*

$$\{ \texttt{true} \} \, safe, \_\_ \ \leftarrow \ \text{PrIC3}_\mathcal{H}(\mathfrak{M}, B, \lambda) \, \{ \, safe \ \Longrightarrow \ Pr^{max}(s_I \models \Diamond B) \ \leq \ \lambda \}$$

PrIC3$_\mathcal{H}$ Terminates for Unsafe MDPs. If the MDP is unsafe, then there exists a step-bound n, such that $Pr^{max}(s_I \models \Diamond^{\leq n} B) > \lambda$. Furthermore, any sound implementation of Strengthen$_\mathcal{H}$ (cf. Definition 4) either immediately terminates PrIC3$_\mathcal{H}$ by returning `false` or restores the PrIC3 invariants for $F_0, \ldots, F_k$. If the former case never arises, then Strengthen$_\mathcal{H}$ will eventually restore the PrIC3 invariants for a frame sequence of length $k = n$. By Lemma 1, we have $F_n[s_I] \geq Pr^{max}(s_I \models \Diamond^{\leq n} B) > \lambda$ contradicting frame-safety.

PrIC3$_\mathcal{H}$ Terminates for Safe MDPs. Standard IC3 terminates on safe finite TSs as there are only finitely many different frames, making every ascending chain of frames eventually stabilize. For us, frames map states to probabilities (Challenge 1), yielding *infinitely many possible frames* even for finite MDPs. Hence, Strengthen$_\mathcal{H}$ need not ever yield a stabilizing chain of frames. If it continuously fails to stabilize while repeatedly reasoning about the same set of states, we give up. PrIC3$_\mathcal{H}$ checks this by comparing the subsystem Strengthen$_\mathcal{H}$ operates on with the one it operated on in the previous loop iteration (l. 8).

Theorem 2. *If* Strengthen$_\mathcal{H}$ *and* Propagate *terminate, then* PrIC3$_\mathcal{H}$ *terminates.*

Recovery Statement 2. *For qual. reachability ($\lambda = 0$), $\mathsf{PrIC3}_{\mathcal{H}}$ never terminates in l. 8.*

$\mathsf{PrIC3}_{\mathcal{H}}$ is Incomplete. Standard IC3 either proves safety or returns `false` and a counterexample—a single path from the initial to a bad state. As single paths are insufficient as counterexamples in MDPs (Challenge 2), $\mathsf{PrIC3}_{\mathcal{H}}$ instead returns a *subsystem* of the MDP $\mathfrak{M}$ provided by $\mathsf{Strengthen}_{\mathcal{H}}$. However, as argued above, we cannot trust $\mathsf{Strengthen}_{\mathcal{H}}$ to provide a stabilizing chain of frames. Reporting `false` thus only means that the given MDP *may* be unsafe; the returned subsystem has to be analyzed further.

The full $\mathsf{PrIC3}$ algorithm presented in Sect. 5 addresses this issue. Exploiting the subsystem returned by $\mathsf{PrIC3}_{\mathcal{H}}$, $\mathsf{PrIC3}$ returns `true` if the MDP is safe; otherwise, it returns `false` and provides a true counterexample witnessing that the MDP is unsafe.

Example 2. We conclude this section with two example executions of $\mathsf{PrIC3}_{\mathcal{H}}$ on a simplified version of the MDP in Fig. 1. Assume that action b has been removed. Then, for every state, exactly one action is enabled, i.e., we consider a Markov chain. Figure 2 depicts the frame sequences computed by $\mathsf{PrIC3}_{\mathcal{H}}$ (for a reasonable $\mathcal{H}$) on that Markov chain for two thresholds: $5/9 = \mathrm{Pr}^{\max}(s_0 \models \Diamond B)$ and $9/10$. In particular, notice that *proving the coarser bound of $9/10$ requires fewer frames than proving the exact bound of $5/9$*.   △

It.	1	2		3			4				5				
F_i	F_1	F_1	F_2	F_1	F_2	F_3	F_1	F_2	F_3	F_4	F_1	F_2	F_3	F_4	F_5
s_0	5/9	5/9	5/9	5/9	5/9	5/9	5/9	5/9	5/9	5/9	5/9	5/9	5/9	5/9	5/9
s_1	1	11/18	1	11/18	11/18	1	11/18	11/18	11/18	1	11/18	11/18	11/18	11/18	1
s_2	1	1/2	1	1/2	1/2	1	1/2	1/2	1/2	1	1/2	1/2	1/2	1/2	1
s_3	1	1	1	2/3	1	1	2/3	2/3	1	1	2/3	2/3	2/3	1	1
s_4	1	1	1	1	1	1	0	1	1	1	0	0	1	1	1
s_5	1	1	1	1	1	1	1	1	1	1	1	1	1	1	1

(a) Threshold $\lambda = 5/9$

It.	1	2		3			4			
F_i	F_1	F_1	F_2	F_1	F_2	F_3	F_1	F_2	F_3	F_4
s_0	9/10	9/10	9/10	9/10	9/10	9/10	9/10	9/10	9/10	9/10
s_1	1	99/100	1	99/100	99/100	1	99/100	99/100	99/100	1
s_2	1	81/100	1	81/100	81/100	1	81/100	81/100	81/100	1
s_3	1	1	1	1	1	1	1	1	1	1
s_4	1	1	1	0	1	1	0	0	1	1
s_5	1	1	1	1	1	1	1	1	1	1

(b) Threshold $\lambda = 9/10$

Fig. 2. Two runs of $\mathsf{PrIC3}_{\mathcal{H}}$ on the Markov chain induced by selecting action a in Fig. 1. For every iteration, frames are recorded after invocation of $\mathsf{Strengthen}_{\mathcal{H}}$.

4   Strengthening in $\mathsf{PrIC3}_{\mathcal{H}}$

When the main loop of $\mathsf{PrIC3}_{\mathcal{H}}$ has created a new frame $F_k = 1$ in its previous iteration, this frame may violate frame-safety (Definition 3.3) because of $F_k[s_I] = 1 \not\leq \lambda$. The task of $\mathsf{Strengthen}_{\mathcal{H}}$ is to restore the $\mathsf{PrIC3}$ invariants on *all* frames $F_0, \ldots, F_k$. To this end, our first *obligation* is to lower the value in frame $i = k$ for state $s = s_I$ to $\delta = \lambda \in [0, 1]$. We denote such an obligation by (i, s, δ). Observe that implicitly $\delta = 0$ in the qualitative case, i.e., when proving unreachability. An obligation (i, s, δ) is *resolved* by updating the values assigned to state s in *all* frames $F_1, \ldots, F_i$ to at most δ. That is, for all $j \leq i$, we set $F_j[s]$ to the minimum

```
1   Q ← {(k, s_I, λ)} ;
2   while Q not empty do
3   |   (i, s, δ) ← Q.popMin();        /* pop obligation with minimal frame
    |   index */
4   |   if i = 0  ∨  (s ∈ B ∧ δ < 1) then
    |   |   /* possible counterexample given by subsystem
    |   |       consisting of states popped from Q at some point */
5   |   |   return false, __, Q.touched();
    |   /* check whether F_i[s] ← δ violates relative inductivity */
6   |   if ∃a ∈ Act(s) : Φ_a (F_{i-1}) [s] > δ then for such an a
7   |   |   δ_1, ..., δ_n ← H (s, a, δ) ;
8   |   |   {s_1, ..., s_n} ← Succs(s, a);
9   |   |   Q.push ((i - 1, s_1, δ_1), ..., (i - 1, s_n, δ_n), (i, s, δ));
10  |   else /* resolve (i, s, δ) without violating relative
    |   inductivity */
11  |   |   F_1[s] ← min (F_1[s], δ) ; ... ; F_i[s] ← min (F_i[s], δ);
12  end
13  (/* Q empty; all obligations have been resolved */ ) return
    true, F_0, ..., F_k, Q.touched();
```
Algorithm 2: Strengthen$_\mathcal{H}$ $(F_0, \ldots, F_k)$

of δ and the original value $F_j[s]$. Such an update affects neither initiality nor the chain property (Definitions 3.1, 3.2). It may, however, violate relative inductivity (Definition 3.4), i.e., $\Phi(F_{i-1}) \leq F_i$. Before resolving obligation (i, s, δ), we may thus have to further decrease some entries in F_{i-1} as well. Hence, *resolving obligations may spawn additional obligations* which have to be resolved first to maintain relative inductivity. In this section, we present a generic instance of Strengthen$_\mathcal{H}$ meeting its specification (Definition 4) and discuss its correctness.

Strengthen$_\mathcal{H}$ by Example. Strengthen$_\mathcal{H}$ is given by the pseudo code in Algorithm 2; differences to standard IC3 (cf. [23, Fig. 6]) are highlighted in red. Intuitively, Strengthen$_\mathcal{H}$ attempts to recursively resolve all obligations until either both frame-safety and relative inductivity are restored for *all* frames or it detects a *potential counterexample* justifying why it is unable to do so. We first consider an execution where the latter does not arise:

Example 3. We zoom in on Example 2: Prior to the second iteration, we have created the following three frames assigning values to the states s_0, s_5:

$$F_0 = (0, 0, 0, 0, 1), \qquad F_1 = (5/9, 1, 1, 1, 1, 1), \qquad \text{and} \qquad F_2 = 1.$$

To keep track of unresolved obligations (i, s, δ), Strengthen$_\mathcal{H}$ employs a priority queue Q which pops obligations with minimal frame index i first. Our first step is to ensure frame-safety of F_2, i.e., alter F_2 so that $F_2[s_0] \leq 5/9$; we thus initialize the queue Q with the initial obligation $(2, s_0, 5/9)$ (l. 1). To do so, we check whether updating $F_2[s_0]$ to $5/9$ would invalidate relative inductivity (l. 6). This is indeed the case:

$$\Phi\left(F_1\right)[s_0] \;=\; 1/2 \cdot F_1[s_1] + 1/2 \cdot F_1[s_2] \;=\; 1 \not\leq 5/9.$$

To restore relative inductivity, $\mathsf{Strengthen}_{\mathcal{H}}$ spawns one new obligation for each relevant successor of s_0. These have to be resolved before retrying to resolve the old obligation.[5]

In contrast to standard IC3 *, spawning obligations involves finding suitable probabilities* δ (l. 7). In our example this means we have to spawn two obligations $(1, s_1, \delta_1)$ and $(1, s_2, \delta_2)$ such that $1/2 \cdot \delta_1 + 1/2 \cdot \delta_2 \leq 5/9$. There are *infinitely many choices* for δ_1 and δ_2 satisfying this inequality. Assume some heuristic $\mathcal{H}$ chooses $\delta_1 = 11/18$ and $\delta_2 = 1/2$; we push obligations $(1, s_1, 11/18)$, $(1, s_2, 1/2)$, and $(2, s_0, 5/9)$ (ll. 8, 9). In the next iteration, we first pop obligation $(1, s_1, 11/18)$ (l. 3) and find that it can be resolved without violating relative inductivity (l. 6). Hence, we set $F_1[s_1]$ to $11/18$ (l. 11); no new obligation is spawned. Obligation $(1, s_2, 1/2)$ is resolved analogously; the updated frame is $F_1 = (5/9, 11/18, 1/2, 1)$. Thereafter, our initial obligation $(2, s_0, 5/9)$ can be resolved; relative inductivity is restored for F_0, F_1, F_2. Hence, $\mathsf{Strengthen}_{\mathcal{H}}$ returns true together with the updated frames.   △

$\mathsf{Strengthen}_{\mathcal{H}}$ is Sound. Let us briefly discuss why Algorithm 2 meets the specification of a sound implemenation of $\mathsf{Strengthen}_{\mathcal{H}}$ (Definition 4): First, we observe that Algorithm 2 alters the frames—and thus potentially invalidates the PrIC3 invariants—only in l. 11 by resolving an obligation (i, s, δ) with $\Phi\left(F_{i-1}\right)[s] \leq \delta$ (due to the check in l. 6).
Let $F \langle s \mapsto \delta \rangle$ denote the frame F in which $F[s]$ is set to δ, i.e.,

$$F \langle s \mapsto \delta \rangle [s'] \;=\; \begin{cases} \delta, & \text{if } s' = s, \\ F[s'], & \text{otherwise.} \end{cases}$$

Indeed, resolving obligation (i, s, δ) in l. 11 lowers the values assigned to state s to at most δ *without* invalidating the PrIC3 invariants:

Lemma 3. *Let* (i, s, δ) *be an obligation and* $F_0, \ldots, F_i$, *for* $i > 0$, *be frames with* $\Phi\left(F_{i-1}\right)[s] \leq \delta$. *Then* $\mathsf{PrIC3Inv}\left(F_0, \ldots, F_i\right)$ *implies*

$$\mathsf{PrIC3Inv}\left(F_0 \langle s \mapsto \min\left(F_0[s],\, \delta\right)\rangle, \,\ldots,\, F_i \langle s \mapsto \min\left(F_i[s],\, \delta\right)\rangle \right).$$

Crucially, the precondition of Definition 4 guarantees that all PrIC3 invariants except frame safety hold initially. Since these invariants are never invalidated due to Lemma 3, Algorithm 2 is a sound implementation of $\mathsf{Strengthen}_{\mathcal{H}}$ if it restores frame safety whenever it returns true, i.e., once it leaves the loop with an empty obligation queue Q (ll. 12–13). Now, an obligation (i, s, δ) is only popped from Q in l. 3. As (i, s, δ) is added to Q upon reaching l. 9, the size of Q can only ever be reduced (without returning false) by resolving (i, s, δ) in l. 11. Hence, Algorithm 2 does not return true unless it restored frame safety by resolving, amongst all other obligations, the initial obligation (k, s_I, λ). Consequently:

---

[5] We assume that the set $\mathrm{Succs}(s, a) \;=\; \{s' \in S \mid P(s, a, s') > 0\}$ of *relevant a-successors* of state s is returned in some arbitrary, but fixed order.

Lemma 4. *Procedure* Strengthen$_\mathcal{H}$ *is sound, i.e., it satisfies the specification in Definition 4.*

Theorem 3. *Procedure* PrIC3$_\mathcal{H}$ *is sound, i.e., satisfies the specification in Theorem 1.*

We remark that, analogously to standard IC3, resolving an obligation in l. 11 may be accompanied by *generalization*. That is, we attempt to update the values of multiple states at once. Generalization is, however, highly non-trivial in a probabilistic setting. We discuss three possible approaches to generalization in Sect. 6.2.

Strengthen$_\mathcal{H}$ Terminates. We now show that Strengthen$_\mathcal{H}$ as in Algorithm 2 terminates. The only scenario in which Strengthen$_\mathcal{H}$ may not terminate is if it keeps spawning obligations in l. 9. Let us thus look closer at how obligations are spawned: Whenever we detect that resolving an obligation (i, s, δ) would violate relative inductivity for some action a (l. 6), we first need to update the values of the successor states $s_1, \dots, s_n \in \text{Succs}(s, a)$ in frame $i-1$, i.e., we push the obligations $(i-1, s_1, \delta_1), \dots, (i-1, s_n, \delta_n)$ which have to be resolved first (ll. 7–9). It is noteworthy that, for a TS, a single action leads to a single successor state s_1. Algorithm 2 employs a heuristic $\mathcal{H}$ to determine the probabilities required for pushing obligations (l. 7). Assume for an obligation (i, s, δ) that the check in l. 6 yields $\exists a \in \text{Act}(s) : \Phi_a(F_{i-1})[s] > \delta$. Then $\mathcal{H}$ takes s, a, δ and reports some probability δ_j for every a-successor s_j of s. However, an arbitrary heuristic of type $\mathcal{H}: S \times \text{Act} \times [0, 1] \rightarrow [0, 1]^*$ may lead to non-terminating behavior: If $\delta_1, \dots, \delta_n = F_{i-1}[s_1], \dots F_{i-1}[s_n]$, then the heuristic has no effect. It is thus natural to require that an *adequate* heuristic $\mathcal{H}$ yields probabilities such that the check $\Phi_a(F_{i-1})[s] > \delta$ in l. 6 cannot succeed twice for the *same obligation* (i, s, δ) and *same action* a. Formally, this is guaranteed by the following:

Definition 5. *Heuristic $\mathcal{H}$ is* adequate *if the following triple is valid (for any frame F):*

$$\left\{ \, Succs(s, a) = s_1, \dots, s_n \, \right\}$$
$$\delta_1, \dots, \delta_n \; \leftarrow \; \mathcal{H}(s, a, \delta)$$
$$\left\{ \, \Phi_a\left(F \langle s_1 \mapsto \delta_1 \rangle \dots \langle s_n \mapsto \delta_n \rangle\right)[s] \leq \delta \, \right\} \qquad\qquad \triangle$$

Details regarding our implementation of heuristic $\mathcal{H}$ are found in Sect. 6.1.

For an adequate heuristic, attempting to resolve an obligation (i, s, δ) (ll. 3 – 11) either succeeds after spawning it at most $|\text{Act}(s)|$ times or Strengthen$_\mathcal{H}$ returns false. By a similar argument, attempting to resolve an obligation $(i > 0, s, \_)$ leads to at most $\sum_{a \in \text{Act}(s)} |\{s' \in S \mid P(s, a, s') > 0\}|$ other obligations of the form $(i-1, s', \_)$. Consequently, the total number of obligations spawned by Algorithm 2 is bounded. Since Algorithm 2 terminates if all obligations have been resolved (l. 12) and each of its loop iterations either returns false, spawns obligations, or resolves an obligation, we conclude:

Lemma 5. Strengthen$_\mathcal{H}(F_0, \ldots, F_k)$ *terminates for every adequate heuristic* $\mathcal{H}$.

Recovery Statement 3. *Let* $\mathcal{H}$ *be adequate. Then for qualitative reachability* $(\lambda = 0)$, *all obligations spawned by* Strengthen$_\mathcal{H}$ *as in Algorithm 2 are of the form* $(i, s, 0)$.

Strengthen$_\mathcal{H}$ returns `false`. There are two cases in which Strengthen$_\mathcal{H}$ fails to restore the PrIC3 invariants and returns `false`. The first case (the left disjunct of l. 4) is that we encounter an obligation for frame F_0. Resolving such an obligation would inevitably violate *initiality*; analogously to standard IC3, we thus return `false`.

The second case (the right disjunct of l. 4) is that we encounter an obligation (i, s, δ) for a bad state $s \in B$ with a probability $\delta < 1$ (though, obviously, all $s \in B$ have probability $=1$). Resolving such an obligation would inevitably prevents us from restoring *relative inductivity*: If we updated $F_i[s]$ to δ, we would have $\Phi(F_{i-1})[s] = 1 > \delta = F_i[s]$. Notice that, in contrast to standard IC3, this second case *can* occur in PrIC3:

Example 4. Assume we have to resolve an obligation $(i, s_3, 1/2)$ for the MDP in Fig. 1. This involves spawning obligations $(i-1, s_4, \delta_1)$ and $(i-1, s_5, \delta_2)$, where s_5 is a bad state, such that $1/3 \cdot \delta_1 + 2/3 \cdot \delta_2 \leq 1/2$. Even for $\delta_1 = 0$, this is only possible if $\delta_2 \leq 3/4 < 1$. △

Strengthen$_\mathcal{H}$ Cannot Prove Unsafety. If standard IC3 returns `false`, it proves unsafety by constructing a counterexample, i.e., *a single path from the initial state to a bad state*. If PrIC3 returns `false`, there are two possible reasons: *Either* the MDP is indeed unsafe, *or* the heuristic $\mathcal{H}$ at some point selected probabilities in a way such that Strengthen$_\mathcal{H}$ is unable to restore the PrIC3 invariants (even though the MDP might in fact be safe). Strengthen$_\mathcal{H}$ thus only returns a *potential* counterexample which either proves unsafety or indicates that our heuristic was inappropriate.

Counterexamples in our case consist of subsystems rather than a single path (see Challenge 2 and Sect. 5). Strengthen$_\mathcal{H}$ hence returns the set $Q.\text{touched}()$ of all states that eventually appeared in the obligation queue. This set is a conservative approximation, and optimizations as in [1] may be beneficial. Furthermore, in the qualitative case, our potential counterexample subsumes the counterexamples constructed by standard IC3:

Recovery Statement 4. *Let* $\mathcal{H}_0$ *be the adequate heuristic mapping every state to 0. For qual. reachability* $(\lambda = 0)$, *if* success = `false` *is returned by* Strengthen$_{\mathcal{H}_0}(F_0, \ldots, F_k)$, *then* $Q.\text{touched}()$ *contains a path from the initial to a bad state.*[6]

---

[6] $Q.\text{touched}()$ might be restricted to only contain this path by some simple adaptions.

Data: global MDP $\mathfrak{M}$,   set of bad states B,   threshold λ
Result: true iff $\mathrm{Pr}^{\max}(s_I \models \Diamond B) \leq \lambda$

1 $\Omega \leftarrow$ Initialize(); *touched* $\leftarrow \{s_I\}$;
2 **do**
3     $\mathcal{H} \leftarrow$ CreateHeuristic(Ω);   *safe, subsystem* $\leftarrow$ PrIC3$_{\mathcal{H}}()$;
4   **if** *safe* **then return** true ;
5   **if** CheckRefutation(*subsystem*) **then return** false ;
6   *touched* $\leftarrow$ Enlarge(*touched, subsystem*);
7     $\Omega \leftarrow$ Refine$(\Omega, touched)$;
8 **while** *touched* $\neq S$;
9 **return** $\Omega(s_I) \leq \lambda$

Algorithm 3: PrIC3: The outermost loop dealing with possibly imprecise heuristics

5   Dealing with Potential Counterexamples

Recall that our core algorithm PrIC3$_{\mathcal{H}}$ is incomplete for a fixed heuristic $\mathcal{H}$: It cannot give a conclusive answer whenever it finds a potential counterexample for two possible reasons: Either the heuristic $\mathcal{H}$ turned out to be inappropriate or the MDP is indeed unsafe. The idea to overcome the former is to call PrIC3$_{\mathcal{H}}$ finitely often in an outer loop that generates new heuristics until we find an appropriate one: If PrIC3$_{\mathcal{H}}$ still does not report safety of the MDP, then it is indeed unsafe. We do not blindly generate new heuristics, but use the potential counterexamples returned by PrIC3$_{\mathcal{H}}$ to refine the previous one.

Let consider the procedure PrIC3 in Algorithm 3 which wraps our core algorithm PrIC3$_{\mathcal{H}}$ in more detail: First, we create an *oracle* $\Omega: S \to [0,1]$ which (roughly) *estimates* the probability of reaching B for every state. A *perfect oracle* would yield *precise* maximal reachability probabilites, i.e., $\Omega(s) = \mathrm{Pr}^{\max}(s \models \Diamond B)$ for every state s. We construct oracles by user-supplied methods (highlighted in blue). Examples of implementations of all user-supplied methods in Algorithm 3 are discussed in Sect. 7.

Assuming the oracle is good, but not perfect, we construct an adequate heuristic $\mathcal{H}$ selecting probabilities based on the oracle[7] for all successors of a given state: There are various options. The simplest is to pass-through the oracle values. A version that is more robust against noise in the oracle is discussed in Sect. 6. We then invoke PrIC3$_{\mathcal{H}}$. If PrIC3$_{\mathcal{H}}$ reports safety, the MDP is indeed safe by the soundness of PrIC3$_{\mathcal{H}}$.

Check Refutation. If PrIC3$_{\mathcal{H}}$ does not report safety, it reports a subsystem that hints to a *potential* counterexample. Formally, this subsystem is a subMDP of states that were 'visited' during the invocation of Strengthen$_{\mathcal{H}}$.

Definition 6 (subMDP). *Let* $\mathfrak{M} = (S, s_I, \mathrm{Act}, P)$ *be an MDP and let* $S' \subseteq S$ *with* $s_I \in S'$. *We call* $\mathfrak{M}_{S'} = (S', s_I, \mathrm{Act}, P')$ *the* subMDP *induced by* $\mathfrak{M}$ *and* S', *where for all* $s, s' \in S'$ *and all* $a \in \mathrm{Act}$, *we have* $P'(s, a, s') = P(s, a, s')$. $\triangle$

---

[7] We thus assume that heuristic $\mathcal{H}$ invokes the oracle whenever it needs to guess some probability.

A subMDP $\mathfrak{M}_{S'}$ may be substochastic where missing probability mass never reaches a bad state. Definition 1 is thus relaxed: For all states $s \in S'$ we require that $\sum_{s' \in S'} P(s, a, s') \leq 1$.If the subsystem is unsafe, we can conclude that the original MDP $\mathfrak{M}$ is also safe.

Lemma 6. *If $\mathfrak{M}'$ is a subMDP of $\mathfrak{M}$ and $\mathfrak{M}'$ is unsafe, then $\mathfrak{M}$ is also unsafe.*

The role of CheckRefutation is to establish whether the subsystem is indeed a true counterexample or a spurious one. Formally, CheckRefutation should ensure:

$$\{\, \texttt{true} \,\} \; res \leftarrow \mathsf{CheckRefutation}\,(subsystem) \; \{\, res = \texttt{true} \; \Leftrightarrow \; \mathfrak{M}_{subsystem} \text{ unsafe} \,\}.$$

Again, PrIC3 is backward compatible in the sense that a single fixed heuristic is always sufficient when reasoning about reachability ($\lambda = 0$).

Recovery Statement 5. *For qualitative reachability ($\lambda = 0$) and the heuristic $\mathcal{H}_0$ from Recovery Statement 4, PrIC3 invokes its core PrIC3$_\mathcal{H}$ exactly once.*

This statement is true, as PrIC3$_\mathcal{H}$ returns either *safe* or a subsystem containing a path from the initial state to a bad state. In the latter case, CheckRefutation detects that the subsystem is indeed a counterexample which cannot be spurious in the qualitative setting.

We remark that the procedure CheckRefutation invoked in l. 5 is a classical fallback; it runs an (alternative) model checking algorithm, e.g., solving the set of Bellman equations, for the subsystem. In the worst case, i.e., for $S' = S$, we thus solve exactly our problem statement. Empirically (Table 1) we observe that for reasonable oracles the procedure CheckRefutation is invoked on significantly smaller subMDPs. However, in the worst case the subMDP must include *all* paths of the original MDP, and then thus coincides.

Refine Oracle. Whenever we have neither proven the MDP safe nor unsafe, we refine the oracle to prevent generating the same subsystem in the next invocation of PrIC3$_\mathcal{H}$. To ensure termination, oracles should only be refined finitely often. That is, we need some progress measure. The set *touched* overapproximates all counterexamples encountered in some invocation of PrIC3$_\mathcal{H}$ and we propose to use its size as the progress measure. While there are several possibilities to update *touched* through the user-defined procedure Enlarge (l. 6), every implementation should hence satisfy $\{\, \texttt{true} \,\}$ *touched'* $\leftarrow$ Enlarge(*touched*, $\_\_$) $\{\, |touched'| >$ $|touched| \,\}$. Consequently, after finitely many iterations, the oracle is refined with respect to all states. In this case, we may as well rely on solving the characteristic LP problem:

Lemma 7. *The algorithm PrIC3 in Algorithm 3 is sound and complete if Refine(Ω, S) returns a perfect oracle Ω (with S is the set of all states).*

Weaker assumptions on Refine are possible, but are beyond the scope of this paper. Moreover, the above lemma does not rely on the abstract concept that heuristic $\mathcal{H}$ provides suitable probabilities after finitely many refinements.[8]

---

[8] One could of course now also create a heuristic that is trivial for a perfect oracle and invoke PrIC3$_\mathcal{H}$ with the heuristic for the perfect oracle, but there really is no benefit in doing so.

6 Practical PrIC3

So far, we gave a conceptual view on PrIC3, but now take a more practical stance. We detail important features of effective implementations of PrIC3 (based on our empirical evaluation). We first describe an implementation without generalization, and then provide a prototypical extension that allows for three variants of generalization.

6.1 A Concrete PrIC3 Instance Without Generalization

Input. We describe MDPs using the Prism guarded command language[9], exemplified in Fig. 3. States are described by valuations to m (integer-valued) program variables vars, and outgoing actions are described by commands of the form

```
[] guard -> prob1 : update1 & ... & probk : updatek
```

If a state satisfies guard, then the corresponding action with k branches exists; probabilities are given by probi, the successor states are described by updatei, see Fig. 3b.

```
module ex
  c : [0..20] init 0;   f : [0..1] init 0;
  [] c<20 -> 0.1:(f'=1) + 0.9:(c'=c+1); // cmd 1
  [] c<10 -> 0.2:(f'=1) + 0.8:(c'=c+2);
endmodule
```

(a) Prism code snippet

(b) Part of the corresponding MDP

Fig. 3. Illustrative Prism-style probabilistic guarded command language example

Encoding. We encode frames as logical formulae. Updating frames then corresponds to adding conjuncts, and checking for relative inductivity is a satisfiability call. Our encoding is as follows: States are assignments to the program variables, i.e., States $= \mathbb{Z}^m$. We use various uninterpreted functions, to whom we give semantics using appropriate constraints. Frames[10] are represented by uninterpreted functions Frame: States $\to \mathbb{R}$ satisfying Frame $(s) = d$ implies $F[s] \geq d$. Likewise, the Bellman operator is an uninterpreted function Phi: States $\to \mathbb{R}$ such that Phi $(s) = d$ implies $\Phi(F)[s] \geq d$. Finally, we use Bad: States $\to \mathbb{B}$ with Bad (s) iff $s \in B$.

Among the appropriate constraints, we ensure that variables are within their range, bound the values for the frames, and enforce Phi $(s) = 1$ for $s \in B$. We encode the guarded commands as exemplified by this encoding of the first command in Fig. 3:

$$\forall\, s \in \text{States}: \neg\text{Bad}\,(s) \wedge s[c] < 20$$
$$\implies \text{Phi}\,(s) = 0.1 \cdot \text{Frame}\,((s[c], 1)) + 0.9 \cdot \text{Frame}\,((s[c] + 1, s[f])).$$

---

[9] Preprocessing ensures a single thread (module) and no deadlocks.
[10] In each operation, we only consider a single frame.

In our implementation, we optimize the encoding. We avoid the uninterpreted functions by applying an adapted Ackerman reduction. We avoid universal quantifiers, by first observing that we always ask whether a single state is not inductive, and then unfolding the guarded commands in the constraints that describe a frame. That encoding grows linear in the size of the maximal out-degree of the MDP, and is in the quantifier-free fragment of linear arithmetic (QFLRIA).

Heuristic. We select probabilities δ_i by solving the following optimization problem, with variables x_i, $range(x_i) \in [0,1]$, for states $s_i \in \mathrm{Succs}(s,a)$ and oracle Ω[11].

$$\text{minimize} \sum_{\substack{i \\ s_i \notin B}}^{k} \left| \frac{x_i}{\sum_{j=1}^{k} x_j} - \frac{\Omega(s_i)}{\sum_{j=1}^{n} \Omega(s_j)} \right| \quad \text{s.t.} \quad \delta = \sum_{i=1}^{k} P(s,a,s_i) \cdot \begin{cases} 1, & \text{if } s_i \in B, \\ x_i, & \text{else.} \end{cases}$$

The constraint ensures that, if the values x_i correspond to the actual reachability probabilities from s_i, then the reachability from state s is exactly δ. A constraint stating that $\delta \geq \ldots$ would also be sound, but we choose equality as it preserves room between the actual probability and the threshold we want to show. Finally, the objective function aims to preserve the ratio between the suggested probabilities.

Repushing and Breaking Cycles. Repushing [23] is an essential ingredient of both standard IC3 and PrIC3. Intuitively, we avoid opening new frames and spawning obligations that can be deduced from current information. Since repushing generates further obligations in the current frame, its implementation requires that the detection of Zeno-behavior has to be moved from PrIC3$_{\mathcal{H}}$ into the Strengthen$_{\mathcal{H}}$ procedure. Therefore, we track the histories of the obligations in the queue. Furthermore, once we detect a cycle we first try to adapt the heuristic $\mathcal{H}$ locally to overcome this cyclic behavior instead of immediately giving up. This local adaption reduces the number of PrIC3$_{\mathcal{H}}$ invocations.

Extended Queue. In contrast to standard IC3, the obligation queue might contain entries that vary only in their δ entry. In particular, if the MDP is not a tree, it may occur that the queue contains both (i, s, δ) and (i, s, δ') with $\delta > \delta'$. Then, (i, s, δ') can be safely pruned from the queue. Similarly, after handling (i, s, δ), if some fresh obligation $(i, s, \delta'' > \delta)$ is pushed to the queue, it can be substituted with (i, s, δ). To efficiently operationalize these observations, we keep an additional mapping which remains intact over multiple invocations of Strengthen$_{\mathcal{H}}$. We furthermore employed some optimizations for Q.touched() aiming to track potential counterexamples better. After refining the heuristic, one may want to reuse frames or the obligation queue, but empirically this leads to performance degradation as the values in the frames are inconsistent with behavior suggested by the heuristic.

---

[11] If $\max \Omega(s_j) = 0$, we assume $\forall j. \Omega(s_j) = 0.5$. If $\delta = 0$, we omit rescaling to allow $\sum x_j = 0$.

6.2   Concrete PrIC3 with Generalization

So far, frames are updated by changing single entries whenever we resolve obligations (i, s, δ), i.e., we add conjunctions of the form $F_i[s] \leq \delta$. Equivalently, we may add a constraint $\forall s' \in S : F_i[s'] \leq p_{\{s\}}(s')$ with $p_{\{s\}}(s) = \delta$ and $p_{\{s\}} = 1$ for all $s' \neq s$.

Generalization in IC3 aims to update a set G (including s) of states in a frame rather than a single one without invalidating relative inductivity. In our setting, we thus consider a function $p_G \colon G \to [0, 1]$ with $p_G(s) \leq \delta$ that assigns (possibly different) probabilities to all states in G. Updating a frame then amounts to adding the constraint

$$\forall s \in \mathsf{States} \colon s \in G \Longrightarrow \mathsf{Frame}\,(s) \leq p_G(s).$$

Standard IC3 generalizes by iteratively "dropping" a variable, say v. The set G then consists of all states that do not differ from the fixed state s except for the value of v.[12] We take the same approach by iteratively dropping program variables. Hence, p_G effectively becomes a mapping from the value $s[v]$ to a probability. We experimented with four types of functions p_G that we describe for Markov chains. The ideas are briefly outlined below; details are beyond the scope of this paper.

Constant p_G. Setting all $s \in G$ to δ is straightforward but empirically not helpful.

Linear Interpolation. We use a linear function p_G that interpolates two points. The first point $(s[v], \delta)$ is obtained from the obligation (i, s, δ). For a second point, consider the following: Let Com be the unique[13] command active at state s. Among all states in G that are enabled in the guard of Com, we take the state s' in which $s'[v]$ is maximal[14]. The second point for interpolation is then $(s'[v], \Phi\,(F_{i-1})\,[s'])$. If the relative inductivity fails for p_G we do not generalize with p_G, but may attempt to find other functions.

Polynomial Interpolation. Rather than linearly interpolating between two points, we may interpolate using more than two points. In order to properly fit these points, we can use a higher-degree polynomial. We select these points using counterexamples to generalization (CTGs): We start as above with linear interpolation. However, if p_G is not relative inductive, the SMT solver yields a model with state $s'' \in G$ and probability δ'', with s'' violating relative inductivity, i.e., $\Phi\,(F_{i-1})\,[s''] > \delta''$. We call $(s'', \Phi\,(F_{i-1})\,[s''])$ a CTG, and $(s''[v], \Phi\,(F_{i-1})\,[s''])$ is then a further interpolation point, and we repeat.

Technically, when generalizing using nonlinear constraints, we use real-valued arithmetic with a branch-and-bound-style approach to ensure integer values.

---

[12] Formally, $G = \{s' \mid \text{for all } v' \in \mathrm{vars} \setminus \{v\} : s'(v') = s(v')\}$.

[13] Recall that we have a Markov chain consisting of a single module.

[14] This implicitly assumes that v is increased. Adaptions are possible.

Hybrid Interpolation. In polynomial interpolation, we generate high-degree polynomials and add them to the encoding of the frame. In subsequent invocations, reasoning efficiency is drastically harmed by these high-degree polynomials. Instead, we soundly approximate p_G by a piecewise linear function, and use these constraints in the frame.

7   Experiments

We assess how PrIC3 may contribute to the state of the art in probabilistic model checking. We do some early empirical evaluation showing that PrIC3 is feasible. We see ample room for further improvements of the prototype.

Implementation. We implemented a prototype[15] of PrIC3 based on Sect. 6.1 in Python. The input is represented using efficient data structures provided by the model checker Storm. We use an incremental instance of Z3 [47] for each frame, as suggested in [23]. A solver for each frame is important to reduce the time spent on pushing the large frame-encodings. The optimization problem in the heuristic is also solved using Z3. All previously discussed generalizations (none, linear, polynomial, hybrid) are supported.

Oracle and Refinement. We support the (pre)computation of four different types of oracles for the initialization step in Algorithm 3: (1) A perfect oracle solving *exactly* the Bellman equations. Such an oracle is unrealistic, but interesting from a conceptual point. (2) Relative frequencies by recording all visited states during simulation. This idea is a naïve simplification of Q-learning. (3) Model checking with decision diagrams (DDs) and few value iterations. Often, a DD representation of a model can be computed fast, and the challenge is in executing sufficient value iterations. We investigate whether doing few value iterations yields a valuable oracle (and covers states close to bad states). (4) Solving a (pessimistic) LP from BFS partial exploration. States that are not expanded are assumed bad. Roughly, this yields oracles covering states close to the initial states.

To implement Refine (cf. Algorithm 3, l. 7), we create an LP for the subMDP induced by the touched states. For states whose successors are not in the touched states, we add a transition to B labeled with the oracle value as probability. The solution of the resulting LP updates the entries corresponding to the touched states.

For Enlarge (cf. Algorithm 3, l. 6), we take the union of the subsystem and the touched states. If this does not change the set of touched states, we also add its successors.

Setup. We evaluate the run time and memory consumption of our prototype of PrIC3. We choose a combination of models from the literature (BRP [21], ZeroConf [18]) and some structurally straightforward variants of grids (chain, double chain; see [11, Appendix A]). Since our prototype lacks the sophisticated

---

[15] The prototype is available open-source from https://github.com/moves-rwth/PrIC3.

preprocessing applied by many state-of-the-art model checkers, it is more sensitive to the precise encoding of a model, e.g., the number of commands. To account for this, we generated new encodings for all models. All experiments were conducted on an single core of an Intel® Xeon® Platinum 8160 processor. We use a 15 min time-limit and report TO otherwise. Memory is limited to 8GB; we report MO if it is exceeded. Apart from the oracle, all parameters of our prototype remain fixed over all experiments. To give an impression of the run times, we compare our prototype with both the explicit ($\text{Storm}_{\text{sparse}}$) and DD-based ($\text{Storm}_{\text{dd}}$) engine of the model checker Storm 1.4, which compared favourably in QComp [29].

Results. In Table 1, we present the run times for various invocations of our prototype and Oracle 4^{16}. In particular, we give the model name and the number of (non-trivial) states in the particular instance, and the (estimated) actual probability to reach B. For each model, we consider multiple thresholds λ. The next 8 columns report on the four variants of PrIC3 with varying generalization schemes. Besides the scheme with the run times, we report for each scheme the number of states of the largest (last) subsystem that CheckRefutation in Algorithm 3, l. 5 was invoked upon (column $|sub|$). The last two columns report on the run times for Storm that we provide for comparison. In each row, we mark with purple MDPs that are unsafe, i.e., PrIC3 refutes these MDPs for the given threshold λ. We **highlight** the best configurations of PrIC3.

Discussion. Our experiments give a mixed picture on the performance of our implementation of PrIC3. On the one hand, Storm significantly outperforms PrIC3 on most models. On the other hand, PrIC3 is capable of reasoning about huge, yet simple, models with up to 10^{12} states that Storm is unable to analyze within the time and memory limits. There is more empirical evidence that PrIC3 may complement the state-of-the-art:

First, *the size of thresholds matters.* Our benchmarks show that—at least without generalization—more "wiggle room" between the precise maximal reachability probability and the threshold generally leads to a better performance. PrIC3 may thus prove bounds for large models where a precise quantitative reachability analysis is out of scope.

Second, PrIC3 *enjoys the benefits of bounded model checking.* In some cases, e.g., ZeroConf for $\lambda = 0.45$, PrIC3 refutes very fast as it does not need to build the whole model.

Third, if PrIC3 proves the safety of the system, it does so without relying on checking large subsystems in the CheckRefutation step.

Fourth, *generalization is crucial.* Without generalization, PrIC3 is unable to prove safety for any of the considered models with more than 10^3 states. With generalization, however, it can prove safety for very large systems and thresholds close to the exact reachability probability. For example, it proved safety of the

---

[16] We explore $\min\{|S|, 5000\}$ states using BFS and Storm.

Table 1. Empirical results. Run times are in seconds; time out $= 15$ min.

	$|S|$	$\mathrm{Pr}^{\max}(s_I \models \Diamond B)$	λ	w/o	$|sub|$	lin	$|sub|$	pol	$|sub|$	hyb	$|sub|$	Storm$_{\mathrm{sparse}}$	Storm$_{\mathrm{dd}}$
BRP	10^3	0.035	0.1	TO	–	TO	–	TO	–	TO	–	<0.1	0.12
			0.01	**51.3**	324	125.8	324	TO	–	MO	–	<0.1	0.18
			0.005	**10.9**	188	38.3	188	TO	–	MO	–	<0.1	0.1
ZeroConf	10^4	0.5	0.9	TO	–	TO	–	0.4	0	**0.1**	0	<0.1	296.8
			0.52	TO	–	TO	–	0.2	0	**0.2**	0	<0.1	282.6
			0.45	**<0.1**	1	**<0.1**	1	**<0.1**	1	**<0.1**	1	<0.1	300.2
	10^9	~0.55	0.9	TO	–	TO	–	**3.7**	0	MO	–	MO	TO
			0.75	TO	–	TO	–	**3.4**	0	MO	–	MO	TO
			0.52	TO	–	TO	–	TO	–	TO	–	MO	TO
			0.45	**<0.1**	1	**<0.1**	1	**<0.1**	1	**<0.1**	1	MO	TO
Chain	10^3	0.394	0.9	18.8	0	60.2	0	1.2	0	**0.3**	0	<0.1	<0.1
			0.4	20.1	0	55.4	0	**0.9**	0	TO	–	<0.1	<0.1
			0.35	**91.8**	431	119.5	431	TO	–	TO	–	<0.1	<0.1
			0.3	**46.1**	357	64.0	357	TO	–	TO	–	<0.1	<0.1
	10^4	0.394	0.9	TO	–	TO	–	1.6	0	**0.3**	0	<0.1	4.5
			0.4	TO	–	TO	–	**1.4**	0	TO	–	<0.1	4.9
			0.3	TO	–	TO	–	TO	–	TO	–	<0.1	4.9
	10^{12}	0.394	0.9	TO	–	TO	–	**6.4**	0	MO	–	MO	TO
			0.4	TO	–	TO	–	**6.0**	0	MO	–	MO	TO
Double chain	10^3	0.215	0.9	528.1	0	828.8	0	203.3	0	**0.6**	0	<0.1	<0.1
			0.3	588.4	0	TO	–	138.3	0	**0.5**	0	<0.1	<0.1
			0.216	**597.4**	0	TO	–	765.8	0	MO	–	<0.1	<0.1
			0.15	TO	–	TO	–	TO	–	TO	–	<0.1	<0.1
	10^4	0.22	0.3	TO	–	TO	–	17.5	0	**0.5**	0	0.2	2.6
			0.24	TO	–	TO	–	**16.8**	0	MO	–	0.2	2.7
	10^7	2.6E^{-4}	4E^{-3}	TO	–	TO	–	TO	–	MO	–	TO	TO
			2.7E^{-4}	TO	–	TO	–	**281.2**	0	MO	–	TO	TO

Chain benchmark with 10^{12} states for a threshold of 0.4 which differs from the exact reachability probability by 0.006.

Fifth, *there is no best generalization*. There is no clear winner out of the considered generalization approaches. Linear generalization always performs worse than the other ones. In fact, it performs worse than no generalization at all. The hybrid approach, however, occasionally has the edge over the polynomial approach. This indicates that more research is required to find suitable generalizations.

In [11, Appendix A], we also compare the additional three types of oracles (1–3). We observed that only few oracle refinements are needed to prove *safety*; for small models at most one refinement was sufficient. However, this does not hold if the given MDP is unsafe. DoubleChain with $\lambda = 0.15$, for example, and Oracle 2 requires 25 refinements.

8   Conclusion

We have presented PrIC3—the first truly probabilistic, yet conservative, extension of IC3 to quantitative reachability in MDPs. Our theoretical development is accompanied by a prototypical implementation and experiments. We believe there is ample space for improvements including an in-depth investigation of suitable oracles and generalizations.

References

1. Ábrahám, E., Becker, B., Dehnert, C., Jansen, N., Katoen, J.-P., Wimmer, R.: Counterexample generation for discrete-time Markov models: an introductory survey. In: Bernardo, M., Damiani, F., Hähnle, R., Johnsen, E.B., Schaefer, I. (eds.) SFM 2014. LNCS, vol. 8483, pp. 65–121. Springer, Cham (2014). https://doi.org/10.1007/978-3-319-07317-0_3
2. Agha, G., Palmskog, K.: A survey of statistical model checking. ACM Trans. Model. Comput. Simul. **28**(1), 6:1–6:39 (2018)
3. Agrawal, S., Chatterjee, K., Novotný, P.: Lexicographic ranking supermartingales: an efficient approach to termination of probabilistic programs. In: PACMPL 2(POPL), pp. 34:1–34:32 (2018)
4. de Alfaro, L., Kwiatkowska, M., Norman, G., Parker, D., Segala, R.: Symbolic model checking of probabilistic processes using MTBDDs and the kronecker representation. In: Graf, S., Schwartzbach, M. (eds.) TACAS 2000. LNCS, vol. 1785, pp. 395–410. Springer, Heidelberg (2000). https://doi.org/10.1007/3-540-46419-0_27
5. Baier, C., de Alfaro, L., Forejt, V., Kwiatkowska, M.: Model checking probabilistic systems. Handbook of Model Checking, pp. 963–999. Springer, Cham (2018). https://doi.org/10.1007/978-3-319-10575-8_28
6. Baier, C., Hermanns, H., Katoen, J.-P.: The 10,000 facets of MDP model checking. In: Steffen, B., Woeginger, G. (eds.) Computing and Software Science. LNCS, vol. 10000, pp. 420–451. Springer, Cham (2019). https://doi.org/10.1007/978-3-319-91908-9_21
7. Baier, C., Katoen, J.-P.: Principles of Model Checking. MIT Press, Cambridge (2008)
8. Baier, C., Klein, J., Leuschner, L., Parker, D., Wunderlich, S.: Ensuring the reliability of your model checker: interval iteration for markov decision processes. In: Majumdar, R., Kunčak, V. (eds.) CAV 2017. LNCS, vol. 10426, pp. 160–180. Springer, Cham (2017). https://doi.org/10.1007/978-3-319-63387-9_8
9. Barthe, G., Espitau, T., Ferrer Fioriti, L.M., Hsu, J.: Synthesizing probabilistic invariants via Doob's decomposition. In: Chaudhuri, S., Farzan, A. (eds.) CAV 2016. LNCS, vol. 9779, pp. 43–61. Springer, Cham (2016). https://doi.org/10.1007/978-3-319-41528-4_3
10. Bartocci, E., Kovács, L., Stankovič, M.: Automatic generation of moment-based invariants for prob-solvable loops. In: Chen, Y.-F., Cheng, C.-H., Esparza, J. (eds.) ATVA 2019. LNCS, vol. 11781, pp. 255–276. Springer, Cham (2019). https://doi.org/10.1007/978-3-030-31784-3_15
11. Batz, K., Junges, S., Kaminski, B.L., Katoen, J.-P., Matheja, C., Schröer, P.: Pric3: Property directed reachability for MDPS. ArXiv e-prints (2020). https://arxiv.org/abs/2004.14835
12. Biere, A.: Bounded model checking, Handbook of Satisfiability. Frontiers in Artificial Intelligence and Applications, vol. 185, pp. 457–481. IOS Press (2009)
13. Bradley, A.R.: SAT-based model checking without unrolling. In: Jhala, R., Schmidt, D. (eds.) VMCAI 2011. LNCS, vol. 6538, pp. 70–87. Springer, Heidelberg (2011). https://doi.org/10.1007/978-3-642-18275-4_7

14. Brázdil, T., Chatterjee, K., Chmelík, M., Forejt, V., Křetínský, J., Kwiatkowska, M., Parker, D., Ujma, M.: Verification of Markov decision processes using learning algorithms. In: Cassez, F., Raskin, J.-F. (eds.) ATVA 2014. LNCS, vol. 8837, pp. 98–114. Springer, Cham (2014). https://doi.org/10.1007/978-3-319-11936-6_8
15. Chadha, R., Viswanathan, M.: A counterexample-guided abstraction-refinement framework for Markov decision processes. ACM Trans. Comput. Logist. **12**(1), 1:1–1:49 (2010)
16. Chakarov, A., Sankaranarayanan, S.: Probabilistic program analysis with martingales. In: Sharygina, N., Veith, H. (eds.) CAV 2013. LNCS, vol. 8044, pp. 511–526. Springer, Heidelberg (2013). https://doi.org/10.1007/978-3-642-39799-8_34
17. Chakraborty, S., Fried, D., Meel, K.S., Vardi, M.Y.: From weighted to unweighted model counting. In: IJCAI, pp. 689–695. AAAI Press (2015)
18. Cheshire, S., Aboba, B., Guttman, E.: Dynamic configuration of ipv4 link-local addresses. RFC **3927**, 1–33 (2005)
19. Cimatti, A., Griggio, A., Mover, S., Tonetta, S.: Infinite-state invariant checking with IC3 and predicate abstraction. FMSD **49**(3), 190–218 (2016)
20. D'Argenio, P.R., Hartmanns, A., Sedwards, S.: Lightweight statistical model checking in nondeterministic continuous time. In: Margaria, T., Steffen, B. (eds.) ISoLA 2018. LNCS, vol. 11245, pp. 336–353. Springer, Cham (2018). https://doi.org/10.1007/978-3-030-03421-4_22
21. D'Argenio, P.R., Jeannet, B., Jensen, H.E., Larsen, K.G.: Reachability analysis of probabilistic systems by successive refinements. In: de Alfaro, L., Gilmore, S. (eds.) PAPM-PROBMIV 2001. LNCS, vol. 2165, pp. 39–56. Springer, Heidelberg (2001). https://doi.org/10.1007/3-540-44804-7_3
22. Dehnert, C., Junges, S., Katoen, J.-P., Volk, M.: A STORM is coming: a modern probabilistic model checker. In: Majumdar, R., Kunčak, V. (eds.) CAV 2017. LNCS, vol. 10427, pp. 592–600. Springer, Cham (2017). https://doi.org/10.1007/978-3-319-63390-9_31
23. Eén, N., Mishchenko, A., Brayton, R.K.: Efficient implementation of property directed reachability. In: FMCAD, pp. 125–134. FMCAD Inc. (2011)
24. Fränzle, M., Hermanns, H., Teige, T.: Stochastic satisfiability modulo theory: a novel technique for the analysis of probabilistic hybrid systems. In: Egerstedt, M., Mishra, B. (eds.) HSCC 2008. LNCS, vol. 4981, pp. 172–186. Springer, Heidelberg (2008). https://doi.org/10.1007/978-3-540-78929-1_13
25. Gretz, F., Katoen, J.-P., McIver, A.: PRINSYS—On a Quest for Probabilistic Loop Invariants. In: Joshi, K., Siegle, M., Stoelinga, M., D'Argenio, P.R. (eds.) QEST 2013. LNCS, vol. 8054, pp. 193–208. Springer, Heidelberg (2013). https://doi.org/10.1007/978-3-642-40196-1_17
26. Gretz, F., Katoen, J.-P., McIver, A.: Operational versus weakest pre-expectation semantics for the probabilistic guarded command language. Perform. Eval. **73**, 110–132 (2014)
27. Gurfinkel, A., Ivrii, A.: Pushing to the top. In: FMCAD, pp. 65–72. IEEE (2015)
28. Haddad, S., Monmege, B.: Interval iteration algorithm for MDPs and IMDPs. Theor. Comput. Sci. **735**, 111–131 (2018)
29. Hahn, E.M., Hartmanns, A., Hensel, C., Klauck, M., Klein, J., Křetínský, J., Parker, D., Quatmann, T., Ruijters, E., Steinmetz, M.: The 2019 comparison of tools for the analysis of quantitative formal models. In: Beyer, D., Huisman, M., Kordon, F., Steffen, B. (eds.) TACAS 2019. LNCS, vol. 11429, pp. 69–92. Springer, Cham (2019). https://doi.org/10.1007/978-3-030-17502-3_5

30. Hahn, E.M., Hermanns, H., Wachter, B., Zhang, L.: PASS: abstraction refinement for infinite probabilistic models. In: Esparza, J., Majumdar, R. (eds.) TACAS 2010. LNCS, vol. 6015, pp. 353–357. Springer, Heidelberg (2010). https://doi.org/10.1007/978-3-642-12002-2_30

31. Hahn, E.M., Li, Y., Schewe, S., Turrini, A., Zhang, L.: ISCASMC: a web-based probabilistic model checker. In: Jones, C., Pihlajasaari, P., Sun, J. (eds.) FM 2014. LNCS, vol. 8442, pp. 312–317. Springer, Cham (2014). https://doi.org/10.1007/978-3-319-06410-9_22

32. Han, T., Katoen, J.-P., Damman, B.: Counterexample generation in probabilistic model checking. IEEE Trans. Software Eng. **35**(2), 241–257 (2009)

33. Hark, M., Kaminski, B.L., Giesl, J., Katoen, J.-P.: Aiming low is harder: Induction for lower bounds in probabilistic program verification. In: PACMPL 4(POPL), 37:1–37:28 (2020)

34. Hartmanns, A., Hermanns, H.: The modest toolset: an integrated environment for quantitative modelling and verification. In: Ábrahám, E., Havelund, K. (eds.) TACAS 2014. LNCS, vol. 8413, pp. 593–598. Springer, Heidelberg (2014). https://doi.org/10.1007/978-3-642-54862-8_51

35. Hartmanns, A., Kaminski, B.L.: Optimistic value iteration. CAV. LNCS, Springer (2020). [to appear]

36. Hassan, Z., Bradley, A.R., Somenzi, F.: Better generalization in IC3. In: FMCAD, pp. 157–164. IEEE (2013)

37. Hermanns, H., Wachter, B., Zhang, L.: Probabilistic CEGAR. In: Gupta, A., Malik, S. (eds.) CAV 2008. LNCS, vol. 5123, pp. 162–175. Springer, Heidelberg (2008). https://doi.org/10.1007/978-3-540-70545-1_16

38. Hoder, K., Bjørner, N.: Generalized property directed reachability. In: Cimatti, A., Sebastiani, R. (eds.) SAT 2012. LNCS, vol. 7317, pp. 157–171. Springer, Heidelberg (2012). https://doi.org/10.1007/978-3-642-31612-8_13

39. Kaminski, B.L.: Advanced Weakest Precondition Calculi for Probabilistic Programs. Ph.D. thesis, RWTH Aachen University, Germany (2019). http://publications.rwth-aachen.de/record/755408/files/755408.pdf

40. Kaminski, B.L., Katoen, J.-P., Matheja, C., Olmedo, F.: Weakest precondition reasoning for expected runtimes of randomized algorithms. J. ACM **65**(5), 30:1–30:68 (2018)

41. Kattenbelt, M., Kwiatkowska, M.Z., Norman, G., Parker, D.: A game-based abstraction-refinement framework for Markov decision processes. FMSD **36**(3), 246–280 (2010)

42. Kozen, D.: A probabilistic PDL. In: STOC, pp. 291–297. ACM (1983)

43. Kwiatkowska, M., Norman, G., Parker, D.: PRISM 4.0: verification of probabilistic real-time systems. In: Gopalakrishnan, G., Qadeer, S. (eds.) CAV 2011. LNCS, vol. 6806, pp. 585–591. Springer, Heidelberg (2011). https://doi.org/10.1007/978-3-642-22110-1_47

44. Lange, T., Neuhäußer, M.R., Noll, T., Katoen, J.-P.: IC3 software model checking. In: STTT, vol. 22, pp. 135–161 (2020)

45. Lassez, J.L., Nguyen, V.L., Sonenberg, L.: Fixed point theorems and semantics: a folk tale. Inf. Process. Lett. **14**(3), 112–116 (1982)

46. McIver, A., Morgan, C.: Abstraction, Refinement and Proof for Probabilistic Systems. Monographs in Computer Science. Springer, New York (2005). https://doi.org/10.1007/b138392

47. de Moura, L., Bjørner, N.: Z3: an efficient SMT solver. In: Ramakrishnan, C.R., Rehof, J. (eds.) TACAS 2008. LNCS, vol. 4963, pp. 337–340. Springer, Heidelberg (2008). https://doi.org/10.1007/978-3-540-78800-3_24

48. Park, D.: Fixpoint induction and proofs of program properties. Machine intelligence **5**, 59–78 (1969)
49. Polgreen, E., Brain, M., Fränzle, M., Abate, A.: Verifying reachability properties in Markov chains via incremental induction. CoRR abs/1909.08017 (2019)
50. Puterman, M.L.: Markov Decision Processes: Discrete Stochastic Dynamic Programming. Wiley Series in Probability and Statistics, Wiley, Hoboken (1994)
51. Quatmann, T., Katoen, J.-P.: Sound value iteration. In: Chockler, H., Weissenbacher, G. (eds.) CAV 2018. LNCS, vol. 10981, pp. 643–661. Springer, Cham (2018). https://doi.org/10.1007/978-3-319-96145-3_37
52. Rabe, M.N., Wintersteiger, C.M., Kugler, H., Yordanov, B., Hamadi, Y.: Symbolic approximation of the bounded reachability probability in large Markov chains. In: Norman, G., Sanders, W. (eds.) QEST 2014. LNCS, vol. 8657, pp. 388–403. Springer, Cham (2014). https://doi.org/10.1007/978-3-319-10696-0_30
53. Seufert, T., Scholl, C.: Sequential verification using reverse PDR. MBMV. pp. 79–90. Shaker Verlag (2017)
54. Suenaga, K., Ishizawa, T.: Generalized property-directed reachability for hybrid systems. In: Beyer, D., Zufferey, D. (eds.) VMCAI 2020. LNCS, vol. 11990, pp. 293–313. Springer, Cham (2020). https://doi.org/10.1007/978-3-030-39322-9_14
55. Takisaka, T., Oyabu, Y., Urabe, N., Hasuo, I.: Ranking and repulsing supermartingales for reachability in probabilistic programs. In: Lahiri, S.K., Wang, C. (eds.) ATVA 2018. LNCS, vol. 11138, pp. 476–493. Springer, Cham (2018). https://doi.org/10.1007/978-3-030-01090-4_28
56. Vazquez-Chanlatte, M., Rabe, M.N., Seshia, S.A.: A model counter's guide to probabilistic systems. CoRR abs/1903.09354 (2019)
57. Wimmer, R., Braitling, B., Becker, B.: Counterexample generation for discrete-time markov chains using bounded model checking. In: Jones, N.D., Müller-Olm, M. (eds.) VMCAI 2009. LNCS, vol. 5403, pp. 366–380. Springer, Heidelberg (2008). https://doi.org/10.1007/978-3-540-93900-9_29

Synthesis

Good-Enough Synthesis

Shaull Almagor[1]([⊠])[iD] and Orna Kupferman[2][iD]

[1] Department of Computer Science, Technion, Haifa, Israel
shaull@cs.technion.ac.il
[2] School of Computer Science and Engineering, The Hebrew University,
Jerusalem, Israel
orna@cs.huji.ac.il

Abstract. We introduce and study *good-enough synthesis* (GE-synthesis) – a variant of synthesis in which the system is required to satisfy a given specification ψ only when it interacts with an environments for which a satisfying interaction exists. Formally, an input sequence x is *hopeful* if there exists some output sequence y such that the induced computation $x \otimes y$ satisfies ψ, and a system GE-realizes ψ if it generates a computation that satisfies ψ on all hopeful input sequences. GE-synthesis is particularly relevant when the notion of correctness is *multi-valued* (rather than Boolean), and thus we seek systems of the highest possible quality, and when synthesizing *autonomous systems*, which interact with unexpected environments and are often only expected to do their best.

We study GE-synthesis in Boolean and multi-valued settings. In both, we suggest and solve various definitions of GE-synthesis, corresponding to different ways a designer may want to take hopefulness into account. We show that in all variants, GE-synthesis is not computationally harder than traditional synthesis, and can be implemented on top of existing tools. Our algorithms are based on careful combinations of nondeterministic and universal automata. We augment systems that GE-realize their specifications by monitors that provide satisfaction information. In the multi-valued setting, we provide both a worst-case analysis and an expectation-based one, the latter corresponding to an interaction with a stochastic environment.

1   Introduction

Synthesis is the automated construction of a system from its specification: given a specification ψ, typically by a linear temporal logic (LTL) formula over sets I and O of input and output signals, the goal is to construct a finite-state system that satisfies ψ [9,20]. At each moment in time, the system reads an assignment, generated by the environment, to the signals in I, and responds with an assignment to the signals in O. Thus, with every input sequence, the system associates an output sequence. The system *realizes* ψ if ψ is satisfied in all the interactions of the system, with all environments [5].

S. Almagor—Supported by the European Union's Horizon 2020 research and innovation programme under the Marie Skłodowska-Curie grant agreement No. 837327.

O. Kupferman—Supported in part by the Israel Science Foundation, grant No. 2357/19.

S. K. Lahiri and C. Wang (Eds.): CAV 2020, LNCS 12225, pp. 541–563, 2020.
https://doi.org/10.1007/978-3-030-53291-8_28

In practice, the requirement to satisfy the specification in all environments is often too strong. Accordingly, it is common to add assumptions on the behavior of the environment. An assumption may be direct, say given by an LTL formula that restricts the set of possible input sequences [8], less direct, say a bound on the size of the environment [13] or other resources it uses, or conceptual, say rationality from the side of the environment, which may have its own objectives [11,14]. We introduce and study a new type of relaxation of the requirement to satisfy the specification in all environments. The idea behind the relaxation is that if an environment is such that no system can interact with it in a way that satisfies the specification, then we cannot expect our system to succeed. In other words, the system has to satisfy the specification only when it interacts with environments in which this mission is possible. This is particularly relevant when synthesizing *autonomous systems*, which interact with unexpected environments and often replace human behavior, which is only expected to be *good enough* [28], and when the notion of correctness is multi-valued (rather than Boolean), and thus we seek *high-quality* systems.

Before we explain the relaxation formally, let us consider a simple example, and we start with the Boolean setting. Let $I = \{req\}$ and $O = \{grant\}$. Thus, the system receives requests and generates grants. Consider the specification $\psi = \mathsf{GF}(req \wedge grant) \wedge \mathsf{GF}(\neg req \wedge \neg grant)$. Clearly, ψ is not realizable, as an input sequence need not satisfy $\mathsf{GF}\,req$ or $\mathsf{GF}\neg req$. However, a system that always generates a grant upon (and only upon) a request, GE-*realizes* ψ, in the sense that for every input sequence, if there is some interaction with it with which ψ is satisfied, then our system generates such an interaction.

Formally, we model a system by a strategy $f : (2^I)^+ \to 2^O$, which given an input sequence $x = i_0 \cdot i_1 \cdot i_2 \cdots \in (2^I)^\omega$, generates an output sequence $f(x) = f(i_0) \cdot f(i_0 \cdot i_1) \cdot f(i_0 \cdot i_1 \cdot i_2) \cdots \in (2^O)^\omega$, inducing the computation $x \otimes f(x) = (i_0 \cup f(i_0)) \cdot (i_i \cup f(i_0 \cdot i_1)) \cdot (i_2 \cup f(i_0 \cdot i_1 \cdot i_2)) \cdots \in (2^{I \cup O})^\omega$, obtained by "merging" x and $f(x)$. In traditional realizability, a system realizes ψ if ψ is satisfied in all environments. Formally, for all input sequences $x \in (2^I)^\omega$, the computation $x \otimes f(x)$ satisfies ψ. For our new notion, we first define when an input sequence $x \in (2^I)^\omega$ is *hopeful*, namely there is an output sequence $y \in (2^O)^\omega$ such that the computation $x \otimes y$ satisfies ψ. Then, a system GE-*realizes* ψ if ψ is satisfied in all interactions with hopeful input sequences. Formally, for all $x \in (2^I)^\omega$, if x is hopeful, then the computation $x \otimes f(x)$ satisfies ψ.

Since LTL is Boolean, synthesized systems are correct, but there is no reference to their quality. This is a crucial drawback, as designers would be willing to give up manual design only if automated-synthesis algorithms return systems of comparable quality. Addressing this challenge, researchers have developed quantitative specification formalisms. For example, in [4], the input to the synthesis problem includes also Mealy machines that grade different realizing systems. In [1], the specification formalism is the multi-valued logic LTL[$\mathcal{F}$], which augments LTL with quality operators. The satisfaction value of an LTL[$\mathcal{F}$] formula is a real value in $[0, 1]$, where the higher the value, the higher the quality in which the computation satisfies the specification. The quality operators in $\mathcal{F}$ can prioritize and weight different scenarios. The synthesis algorithm for LTL[$\mathcal{F}$] seeks systems with a highest possible satisfaction value. One can consider either a worst-case approach, where the satisfaction value of a system is the satisfaction value of its computation with the lowest satisfaction value [1], or a stochastic approach, where it is the expected satisfaction value, given a distribution of the inputs [2].

Consider, for example, an acceleration controller of an autonomous car. Normally, the car should maintain a relatively constant speed. However, in order to optimize travel time, if a long stretch of road is visible and is identified as low-risk, the car should accelerate. Conversely, if an obstacle or some risk factor is identified, the car should decelerate. Clearly, the car cannot accelerate and decelerate at the same time. We capture this desired behavior with the following LTL[$\mathcal{F}$] formula over the inputs $\{safe, obs\}$ and outputs $\{acc, dec\}$:

$$\psi = \mathsf{G}(safe \rightarrow (acc \oplus_{\frac{2}{3}} \mathsf{X}acc)) \wedge \mathsf{G}(obs \rightarrow (dec \oplus_{\frac{3}{4}} \mathsf{X}dec)) \wedge \mathsf{G}(\neg(acc \wedge dec)).$$

Thus, in order to get satisfaction value 1, each detection of a safe stretch should be followed by an acceleration during two transactions, with a preference to the first (by the semantics of the weighted average $\oplus_\lambda$ operator, the satisfaction value of $safe \rightarrow (acc \oplus_{\frac{2}{3}} \mathsf{X}acc)$ is 1 when $safe$ is followed by two accs, $\frac{2}{3}$ when it is followed by one acc, and $\frac{1}{3}$ if it is followed by one acc with a delay), and each detection of an obstacle should be followed by a deceleration during two transactions, with a (higher) preference to the first. Clearly, ψ is not realizable with satisfaction value 1, as for some input sequences, namely those with simultaneous or successive occurrences of $safe$ and obs, it is impossible to respond with the desired patterns of acceleration or declaration. Existing frameworks for synthesis cannot handle this challenge. Indeed, we do not want to add an assumption about $safe$ and obs occurring far apart. Rather, we want our autonomous car to behave in an optimal way also in problematic environments, and we want, when we evaluate the quality of a car, to take into an account the challenge posed by the environment. This is exactly what high-quality GE-synthesis does: for each input sequence, it requires the synthesized car to obtain the maximal satisfaction value that is possible for that input sequence.

We show that in the Boolean setting, GE-synthesis can be reduced to synthesis of LTL with quantification of atomic propositions [26]. Essentially, GE-synthesis of ψ amounts to synthesis of $(\exists O.\psi) \rightarrow \psi$. We show that by carefully switching between nondeterminisitc and universal automata, we can solve the GE-synthesis problem in doubly-exponential time, thus it is not harder than traditional synthesis. Also, our algorithm is *Safraless*, thus no determinization and parity games are needed [15,17].

A drawback of GE-synthesis is that we do not actually know whether the specification is satisfied. We describe two ways to address this drawback. The first goes beyond providing satisfaction information and enables the designer to partition the specification into a *strong* component, which is guaranteed to be satisfied in all environments, and a *weak* component, which is guaranteed to be satisfied only in hopeful ones. The second way augments GE-realizing systems by "satisfaction indicators". For example, we show that when a system is lucky to interact with an environment that generates a prefix of an input sequence such that, when combined with a suitable prefix of an output sequence, the specification becomes realizable, then GE-synthesis guarantees that the system indeed responds with a suitable prefix of an output sequence. Moreover, it is easy to add to the system a monitor that detects such prefixes, thus indicating that the specification is going to be satisfied in all environments. Additional monitors we suggest detect prefixes after which the satisfaction becomes valid or unsatisfiable.

We continue to the quantitative setting. We parameterize hope by a satisfaction value $v \in [0, 1]$ and say that an input sequence $x \in (2^I)^\omega$ is v-hopeful for an LTL[$\mathcal{F}$] formula ψ if an interaction with it can generate a computation that satisfies ψ with value at least v. Formally, there is an output sequence $y \in (2^O)^\omega$ such that $[\![x \otimes y, \psi]\!] \geq v$, where for a computation $w \in (2^{I \cup O})^\omega$, we use $[\![w, \psi]\!]$ to denotes the satisfaction value of ψ in w. As we elaborate below, while the basic idea of GE-synthesis, namely "input sequences with a potential to high quality should realize this potential" is as in the Boolean setting, there are several ways to implement this idea.

We start with a worst-case approach. There, a strategy $f : (2^I)^+ \to 2^O$ GE-realizes an LTL[$\mathcal{F}$] formula ψ if for all input sequences $x \in (2^I)^\omega$, if x is v-hopeful, then $[\![x \otimes f(x), \psi]\!] \geq v$. The requirement can be applied to a threshold value or to all values $v \in [0, 1]$. For example, our autonomous car controller has to achieve satisfaction value 1 in roads with no simultaneous or successive occurrences of *safe* and *obs*, and value $\frac{3}{4}$ in roads that violate the latter only with some *obs* followed by *safe*. We then argue that the situation is similar to that of *high-quality assume guarantee synthesis* [3], where richer relations between a quantitative assumption and a quantitative guarantee are of interest. In our case, the assumption is the hopefulness level of the input sequence, namely $[\![x, \exists O.\psi]\!]$, and the guarantee is the satisfaction value of the specification in the generated computation, namely $[\![x \otimes f(x), \psi]\!]$. When synthesizing, for example, a robot controller (e.g., vacuum cleaner) in a building, the doors to rooms are controlled by the environment, whereas the movement of the robot by the system. A measure of the performance of the robot has to take into an account both the number of "hopeful rooms", namely these with an open door – a projection of this number on [0, 1] serves as the assumption, and the number of room cleaned – which induces the guarantee. We assume that the desired relation between the assumption and the guarantee is given by a function comb : $[0, 1] \times [0, 1] \to [0, 1]$, which can capture implication, difference, or ratio.

We continue with an analysis of the expected performance of the system. We do so by assuming a stochastic environment, with a known distribution on the input sequences. We introduce and study two measures for high-quality GE-synthesis in a stochastic environment. In the first, termed *expected GE-synthesis*, all input sequences are sampled, yet the satisfaction value in each input sequence takes its hopefulness level into account, for example by a comb function as in the assume-guarantee setting. In the second, termed *conditional expected*

GE-*synthesis*, only hopeful input sequences are sampled. For both approaches, our synthesis algorithm is based on the high-quality LTL[$\mathcal{F}$] synthesis algorithm of [2], which is based on an analysis of deterministic automata associated with the different satisfaction values of the LTL[$\mathcal{F}$] specification. Here too, the complexity stays doubly exponential. In addition, we extend the synthesized systems with guarantees for satisfaction and monitors indicating satisfaction in various satisfaction levels.

2 Preliminaries

Consider two finite sets I and O of input and output signals, respectively. For two words $x = i_0 \cdot i_1 \cdot i_2 \cdots \in (2^I)^\omega$ and $y = o_0 \cdot o_1 \cdot o_2 \cdots \in (2^I)^\omega$, we define $x \otimes y$ as the word in $(2^{I \cup O})^\omega$ obtained by merging x and y. Thus, $x \otimes y = (i_0 \cup o_0) \cdot (i_1 \cup o_1) \cdot (i_2 \cup o_2) \cdots$. The definition is similar for finite x and y of the same length. For a word $w \in (2^{I \cup O})^\omega$, we use $w_{|I}$ to denote the projection of w on I. In particular, $(x \otimes y)_{|I} = x$.

A *strategy* is a function $f : (2^I)^+ \to 2^O$. Intuitively, f models the interaction of a system that generates in each moment in time a letter in 2^O with an environment that generates letters in 2^I. For an input sequence $x = i_0 \cdot i_1 \cdot i_2 \cdots \in (2^I)^\omega$, we use $f(x)$ to denote the output sequence $f(i_0) \cdot f(i_0 \cdot i_1) \cdot f(i_0 \cdot i_1 \cdot i_2) \cdots \in (2^O)^\omega$. Then, $x \otimes f(x) \in (2^{I \cup O})^\omega$ is the *computation* of f on x. Note that the environment initiates the interaction, by inputting i_0. Of special interest are *finite-state strategies*, induced by finite state transducers. Formally, an *I/O-transducer* is $\mathcal{T} = \langle I, O, S, s_0, M, \tau \rangle$, where S is a finite set of states, $s_0 \in S$ is an initial state, $M : S \times 2^I \to S$ is a transition function, and $\tau : S \to 2^O$ is a labelling function. For $x = i_0 \cdot i_1 \cdot i_2 \cdots \in (2^I)^*$, let $M^*(x)$ be the state in S that $\mathcal{T}$ reaches after reading x. Thus is, $M^*(\epsilon) = s_0$ and for every $j \geq 0$, we have that $M^*(i_0 \cdot i_1 \cdot i_2 \cdots i_j) = M(M^*(i_0 \cdot i_1 \cdot i_2 \cdots i_{j-1}), i_j)$. Then, $\mathcal{T}$ induces the strategy $f_{\mathcal{T}} : (2^I)^+ \to 2^O$, where for every $x \in (2^I)^+$, we have that $f_{\mathcal{T}}(x) = \tau(M^*(x))$. We use $\mathcal{T}(x)$ and $x \otimes \mathcal{T}(x)$ to denote the output sequence and the computation of $\mathcal{T}$ on x, respectively, and talk about $\mathcal{T}$ realizing a specification, referring to the strategy $f_{\mathcal{T}}$.

We specify on-going behaviors of reactive systems using the *linear temporal logic* LTL [19]. Formulas of LTL are constructed from a set AP of atomic proposition using the usual Boolean operators and temporal operators like G ("always"), F ("eventually"), X ("next time"), and U ("until"). Each LTL formula ψ defines a language $L(\psi) = \{w : w \models \psi\} \subseteq (2^{AP})^\omega$. We also use *automata on infinite words* for specifying and reasoning about on-going behaviors. We use automata with different branching modes (nondeterministic, where some run has to be accepting; universal, where all runs have to be accepting; and deterministic, where there is a single run) and different acceptance conditions (Büchi, co-Büchi, and parity). We use the three letter acronyms NBW, UCW, DPW, and DFW, to refer to nondeterministic Büchi, universal co-Büchi, deterministic parity, and deterministic finite word automata, respectively. Given an LTL formula ψ over AP, one can constructs an NBW $\mathcal{A}_\psi$ with at most $2^{O(|\psi|)}$ states such that $L(\mathcal{A}_\psi) = L(\psi)$ [27]. Constructing an NBW for $\neg\psi$ and then dualizing it, results in a UCW for $L(\psi)$, also with at most $2^{O(|\psi|)}$ states. Determinization [23] then leads to a DPW for $L(\psi)$ with at at most $2^{2^{O(|\psi|)}}$ states and index $2^{O(|\psi|)}$. For full definitions of LTL, automata, and their relation, see [12].

Consider an LTL formula ψ over $I \cup O$. We say that ψ is *realizable* if there is a finite-state strategy $f : (2^I)^+ \to 2^O$ such that for all $x \in (2^I)^\omega$, we have that $x \otimes f(x) \models \psi$. That is, the computation of f on every input sequence satisfies ψ. We say that a word $x \in (2^I)^\omega$ is *hopeful* for ψ if there is $y \in (2^O)^\omega$ such that $x \otimes y \models \psi$. Then, we say that ψ is *good-enough realizable* (GE-realizable, for short) if there is a finite-state strategy $f : (2^I)^+ \to 2^O$ such that for every $x \in (2^I)^\omega$ that is hopeful for ψ, we have that $x \otimes f(x) \models \psi$. That is, if there is some output sequence whose combination with x satisfies ψ, then the computation of f on x satisfies ψ. The LTL GE-synthesis problem is then to decide whether a given LTL formula is GE-realizable, and if so, to return a transducer that GE-realizes it. Clearly, every realizable specification is GE-realizable – by the same transducer. We say that ψ is *universally satisfiable* if all input sequences are hopeful for ψ. It is easy to see that for universally satisfiable specifications, realizability and GE-realizability coincide. On the other hand, as demonstrated in Sect. 1, there are specifications that are not realizable and are GE-realizable.

Example 1. Let $I = \{p\}$ and $O = \{q\}$. Consider the specification $\psi = \mathsf{GF}((\mathsf{X}p) \wedge q) \wedge \mathsf{GF}((\mathsf{X}\neg p) \wedge \neg q)$. Clearly, ψ is not realizable, as an input sequence $x \in (2^I)^\omega$ is hopeful for ψ iff $x \models \mathsf{GF}p \wedge \mathsf{GF}\neg p$. Since the system has to assign a value to q before it knowns the value of $\mathsf{X}p$, it seems that ψ is also not GE-realizable. As we show below, however, the specification ψ is GE-realizable. Intuitively, it follows from the fact that hopeful input sequences consists of alternating p-blocks and $(\neg p)$-blocks. Then, by outputting $\neg q$ in p-blocks and outputting q in $(\neg p)$-blocks, the system guarantees that each last position in a $(\neg p)$-block satisfies $q \wedge \mathsf{X}p$ and each last position in a p-block satisfies $(\neg q) \wedge \mathsf{X}p$. Formally, ψ is GE-realized by the transducer $\mathcal{T} = \langle \{p\}, \{q\}, \{s_0, s_1\}, s_0, M, \tau \rangle$, where $M(s_0, \emptyset) = M(s_1, \emptyset) = s_0$, $M(s_0, \{p\}) = M(s_1, \{p\}) = s_1$, $\tau(s_0) = \{q\}$, and $\tau(s_1) = \emptyset$.   □

3   LTL Good-Enough Synthesis

Recall that a strategy $f : (2^I)^+ \to 2^O$ GE-realizes an LTL formula ψ if its computations on all hopeful input sequences satisfy ψ. Thus, for every input sequence $x \in (2^I)^\omega$, either $x \otimes y \not\models \psi$ for all $y \in (2^O)^\omega$, or $x \otimes f(x) \models \psi$. The above suggests that algorithms for solving LTL GE-synthesis involve existential and universal quantification over the behavior of output signals. The logic EQLTL extends LTL by allowing existential quantification over atomic propositions [26]. We refer here to the case the atomic propositions are the signals in $I \cup O$, and the signals in O are existentially quantified. Then, an EQLTL formula is of the form $\exists O.\psi$, and a computation $w \in (2^{I \cup O})^\omega$ satisfies $\exists O.\psi$ iff there is $y \in (2^O)^\omega$ such that $w_{|I} \otimes y \models \psi$. Dually, AQLTL extends LTL by allowing universal quantification over atomic propositions. We consider here formulas of the form

$\forall O.\psi$, which are equivalent to $\neg \exists O.\neg \psi$. Indeed, a computation $w \in (2^{I \cup O})^\omega$ satisfies $\forall O.\psi$ iff for all $y \in (2^O)^\omega$, we have that $w_{|I} \otimes y \models \psi$. Note that in both the existential and universal cases, the O-component of w is ignored. Accordingly, we sometimes interpret EQLTL and AQLTL formulas with respect to input sequences $x \in (2^I)^\omega$. Also note that both EQLTL and AQLTL increase the expressive power of LTL. For example, the EQLTL formula $\exists q.q \wedge \mathsf{X} \neg q \wedge \mathsf{G}(q \leftrightarrow \mathsf{XX}q) \wedge \mathsf{G}(q \rightarrow p)$ states that p holds in all even positions of the computation, which cannot be specified in LTL [29].

Theorem 1. *The LTL* GE-*synthesis problem is 2EXPTIME-complete.*

Proof. We start with the upper bound. Given an LTL formula ψ over $I \cup O$, we describe an algorithm that returns a transducer $\mathcal{T}$ that GE-realizes ψ, or declares that no such transducer exists.

It is not hard to see that $\mathcal{T}$ GE-realizes ψ iff $\mathcal{T}$ realizes $\varphi = \psi \vee \forall O.\neg \psi$. Indeed, an input sequence $x \in (2^I)^\omega$ is hopeful for ψ iff $x \models \exists O.\psi$, and so the specification φ requires all hopeful input sequences to satisfy ψ. A naive construction of an NBW for φ involves a universal projection of the signals in O in an automaton for $\neg \psi$, and results in an NBW that is doubly exponential. In order to circumvent the extra exponent, we construct an NBW $\mathcal{A}_{\neg \varphi}$ for $\neg \varphi$, and then dualize it to get a UCW for φ, as follows.

Let $\mathcal{A}_{\neg \psi}$ be an NBW for $L(\neg \psi)$ and $\mathcal{A}_{\exists O.\psi}$ be an NBW for $L(\exists O.\psi)$. Thus, $\mathcal{A}_{\exists O.\psi}$ is obtained from an NBW $\mathcal{A}_\psi$ for $L(\psi)$ by existentially projecting its transitions on 2^I. In more details, if $\mathcal{A}_\psi = \langle 2^{I \cup O}, Q, Q_0, \delta, \alpha \rangle$, then $\mathcal{A}_{\exists O.\psi} = \langle 2^{I \cup O}, Q, Q_0, \delta', \alpha \rangle$, where for all $q \in Q$ and $i \cup o \in 2^{I \cup O}$, we have $\delta'(q, \sigma) = \bigcup_{o \in 2^O} \{\delta(q, (\sigma \cap I) \cup o)\}$.

Let $\mathcal{A}_{\neg \varphi}$ be an NBW for the intersection of $\mathcal{A}_{\neg \psi}$ and $\mathcal{A}_{\exists O.\psi}$. We can define $\mathcal{A}_{\neg \varphi}$ as the product of $\mathcal{A}_{\neg \psi}$ and $\mathcal{A}_{\exists O.\psi}$, possibly using the generalized Büchi acceptance condition (see Remark 1), thus its size is exponential in ψ. The language of $\mathcal{A}_{\neg \varphi}$ is then $\{w \in (2^{I \cup O})^\omega : w \not\models \psi$ and $w \models \exists O.\psi\}$. We then solve usual synthesis for the complementing UCW. Its language is $\{w \in (2^{I \cup O})^\omega : w \models \psi$ or $w \models \forall O.\neg \psi\}$, as required. By [17], the synthesis problem for UCW can be solved in EXPTIME, and we are done.

The lower bound follows from the 2EXPTIME-hardness of LTL realizability [22]. The hardness proof there constructs, given a 2EXPTIME Turing machine M, an LTL formula ψ that is realizable iff M accepts the empty tape. Since all input sequences are hopeful for ψ, realizability and GE-realizability coincide, and we are done.   □

Note that working with a UCW not only handles the universal quantification for free but also has the advantage of a Safraless synthesis algorithm – no determinization and parity games are needed [15,17]. Also note that the algorithm we suggest in the proof of Theorem 1 can be generalized to handle specifications that are arbitrary positive Boolean combinations of EQLTL formulas.

Remark 1 [**Products and optimizations**]. Throughout the paper, we construct products of automata whose state space is $2^{cl(\psi)}$, and states correspond to maximal consistent subsets of $cl(\psi)$, possibly in the scope of an existential quantifier of O. Accordingly, the product can be minimized to include only consistent pairs. Also, since traditional-synthesis algorithms, in particular the Safraless algorithms we use, can handle automata with *generalized* Büchi and co-Büchi acceptance condition, we need only one copy of the product.   □

Remark 2 [**Determinancy of the GE-synthesis game**]. Determinancy of games implies that in traditional synthesis, a specification ψ is not I/O-realizable iff $\neg\psi$ is O/I-realizable This is useful, for example when we want to synthesize a transducer of a bounded size and proceed simultaneously, aiming to synthesize either a system transducer that realizes ψ or an environment transducer that realizes $\neg\psi$ [17]. For GE-synthesis, simple dualization does not hold, but we do have determinancy in the sense that $(\exists O.\psi) \rightarrow \psi$ is not I/O-realizable iff $(\exists O.\psi) \wedge \neg\psi$ is O/I-realizable. Accordingly, ψ is not GE-realizable iff the environment has a strategy that generates, for each output sequence $y \in (2^O)^\omega$, a helpful input sequence $x \in (2^I)^\omega$ such that $x \otimes y \models \neg\psi$. In the full version, we formalize and study this duality further.   □

4   Guarantees in Good-Enough Synthesis

A drawback of GE-synthesis is that we do not actually know whether the specification is satisfied. In this section we describe two ways to address this drawback. The first way goes beyond providing satisfaction information and enables the designer to partition the specification into to a *strong* component, which should be satisfied in all environments, and a *weak* component, which should be satisfied only in hopeful ones. The second way augments GE-realizing transducers by flags, raised to indicate the status of the satisfaction.

4.1   GE-Synthesis with a Guarantee

Recall that GE-realizability is suitable especially in settings where we design a system that has to do its best in all environments. GE-synthesis with a guarantee is suitable in settings where we want to make sure that some components of the specification are satisfied in all environment. Accordingly, a specification is an LTL formula $\psi = \psi_{strong} \wedge \psi_{weak}$. When we GE-*synthesize* ψ_{weak} *with guarantee* ψ_{strong}, we seek a transducer T that realizes ψ_{strong} and GE-realizes ψ_{weak}. Thus, for all input sequences $x \in (2^I)^\omega$, we have that $x \otimes T(x) \models \psi_{strong}$, and if x is hopeful for ψ_{weak}, then $x \otimes T(x) \models \psi_{strong}$.

Theorem 2. *The LTL GE-synthesis with guarantee problem is 2EXPTIME-complete.*

Proof. Consider an LTL formula $\psi = \psi_{strong} \wedge \psi_{weak}$ over $I \cup O$. It is not hard to see that a transducer T GE-realizes ψ_{weak} with guarantee ψ_{strong} iff T realizes $\varphi = \psi_{strong} \wedge ((\exists O.\psi_{weak}) \rightarrow \psi_{weak})$. We can then construct a UCW $\mathcal{A}_\varphi$ for $L(\varphi)$ by dualizing an NBW for its negation $\neg\psi_{strong} \vee ((\exists O.\psi_{weak}) \wedge \neg\psi_{weak})$, which can be constructed using techniques similar to those in the proof of Theorem 1. We then proceed with standard synthesis for $\mathcal{A}_\varphi$. Note that the approach is Safraless. Taking an empty (that is, True) guarantee, a lower bound follows from the 2EXPTIME-hardness of LTL GE-synthesis.   □

4.2   Flags by a GE-Realizing Transducer

For a language $L \subseteq (2^{I \cup O})^\omega$ and a finite word $w \in (2^{I \cup O})^*$, let $L^w = \{w' \in (2^{I \cup O})^\omega : w \cdot w' \in L\}$. That is, L^w is the language of suffixes of words in L that have w as a prefix. We say that a word $w \in (2^{I \cup O})^*$ is *green for* L if L^w is realizable. Then, a word $x \in (2^I)^*$ is *green for* L if there is $y \in (2^O)^*$ such that $x \otimes y$ is green for L. When a system is lucky to interact with an environment that generates a green input sequence, we want the system to react in a way that generates a green prefix, and then realizes the specification. Formally, we say that a strategy $f : (2^I)^+ \to 2^O$ *green realizes* L if for every $x \in (2^I)^+$, if x is green for L, then $x \otimes f(x)$ is green for L.[1,2] We say that a word $w \in (2^{I \cup O})^*$ is *light green for* L if L^w is universally satisfiable, thus all input sequences are hopeful for L^w. A word $x \in (2^I)^*$ is *light green for* L if there is $y \in (2^O)^*$ such that $x \otimes y$ is light green for L. It is not hard to see that for GE-realizable languages, green and light green coincide. Indeed, if L is universally satisfiable and GE-realizable, then L is realizable.

Theorem 3. GE-*realizability is strictly stronger than green realizability.*

Proof. We first prove that every strategy $f : (2^I)^+ \to 2^O$ that GE-realizes a specification ψ also green realizes ψ. Consider $x \in (2^I)^+$ that is green for ψ. By definition, there is $y \in (2^O)^+$ such that $L^{x \otimes y}$ is realizable. Then, for every $x' \in (2^I)^\omega$, there is $y' \in (2^O)^\omega$ such that $x' \otimes y'$ in $L^{x \otimes y}$. Hence, for every $x' \in (2^I)^\omega$, we have that $x \cdot x'$ is hopeful. Therefore, as f GE-realizes ψ, we have that $(x \cdot x') \otimes f(x \cdot x') \models \psi$. Thus, $x \otimes f(x)$ is green, and so f green realizes ψ.

We continue and describe a specification that is green realizable and not GE-realizable. Let $I = \{p\}$ and $O = \{q\}$. Consider the specification $\psi = \mathsf{G}((\mathsf{X}p) \leftrightarrow q)$. Clearly, ψ is not realizable, as the system has to commit a value for q before a value for $\mathsf{X}p$ is known. Likewise, no word $w \in (2^{I \cup O})^*$ is green for ψ, and so no finite input sequence $x \in (2^I)^*$ is green for ψ. Hence, every strategy (vacuously) green realizes ψ. On the other hand, for every input sequences $x \in (2^I)^\omega$ there is an output sequence $y \in (2^O)^\omega$ such that $x \otimes y \models \psi$. Thus, all input sequences are hopeful for ψ. Thus, synthesis and GE-synthesis coincide for ψ, which is not GE-realizable.   □

Theorem 3 brings with it two good news. The first is that a GE-realizing transducer has the desired property of being also green realizing. The second has

---

[1] Note that while the definition of green realization does not refer to ϵ directly, we have that ϵ is green iff L is realizable, in which case all $x \in (2^I)^*$ are green.

[2] While synthesis corresponds to finding a winning strategy for the system, green synthesis can be viewed as a subgame-perfect best-response strategy, where the system does its best in every subgame, even if it loses the overall game.

to do with our goal of providing the user with information about the satisfaction status, in particular raising a green flag whenever a green prefix is detected. By Theorem 3, such a flag indicates that the computation generated by our GE-realizing transducer satisfies the specification. A naive way to detect green prefixes for a specification ψ is to solve the synthesis problem for ψ by solving a game on top of a DPW $\mathcal{D}_\psi$ for ψ. The winning positions in the game are states in $\mathcal{D}_\psi$. By defining them as accepting states, we can obtain from $\mathcal{D}_\psi$ a DFW for green prefixes. Then, we run this DFW in parallel with the GE-realizing transducer, and raise the green flag whenever a green prefix is detected. This, however, requires a generation of $\mathcal{D}_\psi$ and a solution of parity games. Below we describe a much simpler way, which makes use of the fact that our transducer GE-realizes the specification.

Recall that if L is universally satisfiable and GE-realizable, then L is realizable. Accordingly, given a transducer $\mathcal{T}$ that GE-realizes ψ, we can augment it with green flags by running in parallel a DFW that detects light-green prefixes. As we argue below, constructing such a DFW only requires an application of the subset construction on top of an NBW for the existential projection of ψ on 2^I.

Lemma 1. *Given an LTL formula ψ over $I \cup O$, we can construct a DFA $\mathcal{S}$ of size $2^{2^{O(|\psi|)}}$ such that $L(\mathcal{S}) = \{x \in (2^I)^* : x \text{ is light green for } L(\psi)\}$.*

Proof. Let $\mathcal{A}_\psi = \langle 2^{I \cup O}, Q, \delta, Q_0, \alpha \rangle$ be an NBW for $L(\psi)$, and let $\mathcal{B}_\psi = \langle 2^I, Q, \delta', Q_0, \alpha \rangle$ be its existential projection on 2^I. Thus, for every $q \in Q$ and $i \in 2^I$, we have $\delta'(q, i) = \bigcup_{o \in 2^O} \delta(q, i \cup o)$. We define the DFW $\mathcal{S} = \langle 2^I, 2^Q, M, \{Q_0\}, F \rangle$, where M follows the subset construction of $\mathcal{B}_\psi$: for every $S \in 2^Q$ and $i \in 2^I$, we have $M(S, i) = \bigcup_{s \in S} \delta'(s, i)$. Then, $F = \{S \in 2^Q : L(\mathcal{B}_\psi^S) = (2^I)^\omega\}$. Observe that $\mathcal{S}$ rejects $x \in (2^I)^*$ iff there is $x' \in (2^I)^\omega$ such that for all $y \in (2^O)^*$ and $y' \in (2^O)^\omega$, no state in $\delta(Q_0, x \otimes y)$ accepts $x' \otimes y'$. Thus, $\mathcal{S}$ rejects x iff x is not light green, and accepts it otherwise. Note that the definition of F involves universality checking, possibly via complementation, yet no determinization is required, and the size of $\mathcal{S}$ is $2^{2^{O(|\psi|)}}$. □

Note that once we reach an accepting state in $\mathcal{S}$, we can make it an accepting loop. Indeed, once a green prefix is detected, then all prefixes that extend it are green. Accordingly, once the green flag is raised, it stays up. Also note that if an input sequence is not hopeful for ψ, then none of its prefixes is light green for ψ. The converse, however, is not true: an input sequence may be hopeful and still have no light green prefixes. For example, taking $I = \{p\}$, the input sequence $\{p\}^\omega$ is hopeful for Gp, yet none of its prefixes is green light, as it can be extended to an input sequence with $\neg p$.

Green flags provide information about satisfaction. Two additional flags of interest are related to safety and co-safety properties:

- A word $w \in (2^{I \cup O})^*$ is *red for L* if $L^w = \emptyset$. A word $x \in (2^I)^*$ is *red for L* if for all $y \in (2^O)^*$, we have that $x \otimes y$ is red for L. Thus, when the environment generates x, then no matter how the system responds, L is not satisfied.

– a word $w \in (2^{I \cup O})^*$ is *blue for* L when $L^w = (2^{I \cup O})^\omega$, and then define a word $x \in (2^I)^*$ as *blue for* L if there is $y \in (2^O)^*$ such that $x \otimes y$ is blue for L. Thus, when the environment generates x, the system can respond in a way that guarantees satisfaction no matter how the interaction continues.

A monitor that detects red and blue prefixes for L can be added to a transducer that GE-realizes L. As has been the case with the monitor for green prefixes, its construction is based on applying the subset construction on an NBW for L [16]. Also, once a red or blue flag is raised, it stays up. In a way analogous to green realizability, we seek a transducer that GE-realizes the specification and generates a red prefix only if all interactions generate a red prefix, and generates a blue prefix whenever this is possible. In the full version, we show that while GE-realization implies *red realization*, it may conflict with *blue realization*.

5 High-Quality Good-Enough Synthesis

GE-synthesis is of special interest when the satisfaction value of the specification is multi-valued, and we want to synthesize high-quality systems. We start by defining the multi-valued logic LTL[$\mathcal{F}$], which is our multi-valued specification formalism. We then study LTL[$\mathcal{F}$] GE-synthesis, first in a worst-case approach, where the satisfaction value of a transducer is the satisfaction value of its computation with the lowest satisfaction value, and then in a stochastic approach, where it is the expected satisfaction value, given a distribution of the inputs.

5.1 The Logic LTL[$\mathcal{F}$]

Let AP be a set of Boolean atomic propositions and let $\mathcal{F} \subseteq \{f : [0,1]^k \to [0,1] : k \in \mathbb{N}\}$ be a set of *quality operators*. An LTL[$\mathcal{F}$] formula is one of the following:

– True, False, or p, for $p \in AP$.
– $f(\psi_1, ..., \psi_k)$, $\mathsf{X}\psi_1$, or $\psi_1 \mathsf{U} \psi_2$, for LTL[$\mathcal{F}$] formulas $\psi_1, \ldots, \psi_k$ and a function $f \in \mathcal{F}$.

The semantics of LTL[$\mathcal{F}$] formulas is defined with respect to infinite computations over AP. For a computation $w = w_0, w_1, \ldots \in (2^{AP})^\omega$ and position $j \geq 0$, we use w^j to denote the suffix $w_j, w_{j+1}, \ldots$. The semantics maps a computation w and an LTL[$\mathcal{F}$] formula ψ to the *satisfaction value* of ψ in w, denoted $[\![w, \psi]\!]$. The satisfaction value is in $[0, 1]$ and is defined inductively as follows.

– $[\![w, \mathsf{True}]\!] = 1$ and $[\![w, \mathsf{False}]\!] = 0$.
– For $p \in AP$, we have that $[\![w, p]\!] = 1$ if $p \in w_0$, and $[\![w, p]\!] = 0$ if $p \notin w_0$.
– $[\![w, f(\psi_1, ..., \psi_k)]\!] = f([\![w, \psi_1]\!], ..., [\![w, \psi_k]\!])$.
– $[\![w, \mathsf{X}\psi_1]\!] = [\![w^1, \psi_1]\!]$.
– $[\![w, \psi_1 \mathsf{U} \psi_2]\!] = \max_{i \geq 0}\{\min\{[\![w^i, \psi_2]\!], \min_{0 \leq j < i}[\![w^j, \psi_1]\!]\}\}$.

The logic LTL can be viewed as LTL[$\mathcal{F}$] for $\mathcal{F}$ that models the usual Boolean operators. In particular, the only possible satisfaction values are 0 and 1. We abbreviate common functions as described below. Let $x, y, \lambda \in [0, 1]$. Then,

- $\neg x = 1 - x$
- $x \vee y = \max\{x, y\}$
- $x \wedge y = \min\{x, y\}$
- $x \rightarrow y = \max\{1 - x, y\}$
- $\nabla_\lambda x = \lambda \cdot x$
- $x \oplus_\lambda y = \lambda \cdot x + (1 - \lambda) \cdot y$

The realizability problem for $\mathrm{LTL}[\mathcal{F}]$ is an optimization problem: For an $\mathrm{LTL}[\mathcal{F}]$ specification ψ and a transducer $\mathcal{T}$, we define the satisfaction value of ψ in $\mathcal{T}$, denoted $[\![\mathcal{T}, \psi]\!]$, by $\min\{[\![x \otimes \mathcal{T}(x), \psi]\!] : x \in (2^I)^\omega\}$, namely the satisfaction value of ψ in the worst-case. Then, the synthesis problem is to find, given ψ, a transducer that maximizes its satisfaction value. Moving to a decision problem, given ψ and a threshold value $v \in [0, 1]$, we say that ψ is v-*realizable* if there exists a transducer $\mathcal{T}$ such that $[\![\mathcal{T}, \psi]\!] \geq v$, and the synthesis problem is to find, given ψ and v, a transducer $\mathcal{T}$ that v-realizes ψ.

For an $\mathrm{LTL}[\mathcal{F}]$ formula ψ, let $V(\psi)$ be the set of possible satisfaction values of ψ in arbitrary computations. Thus, $V(\psi) = \{[\![w, \psi]\!] : w \in (2^{AP})^\omega\}$.

Theorem 4 [1]. *Consider an* $\mathrm{LTL}[\mathcal{F}]$ *formula* ψ.

- $|V(\psi)| \leq 2^{|\psi|}$.
- *For every predicate* $P \subseteq [0, 1]$, *there exists an NBW* $\mathcal{A}_\psi^P$ *such that* $L(\mathcal{A}_\psi^P) = \{w : [\![w, \psi]\!] \in P\}$. *Furthermore,* $\mathcal{A}_\psi^P$ *has at most* $2^{O(|\psi|^2)}$ *states* [1].

As with LTL, we define the existential and universal extensions $\mathrm{EQLTL}[\mathcal{F}]$ and $\mathrm{AQLTL}[\mathcal{F}]$ of $\mathrm{LTL}[\mathcal{F}]$. Here too, we consider the case $AP = I \cup O$, with the signals in O being quantified. Then, $[\![w, \exists O.\psi]\!] = \max_{y \in (2^O)^\omega}\{[\![w_{|I} \otimes y, \psi]\!]\}$ and $[\![w, \forall O.\psi]\!] = \min_{y \in (2^O)^\omega}\{[\![w_{|I} \otimes y, \psi]\!]\}$.

Remark 3 [**On the semantics of** $\mathrm{EQLTL}[\mathcal{F}]$]. It is tempting to interpret an expression like $[\![w, \exists O.\psi]\!] \leq v$ as "there exists an output sequence y such that $[\![w_I \otimes y, \psi]\!] \leq v$". By the semantics of $\exists O.\psi$, however, $[\![w, \exists O.\psi]\!] \leq v$ actually means that $\max_{y \in (2^O)^\omega} [\![w_I \otimes y, \psi]\!] \leq v$. Thus, the correct interpretation is "for all output sequences y, we have that $[\![w_I \otimes y, \psi]\!] \leq v$".   □

5.2 $\mathrm{LTL}[\mathcal{F}]$ GE-Synthesis

For a value $v \in [0, 1]$, we say that x is v-*hopeful for* ψ if there is $y \in (2^O)^\omega$ such that $[\![x \otimes y, \psi]\!] \geq v$. We study two variants of $\mathrm{LTL}[\mathcal{F}]$ GE-synthesis:

- In $\mathrm{LTL}[\mathcal{F}]$ GE-*synthesis with a threshold*, the input is an $\mathrm{LTL}[\mathcal{F}]$ formula ψ and a value $v \in [0, 1]$, and the goal is to generate a transducer whose computation on every input sequence that is v-hopeful has satisfaction value at least v. Formally, a function $f : (2^I)^+ \rightarrow 2^O$ GE-realizes ψ with threshold v if for every $x \in (2^I)^\omega$, if x is v-hopeful, then $[\![x \otimes f(x), \psi]\!] \geq v$.
- In $\mathrm{LTL}[\mathcal{F}]$ GE-*synthesis*, the input is an $\mathrm{LTL}[\mathcal{F}]$ formula ψ, and the goal is to generate a transducer whose computation on every input sequence has the highest possible satisfaction value for this input sequence. Formally, a function $f : (2^I)^+ \rightarrow 2^O$ GE-realizes ψ if for every $x \in (2^I)^\omega$ and value $v \in [0, 1]$, if x is v-hopeful, then $[\![x \otimes f(x), \psi]\!] \geq v$.

In the Boolean case, the two variants coincide, taking $v = 1$. Indeed, then, for every $x \in (2^I)^\omega$, if x is hopeful, then $x \otimes f(x)$ has to satisfy ψ. We note that GE-realization with a threshold is not monotone, in the sense that decreasing the threshold need not lead to GE-realization. Indeed, the lower is the threshold v, the more input sequences are v-helpful (see Example 2). Accordingly, we do not search for a maximal threshold, and rather may ask about a desired threshold or about GE-synthesis without a threshold.

Solving the GE-synthesis problem, a naive combination of the automata construction of Theorem 4 with the projection technique of Theorem 1, corresponds to an erroneous semantics of EQLTL$[\mathcal{F}]$, as noted in Remark 3. Before describing our construction, it is helpful to state the correct (perhaps less intuitive) interpretation of existential and universal quantification in the quantitative setting:

Lemma 2. *For every* LTL$[\mathcal{F}]$ *formula ψ and an input sequence $x \in (2^I)^\omega$, we have that $[\![x, \exists O.\psi]\!] = 1 - [\![x, \forall O.\neg\psi]\!]$. Accordingly, for every value $v \in [0,1]$, we have that $[\![x, \exists O.\psi]\!] < v$ iff $[\![x, \forall O.\neg\psi]\!] > 1 - v$.*

Proof. By definition, $[\![x, \exists O.\psi]\!] = \max_{y \in (2^O)^\omega} [\![x \otimes y, \psi]\!] = 1 - \min_{y \in (2^O)^\omega} 1 - [\![x \otimes y, \psi]\!] = 1 - \min_{y \in (2^O)^\omega} [\![x \otimes y, \neg\psi]\!] = 1 - [\![x, \forall O.\neg\psi]\!]$. Then, $[\![x, \exists O.\psi]\!] < v$ iff $1 - [\![x, \exists O.\psi]\!] > 1 - v$ iff $[\![x, \forall O.\neg\psi]\!] > 1 - v$. $\square$

Consider an LTL$[\mathcal{F}]$ formula ψ, a value $v \in [0,1]$, and an input sequence $x \in (2^I)^\omega$. Recall that x is v-hopeful for ψ if there is $y \in (2^O)^\omega$ such that $[\![x \otimes y, \psi]\!] \geq v$. Equivalently, $[\![x, \exists O.\psi]\!] \geq v$. Indeed, $[\![x, \exists O.\psi]\!] = \max_{y \in (2^O)^\omega} [\![x \otimes y, \psi]\!]$, which is greater or equal to v iff there is $y \in (2^O)^\omega$ such that $[\![x \otimes y, \psi]\!] \geq v$. Hence, x is not v-hopeful for ψ if $[\![x, \exists O.\psi]\!] < v$. Equivalently, by Lemma 2, $[\![x, \forall O.\neg\psi]\!] > 1 - v$. Accordingly, for a strategy $f : (2^I)^+ \to 2^O$, an input sequence $x \in (2^I)^\omega$, and a value $v \in [0,1]$, we say that f is v-*good for x with respect to* ψ, if $[\![x \otimes f(x), \psi]\!] \geq v$ or $[\![x, \forall O.\neg\psi]\!] > 1 - v$.

Example 2. Let $I = \{p\}$ and $O = \{q\}$. Consider the LTL$[\mathcal{F}]$ formula $\psi = (\nabla_{\frac{1}{4}} p \vee \nabla_{\frac{1}{2}} q)$. Checking for which values v a strategy f is v-good for x with respect to ψ, we examine whether $[\![x \otimes f(x), \nabla_{\frac{1}{4}} p \vee \nabla_{\frac{1}{2}} q]\!] \geq v$ or $[\![x, \forall q.\neg(\nabla_{\frac{1}{4}} p \vee \nabla_{\frac{1}{2}} q)]\!] > 1 - v$. Since ψ refers only to the first position in the computation, it is enough to examine x_0 and $f(x_0)$. For example, if $x_0 = \emptyset$ and $f(x_0) = \emptyset$, then $[\![x \otimes f(x), \nabla_{\frac{1}{4}} p \vee \nabla_{\frac{1}{2}} q]\!] = 0$, $[\![x, \exists q.\nabla_{\frac{1}{4}} p \vee \nabla_{\frac{1}{2}} q]\!] = \max\{0, \frac{1}{2}\} = \frac{1}{2}$, and $[\![x, \forall q.\neg(\nabla_{\frac{1}{4}} p \vee \nabla_{\frac{1}{2}} q)]\!] = \min\{1, 1 - \frac{1}{2}\} = \frac{1}{2}$. Hence, f is v-good for x with respect to ψ if $v = 0$ or $v > \frac{1}{2}$, thus $v \in \{0\} \cup (\frac{1}{2}, 1]$. Similarly, we have the following.

- If $x_0 = \emptyset$ and $f(x_0) = \{q\}$ then f is v-good for x when $v \in [0, 1]$.
- If $x_0 = \{p\}$ and $f(x_0) = \emptyset$ then f is v-good for x when $v \in [0, \frac{1}{4}] \cup (\frac{1}{2}, 1]$.
- If $x_0 = \{p\}$ and $f(x_0) = \{q\}$ then f is v-good for x when $v \in [0, 1]$.

Theorem 5. *The* LTL$[\mathcal{F}]$ GE-*synthesis with threshold problem is 2EXPTIME-complete.*

Proof. We show we can adjust the upper bound described in the proof of Theorem 1 to the multi-valued setting. Given an LTL[$\mathcal{F}$] formula ψ over $I \cup O$ and a threshold $v \in [0, 1]$, we describe an algorithm that returns a transducer $\mathcal{T}$ that GE-realizes ψ with threshold v, or declares that no such transducer exists.

By definition, we have that $\mathcal{T}$ GE-realizes ψ with threshold v if for every input sequence x, we have that $f_{\mathcal{T}}$ is v-good for x with respect to ψ. Thus, $[\![x \otimes f_{\mathcal{T}}(x), \psi]\!] \geq v$ or $[\![x, \forall O. \neg \psi]\!] > 1 - v$. We construct a UCW whose language is $\{w \in (2^{I \cup O})^{\omega} : [\![w, \psi]\!] \geq v$ or $[\![w, \forall O. \neg \psi]\!] > 1 - v\}$.

Let $\mathcal{A}_{\psi}^{<v}$ be an NBW for $\{w : [\![w, \psi]\!] < v\}$ and $\mathcal{A}_{\exists O. \psi}^{\geq v}$ be an NBW for $\{w : [\![w, \exists O. \psi]\!] \geq v\}$. Thus, $\mathcal{A}_{\exists O. \psi}^{\geq v}$ is obtained from an NBW $\mathcal{A}_{\psi}^{\geq v}$ for $\{w : [\![w, \psi]\!] \geq v\}$ by existentially projecting its transitions on 2^I. By Theorem 4, both $\mathcal{A}_{\psi}^{<v}$ and $\mathcal{A}_{\exists O. \psi}^{\geq v}$ are of size exponential in ψ.

Let $\mathcal{B}_{\psi}^{v}$ be an NBW for the intersection of $\mathcal{A}_{\psi}^{<v}$ and $\mathcal{A}_{\exists O. \psi}^{\geq v}$. The language of $\mathcal{B}_{\psi}^{v}$ is then $\{w \in (2^{I \cup O})^{\omega} : [\![w, \psi]\!] < v$ and $[\![w, \exists O. \psi]\!] \geq v\}$. We then solve usual synthesis for the complementing UCW, whose language is $\{w \in (2^{I \cup O})^{\omega} : [\![w, \psi]\!] \geq v$ or $[\![w, \forall O. \neg \psi]\!] > 1 - v\}$, as required. By [17], the synthesis problem for UCW can be solved in EXPTIME.

The lower bound follows from the 2EXPTIME-hardness of LTL GE-realizability. □

Theorem 6. *The* LTL[$\mathcal{F}$] *GE-synthesis problem is 2EXPTIME-complete.*

Proof. We start with the upper bound. Given an LTL[$\mathcal{F}$] specification ψ over $I \cup O$, we describe an algorithm that returns a transducer $\mathcal{T}$ that GE-realizes ψ or declares that no such transducer exists.

As discussed above, a transducer $\mathcal{T}$ GE-realizes ψ iff for every input sequence $x \in (2^I)^{\omega}$ and value $v \in [0, 1]$, we have that $f_{\mathcal{T}}$ is v-good for x with respect to ψ. Accordingly, we construct a UCW whose language is $\bigcap_{v \in V(\psi)} \{w \in (2^{I \cup O})^{\omega} : [\![w, \psi]\!] \geq v$ or $[\![w, \forall O. \neg \psi]\!] > 1 - v\}$.

For $v \in V(\psi)$, let $\mathcal{B}_{\psi}^{v}$ be an NBW for $\{w : [\![w, \neg \psi]\!] \geq v$ and $[\![w, \exists O. \psi]\!] \geq v\}$, as constructed in the proof of Theorem 5, and let $\mathcal{B}$ be the union of $\mathcal{B}_{\psi}^{v}$ for all $v \in V(\psi)$. By Theorem 4, the size of $V(\psi)$ is exponential in ψ, and thus so is the size of $\mathcal{B}$. We then solve usual synthesis for the complementing UCW, whose language is as required. By [17], the synthesis problem for UCW can be solved in EXPTIME. The lower bound follows from the 2EXPTIME-hardness of LTL GE-realizability. □

Remark 4 [**Tuning hope down**]. The quantitative setting allows the designer to tune down "satisfaction by hoplessness": rather than synthesizing $\psi \vee \forall O. \neg \psi$, we can have a factor λ and synthesize $\psi \vee \nabla_{\lambda} \forall O. \neg \psi$. In Sect. 5.3 below we study additional ways to refer to hopefulness levels.

5.3   LTL[$\mathcal{F}$]   Assume-Guarantee GE-Synthesis

In Sect. 5.2, we seek a transducer $\mathcal{T}$ such that for a given or for all values $v \in [0, 1]$ and input sequences $x \in (2^I)^{\omega}$, if $[\![x, \exists O. \psi]\!] \geq v$ then $[\![x \otimes \mathcal{T}(x), \psi]\!] \geq v$. In this section we measure the quality of a transducer $\mathcal{T}$ by analyzing richer relations between $[\![x, \exists O.\psi]\!]$ and $[\![x \otimes \mathcal{T}(x), \psi]\!]$. The setting has the flavor of quantitative assume-guarantee synthesis [3]. There, the specification consists of a multi-valued assumption A, which in our case is $\exists O.\psi$, and a multi-valued guarantee G, which is our case is ψ.

There are different ways to analyze the relation between $[\![x, \exists O.\psi]\!]$ and $[\![x \otimes \mathcal{T}(x), \psi]\!]$. To this end, we assume that we are given a function comb : $[0, 1] \times [0, 1] \rightarrow [0, 1]$ that given the satisfaction values of $\exists O.\psi$ and of ψ, outputs a combined satisfaction value. We assume that comb is decreasing in the first component and increasing in the second component. This corresponds to the intuition that a lower satisfaction value of $\exists O.\psi$ and a higher satisfaction value of ψ both yield a higher overall score. Also, since $[\![x, \exists O.\psi]\!] \geq [\![x \otimes \mathcal{T}(x), \psi]\!]$ for all $x \in (2^I)^\omega$, we assume that the first component is greater than or equal to the second. Finally, we require comb to be efficiently computed. Some natural comb functions include:

- The quantitative implication function: $\text{comb}(A, G) = \max\{1 - A, G\}$. This captures the quantitative notion of the implication $(\exists O.\psi) \rightarrow \psi$.
- The (negated) difference function: $\text{comb}(A, G) = 1 - (A - G)$. This captures how far the satisfaction value for the given computation is from the best satisfaction value. Since $A \geq G$, the range of the function is indeed $[0, 1]$.
- The ratio function, given by some normalization to $[0, 1]$ of the function $\text{comb}(A, G) = \frac{G}{A}$, which captures the "relative success" with respect to the best possible satisfaction value.

The choice of an appropriate comb function depends on the setting. Implication is in order when harsh environments may outweigh the actual performance of the system. For example, if our specification measures the uptime of a server in a cluster, then environments that cause very frequent power failures render the server unusable, as the overhead of reconnecting it outweighs its usefulness. In such a case, being shut down is better than continuously trying to reconnect, and so we give a higher satisfaction value for the server being down, which depends only on the environment. Then, as demonstrated with the cleaning robot in Sect. 1, the difference and ratio functions are fairly natural when measuring "realization of potential". We now describe a more detailed example when these measures are in order.

Example 3. Consider a controller for an elevator in an n-floor building. The environment sends to the controller requests, by means of a truth assignment to $I = \{1, \ldots, n\}$, indicating the subset of floors in which the elevator is requested. Then, the controller assigns values to $O = \{up, down\}$, directing the elevator to go up, go down, or stay. The satisfaction value of the specification ψ reflects the waiting time of the request with the slowest response: it is 0 when this time is more than $2n$, and is 1 when the slowest request is granted immediately. Sure enough, there is no controller that attains satisfaction value 1 on all input sequences, and so ψ is not realizable with satisfaction value 1. Also, adding assumptions about the behavior of the environment is not of much interest. Using

AG GE-realizability, we can synthesize a controller that behaves in an optimal way. For example, using the difference function, we measure the performance of the controller on an input sequence $x \in (2^I)^\omega$ with respect to the best possible performance on x. Note that such a best performance needs a look-ahead on requests yet to come, which is indeed the satisfaction value of $\exists O.\psi$ in x. Thus, the assumption $[x, \exists O.\psi]$ actually gives us the performance of a good-enough *off-line* controller. Accordingly, using the ratio function, we can synthesize a system with the best *competitive ratio* for an on-line interaction [7].   □

Given an LTL[$\mathcal{F}$] formula ψ and a function comb, we define the GE-*AG-realization value* of ψ in a transducer $\mathcal{T}$ by $\min\{\text{comb}([x, \exists O.\psi], [x \otimes \mathcal{T}(x), \psi]) : x \in (2^I)^\omega\}$. Then, our goal in *AG* GE-*realizability* is to find, given an LTL[$\mathcal{F}$] formula ψ and a function comb, the maximal value $v \in [0, 1]$ such that there exists a transducer $\mathcal{T}$ whose AG GE-realization value of ψ is v. The *AG* GE *-synthesis* problem is then to find such a transducer.

We start by solving the decision version of AG GE-realizability.

Theorem 7. *The problem of deciding, given an* LTL[$\mathcal{F}$] *formula ψ, a function* comb, *and a threshold $v \in [0, 1]$, whether there exists a transducer $\mathcal{T}$ whose AG* GE-*realization value of ψ is v, is 2EXPTIME-complete.*

Proof. Recall that $V(\psi)$ is the set of possible satisfaction values of ψ (and hence of $\exists O.\psi$), and that by Theorem 4, we have that $|V(\psi)| \leq 2^{|\psi|}$. Let $G_v = \{\langle v_1, v_2 \rangle \in V(\psi) \times V(\psi) : \text{comb}(v_1, v_2) \geq v\}$. Intuitively, G is the set of satisfaction-value pairs $\langle [w, \exists O.\psi], [w, \psi] \rangle$ that are allowed to be generated by a transducer whose AG GE-realization value of ψ is at least v. By definition, AG GE-realization of ψ with value v coincides with realization of the language $L_v = \{w \in (2^{I \cup O})^\omega : \text{comb}([w, \exists O.\psi], [w, \psi]) \geq v\}$. By the monotonicity assumption on comb, for every $\langle v_1, v_2 \rangle \in G_v$, we have that $\langle v_1', v_2' \rangle \in G$ for every $v_1' \leq v_1$ and $v_2' \geq v_2$. Hence, we can write $L_v = \bigcup_{\langle v_1, v_2 \rangle \in G_v} \{w \in (2^{I \cup O})^\omega : [w, \exists O.\psi] \leq v_1 \text{ and } [w, \psi] \geq v_2\}$, and proceed to construct an NBW for L_v by taking the union of NBWs $\mathcal{A}_{v_1, v_2}$ for all $\langle v_1, v_2 \rangle \in G_v$, each of which is the product of NBWs $\mathcal{A}_{\exists O.\psi}^{\leq v_1}$ and $\mathcal{A}_{\psi}^{\geq v_2}$, as in the proof of Theorem 5.

Aiming to proceed Safralessly, we can also construct a UCW for L_v, as follows. First, note that by the monotonicity of comb, for every $\langle v_1, v_2 \rangle \in V(\psi) \times V(\psi)$ we have that $\langle v_1, v_2 \rangle \in G_v$ iff for every $\langle u_1, u_2 \rangle \in V(\psi) \times V(\psi) \setminus G_v$, we have that $v_1 < u_1$ or $v_2 > u_2$. Hence, $L_v = \bigcap_{\langle u_1, u_2 \rangle \in V(\psi) \times V(\psi) \setminus G_v} \{w \in (2^{I \cup O})^\omega : [w, \exists O.\psi] < u_1 \text{ or } [w, \psi] > u_2\}$, and so by dualization we have $(2^{I \cup O})^\omega \setminus L_v = \bigcup_{\langle u_1, u_2 \rangle \in V(\psi) \times V(\psi) \setminus G_v} \{w \in (2^{I \cup O})^\omega : [w, \exists O.\psi] \geq u_1 \text{ and } [w, \psi] \leq u_2\}$. Hence, we can obtain a UCW for L_v by dualizing an NBW that is the union of NBWs $\mathcal{A}_{u_1, u_2}$, for all $\langle u_1, u_2 \rangle \in V(\psi) \times V(\psi) \setminus G_v$, each of which is the product of NBWs $\mathcal{A}_{\exists O.\psi}^{\geq u_1}$ and $\mathcal{A}_{\psi}^{\leq u_2}$.

Observe that in all cases, the size of the NBW is $2^{O(|\psi|)}$. Indeed, there are at most $2^{2|\psi|}$ pairs in the union, and, by Theorem 4, the size of the NBW for each pair is $2^{O(|\psi|)}$.

The lower bound follows from the 2EXPTIME-hardness of LTL GE-realizability.   □

By Theorem 4, the number of possible satisfaction values for ψ is at most $2^{|\psi|}$. Thus, the number of possible values for $\mathsf{comb}(A, G)$, where A and G are satisfaction values of ψ, is at most $2^{2|\psi|}$. Using binary search over the image of comb, we can use Theorem 7 to obtain the following.

Corollary 1. *The AG GE-synthesis problem can be solved in doubly-exponential time.*

Remark 5 [**GE-synthesis as a special case of AG GE-synthesis**]. The two approaches taken in Sect. 5.2 can be captured by an appropriate comb function. Indeed, for GE-synthesis with a threshold, we can use the function comb with $\mathsf{comb}(A, G) = 1$ if $A \geq v \to G \geq v$, and $\mathsf{comb}(A, G) = 0$ otherwise. For GE-synthesis (without a threshold), we can use the function comb with $\mathsf{comb}(A, G) = 1$ if $A = G$, and $\mathsf{comb}(A, G) = 0$ otherwise (recall that $A \geq G$ by definition). However, the solution described in Sect. 5.2 is simpler than the one described here for the general case. $\qquad\qquad\square$

5.4   LTL[$\mathcal{F}$] GE-Synthesis in Stochastic Environments

The setting of LTL[$\mathcal{F}$] GE-synthesis studied in Sects. 5.2 and 5.3 takes the different satisfaction values into an account, but is binary, in the sense that a specification is either (possibly AG) GE-realizable, or is not. In particular, in case the specification is not GE-realizable, synthesis algorithms only return "no". In this section we add a quantitative measure also to the underlying realizability question. We do so by assuming a stochastic environment, with a known distribution on the inputs sequences, and analyzing the expected performance of the system.

For completeness, we remind the reader of some basics of probability theory. For a comprehensive reference see e.g., [25]. Let Σ be a finite alphabet, and let ν be some *probability distribution* over Σ^ω. For example, in the uniform distribution over $(2^I)^\omega$, the probability space is induced by sampling each letter with probability $2^{-|I|}$, corresponding to settings in which each signal in I always holds in probability $\frac{1}{2}$. We assume ν is given by a finite Markov Decision Process (MDP). That is, ν is induced by the distribution of each letter $i \in 2^I$ at each time step, determined by a finite stochastic control process that takes into account also the outputs generated by the system (see [2] for the precise model). A *random variable* is then a function $X : \Sigma^\omega \to \mathbb{R}$. When X has a finite image V, which is the case in our setting, its *expected value* is $\mathbb{E}[X] = \sum_{v \in V} v \cdot \Pr(X^{-1}(v))$. Intuitively, $\mathbb{E}[X]$ is the "average" value that X attains. Next, consider an *event* $E \subseteq \Sigma^\omega$. The *conditional expectation of* X *with respect to* E is $\mathbb{E}[X|E] = \frac{\mathbb{E}[\mathbb{1}_E X]}{\Pr(E)}$, where $\mathbb{1}_E X$ is the random variable that assigns $X(w)$ to $w \in E$ and 0 to $w \notin E$. Intuitively, $\mathbb{E}[X|E]$ is the average value that X attains when restricting to words in E, and normalizing according to the probability of E itself.

We continue and review the *high-quality synthesis problem* [2], where the GE variant is not considered. There, the environment is assumed to be stochastic and we care for the expected satisfaction value of an LTL[$\mathcal{F}$] specification in the computations of a transducer $\mathcal{T}$, assuming some given distribution on the inputs sequences. Formally, let $X_{\mathcal{T},\psi} : (2^I)^\omega \to \mathbb{R}$ be a random variable that assigns each sequence $x \in (2^I)^\omega$ of input signals with $[\![\mathcal{T}(x), \psi]\!]$. Then, when the sequences in $(2^I)^\omega$ are sampled according to a given distribution ν of $(2^I)^\omega$, we define $[\![\mathcal{T}, \psi]\!]^\nu = \mathbb{E}[X_{\mathcal{T},\psi}]$. Since ν is fixed, we omit it from the notation and use $[\![\mathcal{T}, \psi]\!]$ in the following.

Remark 6 [**Relating LTL GE-synthesis with stochastic LTL[$\mathcal{F}$] synthesis**] Given an LTL formula ψ, we can view it as an LTL[$\mathcal{F}$] formula with possible satisfaction values $\{0, 1\}$, apply to it high-quality synthesis *a-la* [2], and find a transducer $\mathcal{T}$ that maximizes $\mathbb{E}[X_{\mathcal{T},\psi}]$. An interesting observation is that if $\mathcal{T}$ GE-realizes ψ, then it also maximizes $\mathbb{E}[X_{\mathcal{T},\psi}]$. Indeed, all input sequences that can contribute to the expected satisfaction value, do so.   □

We introduce and study two measures for high-quality synthesis in a stochastic environment. In the first, termed *expected GE-synthesis*, all input sequences are sampled, yet the satisfaction value in each input sequence takes its hopefulness level into account. In the second, termed *conditional expected GE-synthesis*, only hopeful input sequences are sampled.

We start with expected GE-synthesis. There, instead of associating each sequence $x \in (2^I)^\omega$ with $[\![x \otimes \mathcal{T}(x), \psi]\!]$, we associate it with $X^{\mathrm{comb}}_{\mathcal{T},\psi} = \mathrm{comb}([\![x, \exists O.\psi]\!], [\![x \otimes \mathcal{T}(x), \psi]\!]\}$, where comb is as described in Sect. 5.3, thus capturing the assume-guarantee semantics of quantitative GE-synthesis. Then, we define $[\![\mathcal{T}, \psi]\!]^{\mathrm{comb}} = \mathbb{E}[X^{\mathrm{comb}}_{\mathcal{T},\psi}]$. For example, taking comb as implication, we have $X^{\mathrm{comb}}_{\mathcal{T},\psi} = \max\{[\![x \otimes \mathcal{T}(x), \psi]\!], [\![x, \forall O.\neg\psi]\!]\}$, capturing the semantics of $(\exists O.\psi) \to \psi$.

Then, in conditional expected GE-synthesis, we consider $\exists O.\psi$ as an environment assumption, and factor it in using conditional expectation, parameterized by a threshold $v \in [0, 1]$. Formally, let $\exists O.\psi \geq v$ denote the event $\{x \in (2^I)^\omega : [\![x, \exists O.\psi]\!] \geq v\}$. Then, we define $[\![\mathcal{T}, \psi]\!]^{\mathrm{cond}(v)} = \mathbb{E}[X_{\mathcal{T},\psi} | \exists O.\psi \geq v]$, assuming the event $\exists O.\psi \geq v$ has a strictly positive probability.

In [2], it is shown that the high-quality synthesis problem can be solved in doubly-exponential time, also in the presence of environment assumptions. In the solution, the first step is the translation of the involved formulas to DPWs. In order to extract from [2] the results relevant to us, we describe them by means of *discrete quantitative specifications*, defined as follows. A discrete quantitative specification Ψ over $I \cup O$ is given by means of a sequence $\mathcal{A}_1, \ldots, \mathcal{A}_n$ of DPWs, with $(2^{I \cup O})^\omega = L(\mathcal{A}_1) \supseteq L(\mathcal{A}_2) \supseteq \ldots \supseteq L(\mathcal{A}_n)$, and sequence $0 \leq v_1 < \ldots < v_n \leq 1$ of values. For every $w \in (2^{I \cup O})^\omega$, the satisfaction value of w in Ψ, denoted $[\![w, \Psi]\!]$, is $\max\{v_i : w \in L(\mathcal{A}_i)\}$. We refer to n as the depth of Ψ.

Theorem 8 ([2]). *Consider a discrete quantitative specification Ψ over $I \cup O$. Let n be its depth and m be the size of the largest DPW in Ψ. For a transducer $\mathcal{T}$, let $X_{\mathcal{T}}$ be a random variable that assigns a word $x \in (2^I)^\omega$ with $[\![x \otimes \mathcal{T}(x), \Psi]\!]$.*

1. *We can synthesize a transducer $\mathcal{T}$ that maximizes $\mathbb{E}[X_{\mathcal{T}}]$ in time m^n.*

2. *Given a DPW $\mathcal{B}$ over 2^I such that $\Pr(L(\mathcal{B})) > 0$, we can synthesize a transducer $\mathcal{T}$ that maximizes $\mathbb{E}[X_\mathcal{T}|\mathcal{B}]$ in time $m^n \cdot k$, where k is the size of $\mathcal{B}$.*

We can now state the main results of this section.

Theorem 9. *Consider an* LTL[$\mathcal{F}$] *formula ψ.*

1. *Given a function* comb, *we can find in doubly-exponential time a transducer that maximizes $[\![\mathcal{T}, \psi]\!]^{\text{comb}}$.*
2. *Given a threshold $v \in [0, 1]$, we can find in doubly-exponential time a transducer that maximizes $[\![\mathcal{T}, \psi]\!]^{\text{cond}(v)}$.*

Proof. Let $v_1 < v_2 < \ldots < v_n$ be the possible satisfaction values of ψ (and hence also of $\exists O.\psi$ and of $\forall O.\psi$). By Theorem 4, we have that $n \leq 2^{|\psi|}$. For each v_i, we can construct a DPW $\mathcal{D}^{\geq v_i}_{\text{comb}(\exists O.\psi,\psi)}$ as in Theorem 7. It is not hard to see that the discrete quantitative specification given by the DPWs $\mathcal{D}^{\geq v_i}_{\text{comb}(\exists O.\psi,\psi)}$ and the values v_i, for $1 \leq i \leq n$, is qual to the specification $\text{comb}(\exists O.\psi, \psi)$. Thus, by Theorem 8 (1), we can find a transducer that maximizes $\mathbb{E}[X_\mathcal{T}]$ in time $(2^{2^{O(|\psi|)}})^{2^{|\psi|}} = 2^{2^{O(|\psi|)}}$.

Next, given $v \in [0, 1]$, we can check whether $\Pr(\exists O.\psi > v) > 0$, for example by converting a DPW $\mathcal{D}^{\geq v}_{\exists O.\psi}$ to an MDP, and reasoning about its Ergodic-components. Then, by Theorem 8 (2), we can find a transducer that maximizes $\mathbb{E}[X_\mathcal{T}|\exists O\psi > v]$, in time $(2^{2^{O(|\psi|)}})^{2^{|\psi|}} \cdot 2^{2^{O(\psi)}} = 2^{2^{O(|\psi|)}}$. □

Corollary 2. *The (possibly conditional) expected* GE-*synthesis problem for* LTL[$\mathcal{F}$] *can be solved in doubly-exponential time.*

5.5   Guarantees in High-Quality GE-Synthesis

As in the Boolean setting, also in the high-quality one we would like to add to a GE-realizing transducer guarantees and indications about the satisfaction level. As we detail below, the quantitative setting offers many possible ways to do so.

High-Quality GE-Synthesis with Guarantees. We consider specifications of the form $\psi = \psi_{strong} \wedge \psi_{weak}$, where essentially, we seek a transducer that realizes ψ_{strong} and (possibly AG) GE-realizes ψ_{weak}. Maximizing the realization value of ψ_{strong} may conflict with maximizing the GE-realization value of ψ_{weak}, and there are different ways to trade-off the two goals. Technically, in the decision-problem variant, we are given two thresholds $v_1, v_2 \in [0, 1]$, and we seek a transducer $\mathcal{T}$ that realizes ψ_{strong} with value at least v_1, and GE-realizes ψ_{weak} with value at least v_2. Then, one may start, for example, by maximizing the value v_1, and then find the maximal value v_2 that may be achieved simultaneously. Alternatively, one may prefer to maximize v_2, or some other combination of v_1 and v_2. Also, it is possible to decompose ψ further, to several strong and weak components, each with its desired threshold.

The solutions in the different settings all involve a construction of a UCW $\mathcal{A}^{\geq v_1}_{\psi_{strong}}$, and its product with the automata constructed in the solutions for the different GE-synthesis variants. We thus have the following. We note that when the solution for ψ_{weak} is Safraless, we can use a UCW for ψ_{strong} to maintain a Safraless construction.

Theorem 10. *The problem of* LTL[$\mathcal{F}$] *high-quality* GE-*synthesis with a guarantee can be solved in doubly-exponential time.*

Flags by a High-Quality GE-Realizing Transducer. In the quantitative setting, we parameterized the flags raised by the GE-realizing transducer by values in $[0, 1]$, indicating the announced satisfaction level. Thus, rather than talking about prefixes being green, red, or blue, we talk about them being v-green, v-red, and v-blue, for $v \in [0, 1]$, which essentially means that a satisfaction value of at least v is guarantees (in green and blue flags) or is impossible (in red ones). We can think of those as "degrees" of green, red, and blue. Below, we formalize this intuition and argue that even an augmentation of a transducer that GE-realizes ψ by flags for all values in $V(\psi)$ leaves the problem in doubly-exponential time.

A *quantitative language* over $2^{I \cup O}$ is $L : (2^{I \cup O})^\omega \to [0, 1]$. For a quantitative language L and a word $w \in (2^{I \cup O})^*$, we define L^w as the quantitative language where for all $w' \in (2^{I \cup O})^\omega$, we have $L^w(w') = L(w \cdot w')$. For a value $v \in [0, 1]$, a word $w \in (2^{I \cup O})^*$ is v-*green for* L if L^w is v-realizable. That is, there is a transducer $\mathcal{T}$ such that $[\![T, L^w]\!] \geq v$. A word $x \in (2^I)^*$ is v-*green for* L if there is $y \in (2^O)^*$ such that $x \otimes y$ is v-green for L. Thus, when the environment generates x, the system can respond in a way that would guarantee v-realizability. Finally, we say that L is *green realizable* if there is a strategy $f : (2^I)^+ \to 2^O$ that for every threshold v and for every input $x \in (2^I)^+$ that is v-green for L, we have that $x \otimes f(x)$ is v-green for L. It is not hard to see that Theorem 3 carries over to the quantitative setting, thus quantitative optimal realizability is strictly stronger than quantitative green realizability. In particular, if a transducer $\mathcal{T}$ optimally realizes an LTL[$\mathcal{F}$] formula ψ, then $\mathcal{T}$ also green realizes ψ. In the full version, we describe quantitative definitions also for red and blue prefixes, and describe monitors for the detection of the various types of prefixes.

6   Discussion

We introduced and solved several variants of GE-synthesis. Our complexity results are tight and show that GE-synthesis is not more complex than traditional synthesis. In practice, however, traditional synthesis algorithms do not scale well, and much research is devoted for the development of methods and heuristics for coping with the implementation challenges of synthesis. A natural future research direction is to extend these heuristics and methods for GE-synthesis. We mention here two specific examples.

Efficient synthesis algorithms have been developed for fragments of LTL [21]. Most notable is the *GR(1) fragment* [18], which supports assume-guarantee reasoning, and for which synthesis has an efficient symbolic solution. Adding existential quantification to GR(1) specifications, which is how we handled LTL

GE-synthesis, is not handled by its known algorithms, and is an interesting challenge. The success of SAT-based model-checking have led to the development of SAT-based synthesis algorithms [6], where the synthesis problem is reduced to satisfiability of a QBF formula. The fact the setting already includes quantifiers suggests it can be extended to GE-synthesis. A related effort is *bounded synthesis* algorithms [13,24], where the synthesized systems are assumed to be of a bounded size and can be represented symbolically [10].

References

1. Almagor, S., Boker, U., Kupferman, O.: Formalizing and reasoning about quality. J. ACM **63**(3), 24:1–24:56 (2016)
2. Almagor, S., Kupferman, O.: High-quality synthesis against stochastic environments. In: Proceedings of 25th Annual Conference of the European Association for Computer Science Logic, LIPIcs, vol. 62, pp. 28:1–28:17 (2016)
3. Almagor, S., Kupferman, O., Ringert, J.O., Velner, Y.: Quantitative assume guarantee synthesis. In: Majumdar, R., Kunčak, V. (eds.) CAV 2017. LNCS, vol. 10427, pp. 353–374. Springer, Cham (2017). https://doi.org/10.1007/978-3-319-63390-9_19
4. Bloem, R., Chatterjee, K., Henzinger, T.A., Jobstmann, B.: Better quality in synthesis through quantitative objectives. In: Bouajjani, A., Maler, O. (eds.) CAV 2009. LNCS, vol. 5643, pp. 140–156. Springer, Heidelberg (2009). https://doi.org/10.1007/978-3-642-02658-4_14
5. Bloem, R., Chatterjee, K., Jobstmann, B.: Graph games and reactive synthesis. Handbook of Model Checking, pp. 921–962. Springer, Cham (2018). https://doi.org/10.1007/978-3-319-10575-8_27
6. Bloem, R., Egly, U., Klampfl, P., Könighofer, R., Lonsing, F.: Sat-based methods for circuit synthesis. In: Proceedings of 14th International Conference on Formal Methods in Computer-Aided Design, pp. 31–34. IEEE (2014)
7. Borodin, A., El-Yaniv, R.: Online Computation and Competitive Analysis. Cambridge University Press, New York (1998)
8. Chatterjee, K., Henzinger, T.A., Jobstmann, B.: Environment assumptions for synthesis. In: van Breugel, F., Chechik, M. (eds.) CONCUR 2008. LNCS, vol. 5201, pp. 147–161. Springer, Heidelberg (2008). https://doi.org/10.1007/978-3-540-85361-9_14
9. Church, A.: Logic, arithmetics, and automata. In: Proceedings of International Congress of Mathematicians, vol. 1962, pp. 23–35. Institut Mittag-Leffler (1963)
10. Ehlers, R.: Symbolic bounded synthesis. In: Touili, T., Cook, B., Jackson, P. (eds.) CAV 2010. LNCS, vol. 6174, pp. 365–379. Springer, Heidelberg (2010). https://doi.org/10.1007/978-3-642-14295-6_33
11. Fisman, D., Kupferman, O., Lustig, Y.: Rational synthesis. In: Esparza, J., Majumdar, R. (eds.) TACAS 2010. LNCS, vol. 6015, pp. 190–204. Springer, Heidelberg (2010). https://doi.org/10.1007/978-3-642-12002-2_16
12. Kupferman, O.: Automata theory and model checking. In: Clarke, E., Henzinger, T., Veith, H., Bloem, R. (eds.) Handbook of Model Checking, pp. 107–151. Springer, Cham (2018). https://doi.org/10.1007/978-3-319-10575-8_4
13. Kupferman, O., Lustig, Y., Vardi, M.Y., Yannakakis, M.: Temporal synthesis for bounded systems and environments. In: Proceedings of 28th Symposium on Theoretical Aspects of Computer Science, pp. 615–626 (2011)

14. Kupferman, O., Perelli, G., Vardi, M.Y.: Synthesis with rational environments. Ann. Math. Artif. Intell. **78**(1), 3–20 (2016). https://doi.org/10.1007/s10472-016-9508-8

15. Kupferman, O., Piterman, N., Vardi, M.Y.: Safraless compositional synthesis. In: Ball, T., Jones, R.B. (eds.) CAV 2006. LNCS, vol. 4144, pp. 31–44. Springer, Heidelberg (2006). https://doi.org/10.1007/11817963_6

16. Kupferman, O., Vardi, M.Y.: Model checking of safety properties. Formal Methods Syst. Des. **19**(3), 291–314 (2001). https://doi.org/10.1023/A:1011254632723

17. Kupferman, O., Vardi, M.Y.: Safraless decision procedures. In: Proceedings of 46th IEEE Symposium on Foundations of Computer Science, pp. 531–540 (2005)

18. Piterman, N., Pnueli, A., Sa'ar, Y.: Synthesis of reactive(1) designs. In: Emerson, E.A., Namjoshi, K.S. (eds.) VMCAI 2006. LNCS, vol. 3855, pp. 364–380. Springer, Heidelberg (2005). https://doi.org/10.1007/11609773_24

19. Pnueli, A.: The temporal semantics of concurrent programs. Theor. Comput. Sci. **13**, 45–60 (1981)

20. Pnueli, A., Rosner, R.: On the synthesis of a reactive module. In: Proceedings of 16th ACM Symposium on Principles of Programming Languages, pp. 179–190 (1989)

21. Alur, R., La Torre, S., Madhusudan, P.: Playing games with boxes and diamonds. In: Amadio, R., Lugiez, D. (eds.) CONCUR 2003. LNCS, vol. 2761, pp. 128–143. Springer, Heidelberg (2003). https://doi.org/10.1007/978-3-540-45187-7_8

22. Rosner, R.: Modular synthesis of reactive systems. Ph.D thesis, Weizmann Institute of Science (1992)

23. Safra, S.: On the complexity of ω-automata. In: Proceedings of 29th IEEE Symposium on Foundations of Computer Science, pp. 319–327 (1988)

24. Schewe, S., Finkbeiner, B.: Bounded synthesis. In: Namjoshi, K.S., Yoneda, T., Higashino, T., Okamura, Y. (eds.) ATVA 2007. LNCS, vol. 4762, pp. 474–488. Springer, Heidelberg (2007). https://doi.org/10.1007/978-3-540-75596-8_33

25. Sheldon, R.: A First Course in Probability. Pearson Education India, Delhi (2002)

26. Sistla, A.P., Vardi, M.Y., Wolper, P.: The complementation problem for Büchi automata with applications to temporal logic. Theor. Comput. Sci. **49**, 217–237 (1987)

27. Vardi, M.Y., Wolper, P.: Reasoning about infinite computations. Inf. Comput. **115**(1), 1–37 (1994)

28. Winnicott, D.W.: Playing and Reality. Penguin, Harmondsworth (1971)

29. Wolper, P.: Temporal logic can be more expressive. In: Proceedings of 22nd IEEE Symposium on Foundations of Computer Science, pp. 340–348 (1981)

Synthesizing JIT Compilers
for In-Kernel DSLs

Jacob Van Geffen[1(✉)], Luke Nelson[1], Isil Dillig[2], Xi Wang[1],
and Emina Torlak[1]

[1] University of Washington, Seattle, USA
jsvg@cs.washington.edu
[2] University of Texas at Austin, Austin, USA

Abstract. Modern operating systems allow user-space applications to
submit code for kernel execution through the use of in-kernel domain specific languages (DSLs). Applications use these DSLs to customize system
policies and add new functionality. For performance, the kernel executes
them via just-in-time (JIT) compilation. The correctness of these JITs
is crucial for the security of the kernel: bugs in in-kernel JITs have led
to numerous critical issues and patches.

This paper presents JitSynth, the first tool for synthesizing verified JITs for in-kernel DSLs. JitSynth takes as input interpreters for
the source DSL and the target instruction set architecture. Given these
interpreters, and a mapping from source to target states, JitSynth synthesizes a verified JIT compiler from the source to the target. Our key
idea is to formulate this synthesis problem as one of synthesizing a per-
instruction compiler for *abstract register machines*. Our core technical
contribution is a new *compiler metasketch* that enables JitSynth to
efficiently explore the resulting synthesis search space. To evaluate Jit-
Synth, we use it to synthesize a JIT from eBPF to RISC-V and compare
to a recently developed Linux JIT. The synthesized JIT avoids all known
bugs in the Linux JIT, with an average slowdown of 1.82× in the performance of the generated code. We also use JitSynth to synthesize JITs
for two additional source-target pairs. The results show that JitSynth
offers a promising new way to develop verified JITs for in-kernel DSLs.

Keywords: Synthesis · Just-in-time compilation · Symbolic execution

1 Introduction

Modern operating systems (OSes) can be customized with user-specified programs that implement functionality like system call whitelisting, performance
profiling, and power management [11,12,24]. For portability and safety, these
programs are written in restricted domain-specific languages (DSLs), and the
kernel executes them via interpretation and, for better performance, just-in-time
(JIT) compilation. The correctness of in-kernel interpreters and JITs is crucial
for the reliability and security of the kernel, and bugs in their implementations

ⓒ The Author(s) 2020
S. K. Lahiri and C. Wang (Eds.): CAV 2020, LNCS 12225, pp. 564–586, 2020.
https://doi.org/10.1007/978-3-030-53291-8_29

have led to numerous critical issues and patches [15,30]. More broadly, embedded DSLs are also used to customize—and compromise [6,18]—other low-level software, such as font rendering and anti-virus engines [8]. Providing formal guarantees of correctness for in-kernel DSLs is thus a pressing practical and research problem with applications to a wide range of systems software.

Prior work has tackled this problem through interactive theorem proving. For example, the Jitk framework [40] uses the Coq interactive theorem prover [38] to implement and verify the correctness of a JIT compiler for the classic Berkeley Packet Filter (BPF) language [24] in the Linux kernel. But such an approach presents two key challenges. First, Jitk imposes a significant burden on DSL developers, requiring them to implement both the interpreter and the JIT compiler in Coq, and then manually prove the correctness of the JIT compiler with respect to the interpreter. Second, the resulting JIT implementation is extracted from Coq into OCaml and cannot be run in the kernel; rather, it must be run in user space, sacrificing performance and enlarging the trusted computing base (TCB) by relying on the OCaml runtime as part of the TCB.

This paper addresses these challenges with JITSYNTH, the first tool for synthesizing verified JIT compilers for in-kernel DSLs. JITSYNTH takes as input interpreters for the source DSL and the target instruction set architecture (ISA), and it synthesizes a JIT compiler that is guaranteed to transform each source program into a semantically equivalent target program. Using JITSYNTH, DSL developers write no proofs or compilers. Instead, they write the semantics of the source and target languages in the form of interpreters and a mapping from source to target states, which JITSYNTH trusts to be correct. The synthesized JIT compiler is implemented in C; thus, it can run directly in the kernel.

At first glance, synthesizing a JIT compiler seems intractable. Even the simplest compiler contains thousands of instructions, whereas existing synthesis techniques scale to tens of instructions. To tackle this problem in our setting, we observe that in-kernel DSLs are similar to ISAs: both take the form of bytecode instructions for an *abstract register machine*, a simple virtual machine with a program counter, a few registers, and limited memory store [40]. We also observe that in practice, the target machine has at least as many resources (registers and memory) as the source machine; and that JIT compilers for such abstract register machines perform register allocation statically at compile time. Our main insight is that we can exploit these properties to make synthesis tractable through *decomposition* and *prioritization*, while preserving soundness and completeness.

JITSYNTH works by decomposing the JIT synthesis problem into the problem of synthesizing individual *mini compilers* for every instruction in the source language. Each mini compiler is synthesized by generating a *compiler metasketch* [7], a set of ordered sketches that collectively represent *all* instruction sequences in the target ISA. These sketches are then solved by an off-the-shelf synthesis tool based on reduction to SMT [39]. The synthesis tool ensures that the target instruction sequence is semantically equivalent to the source instruction, according to the input interpreters. The order in which the sketches are explored is key to making this search practical, and JITSYNTH contributes two techniques for biasing the search towards tightly constrained, and therefore tractable, sketches that are likely to contain a correct program.

First, we observe that source instructions can often be implemented with target instructions that access the same parts of the state (e.g., only registers). Based on this observation, we develop *read-write sketches*, which restrict the synthesis search space to a subset of the target instructions, based on a sound and precise summary of their semantics. Second, we observe that hand-written JITs rely on pseudoinstructions to generate common target sequences, such as loading immediate (constant) values into registers. We use this observation to develop *pre-load sketches*, which employ synthesized pseudoinstructions to eliminate the need to repeatedly search for common target instruction subsequences.

We have implemented JITSYNTH in Rosette [39] and used it to synthesize JIT compilers for three widely used in-kernel DSLs. As our main case study, we used JITSYNTH to synthesize a RISC-V [32] compiler for extended BPF (eBPF) [12], an extension of classic BPF [24], used by the Linux kernel. Concurrently with our work, Linux developers manually built a JIT compiler for the same source and target pair, and a team of researchers found nine correctness bugs in that compiler shortly after its release [28]. In contrast, our JIT compiler is verified by construction; it supports 87 out of 102 eBPF instructions and passes all the Linux kernel tests within this subset, including the regression tests for these nine bugs. Our synthesized compiler generates code that is 5.24× faster than interpreted code and 1.82× times slower than the code generated by the Linux JIT. We also used JITSYNTH to synthesize a JIT from libseccomp [10], a policy language for system call whitelisting, to eBPF, and a JIT from classic BPF to eBPF. The synthesized JITs avoid previously found bugs in the existing generators for these source target pairs, while incurring, on average, a 2.28–2.61× slowdown in the performance of the generated code.

To summarize, this paper makes the following contributions:

1. JITSYNTH, the first tool for synthesizing verified JIT compilers for in-kernel DSLs, given the semantics of the source and target languages as interpreters.
2. A novel formulation of the JIT synthesis problem as one of synthesizing a per-instruction compiler for *abstract register machines*.
3. A novel *compiler metasketch* that enables JITSYNTH to solve the JIT synthesis problem with an off-the-shelf synthesis engine.
4. An evaluation of JITSYNTH's effectiveness, showing that it can synthesize verified JIT compilers for three widely used in-kernel DSLs.

The rest of this paper is organized as follows. Section 2 illustrates JITSYNTH on a small example. Section 3 formalizes the JIT synthesis problem for in-kernel DSLs. Section 4 presents the JITSYNTH algorithm for generating and solving compiler metasketches. Section 5 provides implementation details. Section 6 evaluates JITSYNTH. Section 7 discusses related work. Section 8 concludes.

2   Overview

This section provides an overview of JITSYNTH by illustrating how it synthesizes a toy JIT compiler (Fig. 1). The source language of the JIT is a tiny subset of

instruction	description	semantics
eBPF (subset):		
addi32 *dst, imm32*	32-bit add (high 32 bits cleared)	$R[dst] \leftarrow 0^{32} \oplus (\text{extract}(31,0,R[dst]) + imm32)$
RISC-V (subset):		
lui *rd, imm20*	load upper immediate	$R[rd] \leftarrow \text{sext}64(imm20 \oplus 0^{12})$
addiw *rd, rs, imm12*	32-bit register-immediate add	$R[rd] \leftarrow \text{sext}64(\text{extract}(31,0,R[rs]) + \text{sext}32(imm12))$
add *rd, rs1, rs2*	register-register add	$R[rd] \leftarrow R[rs1] + R[rs2]$
slli *rd, rs, imm6*	register-immediate left shift	$R[rd] \leftarrow rs << (0^{58} \oplus imm6)$
srli *rd, rs, imm6*	register-immediate logical right shift	$R[rd] \leftarrow rs >> (0^{58} \oplus imm6)$
lb *rd, rs, imm12*	load byte from memory	$R[rd] \leftarrow \text{sext}64(M[R[rs] + \text{sext}64(imm12)])$
sb *rs1, rs2, imm12*	store byte to memory	$M[R[rs1] + \text{sext}64(imm12)] \leftarrow \text{extract}(7,0,R[rs2])$

Fig. 1. Subsets of eBPF and RISC-V used as source and target languages, respectively, in our running example: $R[r]$ denotes the value of register r; $M[a]$ denotes the value at memory address a; $\oplus$ denotes concatenation of bitvectors; superscripts (e.g., 0^{32}) denote repetition of bits; $sext32(x)$ and $sext64(x)$ sign-extend x to 32 and 64 bits, respectively; and extract(i, j, x) produces a subrange of bits of x from index i down to j.

eBPF [12] consisting of one instruction, and the target language is a subset of 64-bit RISC-V [32] consisting of seven instructions. Despite the simplicity of our languages, the Linux kernel JIT used to produce incorrect code for this eBPF instruction [27]; such miscompilation bugs not only lead to correctness issues, but also enable adversaries to compromise the OS kernel by crafting malicious eBPF programs [40]. This section shows how JITSYNTH can be used to synthesize a JIT that is verified with respect to the semantics of the source and target languages.

In-Kernel Languages. JITSYNTH expects the source and target languages to be a set of instructions for manipulating the state of an *abstract register machine* (Sect. 3). This state consists of a program counter (*pc*), a finite sequence of general-purpose registers (*reg*), and a finite sequence of memory locations (*mem*), all of which store bitvectors (i.e., finite precision integers). The length of these bitvectors is defined by the language; for example, both eBPF and RISC-V store 64-bit values in their registers. An instruction consists of an *opcode* and a finite set of *fields*, which are bitvectors representing either register identifiers or immediate (constant) values. For instance, the addi32 instruction in eBPF has two fields: *dst* is a 4-bit value representing the index of the output register, and *imm32* is a 32-bit immediate. (eBPF instructions may have two additional fields *src* and *off*, which are not shown here as they are not used by addi32). An abstract register machine for a language gives meaning to its instructions: the machine consumes an instruction and a state, and produces a state that is the result of executing that instruction. Figure 1 shows a high-level description of the abstract register machines for our languages.

JITSYNTH *Interface.* To synthesize a compiler from one language to another, JITSYNTH takes as input their syntax, semantics, and a mapping from source to target states. All three inputs are given as a program in a *solver-aided host language* [39]. JITSYNTH uses Rosette as its host, but the host can be any language with a symbolic evaluation engine that can reduce the semantics of host programs to SMT constraints (e.g., [37]). Figure 2 shows the interpreters for the source and target languages (i.e., emulators for their abstract register machines), as well as the state-mapping functions regST, pcST, and memST that JITSYNTH uses to determine whether a source state σ_S is equivalent to a target state σ_T. In particular, JITSYNTH deems these states equivalent, denoted by $\sigma_S \cong \sigma_T$, whenever $reg(\sigma_T)[\text{regST}(r)] = reg(\sigma_S)[r]$, $pc(\sigma_T) = \text{pcST}(pc(\sigma_S))$, and $mem(\sigma_T)[\text{memST}(a)] = mem(\sigma_S)[a]$ for all registers r and memory addresses a.

```
(struct state (regs mem pc) #:transparent)    ; Abstract register machine state.
                                              ; Input 1/3: toy eBPF.
(struct ebpf-insn (opcode dst src off imm))   ;  - eBPF instruction format;
(define (ebpf-interpret insn st)              ;  - eBPF interpreter for addi32.
  (define-match (ebpf-insn op dst _ _ imm) insn) ;
    (case op                                  ; Note: addi32 does not use the src
      [(addi32)                               ; and off fields.
       (state
        (reg-set st dst (concat (bv 0 32) (bvadd (extract 31 0 (reg-ref st dst)) imm)))
        (state-mem st)
        (bvadd (state-pc st) (bv 1 64)))]))
                                              ; Input 2/3: toy RISC-V.
(struct rv-insn (opcode rd rs1 rs2 imm))      ;  - RISC-V instruction format;
(define (rv-interpret insn st)                ;  - RISC-V interpreter.
  (define-match (rv-insn op rd rs1 rs2 imm) insn)
    (case op
      [(lui)
       (state
        (reg-set st rd (sext64 (concat imm (bv 0 12))))
        (state-mem st)
        (bvadd (state-pc st) (bv 4 64)))] ...))
                                              ; Input 3/3: state mapping functions.
(define (regST r)                             ;  - Register mapping:
  (cond [(equal? r (bv 0 4)) (bv 15 5)] ...)) ;    - eBPF r0 -> RISC-V x15, ...;
(define (memST a) a)                          ;  - Memory mapping is the identity.
(define (pcST pc) (bvshl pc (bv 2 64)))       ;  - PC mapping.
```

Fig. 2. Snippets of inputs to JITSYNTH: the interpreters for the source (eBPF) and and target (RISC-V) languages and state-mapping functions.

Decomposition into Per-instruction Compilers. Given these inputs, JITSYNTH generates a *per-instruction compiler* from the source to the target language. To ensure that the resulting compiler is correct (Theorem 1), and that one will be found if it exists (Theorem 2), JITSYNTH puts two restrictions on its inputs. First, the inputs must be self-finitizing [39], meaning that both the interpreters and the mapping functions must have a finite symbolic execution tree when applied to symbolic inputs. Second, the target machine must have at least as many registers and memory locations as the source machine; these storage cells must be as wide as those of the source machine; and the state-mapping functions (pcST, regST, and memST) must be injective. Our toy inputs satisfy these restrictions, as do the real in-kernel languages evaluated in Sect. 6.

Synthesis Workflow. JITSYNTH generates a per-instruction compiler for a given source and target pair in two stages. The first stage uses an optimized *compiler metasketch* to synthesize a mini compiler from every instruction in the source language to a sequence of instructions in the target language (Sect. 4).

The second stage then simply stitches these mini compilers into a full C compiler using a trusted outer loop and a switch statement. The first stage is a core technical contribution of this paper, and we illustrate it next on our toy example.

Metasketches. To understand how JITSYNTH works, consider the basic problem of determining if every addi32 instruction can be emulated by a sequence of k instructions in toy RISC-V. In particular, we are interested in finding a program $C_{\mathtt{addi32}}$ in our host language (which JITSYNTH translates to C) that takes as input a source instruction $s = \mathtt{addi32}\ dst, imm32$ and outputs a semantically equivalent RISC-V program $t = [t_1, \ldots, t_k]$. That is, for all $dst, imm32$, and for all equivalent states $\sigma_S \cong \sigma_T$, we have $run(s, \sigma_S, \mathtt{ebpf\text{-}interpret}) \cong run(t, \sigma_T, \mathtt{rv\text{-}interpret})$, where $run(e, \sigma, f)$ executes the instruction interpreter f on the sequence of instructions e, starting from the state σ (Definition 3).

We can solve this problem by asking the host synthesizer to search for $C_{\mathtt{addi32}}$ in a space of candidate mini compilers of length k. We describe this space with a syntactic template, or a *sketch*, as shown below:

```
(define (compile-addi32 s)       ; Returns a list of k instruction holes, to be
  (define dst (ebpf-insn-dst s)) ; filled with toy RISC-V instructions. Each
  (define imm (ebpf-insn-imm s)) ; hole represents a set of choices, defined
  (list (??insn dst imm) ...))   ; by the ??insn procedure.
(define (??insn . sf)            ; Takes as input source instruction fields and
  (define rd  (??reg sf))        ; uses them to construct target field holes.
  (define rs1 (??reg sf))        ; ??reg and ??imm field holes are bitvector
  (define rs2 (??reg sf))        ; expressions over sf and arbitrary constants.
  (choose*                       ; Returns an expression that chooses among
    (rv-insn lui rd rs1 rs2 (??imm 20 sf))  ; lui, addiw,
    ...                          ; ..., and
    (rv-insn sb  rd rs1 rs2 (??imm 12 sf)))); sb instructions.
```

Here, (??insn dst imm) stands for a missing expression—a hole—that the synthesizer needs to fill with an instruction from the toy RISC-V language. To fill an instruction hole, the synthesizer must find an expression that computes the value of the target instruction's fields. JITSYNTH limits this expression language to bitvector expressions (of any depth) over the fields of the source instruction and arbitrary bitvector constants.

Given this sketch, and our correctness specification for $C_{\mathtt{addi32}}$, the synthesizer will search the space defined by the sketch for a program that satisfies the specification. Below is an example of the resulting toy compiler from eBPF to RISC-V, synthesized and translated to C by JITSYNTH (without the outer loop):

```
void compile(struct bpf_insn *insn, struct rv_insn *tgt_prog) {
  switch (insn->op) {
  case BPF_ADDI32:
    tgt_prog[0] = /* lui   x6, extract(19, 0, (imm + 0x800) >> 12) */
      rv_lui(6, extract(19, 0, (insn->imm + 0x800) >> 12));
    tgt_prog[1] = /* addiw x6, x6, extract(11, 0, imm) */
      rv_addiw(6, 6, extract(11, 0, insn->imm));
    tgt_prog[2] = /* add   rd, rd, x6 */
      rv_add(regmap(insn->dst), regmap(insn->dst), 6);
    tgt_prog[3] = /* slli  rd, rd, 32 */
      rv_slli(regmap(insn->dst), regmap(insn->dst), 32);
    tgt_prog[4] = /* srli  rd, rd, 32 */
      rv_srli(regmap(insn->dst), regmap(insn->dst), 32);
    break;
  }
}
```

Once we know how to synthesize a compiler of length k, we can easily extend this solution into a naive method for synthesizing a compiler of any length.

We simply enumerate sketches of increasing lengths, $k = 1, 2, 3, \ldots$, invoke the synthesizer on each generated sketch, and stop as soon as a solution is found (if ever). The resulting ordered set of sketches forms a metasketch [7]—i.e., a search space and a strategy for exploring it—that contains all candidate mini compilers (in a subset of the host language) from the source to the target language. This naive metasketch can be used to find a mini compiler for our toy example in 493 min. However, it fails to scale to real in-kernel DSLs (Sect. 6), motivating the need for JITSYNTH's optimized compiler metasketches.

Compiler Metasketches. JITSYNTH optimizes the naive metasketch by extending it with two kinds of more tightly constrained sketches, which are explored first. A constrained sketch of size k usually contains a correct solution of a given size if one exists, but if not, JITSYNTH will eventually explore the naive sketch of the same length, to maintain completeness. We give the intuition behind the two optimizations here, and present them in detail in Sect. 4.

First, we observe that practical source and target languages include similar kinds of instructions. For example, both eBPF and RISC-V include instructions for adding immediate values to registers. This similarity often makes it possible to emulate a source instruction with a sequence of target instructions that access the same part of the state (the program counter, registers, or memory) as the source instruction. For example, addi32 reads and writes only registers, not memory, and it can be emulated with RISC-V instructions that also access only registers. To exploit this observation, we introduce *read-write sets*, which summarize, soundly and precisely, how an instruction accesses state. JITSYNTH uses these sets to define *read-write sketches* for a given source instruction, including only target instructions that access the state in the same way as the source instruction. For instance, a read-write sketch for addi32 excludes both lb and sb instructions because they read and write memory as well as registers.

Second, we observe that hand-written JITs use pseudoinstructions to simplify their implementation of mini compilers. These are simply subroutines or macros for generating target sequences that implement common functionality. For example, the Linux JIT from eBPF to RISC-V includes a pseudoinstruction for loading 32-bit immediates into registers. JITSYNTH mimics the way hand-written JITs use pseudoinstructions with the help of *pre-load sketches*. These sketches first use a synthesized pseudoinstruction to create a sequence of concrete target instructions that load source immediates into scratch registers; then, they include a compute sequence comprised of read-write instruction holes. Applying these optimizations to our toy example, JITSYNTH finds a mini compiler for addi32 in 5 s—a roughly 6000× speedup over the naive metasketch.

3   Problem Statement

This section formalizes the compiler synthesis problem for in-kernel DSLs. We focus on JIT compilers, which, for our purposes, means one-pass compilers [11]. To start, we define *abstract register machines* as a way to specify the syntax and semantics of in-kernel languages. Next, we formulate our compiler synthesis problem as one of synthesizing a set of sound *mini compilers* from a single source instruction to a sequence of target instructions. Finally, we show that these mini compilers compose into a sound JIT compiler, which translates every source program into a semantically equivalent target program.

Abstract Register Machines. An abstract register machine (ARM) provides a simple interface for specifying the syntax and semantics of an in-kernel language. The syntax is given as a set of abstract instructions, and the semantics is given as a transition function over instructions and machine states.

An *abstract instruction* (Definition 1) defines the name (op) and type signature ($\mathcal{F}$) of an operation in the underlying language. For example, the abstract instruction ($addi32, r \mapsto Reg, imm32 \mapsto BV(32)$) specifies the name and signature of the addi32 operation from the eBPF language (Fig. 1). Each abstract instruction represents the (finite) set of all *concrete instructions* that instantiate the abstract instruction's parameters with values of the right type. For example, addi32 0, 5 is a concrete instantiation of the abstract instruction for addi32. In the rest of this paper, we will write "instruction" to mean a concrete instruction.

Definition 1 (Abstract and Concrete Instructions). *An abstract instruction ι is a pair $(op, \mathcal{F})$ where op is an opcode and $\mathcal{F}$ is a mapping from fields to their types. Field types include Reg, denoting register names, and $BV(k)$, denoting k-bit bitvector values. The abstract instruction ι represents all concrete instructions $p = (op, F)$ with the opcode op that bind each field $f \in dom(\mathcal{F})$ to a value $F(f)$ of type $\mathcal{F}(f)$. We write $P(\iota)$ to denote the set of all concrete instructions for ι, and we extend this notation to sets of abstract instructions in the usual way, i.e., $P(\mathcal{I}) = \bigcup_{\iota \in \mathcal{I}} P(\iota)$ for the set $\mathcal{I}$.*

Instructions operate on machine *states* (Definition 2), and their semantics are given by the machine's *transition function* (Definition 3). A machine state consists of a program counter, a map from register names to register values, and a map from memory addresses to memory values. Each state component is either a bitvector or a map over bitvectors, making the set of all states of an ARM finite. The transition function of an ARM defines an interpreter for the ARM's language by specifying how to compute the output state for a given instruction and input state. We can apply this interpreter, together with the ARM's *fuel function*, to define an *execution* of the machine on a program and an initial state. The fuel function takes as input a sequence of instructions and returns a natural number that bounds the number of steps (i.e., state transitions) the machine can make to execute the given sequence. The inclusion of fuel models the requirement of in-kernel languages for all program executions to terminate [40]. It also enables us to use symbolic execution to soundly reduce the semantics of these languages to SMT constraints, in order to formulate the synthesis queries in Sect. 4.5.

Definition 2 (State). *A state σ is a tuple (pc, reg, mem) where pc is a value, reg is a function from register names to values, and mem is a function from memory addresses to values. Register names, memory addresses, and all values* *are finite-precision integers, or bitvectors. We write $|\sigma|$ to denote the size of the state σ. The size $|\sigma|$ is defined to be the tuple $(r, m, k_{pc}, k_{reg}, k_{mem})$, where r is the number of registers in σ, m is the number of memory addresses, and k_{pc}, k_{reg}, and k_{mem} are the width of the bitvector values stored in the pc, reg, and mem, respectively. Two states have the same size if $|\sigma_i| = |\sigma_j|$; one state is smaller than another, $|\sigma_i| \leq |\sigma_j|$, if each element of $|\sigma_i|$ is less than or equal to the corresponding element of $|\sigma_j|$.*

Definition 3 (Abstract Register Machines and Executions). *An abstract register machine $\mathcal{A}$ is a tuple $(\mathcal{I}, \Sigma, \mathcal{T}, \Phi)$ where $\mathcal{I}$ is a set of abstract instructions, Σ is a set of states of the same size, $\mathcal{T} : P(\mathcal{I}) \to \Sigma \to \Sigma$ is a transition function from instructions and states to states, and $\Phi : List(P(\mathcal{I})) \to \mathbb{N}$ is a fuel function from sequences of instructions to natural numbers. Given a state $\sigma_0 \in \Sigma$ and a sequence of instructions $\boldsymbol{p}$ drawn from $P(\mathcal{I})$, we define the execution of $\mathcal{A}$ on $\boldsymbol{p}$ and σ_0 to be the result of applying $\mathcal{T}$ to $\boldsymbol{p}$ at most $\Phi(\boldsymbol{p})$ times. That is, $\mathcal{A}(\boldsymbol{p}, \sigma_0) = run(\boldsymbol{p}, \sigma_0, \mathcal{T}, \Phi(\boldsymbol{p}))$, where*

$$run(\boldsymbol{p}, \sigma, \mathcal{T}, k) = \begin{cases} \sigma, & \text{if } k = 0 \text{ or } pc(\sigma) \notin [0, |\boldsymbol{p}|) \\ run(\boldsymbol{p}, \mathcal{T}(\boldsymbol{p}[pc(\sigma)], \sigma), \mathcal{T}, k - 1), & \text{otherwise.} \end{cases}$$

Synthesizing JIT Compilers for ARMs. Given a source and target ARM, our goal is to synthesize a one-pass JIT compiler that translates source programs to semantically equivalent target programs. To make synthesis tractable, we fix the structure of the JIT to consist of an outer loop and a switch statement that dispatches compilation tasks to a set of *mini compilers* (Definition 4). Our synthesis problem is therefore to find a sound mini compiler for each abstract instruction in the source machine (Definition 5).

Definition 4 (Mini Compiler). *Let $\mathcal{A}_S = (\mathcal{I}_S, \Sigma_S, \mathcal{T}_S, \Phi_S)$ and $\mathcal{A}_T = (\mathcal{I}_T, \Sigma_T, \mathcal{T}_T, \Phi_T)$ be two abstract register machines, $\cong$ an equivalence relation on their states Σ_S and Σ_T, and $C : P(\iota) \to List(P(\mathcal{I}_T))$ a function for some $\iota \in \mathcal{I}_S$. We say that C is a sound mini compiler for ι with respect to $\cong$ iff*

$$\forall \sigma_S \in \Sigma_S, \ \sigma_T \in \Sigma_T, \ p \in P(\iota). \ \sigma_S \cong \sigma_T \Rightarrow \mathcal{A}_S(p, \sigma_S) \cong \mathcal{A}_T(C(p), \sigma_T)$$

Definition 5 (Mini Compiler Synthesis). *Given two abstract register machines $\mathcal{A}_S = (\mathcal{I}_S, \Sigma_S, \mathcal{T}_S, \Phi_S)$ and $\mathcal{A}_T = (\mathcal{I}_T, \Sigma_T, \mathcal{T}_T, \Phi_T)$, as well as an equivalence relation $\cong$ on their states, the mini compiler synthesis problem is to generate a sound mini compiler C_ι for each $\iota \in \mathcal{I}_S$ with respect to $\cong$.*

The general version of our synthesis problem, defined above, uses an arbitrary equivalence relation $\cong$ between the states of the source and target machines to determine if a source and target program are semantically equivalent. JIT-SYNTH can, in principle, solve this problem with the naive metasketch described in Sect. 2. In practice, however, the naive metasketch scales poorly, even on small languages such as toy eBPF and RISC-V. So, in this paper, we focus on source and target ARMs that satisfy an additional assumption on their state equivalence relation: it can be expressed in terms of injective mappings from source to target states (Definition 6). This restriction enables JITSYNTH to employ optimizations (such as pre-load sketches described in Sect. 4.4) that are crucial to scaling synthesis to real in-kernel languages.

Definition 6 (Injective State Equivalence Relation). *Let $\mathcal{A}_S$ and $\mathcal{A}_T$ be abstract register machines with states Σ_S and Σ_T such that $|\sigma_S| \leq |\sigma_T|$ for all $\sigma_S \in \Sigma_S$ and $\sigma_T \in \Sigma_T$. Let $\mathcal{M}$ be a state mapping $(\mathcal{M}_{pc}, \mathcal{M}_{reg}, \mathcal{M}_{mem})$ from Σ_S and Σ_T, where $\mathcal{M}_{pc}$ multiplies the program counter of the states in Σ_S by a constant factor, $\mathcal{M}_{reg}$ is an injective map from register names in Σ_S to those in Σ_T, and $\mathcal{M}_{mem}$ is an injective map from memory addresses in Σ_S to those in Σ_T. We say that two states $\sigma_S \in \Sigma_S$ and $\sigma_T \in \Sigma_T$ are equivalent according to $\mathcal{M}$, written $\sigma_S \cong_\mathcal{M} \sigma_T$, iff $\mathcal{M}_{pc}(pc(\sigma_S)) = pc(\sigma_T)$, $reg(\sigma_S)[r] = reg(\sigma_T)[\mathcal{M}_{reg}(r)]$ for all register names $r \in dom(reg(\sigma_S))$, and $mem(\sigma_S)[a] = mem(\sigma_T)[\mathcal{M}_{mem}(a)]$ for all memory addresses $a \in dom(mem(\sigma_S))$. The binary relation $\cong_\mathcal{M}$ is called an* injective state equivalence relation *on $\mathcal{A}_S$ and $\mathcal{A}_T$.*

Soundness of JIT Compilers for ARMs. Finally, we note that a JIT compiler composed from the synthesized mini compilers correctly translates every source program to an equivalent target program. We formulate and prove this theorem using the Lean theorem prover [25].

Theorem 1 (Soundness of JIT compilers). *Let $\mathcal{A}_S = (\mathcal{I}_S, \Sigma_S, \mathcal{T}_S, \Phi_S)$ and $\mathcal{A}_T = (\mathcal{I}_T, \Sigma_T, \mathcal{T}_T, \Phi_T)$ be abstract register machines, $\cong_\mathcal{M}$ an injective state equivalence relation on their states such that $M_{pc}(pc(\sigma_S)) = N_{pc}pc(\sigma_S)$, and $\{C_1, \ldots, C_{|\mathcal{I}_S|}\}$ a solution to the mini compiler synthesis problem for $\mathcal{A}_S$, $\mathcal{A}_T$, and $\cong_\mathcal{M}$ where $\forall s \in P(\iota)$. $|C_i(s)| = N_{pc}$. Let $\mathcal{C} : P(\mathcal{I}_S) \rightarrow List(P(\mathcal{I}_T))$ be a function that maps concrete instructions $s \in P(\iota)$ to the compiler output $C_\iota(s)$ for $\iota \in \mathcal{I}_S$. If $s = s_1, \ldots, s_n$ is a sequence of concrete instructions drawn from $\mathcal{I}_S$, and $t = \mathcal{C}(s_1) \cdot \ldots \cdot \mathcal{C}(s_n)$ where $\cdot$ stands for sequence concatenation, then $\forall \sigma_S \in \Sigma_S, \sigma_T \in \Sigma_T$. $\sigma_S \cong_\mathcal{M} \sigma_T \Rightarrow \mathcal{A}_S(s, \sigma_S) \cong_\mathcal{M} \mathcal{A}_T(t, \sigma_T)$.*

4   Solving the Mini Compiler Synthesis Problem

This section presents our approach to solving the mini compiler synthesis problem defined in Sect. 3. We employ syntax-guided synthesis [37] to search for an implementation of a mini compiler in a space of candidate programs. Our core contribution is an effective way to structure this space using a *compiler metasketch*. This section presents our algorithm for generating compiler metasketches, describes its key subroutines and optimizations, and shows how to solve the resulting sketches with an off-the-shelf synthesis engine.

4.1   Generating Compiler Metasketches

JITSYNTH synthesizes mini compilers by generating and solving *metasketches* [7]. A metasketch describes a space of candidate programs using an ordered set of syntactic templates or *sketches* [37]. These sketches take the form of programs with missing expressions or *holes*, where each hole describes a finite set of candidate completions. JITSYNTH sketches are expressed in a *host language* $\mathcal{H}$ that serves both as the implementation language for mini compilers and the specification language for ARMs. JITSYNTH expects the host to provide a synthesizer for completing sketches and a symbolic evaluator for reducing ARM semantics to SMT constraints. JITSYNTH uses these tools to generate optimized metasketches for mini compilers, which we call *compiler metasketches*.

Figure 3 shows our algorithm for generating compiler metasketches. The algorithm, CMS, takes as input an abstract source instruction ι for a source machine $\mathcal{A}_S$, a target machine $\mathcal{A}_T$, and a state mapping $\mathcal{M}$ from $\mathcal{A}_S$ to $\mathcal{A}_T$. Given these inputs, it lazily enumerates an infinite set of *compiler sketches* that collectively represent the space of all straight-line bitvector programs from $P(\iota)$ to $List(P(\mathcal{I}_T))$. In particular, each compiler sketch consists of k target *instruction holes*, constructed from field holes that denote bitvector expressions (over the fields of ι) of depth d or less. For each length k and depth d, the CMS loop generates three kinds of compiler sketches: the *pre-load*, the *read-write*, and the *naive* sketch. The naive sketch (Sect. 4.2) is the most general, consisting of all candidate mini compilers of length k and depth d. But it also scales poorly, so CMS first yields the pre-load (Sect. 4.4) and read-write (Sect. 4.3) sketches. As we will see later, these sketches describe a subset of the programs in the naive sketch, and they are designed to prioritize exploring small parts of the search space that are likely to contain a correct mini compiler for ι, if one exists.

```
1: function CMS(ι, A_S, A_T, M)                           ▷ ι ∈ I_S, A_S = (I_S, ...)
2:     for n ∈ Z⁺ do                          ▷ Lazily enumerates all compiler sketches
3:         for k ∈ [1, n], d = n − k do                    ▷ of length k and depth d,
4:             yield PLD(k, d, ι, A_S, A_T, M)          ▷ yielding the pre-load sketch first,
5:             yield RW(k, d, ι, A_S, A_T, M)               ▷ read-write sketch next, and
6:             yield NAIVE(k, d, ι, A_S, A_T, M)            ▷ the most general sketch last.
```

Fig. 3. Compiler metasketch for the abstract source instruction ι, source machine $\mathcal{A}_S$, target machine $\mathcal{A}_T$, and state mapping $\mathcal{M}$ from $\mathcal{A}_S$ to $\mathcal{A}_T$.

4.2   Generating Naive Sketches

The most general sketch we consider, $\text{NAIVE}(k, d, \iota, \mathcal{A}_S, \mathcal{A}_T, \mathcal{M})$, is shown in Fig. 4. This sketch consists of k instruction holes that can be filled with any instruction from $\mathcal{I}_T$. An instruction hole chooses between expressions of the form (op_T, H), where op_T is a target opcode, and H specifies the field holes for that opcode. Each field hole is a bitvector expression (of depth d) over the fields of the input source instruction and arbitrary bitvector constants. This lets target instructions use the immediates and registers (modulo $\mathcal{M}$) of the source instruction, as well as arbitrary constant values and register names. Letting field holes include constant register names allows the synthesized mini compilers to use target registers unmapped by $\mathcal{M}$ as temporary, or scratch, storage. In essence, the naive sketch describes all straight-line compiler programs that can make free use of standard C arithmetic and bitwise operators, as well as scratch registers.

The space of such programs is intractably large, however, even for small inputs. For instance, it includes at least 2^{350} programs of length $k = 5$ and depth $d \leq 3$ for the toy example from Sect. 2. JITSYNTH therefore employs two effective heuristics to direct the exploration of this space toward the most promising candidates first, as defined by the read-write and pre-load sketches.

```
1:  function NAIVE(k, d, ι, A_S, A_T, M)                    ▷ ι ∈ I_S, A_S = (I_S, ...)
2:      (op, F) ← ι, (I_T, ...) ← A_T            ▷ Source instruction, target instructions.
3:      p ← FreshId()                            ▷ Identifier for the compiler's input.
4:      body ← []                          ▷ The body of the compiler is a sequence
5:      for 0 ≤ i < k do                              ▷ of k target instruction holes.
6:          I ← {}                      ▷ The set I of choices for a target instruction hole
7:          for (op_T, F_T) ∈ I_T do              ▷ includes all instructions from I_T.
8:              E ← {Expr(p.f, M) | f ∈ dom(F)}       ▷ Any source field can appear in
9:              H ← {f ↦ Field(F_T(f), d, E) | f ∈ dom(F_T)}   ▷ a target field hole, and
10:             I ← I ∪ {Expr((op_T, H), M)}          ▷ any constant register or value.
11:         body ← body · [Choose(I)]          ▷ Append a hole over I to the body.
12:     return Expr((λp ∈ P(ι) . body), M)        ▷ A mini compiler sketch for ι.
```

Fig. 4. Naive sketch of length k and maximum depth d for $ι$, A_S, A_T, and $\mathcal{M}$. Here, *Expr* creates an expression in the host language, using $\mathcal{M}$ to map from source to target register names and memory addresses; *Choose(E)* is a hole that chooses an expression from the set E; and *Field(τ, d, E)* is a hole for a bitvector expression of type $τ$ and maximum depth d, constructed from arbitrary bitvector constants and expressions E.

4.3   Generating Read-Write Sketches

The read-write sketch, $RW(k, d, ι, A_S, A_T, \mathcal{M})$, is based on the observation that many practical source and target languages provide similar functionality, so a source instruction $ι$ can often be emulated with target instructions that access the same parts of the state as $ι$. For example, the `addi32` instruction from eBPF reads and writes only registers (not, e.g., memory), and it can be emulated with RISC-V instructions that also touch only registers (Sect. 2). Moreover, note that the semantics of `addi32` ignores the values of its *src* and *off* fields, and that the target RISC-V instructions do the same. Based on these observations, our optimized sketch for `addi32` would therefore consists of instruction holes that allow only register-register instructions, with field holes that exclude *src* and *off*. We first formalize this intuition with the notion of *read and write sets*, and then describe how JITSYNTH applies such sets to create RW sketches.

Read and Write Sets. Read and write sets provide a compact way to summarize the semantics of an abstract instruction ι. This summary consists of a set of *state labels*, where a state label is one of L_{reg}, L_{mem}, and L_{pc} (Definition 7). Each label in a summary set represents a state component (registers, memory, or the program counter) that a concrete instance of ι may read or write during some execution. We compute three such sets of labels for every ι: the read set $Read(\iota)$, the write set $Write(\iota)$, and the write set $Write(\iota, f)$ for each field f of ι. Figure 5 shows these sets for the toy eBPF and RISC-V instructions.

ι	$Read(\iota)$	$Write(\iota)$	$Write(\iota, field)$
addi32	$\{L_{reg}\}$	$\{L_{reg}\}$	*imm*: $\{L_{reg}\}$; *off*: $\emptyset$; *src*: $\emptyset$; *dst*: $\{L_{reg}\}$
lui	$\{L_{reg}\}$	$\{L_{reg}\}$	*rd*: $\{L_{reg}\}$; *imm20*: $\{L_{reg}\}$
sb	$\{L_{reg}\}$	$\{L_{mem}\}$	*rs1*: $\{L_{mem}\}$; *rs2*: $\{L_{mem}\}$; *imm12*: $\{L_{mem}\}$

Fig. 5. Read and write sets for the addi32, lui, and sb instructions from Fig. 1.

The read set $Read(\iota)$ specifies which components of the input state may affect the execution of ι (Definition 8). For example, if $Read(\iota)$ includes L_{reg}, then some concrete instance of ι produces different output states when executed on two input states that differ only in register values. The write set $Write(\iota)$ specifies which components of the output state may be affected by executing ι (Definition 9). In particular, if $Write(\iota)$ includes L_{reg} (or L_{mem}), then executing some concrete instance of ι on an input state produces an output state with different register (or memory) values. The inclusion of L_{pc} is based on a separate condition, designed to distinguish jump instructions from fall-through instructions. Both kinds of instructions change the program counter, but fall-through instructions always change it in the same way. So, $L_{pc} \in Write(\iota)$ if two instances of ι can write different values to the program counter. Finally, the field write set, $Write(\iota, f)$, specifies the parts of the output state are affected by the value of the field f; $L_n \in Write(\iota, f)$ means that two instances of ι that differ only in f can produce different outputs when applied to the same input state.

JITSYNTH computes all read and write sets from their definitions, by using the host symbolic evaluator to reduce the reasoning about instruction semantics to SMT queries. This reduction is possible because we assume that all ARM interpreters are self-finitizing, as discussed in Sect. 2.

Definition 7 (State Labels). *A state label is an identifier L_n where n is a state component, i.e., $n \in \{reg, mem, pc\}$. We write N for the set of all state components, and $\mathcal{L}$ for the set of all state labels. We also use state labels to access the corresponding state components: $L_n(\sigma) = n(\sigma)$ for all $n \in N$.*

Definition 8 (Read Set). *Let $\iota \in \mathcal{I}$ be an abstract instruction in $(\mathcal{I}, \Sigma, \mathcal{T}, \Phi)$. The read set of ι, $Read(\iota)$, is the set of all state labels $L_n \in \mathcal{L}$ such that $\exists p \in P(\iota). \exists L_w \in Write(\iota). \exists \sigma_a, \sigma_b \in \Sigma. (L_n(\sigma_a) \neq L_n(\sigma_b) \wedge (\bigwedge_{m \in N \setminus \{n\}} L_m(\sigma_a) = L_m(\sigma_b)) \wedge L_w(\mathcal{T}(p, \sigma_a)) \neq L_w(\mathcal{T}(p, \sigma_b))).*

Definition 9 (Write Set). *Let $\iota \in \mathcal{I}$ be an abstract instruction in $(\mathcal{I}, \Sigma, \mathcal{T}, \Phi)$. The* write set *of ι, $Write(\iota)$, includes the state label $L_n \in \{L_{reg}, L_{mem}\}$ iff $\exists p \in P(\iota). \exists \sigma \in \Sigma. L_n(\sigma) \neq L_n(\mathcal{T}(p, \sigma))$, and it includes the state label L_{pc} iff $\exists p_a, p_b \in P(\iota). \exists \sigma \in \Sigma. L_{pc}(\mathcal{T}(p_a, \sigma)) \neq L_{pc}(\mathcal{T}(p_b, \sigma))$.*

Definition 10 (Field Write Set). *Let f be a field of an abstract instruction $\iota = (op, \mathcal{F})$ in $(\mathcal{I}, \Sigma, \mathcal{T}, \Phi)$. The* write set *of ι and f, $Write(\iota, f)$, includes the state label $L_n \in \mathcal{L}$ iff $\exists p_a, p_b \in P(\iota). \exists \sigma \in \Sigma. (p_a.f \neq p_b.f) \wedge (\bigwedge_{g \in dom(\mathcal{F}) \setminus \{f\}} p_a.g = p_b.g) \wedge L_n(\mathcal{T}(p_a, \sigma)) \neq L_n(\mathcal{T}(p_b, \sigma))$, where $p.f$ denotes $F(f)$ for $p = (op, F)$.*

Using Read and Write Sets. Given the read and write sets for a source instruction ι and target instructions $\mathcal{I}_T$, JITSYNTH generates the RW sketch of length k and depth d by modifying the NAIVE algorithm (Fig. 4) as follows. First, it restricts each target instruction hole (line 7) to choose an instruction $\iota_T \in \mathcal{I}_T$ with the same read and write sets as ι, i.e., $Read(\iota) = Read(\iota_T)$ and $Write(\iota) = Write(\iota_T)$. Second, it restricts the target field holes (line 9) to use the source fields with the matching field write set, i.e., the hole for a target field f_T uses the source field f when $Write(\iota_T, f_t) = Write(\iota, f)$. For example, given the sets from Fig. 5, the RW instruction holes for addi32 exclude sb but include lui, and the field holes for lui use only the *dst* and *imm* source fields. More generally, the RW sketch for addi32 consists of register-register instructions over *dst* and *imm*, as intended. This sketch includes 2^{290} programs of length $k = 5$ and depth $d \leq 3$, resulting in a 2^{60} fold reduction in the size of the search space compared to the NAIVE sketch of the same length and depth.

4.4   Generating Pre-load Sketches

The pre-load sketch, PLD $(k, d, \iota, \mathcal{A}_S, \mathcal{A}_T, \mathcal{M})$, is based on the observation that hand-written JITs use macros or subroutines to generate frequently used target instruction sequences. For example, compiling a source instruction with immediate fields often involves loading the immediates into scratch registers, and hand-written JITs include a subroutine that generates the target instructions for performing these loads. The pre-load sketch shown in Fig. 6 mimics this structure.

In particular, PLD generates a sequence of m concrete instructions that load the (used) immediate fields of ι, followed by a sequence of $k - m$ instruction holes. The instruction holes can refer to both the source registers (if any) and the scratch registers (via the arbitrary bitvector constants included in the *Field* holes). The function $Load(Expr(p.f), \mathcal{A}_T, \mathcal{M})$ returns a sequence of target instructions that load the immediate $p.f$ into an unused scratch register. This function itself is synthesized by JITSYNTH using a variant of the RW sketch.

As an example, the pre-load sketch for addi32 consists of two *Load* instructions (lui and addiw in the generated C code) and $k - 2$ instruction holes. The holes choose among register-register instructions in toy RISC-V, and they can refer to the *dst* register of addi32, as well as any scratch register. The resulting sketch includes 2^{100} programs of length $k = 5$ and depth $d \leq 3$, providing a 2^{190} fold reduction in the size of the search space compared to the RW sketch.

```
1: function PLD(k, d, ι, A_S, A_T, M)                    ▷ ι ∈ I_S, A_S = (I_S, ...)
2:    (op, F) ← ι, (I_T, ...) ← A_T          ▷ Source instruction, target instructions.
3:    p ← FreshId()                 ▷ Identifier for the compiler's input source instruction.
4:    body ← []                     ▷ The body of the compiler is a sequence with 2 parts:
5:    imm ← {f | F(f) = BV(k) and Write(ι, f) ≠ ∅}        ▷ (1) Load each relevant
6:    for f ∈ imm do                       ▷ source immediate into a free scratch register
7:        body ← body · Load(Expr(p.f), A_T, M) ▷ using the load pseudoinstruction.
8:    m ← |body|                         ▷ Let m be the length of the load sequence.
9:    if m ≥ k or m = 0 then return ⊥    ▷ Return the empty sketch if m ∉ (0..k).
10:   for m ≤ i < k do    ▷ (2) Create k − m target instruction holes, where the set
11:       I ← {}                      ▷ I of choices for a target instruction hole includes
12:       for ι_T ∈ I_T, ι_T = (op_T, F_T) do ▷ all instructions from I_T that read-write
13:           rw_T ← Read(ι_T) × Write(ι_T)      ▷ the same state as ι or just registers.
14:           if rw_T = Read(ι) × Write(ι) or rw_T ⊆ {L_reg} × {L_reg} then
15:               regs ← {f | F(f) = Reg and Write(ι, f) ≠ ∅}        ▷ Any relevant
16:               E ← {Expr(p.f, M) | f ∈ regs}      ▷ source register can appear in
17:               H ← {f ↦ Field(F_T(f), d, E) | f ∈ dom(F_T)}  ▷ a target field hole,
18:               I ← I ∪ {Expr((op_T, H), M)}  ▷ and any constant register or value.
19:           body ← body · [Choose(I)]          ▷ Append a hole over I to the body.
20:   return Expr((λp ∈ P(ι) . body), M)         ▷ A mini compiler sketch for ι.
```

Fig. 6. Pre-load sketch of length k and maximum depth d for $ι$, A_S, A_T, and M. The $Load(E, A_T, M)$ function returns a sequence of target instructions that load the immediate value described by the expression E into an unused scratch register; see Fig. 4 for descriptions of other helper functions.

4.5   Solving Compiler Metasketches

JITSYNTH solves the metasketch $CMS(ι, A_S, A_T, M)$ by applying the host synthesizer to each of the generated sketches in turn until a mini compiler is found. If no mini compiler exists in the search space, this synthesis process runs forever. To check if a sketch S contains a mini compiler, JITSYNTH would ideally ask the host synthesizer to solve the following query, derived from Definitions 4–6:

$$\exists C \in S. \ \forall \sigma_S \in \Sigma_S, \ \sigma_T \in \Sigma_T, \ p \in P(ι).\sigma_S \cong_M \sigma_T \Rightarrow A_S(p, \sigma_S) \cong_M A_T(C(p), \sigma_T)$$

But recall that the state equivalence check $\cong_M$ involves universally quantified formulas over memory addresses and register names. In principle, these innermost quantifiers are not problematic because they range over finite domains (bitvectors) so the formula remains decidable. In practice, however, they lead to intractable SMT queries. We therefore solve a stronger soundness query (Definition 11) that pulls these quantifiers out to obtain the standard $\exists\forall$ formula with a quantifier-free body. The resulting formula can be solved with CEGIS [37], without requiring the underlying SMT solver to reason about quantifiers.

Definition 11 (Strongly Sound Mini Compiler). *Let* $A_S = (I_S, \Sigma_S, T_S, \Phi_S)$ *and* $A_T = (I_T, \Sigma_T, T_T, \Phi_T)$ *be two abstract register machines,* $\cong_M$ *an injective state equivalence relation on their states* Σ_S *and* Σ_T, *and* $C : P(ι) \rightarrow$

$List(P(\mathcal{I}_T))$ *a function for some* $\iota \in \mathcal{I}_S$. *We say that* C *is a* strongly sound mini compiler *for* $\iota_\mathcal{M}$ *with respect to* $\cong$ *iff*

$$\forall \sigma_S \in \Sigma_S, \ \sigma_T \in \Sigma_T, \ p \in P(\iota), \ a \in dom(mem(\sigma_S)), \ r \in dom(reg(\sigma_S)).$$
$$\sigma_S \cong_{\mathcal{M},a,r} \sigma_T \Rightarrow \mathcal{A}_S(p, \sigma_S) \cong_{\mathcal{M},a,r} \mathcal{A}_T(C(p), \sigma_T)$$

where $\cong_{\mathcal{M},a,r}$ *stands for the* $\cong_\mathcal{M}$ *formula with* a *and* r *as free variables.*

The JITSYNTH synthesis procedure is sound and complete with respect to this stronger query (Theorem 2). The proof follows from the soundness and completeness of the host synthesizer, and the construction of the compiler metasketch. We discharge this proof using Lean theorem prover [25].

Theorem 2 (Strong soundness and completeness of JITSYNTH**).** *Let* $C = \mathrm{CMS}(\iota, \mathcal{A}_S, \mathcal{A}_T, \mathcal{M})$ *be the compiler metasketch for the abstract instruction* ι, *machines* $\mathcal{A}_S$ *and* $\mathcal{A}_T$, *and the state mapping* $\mathcal{M}$. *If* JITSYNTH *terminates and returns a program* C *when applied to* C, *then* C *is a strongly sound mini compiler for* ι *and* $\mathcal{A}_T$ *(soundness). If there is a strongly sound mini compiler in the most general search space* $\{\mathrm{NAIVE}(k, d, \iota, \mathcal{A}_S, \mathcal{A}_T, \mathcal{M}) \mid k, d \in \mathbb{N}\}$, *then* JITSYNTH *will terminate on* C *and produce a program (completeness).*

5 Implementation

We implemented JITSYNTH as described in Sect. 2 using Rosette [39] as our host language. Since the search spaces for different compiler lengths are disjoint, the JITSYNTH implementation searches these spaces in parallel [7]. We use $\Phi(p) = \texttt{length}(p)$ as the fuel function for all languages studied in this paper. This provides sufficient fuel for evaluating programs in these languages that are accepted by the OS kernel. For example, the Linux kernel requires eBPF programs to be loop-free, and it enforces this restriction with a conservative static check; programs that fail the check are not passed to the JIT [13].

6 Evaluation

This section evaluates JITSYNTH by answering the following research questions:

RQ1: Can JITSYNTH synthesize correct and performant compilers for real-world source and target languages?
RQ2: How effective are the sketch optimizations described in Sect. 4?

6.1 Synthesizing Compilers for Real-World Source-Target Pairs

To demonstrate the effectiveness of JITSYNTH, we applied JITSYNTH to synthesize compilers for three different source-target pairs: eBPF to 64-bit RISC-V, classic BPF to eBPF, and libseccomp to eBPF. This subsection describes our results for each of the synthesized compilers.

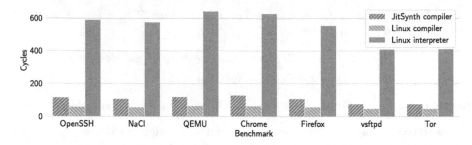

Fig. 7. Execution time of eBPF benchmarks on the HiFive Unleashed RISC-V development board, using the existing Linux eBPF to RISC-V compiler, the JITSYNTH compiler, and the Linux eBPF interpreter. Measured in processor cycles.

eBPF to RISC-V. As a case study, we applied JITSYNTH to synthesize a compiler from eBPF to 64-bit RISC-V. It supports 87 of the 102 eBPF instruction opcodes; unsupported eBPF instructions include function calls, endianness operations, and atomic instructions. To validate that the synthesized compiler is correct, we ran the existing eBPF test cases from the Linux kernel; our compiler passes all test cases it supports. In addition, our compiler avoids bugs previously found in the existing Linux eBPF-to-RISC-V compiler in Linux [27]. To evaluate performance, we compared against the existing Linux compiler. We used the same set of benchmarks used by Jitk [40], which includes system call filters from widely used applications. Because these benchmarks were originally for classic BPF, we first compile them to eBPF using the existing Linux classic-BPF-to-eBPF compiler as a preprocessing step. To run the benchmarks, we execute the generated code on the HiFive Unleashed RISC-V development board [35], measuring the number of cycles. As input to the filter, we use a system call number that is allowed by the filter to represent the common case execution.

Figure 7 shows the results of the performance evaluation. eBPF programs compiled by JITSYNTH JIT compilers show an average slowdown of 1.82× compared to programs compiled by the existing Linux compiler. This overhead results from additional complexity in the compiled eBPF jump instructions. Linux compilers avoid this complexity by leveraging bounds on the size of eBPF jump offsets. JITSYNTH-compiled programs get an average speedup of 5.24× compared to interpreting the eBPF programs. This evidence shows that JITSYNTH can synthesize a compiler that outperforms the current Linux eBPF interpreter, and nears the performance of the Linux compiler, while avoiding bugs.

Classic BPF to eBPF. Classic BPF is the original, simpler version of BPF used for packet filtering which was later extended to eBPF in Linux. Since many applications still use classic BPF, Linux must first compile classic BPF to eBPF as an intermediary step before compiling to machine instructions. As a second case study, we used JITSYNTH to synthesize a compiler from classic BPF to eBPF. Our synthesized compiler supports all classic BPF opcodes. To evaluate performance, we compare against the existing Linux classic-BPF-to-eBPF

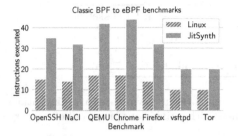

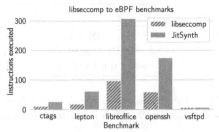

Fig. 8. Performance of code generated by JITSYNTH compilers compared to existing compilers for the classic BPF to eBPF benchmarks (left) and the libseccomp to eBPF benchmarks (right). Measured in number of instructions executed.

compiler. Similar to the RISC-V benchmarks, we run each eBPF program with input that is allowed by the filter. Because eBPF does not run directly on hardware, we measure the number of instructions executed instead of processor cycles.

Figure 8 shows the performance results. Classic BPF programs generated by JITSYNTH compilers execute an average of 2.28× more instructions than those compiled by Linux.

Libseccomp to eBPF. libseccomp is a library used to simplify construction of BPF system call filters. The existing libseccomp implementation compiles to classic BPF; we instead choose to compile to eBPF because classic BPF has only two registers, which does not satisfy the assumptions of JITSYNTH. Since libseccomp is a library and does not have distinct instructions, libseccomp itself does not meet the definition of an abstract register machine; we instead introduce an intermediate libseccomp language which does satisfy this definition. Our full libseccomp to eBPF compiler is composed of both a trusted program to translate from libseccomp to our intermediate language and a synthesized compiler from our intermediate language to eBPF.

To evaluate performance, we select a set of benchmark filters from real-world applications that use libseccomp, and measure the number of eBPF instructions executed for an input the filter allows. Because no existing compiler exists from libseccomp to eBPF directly, we compare against the composition of the existing libseccomp-to-classic-BPF and classic-BPF-to-eBPF compilers.

Figure 8 shows the performance results. libseccomp programs generated by JITSYNTH execute 2.61× more instructions on average compared to the existing libseccomp-to-eBPF compiler stack. However, the synthesized compiler avoids bugs previously found in the libseccomp-to-classic-BPF compiler [16].

6.2 Effectiveness of Sketch Optimizations

In order to evaluate the effectiveness of the search optimizations described in Sect. 4, we measured the time JITSYNTH takes to synthesize each of the three compilers with different optimizations enabled. Specifically, we run JITSYNTH in

Compiler	NAIVE sketch	RW sketch	PLD sketch
eBPF to RISC-V	X	X	44.4h
classic BPF to eBPF	X	X	1.2h
libseccomp to eBPF	4.0h	43.5m	7.1m

Fig. 9. Synthesis time for each source-target pair, broken down by set of optimizations used in the sketch. An X indicates that synthesis either timed out or ran out of memory.

three different configurations: (1) using NAIVE sketches, (2) using RW sketches, and (3) using PLD sketches. For each configuration, we ran JITSYNTH with a timeout of 48 hours (or until out of memory). Figure 9 shows the time to synthesize each compiler under each configuration. Note that these figures do not include time spent computing read and write sets, which takes less than 11 min for all cases. Our results were collected using an 8-core AMD Ryzen 7 1700 CPU with 16 GB memory, running Racket v7.4 and the Boolector [29] solver v3.0.1-pre.

When synthesizing the eBPF-to-RISC-V compiler, JITSYNTH runs out of memory with NAIVE sketches, reaches the timeout with RW sketches, and completes synthesis with PLD sketches. For the classic-BPF-to-eBPF compiler, JITSYNTH times out with both NAIVE sketches and RW sketches. JITSYNTH only finishes synthesis with PLD sketches. For the libseccomp-to-eBPF compiler, all configurations finish, but JITSYNTH finishes synthesis about 34× times faster with PLD sketches than with NAIVE sketches. These results demonstrate that the techniques JITSYNTH uses are essential to the scalability of JIT synthesis.

7   Related Work

JIT Compilers for In-kernel Languages. JIT compilers have been widely used to improve the extensibility and performance of systems software, such as OS kernels [8,11,12,26]. One notable system is Jitk [40]. It builds on the CompCert compiler [20] to compile classic BPF programs to machine instructions. Both Jitk and CompCert are formally verified for correctness using the Coq interactive theorem prover. Jitk is further extended to support eBPF [36]. Like Jitk, JITSYNTH provides formal correctness guarantees of JIT compilers. Unlike Jitk, JITSYNTH does not require developers to write either the implementation or proof of a JIT compiler. Instead, it takes as input interpreters of both source and target languages and state-mapping functions, using automated verification and synthesis to produce a JIT compiler.

An in-kernel extension system such as eBPF also contains a *verifier*, which checks for safety and termination of input programs [13,40]. JITSYNTH assumes a well-formed input program that passes the verifier and focuses on the correctness of JIT compilation.

Synthesis-Aided Compilers. There is a rich literature that explores generating and synthesizing peephole optimizers and superoptimizers based on a given ISA or language specification [4,9,14,17,23,33,34]. Bansal and Aiken described a PowerPC-to-x86 binary translator using peephole superoptimization [5]. Chlorophyll [31] applied synthesis to a number of compilation tasks for the GreenArrays GA144 architecture, including code partitioning, layout, and generation. JITSYNTH bears the similarity of translation between a source-target pair of languages and shares the challenge of scaling up synthesis. Unlike existing work, JITSYNTH synthesizes a *compiler* written in a host language, and uses compiler metasketches for efficient synthesis.

Compiler Testing. Compilers are complex pieces of software and are known to be difficult to get right [22]. Recent advances in compiler testing, such as Csmith [41] and EMI [42], have found hundreds of bugs in GCC and LLVM compilers. Alive [19,21] and Serval [28] use automated verification techniques to uncover bugs in the LLVM's peephole optimizer and the Linux kernel's eBPF JIT compilers, respectively. JITSYNTH complements these tools by providing a correctness-by-construction approach for writing JIT compilers.

8   Conclusion

This paper presents a new technique for synthesizing JIT compilers for in-kernel DSLs. The technique creates per-instruction compilers, or compilers that independently translate single source instructions to sequences of target instructions. In order to synthesize each per-instruction compiler, we frame the problem as search using compiler metasketches, which are optimized using both read and write set information as well as pre-synthesized load operations. We implement these techniques in JITSYNTH and evaluate JITSYNTH over three source and target pairs from the Linux kernel. Our evaluation shows that (1) JITSYNTH can synthesize correct and performant compilers for real in-kernel languages, and (2) the optimizations discussed in this paper make the synthesis of these compilers tractable to JITSYNTH. As future in-kernel DSLs are created, JITSYNTH can reduce both the programming and proof burden on developers writing compilers for those DSLs. The JITSYNTH source code is publicly available at https://github.com/uw-unsat/jitsynth.

References

1. Proceedings of the 12th International Conference on Architectural Support for Programming Languages and Operating Systems (ASPLOS), October 2006
2. Proceedings of the 32nd ACM SIGPLAN Conference on Programming Language Design and Implementation (PLDI), June 2011
3. Proceedings of the 35th ACM SIGPLAN Conference on Programming Language Design and Implementation (PLDI), June 2014

4. Bansal, S., Aiken, A.: Automatic generation of peephole superoptimizers. In: Proceedings of the 12th International Conference on Architectural Support for Programming Languages and Operating Systems (ASPLOS) [1], pp. 394–403 (2006)

5. Bansal, S., Aiken, A.: Binary translation using peephole superoptimizers. In: Proceedings of the 8th USENIX Symposium on Operating Systems Design and Implementation (OSDI), San Diego, CA, pp. 177–192, December 2008

6. Blazakis, D.: Interpreter exploitation: Pointer inference and JIT spraying. In: Black Hat DC, Arlington, VA, February 2010

7. Bornholt, J., Torlak, E., Grossman, D., Ceze, L.: Optimizing synthesis with metasketches. In: Proceedings of the 43rd ACM Symposium on Principles of Programming Languages (POPL), St. Petersburg, FL, pp. 775–788, January 2016

8. Chen, H., et al.: Security bugs in embedded interpreters. In: Proceedings of the 4th Asia-Pacific Workshop on Systems, 6 p. Singapore (2013)

9. Davidson, J.W., Fraser, C.W.: Automatic generation of peephole optimizations. In: Proceedings of the SIGPLAN Symposium on Compiler Construction, Montreal, Canada, pp. 111–116, June 1984

10. Edge, J.: A library for seccomp filters, April 2012. https://lwn.net/Articles/494252/

11. Engler, D.R.: VCODE: a retargetable, extensible, very fast dynamic code generation system. In: Proceedings of the 17th ACM SIGPLAN Conference on Programming Language Design and Implementation (PLDI), Philadephia, PA, pp. 160–170, May 1996

12. Fleming, M.: A thorough introduction to eBPF, December 2017. https://lwn.net/Articles/740157/

13. Gershuni, E., et al.: Simple and precise static analysis of untrusted Linux kernel extensions. In: Proceedings of the 40th ACM SIGPLAN Conference on Programming Language Design and Implementation (PLDI), Phoenix, AZ , pp. 1069–1084, June 2019

14. Gulwani, S., Jha, S., Tiwari, A., Venkatesan, R.: Synthesis of loop-free programs. In: Proceedings of the 32nd ACM SIGPLAN Conference on Programming Language Design and Implementation (PLDI) [2], pp. 62–73 (2011)

15. Horn, J.: Issue 1454: arbitrary read+write via incorrect range tracking in eBPF, January 2018. https://bugs.chromium.org/p/project-zero/issues/detail?id=1454

16. Horn, J.: libseccomp: incorrect compilation of arithmetic comparisons, March 2019. https://bugs.chromium.org/p/project-zero/issues/detail?id=1769

17. Joshi, R., Nelson, G., Randall, K.: Denali: a goal-directed superoptimizer. In: Proceedings of the 23rd ACM SIGPLAN Conference on Programming Language Design and Implementation (PLDI), Berlin, Germany, pp. 304–314, June 2002

18. Kocher, P., et al.: Spectre attacks: exploiting speculative execution. In: Proceedings of the 40th IEEE Symposium on Security and Privacy, San Francisco, CA, pp. 19–37, May 2019

19. Lee, J., Hur, C.K., Lopes, N.P.: AliveInLean: a verified LLVM peephole optimization verifier. In: Proceedings of the 31st International Conference on Computer Aided Verification (CAV), New York, NY, pp. 445–455, July 2019

20. Leroy, X.: Formal verification of a realistic compiler. Commun. ACM **52**(7), 107–115 (2009)

21. Lopes, N.P., Menendez, D., Nagarakatte, S., Regehr, J.: Provably correct peephole optimizations with alive. In: Proceedings of the 36th ACM SIGPLAN Conference on Programming Language Design and Implementation (PLDI), Portland, OR, pp. 22–32, June 2015

22. Marcozzi, M., Tang, Q., Donaldson, A., Cadar, C.: Compiler fuzzing: how much does it matter? In: Proceedings of the 2019 Annual ACM Conference on Object-Oriented Programming, Systems, Languages, and Applications (OOPSLA), Athens, Greece, October 2019

23. Massalin, H.: Superoptimizer: a look at the smallest program. In: Proceedings of the 2nd International Conference on Architectural Support for Programming Languages and Operating Systems (ASPLOS), Palo Alto, CA, pp. 122–126, October 1987

24. McCanne, S., Jacobson, V.: The BSD packet filter: a new architecture for user-level packet capture. In: Proceedings of the Winter 1993 USENIX Technical Conference, San Diego, CA, pp. 259–270, January 1993

25. de Moura, L., Kong, S., Avigad, J., van Doorn, F., von Raumer, J.: The lean theorem prover (system description). In: Felty, A.P., Middeldorp, A. (eds.) CADE 2015. LNCS (LNAI), vol. 9195, pp. 378–388. Springer, Cham (2015). https://doi.org/10.1007/978-3-319-21401-6_26

26. Myreen, M.O.: Verified just-in-time compiler on x86. In: Proceedings of the 37th ACM Symposium on Principles of Programming Languages (POPL), pp. 107–118. Association for Computing Machinery, New York, January 2010

27. Nelson, L.: bpf, riscv: clear high 32 bits for ALU32 add/sub/neg/lsh/rsh/arsh, May 2019. https://git.kernel.org/pub/scm/linux/kernel/git/torvalds/linux.git/commit/?id=1e692f09e091

28. Nelson, L., Bornholt, J., Gu, R., Baumann, A., Torlak, E., Wang, X.: Scaling symbolic evaluation for automated verification of systems code with serval. In: Proceedings of the 27th ACM Symposium on Operating Systems Principles (SOSP), Huntsville, Ontario, Canada, pp. 225–242, October 2019

29. Niemetz, A., Preiner, M., Biere, A.: Boolector 20 system description. J. Satisfiabil. Boolean Model. Comput. 9, 53–58 (2014). (published 2015)

30. Paul, M.: CVE-2020-8835: linux kernel privilege escalation via improper eBPF program verification, April 2020. https://www.thezdi.com/blog/2020/4/8/cve-2020-8835-linux-kernel-privilege-escalation-via-improper-ebpf-program-verification

31. Phothilimthana, P.M., Jelvis, T., Shah, R., Totla, N., Chasins, S., Bodik, R.: Chlorophyll: synthesis-aided compiler for low-power spatial architectures. In: Proceedings of the 35th ACM SIGPLAN Conference on Programming Language Design and Implementation (PLDI) [3], pp. 396–407 (2014)

32. RISC-V Foundation: The RISC-V Instruction Set Manual, Volume I: Unprivileged ISA, Document Version 2019121, December 2019

33. Sasnauskas, R., et al.: Souper: a synthesizing superoptimizer, November 2017. https://arxiv.org/abs/1711.04422

34. Schkufza, E., Sharma, R., Aiken, A.: Stochastic superoptimization. In: Proceedings of the 18th International Conference on Architectural Support for Programming Languages and Operating Systems (ASPLOS), Houston, TX, pp. 305–316, March 2013

35. SiFive: SiFive FU540-C000 manual, v1p0, April 2018. https://www.sifive.com/boards/hifive-unleashed

36. Sobel, L.: eJitk: extending Jitk to eBPF, May 2015. https://css.csail.mit.edu/6.888/2015/papers/ejitk_sobel.pdf

37. Solar-Lezama, A., Tancau, L., Bodik, R., Seshia, S., Saraswat, V.: Combinatorial sketching for finite programs. In: Proceedings of the 12th International Conference on Architectural Support for Programming Languages and Operating Systems (ASPLOS) [1], pp. 404–415 (2006)

38. The Coq Development Team: The Coq Proof Assistant, version 8.9.0, January 2019. https://doi.org/10.5281/zenodo.2554024
39. Torlak, E., Bodik, R.: A lightweight symbolic virtual machine for solver-aided host languages. In: Proceedings of the 35th ACM SIGPLAN Conference on Programming Language Design and Implementation (PLDI) [3], pp. 530–541 (2014)
40. Wang, X., Lazar, D., Zeldovich, N., Chlipala, A., Tatlock, Z.: Jitk: a trustworthy in-kernel interpreter infrastructure. In: Proceedings of the 11th USENIX Symposium on Operating Systems Design and Implementation (OSDI), Broomfield, CO, pp. 33–47, October 2014
41. Yang, X., Chen, Y., Eide, E., Regehr, J.: Finding and understanding bugs in C compilers. In: Proceedings of the 32nd ACM SIGPLAN Conference on Programming Language Design and Implementation (PLDI) [2], pp. 283–294 (2011)
42. Zhang, Q., Sun, C., Su, Z.: Skeletal program enumeration for rigorous compiler testing. In: Proceedings of the 38th ACM SIGPLAN Conference on Programming Language Design and Implementation (PLDI), Barcelona, Spain, pp. 347–361 June 2017

Program Synthesis Using Deduction-Guided Reinforcement Learning

Yanju Chen[1]([✉]), Chenglong Wang[2], Osbert Bastani[3], Isil Dillig[4], and Yu Feng[1]([✉])

[1] University of California, Santa Barbara, Santa Barbara, CA 93106, USA
{yanju,yufeng}@cs.ucsb.edu
[2] University of Washington, Seattle, WA 98115, USA
clwang@cs.washington.edu
[3] University of Pennsylvania, Philadelphia, PA 19104, USA
obastani@seas.upenn.edu
[4] The University of Texas at Austin, Austin, TX 78712, USA
isil@cs.utexas.edu

Abstract. In this paper, we present a new program synthesis algorithm based on reinforcement learning. Given an initial policy (i.e. statistical model) trained off-line, our method uses this policy to guide its search and gradually improves it by leveraging feedback obtained from a deductive reasoning engine. Specifically, we formulate program synthesis as a reinforcement learning problem and propose a new variant of the *policy gradient* algorithm that can incorporate feedback from a deduction engine into the underlying statistical model. The benefit of this approach is two-fold: First, it combines the power of deductive and statistical reasoning in a unified framework. Second, it leverages deduction not only to *prune* the search space but also to *guide* search. We have implemented the proposed approach in a tool called CONCORD and experimentally evaluate it on synthesis tasks studied in prior work. Our comparison against several baselines and two existing synthesis tools shows the advantages of our proposed approach. In particular, CONCORD solves 15% more benchmarks compared to NEO, a state-of-the-art synthesis tool, while improving synthesis time by 8.71× on benchmarks that can be solved by both tools.

1 Introduction

Due to its potential to significantly improve both programmer productivity and software correctness, *automated program synthesis* has gained enormous popularity over the last decade. Given a high-level specification of user intent, most modern synthesizers perform some form of backtracking search in order to find a

---

This work was sponsored by the National Science Foundation under agreement number of 1908494, 1811865 and 1910769.

S. K. Lahiri and C. Wang (Eds.): CAV 2020, LNCS 12225, pp. 587–610, 2020.
https://doi.org/10.1007/978-3-030-53291-8_30

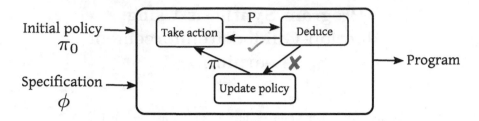

Fig. 1. Overview of our synthesis algorithm

program that satisfies the specification. However, due to the enormous size of the search space, synthesizers additionally use at least one of two other techniques, namely deduction and statistical reasoning, to make this approach practical. For example, many recent synthesis techniques use lightweight program analysis or logical reasoning to significantly prune the search space [18,19,39,53]. On the other hand, several recent approaches utilize a statistical model (trained off-line) to bias the search towards programs that are more likely to satisfy the specification [2,4,7,19]. While both deductive and statistical reasoning have been shown to dramatically improve synthesis efficiency, a key limitation of existing approaches is that they do not tightly combine these two modes of reasoning. In particular, although logical reasoning often provides very useful feedback at synthesis time, existing synthesis algorithms do not leverage such feedback to improve their statistical model.

In this paper, we propose a new synthesis algorithm that meaningfully combines deductive and statistical reasoning. Similar to prior techniques, our approach starts with a statistical model (henceforth called a *policy*) that is trained off-line on a representative set of training problems and uses this policy to guide search. However, unlike prior techniques, our method *updates* this policy on-line at synthesis time and gradually improves the policy by incorporating feedback from a deduction engine.

To achieve this tight coupling between deductive and statistical reasoning, we formulate syntax-guided synthesis as a reinforcement learning (RL) problem. Specifically, given a context-free grammar for the underlying DSL, we think of partial (i.e., incomplete) programs in this DSL as states in a Markov Decision Process (MDP) and actions as grammar productions. Thus, a *policy* of this MDP specifies how a partial program should be extended to obtain a more specific program. Then, the goal of our reinforcement learning problem is to improve this policy over time as some partial programs are proven infeasible by an underlying deduction engine.

While the framework of reinforcement learning is a good fit for our problem, standard RL algorithms (e.g., policy gradient) typically update the policy based on feedback received from states that have *already* been explored. However, in the context of program synthesis, deductive reasoning can also provide feedback about states that have *not* been explored. For example, given a partial program that is infeasible, one can analyze the root cause of failure to infer *other* infeasible programs [18,54]. To deal with this difficulty, we propose an *off-policy* reinforcement learning algorithm that can improve the policy based on such additional feedback from the deduction engine.

As shown schematically in Fig. 1, our synthesis algorithm consists of three conceptual elements, indicated as "Take action", "Deduce", and "Update policy". Given the current policy π and partial program P, "Take action" uses π to expand P into a more complete program P'. Then, "Deduce" employs existing deductive reasoning techniques (e.g., [18,32]) to check whether P' is feasible with respect to the specification. If this is not the case, "Update policy" uses the feedback provided by the deduction engine to improve π. Specifically, the policy is updated using an off-policy variant of the *policy gradient* algorithm, where the gradient computation is adapted to our unique setting.

We have implemented the proposed method in a new synthesis tool called CONCORD and empirically evaluate it on synthesis tasks used in prior work [2,18]. We also compare our method with several relevant baselines as well as two existing synthesis tools. Notably, our evaluation shows that CONCORD can solve 15% more benchmarks compared to NEO (a state-of-the-art synthesis tool), while being 8.71× faster on benchmarks that can be solved by both tools. Furthermore, our ablation study demonstrates the empirical benefits of our proposed reinforcement learning algorithm.

To summarize, this paper makes the following key contributions:

- We propose a new synthesis algorithm based on reinforcement learning that tightly couples statistical and deductive reasoning.
- We describe an off-policy reinforcement learning technique that uses the output of the deduction engine to gradually improve its policy.
- We implement our approach in a tool called CONCORD and empirically demonstrate its benefits compared to other state-of-the-art tools as well as ablations of our own system.

The rest of this paper is structured as follows. First, we provide some background on reinforcement learning and MDPs (Sect. 2) and introduce our problem formulation in Sect. 3. After formulating the synthesis problem as an MDP in Sect. 4, we then present our synthesis algorithm in Sect. 5. Sections 6 and 7 describe our implementation and evaluation respectively. Finally, we discuss related work and future research directions in Sect. 8 and 9.

2 Background on Reinforcement Learning

At a high level, the goal of reinforcement learning (RL) is to train an agent, such as a robot, to make a sequence of decisions (e.g., move up/down/left/right) in order to accomplish a task. All relevant information about the environment and the task is specified as a *Markov decision process (MDP)*. Given an MDP, the goal is to compute a policy that specifies how the agent should act in each state to maximize their chances of accomplishing the task.

In the remainder of this section, we provide background on MDPs and describe the policy gradient algorithm that our method will build upon.

Markov Decision Process. We formalize a *Markov decision process (MDP)* as a tuple $\mathcal{M} = (\mathcal{S}, \mathcal{S}_I, \mathcal{S}_T, \mathcal{A}, \mathcal{F}, \mathcal{R})$, where:

- $\mathcal{S}$ is a set of *states* (e.g., the robot's current position),
- $\mathcal{S}_I$ is the initial state distribution,
- $\mathcal{S}_T$ is a set of the final states (e.g., a dead end),
- $\mathcal{A}$ is a set of actions (e.g., move up/down/left/right),
- $\mathcal{F} : \mathcal{S} \times \mathcal{A} \to \mathcal{S}$ is a set of transitions,
- $\mathcal{R} : \mathcal{S} \to \mathbb{R}$ is a reward function that assigns a reward to each state (e.g., 1 for reaching the goal and 0 otherwise).

In general, transitions in an MDP can be stochastic; however, for our setting, we only consider deterministic transitions and rewards.

Policy. A policy for an MDP specifies how the agent should act in each state. Specifically, we consider a (stochastic) *policy* $\pi : \mathcal{S} \times \mathcal{A} \to \mathbb{R}$, where $\pi(S, A)$ is the probability of taking action A in state S. Alternatively, we can also think of π as a mapping from states to distributions over actions. Thus, we write $A \sim \pi(S)$ to denote that action A is sampled from the distribution for state s.

Rollout. Given an MDP $\mathcal{M}$ and policy π, a *rollout* is a sequence of state-action-reward tuples obtained by sampling an initial state and then using π to make decisions until a final state is reached. More formally, for a rollout of the form:

$$\zeta = ((S_1, A_1, R_1), ..., (S_{m-1}, A_{m-1}, R_{m-1}), (S_m, \varnothing, R_m)),$$

we have $S_m \in \mathcal{S}_T$, $S_1 \sim \mathcal{S}_I$ (i.e., S_1 is sampled from an initial state), and, for each $i \in \{1, ..., m-1\}$, $A_i \sim \pi(S_i)$, $R_i = \mathcal{R}(S_i)$, and $S_{i+1} = \mathcal{F}(S_i, A_i)$.

In general, a policy π induces a distribution $\mathcal{D}_\pi$ over the rollouts of an MDP $\mathcal{M}$. Since we assume that MDP transitions are deterministic, we have:

$$\mathcal{D}_\pi(\zeta) = \prod_{i=1}^{m-1} \pi(S_i, A_i).$$

RL Problem. Given an MDP $\mathcal{M}$, the goal of reinforcement learning is to compute an *optimal* policy π^* for $\mathcal{M}$. More formally, π^* should maximize *cumulative expected reward*:

$$\pi^* = \arg \max_\pi J(\pi)$$

where the *cumulative expected reward* $J(\pi)$ is computed as follows:

$$J(\pi) = \mathbb{E}_{\zeta \sim \mathcal{D}_\pi} \left[\sum_{i=1}^{m} R_i \right]$$

Policy Gradient Algorithm. The *policy gradient algorithm* is a well-known RL algorithm for finding optimal policies. It assumes a parametric policy family π_θ with parameters $\theta \in \mathbb{R}^d$. For example, π_θ may be a deep neural network (DNN), where θ denotes the parameters of the DNN. At a high level, the policy gradient algorithm uses the following theorem to optimize $J(\pi_\theta)$ [48]:

Theorem 1. *We have*

$$\nabla_\theta J(\pi_\theta) = \mathbb{E}_{\zeta \sim \mathcal{D}_{\pi_\theta}}[\ell(\zeta)] \qquad where \qquad \ell(\zeta) = \sum_{i=1}^{m-1} \left(\sum_{j=i+1}^{m} R_j \right) \nabla_\theta \log \pi_\theta(S_i, A_i). \tag{1}$$

In this theorem, the term $\nabla_\theta \log \pi_\theta(S_i, A_i)$ intuitively gives a direction in the parameter space that, when moving the policy parameters towards it, increases the probability of taking action A_i at state S_i. Also, the sum $\sum_{j=i+1}^{m} R_j$ is the total future reward after taking action A_i. Thus, $\ell(\zeta)$ is just the sum of different directions in the parameter space weighted by their corresponding future reward. Thus, the gradient $\nabla_\theta J(\pi_\theta)$ moves policy parameters in a direction that increases the probability of taking actions that lead to higher rewards.

Based on this theorem, we can estimate the gradient $\nabla_\theta J(\pi_\theta)$ using rollouts sampled from $\mathcal{D}_{\pi_\theta}$:

$$\nabla_\theta J(\pi_\theta) \approx \frac{1}{n} \sum_{k=1}^{n} \ell(\zeta^{(k)}), \tag{2}$$

where $\zeta^{(k)} \sim \mathcal{D}_{\pi_\theta}$ for each $k \in \{1, ..., n\}$. The policy gradient algorithm uses stochastic gradient ascent in conjunction with Eq. (2) to maximize $J(\pi_\theta)$ [48].

3   Problem Formulation

In this paper, we focus on the setting of syntax-guided synthesis [1]. Specifically, given a domain-specific language (DSL) L and a specification ϕ, our goal is to find a program in L that satisfies ϕ. In the remainder of this section, we formally define our synthesis problem and clarify our assumptions.

DSL. We assume a domain-specific language L specified as a context-free grammar $L = (V, \Sigma, R, S)$, where V, Σ denote non-terminals and terminals respectively, R is a set of productions, and S is the start symbol.

Definition 1 (Partial program). *A partial program P is a sequence $P \in (\Sigma \cup V)^*$ such that $S \overset{*}{\Rightarrow} P$ (i.e., P can be derived from S via a sequence of productions). We refer to any non-terminal in P as a hole* hole, *and we say that P is* complete *if it does not contain any holes.*

$$S \rightarrow N \mid L$$
$$N \rightarrow 0 \mid \ldots \mid 10 \mid x_i$$
$$L \rightarrow x_i \mid \texttt{take}(L, N) \mid \texttt{drop}(L, N) \mid \texttt{sort}(L)$$
$$\mid \texttt{reverse}(L) \mid \texttt{add}(L, L) \mid \texttt{sub}(L, L) \mid \texttt{sumUpTo}(L)$$

Fig. 2. A simple programming language used for illustration. Here, `take` (resp. `drop`) keeps (resp. removes) the first N elements in the input list. Also, `add` (resp. `sub`) compute a new list by adding (resp. subtracting) elements from the two lists pair-wise. Finally, `sumUpTo` generates a new list where the i'th element in the output list is the sum of all previous elements (including the i'th element) in the input list.

Given a partial program P containing a hole H, we can fill this hole by replacing H with the right-hand-side of any grammar production r of the form $H \rightarrow e$. We use the notation $P \xrightarrow{r} P'$ to indicate that P' is the partial program obtained by replacing the first occurrence of H with the right-hand-side of r, and we write $\text{FILL}(P, r) = P'$ whenever $P \xrightarrow{r} P'$.

Example 1. Consider the small programming language shown in Fig. 2 for manipulating lists of integers. The following partial program P over this DSL contains three holes, namely L_1, L_2, N_1:

$$\texttt{add}(L_1, \texttt{take}(L_2, N_1))$$

Now, consider the production $r \equiv L \rightarrow \texttt{reverse}(L)$. In this case, $\text{FILL}(P, r)$ yields the following partial program P':

$$\texttt{add}(\texttt{reverse}(L_1), \texttt{take}(L_2, N_1))$$

Program Synthesis Problem. Given a specification ϕ and language $L = (V, \Sigma, R, S)$, the goal of program synthesis is to find a *complete* program P such that $S \xrightarrow{*} P$ and P satisfies ϕ. We use the notation $P \models \phi$ to indicate that P is a complete program that satisfies specification ϕ.

Deduction Engine. In the remainder of this paper, we assume access to a *deduction engine* that can determine whether a partial program P is *feasible* with respect to specification ϕ. To make this more precise, we introduce the following notion of feasibility.

Definition 2 (Feasible partial program). *Given a specification ϕ and language $L = (V, \Sigma, R, S)$, a partial program P is said to be* feasible *with respect to ϕ if there exists any complete program P' such that $P \xrightarrow{*} P'$ and $P' \models \phi$.*

In other words, a feasible partial program can be refined into a complete program that satisfies the specification. We assume that our deduction oracle over-approximates feasibility. That is, if P is feasible with respect to specification ϕ, then $\text{DEDUCE}(P, \phi)$ should report that P is feasible but not necessarily vice versa. Note that almost all deduction techniques used in the program synthesis literature satisfy this assumption [18, 19, 21, 27, 53].

Example 2. Consider again the DSL from Fig. 2 and the specification ϕ defined by the following input-output example:

$$[65, 2, 73, 62, 78] \mapsto [143, 129, 213, 204, 345]$$

The partial program $\mathtt{add}(\mathtt{reverse}(x), \mathtt{take}(x, N))$ is infeasible because, no matter what production we use to fill non-terminal N, the resulting program cannot satisfy the provided specification for the following reason:

- Given a list l and integer n where $n < length(l)$, $\mathtt{take}(l, n)$ returns the first n elements in l. Thus, the length of $\mathtt{take}(l, n)$ is smaller than that of l.
- The construct $\mathtt{reverse}(l)$ reverses its input; thus, the size of the output list is the same as its input.
- Finally, $\mathtt{add}(l_1, l_2)$ constructs a new list by adding the elements of its input lists pair-wise. Thus, $\mathtt{add}$ expects the two input lists to be the same size.
- Since the outputs of $\mathtt{reverse}$ and $\mathtt{take}$ do not have the same size, we cannot combine them using $\mathtt{add}$.

Several techniques from prior work (e.g., [18,19,39,53]) can prove the infeasibility of such partial programs by using an SMT solver (provided specifications are given for the DSL constructs).

Beyond checking feasibility, some deduction techniques used for synthesis can also provide additional information [18,32,54]. In particular, given a partial program P that is infeasible with respect to specification ϕ, several deduction engines can generate a set of other infeasible partial programs $P_1, \ldots, P_n$ that are infeasible for the same reason as P. To unify both types of feedback, we assume that the output of the deduction oracle $\mathcal{O}$ is a set S of partial programs such that S is empty if and only if $\mathcal{O}$ decides that the partial program is feasible.

This discussion is summarized by the following definition:

Definition 3 (Deduction engine). *Given a partial program P and specification ϕ, $\text{DEDUCE}(P, \phi)$ yields a set of partial programs S such that (1) if $S \neq \varnothing$, then P is infeasible, and (2) for every $P' \in S$, it must be the case that P' is infeasible with respect to ϕ.*

Example 3. Consider again the same infeasible partial program P given in Example 2. Since $\mathtt{drop}(l, n)$ drops the first n elements from list l (where $n < length(l)$), it also produces a list whose length is smaller than that of the input. Thus, the following partial program P' is also infeasible for the same reason as P:

$$P' \equiv \mathtt{add}(\mathtt{reverse}(x), \mathtt{drop}(x, N))$$

Thus, $\text{DEDUCE}(P, \phi)$ may return the set $\{P, P'\}$.

4   MDP Formulation of Deduction-Guided Synthesis

Given a specification ϕ and language $L = (V, \Sigma, R, S)$, we can formulate the program synthesis problem as an MDP $\mathcal{M}_\phi = (\mathcal{S}, \mathcal{S}_I, \mathcal{S}_T, \mathcal{A}, \mathcal{F}, \mathcal{R})$, where:

- States $\mathcal{S}$ include all partial programs P such that $S \overset{*}{\Rightarrow} P$ as well as a special label $\bot$ indicating a syntactically ill-formed partial program
- $\mathcal{S}_I$ places all probability mass on the empty program S, i.e.,

$$\mathcal{S}_I(P) = \begin{cases} 1 \text{ if } P = S \\ 0 \text{ if } P \neq S \end{cases}$$

- $\mathcal{S}_T$ includes complete programs as well as infeasible partial programs, i.e.,

$$P \in \mathcal{S}_T \iff \text{IsComplete}(P) \lor \text{Deduce}(P, \phi) \neq \varnothing \lor P = \bot$$

- Actions $\mathcal{A}$ are exactly the productions R for the DSL
- Transitions $\mathcal{F}$ correspond to filling a hole using some production i.e.,

$$\mathcal{F}(P,\ r = (H \to e)) = \begin{cases} \bot & \text{if } H \text{ is not a hole in } P \\ \text{Fill}(P, r) & \text{otherwise} \end{cases}$$

- The reward function penalizes infeasible programs and rewards correct solutions, i.e.,

$$\mathcal{R}(P) = \begin{cases} 1 & \text{if } P \models \phi \\ -1 & \text{if } P = \bot \lor \text{Deduce}(P, \phi) \neq \varnothing \lor (\text{IsComplete}(P) \land P \not\models \phi) \\ 0 & \text{otherwise.} \end{cases}$$

Observe that our reward function encodes the goal of synthesizing a complete program P that satisfies ϕ, while avoiding the exploration of as many infeasible programs as possible. Thus, if we have a good policy π for this MDP, then a rollout of π is likely to correspond to a solution of the given synthesis problem.

Example 4. Consider the same specification (i.e., input-output example) ϕ from Example 2 and the DSL from Example 1. The partial program

$$P \equiv \texttt{add}(\texttt{reverse}(x), \texttt{take}(x, N))$$

is a terminal state of $\mathcal{M}_\phi$ since $\text{Deduce}(P, \phi)$ yields a non-empty set, and we have $\mathcal{R}(P) = -1$. Thus, the following sequence corresponds to a rollout of $\mathcal{M}_\phi$:

$(S, S \to L, 0),\ (L, L \to \texttt{add}(L, L), 0),\ (\texttt{add}(L_1, L_2), L \to \texttt{reverse}(L), 0)$
$(\texttt{add}(\texttt{reverse}(L_1), L_2), L \to x, 0),\ (\texttt{add}(\texttt{reverse}(x), L), L \to \texttt{take}(L, N), 0)$
$(\texttt{add}(\texttt{reverse}(x), \texttt{take}(L, N)), L \to x, 0), (\texttt{add}(\texttt{reverse}(x), \texttt{take}(x, N)), \varnothing, -1).$

Simplified Policy Gradient Estimate for $\mathcal{M}_\phi$. Since our synthesis algorithm will be based on policy gradient, we will now derive a simplified policy gradient for our MDP $\mathcal{M}_\phi$. First, by construction of $\mathcal{M}_\phi$, a rollout ζ has the form

$$(P_1, r_1, 0), ..., (P_m, \varnothing, q)$$

where $q = 1$ if $P_m \models \phi$ and $q = -1$ otherwise. Thus, the term $\ell(P)$ from Eq. 1 can be simplified as follows:

$$\ell(P_m) = \sum_{i=1}^{m-1} q \cdot \nabla_\theta \log \pi_\theta(P_i, r_i), \tag{3}$$

where $P_m \sim \mathcal{D}_{\pi_\theta}$ is a final state (i.e., complete program or infeasible partial program) sampled using π_θ. Then, Eq. 1 is equivalently

$$\nabla_\theta J(\pi_\theta) \approx \frac{1}{n} \sum_{k=1}^{n} \ell(P^{(k)}), \tag{4}$$

where $P^{(k)} \sim \mathcal{D}_{\pi_\theta}$ for each $k \in \{1, ..., n\}$.

5 RL-Based Synthesis Algorithm

In this section, we describe our synthesis algorithm based on reinforcement learning. Our method is an *off-policy* variant of the standard (on-policy) policy gradient algorithm and incorporates additional feedback – in the form of other infeasible programs – provided by the deduction engine when improving its policy parameters. We first give a high-level overview of the synthesis algorithm and then explain how to update the policy.

5.1 Overview of Synthesis Algorithm

Our RL-based synthesis algorithm is presented in Fig. 3. In addition to specification ϕ and domain-specific language L, this algorithm also takes as input an initial policy π_0 that has been trained off-line on a representative set of training problems.[1] In each iteration of the main synthesis loop, we first obtain a rollout of the current policy by calling the GETROLLOUT procedure at line 7. Here, each rollout either corresponds to a complete program P or an infeasible partial program. If P is complete *and* satisfies the specification, we return it as a solution in line 8. Otherwise, we use feedback $\mathcal{C}$ provided by the deduction engine to improve the current policy (line 9). In the following subsections, we explain the GETROLLOUT and UPDATEPOLICY procedures in more detail.

5.2 Sampling Rollouts

The GETROLLOUT procedure iteratively expands a partial program, starting from the start symbol S of the grammar (line 11). In each iteration (lines 12–19), we first check whether the current partial program P is feasible by calling DEDUCE. If P is infeasible (i.e., $\mathcal{C}$ is non-empty), then we have reached a terminal

---

[1] We explain how to train this initial policy in Sect. 6.

```
 1: procedure SYNTHESIZE(L, φ, π₀)
 2:     input: Domain-specific language L = (V, Σ, R, S)
 3:     input: Specification φ; initial policy π₀
 4:     output: Complete program P such that P ⊨ φ

 5:     πθ ← π₀
 6:     while true do
 7:         (P, C) ← GETROLLOUT(L, φ, πθ)
 8:         if C = ∅ then return P
 9:         else πθ ← UPDATEPOLICY(πθ, C)

10: procedure GETROLLOUT(L, φ, πθ)
11:     P ← S
12:     while true do
13:         C ← DEDUCE(P, φ)
14:         if C ≠ ∅ then return (P, C)
15:         choose  r ∼ πθ(P) ∧ LHS(r) ∈ HOLES(P)
16:         P ← FILL(P, r)
17:         if ISCOMPLETE(P) then
18:             if  P ⊨ φ then return (P, ∅)
19:             else return (P, {P})

20: procedure UPDATEPOLICY(πθ, C)
21:     for k ∈ {1, ..., n'} do
22:         P^(k) ∼ Uniform(C)
```

$$23: \quad \theta' \leftarrow \theta + \eta \sum_{k=1}^{n'} \ell(P^{(k)}) \cdot \frac{\mathcal{D}_{\pi_\theta}(P^{(k)})}{1/|\mathcal{C}|}$$

```
24:     return πθ'
```

Fig. 3. Deduction-guided synthesis algorithm based on reinforcement learning

state of the MDP; thus, we return P as the final state of the rollout. Otherwise, we continue expanding P according to the current policy π_θ. Specifically, we first sample an action (i.e., grammar production) r that is applicable to the current state (i.e., the left-hand-side of r is a hole in P), and, then, we expand P by calling the FILL procedure (defined in Sect. 3) at line 16. If the resulting program is complete, we have reached a terminal state and return P; otherwise, we continue expanding P according to the current policy.

5.3   Improving the Policy

As mentioned earlier, our algorithm improves the policy by using the feedback $\mathcal{C}$ provided by the deduction engine. Specifically, consider an infeasible program P explored by the synthesis algorithm at line 7. Since DEDUCE(P, ϕ) yields a set of infeasible programs, for every program $P' \in \mathcal{C}$, we know that the reward should be -1. As a consequence, we should be able to incorporate the rollout used to construct P into the policy gradient estimate based on Eq. (3). However, the challenge to doing so is that Eq. (4) relies on *on-policy* samples – i.e., the programs $P^{(k)}$ in Eq. (4) must be sampled using the current policy π_θ. Since $P' \in C$ is not sampled using π_θ, we cannot directly use it in Eq. (4).

Instead, we use *off-policy* RL to incorporate P' into the estimate of $\nabla_\theta J(\pi_\theta)$ [28]. Essentially, the idea is to use *importance weighting* to incorporate data sampled from a different distribution than $\mathcal{D}_{\pi_\theta}$. In particular, suppose we are given a distribution $\tilde{\mathcal{D}}$ over final states. Then, we can derive the following gradient:

$$\nabla_\theta J(\pi_\theta) = \mathbb{E}_{P \sim \mathcal{D}_{\pi_\theta}}[\ell(P)] \tag{5}$$

$$= \mathbb{E}_{P \sim \tilde{\mathcal{D}}}\left[\ell(P) \cdot \frac{\mathcal{D}_{\pi_\theta}(P)}{\tilde{\mathcal{D}}(P)}\right]$$

Intuitively, the *importance weight* $\frac{\mathcal{D}_{\pi_\theta}(P)}{\tilde{\mathcal{D}}(P)}$ accounts for the fact that P is sampled from the "wrong" distribution.

Now, we can use the distribution $\tilde{\mathcal{D}} = \text{Uniform}(\text{DEDUCE}(P', \phi))$ for a randomly sampled final state $P' \sim \mathcal{D}_{\pi_\theta}$. Thus, we have[2]:

Theorem 2. *The policy gradient is*

$$\nabla_\theta J(\pi_\theta) = \mathbb{E}_{P' \sim \mathcal{D}_{\pi_\theta}, P \sim Uniform(\text{DEDUCE}(P', \phi))}\left[\ell(P) \cdot \frac{\mathcal{D}_{\pi_\theta}(P)}{1/|\text{DEDUCE}(P', \phi)|}\right]. \tag{6}$$

Proof. Note that

$$\nabla_\theta J(\pi_\theta) = \mathbb{E}_{P' \sim \mathcal{D}_{\pi_\theta}}[\nabla_\theta J(\pi_\theta)]$$

$$= \mathbb{E}_{P' \sim \mathcal{D}_{\pi_\theta}, P \sim Uniform(\text{DEDUCE}(P', \phi))}\left[\ell(P) \cdot \frac{\mathcal{D}_{\pi_\theta}(P)}{1/|\text{DEDUCE}(P', \phi)|}\right],$$

as claimed.   □

The corresponding estimate of $\nabla_\theta J(\pi_\theta)$ is given by the following equation:

$$\nabla_\theta J(\theta) \approx \frac{1}{n}\sum_{k=1}^{n}\frac{1}{n'}\sum_{k'=1}^{n'}\ell(P^{(k,k')}) \cdot \frac{\mathcal{D}_{\pi_\theta}(P^{(k,k')})}{1/|\text{DEDUCE}(P^{(k)}, \phi)|},$$

where $P^{(k)} \sim \tilde{\mathcal{D}}$ and $P^{(k,k')} \sim \text{Uniform}(\text{DEDUCE}(P^{(k)}, \phi))$ for each $k \in \{1, ..., n\}$ and $k' \in \{1, ..., n'\}$. Our actual implementation uses $n = 1$, in which case this equation can be simplified to the following:

$$\nabla_\theta J(\theta) \approx \frac{1}{n'}\sum_{k'=1}^{n'}\ell(P) \cdot \frac{\mathcal{D}_{\pi_\theta}(P^{(k')})}{1/|\text{DEDUCE}(P, \phi)|}, \tag{7}$$

---

[2] Technically, importance weighting requires that the support of $\tilde{\mathcal{D}}$ contains the support of $\mathcal{D}_{\pi_\theta}$. We can address this issue by combining $\tilde{\mathcal{D}}$ and $\mathcal{D}_{\pi_\theta}$—in particular, take $\tilde{\mathcal{D}}(P) = (1 - \epsilon) \cdot \text{Uniform}(\text{DEDUCE}(P', \phi))(P) + \epsilon \cdot \mathcal{D}_{\pi_\theta}(P)$, for any $\epsilon > 0$.

where $P \sim \tilde{D}$ and $P^{(k')} \sim \text{Uniform}(\text{DEDUCE}(P, \phi))$ for each $k' \in \{1, ..., n'\}$.

Now, going back to our synthesis algorithm from Fig. 3, the UPDATEPOLICY procedure uses Eq. 7 to update the policy parameters θ. Specifically, given a set $\mathcal{C}$ of infeasible partial programs, we first sample n' programs $P^{(1)}, \ldots, P^{(n')}$ from $\mathcal{C}$ uniformly at random (line 22). Then, we use the probability of each $P^{(k)}$ being sampled from the current distribution $\mathcal{D}_{\pi_\theta}$ to update the policy parameters to a new value θ' according to Eq. 7.

Example 5. Suppose that the current policy assigns the following probabilities to these state, action pairs:

$$\pi_\theta((\text{add}(\text{reverse}(x), L)), L \rightarrow \text{take}(L, N)) = 0.3$$
$$\pi_\theta((\text{add}(\text{reverse}(x), L)), L \rightarrow \text{drop}(L, N)) = 0.3$$
$$\pi_\theta((\text{add}(\text{reverse}(x), L)), L \rightarrow \text{sumUpTo}(L)) = 0.1$$

Furthermore, suppose that we sample the following rollout using this policy:

$$P \equiv \text{add}(\text{reverse}(x), \text{take}(x, N)),$$

This corresponds to an infeasible partial program, and, as in Example 3, DEDUCE(P, ϕ) yields $\{P, P'\}$ where $P' \equiv \text{add}(\text{reverse}(x), \text{drop}(x, N))$. Using the gradients derived by Eq. 7, we update the policy parameters θ to θ'. The updated policy now assigns the following probabilities to the same state, action pairs:

$$\pi_{\theta'}((\text{add}(\text{reverse}(x), L)), L \rightarrow \text{take}(L, N)) = 0.15$$
$$\pi_{\theta'}((\text{add}(\text{reverse}(x), L)), L \rightarrow \text{drop}(L, N)) = 0.15$$
$$\pi_{\theta'}((\text{add}(\text{reverse}(x), L)), L \rightarrow \text{sumUpTo}(L)) = 0.2$$

Observe that the updated policy makes it less likely that we will expand the partial program $\text{add}(\text{reverse}(x), L))$ using the drop production in addition to the take production. Thus, if we reach the same state $\text{add}(\text{reverse}(x), L)$ during rollout sampling in the next iteration, the policy will make it more likely to explore the sumUpTo production, which does occur in the desired program

$$\text{add}(\text{reverse}(x), \text{sumUpTo}(x))$$

that meets the specification from Example 2.

6   Implementation

We have implemented the proposed algorithm in a new tool called CONCORD written in Python. In what follows, we elaborate on various aspects of our implementation.

6.1 Deduction Engine

CONCORD uses the same deduction engine described by Feng et al. [18]. Specifically, given a partial program P, CONCORD first generates a specification φ of P by leveraging the abstract semantics of each DSL construct. Then, CONCORD issues a satisfiability query to the Z3 SMT solver [15] to check whether φ is consistent with the provided specification. If it is not, this means that P is infeasible, and CONCORD proceeds to infer other partial programs that are also infeasible for the same reason as P. To do so, CONCORD first obtains an unsatisfiable core ψ for the queried formula, and, for each clause c_i of ψ originating from DSL construct f_i, it identifies a set S_i of other DSL constructs whose semantics imply c_i. Finally, it generates a set of other infeasible programs by replacing all f_i's in the current program with another construct drawn from its corresponding set S_i.

6.2 Policy Network

Architecture. As shown by Fig. 4, CONCORD represents its underlying policy using a deep neural network (DNN) $\pi_\theta(r \mid P)$, which takes as input the current state (i.e., a partial program P) and outputs a probability distribution over actions (i.e., productions r in the DSL). We represent each program P as a flat sequence of statements and use a recurrent neural network (RNN) architecture, as this is a natural choice for sequence inputs. In particular, our policy network is a gated recurrent unit (GRU) network [13], which is a state-of-the-art RNN architecture. Our policy network has one hidden layer with 256 neurons; this layer is sequentially applied to each statement in the partial program together with the latent vector from processing the previous statement. Once the entire partial program P has been encoded into a vector, π_θ has a final layer that outputs a distribution over DSL productions r based on this vector.

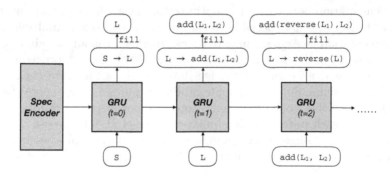

Fig. 4. The architecture of the policy network showing how to roll out the partial program in Example 4.

Pretraining the Initial Policy. Recall from Sect. 5 that our synthesis algorithm takes a input an *initial policy network* that is updated during the synthesis process. One way to initialize the the policy network would be to use a standard random initialization of the network weights. However, a more effective alternative is to *pretrain* the policy on a benchmark suite of program synthesis problems [44]. Specifically, consider a representative training set X_{train} of synthesis problems of the form (ϕ, P), where ϕ is the specification and P is the desired program. To obtain an initial policy, we augment our policy network to take as input an encoding of the specification ϕ for the current synthesis problem – i.e., it has the form $\pi_\theta(r \mid P, \phi)$.[3] Then, we use supervised learning to train π_θ to predict P given ϕ—i.e.,

$$\theta^0 = \arg\max_\theta \sum_{(\phi,P)\in X_{\text{train}}} \sum_{i=1}^{|P|-1} \pi_\theta(r_i \mid P_i, \phi).$$

We optimize θ using stochastic-gradient descent (SGD) on this objective.

Given a new synthesis problem ϕ, we use π_{θ^0} as the initial policy. Our RL algorithm then continues to update the parameters starting from θ^0.

6.3 Input Featurization

As standard, we need a way to featurize the inputs to our policy network – i.e., the statements in each partial program P, and the specification ϕ. Our current implementation assumes that statements are drawn from a finite set and featurizes them by training a different embedding vector for each kind of statement. While our general methodology can be applied to different types specifications, our implementation featurizes the specification under the assumption that it consists of input-output examples and uses the same methodology described by Balog et al. [2].

6.4 Optimizations

Our implementation performs a few optimization over the algorithm presented in Sect. 5. First, since it is possible to sample the same rollout multiple times, our implementation uses a hash map to check whether a rollout has already been explored. Second, in different invocations of the GETROLLOUT procedure from Fig. 3, we may end up querying the feasibility of the same state (i.e., partial program) *many* times. Since checking feasibility requires a potentially-expensive call to the SMT solver, our implementation also memoizes the results of feasibility checks for each state. Finally, similar to Chen et al. [11], we use a 3-model ensemble to alleviate some of the randomness in the synthesis process and return a solution as soon as one of the models in the ensemble finds a correct solution.

7   Evaluation

In this section, we describe the results from our experimental evaluation, which is designed to answer the following key research questions:

---

[3] Including the specification as an input to π_θ is unnecessary if we do not use pretraining, since ϕ does not change for a single synthesis problem.

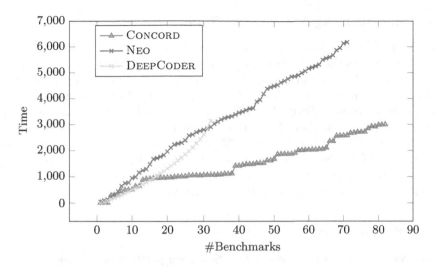

Fig. 5. Comparison between CONCORD, NEO, and DEEPCODER

1. How does CONCORD compare against existing synthesis tools?
2. What is the impact of updating the statistical model during synthesis? (i.e., is reinforcement learning actually useful)?
3. How important is the proposed off-policy RL algorithm compared to standard policy gradient?
4. How important is it to get feedback from the deduction engine when updating the policy?

Benchmarks. We evaluate the proposed technique on a total of 100 synthesis tasks used in prior work [2, 18]. Specifically, these synthesis tasks require performing non-trivial transformations and computations over lists using a functional programming language. Since these benchmarks have been used to evaluate both NEO [18] and DEEPCODER [2], they provide a fair ground for comparing our approach against two of the most closely-related techniques. In particular, note that DEEPCODER uses a pre-trained deep neural network to guide its search, whereas NEO uses both statistical and logical reasoning (i.e., statistical model to guide search and deduction to prune the search space). However, unlike our proposed approach, neither NEO nor DEEPCODER update their statistical model during synthesis time.

Training. Recall that our algorithm utilizes a pre-trained initial policy. To generate the initial policy, we use the same methodology described in DeepCoder [2] and adopted in NEO [18]. Specifically, we randomly generate both programs and inputs, and we obtain the corresponding output by executing the program. Then, we train the DNN model discussed in Sect. 6 on the Google Cloud Platform with a 2.20 GHz Intel Xeon CPU and an NVIDIA Tesla K80 GPU using 16 GB of memory.

7.1   Comparison Against Existing Tools

To answer our first research question, we compare CONCORD against both NEO and DeepCoder on the 100 synthesis benchmarks discussed earlier. The result of this comparison is shown in Fig. 5, which plots the number of benchmarks solved within a given time limit for each of the three tools. As we can see from this figure, CONCORD outperforms DEEPCODER and NEO both in terms of synthesis time as well as the number of benchmarks solved within the 5-min time limit. In particular, CONCORD can solve 82% of these benchmarks with an average running time of 36 s, whereas NEO (resp. DEEPCODER) solves 71% (resp. 32%) with an average running time of 99 s (resp. 205 s). Thus, we believe these results answer our first research question in a positive way.

7.2   Ablation Study

To answer our remaining research questions, we perform an ablation study in which we compare CONCORD against three variants:

- **Concord-noRL:** This variant does not use reinforcement learning to update its policy during synthesis. However, it still uses the pre-trained policy to guide search, and it also uses deduction to prune infeasible partial programs. In other words, Concord-noRL is the same as the synthesis algorithm from Fig. 3 but it does not invoke the `UpdatePolicy` procedure to improve its policy during synthesis.
- **Concord-NoDeduce:** This variant uses reinforcement learning; however, it does not incorporate feedback from the deduction engine. That is, rather than checking feasibility of partial programs, it instead samples complete programs and uses the percentage of passing input-output examples as the reward signal. Note that this variant of CONCORD essentially corresponds to the technique proposed by Si et al. [44].[4]
- **Concord-StandardPG:** Recall that our algorithm uses an off-policy variant of the standard policy gradient algorithm to incorporate additional feedback from the deduction engine. To evaluate the benefit of our proposed approach, we created a variant called Concord-StandardPG that uses the standard (i.e., on-policy) policy gradient algorithm. In other words, ConcordStandardPG implements the same synthesis algorithm from Fig. 3 except that it uses Theorem 1 to update θ instead of Theorem 2.

The results from this evaluation are summarized in Table 1. Here, the first column labeled "# solved" shows the number of solved benchmarks, and the second column shows percentage improvement over NEO in terms of benchmarks solved. The third column shows average synthesis time for benchmarks that can

---

[4] We reimplement the RL algorithm proposed in [44] since we cannot directly compare against their tool. Specifically, the policy network in their implementation is tailored to their problem domain.

Table 1. Results of ablation study result comparing different variants.

	# solved	Delta to NEO	Avg. time (s)	Speedup over NEO
CONCORD-noRL	56	−21%	48	1.63×
CONCORD-NoDeduce	65	−8%	21	3.66×
CONCORD-StandardPG	65	−8%	27	2.88×
CONCORD	82	+15%	9	8.71×

be solved by *all* variants and NEO. Finally, the last column shows speed-up in terms of synthesis time compared to NEO.

As we can see from this table, all variants are significantly worse than CONCORD in terms of the number of benchmarks that can be solved within a 5-min time limit[5]. Furthermore, as we can see from the column labeled "Delta to NEO", all of our proposed ideas are important for improving over the state-of-the-art, as NEO outperforms all three variants but not the full CONCORD system, which solves 15% more benchmarks compared to NEO.

Next, looking at the third column of Table 1, we see that all three variants of CONCORD are significantly slower compared to CONCORD in terms of synthesis time. While both CONCORD and all of its variants outperform NEO in terms of synthesis time (for benchmarks solved by all tools), CONCORD by far achieves the greatest speed-up over NEO.

In summary, the results from Table 1 highlight that all of our proposed ideas (i.e., (1) improving policy at synthesis time; (2) using feedback from deduction; and (3) off-policy RL) make a significant difference in practice. Thus, we conclude that the ablation study positively answers our last three research questions.

8   Related Work

In this section, we survey prior work that is closely related to the techniques proposed in this paper.

Program Synthesis. Over the past decade, there has been significant interest in automatically synthesizing programs from high-level expressions of user intent [2,6,21,23,25,39,40,46]. Some of these techniques are geared towards computer end-users and therefore utilize informal specifications such as input-output examples [23,40,50], natural language [24,42,55,56], or a combination of both [10,12]. On the other hand, program synthesis techniques geared towards programmers often utilize additional information, such as a program sketch [17,36,46,49] or types [33,39] in addition to test cases [20,30] or logical specifications [6,49]. While the synthesis methodology proposed in this paper

---

[5] To understand the improvement brought by the pre-trainedd policy, we also conduct a baseline experiment by using randomly initialized policy in CONCORD. Given the setting, CONCORD can solve as many as 27% of the benchmarks in the given 5-min time limit.

can, in principle, be applied to a broad set of specifications, the particular featurization strategy we use in our implementation is tailored towards input-output examples.

Deduction-Based Pruning. In this paper, we build on a line of prior work on using deduction to prune the search space of programs in a DSL [18,19,21,39,53]. Some of these techniques utilize type-information and type-directed reasoning to detect infeasible partial programs [20–22,37,39]. On the other hand, other approaches use some form of lightweight program analysis to prune the search space [18,19,53]. Concretely, BLAZE uses abstract interpretation to build a compact version space representation capturing the space of all feasible programs [53]; MORPHEUS [19] and NEO [18] utilize logical specifications of DSL constructs to derive specifications of partial programs and query an SMT solver to check for feasibility; SCYTHE [50] and VISER [51] use deductive reasoning to compute approximate results of partial programs to check their feasibility. Our approach learns from deduction feedback to improve search efficiency. As mentioned in Sect. 6, the deductive reasoning engine used in our implementation is similar to the latter category; however, it can, in principle, be used in conjunction with other deductive reasoning techniques for pruning the search space.

Learning from Failed Synthesis Attempts. The technique proposed in this paper can utilize feedback from the deduction engine in the form of other infeasible partial programs. This idea is known as *conflict-driven learning* and has been recently adopted from the SAT solving literature [5,57] to program synthesis [18]. Specifically, NEO uses the unsat core of the program's specification to derive other infeasible partial programs that share the same root cause of failure, and, as described in Sect. 6, we use the same idea in our implementation of the deduction engine. While we use logical specifications to infer other infeasible programs, there also exist other techniques (e.g., based on testing [54]) to perform this kind of inference.

Machine Learning for Synthesis. This paper is related to a long line of work on using machine learning for program synthesis. Among these techniques, some of them train a machine learning model (typically a deep neural network) to directly predict a full program from the given specification [12,16,34,35]. Many of these approaches are based on sequence-to-sequence models [47], sequence to tree models [56], or graph neural networks [41] commonly used in machine translation.

A different approach, sometimes referred to as *learning to search*, is to train a statistical model that is used to *guide* the search rather than directly predict the target program. For example, DeepCoder [2] uses a deep neural network (DNN) to predict the most promising grammar productions to use for the given input-output examples. Similarly, R3NN [38] and NGDS [26] use DNNs to predict the most promising grammar productions conditioned on both the specification and the current partial program. In addition, there has been work on using concrete program executions on the given input-output examples to guide the DNN [11,52]. Our technique for pretraining the initial policy network is based on the same ideas as these supervised learning approaches; however, their initial policies do not change during the synthesis algorithm, whereas we continue to update the policy using RL.

While most of the work at the intersection of synthesis and machine learning uses *supervised learning* techniques, recent work has also proposed using reinforcement learning to speed up syntax-guided synthesis [8,29,31,44] These approaches are all on-policy and do not incorporate feedback from a deduction engine. In contrast, in our problem domain, rewards are very sparse in the program space, which makes exploration highly challenging in a on-policy learning setting. Our approach addresses this problem using off-policy RL to incorporate feedback from the deduction engine. Our ablation study results demonstrate that our off-policy RL is able to scale to more complex benchmarks.

Reinforcement Learning for Formal Methods. There has been recent interest in applying reinforcement learning (RL) to solve challenging PL problems where large amounts of labeled training data are too expensive to obtain. For instance, Si et al. use graph-based RL to automatically infer loop invariants [43], Singh et al. use Q-learning (a different RL algorithm) to speed up program analysis based on abstract interpretation [45], Dai et al. [14] uses meta-reinforcement learning for test data generation, and Chen et al. [9] uses RL to speed up relational program verification. However, these approaches only use RL offline to pretrain a DNN policy used to guide search. In contrast, we perform reinforcement learning online during synthesis. Bastani et al. has used an RL algorithm called Monte-carlo tree search (MCTS) to guide a specification inference algorithm [3]; however, their setting does not involve any kind of deduction.

9   Conclusion and Future Work

We presented a new program synthesis algorithm based on reinforcement learning. Given an initial policy trained off-line, our method uses this policy to guide its search at synthesis time but also gradually improves this policy using feedback obtained from a deductive reasoning engine. Specifically, we formulated program synthesis as a reinforcement learning problem and proposed a new variant of the *policy gradient* algorithm that is better suited to solve this problem. In addition, we implemented the proposed approach in a new tool called CONCORD and evaluated it on 100 synthesis tasks taken from prior work. Our evaluation shows that CONCORD outperforms a state-of-the-art tool by solving 15% more benchmarks with an average speedup of 8.71×. In addition, our ablation study highlights the advantages of our proposed reinforcement learning algorithm.

There are several avenues for future work. First, while our approach is applicable to different DSLs and specifications, our current implementation focuses on input-output examples. Thus, we are interested in extending our implementation to richer types of specifications and evaluating our method in application domains that require such specifications. Another interesting avenue for future work is to integrate our method with other types of deductive reasoning engines.

In particular, while our deduction method is based on SMT, it would be interesting to try other methods (e.g., based on types or abstract interpretation) in conjunction with our proposed RL approach.

References

1. Alur, R., et al.: Syntax-guided synthesis. IEEE (2013)
2. Balog, M., Gaunt, A.L., Brockschmidt, M., Nowozin, S., Tarlow, D.: DeepCoder: learning to write programs. In: Proceedings of International Conference on Learning Representations. OpenReview (2017)
3. Bastani, O., Sharma, R., Aiken, A., Liang, P.: Active learning of points-to specifications. In: Proceedings of the 39th ACM SIGPLAN Conference on Programming Language Design and Implementation, pp. 678–692 (2018)
4. Bavishi, R., Lemieux, C., Fox, R., Sen, K., Stoica, I.: AutoPandas: neural-backed generators for program synthesis. PACMPL 3(OOPSLA), 168:1–168:27 (2019)
5. Biere, A., Heule, M., van Maaren, H., Walsh, T.: Conflict-driven clause learning SAT solvers. In: Handbook of Satisfiability. Frontiers in Artificial Intelligence and Applications, pp. 131–153 (2009)
6. Bornholt, J., Torlak, E.: Synthesizing memory models from framework sketches and litmus tests. In: Proceedings of the 38th ACM SIGPLAN Conference on Programming Language Design and Implementation, PLDI 2017, Barcelona, Spain, 18–23 June 2017, pp. 467–481 (2017)
7. Brockschmidt, M., Allamanis, M., Gaunt, A.L., Polozov, O.: Generative code modeling with graphs. In: ICLR (2019)
8. Bunel, R., Hausknecht, M., Devlin, J., Singh, R., Kohli, P.: Leveraging grammar and reinforcement learning for neural program synthesis. In: ICLR (2018)
9. Chen, J., Wei, J., Feng, Y., Bastani, O., Dillig, I.: Relational verification using reinforcement learning. PACMPL 3(OOPSLA), 14:11–14:130 (2019)
10. Chen, Q., Wang, X., Ye, X., Durrett, G., Dillig, I.: Multi-modal synthesis of regular expressions (2019)
11. Chen, X., Liu, C., Song, D.: Execution-guided neural program synthesis. In: ICLR (2018)
12. Chen, Y., Martins, R., Feng, Y.: Maximal multi-layer specification synthesis. In: Proceedings of the ACM Joint Meeting on European Software Engineering Conference and Symposium on the Foundations of Software Engineering, ESEC/SIGSOFT FSE 2019, Tallinn, Estonia, 26–30 August 2019, pp. 602–612 (2019)
13. Cho, K., et al.: Learning phrase representations using RNN encoder-decoder for statistical machine translation. arXiv preprint arXiv:1406.1078 (2014)
14. Dai, H., Li, Y., Wang, C., Singh, R., Huang, P., Kohli, P.: Learning transferable graph exploration. In: Advances in Neural Information Processing Systems 32: Annual Conference on Neural Information Processing Systems 2019, NeurIPS 2019, Vancouver, BC, Canada, 8–14 December 2019, pp. 2514–2525 (2019). http://papers.nips.cc/paper/8521-learning-transferable-graph-exploration
15. de Moura, L., Bjørner, N.: Z3: an efficient SMT solver. In: Ramakrishnan, C.R., Rehof, J. (eds.) TACAS 2008. LNCS, vol. 4963, pp. 337–340. Springer, Heidelberg (2008). https://doi.org/10.1007/978-3-540-78800-3_24
16. Devlin, J., Uesato, J., Bhupatiraju, S., Singh, R., Mohamed, A.R., Kohli, P.: RobustFill: neural program learning under noisy I/O. In: Proceedings of the 34th International Conference on Machine Learning, vol. 70, pp. 990–998. JMLR.org (2017)

17. Ellis, K., Ritchie, D., Solar-Lezama, A., Tenenbaum, J.: Learning to infer graphics programs from hand-drawn images. In: Advances in Neural Information Processing Systems, pp. 6059–6068 (2018)
18. Feng, Y., Martins, R., Bastani, O., Dillig, I.: Program synthesis using conflict-driven learning. In: Proceedings of Conference on Programming Language Design and Implementation, pp. 420–435 (2018)
19. Feng, Y., Martins, R., Van Geffen, J., Dillig, I., Chaudhuri, S.: Component-based synthesis of table consolidation and transformation tasks from examples. In: Proceedings of Conference on Programming Language Design and Implementation, pp. 422–436. ACM (2017)
20. Feng, Y., Martins, R., Wang, Y., Dillig, I., Reps, T.: Component-based synthesis for complex APIs. In: Proceedings of Symposium on Principles of Programming Languages, pp. 599–612. ACM (2017)
21. Feser, J.K., Chaudhuri, S., Dillig, I.: Synthesizing data structure transformations from input-output examples. In: Proceedings of the 36th ACM SIGPLAN Conference on Programming Language Design and Implementation, Portland, OR, USA, 15–17 June 2015, pp. 229–239 (2015)
22. Frankle, J., Osera, P., Walker, D., Zdancewic, S.: Example-directed synthesis: a type-theoretic interpretation. In: Proceedings of the 43rd Annual ACM SIGPLAN-SIGACT Symposium on Principles of Programming Languages, POPL 2016, St. Petersburg, FL, USA, 20–22 January 2016, pp. 802–815 (2016)
23. Gulwani, S.: Automating string processing in spreadsheets using input-output examples. In: Proceedings of Symposium on Principles of Programming Languages, pp. 317–330. ACM (2011)
24. Iyer, S., Konstas, I., Cheung, A., Zettlemoyer, L.: Mapping language to code in programmatic context. In: Proceedings of the 2018 Conference on Empirical Methods in Natural Language Processing, Brussels, Belgium, 31 October–4 November 2018, pp. 1643–1652 (2018). https://www.aclweb.org/anthology/D18-1192/
25. Jha, S., Gulwani, S., Seshia, S.A., Tiwari, A.: Oracle-guided component-based program synthesis. In: Proceedings of International Conference on Software Engineering, pp. 215–224. ACM/IEEE (2010)
26. Kalyan, A., Mohta, A., Polozov, O., Batra, D., Jain, P., Gulwani, S.: Neural-guided deductive search for real-time program synthesis from examples. In: 6th International Conference on Learning Representations, ICLR 2018, Vancouver, BC, Canada, 30 April–3 May 2018, Conference Track Proceedings (2018). https://openreview.net/forum?id=rywDjg-RW
27. Lee, M., So, S., Oh, H.: Synthesizing regular expressions from examples for introductory automata assignments. In: Proceedings of the 2016 ACM SIGPLAN International Conference on Generative Programming: Concepts and Experiences, pp. 70–80 (2016)
28. Levine, S., Koltun, V.: Guided policy search. In: International Conference on Machine Learning, pp. 1–9 (2013)
29. Liang, C., Norouzi, M., Berant, J., Le, Q.V., Lao, N.: Memory augmented policy optimization for program synthesis and semantic parsing. In: Advances in Neural Information Processing Systems 31: Annual Conference on Neural Information Processing Systems 2018, NeurIPS 2018, Montréal, Canada, 3–8 December 2018, pp. 10015–10027 (2018). http://papers.nips.cc/paper/8204-memory-augmented-policy-optimization-for-program-synthesis-and-semantic-parsing
30. Long, F., Amidon, P., Rinard, M.: Automatic inference of code transforms for patch generation. In: Proceedings of the 2017 11th Joint Meeting on Foundations of Software Engineering, pp. 727–739 (2017)

31. Mao, J., Gan, C., Kohli, P., Tenenbaum, J.B., Wu, J.: The neuro-symbolic concept learner: interpreting scenes, words, and sentences from natural supervision. In: 7th International Conference on Learning Representations, ICLR 2019, New Orleans, LA, USA, 6–9 May 2019 (2019). https://openreview.net/forum?id=rJgMlhRctm

32. Martins, R., Chen, J., Chen, Y., Feng, Y., Dillig, I.: Trinity: an extensible synthesis framework for data science. Proc. VLDB Endow. **12**(12), 1914–1917 (2019)

33. Miltner, A., Maina, S., Fisher, K., Pierce, B.C., Walker, D., Zdancewic, S.: Synthesizing symmetric lenses. Proc. ACM Program. Lang. **3**(ICFP), 1–28 (2019)

34. Neelakantan, A., Le, Q.V., Abadi, M., McCallum, A., Amodei, D.: Learning a natural language interface with neural programmer. In: 5th International Conference on Learning Representations, ICLR 2017, Toulon, France, 24–26 April 2017, Conference Track Proceedings (2017). https://openreview.net/forum?id=ry2YOrcge

35. Neelakantan, A., Le, Q.V., Sutskever, I.: Neural programmer: inducing latent programs with gradient descent. In: 4th International Conference on Learning Representations, ICLR 2016, San Juan, Puerto Rico, 2–4 May 2016, Conference Track Proceedings (2016). http://arxiv.org/abs/1511.04834

36. Nye, M.I., Hewitt, L.B., Tenenbaum, J.B., Solar-Lezama, A.: Learning to infer program sketches. In: Proceedings of the 36th International Conference on Machine Learning, ICML 2019, Long Beach, California, USA, 9–15 June 2019, pp. 4861–4870 (2019). http://proceedings.mlr.press/v97/nye19a.html

37. Osera, P., Zdancewic, S.: Type-and-example-directed program synthesis. In: Proceedings of the 36th ACM SIGPLAN Conference on Programming Language Design and Implementation, Portland, OR, USA, 15–17 June 2015, pp. 619–630 (2015)

38. Parisotto, E., Mohamed, A.R., Singh, R., Li, L., Zhou, D., Kohli, P.: Neuro-symbolic program synthesis. In: ICLR (2017)

39. Polikarpova, N., Kuraj, I., Solar-Lezama, A.: Program synthesis from polymorphic refinement types. In: Proceedings of Conference on Programming Language Design and Implementation, pp. 522–538 (2016)

40. Polozov, O., Gulwani, S.: FlashMeta: a framework for inductive program synthesis. In: Proceedings of the 2015 ACM SIGPLAN International Conference on Object-Oriented Programming, Systems, Languages, and Applications, OOPSLA 2015, Part of SPLASH 2015, Pittsburgh, PA, USA, 25–30 October 2015, pp. 107–126 (2015)

41. Shin, E.C., Allamanis, M., Brockschmidt, M., Polozov, A.: Program synthesis and semantic parsing with learned code idioms. In: Advances in Neural Information Processing Systems, pp. 10824–10834 (2019)

42. Shin, R., Allamanis, M., Brockschmidt, M., Polozov, O.: Program synthesis and semantic parsing with learned code idioms. In: NeurIPS (2019)

43. Si, X., Dai, H., Raghothaman, M., Naik, M., Song, L.: Learning loop invariants for program verification. In: Advances in Neural Information Processing Systems 31: Annual Conference on Neural Information Processing Systems 2018, NeurIPS 2018, Montréal, Canada, 3–8 December 2018, pp. 7762–7773 (2018)

44. Si, X., Yang, Y., Dai, H., Naik, M., Song, L.: Learning a meta-solver for syntax-guided program synthesis. In: 7th International Conference on Learning Representations, ICLR 2019, New Orleans, LA, USA, 6–9 May 2019 (2019)

45. Singh, G., Püschel, M., Vechev, M.T.: Fast numerical program analysis with reinforcement learning. In: Computer Aided Verification - 30th International Conference, CAV 2018, Held as Part of the Federated Logic Conference, FloC 2018, Oxford, UK, 14–17 July 2018, Proceedings, Part I, pp. 211–229 (2018)

46. Solar-Lezama, A., Tancau, L., Bodík, R., Seshia, S.A., Saraswat, V.A.: Combinatorial sketching for finite programs. In: Proceedings of the 12th International Conference on Architectural Support for Programming Languages and Operating Systems, ASPLOS 2006, San Jose, CA, USA, 21–25 October 2006, pp. 404–415 (2006)
47. Sutskever, I., Vinyals, O., Le, Q.V.: Sequence to sequence learning with neural networks. In: Advances in Neural Information Processing Systems, pp. 3104–3112 (2014)
48. Sutton, R.S., McAllester, D.A., Singh, S.P., Mansour, Y.: Policy gradient methods for reinforcement learning with function approximation. In: Advances in Neural Information Processing Systems, pp. 1057–1063 (2000)
49. Torlak, E., Bodík, R.: A lightweight symbolic virtual machine for solver-aided host languages. In: ACM SIGPLAN Conference on Programming Language Design and Implementation, PLDI 2014, Edinburgh, United Kingdom, 09–11 June 2014, pp. 530–541 (2014)
50. Wang, C., Cheung, A., Bodik, R.: Synthesizing highly expressive SQL queries from input-output examples. In: Proceedings of Conference on Programming Language Design and Implementation, pp. 452–466. ACM (2017)
51. Wang, C., Feng, Y., Bodík, R., Cheung, A., Dillig, I.: Visualization by example. PACMPL 4(POPL), 49:1–49:28 (2020). https://doi.org/10.1145/3371117
52. Wang, C., Huang, P., Polozov, A., Brockschmidt, M., Singh, R.: Execution-guided neural program decoding. CoRR abs/1807.03100 (2018). http://arxiv.org/abs/1807.03100
53. Wang, X., Dillig, I., Singh, R.: Program synthesis using abstraction refinement. In: Proceedings of Symposium on Principles of Programming Languages, pp. 63:1–63:30. ACM (2018)
54. Wang, Y., Dong, J., Shah, R., Dillig, I.: Synthesizing database programs for schema refactoring. In: Proceedings of the 40th ACM SIGPLAN Conference on Programming Language Design and Implementation, PLDI 2019, Phoenix, AZ, USA, 22–26 June 2019, pp. 286–300 (2019)
55. Yaghmazadeh, N., Wang, Y., Dillig, I., Dillig, T.: SQLizer: query synthesis from Natural Language. In: Proceedings of International Conference on Object-Oriented Programming, Systems, Languages, and Applications, pp. 63:1–63:26. ACM (2017)
56. Yu, T., Yasunaga, M., Yang, K., Zhang, R., Wang, D., Li, Z., Radev, D.: SyntaxSQLNet: syntax tree networks for complex and cross-domain text-to-SQL task. In: Proceedings of EMNLP. Association for Computational Linguistics (2018)
57. Zhang, L., Madigan, C.F., Moskewicz, M.W., Malik, S.: Efficient conflict driven learning in Boolean satisfiability solver. In: Proceedings of International Conference on Computer-Aided Design, pp. 279–285. IEEE Computer Society (2001)

Manthan: A Data-Driven Approach for Boolean Function Synthesis

Priyanka Golia[1,2]([✉]), Subhajit Roy[1], and Kuldeep S. Meel[2]

[1] Computer Science and Engineering, Indian Institute of Technology Kanpur, Kanpur, India
{pgolia,subhajit}@cse.iitk.ac.in
[2] School of Computing, National University of Singapore, Singapore, Singapore
meel@comp.nus.edu.sg

Abstract. Boolean functional synthesis is a fundamental problem in computer science with wide-ranging applications and has witnessed a surge of interest resulting in progressively improved techniques over the past decade. Despite intense algorithmic development, a large number of problems remain beyond the reach of the state of the art techniques.

Motivated by the progress in machine learning, we propose Manthan, a novel data-driven approach to Boolean functional synthesis. Manthan views functional synthesis as a classification problem, relying on advances in constrained sampling for data generation, and advances in automated reasoning for a novel proof-guided refinement and provable verification. On an extensive and rigorous evaluation over 609 benchmarks, we demonstrate that Manthan significantly improves upon the current state of the art, solving 356 benchmarks in comparison to 280, which is the most solved by a state of the art technique; thereby, we demonstrate an increase of 76 benchmarks over the current state of the art. Furthermore, Manthan solves 60 benchmarks that none of the current state of the art techniques could solve. The significant performance improvements, along with our detailed analysis, highlights several interesting avenues of future work at the intersection of machine learning, constrained sampling, and automated reasoning.

1 Introduction

Given an existentially quantified Boolean formula $\exists Y F(X, Y)$ over the set of variables X and Y, the problem of Boolean functional synthesis is to compute a vector of Boolean functions, denoted by $\Psi(X) = \langle \psi_1(X), \psi_2(X), \ldots, \psi_{|Y|}(X) \rangle$, and referred to as Skolem function vector, such that $\exists Y F(X, Y) \equiv F(X, \Psi(X))$. In the context of applications, the sets X and Y are viewed as inputs and outputs, and the formula $F(X, Y)$ is viewed as a functional specification capturing the relationship between X and Y, while the Skolem function vector $\Psi(X)$ allows one to determine the value of Y for the given X by evaluating Ψ. The study of

---

The open source tool is available at https://github.com/meelgroup/manthan.

© The Author(s) 2020
S. K. Lahiri and C. Wang (Eds.): CAV 2020, LNCS 12225, pp. 611–633, 2020.
https://doi.org/10.1007/978-3-030-53291-8_31

Boolean functional synthesis traces back to Boole [12], and over the decades, the problem has found applications in a wide variety of domains such as certified QBF solving [8,9,36,41], automated program repair [27], program synthesis [44], and cryptography [35].

Theoretical investigations have demonstrated that there exist instances where Boolean functional synthesis takes super-polynomial time. On the other hand, practical applicability has necessitated the development of algorithms with progressively impressive scaling. The algorithmic progress for Boolean functional synthesis has been driven by a diverse set of techniques: (i) the usage of incremental determinization employing the several heuristics in state-of-the-art Conflict Driven Clause Learning (CDCL) solvers [41], (ii) usage of decomposition techniques employing the progress in knowledge compilation [6,19,28,45], and (iii) Counter-Example Guided Abstraction Refinement (CEGAR)-based techniques relying on usage of SAT solvers as black boxes [4–6,28]. While the state of the art techniques are capable of handling problems of complexity beyond the capability of tools a decade ago, the design of scalable algorithms capable of handling industrial problems remains the holy grail.

In this work, we take a step towards the above goal by proposing a novel approach, called Manthan, at the intersection of machine learning, constrained sampling, and automated reasoning. Motivated by the unprecedented advances in machine learning, we view the problem of functional synthesis through the lens of multi-class classification aided by the generation of the data via constrained sampling and employ automated reasoning to certify and refine the learned functions. To this end, the architecture of Manthan comprises of the following three novel techniques:

Data Generation. The state of the art machine learning techniques use training data represented as a set of samples where each sample consists of valuations to features and the corresponding label. In our context, we treat X as the features and Y as labels. Unlike the standard setup of machine learning wherein for each assignment to X, there is a unique label, i.e. assignment to Y, the relationship between X and Y is captured by a relation and not necessarily a function. To this end, we design a weighted sampling strategy to generate a *representative* data set that can be fitted using a *compactly sized* classifier. The weighted sampling strategy, implemented using state of the constrained sampler, seeks to uniformly sample input variables (X) while biasing the valuations of output variables towards a particular value.

Dependency-Driven Classifier for Candidates. Given training data viewed as a valuation of *features* (X) and their corresponding labels (Y), a natural approach from machine learning perspective would be to perform multi-class classification to obtain $Y = h(X)$, where h is a symbolic representation of the learned classifier. Such an approach, however, can not ensure that h can be expressed as a vector of Boolean functions. To this end, we design a dependency aware classifier to construct a vector of decision trees corresponding to each Y_i, wherein each decision tree is expressed as a Boolean function.

Proof-Guided Refinement. Since machine learning techniques often produce good but inexact approximations, we augment our method with automated reasoning techniques to verify the correctness of decision tree-based candidate Skolem functions. To this end, we perform a counterexample driven refinement approach for candidate Skolem functions.

To fully utilize the impressive test accuracy attained by machine learning models, we design a *proof-guided refinement* approach that seeks to identify and apply *minor* repairs to the candidate functions, in an iterative manner, until we converge to a provably correct Skolem function vector. In a departure from prior approaches utilizing the Shannon expansion and self-substitution, we first use a MaxSAT solver to determine potential repair candidates, and employ unsatisfiability cores obtained from the infeasibility proofs capturing the reason for current candidate functions to meet the specification, to construct a *good repair*.

Finally, We perform an extensive evaluation over a diverse set of benchmarks with state-of-the-art tools, viz. C2Syn [4], BFSS [5], and CADET [39]. Of 609 benchmarks, Manthan is able to solve 356 benchmarks while C2Syn, BFSS, and CADET solve 206, 247, and 280 benchmarks respectively. Significantly, Manthan can solve 60 benchmarks beyond the reach of all the other existing tools extending the reach of functional synthesis tools. We then perform an extensive empirical evaluation to understand the impact of different design choices on the performance of Manthan. Our study reveals several surprising observations arising from the inter-play of machine learning and automated reasoning.

Manthan owes its runtime performance to recent advances in machine learning, constrained sampling, and automated reasoning. Encouraged by Manthan's scalability, we will seek to extend the above approach to related problem domains such as automated program synthesis, program repair, and reactive synthesis.

The rest of the paper is organized as follows: We first introduce notations and preliminaries in Sect. 2. We then discuss the related work in Sect. 3. In Sect. 4 we present an overview of Manthan and give an algorithmic description in Section 5. We then describe the experimental methodology and discuss results in Sect. 6. Finally, we conclude in Sect. 7.

2 Notations and Preliminaries

We use lower case letters (with subscripts) to denote propositional variables and upper case letters to denote a subset of variables. The formula $\exists Y F(X, Y)$ is existentially quantified in Y, where $X = \{x_1, \cdots, x_n\}$ and $Y = \{y_1, \cdots, y_m\}$. For notational clarity, we use F to refer to $F(X, Y)$ when clear from the context. We denote $Vars(F)$ as the set of variables appearing in $F(X, Y)$. A literal is a boolean variable or its negation. We often abbreviate universally (resp. existentially) quantified variables as universal (resp. existential) variables.

A *satisfying assignment* of a formula $F(X, Y)$ is a mapping $\sigma : Vars(F) \rightarrow \{0, 1\}$, on which the formula evaluates to True. For $V \subseteq Vars(F)$, $\sigma[V]$ represents the truth values of variables in V in a satisfying assignment σ of F.

We denote the set of all witnesses of F as R_F. For a formula in conjunctive normal form, the *unsatisfiable core*(UnsatCore) is a subset of clauses of the formula for which no satisfying assignment exists.

We use $F(X,Y)|_{y_i=b}$ to denote *substitutions*: a formula obtained after substituting every occurrence of y_i in $F(X,Y)$ by b, where b can be a constant (0 or 1) or a formula. The operator *ite(condition,exp1,exp2)* is used to represent the if-else case: if the *condition* is true, then it returns *exp1*, else it returns *exp2*.

A variable y_i is considered as a *positive unate* if and only if $F(X,Y)|_{y_i=0} \wedge \neg F(X,Y)|_{y_i=1}$ is UNSAT and a *negative unate* if and only if $F(X,Y)|_{y_i=1} \wedge \neg F(X,Y)|_{y_i=0}$ is UNSAT [5].

Given a function vector $\langle \psi_1, \ldots, \psi_m \rangle$ for the vector of variables $\langle y_1, \ldots y_m \rangle$ such that ψ_i is the function corresponding to y_i, we say that there exists a partial order $\prec_d$ over the variables $\{y_1, \ldots y_m\}$ such that $y_i \prec_d y_j$ if ψ_i depends on y_j.

In decision tree learning, a fraction of incorrectly assigned labels refer to the *impurity*. We use Gini Index [38] as a measure of *impurity* for a class label. The *impurity decrease* at a node is the difference of its impurity to the mean of impurities of its children. The *minimum impurity decrease* is a hyper-parameter used to control the maximum allowable impurity at the leaf nodes, thereby providing a lever for how closely the classifier fits the training data.

Given a propositional formula $F(X,Y)$ and a weight function $W(\cdot)$ assigning non-negative weights to every literal, we refer to the *weight* of a satisfying assignment σ, denoted as $W(\sigma)$, as the product of weights of all the literals appearing in σ, i.e., $W(\sigma) = \prod_{l \in \sigma} W(l)$. A *sampler* $\mathcal{A}(\cdot, \cdot)$ is a probabilistic generator that guarantees $\forall \sigma \in R_F$, $\Pr[\mathcal{A}(F, \text{Bias}) = \sigma] \propto W(\sigma)$.

We use a function Bias that takes a mapping from a sequence of variables to the desired weights of their positive literals, and assigns corresponding weights to each of the positive literals. We use a simpler notation, Bias(a,b) to denote that positive literals corresponding to all universal variables are assigned a weight a and positive literals corresponding to all existential variables are assigned a weight b. For example, Bias(0.5, 0.9) assigns a weight of 0.5 to the positive literals of the universally quantified variables and 0.9 to the positive literals of the existentially quantified variables.

Problem Statement: Given a Boolean specification $F(X,Y)$ between set of inputs $X = \{x_1, \cdots, x_n\}$ and vector of outputs $Y = \langle y_1, \cdots, y_m \rangle$, the problem of *Skolem function synthesis* is to synthesize a function vector $\Psi = \langle \psi_1(X), \cdots, \psi_m(X) \rangle$ such that $y_i \leftrightarrow \psi_i(X)$ and $\exists Y F(X,Y) \equiv F(X, \Psi)$. We refer to Ψ as the *Skolem function vector* and ψ_i as the *Skolem function* for y_i.

A variable y_i is called self-substituted variable, if the Skolem function ψ_i corresponding to y_i is set to $F(X,Y)|_{y_i=1}$ [19].

Given a formula $\exists Y F(X,Y)$ and a Skolem function vector Ψ, we refer to $E(X,Y,Y')$ as an *error formula* [28], where $Y' = \{y'_1, \cdots, y'_{|Y|}\}$, and $Y' \neq Y$.

$$E(X,Y,Y') = F(X,Y) \wedge \neg F(X,Y') \wedge (Y' \leftrightarrow \Psi) \qquad (1)$$

We use the following theorems from prior work:

Theorem 1 ([28]). Ψ is a Skolem function if and only if $E(X, Y, Y')$ is UNSAT.

Theorem 2 ([5]). If y_i is positive(resp negative) unate in $F(X, Y)$, then $\psi_i = 1$ (resp $\psi_i = 0$) is the Skolem function for y_i.

3   Related Work

The origins of the problem of Boolean functional synthesis traces back to Boole's seminal work [12], which was subsequently rigorously pursued, albeit focused on decidability, by Lowenheim and Skolem [33]. The complexity theoretic studies have shown that there exist instances where Boolean functional synthesis takes super polynomial time and was also shown that there exist instances for which polynomial size Skolem function vector does not suffice unless Polynomial Hierarchy (PH) collapses [5].

Motivated by the success of the CEGAR (Counter-Example Guided Abstraction Refinement) approach in model checking, CEGAR-based approaches have been pursued in the context of synthesis as well, where the key idea is to use a Conflict-Driven Clause Learning (CDCL) SAT solver to verify and refine the candidate Skolem functions [4–6,28].

Another line of work has focused on the representation of specification, i.e., $F(X, Y)$, in representations that are amenable to efficient synthesis for a class of functions. The early approaches focused on ROBDD representation building on the functional composition approach proposed by Balabanov and Jiang [8]. Building on Tabajara and Vardi's ROBDD-based approach [45], Chakraborty et al. extended the approach to factored specifications [14]. It is worth mentioning that factored specifications had earlier been pursued in the context of CEGAR-based approaches. Motivated by the success of knowledge compilation in the field of probabilistic reasoning, Akshay et al. achieved a significant breakthrough over a series of papers [5,6,28] to propose a new negation normal form, SynNNF [4]. The generalization and a functional specification presented in SynNNF is amenable to efficient functional synthesis [4]. Another line of work focused on the usage of *incremental determinization* to incrementally construct the Skolem functions [25,30,36,39,41].

Several approaches have been proposed for the particular case when the specification, $\exists Y F(X, Y)$ is valid, i.e., $\forall X \exists Y F(X, Y)$ is True. Inspired by the sequential relational decomposition, Chakraborty et al. [14] recently proposed an approach focused on viewing each CNF clause of the specification consisting of *input and output* clauses and employing a *cooperation*-based strategy. The progress in modern CDCL solvers has led to an exploration of usage of heuristics for problems in complexity classes beyond NP. This has led to work on the extraction of Skolem functions from the proofs constructed for the formulas expressed as $\forall X \exists Y F(X, Y)$ [8,9].

The performance of Manthan crucially depends on its ability to employ constrained sampling, which has witnessed a surge of interest with approaches

ranging from those based on hashing-based techniques [15], knowledge compilation [24,42], augmentation of SAT solvers with heuristics [43].

The recent success of machine learning has led to several attempts to the
usage of machine learning in several related synthesis domains such as program
synthesis [7], invariant generation, decision-tree for functions in Linear Integer Arithmetic theory using pre-specified examples [18], strategy synthesis for
QBF [26]. Use of data-driven approaches for invariant synthesis has been investigated in the ICE learning framework [17,20,21] aimed with data about the
program behavior from test executions, it proposes invariants by learning from
data, checks for inductiveness and, on failure, extend the data by the generated counterexamples. The usage of proof-artifacts such as unsat cores has been
explored in verification since early 2000s [23] and in program repair in Wolver-
ine [46], while MaxSAT has been used in program debugging in [10,29].

4   Manthan: An overview

In this section, we provide an overview of our proposed framework, Manthan,
before divulging into core algorithmic details in the following section. Manthan
takes in a function specification, represented as $F(X, Y)$, and returns a Skolem
function vector $\Psi(X)$ such that $\exists Y F(X, Y) \equiv F(X, \Psi(X))$. As shown in Fig. 1
Manthan consists of following three phases:

1. **Preprocess** employs state-of-the-art pre-processing techniques on F to compute a partial Skolem function vector.
2. **LearnSkF** takes in the pre-processed formula and uses constrained samplers,
   and classification techniques to compute candidate Skolem functions for all
   the variables in Y.
3. **Refine** performs verification and proof-guided refinement procedure wherein
   a SAT solver is employed to verify the correctness of candidate functions and
   a MaxSAT solver in conjunction with a SAT solver is employed to refine the
   candidate functions until the entire candidate Skolem function vector passes
   the verification check.

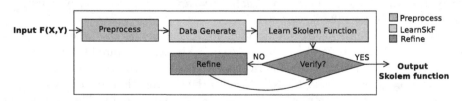

Fig. 1. Overview of Manthan

We now provide a high-level description of different phases to highlight
the technical challenges, which provides context for several algorithmic design
choices presented in the next section.

4.1   Phase 1: **Preprocess**

Preprocess focuses on pre-processing of the formula to search for unates among the variables in Y; if y_i is positive (resp. negative) unate, then $\psi_i = 1$(resp. 0) suffices as a Skolem function. We employ the algorithmic routine proposed by Akshay et al. [5] to drive this preprocessing.

4.2   Phase 2: **LearnSkF**

LearnSkF views the problem of functional synthesis through the lens of machine learning where the learned machine learning model for classification of a variable y_i can be viewed as a candidate Skolem function for y_i. We gather training data about the function's behavior by exploiting the progress in constrained sampling to sample solutions of $F(X,Y)$. Recall that $F(X,Y)$ defines a relation (and not necessarily a function) between X and Y, and the machine learning techniques typically assume the existence of function between features and labels, necessitating the need for sophisticated sampling strategy as discussed below. Moving on to features and labels, since we want to learn Y in terms of X, we view X as a set of features while assignments to Y as a set of class labels.

The off-the-shelf classification techniques typically require that the size of training data is several times larger than the size of possible class labels, which would be prohibitively large for the typical problems involving more than thousand variables. To mitigate the requirement of large training data, we make note of two well-known observations in functional synthesis literature: (1) the Skolem function ψ_i for a variable y_i typically does not depend on all the variables in X, (2) A Skolem function vector Ψ where ψ_i depends on variable y_j is a valid vector if the Skolem function ψ_j is not dependent on y_i (i.e., acyclic dependency), i.e., there exists a partial order $\prec_d$ over $\{y_1, \ldots y_m\}$.

The above observations lead us to design an algorithmic procedure where we learn candidate Skolem functions as decision trees in an iterative manner, i.e., one y_i at a time, thereby allowing us to constrain ourselves to the binary classification. The learned classifier can then be represented as the disjunction of all the paths from the root to the leaves in the learnt decision tree. We update the set of possible features for a given y_i depending on the candidate functions generated so far, i.e., valuation of X variables and Y variables, which are not dependent on y_i. Finally, we compute the candidate Skolem function for y_i as the disjunction of labels along edges for all the paths from the root to leaf nodes with label 1. Once, we have the candidate Skolem function vector Ψ, we obtain a valid linear extension, *TotalOrder*, of the partial order $\prec_d$ in accordance to Ψ.

Before moving on to the next phase, we return to the formulation of sampling. The past few years have witnessed the design of uniform [15,42], and weighted samplers [24], and one wonders what kind of sampler should we choose to generate samples for training data. A straightforward choice would be to perform uniform sampling over X and Y, but the relational nature of specification, F, between X and Y offers interesting challenges and opportunities. Recall while F specifies a relation between X and Y, we are interested in a Skolem function, and we would like to tailor our sampling subroutines to allow discovery of Skolem functions with *small* description given the relationship between description and sample complexity. To this end, consider $X = \{x_1, x_2\}$ and $Y = \{y_1\}$, and let $F := (x_1 \vee x_2 \vee y_1)$. Note that F has 7 solutions over $X \cup Y$, out of which $y_1 = 0$ appears in 3 solutions while $y_1 = 1$ appears in 4. Also, note that there are several possible Skolem functions such as $y_1 = \neg(x_1 \wedge x_2)$. Now, if we uniformly sample solutions of F over x_1, x_2, y_1, i.e. Bias(0.5, 0.5), we would see (almost) equal number of samples with $y_1 = 0$ and $y_1 = 1$. A closer look at F reveals that it is possible to construct a Skolem function by knowing that the only case where y_1 cannot be assigned 0 is when $x_1 = x_2 = 0$. To encode this intuition, we propose a novel idea of collecting samples with weighted sampling, i.e., Bias(0.5, q) where q is chosen in a multi-step process of first drawing a small set of samples with both $q = 0.9$ and $q = 0.1$, and then drawing rest of the samples by fixing the value of q following analysis of an initial set of samples. To the best of our knowledge, this is the first application of weighted sampling in the context of synthesis, and our experimental results point to several interesting avenues of future work.

4.3   Phase 3: Refine

The candidate Skolem functions generated in LearnSkF may not always be the actual Skolem functions. Hence, we require a *verification* check to see if candidate Skolem functions are indeed correct; if not, the generated counterexample can be used to *repair* it. The verification query constructs an *error formula* $E(X, Y, Y')$ (Formula 1): if unsatisfiable, the candidate Skolem function vector is indeed a Skolem function vector and the procedure can terminate; else, when $E(X, Y, Y')$ is SAT, the solution of $E(X, Y, Y')$ is used to identify and refine the erring functions among the candidate Skolem function vector.

In contrast to prior techniques that apply Shannon expansion or self-substitution, the refinement strategy in Manthan is guided by the view that the candidate function vector from the LearnSkF phase is *almost correct*, and hence, attempts to identify and apply a series of *minor* repairs to the erring functions to arrive at the correct Skolem function vector. To this end, Manthan uses two key techniques: *fault localization* and *repair synthesis*. Let us assume that σ is a satisfying assignment of $E(X, Y, Y')$ and referred to as counterexample for the current candidate Skolem function vector Ψ.

Fault Localization. In order to identify the initial candidates to repair for the counterexample σ, Manthan attempts to identify a small number of Skolem functions (correspondingly Y variables) whose outputs must undergo a change for the formula to behave correctly on σ; in other words, it makes a best-effort attempt to ensure that most of the Skolem functions (correspondingly Y variables) can retain their current output on σ while satisfying the formula. Manthan encodes this problem as a partial MaxSAT query with $F(X, Y) \wedge (X \leftrightarrow \sigma[X])$ as a hard constraint and $(Y \leftrightarrow \sigma[Y'])$ as soft constraints. All Y variables whose valuation constraint $(Y \leftrightarrow \sigma[Y'])$ does not hold in the MaxSAT solution are identified as erring Skolem functions that may need to be repaired.

Repair Synthesis. Let y_k be the variable corresponding to the erring function, ψ_k, identified in the previous step. To synthesize a repair for the function, Manthan applies a proof-guided strategy: it constructs a formula $G_k(X, Y)$, such that if $G_k(X, Y)$ is unsatisfiable then ψ_k must undergo a change. The Unsat-Core of $G_k(X, Y)$ provides a *reason* that explains the discrepancy between the specification and the current Skolem function.

$$G_k(X, Y) = (y_k \leftrightarrow \sigma[y_k']) \wedge F(X, Y) \wedge (X \leftrightarrow \sigma[X]) \wedge (\hat{Y} \leftrightarrow \sigma[\hat{Y}])$$
$$\text{where } \hat{Y} \subset Y \text{ and } \hat{Y} = \{ TotalOrder[index(y_k) + 1], \cdots, TotalOrder[|Y|]\} \quad (2)$$

Manthan uses the UnsatCore to constructs a *repair formula*, say β, as a conjunction over literals in the unsatisfiable core; if ψ_k is *true* with the current valuation of X and $\hat{Y}$, Manthan updates the function ψ_k by conjoining it with the negation of repair formula ($\psi_k \leftarrow \psi_k \wedge \neg\beta$); otherwise, Manthan updates the function ψ_k, by disjoining it with the repair formula ($\psi_k \leftarrow \psi_k \vee \beta$).

Self-substitution for Poorly Learnt Functions. Some Skolem functions are difficult to learn through data. In our implementation, the corresponding variables escape the LearnSkF phase with poor candidate functions, thereby requiring a long sequence of incremental repairs for convergence. To handle such scenarios, we make the following observation: though synthesizing Skolem functions via self-substitution [19] can lead to an exponential blowup in the worst case, it is inexpensive if the number of variables synthesized via this technique is small. We use this observation to quickly synthesize a Skolem function for an erring variable if we detect its candidate function is poor (detected by comparing the number of times it enters refinement against an empirically determined threshold). Of course, this heuristic does not scale well if the number of such variables is large; in our experiments, we found less than 20% of the instances solved required self-substitution, and for over 75% of these instances, only one variable needed self-substitution. We elaborate more on the empirical evidence on the success of this heuristic in Sect. 6. A theoretical understanding of the learnability of Boolean functions from data seems to be an interesting direction for future work.

5   Manthan: Algorithmic Description

In this section, we present a detailed algorithmic description of Manthan, whose pseudocode is presented in Algorithm 1. Manthan takes in a formula $F(X, Y)$ as input and returns a Skolem vector Ψ. The algorithm starts off by preprocessing (line 1) the formula $F(X, Y)$ to get the unates (U) and their corresponding Skolem functions (Ψ). Next, it invokes the sampler (line 2) to collect a set of samples(Σ) as training data for the learning phase.

For each of the existential variables that are not unates, Manthan attempts to learn candidate Skolem functions (lines 4–5). To generate a variable order,

---

Algorithm 1: Manthan($F(X, Y)$)

---

1 $\Psi, U \leftarrow$ Preprocess($F(X, Y)$)
2 $\Sigma \leftarrow$ GetSamples($F(X, Y)$)
3 $D \leftarrow \emptyset$
4 **foreach** $y_j \in Y \setminus U$ **do**
5 | $\psi_j, D \leftarrow$ CandidateSkF($\Sigma, F(X, Y), y_j, D$)
6 $TotalOrder \leftarrow$ FindOrder(D)
7 **repeat**
8 | $E(X, Y, Y') \leftarrow F(X, Y) \wedge \neg F(X, Y') \wedge (Y' \leftrightarrow \Psi)$
9 | $ret, \sigma \leftarrow$ CheckSat($E(X, Y, Y')$)
10 | **if** $ret = SAT$ **then**
11 | | $\Psi \leftarrow$ RefineSkF($F(X, Y), \Psi, \sigma, TotalOrder$)
12 **until** $ret = UNSAT$
13 $\Psi \leftarrow$ Substitute($F(X, Y), \Psi, TotalOrder$)
14 **return** Ψ

CandidateSkF uses a collection of sets $d_1, \cdots, d_{|Y|} \in D$, such that $y_i \in d_j$ indicates that y_j depends on y_i. Next, the FindOrder routine (line 6) construct *TotalOrder* of the Y variables in accordance to the dependencies in D. The verification and refinement phase (line 8) commences by constructing the error formula and launching the verification check (line 9). If the error formula is satisfiable, the counterexample model (σ) is used to refine the formula. Once the verification check is successful, the refinement phase ends and the subroutine Substitute is invoked to recursively substitute all $y_i \in Y$ appearing in Skolem functions with their corresponding Skolem functions such that only X variables entirely describe all Skolem functions. The strict variable ordering enforced above ensures that Substitute always succeeds and does not get stuck in a cycle. Finally, the Skolem function vector Ψ is returned.

It is worth noting that Manthan can successfully solve an instance without having to necessarily execute all the phases. In particular, if $U = Y$, then Manthan terminates after Preprocess (i.e., line 1). Similarly, if the CheckSat return UNSAT during the first iteration of loop (lines 8–11), then Manthan does not invoke RefineSkF.

We now discuss each subroutine in detail. The pseudocode for Preprocess, GetSamples and Substitute is deferred to technical report [22].

Preprocess: We perform the pre-processing step as described in [5], which performs SAT queries on the formulas constructed as specified in Theorem 2.

GetSamples: GetSamples takes $F(X, Y)$ as input and returns a subset of satisfying assignments of $F(X, Y)$. GetSamples first generates a small set of samples (500) with Bias(0.5, 0.9) and calculates m_i for all y_i, m_i is a ratio of number of samples with y_i being 1 to the total number of samples. Similarity, GetSamples generates 500 samples with Bias(0.5, 0.1) and calculates n_i for all y_i, n_i is a ratio

---

Algorithm 2: CandidateSkF$(\Sigma, F(X, Y), y_j, D)$

---

1   $featset \leftarrow X$
2   **foreach** $y_k \in Y \setminus y_j$ **do**
3   **if** $y_j \notin d_k$ **then**
4       $featset \leftarrow featset \cup y_k$ /* if y_k is not dependent on y_j */
5   $feat, lbl \leftarrow \Sigma_{\downarrow featset}, \Sigma_{\downarrow y_j}$
6   $t \leftarrow$ CreateDecisionTree$(feat, lbl)$
7   **foreach** $n \in$ LeafNodes(t) **do**
8   **if** $Label(n) = 1$ **then**
9       $\pi \leftarrow$ Path$(t, root, n)$
10       $\psi_j \leftarrow \psi_j \vee \pi$
11   **foreach** $y_k \in \psi_j$ **do**
12     $d_j \leftarrow d_j \cup y_k \cup d_k$
13   **return** ψ_j, D

---

of number of samples with y_i being 0 to the total number of samples. Finally, GetSamples generates required number of samples with Bias$(0.5, q)$; for a y_i, q is m_i if both m_i and n_i are in range 0.35 to 0.65, else q is 0.9.

CandidateSkF: CandidateSkF, presented in Algorithm 2, assumes access to following three subroutines:

1. CreateDecisionTree takes the feature and label sets as input (training data) and returns a decision tree t. We use the ID3 algorithm [38] to construct a decision tree t where the internal node of t represents a feature on which a decision is made, the branches represent partitioning of the training data on the decision, and the leaf nodes represent the classification outcomes (i.e class labels). The ID3 algorithm iterates over the training data, and in each iteration, it selects a new attribute to extend the tree by a new decision node: the selected attribute is one that causes the maximum drop in the impurity of the resulting classes; we use Gini Index [38] as the measure of impurity. The algorithm, then, extends the tree by the selected decision and continues extending building the tree. The algorithm terminates on a path if either it exhausts all attributes for decisions, or the impurity of the resulting classes drop below a (user-specified) impurity decrease parameter.
2. Label takes a leaf node of the decision tree as input and returns the class label corresponding to the node.
3. Path takes a tree t and two nodes of t (node a and node b) as input and outputs a conjunction of literals in the path from node a to node b in t.

As we seek to learn Boolean functions, we employ binary classifiers with class labels 0 and 1. CandidateSkF shows our algorithm for extracting a Boolean function from the decision trees: lines 2–4 find a feature set (*featset*) to predict y_j. The feature set includes all X variables and the subset of Y variables that are not dependent on y_j. CandidateSkF creates decision tree t using samples Σ over the feature set. Lines 7–10 generate candidate Skolem function ψ_j by iterating over all the leaf nodes of t. In particular, if a leaf node is labeled with 1, the candidate function is updated by disjoining with the formula returned by sub-routine Path. CandidateSkF also updates d_j in D, d_j is set of all Y variables on which, y_j depends. If y_j depends on y_k, then by transitivity y_j also depends on d_k; in line 12, CandidateSkF updates d_j accordingly.

FindOrder: FindOrder takes D as an input to output a valid linear extension of the partial order $\prec_d$ defined over $\{y_1, \ldots y_m\}$ with respect to the candidate Skolem function vector Ψ.

Algorithm 3: RefineSkF($F(X,Y), \Psi, \sigma, TotalOrder$)

1   $H \leftarrow F(X,Y) \wedge (X \leftrightarrow \sigma[X]); S \leftarrow (Y \leftrightarrow \sigma[Y'])$
2   $Ind \leftarrow$ MaxSATList(H, S)
3   **foreach** $y_k \in Ind$ **do**
4     $\hat{Y} \leftarrow \{TotalOrder[index(y_k)+1], \cdots, TotalOrder[|Y|]\}$
5   **if** $CheckSubstitute(y_k)$ **then**
6       $\psi_k \leftarrow$ DoSelfSubstitution($F(X,Y), y_k, Y \setminus \hat{Y}$)
7   **else**
8       $G_k \leftarrow (y_k \leftrightarrow \sigma[y_k']) \wedge F(X,Y) \wedge (X \leftrightarrow \sigma[X]) \wedge (\hat{Y} \leftrightarrow \sigma[\hat{Y}])$
9       $ret, \rho \leftarrow$ CheckSat(G_k)
10   **if** $ret = UNSAT$ **then**
11        $C \leftarrow$ FindCore(G_k)
12        $\beta \leftarrow \bigwedge_{l \in C} ite((\sigma[l]=1), l, \neg l)$
13        $\psi_k \leftarrow ite((\sigma[y_k']=1), \psi_k \wedge \neg\beta, \psi_k \vee \beta)$
14   **else**
15   **foreach** $y_t \in Y \setminus \hat{Y}$ **do**
16   **if** $\rho[y_t] \neq \sigma[y_t']$ **then**
17          $Ind \leftarrow Ind.Append(y_t)$
18       $\sigma[y_k] \leftarrow \sigma[y_k']$
19   **return** Ψ

RefineSkF: RefineSkF is invoked with a counterexample σ. RefineSkF first performs *fault localization* to find the initial set of erring candidate functions; to this end, it calls the MaxSATList subroutine (line 2) with $F(X,Y) \wedge (X \leftrightarrow \sigma[X])$ as hard-constraints and $(Y \leftrightarrow \sigma[Y])$ as soft-constraints. MaxSATList employs a MaxSAT solver to find the solution that satisfies all the hard constraints and maximizes the number of satisfied soft constraints, and then returns a list (Ind) of Y variables such that for each of the variables appearing in (Ind) the corresponding soft-constraint was not satisfied by the optimal solution returned by MaxSAT solver.

Since candidate Skolem function corresponding to the variables in Ind needs to refine, RefineSkF now attempts to synthesize a repair for each of these candidate Skolem functions. Repair synthesis loop (lines 3–19) starts off by collecting the set of Y variables, $\hat{Y}$, on which y_k of Ind can depend on as per the ordering constraints (line 4). Next, it invokes the subroutine CheckSubstitute, which returns True if the candidate function corresponding to y_k has been refined more than a chosen threshold times (fixed to 10 in our implementation), and the corresponding decision tree constructed during execution CandidateSkF has exactly one node. If CheckSubstitute returns true, RefineSkF calls DoSelfSubstitution to perform self-substitution. DoSelfSubstitution takes a formula $F(X,Y)$, an existentially quantified variable y_k and a list of variables which depends on y_k and performs self substitution of y_k with constant 1 in the formula $F(X,Y)$ [28].

If CheckSubstitute returns false, RefineSkF attempts a proof-guided repair for y_k. RefineSkF calls CheckSat in line 9 on G_k, which corresponds to formula 2: if G_k is SAT, then CheckSat returns a satisfying assignment(ρ) of G_k in σ, else CheckSat returns unsatisfiable in the result, ret.

1. If ret is UNSAT, we proceed to refine ψ_k such that for $\psi_k(X \mapsto \sigma[X], \hat{Y} \mapsto \sigma[\hat{Y}]) = \sigma[y_k]$. Ideally, we would like to apply a refinement that generalizes to potentially other counter-examples, i.e. solutions of $E(X, Y, Y')$. To this end, RefineSkF calls FindCore with G_k; FindCore returns the list of variables (C) that occur in the clauses of UnsatCore of G_k. Accordingly, the algorithm constructs a *repair formula* β as a conjunction of literals in σ corresponding to variables in C (line 12). If $\sigma[y'_k]$ is 1, then ψ_k is ψ_k with conjunction of negation of β and if $\sigma[y'_k]$ is 0, then ψ_k is ψ_k with disjunction of β.
2. If ret is SAT and ρ is a satisfying assignment of G_k, then there exists a Skolem function vector such that the value of ψ_k agrees with $\sigma[y_k]$ for the valuation of X and $\hat{Y}$ set to $\sigma[X]$ and $\sigma[\hat{Y}]$. However, for any $y_t \in Y \setminus \hat{Y}$ if $\sigma[y'_t] \neq \rho[y'_t]$, then for such a y_t, the Skolem function corresponding to y_t may need to refine . Therefore, RefineSkF adds y_t to list of candidates to refine, Ind. Note that since $\sigma \models E(X, Y, Y')$, there exists at least one iteration of the loop (lines 3–18) where ret is UNSAT.

Substitute: To return the Skolem functions in terms of only X, Manthan invokes Substitute subroutine. For each y_j of Y variable, Substitute consider Y variables that occurs later in $TotalOrder$ as $\hat{Y}$. Then, for each y_i of $\hat{Y}$; it substitutes corresponding Skolem function ψ_i in the Skolem function ψ_j of y_j.

An example to illustrate our algorithm is deferred to the technical report [22].

6 Experimental Results

We evaluate the performance of Manthan on the union of all the benchmarks employed in the most recent works [4,5],which includes 609 benchmarks from different sources: Prenex-2QBF track of QBFEval-17 [2], QBFEval-18 [3], disjunctive [6], arithmetic [45] and factorization [6]. We ran all the tools as per the specification laid out by their authors. We used Open-WBO [34] for our MaxSAT queries and PicoSAT [11] to compute UnsatCore. We used PicoSAT for its ease of usage and we expect further performance improvements by upgrading to one of the state of the art SAT solvers. We have used the Scikit-Learn [37] to create decision trees in LearnSkF phase of Manthan. We have also used ABC [31] to represent and manipulate Boolean functions. To allow for the input formats supported by the different tools, we use the utility scripts available with the BFSS distribution [5] to convert each of the instances to both QDIMACS and Verilog formats. For Manthan, unless otherwise specified, we set the number of samples according to heuristic based on $|Y|$ as described in Sect. 6.3 and minimum impurity decrease to 0.005. All our experiments were conducted on a high-performance computer cluster with each node consisting of a E5-2690 v3 CPU with 24 cores and 96 GB of RAM, with a memory limit set to 4 GB per core. All tools were run in a single-threaded mode on a single core with a timeout of 7200 s.

The objective of our experimental evaluation was two-fold: to understand the impact of various design choices on the runtime performance of Manthan and to perform an extensive comparison of runtime performance vis-a-vis state of the art synthesis tools. In particular, we sought to answer the following questions:

1. How does the performance of Manthan compare with state of the functional synthesis engines?
2. How do the usage of different sampling schemes and the quality of samplers impact the performance of Manthan?
3. What is the impact of LearnSkF on the performance of Manthan?
4. What is the distribution of the time spent in each phase of Manthan?
5. How does using MaxSAT solver to identify the potential erring Skolem functions impacts on the performance of Manthan?
6. How does employing self-substitution for some Skolem functions impact Manthan?

We observe that Manthan significantly improves upon state of the art, and solves 356 benchmarks while the state of the art tool can only solve 280; in particular, Manthan solves 60 more benchmarks that could not be solved by any of the state of the art tools. To put the runtime performance statistics in a broader context, the number of benchmarks solved by techniques developed over the past five years range from 206 to 280, i.e., a difference of 74, which is same as an increase of 76 (i.e., from 280 to 356) due to Manthan.

Our experimental evaluation leads to interesting conclusions and several directions for future work. We observe that the performance of Manthan is sensitive to different sampling schemes and the underlying samplers; in fact, we found that biased sampling yields better results than uniform sampling. This raises interesting questions on the possibility of designing specialized samplers for this task. Similarly, we observe interesting trade offs between the number of samples and the minimum impurity decrease in LearnSkF. The diversity of our extensive benchmark suite produces a nuanced picture with respect to time distribution across different phases, highlighting the critical nature of each of the phases to the performance of Manthan. Manthan shows significant performance improvement by using MaxSAT solver to identify candidates to refine. Manthan also has significant performance improvement with self substitution in terms of the required number of refinements.

6.1   Comparison with Other Tools

We now present performance comparison of Manthan with the current state of the art synthesis tools, BFSS [5], C2Syn [4], BaFSyn [14] and the current state of the art 2-QBF solvers CADET [39],CAQE [40] and DepQBF [32]. The certifying 2-QBF solver produces QBF certificates, that can be used to extract Skolem functions [8]. Developers of BaFSyn and DepQBF confirmed that the tools produce Skolem function for only valid instances, i.e. when $\forall X \exists Y F(X, Y)$ is valid. Note that the current version of CAQE does not support certification and we have used CAQE version 2 for the experiments after consultation with the developers of CAQE.

Table 1. No. of benchmarks solved by different tools

Total	BaFSyn	CAQE	DepQBF	C2Syn	BFSS	CADET	Manthan	All tools
609	13	54	59	206	247	280	**356**	476

We present the number of instances solved Table 1. Out of 609 benchmarks, the most number of instances solved by any of the remaining techniques is 280 while Manthan is able to solve 356 instances – a significant improvement over state of the art. We will focus on top 4 synthesis tools from Table 1 for further analysis.

For a deeper analysis of runtime behavior, we present the cactus plot in Fig. 2: the number of instances are shown on the x-axis and the time taken on the y-axis; a point (x, y) implies that a solver took less than or equal to y seconds to find Skolem function of x instances on a total of 609 instances. An interesting behavior predicted by cactus plot and verified upon closer analysis is that for instances that can be solved by most of the tools, the initial overhead due to a multi-phase approach may lead to relatively larger runtime for Manthan. However, with the rise in empirically observed hardness of instances, one can observe the strengths of the multi-phase approach. Overall, Manthan solves 76 more instances than the rest of the remaining techniques.

We show a pairwise comparison of Manthan vis-a-vis other techniques in Table 2. The second row of the table lists the number of instances that were solved by the technique in the corresponding column but not by Manthan while the third row lists the number of instances that were solved by Manthan but not the corresponding technique. First, we observe that Manthan solves 163, 194, and 187 instances that are not solved by C2Syn, BFSS, and CADET respectively. Though

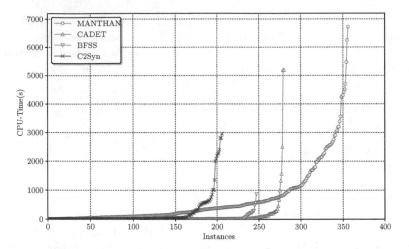

Fig. 2. Manthan versus competing tools for Skolem function synthesis

Table 2. Manthan vs other state-of-the-art tools

		C2Syn	BFSS	CADET	All Tools
Manthan	Less	13	85	111	122
	More	**163**	**194**	**187**	**60**

BFSS and CADET solve more than 80 instances that Manthan does not solve, they are not complementary; there are only 121 instances that can be solved by either BFSS or CADET but Manthan fails to solve. A closer analysis of Manthan's performance on these instances revealed that the decision trees generated by CandidateSkF were shallow, which is usually a sign of significant under-fitting. On the other hand, there are 130 instances that Manthan solves, but neither CADET nor BFSS can solve. These instances have high dependencies between variables that Manthan can infer from the samples en route to predicting good candidate Skolem functions. Akshay et al. [4] suggest that C2Syn is an orthogonal approach to BFSS. Manthan solves 81 instances that neither C2Syn nor BFSS is able to solve, and these tools together solve 86 instances that Manthan fails to solve. Overall, Manthan solves **60** instances beyond the reach of any of the above state of the art tools.

6.2   Impact of the Sampling Scheme

To analyze the impact of the adaptive sampling and the quality of distributions generated by underlying samplers, we augmented Manthan with samples drawn from different samplers for adaptive and non-adaptive sampling. In particular, we employed QuickSampler [16], KUS [42], UniGen2 [15], and BiasGen[1]. The

---
[1] BiasGen is developed by Mate Soos and Kuldeep S. Meel, and is pending publication.

samplers KUS and UniGen2 could only produce samples for mere 14 and 49 benchmarks respectively within a timeout of 3600 s. Hence, we have omitted KUS and UniGen2 from further analysis. We also experimented with a naive enumeration of solution using off-the-shelf SAT solver, CryptoMiniSat [43]. It is worth noting that QuickSampler performs worse than BiasGen for uniformity testing using Barbarik [13]. In our implementation, we had to turn off the validation phase of QuickSampler to allow generation number of samples within a reasonable time. To statistically validate our intuition described in Sect. 4, we performed adaptive sampling using BiasGen. We use AdaBiasGen to refer to the adaptive sampling implementation.

Table 3 presents the performance of Manthan with different samplers listed in Column 1. The columns 2, 3, and 4 lists the number of instances that were solved during the execution of respective phases: Preprocess, LearnSkF, and Refine. Finally, column 5 lists the total number of instances solved. Two important findings emerge from Table 3: Firstly, as the quality of samplers improve, so does the performance of Manthan. In particular, we observe that with the improvement in the quality of samples leads to Manthan solving more instances in LearnSkF. Secondly, we see a significant increase in the number of instances that can be solved due to LearnSkF with samples from AdaBiasGen. It is worth remarking that one should view the adaptive scheme proposed in Sect. 4 to be a proof of concept and our results will encourage the development of more complex schemes.

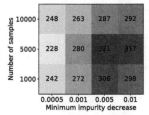

Fig. 3. Heatmap of # instances solved. (Color figure online)

Sampler	No. of instances solved			#Solved
	Preprocess	LearnSkF	Refine	
CryptoMiniSat	66	14	191	271
QuickSampler	66	28	181	275
BiasGen	66	51	228	345
AdaBiasGen	66	66	224	**356**

Table 3. Manthan with different samplers

6.3   Impact of LearnSkF

To analyze the impact of different design choices in LearnSkF, we analyzed the performance of Manthan for different samples (1000, 5000 and 10000) generated by GetSamples and for different choices of minimum impurity decrease (0.001, 0.005, 0.0005). Figure 3 shows a heatmap on the number of instances solved on each combination of the hyperparameters; the closer the color of a cell is to the red end of the spectrum, the better the performance of Manthan.

At the first look, Fig. 3 presents a puzzling picture: It seems that increasing the number of samples does not improve the performance of Manthan. On a closer analysis, we found that the increase in the number of samples leads to an increase in the runtime of CandidateSkF but without significantly increasing the number of instances solved during LearnSkF. The runtime of CandidateSkF is dependent on the number of samples and $|Y|$. On the other hand, we see an interesting trend with respect to minimum impurity decrease where the performance first improves and then degrades. A plausible explanation for such a behavior is that with an increase in *minimum impurity decrease*, the generated decision trees tend to underfit while significantly low values of *minimum impurity decrease* lead to overfitting. We intend to study this in detail in the future.

Based on the above observations, we set the value of minimum impurity decrease to 0.005 and set the number of samples to (1) 10000 for $|Y| < 1200$, (2) 5000 for $1200 < |Y| \leq 4000$, and (3) 1000 for $|Y| > 4000$.

6.4   Division of Time Taken Across Different Phases

To analyze the time taken by different phases of Manthan across different categories of the benchmarks, we normalize the time taken for each of the four core subroutines, Preprocess, GetSamples, CandidateSkF, and RefineSkF, for every benchmark that was solved by Manthan such that the sum of time taken for each benchmark is 1. We then compute the mean of the normalized times across different categories instances. Figure 4 shows the distribution of mean normalized times for different categories: Arithmetic, Disjunction, Factorization, QBFEval, and all the instances.

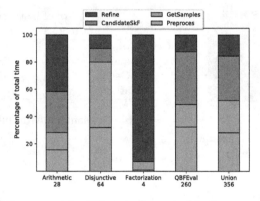

Fig. 4. Fraction of time spent in different phases in Manthan over different classes of benchmarks. (Color figure online)

The diversity of our benchmark suite shows a nuanced picture and shows that the time taken by different phases strongly depends on the family of instances. For example, the disjunctive instances are particularly hard to sample and an improvement in the sampling techniques would lead to significant performance gains. On the other hand, a significant fraction of runtime is spent in the CandidateSkF subroutine indicating the potential gains due to improvement in decision tree generation routines. In all, Fig. 4 identifies the categories of instances that would benefit from algorithmic and engineering improvements in Manthan's different subroutines.

6.5 Impact of Using MaxSAT

In RefineSkF, Manthan invokes the MaxSATList subroutine, which calls MaxSAT solver to identify the potential erring Skolem functions. To observe the impact of using MaxSAT solver to identify the candidates to refine, we did an experiment with Manthan, without MaxSATList subroutine call. For all y_i, where $\sigma[y_i] \neq \sigma[y_i']$ were considered as candidates to refine. Manthan without MaxSATList subroutine call solved 204 instances that represents a significant drop in the number of solved instances by Manthan with MaxSATList subroutine.

6.6 Impact of Self-substitution

To understand the impact of self-substitution, we profile the behavior of candidate Skolem functions with respect to number of refinements for two of our benchmarks; *pdtpmsmiim-all-bit* and *pdtpmsmiim*. In Fig. 5, we use histograms with the number of candidate Skolem functions on y-axis and required number of refinements on x-axis. A bar of height a i.e $y = a$ at b i.e $x = b$ in Fig. 5 represents that a candidate Skolem functions converged in b refinements. The histograms show that only a few Skolem functions require a large number of refinements: the tiny bar towards the right end in Fig. 5a represents that for the benchmark *pdtpmsmiim-all-bit* only 1 candidate Skolem function required more than 60 refinements whereas all other candidate Skolem functions needed less than 15 refinements. Similarly, for the benchmark *pdtpmsmiim*, Fig. 5b shows that only 1 candidate Skolem function was refined more than 15 times, whereas all other Skolem functions required less than 5 refinements. We found similar behaviors in many of our other benchmarks.

Based on the above trend and an examination of the decision trees corresponding to these instances, we hypothesize that some Skolem functions are hard to learn through data. For such functions, the candidate Skolem function generated from the data-driven phase in Manthan tends to be poor, and hence Manthan requires a long series of refinements for convergence. Since our refinement algorithm is designed for small, efficient corrections, we handle such hard to learn Skolem functions by synthesizing via self-substitution. Manthan detects such functions via a threshold on the number of refinements, which is empirically determined as 10, to identify hard to learn instances and sets them up for self-substitution.

In our experiments, we found 75 instances out of 356 solved instances required self-substitution, and for 51 of these 75 instances, only one variable undergoes self-substitution. Table 4 shows the impact of self-substitution for five of our benchmarks: Manthan has significant performance improvement with self-substitution in terms of the required number of refinements, which in turns affects the overall time. Note that Manthan can refine multiple candidates in a single RefineSkF call. For the first four benchmarks, all the other Skolem function

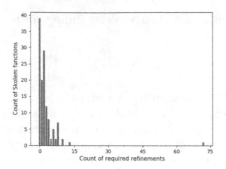 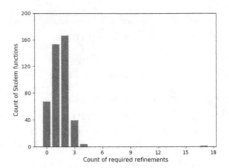

(a) Benchmark *pdtpmsmiim-all-bit:* plot for no. of Skolem functions vs required no. of refinements

(b) Benchmark *pdtpmsmiim:* plot for no. of Skolem functions vs required no. of refinements

Fig. 5. The plots to show the required number of refinements for the candidate Skolem functions.

except the poor candidates were synthesized earlier than 10 refinement iteration, and at the 10th refinement iteration the poor candidate functions hit our threshold for self-substitution. Taking the case of the last benchmark, all the other Skolem functions for it were synthesized earlier than 40 refinement cycles, and the last 16 iterations were only needed for 2 of the poor candidate functions to hit our threshold for self-substitution. Note that self-substitution can lead to an exponential blowup in the size of the formula, but it works quite well in our design as most Skolem functions are learnt quite well in the LearnSkF phase.

Table 4. Manthan : Impact of self substitution

Benchmarks $\exists Y F(X, Y)$	$|X|$	$|Y|$	No. of Refinements		Time(s)	
			Self-Substitution		Self-Substitution	
			Without	With	Without	With
kenflashpo2-all-bit	71	32	319	10	35.88	19.22
eijkbs1512	316	29	264	10	42.88	32.35
pdtpmsmiim-all-bit	429	30	313	10	72.75	36.08
pdtpmssfeistel	1510	68	741	10	184.11	115.07
pdtpmsmiim	418	337	127	56	1049.29	711.48

7   Conclusion

Boolean functional synthesis is a fundamental problem in Computer Science with a wide variety of applications. In this work, we propose a novel data-driven approach to synthesis that employs constrained sampling techniques for generation of data, machine learning for candidate Skolem functions, and automated reasoning to verify and refine to generate Skolem functions. Our approach achieves significant performance improvements. As pointed out in Sects. 5 and 6, our work opens up several interesting directions for future work at the intersection of machine learning, constrained sampling, and automated reasoning.

Acknowledgment. We are grateful to the anonymous reviewers and Dror Fried for constructive comments that significantly improved the final version of the paper. We are grateful to Mate Soos for tweaking BiasGen to support Manthan. We are indebted to S. Akshay, Supratik Chakraborty, and Shetal Shah for their patient responses to our tens of queries regarding prior work.

This work was supported in part by National Research Foundation Singapore under its NRF Fellowship Programme [NRF-NRFFAI1-2019-0004] and AI Singapore Programme [AISG-RP-2018-005], and NUS ODPRT Grant [R-252-000-685-13]. The computational work for this article was performed on resources of the National Supercomputing Centre, Singapore: https://www.nscc.sg [1].

References

1. ASTAR, NTU, NUS, SUTD: National Supercomputing Centre (NSCC) Singapore (2018). https://www.nscc.sg/about-nscc/overview/
2. QBF solver evaluation portal 2017. http://www.qbflib.org/qbfeval17.php
3. QBF solver evaluation portal 2018. http://www.qbflib.org/qbfeval18.php
4. Akshay, S., Arora, J., Chakraborty, S., Krishna, S., Raghunathan, D., Shah, S.: Knowledge compilation for boolean functional synthesis. In: Proc. of FMCAD (2019)
5. Akshay, S., Chakraborty, S., Goel, S., Kulal, S., Shah, S.: What's hard about boolean functional synthesis? In: Proc. of CAV (2018)
6. Akshay, S., Chakraborty, S., John, A.K., Shah, S.: Towards parallel boolean functional synthesis. In: Proc. of TACAS (2017)
7. Alur, R., Bodik, R., Juniwal, G., Martin, M.M., Raghothaman, M., Seshia, S.A., Singh, R., Solar-Lezama, A., Torlak, E., Udupa, A.: Syntax-guided synthesis. In: Proc. of FMCAD (2013)
8. Balabanov, V., Jiang, J.H.R.: Resolution proofs and skolem functions in QBF evaluation and applications. In: Proc. of CAV (2011)
9. Balabanov, V., Jiang, J.H.R.: Unified QBF certification and its applications. In: Proc. of FMCAD (2012)
10. Bavishi, R., Pandey, A., Roy, S.: To be precise: regression aware debugging. In: Proc. of OOPSLA (2016)
11. Biere, A.: PicoSAT essentials. Proc. of JSAT (2008)
12. Boole, G.: The mathematical analysis of logic. Philosophical Library (1847)
13. Chakraborty, S., Meel, K.S.: On testing of uniform samplers. In: Proc. of AAAI (2019)

14. Chakraborty, S., Fried, D., Tabajara, L.M., Vardi, M.Y.: Functional synthesis via input-output separation. In: Proc. of FMCAD (2018)
15. Chakraborty, S., Meel, K.S., Vardi, M.Y.: Balancing scalability and uniformity in SAT witness generator. In: Proc. of DAC (2014)
16. Dutra, R., Laeufer, K., Bachrach, J., Sen, K.: Efficient sampling of SAT solutions for testing. In: Proc. of ICSE (2018)
17. Ezudheen, P., Neider, D., D'Souza, D., Garg, P., Madhusudan, P.: Horn-ICE learning for synthesizing invariants and contracts. In: Proc. of OOPSLA (2018)
18. Fedyukovich, G., Gupta, A.: Functional synthesis with examples. In: Proc. of CP (2019)
19. Fried, D., Tabajara, L.M., Vardi, M.Y.: BDD-based boolean functional synthesis. In: Proc. of CAV (2016)
20. Garg, P., Löding, C., Madhusudan, P., Neider, D.: ICE: A robust framework for learning invariants. In: Proc. of CAV (2014)
21. Garg, P., Neider, D., Madhusudan, P., Roth, D.: Learning invariants using decision trees and implication counterexamples. In: Proc. of POPL (2016)
22. Golia, P., Roy, S., Meel, K.S.: Manthan: A data driven approach for boolean function synthesis (2020). https://arxiv.org/abs/2005.06922
23. Grumberg, O., Lerda, F., Strichman, O., Theobald, M.: Proof-guided underapproximation-widening for multi-process systems. In: Proc. of POPL (2005)
24. Gupta, R., Sharma, S., Roy, S., Meel, K.S.: WAPS: Weighted and projected sampling. In: Proc. of TACAS (2019)
25. Heule, M.J., Seidl, M., Biere, A.: Efficient extraction of skolem functions from QRAT proofs. In: Proc. of FMCAD (2014)
26. Janota, M.: Towards generalization in QBF solving via machine learning. In: Proc. of AAAI (2018)
27. Jo, S., Matsumoto, T., Fujita, M.: SAT-based automatic rectication and debugging of combinational circuits with lut insertions. Proc. of IPSJ T-SLDM (2014)
28. John, A.K., Shah, S., Chakraborty, S., Trivedi, A., Akshay, S.: Skolem functions for factored formulas. In: Proc. of FMCAD (2015)
29. Jose, M., Majumdar, R.: Cause clue clauses: error localization using maximum satisfiability. In: Proc. of PLDI (2011)
30. Jussila, T., Biere, A., Sinz, C., Kröning, D., Wintersteiger, C.M.: A first step towards a unified proof checker for QBF. In: Proc. of SAT (2007)
31. Logic, B., Group, V.: ABC: A system for sequential synthesis and verification. http://www.eecs.berkeley.edu/~alanmi/abc/
32. Lonsing, F., Egly, U.: Depqbf 6.0: A search-based QBF solver beyond traditional QCDCL. In: Proc. of CADE (2017)
33. Löwenheim, L.: Über die auflösung von gleichungen im logischen gebietekalkul. Mathematische Annalen (1910)
34. Martins, R., Manquinho, V., Lynce, I.: Open-WBO: A modular MaxSAT solver. In: Proc. of SAT (2014)
35. Massacci, F., Marraro, L.: Logical cryptanalysis as a SAT problem. Journal of Automated Reasoning (2000)
36. Niemetz, A., Preiner, M., Lonsing, F., Seidl, M., Biere, A.: Resolution-based certificate extraction for QBF. In: Proc. of SAT (2012)
37. Pedregosa, F., Varoquaux, G., Gramfort, A., Michel, V., Thirion, B., Grisel, O., Blondel, M., Prettenhofer, P., Weiss, R., Dubourg, V., Vanderplas, J., Passos, A., Cournapeau, D., Brucher, M., Perrot, M., Duchesnay, E.: Scikit-learn: Machine Learning in Python. Proc. of Machine Learning Research (2011)

38. Quinlan, J.R.: Induction of decision trees. Proc. of Machine learning (1986)
39. Rabe, M.N.: Incremental determinization for quantier elimination and functional synthesis. In: Proc. of CAV (2019)
40. Rabe, M.N., Tentrup, L.: CAQE: A certifying QBF solver. In: Proc. of FMCAD (2015)
41. Rabe, M.N., Tentrup, L., Rasmussen, C., Seshia, S.A.: Understanding and extending incremental determinization for 2QBF. In: Proc. of CAV (2018)
42. Sharma, S., Gupta, R., Roy, S., Meel, K.S.: Knowledge compilation meets uniform sampling. In: Proc. of LPAR (2018)
43. Soos, M.: msoos/cryptominisat (2019). https://github.com/msoos/cryptominisat
44. Srivastava, S., Gulwani, S., Foster, J.S.: Template-based program verication and program synthesis. STTT (2013)
45. Tabajara, L.M., Vardi, M.Y.: Factored boolean functional synthesis. In: Proc. of FMCAD (2017)
46. Verma, S., Roy, S.: Synergistic debug-repair of heap manipulations. In: Proc. of ESEC/FSE (2017)

Decidable Synthesis of Programs
with Uninterpreted Functions

Paul Krogmeier$^{(\boxtimes)}$ (iD), Umang Mathur(iD), Adithya Murali(iD), P. Madhusudan,
and Mahesh Viswanathan

University of Illinois at Urbana-Champaign, Champaign, USA
{paulmk2,umathur3,adithya5,madhu,vmahesh}@illinois.edu

Abstract. We identify a decidable synthesis problem for a class of programs of unbounded size with conditionals and iteration that work over infinite data domains. The programs in our class use uninterpreted functions and relations, and abide by a restriction called coherence that was recently identified to yield decidable verification. We formulate a powerful grammar-restricted (syntax-guided) synthesis problem for coherent uninterpreted programs, and we show the problem to be decidable, identify its precise complexity, and also study several variants of the problem.

1 Introduction

Program synthesis is a thriving area of research that addresses the problem of automatically constructing a program that meets a user-given specification [1,21,22]. Synthesis specifications can be expressed in various ways: as input-output examples [19,20], temporal logic specifications for reactive programs [44], logical specifications [1,4], etc. Many targets for program synthesis exist, ranging from transition systems [31,44], logical expressions [1], imperative programs [51], distributed transition systems/programs [38,43,45], filling holes in programs [51], or repairs of programs [49].

A classical stream of program synthesis research is one that emerged from a problem proposed by Church [13] in 1960 for Boolean circuits. Seminal results by Büchi and Landweber [9] and Rabin [48] led to a mature understanding of the problem, including connections to infinite games played on finite graphs and automata over infinite trees (see [18,32]). Tractable synthesis for temporal logics like LTL, CTL, and their fragments was investigated and several applications for synthesizing hardware circuits emerged [6,7].

In recent years, the field has taken a different turn, tackling synthesis of programs that work over infinite domains such as strings [19,20], integers [1,51], and heaps [47]. Typical solutions derived in this line of research involve (a) bounding the class of programs to a finite set (perhaps iteratively increasing the class) and (b) searching the space of programs using techniques like symmetry-reduced enumeration, SAT solvers, or even random walks [1,4], typically guided

Paul Krogmeier and Mahesh Viswanathan are partially supported by NSF CCF 1901069. Umang Mathur is partially supported by a Google PhD Fellowship.

S. K. Lahiri and C. Wang (Eds.): CAV 2020, LNCS 12225, pp. 634–657, 2020.
https://doi.org/10.1007/978-3-030-53291-8_32

by counterexamples (CEGIS) [28,34,51]. Note that iteratively searching larger classes of programs allows synthesis engines to find a program if one exists, but it does not allow one to conclude that there is no program that satisfies the specification. Consequently, in this stream of research, decidability results are uncommon (see Sect. 7 for some exceptions in certain heavily restricted cases).

In this paper we present, to the best of our knowledge, the first decidability results for program synthesis over a natural class of programs with iteration/recursion, having arbitrary sizes, and which work on infinite data domains. In particular, we show decidable synthesis of a subclass of programs that use uninterpreted functions and relations.

Our primary contribution is a decidability result for realizability and synthesis of a restricted class of imperative *uninterpreted* programs. Uninterpreted programs work over infinite data models that give arbitrary meanings to their functions and relations. Such programs satisfy their assertions if they hold along all executions for *every* model that interprets the functions and relations. The theory of uninterpreted functions and relations is well studied—classically, in 1929, by Gödel, where completeness results were shown [5] and, more recently, its decidable quantifier-free fragment has been exploited in SMT solvers in combination with other theories [8]. In recent work [39], a subclass of uninterpreted programs, called *coherent* programs, was identified and shown to have a decidable verification problem. Note that in this verification problem there are no user-given loop invariants; the verification algorithm finds inductive invariants and proves them automatically in order to prove program correctness.

In this paper, we consider the synthesis problem for coherent uninterpreted programs. The user gives a *grammar* $\mathcal{G}$ that generates well-formed programs in our programming language. The grammar can force programs to have **assert** statements at various points which collectively act as the specification. The program synthesis problem is then to construct a coherent program, if one exists, conforming to the grammar $\mathcal{G}$ that satisfies all assertions in all executions when running on *any* data model that gives meaning to function and relation symbols.

Our primary result is that the realizability problem (checking the existence of a program conforming to the grammar and satisfying its assertions) is decidable for coherent uninterpreted programs. We prove that the problem is 2EXPTIME-complete. Further, whenever a correct coherent program that conforms to the grammar exists, we can synthesize one. We also show that the realizability/synthesis problem is undecidable if the coherence restriction is dropped. In fact we show a stronger result that the problem is undecidable even for synthesis of *straight-line* programs (without conditionals and iteration)!

Coherence of programs is a technical restriction that was introduced in [39]. It consists of two properties, both of which were individually proven to be essential for ensuring that program verification is decidable. Intuitively, the restriction demands that functions are computed on any tuple of terms only once and that assumptions of equality come early in the executions. In more recent work [41], the authors extend this decidability result to handle map updates, and applied it to memory safety verification for a class of heap-manipulating programs on forest data-structures, demonstrating that the restriction of coherence is met in practice by certain natural and useful classes of programs.

Note that automatic synthesis of correct programs over infinite domains demands that we, at the very least, can automatically verify the synthesized program to be correct. The class of coherent uninterpreted programs identified in the work of [39] is the only natural class of programs we are aware of that has recursion and conditionals, works over infinite domains, and admits decidable verification. Consequently, this class is a natural target for proving a decidable synthesis result.

The problem of synthesizing a program from a grammar with assertions is a powerful formulation of program synthesis. In particular, the grammar can be used to restrict the space of programs in various ways. For example, we can restrict the space syntactically by disallowing while loops. Or, for a fixed n, by using a set of Boolean variables linear in n and requiring a loop body to strictly increment a counter encoded using these variables, we can demand that loops terminate in a linear/polynomial/exponential number of iterations. We can also implement loops that do not always terminate, but terminate only when the data model satisfies a particular property, e.g., programs that terminate only on finite list segments, by using a skeleton of the form: **while** $(x \neq y)\{ \dots ; x := \mathbf{next}(x)\}$. Grammar-restricted program synthesis can express the synthesis of programs with holes, used in systems like SKETCH [50], where the problem is to fill holes using programs/expressions conforming to a particular grammar so that the assertions in the program hold. Synthesizing programs or expressions using restricted grammars is also the cornerstone of the intensively studied SyGuS (syntax-guided synthesis) format [1,52][1].

The proof of our decidability result relies on tree automata, a callback to classical theoretical approaches to synthesis. The key idea is to represent programs as trees and build automata that accept trees corresponding to correct programs. The central construction is to build a two-way alternating tree automaton that accepts *all* program trees of coherent programs that satisfy their assertions. Given a grammar $\mathcal{G}$ of programs (which has to satisfy certain natural conditions), we show that there is a regular set of program trees for the language of allowed programs $L(\mathcal{G})$. Intersecting the automata for these two regular tree languages and checking for emptiness establishes the upper bound. Our constructions crucially use the automaton for verifying coherent uninterpreted programs in [39] and adapt ideas from [35] for building two-way automata over program trees. Our final decision procedure is doubly-exponential in the number of program variables and *linear* in the size of the grammar. We also prove a matching lower bound by reduction from the acceptance problem for alternating exponential-space Turing machines. The reduction is non-trivial in that programs (which correspond to runs in the Turing machine) must simulate sequences of configurations, each of which is of exponential size, by using only polynomially-many variables.

---

[1] Note, however, that both SKETCH and SyGuS problems are defined using functions and relations that are interpreted using standard theories like arithmetic, etc., and hence of course do not have decidable synthesis.

Recursive Programs, Transition Systems, and Boolean Programs: We study three related synthesis problems. First, we show that our results extend to synthesis of call-by-value *recursive* uninterpreted programs (with a fixed number of functions and fixed number of local/global variables). This problem is also 2EXPTIME-complete but is more complex, as even single executions simulated on the program tree must be split into separate copies, with one copy executing the summary of a function call and the other proceeding under the assumption that the call has returned in a summarized state.

We next examine a synthesis problem for *transition systems*. Transition systems are similar to programs in that they execute similar kinds of atomic statements. We allow the user to restrict the set of allowable executions (using regular sets). Despite the fact that this problem seems very similar to program synthesis, we show that it is an *easier* problem, and coherent transition system realizability and synthesis can be solved in time exponential in the number of program variables and polynomial in the size of the automata that restrict executions. We prove a corresponding lower bound to establish EXPTIME-completeness of this problem.

Finally, we note that our results also show, as a corollary, that the grammar-restricted realizability/synthesis problem for Boolean programs (resp. execution-restricted synthesis problem for Boolean transition systems) is decidable and is 2EXPTIME-complete (resp. EXPTIME-complete). These results for Boolean programs are themselves new. The lower bound results for these problems hence show that coherent program/transition-system synthesis is not particularly harder than Boolean program synthesis for uninterpreted programs. Grammar-restricted Boolean program synthesis is an important problem which is addressed by many practical synthesis systems like Sketch [50].

Due to space restrictions, we present only proof gists for main results in the paper. All the complete proofs can be found in our technical report [30].

2   Examples

We will begin by looking at several examples to gain some intuition for uninterpreted programs.

Example 1. Consider the program in Fig. 1 (left). This program has a *hole* '⟨⟨ ?? | Cannot ... ⟩⟩' that we intend to fill with a sub-program so that the entire program (together with the contents of the hole) satisfies the assertion at the end. The sub-program corresponding to the hole is allowed to use the variable cipher as well as some additional variables $y_1, \ldots, y_n$ (for some fixed n), but is not allowed to refer to key or secret in any way. Here we also restrict the hole to exclude while loops. This example models the encryption of a secret message secret with a key key. The assumption in the second line of the program models

```
cipher := enc(secret, key);            assume(T ≠ F);
assume(secret = dec(cipher, key));     if (x = T) then b := T else b := F;
⟨⟨ ?? | Cannot refer to secret or key⟩⟩;   ⟨⟨ ?? | Cannot refer to x or b⟩⟩;
assert(z = secret)                     assert(y = b)
```

Decrypting a ciphertext   Synthesis with incomplete information

Fig. 1. Examples of programs with holes

the fact that the secret message can be decrypted from `cipher` and `key`. Here, the functions `enc` and `dec` are *uninterpreted functions*, and thus the program we are looking for is an *uninterpreted program*. For such a program, the assertion "assert(z = secret)" holds at the end if it holds for *all models*, i.e, for all interpretations of `enc` and `dec` and for all initial values of the program variables `secret`, `key`, `cipher`, and $y_1, \ldots, y_n$. With this setup, we are essentially asking whether a program that does not have access to `key` can recover `secret`. It is not hard to see that there is no program which satisfies the above requirement. The above modeling of keys, encryption, nonces, etc. is common in algebraic approaches to modeling cryptographic protocols [15,16].

Example 2. The program in Fig. 1 (right) is another simple example of an unrealizable specification. The program variables here are x, b, and y. The hole in this partial program is restricted so that it cannot refer to x or b. It is easy to phrase the question for synthesis of the complete program in terms of a grammar. The restriction on the hole ensures that the synthesized code fragment can neither directly check if x = T, nor indirectly check via b. Consequently, it is easy to see that there is no program for the hole that can ensure y is equal to b. We remark that the code at the hole, apart from not being allowed to examine some variables, is also implicitly prohibited from looking at the control path taken to reach the hole. If we could synthesize two different programs depending on the control path taken to reach the hole, then we could set y := T when the **then**-branch is taken and set y := F when the **else**-branch is taken. Program synthesis requires a control-flow independent decision to be made about how to fill the hole. In this sense, we can think of the hole as having only *incomplete information* about the executions for which it must be correct. This can be used to encode specifications using complex ghost code, as we show in the next examples. In Sect. 6, we explore a slightly different synthesis problem, called *transition system synthesis*, where holes can be differently instantiated based on the history of an execution.

Example 3. In this example, we model the synthesis of a program that checks whether a linked list pointed to by some node x has a key k. We model a *next* pointer with a unary function `next` and we model locations using elements in the underlying data domain.

Our formalism allows only for **assert** statements to specify desired program properties. In order to state the correctness specification for our desired list-search program, we interleave *ghost code* into the program skeleton; we distinguish ghost code fragments by enclosing them in ⌐dashed boxes⌐ . The skeleton in Fig. 2 has a loop that advances the pointer variable x along the list until NIL is reached. We model NIL with an immutable program variable. The first hole '$\langle\langle$??⓪ $\rangle\rangle$' before the **while**-loop and the second hole '$\langle\langle$??② $\rangle\rangle$' within the **while**-loop need to be filled so that the assertion at the end is satisfied. We use three ghost variables in the skeleton: g_{ans}, $g_{witness}$, and g_{found}. The ghost variable g_{ans} evaluates to whether we expect to find k in the list or not, and hence at the end the skeleton asserts that the Boolean variable b computed by the holes is precisely g_{ans}. The holes are restricted to not look at the ghost variables.

Now, notice that the skeleton needs to *check* that the answer g_{ans} is indeed correct. If g_{ans} is not T, then we add the assumption that key(x) $\neq$ k in each iteration of the loop, hence ensuring the key is not present. For ensuring correctness in the case g_{ans} = T, we need two more ghost variables $g_{witness}$ and g_{found}. The variable $g_{witness}$ witnesses the precise location in the list that holds the key k, and variable g_{found} indicates whether the location at $g_{witness}$ belongs to the list pointed to by x. Observe that this specification can be realized by filling '$\langle\langle$??⓪ $\rangle\rangle$' with "b := F" and '$\langle\langle$??② $\rangle\rangle$' with "**if** key(x) = k **then** b := T", for instance. Furthermore, this program is *coherent* [39] and hence our decision procedure will answer in the affirmative and synthesize code for the holes.

```
assume(T ≠ F);
⌐g_found := F;⌐
⟨⟨ ??⓪ ⟩⟩;
while(x ≠ NIL) {
 ⌐if (g_ans ≠ T) then⌐
 ⌐    assume(key(x) ≠ k);⌐
 ⌐else if (g_witness = x) then {⌐
 ⌐    assume (key(x) = k);⌐
 ⌐    g_found := T;⌐
 ⌐};⌐
   ⟨⟨ ??② ⟩⟩;
   x := next(x);
}
⌐assume (g_ans = T ⇒ g_found = T);⌐
assert b = T ⟺ g_ans = T
```

Fig. 2. Skeleton with ghost code

In fact, our procedure will synthesize a representation for *all* possible ways to fill the holes (thus including the solution above) and it is therefore possible to enumerate and pick specific solutions. It is straightforward to formulate a grammar which matches this setup. As noted, we must stipulate that the holes do not use the ghost variables.

Example 4. Consider the same program skeleton as in Example 3, but let us add an assertion at the end: "**assert** (b = T $\Rightarrow$ z = $g_{witness}$)", where z is another program variable. We are now demanding that the synthesized code also find a location z, whose key is k, that is equal to the ghost location $g_{witness}$, which is guessed nondeterministically at the beginning of the program. This specification is *unrealizable*: for a list with multiple locations having the key k, no matter what the program picks we can always take $g_{witness}$ to be the *other* location with key k in the list, thus violating the assertion. Our decision procedure will report in the negative for this specification.

Example 5 (Input/Output Examples). We can encode input/output examples by adding a sequence of assignments and assumptions that define certain models at the beginning of the program grammar. For instance, the sequence of statements in Fig. 3 defines a linked list of two elements with different keys.

We can similarly use special variables to define the output that we expect in the case of each model. And as we saw in the ghost code of Fig. 2, we can use fresh variables to introduce nondeterministic choices, which the grammar can use to pick an example model nondeterministically. Thus when the synthesized program is executed on the chosen model it computes the expected answer. This has the effect of requiring a solution that generalizes across models. See [30] for a more detailed example.

```
assume(x₁ ≠ NIL);
x₂ := next(x₁);
assume(x₂ ≠ NIL);
assume(next(x₂) = NIL);
k₁ := key(x₁);
k₂ := key(x₂);
assume(k₁ ≠ k₂)
```

Fig. 3. An example model

3 Preliminaries

In this section we define the syntax and semantics of uninterpreted programs and the *(grammar-restricted) uninterpreted program synthesis* problem.

Syntax. We fix a first order signature $\Sigma = (\mathcal{F}, \mathcal{R})$, where $\mathcal{F}$ and $\mathcal{R}$ are sets of function and relation symbols, respectively. Let V be a finite set of program variables. The set of programs over V is inductively defined using the following grammar, with $f \in \mathcal{F}$, $R \in \mathcal{R}$ (with f and R of the appropriate arities), and $x, y, z_1, \ldots, z_r \in V$.

$$\langle stmt \rangle_V ::= \mathbf{skip} \mid x := y \mid x := f(z_1, \ldots, z_r) \mid$$
$$\mathbf{assume}\,(\langle cond \rangle_V) \mid \mathbf{assert}\,(\langle cond \rangle_V) \mid \langle stmt \rangle_V \,;\, \langle stmt \rangle_V \mid$$
$$\mathbf{if}\,(\langle cond \rangle_V)\,\mathbf{then}\,\langle stmt \rangle_V\,\mathbf{else}\,\langle stmt \rangle_V \mid \mathbf{while}\,(\langle cond \rangle_V)\,\langle stmt \rangle_V$$
$$\langle cond \rangle_V ::= x = y \mid R(z_1, \ldots, z_r) \mid \langle cond \rangle_V \vee \langle cond \rangle_V \mid \neg \langle cond \rangle_V$$

Without loss of generality, we can assume that our programs do not use relations (they can be modeled with functions) and that every condition is either an equality or disequality between variables (arbitrary Boolean combinations can be modeled with nested **if−then−else**). When the set of variables V is clear from context, we will omit the subscript V from $\langle stmt \rangle_V$ and $\langle cond \rangle_V$.

Program Executions. An execution over V is a finite word over the alphabet

$$\Pi_V = \{ \text{``}x := y\text{''}, \text{``}x := f(\bar{z})\text{''}, \text{``}\mathbf{assume}(x = y)\text{''}, \text{``}\mathbf{assume}(x \neq y)\text{''},$$
$$\text{``}\mathbf{assert}(\bot)\text{''} \mid x, y \in V, \bar{z} \in V^r, f \in \mathcal{F} \}.$$

The set of *complete executions* for a program p over V, denoted $\mathsf{Exec}(p)$, is a regular language. See [30] for a straightforward definition. The set $\mathsf{PExec}(p)$ of *partial executions* is the set of prefixes of complete executions in $\mathsf{Exec}(p)$. We refer to partial executions as simply *executions*, and clarify as needed when the distinction is important.

Semantics. The semantics of executions is given in terms of data models. A data model $\mathcal{M} = (U, \mathcal{I})$ is a first order structure over Σ comprised of a universe U and an interpretation function $\mathcal{I}$ for the program symbols. The semantics of an execution π over a data model $\mathcal{M}$ is given by a configuration $\sigma(\pi, \mathcal{M}) : V \to U$ which maps each variable to its value in the universe U at the end of π. This notion is straightforward and we skip the formal definition (see [39] for details). For a fixed program p, any particular data model corresponds to at most one complete execution $\pi \in \text{Exec}(p)$.

An execution π is *feasible* in a data model $\mathcal{M}$ if for every prefix $\rho = \rho' \cdot \textbf{assume}(x \sim y)$ of π (where $\sim \in \{=, \neq\}$), we have $\sigma(\rho', \mathcal{M})(x) \sim \sigma(\rho', \mathcal{M})(y)$. Execution π is said to be *correct* in a data model $\mathcal{M}$ if for every prefix of π of the form $\rho = \rho' \cdot \textbf{assert}(\bot)$, we have that ρ' is not feasible, or *infeasible* in $\mathcal{M}$. Finally, a program p is said to be *correct* if for all data models $\mathcal{M}$ and executions $\pi \in \text{PExec}(p)$, π is correct in $\mathcal{M}$.

3.1   The Program Synthesis Problem

We are now ready to define the program synthesis problem. Our approach will be to allow users to specify a grammar and ask for the synthesis of a program from the grammar. We allow the user to express specifications using *assertions* in the program to be synthesized.

Grammar Schema and Input Grammar. In our problem formulation, we allow users to define a grammar which conforms to a schema, given below. The input grammars allow the usual context-free power required to describe proper nesting/bracketing of program expressions, but disallow other uses of the context-free power, such as *counting statements*.

For example, we disallow the grammar in Fig. 4. This grammar has two non-terminals S (the start symbol) and T. It generates programs with a conditional that has the *same* number of assignments in the **if** and **else** branches. We assume a countably infinite set PN of nonterminals and a countably infinite set PV of program variables. The grammar schema $\mathcal{S}$ over PN and PV is an infinite collection of productions:

$$S \to \textbf{if}\,(\text{x} = \text{y})$$
$$\qquad \textbf{then}\,\text{u} := \text{v}\; T\,\text{u} := \text{v}$$
$$T \to \textbf{else}$$
$$T \to ;\,\text{u} := \text{v}\;\; T\;\; \text{u} := \text{v}\,;$$

Fig. 4. Grammar with counting

$$S = \left\{ \begin{array}{ll} \text{``}P \to x := y\text{''},\; \text{``}P \to x := f(\overline{z})\text{''}, \\ \text{``}P \to \textbf{assume}(x \sim y)\text{''},\; \text{``}P \to \textbf{assert}(\bot)\text{''}, \\ \text{``}P \to \textbf{skip}\text{''},\; \text{``}P \to \textbf{while}\,(x \sim y)\,P_1\text{''}, \\ \text{``}P \to \textbf{if}\,(x \sim y)\,\textbf{then}\,P_1\,\textbf{else}\,P_2\text{''},\; \text{``}P \to P_1; P_2\text{''} \end{array} \middle| \begin{array}{l} P, P_1, P_2 \in PN \\ x, y \in PV, \overline{z} \in PV^r \\ \sim \in \{=, \neq\} \end{array} \right\}$$

An *input grammar* $\mathcal{G}$ is any finite subset of the schema $\mathcal{S}$, and it defines a set of programs, denoted $L(\mathcal{G})$. We can now define the main problem addressed in this work.

Definition 1 (Uninterpreted Program Realizability and Synthesis).
Given an input grammar $\mathcal{G}$, the realizability problem is to determine whether there is an uninterpreted program $p \in L(\mathcal{G})$ such that p is correct. The synthesis problem is to determine the above, and further, if realizable, synthesize a correct program $p \in L(\mathcal{G})$.

Example 6. Consider the program with a hole from Example 1 (Fig. 1, left). We can model that synthesis problem in our framework with the following grammar.

$$S \to P_1; P_2; P_{\langle\langle ??\rangle\rangle}; P_3 \qquad\qquad P_{\langle\langle ??\rangle\rangle} \to \langle stmt\rangle_{V_{\langle\langle ??\rangle\rangle}}$$
$$P_1 \to \text{``cipher := enc(secret, key)''} \qquad P_3 \to \text{``assert(z = secret)''}$$
$$P_2 \to \text{``assume(secret = dec(cipher, key))''}$$

Here, $V_{\langle\langle ??\rangle\rangle} = \{\text{cipher}, \text{y}_1, \ldots, \text{y}_n\}$ and the grammar $\langle stmt\rangle_{V_{\langle\langle ??\rangle\rangle}}$ is that of Sect. 3, restricted to loop-free programs. Any program generated from this grammar indeed matches the template from Fig. 1 (left) and any such program is correct if it satisfies the last assertion for all models, i.e., all interpretations of the function symbols enc and dec and for all initial values of the variables in $V = V_{\langle\langle ??\rangle\rangle} \cup \{\text{key}, \text{secret}\}$.

4 Undecidability of Uninterpreted Program Synthesis

Since verification of uninterpreted programs with loops is undecidable [39, 42], the following is immediate.

Theorem 1. *The uninterpreted program synthesis problem is undecidable.*

We next consider synthesizing loop-free uninterpreted programs (for which verification reduces to satisfiability of quantifier-free EUF) from grammars conforming to the following schema:

$$\mathcal{S}_{\text{loop-free}} = \mathcal{S} \setminus \{\text{``}P \to \textbf{while}\,(x \sim y)\ P_1\text{''} \mid P, P_1 \in PN,\ x, y \in PV, \sim \in \{=, \neq\}\}$$

Theorem 2. *The uninterpreted program synthesis problem is undecidable for the schema $\mathcal{S}_{loop\text{-}free}$.*

This is a corollary of the following stronger result: synthesis of *straight-line uninterpreted programs* (conforming to schema $\mathcal{S}_{\text{SLP}}$ below) is undecidable.

$$\mathcal{S}_{\text{SLP}} = \mathcal{S}_{\text{loop-free}} \setminus \{\text{``}P \to \textbf{if}(x \sim y)\,\textbf{then}\,P_1\,\textbf{else}\,P_2\text{''} \mid P, P_1, P_2 \in PN,$$
$$x, y \in PV, \sim \in \{=, \neq\}\}$$

Theorem 3. *The uninterpreted program synthesis problem is undecidable for the schema $\mathcal{S}_{SLP}$.*

In summary, program synthesis of even straight-line uninterpreted programs, which have neither conditionals nor iteration, is already undecidable. The notion of *coherence* for uninterpreted programs was shown to yield decidable verification in [39]. As we'll see in Sect. 5, restricting to coherent programs yields decidable synthesis, even for programs with conditionals *and* iteration.

5   Synthesis of Coherent Uninterpreted Programs

In this section, we present the main result of the paper: grammar-restricted program synthesis for uninterpreted *coherent* programs [39] is decidable. Intuitively, coherence allows us to maintain congruence closure in a streaming fashion when reading a coherent execution. First we recall the definition of coherent executions and programs in Sect. 5.1 and also the algorithm for verification of such programs. Then we introduce the synthesis procedure, which works by constructing a two-way alternating tree automaton. We briefly discuss this class of tree automata in Sect. 5.2 and recall some standard results. In Sects. 5.3, 5.4 and 5.5 we describe the details of the synthesis procedure, argue its correctness, and discuss its complexity. In Sect. 5.6, we present a tight lower bound result.

5.1   Coherent Executions and Programs

The notion of coherence for an execution π is defined with respect to the *terms* it computes. Intuitively, at the beginning of an execution, each variable $x \in V$ stores some constant term $\widehat{x} \in C$. As the execution proceeds, new terms are computed and stored in variables. Let Terms_Σ be the set of all ground terms defined using the constants and functions in Σ. Formally, the term corresponding to a variable $x \in V$ at the end of an execution $\pi \in \Pi_V^*$, denoted $\mathsf{T}(\pi, x) \in \mathsf{Terms}_\Sigma$, is inductively defined as follows. We assume that the set of constants C includes a designated set of *initial* constants $\widehat{V} = \{\widehat{x} \mid x \in V\} \subseteq C$.

$$
\begin{aligned}
\mathsf{T}(\varepsilon, x) &= \widehat{x} & x \in V \\
\mathsf{T}(\pi \cdot \text{``}x := y\text{''}, x) &= \mathsf{T}(\pi, y) & x, y \in V \\
\mathsf{T}(\pi \cdot \text{``}x := f(z_1, \dots, z_r)\text{''}, x) &= f(\mathsf{T}(\pi, z_1), \dots, \mathsf{T}(\pi, z_r)) \; x, z_1, \dots, z_r \in V \\
\mathsf{T}(\pi \cdot a, x) &= \mathsf{T}(\pi, x) & \text{otherwise}
\end{aligned}
$$

We will use $\mathsf{T}(\pi)$ to denote the set $\{\mathsf{T}(\pi', x) \mid x \in V, \pi' \text{ is a prefix of } \pi\}$.

A related notion is the set of *term equality assumptions* that an execution accumulates, which we formalize as $\alpha : \pi \to \mathcal{P}(\mathsf{Terms}_\Sigma \times \mathsf{Terms}_\Sigma)$, and define inductively as $\alpha(\varepsilon) = \varnothing$, $\alpha(\pi \cdot \text{``}\mathbf{assume}(x = y)\text{''}) = \alpha(\pi) \cup \{(\mathsf{T}(\pi, x), \mathsf{T}(\pi, y))\}$, and $\alpha(\pi \cdot a) = \alpha(\pi)$ otherwise.

For a set of term equalities $A \subseteq \mathsf{Terms}_\Sigma \times \mathsf{Terms}_\Sigma$, and two ground terms $t_1, t_2 \in \mathsf{Terms}_\Sigma$, we say t_1 and t_2 are *equivalent modulo* A, denoted $t_1 \cong_A t_2$, if $A \models t_1 = t_2$. For a set of terms $S \subseteq \mathsf{Terms}_\Sigma$, and a term $t \in \mathsf{Terms}_\Sigma$ we write $t \in_A S$ if there is a term $t' \in S$ such that $t \cong_A t'$. For terms $t, s \in \mathsf{Terms}_\Sigma$, we say s is a *superterm modulo* A of t, denoted $t \preceq_A s$ if there are terms $t', s' \in \mathsf{Terms}_\Sigma$ such that $t \cong_A t'$, $s \cong_A s'$ and s' is a superterm of t'.

With the above notation in mind, we now review the notion of coherence.

Definition 2 (Coherent Executions and Programs [39]). *An execution $\pi \in \Pi_V^*$ is said to be* coherent *if it satisfies the following two conditions.*

Memoizing. *Let $\rho = \rho' \cdot \text{``}x := f(\overline{y})\text{''}$ be a prefix of π. If $t_x = \mathsf{T}(\rho, x) \in_{\alpha(\rho')} \mathsf{T}(\rho')$, then there is a variable $z \in V$ such that $t_x \cong_{\alpha(\rho')} t_z$, where $t_z = \mathsf{T}(\rho', z)$.*

Early Assumes. *Let* $\rho = \rho' \cdot$ *"$\textbf{assume}(x = y)$" be a prefix of* π, $t_x = T(\rho', x)$ *and* $t_y = T(\rho', y)$. *If there is a term* $s \in T(\rho')$ *such that either* $t_x \preccurlyeq_{\alpha(\rho')} s$ *or* $t_y \preccurlyeq_{\alpha(\rho')} s$, *then there is a variable* $z \in V$ *such that* $s \cong_{\alpha(\rho')} t_z$, *where* $t_z = T(\rho', z)$.

A program p is coherent if every complete execution $\pi \in \textsf{Exec}(p)$ *is coherent.*

The following theorems due to [39] establish the decidability of verifying coherent programs and also of checking if a program is coherent.

Theorem 4 ([39]). *The verification problem for coherent programs, i.e. checking if a given uninterpreted coherent program is correct, is decidable.*

Theorem 5 ([39]). *The problem of checking coherence, i.e. checking if a given uninterpreted program is coherent, is decidable.*

The techniques used in [39] are automata theoretic. They allow us to construct an automaton $\mathcal{A}_{\text{exec}}^{\leftrightsquigarrow}$[2], of size $O(2^{\text{poly}(|V|)})$, which accepts all coherent executions that are also correct.

To give some intuition for the notion of coherence, we illustrate simple example programs that are not coherent. Consider program p_0 below, which is not coherent because it fails to be memoizing.

$$p_0 \quad \triangleq \quad \texttt{x := f(y); x := f(x); z := f(y)}$$

The first and third statements compute $f(\hat{y})$, storing it in variables x and z, respectively, but the term is *dropped* after the second statement and hence is not contained in any program variable when the third statement executes. Next consider program p_1, which is not coherent because it fails to have early assumes.

$$p_1 \quad \triangleq \quad \texttt{x := f(w); x := f(x); y := f(z); y := f(y); assume(w = z)}$$

Indeed, the assume statement is not early because superterms of w and z, namely $f(\hat{w})$ and $f(\hat{z})$, were computed and subsequently dropped before the assume.

Intuitively, the coherence conditions are necessary to allow equality information to be tracked with finite memory. We can make this stark by tweaking the example for p_1 above as follows.

$$p_1' \quad \triangleq \quad \texttt{x := f(w);} \underbrace{\texttt{x := f(x)} \cdots \texttt{x := f(x)}}_{n \text{ times}}\texttt{;}$$

$$\texttt{y := f(z);} \underbrace{\texttt{y := f(y)} \cdots \texttt{y := f(y)}}_{n \text{ times}}\texttt{; assume(w = z)}$$

Observe that, for large n (e.g. $n > 100$), many terms are computed and dropped by this program, like $f^{42}(\hat{x})$ and $f^{99}(\hat{y})$ for instance. The difficulty with this

---

[2] We use superscripts '$\leftrightsquigarrow$' and '$\wedge$' for word and tree automata, respectively.

program, from a verification perspective, is that the assume statement entails equalities between many terms which have not been kept track of. Imagine trying to verify the following program

$$p_2 \;\stackrel{\Delta}{=}\; p_1'; \; \mathbf{assert}(\mathtt{x} = \mathtt{y})$$

Let $\pi_{p_1'} \in \mathsf{Exec}(p_1')$ be the unique complete execution of p_1'. If we examine the details, we see that $t_x = \mathsf{T}(\pi_{p_1'}, x) = f^{101}(\widehat{w})$ and $t_y = \mathsf{T}(\pi_{p_1'}, y) = f^{101}(\widehat{z})$. The assertion indeed holds because $t_x \cong_{\{(\widehat{w}, \widehat{z})\}} t_y$. However, to keep track of this fact requires remembering an arbitrary number of terms that grows with the size of the program. Finally, we note that the coherence restriction is met by many single-pass algorithms, e.g. searching and manipulation of lists and trees.

5.2 Overview of the Synthesis Procedure

Our synthesis procedure uses tree automata. We consider tree representations of programs, or *program trees*. The synthesis problem is thus to check if there is a program tree whose corresponding program is coherent, correct, and belongs to the input grammar $\mathcal{G}$.

The synthesis procedure works as follows. We first construct a top-down tree automaton $\mathcal{A}_{\mathcal{G}}^\wedge$ that accepts the set of trees corresponding to the programs generated by $\mathcal{G}$. We next construct another tree automaton $\mathcal{A}_{\mathrm{cc}}^\wedge$, which accepts all trees corresponding to programs that are <u>c</u>oherent and <u>c</u>orrect. $\mathcal{A}_{\mathrm{cc}}^\wedge$ is a two-way alternating tree automaton that simulates all executions of an input program tree and checks that each is both correct and coherent. In order to simulate longer and longer executions arising from constructs like **while**-loops, the automaton traverses the input tree and performs multiple passes over subtrees, visiting the internal nodes of the tree many times. We then translate the two-way alternating tree automaton to an equivalent (one-way) nondeterministic top-down tree automaton by adapting results from [33,53] to our setting. Finally, we check emptiness of the intersection between this top-down automaton and the grammar automaton $\mathcal{A}_{\mathcal{G}}^\wedge$. The definitions for trees and the relevant automata are standard, and we refer the reader to [14] and to our technical report [30].

5.3 Tree Automaton for Program Trees

Every program can be represented as a tree whose leaves are labeled with basic statements like "$x := y$" and whose internal nodes are labeled with constructs like **while** and **seq** (an alias for the sequencing construct ';'), which have subprograms as children. Essentially, we represent the set of programs generated by an input grammar $\mathcal{G}$ as a regular set of program trees, accepted by a nondeterministic top-down tree automaton $\mathcal{A}_{\mathcal{G}}^\wedge$. The construction of $\mathcal{A}_{\mathcal{G}}^\wedge$ mimics the standard construction for tree automata that accept *parse trees* of context free grammars. The formalization of this intuition is straightforward, and we refer the reader to [30] for details. We note the following fact regarding the construction of the acceptor of program trees from a particular grammar $\mathcal{G}$.

Lemma 1. *$\mathcal{A}_{\mathcal{G}}^\wedge$ has size $O(|\mathcal{G}|)$ and can be constructed in time $O(|\mathcal{G}|)$.*   □

5.4   Tree Automaton for Simulating Executions

We now discuss the construction of the two-way alternating tree automaton $\mathcal{A}_{cc}^{\mathbb{A}}$ that underlies our synthesis procedure. A two-way alternating tree automaton consists of a finite set of states and a transition function that maps tuples (q, m, a) of state, incoming direction, and node labels to positive Boolean formulas over pairs (q', m') of next state and next direction. In the case of our binary program trees, incoming directions come from $\{D, U_L, U_R\}$, corresponding to coming down from a parent, and up from left and right children. Next directions come from $\{U, L, R\}$, corresponding to going up to a parent, and down to left and right children.

The automaton $\mathcal{A}_{cc}^{\mathbb{A}}$ is designed to accept the set of all program trees that correspond to correct and coherent programs. This is achieved by ensuring that a program tree is accepted precisely when all executions of the program it represents are accepted by the word automaton $\mathcal{A}_{exec}^{\cdots}$ (Sect. 5.1). The basic idea behind $\mathcal{A}_{cc}^{\mathbb{A}}$ is as follows. Given a program tree T as input, $\mathcal{A}_{cc}^{\mathbb{A}}$ traverses T and explores all the executions of the associated program. For each execution σ, $\mathcal{A}_{cc}^{\mathbb{A}}$ keeps track of the state that the word automaton $\mathcal{A}_{exec}^{\cdots}$ would reach after reading σ. Intuitively, an accepting run of $\mathcal{A}_{cc}^{\mathbb{A}}$ is one which never visits the unique rejecting state of $\mathcal{A}_{exec}^{\cdots}$ during simulation.

We now give the formal description of $\mathcal{A}_{cc}^{\mathbb{A}} = (Q^{cc}, I^{cc}, \delta_0^{cc}, \delta_1^{cc}, \delta_2^{cc})$, which works over the alphabet Γ_V described in Sect. 5.3.

States. Both the full set of states and the initial set of states for $\mathcal{A}_{cc}^{\mathbb{A}}$ coincide with those of the word automaton $\mathcal{A}_{exec}^{\cdots}$. That is, $Q^{cc} = Q^{exec}$ and $I^{cc} = \{q_0^{exec}\}$, where q_0^{exec} is the unique starting state of $\mathcal{A}_{exec}^{\cdots}$.

Transitions. For intuition, consider the case when the automaton's control is in state q reading an internal tree node n with one child and which is labeled by $a =$ "**while**$(x = y)$". In the next step, the automaton simultaneously performs two transitions corresponding to two possibilities: entering the loop after assuming the guard "$x = y$" to be true and exiting the loop with the guard being false. In the first of these simultaneous transitions, the automaton moves to the left child $n \cdot L$, and its state changes to q_1', where $q_1' = \delta^{exec}(q, \text{"}\mathbf{assume}(x = y)\text{"})$. In the second simultaneous transition, the automaton moves to the parent node $n \cdot U$ (searching for the next statement to execute, which follows the end of the loop) and changes its state to q_2', where $q_2' = \delta^{exec}(q, \text{"}\mathbf{assume}(x \neq y)\text{"})$. We encode these two possibilities as a *conjunctive* transition of the two-way alternating automaton. That is, $\delta_1^{cc}(q, m, a) = ((q_1', L) \wedge (q_2', U))$.

For every i, m, a, we have $\delta_i(q_{\mathsf{reject}}, m, a) = \bot$, where q_{reject} is the unique, absorbing rejecting state of $\mathcal{A}_{exec}^{\cdots}$. Below we describe the transitions from all other states $q \neq q_{\mathsf{reject}}$. All transitions $\delta_i(q, m, a)$ not described below are $\bot$.

Transitions from the Root. At the root node, labeled by "**root**", the automaton transitions as follows:

$$\delta_1^{cc}(q, m, \mathbf{root}) = \begin{cases} (q, L) & \text{if } m = D \\ \mathbf{true} & \text{otherwise} \end{cases}$$

A two-way tree automaton starts in the configuration where m is set to D. This means that in the very first step the automaton moves to the child node (direction L). If the automaton visits the root node in a subsequent step (marking the completion of an execution), then all transitions are enabled.

Transitions from Leaf Nodes. For a leaf node with label $a \in \Gamma_0$ and state q, the transition of the automaton is $\delta_0^{cc}(q, D, a) = (\delta^{exec}(q, a), U)$. That is, when the automaton visits a leaf node from the parent, it simulates reading a in $\mathcal{A}_{exec}^{\cdots}$ and moves to the resulting state in the parent node.

Transitions from "while" Nodes. As described earlier, when reading a node labeled by "**while**$(x \sim y)$", where $\sim \in \{=, \neq\}$, the automaton simulates both the possibility of entering the loop body as well as the possibility of exiting the loop. This corresponds to a conjunctive transition:

$$\delta_1^{cc}(q, m, \text{"\textbf{while}}(x \sim y)\text{"}) = (q', L) \wedge (q'', U)$$
$$\text{where } q' = \delta^{exec}(q, \text{"\textbf{assume}}(x \sim y)\text{"})$$
$$\text{and } q'' = \delta^{exec}(q, \text{"\textbf{assume}}(x \not\sim y)\text{"})$$

Above, $\not\sim$ refers to " $=$ " when $\sim$ is " $\neq$ ", and vice versa. The first conjunct corresponds to the execution where the program enters the loop body (assuming the guard is true), and thus control moves to the left child of the current node, which corresponds to the loop body. The second conjunct corresponds to the execution where the loop guard is false and the automaton moves to the parent of the current tree node. Notice that, in both the conjuncts above, the direction in which the tree automaton moves does not depend on the last move m of the state. That is, no matter how the program arrives at a **while** statement, the automaton simulates both the possibilities of entering or exiting the loop body.

Transitions from "ite" Nodes. At a node labeled "ite$(x \sim y)$", when coming down the tree from the parent, the automaton simulates both branches of the conditional:

$$\delta_2^{cc}(q, D, \text{"ite}(x \sim y)\text{"}) = (q', L) \wedge (q'', R)$$
$$\text{where } q' = \delta^{exec}(q, \text{"\textbf{assume}}(x \sim y)\text{"})$$
$$\text{and } q'' = \delta^{exec}(q, \text{"\textbf{assume}}(x \not\sim y)\text{"})$$

The first conjunct in the transition corresponds to simulating the word automaton on the condition $x \sim y$ and moving to the left child, i.e. the body of the **then** branch. Similarly, the second conjunct corresponds to simulating the word automaton on the negation of the condition and moving to the right child, i.e. the body of the **else** branch.

Now consider the case when the automaton moves *up* to an **ite** node from a child node. In this case, the automaton moves up to the parent node (having completed simulation of the **then** or **else** branch) and the state q remains unchanged:

$$\delta_2^{cc}(q, m, \text{“ite}(x \sim y)\text{”}) = (q, U) \quad m \in \{U_L, U_R\}$$

Transitions from *“seq”* ***Nodes.*** In this case, the automaton moves either to the left child, the right child, or to the parent, depending on the last move. It does not change the state component. Formally,

$$\delta_2^{cc}(q, m, \text{“seq”}) = \begin{cases} (q, L) \text{ if } m = D \\ (q, R) \text{ if } m = U_L \\ (q, U) \text{ if } m = U_R \end{cases}$$

The above transitions match the straightforward semantics of sequencing two statements $s_1; s_2$. If the automaton visits from the parent node, it next moves to the left child to simulate s_1. When it finishes simulating s_1, it comes up from the left child and enters the right child to begin simulating s_2. Finally, when simulation of s_2 is complete, the automaton moves to the parent node, exiting the subtree.

The following lemma asserts the correctness of the automaton construction and states its complexity.

Lemma 2. $\mathcal{A}_{cc}^{\Lambda}$ *accepts the set of all program trees corresponding to correct, coherent programs. It has size $|\mathcal{A}_{cc}^{\Lambda}| = O(2^{\text{poly}(|V|)})$, and can be constructed in $O(2^{\text{poly}(|V|)})$ time.*   □

5.5   Synthesis Procedure

The rest of the synthesis procedure goes as follows. We first construct a nondeterministic top-down tree automaton $\mathcal{A}_{cc\text{-td}}^{\Lambda}$ such that $L(\mathcal{A}_{cc\text{-td}}^{\Lambda}) = L(\mathcal{A}_{cc}^{\Lambda})$. An adaptation of results from [33,53] ensures that $\mathcal{A}_{cc\text{-td}}^{\Lambda}$ has size $|\mathcal{A}_{cc\text{-td}}^{\Lambda}| = O(2^{2^{\text{poly}(|V|)}})$ and can be constructed in time $O(2^{2^{\text{poly}(|V|)}})$. Next we construct a top-down nondeterministic tree automaton $\mathcal{A}^{\Lambda}$ such that $L(\mathcal{A}^{\Lambda}) = L(\mathcal{A}_{cc\text{-td}}^{\Lambda}) \cap L(\mathcal{A}_{\mathcal{G}}^{\Lambda}) = L(\mathcal{A}_{cc}^{\Lambda}) \cap L(\mathcal{A}_{\mathcal{G}}^{\Lambda})$, with size $|\mathcal{A}^{\Lambda}| = O(2^{2^{\text{poly}(|V|)}} \cdot |\mathcal{G}|)$ and in time $O(|\mathcal{A}_{cc\text{-td}}^{\Lambda}| \cdot |\mathcal{A}_{\mathcal{G}}^{\Lambda}|) = O(2^{2^{\text{poly}(|V|)}} \cdot |\mathcal{G}|)$. Finally, checking emptiness of $\mathcal{A}^{\Lambda}$ can be done in time $O(|\mathcal{A}^{\Lambda}|) = O(2^{2^{\text{poly}(|V|)}} \cdot |\mathcal{G}|)$. If non-empty, a program tree can be constructed.

This gives us the central upper bound result of the paper.

Theorem 6. *The grammar-restricted synthesis problem for uninterpreted coherent programs is decidable in 2EXPTIME, and in particular, in time doubly exponential in the number of variables and linear in the size of the input grammar. Furthermore, a tree automaton representing the set of all correct coherent programs that conform to the grammar can be constructed in the same time.*   □

5.6 Matching Lower Bound

Our synthesis procedure is optimal. We prove a 2EXPTIME lower bound for the synthesis problem by reduction from the 2EXPTIME-hard acceptance problem of *alternating* Turing machines (ATMs) with exponential space bound [12]. Full details of the reduction can be found in [30].

Theorem 7. *The grammar-restricted synthesis problem for coherent uninterpreted programs is* 2EXPTIME-*hard.*

6 Further Results

In this section, we give results for variants of uninterpreted program synthesis in terms of transition systems, Boolean programs, and recursive programs.

6.1 Synthesizing Transition Systems

Here, rather than synthesizing programs from grammars, we consider instead the synthesis of transition systems whose executions must belong to a regular set. Our main result is that the synthesis problem in this case is EXPTIME-complete, in contrast to grammar-restricted program synthesis which is 2EXPTIME-complete.

Transition System Definition and Semantics. Let us fix a set of program variables V as before. We consider the following finite alphabet

$$\Sigma_V = \{ \text{``}x := y\text{''}, \text{``}x := f(\bar{z})\text{''}, \text{``}\mathbf{assert}(\bot)\text{''}, \text{``}\mathbf{check}(x = y)\text{''} \mid x, y, \in V, \bar{z} \in V^r \}$$

Let us define $\Gamma_V \subseteq \Sigma_V$ to be the set of all elements of the form "$\mathbf{check}(x = y)$", where $x, y \in V$. We refer to the elements of Γ_V as *check* letters.

A (deterministic) transition system TS over V is a tuple $(Q, q_0, H, \lambda, \delta)$, where Q is a finite set of states, $q_0 \in Q$ is the initial state, $H \subseteq Q$ is the set of halting states, $\lambda : Q \to \Sigma_V$ is a labeling function such that for any $q \in Q$, if $\lambda(q) = \text{``}\mathbf{assert}(\bot)\text{''}$ then $q \in H$, and $\delta : (Q \setminus H) \to Q \cup (Q \times Q)$ is a transition function such that for any $q \in Q \setminus H$, $\delta(q) \in Q \times Q$ iff $\lambda(q) \in \Gamma_V$.

We define the semantics of a transition system using the set of executions that it generates. A *(partial) execution* π of a transition system $TS = (Q, q_0, H, \lambda, \delta)$ over variables V is a finite word over the induced execution alphabet Π_V (from Sect. 3) with the following property. If $\pi = a_0 a_1 \ldots a_n$ with $n \geq 0$, then there exists a sequence of states $q_{j_0}, q_{j_1}, \ldots, q_{j_n}$ with $q_{j_0} = q_0$ such that $(0 \leq i \leq n)$:

- If $\lambda(q_{j_i}) \notin \Gamma_V$ then $a_i = \lambda(q_{j_i})$, and if $i < n$ then $q_{j_{i+1}} = \delta(q_{j_i})$.
- Otherwise $\begin{cases} \text{either} & a_i = \text{``}\mathbf{assume}(x = y)\text{''} \text{ and } i < n \Rightarrow q_{j_{i+1}} = \delta(q_{j_i}) \downharpoonright_1, \\ \text{or} & a_i = \text{``}\mathbf{assume}(x \neq y)\text{''} \text{ and } i < n \Rightarrow q_{j_{i+1}} = \delta(q_{j_i}) \downharpoonright_2 \end{cases}$

In the above, we denote pair projection with $\lfloor$, i.e., $(t_1, t_2) \lfloor_i = t_i$, where $i \in \{1, 2\}$. A *complete execution* is an execution whose corresponding final state (q_n above) is in H. For any transition system TS, we denote the set of its executions by $\mathsf{Exec}(TS)$ and the set of its complete executions by $\mathsf{CompExec}(TS)$. The notions of *correctness* and *coherence* for transition systems are identical to their counterparts for programs.

The Transition System Synthesis Problem. We consider transition system specifications that place restrictions on executions (both partial and complete) using two regular languages S and R. Executions must belong to the first language S (which is prefix-closed) and all complete executions must belong to the second language R. A specification is given as two deterministic automata $\mathcal{A}_S^{\cdots}$ and $\mathcal{A}_R^{\cdots}$ over executions, where $L(\mathcal{A}_S^{\cdots}) = S$ and $L(\mathcal{A}_R^{\cdots}) = R$. For a transition system TS and specification automata $\mathcal{A}_S^{\cdots}$ and $\mathcal{A}_R^{\cdots}$, whenever $\mathsf{Exec}(TS) \subseteq L(\mathcal{A}_S^{\cdots})$ and $\mathsf{CompExec}(TS) \subseteq L(\mathcal{A}_R^{\cdots})$ we say that TS satisfies its (syntactic) specification. Note that this need not entail correctness of TS. Splitting the specification into partial executions S and complete executions R allows us, among other things, to constrain the executions of non-halting transition systems.

Definition 3 (Transition System Realizability and Synthesis). *Given a finite set of program variables V and deterministic specification automata $\mathcal{A}_S^{\cdots}$ (prefix-closed) and $\mathcal{A}_R^{\cdots}$ over the execution alphabet Π_V, decide if there is a correct, coherent transition system TS over V that satisfies the specification. Furthermore, produce one if it exists.*

Since programs are readily translated to transition systems (of similar size), the transition system synthesis problem seems, at first glance, to be a problem that ought to have similar complexity. However, as we show, it is crucially different in that it allows the synthesized transition system to have *complete information* of past commands executed at any point. We will observe in this section that the transition system synthesis problem is EXPTIME-complete.

To see the difference between program and transition system synthesis, consider program skeleton P from Example 2 in Sect. 2. The problem is to fill the hole in P with either y := T or y := F. Observe that when P executes, there are *two* different executions that lead to the hole. In grammar-restricted program synthesis, the hole must be filled by a sub-program that is executed *no matter how the hole is reached*, and hence no such program exists. However, when we model this problem in the setting of transition systems, the synthesizer is able to produce transitions that depend on how the hole is reached. In other words, it does not fill the hole in P with *uniform* code. In this sense, in grammar-restricted program synthesis, programs have *incomplete information* of the past. We crucially exploited this difference in the proof of 2EXPTIME-hardness for grammar-restricted program synthesis (see [30]). No such incomplete information can be enforced by regular execution specifications in transition system synthesis, and indeed the problem turns out to be easier: transition system realizability and synthesis are EXPTIME-complete.

Theorem 8. *Transition system realizability is decidable in time exponential in the number of program variables and polynomial in the size of the automata $\mathcal{A}_S^{\cdots}$ and $\mathcal{A}_R^{\cdots}$. Furthermore, the problem is* EXPTIME-*complete. When realizable, within the same time bounds we can construct a correct, coherent transition system whose partial and complete executions are in $L(\mathcal{A}_S^{\cdots})$ and $L(\mathcal{A}_R^{\cdots})$, respectively.*

6.2 Synthesizing Boolean Programs

Here we observe corollaries of our results when applied to the more restricted problem of synthesizing Boolean programs.

In Boolean program synthesis we interpret variables in programs over the Boolean domain $\{T, F\}$, and we disallow computations of uninterpreted functions and the checking of uninterpreted relations. Standard Boolean functions like $\wedge$ and $\neg$ are instead allowed, but note that these can be modeled using conditional statements. We allow for *nondeterminism* with a special assignment "$b := *$", which assigns b nondeterministically to T or F. As usual, a program is correct when it satisfies all its assertions.

Synthesis of Boolean programs can be reduced to uninterpreted program synthesis using two special constants T and F. Each nondeterministic assignment is modeled by computing a **next** function on successive nodes of a linked list, accessing a nondeterministic value by computing **key** on the current node, and assuming the result is either T or F. Since uninterpreted programs must satisfy assertions in all models, this indeed captures nondeterministic assignment. Further, every term ever computed in such a program is equivalent to T or F (by virtue of the interleaved **assume** statements), making the resulting program coherent. The 2EXPTIME upper bound for Boolean program synthesis now follows from Theorem 6. We further show that, perhaps surprisingly, the 2EXPTIME lower bound from Sect. 5 can be adapted to prove 2EXPTIME-hardness of Boolean program synthesis.

Theorem 9. *The grammar-restricted synthesis problem for Boolean programs is* 2EXPTIME-*complete, and can be solved in time doubly-exponential in the number of variables and linear in the size of the input grammar.*   □

Thus synthesis for coherent uninterpreted programs is no more complex than Boolean program synthesis, establishing decidability and complexity of a problem which has found wide use in practice—for instance, the synthesis tool SKETCH solves precisely this problem, as it models integers using a small number of bits and allows grammars to restrict programs with holes.

6.3 Synthesizing Recursive Programs

We extend the positive result of Sect. 5 to synthesize coherent recursive programs. The setup for the problem is very similar. Given a grammar that identifies a class of recursive programs, the goal is to determine if there is a program in the grammar that is coherent and correct.

The syntax of recursive programs is similar to the non-recursive case, and we refer the reader to [30] for details. In essence, programs are extended with a new function call construct. Proofs are similar in structure to the non-recursive case, with the added challenge of needing to account for recursive function calls and the fact that $\mathcal{A}_{exec}^{...}$ becomes a (visibly) pushdown automaton rather than a standard finite automaton. This gives a 2EXPTIME algorithm for synthesizing recursive programs; a matching lower bound follows from the non-recursive case.

Theorem 10. *The grammar-restricted synthesis problem for uninterpreted coherent recursive programs is 2EXPTIME-complete. The algorithm is doubly exponential in the number of program variables and linear in the size of the input grammar. Furthermore, a tree automaton representing the set of all correct, coherent recursive programs that conform to the grammar can be constructed in the same time.*

7   Related Work

The automata and game-theoretic approaches to synthesis date back to a problem proposed by Church [13], after which a rich theory emerged [9,18,32,48]. The problems considered in this line of work typically deal with a system reacting to an environment interactively using a finite set of signals over an infinite number of rounds. Tree automata over infinite *trees*, representing strategies, with various infinitary acceptance conditions (Büchi, Rabin, Muller, parity) emerged as a uniform technique to solve such synthesis problems against temporal logic specifications with optimal complexity bounds [31,38,44,45]. In this paper, we use an alternative approach from [35] that works on *finite* program trees, using two-way traversals to simulate iteration. The work in [35], however, uses such representations to solve synthesis problems for programs over a fixed finite set of Boolean variables and against LTL specifications. In this work we use it to synthesize coherent programs that have finitely many variables working over infinite domains endowed with functions and relations.

While decidability results for program synthesis beyond finite data domains are uncommon, we do know of some results of this kind. First, there are decidability results known for synthesis of tranducers with registers [29]. Transducers interactively read a stream of inputs and emit a stream of outputs. Finite-state tranducers can be endowed with a set of registers for storing inputs and doing only equality/disequality comparisons on future inputs. Synthesis of such transducers for temporal logic specifications is known to be decidable. Note that, although the data domain is infinite, there are no functions or relations on data (other than equality), making it a much more restricted class (and grammar-based approaches for syntactically restricting transducers has not been studied). Indeed, with uninterpreted functions and relations, the synthesis problem is undecidable (Theorem 1), with decidability only for coherent programs. In [11], the authors study the problem of synthesizing uninterpreted terms from a grammar that satisfy a first-order specification. They give various decidability and undecidability results. In contrast, our results are for programs with conditionals and iteration (but restricted to coherent programs) and for specifications using assertions in code.

Another setting with a decidable synthesis result over unbounded domains is work on strategy synthesis for linear arithmetic *satisfiability* games [17]. There it is shown that for a satisfiability game, in which two players (SAT and UNSAT) play to prove a formula is satisfiable (where the formula is interpreted over the theory of linear rational arithmetic), if the SAT player has a winning strategy then a strategy can be synthesized. Though the data domain (rationals) is infinite, the game consists of a finite set of interactions and hence has no need for recursion. The authors also consider reachability games where the number of rounds can be unbounded, but present only sound and incomplete results, as checking who wins in such reachability games is undecidable.

Tree automata techniques for accepting finite parse trees of programs was explored in [37] for synthesizing reactive programs with variables over finite domains. In more recent work, automata on finite trees have been explored for synthesizing data completion scripts from input-output examples [55], for accepting programs that are verifiable using abstract interpretations [54], and for relational program synthesis [56].

The work in [36] explores a decidable logic with $\exists^* \forall^*$ prefixes that can be used to encode synthesis problems with background theories like arithmetic. However, encoding program synthesis in this logic only expresses programs of finite size. Another recent paper [27] explores sound (but incomplete) techniques for showing unrealizability of syntax-guided synthesis problems.

8   Conclusions

We presented foundational results on synthesizing coherent programs with uninterpreted functions and relations. To the best of our knowledge, this is the first natural decidable program synthesis problem for programs of arbitrary size which have iteration/recursion, and which work over infinite domains.

The field of program synthesis lacks theoretical results, and especially decidability results. We believe our results to be the first of their kind to fill this lacuna, and we find this paper exciting because it bridges the worlds of program synthesis and the rich classical synthesis frameworks of systems over finite domains using tree automata [9,18,32,48]. We believe this link could revitalize both domains with new techniques and applications.

Turning to practical applications of our results, several questions require exploration in future work. First, one might question the utility of programs that verify only with respect to uninterpreted data domains. Recent work [10] has shown that verifying programs using uninterpreted abstractions can be extremely effective in practice for proving programs correct. Also, recent work by Mathur et al. [40] explores ways to add *axioms* (such as commutativity of functions, axioms regarding partial orders, etc.) and yet preserve decidability of verification. The methods used therein are compatible with our technique, and we believe our results can be extended smoothly to their decidable settings. A more elaborate way to bring in complex theories (like arithmetic) would be to marry our technique with the *iterative* automata-based software verification technique pioneered by work behind the ULTIMATE tool [23–26]; this won't yield decidable synthesis, but still could result in *complete* synthesis procedures.

The second concern for practicality is the coherence restriction. There is recent work by Mathur et al. [41] that shows single-pass heap-manipulating programs respect a (suitably adapted) notion of coherence. Adapting our technique to this setting seems feasible, and this would give an interesting application of our work. Finally, it is important to build an implementation of our procedure in a tool that exploits pragmatic techniques for constructing tree automata, and the techniques pursued in [54–56] hold promise.

References

1. Alur, R., et al.: Syntax-guided synthesis. In: Dependable Software Systems Engineering, NATO Science for Peace and Security Series, D: Information and Communication Security, vol. 40, pp. 1–25. IOS Press (2015)
2. Alur, R., Madhusudan, P.: Visibly pushdown languages. In: Proceedings of the Thirty-sixth Annual ACM Symposium on Theory of Computing, STOC 2004, pp. 202–211. ACM, New York (2004). https://doi.org/10.1145/1007352.1007390
3. Alur, R., Madhusudan, P.: Adding nesting structure to words. J. ACM **56**(3), 16:1–16:43 (2009). https://doi.org/10.1145/1516512.1516518
4. Alur, R., Singh, R., Fisman, D., Solar-Lezama, A.: Search-based program synthesis. Commun. ACM **61**(12), 84–93 (2018). https://doi.org/10.1145/3208071
5. Bauer-Mengelberg, S.: über die vollständigkeit des logikkalküls. J. Symb. Log. **55**(1), 341–342 (1990). https://doi.org/10.2307/2274974
6. Bloem, R., Galler, S.J., Jobstmann, B., Piterman, N., Pnueli, A., Weiglhofer, M.: Specify, compile, run: hardware from PSL. Electr. Notes Theor. Comput. Sci. **190**(4), 3–16 (2007). https://doi.org/10.1016/j.entcs.2007.09.004
7. Bloem, R., Jobstmann, B., Piterman, N., Pnueli, A., Sa'ar, Y.: Synthesis of reactive(1) designs. J. Comput. Syst. Sci. **78**(3), 911–938 (2012). https://doi.org/10.1016/j.jcss.2011.08.007
8. Bradley, A.R., Manna, Z.: The Calculus of Computation: Decision Procedures with Applications to Verification. Springer, Heidelberg (2007). https://doi.org/10.1007/978-3-540-74113-8
9. Buchi, J.R., Landweber, L.H.: Solving sequential conditions by finite-state strategies. Trans. Am. Math. Soc. **138**, 295–311 (1969). https://doi.org/10.2307/1994916
10. Bueno, D., Sakallah, K.A.: euforia: complete software model checking with uninterpreted functions. In: Enea, C., Piskac, R. (eds.) VMCAI 2019. LNCS, vol. 11388, pp. 363–385. Springer, Cham (2019). https://doi.org/10.1007/978-3-030-11245-5_17
11. Caulfield, B., Rabe, M.N., Seshia, S.A., Tripakis, S.: What's decidable about syntax-guided synthesis? CoRR abs/1510.08393 (2015)
12. Chandra, A.K., Kozen, D.C., Stockmeyer, L.J.: Alternation. J. ACM **28**(1), 114–133 (1981). https://doi.org/10.1145/322234.322243
13. Church, A.: Application of recursive arithmetic to the problem of circuit synthesis. Summaries of talks presented at the Summer Institute for Symbolic Logic Cornell University, 1957, 2nd edn., J. Symb. Log. **28**(4), 30–50. 3a–45a. (1960)

14. Comon, H., et al.: Tree automata techniques and applications (2007). https://tata.gforge.inria.fr. Accessed 29 Jun 2020
15. Dolev, D., Yao, A.: On the security of public key protocols. IEEE Trans. Inf. Theory **29**(2), 198–208 (1983). https://doi.org/10.1109/TIT.1983.1056650
16. Durgin, N., Lincoln, P., Mitchell, J., Scedrov, A.: Multiset rewriting and the complexity of bounded security protocols. J. Comput. Secur. **12**(2), 247–311 (2004). https://doi.org/10.3233/JCS-2004-12203
17. Farzan, A., Kincaid, Z.: Strategy synthesis for linear arithmetic games. PACMPL **2**(POPL), 61:1–61:30 (2018). https://doi.org/10.1145/3158149
18. Grädel, E., Thomas, W., Wilke, T. (eds.): Automata, Logics, and Infinite Games: A Guide to Current Research [outcome of a Dagstuhl seminar, February 2001]. Lecture Notes in Computer Science, vol. 2500. Springer, Heidelberg (2002). https://doi.org/10.1007/3-540-36387-4
19. Gulwani, S.: Automating string processing in spreadsheets using input-output examples. In: POPL, pp. 317–330. ACM (2011). https://doi.org/10.1145/1925844.1926423
20. Gulwani, S., Harris, W.R., Singh, R.: Spreadsheet data manipulation using examples. Commun. ACM **55**(8), 97–105 (2012). https://doi.org/10.1145/2240236.2240260
21. Gulwani, S., Hernández-Orallo, J., Kitzelmann, E., Muggleton, S.H., Schmid, U., Zorn, B.G.: Inductive programming meets the real world. Commun. ACM **58**(11), 90–99 (2015). https://doi.org/10.1145/2736282
22. Gulwani, S., Polozov, O., Singh, R.: Program synthesis. Found. Trends Program. Lang. **4**(1–2), 1–119 (2017)
23. Heizmann, M., et al.: Ultimate automizer with smtinterpol. In: Piterman, N., Smolka, S.A. (eds.) TACAS 2013. LNCS, vol. 7795, pp. 641–643. Springer, Berlin Heidelberg, Berlin, Heidelberg (2013). https://doi.org/10.1007/978-3-642-36742-7_53
24. Heizmann, M., Hoenicke, J., Podelski, A.: Refinement of trace abstraction. In: Palsberg, J., Su, Z. (eds.) SAS 2009. LNCS, vol. 5673, pp. 69–85. Springer, Heidelberg (2009). https://doi.org/10.1007/978-3-642-03237-0_7
25. Heizmann, M., Hoenicke, J., Podelski, A.: Nested interpolants. In: Proceedings of the 37th Annual ACM SIGPLAN-SIGACT Symposium on Principles of Programming Languages, POPL 2010, pp. 471–482. ACM, New York (2010). https://doi.org/10.1145/1706299.1706353
26. Heizmann, M., Hoenicke, J., Podelski, A.: Software model checking for people who love automata. In: Sharygina, N., Veith, H. (eds.) CAV 2013. LNCS, vol. 8044, pp. 36–52. Springer, Heidelberg (2013). https://doi.org/10.1007/978-3-642-39799-8_2
27. Hu, Q., Breck, J., Cyphert, J., D'Antoni, L., Reps, T.: Proving unrealizability for syntax-guided synthesis. In: Dillig, I., Tasiran, S. (eds.) CAV 2019. LNCS, vol. 11561, pp. 335–352. Springer, Cham (2019). https://doi.org/10.1007/978-3-030-25540-4_18
28. Jha, S., Seshia, S.A.: A theory of formal synthesis via inductive learning. Acta Inf. **54**(7), 693–726 (2017). https://doi.org/10.1007/s00236-017-0294-5
29. Khalimov, A., Maderbacher, B., Bloem, R.: Bounded synthesis of register transducers. In: Lahiri, S.K., Wang, C. (eds.) ATVA 2018. LNCS, vol. 11138, pp. 494–510. Springer, Cham (2018). https://doi.org/10.1007/978-3-030-01090-4_29
30. Krogmeier, P., Mathur, U., Murali, A., Madhusudan, P., Viswanathan, M.: Decidable synthesis of programs with uninterpreted functions. CoRR abs/1910.09744 (2019). http://arxiv.org/abs/1910.09744

31. Kupferman, O., Madhusudan, P., Thiagarajan, P.S., Vardi, M.Y.: Open systems in reactive environments: control and synthesis. In: Palamidessi, C. (ed.) CONCUR 2000. LNCS, vol. 1877, pp. 92–107. Springer, Heidelberg (2000). https://doi.org/10.1007/3-540-44618-4_9

32. Kupferman, O., Piterman, N., Vardi, M.Y.: An automata-theoretic approach to infinite-state systems. In: Manna, Z., Peled, D.A. (eds.) Time for Verification. LNCS, vol. 6200, pp. 202–259. Springer, Heidelberg (2010). https://doi.org/10.1007/978-3-642-13754-9_11

33. Kupferman, O., Vardi, M.Y.: An automata-theoretic approach to reasoning about infinite-state systems. In: Emerson, E.A., Sistla, A.P. (eds.) CAV 2000. LNCS, vol. 1855, pp. 36–52. Springer, Heidelberg (2000). https://doi.org/10.1007/10722167_7

34. Löding, C., Madhusudan, P., Neider, D.: Abstract learning frameworks for synthesis. In: Chechik, M., Raskin, J.F. (eds.) LTACAS 2016. LNCS, vol. 9636, pp. 167–185. Springer, Heidelberg (2016). https://doi.org/10.1007/978-3-662-49674-9_10

35. Madhusudan, P.: Synthesizing reactive programs. In: CSL. LIPIcs, vol. 12, pp. 428–442. Schloss Dagstuhl - Leibniz-Zentrum fuer Informatik (2011). https://doi.org/10.4230/LIPIcs.CSL.2011.428

36. Madhusudan, P., Mathur, U., Saha, S., Viswanathan, M.: A decidable fragment of second order logic with applications to synthesis. In: Ghica, D., Jung, A. (eds.) 27th EACSL Annual Conference on Computer Science Logic (CSL 2018). Leibniz International Proceedings in Informatics (LIPIcs), vol. 119, pp. 31:1–31:19. Schloss Dagstuhl-Leibniz-Zentrum fuer Informatik, Dagstuhl (2018). https://doi.org/10.4230/LIPIcs.CSL.2018.31

37. Madhusudan, P., Parlato, G.: The tree width of auxiliary storage. In: Proceedings of the 38th Annual ACM SIGPLAN-SIGACT Symposium on Principles of Programming Languages, POPL 2011, pp. 283–294. ACM, New York (2011). https://doi.org/10.1145/1926385.1926419

38. Madhusudan, P., Thiagarajan, P.S.: Distributed controller synthesis for local specifications. In: Orejas, F., Spirakis, P.G., van Leeuwen, J. (eds.) ICALP 2001. LNCS, vol. 2076, pp. 396–407. Springer, Heidelberg (2001). https://doi.org/10.1007/3-540-48224-5_33

39. Mathur, U., Madhusudan, P., Viswanathan, M.: Decidable verification of uninterpreted programs. Proc. ACM Program. Lang. 3(POPL), 46:1–46:29 (2019). https://doi.org/10.1145/3290359

40. Mathur, U., Madhusudan, P., Viswanathan, M.: What's decidable about program verification modulo axioms? In: Biere, A., Parker, D. (eds.) TACAS 2020. LNCS, vol. 12079, pp. 158–177. Springer, Cham (2020). https://doi.org/10.1007/978-3-030-45237-7_10

41. Mathur, U., Murali, A., Krogmeier, P., Madhusudan, P., Viswanathan, M.: Deciding memory safety for single-pass heap-manipulating programs. Proc. ACM Program. Lang. 4(POPL), 1–29 (2019). https://doi.org/10.1145/3371103

42. Müller-Olm, M., Rüthing, O., Seidl, H.: Checking herbrand equalities and beyond. In: Cousot, R. (ed.) VMCAI 2005. LNCS, vol. 3385, pp. 79–96. Springer, Heidelberg (2005). https://doi.org/10.1007/978-3-540-30579-8_6

43. Muscholl, A., Walukiewicz, I.: Distributed synthesis for acyclic architectures. In: FSTTCS. LIPIcs, vol. 29, pp. 639–651. Schloss Dagstuhl - Leibniz-Zentrum fuer Informatik (2014). https://doi.org/10.4230/LIPIcs.FSTTCS.2014.639

44. Pnueli, A., Rosner, R.: On the synthesis of a reactive module. In: POPL, pp. 179–190. ACM Press (1989). https://doi.org/10.1145/75277.75293

45. Pnueli, A., Rosner, R.: Distributed reactive systems are hard to synthesize. In: FOCS, pp. 746–757. IEEE Computer Society (1990). https://doi.org/10.1109/FSCS.1990.89597

46. Post, E.L.: A variant of a recursively unsolvable problem. Bull. Amer. Math. Soc. **52**(4), 264–268 (1946). https://doi.org/10.1090/S0002-9904-1946-08555-9

47. Qiu, X., Solar-Lezama, A.: Natural synthesis of provably-correct data-structure manipulations. PACMPL **1**(OOPSLA), 65:1–65:28 (2017). https://doi.org/10.1145/3133889

48. Rabin, M.O.: Automata on Infinite Objects and Church's Problem. American Mathematical Society, Boston (1972)

49. Singh, R., Gulwani, S., Solar-Lezama, A.: Automated feedback generation for introductory programming assignments. SIGPLAN Not. **48**(6), 15–26 (2013). https://doi.org/10.1145/2499370.2462195

50. Solar-Lezama, A.: Program sketching. Int. J. Softw. Tools Technol. Transf. **15**(5), 475–495 (2013). https://doi.org/10.1007/s10009-012-0249-7

51. Solar-Lezama, A., Tancau, L., Bodík, R., Seshia, S.A., Saraswat, V.A.: Combinatorial sketching for finite programs. In: ASPLOS, pp. 404–415. ACM (2006). https://doi.org/10.1145/1168857.1168907

52. SyGuS: Syntax guided synthesis. https://sygus.org/

53. Vardi, M.Y.: Reasoning about the past with two-way automata. In: Larsen, K.G., Skyum, S., Winskel, G. (eds.) ICALP 1998. LNCS, vol. 1443, pp. 628–641. Springer, Heidelberg (1998). https://doi.org/10.1007/BFb0055090

54. Wang, X., Dillig, I., Singh, R.: Program synthesis using abstraction refinement. Proc. ACM Program. Lang. **2**(POPL), 63:1–63:30 (2017). https://doi.org/10.1145/3158151

55. Wang, X., Gulwani, S., Singh, R.: FIDEX: filtering spreadsheet data using examples. In: Proceedings of the 2016 ACM SIGPLAN International Conference on Object-Oriented Programming, Systems, Languages, and Applications, OOPSLA 2016, pp. 195–213. ACM, New York (2016). https://doi.org/10.1145/2983990.2984030

56. Wang, Y., Wang, X., Dillig, I.: Relational program synthesis. Proc. ACM Program. Lang. **2**(OOPSLA), 155:1–155:27 (2018). https://doi.org/10.1145/3276525

Must Fault Localization for Program Repair

Bat-Chen Rothenberg and Orna Grumberg$^{(\boxtimes)}$

Technion - Israel Institute of Technology, Haifa, Israel
{batg,orna}@cs.technion.ac.il

Abstract. This work is concerned with fault localization for automated program repair.

We define a novel concept of a *must* location set. Intuitively, such a set includes at least one program location from every repair for a bug. Thus, it is impossible to fix the bug without changing at least one location from this set. A fault localization technique is considered a *must* algorithm if it returns a must location set for every buggy program and every bug in the program. We show that some traditional fault localization techniques are not must.

We observe that the notion of must fault localization depends on the chosen repair scheme, which identifies the changes that can be applied to program statements as part of a repair. We develop a new algorithm for fault localization and prove that it is *must* with respect to commonly used schemes in automated program repair.

We incorporate the new fault localization technique into an existing mutation-based program repair algorithm. We exploit it in order to prune the search space when a buggy mutated program has been generated. Our experiments show that must fault localization is able to significantly speed-up the repair process, without losing any of the potential repairs.

1 Introduction

Fault localization and automated program repair have long been combined. Traditionally, given a buggy program, fault localization suggests locations in the program that might be the cause of the bug. Repair then attempts to change those suspicious locations in order to eliminate the bug.

Bad fault localization may cause a miss of potential repairs, if it is too restrictive, or cause an extra work, if it is too permissive. Studies have shown that for test-based repair imprecise fault localizations happen very often in practice [27]. This identifies the need for fault localization that can narrow down the space of candidates while still promising not to lose potential causes for a bug.

In this work, we define the concept of a *must* location set. Intuitively, such a set includes at least one location from every repair for the bug. Thus, it *must* be

This research was partially supported by the Technion Hiroshi Fujiwara cyber security research center and the Israel cyber bureau and partially by the Israel Science Foundation.

S. K. Lahiri and C. Wang (Eds.): CAV 2020, LNCS 12225, pp. 658–680, 2020.
https://doi.org/10.1007/978-3-030-53291-8_33

used for repair. In other words, **it is impossible to fix the bug using only locations outside this set**. A fault localization technique is considered a *must* algorithm if it returns a must location set for every buggy program and every bug in the program.

To demonstrate the importance of the *must* notion, consider the program in Fig. 1 for computing the absolute value of a variable x. The program is buggy since the assertion in location 4 is violated when initially x = -1. Intuitively, a good repair would replace the condition (x < -1) in location 2 with condition x <= -1. Our must fault localization, defined formally in the paper, will include location 2 in the must location set. In contrast, the fault localization techniques defined for instance in [14,21] do not include 2 in their location sets: They are not must and may miss optional repairs.

Our first observation regarding must notions is that their definition should take into account the *repair scheme* under consideration. A repair scheme identifies the changes that can be applied to program statements as part of a repair. A scheme can allow, for instance, certain syntactic changes in a condition (e.g. replacing < with >) or in the right-hand-side expression of an assignment (e.g. replacing + by -). A particular location set can be a *must* set using one scheme, but non-*must* using another. We further discuss this observation when presenting our formal definition of a must fault localization.

The setting of our work is as follows. Our approach is formula-based rather than test-based. We handle simple C-programs, with specification given as assertions in the code. Similarly to bounded model checking tools (e.g. [8]), the program and the negated specification are translated to a set of constraints, whose conjunction forms the *program formula*. This formula is satisfiable if and only if the program violates an assertion, in which case a satisfying assignment (also called a *model*) is returned.

We focus on a simple repair scheme of syntactic changes, as described above. We assume that the user prefers repairs that are as close to the original program as possible and will want to get several repair suggestions. Thus, we return *all minimal repairs* (minimal in the number of changes applied to the program code).

Once the notion of must fault localization is defined, we develop a new algorithm for fault localization and prove that it is *must* with respect to syntactic mutation schemes. The input to the algorithm is a program formula φ and a model μ for φ, representing a buggy execution of the program. Our approach is based on a dynamic-slicing-like algorithm that computes dependencies.

For a variable v in φ, its slice F is computed based on dynamic dependencies among variables in φ, whose values influence the value of v in μ. Informally, F is a must location set that contains all assignment to the variables that v depends upon. Some assignment from F thus must be changed in order to eliminate the bug associated with μ.

We incorporated the new fault localization technique into an existing mutation-based program repair algorithm [38]. In [38], the repair scheme is based on a predefined set of mutations. Given a buggy program P, the goal of the algorithm is to return all minimal repairs for P. The algorithm goes through iterations of generate-validate, where the generate part produces a mutated program of P and the validate part checks whether it is bounded-correct. The bottleneck of the algorithm is the size of the search space, consisting of all possible mutated programs of P. In [38], the search space has been pruned when the generated mutated program has been successfully validated. No pruning has been applied otherwise.

In this work, we exploit our novel *must* fault localization in order to prune the search space when a buggy mutated program P' has been generated (i.e. validation failed). In this case, we compute the *must* location set F of P'. We can now prune from the search space any mutated program whose F locations are identical to those of P'. This is because, by the property of *must* location set, it is guaranteed that the bug cannot be repaired without changing a location in F. Thus, a large set of buggy mutated programs is pruned, without the need for additional validation and without losing any minimally repaired program. It should be noted that the smaller F is, the larger the pruned set is. Our experimental results confirm the effectiveness of this pruning by showing significant speedups.

To summarize, the contributions of this work are:

1. We define a novel notion of *must* fault localization with respect to a repair scheme. We show that many of the formula-based techniques are not must.
2. We present a novel fault localization technique and prove that it is *must* for the scheme of syntactic mutations. Our technique also has other advantages, such as low-complexity and incrementality.
3. We show how our new fault localization technique can be incorporated into an existing mutation-based program repair algorithm for pruning its search space. The technique is applied iteratively, whenever a generated mutated program is found to be incorrect.
4. We implemented the algorithm of repair with fault localization as part of the open source tool AllRepair. Our experimental results show that fault-localization is able to significantly speed-up the repair process, without losing any of the potential repairs.

2   Motivating Example

Figure 1 presents a simple program for computing the absolute value of a variable x. The result is computed in the variable **abs**, and the specification states, using an assertion on line 4, that in the end **abs** should always be non-negative. Unfortunately, the program

```
     procedure absValue(x)
1:   abs := x
2:   if x < -1 then
3:       abs := -x
4:   assert (abs >= 0)
```

Fig. 1. A buggy program

has a bug. The true branch of the if is intended to flip the sign of x whenever x is negative, but it accidentally misses the case where x is -1. As a result, if x is -1, the wrong branch of the if is taken, and the assertion is reached with $abs = -1$, which causes a violation.

Clearly, it is desirable that line number 2 be returned when running fault localization on this bug, as a human written repair is likely to change the condition on this line from x < −1 to x <= −1 or x < 0. But, as we will show next, some of the existing formula-based fault localization techniques do not include this line in their result.

The error trace representing the bug for input $I = \{x \leftarrow -1\}$ is $\pi = < 1, 2, 4 >$ (this is the sequence of program locations visited when executing the program on I). The MAX-SAT-based fault localization technique of [21] and the error-invariant-based technique of [14] use a formula called the *extended trace formula* in order to find faulty statements along the error trace. The extended trace formula for the bug in question is

$$\underbrace{(x = -1)}_{\text{Input}} \wedge \underbrace{(abs = x) \wedge (x \geq -1)}_{\text{Computation}} \wedge \underbrace{(abs \geq 0)}_{\text{Assertion}}$$

This formula encodes three things: a) that the input remains I, b) that the computation is as the trace dictates, and, c) that the assertion holds at the end. Therefore, the formula is unsatisfiable. Both [21] and [14] intuitively look for explanations of its unsatisfiability, and therefore decide that the statement $(x \geq -1)$ on line 2 is irrelevant; The formula remains unsatisfiable even if the constraint $(x \geq -1)$ is removed.

Even the method of [6], which suggests a flow-sensitive encoding of the extended trace formula, with the goal of including all statements affecting control-flow decisions that are relevant to the bug, classifies the statement on line 2 as irrelevant. This is because the error trace does not include any location from the body of the branch that was taken (in our case it is the else branch, which is empty), in which case the flow-sensitive formula remains identical to the traditional formula.

The dynamic slicing method of [2,23] also fails to include line 2 in its result. This method computes the set of statements influencing the evaluation of the assertion along the trace, using data and control dependency relations. A statement st_1 is data dependent on st_2 iff st_1 uses a variable x, and st_2 is the last to assign a value to x along the trace. In our example, the assertion on line 4 is data dependent only on the statement in line 1, which in itself is not data dependent on any other statement. A statement st_1 is control dependent on a conditional statement st_2 iff st_1 is inside the body of either branch of st_2. None of the statements along our error trace is control dependent on another statement. The slice, which is the set of lines returned, is computed using the transitive closure of these relations. Thus, for our example, only line 1 is part of the slice.

In this example, we have seen how many different fault localization techniques fail to include a statement that is relevant, i.e., where a modification could be made for the bug to be fixed. In contrast, the set of locations returned by our technique for this example is $\{1, 2\}$. The fact that our technique includes line 2 is not a coincidence: We show that, intuitively, whenever a repair can be made by making changes to a single line, this line *must* be included in the result.

proc. foo(x, w)	proc. simFoo(x, w)	proc. SSAFoo(x, w)	$\varphi_{foo} = \{$
1: t := 0	t := 0	t0 := 0	$t_0 = 0,$
2: y := x - 3	y := x - 3	y0 := x0 - 3	$y_0 = x_0 - 3,$
3: z := x + 3	z := x + 3	z0 := x0 + 3	$z_0 = x_0 + 3,$
4: if (w > 3) then	g := w > 3	g0 := w0 > 3	$g_0 = w_0 > 3,$
5: t := z + w	if (g) then	t1 := z0 + w0	$t_1 = z_0 + w_0,$
6: assert (t < x)	t := z + w	assert (g0 $\rightarrow$ t1 < x0)	
7: y := y + 10	assert (t < x)	y1 := y0 + 10	$y_1 = y_0 + 10,$
8: assert (y > z)	y := y + 10	t2 := g0 ? t1 : t0	$t_2 = ite(g_0, t_1, t_0),$
	assert (y > z)	y2 := g0 ? y1 : y0	$y_2 = ite(g_0, y_1, y_0),$
		assert (y2 > z0)	$\neg(y2 > z0) \lor \neg(g0 \rightarrow t1 < x0)$
			$\}$

Fig. 2. Example of the translation process of a simple program

In general, whenever a repair can be made by making changes to a set of lines, at least one of them must be included in the result.

3   Preliminaries

3.1   Programs and Error Traces

For our purposes, a *program* is a sequential program composed of standard statements: assignments, conditionals, loops and function calls, all with their standard semantics. Each statement is located at a certain *location* (or *line*) l_i, and all statements are defined over the set of program variables X.

In addition to the standard statements, a program may also contain *assume* statements of the form `assume(bexpr)`, and *assert* statements of the form `assert(bexpr)`. In both cases `bexpr` is a boolean expression over X. If an assume or an assert statement is located in l_i, execution of the program stops whenever location l_i is reached in a state where `bexpr` is evaluated to false. In the case of an assertion, this early termination has the special name *assertion violation*, and it is an indication that an error has occurred.

A program P has a *bug on input* I if an assertion violation occurs during the execution of P on I. Otherwise, the program is *correct for* I.[1] Whenever P has a bug on I, this bug is associated with an *error trace*, which is the sequence of statements visited during the execution of P on I.

3.2   From Programs to Program Formulas

In this section we explain how a program is translated into a set of constraints, whose conjunction constitutes the program formula. In addition to constraints representing assignments and conditionals, such a formula includes constraints representing assumptions and a constraint representing the negated conjunction of all assertions. Thus, a satisfying assignment (a *model*) of the program formula

---

[1] Alternatively, one could assume to know the desired output of the program for I and define a bug on I as a case where the program outputs the wrong value for I.

represents an execution of the program that satisfies all assumption but violates at least one assertion. Such an execution is a *counterexample*.

The translation, following [8], goes through four stages. We refer to the example in Fig. 2 to demonstrate certain steps.

1. Simplification: Complex constructs of the language are replaced with equivalent simpler ones. Also, branch conditions are replaced with fresh boolean variables. In the example, the `if` condition (`w > 3`) is assigned to a fresh boolean variable `g`. Branching is then done based on the value of `g`, instead of (`w > 3`).
2. Unwinding: The body of each loop and each function is inlined wb times. The set of executions of the new program is called the wb-executions of P.
3. Conversion to SSA: The program is converted to static single assignment (SSA) form, which means that each variable in the new program is assigned at most once. This is done by replacing all variables with indexed variables, and increasing the index of a variable whenever it appears on the left-hand-side of an assignment. In the example, the first assignment to `t` is replaced by an assignment to `t0` and the second, by an assignment to `t1`. Since `t` is assigned inside a conditional statement and is used after the statement, the if-then-else assignment `t2 := g0?t1:t0` is inserted in order to determine which copy of `t` should be used after the conditional statement. These special if-then-else assignments are called Φ-*assignments*. In the example, there is also a Φ-assignment for `y` (`y2=g0?y1:y0`).

   Note that, assertions are also expressed by means of indexed variables. The specific indices in the assertion indicate the location in the execution in which the assertion is checked. In addition, if an assumption or an assertion is located within an `if` statement with branch condition g, then it is implied by g if it is within the **then** part of the `if` and is implied by $\neg g$, if it is within the **else** part. In the example, `assert (t < x)` is encoded by $(g_0 \rightarrow t_1 < x_0)$.
4. Conversion to SMT constraints: Once the program is in SSA form, conversion to SMT is straightforward: An assignment `x:=e` is converted to the constraint $x = e$; A Φ-assignment `x:= b?x1:x2` is converted to the constraint $(x = ite(b, x_1, x_2))$, which is an abbreviation of $((b \wedge x = x_1) \vee (\neg b \wedge x = x_2))$; An assume statement `assume(bexpr)` is converted to the constraint `bexpr`, and an assert statement `assert(bexpr)` is converted to the constraint `¬bexpr` (since a model of the SMT formula should correspond to an assertion violation).

   If the program includes several assertions, then they are converted to one constraint, representing the negation of their conjunction. In the example, the two assertions are converted to the following constraint:

$$\neg(y2 > z0) \vee \neg(g0 \rightarrow t1 < x0).$$

We say that a constraint *encodes* the statement it came from and we partition constraints into three sets, S_{assign}, S_{phi} and S_{demand}, based on what they encode. S_{assign} contains constraints encoding assignments, including those originated from assigning a fresh boolean variable with a branching condition;

S_{phi} - encoding Φ-assignments; and S_{demand} - encoding demands from assert and assume statements. In particular, it encodes the negated conjunction of all assertions.

The triple $(S_{assign}, S_{phi}, S_{demand})$ is called a *program constraint set*. The program constraint set we get from a program P when using wb as an unwinding bound is denoted CS_P^{wb}. The *program formula* φ_P^{wb}, is the conjunction of all constraints in all three sets of CS_P^{wb}:

$$\varphi_P^{wb} = (\bigwedge_{s \in S_{assign}} s) \wedge (\bigwedge_{s \in S_{phi}} s) \wedge (\bigwedge_{s \in S_{demand}} s).$$

Theorem 1 ([9]). *A program P is wb-violation free iff the formula φ_P^{wb} is unsatisfiable.*

For simplicity of notation, in the rest of the paper we omit the superscript wb.

Since the program formula is the result of translating an SSA program, the formula is defined over indexed variables. Further, each constraint in S_{assign} corresponds to the single variable, which is assigned in the statement encoded by the constraint.

4   Must Fault Localization

In this section, we precisely define when a location should be considered relevant for a bug. This definition is motivated by a repair perspective, taking into account which changes can be made to statements in order to repair a bug.

In order to define the changes allowed, we use repair schemes. A *repair scheme* S is a function from statements to sets of statements. An S-*patch* for a program P is a set of pairs of location and statement $\{(l_1, st_1^r), \cdots, (l_k, st_k^r)\}$, for which the following holds: for all $1 \leq i \leq k$, let st_i be the statement in location l_i in P, then $st_i^r \in S(st_i)$. The patch is said to be *defined over* the set of locations $\{l_1, \cdots, l_k\}$. Applying an S-*patch* τ to a program P means replacing for every location l_i in τ, the statement st_i with st_i^r. This results in an S-*patched* program of P. The set of all S-*patched* programs created from a program P is the S-*search space* of P.

Let P be a program with a bug on input I, and S be a repair scheme. An S-*repair* for I is an S-patched program that is correct for I. An S-*repairable set* is a set of locations F such that there exists an S-repair defined over F. An S-repairable set is *minimal* if removing any location from it makes it no longer an S-repairable set. A location is S-*relevant* if it is a part of a minimal S-repairable set.[2]

In this paper, we focus on two repair schemes that are frequently used for automated program repair: the arbitrary scheme (S_{arb}) and the mutation scheme (S_{mut}). Both schemes only manipulate program expressions, but the

---

[2] We sometimes omit S from notations where S is clear from context.

mutation scheme is more restrictive than the arbitrary scheme: $\mathcal{S}_{arb}(st)$ is the set of all options to replace the expression of st^3 with an arbitrary expression, while $\mathcal{S}_{mut}(st)$ only contains statements where the expression in st is mutated according to a set of simple syntactic rules. The rules we consider are replacing a + operator with a - operator, and vice versa, replacing a < operator with a > operator, and vice versa, and increasing or decreasing a numerical constant by 1.[4]

Example 1. In this example we demonstrate how different repair schemes define different sets of relevant locations. Consider again the foo program from Fig. 2. This program has a bug on input $I = \mathtt{x} \leftarrow 0, \mathtt{w} \leftarrow 0$. The error trace associated with the bug is $\langle 1, 2, 3, 4, 8 \rangle$ (the assertion on line 8 is violated).

The location set $\{3, 4\}$ is a minimal $\mathcal{S}_{mut}$-repairable set: It is an $\mathcal{S}_{mut}$-repairable set because applying the $\mathcal{S}_{mut}$-patch $\{(3, \mathtt{z:=x-3}), (4, \mathtt{w<3})\}$, results in an $\mathcal{S}_{mut}$-patched program that is correct for I. This set is also minimal, because none of the $\mathcal{S}_{mut}$-patches defined over $\{3\}$ or $\{4\}$ alone is an $\mathcal{S}_{mut}$-repair for I: Each one of the $\mathcal{S}_{mut}$-patches $\{(3, \mathtt{z:=x-3})\}, \{(3, \mathtt{z:=x+4})\}, \{(3, \mathtt{z:=x+2})\}$, $\{(4, \mathtt{w<3})\}, \{(4, \mathtt{w>4})\}, \{(4, \mathtt{w>2})\}$ results in an assertion violation for I.

On the other hand, $\{3, 4\}$ is *not* a minimal $\mathcal{S}_{arb}$-repairable set: For example, the $\mathcal{S}_{arb}$-patch $\{(3, \mathtt{z:=-6})\}$ is an $\mathcal{S}_{arb}$-repair for I. Note that, the $\mathcal{S}_{arb}$-patch only needs to repair the bug, and not the program. That is, it is sufficient that there is no assertion violation on the specific input I, even though an assertion could be violated in the $\mathcal{S}_{arb}$-patched program on another input.

The set of all minimal $\mathcal{S}_{arb}$-*repairable sets* is $\{\{2\}, \{3\}, \{4, 5\}\}$. Therefore, the set of $\mathcal{S}_{arb}$-relevant statements is $\{2, 3, 4, 5\}$. The set of all minimal $\mathcal{S}_{mut}$-*repairable sets* is $\{\{2, 3\}, \{3, 4\}\}$. Therefore, the set of $\mathcal{S}_{mut}$-relevant statements is $\{2, 3, 4\}$.

Fault localization should focus the programmer's attention on locations that are relevant for the bug. But, returning the exact set of $\mathcal{S}$-*relevant* locations, as defined above, can be computationally hard. In practice, what many fault localization algorithms return is a set of locations that *may* be relevant: The returned locations have a higher chance of being $\mathcal{S}$-relevant than those who are not, but there is no guarantee that all returned locations are $\mathcal{S}$-relevant, nor that all $\mathcal{S}$-relevant locations are returned. We call such an algorithm *may fault localization*. In contrast, we define *must fault localization*, as follows:

Definition 1 ($\mathcal{S}$-must location set). *An $\mathcal{S}$-must location set is a set of locations that contains at least one location from each minimal $\mathcal{S}$-repairable set.*[5]

---

[3] If st is an assignment, its expression is its right-hand-side. If st is a conditional statement, its expression is its condition.

[4] This simple definition of the mutation scheme is used only for simplicity of presentation. Our implementation supports a much richer set of mutation rules, as explained in Sect. 7.

[5] This is, in fact, a hitting set of the set of all minimal $\mathcal{S}$-repairable sets.

Definition 2 (S-must fault localization). *An S-must fault localization algorithm is an algorithm that for every program P and every buggy input I, returns an S-must location set.*

Note that, an S-must location set is not required to contain all S-relevant locations, but only one location from each minimal S-repairable set. Still, this is a powerful notion since it guarantees that no repair is possible without including at least one element from the set.

Also note, that the set of all locations visited by P during its execution on I is always an S-must location set. This is because any S-patch where none of these locations is included is definitely **not** an S-repair, since the same assertion will be violated along the same path. However, this set of locations may not be minimal. In the sequel, we aim at finding small S-must location sets.

Example 2. Continuing the previous example, the set $\{2,3,4\}$ is an S_{arb}-must location set, and also an S_{mut}-must location set. In contrast, the set $\{2,3\}$ is only an S_{mut}-must location set, but not an S_{arb}-must location set, since it does not contain any location from the S_{arb}-minimal repairable set $\{4,5\}$. The set $\{2\}$ is neither an S_{arb}-must location set nor an S_{mut}-must location set.

Example 3. Consider again the `absValue` procedure of Fig. 1. The set $\{2\}$ is an S_{mut}-minimal repairable set and an S_{arb}-minimal repairable set for the bug in question. Therefore, we can say that all algorithms that were shown in Sect. 2 not to include the location 2 in their result [2,6,14,21,23], are neither S_{arb}-must nor S_{mut}-must fault localization algorithms.

5 Fault Localization Using Program Formula Slicing

In this section we formally define the notion of slicing. Based on this, we present an algorithm for computing must fault localization for S_{arb} and S_{mut}.

5.1 Program Formula Slicing

A central building block in our fault localization technique is *slicing*. But, we do not define slicing in terms of the program directly, but in terms of the program formula representing it, instead. The input to the slicing algorithm is a program formula φ, a model μ of it, and a variable v. Recall that φ is a conjunction of constraints from S_{assign}, S_{phi} and S_{demand} (see Sect. 3.2). The goal of the slicing algorithm is to compute the *slice* of the variable v with respect to φ and μ. Intuitively, this slice includes the set of all constraints that influence the value v gets in μ.

Similar to traditional slicing, it is easy to define the slice as the reflexive-transitive closure of a dependency relation. But, unlike traditional slicing, which defines dependencies between statements, our dependency relation is between variables of the formula. These variables are indexed. Each originates from a variable of the underlying SSA program, where it was assigned at most once.

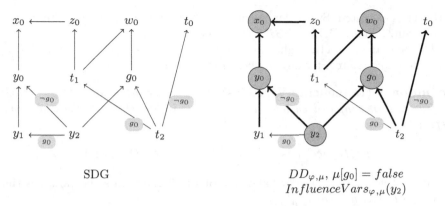

SDG ⟶ $DD_{\varphi,\mu}, \mu[g_0] = false$
$InfluenceVars_{\varphi,\mu}(y_2)$

Fig. 3. Illustration of the static and dynamic dependency relations of the `foo` procedure

We refer to variables never assigned as *input variables*, and denote the set containing them by *InputVars*. A variable v that was assigned once is called a *computed variable*, and the (unique) constraint encoding the assignment to it is denoted $Assign(v)$. The set of all computed variables is denoted $ComputedVars$. We also denote by $vars(e)$ the set of variables that appear in a formula or expression e.

Definition 3 (Static Dependency). *The static dependency relation of a program formula φ is $SD_\varphi \subseteq vars(\varphi) \times vars(\varphi)$ s.t.*

$$SD_\varphi = \{(v_1, v_2) \mid \exists e \text{ s.t. } (v_1 = e) \in S_{assign}, v_2 \in vars(e)\} \cup$$

$$\{(v, b), (v, v_1), (v, v_2) \mid (v = ite(b, v_1, v_2)) \in S_{phi}\}$$

.

The left-hand-side of Fig. 3 presents the graph for the static dependency relation of the `foo` procedure of Fig. 2. The nodes in the graph are (indexed) variables and there is an arrow from v_1 to v_2 iff $(v_1, v_2) \in SD_\varphi$.

Definition 4 (Dynamic Dependency). *The dynamic dependency relation of a program formula φ and a model μ of φ is $DD_{\varphi,\mu} \subseteq vars(\varphi) \times vars(\varphi)$ s.t.*

$$DD_{\varphi,\mu} = \{(v, v_1) \mid \exists b, v_2 \text{ s.t. } (v = ite(b, v_1, v_2)) \in S_{phi}, \ \mu[b] = true\}$$

$$\cup \{(v, v_2) \mid \exists b, v_1 \text{ s.t. } (v = ite(b, v_1, v_2)) \in S_{phi}, \ \mu[b] = false\}$$

$$\cup \{(v, b) \mid \exists v_1, v_2 \text{ s.t. } (v = ite(b, v_1, v_2)) \in S_{phi}\}$$

$$\cup \{(v, v_1) \mid \exists e \text{ s.t. } (v = e) \in S_{assign}, v_1 \in vars(e)\}$$

Note that, dynamic dependency includes only dependencies that coincide with the specific model μ, which determines whether the `then` or the `else` direction of the `if` is executed. Static dependency, on the other hand, takes both options into account. Thus, $DD_{\varphi,\mu} \subseteq SD_\varphi$ for every model μ.

The bold arrows on the right-hand-side of Fig. 3 represent the relation $DD_{\varphi,\mu}$ of the `foo` procedure, for any μ where $\mu[g_0] = false$.

Definition 5 (Influencing Variables). *Given a program formula φ, a model μ of it, and a computed variable v, the set of influencing variables of v with respect to φ and μ is:*

$$InfluenceVars_{\varphi,\mu}(v) = \{v' \mid (v, v') \in (DD_{\varphi,\mu})^*\}$$

The circled nodes on the right-hand-side of Fig. 3 represents the variables that belong to $InfluenceVars_{\varphi,\mu}(y_2)$.

Definition 6 (Program Formula Slice). *Given a program formula φ, a model μ of it, and a computed variable v, the program formula slice of v with respect to φ and μ is:*

$$Slice_{\varphi,\mu}(v) = \{Assign(v') \mid v' \in (InfluenceVars_{\varphi,\mu}(v) \cap ComputedVars)\}$$

Thus, intuitively, $Slice_{\varphi,\mu}(v)$ includes all constraints (in SSA form) encoding assignments that influence the value of v in μ. More precisely, when considering the conjunction of only the constraints of $Slice_{\varphi,\mu}(v)$, as long as the value of all input variables remains the same as in μ, the value of v will remain the same as well. This is formalized in the following theorem, whose proof can be found in the full version [39].

Theorem 2. *For every φ, μ and v, the following holds:*

$$\left[\bigwedge_{c \in Slice_{\varphi,\mu}(v)} c \wedge \bigwedge_{v_i \in InputVars} (v_i = \mu[v_i]) \right] \implies (v = \mu[v])$$

Continuing with our example of `foo` procedure,

$$Slice_{\varphi,\mu}(y_2) = \{\ y_2 = ite(g_0, y_1, y_0),\ y_0 = x_0 - 3,\ g_0 = w_0 > 3\}.$$

5.2   Computing the Program Formula Slice

The computation of the program formula slice is composed of two steps. In the first step, we build a graph based on the static dependency relation, SD_φ. In the second step, we compute the slice $Slice_{\varphi,\mu}(v)$ by computing the set of nodes reachable from v in this graph, using a customized reachability algorithm, which makes use of the model μ.

The graph built during the first step is called the *Static Dependency Graph (SDG)* of φ. Nodes of this graph are variables of φ and edges are the static dependencies of SD_φ. Edges are annotated using the function ψ, mapping every static dependency (v, v') to a boolean formula such that $(v, v') \in DD_{\varphi,\mu}$ iff

$\mu \models \psi[(v, v')]$. Specifically, for every constraint of the form $(v = ite(b, v_1, v_2))$ in S_{phi}, the edge (v, v_1) is annotated with b and the edge (v, v_2) is annotated with $\neg b$. All other edges of the graph are annotated with *true*. See the left-hand-side of Fig. 3. For simplicity all *true* annotations are omitted.

The algorithm for the second step is presented in Algorithm 1. This algorithm gets a program formula φ, its SDG, a model μ of φ, and a variable v, and computes $Slice_{\varphi,\mu}(v)$. First, the set $InfluenceVars_{\varphi,\mu}(v)$ is computed as the set of nodes reachable from v in SDG, except that the reachability algorithm traverses an edge (v, v') only if $\mu \models \psi[(v, v')]$. Thus, an edge (v, v') is traversed iff $(v, v') \in DD_{\varphi,\mu}$, which means that the set of reachable nodes computed this way is in fact $InfluenceVars_{\varphi,\mu}(v)$. Finally, the slice $Slice_{\varphi,\mu}(v)$ is the set of constraints encoding assignments to variables in $InfluenceVars_{\varphi,\mu}(v)$.

Algorithm 1. Compute The Program Formula Slice

Input: a program formula φ, its SDG, a model μ of φ and a variable v.

Output: $Slice_{\varphi,\mu}(v)$.

Procedure
$ComputeSlice(\varphi, SDG, \mu, v)$
1: $V := \emptyset$
2: $ModelBasedDFS(SDG, v, \mu, V)$
3: $Slice := \{Assign(v') \mid v' \in V\}$
4: **return** $Slice$

Procedure
$ModelBasedDFS(SDG, v, \mu, V)$
1: $V := V \cup \{v\}$
2: **for** $(v, w) \in E$ s.t. $\mu \models \psi[(v, w)]$ **do**
3:     **if** $w \notin V$ **then**
4:         $ModelBasedDFS(SDG, w, \mu, V)$

Algorithm 2. FOrmula-Slicing-Fault-Localization (FOSFL)

Input: A program formula φ of a program P, and a model μ of φ.

Output: A set of statements F of P.

Procedure $FOSFL(\varphi, \mu)$
1: $SDG := ComputeDependencyGraph(\varphi)$
2: demandFormula $:= \bigwedge_{c \in S_{demand}} c$
3: $V := ImportantVars(\text{demandFormula}, \mu)$
4: $S := \emptyset$
5: **for** $v \in V$ **do**
6:     $S := S \cup ComputeSlice(\varphi, SDG, \mu, v)$
7: $F := \emptyset$
8: **for** $c \in S \cap S_{assign}$ **do**
9:     $F := F \cup \{Origin(c)\}$
10: **return** F

5.3 The Fault Localization Algorithm

Our fault localization algorithm is presented in Algorithm 2. The input to this algorithm is a program formula φ of a program P, and a model μ of φ. The model μ represents a buggy execution of P on an input I, and the algorithm returns a set of locations, F, that is an S_{mut}-must location set.

As before, we assume to know the origin of constraints in φ, and use the sets S_{assign}, S_{phi} and S_{demand}. Furthermore, here we also assume that for every constraint $c \in S_{assign}$, we know exactly which program statement it came from. We call this statement the *origin* of c, and denote it by $Origin(c)$.

As a first step, the algorithm computes a set of variables V by calling the procedure $ImportantVars$. This procedure receives an SMT formula φ and a model μ of φ, and reduces μ to a partial model of φ. A *partial model* of φ w.r.t. μ is a partial mapping from variables of the formula to values, which is consistent with μ and is sufficient to satisfy the formula. For example, for the formula $\varphi = (a = 0 \vee b = 0)$ and the model $\mu = \{a \mapsto 0, b \mapsto 1\}$, the valuation $\{a \mapsto 0\}$ is a partial model of φ. Procedure $ImportantVars$ will return the set of variables that appear in the partial model ($\{a\}$ in our example). Details of this procedure are presented in the full version [39].

The formula passed to $ImportantVars$ in our case is the conjunction of all demands in S_{demand}. Recall that the set S_{demand} contains constraints encoding all conditions that need to be met for an assertion violation to happen: Conditions from assumptions appear as is, while conditions from assertions are negated and disjuncted (See Fig. 2. The last constraint on the right-hand-side represents the disjunction of the negated assertions). Therefore, the set of variables V, returned by $ImportantVars$, is such that as long as their values in μ remain the same, this conjunction will still be satisfied, which means that an assertion violation will still occur.

To make sure that their values do *not* remain the same, we use slicing: The algorithm proceeds by computing the program formula slice for each of the variables in V using Algorithm 1. All slices are united into the combined set S. This set represents all constraints that if remain the same, then *all* the variables in V maintain their value. Thus, at least one element from S must be included in any repair.

Note that, by first applying $ImportantVars$, we reduce the number of variables whose value should be preserved in order to maintain the bug. The smaller this number, the smaller F is. We will explain the usefulness of a small F in Sect. 6.

Finally, we need to translate the constraints in S back to statements of P. Because of how the slicing algorithm works, constraints in S may belong to either S_{assign} or S_{phi}. If they belong to S_{phi}, we ignore them, because they encode the control-flow structure of the program, rather than a particular statement. Otherwise, we add the origin of the constraint, which is a statement of the program, to the set of returned locations, F. Note that, several different constraints may have the same origin, for example due to loop unwinding. In such a case, it is sufficient for one constraint encoding the statement st to be included in S, for st to be included in F. A proof for the following theorem can be found in the full version [39].

Theorem 3. *Algorithm FOSFL is an S_{arb}-must and also an S_{mut}-must fault localization algorithm.*

5.4 Incremental Fault Localization

It is often necessary to apply fault localization to several bugs in the same program, or even to several programs with different bugs. Therefore, it is desired that the fault localization algorithm be *incremental*, which means that the computation effort of each fault localization attempt should be proportional to the changes made from the previous attempt. In other words, we should avoid recomputation whenever possible, taking advantage of the fact that the program remains the same, or at least remains similar.

Algorithm FOSFL can be easily made incremental for the case of different bugs of the same program. In this case, several successive calls are made to the algorithm using the same program formula φ, but with different models of it. Since the static dependency relation SD_φ depends solely on the program formula, and not on the model, we can avoid re-computing the SDG for each call. Instead, we can compute the SDG once, upfront, and whenever FOSFL is called, simply skip the first line. We call the incremental version of FOSFL Incremental-Formula-Slicing-Fault-Localization (I-FOSFL).

Note that I-FOSFL is useful not only for fault localization of different bugs of the same program, but also whenever the SDG remains the same during successive fault localization calls. This is the case when considering different mutated programs P' of the same program P, since every change to P' replaces an expression e with an expression e' over the same variables. Thus, the SDG remains the same, since the static dependency relation, in fact, only depends on $vars(e)$, and not on e itself[6].

6 Program Repair with Iterative Fault Localization

In [38], a mutation-based algorithm for program repair, named ALLREPAIR, was presented. This algorithm uses the mutation scheme in order to repair programs with respect to assertions in the code. Unlike fault localization, where the motivation is repairing a bug for a specific input, program repair aims at repairing the program for *all* inputs. To avoid confusion, we refer to a repair for all inputs as a *full repair*. In [38], the notion of a *full repair* is bounded: loops are unwound wb times, and a program is considered *fully repaired* if no assertion is violated along executions with at most wb unwindings. A program that is not fully repaired is said to be *buggy*. For the rest of this section, we refer to an S_{mut}-patch as a patch, and to an S_{mut}-patched program as a mutated program.

As its name implies, the goal of ALLREPAIR is to obtain all *minimal* fully repaired mutated programs, where minimality refers to the patch used in the program. It goes through an iterative generate-validate process. The generate phase chooses a mutated program from the search space, and the validate phase checks whether this program is fully repaired, by solving its program formula. The mutated program is fully repaired iff the formula is unsatisfiable.

The generate-validate process is realized using an interplay between a SAT solver and an SMT solver. The SAT solver is used for the generate stage. For every mutation M and line l, there is a boolean variable $B_M(l)$, which is true if and only if mutation M is applied to line l. A boolean formula is constructed and sent to the SAT solver, where each satisfying assignment corresponds to a program in the search space. The SMT solver is used for the validate stage. The program formula of the mutated program is solved to check if it is buggy

---

[6] This is true for S_{mut} but not for S_{arb}, since the latter allows to replace an expression e with an expression e' over different variables.

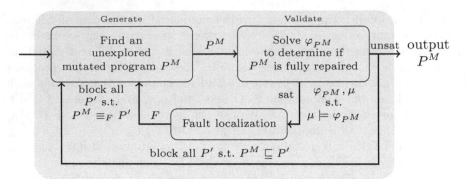

Fig. 4. Algorithm FL-ALLREPAIR: Mutation-based program repair with iterative fault localization. The notation $P^M \equiv_F P'$ means that P^M and P' agree on the content of all locations in F. The notation $P^M \sqsubseteq P'$ means that the patch used for creating P' is a superset of the patch used for creating P^M.

or not. To achieve minimality, when a mutated program created using a patch τ is fully repaired, every mutated program created using a patch τ', with $\tau \subseteq \tau'$, is blocked.

Example 4. Let P^M be a fully repaired mutated program obtained by applying the patch τ, consisting of mutating line l_1 using mutation M_1 and mutating line l_2 using mutation M_2. Then blocking any superset of τ will we done by adding to the boolean formula representing the search space, the blocking clause $\neg(B_{M_1}(l_1) \wedge B_{M_2}(l_2))$, which means "either do not apply M_1 to l_1 or do not apply M_2 to l_2". This clause blocks any mutated program with $\tau \subseteq \tau'$.

Blocking such programs prunes the search space, but only in a limited way. No pruning occurs when the mutated program is buggy.

In this paper, we extend the algorithm of [38] with a fault localization component. The goal of the new component is to prune the search space by identifying sets of mutated programs that are buggy, without inspecting each of the individual programs in the set.

Figure 4 shows the program repair algorithm with the addition of fault localization. In the new algorithm, called FL-ALLREPAIR, whenever a mutated program is found to be buggy during the validation step, its program formula is passed to the fault localization component along with the model obtained when solving the formula. The fault localization component returns a set of locations F, following the I-FOSFL algorithm. Since this set is guaranteed to be an S_{mut}-must location set, at least one of the locations in it should be changed for the bug to be fixed. Consequently, all mutated programs in which all locations from F remain unchanged are blocked from being explored in the future. As before, blocking is done by adding a blocking clause that disallows such programs.

Example 5. Let P^M be a buggy mutated program for which F consists of $\{l_1, l_2, l_3\}$, where l_1 was mutated with M_1, l_2 was not mutated, and l_3 was mutated with M_3. The blocking clause $\neg B_{M_1}(l_1) \vee \neg B_{Original}(l_2) \vee \neg B_{M_3}(l_3)$ will be added to the boolean formula representing the search space of mutated programs. It restricts the search space to those mutated programs that either do not apply mutation M_1 to l_1, or do mutate l_2 or do not apply M_3 to l_3. This will prune from the search space all mutated programs which are identical to P^M on the locations in F. Note that smaller F will result in a larger set of pruned programs.

Proposition 1. *Algorithm* FL-ALLREPAIR *is sound and complete.*

7   Experimental Results

We have implemented our fault localization technique and its integration with mutated-based program repair in the tool ALLREPAIR, available at https://github.com/batchenRothenberg/AllRepair. In this section, we present experiments evaluating the contribution of the new fault localization component to the program repair algorithm. We refer to the algorithm of [38], without fault localization, as AllRepair, and to the algorithm presented in this paper as FL-AllRepair. Both algorithms search for minimal wb-violation free programs, and both are sound and complete. Thus, for every buggy program and every bound wb, both algorithms will eventually produce the same list of repairs.

The difference between the algorithms lies in the repair loop. In case a mutated program is found to be buggy, the AllRepair algorithm will only block the one program, while the FL-AllRepair algorithm might block a set of programs. Therefore, the number of repair iterations required to cover the search space can only decrease using the FL-AllRepair algorithm. On the other hand, the cost of each iteration with fault localization is strictly higher than without it. Our goal in this evaluation is to check if the use of fault localization pays off. That is, to check if repairs are produced faster using FL-AllRepair than using AllRepair.

Benchmarks. For our evaluation, we have used programs from two benchmarks: TCAS and Codeflaws. The TCAS benchmark is part of the Siemens suite [12], and is frequently used for program repair evaluation [5,34,38]. The TCAS program implements a traffic collision avoidance system for aircrafts, and consists of approximately 180 lines of code. We have used all 41 faulty versions of the benchmark in our experiments.

The Codeflaws benchmark [41] is also a well-known and widely used benchmark for program repair. Programs in this benchmark are taken from buggy user submissions to the programming contest site Codeforces[7]. In each program, a user tries to solve a programming problem published as part of a contest on the site. The programming problems are varied, and also the users have a diverse level of expertise. The benchmark also provides correct versions for all buggy versions, which are used to classify bug types by computing the syntactic difference. For our experiments we randomly chose 13 buggy versions classified with bug types that can be fixed using mutations. The size of the chosen programs ranges from 17 to 44 lines of code.

---

[7] http://codeforces.com/.

Mutations. The mutations used in ALLREPAIR (and accordingly in FL-AllRepair) is a subset of the mutations used in [37]. We define two *mutation levels*, where level 1 contains only a subset of the mutations available in level 2. Thus, level 1 involves easier computation but may fail more often in finding repairs.

Table 1 shows the list of mutations used in each mutation level. For example, for the category of arithmetic operator replacement, in mutation level 1, the table specifies two sets: $\{+, -\}$ and $\{/, \%\}$. This means that a $+$ can be replaced by a $-$, and vice versa, and that the operators $/, \%$ can be replaced with each other. Constant manipulation mutations

Level 1	Level 2
$\{+, -\}, \{/, \%\}$	$\{+, -, *\}, \{/, \%\}$
$\{>, >=\},$ $\{<, <=\}$	$\{>, >=, <, <=\}, \{==, !=\}$
$\{\|\|, \& \& \}$	
$\{>>, <<\},\{\&, \|, \hat{}\}$	
	$C \to C +1, C \to C -1, C \to -C,$ $C \to 0$

Table 1. Partition of mutations to levels

apply to a numeric constant and include increasing its value by 1 ($C \to C +1$), decreasing it by 1 ($C \to C -1$), setting it to 0 ($C \to 0$) and changing its sign ($C \to -C$).

Setting. All of our experiments were run on a Linux 64-bit Ubuntu 16.0.4 virtual machine with 1 CPU, 4 GB of RAM and 40 GB of storage, provided using the VMWARE vRA service[8]. For each of the buggy versions in our benchmarks we have experimented with both mutation levels 1 and 2. For the Codeflaws benchmarks we additionally experimented with different unwinding bounds: 2 (entering the loop once), 5, 8 and 10. This experiment is irrelevant to the TCAS benchmarks since the TCAS program does not contain loops or recursive calls. Overall we had 186 combinations of buggy programs, mutation levels and unwinding bounds. We refer to each such combination as an *input*. For each input, we run both the AllRepair and the FL-AllRepair algorithms with a timeout of 10 minutes and a mutation size limit of 2 (i.e., at most two mutations could be applied at once).

7.1 Results

In total, 131 different repairs were found during our experiments, for 60 different inputs (for several inputs there was more than one possible repair). In this count, we treat repairs fixing the same program in the same way as different, if they were produced using different mutation levels or unwinding bounds. This is because our evaluation is concerned with the time to find these repairs, and both the mutation level and the unwinding bound greatly influence this time.

Because the time to produce a repair sometimes varied in several orders of magnitude depending on the input, we have chosen to split repairs into three categories: fast, intermediate, and slow, and examine the time difference separately for each category. Splitting repairs to categories was done according to the time it took to find them using the AllRepair algorithm. If that time was

---

[8] https://www.vmware.com/il/products/vrealize-automation.html.

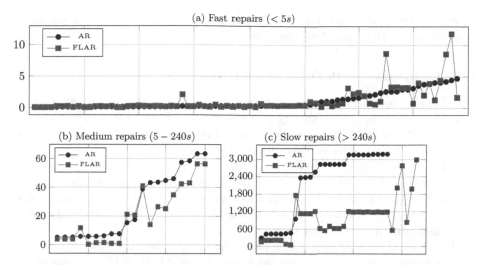

Fig. 5. Time to find each repair using AllRepair (AR) and FL-AllRepair (FLAR). Each x value represents a single repair, and the corresponding y values represent the time, in seconds, it took to find that repair using both algorithms. Note that the graphs differ in the y axis scale.

under 5 seconds, the repair was considered fast. If it was over 4 minutes, it was considered slow, and otherwise it was considered intermediate.

Figure 5 shows a comparison of the time, in seconds, it took to find repairs in both algorithms. There are three graphs, according to our three categories. In all graphs, each x value represents a single repair, where the corresponding blue dot in the y axis represents the time it took to find that repair using AllRepair, and the red square represents the time using FL-AllRepair. So, whenever the blue dot is above the red square, FL-AllRepair was faster in finding that repair, and the y difference represents the time saved.

For the fast category (Fig. 5a), there is no clear advantage to FL-AllRepair. The majority of the repairs in this category are produced in less than a second using both algorithms. For the remaining repairs, there appears to be as many cases where FL-AllRepair is faster as when it is slower. But, in all cases where there is a time difference, in either direction, it is only of a few seconds.

For the intermediate category (Fig. 5b), the advantage of FL-AllRepair is starting to become clear. There are now only 4 repairs (out of 20) for which FL-AllRepair is slower. Also, on average, it is slower by 4 seconds, but faster by 10 seconds. Finally, for the slow category (Fig. 5c), there is an obvious advantage to FL-AllRepair. First, it is able to find 6 repairs *exclusively*, while AllRepair reaches a time-out. Also, for the remaining 27 repairs, FL-AllRepair is faster in all cases but one. The time difference is now also very significant: FL-AllRepair is faster by 1512 seconds (around 25 minutes) on average.

To sum up, the results show that in many cases our algorithm FL-AllRepair is able to save time in finding repairs. The savings are especially significant in cases where it takes a long time to produce the repair using the original AllRepair algorithm, and these are the cases where time savings are most needed.

7.2   Comparison with Other Repair Methods

The TCAS benchmark was recently used also in [34], where ALLREPAIR's performance was compared to that of four other automated repair tools: ANGELIX [29], GENPROG [26], FORENSIC [5] and MAPLE [34]. ALLREPAIR was found to be faster by an order of magnitude than all of the compared tools, taking only 16.9 seconds to find a repair on average, where the other tools take 1540.7, 325.4, 360.1, and 155.3 seconds, respectively. Since in our experiments on TCAS FL-ALLREPAIR was faster than ALLREPAIR on average (and even when it was slower it was only by a few seconds), we conclude that FL-ALLREPAIR also compares favorably to these other tools.

In terms of repairability, the repair scheme used by ALLREPAIR (and FL-ALLREPAIR) is limited compared to the other tools: ALLREPAIR only uses mutations on expressions while ANGELIX, FORENSIC and MAPLE allow replacing an expression with a template (e.g., a linear combination of variables), which is then filled out to create a repair. GENPROG allows modifying a statement as well as deleting it or adding a statement after it. Therefore, the other tools are inherently capable of producing repairs in more cases than ALLREPAIR.

In the case of TCAS, the study showed that ALLREPAIR is able to find repairs for 18 versions (a result that we confirm in our experiments as well), while ANGELIX, GENPROG, FORENSIC and MAPLE found 32, 11, 23 and 26, respectively. But, what the study also showed, is that in repair methods that are based on tests, in many cases the repair found only adhered to the test-suite, but was not correct when inspected manually. When counting only correct repairs, ALLREPAIR finds repairs for 18 versions (all of ALLREPAIRs repairs are correct), while ANGELIX, GENPROG, FORENSIC and MAPLE find 9, 0, 15 and 26, respectively. Since FL-ALLREPAIR is able to find all repairs found by ALLREPAIR, the same results also apply to FL-ALLREPAIR.

8   Related Work

Dynamic slicing has been widely used for fault localization in the past [16, 36, 43, 45–47]. But, as we have seen, traditional notations of dynamic slicing [2, 23] are not must (with respect to neither of the presented schemes), and thus, the above techniques may fail to include relevant locations in their results.

Other approaches for fault localization include spectrum-based (SBFL) [1, 13, 20, 31, 44], mutation-based (MBFL) [15, 18, 30, 35] and formula-based (FBFL) [7, 14, 17, 21, 40]. Both SBFL and MBFL techniques compute the suspiciousness of a statement using coverage information from failing and passing test executions. MBFL uses, in addition, information on how test results change after applying different mutations to the program. Both SBFL and MBFL techniques can be seen as may fault localization techniques, in nature: they return locations that *are likely* to be relevant to the failing execution, based on all executions. We see may fault localization techniques as orthogonal to ours (and to must fault localization techniques in general), since in the trade-off between returning a small set of locations, and returning one that is guaranteed to contain all relevant statements, may techniques prefer the first, while must techniques prefer the second. In the context of repair, there are interesting applications for both.

FBFL techniques represent an error trace using an SMT formula and analyze it to find suspicious locations. These techniques include using error invariants [6,14,17,40], maximum satisfiability [21,24,25], and weakest preconditions [7]. What we were able to show in this paper, is that the methods of [6,14,21] are not must. In contrast, we believe (though we do not prove it) that the methods of [7,24,25] are must. But, what [7,24,25] have in common is that they use the semantics of the error trace or the program. Though semantic information can help to further minimize the number of suspicious locations, retrieving it involves using expensive solving-based procedures. Our approach, on the other hand, uses only syntactic information, which makes the fault localization computation relatively cheap; No SMT solving is needed. Thus, these approaches can be seen as complementary to ours.

In the literature there is also a wide range of techniques for automated program repair using formal methods [4,10,19,22,29,32,33,42]. Both [11] and [37] also use fault localization followed by applying mutations for repair. But, unlike this work, fault localization is applied only for the original program. Also, neither the Tarantula fault localization used in [11] nor the dynamic slicing used in [37] carries the guarantee of being a must fault localization. The tool MUT-APR [3] fixes binary operator faults in C programs, but only targets faults that require one line modification. The tools FORENSIC [5] and MAPLE [34] repair C programs with respect to a formal specification, but they do so by replacing expressions with templates, which are then patched and analysed. SEMGRAFT [28] conducts repair with respect to a reference implementation, but relies on tests for SBFL fault localization of the original program.

9   Conclusion

In this work we define a novel notion of *must* fault localization, that carefully identifies program locations that are relevant for a bug, so that the set is sufficiently small but is guaranteed not to miss desired repairs. We also show that the notion of *must* fault localization should be defined with respect to the repair scheme in use. We show that our notion of must fault localization is particularly useful in pruning the search space of a specific mutation-based repair algorithm.

To the best of our knowledge, we are the first to investigate the widely-used notion of fault localization and to suggest criteria for evaluating its different implementation.

References

1. Abreu, R., Zoeteweij, P., Van Gemund, A.J.C.: An evaluation of similarity coefficients for software fault localization. In: Proceedings of the 12th Pacific Rim International Symposium on Dependable Computing, PRDC 2006, pp. 39–46 (2006)
2. Agrawal, H., Horgan, J.R.: Dynamic Program Slicing. In: PLDI, pp. 246–256 (1990)
3. Assiri, F.Y., Bieman, J.M.: MUT-APR: MUTation-based automated program repair research tool. In: Arai, K., Kapoor, S., Bhatia, R. (eds.) FICC 2018. AISC, vol. 887, pp. 256–270. Springer, Cham (2019). https://doi.org/10.1007/978-3-030-03405-4_17
4. Attie, P.C., Dak, K., Bab, A.L., Sakr, M.: Model and program repair via SAT solving. ACM Trans. Embed. Comput. Syst. **17**(2), 1–25 (2017)
5. Bloem, R., Drechsler, R., Fey, G., Finder, A., Hofferek, G., Könighofer, R., Raik, J., Repinski, U., Sülflow, A.: FoREnSiC– an automatic debugging environment for C programs. In: Biere, A., Nahir, A., Vos, T. (eds.) HVC 2012. LNCS, vol. 7857, pp. 260–265. Springer, Heidelberg (2013). https://doi.org/10.1007/978-3-642-39611-3_24
6. Christ, J., Ermis, E., Schäf, M., Wies, T.: Flow-sensitive fault localization. In: Giacobazzi, R., Berdine, J., Mastroeni, I. (eds.) VMCAI 2013. LNCS, vol. 7737, pp. 189–208. Springer, Heidelberg (2013). https://doi.org/10.1007/978-3-642-35873-9_13
7. Christakis, M., Heizmann, M., Mansur, M.N., Schilling, C., Wüstholz, V.: Semantic fault localization and suspiciousness ranking. In: Vojnar, T., Zhang, L. (eds.) TACAS 2019. LNCS, vol. 11427, pp. 226–243. Springer, Cham (2019). https://doi.org/10.1007/978-3-030-17462-0_13
8. Clarke, E., Kroening, D., Lerda, F.: A tool for checking ANSI-C programs. In: Jensen, K., Podelski, A. (eds.) TACAS 2004. LNCS, vol. 2988, pp. 168–176. Springer, Heidelberg (2004). https://doi.org/10.1007/978-3-540-24730-2_15
9. Clarke, E., Kroening, D., Yorav, K.: Behavioral consistency of C and Verilog programs using bounded model checking. In: Proceedings of the Design Automation Conference, 2003, pp. 368–371. IEEE (2003)
10. D'Antoni, L., Samanta, R., Singh, R.: QLOSE: program repair with quantitative objectives. In: Chaudhuri, S., Farzan, A. (eds.) CAV 2016. LNCS, vol. 9780, pp. 383–401. Springer, Cham (2016). https://doi.org/10.1007/978-3-319-41540-6_21
11. Debroy, V., Wong, W.E.: Using mutation to automatically suggest fixes for faulty programs. In: 2010 Third International Conference on Software Testing, Verification and Validation (ICST), pp. 65–74. IEEE (2010)
12. Do, H., Elbaum, S., Rothermel, G.: Supporting controlled experimentation with testing techniques: an infrastructure and its potential impact. Empir. Softw. Eng. **10**(4), 405–435 (2005)
13. Eric Wong, W., Debroy, V., Choi, B.: A family of code coverage-based heuristics for effective fault localization. J. Syst. Softw. **83**(2), 188–208 (2010)
14. Ermis, E., Schäf, M., Wies, T.: Error invariants. In: Giannakopoulou, D., Méry, D. (eds.) FM 2012. LNCS, vol. 7436, pp. 187–201. Springer, Heidelberg (2012). https://doi.org/10.1007/978-3-642-32759-9_17
15. Gong, P., Zhao, R., Li, Z.: Faster mutation-based fault localization with a novel mutation execution strategy. In: Proceedings of the 2015 IEEE 8th International Conference on Software Testing, Verification and Validation Workshops, ICSTW 2015, pp. 1–10. IEEE (2015)

16. Hofer, B., Wotawa, F.: Spectrum enhanced dynamic slicing for better fault localization. ECAI **242**, 420–425 (2012)
17. Holzer, A., Schwartz-Narbonne, D., Tabaei Befrouei, M., Weissenbacher, G., Wies, T.: Error invariants for concurrent traces. In: Fitzgerald, J., Heitmeyer, C., Gnesi, S., Philippou, A. (eds.) FM 2016. LNCS, vol. 9995, pp. 370–387. Springer, Cham (2016). https://doi.org/10.1007/978-3-319-48989-6_23
18. Hong, S., Lee, B., Kwak, T., Jeon, Y., Ko, B., Kim, Y., Kim, M.: Mutation-based fault localization for real-world multilingual programs. In: ASE, pp. 464–475 (2015)
19. Jobstmann, B., Griesmayer, A., Bloem, R.: Program repair as a game. In: Etessami, K., Rajamani, S.K. (eds.) CAV 2005. LNCS, vol. 3576, pp. 226–238. Springer, Heidelberg (2005). https://doi.org/10.1007/11513988_23
20. Jones, J., Harrold, M., Stasko, J.: Visualization for fault localization. In: Proceedings of ICSE 2001 Workshop on Software Visualization, pp. 71–75 (2001)
21. Jose, M., Majumdar, R.: Cause clue clauses: error localization using maximum satisfiability. In: PLDI, pp. 437–446 (2011)
22. Kneuss, E., Koukoutos, M., Kuncak, V.: Deductive program repair. In: Kroening, D., Păsăreanu, C.S. (eds.) CAV 2015. LNCS, vol. 9207, pp. 217–233. Springer, Cham (2015). https://doi.org/10.1007/978-3-319-21668-3_13
23. Korel, B., Laski, J.: Dynamic program slicing. Inf. Process. Lett. **29**, 155–163 (1988)
24. Lamraoui, S.-M., Nakajima, S.: A formula-based approach for automatic fault localization of multi-fault programs. J. Inf. Process. **24**, 88–98 (2016)
25. Lamraoui, S.-M., Nakajima, S., Hosobe, H.: Hardened flow-sensitive trace formula for fault localization. In: ICECCS (2015)
26. Le Goues, C., Nguyen, T., Forrest, S., Weimer, W.: GenProg: a generic method for automatic software repair. IEEE Trans. Softw. Eng. **38**(1), 54–72 (2012)
27. Liu, K., Koyuncu, A., Bissyande, T.F., Kim, D., Klein, J., Le Traon, Y.: You cannot fix what you cannot find! An investigation of fault localization bias in benchmarking automated program repair systems. In: ICST, pp. 102–113 (2019)
28. Mechtaev, S., Nguyen, M.-D., Noller, Y., Grunske, L., Roychoudhury, A.: Semantic program repair using a reference implementation. In: ICSE (2018)
29. Mechtaev, S., Yi, J., Roychoudhury, A.: Angelix: scalable multiline program patch synthesis via symbolic analysis. In: ICSE (2016)
30. Moon, S., Kim, Y., Kim, M., Yoo, S.: Ask the mutants: mutating faulty programs for fault localization. In: ICST (2014)
31. Naish, L., Lee, H.J., Ramamohanarao, K.: A model for spectra-based software diagnosis. ACM Trans. Softw. Eng. Methodol. **20**(3), 1–32 (2011)
32. Nguyen, H.D.T., Qi, D., Roychoudhury, A., Chandra, S.: SemFix: program repair via semantic analysis. In: Proceedings of the 2013 International Conference on Software Engineering, pp. 772–781. IEEE Press (2013)
33. Nguyen, T.V., Weimer, W., Kapur, D., Forrest, S.: Connecting program synthesis and reachability: automatic program repair using test-input generation. In: Legay, A., Margaria, T. (eds.) TACAS 2017. LNCS, vol. 10205, pp. 301–318. Springer, Heidelberg (2017). https://doi.org/10.1007/978-3-662-54577-5_17
34. Nguyen, T.-T., Ta, Q.-T., Chin, W.-N.: Automatic program repair using formal verification and expression templates. In: Enea, C., Piskac, R. (eds.) VMCAI 2019. LNCS, vol. 11388, pp. 70–91. Springer, Cham (2019). https://doi.org/10.1007/978-3-030-11245-5_4
35. Papadakis, M., Traon, Y.L.: Metallaxis-FL: mutation-based fault localization. Softw. Test. Verif. Reliab. **21**(3), 195–214 (2015)

36. Qian, J., Xu, B.: Scenario oriented program slicing. In: Proceedings of the ACM Symposium on Applied Computing, pp. 748–7752 (2008)
37. Repinski, U., Hantson, H., Jenihhin, M., Raik, J., Ubar, R., Guglielmo, G.D., Pravadelli, G., Fummi, F.: Combining dynamic slicing and mutation operators for ESL correction. In: 2012 17th IEEE European Test Symposium (ETS), pp. 1–6. IEEE (2012)
38. Rothenberg, B.-C., Grumberg, O.: Sound and complete mutation-based program repair. In: Fitzgerald, J., Heitmeyer, C., Gnesi, S., Philippou, A. (eds.) FM 2016. LNCS, vol. 9995, pp. 593–611. Springer, Cham (2016). https://doi.org/10.1007/978-3-319-48989-6_36
39. Rothenberg, B.-C., Grumberg, O.: Must fault localization for program repair. https://batg.cswp.cs.technion.ac.il/wp-content/uploads/sites/78/2020/05/MustFaultLocalizationForProgramRepairCav2020.pdf, May 2020. A full version of the CAV 2020 paper of the same title
40. Schäf, M., Schwartz-Narbonne, D., Wies, T.: Explaining inconsistent code. In: ESEC/FSE, pp. 521–531 (2013)
41. Tan, S.H., Yi, J., Yulis, Mechtaev, S., Roychoudhury, A.: Codeflaws: A programming competition benchmark for evaluating automated program repair tools. In: Proceedings of the 2017 IEEE/ACM 39th International Conference on Software Engineering Companion, ICSE-C 2017, pp. 180–182 (2017)
42. von Essen, C., Jobstmann, B.: Program repair without regret. Form. Methods Syst. Des. **47**(1), 26–50 (2015). https://doi.org/10.1007/s10703-015-0223-6
43. Wang, Y., Patil, H., Pereira, C., Lueck, G., Gupta, R., Neamtiu, I.: DrDebug: deterministic replay based cyclic debugging with dynamic slicing. In: Proceedings of the 12th ACM/IEEE International Symposium on Code Generation and Optimization, CGO 2014, pp. 98–108 (2014)
44. Wong, W.E., Debroy, V., Gao, R., Li, Y.: The DStar method for effective software fault localization. IEEE Trans. Reliab. **63**(1), 290–308 (2014)
45. Wotawa, F.: Fault localization based on dynamic slicing and hitting-set computation. In: Proceedings of the International Conference on Quality Software, pp. 161–170 (2010)
46. Zhang, X., Gupta, N., Gupta, R.: A study of effectiveness of dynamic slicing in locating real faults. Empir. Softw. Eng. **12**(2), 143–160 (2007)
47. Zhang, X., Gupta, N., Gupta, R.: Locating faulty code by multiple points slicing. Softw. Pract. Exp. **39**(7), 661–699 (2007)

Author Index

Albert, Elvira   I-177
Almagor, Shaull   II-541
Arcak, Murat   I-556

Backes, John   I-165
Bak, Stanley   I-3, I-18, I-66
Barrett, Clark   I-137, I-403
Bastani, Osbert   II-587
Batz, Kevin   II-512
Baumeister, Jan   II-28
Bazille, Hugo   II-304
Bendík, Jaroslav   I-439
Beneš, Nikola   I-569
Berdine, Josh   II-225
Berrueco, Ulises   I-165
Beyer, Dirk   II-165
Blackshear, Sam   I-137
Blahoudek, František   II-15, II-421
Blondin, Michael   II-372
Bray, Tyler   I-165
Brázdil, Tomáš   II-421
Brim, Daniel   I-165
Brim, Luboš   I-569
Brotherston, James   II-203
Buiras, Pablo   I-225
Büning, Julian   I-376

Češka, Milan   I-653
Chang, Kai-Chieh   I-543
Chatterjee, Krishnendu   II-398
Chau, Calvin   I-653
Cheang, Kevin   I-137
Chen, Mingshuai   II-327
Chen, Xin   I-582
Chen, Yanju   II-587
Chen, YuTing   II-101
Chiu, Johnathan   I-122
Çirisci, Berk   I-350
Cook, Byron   I-165
Costa, Diana   II-203

D'Antoni, Loris   II-3
Dai, Hanjun   II-151

Dai, Liyun   I-415
Daly, Ross   I-403
Dang, Hoang-Hai   II-225
Devonport, Alex   I-556
Dill, David L.   I-137
Dillig, Isil   II-564, II-587
Donovick, Caleb   I-403
Dreyer, Derek   II-225
Dross, Claire   II-178
Dullerud, Geir E.   II-448
Duret-Lutz, Alexandre   II-15
Dwyer, Matthew B.   I-97

Elbaum, Sebastian   I-97
Elboher, Yizhak Yisrael   I-43
Enea, Constantin   I-350
Esparza, Javier   II-372

Fan, Chuchu   I-629
Farzan, Azadeh   I-350
Feng, Shenghua   II-327
Feng, Yu   II-587
Finkbeiner, Bernd   II-28, II-40, II-64
Fremont, Daniel J.   I-122

Gacek, Andrew   I-165
Gan, Ting   I-415
Genest, Blaise   II-304
Gieseking, Manuel   II-64
Gocht, Stephan   I-463
Golia, Priyanka   II-611
Gopinathan, Kiran   II-279
Gordillo, Pablo   I-177
Gottschlich, Justin   I-43
Grieskamp, Wolfgang   I-137
Grumberg, Orna   II-658
Guanciale, Roberto   I-225
Gurfinkel, Arie   II-101

Haas, Thomas   II-349
Hahn, Christopher   II-40
Hanrahan, Pat   I-403
Hartmanns, Arnd   II-488

Hasuo, Ichiro   II-349
Hecking-Harbusch, Jesko   II-64
Helfrich, Martin   II-3, II-372
Henzinger, Thomas A.   I-275
Herbst, Steven   I-403
Hobbs, Kerianne   I-66
Hobor, Aquinas   II-203
Hofmann, Jana   II-40
Horowitz, Mark   I-403
Houshmand, Farzin   I-324
Huang, Chao   I-543
Hunt Jr., Warren A.   I-485

Jaber, Nouraldin   I-299
Jacobs, Swen   I-225, I-299
Jagannathan, Suresh   I-251
Jegourel, Cyrille   II-304
Jhala, Ranjit   I-165
Johnson, Taylor T.   I-3, I-18, I-66
Junges, Sebastian   II-512

Kadlecaj, Jakub   I-569
Kaminski, Benjamin Lucien   II-488, II-512
Kanig, Johannes   II-178
Katoen, Joost-Pieter   II-398, II-512
Katz, Guy   I-43
Khaled, Mahmoud   I-556, II-461
Klimis, Vasileios   II-126
Kölbl, Martin   I-529
Kragl, Bernhard   I-275
Křetínský, Jan   II-3, I-653
Krogmeier, Paul   II-634
Kučera, Antonín   II-372
Kulkarni, Milind   I-299
Kupferman, Orna   II-541
Kwiatkowska, Marta   II-475

Laprell, David   I-376
Lavaei, Abolfazl   II-461
Lesani, Mohsen   I-324
Leue, Stefan   I-529
Li, Xiao   I-324
Li, Xuandong   I-582
Lin, Chung-Wei   I-543
Lin, Wang   I-582
Lindner, Andreas   I-225
Luckow, Kasper   I-165

Madhusudan, P.   II-634
Mann, Makai   I-403
Manzanas Lopez, Diego   I-3
Margineantu, Dragos D.   I-122
Matheja, Christoph   II-512
Mathur, Umang   II-634
McLaughlin, Sean   I-165
McMillan, Kenneth L.   II-190
Meel, Kuldeep S.   I-439, I-463, II-611
Menon, Madhav   I-165
Meyer, Philipp J.   II-372
Miller, Kristina   I-629
Mitra, Sayan   I-629
Mukherjee, Prasita   I-251
Murali, Adithya   II-634
Musau, Patrick   I-3
Mutluergil, Suha Orhun   I-350

Nagar, Kartik   I-251
Naik, Aaditya   II-151
Naik, Mayur   II-151
Nelson, Luke   II-564
Nemati, Hamed   I-225
Nguyen, Luan Viet   I-3
Norman, Gethin   II-475
Novotný, Petr   II-421

O'Hearn, Peter   II-225
Olderog, Ernst-Rüdiger   II-64
Ornik, Melkior   II-421
Osipychev, Denis   I-122

Padon, Oded   II-190
Parisis, George   II-126
Park, Daejun   I-151
Park, Junkil   I-137
Parker, David   II-475
Pastva, Samuel   I-569
Peebles, Daniel   I-165
Peng, Chao   I-582
Phalakarn, Kittiphon   II-349
Pugalia, Ujjwal   I-165

Qadeer, Shaz   I-137, I-275

Raad, Azalea   II-225
Ramneantu, Emanuel   II-3
Reus, Bernhard   II-126

Rodríguez, César I-376
Roohi, Nima II-448
Rosu, Grigore I-151
Rothenberg, Bat-Chen II-658
Roy, Subhajit II-611
Rubio, Albert I-177
Rungta, Neha I-165

Šafránek, David I-569
Sahai, Shubham I-201
Samanta, Roopsha I-299
Sankaranarayanan, Sriram I-604, II-327
Santos, Gabriel II-475
Schemmel, Daniel I-376
Schett, Maria A. I-177
Schirmer, Sebastian II-28
Schlesinger, Cole I-165
Schodde, Adam I-165
Schröer, Philipp II-512
Schwenger, Maximilian II-28
Sergey, Ilya II-279
Seshia, Sanjit A. I-122, II-255
Setaluri, Rajsekhar I-403
Shoham, Sharon II-101
Shriver, David I-97
Si, Xujie II-151
Siegel, Stephen F. II-77
Sinha, Rohit I-201
Slivovsky, Friedrich I-508
Slobodova, Anna I-485
Song, Le II-151
Soos, Mate I-463
Soudjani, Sadegh II-461
Spiessl, Martin II-165
Stanley, Daniel I-403
Strejček, Jan II-15
Subramanyan, Pramod I-201
Sun, Jun II-304

Takisaka, Toru II-349
Tanuku, Anvesh I-165
Temel, Mertcan I-485
Tentrup, Leander II-40

Thangeda, Pranay II-421
Topcu, Ufuk II-421
Torens, Christoph II-28
Torlak, Emina II-564
Tran, Hoang-Dung I-3, I-18, I-66
Truong, Lenny I-403

Van Geffen, Jacob II-564
Varming, Carsten I-165
Vazquez-Chanlatte, Marcell II-255
Vediramana Krishnan, Hari Govind II-101
Villard, Jules II-225
Viswanathan, Deepa I-165
Viswanathan, Mahesh II-448, II-634

Wagner, Christopher I-299
Wang, Chenglong II-587
Wang, Xi II-564
Wang, Yu II-448
Wehrle, Klaus I-376
Weininger, Maximilian II-3, II-398
West, Matthew II-448
Wickerson, John II-203
Wies, Thomas I-529
Winkler, Tobias II-398

Xia, Bican I-415
Xiang, Weiming I-3, I-18
Xu, Dong I-97
Xue, Bai I-415, II-327

Yan, Yihao II-77
Yang, Xiaodong I-3
Yang, Zhengfeng I-582

Zamani, Majid I-556, II-461
Zhan, Naijun I-415, II-327
Zhang, Keyi I-403
Zhang, Yi I-151
Zhang, Yifang I-582
Zhong, Jingyi Emma I-137
Zhu, Qi I-543
Zohar, Yoni I-137

Printed in the United States
by Bookmasters

Printed in the United States
By Bookmasters